D1073874

FINANCIAL ANALYST'S HANDBOOK I

Portfolio Management

FINANCIAL ANALYST'S HANDBOOK I

Methods, Theory, and Portfolio Management

Edited by
SUMNER N. LEVINE
State University of New York
Stony Brook, New York

1975

DOW JONES-IRWIN, INC. *Homewood, Illinois 60430*

First Printing, February 1975

Library of Congress Cataloging in Publication Data

Levine, Sumner N.
Financial analyst's handbook.
CONTENTS: v. 1. Portfolio management.—v. 2. Analysis by industry.
1. Investments. I. Title.
HG4521.L625 332.6 74–81386
ISBN 0-87094-082-1 (v. 1)

Printed in the United States of America

Preface

THIS TWO PART HANDBOOK is intended as a comprehensive guide to the principles and procedures necessary for successful investment management. Security analysts, portfolio managers, corporate financial officers and other professional investors will find these volumes a convenient and authoritative source of information.

The Handbook was originally conceived as a single volume reference. However, the enthusiasm of a singularly capable group of editors and contributors soon overwhelmed the original scenario and the project grew like Topsy. The coverage was increased and a number of contributions turned out to be longer than originally planned. Many of these more extensive sections contained much valuable information not readily found elsewhere. Rather than implore our contributors to cut and prune their sections to accommodate the confines of a single volume Handbook, it was decided to expand the book into two volumes. The first volume provides a discipline oriented coverage of investments while the second deals with the analysis of specific industries.

Because of the rapidly changing hues of the investment landscape, we expect that both volumes will find considerable use by analysts. Such is the tempo of events, that on one occasion the analyst may find it necessary to undertake an in-depth analysis of a specific industry, and hence refer to Volume II, while on another occasion he may seek guidance in Volume I for a critical evaluation of special situations, foreign securities, or municipal bonds. Each section provides the analyst with the expertise of authorities who have devoted years to their subject.

A few words should be devoted to the organization and some special features of Volume I. The first sections take cognizance of the growing complexity of government regulations as they impinge on the profession. Recognition is also given to the increasing importance of the examinations administered by the Institute of Chartered Financial Analysts.

Comprehensive coverage is given to the characteristics and analysis of both long term and short term investment vehicles. Indeed, we have leaned over backward in this regard and have included substantial information on special situations, foreign securities, and even venture capital investments. Who can foresee future investment opportunities?

The sections on the Analysis of Financial Reports contain a number of special features. Because of the frequent need to compute earnings per share, we have included, in full, APB Opinion 15, together with relevant supporting material. Another feature worthy of comment is an up-dated outline of the 10-K form. Study of this 10-K form section will inform the analyst what information is available and where in the 10-K form it can be found.

The sections on Economic Analysis and Timing also contain a number of useful features. A very complete account is given of the Federal Reserve System since, as every analyst is well aware, the securities markets exhibit an almost instantaneous reflex reaction to significant changes in the Fed's policies. Also included is a detailed section on the interpretation of National Income and Balance of Payments Accounts. It should be noted too, that technical analysis has also been given its day in court. A useful appendix to the latter section will provide the user with detailed definitions of the more commonly used market averages.

Quantitative methods are presented at a level which should be accessible to most analysts. In order to enhance the usefulness of these sections, fairly comprehensive tables of the more widely used compound interest functions have been provided.

Considerable space has been given to Portfolio Management and Theories. The field of capital market theory has experienced an explosive development in recent years. As with most new ideas, some of these developments (efficient markets, random walk, and others) have been the subject of considerable controversy. One point seems clear, however, it is not enough for analysts to evaluate a company, an industry and even future economic trends, as important as these matters may be. He must also attempt to determine whether the market has already discounted his prognostications; for what one analyst knows, so may others. In any case, a broad spectrum of views concerning portfolio management has also been provided, including a section which gives a very comprehensive and objective assessment of current opinions.

The second volume of the Handbook covers the analysis of specific industries. The material in this volume is intended to provide examples of how leading industry specialists proceed. A large selection of industries is represented. The coverage is not exhaustive since it is assumed that the reader has a good familiarity with security analysis: Each section emphasizes only the specific considerations relevant to the industry. Contributors have attempted to point out the economic, social, marketing, regulatory, taxation, accountancy, and other considerations of significance in each instance. The length of the sections varies and is not necessarily proportional to the economic significance of the industry. This is due, in part, to a contributor's style and emphasis, but it also reflects the nature of the industry. For example, somewhat more space is given to highly regulated industries with rather special accounting practices (banking, insurance, and utilities) than is given to the manufacturing industries.

Familiarity with key government and trade publications is a vital aspect of investment analysis. Several sections are devoted to information sources including one on site visits. A list of some of the more important trade publications relating to a variety of industries has been included. Such publications number in the thousands, and complete listings are available in the compendia referred to in the section on Information Sources.

Security analysis and the management of investments is surely one of the more exciting and, we hasten to add, precarious professions. Perhaps it may be likened to cardiac surgery; a vital and necessary business involving substantial survival risks. We hope that the information provided in these volumes will help the user reduce his risk and increase his returns—more we cannot wish fellow analysts.

January 1975 SUMNER N. LEVINE

Contributors

Peter L. Anker, C.F.A. First Vice President, Smith, Barney & Co., Incorporated, New York, New York.

James Balog Chairman of the Board, William D. Witter, Inc., New York, New York.

W. Scott Bauman, D.B.A., C.F.A. Executive Director, The Institute of Chartered Financial Analysts and The Darden Graduate School of Business Administration, University of Virginia, Charlottesville, Virginia.

Nathan Belfer, Ph.D., C.F.A. Vice President, Wood, Struthers & Winthrop, Inc., New York, New York.

Martin Benis, Ph.D., C.P.A. Baruch College, The City University of New York, New York, New York.

Peter L. Bernstein Peter L. Bernstein, Inc., New York, New York.

Robert P. Black, Ph.D. First Reserve Bank of Richmond, Richmond, Virginia.

Charles P. Bonini, Ph.D. Graduate School of Business, Stanford University, Stanford, California.

Clarence W. Brown Senior Investment Analyst, H. C. Wainwright & Co.. New York, New York.

Jerome H. Buff, C.F.A. First Vice President, Smith, Barney & Co., Incorporated, New York, New York.

Gordon L. Calvert, J.D. Vice President and General Counsel (Washington), The New York Stock Exchange, Washington, D.C.

Arthur K. Carlson Vice President, First National City Bank, New York, New York.

Glenelg P. Caterer, C.F.A. Advisor to Corporate Information Committee, Financial Analysts Federation, New York, New York.

David C. Cates President, David C. Cates & Co., Inc., New York, New York.

Abraham Charnes, Ph.D. Center for Cybernetic Studies, University of Texas at Austin, Austin, Texas.

William E. Chatlos Principal, Georgeson & Co., New York, New York.

George H. Cleaver First Vice President, White, Wild & Co., Incorporated, New York, New York.

Stuart H. Clement, Jr., C.F.A. Ernst & Company, Rye, New York.

Jerome B. Cohen, Ph.D. Senior Editor, *Bankers Magazine,* and Emeritus Professor of Finance, Baruch College, The City University of New York, New York, New York.

William W. Cooper, Ph.D. School of Urban and Public Affairs, Carnegie Mellon University, Pittsburgh, Pennsylvania.

Thomas J. Donnelly, C.F.A. Vice President, Kuhn, Loeb & Co., New York, New York.

Edwin J. Elton, Ph.D. Graduate School of Business Administration, New York University, New York, New York.

Herbert E. Goodfriend Vice President—Research, Paine, Webber, Jackson & Curtis, Inc., New York, New York.

Eileen M. Gormley, C.F.A. Vice President and Senior Institutional Analyst, Thomson & McKinnon Auchincloss Kohlmeyer, Inc., New York, New York.

Martin J. Gruber, Ph.D. Graduate School of Business Administration, New York University, New York, New York.

Charles H. Hanneman, C.F.A. Vice President, Argus Research Corporation, New York, New York.

David R. Hathaway Vice President, Director of Technology Research, G. A. Saxton & Co., Inc., New York, New York.

Erich A. Helfert, D.B.A. Assistant to the President, Crown Zellerbach, San Francisco, California.

Kenneth Hollister, C.F.A. Vice President, Dean Witter & Co., Inc., New York, New York.

Arvid F. Jouppi Senior Vice President, Delafield Childs, Inc., New York, New York.

Robert A. Kavesh, Ph.D. Graduate School of Business Administration, New York University, New York, New York.

Martin A. Keane, Ph.D. Research Laboratories, General Motors Corporation, Warren, Michigan.

Saul B. Klaman, Ph.D. Vice President and Chief Economist, National Association of Mutual Savings Banks, New York, New York.

Dennis A. Kraebel Manager of Preferred Stock Trading, Donaldson, Lufkin & Jenrette, New York, New York.

Charles D. Kuehner, Ph.D., C.F.A. Director—Security Analysis and Investor Relations, American Telephone & Telegraph Co., New York, New York.

Dennis H. Leibowitz Partner, Coleman and Company, New York, New York.

Martin L. Leibowitz, Ph.D. Vice President and Director of Investment Systems, Salomon Brothers, New York, New York.

Sumner N. Levine, Ph.D. State University of New York, Stony Brook, New York.

A. Michael Lipper, C.F.A. Lipper Analytical Services, Inc., Westfield, New Jersey.

Herbert W. McNulty Senior Security Analyst, Hornblower & Weeks-Hemphill, Noyes, Inc., New York, New York.

Joseph A. Mauriello, Ph.D., C.P.A. Graduate School of Business Administration, New York University, New York, New York.

Rose Mayerson Security Analyst, Bear, Stearns & Co., New York, New York.

Sylvia Mechanic Business Librarian, Brooklyn Public Library, Brooklyn, New York.

Edmund A. Mennis, Ph.D., C.F.A. Senior Vice President and Chairman of the Investment Policy Committee, Security Pacific National Bank, Los Angeles, California.

Robert D. Milne, C.F.A. Partner, Boyd, Watterson & Co., Cleveland, Ohio.

Francis A. Mlynarczyk, Jr. Investment Officer, First National City Bank, New York, New York.

Franco Modigliani, Ph.D. Sloan School of Management, Massachusetts Institute of Technology, Cambridge, Massachusetts.

Geoffrey H. Moore, Ph.D. Vice President-Research, National Bureau of Economic Research, Inc., New York, and Senior Research Fellow, Hoover Institution, Stanford University, Stanford, California.

J. Kendrick Noble, Jr., C.F.A. Vice President, Auerbach, Pollack, and Richardson, Inc., New York, New York.

William C. Norby, C.F.A. Senior Vice President, Duff, Anderson & Clark, Inc., Chicago, Illinois.

Thomas L. Owen Vice President, National Securities and Research Corporation, New York, New York.

Jackson Phillips, Ph.D. Vice President and Director, Municipal Bonds Research Division, Moody's Investors Service, Inc., New York, New York.

Robert B. Platt, Ph.D. Economist, Delafield Childs, Inc., New York, New York.

Gerald A. Pogue, Ph.D. Baruch College, The City University of New York, New York, New York.

B. U. Ratchford, Ph.D. First Reserve Bank of Richmond, Richmond, Virginia.

Robert B. Ritter Institutional Research, L. F. Rothschild & Co., New York, New York.

Benjamin Rosen Director of Research, Coleman and Company, New York, New York.

Terry W. Rothermel, Ph.D. Arthur D. Little, Inc., Cambridge, Massachusetts.

Stanley M. Rubel President, S. M. Rubel and Company, The Vencap Fund, Chicago, Illinois.

Jack Rubinson Assistant Director of Research, National Association of Mutual Savings Banks, New York, New York.

Alfred S. Rudd Standard & Poor's Corporation, New York, New York.

Maurece Schiller Goleta, California.

Peter A. Schulkin, Ph.D. Director of Research, National Association of Real Estate Investment Trusts, Washington, D.C.

Ira O. Scott, Jr., Ph.D. Executive Vice President, Savings Banks Association of New York State, New York, New York.

Alan R. Shaw Vice President and a Director of Research, Harris, Upham & Co., Inc., New York, New York.

Ruben Shohet, C.F.A. First Vice President and Director, Drexel Burnham and Co., Incorporated, New York, New York.

Irwin W. Silverberg, C.F.A. Vice President, Loeb, Rhoades & Co., New York, New York.

Aubrey N. Snellings, Ph.D. First Reserve Bank of Richmond, Richmond, Virginia.

Beryl W. Sprinkel, Ph.D. Executive Vice President and Economist, Harris Trust and Savings Bank, Chicago, Illinois.

William A. Spurr, Ph.D. Graduate School of Business, Stanford University, Stanford, California.

Samuel S. Stewart, Jr., Ph.D. College of Business, The University of Utah, Salt Lake City, Utah.

Dorothy Hennessy Sussman Vice President-Librarian, Goldman, Sachs & Co., New York, New York.

David C. Sutliff, C.F.A. Vice President, E. F. Hutton & Company, Inc., New York, New York.

David H. Talbot Vice President, William D. Witter, Inc., New York, New York.

Jack L. Treynor Editor, *Financial Analyst's Journal,* New York, New York.

Daniel Turov Warrant and Convertible Securities Analyst, Thomson & McKinnon Auchincloss Kohlmeyer, Inc., New York, New York.

James E. Wheeler, Ph.D. Graduate School of Business Administration, University of Michigan, Ann Arbor, Michigan.

Roger B. Wilson, C.F.A. Manager of Investor Relations, Continental Can Company, New York, New York.

Contents

VOLUME I METHODS, THEORY, AND PORTFOLIO MANAGEMENT

Part I Introduction

Part II Investment Vehicles

VOLUME II ANALYSIS BY INDUSTRY

Part I Introduction

Part II Analysis by Industry Categories

Part III Information Sources

PART I

Introduction

1

Overview of Financial Analysis

WILLIAM C. NORBY, C.F.A.
Senior Vice President
Duff, Anderson & Clark, Inc.
Chicago, Illinois

THE ROLE OF THE FINANCIAL ANALYST IN THE INVESTMENT PROCESS

FINANCIAL ANALYSIS is an exciting occupation. Its subject matter encompasses not only business and finance but also science, government, and society around the world. Its perspective is both broad and deep. It is future oriented. It has a strong influence on the direction of capital investment and hence on the shape of business and industry. It employs a wide diversity of analytical techniques including economics, mathematics, accounting, and psychology. No wonder financial analysis holds such fascination for so many able people.

The Financial Analyst

The term *financial analyst* has broad usage throughout business and government to identify anyone who analyzes financial data for internal or external purposes such as capital expenditure programs, current operating budgets, or long-term financial plans. This book is concerned with financial analysis *as related to security investments*. In this context it is synonymous with *security analyst* or *investment analyst*—that is, one who analyzes securities and makes recommendations thereon.

Even within the field of investment, financial analysis is sometimes used to describe the entire field of investment management but at other times is confined to the narrower function of company and industry analysis. Continuing the definition then, this book uses the term financial analysis *as comprehending the entire function of securities investment management,* including both analysis of companies and industries and the management of investment portfolios.

A financial analyst thus is one who: (1) analyzes companies and industries and makes recommendations thereon, or (2) as a principal or advisor selects securities for purchase or sale in an investment portfolio to achieve the objectives of the fund, or (3) manages all or part of the organization responsible for those functions.

These functions have been a part of the investment process since the beginning, but they have become increasingly specialized and institutionalized in the postwar period coincident with the expansion of savings intermediaries, increased capital investment in a growing economy, and a rising confidence in common stocks as a medium of investment. These developments stimulated a rapid growth in the emerging profession of financial analysis. Today the typical profile of the financial analyst is that of a relatively young and well-educated man who has moved up in his organization fairly quickly. His mean age is 41 years but 36 percent are under 35. A high educational attainment is indicated by the fact that over 90 percent have college degrees and half have one or more graduate degrees. The average experience in investments is almost 13 years. More than 40 percent of financial analysts have attained a high organizational level—either vice president or above in the corporate sector, or partner in the noncorporate sector. Women have been attracted to the field in recent years, but as yet they number only 5 percent of the total.[1]

The Investment Process

The investment decision process may be thought of as a three-legged stool. One leg is the analysis of the company and its securities and of the industry in which it operates. The second is the assessment of the economic environment which includes the business outlook, financial markets and interest rates, and international trade and finance. The third is the portfolio decision in which these two streams of information are integrated into an investment appraisal related to the objectives of the fund. Portfolio decisions sort out expected rates of return (income and appreciation) relative to risk as the portfolio manager seeks that combination of securities which will produce the highest total return available within the risk constraints established for the fund. In this continual

[1] William C. Norby, *Compensation in Professional Investment Research and Management* (New York: The Financial Analysts Federation, 1972), p. 8. This study was based on a survey of members of the Financial Analysts Federation in October 1971. The federation's membership (13,500 at the time of the survey; about 14,000 at the beginning of 1974) is considered to encompass substantially all financial analysts in the United States and Canada.

winnowing process, investment funds tend to flow toward the most favorably situated companies and industries and away from the weaker and less promising areas. Economic theory tells us that this free market direction of investment capital leads to the most efficient employment of scarce economic resources.

The financial analyst plays a key role in this capital allocation process. As a security analyst he studies and selects industries and companies, interacting with the economist who provides the general economic framework. As a portfolio manager he integrates the work of the economist on the outlook for business and the financial markets with the securities recommendations of the analyst to make portfolio selections. These roles are interdependent; each contributes a necessary element to the investment decision.

Company and Industry Analysis

Subsequent chapters in this book will examine in detail the methodology of analyzing companies and their securities. It is useful here, where we are broadly defining the functions of the financial analyst, to put that methodology in broad perspective. The primary objective of any security analysis is the determination of future earning power because earning power is the source of cash flow to the investor (interest or dividends). Capitalized earning power is the primary basis of wealth. In the long run, the quality of any security rests on earning power and so the essentials of analysis are the same for all types of securities although the areas of emphasis may differ. Investment analysis concentrates largely on common stocks to which the residual earnings accrue and therefore where change and risk are greatest.

The methodology of investment analysis is directed to identifying change and change in the rate of change in the earning power and financial position of a company. A typical analysis begins with a review of the company's history, products, markets, operations, earnings, and financial position. Data for the firm are then related to information about the industry in which it operates, to its competitors within that industry, and to the general economy in order to determine the dynamic relationships between the firm and its environment. Analysis of the individual firm must also encompass management and its decision-making philosophy, marketing capabilities, production facilities, and changes in all of these elements as they have occurred over time.

The many elements of an investment analysis must be summarized and expressed in quantitative terms. Investors generally consider net earnings as the best measure of a company's performance and the indicator of value in most continuing enterprises. The quality of earnings is tested by the concepts of normality (i.e., what a company might earn under normal economic conditions absent strikes, floods, wars, and the like); extraordinary earnings from special nonrecurring events in the company; the trend over a 5- or 10-year period or a succession of business cycles; and stability or variability from year to year around the trend line.

All these facets of earnings add up to the concept of *earning power* which may be defined as the ability of the company to produce continuing earnings from the operating assets of the business over a period of years. It encompasses the foregoing concepts of normality, stability, and growth. It is not fixed but will change with changes in management, the life cycle of industries, and other long-term factors. Investors are constantly on the alert to catch incipient shifts in the direction of earning power, and consequently, even small variations in earnings, depending upon their cause, can have a magnified impact on investor expectations.

This historical record is the basis for an evaluation of management's ability to plan and to take advantage of economic opportunity or defend against economic adversity. It also is the basis for the analyst's estimate of earning power over future periods—one, three, and perhaps five years. The estimating process moves from the general to the particular, starting with the outlook for the economy and the industry. Detailed analysis of new markets, new capital investment, new technology, regulatory changes, price trends, and many other factors follows. Their impact on the company is measured through the financial statements. The analytical conclusion usually is cast in the form of a forecast of earnings, dividends, and financial requirements for the period ahead. In a dynamic economy, the margin of error in such forecasts is bound to be considerable, but nevertheless, investors base their decisions on expectations of the future.

This kind of future-oriented information is not readily available to the analyst in convenient brochures or corporate plans. Much of it must be pieced together from various sources, making inferences based on past experience. Projective information is subject to considerable error and must be checked against other information. Thus the task of the analyst is difficult and strenuous. Ingenuity is required to collect and organize all of this data. Yet these analytical procedures must be repeated many times since the investor is faced with continually shifting investment alternatives. Investment analysis is comparative between companies in the same industry, between different industries, and over time.

Portfolio Management

The methodology of portfolio management lagged behind economic and security analysis as a discipline but in recent years has developed rapidly. If all the portfolio manager had to do was select the companies with the most optimistic earnings projections, his task would be relatively easy. In fact, it is far more complex.

First, he must indeed weigh the evaluations and projections of several security analysts to develop an array of estimated future returns and attendant risks. Individual security analysts are skilled in regard to companies and industries they follow, while the portfolio manager (or perhaps the research director) must integrate these segments into a comparative list of all securities followed.

Second, the portfolio manager must temper the collective outlook for individual companies with macroeconomic factors provided by the economist. This is especially important at turning points in the economic cycle, since impending change is usually perceived in macro factors before it appears in individual companies. Hopefully, the security analyst has also been able to sense economic change and apply it to his estimates, but the portfolio manager (or the chief investment executive in large organizations) must insure that this integration is complete.

Third, the portfolio manager must consider financial markets. There is no simple sequence of earnings changes and market price changes. Various security instruments compete with each other for investment funds—bonds versus stocks, short-term notes versus long-term bonds, or bonds versus mortgages. To some degree, the price of each security is affected by supply and demand within its sector of the market, but the sectors are interconnected so that developments in one sector affect all others. Therefore the portfolio manager must take into account all developments in the financial markets, such as the structure of interest rates, monetary policy, and the volume of new offerings of stocks and bonds.

The portfolio manager may sometimes avail himself of so-called technical analysis. Technical analysis attempts to infer the supply and demand conditions for a stock or for the market as a whole from the pattern of price movements, trading volume, short position, and the like. This is thought to be a more direct approach to predicting price than analysis of the underlying economic and investment factors, but numerous statistical studies indicate that technical analysis does not produce results significantly different from chance. Technical analysis is not usually considered a part of the discipline of investment analysis and management, but because of the widespread interest in the subject, it is discussed in a later chapter in this handbook.

Finally, all of these investment and economic factors must be related to the objectives of the fund and the amount of risk it can accept. The manager selects from the broad array of investment opportunities those securities that are expected to provide the best relative returns (income and appreciation) within the risk constraints, i.e., the acceptable degree of uncertainty of the returns. The decision might be a combination of treasury bills and commercial paper for low return and low risk at one end of the spectrum or common stocks of a diversified list of small, fast growing, high-technology companies for high potential return and high risk at the opposite end of the spectrum. And since these factors are constantly changing, the portfolio manager must monitor the financial markets and investment opportunities to continually optimize portfolio return and risk.

Ancillary Functions of the Financial Analyst

From the foregoing brief sketch we can readily see that the financial analyst—either the security analyst or the portfolio manager—engages in a rigorous and demanding intellectual endeavor in his primary function of allocating investment funds. In the process he serves other important functions tangential to portfolio management.

The security analyst is frequently a reporter and interpreter of corporate financial information to a wider investing public. This is particularly true of analysts with brokerage firms, since their reports are publicly distributed. The security analyst reports on a current basis factual and interpretive corporate information which is frequently more understandable than the company's own reports. Although the analyst's primary responsibility is to his clients rather than to a more general investing public, his reports must be prepared with the same standard for accuracy and completeness of the facts and objectivity of his interpretation that is required for general publication.

The experienced financial analyst has a breadth and depth of comparative knowledge of company finance and financial markets which can make him an especially valuable advisor to corporations on mergers and acquisitions, capital structures, new financing, and valuations. Such work may be performed on a professional fee basis or as a supplementary service to important clients of the firm.

Similarly, experienced investment managers may be retained to consult with large investors on the organization structure for management of their funds, or on the criteria for determination of investment objectives, or on the measurement of investment results. These subjects are appropriate aspects of the broad function of investment management. Both financial analysts and econometricians have contributed to the newly developing disciplines supporting these subjects.

Is Financial Analysis a Professional Discipline?

The complexities of investment decision making as suggested in this brief summary confirm the status of present-day investment research and management as a professional discipline. Yet when we observe the ups and downs of the stock market or the seeming perverse responses of stock prices to company developments, we might well ask whether the net impact of all of this analytical effort on the stock market is any greater than almost 50 years ago, when investment analysis first gained identity as a specialized activity.

In the final analysis, prices of securities, especially common stocks, attempt to discount expected future returns. The future is unknowable, and we can only speculate on the outcome of events based on the best information available. While we attempt to apply rigorous discipline to this speculation, human emotions also play a role in market trends. The two emotions which tend to dominate investors are greed and fear—among the most powerful known to man. As a result of these psychological elements, market prices show wide dispersion around the trend line of value. There would seem to be room for another intellectual discipline in the panoply of investment management, namely the psychology of markets, for we find ever present in financial markets the twin strands of "logical" investment analysis and "illogical" investor emotions.

These twin strands are reflected in the following summary of views of business executives as issuers of corporate reports:

> While security analysts in particular were regarded as the focal point of the financial community audience, their rights to financial information were viewed in sharply differing ways. They were portrayed on the one hand as public servants interpreting business performance for the layman, and on the other as incompetent and ruthless profiteers seeking only to "find a reason to trade." Despite this divergence, managements, on balance, regarded the power of this audience as significant and failure to recognize its needs was seen as shortsighted.[2]

Clearly the profession of financial analysis must aim to further expand and deepen its discipline in the public interest and to submerge illogical emotions and "incompetent and ruthless profiteers."

CAREER PATHS OF FINANCIAL ANALYSTS

The career opportunities open to the financial analyst can be best understood in the context of the institutional structure of investment management. Professional financial analysis occurs almost entirely in an institutional setting. After giving an overview of the institutional framework, the specialized facets of investment research and portfolio management will be described in detail. Finally compensation will be sum-

---

[2] Booz Allen & Hamilton, *The Businessman's View of the Purposes of Financial Reporting* (New York: Financial Executives Research Foundation, 1973), p. 13.

marized. This section is based largely on two studies of the Financial Analysts Federation.[3]

Overview of Institutional Structure of Investment Management

While investment research of some sort has always been an aspect of investment management, the first professional organization did not appear until 1925, when the Investment Analysts Society of Chicago was organized. However, research did not begin to achieve independent stature until the advent of increased corporate disclosure stemming from the Securities Acts of 1933 and 1934, and rapid growth did not begin until after World War II.

Development of investment research has proceeded in tandem at both institutional investors and broker-dealers during the postwar period. The larger investing institutions, such as banks, mutual funds, and advisory firms, were the first to go beyond published reports to visit company managements and do other field work, and to practice industry specialization. Prior to the early 1950 brokerage research was generally limited to elementary statistical comparisons and answering questions; the primary sources were the financial services and an occasional call to company management. Research was neither intensive nor continuous. Specialization by industry was rare, being practiced only by a few investment houses largely, but not entirely, retail oriented.

Starting in the mid-1950s specialized institutional brokerage firms started to appear. These firms covered industries intensively and on a continuing basis and aimed largely at institutional markets. By the early 1960s the universe of brokerage houses doing intensive continuing research had expanded substantially.

Concurrently the research staffs of major investing institutions continued to grow, and more institutions moved into the major size category. The growth in staff was not commensurate with the growth in assets and rising standards of investment performance, however, and so increasing use was made of the greatly expanded institutional research services of broker-dealer firms. The larger institutions utilized broker research to supplement field work by their in-house staffs and also to originate new investment ideas. The expansion of assets, coupled with some increase in turnover, provided ample commission dollars to pay for this research and created incentives for rapid expansion of broker-dealer research.

As institutionalized savings spread more widely through the economy and the acceptability of common stocks continued to grow, many new and smaller investing institutions entered the investment management field. They were able to meet their requirements for basic investment re-

---

[3] Walter P. Stern and William C. Norby, "Investment Research and Market Structure—Today and Tomorrow," *Financial Analysts Journal*, January–February 1972; and Norby, *Compensation in Professional Investment Research*.

search through the services of broker-dealers. Typically the staffs of such organizations consisted of one to a few analysts to digest and check outside research reports, and several portfolio managers. Commission dollars generated by funds under their management were sufficient to acquire the necessary research services from brokers and thereby keep internal overhead costs low.

The "performance era" of 1967–69 lowered research discipline substantially on the part of both brokers and institutions. Many smaller securities houses entered the institutional business by covering new industries, "concept stocks," and a variety of other investment vehicles which grew up in this speculative period. This was facilitated by the great increase in "soft" dollars available as institutional turnover increased rapidly and the spreading use of the "give-up."

As the search for new common stocks spread to smaller companies, some strong regional broker firms perceived an opportunity to provide specialized research of institutional caliber on companies in their region. This service enabled them to develop commission business with institutional investors outside of their region.

The market decline of 1969–70 brought about some change in attitudes of institutional investors. The shake out of performance stocks led them to rely somewhat more on their internal sources, and many institutional investors increased their analytical staffs between 1970 and 1973. Nonetheless they continued to utilize broker research because the commission dollars available were ample. In 1970 there was much shifting of research personnel in the broker-dealer community and probably a net reduction in number, but in 1971, some rebuilding of broker research staffs occurred.

The 1973 market decline and the ensuing financial crisis in the brokerage industry has brought further changes. The consolidation of brokerage firms and the drive to reduce overhead costs have reduced the size and number of research staffs in the brokerage industry. Institutional quality research has been maintained reasonably well, but regional and small company research has been sharply curtailed due to evident lack of investor interest. Research for retail clients has also been curtailed.

To some extent these recent developments are typical of the highly volatile brokerage industry, but they portend a longer run shift in the structure of investment research which cannot yet be fully evaluated.

The market pattern of 1970–73 has also produced shifts in the structure of investment management. Bank trust departments, by far the largest sector of funds under management, regained stature during this period as their investment results were generally more favorable than other types. This reflects their tendency to concentrate on the large capitalization growth companies which performed well in the market, and their efforts to modernize their investment management organizations. Mutual funds as a group experienced continuous net redemptions as their investment results suffered in comparison with market averages. The new small institutional advisory firms seem to have survived for the most part, but the rate of new entrants has dropped. In any case, the size of funds under institutional management today is so large that structural change comes slowly.

Employment and Compensation Profile of Analysts

The overall structure of institutional investment can be described in terms of the membership of the Financial Analysts Federation. The aforementioned survey in late 1971 showed the following:

One third of all members work for broker-dealers and 62 percent for institutional investors such as banks (25 percent), investment counselors, insurance companies, mutual funds, and others.

By function, 43 percent are engaged in research and analysis; 25 percent, in portfolio managment; and 11 percent have executive responsibility for the investment function. The balance are salesmen, economists, and academicians.

About half of all research members are employed by broker-dealers. Research is heavily concentrated in New York, which accounts for 49 percent of all research members.

Portfolio management members are more dispersed. Only 19 percent of portfolio management members work in New York, while about 26 percent are in Boston, Chicago, San Francisco, and Philadelphia. Trust investment accounts for 38 percent of such members, other institutional investors together total 48 percent, while brokers employ only 8 percent.

This profile has probably changed marginally in the last two years but is still broadly representative.

In terms of career paths, the normal progression is from entry as an investment analyst up through research to supervisory responsibilities and director of research. Some analysts may develop substantial seniority

TABLE 1

Age, Experience, and Function (mean years)*

	Age	*Experience*
Analyst	36.3	9.2
Supervising analyst	39.3	12.8
Director of research	41.8	15.2
Portfolio manager	39.5	12.2
Supervisor portfolio management	41.4	14.7
Director portfolio management	45.1	18.3
Chief investment executive	45.5	17.9

* Norby, *Compensation in Professional Investment Research*

as specialists without supervisory responsibilities. Lateral moves may be made from research to portfolio management and then by normal progression to director of portfolio management. Progression is often fairly rapid, and beyond the entry level positions there is not much difference in age or experience in the managerial positions. (See Table 1.)

Structure of Investment Research

Investment research is a fixed cost function and therefore tends to be concentrated in larger institutions and firms. Most large research departments are located in the major financial centers. Almost half of research is performed by brokers whose product is distributed over a more widely dispersed portfolio management function. Brokers are compensated largely by commissions. This arrangement enables institutions to gear their investment management costs more directly to the volume of funds under management and to reduce fixed research costs. This structure of investment research may change if the brokerage industry continues under economic pressure or when fixed minimum commissions are abolished.[4]

Broker investment research covers a broad range of activities designed to provide the investor or portfolio manager with information and ideas for investment decision making. There are probably some 10 to 20 firms which consider themselves "broad service" institutional firms; some 40–50 more specialized firms including regional firms and small firms covering a few industries intensively; and an additional 10 to 20 largely retail houses with a small institutional group.[5]

Many other brokerage firms offer so-called retail research. This is less intensive research drawn largely from secondary sources such as other brokers' reports and statistical services, but supplemented with an occasional company check.

Among institutional investors, many large banks, a few of the large advisory firms and mutual funds, and some of the insurance companies maintain large research staffs although there is somewhat less emphasis on original field work or company contact and more on evaluating the flow of investment information from outside sources. A number of large banks have begun to offer their investment research materials to other institutions for a fee either in cash or deposit balances.

The research staffs of medium and smaller institutional investors rely largely on outside sources for information and confine their efforts to assimilation and evaluation. They will do occasional original research on special situations or important concentrations.

---

[4] Chairman Garrett of the SEC announced the present intention of the SEC to end fixed commissions by April 1975. *Wall Street Journal,* October 4, 1973.

[5] Data as of late 1971. The numbers had declined somewhat by mid-1974.

Most research departments of any size are organized by industry specialties, and many analysts are classified as specialists in one or more industries. It is probable that each major industry grouping has some three to six key analysts, well known in the field, at leading brokers and perhaps one or two at leading institutions. There may be another 20 to 30 industry specialists spread around various brokerage firms and a number of larger institutions. Other analysts are generalists, applying standard research techniques to a variety of companies over a period of time.

No research staff is really large. In the largest institutions, with $4 to $12 billion of funds under management, the number of analysts doing specific industry and company work does not exceed 30 to 40. In organizations with $1 to $3 billion under management, these analysts will number 20 to 25. In medium-sized and smaller organizations, the typical number will be three to seven, and some may rely entirely on outside sources for company and industry information.

Research staffs in broker-dealer firms doing institutional research show a similar size range with the exception of one firm having a larger staff for both institutional and retail research. The SEC Institutional Investor Study showed that research expenses attributable to commission business for all NYSE member firms was only 1.4 percent of all commission expenses. However, the expense ratio for the median institutional firm was 3.3 percent (with some up to 10–15 percent) but only 1.0 percent for the retail firm.[6]

It is evident that broker institutional research now makes an important contribution to the investment management function of institutional investors. The research-for-commission-dollars system is embedded in their costs and operations, although reliance on it varies among institutions, primarily by size.

The intensive specialization of top industry analysts makes it economic for them to work in an organization serving more than one institution. Many institutional users of broker research regard the work of these specialists as excellent. Frequently they allocate commission dollars to these individual analysts rather than to the firm as such and often follow them as they move from one firm to another.

The largest banks, insurance companies, and investment counselors rely on broker research for 5 to 35 percent of their total research input (based on informed judgment since this is hard to quantify). They value broker research for the stimulus of new ideas and the work of particular industry specialists.

Medium-sized organizations of all types, with management responsibility for $250 million to $2 billion of investment funds, may rely on

---

[6] Securities and Exchange Commission, *Institutional Investor Study Report,* 1971, p. 2,265.

broker research for up to 75 percent of total research input. For the smallest organizations, the degree of reliance may be even higher. Most smaller organizations rate broker research a "significant addition."

Specialized research services available on a fee basis provide only a small fraction of research input—typically 5 to 10 percent. Today there are only two independent firms whose principal business is investment research on a cash fee basis. There are a few exceptions where fee services provide up to 50 percent of input with broker research the balance. There are a few isolated cases of cash fee—i.e., "hard dollar"—payments for broker research and also a few cases on nonbroker research for commissions through "soft dollar" conduits, i.e., brokers.

Will the structure of investment research change in the evolving structure of the brokerage industry due to economic pressure and competitive determination of commissions? The FAF study indicated that most broker-dealers would continue to provide present research services in order to maintain industry position. Research is an important marketing tool. Most large institutional investors, especially those acting as fiduciaries, have indicated that, given "best execution," they would continue to allocate business on the basis of research services. Some institutions such as endowment and pension funds and insurance companies might place some business at higher than pure transaction cost as compensation for research. Typically, these are organizations without a large internal staff which pay commissions out of their own resources. Thus there appears to be sufficient common ground in the present hopes or intentions of institutional investors and broker-dealers to warrant supposing that some broker research will continue to be a viable service and that investors will be willing to pay for it through the commission structure. But, until these considerations interact in the marketplace, no confident prediction can be made.

Should there be, contrary to expectation, a sharp curtailment of brokerage research, institutional investors have a combination of alternatives. These alternatives are: purchase of fee services either (1) from present institutional brokers or (2) from new research consulting groups which might be formed or (3) expansion of the internal research staff.

The financial feasibility of these alternatives varies largely by size of institution. Many large and medium-size institutions would have no problem in utilizing these alternatives, assuming that structural changes were phased in over a period of time. A good many smaller institutional investors of all types, which are now heavily dependent on the present broker-research-for-commissions system, might have some difficulty in moving to any of these alternatives, all of which require the displacement of variable costs with fixed costs, a change that is more burdensome for the smaller firm.

The financial analyst would be well advised to understand and follow these possible structural changes in investment research as they may affect his career development.

Structure of Portfolio Management

Most portfolio managers begin their investment careers in investment research and after several years of training move across to portfolio management. In banks and counseling firms where there are many client accounts to manage, the portfolio manager will have 10 to 50 accounts assigned to him depending on their size and complexity. He will have relatively little discretion to deviate from institutional policy. In due course he may supervise several portfolio managers and finally, in large organizations, may become the director of portfolio management or chief investment executive. In these positions, he will be concerned largely with development of policy rather than actual management of accounts.

In such institutional investors as insurance companies there are only one or a few accounts to manage, and portfolio managers will tend to be both policy makers and managers. There will be little of the hierarchal organization necessary to administer a multiplicity of accounts. Consequently over 60 percent of portfolio managers are employed by banks and counseling firms. Brokers also provide portfolio management services and employ over 8 percent of portfolio managers.

Only 19 percent of portfolio managers are located in New York, in contrast to 49 percent of investment analysts. Other concentrations of portfolio managers occur in Boston and Chicago, but otherwise they are more widely dispersed, reflecting the decentralization of investment funds throughout the country.

Compensation

The best information available on compensation in investment research and management is the Financial Analysts Federation (FAF) survey of October 1971. General trends in compensation since then make the actual figures obsolete, but the compensation *structure* can be assumed to be still indicative. The comparative data may be useful to financial analysts in their career planning.

Investment research and management is a highly compensated professional activity. The median salary in 1971 was almost $27,000. Close to one fourth made $40,000 or more and about 15 percent received $50,000 and above. The range was great—from under $10,000 to over $100,000.

There is a wide diversity in compensation by type of employer, functional responsibility, and geographic location. Such factors as age, experience, and education are also present, as in any similar professional group. By type of business, brokerage-investment banking is the most remunerative and trust investment the least, with a spread in median salaries from $33,660 for brokers to $19,700 for bank trust departments. Geographically, New York shows the highest median compensation, but Boston and Chicago also rank relatively high. Investment research and portfolio management are approximately equal at the first two levels, but research is more highly compensated at the director level. Directors of research and New York Stock Exchange supervising analysts show the highest compensation in the entire field with medians of $43,000 and third quartiles of $65,000.

Compensation normally tends to rise with experience and investment management is no exception. Most of the rise takes place in the first 15 years, after which there is a further slight gain and then a leveling off.

PROFESSIONAL ORGANIZATION AND DEVELOPMENT

Individuals engaged in a common pursuit usually find it worthwhile to band together for mutual advantage in the performance of their work and to enhance their status as an occupational group. Financial analysts are no exception. Much thought and organization effort has been invested in establishing financial analysts as a professional body with a public identity.

The analyst interested in his own advancement and concerned for the public recognition of his occupation will find it worthwhile to participate in the activities of the professional organization, which for financal analysis and investment management is the Financial Analysts Federation and its constituent bodies. Since substantially all eligible analysts and most portfolio managers are members, the new analyst entering the profession should be familiar with its structure and activities and how they relate to professionalism.

The Attributes of a Profession

The first attribute of a profession is a common body of knowledge that has an intellectual content which can be mastered only after a period of study. We often use the term "profession" loosely to refer to baseball players, or politicians, or lawyers, or investment managers. Sometimes the term simply means that one is doing something on a full-time basis for pay rather than on a part-time, amateur basis. Sometimes it means that the person excels at the activity and at the same time is knowledgeable as to its structure and techniques.

In regard to investment management or financial analysis, we should use profession in the strict sense as a subject of some difficulty requiring training and study to master. It is often argued that investment management is an art and not a science and that one can be successful without any particular training simply because he has a certain shrewdness or insight. Fortuitous events do play an important role in investment success but certainly one should not hold himself out to serve the public on this basis. And when we speak of something as "art," we usually overlook the fact that the artist has indeed gone through a long period of training and study and has mastered the basic techniques of his art before he undertakes his own self-expression. It is somewhat the same in investment management.

The second attribute of a profession is qualification for entry to practice before the public. The legal qualifications for financial analysis-investment management have been minimal and not subject oriented, in contrast to law, accounting, or medicine for example. Supervising research analysts of New York Stock Exchange member firms are required to be qualified as such and investment advisers must register with the Securities and Exchange Commission. Otherwise anyone can hold himself out to be a financial analyst.

Qualification for entry presumes mastery of the body of knowledge. An individual can give evidence of his mastery of the body of knowledge in various ways. One is through an examination program. However, an examination program by itself is not sufficient in the investment field. Practical experience in research or portfolio management is also desirable to assure thorough training, for not all investment knowledge can be reduced to book learning and examination.

The third important attribute of a profession is a code of ethics and professional conduct which the members understand and apply in the daily conduct of their affairs. As members of a professional group they hold themselves out to the public to follow that code and to be subject to professional discipline for infractions.

A fourth attribute of a profession is service to society above monetary gain; a belief or a goal beyond making a living. In law we think of justice; in medicine, life and health. In investment management and financial analysis, the public service element is more difficult to define since the apparent objective is an increase in personal or institutional wealth. It can be argued that professional financial analysis improves the efficiency of the capital allocation function in the economy by enhancing the quality of judgments which direct savings flows. This is a worthy but abstract goal and it must be conceded that the investment process of necessity will always have an element of speculative gain which seems antithetical to service.

The fifth attribute is public recognition. The public must know about, understand, and respect the profession and the members must live up to the image of the profession. Financial analysis has gained much public recognition in the last 25 years but not yet to the same extent as, say, law or accounting.

Not all of these rigorous requirements for true professional status have been met but in early 1974, after active debate, financial analysts adopted significant measures in furtherance of that objective. These will be explained in the context of the Financial Analysts Federation. Whether the ultimate goal can be attained will be known only in the future but in a larger sense the striving for professional status may be just as important as its achievement. It is in striving for larger goals that we make progress by setting a tone, raising standards, enhancing competance, and expanding knowledge.

The Financial Analysts Federation

The Financial Analysts Federation is an organization of member societies located in 46 cities in the United States and Canada. The Federation is governed by a board of directors and officers elected by delegates appointed by the societies. An analyst can become a regular member in a society if he is engaged in investment research, portfolio management, or certain ancillary functions, and has completed three years experience in these qualifying activities. Some societies admit provisional or junior members upon completion of two years work as an analyst.

There are many important activities that comprise a professional organization—information and service, education, enlargement of the relevant body of knowledge, and promotion of the public interest. Specific activities of the FAF and its constituent societies provide examples of these professional endeavors.

Information and Service. The society meetings and periodic FAF conferences are the principal public forums at which corporate executives report to investors on their progress. Other meetings provide information on industries, or special topics such as the "energy crisis," or new techniques of portfolio management. Over the course of a year these programs provide a vast flow of information to professional investors.

Education. Continuing education is an obligation of every professional because new techniques of analysis and management are constantly appearing. Of course, the nature of the work itself and of many information programs is educational in a sense. Formal programs available to members include an annual seminar in association with the University of Chicago Graduate School of Business, a Canadian seminar in association with the University of Western Ontario, and a workshop for portfolio managers at Harvard Graduate School of Business Administration.

Body of Knowledge. Much of the research and thought is done by individual practitioners and by academicians. Up to this time the Federation has not sponsored major research projects. However its *Financial Analysts Journal* is the leading professional journal in the field and every FAF member receives a subscription. Almost all of the ideas that have become permanent additions to the body of knowledge have appeared in the *Journal* at one time or another.

Promotion of the Public Interest. The public interest is not always easy to identify; inevitably there are many conflicts of interest and divided loyalties in business and finance. One area of the public interest on which investment analysts and managers can agree, regardless of their business affiliation, is full and fair disclosure of corporate information to the investor. This is the primary thrust of the legislation that established the Securities and Exchange Commission.

The efforts of the FAF and of individual analysts have contributed much to the improvement of corporate disclosure. The FAF Corporate Information Committee for many years has evaluated company reports and sought more and better quality information about important aspects of the company's business. Its Financial Accounting Policy Committee has recommended changes in accounting policies to the accounting profession to ensure more accurate measurement of corporate earnings.

Through FAF position papers, the views of financial analysts on corporate disclosure issues are presented to regulatory bodies. In 1973, for example, the Federation recommended to the SEC some guidelines on the definition and disclosure of inside information. This is a subject of great concern to individual analysts as well as to the investing public at large.

In these cases the real interests of professional investment managers and the public at large are the same. This fortunate curcumstance, if effectively articulated by analysts and their organization, can serve to enhance the stature of the profession and give members a greater voice in financial affairs. All benefit when analysts can give thought and consideration to broad questions and speak out with their views.

The FAF Plan for Professional Self-Regulation

In becoming a member of a constituent society, the analyst commits himself to know and follow the Code of Ethics and Standards of Professional Conduct adopted by the society and the Federation. These are reproduced in their entirety in Appendix A and every analyst should be familiar with them.

While analysts as a group have demonstrated exemplary conduct, there have been isolated failures to meet these standards. Enforcement has been the responsibility of the societies rather than the FAF and has been ineffective because it is difficult and burdensome. Consequently, during 1974, the FAF and its member societies actively debated alternative methods of strengthening enforcement proceedures. At its 1974 annual meeting, FAF Delegates adopted a plan for self-regulation of professional conduct on a national basis. The three key features of this plan are:

Enforcement of Standards. Means of effective enforcement of standards of practice and ethics are provided by:

a. a "dual membership" plan by which regular and junior members of electing societies become direct "fellows" and "juniors" of the FAF in addition to being members of the society, and
b. establishment of a national centralized Professional Conduct Committee which will investigate and adjudicate possible violations of standards of professional conduct by fellows and juniors.

Standards of Practice. The "Investment Analysis Standards Board" was established to review continuously the standards of practice and ethics of the profession. It supersedes and greatly expands the work of the Professional Ethics Committee.

Entry Standards. Commencing July 1, 1976, in order to become a regular member of a member society or a Fellow of the FAF, an applicant must have passed Chartered Financial Analysts Examination I. This means that applicants will be required to demonstrate certain minimum professional knowledge before being eligible for membership.[7]

This plan will give the Federation direct responsibility for those individual members who become fellows of the FAF and in due course, by a complex process, these should be substantially all regular members of societies. The staff and resources of the FAF will provide stronger support to the Professional Conduct Committee for disciplinary proceedings. Through the new Standards Board, there will be continuous development of standards of practice in financial analysis. Most important is the establishment of an examination for entry. Thus, the FAF plan marks substantial forward movement toward full public recognition of the profession. It is hoped that the designations of *FAF Fellow* and *Chartered Financial Analyst* will become well known and widely used marks of distinction in the field, and necessary for individual recognition.

Self-regulation has proven difficult in almost all professional fields. The FAF plan does not have the force of law and cannot prohibit an individual from practicing financial analysis—although not as a society member. If, however, public recognition of FAF Fellows and C.F.A.s makes these designations sine qua non for public practice, then society membership will become necessary for entry to the profession and self regulation could work. Should this expectation prove optimistic, then some form of government involvement might become necessary.

---

[7] From letter of E. H. Vaughn Jr., chairman, The Financial Analysts Federation, to the members dated May 15, 1974.

The Institute of Chartered Financial Analysts

After years of debate and discussion within the FAF on professionalism and a professional designation, the Institute of Chartered Financial Analysts was established by the Federation in 1962. Its purpose was to develop an examination program leading to the award of the professional designation of Chartered Financial Analyst or C.F.A. The first C.F.A.s were awarded in 1963 and ten years later over 3,200 analysts held this designation. Another 3,000 were registered in the study program.

The C.F.A. designation connotes high achievement in mastery of the body of knowledge of financial analysis and a commitment to high standards of professional conduct. It is not yet a requirement for public practice, as is a CPA certificate for example, but is a foundation for such legal sanction in the future.

The Institute is now an independent organization within the Financial Analysts Federation. Its principal functions are to administer the examination program and maintain the ethical standards of C.F.A.s. It has a Code of Ethics and Standards of Professional Conduct similar to those of the FAF shown in Appendix A. It also publishes the *C.F.A. Digest*, a quarterly summary of important academic articles on aspects of financial analysis. All C.F.A.s become members of the Institute, and since they already are members of a society, there is a close identity of interest between the FAF and the Institute.

For the new financial analyst the examination program is the key aspect of the Institute of Chartered Financial Analysts. Three examinations, taken at intervals of at least a year, must be passed in order to receive the C.F.A. designation. In addition, the candidate must conform to the Code of Ethics and Standards of Professional Conduct, must be engaged in a qualifying aspect of financial analysis as related to security investment, and (for Examinations II and III) must be a member in good standing of a constituent society. The examinations are given once each year in June and require about 5½ hours each.

Altogether these requirements probably are the most rigorous of any professional designation. They combine comprehensive examinations with a lengthy experience requirement in well-defined activities in financial analysis. The examinations are not easy; failure rates range between 25 percent and 35 percent on each examination. The experience requirement is a practical minimum of five years, which is longer than any other similar professional qualification program and is one of the strengths of the C.F.A. program.

The occupational definitions are carefully applied to insure that the experience is in acceptable aspects of financial analysis and investment management. There are many closely allied activities in the investment business, such as sales or underwriting, which require some degree of analytical ability as well as other skills. However, none of these activities require a consistent application of the techniques of investment research and management, and it is for that reason that these individuals are not considered eligible for the C.F.A. program. There is no question that many of them, with an appropriate study program, might be able to pass the examinations. However, they would not have evidenced the complete commitment to the field of investment research and management or perhaps would not be committed to the C.F.A. ethical standards. Therefore it would not be fair then for them to hold themselves out as professional investment managers along with those who are fully qualified.

The C.F.A. Examinations[8]

The examination program is worth review by the new financial analyst seeking an outline of the fields of study. There are five basic areas: (1) accounting, (2) economics, (3) financial analysis, (4) portfolio management, and (5) ethical standards. Each area is covered in all three examinations, but initial emphasis in Examination I is on principles and techniques. Examination II places more emphasis on analytical use of these techniques; Examination III moves on to policy applications. A schematic outline of the subject matter of the examination program and information on the contents appears in Appendix B.

The Institute has prepared study guides, supplemental readings, and textbook references which together make up a graduate course of study in financial analysis. The serious student will find these materials valuable as he pursues his career in financial analysis.

Financial Analysts on an International Scale

We conclude this chapter with the observation that professional financial analysis and investment management has become worldwide in scope. This development came later abroad than it did in North America, but now analysts societies circle the globe. As capital markets become increasingly international in character, standards of financial analysis and corporate reporting must become more uniform from country to country if investment funds are to flow freely and confidently. The accounting profession has taken initial steps toward international standards, and this movement is bound to accelerate in the next five years.

Financial analysts are developing an organization structure which will enable them to move in the same direction. There is a European Federation of Financial Analysts Societies composed of societies in 10

---

[8] A sample set of C.F.A. examinations is given in Appendix C.

countries. There are active societies in Japan, Australia, and South Africa. A society has been formed in Brazil where there is a newly developing capital market. These analyst organizations are already cooperating on projects such as field trips, and an international congress of analysts' organizations is likely to develop within a few years in concert with the increase in international capital movements.

A financial analyst can take pride in the professional growth of his profession in the past 26 years, but still more exciting opportunities lie ahead!

APPENDIX A: Code of Ethics and Standards of Professional Conduct of the Financial Analysts Federation

CODE OF ETHICS

WHEREAS, the profession of financial analysis has evolved because of the increasing public need for competent, objective and trustworthy advice with regard to investments and financial management; and

WHEREAS, those engaged in this profession have joined together in an organization known as The Financial Analysts Federation; and

WHEREAS, despite a wide diversity of interest among analysts employed by banks, brokers and security dealers, investment advisory organizations, financial relations counselors, insurance companies, investment companies, investment trusts, pension trusts and other institutional investors and corporate bodies, there are nevertheless certain fundamental standards of conduct which should be common to all engaged in the profession of financial analysis and accepted and maintained by them; and

WHEREAS, the members of The Financial Analysts Federation adopted a Code of Ethics and Standards on May 20, 1962, and it is now deemed appropriate to make certain amendments to this Code.

NOW, THEREFORE, the members of The Financial Analysts Federation hereby adopt on October 19, 1969, the following Code of Ethics, and Standards of Professional Conduct:

A financial analyst should conduct himself with integrity and dignity and encourage such conduct by others in the profession.

A financial analyst should act with competence and strive to maintain and improve his competence and that of others in the profession.

A financial analyst should use proper care and exercise independent professional judgment.

STANDARDS OF PROFESSIONAL CONDUCT

1. The financial analyst shall conduct himself and encourage the practice of financial analysis in a manner that shall reflect credit on himself and on the profession. The financial analyst shall have and maintain knowledge of and shall comply strictly with all federal, state and provincial laws as well as with all rules and regulations of any governmental agency governing his activities. The financial analyst also shall comply strictly with the rules and regulations of the stock exchanges and of the National Association of Securities Dealers if he, or his employer, is a member of these organizations.

2. The financial analyst shall ascertain that his employer is aware of the existence and content of the Code of Ethics and of these Standards of Professional Conduct.

3. The financial analyst shall conduct himself in such manner that transactions for his customers, clients, or employer have priority over personal transactions, that personal transactions do not operate adversely to their interests, and that he act with impartiality. Thus, if an analyst has decided to make a recommendation as to the purchase or sale of a security, he shall give his customers, clients, and employer adequate opportunity to act on such recommendation before acting on his own behalf.

4. The financial analyst shall, in addition to the requirements of disclosure required by law and rules and regulations of organizations governing his activities, when making recommendations, disclose to his customers, clients, and employer any material conflict of interest relating to him and any material beneficial ownership of the securities involved which could reasonably be expected to impair his ability to render unbiased and objective advice.

5. The financial analyst shall be objective in his opinions in advising his customers, clients, and employer, and when making a recommendation must have a basis which can be substantiated as reasonable. He must be accurate and complete when reporting facts.

6. The financial analyst shall inform his customers, clients, and employer of compensation arrangements in connection with his services to them which are in addition to compensation from his employer or from the customer or client for such services.

7. The financial analyst shall not pay any consideration to others for recommending his services unless such arrangement has been appropriately disclosed.

8. The financial analyst shall not undertake independent practice for compensation in competition with his employer unless he has received written consent from both his employer and the person for whom he undertakes independent employment.

9. The financial analyst shall not, in the preparation of material for distribution to customers, clients, or the general public, copy or use in substantially the same form material prepared by other persons without acknowledging its use and identifying the name of the author or publisher of such material.

APPENDIX B: The C.F.A. Candidate Study Program*

The Specific content of the C.F.A. study materials and examinations are subject to modifications in order to keep pace with changing emphases and techniques in financial analysis.*

Candidates who have been approved for a particular study program and who have paid the applicable enrollment fee will receive a Study Guide containing a detailed reading list prepared specifically for C.F.A. candidates.

---

* In Canada, examinations for C.F.A. candidates will recognize the differences in regulatory procedures.

Source: The Institute of Chartered Financial Analysts, *C.F.A. Study Programs, 1973–74*, pp. 6–9.

There is no additional charge to such candidates for this material. A limited number of copies is available for purchase by non-candidates.

While the Institute itself does not offer classroom-type courses of instruction, it does assist in the organization of local study groups in conjunction with the C.F.A. Educational Coordinators of local analyst societies and universities. Of special assistance to candidates are the Study Guides, textbooks, and books of readings published periodically by the Institute.

The C.F.A. is awarded to those candidates who have successfully completed the examinations and other requirements established by The Institute of Chartered Financial Analysts. The candidate must pass three examinations: Examination I—Investment Principles; Examination II—Applied Financial Analysis; and Examination III—Investment Management.

The Main objective of the C.F.A. Candidate Study Program and examination series is to assure the investing public, employers, and fellow analysts that a C.F.A. possesses at least the fundamental knowledge necessary to practice his profession. There are seven basic topical areas extending through the study series: Economics, Financial Accounting, Quantitative Techniques, Fixed Income Securities Analysis, Equity Securities Analysis, Portfolio Management, and Professional Standards. The C.F.A. study program necessarily continues to be of an evolutionary nature, reflecting as it does the changing emphasis and techniques of financial analysis and portfolio management in the dynamic economies of the United States and Canada. The logic and objectives of the program may best be illustrated by the following brief review of the seven main subject areas. More specific study guidance to candidates is provided in each of the three Study Guides published annually by the Institute.

The C.F.A. Competency Standards

Although the subject matter and skills needed by a C.F.A. continue to evolve the principal areas and topics to be mastered by C.F.A. candidates are suggested by the topic areas described below and listed in the *General Topical Outline*. The candidate level I study program is designed for the junior analyst, while the program at levels II and III is intended for analysts at progressively more advanced stages of professional development. Consequently, the candidate study program emphasizes the continuity of required subject matter over the three different levels as well as a progression to higher levels of sophistication involving more complex financial problems. In addition, at the progressively more advanced levels, the experienced candidate is expected to deal with an expanded number of topics.

Area One—Economics

Pre-Candidate Requirements. The candidate should be familiar with the basic principles of macroeconomics and the monetary system. The analyst should have minimum knowledge equivalent to one academic year of principles of economics as reflected in an elementary economics textbook. The examination, however, emphasizes practical application of economic concepts rather than abstract economic and monetary theories.

Candidate Level I. The candidate should be familiar with the tools of economic analysis and forecasting and have a perspective of the history of economic and industrial activity and of the structure of money and capital markets. Primary emphasis is placed on the relevance and application of economics to the practice of financial analysis as related to securities investment.

Candidate Level II. The candidate should be able to apply the basic economic techniques and concepts, studied under candidate level I, to an evaluation of the prospects for specific industries and companies. Emphasis is placed on forecasting broad economic forces and understanding their implications for forecasts of interest rates, aggregate corporate earnings, and equity prices.

Candidate Level III. At this level, the candidate should be able to interpret economic conditions, government policies and actions and their effects on growth, inflation, and employment. The analyst is expected to understand the implications of these policies and conditions and to relate them to the conduct of a penetrating analysis of aggregate corporate earnings, of earnings trends in specific industries and companies, of interest rates, and of security prices. This analysis should be used to formulate investment policy decisions.

Area Two—Financial Accounting

Pre-Candidate Requirements. The candidate should understand the basic principles of accounting equivalent to at least one year of college level accounting.

Candidate Level I. A candidate should be able to apply accounting principles and techniques to basic financial analysis. Emphasis is placed on skill in using published accounting data, including corporate financial statements and reports, in a meaningful analysis of the firm.

Candidate Level II. The candidate should have a sufficiently thorough understanding of financial accounting, including such complex areas of accounting as mergers, acquisitions, asset valuation, and pension plans, to interpret financial statements for use in the proper evaluation of companies and securities. Candidates are expected to be familiar with current opinions and decisions of the FASB, AICPA, and regulatory authorities.

Candidate Level III. In addition to the knowledge required at levels I and II, the candidate is expected to be able to relate accounting data to the investment decision-making process with emphasis on portfolio management.

Area Three—Quantitative Techniques

Pre-Candidate Requirements. It is assumed that the candidate has some knowledge of elementary statistics and basic mathematics.

Candidate Level I. The candidate should have a sufficient understanding of elementary statistics, mathematics of finance, and probability theory to be able to work with statistical data and apply a knowledge of statistical techniques to basic problems in finance and in financial analysis.

Candidate Level II. In addition to the knowledge at level I, a candidate is expected to be familiar with more advanced techniques such as hypothesis testing, and simple and multiple regression and correlation analysis, and to be able to apply these techniques to problems of financial projections, portfolio analysis, and security valuation and risk.

Candidate III. At this further advanced level, the candidate is expected to understand the application of more sophisticated statistical techniques and systems to problems in financial analysis, capital markets, and portfolio selection.

Area Four—Fixed-Income Securities

Pre-Candidate Requirements. The candidate is assumed to have the equivalent of at least two years of college exposure to business administration, including business finance, corporate financial analysis, and either money and banking or money and capital markets.

Candidate Level I. The candidate is expected to be able to analyze and understand the basic features and characteristics of various fixed-income securities, such as preferred stocks, corporate bonds, and national and local government bonds, including convertible securities. The analyst should be able to determine the basic investment quality and value of such securities in terms of yield and exposure to the risk of corporate illiquidity and insolvency. The candidate should understand the basic nature and cause of bond price fluctuations and the exposure of fixed income securities to interest rate risk and purchasing power risk.

Candidate Level II. At this level, the candidate should have an understanding of the financial and investment implications of all of the usual elements and characteristics commonly present in fixed income securities. The candidate is expected to be able to conduct a penetrating analysis of government and corporate issuers and of the major types of fixed income securities. In the selection of such securities, the analyst should understand the implications of the interest rate structure or yield spreads, and of the term structure of interest rates or yield curve. The candidate should be able to analyze bond swaps and problems of marketability.

Candidate Level III. In addition to the knowledge required at levels I and II, emphasis at this level is placed on the management of fixed income securities in a portfolio situation and their suitability to objectives and constraints of different investors under changing economic and market conditions.

Area Five—Equity Securities Analysis

Pre-Candidate Requirements. The prerequisite requirements for the candidate correspond to those under Area Four, above.

Candidate Level I. The candidate should have the ability to conduct a relatively basic appraisal and evaluation of industries and companies from a financial and investment point of view. The analyst should be able to understand and interpret ordinary types of financial data and demonstrate an ability to appraise the risks and values of common stocks, warrants, rights, and options.

Candidate Level II. Emphasis is placed on a rigorous and complete appraisal and evaluation of industries, companies and their common stocks with respect to their current position and outlook, and on an appreciation of the investment implications of such an analysis for different investors. The candidate should be able to apply the techniques of security analysis including quantitative measures for valuation and risk, and the analyst should have an appreciation of controversial issues in capital market theory.

Candidate Level III. In addition to the requirements at prior levels, emphasis is placed on the analysis and selection of equities consistent with the financial circumstances of different types of individual and institutional investors and consistent with changing economic and market environments.

Area Six—Portfolio Management

Pre-Candidate Requirements. Because the task of portfolio and investment management involves to a considerable extent the integration of economics, financial accounting, quantitative techniques, and security analysis, the pre-candidate requirements for this area are the same as those for the five areas previously specified.

Candidate Level I. The candidate is expected to understand the basic financial circumstances of different individual and institutional investors, to be able to formulate appropriate fundamental portfolio account objectives and constraints and to be able to select specific investment instruments that are suitable for such portfolios.

Candidate Level II. The candidate should, at this level, be able to construct portfolios and to formulate portfolio strategies based on the candidate's analysis of the outlook of the economy and of conditions in the securities markets. Emphasis is placed on security selection, concepts of diversification, risk, return, and modern portfolio and capital market theory.

Candidate Level III. Based on knowledge gained at previous levels and in the other topical areas, the candidate is expected to interrelate economic and market conditions, securities analysis, analysis of the requirements of individual and institutional investors, and portfolio concepts, and be able to develop suitable investment policies and construct appropriate portfolios. The candidate should have an understanding of the investment management process including how to organize and implement the security analysis and portfolio management effort and how to evaluate the results.

Area Seven—Ethical and Professional Standards

Pre-Candidate Requirements. Candidates are required to show evidence of sound character and to agree, in writing, to abide by the I.C.F.A. Code of Ethics, Standards of Professional Conduct, and related rules at the time of candidate registration. Character references are an integral part of the registration requirement. Violations of professional standards may cause suspension from the candidate program or revocation of the charter.

Candidate Level I. The candidate should be familiar with ethical and professional standards and security laws and regulations and be able to deal

The C.F.A. Candidate Study Program—General Topical Outlines

Candidate Level
I II III

ECONOMICS

Tools of analysis and forecasting:
- —National income accounts
- —Flow of funds and money supply indicators
- —Input-output analysis
- —Leading indicators

Historical and structural perspective:
- —Economic trends and cycles
- —Flow of funds and relationship to national income accounts
- —Economic price indexes
- —Aggregate profit trends by types
- —Trends and cycles in stock prices and interest rates

Forecasting broad economic forces:
- —Quantitative and qualitative aspects of forecasts
- —Implications for forecasts of:
  - interest rates and the structure of interest rates
  - corporate profits and earnings of stock price indexes
  - aggregate equity price indexes
  - industry and company prospects

Economic policy:
- —Government policies and actions regarding:
  - growth, inflation and employment
  - monetary and fiscal policies
  - social goals
  - antitrust and industry regulation
  - international policy, including balance of payments
- —Implications of policy decisions for:
  - profit outlook
  - interest rates
  - equity prices
  - industry and company analysis

Candidate Level
I II III

FINANCIAL ACCOUNTING

Principles and construction of accounting statements:
- —Income statements
- —Balance sheets
- —Sources and uses of funds

Content and usefulness of accounting reports to regulatory agencies

Financial analysis of accounting statements:
- —Adjustments for comparability
- —Ratio analysis
- —Adjustments for subsidiaries, affiliates and foreign operations
- —Stock splits and dividends
- —Rights, warrants and convertible securities
- —Effect of price level changes

Areas of judgment:
- —Inventories
- —Depreciation
- —Tax treatment
- —Intangibles
- —Consolidation
- —Acquisitions and mergers
- —Deferred assets and liabilities
- —Off balance sheet financing
- —Pension plans

Current accounting principles and practices:
- —AICPA and FASB opinions
- —Regulatory decisions

The C.F.A. Candidate Study Program—*Continued*

Candidate Level
I II III

APPLICATION OF QUANTITATIVE TECHNIQUES

Elementary statistics:
—Averages and measures of dispersion
Mathematics of finance:
—Compound growth
—Present value of stocks and bonds
—Performance measurement techniques
Probability theory:
—Expected values
—Strategies
Hypothesis testing:
—Sample testing and confidence limits
—Analysis of variance
Simple and multiple regression and correlation
Matrix algebra
Mathematical programming in portfolio theory
Applications of computer systems to financial analysis

TECHNIQUES OF ANALYSIS—FIXED INCOME SECURITIES

Classification of fixed income securities:
—By issuer
—By maturity, if any
—By security
—By contractual obligation
—By tax status
—Convertible features, if any
Special characteristics:
—Call features
—Sinking fund provisions
—Security
—Protective covenants
—Taxable features
Fixed income security selection and management:
—Quality ratings
—Interest or preferred dividend coverage, past and future
—Coupon and maturity
—New issues, discount and premium bonds
—The yield curve and interest rate structure
—Marketability
—Bond swaps

Candidate Level
I II III

TECHNIQUES OF ANALYSIS—EQUITY SECURITIES

Sources of information

Financial instruments:
—Stocks, warrants, rights, options

Industry appraisal and evaluation:
—Interindustry competition, supply-demand, product prices, costs and profits
—Security market evaluation of profits, historical and projected

Company appraisal and evaluation:
—Sales volume, product prices, product research, intraindustry competition
—Ratio analysis-balance sheet and income statement and analysis of corporate profitability, liquidity, solvency, operating and financial leverage
—Management appraisal
—Earnings and dividend evaluation and projection, near and long-term
—Valuation techniques-long and short-term:
discounted cash flow
earnings multiplies, absolute and relative
growth stock valuation
—Risk analysis-quantitative and qualitative
—Efficient capital market hypothesis

The C.F.A. Candidate Study Program—*Continued*

Objective of Analysis—Portfolio Management

Topic	Candidate Level I	II	III
Investor Objectives and constraints: —Individuals —Institutions: investment companies foundations and endowment funds pension funds and profit sharing plans trust funds property and liability insurance companies life insurance companies commercial banks	X	X	X
Portfolio strategy and construction —Policy inputs: assumptions regarding the short and long-term outlook for the economy and the securities markets types of investments to be used regarding quality, liquidity, risk and other characteristics portfolio diversification by type of investment and diversification by industry		X	X
—Account objectives and constraints: specific definition of objectives, e.g., risk and return, liquidity requirements, legal and regulatory constraints the time horizon for the investment aggressive and speculative properties —Investment selection: selection of specific investments suitable for objectives comparative evaluation of alternative investments	X	X	X
—Modern portfolio theory and the construction of "efficient portfolios"		X	X
—Tax planning —Execution of purchases and sales —Evaluation of account performance			X

Conduct of Analysis—Ethical and Professional Standards, Securities Laws and Regulations

Topic	Candidate Level I	II	III
Ethical standards and professional responsibilities: —Public —Customers and clients —Employers —Associates —Other analysts —Corporate management —Other sources of information treatment of ethical issues: —Identification of ethical problems	X	X	X
—Administration of ethical policies —Changing structure of financial markets and the participants therein and the consequent development of new ethical issues			X
Security laws and regulations: —Nature and applicability of fiduciary standards —Pertinent laws and regulations —Treatment of insider information	X	X	X

with these standards as they pertain to his responsibilities with the public, clients, employer, his fellow analysts, and corporate management.

Candidate Level II. The candidate should be able to identify poor professional practices and violations of standards in a variety of areas, including conflicts of interest and use of insider information, and to understand appropriate corrective actions.

Candidate Level III. The candidate should understand how to administer a program of professional and ethical standards within an organization in terms of internal disciplinary controls and of compliance with the I.C.F.A. standards and rules and security laws and regulations. The candidate should understand the full meaning of the public interest, professionalism of financial analysts, and ethical issues associated with changes in the financial system.

Eligibility Requirements for C.F.A. Candidates

C.F.A. Candidate Level I

Education: A candidate should have a bachelor's degree from an accredited academic institution. In the absence of a degree, other educational training or work experience may be accepted for C.F.A. candidacy. The candidate must submit credentials in proper form evidencing his education.

Occupation and Experience: In order to qualify for this examination, the candidate must be currently and primarily engaged in the occupation of financial analysis as related to securities investment as outlined on page 15 and must have completed *at least* one year of experience in one or more of these occupational categories by the end of the calendar year preceding the year in which the examination is to be taken.

C.F.A. Candidate Level II

Occupation and Experience: In order to qualify for this examination, the candidate must be currently and primarily engaged in the occupation of financial analysis as related to securities investment as outlined on page 15 and must have completed *at least* three years of experience in one or more of these occupational categories by the end of the calendar year preceding the year in which the examination is to be taken.

Society Membership: A candidate must be a member in good standing of a constituent society of The Financial Analysts Federation. Membership in a constituent society must be obtained by April 15 of the year in which the examination is to be taken.

C.F.A. Candidate Level III

Occupation and Experience: In order to qualify for this examination, the candidate must be currently and primarily engaged in the occupation of financial analysis as related to securities investment as outlined on page 15 and must have completed *at least* five years of experience in one or more of these occupational categories by the end of the calendar year preceding the year in which the examination is to be taken.

Society Membership: A candidate must be a member in good standing of a constituent society of The Financial Analysts Federation.

C.F.A. Occupation and Experience Requirement

A candidate for the C.F.A. designation must be currently and primarily engaged in the occupation of financial analysis *as related to securities investment.* This statement is sufficiently comprehensive to include the following occupational categories:

a. A person who is engaged in financial analysis as related to securities investment for a bank, insurance company, investment counsel firm, investment company, securities firm, financial publishing house, or other similar organization.
b. A person occupying the position of professor (including assistant and associate professors) or dean of a college or university who is currently teaching or conducting research in the field of securities investment.
c. A person engaged as an economist in the field of financial analysis as related to securities investment.
d. A person who is engaged in portfolio management.
e. A person who is engaged in financial analysis as related to securities investment for a public agency.
f. A person who is engaged in financial analysis as related to securities investment for a corporate pension, profit sharing, or similar fund.
g. A person who previously would have qualified for candidacy as a financial analysts or portfolio manager, but is curently engaged in the professional supervision of financial analysts or portfolio managers as related to securities investment.

Change in Employment Status

In order to meet the occupational requirement for C.F.A. candidacy, it shall be the responsibility of a C.F.A. candidate to notify the Institute immediately of any change or termination in his company affiliation or position, *giving the details of the duties involved in the new position.* The candidate should include the *date* on which he terminated his previous employment and the effective *date* of his new affiliation.

Ethical Standards

The professional conduct, of a candidate must conform to the Institute's *Code of Ethics* and *Standards of Professional Conduct.* The Institute will obtain confidential reports on each candidate.

APPENDIX C: Recent I.C.F.A. Examinations

C. F. A.
Examination I
Section 1

THE INSTITUTE OF CHARTERED FINANCIAL ANALYSTS

C. F. A.
EXAMINATION I

(June 9, 1973)

SECTION 1

9:45 A.M. – 12:00 P.M.

There are five questions in this section of the examination. The weighting used to grade each question is equal to the amount of time allocated to answering each question.

The time allocated for answering each question is:

Questions	Minutes
1	60
2	20
3	25
4	15
5	15
Total	135

INSTRUCTIONS TO CANDIDATES

1. All questions must be answered.
2. Write legibly and in ink.
3. Begin each question on a new page.
4. Write your identification number in the two spaces indicated on the front cover of your answer book. Fill in the other required information on the cover of your answer book.

I-1-2

1. Zeller's Limited and Metropolitan Stores of Canada Limited are two medium-sized department and variety store chains which operate across Canada. Table I below shows the net sales of each of these companies, the value of retail trade and Canadian Disposable Personal Income.

   (a) Based solely on the data in Table I, **characterize** the growth and stability of retail sales, the value of retail trade, and the relative position of Zeller's and Metropolitan in the Canadian retail industry. **Illustrate** your conclusions numerically by using 1962, 1966, and 1971 statistics.

   (15 minutes)

TABLE I

Year	Net Sales* (Current $ in Millions) Zeller's	Metropolitan	Canadian Value of Retail Trade** ($ Billion)	Canadian Disposable Personal Income ($ Billion)
1971	201.4	75.7	30.6	58.9
1970	176.6	69.0	28.0	53.6
1969	157.6	64.7	27.3	50.5
1968	142.9	60.7	25.4	46.4
1967	132.7	50.0	23.8	41.7
1966	117.2	37.7	22.4	38.6
1965	102.8	32.7	21.0	35.0
1964	86.0	28.8	20.1	31.6
1963	74.0	25.9	18.8	29.9
1962	68.8	23.2	17.9	28.1
1960	--	--	16.5	24.8
1955	--	--	13.1	18.2

*Fiscal years end January 31 of the following calendar year.

**Includes automobile sales at retail.

Zeller's Limited, directly and through subsidiaries, operates a chain of department and variety stores across Canada and offers credit facilities to its customers. In mid-1972, there were 62 suburban department stores and 84 variety stores in operation. W. T. Grant Co. owns 50% of the company's common stock and thus Zeller's has access to the experience of Grant in matters of real estate, store development and general administration. The company added eleven new department stores in the 1972-73 fiscal year and the same number is expected to be opened in the 1973-74 fiscal year. Variety store operations are being phased out. The merchandise sold ranges from high-turnover variety items to clothing, camper trailers and camping supplies, floor coverings, major appliances, home entertainment units, cameras, sporting goods, and home furnishings. In addition, auto service bays, food service, beauty salons, etc., are offered.

I-1-3

Metropolitan Stores of Canada Limited, directly and through subsidiaries, operates a chain of 171 variety and junior department stores in all provinces of Canada. At January 31, 1973, there were 171 stores in operation, with twenty stores opened February 1, 1972 through January 31, 1973. An aggressive expansion program is planned for future years. The more important merchandise handled includes textiles, ladies dresses, infants wear, sports wear, mens' and boys' wear, notions, toys, toiletry and crockery items. Restaurants and bakeries operated at many locations.

Both companies write-off store opening expenses as incurred.

(b) Using the information below and in Table II, on the following page, compare the progress of the two companies from 1962 to 1972 and their respective positions at January 31, 1972.

(25 minutes)

The following paragraph summarizes the appraisal of the retail store industry by a prominent Canadian research-oriented brokerage house early in 1973:

> In 1972, we estimate that total retail sales, excluding autos and fuel oil sales, were up 11%. This compares with the annual average increase from 1967-72 of only 7.7% . . . . Our estimate of a 9½% increase in retail trade in 1973, excluding autos and fuel, is a very bouyant one and above the five year average gain. Our estimate assumes a decrease in the rate of personal savings, which was extremely high last year, and some further stimulus to the economy by the federal government to combat the high level of unemployment . . . .
>
> The expected continued growth in the merchandising sector in 1973 will help minimize the adverse effect that some investors have been anticipating from the rapid store expansion programs being undertaken by many of the major retailing companies . . . . We do not feel that overstoring is going to be a universal problem though some areas of the country may periodically experience some overstoring. Probably a more difficult obstacle to overcome will be rising costs, particularly labor costs. This factor, combined with a continuing price awareness by the consumer, may tend to further enhance the price advantages that genuine discounters are able to offer consumers . . . .
>
> The merchandising sector has been popular with investors for almost two years now and as a result, multiples are generally high reflecting investors anticipation of the good results that 1972 is expected to provide, particularly in the fourth quarter. The earnings outlook for most companies continues to be favorable in 1973, but it is unlikely that these prospects will stimulate upward multiple revision for this group generally. The long-term economic outlook to the mid-1970's for merchandisers is attractive considering the forecasts produced by the Economic Council of Canada; thus the earnings multiples for this group are probably quite realistic for the longer-term view . . . . We do not feel that this is the time for portfolios to move out of the merchandising field as their outlook over the next two or three years continues to be favorable.

(Question 1 continues on next page)

I-1-4

TABLE II

Zeller's Limited vs. Metropolitan Stores

Year (1)	Earned on Net Worth Zel %	Met %	Oper. Profit Margin Zel %	Met %	Asset Turnover Zel X	Met X	Total Debt: Net Worth Zel %	Met %	Current Ratio Zel X	Met X	Acid Test Ratio Zel X	Met X	Sales per Store ($ Million) Zel $	Met $
1973	-	-	-	-	-	-	-	-	-	-	-	-	-	-
1972	-	-	-	-	-	-	-	-	-	-	-	-	-	-
1971	15.7	13.1	8.2	8.0	2.1	2.2	88.8	57.2	3.5	2.0	1.9	.3	1.47	.48
1970	16.6	11.1	9.4	5.7	2.1	2.0	82.3	75.9	2.5	1.7	1.3	.4	1.37	.44
1969	16.5	11.1	9.7	6.9	2.2	2.0	72.1	79.5	3.1	1.6	1.9	.3	1.32	.40
1968	17.0	12.0	9.9	7.6	2.1	1.9	79.5	88.0	3.0	1.5	1.8	.3	1.20	.39
1967	18.1	12.5	10.3	8.0	2.3	1.7	73.3	89.0	3.7	1.5	2.2	.3	1.19	.34
1966	16.3	10.1	8.8	7.8	2.2	1.8	76.7	90.9	4.0	2.0	2.3	.2	1.07	.29
1965	15.9	10.4	8.8	7.8	2.3	1.6	67.1	100.6	3.0	2.0	1.7	.2	.97	.26
1964	12.7	8.7	7.7	7.1	2.3	1.5	55.0	112.5	4.2	1.9	2.3	.1	.84	.25
1963	9.6	8.0	6.1	6.9	2.2	1.4	54.4	102.3	4.6	2.4	2.4	.2	.74	.23
1962	8.9	7.7	5.7	7.5	2.1	1.4	54.0	103.7	4.9	2.6	2.4	.3	.69	.21
1961	9.1	4.2	5.8	4.8	2.2	1.4	38.0	107.7	3.1	3.0	1.4	.4	.67	.24

Year (1)	Sales per Share Zel $	Met $	Earnings per Share Zel $	Met $	Dividends per Share Zel $	Met $	Payout Ratio Zel %	Met %	Price/Earn. Ratio Zel X	Met X	Div. Yield on Common Zel %	Met %
1973 e	-	-	.96	1.60	.35	.28	36.5	17.5	-	-	-	-
1972 e	-	-	.81	1.30	.30	.24	37.0	18.5	20.4	15.8	2.1	1.5
1971	15.86	29.58	.61	1.00	.28	.10	45.9	10.0	26.7	14.9	1.7	0.7
1970	13.94	26.96	.59	.73	.26	Nil	44.0	Nil	18.6	12.0	2.4	Nil
1969	12.47	25.27	.53	.65	.24	"	45.3	"	25.3	20.8	1.8	"
1968	11.36	23.71	.50	.65	.22	"	44.0	"	26.3	23.0	1.7	"
1967	10.53	19.55	.48	.54	.18	"	36.5	"	17.9	16.1	2.0	"
1966	9.48	14.75	.37	.45	.15	"	40.5	"	17.4	11.6	2.3	"
1965	8.38	12.77	.33	.33	.13	"	37.9	"	14.9	11.3	2.5	"
1964	7.07	11.24	.23	.24	.10	"	43.5	"	13.1	13.1	3.3	"
1963	6.12	10.14	.15	.21	.09	"	58.0	"	14.7	12.7	3.9	"
1962	5.71	9.06	.13	.18	.09	"	66.9	"	15.7	15.1	4.3	"
1961	5.23	9.32	.13	.03	.09	"	66.9	"	18.5	18.6	3.6	"

COMPOUND GROWTH RATES

Years (1)	Sales Per Share Common Zel	Met	Earnings per Share Common Zel	Met	Dividends per Share Common Zel	Met
1961-71	11.7%	12.2%	16.7%	42.0%	12.0%	N.A.
1964-71	12.2%	14.8%	15.1%	22.6%	15.7%	N.A.
1968-71	11.7%	7.6%	7.0%	15.4%	8.3%	N.A.

(1) Fiscal years end January 31 of the following calendar year
e - Estimates
N.A. - Not applicable

I-1-5

(c) As the manager of a medium-sized pension fund, you are planning to make a new commitment of up to $250,000 in the Canadian department store industry. Early in January, 1973, you are considering the stocks of these two companies. There is room for one—but not both—of these stocks. Price data is as follows:

Market Close	Zeller's	Metropolitan
1/19/73	19½	25¾
Range of Market		
Year 1972	20-13	25-16

Based on the information supplied in (a), (b), and (c) above, state which of the two stocks you would have selected for inclusion in the portfolio of January 31, 1973. Explain. (Ignore interest equalization tax in this problem.)

(20 minutes)

2. Ed Updike has been an analyst for two years in a medium-sized brokerage firm. The firm derives its business primarily from retail accounts but is now making an effort to gain institutional clients. He has completed a review of ABC Corporation, a small company in one of the industries he follows, and is reporting to his supervisor and research manager, Mr. Owens. In his verbal report, Updike has concluded that there is little likelihood of future improvement in ABC's record of below-average sales and earnings growth within its industry, and that ABC's stock is unattractive as an investment. The stock has been strong recently.

Owens tells Updike that his conclusion regarding the continued slow sales growth is incorrect. Owens' argument rests on his knowledge that one of ABC's new product development projects has been successful. Owens cites another brokerage firm's recent buy recommendation as the source of that information. The meeting ends with Owens asking Updike to read that recommendation and then to prepare his own buy recommendation on ABC stock.

(a) Identify those provisions of the *C.F.A. Code of Ethics* and *Standards of Professional Conduct* which are pertinent to this situation.

(8 minutes)

(b) Based on your answer in (a) above, state what action Updike should take on Owens' request. Explain your reasons.

(12 minutes)

(Please Turn Page)

I-1-6

3. Company A's common stock had a market value of $72.00 immediately prior to the announcement of a merger with Company B. There were 6,100,000 shares outstanding and earnings just reported were $3.50 per share.

Company B had 800,000 shares of common stock outstanding. Immediately prior to the merger announcement, its stock sold at 10 times most recent earnings per share.

Company A acquired Company B on a pooling of interests basis with Company A being the surviving corporation. Company A exchanges one share of its stock for three shares of B's stock. The exchange ratio was determined solely on the basis of the market prices of the two stocks immediately prior to the merger announcement.

(a) **Calculate** the per share earnings of Company A after the merger.

(20 minutes)

(b) Based on your calculation in (a) for Company A, **explain** why post-merger EPS for Company A differs from its pre-merger EPS.

(5 minutes)

4. The following tabulation gives pertinent data on the bonds of two electric utility companies early in January, 1973. Both of these bonds are rated Aa by Moody's. The yield to maturity for Moody's Aa-rated Utility Bond Index was 7.40% at this time.

Bond No. 1 - Toledo Edison - First 9s of 11/1/2000

Bond No. 2 - Pacific Gas and Electric - First 4 1/4s of 6/1/1995

	Bond No. 1	Bond No. 2
Current Price	110 1/4	68
First Call Date	11/1/75	Currently callable
Call Price	107.33	103.39
Yield to First Call Date	7.36%	Not applicable
Yield to Maturity	8.07%	7.12%

Discuss the price fluctuations of these two bonds if the interest rate on Moody's Aa-rated utility bonds:

(a) Decreases to 6.40%.

(b) Increases to 8.40%.

(15 minutes)

I-1-7

5. Corporate management has considerable freedom of action in selecting from generally acceptable accounting procedures that have a material effect on reported results. **List 5** such procedures relating to different areas of accounting, and **explain** in a sentence or two how each might be used to report higher current earnings per share.

(15 minutes)

END OF SECTION 1

C. F. A.
Examination I
Section 2

THE INSTITUTE OF CHARTERED FINANCIAL ANALYSTS

C. F. A.
EXAMINATION I

(June 9, 1973)

SECTION 2

1:45 P.M. – 4:45 P.M.

There are six questions in this section of the examination. The weighting used to grade each question is equal to the amount of time allocated to answering each question.

The time allocated for answering each question is:

Questions	Minutes
1	20
2	25
3	20
4	30
5	35
6	50
Total	180

INSTRUCTIONS TO CANDIDATES

1. All questions must be answered.

2. Write legibly and in ink.

3. Begin each question on a new page.

4. Write your identification number in the two spaces indicated on the front cover of your answer book. Fill in the other required information on the cover of your answer book.

I-2-2

1. A linear regression study was made using a sample of 72 common stocks over an eight year period. The following variables and equations were used:

   The dependent variable Y = the annual rate of return (market price change and dividends) for each stock.

   The independent variable X = the annual growth rate in earnings per share for each stock.

$$Y = a + bX$$

The results of the study produced these findings:

The intercept $\underline{a} = 0.05$

The slope $\underline{b} = 1.17$

The standard error of estimate $S_{y.x} = 0.08$

The coefficient of correlation $r = 0.67$

The coefficient of determination $R^2 = 0.45$

The average annual rate of return for the average stock in the group was 0.12 (12%).

(a) Describe the relationship which existed between rate of return and the growth rate of EPS for this 72 stock sample.

(10 minutes)

(b) State how well this equation explains the relationship between rate of return and growth of EPS for this sample. Discuss in statistical terms.

(10 minutes)

2. The United States International Balance of Payments has deteriorated in the last decade.

(a) List the major factors contributing to the declining strength of the dollar.

(10 minutes)

(b) Beginning in 1971, discuss briefly the changes which have been made in the effort to reverse the adverse trend in the U. S. Balance of Payments.

(15 minutes)

I-2-3

3. Following are financial data for three corporations. Select the most attractive investment under stated assumptions. Dividend payout ratios and P/E ratios will remain constant. The growth rate in earnings per share from 1967 through 1972 is presumed to continue indefinitely. Investor's required rate of return is adjusted for the different risk characteristics of each security. Show all calculations.

	Albemarle Co.		Nelson Co.		Orange Co.	
	1967	1972	1967	1972	1967	1972
Earnings per share	$2.00	$ 2.94	$2.30	$ 3.70	$1.20	$ 2.10
Current market price		40.00		60.00		40.00
Current dividend rate		1.60		1.80		1.00
Investor's required rate of return		10%		12%		14%

Compound Sum of $1 for N Years

Year	6%	7%	8%	9%	10%	12%	14%	16%
4	1.26	1.31	1.36	1.41	1.46	1.57	1.69	1.81
5	1.34	1.40	1.47	1.54	1.61	1.76	1.93	2.01
6	1.42	1.50	1.59	1.68	1.77	1.97	2.20	2.44

Compound Sum of an Annuity of $1 for N Years

Year	6%	7%	8%	9%	10%	12%	14%	16%
4	4.64	4.75	4.87	4.99	5.11	5.35	5.61	5.88
5	5.98	6.15	6.34	6.52	6.72	7.12	7.54	7.98
6	7.39	7.65	7.92	8.20	8.49	9.09	9.73	10.41

(20 minutes)

(Please Turn Page)

I-2-4

4. Based on the information below, **outline** and **explain** briefly your recommendations as an investment counselor in each of the following cases. Also, **list** what additional information you would like to have.

    (a) Mr. Adams, aged 40, with a wife and two teen-age children, approaches you with the following questions:

    "I have been investing in stocks for the past ten years. Recently I've been having doubts about placing all of my investment funds there. I have about $100,000 in stocks and own my home. I am gainfully employed. What do you suggest about bonds as an investment vehicle?"

    (15 minutes)

    (b) A recently divorced woman, age 32, with one child seven years old teaches technical writing at a large university. The university has a retirement program and a group insurance program covering life insurance, basic medical and major medical expenses. She participates in both of these programs. In the divorce settlement, she was awarded the home and furnishings worth $50,000 and cash of $30,000. In addition, the husband was required to pay her a total of $50,000 in installments of $4,000 per year for the first five years and $3,000 a year for the following ten years. She can live on her salary. She does not understand investments, but she wishes to invest aggressively.

    (15 minutes)

5. Badger Company is being organized to manufacture and sell a product which is produced on machines each having an installed cost of $300, a life of three years, and zero salvage value. Pre-depreciation pre-tax income from each machine is $200 per year. The company plans to install one machine each year in the first three years but none thereafter. The effective tax rate on income is fifty percent.

    The company is considering different methods for the treatment of depreciation expense and income accrual in reporting to stockholders. The data in Table I show results using straight-line depreciation, and Table II shows results using sum-of-the-year's digits depreciation.

I-2-5

Table I
Straight-Line Depreciation

	Year 1	2	3	4	5
Pre-depreciation pre-tax income	200	400	600	400	200
Depreciation expense:					
Machine No. 1	100	100	100		
Machine No. 2	-	100	100	100	
Machine No. 3	-	-	100	100	100
Total Depreciation Expense	100	200	300	200	100
Pre-tax income	100	200	300	200	100
Tax on income - 50%	50	100	150	100	50
Net Income	50	100	150	100	50

Table II
Sum-of-the-Year's Digits Depreciation

	Year 1	2	3	4	5
Pre-depreciation pre-tax income	200	400	600	400	200
Depreciation expense:					
Machine No. 1	150	100	50		
Machine No. 2	-	150	100	50	
Machine No. 3	-	-	150	100	50
Total Depreciation Expense	150	250	300	150	50
Pre-tax income	50	150	300	250	150
Tax on income - 50%	25	75	150	125	75
Net Income	25	75	150	125	75

(a) Explain why Badger Company might use the sum-of-the-year's digits method of depreciation instead of straight-line depreciation.

(10 minutes)

(b) Suppose Badger Company were to use "flow-through accounting." Using the data in the above tables, calculate the income after taxes in each of the five years.

(10 minutes)

(c) Explain the "normalizing method" of determining depreciation, using the data supplied above.

(10 minutes)

(d) Identify the advantages and disadvantages of the "normalizing method" of depreciation compared to the use of "flow-through accounting."

(5 minutes)

(Please Turn Page)

I-2-6

6. **SHORT ANSWER QUESTIONS**

(4 Questions – 50 minutes)

Answer briefly **ALL** of the following questions. (The answers must appear on consecutive pages in the answer book.)

6-1. These data are for the Cavalier Company:

Ratio	Forecasted 5 Year Average
Pre-tax operating income (loss) / Sales	15.5%
Pre-tax non-operating income (loss) / Sales	(1.5%)
Sales / Operating assets	1.3
Income taxes / Net income before taxes	50%
Dividends / Net income	40%
Operating assets / Shareholder's equity	1.4

Based on these data, calculate the expected growth rate of earnings per share for this company. Show all calculations.

(10 minutes)

6-2. APB Opinion No. 15 covers the calculation of earnings per share.

(a) In accordance with the Opinion, **list** four categories of common stock equivalents which must be used to determine primary earnings per share.

(10 minutes)

(b) **Explain** how primary EPS is modified to determine fully diluted earnings per share.

(5 minutes)

I-2-7

6-3. The variance, standard deviation and coefficient of variation have been calculated for these numbers: 2, 3, 5, 7, 8.

$$\text{Variance} = \frac{(2-5)^2 + (3-5)^2 + (5-5)^2 + (7-5)^2 + (8-5)^2}{5} =$$

$$\frac{(-3)^2 + (-2)^2 + 2^2 + 3^2}{5} = \frac{26}{5}$$

$$\text{Standard Deviation} = \sqrt{\frac{26}{5}}$$

$$\text{Coefficient of Variation} = \frac{\sqrt{\frac{26}{5}}}{5}$$

(a) **Explain** what analytical purpose is served by these statistical measures.

(5 minutes)

(b) **Identify** one useful application in financial analysis for each of these statistical concepts.

(5 minutes)

6-4. "An analysis of the growth record and growth prospects of an industry or a company frequently can be conducted within the framework of the so-called 'industrial life cycle.' Many students of economic history have argued that industries, like people, go through fairly well-defined stages of development."

(a) **Explain** what is meant by the concept of the "industrial life cycle" of a company or an industry.

(5 minutes)

(b) **Explain** the implications of this approach for achieving investment success.

(5 minutes)

(c) **Explain** the limitations of this concept.

(5 minutes)

END OF SECTION 2

C. F. A.
Examination II
Section 1

THE INSTITUTE OF CHARTERED FINANCIAL ANALYSTS

C. F. A.
EXAMINATION II

(June 9, 1973)

SECTION 1

9:45 A.M. – 12:00 P.M.

Five questions must be answered in this section of the examination. You may choose between Question 5 or 6, but you must answer Questions 1 through 4. The weighting used to grade each question is equal to the amount of time allocated to answering each question.

The time allocated for answering each question is:

Questions		Minutes
1		25
2		30
3		30
4		30
5 or 6		20
	Total	135

INSTRUCTIONS TO CANDIDATES

1. Questions 1 through 4 must be answered. Answer either question 5 or 6, but not both.

2. Write legibly and in ink.

3. Begin each question on a new page.

4. Write your identification number in the two spaces indicated on the front cover of your answer book. Fill in the other required information on the cover of your answer book.

II-1-2

1. The following quotation from an article written by Leopold Bernstein highlights the issue concerning the use of reserves to recognize future costs and losses—are they valid or merely a means of further clouding reports?

"The growing use of reserves for future costs and losses impairs the significance of periodically reported income and should be viewed with skepticism by the analyst of financial statements. That is especially true when the reserves are established in years of heavy losses, when they are established in an arbitrary amount designed to offset an extraordinary gain, or when they otherwise appear to have as their main purpose the relieving of future income of expenses properly chargeable to it.

"The basic justification in accounting for the recognition of future losses stems from the doctrine of conservatism which, according to one popular application, means that one should anticipate no gains, but take all the losses one can clearly see as already incurred."

(a) Discuss the merits of Bernstein's arguments and apprehensions.

(b) Explain how such information may be factored into your review of past trends, the estimates of future earnings, and valuation of the common stock.

(25 minutes)

II-1-3

2. Three years ago, you established an investment counseling organization which achieved substantial success in the bull market from mid-1970 through 1972. A brokerage firm, which includes several of your friends, has recently established an advisory service for corporations to recommend the types of managers which should be used in handling their pension accounts. Both you and the principals of the brokerage firm are C.F.A.'s.

Two members of this brokerage firm recently informed you that your record was good–but not more spectacular than several other counseling organizations. They pointed out that their work necessitated making many contacts and numerous presentations–many of which did not result in a new business relationship. After many inferences, it became evident that their recommendations about your management ability were somewhat dependent upon your willingness to provide them with substantial brokerage commissions.

This brokerage firm was continuing a modest research effort and had, in past years, been valuable in helping you select stocks for customers.

Because you and your associates realize that the amount of your future counseling business may be dependent upon the recommendations of these "advisors," you and your associates decided to discuss the entire situation and any ethical problems which were inherent in it.

(a) Review the situation as it pertains to the *C.F.A. Code of Ethics* and *Standards of Professional Conduct.*

(b) List and explain your recommendations for handling the situation as a principal of the investment counseling organization.

(30 minutes)

(PLEASE TURN PAGE)

II-1-4

3. Robert Graham has come to your office for investment counseling. You have been acquainted socially with him and his family for several years, but only today were you told of the details concerning his family situation. He is 38 years old, is married and has three children. The oldest child, a 10 year old boy, has a physical deformity which may limit his work potential. Mr. Graham is concerned that his son may need some type of income supplement for the remainder of his life. The other two children, a boy and a girl, appear to be doing well in school; Graham expects that each will go to college. He carries a $40,000 ordinary life policy on himself and $15,000 on his wife.

   Robert Graham has an executive position with a small manufacturing corporation. He earns $35,000 per year, from which he is saving approximately $3,000 annually at the present time—but savings are becoming increasingly more difficult as he tries to meet some of the social obligations which have been necessary in the business. He feels his job is very secure and enjoys working for the company, but any chance of advancement is limited. He expects regular though modest salary increases but no promotions. Mrs. Graham's mother, age 58, recently became paralyzed and has limited financial resources. Mr. Graham believes that she will need approximately $3,000 per year for the remainder of her life.

   The parents of Mr. Graham were recently killed in an automobile accident and he inherited $200,000. The inheritance is in savings accounts and readily marketable securities.

   (a) Outline your recommendation for a general investment plan for Robert Graham.

   (b) Indicate the type of investments (not necessarily the specific securities) which would suit his needs and requirements best.

   (c) List and discuss the factors which you must consider in making these decisions.

(30 minutes)

II-1-5

4. "There are those who believe that the time is at hand to abandon the experiment with controls and to rely entirely on monetary and fiscal restraint to restore a stable price level. This prescription has great intellectual appeal; unfortunately, it is impractical." (Arthur Burns, Chairman of the Federal Reserve Board of Governors, December 29, 1972).

   (a) **State** the intellectual appeal of using only monetary and fiscal policies.

   (b) **Explain** why Mr. Burns thinks it is "impractical" to rely only on monetary and fiscal policies in 1973.

   (c) **Discuss** briefly "Phase III" and evaluate its potential effect on controlling wages and prices, and on corporate profits.

(30 minutes)

(PLEASE TURN PAGE)

II-1-6

(ANSWER EITHER NO. 5 OR NO. 6. IF BOTH ARE ANSWERED, ONLY THE FIRST ANSWER APPEARING IN THE ANSWER BOOK WILL BE GRADED.)

5. The chart below is a schematic illustration showing the historical relationship between rate of return on bonds and stocks. It shows a probability distribution of rate of return with the rates on the horizontal axis, and the probabilities on the vertical axis. (The probabilities are based on the frequencies of observed occurances.) Assume that distribution "A" represents AAA-rated corporate bonds, while distribution "B" represents the rate of return on the common stocks of large, established corporations.

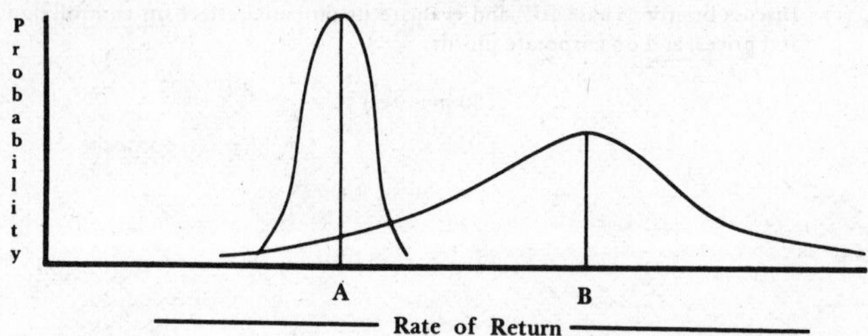

(a) **Reproduce** the chart in your answer book. For each type of security listed below (C, D, and E), **place** a vertical line to indicate the mean and **sketch** the shape (width and height) of the frequency distribution. **Label** with the appropriate letter.

Type of Security	Letter
Long-term U. S. Treasury bonds	C
Common stock warrants	D
Convertible bonds	E

(b) **Justify** your answer to (a) above by **discussing** each type (C, D, and E) in terms of its expected return and dispersion of returns relative to securities A and B. **Explain** your placement of distribution C, D, and E.

(20 minutes)

II-1-7

6. (ANSWER EITHER NO. 5 OR NO. 6. IF BOTH ARE ANSWERED, ONLY THE FIRST ANSWER APPEARING IN THE ANSWER BOOK WILL BE GRADED.)

You are managing a $100 million pension fund portfolio and have received the following probability distribution, based on an econometric model, for the expected one-year total return (including income) on the Standard and Poor's 500 Index.

Market Prediction	One-year Total Return S&P 500	Probability
I	+20%	0.15
II	+10%	0.30
III	+ 5%	0.20
IV	- 5%	0.20
V	- 10%	0.10
VI	- 20%	0.05
		1.00

There are three possible portfolio strategies available, A, B, and C. Under each portfolio strategy is displayed the percentage return for each of the three market predictions.

PORTFOLIO STRATEGY

Market Prediction	A	B	C
I	7%	50%	20%
II	7	30	12
III	7	10	10
IV	7	-10	4
V	7	-25	0
VI	7	-40	-8

(a) State the expected one-year total return for the S&P 500. Compare this return with the mode of the distribution, explaining the difference, if any.

(b) Assuming that you are an expected-value decision maker (linear utility curve), select the proper strategy. Explain.

(c) Assuming a "risk-averter" utility curve, select the proper strategy. Explain.

(20 minutes)

(END OF SECTION 1)

C. F. A.
Examination II
Section 2

THE INSTITUTE OF CHARTERED FINANCIAL ANALYSTS

C. F. A.
EXAMINATION II

(June 9, 1973)

SECTION 2

1:45 P. M. – 4:45 P. M.

There are three questions in this section of the examination. The weighting used to grade each question is equal to the amount of time allocated to answering each question.

The time allocated for answering each question is:

Questions		Minutes
1		60
2		60
3		60
	Total	180

INSTRUCTIONS TO CANDIDATES

1. All questions must be answered.

2. Write legibly and in ink.

3. Begin each question on a new page.

4. Write your identification number in the two spaces indicated on the front cover of your answer book. Fill in the other required information on the cover of your answer book.

II-2-2

This section of the examination consists of 3 questions based upon:

1. the annual report of Walt Disney Productions (enclosed)

2. a research memorandum (accompanying the questions).

Base your answers on the information contained in these materials.

1. You have been granted a one-half hour interview with the top management of Walt Disney Productions. You may presume that those present will be able to answer your questions concerning the company and its operations, but you wish to concentrate on basic policy-level topics, since another interview with the financial staff has been arranged for later in the day.

   (a) **List** the subjects you would try to cover pertaining to this annual report and the particular questions which you feel would be most important from the standpoint of a stockholder.

   (b) **State** your reasons for asking these questions.

(60 minutes)

II-2-3

2.

MEMORANDUM

To: Herbert Standish, Research Director

Date: March 15, 1973

From: Lawrence Miller, Staff Analyst

Subject: An Analysis of Research Reports on Walt Disney Productions

This analysis summarizes two of the better research reports published in February on Walt Disney Productions. In brief, Report A continues to rank the stock as a "definite candidate for accumulation" while Report B states purchase of Disney should be deferred at this time "in light of the possibility of poor first-half earnings."

Both reports discussed four major areas to provide a rationale for their recommendations:

(1) Earnings
(2) Motion Pictures and T. V.
(3) Parks
(4) Ancillary Operations

REPORT A: DEFINITE CANDIDATE FOR ACCUMULATION

(1) Earnings:

(a) First quarter earnings down from $0.19 in the prior year to $0.18.

(b) Table 2 (under Financial Data) indicates a 17.9% increase in revenues but a 6.1% reduction in net income for the first quarter.

(c) Second quarter earnings could be lower than in prior years.

(d) We anticipate earnings of $1.65 - $1.70 for fiscal 1973 (down from our previous $1.80 forecast), but still a 19% annual gain.

(e) Long-term growth is expected to be in the area of 15% to 20% per year.

(PLEASE TURN PAGE)

II-2-4

(2) Motion Pictures and T. V.:

(a) Disney continues to regard motion pictures and T. V. as its main business.

(b) Revenues from these sources should increase but there should be a small decline in profit margins.

(c) *Mary Poppins,* Disney's most successful film, is scheduled for reissue in mid-1973.

(d) It will be difficult to attain last year's income in this area because of the great success Disney had with foreign films in 1972.

(e) Disney will release one more motion picture this year than it did last year.

(f) Disney, over the years, has been the most successful motion picture production company. It is important to realize that quarterly earnings from motion pictures are quite volatile.

(g) The company's major motion picture release, *Snowball Express,* is going well and the company forecasts about $7,000,000 in revenue from it.

(3) Parks:

(a) There is "no convincing evidence that things are not going well at Walt Disney World."

(b) Attendance at Walt Disney World is up 5-6%, less than the 10% forecast. Local attendance is down, but there were record crowds of out-of-state visitors at Christmas-time.

(c) Attendance at Disney World is expected to reach 12 million and per capita expenditures are rising at roughly a 6% rate.

(d) Disneyland attendance was up 10% last year over the previous year and per capita expenditures were up. The corporation is expecting a 5% attendance increase and 5% increase in expenditures per capita for 1973.

(4) Ancillary Activities:

(a) Disney has announced a residential development of conventional homes.

(b) Continued development of the company's vast Florida land holding is expected.

(c) Long-term growth in ancillary activities is expected but no significant impact is anticipated for 1973

II-2-5

REPORT B: PURCHASE SHOULD BE DEFERRED AT THIS TIME

(1) Earnings:

Overall evaluation: $1.60 EPS forecast. This long-term forecast is for 20-25% annual rate of growth. Current problems are unrelated to areas of expected future growth.

(a) Films dominate near-term prospects

- Foreign films are down compared to last year
- There is one less film in the first quarter for the domestic market compared to last year.

(b) Nevertheless, increases were shown at Walt Disney World, at Disneyland, and in the ancillary activities. The long-term prospects are exciting.

(2) Motion Pictures and T.V.:

Overall evaluation: Films dominate earnings in the first two quarters of the year. EPS from films will be flat to up moderately compared to last year.

(a) While first quarter EPS is affected by fewer films than last year, the second quarter will benefit from one added film. Also, the fourth quarter reissue of *Mary Poppins* (with no negative costs to be amortized) is expected to have a substantial positive affect on EPS.

(b) No precise breakdown on the impact of the decline in foreign film earnings is available, but the impact will lessen throughout the year.

(3) Parks:

Overall evaluation: Parks dominate earnings in the third and fourth quarters. Increases here will offset possible declines or flat performance in other areas of operations.

(a) Walt Disney World attendance is up 6% during the first quarter, with a 10% increase expected for the year. Spending per capita could be up 5-10%. Revenues will also benefit from the increase in ticket price. Revenues will also benefit from the increase in ticket price. Revenues are expected to be $160-$180 million. Operating margins may hit 17% this year, compared to 13% last year, with 23-25% in the future.

(b) Disneyland attendance is up 19% in the first quarter. A 3-4% increase is expected for the year. Revenues will be up 5-6%. No change in profitability is expected.

(4) Ancillary Activities:

Overall evaluation: A 20% gain this year in both revenues and earnings.

(PLEASE TURN PAGE)

II-2-6

FINANCIAL DATA FROM REPORTS A AND B

TABLE 1

1972-73 Range	Recent Price	Indicated Dividend	Yield	1972 Earnings Per Share	Common Shares Outstanding	Market Value ($ Million)
124-66	$104	$0.12	0.1%	$1.41	28,564,000	$2,970

TABLE 2

	First Quarter of Fiscal Year Ended		
	12/31/72	12/31/71	% Change
Revenues (000)	$68,916	$58,433	+ 17.9
Cost and Expenses (000)	60,442	48,880	+ 23.7
Net Income (000)	5,024	5,353	- 6.1
After-tax Margin	7.3%	9.2%	
Earnings Per Share	$ 0.18	$ 0.19	- 5.3

TABLE 3

	Report A	Report B
Estimated EPS - 1973	$1.65 - 1.70	$ 1.60
Estimated EPS - 1974	$1.95 - 2.00	N.A.*
P/E Ratio - Recent	74	74
P/E Estimated - 1973	62	65
P/E Estimated - 1974	53	N.A.*

*Not Available

End of Memorandum

II-2-7

The above memorandum was prepared by Lawrence Miller, an analyst in your research department:

(a) **State** your opinion of the recommendations, based on the 1972 Annual Report and the memorandum.

(b) **State** the various methods which could be used in placing a value on the stock. **Explain.**

(c) **State** the time horizon that you are using for each valuation method. **Explain.**

(d) **Compute** the return on total capitalization for 1972 and **discuss** its significance.

(60 minutes)

3. In preparing for your interview with Disney's financial staff, **review** those areas in the annual report which could be presented in greater detail. After reading the financial statements, the letter to stockholders on pages 28 and 29, the Summary of Significant Accounting Policies on page 30, the Notes to Consolidated Financial Statements on pages 36 and 37, and the historical material on pages 38 and 39, **list** the factors which, in your opinion, need close appraisal and will provide the basis for your questioning. **Explain** carefully using numerical data to **substantiate** your reasoning where it is appropriate.

(60 minutes)

END OF SECTION 2

C. F. A.
Examination III
Section 1

THE INSTITUTE OF CHARTERED FINANCIAL ANALYSTS

C. F. A.
EXAMINATION III

(June 9, 1973)

SECTION 1

9:45 A.M. - 12:00 P.M.

There are five questions in this section of the examination. The weighting used to grade each question is equal to the amount of time allocated to answering each question.

The time allocated for answering each question is:

Questions	Minutes
1	30
2	30
3	25
4	30
5	20
Total	135

INSTRUCTIONS TO CANDIDATES

1. All questions must be answered.
2. Write legibly and in ink.
3. Begin each question on a new page.
4. Write your identification number in the two spaces indicated on the front cover of your answer book. Fill in the other required information on the cover of your answer book.

III-1-2

1. During 1972 the United States imported about $7 billion more goods than it exported. This trade deficit was much larger than had been expected after the realignment of currencies at the Smithsonian meeting in December, 1971. A rather prompt reversal in the deterioration of the trade balance had been expected.

   Identify and **discuss** the factors which were present in the world and U. S. economies that negated or slowed the "expected" effect of devaluation.

(30 minutes)

2.

GREAT LAKES MANUFACTURING COMPANY
Lorain, Ohio 44120

March 31, 1973

Mr. Arthur G. Hopewell
Vice President, Trust Department
Ohio State Bank and Trust Company
Cleveland, Ohio

Dear Art:

Your year-end report on the performance and status of our pension fund was reviewed at yesterday's meeting of the Pension Fund Advisory Committee of the Board of Directors. A serious question was raised about the continued shift to common stocks.

Under policies you have been following, and with which the Committee has concurred, the bank has raised the percentage of common stocks in the fund from 40 to 75 percent (at market) over the last ten years. The question we would like to discuss with you at our April 15th meeting is whether this policy should be reversed, or at a minimum modified to place all new money (contributions plus investment income) in bonds. Based on the past five years, our rate of return on common stocks appears to be lower than the return now available on high-grade bonds (7¼%-7½%). From your year-end report:

III-1-3

Overall Rate of Return (% per annum)

	Great Lakes Mfg. Common Stock Fund	S & P 425 Industrials
1967-72	6.9	6.5
1962-72	8.5	8.4

As you know from the actuary's report, a copy of which you received, the forecast for excess of contributions over outlays will slow from its present rate of 20 percent to 10 percent over the next ten years.

We look forward to seeing you shortly.

Sincerely,

James S. Gans

James S. Gans
Vice President - Finance

(a) **State** your recommendation to the Committee.

(b) **Substantiate** your recommendation by **discussing** the major points, pro and con.

(30 minutes)

3. As a highly respected senior investment official in the financial community, you have been approached by the chief executive officer of one of the largest industrial corporations in the world. He has asked for your advice about the establishment of a corporate policy to estimate earnings, as permitted by SEC rulings.

Prepare a carefully reasoned recommendation **discussing** points in favor of and opposed to such a policy.

(25 minutes)

(PLEASE TURN PAGE)

III-1-4

4. The trust department of Inner City Bank has decided to monitor the investment performance of its portfolio managers due to a recent increase in the number of performance-related complaints from clients. As Director of Portfolio Management of the bank, you are reviewing two performance measurement techniques proposed by a committee established to investigate the problem and to recommend solutions. A basic stumbling block has arisen because the bank's clients require portfolios with a diversity of investment objectives.

   One group has proposed that the portfolio performance be measured by comparing portfolio performance with the performance achieved by the market as a whole. In its opinion, this approach should be sufficient since most investors normally relate their portfolio's performance to that of the general market.

   An opposing body of opinion—led by several "beta theorists"—argues that the general market approach does not adequately take into account the degree of risk assumed by portfolio managers in achieving performance.

   (a) **Describe** how the beta theorists might take investment risk into consideration by **outlining** a possible portfolio performance measurement technique.

   (b) **Discuss** briefly some of the weaknesses of the measurement technique described in (a) above.

   (c) Without using either the "beta technique" or the general market approach, **outline** another approach to the measurement of performance.

(30 minutes)

5. Several commentators on the state of the bond market during 1972 and early 1973 have pointed to the increased activity in the secondary market, much of it due to the greater emphasis placed on bond performance by institutional investors.

   Cite at least **four** different kinds of trades or switches that are used by bond investors (not necessarily within the last 12 to 15 months) who attempt to increase "performance." **Explain** clearly how each, if successful, will benefit a portfolio.

(20 minutes)

END OF SECTION 1

C. F. A.
Examination III
Section 2

THE INSTITUTE OF CHARTERED FINANCIAL ANALYSTS

C. F. A.
EXAMINATION III

(June 9, 1973)

SECTION 2

1:45 P.M. - 4:45 P.M.

There are five questions in this section of the examination. The weighting used to grade each question is equal to the amount of time allocated to answering each question.

The time allocated for answering each question is:

Questions	Minutes
1	30
2	60
3	35
4	25
5	30
	180

INSTRUCTIONS TO CANDIDATES

1. All questions must be answered.
2. Write legibly and in ink.
3. Begin each question on a new page.
4. Write your identification number in the two spaces indicated on the front cover of your answer book. Fill in the other required information on the cover of your answer book.

III-2-2

1. Arnold Hornby is the head of research and a partner of a medium-sized investment counseling organization located in a large eastern city. Most of the firm's accounts are managed with the firm having full discretion for transactions. Peter Spencer, the youngest of the firm's four analysts, rushes into Mr. Hornby's office and makes this statement:

   > "Let's get on the wire to account managers and sell General Manufacturing out of all accounts right now—I've just received some very unfavorable news. The salesman for one of our prime brokers is friendly with an outside director of that company who told him that development costs on their new product are running much higher than expected, earnings for 1973 will be sharply lower than the $3.20 that most people are using, and that, in addition, the new product is likely to be abandoned soon. The stock has been selling pretty full even on the $3.20, with a lot of hope given to the long run potential of the new product. When this news gets generally known that stock is going to plummet. We have an obligation to our clients to get them out now!"

   Mr. Hornby knows that Peter keeps in touch with the treasurer of General Manufacturing on a regular basis.

   Discuss thoroughly what Mr. Hornby should do.

   (30 minutes)

2. The El Camino Press publishes a daily newspaper in a medium-sized U. S. city. Its printing press is more than ten years old and will need replacement in about ten years. The estimated replacement cost will be $4,000,000 in ten years, including building renovations needed to accommodate the press. The best estimates are that the salvage value of the printing press will be $200,000 ten years from now.

   The management of El Camino Press has decided that depreciation on the old equipment and building will be funded into an investment account, with augmentation from retained earnings annually. The depreciation charges can provide $100,000 annually, while an average of $50,000 annually is available from after-tax operating earnings. The El Camino Press is a corporation, and usually has a net income before tax

III-2-3

in excess of $100,000. It is owned by a relatively small number of civic-minded citizens who are not primarily interested in large dividends each year, but who think that some cash payment should be made. The editor-publisher draws an adequate salary.

The portfolio accumulated to date is listed below:

	Approx. Mkt. Value	Est. Income
100 shrs. I.B.M. common	$ 43,000	$ 560
400 shrs. Gulf Oil common	10,400	600
400 shrs. U.S. Steel common	12,000	640
1,200 shrs. Sears, Roebuck common	133,000	1,680
100 shrs. Merck common	9,600	118
500 shrs. General Motors common	36,000	2,225
1,000 shrs. Litton Industries common	10,000	---
$100,000 P.V. U.S. Treas. 6¼%, 2-15-78	99,000	6,250
$100,000 P.V. G.M.A.C. 7¼%, 3-1-95	99,000	7,250
Total	$452,000	$19,323

In making the analysis, ignore the capital gains already in the portfolio. Otherwise, assume a capital gains tax rate of 25%.

(a) Without performing the calculations, **outline** in detail the analytic approach you would use in determining the capital accumulations required for the printing press and building improvements.

(b) **Perform** the calculations outlined in (a) above.

(c) **Present** a general long-range investment plan, including any specific changes you would make now to implement the plan. **Explain** carefully all of your reasoning. (You need not name specific securities for purchase. Instead, **indicate** classes and types; bonds, preferreds, and commons by industry or other category.

(60 minutes)

(PLEASE TURN PAGE)

III-2-4

3. On January 17, 1973, the following new issues were publicly offered by underwriting syndicates:

(a) Vermont Yankee Nuclear Power Corporation 7.70%
First Mortgage Bonds due January 15, 1998 --
$20 million
Offered at 101.375 to yield 7.58% to maturity
Rated "A"
Redeemable on 1/15/78 beginning at $107.26.

(b) Vermont Yankee Nuclear Power Corporation 7.48%
Cumulative Preferred stock -- 250,000 shares,
$100 par value
Offered at 101.355 per share to yield 7.38%
Rated "BBB"
Redeemable on 3/1/75 beginning at par

(c) State of New York General Obligations (a tax-exempt security)
due serially February 1, 1990-95
Offered as part of a $129,500,000 issue of serial
bonds due 1974 to 2003
Rated "AA"
Non-redeemable prior to maturity

Amount	Year of Maturity	Coupon	Price	Yield to Maturity
$4,975,000	1990	4.75%	99.42	4.80%
4,975,000	1991	4.80	100	4.80
4,975,000	1992	4.80	99.79	4.85
4,975,000	1993	4.80	99.79	4.85
900,000	1994	4.90	100	4.90
900,000	1995	4.90	100	4.90

(d) Pan American World Airways, Inc. 7½%
Convertible Subordinated Debentures due
January 15, 1998 -- $75 million
Offered at 100 to yield 7.50% to maturity
Rated "B"

III-2-5

Convertible on and after January 16, 1975 into common stock. The initial conversion price equals 80% of the market price–but the initial conversion price may not be less than $7.00 or more than $13.50 per share.

Not redeemable prior to February 1, 1976: then at 107-1/2. Market price of common stock on 1/17/73: 9-1/8.

Common Price Range		Earnings Per Share
1968	30 - 19-1/2	$1.46
1969	31-3/4 - 11-3/8	.77 (deficit)
1970	14-1/2 - 8	1.38 (deficit)
1971	20-1/4 - 9-1/2	1.19 (deficit)
1972	17-3/4 - 8-5/8	.72 (deficit)

As head of a portfolio management unit in a large investment counseling firm, you are responsible for a number of accounts with varying investment objectives and requirements. These include:

- individual clients whose investment assets range from moderate to large size
- educational endowment funds
- a $10 million pension fund
- the $15 million investment portfolio of a rapidly-growing and profitable casualty insurance company.

Your firm's established policy is to make continuous use of fixed-income securities rather than investing entirely in equities. At a meeting early in January, 1973, the management committee of the firm advised all portfolio managers that, while there were some uncertainties in the outlook for the bond market, the acquisition of fixed-income securities would be approved, consistent with on-going investment programs for the accounts under supervision.

Discuss the suitability and attractiveness of each of the four newly-issued securities for each type of client listed above.

(35 minutes)

(PLEASE TURN PAGE)

III-2-6

4. "The principal question on the economic outlook for 1973 is not whether, but how fast, output and employment will expand. For policy, there are two issues. The first is to find and implement the set of policy actions which will maximize the likelihood that the economy will move to its full potential level of output and employment. The second is to do so in ways that will serve both to eliminate the vestiges of the post-1965 inflation and to place the economy squarely on a sustainable path of subsequent non-inflationary growth.

"This is an ambitious set of policy goals, but there is a good prospect of achieving them, or at least approaching them closely. The year ahead is the first in a long time in which there is reasonable hope of closing in on full prosperity without serious inflation and without war."*

**Economic Report of the President,* 1973, p. 71.

Identify the fiscal and monetary actions, excluding "Phase III" controls, which the *Report* recommends for realizing these goals. **Explain** the impact that each of these fiscal and monetary actions is expected to have on the stock market and the bond market.

(25 minutes)

5. As senior vice-president of the trust investment division of a large commercial bank, you are chairing a meeting of the investment committee in March, 1973. The vice-president for research holds a viewpoint regarding investment policy which is the polar opposite of the view held by the vice-president for portfolio management. The research V. P. wants to stress basic stocks of the type in Group A below, which was recently prepared by an analyst on his staff. The portfolio management V. P. wants to continue to stress the leading high-quality growth stocks such as those in Group B below.

   (a) **Summarize** carefully the case which can be made for each of the two viewpoints.

   (b) **Discuss** in detail how you would resolve the two viewpoints, and **substantiate** your reasoning.

III-2-7

	Group A			Group B		
	Am.Elec.Power	G.M.	Goodyear	Avon	Coca Cola	IBM
EPS Growth Rate						
Average Past 10 Years	6.3%	0.2%	8.4%	18.1%	14.1%	15.3%
Average Next 5 Years (estimate)	4%-6%	4%-6%	4%-6%	14%-16%	10%-12%	12%-15%
Dividends						
Payout Ratio	68%	59%	35%	65%	51%	49%
Current Yield	6.7%	6.0%	3.4%	1.0%	1.1%	1.2%
Return on Equity						
Average Past 5 Years	11.9%	16.0%	12.2%	34.3%	23.8%	18.6%
Price/Earnings Ratio						
Average Past 10 Years	19	15	15	43	31	41
Current	10	9	9	56	40	34

(30 minutes)

END OF SECTION 2

2

Inside Information and the Analyst

WILLIAM E. CHATLOS
Principal
Georgeson & Co.
New York, New York

An area of rapidly growing concern for the analyst is liability under the various antifraud provisions of the federal securities law and in particular Rule 10b–5. Applications of Rule 10b–5 now appear quite frequently in reported cases and represent about one third of all current cases, both public and private, under the whole array of SEC statutes. This dramatic increase in the number of cases being brought before the courts or the commission is attributable, in significant part, to the loss of small investor confidence in the market system due to repeated violations of the rules covering material nonpublic information.

In the Treasury Department's recently released report entitled *Public Policy for American Capital Markets,* George P. Schultz, former Secretary of the Treasury, points out that "The loss of public confidence in our securities markets can be directly attributed to the relatively low returns on equity investment in recent years and to the feeling that institutions have an advantage over individual investors." Put another way, the average investor simply feels that he cannot compete equitably in the marketplace if he does not have access to the same lexicon of information that his more formidable counterparts do. As is typical of our democratic system, these feelings have been transformed into actions to bring the courts and the administrative agencies to full bearance on this now popularly perceived problem of the day. In this environment, analysts face increasingly serious difficulties in going about their ordinary tasks. Bradford Cook, former chairman of the SEC, has stated emphatically that the commission intends to become much more stringent in its dealings with analysts. In a recent decision, an industry specialist in the research department at Merrill Lynch, Pierce, Fenner & Smith received a formal censure and 60 days' suspension without pay for selectively distributing inside information. Also, there is the now famous *Equity Funding* case in which analyst Raymond Dirks was indicted for inadvertently committing a fraud while attempting to uncover and expose fraudulent activities which had been committed by others. Fortunately, thus far, citations of actual incidences of infractions by analysts have been few. But the momentum of court and commission activities indicates that there will be an increasing amount of accountability on the part of the professional financial analyst. In addition to civil penalties such as censure and suspension, criminal penalties of up to $10,000 or two years in jail are specified in the 1934 act for willful violation of the act and rules like 10b–5 issued under it.

As it stands now, the analyst in the course of his everyday work can, inadvertently or otherwise, come into the possession of material nonpublic information and in so doing becomes exposed to action from many sources if it can be determined or inferred that he has distributed or used this information. The action can come from the SEC through the initiation of proceedings for suspension, license revocation, and so forth, by the courts through injunction, by his own or his company's clients for issuing misleading advice or discrimination in issuing advice, by an issuer company or its shareholders claiming misappropriated company property, and by buyers and sellers of particular securities at the time when the information is possessed, distributed, or used alleging damages on the basis of same.

While total protection for the analyst is impossible, especially at present when there is as yet no definitive set of guidelines on what is specifically permitted and prohibited, there are reasonable considerations that the prudent analyst should make in order to effectively protect both himself and his profession. In addition, the survival of the marketplace will depend, in no small way, on the curtailment of the frequency of abuse of inside information by individuals and organizations occupying a favored position not available to all.

The next few years will determine direction of rule 10b–5's development. What we endeavor to do here, during this intervening period, when the SEC is developing the definitive set of guidelines on the responsibilities and obligations imposed by the rule is to sketch a general picture of where some of the lines have been drawn and where they may be drawn in the future. The area of greatest need for the analyst is a delineation of what separates good analytical inquiry from inside information. Many who seek useful private information are not fully informed of the intricacies of securities law and their responsibilities under such law. All that we have at present is a spectrum on one end of which there appears an emerging body of case law with citations of specific infractions of Rule 10b–5 with their far-reaching implications. At the other end of the spectrum, we have a host of real, everday hypothetical situations involving bona fide research and analysis, not yet determined as lawful or otherwise. The entire scope of the rule has not yet been fully defined but its growing implications for the analyst are outstanding. In the brief space of this chapter, we shall attempt to describe some of the more obvious practical considerations which the analyst should entertain in the course of his work.

The term *insider* has been defined in a number of ways but has come to include any person with material information not yet disclosed to the public. The question of exactly what constitutes inside information is a more difficult one. The two major elements are materiality and publicity. Under what circumstances is information material and when is it considered to be public? Although, as yet, there is no universal agreement as to what exactly constitutes liability for the analyst under rule 10b–5, it can be safely said that the potential for liability exists when an analyst distributes or uses information in his possession which is (1) material, (2) nonpublic, (3) known to be nonpublic and possibly obtained improperly, and (4) a factor in a decision to act. Information is material when in and of itself it would reasonably be expected to have a marked impact on the stock or would be considered important by the average investor in making his decision to buy or sell a security. Information is nonpublic when it has not been channeled through any of the various mass media or when knowledge of such information is in the possession of an extremely limited number of individuals. Information is obtained improperly when it is of a confidential nature, and is transmitted or received by unauthorized or unethical means. Information is a factor in a decision to act when it is received before the execution of such actions, and when it has some bearing or relevance to that which is acted upon.

In order to present as clear a picture as is possible of both the nature and direction of the law, it is necessary to undertake a brief examination of some of the more significant cases which have come before the court and the commission. Insofar as the judicial decisions are concerned, it should be noted that most have been on the pleadings. Typically then, a 10b–5 decision has been only a holding by the court that a cause of action has been stated well enough to withstand a motion to dismiss. This is far from a decision on the merits, where adequate proof of the relevant assertions has been made. It should also be noted that most of 10b–5 law has come from the district courts. The circuit courts have come to approve many of their principles, but many remain unconfirmed by any higher court, and as of this writing the Supreme Court has yet to speak on 10b–5.

The SEC has been the initiator in three landmark cases under the rule. The first is the *Cady Roberts* case of 1961 where a quarterly dividend was reduced and one of the directors ordered a trade in advance of public dissemination. The second case was the now famous *Texas Gulf Sulfur* case of 1968 where directors and officers and employees of the company purchased large amounts of shares and calls and tipped off others to do the same in advance of a public announcement regarding a mineral discovery. The third was the 1968 matter involving Merrill Lynch, Pierce, Fenner & Smith where the employees of that firm received information as prospective underwriters of an issuing company which was used to trade with and distribute to others for the same purposes prior to public disclosure.

In the *Cady Roberts & Company* case a partner in a brokerage house heard of an impending dividend cut from one of the company's directors.[1] Trading had taken place before the news of the dividend reduction had reached the market. In this case, a special relationship with the source of information was determined. It was also determined that the information was properly designated for corporate purposes alone. It was determined, therefore, that there was an "inherent unfairness" in using information for a purpose other than that for which it was intended. It was reasoned that analytically the obligation to disclose material public information prior to trading rests on two principal elements; first, the existence of a relationship giving access directly or indirectly to information intended to be available only for a corporate purpose and not for the personal benefit of any individual and, second, the inherent unfairness involved where a party takes advantage of such information knowing it is unavailable to those with whom he is dealing (in the market).

In the case of the *Securities and Exchange Commission* v. *Texas Gulf Sulfur Company*,[2] the information involved knowledge of a discovery of a substantial, commercially exploitable mineral deposit on a piece of company owned land. Officers and directors of the company who became aware of this discovery purchased the company's stock in the market before the information was made public. When the information finally became public, the market knew that the value of the company's assets and its earning power would become substantially augmented and the price of the stock adjusted to reflect the increase in the value of the company. Purchase of the stock by directors and officers of the company, under these circumstances, violated the antifraud provision of rule 10b–5, and the court's decision confirmed judicially the Cady Roberts' rule that trading with material undisclosed information violated 10b–5. In addition, the Texas Gulf decision made new law by determining that tipping, the selective transmission of material inside information,

---

[1] In the matter of *Cady Roberts & Co.*, 40 Securities and Exchange Commission 907, 912 (1961).

[2] *Securities and Exchange Commission* v. *Texas Gulf Sulfur Co.* 401 F.2d 833, 849 (2d Cir. 1968).

was a violation of the law. This case also initiated the classic discussion about proximity to the originating source of information as a determinant of liability. "As information becomes more diffuse in terms of its specificity and its remoteness from a corporate source, the appropriateness of applying Rule 10b–5 diminishes."[3]

The case of *Investors Management Co., Inc.* (Merrill Lynch–Douglas)[4] was the first where the commission held a tippee in violation of rule 10b–5. In this instance, it was determined the information was nonpublic because it was not available to investors generally; some analysts had reached negative conclusions regarding Douglas' profitability, but the information passed out by Merrill Lynch was much more specific than that which was generally possessed by the investment community at the time. It was also determined that the tippees either knew or should have known that the information was from an inside source. That source was a prospective underwriter for a proposed Douglas debenture offering. Finally, it was determined that the tippees knew or should have known that the information was inside nonpublic information intended for corporate purposes only and not for external distribution. Conclusions handed down in this case included a set of general guides for disclosure which encouraged discussion between management and analysts while stressing the need for adequate and timely disclosure of any material nonpublic corporate information which might come out during the course of such discussions. This case was the first instance where the SEC considered whether tippees are subject to prohibitions on trading and distribution when they receive material nonpublic information about a company. The SEC said that liability can be incurred if the tippees "know or have reason to know that [the information] was nonpublic and had been obtained improperly by selective revelation or otherwise."[5] Since this case, the term *insiders* has come to include those persons who come into possession of inside information even though they do not fall within the traditional categories of insiders.

The case involving Faberge Inc. was another clear example of an instance in which information about a company came into the possession, use, or distribution of certain individuals but had not been generally disclosed.[6] Had it been disseminated, it would have likely affected the market price of the company's stock because it would have been considered important by reasonable investors in determining their position. What specifically happened in this instance was that a report for a third quarter became known to the company's vice president of finance and this report indicated a substantial loss for the third quarter

[3] Ibid.

[4] In the matter of *Investors Management Co., Inc. et al.* (Securities and Exchange Act Release No. 9267. Investment Advisers Act Release No. 289. July 29, 1971.)

[5] Ibid.

[6] In the matter of Faberge, Inc. (Release No. 34–10174, May 25, 1973).

due to disappointing sales. The information was transmitted privately through telephone calls between the vice president and a number of persons who consequently acted on the basis of it and effected large sales of the stock of the company. The formal public dissemination of the information via communications wire systems was not made until some time after this preliminary selective disclosure.

Another case similar to that of the *Faberge* case was that of the *SEC* v. *Lum's Inc.*[7] In this instance the president of the company had informed a group of security analysts in a seminar that the company's earnings would fall within a certain definite range. Some time later he revised his estimate sharply downward. The information was telephoned to an employee in a Wall Street firm who, in turn, telephoned it to a portfolio manager who informed another portfolio manager of the same firm. Both subsequently sold their entire holdings in the company. Later in the day, when revised earnings were publicly released, the stock dropped substantially in price. Many of the individuals involved in this chain of selective distribution and use of what was material non-public information were found by the court to be involved in a common enterprise to misuse confidential information.

In a case involving Bausch & Lomb, actions were commenced through the SEC against the company, its chairman of the board, certain Wall Street brokerage firms, and others.[8] The actions alleged, among other things, violation of disclosure requirements under federal securities laws. It was alleged that various individuals failed to make timely public disclosure of adverse information and made disclosure of certain information including projected earnings of the company on a selected basis. This information was subsequently used by others to effect sales prior to its dissemination to the public. During 1973, the SEC commenced action against the company and others relating to these same events and seeking injunctive relief.

One of the most recent additions to the body of case law has been a case involving Liggett & Myers Inc.[9] The diversified tobacco and consumer products company was enjoined, upon consent, for violating an antifraud provision of federal securities laws. The SEC had charged that L & M's director of corporate communication gave several security analysts nonpublic inside information about a decline in the company's earnings before the figures were made public. The disclosure, in this instance, was alleged to have triggered trading activity by the analysts' firm and their clients.

---

[7] *Securities and Exchange Commission* v. *Lum's Inc.* —F. Supp.— (S.D. N.Y. 1972) 70 Civ. 5280 (HRT) CCH Fed. Sec. Law Reports, #93659.

[8] *Hawk Industries Inc. et al.* v. *Bausch & Lomb, Inc. et al.* 59 F.R.D. 619 (S.D. N.Y. 1973).

[9] *Securities and Exchange Commission* v. *Liggett & Myers, Inc. et al.* (S.D. N.Y. 1973) 73 Civ. 2796, CCH #94204.

The *Equity Funding* case was another case where infraction of rule 10b-5 occurred as a result of tipping.[10] An analyst received a rumor in a phone call from a disgruntled former employee of the company. The rumor was that at least 66 percent of the total underwriting of the company's insurance operation was bogus. While the analyst investigated what he termed "sensational rumors," he discussed those rumors with various clients who began to unload their stock. News of the scandal did not become public until three weeks later, long after several large accounts, with whom the analyst had been in contact, dumped their stock. The analyst contended that unsubstantiated rumors cannot be considered inside information and that to publicly disseminate such "hearsay information" would have been irresponsible and improper. Essentially, he was caught in the middle of an incredible predicament. First, he was trying to learn the truth behind the rumor of fraud. Second, he was trying to keep his institutional clients informed of what he had learned. Third, he wanted to expose the fraud to the public. Unfortunately, because of his ignorance of the finer points of the law with regard to material information, he got himself into considerable difficulty. Partly as the result of this case, the New York Stock Exchange stated on May 10, 1973, that analysts have "an obligation to the public which must take precedence over the duty to clients or employers".[11]

Liability under the law has been determined to exist even in cases where the information distributed and acted upon is misleading and inaccurate. An example of this is the recent case involving Merrill Lynch, Pierce, Fenner & Smith and sales of Scientific Control Corporation stock.[12] In this instance, Merrill Lynch allegedly disseminated research reports and wire flashes which contained erroneous information about the company. The commission determined that despite the fact the information selectively disseminated was misleading and inaccurate, Merrill Lynch was nevertheless culpable for the misuse of inside material information.

The case of the *SEC* v. *Shapiro* involved a proposed merger between two companies (Harvey's Stores Inc. and Ridge Manor Development Corporation), in which two financial analysts acting as consultants encouraged the merger while at the same time accumulating shares of stock in both companies.[13] While the merger did not go through and the defendants subsequently contended that their knowledge of the negotiations was therefore not material, the court still determined that they were guilty of abusing material nonpublic information.

---

[10] *Securities and Exchange Commission* v. *Equity Funding Corp. of America* (C.D.C. 1973) 73 Civ. 714, CCH #79417.

[11] New York Stock Exchange release dated May 10, 1973.

[12] In the matter of Merrill Lynch, Pierce, Fenner and Smith, Inc., Exchange Act release 10233, June 22, 1973.

[13] *Securities and Exchange Commission* v. *Shapiro et al.* 348 F. Supp. 46 (S.D. N.Y. 1972).

Once it was established by the commission that there were limitations on trading by both corporations and their employees during any period of material nondisclosure, two extensions of the law followed logically—liability of tippors and tippees. It became clear that a corporate official or employee who was not allowed to benefit directly from the use of material undisclosed information should not be able to benefit indirectly by passing on the information to someone else for the same purpose. This was determined to be a violation in the *Texas Gulf Sulfur* case.[14] While in that case the commission proceeded only against the tippor, the commission subsequently held that the tippee is equally bound to refrain from the use of material undisclosed information, at least under circumstances in which the tippee has reason to know the information is nonpublic and improperly obtained. In the broadest terms, the tippee's responsibilities depend upon how the information was acquired, from whom it was acquired, how reliable it was, whether he reasonably believed it was already public, and his degree of financial sophistication. Naturally, this is a very unsettled environment with many potentially conflicting viewpoints. There will be questions of fact in each case which must come to bear on any determination.

Separate from the distinction of tippor as corporate insider is that of the *outside-insider*. Corporate personnel are not the only persons having access to confidential corporate information for legitimate purposes. Such information is obtained by many other persons including analysts, underwriters, lawyers, accountants, government officials, investor relations counselors, and financial printers. While these people have little, if any, control over the disclosure machinery, if they trade upon such information or distribute it in an unauthorized way, they can violate rules of expected confidentiality. It follows logically, then, that they are also bound in a way that is similar to the way corporate officials are bound. Under present circumstances, the analyst should also be wary of using material nonpublic information which comes to him from outside the company, but which he has reason to believe comes from the company itself. Although less risky than information coming directly from the company, it still carries possible violation and liability implications.

In the *Texas Gulf* case as well as the *Investors Management Co.* case and the *Faberge* case, the court determined that the tippee who does trade upon such information is a participant after the fact in the tipping corporate official's breach of fiduciary duty and so may be held responsible for the consequences of any illicit trading activity. A separate but related issue is whether or not a tippor can be held liable for the trades of a tippee, on the theory that such instances fall into the same category as conspiracy or aiding and abetting.

Under certain circumstances, more commonly referred to as the "mosaic" pattern, a securities analyst or other professional obtains from

[14] *Securities and Exchange Commission* v. *Texas Gulf Sulfur Co.*

the sources within an issuer items of information which standing alone would not be material, but which become significant to the security analyst in light of his familiarity with the full mosaic of individual bits of information about that particular issuer or its industry. This is obviously a result of the application of professional expertise which is normally unavailable to the average investor. It seems only right that the analyst's capacity to obtain individually nonsignificant items of information from issuer sources and to utilize this information despite the absence of public dissemination should not be held to be improper or illegal. This type of information is what Philip Loomis, a commissioner of the SEC called "a link in the chain of information." The SEC feels that the kind of research which produces this type of information should not be discouraged. Whether the information is a link in a chain or whether it is one small bit of data which nobody else knows and which gives the recipient a distinctly unfair (potentially illegal) advantage is a fine but important distinction.

While the courts have given certain legal direction as a result of the cases involving inside information, i.e., information originating with the issuer, both the courts and the SEC have been slower in dealing with market information which, while providing the same self-interest advantage, does not fall specifically under the semantic terms associated with materiality in known cases.

> One might conclude that notwithstanding its historical development, thus far, the application of Rule 10b–5 to the unfair use of material nonpublic information should not be restricted to information which emanates from a corporate source, nor need it necessarily deal with a corporate issuer or its affairs. It should apply with equal force to the use of any information in the securities marketplace which either should be or is about to be made public, as long as the publication of the information might effect the decision of a reasonable investor.[15]

If, for example, an analyst has a close relationship with a company giving him possession of certain material nonpublic information, he can become both a tippor and a tippee, subject to legal action even when he, in fact, has done no tipping, but especially, of course, if he has. If his employer or client makes a trade in the issuer company's stock, then he can find that he is in trouble. Another example would be an instance where an analyst is engaged by a company to evaluate a merger or acquisition offer by or for the company. The information he receives in that capacity is inside information, at least that which has not been publicly disseminated. If he passes on the information to friends or clients, both he and they could be potential violators of the law. In

---

[15] Peloso, SEC rule 10b–b5, and outside information, 168N.Y.L.J., December 11, 1972, at 32, 34.

other cases, an analyst may learn that a tender offer for a target company will shortly be made at a premium over the present market price or he may know that some organization or group intends to purchase or sell a sufficiently large number of shares to substantially affect the present market price of a stock. He may, on occasion, learn that a given company may shortly split its stock. Any of these cases could be instances where, if the information is used and/or distributed in advance of public dissemination, the analyst can be held in a violation of the rule.

Let us now consider for a moment the types of liability which might ensue in the course of an analyst issuing his research report. Analysts are, in fact, restricted in the distribution of their own conclusions as a result of analysis. The *Merrill Lynch-Douglas* case is a good example of where selective distribution of a research opinion can be held to be in violation of the SEC rules. Another case, that of *SEC* v. *Alex N. Campbell,* involved a situation where a financial writer, who authored a column which had marked impact, traded on his own recommendation prior to the publication of his column.[16] The case is still under consideration, but the SEC has alleged that the writer was in violation of rule 10b–5.

Let us sketch yet another hypothetical case where infractions of rule 10b–5 can inadvertently occur. Suppose an officer of a company learns from a brokerage firm's analyst interviewing him about his company, that the brokerage firm will shortly publish favorable analysis of his company, including a recommendation to buy the stock. Despite the fact that the report may be based on generally available facts, if the stock is so thinly traded that the appearance of the brokerage report and recommendation is "reasonably certain" to have a substantial impact on the price of the stock, both the officer of the company and the analyst may be in a position where they could be held in violation of rule 10b–5. In this case nothing has happened which affects the value of assets or earning power of the company. However, anyone with advance information as to the brokerage firm's report and recommendation will have an advantage over sellers of the stock who are unaware of the situation. This is just another example of a situation where undisclosed information is market information. In short, information about events or circumstances which affect the market for a company's securities, but which do not necessarily have anything to do with the company's assets or earning power, place the analyst at a potential disadvantage, not only for using and/or distributing such information, but even for the mere possession of it.

It has been argued quite frequently that market information is only important to short-term traders and not so much to long-term investors. It is doubtful, however, that courts will make much of a distinction

[16] *Securities and Exchange Commission* v. *Campbell,* Civil Action 72–1684, (C.D. Cal. 1972).

between market information and information about the company. The case of Texas Gulf Sulfur determined that short-term traders are entitled to the same legal protection that is given to conservative traders.[17]

Among the precautions a prudent analyst should take are the maintenance of careful records, kept as complete as possible, showing the time, source, and character of the information received, the basis for the recommendations, and the time and extent of the distribution of such advice and recommendations. In addition, he should be alert and informed as to what news has already been disseminated about the corporation in question so that he can recognize material nonpublic information when he is confronted with it. If inside information is inadvertently disclosed, he should not allow himself to be compromised in the hope that perhaps the news will slip by unnoticed. News should be disseminated broadly, following at least the minimum guidelines established by the New York Stock Exchange. All rumors should be reported to the appropriate authorities.

The simplest method for an analyst to obtain information concerning a corporation under study is through the use of publicly issued reports, current news reports, and trade publications. In-depth study, however, may involve personal contacts with management, with suppliers, bankers, and other third parties, and possible sources within the analyst's own firm, such as partners who are corporate directors. While verbal communication is necessary and fruitful to the analyst as he probes the company in depth, it is also the most vulnerable and the most difficult to control. Analysts' meetings, splinter group meetings, and especially one-to-one conferences, during which only the analyst and one corporate officer are present, provide fertile ground for planting or inadvertently revealing inside information. It can consist of a mere nod or smile of confirmation. It can be a statement that inadvertently slips out. Nevertheless, the analyst involved has just become an insider.

A suggested protective procedure would be to include a member of the press at all meetings. From a purely logistical standpoint, however, this would obviously be impossible. Not only would the number of meetings have to be severely curtailed as a result of the relatively small number of competent financial reporters available, but one-to-one meetings would become nonexistent. Corporate officers tend to be more formal and constrained in the presence of a member of the press; there is a certain, probably well-warranted, nervousness about possible slips of the tongue (especially concerning personalities) which the press has a great love of publishing and which severely curtails the free give-and-take that small groups have traditionally enjoyed. Those sessions to

---

[17] A fuller description of the SEC's concern with the unfair use of market information appears in Securities and Exchange Act release no. 9950 at 114–29 (January 16, 1973).

which the press is not included tend to have a more conducive business atmosphere. However, these meetings are a perfect opportunity for marginally material information to slip out. In addition, the presence of the press at a meeting is no real defense. The analyst is the expert; if he is not aware of the divulgence of a material fact, how can the member of the press be expected to recognize it?

Regardless of how many analysts are in attendance at such a session, if a material bit of information inadvertently is mentioned, the analysts should not consider the information public. The two alternatives open to him are either to insist upon or arrange for immediate disclosure or to bury the information until the company or someone else releases it. Recommending that the company release the information is perhaps the best choice. Release by an analyst without company authorization could create more legal problems than it would solve. However, it should be considered as a last resort, should all other attempts at prompting public disclosure (including reporting to the SEC or exchange) fail.

A significant problem associated with assuring adequate dissemination of corporate information is that of timing. There is no way of assuring promptness and accuracy. While dissemination is most often sought through the facilities of the major financial news wire services, these do not assure effective dissemination in instances where the wire services are carrying large numbers of releases and are operating under space and time limitations. Perhaps the commission will establish guidelines based on the American Bar Association's suggestions, relating to "waiting periods." These will require those with knowledge of material information to wait until a specified time after dissemination before its distribution or use can be presumptively lawful. In the meantime, the prudent analyst should wait a reasonable length of time after a disclosure, say 24 hours after it has been published on the wire or in the press, in order to be sure that he is not jumping the gun.

Some brief mention should be made in these closing paragraphs about some areas of inquiry for the analyst which have more recently been suggested as areas which fall under the domain of material information. The biggest revelation thus far has been that the seeking out of a firm or person that is the main supplier of an essential part in the production process of a company and asking for information concerning the issuer's orders for parts may be illegal. SEC spokesmen have informally suggested that this type of information could be considered material and nonpublic. Other areas where information could be judged material include information about competitive patterns such as market share, orders and backlogs, sales trends, the significant expansion or curtailment of operations, the status of litigation, extraordinary borrowing, and even, believe it or not, changes in dividend policy and earnings estimates or revisions. This list is by no means complete, either. In the meantime, pending issuance of the definitive guidelines, caution should be exercised in obtaining information in all of these areas.

Indications of the direction of the law thus far point to the objective of achieving equality of information among investors. What is perhaps more realistic is an equal access to that information. This has been termed an "informational access parity" by Harvey Pitt, assistant to the chairman of the SEC.

Until the unlikely time where an effective method of assuring simultaneous receipt of all material information by all interested persons, a strong and healthy capital market will continue to be dependent upon the efforts of security analysts and others to ferret out, analyze, and decipher all of the relevant information that is available in order to make a legitimate profit for themselves and their firm from the application of their resourcefulness and ability in these efforts.

Until precise legal definitions are available, analysts would be well advised to exercise discretion and caution in an attempt to conform not only to the letter of the law and SEC regulations, but also the *intent* and *spirit* of the SEC pronouncements. The advice given by former Chairman William J. Casey of the SEC could well be applied to analysts and should be framed and hung in every financial research department. Speaking about institutional trading, Chairman Casey said that [an analyst] should satisfy himself that all of the information that comes into his possession is available to the public prior to distributing or using it.

3

Securities and Exchange Commission

INTRODUCTION

The Securities and Exchange Commission (SEC) was created by an act of Congress entitled the Securities Exchange Act of 1934. It is an independent, bipartisan, quasi-judicial agency of the United States Government.

The laws administered by the Commission relate in general to the field of securities and finance, and seek to provide protection for investors and the public in their securities transactions. They include (in addition to the Securities Exchange Act of 1934) the Securities Act of 1933 (administered by the Federal Trade Commission until September 1934), the Public Utility Holding Company Act of 1935, the Trust Indenture Act of 1939, the Investment Company Act of 1940, and the Investment Advisers Act of 1940. The Commission also serves as advisor to Federal courts in corporate reorganization proceedings under Chapter X of the National Bankruptcy Act.

Organized July 2, 1934, the Commission is composed of five members not more than three of whom may be members of the same political party. They are appointed by the President, with the advice and consent of the Senate, for 5-year terms, the terms being staggered so that one expires on June 5th of each year. The Chairman is designated by the President.

The Commission's staff is composed of lawyers, accountants, engineers, security analysts and examiners, together with administrative and clerical employees. The staff is divided into Divisions and Offices (including nine Regional Offices), each under charge of officials appointed by the Commission.

The Commission reports annually to the Congress. These reports contain a review of the Commission's administration of the several laws.

SECURITIES ACT OF 1933

This "truth in securities" law has two basic objectives: (*a*) to provide investors with material financial and other information concerning securities offered for public sale; and (*b*) to prohibit misrepresentation, deceit and other fraudulent acts and practices in the sale of securities generally (whether or not required to be registered).

Registration of Securities

The first objective applies to securities offered for public sale by an issuing company or any person in a control relationship to such company. Before the public offering of such securities, a registration statement must be filed with the Commission by the issuer, setting forth the required information. When the statement has become effective, the securities may be sold. The purpose of registration is to provide disclosure of financial and other information on the basis of which investors may appraise the merits of the securities. To that end, investors must be furnished with a prospectus (selling circular) containing the salient data set forth in the registration statement to enable them to evaluate the securities and make informed and discriminating investment decisions.

Exemptions From Registration

The registration requirement applies to securities of both domestic and foreign private issuers, as well as to securities of foreign governments or their instrumentalities. There are, however, certain exemptions from the registration requirement. Among these are: (1) private offerings to a limited number of persons or institutions who have access to the kind of information registration would disclose and who do not propose to redistribute the securities, (2) offerings restricted to the residents of the State in which the issuing company is organized and doing business, (3) securities of municipal, State, Federal and other governmental instrumentalities, of charitable institutions, of banks, and of carriers subject to the Interstate Commerce Act, (4) offerings not in excess of certain specified amounts made in compliance with regulations of the Commission discussed below, and (5) offerings of "small business investment companies" made in accordance with rules and regulations of the Commission. The anti-fraud provisions referred to above, however, apply to all sales of securities involving interstate commerce or the mails, whether or not the securities are exempt from registration.

Purpose of Registration

Registration of securities does not insure investors against loss in their purchase, nor does the Commission have the power to disapprove securities for lack of merit—and it is unlawful to represent otherwise in the sale of securities. The *only* standard which must be met in the registration of securities is an adequate and accurate disclosure of the material facts concerning the company and the securities it proposes to sell. The fairness of the terms of securities (whether price, promoters' or underwriters' profits, or otherwise), the issuing company's prospects for successful operation, and other factors affecting the merits of securities, have no bearing on the question whether securities may be registered.

The purpose of registration is to provide disclosure of these and other important facts so investors may make a realistic appraisal of the merits of the securities and thus exercise an informed judgment in determining whether to purchase them. Assuming proper disclosure, the Commission cannot deny registration or otherwise bar the securities from public sale whether or not the price or other terms of the securities are fair or the issuing company offers reasonable prospects of success. These are factors which the investor must assess for himself in the light of the disclosures provided; and if the facts have been fully and correctly stated, the investor assumes whatever risks may be involved in the purchase of the securities.

Nor does registration guarantee the accuracy of the facts represented in the registration statement and prospectus. The law does, however, prohibit false and misleading statements under penalty of fine or imprisonment, or both. In addition, if an investor suffers loss in the purchase of a registered security, the law provides him with important recovery rights if he can prove that there was incomplete or inaccurate disclosure of material facts in the registration statement or prospectus. These rights must be asserted in an appropriate Federal or State court (not before the Commission, which has no power to award damages); and if such misstatements are proved, the issuing company, its responsible directors and officers, the underwriters, controlling interests, the sellers of the securities, and others (or one or more of such persons) would be liable to the purchaser of the securities for losses sustained in their purchase.

The Registration Process

To facilitate the registration of securities by different types of issuing companies, the Commission has prepared special registration forms which vary in their disclosure requirements to provide disclosure of the essential facts pertinent in a given type of offering while at the same time minimizing the burden and expense of compliance with the law. In general, the registration forms call for disclosure of information such as (1) a description of the registrant's properties and business, (2) a description of the significant provisions of the security to be offered for sale and its relationship to the registrant's other capital securities, (3) information about the management of the registrant, and (4) financial statements certified by independent public accountants.

The registration statement and prospectus become public immediately on filing with the Commission; but it is unlawful to sell the securities until the effective date. After the filing of the registration statement, the securities may be offered orally or by certain summaries of the information in the registration statement as permitted by rules of the Commission. The Act provides that registration statements shall become effective on the 20th day after filing (or on the 20th day after the filing of the last amendment thereto); but the Commission, in its discretion, may advance the effective date if, considering the adequacy of information theretofore publicly available, the ease with which the facts about the new offering can be disseminated and understood, and the interests of investors and the public, such action is deemed appropriate.

Registration statements are examined by the Division of Corporation Finance for compliance with the disclosure requirements. If a statement appears to be materially incomplete or inaccurate, the registrant usually is informed by letter and given an opportunity to file correcting or clarifying amendments. The Commission however, has authority to refuse or suspend the effectiveness of any registration statement if it finds, after hearing, that material representations are misleading, inaccurate or incomplete. Accordingly, if material deficiencies in a registration statement appear to stem from a deliberate attempt to conceal and mislead, or if the deficiencies otherwise are of such nature as not to lend themselves readily to correction through the informal letter process, the Commission may conclude that it is in the public interest to resort to a hearing to develop the facts by evidence and to determine on the evidence whether a stop order should issue refusing or suspending effectiveness of the statement.

A stop order is not a permanent bar to the effectiveness of the registration statement or sale of the securities, for the order must be lifted and the statement declared effective if amendments are filed correcting the statement in accordance with the stop order decision. The Commission may issue stop orders after the sale of securities has been commenced or completed. Although losses which may have been suffered in the purchase of securities are not restored to investors by the stop order, the Commission's decision and the evidence on which it is based may serve to put investors on notice of their rights and aid in their own recovery suits.

This examination process naturally contributes to the general reliability of the registration disclosures—but it does not give positive assurance of the accuracy of the facts reported. Even if such a verification of the facts were possible, the task, if not actually prohibitive, would involve such a tremendous undertaking (both in time and money) as to seriously impede the financing of business ventures through the public sale of securities.

Small Issue Exemption

Among the special exemptions from the registration requirement is one adopted by Congress as an aid primarily to small business. The law provides that offerings of securities not exceeding $500,000 in amount may be exempted from registration, subject to such conditions as the Commission prescribes for the protection of investors. The Commission's Regulation A permits certain domestic and Canadian companies to make exempt offerings not exceeding $500,000 in amount. Offerings on behalf of controlling persons are limited in amount to $100,000 for each such person, not to exceed $500,000 in all. Offerings on behalf of persons other than an Issuer or its affiliates are limited to $100,000 for each such person, not to exceed a total of $300,000, which is not included in the $500,000 ceiling limitation. Under certain circumstances an estate may offer up to $500,000 of securities. The exemption is available provided certain specified conditions are met, including the prior filing of a "Notification" with the appropriate Regional Office of the Commission and the use of an offering circular containing certain basic information in the sale of the securities. A similar regulation is available for offerings not exceeding $500,000 by small business investment companies licensed by the Small Business Administration. Other exemptions of a more limited nature are available for other types of offerings.

Interpretations and Rulemaking

As a part of its activities under this Act, the Division of Corporation Finance also renders administrative interpretations of the law and regulations thereunder to members of the public, prospective registrants and others, to help them decide legal questions about the application of the law and the regulations to particular situations and to aid them in complying with the law. This advice, for example, might include an informal expression of opinion about whether the offering of a particular security is subject to the registration requirements of the law and, if so, advice as to compliance with the disclosure requirements of the applicable registration form. Other Divisions render similar advice and assistance.

The Commission's objective of effective disclosure with a minimum of burden and expense calls for constant review of the practical operation of the rules and registration forms adopted by it. If experience shows that a particular requirement fails to achieve its objective, or if a rule appears unduly burdensome in relation to the benefits resulting from the disclosure provided, the Division of Corporation Finance presents the problem to the Commission for consideration of possible modification of the rule or other requirement. Many suggestions for rule modification follow extensive consultation with industry representatives and others affected. In addition, the Commission normally gives advance public notice of proposals for the adoption of new or amended rules or registration forms and affords opportunity for interested members of the public to comment thereon. The same procedure is followed under the other Acts administered by the Commission.

The scope and importance of the Commission's work in the accounting field under the several statutes are discussed below under "Office of the Chief Accountant."

Fraud Prohibitions

Generally speaking, the fraud prohibitions of the Securities Act are similar to those contained in the Securities Exchange Act of 1934, under which topic the Commission's investigation and enforcement activities are discussed.

SECURITIES EXCHANGE ACT OF 1934

By this Act, Congress extended the "disclosure" doctrine of investor protection to securities listed and registered for public trading on our national securities exchanges; and the enactment in August 1964 of the Securities Acts Amendments of 1964 applied the disclosure and reporting provisions to equity securities of hundreds of companies traded over-the-counter (if their assets exceed $1 million and their shareholders number 500 or more).

Corporate Reporting

Companies which seek to have their securities listed and registered for public trading on such an exchange must file a registration application with the exchange and the Commission. A similar registration form must be filed by companies whose equity securities are traded over-the-counter if they meet the size test referred to. The Commission's rules prescribe the nature and content of these registration statements, including certified financial statements. These data are generally comparable to, but less extensive than, the disclosures required in Securities Act registration statements. Following the registration of their securities, such companies must file annual and other periodic reports to keep current the information contained in the original filing.

Since trading by and between public investors, whether involving listed or over-the-counter securities, involves transactions between holders of outstanding securities (not an offer of securities for sale by the issuing company), there is no provision for dissemination of the reported data to investors through use of a prospectus or similar medium. However, the reported information is available for public inspection, both at the offices of the Commission and the exchanges. It is also used extensively by publishers of securities manuals, securities advisory services, investment advisers, trust departments, brokers and dealers in securities, and similar agencies, and thus obtains widespread dissemination. In addition, as indicated below, copies of any of the reported data may be obtained from the Commission at nominal cost.

The law prescribes penalties for filing false statements and reports with the Commission, as well as provision for recovery by investors who suffer losses in the purchase or sale of registered securities in reliance thereon.

Proxy Solicitations

Another provision of this law governs the solicitation of proxies (votes) from holders of registered securites (both listed and over-the-counter), whether for the election of directors or for approval of other corporate action. In any such solicitation, whether by the management or minority groups, disclosure must be made of all material facts concerning the matters on which such holders are asked to vote; and they must be afforded an opportunity to vote "Yes" or "No" on each matter. Where a contest for control of the management of a corporation is involved, the rules require disclosure of the names and interests of all "participants" in the proxy contest. Holders of such securities thus are enabled to vote intelligently on corporate actions requiring their approval. The Commission's rules require that proposed proxy material be filed in advance for examination by the Commission for compliance with the disclosure requirements.

Tender Offer Solicitations

In 1968, Congress amended the Exchange Act to extend its reporting and disclosure provisions to situations where control of a company is sought through a tender offer or other planned stock acquisition of over 10 percent of a company's equity securities. The amount was reduced to 5 percent by an amendment in 1970. These amendments and Commission rules thereunder require disclosure of pertinent information, by the person seeking to acquire over 5 percent of the company's securities by direct purchase or by tender offer, as well as by any persons soliciting shareholders to accept or reject a tender offer. Thus, as with the proxy rules, public investors who hold stock in the subject corporation may now make informed decisions on take-over bids.

Insider Trading

The protection provided the investing public through disclosure of financial and related information concerning the securities of registered companies, is supplemented by provisions of the law designed to curb misuse of corporate information not available to the general public. To that end, each officer and director of such a company, and each beneficial owner of more than 10 percent of its registered equity securities, must file an initial report with the Commission (and with the exchange on which the stock may be listed) showing his holdings of each of the company's equity securities. Thereafter, they must file reports for any month during which there was any change in such holdings. In addition, the law provides that profits obtained by them from purchases and sales (or sales and purchases) of such equity securities within any 6 months' period may be recovered by the company or by any security holder on its behalf. This recovery right must be asserted in the appropriate United States District Court. Such "insiders" are also prohibited from making short sales of their companies' equity securities.

Margin Trading

The statute also contains provisions governing margin trading in securities. It authorizes the Board of Governors of the Federal Reserve System to set limitations on the amount of credit which may be extended for the purpose of purchasing or carrying securities. The objective is to restrict the excessive use of the nation's credit in the securities markets. While the credit restrictions are set by the Board, investigation and enforcement is the responsibility of the Commission.

Market Surveillance

The Securities Exchange Act also provides a system for regulating securities trading practices in both the exchange and the over-the-counter markets. In general, transactions in securities which are effected otherwise than on national securities exchanges are said to take place "over the counter." Designed to protect the interests of investors and the public, these provisions seek to curb misrepresentations and deceit, market manipulation and other fraudulent acts and practices and to establish and maintain just and equitable principles of trade conducive to the maintenance of open, fair and orderly markets.

While these provisions of the law establish the general regulatory pattern, the Commission is responsible for promulgating rules and regulations for their implementation. Thus, the Commission has adopted regulations which, among other things, (1) define acts or practices which constitute a "manipulative or deceptive device or contrivance" prohibited by the statute, (2) regulate short selling, stabilizing transactions and similar matters, (3) regulate the hypothecation of customers' securities and (4) provide safeguards with respect to the financial responsibility of brokers and dealers.

Registration of Exchanges and Securities Associations

In addition, the law requires registration with the Commission of (1) "national securities exchanges" (those having a substantial securities trading volume); and (2) brokers and dealers who conduct an over-the-counter securities business in interstate commerce.

To obtain registration, exchanges must show that they are so organized as to be able to comply with the provisions of the statute and the rules and regulations of the Commission and that their rules contain provisions which are just and adequate to insure fair dealing and to protect investors. Among other things, exchange rules must provide for the expulsion, suspension or other disciplining of members for conduct inconsistent with just and equitable principles of trade.

While the law contemplates that exchanges shall have full opportunity to establish self-regulatory measures insuring fair dealing and the protection of investors, it empowers the Commission by order, rule or regulation to "alter or supplement" the rules of exchanges with respect to various phases of their activities and trading practices if necessary to effectuate the statutory objective. For the most part, exchange rules and revisions thereof, suggested by exchanges or by the Commission, reach their final form after discussions between representatives of the exchange and the Commission without resort to formal proceedings.

By an amendment to the law enacted in 1938, Congress also provided for creation of a self-policing body among over-the-counter brokers and dealers. This measure authorizes the registration with the Commission of an association of such brokers and dealers provided it is so organized as:

> "to prevent fraudulent and manipulative acts and practices, to promote just and equitable principles of trade, to provide safeguards against unreasonable rates of commissions or other charges, and, in general, to protect investors and the public interest, and to remove impediments to and perfect the mechanism of a free and open market . . ."

To enforce these objectives, the rules of such an association also must provide for the disciplining of members (including suspension or expulsion) for misconduct. The establishment, maintenance and enforcement of a voluntary code of business ethics is one of the principal features of this provision of the law. (Only one such association, the National Association of Securities Dealers, Inc., is registered with the Commission under this provision of the law.)

Not all broker-dealer firms are members of the NASD; thus, some are not subject to supervision and control by that agency. To equalize the regulatory pattern, Congress provided in the 1964 Amendments that the Commission should undertake to establish investor safeguards applicable to non-NASD firms comparable to those applicable to NASD members. Among the controls adopted by the Commission is a requirement that persons associated with non-NASD firms meet certain qualification standards similar to those applied by the NASD to its members.

Broker-Dealer Registration

Applications for registration as broker-dealers and amendments thereto are examined by the Office of Registrations and Reports with the assistance of the Division of Market Regulation. The registration of brokers and dealers engaged in an interstate over-the-counter securities business also is an important phase of the regulatory plan of the Act. They must conform their business practices to the standards prescribed in the law and the Commission's regulations for the protection of investors (as well as to the fair trade practice rules of their association); in addition, as will be seen later, they may violate these regulations only at the risk of possible loss of registration with the Commission and the right to continue to conduct an interstate securities business, or of suspension or expulsion from the association and of the benefits of such membership. (The broker-dealer registration requirement does not apply to firms engaged solely in a municipal securities business.)

Investigation and Enforcement

It is the duty of the Commission under the laws it administers to investigate complaints or other indications of possible law violations in securities transactions, most of which arise under the Securities Act of 1933 and the Securities Exchange Act of 1934. Investigation and enforcement work is the primary responsibility of the Commission's Regional Offices, subject to review and direction by the Division of Enforcement.

Most of the Commission's investigations are conducted privately, the facts being developed to the fullest extent possible through informal inquiry, interviewing of witnesses, examination of brokerage records and other documents, reviewing and trading data and similar means. The Commission however, is empowered to issue subpoenas requiring sworn testimony and the production of books, records and other documents pertinent to the subject matter under investigation; in the event of refusal to respond to a subpoena, the Commission may apply to a Federal court for an order compelling obedience thereto.

Inquiries and complaints of investors and the general public provide one of the primary sources of leads for detection of law violations in securities transactions. Another is the surprise inspections by Regional Offices of the books and records of brokers and dealers to determine whether their business practices conform to the prescribed rules. Still another is the conduct of inquiries into market fluctuations in particular stocks which appear not to be the result of known developments affecting the issuing company or of general market trends.

The more general types of investigations concern the sale without registration of securities subject to the registration requirement of the Securities Act, and misrepresentation or omission of material facts concerning securities offered for sale (whether or not registration is required). The anti-fraud provisions of the law also apply equally to the *purchase* of securities, whether involving outright misrepresentations or the withholding or omission of pertinent facts to which the seller was entitled. For example, it is unlawful in certain situations to purchase securities from another person while withholding material information which would indicate that the securities have a value substantially greater than that at which they are being acquired. Such provisions of the law apply not only to transactions between brokers and dealers and their customers but also to the reacquisition of securities by an issuing company or its "insiders."

Other types of inquiries relate to the manipulation of the market prices of securities; the misappropriation or unlawful hypothecation of customers' funds or securities; the conduct of a securities business while insolvent; the purchase or sale of securities by a broker-dealer, from or to his customers, at prices not reasonably related to the current market prices therefor; and violation by the broker-dealer of his responsibilty to treat his customers fairly.

The most common of the latter type of violation involves the broker-dealer who, on gaining the trust and confidence of a customer and thereby establishing an agency relationship demanding the highest degree of fiduciary duty and care, takes secret profits in his securities transactions with or for the customer over and above the agreed brokerage (agency) commission. For example the broker-dealer may have purchased securities from customers at prices far below, or sold securities to customers at prices far above, their current market prices. In most such cases, the broker-dealer subjects himself to no risk of loss, since his purchases from customers are made only if he can make simultaneous sales of the securities at prices substantially in excess of those paid to the customers, and his sales to customers are made only if he can make simultaneous purchases of the securities at prices substantially lower than those charged the customer. Or the firm may engage in large-scale in-and-out transactions for the customer's account ("churning") to generate increased commissions, usually without regard to any resulting benefit to the customer.

There is a fundamental distinction between a broker and a dealer; and it is important that investors should understand the difference. The *broker* serves as the customer's *agent* in buying or selling securities *for* his customer. As such, he owes the customer the highest fiduciary responsibility and care and may charge only such agency commission as has been agreed to by the customer. On the other hand, a *dealer* acts as a *principal* and buys securities *from* or sell securities *to* his customers. In such transactions, the dealer's profit is measured by the difference between the prices at which he buys and sells securities. Since the dealer is operating for his own account, he normally may not charge the customer a fee or commission for services rendered. Even in the case of such dealer transactions, however, the Commission and the courts have held that the conduct of a securities business carries with it the implied representation that customers will be dealt with fairly and that dealers may not enter into transactions with customers at prices not reasonably related to the prevailing market. The law requires that there be delivered to the customer a written "confirmation" of each transaction disclosing whether the securities firm is acting as a principal for its own account or as an agent for the customer (and, if the latter, the broker's compensation from all sources).

Statutory Sanctions

It should be understood that Commission investigations (which for the most part are conducted in private) are essentially fact finding inquiries. The facts so developed by the staff are considered by the Commission only in determining whether there is *prima facie* evidence of a law violation and whether an action should be commenced to determine whether, in fact, a violation actually occurred and, if so, whether some sanction should be imposed.

Assuming that the facts show possible fraud or other law violation, the laws provide several courses of action or remedies which the Commission may pursue:

a. *Civil injunction.* The Commission may apply to an appropriate United States District Court for an order enjoining those acts or practices alleged to violate the law or Commission rules.

b. *Criminal prosecution.* If fraud or other willful law violation is indicated, the Commission may refer the facts to the Department of Justice with a recommendation for criminal prosecution of the offending persons. That Department, through its local United States Attorneys (who frequently are assisted by Commission attorneys), may present the evidence to a Federal grand jury and seek an indictment.

c. *Administrative remedy.* The Commission may, after hearing, issue orders suspending or expelling members from exchanges or the over-the-counter dealers association; denying, suspending or revoking the registrations of broker-dealers; or censuring individuals for misconduct or barring them (temporarily or permanently) from employment with a registered firm.

Broker-Dealer Revocations

All of these sanctions may be applied to any person who engages in securities transactions violative of the law, whether or not he is engaged in the securities business. However, the administrative remedy is generally only invoked in the case of exchange or association members, registered brokers or dealers, or individuals who may associate with any such firm. In any such administrative proceeding, the Commission issues an order specifying the acts or practices alleged to have been committed in violation of law and directing that a hearing be held for the purpose of taking evidence thereon. At the hearing, counsel for the Division of Enforcement (normally a Regional Office attorney) undertakes to establish for the record those facts which support the charge of law violation, and the respondents have full opportunity to cross-examine witnesses and to present evidence in defense. The procedure followed in the conduct of such proceedings is discussed below under "Administrative Proceedings." If the Commission in its ultimate decision of the case finds that the respondents violated the law, it may take remedial action as indicated above. Such action may effectively bar a firm from the conduct of a securities business in interstate commerce or on exchanges, or an individual from association with a registered firm—subject to the respondents' right to seek judicial review of the decision by the appropriate United States Court of Appeals.

In its investigation and enforcement actions, the Commission cooperates closely with other Federal, State and local law enforcement officials, as well as with such private agenices as the Better Business Bureaus.

The many instances in which these sanctions of the law have been invoked present a formidable record. However, of perhaps greater significance to the investing public is the deterrent or prophylactic effect of the very existence of the fraud prohibitions of the law and the Commission's powers of investigation and enforcement. These provisions of the law, coupled with the disclosure requirements applicable to new security offerings and to other registered securities, tend to inhibit fraudulent stock promotions and operations. They also have a tendency to increase public confidence in securities as an investment medium, thus facilitating financing through the public sale of securities, which contributes to the industrial growth of the nation.

Commission Not a Collection Agency

Communications from the investing public are very helpful to the Commission in connection with its statutory duties and the Commission appreciates receiving them. However, because the Commission receives many inquiries and complaints from investors urging it to intercede in their behalf in an attempt to recover losses in the purchase of securities, it is appropriate to point out that the

Commission in no sense is to be considered a collection agency. While the laws provide investors with important recovery rights if they have been defrauded, and although the Commission's administration of the laws operates in many instances to uncover facts indicating the possible existence of such rights, recovery may be sought only through the assertion of claims by investors before a court of competent jurisdiction. Further, the Commission cannot give advice as to the merits of securities, whether or not they are registered. Through enactment of the securities laws Congress sought to provide disclosure of much of the basic information on which the merits of particular securities, and the risks inherent in their purchase, might be realistically appraised. But the responsibility for examining the information and determining the investment merit of securities and the risks involved in their purchase rests with the investor.

Administrative Interpretations and Rulemaking

As previously indicated, the Commission not only consults and advises with industry representatives and others concerning legal interpretative problems arising under the securities laws and with respect to the adoption of new or amended rules and regulations, but also gives public notice of suggested rules and invites comments and criticisms which are considered in determining the nature and scope of rules to be adopted. The Commission constantly reviews its rules in light of the experience gained in their administration, to the end that they will provide maximum investor protection with a minimum of interference with the proper functioning of the securities markets.

The examination of the periodic report and proxy statements of companies whose shares are listed or traded over-the-counter (except those of investment companies), as well as the reports of insiders, is conducted by the Division of Corporation Finance, while the investigative, enforcement and regulatory work under this law is carried on by the Division of Trading and Markets, assisted by Regional Offices—both under supervision and direction of the Commission.

PUBLIC UTILITY HOLDING COMPANY ACT OF 1935

Purpose of Act

This statute was enacted by Congress to correct the many abuses which Congressional inquiries had disclosed in the financing and operation of electric and gas public-utility holding-company systems.

When the Act became law in 1935, some 15 holding-company systems controlled 80 percent of all electric energy generation, 98.5 percent of all transmission of electric energy across State lines, and 80 percent of all natural-gas pipeline mileage in the United States. Many of the huge utility empires then in existence controlled subsidiaries operating in many widely-separated States and which had no economic or functional relationship to each other. Holding companies were pyramided layer upon layer, many of them serving no useful or economic purpose; and many systems had very complicated corporate and capital structures, with control often lodged in junior securities having little or no equity. These conditions ranked high among the abuses which the Act was designed to correct.

Registration

Interstate holding-companies which are engaged through their subsidiaries in the electric-utility business or in the retail distribution of natural or manufactured gas are subject to regulation under the statute. The Act requires that they register with the Commission and file initial and periodic reports containing detailed data about the organization, financial structure and operations of each such holding company and of its subsidiaries. Once the holding companies are registered, they and their subsidiaries become subject to regulation by the Commission in accordance with statutory standards designed for the protection of investors, consumers, and the public interest. If, however, a holding company or a subsidiary thereof meets certain specifications, it may be exempted from part or all the duties and obligations otherwise imposed on it by statute.

Integration and Simplification

From the standpoint of their impact on the electric and gas utility industries, the most important provisions of the Act are its requirements for the physical integration and corporate simplification of holding-company systems. The integration standards of the statute restrict a holding company's operations to an "integrated utility system," which is defined in the Act as one capable of economical operation as a single coordinated system confined to a single area or region in one or more states and not so large as to impair (considering the state of the art) the advantages of localized management, efficient operation and effectiveness of local regulation. Additional systems or incidental businesses are retainable only under certain limited conditions. The corporate simplification provisions of the Act require action to insure that the capital structure and the continued existence of any company in a holding-company system do not unduly or unnecessarily complicate the corporate structure of the system or unfairly or inequitably distribute voting power among security holders of the system.

The integration and simplification provisions of the Act direct the Commission to determine what action, if any, must be taken by registered holding companies and their subsidiaries to comply with these requirements; and the Commission may apply to Federal courts for orders compelling compliance with Commission directives made on the basis of such determinations. However, many divestments of nonretainable subsidiaries and properties, recapitalizations, dissolutions of companies and other adjustments required to comply with the Act have been accomplished by the holding-company systems through voluntary reorganization plans for which the Act also provides. If a voluntary plan is found by the Commission to be fair and equitable to all affected persons and to be necessary to further the objectives of the Act, the Commission may approve the plan. Thereafter, if the company requests, the Commission applies to a Federal district court for an order approving the plan and directing its enforcement. All interested persons, including State commissions and other governmental agencies, are accorded full opportunity to be heard in proceedings before the Commission and before the Federal courts.

The overall effect of the Commission's administration of the integration and simplification provisions of the law has been far-reaching and unparalleled.

During the 34 year period from 1938 to 1972, about 2,500 companies have been subject to the Act as registered holding companies or subsidiaries thereof at one time or another. Included in this total were over 227 holding companies, 1,046 electric and gas utility companies and 1,210 other companies engaged in a wide variety of pursuits. Among the latter were brick works, laundries, experimental orchards, motion picture theaters and even a baseball club. Today the picture is strikingly different. Only 17 active holding company systems are now registered. They are comprised of 13 registered holding companies which function solely as holding companies, 7 holding companies which also are engaged in utility operations, 91 electric and/or gas subsidiary companies, 57 nonutility subsidiaries and 16 inactive companies, making a total of 184 companies with aggregate assets of $19 billion. Further, these 17 systems now account for only about one-fifth of the aggregate assets of the privately-owned electric and gas utility and gas pipeline industries of the nation. Most electric and gas utility companies, which formerly were associated with registered holding companies, now operate as independent concerns.

The Commission's Continuing Jurisdiction

In enacting the statute, the Congress recognized that certain electric-utility holding company systems and certain groups of gas utility and transmission companies, which constitute physically integrated systems and are not too large or scattered to meet the integration and simplication requirements of the Act, may offer operating economies and other advantages which justify the continuation of holding-company control. Thus, the 17 systems referred to above are expected to be subject to the regulatory provisions of the Act for the indefinite future.

Financing Transactions

The issue and sale of securities by holding companies and their subsidiaries are subject to regulation by the Commission under prescribed standards of the law. The tests which a proposed security issue must meet are: (1) the security must be reasonably adapted to the security structure of the issuer and of other companies in the same holding company system; (2) the security must be reasonably adapted to the earning power of the company; (3) the proposed issue must be necessary and appropriate to the economical and efficient operation of the company's business; (4) the fees, commissions and other remuneration paid in connection with the issue must not be unreasonable; and (5) the terms and conditions of the issue or sale of the security must not be detrimental to the public interest or the interest of investors or consumers. In certain cases where there has been an approval by a State regulatory commission, the law directs the Commission to exempt security issues of subsidiary companies, subject to imposition of such terms and conditions as the Commission may deem necessary for the protection of investors or consumers.

To implement these objectives and to eliminate investment banker control and assure maintenance of competitive conditions as required, the Commission has promulgated a rule requiring (with certain exceptions) that in the sale of new securities by registered holding companies and their subsidiaries, as well as in the sale by such holding companies of securities held in their investment portfolio, the issuer or seller shall invite sealed competitive bids for the securities.

Purchases and Sales of Utility Securities and Properties

The acquisition of securities and utility assets by holding companies and their subsidiaries may not be authorized by the Commission unless the following standards are met:

1. The acquisition must not tend toward interlocking relations or concentration of control to an extent detrimental to the public interest or the interest of investors or consumers;
2. Any consideration paid for the acquisition, including fees, commissions and other remuneration, must not be unreasonable;
3. The acquisition must not complicate the capital structure of the holding company system;
4. The acquisition must not be otherwise detrimental to the public interest or the interest of investors or consumers, or to the proper functioning of the holding company system; and
5. The acquisition must tend toward the economic and efficient development of an integrated public utility system.

Sales of utility assets or securities may not be made in contravention of Commission rules and orders regarding the consideration to be received, maintenance of competitive conditions, fees and commissions, disclosure of interest and similar matters.

Other Regulatory Provisions

Other phases of the Act provide for the regulation of dividend payments (in circumstances where such payments might result in corporate abuses), intercompany loans, solicitation of proxies, consents and other authorizations, and insiders' trading. "Upstream" loans from subsidiaries to their parents and "upstream" or "cross-stream" loans from public-utility companies to any holding company in the same holding-company system are expressly forbidden. The Act also requires that all services performed for any company in a holding-company system by a service company in that system be rendered at cost fairly and equitably allocated. Thus, the Act deals effectively with the problem of excessive service charges levied on operating electric and gas companies by their parent holding companies, a problem with which State commissions had experienced considerable difficulty.

Administrative Interpretations and Advice

The Commission is assisted in the administration of the Holding Company Act by its Division of Corporate Regulation, which analyzes legal, financial, accounting, engineering and other problems arising under the Act. The Division participates in hearings to develop the factual records; where necessary, files briefs and participates in oral arguments before the Commission; and makes recommendations with respect to the Commission's findings and decisions in cases which arise in the administration of the law. All hearings are conducted in accordance with the Commission's Rules of Practice discussed below under

"Administrative Proceedings." The Division also confers with and renders advisory assistance to holding-company representatives to aid in the solution of their problems under the Act.

TRUST INDENTURE ACT OF 1939

This Act applies in general to bonds, debentures, notes, and similar debt securities offered for public sale which are issued pursuant to trust indentures under which more than $1 million of securities may be outstanding at any one time. Even though such securities may be registered under the Securities Act, they may not be offered for sale to the public unless the trust indenture conforms to specified statutory standards of this Act designed to safeguard the rights and interests of the purchasers.

The Act was passed after studies by the Commission had revealed the frequency with which trust indentures failed to provide minimum protections for security holders and absolved so-called trustees from minimum obligations in the discharge of their trusts. It requires that the indenture trustee be free of conflicting interests which might interfere with the faithful exercise of its duties in behalf of the purchasers of the securities. It requires also that the trustee be a corporation with minimum combined capital and surplus; imposes high standards of conduct and responsibility on the trustee; precludes preferential collection of certain claims owing to the trustee by the issuer in the event of default; provides for the issuer's supplying evidence to the trustee of compliance with indenture terms and conditions such as those relating to the release or substitution of mortgaged property, issuance of new securities or satisfaction of the indenture; and provides for reports and notices by the trustee to security holders. Other provisions of the Act prohibit impairment of the security holders' right to sue individually for principal and interest except under certain circumstances, and require the maintenance of a list of security holders which may be used by them to communicate with each other regarding their rights as security holders.

Applications for qualification of trust indentures are examined by the Division of Corporation Finance for compliance with the applicable requirements of the law and the Commission's rules thereunder.

INVESTMENT COMPANY ACT OF 1940

This legislation, together with the Investment Advisers Act of 1940, discussed below, resulted from a study of the activities of investment companies and investment advisers conducted by the Commission pursuant to direction of Congress contained in the Holding Company Act. The results of this study were reported to Congress in a series of reports filed in 1938, 1939 and 1940, the legislation being supported both by the Commission and the investment company industry.

Under this Act, the activities of companies engaged primarily in the business of investing, reinvesting and trading in securities and whose own securities are offered and sold to and held by the investing public, are subject to certain statutory prohibitions and to Commission regulation in accordance with prescribed standards deemed necessary to protect the interests of investors and the public.

It is important for investors to understand, however, that the Commission does not supervise the investment activities of these companies and that regulation by the Commission does not imply safety of investment in such companies.

In addition to a requirement that such companies register with the Commission,* the law requires disclosure of their financial condition and investment policies to afford investors full and complete information about their activities; prohibits such companies from changing the nature of their business or their investment policies without the approval of the stockholders; bars persons guilty of security frauds from serving as officers and directors; prevents underwriters, investment bankers or brokers from constituting more than a minority of the directors of such companies; requires management contracts (and material changes therein) to be submitted to security holders for their approval; prohibits transactions between such companies and their directors, officers, or affiliated companies or persons, except on approval by the Commission as being fair and involving no overreaching; forbids the issuance of senior securities by such companies except under specified conditions and upon specified terms; and prohibits pyramiding of such companies and cross-ownership of their securities.

Other provisions relate to sales and repurchases of securities issued by investment companies, exchange offers, and other activities of investment companies, including special provisions for periodic payment plans and face-amount certificate companies.

With respect to plans of reorganization of investment companies, the Commission is authorized to prepare advisory reports as to the fairness of their terms and provisions if requested by the company or 25 percent of its stockholders; and it may institute court proceedings to enjoin a plan of reorganization if it appears grossly unfair to security holders. The Commission may also institute court action to remove management officials who may be guilty of gross misconduct or gross abuse of trust.

The securities of investment companies are also required to be registered under the Securities Act; and the companies must file periodic reports and are subject to the Commission's proxy and "insider" trading rules.

The Division of Corporate Regulation assists the Commission in the administration of this law, as well as the processing of investment company registration statements under the Securities Act as well as their proxy statements and periodic reports.

INVESTMENT ADVISERS ACT OF 1940

This law establishes a pattern of regulation of investment advisers which is similar in many respects to Securities Exchange Act provisions governing the conduct of brokers and dealers. It requires, with certain exceptions, that persons or firms who engage for compensation in the business of advising others about

*A list of registered investment companies, showing their classification, assets size and location, may be purchased from the Commission in photocopy form (cost furnished upon request).

their securities transactions shall register with the Commission and conform their activities to statutory standards designed to protect the interests of investors.

The registration of investment advisers may be denied, suspended or revoked by the Commission if, after notice and hearing, it finds that a statutory disqualification exists and that such action is in the public interest. Disqualifications include a conviction for certain financial crimes or securities violations, the existence of injunctions based on such activities, a conviction for violation of the Mail Fraud Statute, the wilfull filing of false reports with the Commission, and wilfull violations of this Act, the Securities Act or the Securities Exchange Act. In addition to the administrative sanction of denial, suspension or revocation, the Commission may obtain injunctions restraining violations of this law and may recommend prosecution by the Department of Justice for fraudulent misconduct or wilfull violation ot the law or rules of the Commission thereunder.

The law contains anti-fraud provisions, and it empowers the Commission to adopt rules defining fraudulent, deceptive or manipulative acts and practices and designed to prevent such activities. It also requires that investment advisers disclose the nature of their interest in transactions executed for their clients; and, in effect, it prevents the assignment of investment advisory contracts without the client's consent. The law also imposes on investment advisers subject to the registration requirement the duty to maintain books and records in accordance with such rules as may be prescribed by the Commission, and it authorizes the Commission to conduct inspections of such books and records.

The Commission is aided in the administration of this law by the Office of Registrations and Reports and the Division of Investment Management Regulation.

BANKRUPTCY ACT, CHAPTER X

Under Chapter X, the Commission serves as adviser to United States district courts in connection with proceedings for the reorganization of debtor corporations in which there is a substantial public interest. It participates as a party to these proceedings, either at the request or with the approval of the courts. It renders independent, expert advice and assistance to the courts, which do not maintain their own staffs of expert consultants.

Representatives of the Commission follow closely the progress of reorganization proceedings in which it is a participant, and confer with the court-appointed trustees and their counsel and with other interested parties in the s tion of the various problems which arise in the administration of the affairs of the debtor corporation and in the formulation of plans of reorganization. In addition to the advice and assistance which the Commission renders, both to the court and to the parties, in connection with the preparation of plans of reorganization, the Commission also presents its views and recommendations on such matters as the qualifications and independence of trustees and their counsel, fee allowances to the various parties, including the trustees and their counsel, sales of properties and other assets, interim distributions to security holders, and other financial or legal matters. The Commission has no independent right of appeal from court rulings.

Of primary importance is the Commission's assistance in the formulation of plans of reorganization of the debtor corporation which will provide fair and equitable treatment to the various creditors and other security holders and which will help to assure that the corporation will emerge from bankruptcy in a sound financial condition and able to carry on without the continued threat of bankruptcy. Underlying the Commission's recommendations concerning the fairness and feasibility of reorganization plans, is a thorough study and analysis of the debtor's past operations, its financial condition, its past earnings record and prospective future earning power, its competitive position in the particular industry, and related matters. In cases in which the scheduled liabilities of the debtor exceed $3 million, the plan of reorganization must be, and in other cases may be, referred by the court to the Commission for preparation of an advisory report on the fairness and feasibility of the plan. This advisory report is filed with the court for its assistance and is distributed among the creditors and security holders to enable them to exercise an informed judgment in considering whether to vote for or against acceptance of the plan. In cases where no formal advisory report is prepared, the Commission's views are stated orally at the hearing on the plan before the court.

Because of the predominantly local character of reorganization cases, court appearances, consultations with the parties, investigations and examinations are handled primarily by the Commission's Regional Offices, subject to supervision by the Division of Corporate Regulation and approval by the Commission.

ADMINISTRATIVE PROCEEDINGS

All formal administrative proceedings of the Commission are conducted in accordance with its Rules of Practice, which conform to the Administrative Procedure Act and are designed to establish procedural, "due process" safeguards which will protect the rights and interests of parties to each such proceeding. Among these are requirements for timely notice of the proceeding and for a sufficient specification of the issues or charges involved to enable each of the parties adequately to prepare his case. All parties, including counsel for the interested Division or Office of the Commission, may appear at the hearing and present evidence and cross-examine witnesses in much the same manner as in the ordinary trial of court actions. In addition, other interested persons may be permitted to intervene or be given limited rights of participation. In some cases, the relevant facts may be stipulated in lieu of the conduct of an evidentiary hearing.

Hearings are conducted before a Hearing Officer who is normally an Administrative Law Judge appointed by the Commission; he serves independently of the interested Division or Office and rules on the admissibility of evidence and on other issues arising during the course of the hearing. At the conclusion of the hearing, the parties and participants may urge, in writing, specific findings of fact and conclusions of law for adoption by the Hearing Officer. Thereupon, the Hearing Officer prepares and files an initial decision (unless waived), setting forth his conclusions as to the facts established by the evidence and including an order disposing of the issues involved in the proceeding. Copies of the initial decision are served on the parties and participants, who may seek Commission review thereof. If review is not sought and the Commission does not order review on its own motion, the initial decision becomes final and the Hearing Officer's order becomes effective.

In the event of Commission review of the initial decision, the parties and participants may file briefs and be heard in oral argument before the Commission. On the basis of an independent review of the record, the Commission prepares and issues its own decision; the Office of Opinions and Review aids the Commission in this decisional process. The laws provide that any person or firm aggrieved by a decision or order of the Commission may seek review thereof by the appropriate United States court of appeals. The initial decisions of Hearing Officers as well as the Commission's decisions are made public. Copies of Commission decisions and announcements that the initial decisions of Hearing Officers have become final also are distributed to the Commission's mailing lists. Ultimately, the Commission's decisions (as well as initial decisions which have become final and are of precedential significance) are printed by the Government Printing Office and published in the Commission's "Decisions and Reports"

OFFICE OF THE GENERAL COUNSEL

The General Counsel is the chief legal officer of the Commission. The duties of his office include representing the Commission in judicial proceedings; handling legal matters which cut across the lines of work of the several operating Divisions; and providing advice and assistance to the Commission, its operating Divisions, and Regional Offices with respect to statutory interpretation, rulemaking, legislative matters and other legal problems, public or private investigations, and Congressional hearings and investigations. The Office also reviews cases where criminal prosecution is recommended. The General Counsel directs and supervises all contested civil litigation (except United States district court proceedings under Chapter X of the Bankruptcy Act) and represents the Commission in all cases in the appellate courts, filing briefs and presenting oral arguments in behalf of the Commission. In addition, in cases between private parties involving the statutes the Commission administers, the Office represents the Commission where it participates as a friend of the court in cases involving legal issues of general importance.

The Commission from time to time recommends revisions in the statutes which it administers. In addition, it prepares comments on any proposed legislation which might affect its work or where it is asked for its views by Congressional Committees. The Office of the General Counsel, together with the Division assisting the Commission in the function which may be affected by such legislation, prepares this legislative material.

OFFICE OF THE CHIEF ACCOUNTANT

The Chief Accountant is the Commission's chief consulting officer on accounting matters, advising the Commission with respect to accounting problems which arise in the administration of the Acts, particularly in matters involving new accounting policy determination. The Chief Accountant has general supervision over the execution of Commission policy with respect to the accounting principles and procedures applicable to the financial statements filed with the Commission and to the auditing standards and practices observed by the independent public accountants who examine and render an opinion on these statements.

A major objective of the Commission has been to improve accounting and auditing standards and to maintain high standards of professional conduct by the independent accountants through cooperation with the accounting profession and by the rule-making process. In furtherance of this policy the Chief Accountant consults with representatives of the accounting profession regarding the promulgation of new or revised accounting and auditing standards and drafts rules and regulations which prescribe requirements for financial statements. Many of the rules are embodied in a basic accounting regulation entitled Regulation S–X adopted by the Commission which, together with a number of opinions issued as "Accounting Series Releases," governs the form and content of most of the financial statements filed with it.

The Chief Accountant also has supervisory responsibility for the drafting of uniform systems of accounts for public utility holding companies, mutual service companies and subsidiary service companies under the Holding Company Act; for accounting requirements for investment and broker-dealer companies; and for the general administration of those systems and accounting requirements.

The Chief Accountant administers the Commission's rules which require that accountants who examine financial statements filed with it be independent of their clients, and makes recommendations on cases arising under the Commission's Rules of Practice which specify that an accountant may be denied the privilege of practicing before the Commission because of lack of character or integrity or qualifications to represent others, or because of unethical or unprofessional conduct. He also supervises the procedures followed in accounting investigations conducted by the Commission's staff.

OFFICE OF ECONOMIC RESEARCH

The principal functions of this Office are three-fold: (1) to assist the Commission by analyzing legal, economic and industrial developments affecting the securities markets and by recommending to the Commission the institution or modification of programs commensurate with such developments; (2) to prepare statistical data and analyses related to the capital markets for Commission use as well as for general economic analysis and (3) to compile and publish data furnished to the general public as part of the overall Government statistical program.

Some of the more important projects of this office include: (1) development of analytical framework for anticipating developments in the securities industry and a continuing analysis of the economic and financial condition of the securities industry; (2) analysis of the impact of competitive rates on the economic and legal structure of the securities industry and on the investment process; (3) review of trends in corporate capital structure; (4) analysis of trends in capital markets worldwide, the impact of internationalization of these markets; and (5) continued study as to the role of self-regulation in the securities industry, and the possible need for change in regulatory rules or the industry itself to make the capital markets more efficient.

The Office of Management and Budget has designated the Commission as the agency best suited to make and publish certain financial studies including: (a) The Net Working Capital of Nonfinancial Corporations; (b) The financial activities of Private Noninsured Pension Funds and (c) New Security Offerings and related studies.

PUBLIC INFORMATION

Financial and other data included in registration statements, reports, applications and similar documents filed with the Commission are available for inspection in the Public Reference Room of the Commission's Headquarters Office in Washington, D.C. Copies of portions or all of any such public document may be obtained at nominal cost (the amount of the fee is established by an annual contract between the Commission and the copier who reproduces the documents. Estimates as to the cost of copies of specific reports or other information may be obtained on request to the Section of Public Reference, Office of Records and Service, Securities and Exchange Commission, Washington, D.C. 20549.

Current annual and other periodic reports (including financial statements) filed by companies whose securities are listed on exchanges also are available for inspection in the Commission's New York, Chicago and San Francisco Regional Offices, as are the registration statements (and subsequent reports) filed by those companies whose securities are traded over-the-counter which register under the 1964 Amendments to the Exchange Act. Moreover, if the issuer's principal office is located in the area served by the Atlanta, Boston, Denver, Fort Worth or Seattle Regional Office, its filings also may be examined at the particular Regional Office in question. In addition, prospectuses covering recent public offerings of securities registered under the Securities Act may be examined in all Regional Offices; and copies of broker-dealer and investment adviser registrations, as well as Regulation A notifications and offering circulars, may be examined in the particular Regional Office in which they were filed.

PUBLICATIONS

The publications described below are compiled by the Commission but printed and sold by the Superintendent of Documents. Requests for single copies or subscriptions, accompanied by the correct remittance, should be addressed to the Superintendent of Documents, United States Government Printing Office, Washington, D.C. 20402. THE COMMISSION DOES NOT MAINTAIN A MAILING LIST FOR THESE PUBLICATIONS.

NEWS DIGEST. A daily report of Commission announcements, decisions, orders, rules and rule proposals, current reports and applications filed, and litigation developments.

SEC DOCKET. A weekly compilation of the full texts of SEC releases under the following Acts: Securities Act, Securities Exchange Act, Public Utility Holding Company Act, Trust Indenture Act, Investment Advisers Act, and Investment Company Act. Also included will be the full texts of Accounting series releases, corporate reorganization releases, and litigation releases.

OFFICIAL SUMMARY.

A monthly summary of security transactions and holdings reported under the provisions of the Securities Exchange Act of 1934, the Public Utility Holding Company Act of 1935, and the Investment Company Act of 1940 by officers, directors, and certain other persons.

STATISTICAL BULLETIN.

A weekly publication containing data on odd lot and round lot transactions, block distributions, working capital of U.S. corporations, assets of noninsured pension funds, 144 filings, and 8æ reports.

ACTS AND RULES AND REGULATIONS:

Rules of Practice and Rules Relating to Investigations and Code of Behavior Governing Ex Parte Communications Between Persons Outside the Commission and Decisional Employees.

Securities Act of 1933.

Rules and Regulations under the 1933 Act.

Securities Exchange Act of 1934.

Rules and Regulations under the 1934 Act.

Public Utility Holding Company Act of 1935.

Rules and Regulations under the 1935 Act.

Trust Indenture Act of 1939 and Rules and Regulations.

Investment Company Act of 1940.

Rules and Regulations under the Investment Company Act.

Investment Advisers Act of 1940 and Rules and Regulations.

Chapter X, National Bankruptcy Act,

Regulation S–X (form and content of financial statements under 1933, 1934, 1935 Acts and Investment Company Act of 1940).

ACCOUNTING SERIES RELEASES:

Compilation of Releases Nos. 1-112, inclusive.

Compilation of Releases Dealing with Matters Frequently Arising under the Securities Act of 1933.

Compilations of Releases Dealing with matters arising under the Securities Exchange Act of 1934 and Investment Advisers Act of 1940.

Compilation of Releases Dealing with matters arising under the Investment Company Act of 1940.

SEC ANNUAL REPORT TO CONGRESS:

First through Thirty-fourth (out of print) (Available only for reference purposes in SEC Washington, D.C., and Regional Offices.)

SEC JUDICIAL DECISIONS (Buckram bound)—Vols. 1–5, covering period 1934–48, available only for reference purposes in SEC Washington, D.C., and Regional Offices.

SEC DECISIONS AND REPORTS (Buckram bound)—Vols. 1–41, covering period 1934–64, available only for reference purposes in SEC Washington, D.C., and Regional Offices.

Directory of Companies filing Annual Reports with the Commission under the Securities Exchange Act of 1934. Lists companies alphabetically and classified by industry groups according to the Standard Industrial Classification Manual of the Bureau of the Budget. Published annually.

A Study of Mutual Funds (Prepared for the SEC by the Wharton School of Finance and Commerce) (1962)—595 pages H. Doc. No. 2274 (87th Cong.) (Available only for reference purposes in SEC Washington, D.C., and Regional Offices.)

Report of SEC Special Study of Securities Markets (1963).

Part 6 of the Special Study Report contains the Index to Parts 1, 2, 3, 4 and 5, Tables of statutes, rules, cases, persons or securities mentioned in the Special Study.

Commission Report on Public Policy Implications of Investment Company Growth H. Rept. No. 2337 (89th Cong.), available only for reference purposes in SEC Washington, D.C., and Regional Offices.

Institutional Investor Study Report of the Securities and Exchange Commission (1971)—Eight Parts, H. Doc. No. 64 (92d Cong.).

Part 8 of the said Institutional Investor, containing the Text of the Summary and Conclusions drawn from each of the fifteen chapters of the report.

Study on Unsafe and Unsound Practices of Broker-Dealers, H. Doc. 231, (92nd Cong.)

Report of the Real Estate Advisory Committee to the SEC.

The Financial Collapse of The Penn Central Company, Staff Report of the SEC to the Special Subcommittee on Investigations, August, 1972.

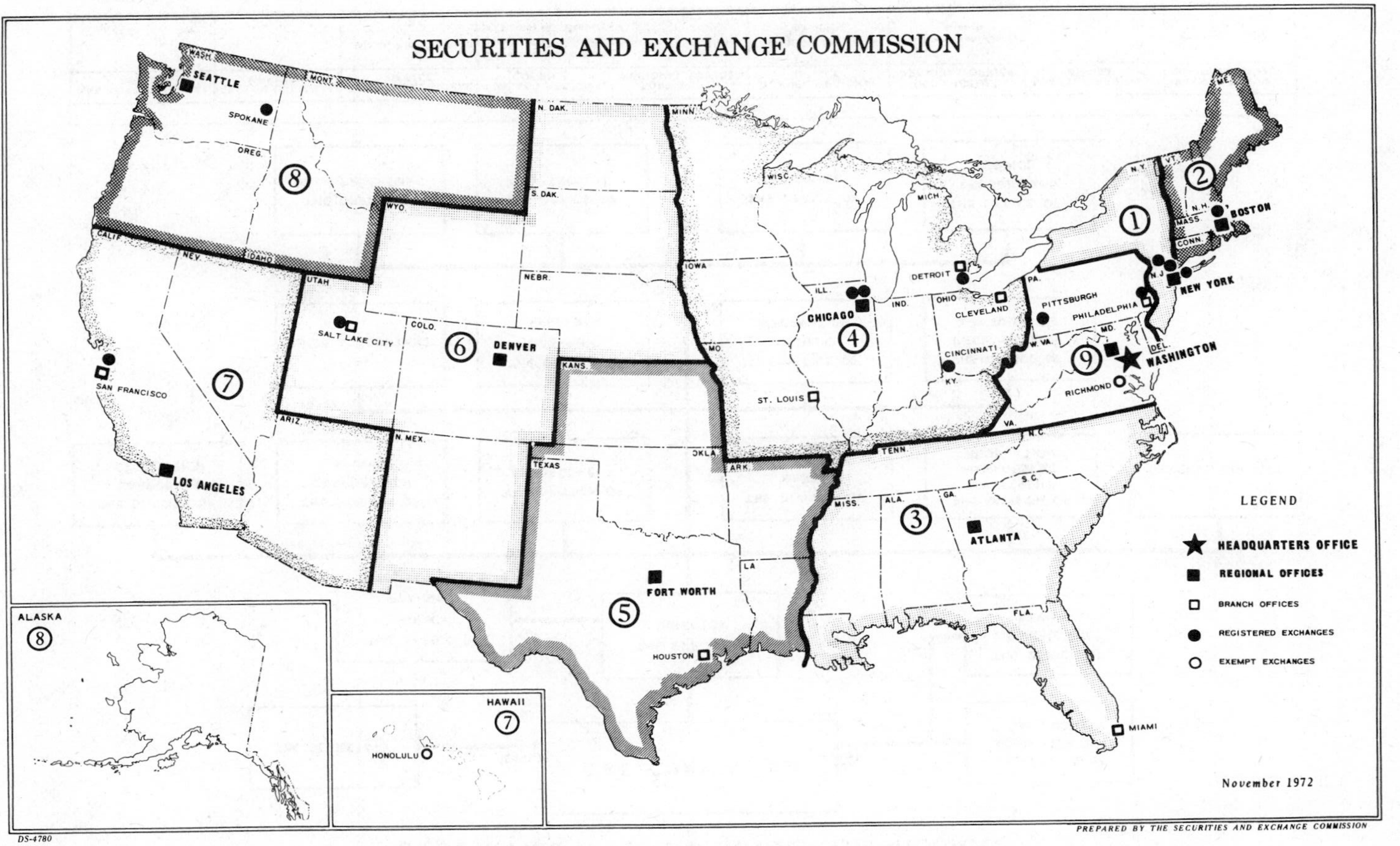
SECURITIES AND EXCHANGE COMMISSION
SEATTLE
SPOKANE
SAN FRANCISCO
LOS ANGELES
SALT LAKE CITY
DENVER
FORT WORTH
HOUSTON
CHICAGO
ST. LOUIS
DETROIT
CLEVELAND
CINCINNATI
PITTSBURGH
PHILADELPHIA
NEW YORK
BOSTON
WASHINGTON
RICHMOND
ATLANTA
MIAMI
ALASKA
HAWAII
HONOLULU
LEGEND
HEADQUARTERS OFFICE
REGIONAL OFFICES
BRANCH OFFICES
REGISTERED EXCHANGES
EXEMPT EXCHANGES
November 1972
PREPARED BY THE SECURITIES AND EXCHANGE COMMISSION
DS-4780

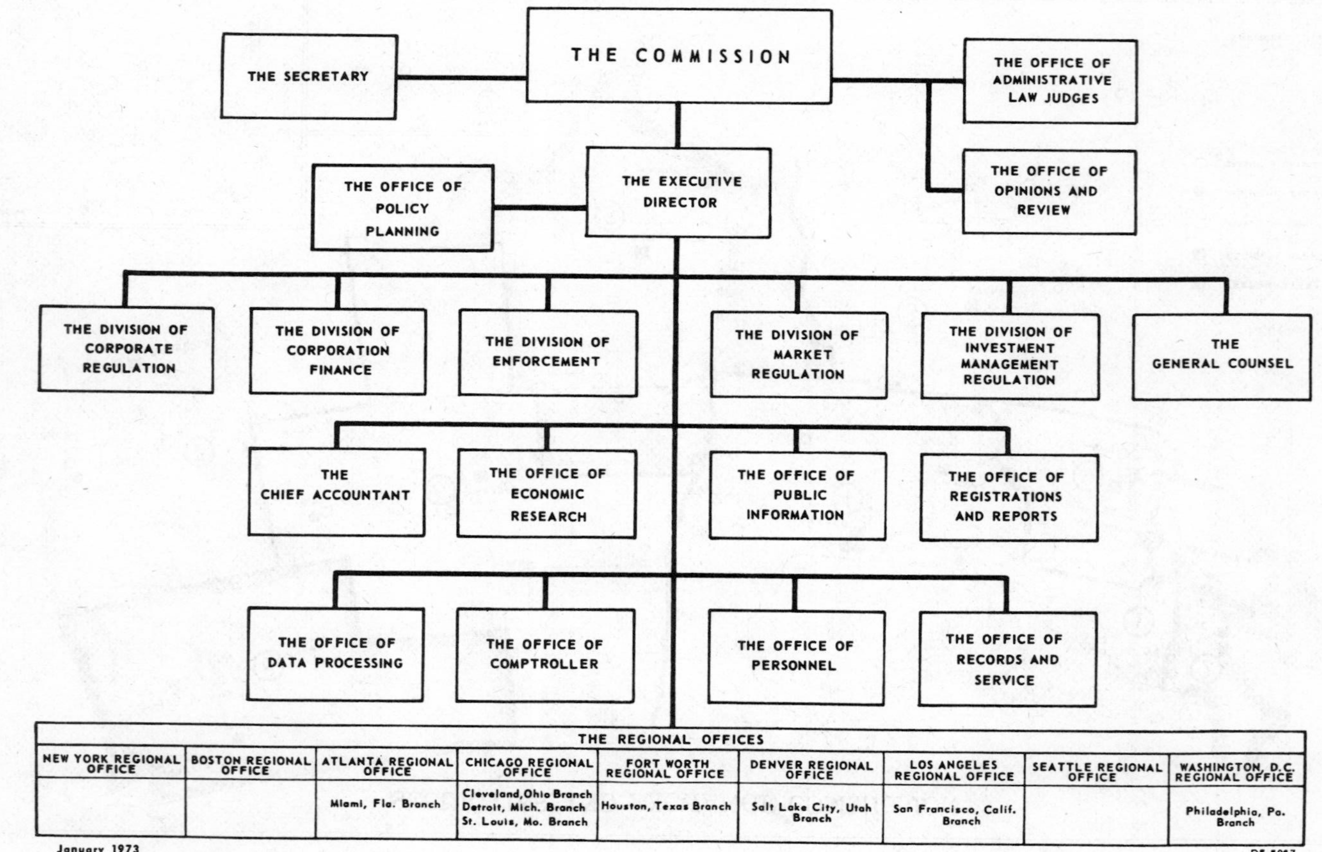
SECURITIES AND EXCHANGE COMMISSION
THE COMMISSION
THE SECRETARY
THE OFFICE OF ADMINISTRATIVE LAW JUDGES
THE OFFICE OF OPINIONS AND REVIEW
THE EXECUTIVE DIRECTOR
THE OFFICE OF POLICY PLANNING
THE DIVISION OF CORPORATE REGULATION
THE DIVISION OF CORPORATION FINANCE
THE DIVISION OF ENFORCEMENT
THE DIVISION OF MARKET REGULATION
THE DIVISION OF INVESTMENT MANAGEMENT REGULATION
THE GENERAL COUNSEL
THE CHIEF ACCOUNTANT
THE OFFICE OF ECONOMIC RESEARCH
THE OFFICE OF PUBLIC INFORMATION
THE OFFICE OF REGISTRATIONS AND REPORTS
THE OFFICE OF DATA PROCESSING
THE OFFICE OF COMPTROLLER
THE OFFICE OF PERSONNEL
THE OFFICE OF RECORDS AND SERVICE
THE REGIONAL OFFICES
NEW YORK REGIONAL OFFICE
BOSTON REGIONAL OFFICE
ATLANTA REGIONAL OFFICE
Miami, Fla. Branch
CHICAGO REGIONAL OFFICE
Cleveland, Ohio Branch
Detroit, Mich. Branch
St. Louis, Mo. Branch
FORT WORTH REGIONAL OFFICE
Houston, Texas Branch
DENVER REGIONAL OFFICE
Salt Lake City, Utah Branch
LOS ANGELES REGIONAL OFFICE
San Francisco, Calif. Branch
SEATTLE REGIONAL OFFICE
WASHINGTON, D.C. REGIONAL OFFICE
Philadelphia, Pa. Branch
January 1973
DS-5067

PART II

Investment Vehicles

4

Common Stock

JEROME B. COHEN, Ph.D.
Senior Editor
Bankers Magazine
Emeritus Professor of Finance
Baruch College, City University of New York

INTRODUCTION

THE ESTIMATED market value of all outstanding corporate stock in the United States, including both common and preferred stock, reached $1,168.5 billion in 1972. See Table 1. There are some 32 million individual shareowners plus several thousand institutions. In a recent year the U.S. capital market facilitated the sale of $14 billion of corporate bonds and $12 billion of corporate stock, while additionally handling billions of dollars of federal, state, and local governmental bonds. Such are the enormous dimensions of our subject.

The last decade saw the emergence of "the cult of equities," and of institutional dominance in the securities markets. In the quarter of a century ending in 1970 (possibly?), two of the most significant trends were the accelerating dominance of institutional activity in equity markets and the increasing extent to which common stock was utilized to achieve portfolio performance objectives. In recent years institutional investors have collectively absorbed not only the entire amount of net new corporate equity issues, but a substantial liquidation of individual stockholdings as well.

The relative importance of institutional activity in the equity markets can be seen by the pattern of trading on the New York Stock Exchange. Institutions and intermediaries accounted for 55.9 percent of the NYSE public trading volume in 1970, and more significantly, for 61.9 percent of the value of all transactions. By contrast, in 1960 the figures were

TABLE 1

Market Value of All Outstanding Corporate Stock in the U.S. (billions of dollars, end of year)

	1964	*1965*	*1966*	*1967*	*1968*	*1969*	*1970*	*1971*	*1972*
Listed stocks (total)	506.8	573.1	514.4	652.7	759.5	682.6	680.7	795.5r	932.1
Domestic companies	486.1	551.7	494.8	627.5	729.1	659.0	656.4	769.4	893.9
Foreign companies	17.7	18.7	16.9	20.9	24.7	18.8	20.5	21.9	33.3
Investment companies	3.0	2.7	2.7	4.3	5.7	4.8	3.8	4.2	4.9
OTC stocks (total)	157.5r	179.8r	166.4r	202.5r	248.3	208.5r	204.0r	246.8r	260.9
Domestic companies	107.5	120.7	105.6	129.2	164.3	119.5	113.7	136.8	161.4
Foreign companies	9.8	11.1	14.8	14.1	14.2	23.7	25.0	28.2r	20.4
Investment companies	40.2r	48.0r	46.0r	59.2r	69.8	65.3r	65.3r	81.8r	79.1
Total traded stock	664.3r	752.9r	680.8r	855.2r	1,007.8	891.1r	884.7r	1,042.3r	1,193.0
Closely held stock	114.9r	130.3r	117.8	147.9	174.3	154.2r	153.1r	180.3r	206.4
Total corporate stock	779.2r	883.2r	798.6r	1,003.1r	1,182.1	1,045.3r	1,037.8r	1,222.6r	1,399.4
Investment companies (–)	43.2r	50.7r	48.7r	63.5r	75.5	70.1r	69.1r	86.0r	84.0
Foreign companies (–)	27.5	29.8	31.7	35.0	38.9	42.5	45.5	50.1r	53.7
Total domestic stock (includes intercorporate holdings)	708.5r	802.7r	718.2	904.6	1,067.7	932.7r	923.2r	1,086.5r	1,261.7
Intercorporate holdings (–)	80.8	93.9	74.7	85.0	99.3	78.3r	74.8r	88.0r	102.2
Total domestic stock (excludes intercorporate holdings)	627.7r	708.8r	643.5	819.6	968.4	854.4	848.4r	998.5r	1,159.5
Portfolio foreign stock	5.3	5.0	4.3	5.2	6.5	7.0	6.4	7.1r	9.0
Total Stock Outstanding	633.0r	713.8r	647.8	824.8	974.9	861.4	854.8r	1,005.6r	1,168.5

Note: r indicates figure is rounded.
Source: *Statistical Bulletin*, Securities and Exchange Commission, April 1973.

31.4 percent and 39.3 percent, respectively. Growing institutional dominance of equity markets had two facets. First, institutional portfolio assets grew more rapidly than the amount of stock available for purchase. For example, the total value of all stock outstanding rose 104 percent between 1960 and 1970, while the assets of noninsured private pension funds rose 193 percent; of state and local retirement funds, 195 percent; of investment companies (mutual funds only), 180 percent; and so on. Secondly, common stockholdings of institutions showed sharp increases throughout the 1950s and 1960s. For example, corporate stock comprised over 67 percent of the assets of noninsured private pension funds at the end of 1971, as compared to 43 percent in 1960, and less than 20 percent in 1952.

A recent study forecast even greater institutional dominance of equity markets in the years ahead. By the year 2000 it was estimated that institutions would own 55 percent of the market value of all common stocks, compared to 34 percent in 1970 and a prospective 36 percent in 1980.[1]

The main reason for the shift to equities was the seeming failure of fixed income investments to produce yields sufficient to offset the inroads of inflation and, on the other hand, the apparent ability of common stocks, *over the long run,* to more than outpace rising prices and the cost of living.

While the dollar lost 85 percent of its value (purchasing power) since 1897, the Dow-Jones industrials were up 1,975 percent. The following tabulation, covering a recent decade, is illuminating:

	Recent Change, 1/1/63–12/31/72
Cost of living	+39.9%
New York Stock Exchange Index	+96.6
Standard & Poor's Index of 500 stocks	+87.1
Dow-Jones Industrial Average	+56.4
Standard & Poor's long-term government bonds	−19.0
Standard & Poor's municipal bonds	−23.6
Standard & Poor's high-grade corporate bonds	−32.2
Standard & Poor's preferred stocks	−36.2

Source: Johnson's Investment Company Charts, Buffalo, New York, 1973.

David L. Babson,[2] in an analysis written near the bottom of the 1970 bear market, indicated that the "net after-inflation return on Single A corporate bonds has consistently been ranging between 2 percent and 2½ percent," as the following tabulation shows:

---

[1] Robert M. Soldofsky, *Institutional Holdings of Common Stock 1900–2000* Ann Arbor, Michigan: Bureau of Business Research, Graduate School of Business Administration, University of Michigan, 1971), p. 209.

[2] Source: *Weekly Staff Letter,* David L. Babson & Co., Inc., Boston, May 27, 1970.

	1970	*1969*	*1968*	*Average 1965–67*	*Average 1955–64*
Bond yields	8.4%	7.4%	6.5%	5.3%	4.3%
Annual inflation rate	6.2	5.4	4.2	3.2	1.6
Net "real" return	2.2%	2.0%	2.3%	2.1%	2.7%

Based on figures such as these, institutions were urged to and did turn to common stock investments. For example, in a study for the Ford Foundation, designed to stimulate educational endowment trustees to take a more aggressive posture, it was noted that:

> Bonds have lost some appeal to investors seeking safety of principal . . . the loss of appeal widens as inflation accelerates.
>
> To be conservative today, one must protect the purchasing power of capital rather than just its dollar value.
>
> Banks are unable to do this when the general price level is rising.[3]

In another study seeking to clarify the responsibilities of endowment trustees, it was said:

> The portfolios of many endowment funds have been far too heavily laden with fixed income securities to resist the relentless erosion of inflation. In a decade when the average price of common stock has risen seven times as fast as the cost of living, and dividends on common stocks three and a half times as fast, many endowments have been exceedingly hard-pressed even to keep abreast of the increase in the cost of living.[4]

The assumption of these and other authors was that common stock investment was an effective hedge against the inroads of inflation whereas bonds were not.

TYPES OF COMMON STOCK

There are a variety of ways of classifying common stock: by issue, by legal status, by degrees of risk, by investment function, and by traditional nomenclature of Wall Street. Consider the customary appellations of the Street. There are blue chip stocks, established growth stocks, newer growth stocks, income stocks, cyclical stocks, speculative stocks, and others. There are high volatility stocks and low volatility shares—high P/E stocks and low P/E stocks. In the loose and flexible

---

[3] *Managing Educational Endowments*, a Report to the Ford Foundation, New York, August 1969, p. 15.

[4] William L. Cary and Craig B. Bright, "The Law and the Lore of Endowment Funds," a Report to the Ford Foundation, New York, March 1969, p. 5.

language of Wall Street, there are both high flyers and low-priced issues. Lines of demarcation between types are not precise and clear, but investors have a general notion of what is meant by each of these imprecise categories.

Blue Chip Stocks

Blue chip stocks are high grade investment quality issues of major companies which have long and unbroken records of earnings and dividend payments. Stocks such as American Telephone & Telegraph, General Motors, Du Pont, Exxon (formerly Standard Oil of New Jersey), Eastman Kodak, and Sears Roebuck, for example, are generally considered to be blue chip shares. The term is generally used to describe the common stock of large, well-established, stable, and mature companies of great financial strength. The term in all probability comes from poker, where blue chips, in contrast to red and white, have the greatest money value.

The blue chips of our era are not necessarily the blue chips of another period. Ever hear of Midvale Steel & Ordinance, Central Leather, International Mercantile Marine, Cambria Steel, Consolidation Coal, Chile Copper, Magnolia Petroleum, American Woolen, Ohio Cities Gas, Virginia Carolina Chemical, Prairie Oil & Gas, Atlantic Gulf & West Indies, American Locomotive, Cuba Cane Sugar, Baldwin Locomotive, Associated Oil, Greene Cananea Copper, American Cotton Oil, and United Verde Extension Mining? They were among the top 100 industrials of 1917. *Forbes* studied the top 100 companies over the last five decades and noted: "Of the top 100 in 1917, only 43 are among the top 100 today. Twenty-eight of 1917's companies have disappeared entirely. Of the top 20 in 1917 only 7 now remain in that corporate eminence."

What constitutes a blue chip does not change over time, but the stocks that qualify do. The railroad issues, once the bluest of the blue chips, no longer qualify. On the other hand, Xerox, which was not considered a blue chip in the early 1950s, does qualify today. Blue chip or high-quality companies, hold important, if not leading, positions in their industries, where they are sometimes pace setters and frequently determine the standards by which other companies in their fields are measured. The companies have foresighted management that has taken steps to insure future growth without jeopardizing current earnings. Policies have been established and implemented to protect the company in an economic reversal. Such companies have the advantage of size—in a recession they should be able to hold their own and then record strong earnings gains in an economic upswing because they have the resources to capitalize on a recovery. Also, their earnings will be sustained during inflationary periods.

Growth Stocks

Many of the blue chips may also be considered *growth stocks;* some, however, are *cyclicals;* and others, *defensive.* A growth stock is one of a company whose sales and earnings are expanding faster than the general economy and faster than the average for the industry. The company is usually aggressive, research minded, plowing back earnings to facilitate expansion. For this reason growth companies, intent on financing their own expansion from retained earnings, pay relatively small dividends and their current yield is generally low. Over time, however, substantial capital gains may accrue from the appreciation of the value of the common as a result of the plowback and expansion.

This may be seen in Table 2 showing a $10,000 portfolio of 10 growth stocks which the Babson Company selected in early 1951 and in which no changes have since been made to rule out hindsight. The 10 growth stock performance is compared to the performance of 30 stocks in the Dow Industrial Average. The investment return of a growth stock consists not only of the difference between original cost and the current price but also of a rising flow of dividends over the years. This often adds up to many times the original investment. For example, the 10 growth stock portfolio has produced total dividend income of $32,343, in addition to $169,046 in capital appreciation. Note also that the market value of the growth stocks was fourfold that of the 30 Dow stocks.

TABLE 2

Performance of 10 Growth Stocks and 30 Dow Stocks, 1950–73

	Market Value		*Cumulative Dividends*		*P/E Ratio*	
	10 Growth Stocks	*30 Dow Stocks*	*10 Growth Stocks*	*30 Dow Stocks*	*Weighted Median Growth*	*Dow*
1950	$ 10,000	$10,000	—	—	10	8
1955	26,732	22,596	$ 2,678	$ 3,761	18	12
1960	65,557	28,495	6,833	8,351	38	19
1965	96.536	44,844	13,999	13,909	28	17
1966	104,336	36,351	15,907	15,302	28	15
1967	139,436	41,876	17,896	16,682	35	14
1968	140,444	43,664	20,092	18,132	35	15
1969	146,301	37,030	22,517	19,701	33	14
1970	129,817	38,814	25,198	21,159	28	14
1971	147,488	41,186	28,007	22,587	32	17
1972	186,664	47,193	30,866	24,080	29	12
Cur.	179,046	41,733	32,343	24,846	28	9

Source: "Long-Term Investing and the 'Two-Tier' Market," *Weekly Staff Letter,* David L. Babson & Co., Inc., Boston, August 16, 1973.

The theme of the 1973 Institutional Investors Conference was "Is Growth Investing Dead?" The main speaker to address this theme was David L. Babson. He said in part:

Is growth dead? Of course, it isn't. Investing for long-term growth is just as alive today as it was 5 years ago, 15 years ago, or 25 years ago.

What's dead and ought to be buried is all the tomfoolery of recent years that has been masquerading under the name of growth investing.

If by growth investing you mean churning a portfolio like some managers have been doing at a rate of 100 percent, 200 percent, or more a year, it's dead all right. Check the past record and you'll find the higher the turnover ratio, the poorer the results.

If by growth investing you mean playing the latest concept stocks with their sky-high P/E ratios, that too, is dead. To convince yourself, you don't have to go back to the performance disasters of 1968–69. Just count up all the fractured fads of 1972–73—the Levitz Furnitures, the Horizon Corporations, the New Process Companies, etc.

If you mean trying for a total return of 15–20 percent each and every year, it isn't dead—it was stillborn. Anyone who thinks he can consistently do twice as well as the S & P 500 has to believe that his judgement is so infallible, his courage so daring, and his luck so fantastic that he will accomplish what no one he knows, including himself, has ever accomplished before.

These phony growth practices have no more connection with real growth investing than the Beatles had with Beethoven. The whole idea behind growth investing is to share—as a partner—in the long-term progress of a group of companies with superior investment characteristics.

Let me list a few of these characteristics which any bona fide growth company must have:

1. A leading position in an attractive business.
2. Top-notch proprietary products, services, or skills.
3. Good pricing flexibility.
4. Ability to develop new products and markets.
5. Low labor costs.
6. High return on equity.
7. Strong financial position.
8. High plow-back ratio.
9. Conservative, sensible accounting.
10. Limited exposure to environmental, social, and political pressures.
11. Relative freedom from import competition.[5]

The performance of a number of growth stocks which meet some but not all of the criteria given above may be seen in Table 3. Note the steady growth in earnings over the 1959–73 period.

It is often the practice to distinguish between large, mature, and stable growth companies and newer, smaller, emerging growth stocks. The former have a track record for growth in earnings per share and price appreciation over long periods of time. The latter may show only

[5] David L. Babson, "Is Growth Investing Dead?" Boston, March 22, 1973.

TABLE 3

The Performance of Some Mature Growth Stocks, 1959–73

	Earnings per Share			*Percent Increase*		*Share Price*		
	1959	*1966*	*1973E*	*1959–1966*	*1966–1973E*	*1959*	*1966*	*Current*
Abbott Labs	$1.18	$2.04	$ 3.30	+ 73	+ 62	23	41	73
Air Products	0.20	0.94	1.67	+ 370	+ 78	10	15	38
American Home	0.34	0.61	1.20	+ 79	+ 97	8	13	42
AMP	0.13	0.41	1.15	+ 224	+185	2	8	38
Colgate	0.49E	0.60E	1.25	+ 22	+108	6	9	30
Dow Chemical	0.95	1.25	2.50	+ 32	+100	27	21	51
Eastman Kodak	0.87	2.15	4.00	+ 147	+ 86	21	61	128
Exxon	2.91	5.06	8.20	+ 74	+ 62	52	71	94
Gillette	1.11	1.75	3.00	+ 58	+ 71	18	37	53
Halliburton	0.99	2.14	4.50	+ 116	+110	14	22	132
Honeywell	2.10	3.07	5.20	+ 46	+ 69	65	74	100
IBM	1.34	3.77	10.00	+ 181	+165	54	131	313
Lilly, Eli	0.37	0.74	2.20	+ 100	+197	10	20	84
Merck	0.47	1.17	2.30	+ 149	+ 97	13	36	89
Minnesota Mining	0.63	1.29	2.50	+ 105	+ 94	24	36	82
National Starch	0.55	1.26	2.45	+ 129	+ 94	11	23	53
Procter & Gamble	0.99	1.74	3.70	+ 76	+113	20	34	99
Provident Life	1.11E	1.75E	4.60	+ 58	+163	16	45	72
Sears	1.50	2.32	4.30	+ 55	+ 85	22	54	95
Xerox	0.04	1.20	3.75	+2900	+213	1	65	148

Note: E indicates figures are estimated.
Source: David L. Babson & Co., Inc., May 24, 1973.

a few years of rapid growth in earnings per share and, having caught the institutional investors' or money managers' attention, may in a bull market sell at from 40 to 60 times earnings, while the mature growth stocks are selling at 20 to 40 times earnings. There is no hard and fast line of demarcation between the two types of growth stock. While there is no simple way of classifying the two types of growth stock, an experienced analyst would place Xerox in one category and Hartz Mountain in the other. Two of the Rowe Price mutual funds exemplify the difference.

The T. Rowe Price Growth Stock Fund leans to large, mature growth companies, while the Rowe Price New Horizons Fund emphasizes the smaller, newer emerging growth companies. The ten largest holdings of the Growth Stock Fund were (in order of dollar market value held as of September 30, 1973) Xerox, IBM, Utah International, Polaroid, S.S. Kresge, National Cash Register, Emery Air Freight, General Telephone and Electronics, Avery Products, and Colonial Penn Group.

The Rowe Price Growth Stock Fund defines a growth stock as:

> A share in a business enterprise which is expected to reach a new peak in earnings per share during each consecutive business cycle. Earnings growth per share should be at a faster rate than the rise in the cost of living to offset the erosion of the purchasing power of the dollar.

In one of its quarterly reports it states:

> We are firmly convinced, however, that over the long term intrinsic value is recognized in the marketplace. Believing that the ultimate determination of value is growth of earnings, we have continuously tried to select a portfolio of companies whose earnings, we believe, will grow faster than the economy and faster than inflation.
>
> We believe that placing emphasis on companies which have demonstrated not only above-average growth of earnings but also *stability* of earnings, has been an important factor in the success of your fund historically. The pattern of earnings growth of portfolio companies has been much more stable than earnings of the popular market indexes. It is in periods of adversity that your portfolio companies have, in the past, shown outstanding relative earnings performance.

The Rowe Price New Horizons Fund concentrates on the newer, smaller growth companies. The 10 largest holdings of the New Horizons Fund (in order of dollar market value held as of September 30, 1973) were Medtronic, Raychem, Longs Drug Stores, Lowe's Companies, Leaseway Transportation, Baker Industries, Hartz Mountain, Petrie Stores, Vetco Offshore Industries, and Wal-Mart Stores. In its prospectus, the New Horizons Fund states:

> The investment objective of Rowe Price New Horizons Fund, Inc. is to increase the shareholder's capital by finding and purchasing a diversified group of growth stocks of the future in these fields before they attain sufficient stature to become attractive to institutional investors. Many of the stocks falling in this category are likely to be shares of relatively small new companies, often unseasoned, and with limited markets.

In one of its quarterly reports, New Horizons states:

> The management of New Horizons lived through a two and one-half year period of disenchantment with the stocks of small growth companies after the bottom of the bear market in 1962. At that time we were one of the few institutions established specifically to invest in small growth companies. Today, however, things are quite different, as many large banks have special situation funds and there are a large number of mutual funds which make such investments. For this reason, we do not anticipate as prolonged a period of disenchantment as in the early 1960s. Even if it should occur, we would not be worried fundamentally since the balance sheets of most of our companies are strong and the majority have sufficiently high returns on invested capital to allow them to finance their growth from internal sources for many years to come.

> In short, we remain optimistic about the prospects for the stocks of good, small companies which can continue to show above-average earnings growth and finance that growth from internal sources.

Growth stock investing then, can range from mature companies with excellent long standing records of expanding sales and earnings, with competent and stable management, and with long, unbroken dividend payment records, such as Bristol-Myers, Eastman Kodak, General Electric, International Business Machines, and Xerox, to newer companies with less maturity and newer appeal, such as Medtronics, MGIC, Walt Disney, McDonald's, Marriott, and Polaroid.

There is again, a very thin line between the obscure but emergent growth stocks, such as those selected by John S. Herold in his "America's Fastest Growing Companies," and purchased by funds, such as New Horizons, and the so-called *performance* or *concept stocks.* These were the popular favorites of the day, zooming across the investment horizons, rising brightly in the firmament for a brief time, and then sinking into nebulous darkness and obscurity.

Fashions In Common Stock

"If you want to make your pile, you have to be in style," wrote Eldon Grimm in the *Financial Analysts Journal,* pointing to the profit possibilities in changing taste patterns in the market. A hot issue during one period may be a dud during the next. Itek shares, for example, rose from 9 to 172 and then fell back to 12. Bausch & Lomb rose from 5 to 95 and then fell back to 17. Mountain Fuel Supply rose from 30 to 106 and then dropped back to 57. Mattel shot up from 2 to 52 and then dropped back to 3. Teledyne went from 4¾ to 71⅞ and then fell to 9½. Kalvar rose to 176½ and then fell to 3½! Syntex has been in and out of favor. From an adjusted price of 5 in 1963, the stock zoomed to a peak of 124¾ in the early part of 1966. By the summer of 1970 it was down to 18½ but recovered to a high of 128½ in 1973. Indeed, its 1973 range ran from a low of 46¼ to a high of 128½.

Grimm noted that fads in common stock change almost as rapidly as clothing styles. You have to be as alert to changes in popularity and psychology as to fundamentals, if not more so, in selecting "performance" or "concept" stocks. For example, during World War I, Bethlehem Steel was in high fashion. It soared from $10 a share in 1914 to $200 just one year later. In the 1920s, talking pictures and radio swept the country and Warner Bros. Pictures shot up from 9¾ in 1927 to 138 in 1928. RCA rose from 12½ in 1922 to 573 in 1929. During the Great Depression and the early New Deal days gold and liquor stocks were in high fashion. The price of the old Homestake Mining stock went from 81 in 1931 to 544 in 1936. With the repeal of Prohibition, National Distillers shot up from 13 in 1932 to 124 a year later.

In recent years, office equipment and electronics stocks, airline and color TV shares have had their periods of popularity. The advent of the computer sent IBM from 40 to 600.[6] Control Data went from $20 to over $174, and then it subsequently fell back down to $28. In color TV, Admiral jumped from 6 to 135 and Motorola rose from 30 to 185. The initial use of jets helped airline stocks soar. Northwest Airlines' earnings rose from $1.11 per share in 1961 to $9.99 per share in 1965, and the stock went from 7 to 171. Delta Airlines' earnings per share rose from 83 cents in 1961 to $3.61 in 1965; the shares rose from 5 to 97.

The spotlight has also touched on office equipment, Burroughs climbing from 12 to 252; hotels and motels, Marriott from 1⅜ to 41; leisure, Walt Disney from 5 to 201¾—and back down to 40½; franchise restaurants, McDonald's from 1 to 76⅞; furniture, Levitz from 1 to 61 and then back down to 3⅜; recreation vehicles, Winnebago Industries from 1 to 48½ and down again to 3 and Skyline from ⅜ to 74 and then to 9⅜; banks, First National City Bank of New York from 17 to 83; cosmetics, Avon Products from 8½ to 140 and then off to 59½; photography, Eastman Kodak from 21¼ to 151¾; beverages, Coca-Cola from 12¼ to 150; health care, Johnson & Johnson from 6 to 133; offshore drilling, Vetco from 4⅝ to 61⅞ and Ocean Drilling from 2⅞ to 70½; oil drilling equipment, Halliburton from 14 to 189; drugs, Schering-Plough from 7¾ to 141¼, Warner Lambert from 17 to 109, Upjohn from 28¾ to 132; and fruit juices, Tropicana from 4 to 60⅜ and down to 17.[7]

Even in the 1973 bear market, certain performance types did well: gold stocks, Dome Mines from 68 to 155, Campbell Red Lake from 35⅞ to 79; semiconductors, National Semi-Conductors from 23 and 108⅝ and Texas Instruments from 74⅜ to 138⅞. The ability to pick next year's performance stocks is a skill akin to alchemy or astrology but much more handsomely rewarded.

Income Stocks

In a category apart from growth stocks, mature or emergent, and also from performance or concept stocks, are *income stocks, cyclical stocks,* and *defensive stocks.* In a period of high interest rates *income* stocks are, in a way, a contradiction in terms, but this is not the case in periods of low interest rates. During the first two decades after World War II, bonds were a disastrous investment medium. As the yields of long-term bonds moved gradually upwards from their all-time lows of the late 1940s, bond prices worked lower, offsetting a large part of the return from interest payments. For example, the American Telephone 3¼'s of 1984, issued at 100 in 1954, dropped 40 points by the end of the sixties. Under such conditions a common stock that yielded

[6] Toward the end of 1973, partly as a result of an unfavorable ruling of the court in an antitrust suit brought by Telex, it fell to 245.

[7] Adjusted when necessary for stock splits.

6 or 7 percent might well have been classified as an income stock. When yields on high-grade bonds, however, reached 8½ percent or even 9 percent, investing in common stock for current income became somewhat questionable. The concept of the income stock survives then from an era of much lower interest rates and bond yields.

Income stocks are those that pay a higher than average current return. They are often sought by the elderly and retired, and by trust funds, pension funds, and university endowments. Choosing income stocks can be a frustrating task. The stock may be paying a high current return because the price has fallen due to uncertainty as to whether the dividend can be maintained in the face of declining earnings; because the stock may be that of a lackluster company in a nongrowth industry; or because the company may be located in a foreign area where there is a large risk due to political instability. Some examples are Roan Consolidated Mines, which extracts copper in Zambia; Free State Geduld, a South African gold producer; Atlas Consolidated Mining and Development, which mines copper in the Philippines; or Telefonos de Mexico. These and others reflect the political factor of a foreign location.

Yet another category of income stocks may be found in the real estate investment trusts, a number of which provide a current return of 10 percent or better. As this is being written, Continental Mortgage Investors sold at a price yielding 14.3 percent in current income; First Mortage Investors sold to yield 23.1 percent; Guardian Mortgage Investors, 17.3 percent; Diversified Mortgage Investors, 17.8 percent; Builders Investment Group, 13.2 percent; and Wells Fargo Mortgage Investors, 13.2 percent.

Focusing investment attention on *current income* is, of course, an inadequate approach in common stock selection. More properly, attention should center on *total return,* which is the addition of current return and capital appreciation over the holding period. From time to time the question is raised as to whether "growth" or "income" shares provide the greater investment return over a period of years. David L. Babson set out to find an answer. In 1951 its staff put together two $10,000 portfolios. Both contained 10 issues with a market value of $1,000 each. One list consisted wholly of companies considered at the time to be growth oriented,[8] while the other consisted wholly of income shares.[9] At the time of selection, the average yield of the income stocks was 30 percent higher than that of the growth list. Obviously, were the selections made today, the choices would be different. However, no

---

[8] The companies were Abbott Laboratories, Celanese, Corning, Dow, Eastman Kodak, Gulf Oil, IBM, Minnesota Mining, Exxon, and Union Carbide.

[9] The income stocks were American Chicle (later Warner-Lambert), American Telephone, American Tobacco, Beneficial Corp., Consolidated Edison, Corn Products (later CPC International), General American Transport, General Foods, International Shoe (later, Interco), and Woolworth.

change was made in either list since 1951 in order to rule out hindsight.

As one would expect, the growth list has shown more capital appreciation. Against the original $10,000 investment, its market value by 1972 was $166,200. In contrast, the income list was worth $49,500. Over the same period, $10,000 in the Dow Jones Industrials (30) would have increased to $40,700. The difference in the income-paying ability of the two portfolios was striking. The 10 growth stocks, which back in 1950 yielded 4.5 percent, as compared with 5.8 percent for the income stocks, by 1972 provided an annual return on cost of 28.6 percent—nearly twice the 15.7 percent yield at cost of the income shares. Since 1950 the growth portfolio provided a total investment return of $184,000 ($156,000 in capital appreciation and $28,000 in dividends). This is three times the income portfolio's overall return of $62,000 ($40,000 in appreciation and $22,000 in dividends). Thus growth stocks over time may well out-perform income stocks in both total return and yield at cost.

Straining for maximum current yield in stocks rather than for total return over time often involves greater risk and less capital appreciation. Often companies have high yields because their shares sell at low prices due to poor prospects and to doubts about continuation of dividends at the then current rate.

Cyclical Stocks

Forbes, in commenting in 1972 on the two-tiered market, declared:

> Probably never before in history has Wall Street had such a split personality. Call a stock a Growth Stock and it sells for 40, 50, or even 60 times earnings. Call it cyclical . . . and it sells for 10 times earnings or less. The market is saying that if General Motors earns $1, that $1 should be capitalized at only $10.90, but if, say, Johnson and Johnson earns $1, it is worth $64. This kind of disparity can go on for a long time, of course, but it can't go on forever.[10]

The favored 50, which constituted the first tier of the two-tiered market, may be seen in Table 4.

Cyclical shares, in Wall Street terminology, refer to stocks of companies whose earnings fluctuate with the business cycle and are accentuated by it. When business conditions improve, the company's profitability is restored and enhanced. The common stock price rises. When conditions deteriorate, business for the cyclical company falls off sharply and its profits are significantly diminished. Industries which are usually regarded as cyclical include steel, cement, paper, machinery and machine tools, automobiles, airlines, railroads, railroad equipment, and building materials.

---

[10] "Statistical Schizophrenia," *Forbes*, August 1, 1972, p. 24.

TABLE 4

Top 50 Stocks, September 30, 1973

RANK BY $ VALUE				STOCKS	$ Value (Millions)	No. Fds. Holding	Number Shares Held	Net Change In Holdings	% Outst. Stk. Held by Fds.
Sept. 30 1968	Dec. 31 1972	June 30 1973	Sept. 30 1973						
1	1	1	1	INTERNATIONAL BUSINESS MACHINES	1819	391	7,049,600	-210,700	4.8
7	4	2	2	EXXON CORPORATION	982	222	10,572,400	+64,300	4.7
2	3	3	3	XEROX CORPORATION	810	190	5,657,400	-64,900	7.2
15	7	4	4	AMERICAN TELEPHONE & TELEGRAPH	711	189	13,666,900	-527,800	2.5
10	6	5	5	EASTMAN KODAK COMPANY	591	179	4,534,900	-94,000	2.8
13	2	7	6	GENERAL MOTORS CORPORATION	570	194	8,513,700	-566,500	3.0
9	11	9	7	BURROUGHS CORPORATION	547	139	2,323,700	+110,300	12.1
37	8	6	8	PHILIP MORRIS, INC.	510	78	4,664,800	-283,600	17.0
42	5	11	9	FORD MOTOR COMPANY	466	117	7,784,000	-415,900	7.8
4	10	8	10	POLAROID CORPORATION	435	100	3,945,100	-123,200	12.0
5	14	10	11	TEXACO INC.	420	150	12,986,300	-361,000	4.8
-	13	16	12	McDONALD'S CORPORATION	387	78	5,505,300	+166,200	13.9
3	27	14	13	ATLANTIC RICHFIELD COMPANY	368	112	3,860,900	-76,400	8.4
29	9	12	14	GENERAL ELECTRIC COMPANY	365	167	5,801,000	-1,116,700	3.2
32	20	18	15	E. I. DU PONT DE NEMOURS	325	112	1,768,800	-10,200	3.7
-	23	20	16	KERR-McGEE CORPORATION	322	64	4,378,800	-86,900	17.9
39	16	22	17	KRESGE (S. S.) COMPANY	313	78	7,519,700	+31,700	6.4
17	15	13	18	AVON PRODUCTS INC.	312	82	3,123,500	+307,700	5.4
-	25	29	19	TEXAS INSTRUMENTS, INC.	311	90	2,587,900	-20,500	11.4
21	17	15	20	MOBIL OIL CORPORATION	308	127	4,896,500	-88,900	4.8
20	21	19	21	MINNESOTA MINING & MANUFACTURING	295	95	3,298,500	-75,400	2.9
31	33	26	22	AETNA LIFE & CASUALTY COMPANY	291	74	3,737,000	+203,700	14.1
-	-	34	23	WEYERHAEUSER COMPANY	267	55	3,803,600	+536,300	5.9
-	32	21	24	WARNER-LAMBERT COMPANY	263	56	5,855,200	+448,200	7.5
-	34	30	25	FIRST NATIONAL CITY CORPORATION	256	70	5,573,000	+431,900	4.7
-	44	23	26	PHILLIPS PETROLEUM	256	84	4,455,200	-138,500	5.9
-	47	37	27	DIGITAL EQUIPMENT CORPORATION	255	78	2,593,300	+345,600	21.9
28	26	17	28	STANDARD OIL OF CALIFORNIA (new)	254	92	7,339,000	-478,200	4.3
-	46	48	29	DEERE & COMPANY	247	96	4,163,000	-87,700	14.3
-	36	31	30	SONY CORPORATION (ADR)	244	63	5,318,900	+320,700	8.0
16	41	38	31	SPERRY RAND CORPORATION	242	90	4,748,000	+328,500	13.8
-	50	24	32	SCHERING-PLOUGH CORPORATION	241	70	3,055,800	-56,700	5.8
-	29	44	33	TRAVELERS CORPORATION	238	74	6,535,000	+296,100	14.5
-	48	27	34	GENERAL TELEPHONE & ELECTRONICS	235	105	7,776,500	+8,400	6.6
25	19	25	35	SEARS, ROEBUCK & COMPANY	232	98	2,366,100	-74,900	1.5
-	-	-	36	**SYNTEX CORPORATION	221	87	2,012,200	+646,300	19.6
-	-	40	37	MONSANTO COMPANY	220	77	3,332,100	-85,100	10.1
-	-	-	38	**HALLIBURTON COMPANY	220	63	1,331,600	+263,100	7.3
14	12	45	39	INTERNATIONAL TELEPHONE & TELEGRAPH	219	104	5,779,000	+163,000	6.0
-	-	-	40	**ALUMINUM CO. OF AMERICA	215	73	2,931,100	+437,100	13.4
-	31	33	41	UNION CARBIDE CORPORATION	213	98	5,435,200	-407,700	8.9
-	-	36	42	UPJOHN COMPANY	208	72	2,428,300	+61,700	8.2
18	24	35	43	WESTINGHOUSE ELECTRIC CORPORATION	206	87	5,608,000	+221,200	6.3
-	39	39	44	GILLETTE COMPANY	202	84	3,228,700	-170,300	10.9
48	-	-	45	**INTERNATIONAL PAPER COMPANY	200	68	4,245,100	+112,000	9.5
-	38	-	46	**UNION PACIFIC CORPORATION	200	41	2,891,300	-174,900	12.8
-	-	-	47	**PHELPS DODGE CORPORATION	198	50	4,128,000	+410,000	20.1
-	-	32	48	ELI LILLY & COMPANY	193	63	2,417,300	+27,500	3.5
-	-	-	49	*AMP INC.	191	45	3,725,700	-20,000	10.1
41	-	42	50	AMERICAN HOME PRODUCTS	190	65	4,477,100	+347,100	2.9

*NEWCOMER **RETURNEE DISPLACED: Bristol-Myers Co. - Imperial Oil Ltd. - Merck & Co. - MGIC Investment - PepsiCo Inc. - Pfizer Inc. - Procter & Gamble Co.

Source: *Vickers Guide to Investment Company Portfolios.*

The two-tiered market, which fell apart in 1973, separated the glamour growth stocks from the cyclicals by sharply different P/E evaluations. For example, at a time when Ford was selling at 9 times earnings, Chrysler at 10 times earnings, Bethlehem Steel at 9.5 times earnings, U.S. Steel at 11 times earnings, Giant Portland Cement at 9.4 times earnings, Crane at 9.3 times earnings, Norfolk & Western Railway at 10 times earnings, Mesta Machine at 9.9 times earnings, and so on, Simplicity Pattern was selling at 51 times earnings, Winnebago Industries at 73 times earnings, Tropicana Products at 54 times earnings, Levitz Furniture at 86 times earnings, Walt Disney Productions at 78 times earnings, and McDonald's at 70 times earnings, to contrast a few.

U.S. Steel, Johns-Manville, General Motors, International Paper, and Anaconda Copper are examples of common stocks which may be classified as *cyclical.* Such stocks may rise sharply in price in the recovery phase of the business cycle and raise dividends, but will tend to decline in price and reduce, or possibly even pass, dividends in the recession phase of the business cycle.

Defensive Stocks. At the opposite pole from cyclical stocks are the so-called *defensive stocks.* By defensive stocks are meant shares of a company which is likely to do better than average, from an earnings and dividend point of view, in a period of deteriorating business. If a recession is feared, a growing interest tends to develop in certain recession-resistant companies. While such stocks lack the glamour of market leaders, they are characterized by a degree of stability desirable when the economy faces a period of uncertainty and decline.

Utility stocks are usually regarded as the best defensive issues, since their slow (5 to 7 percent) but steady growth rate tends to hold up in recession years as well as in boom years. They are sensitive to interest rate changes, falling in price if interest rates rise sharply, and increasing in price if interest rates decline, as they usually do in recession periods. In addition to the electric and gas utilities, the shares of gold mining companies have tended to be effective defensive issues. The price of gold either rises or remains stable during recessions, while the cost of mining may decrease due to lower cost of supplies, less expensive labor, and a better availability of manpower. Also the market demand for gold seems to hold up or even increase in poor years as well as in good ones. No salesmen are needed and no customers are lost since the whole output can easily be sold on world markets.

Other defensive issues are found among companies whose products suffer relatively little in recession periods. These include shares in companies producing tobacco, snuff, soft drinks, gum, candy bars, and other staples. Also companies that provide the essentials of life, particularly food and drugs, tend to hold up well. Packaged food and grocery chain companies are examples.

Speculative Stocks

Minnie Pearl, a fried chicken franchise firm, was renamed Performance Systems and went public in 1968. At that time, the company reported revenues of $13 million and earnings of $3.5 million under an accounting system that counted the total cost of a franchise as income, although only a small percentage was put down in cash. The shares soared to a high of $67 in 1968. By 1972 they sold for six cents a share. This is what Wall Street would call a *speculative stock.*

Webster defines *speculation* as a "transaction or venture the profits of which are conjectural." In this sense all common stock investment is speculative. The purchaser of the shares has no promise, no certainty, that the funds he receives ultimately when he sells the stock will be more, less, or the same as the dollars originally paid. Since they provide a variable rather than a fixed dollar outcome, all common shares are speculative in Webster's sense.

Yet in the flexible parlance of Wall Street, speculative shares or

TABLE 5

Klinker Index

	Recent Price	*High*	*Percent Decline*	*Business*
Acme Missiles & Constr.	0.25	25	99.0	Missile launching sites
AITS	4.00	93	95.7	Travel agency
Airlift Int.	0.37	12	96.8	Airfreight carrier
Alphanumeric	0.87	84	98.9	Computer peripheral equipment
Astrodata	0.50	36	98.6	Electronic data equipment
Beck Indust.	0.12	42	99.7	Leased shoe depts.
Bermec	0.18	31	99.4	Truck leasing, cattle prog.
Borne Chem.	0.12	27	99.5	Textile oils
Cognitronics	2.00	39	94.9	Optical scanning
Commonwealth United	0.15	25	99.4	Conglomerate/theatres
Corporation S	2.00	64	96.9	Data services
Dolly Madison	0.62	47	98.7	Ice cream, furniture
Elcor Chem.	1.25	80	98.4	New sulpher process
Energy Conver. Devices	10.00	155	93.5	Electronic breakthrough
FAS Int.	0.50	63	99.2	Famous artist schools
Farrington	0.04	66	99.9	Optical scanning
Fotochrome	0.62	25	97.5	Film processing
Four Seasons Equity	0.25	49	99.5	Financing nursing homes
Four Seasons Nursing	0.25	91	99.7	Nursing homes
Gale Indust.	0.12	26	99.5	Heat conductive windowpanes
R. Hoe	0.03	60	99.9	Printing presses
King Resources	0.24	34	99.3	Computerized oil development
Liquidonics	3.00	155	98.1	Magnetic door locks
Management Assistance	0.75	46	98.4	Leasing data equipment
Nat'l Student Marketing	1.50	36	95.8	Still trying to determine
Omega Equities	0.07	36	99.8	Questionable ventures
Panacolor	0.37	40	99.1	Color film processing
Performance Systems (i.e. Minnie Pearl)	0.06	24	99.8	Greasy chicken franchiser

Source: Spencer Trask & Co., Inc., December 13, 1971.

speculative stock has a more limited meaning. High flying glamour stocks are speculative; hot new issues and penny oil and mining shares are speculative. The high flying glamour stocks can usually be identified by their very high price earnings ratios. For example, when the Standard & Poor's 500 were selling at 17 times earnings, some of the leading glamour issues were selling at 69.5 times for McDonald's, 68.6 times for Walt Disney, 69 for Memorex, 66 for Baxter Laboratories, and 65.7 for Automatic Data Processing. Speculative buyers of these shares were discounting not only the distant future but possibly the hereafter as well.

At an advanced stage of a bull market, small, little-known companies go public, or small-sized new companies are formed, and offer their low-priced shares to an enormous specuative demand. Prices of new issues soar, doubling or tripling within days or weeks. When a postmortem is undertaken months or years afterwards, the hot new issues are usually either already liquidated, or liquidating, or selling for pennies. One venerable brokerage firm issues a "klinker index," an example of which is shown in Table 5. Notice Four Seasons Nursing Homes was a hot new issue when it went public at $11 a share in May 1968. It soared to more than $100 a share the same year. After a two-for-one split, it shot up again to $90.75 a share in 1969. It went into receivership in 1970, and by 1972, down to 25 cents a share, a number of those associated with the issue were indicted for alleged fraud. Other examples of speculative issues which have had a sad demise are shown in Table 6.

Possibly the lowest level of speculative stocks are the penny mining and oil shares. One broker-dealer specializing in such shares circulated his market report and offers extensively by mail, and his combination packets read like a stamp dealer's. In one report he plugged Trans-Mountain Uranium Company, Globe Hill Mining Company, and Santa Fe International. His description of Trans-Mountain was:

> Trans-Mountain Uranium Co.: Company has ore stockpiled at the Lucky Boy tungsten mine and are anxious to make shipments to the new Min-Con mill located about 14 miles distant. This mill is now in final stages of completion and am told they expected to be ready for milling ores by October 15. However, believe it will take a little extra time before completed. We are all hoping to hear soon that Trans-Mountain is again shipping ore. The shares of stock are low at present price of 2¢.

His combination packet offer was "1,000 Trans-Mountain, 1,000 Santa Fe, and 5,000 Globe Hill Mining" for $63.75 with a bonus of 1,000 United Empire Gold thrown in for each combination packet order.

Thus common stock investment can range from heirloom stocks like the shares of staid and stable First National Bank of Boston, which has

TABLE 6

The Biggest Losers of 1967–70

Company	*1967–70 High*	*Mid-May 1970 Price*	*Percent Drop*
Liquidonics	155	8	95%
Levin-Townsend	68	5	93
Valley Metallurgical	68	5	93
Bio-Dynamics	111	10	91
Ling-Temco-Vought	169	15	91
Unexcelled, Inc.	68	6	91
Susquehanna Corp.	80	8	90
Elcor Chemical	80	9	89
Rucker Co.	66	7	89
Waltham Industries	55	6	89
Perfect Film	82	10	88
Tuco Labs	68	8	88
Conductron	75	10	87
Interphoto	62	8	87
Parvin/Dohrmann	141	19	87
American Export	70	10	86
Graphic Sciences	83	12	86
Home Oil	84	12	86
Gulton Industries	67	10	85
Intersystems	67	11	84
Litton Industries	115	18	84
Tracor, Inc.	75	12	84
TWA	91	15	84
Victor Comptometer	92	15	84
Zapata Norness	87	14	84
Collins Radio	115	20	83
Dennison Mfg.	80	14	83
EG&G	72	12	83
Jefferson Lake Petro	60	10	83
Optical Scanning	145	24	83
Sanders Assoc.	77	13	83
Trans-Lux	84	14	83
Vernitron	52	9	83
Boeing	112	20	82
General Instrument	83	15	82
Iroquois Industries	51	9	82
Lockheed	74	13	82
SCM	77	14	82
Talley Industries	66	12	82
Career Academy	54	10	81
Sunstrand	91	17	81
Keller Ind.	70	14	80
Monogram Ind.	82	16	80
Natomas	130	26	80
St. Paul Railway	69	14	80
Technical Operations	64	13	80
Western Air Lines	59	12	80

Source: Lehman Brothers, 1970.

TABLE 7

A Dozen Good Common Stocks, 1929–32

Company	*1929*	*1932*
Anaconda Copper	174⅞	3
A.T.&T.	310¼	70¼
Chrysler Corporation	87	5
DuPont	503	22
General Motors	224	7⅝
Montgomery Ward	156⅞	3½
New York Central	256½	8¾
Standard Oil of New Jersey	83	19⅞
Standard Oil of California	81⅞	15⅛
Sears, Roebuck	197½	9⅞
U.S. Steel	261¾	21¼
Western Union	272¼	12⅜

Source: Jerome B. Cohen and Arthur W. Hanson, *Personal Finance*, 4th ed. (Homewood, Ill.: Richard D. Irwin, Inc., 1972), p. 677.

paid dividends uninterruptedly for the past 191 years, to Trans-Mountain Uranium at 2¢ a share. Obviously, with so wide a diversity in types of common stock, generalizations are both difficult and hazardous. One that may be ventured, however, is the reply of Bernard Baruch's when he was asked if he would care to comment on the outlook for common stock prices? "They will change," he replied. And, as Tables 7 and 8 show even the best may bow, as each new analyst will learn to his or her chagrin.

TABLE 8

Some Long-Term Disappointments

	Record High		*1973 High*	*Current Price*
American Telephone	75	(1964)	55	50¼
Aluminum Co. of America	133½	(1956)	80½	70⅝
Bethlehem Steel	59⅛	(1959)	35⅝	31⅜
Campbell Soup	43½	(1961)	35	29¼
Con Edison	49¼	(1965)	26	18½
General Motors	113¾	(1965)	84⅝	48¼
Gt. Atlantic & Pacific	70½	(1961)	19	9⅛
Hershey Foods	40¾	(1961)	24¾	12⅞
Lockheed Aircraft	73⅞	(1967)	9⅜	3⅜
R.C.A. Corp.	65½	(1967)	39⅛	16⅞
R. J. Reynolds	89¼	(1961)	55¾	38¾
Scott Paper	47⅞	(1961)	18⅞	13
Sherwin-Williams	76½	(1961)	51⅝	30¾
Singer Co.	129¼	(1962)	73½	35½
Union Carbide	75⅞	(1965)	51¾	31
U.S. Steel	108⅞	(1959)	37½	35½

Source: *New York Times*, December 22, 1973. © 1973 by The New York Times Company. Reprinted by permission.

5

Analysis of Common Stock

JEROME B. COHEN, Ph.D.
Senior Editor, Bankers Magazine
Emeritus Professor of Finance
Baruch College, City University of New York

> *"These questions are very profound, Mr. Dedalus," said the dean. "It is like looking down from the Cliffs of Moher into the depths. Many go down into the depths and never come up. Only the trained diver can go down into those depths and explore them and come to the surface again."—*
>
> JAMES JOYCE—*A Portrait of the Artist as a Young Man.*

Before plumbing the depths of common stock analysis, the aspiring professional, who would ply his or her trade, must navigate the twin Scylla and Charybdis perils of two widely held academic concepts—the efficient market and the random walk (for a complete discussion see Chapter 43). Both combined imply that the security analyst plumbs the depths in vain, for his services can avail little. According to one terse glossary, "an efficient market is one in which prices always fully reflect all available relevant information. Adjustment to new information is virtually instantaneous," while "a random walk implies that there is no discernible pattern of travel (or of stock prices). The size and direction of the next step cannot be predicted from the size and direction of the last or even from all the previous steps. . . . Random walk is a term used in mathematics and statistics to describe a process in which successive changes are statistically independent."[1] Combined, in the words of another authority, "First, the theory (random walk and efficient

[1] See James H. Lorie and Mary T. Hamilton, *The Stock Market: Theories and Evidence* (Homewood, Ill.: Richard D. Irwin, Inc., 1973), pp. 270, 273.

markets) says that new information about a company, its industry, or anything that affects the prospects of the company is disseminated very quickly, once it becomes public. Second, the price of a stock at any particular time represents the judgment of all investors, based on all the information that is public. And third, new information about a company is disseminated randomly over time."[2]

What does all this academic jargon mean for the aspiring security analyst? To many it suggests that he or she is pursuing a career that has no real purpose or function. Why? Because in an efficient market, buyers and sellers factor into their buying and selling decisions all known influences and knowledge, both public and private, that has, is, or will impact upon the price of a security. Since the current price reflects all the known facts, and since prices reflect swiftly any new developments, any digging by a security analyst can add little or nothing to the body of knowledge, which has itself determined the current price of a security. In its strongest form the random walk—efficient market hypothesis argues that past stock prices or earnings cannot be used to forecast future prices or earnings since both series behave randomly and already reflect all knowable facts and information about the market, an industry, a company, stock prices, or the price of a single stock.[3]

Yet all is not lost! It is the thousands of trained security analysts who are the eyes and ears of the efficient market. It is the industrious, probing, prying analyst who ensures that relevant information, and even rumor and hypothesis, is quickly reflected in the current price, and who by the collective weight and chain reaction to prospective trends helps determine the future price. It is the probing analyst, searching for all relevant factors to determine the intrinsic value of a security, who by his actions or recommendations, helps bring a momentarily deviant price to its intrinsic value level.

A VARIETY OF METHODS

"During the last ten years a widening gulf had developed between stock evaluation theories as propounded primarily by academicians, and the practices followed by those who are on the firing line and have to make daily investment decisions," wrote Ralph A. Bing.[4] "The former are on record," he noted, and "their views have been expressed in

[2] See J. Peter Williamson, *Investments: New Analytic Techniques* (New York: Praeger Publishers, 1970), p. 182.

[3] Professor Eugene F. Fama defines an efficient market as "one in which prices always reflect available information." See E. F. Fama, "Efficient Capital Markets: A Review of Theory and Empirical Works," *Journal of Finance,* May 1970; see also Jack L. Treynor, "Efficient Markets and Fundamental Analysis," *Financial Analysts Journal,* March–April 1974.

[4] Ralph A. Bing, CFA, "Survey of Practitioners' Stock Evaluation Methods," *Financial Analysts Journal,* May–June 1971, p. 55.

numerous articles. On the other hand, the man who is confronted with an unending chain of decision-making problems, usually lacks the time to spell out his views in print, and very often has other reasons for not publicizing his evaluation technique. Nevertheless, these men—a 'silent majority' of portfolio managers and securities research heads—occupy a key position in the continuous process of equity evaluation, because values are strongly influenced by those who do the actual evaluating and convert it into buying and selling decisions."

To discern the varying practices and techniques, Bing designed and circulated a questionnaire, listing seven categories of methods and procedures and asking a sample of institutional investment officials to respond. The questionnaire and a tabulation of responses are shown in Figure 1 and Table 1. The table summarizes the answers regarding preference for the six appraisal techniques described in the questionnaire (*a,* indicates top preference; *b,* second; and *c,* third). Since 85 percent of the respondents to Bing's survey used more than one technique, the sum total of the techniques practiced was more than twice the number of respondents. This, of course, indicated an inclination to approach the complex problems of equity appraisals using several techniques, rather than staying rigidly with one. Moreover, some institutions leave considerable leeway in the choice of techniques to their individual analysts. As one of the respondents pointed out: "it is not clear to us that analysts have the same styles, even though they may work for the same organization. . . . The analyst's job remains essentially an unstructured one, and analytical approaches are, therefore, somewhat unstable." Nevertheless it appeared that most of the department heads made their preferred

FIGURE 1

Exhibit—Questionnaire

I. Estimate present value of stock through discounting all future dividends. If yes, how do you select the discount rate(s)?

II. Estimate present value through discounting future dividends plus estimated market value two years out ____ three years out ____ five years out ____. If so, how do you select discount rate?

III. Estimate total future return (dividends plus capital gain) for one year terminal ____ two years terminal ____ three years terminal ____ five years terminal ____ and compare that return with what you consider a normal return for the stock in question.
If so, how do you estimate "normal" return?

IV. Compare present actual p/e multiple (on normalized earnings) with what you consider a normal multiple for the stock in question.

V. Compare price times estimated future earnings (one year out ____ two years out ____ five years out ____) with what you consider a normal multiple of this type.

VI. Compare multiple and growth of individual stock with industry group multiple and growth.

VII. Any other method (kindly explain briefly).
Comments:

. . . .
Signature

TABLE 1

Respondents' Selection of Appraisal Methods

Number of Method in Questionnaire	*Indicated Preference Ranking*					*Percent of 88 Indications*
	a	*b*	*c*	*No Preference*	*Totals*	
I	—	1	—	1	2	2.3%
II	2	—	—	1	3	3.5
III	6	2	1	4	13	14.8
IV	7	8	2	4	21	23.8
V	11	6	3	4	24	27.2
VI	3	6	6	6	21	23.8
Total I to VI	29	23	12	20	84	95.4%
VII (other)	4	—	—	—	4	4.6
Total	33	23	12	20	88	100.0%

Source: Bing, *Stock Evaluation Methods*, p. 56.

appraisal methods sufficiently clear to induce their staff analysts to use, primarily, those methods.

The response summarized in Table 1 indicates that the seemingly simple multiplier techniques—IV, V, and VI—enjoyed the greatest preference. Of the total preferences expressed, 75 percent are concentrated in those three categories. Of the three, No. V, with its built-in estimate of future earnings, was the most popular, closely followed by No. IV (the simple current multiplier-actual versus normal) and No. VI (aimed at multiplier and growth comparisons between the stock in question and its group). At the opposite end of the preference scale, No. I and No. II, incorporating two present value formulas, are all but ignored. These results would seem to indicate a wide gulf between theory and practice. Partly, this would appear to be due to the prevailing short-time horizon of the practitioners surveyed. It is interesting to note in Table 2 that 60 percent extend over a maximum of only two years, as many as 78 percent to a maximum of three years, and none over five years. It would appear that the investment community was primarily concerned with a short range focus of one to three years. This might well account for the relative lack of interest in methods I and II, which tend to have a relatively long-range time horizon.

One of every two respondents gave some indication of how they judged normal investment return, i.e., a normal p/e ratio, or in other words, how they arrived at a yardstick on which to base their investment decisions. The majority of those who answered that question indicated that they derived that yardstick primarily from the historical record of investment returns, or historical p/e multiples, giving more weight to the recent past and considering industry characteristics and risk factors. Some institutions used historical p/e ranges and other factors in order to establish reward-risk ratios; others attempted to quantify their growth

TABLE 2

Indicated Preferences for Time Horizons

Indicated Time Horizon	*Method* II	*Method* III	*Method* V	*Total*	*Percent of 50 Total Indications*
3–6 months	–	1	—	1	2.0%
1 year	–	5	14	19	38.0
2 years	–	5	5	10	20.0
3 years	1	7	1	9	18.0
4 years	–	1	—	1	2.0
5 years	–	1	2	3	6.0
Over 5 years	–	–	–	0	0.0
Undefined	–	2	5	7	14.0
Total	1	22	27	50	100.0%

Source: Bing, *Stock Evaluation Methods*, p. 57.

and p/e forecasts by assigning "confidence factors" in order to bring risk into consideration.

Bing's own preference is for Method III. He says:

> It seems to me that the basis for any equity investment has to be its prospective return—e.g., cash dividends plus capital gains—during the time span envisaged for the investment. This basis is most directly formulated in Method III of the questionnaire, which probably brings out more clearly the hurdles inherent in any rational stock evaluation than other appraisal methods. However, the fundamental problems are, in reality, common to nearly all methods.

First, he notes, there is the problem of estimating future earnings (and dividends), which is basic to all methods, from a fundamental viewpoint. Second, Method III explicitly poses the problem of estimating the potential terminal sales price and the resulting capital gain or loss and is implicit in a number of the other techniques. After making estimates and developing a probable range of future return, there remains the question of how that return compares with what the analyst considers a normal or intrinsic return in order to reach a decision as to whether the stock is an attractive investment or not. This has often implied a value yardstick formed largely by historical experience. Some historical investment return averages will serve as initial reference points, such as the mean return of 9 percent per year (with dividends reinvested), compounded, which Fisher and Lorie arrived at for an equal initial investment in all stocks listed on the New York Stock Exchange from 1926 through 1960,[5] or a mean return of roughly 10 percent

[5] L. Fisher and J. H. Lorie, "Rates of Return on Investments in Common Stocks," *Journal of Business* 37, no. 1 (University of Chicago, January 1964). See also Fisher and Lorie, "Rates of Return on Investments in Common Stocks: The Year-by-Year Record, 1926–1965," *Journal of Business* (University of Chicago, July 1968).

per year for the Dow Jones Industrial Average in the 1959–67 period.[6] Other gauges might be the yields of 8½ or 9 percent available on long-term high-grade bonds or the interest return on risk-free instruments, such as treasury bills, plus an estimated premium for inflation as well as an allowance for the equity risk.

Bing also comments on the widespread use of current and future p/e ratios in institutional equity appraisal, as evidenced by his survey. He assumes that decision-making professionals—in contrast to most amateurs—are perfectly aware of the pitfalls of price-earnings multiples, especially after the collapse of the so-called two-tier market. But, he notes, given estimates of (*a*) a stock's normalized current earning power and pay-out ratio; (*b*) the prospective earnings and dividend growth over the period considered; and (*c*) an informed estimate regarding the prospective terminal p/e ratio, any current p/e ratio may readily be converted into an estimated prospective investment return and vice versa.[7]

To examine the various techniques and problems of common stock analysis in more depth, we turn first to the academic method, or present value estimation.

PRESENT VALUE ESTIMATION[8]

A widely accepted investment theory is that the value of a common stock is equivalent to the *present value* of all future dividends. To calculate the value of a stock on the basis of this theory, it is necessary to estimate the growth rate of the stock's dividend stream and to discount the estimated dividends at a rate which is thought to be appropriate. The present value theory can be applied with practical results to an appraisal of a general index of common stock prices, such as Standard & Poor's industrials, or to estimating the value of individual common stocks.

---

[6] L. Fisher and J. H. Lorie, "Some Studies of Variability of Returns on Investments in Common Stocks, "*Journal of Business* 43, no. 2 (University of Chicago, April 1970).

[7] Bing's illustration: Assume that stock A, currently quoted at 70, is selling at 14 times estimated 1970 earnings of $5.00 per share, and at 10.8 times estimated 1972 earnings of $6.50. Assume further that its current $2.50 dividend rate (50 percent current payout) is expected to remain unchanged through 1972. Assume, finally, that the guessed-at terminal p/e ratio at time of sale, two years from now, is 16, making the sale price 104. Its return on a current purchase will then have consisted of: (1) a capital gain of about 21.5 percent per annum compounded, plus (2) a dividend return of 5 percent per annum (skip compounding), i.e., a total return of approximately 26.5 percent per annum. In other words, under the assumptions made, a current p/e ratio of 14 implies an investment return of over 26 percent per annum. Bing, *Stock Evaluation Methods,* p. 60.

[8] The material and concepts in this section are drawn largely from Jerome B. Cohen, Edward D. Zinbarg, and Arthur Zeikel, *Investment Analysis and Portfolio Management* (Homewood, Ill.: Richard D. Irwin, Inc., 1973), chap. 5. See also Chapter 36 of this volume, which provides a detailed account of the method.

The concept of present value is really quite simple and can be easily illustrated. Assume that A wants to borrow money from B, repayable at a future date. B is willing to make the loan, but feels that, considering the risks involved, he is entitled to a 10 percent annual rate of return. This being the case, how much money will B advance to A on A's note for $10 payable one year hence? The answer is $9.09, because the $10 paid next year provides interest of $.91, which is 10 percent of a $9.09 loan. Thus, $9.09 is the present value of $10 payable one year hence at a discount rate of 10 percent.

And, if A offers a $10 note payable two years hence, how much would B be willing to lend? Answer: $8.26. Ten percent of $8.26 is $.83 (first year's interest); $8.26 plus $.83 = $9.09. Ten percent of $9.09 is $.91 (second year's interest); $9.09 plus $.91 = $10.00. The present value of $10.00 payable two years hence is $8.26 at a discount rate of 10 percent. Table 3 shows the present values of $1 payable in 1 to 50 years at discount rates of 5 to 10 percent. More detailed tables are, of course, available in published form. Note that $1.00 payable 50 years hence is worth only $.09 at a 5 percent discount rate and only $.01 at a 10 percent discount rate. Obviously, the higher the discount rate, the lower the present value.

Assume that future dividends on the stocks in the Standard & Poor's Industrial Stock Price Index will grow at a rate of 5 percent per annum for as far into the future as anyone can imagine. Assume also that investors, as a group, will demand at least an 8 percent rate of return in order to undertake the risks of common stock investment. Recognizing that these assumptions are purely for illustrative purposes, what is the value of S & P's Industrial Index?

There is a simple formula for approximating the present value of perpetual dividend growth at a given discount rate. The formula is:[9]

$$\text{Present value} = \frac{\text{Current dividend rate}}{[(1 + \text{Discount rate}) \div (1 + \text{Growth rate})] - 1}$$

Under our illustrative assumptions this works out as:

$$\frac{\text{Current dividend rate}}{(1.08/1.05) - 1} = \frac{\text{Current dividend rate}}{1.029 - 1} = \frac{\text{Current dividend rate}}{0.029}$$

Thus the formula and the illustrative assumptions tell us that the appropriate current dividend yield of the S & P's Index is 2.9 percent. To

[9] The formula is a reduced form of the equation:

$$\text{Present value} = D + \frac{D(1+g)}{(1+k)} + \frac{D(1+g)^2}{(1+k^2)} + \cdots \frac{D(1+g)^n}{(1+k)^n},$$

where: D = Dividend rate at beginning of period.
g = Growth rate of dividends.
k = Discount rate to be applied to future dividend stream.

TABLE 3

Present Value of $1

Payable in:	Discount Rate 5%	6%	7%	8%	9%	10%
1 year	.952	.943	.935	.926	.917	.909
2	.907	.890	.873	.857	.842	.826
3	.864	.840	.816	.794	.772	.751
4	.823	.792	.763	.735	.708	.683
5	.784	.747	.713	.681	.650	.621
6	.746	.705	.666	.630	.596	.564
7	.711	.665	.623	.583	.547	.513
8	.677	.627	.582	.540	.502	.467
9	.645	.592	.544	.500	.460	.424
10	.614	.558	.508	.463	.422	.386
11	.585	.527	.475	.429	.388	.350
12	.557	.497	.444	.397	.356	.319
13	.530	.469	.415	.368	.326	.290
14	.505	.442	.388	.340	.299	.263
15	.481	.417	.362	.315	.275	.239
16	.458	.394	.339	.292	.252	.218
17	.436	.371	.317	.270	.231	.198
18	.416	.350	.296	.250	.212	.180
19	.396	.331	.277	.232	.194	.164
20	.377	.312	.258	.215	.178	.149
21	.359	.294	.242	.199	.164	.135
22	.342	.278	.226	.184	.150	.123
23	.326	.262	.211	.170	.138	.112
24	.310	.247	.197	.158	.126	.102
25	.295	.233	.184	.146	.116	.092
26	.281	.220	.172	.135	.106	.084
27	.268	.207	.161	.125	.098	.076
28	.255	.196	.150	.116	.090	.069
29	.243	.185	.141	.107	.082	.063
30	.231	.174	.131	.099	.075	.057
31	.220	.164	.123	.092	.069	.052
32	.210	.155	.115	.085	.063	.047
33	.200	.146	.107	.079	.058	.043
34	.190	.138	.100	.073	.053	.039
35	.181	.130	.094	.068	.049	.036
36	.173	.123	.088	.063	.045	.032
37	.164	.116	.082	.058	.041	.029
38	.157	.109	.076	.054	.038	.027
39	.149	.103	.071	.050	.035	.024
40	.142	.097	.067	.046	.032	.022
41	.133	.092	.062	.043	.029	.020
42	.129	.087	.058	.039	.027	.018
43	.123	.082	.055	.037	.025	.017
44	.117	.077	.051	.034	.023	.015
45	.111	.073	.048	.031	.021	.014
46	.106	.069	.044	.029	.019	.012
47	.101	.065	.042	.027	.017	.011
48	.096	.061	.039	.025	.016	.010
49	.092	.058	.036	.023	.015	.009
50	.087	.054	.034	.021	.013	.009

derive the value of the index under these assumptions, we would divide the current dividend rate by 0.029. For example, early in 1972, the indicated dividend rate on S & P's Industrial Index was about $3.20. Dividing by 0.029 produces a value of about 110. Since the actual level of the index was just about 110 early in 1972, we can say that, under our illustrative growth and discount rate assumptions, the actual level of the market represented fair or intrinsic or normal value.

An even simpler version of this formula is available. Instead of dividing (1 + Discount rate) by (1 + Growth rate), we can simply subtract the growth rate from the discount rate. That is, 8 percent minus 5 percent equals 3 percent, which is close enough to 2.9 percent for practical purposes.

To estimate the value of the market more realistically, we need more realistic estimates of (*a*) the growth rate of earnings and dividends and (*b*) an appropriate discount rate. A basic method of arriving at a prospective growth rate is to analyze the past and prospective growth rate of the GNP, considering both real growth as well as an allowance for inflation. Then relate pretax earnings, aftertax earnings, and cash flow, say, of the Standard & Poor's 425 industrials, over time, to the current dollar GNP. Having developed a GNP growth estimate and a reasonable estimate of the growth of earnings, the next step is to examine the relationship between earnings growth and dividend growth to derive an estimate for a dividend growth rate. Since historically dividends on the Standard & Poor's industrials have averaged about 55 percent of reported earnings for several decades, this central tendency has been so persistent that an estimate of a growth rate of dividends can well be based on it.[10] Therefore, we concluded, that if earnings grow at a rate of about 6 percent per annum, dividends should grow correspondingly. Obviously, this will not be the growth rate in every single year. In some years, dividends will grow by 10 percent or more. In other years, dividends may actually be reduced. But the trend is likely to be stable enough to be introduced realistically into a present value calculation.

Choosing an appropriate discount rate is the next step. If we are to discount future dividends on S & P's industrials, we must have a clear idea of the rate of return investors require in order to undertake the risks of common stock investment. Bear in mind that we are here concerned with investors in the aggregate, not any single investor, and that we are considering stocks in the aggregate, as represented by S & P's industrials, and not any specific stock.

There are three approaches that seem useful. First, the annual rate of return on stockholders' equity has typically been about 11–12 percent. But stockholders should not expect this whole rate to be passed on to them. The second factor to be considered comes from the bond market. The rate of return on safe kinds of fixed income investments—long-term government bonds, Aaa and Aa corporate bonds, and savings accounts in savings institutions—has ranged between 4 percent and 9 percent in recent years, averaging 6–7 percent. Clearly, the added risk of owning

---

[10] Bauman declares: "Future earnings and future dividends have a similar influence in determining the investment rate of return or the investment value of common stock, whether one uses a present value dividend model or the traditional earnings multiplier technique. The advantage of the present value model is that it requires the investor to make his assumptions clearly explicit regarding estimates of the quality and rate of growth of earnings and dividends, while traditional techniques permit more vagueness. W. Scott Bauman, "Investment Returns and Present Values," *Financial Analysts Journal*, November–December 1969, p. 117.

common stock justifies a somewhat higher rate of return. The third factor comes from the stock market's own history. During the past half century, the compound rate of return on Standard & Poor's 425 industrials, including dividends and price appreciation, was about 9 percent.

These three factors suggest that a reasonable estimate of the discount rate that should be applied to the 6 percent dividend growth rate previously estimated is less than 11 percent and more than 7 percent. In this context, the historically realized rate of about 9 percent is both intuitively and empirically appealing, though one must admit to some wariness in estimating the future based on the past.

Earlier, a simplified formula was presented for calculating the present value of perpetual dividend growth, at a given discount rate, as:

$$\frac{\text{Current dividend rate}}{(\text{Discount rate}) - (\text{Growth rate})}$$

Using the assumptions previously stated, the value of S & P's industrials, at any point in time, would be their then current dividend rate divided by 3 percent (9 percent discount rate) − (6 percent growth rate). Thus, if the current dividend rate on S & P's industrials were $3, the index should stand at 100. Actually, since our growth rate estimates refer to trends, the dividend rates which should be used in this formula should be trend levels rather than actual current dividends, since the latter may be cyclically high or low. It also may be noted that other reasonable combinations of discount and growth rates would produce somewhat related results. In any such exercise, the analyst must be sure that his assumptions regarding real economic growth, inflation, corporate profit and dividend growth, interest rates, and common stock discount rates are mutually consistent.

Since the concept of the present value of future dividends has proved useful in estimating the value of common stock prices in the aggregate, we turn to application of the concept to the evaluation of individual common stocks.[11]

---

[11] There is, indeed, a vast literature on the subject. See John B. Williams, *Theory of Investment Value* (Cambridge, Mass.: Harvard University Press, 1938); W. Scott Bauman, *Estimating the Present Value of Common Stocks by the Variable Rate Method* (Ann Arbor, Mich.: Bureau of Business Research, University of Michigan, 1963); R. M. Soldofsky and J. T. Murphy, *Growth Yields on Common Stock: Theory and Tables,* rev. ed. (Ames, Iowa: State University of Iowa, Bureau of Business and Economic Research, 1963); N. Molodofsky, C. May, and S. Chottiner, "Common Stock Valuation: Principles, Tables, and Applications," *Financial Analysts Journal,* March–April 1965; Paul F. Wendt, "Current Growth Stock Valuation Methods," *Financial Analysts Journal,* March–April 1965; W. Scott Bauman, "Investment Returns and Present Values," *Financial Analysts Journal,* November–December 1969; Edwin J. Elton and Martin J. Gruber, ed., *Security Evaluation and Portfolio Analysis* (Englewood Cliffs, N.J.: Prentice-Hall, Inc., 1972); James Lorie and Richard Brealey, ed., *Modern Developments in Investment Management* (New York: Praeger Publishers, 1972); and R. A. Brealey and C. Pyle, "The Valuation of Equities," *A Bibliography of Finance and Investments,* Pt. 7 (Cambridge, Mass.: The M.I.T. Press, 1973).

In a number of ways, the present value concept is more difficult to apply to individual common stocks than to stocks in the aggregate. First, it is more difficult to project the growth rate of an individual company than it is to project total corporate growth. Secondly, it is more difficult to select an appropriate discount rate for an individual company's estimated dividend stream than it is to select a rate for all corporations combined. And since the discounting approach has been posited in terms of dividends rather than earnings, it is difficult to deal with the company that does not pay cash dividends.

Theoretically, a corporation cannot grow indefinitely at a faster rate than companies generally, but there are some companies which have managed for a decade or longer to out-perform the average company by a wide margin. IBM is a good example, as is Xerox. IBM has been growing by 10 to 20 percent a year for a number of years. If we try to project its future dividend growth, we know that an ultimate slowdown must be assumed.[12] But the specific pattern of this expected slowdown is difficult to project and yet it will have a major impact on calculated value.

Some advocates of the present value-discounting techniques have attempted to avoid making long-term dividend growth estimates by assuming a selling price some years in the future and discounting it in lieu of the stream of dividends. For example, they may project dividend growth for 10 years and assume some dividend yield at that date. An alternative is to project earnings, assuming a constant dividend payout ratio, and to hypothesize an ultimate price-earnings ratio. Some analysts project earnings and also allow for changes in dividend payout ratios. Since we are dealing, not with absolutes, but with reasonable estimates, these procedures all seem acceptable.

An estimate of the growth potential of a company should be considered in the light of its probability of being reasonably correct. The analyst is likely to feel more confident of an estimate of the future growth of stocks in the aggregate than of a single company's growth. An estimate of the future behavior of a broad aggregate contains a built-in limitation on error—the protection of diversification. An estimate of the future behavior of a single component of the aggregate does not have this hedge and is less likely to be correct, particularly if the estimate is that the component will grow more or less rapidly than the aggregate. Additionally, the projected growth of a company whose past earnings have fluctuated substantially usually contains a greater element of uncertainty than the projected growth of a company with a record of stability.

Present value theory adjusts for uncertainty via the discount rate. The more uncertain the growth projection, the higher the discount rate

[12] For the purposes of our discussion here we will ignore the antitrust suits because (*a*) we do not know their ultimate outcome and (*b*) IBM split up into two or three companies would probably be worth more and do as well as at present.

should be. Investors, in general, are believed to be "risk averters." The appropriate relationship between uncertainty and the discount rate is murky. Thus there are difficulties posed by the need to select different discount rates for different stocks—and even to select different discount rates for different time periods in the growth cycle of any individual stock.

To illustrate the application of the present value technique to the evaluation of a single stock, the example of IBM will be used.[13] In early 1972, before a 5-for-4 split and before the preliminary adverse antitrust decision in the Telex case, IBM was paying a $5.40 per share dividend and selling at about $365. We assumed that the company's dividend rate could be expected to grow at an above-average rate for 20 years beyond 1972 but that the growth rate must slow down gradually during that period, due to increased competition and other factors. Two alternative paths for the rate of dividend growth were assumed—one relatively slower than the other, but both considerably faster than the rate of growth of the average company. These assumptions were:

	Path A (Slow) (*percent per annum*)	*Path B (Rapid)* (*percent per annum*)
1972–77	12%	17%
1977–82	10	13
1982–87	9	11
1987–92	8	8
1992 and beyond	6	6

As for the discount rate to be applied to these streams of dividends, we assumed that the market demanded a 10 percent per annum rate of return as long as the company's growth rate is above average. Once the growth rate becomes average, however, we assumed that the discount rate would drop to 9 percent, the rate used in our analysis of the S & P's industrials.

Admittedly, these are large assumptions, but the present value technique requires that assumptions of this character be made. Indeed, the fact that the assumptions are so heroic illustrates the difficulty of applying the present value technique to individual stock appraisals. The effort may be useful but it is not simple. Given the stated assumptions, however, the following calculations emerged:

1. The first two columns of Table 4 show the progression of dividends under the two growth paths. Note that the dividend grows to between $34.65 and $54.01 by 1992.

2. The third and fourth columns of Table 4 show the present values, in 1972, of each year's dividend, at a 10 percent discount rate. The sum of these present values ranges between $119 and $163.

[13] See Cohen, Zinbarg, and Zeikel, *Investment Analysis and Portfolio Management*, pp. 235–38.

TABLE 4

Present Value of Dividend Stream of IBM Common Stock, 1972–92 (based on assumptions outlined in text)

Year	*Dividends*		*Discounted Value of Dividends in 1972 at 10 Percent Discount Rate*	
	Path A	*Path B*	*Path A*	*Path B*
1972	$ 5.40	$ 5.40	$ 5.40	$ 5.40
1973	6.05	6.32	5.50	5.74
1974	6.77	7.39	5.59	6.10
1975	7.59	8.65	5.70	6.50
1976	8.50	10.12	5.81	6.91
1977	9.52	11.84	5.91	7.35
1978	10.47	13.38	5.91	7.55
1979	11.52	15.12	5.91	7.76
1980	12.67	17.08	5.91	7.98
1981	13.93	19.30	5.91	8.18
1982	15.33	21.81	5.91	8.42
1983	16.71	24.21	5.85	8.47
1984	18.21	26.88	5.81	8.57
1985	19.85	29.83	5.76	8.65
1986	21.63	33.11	5.69	8.71
1987	23.58	36.76	5.64	8.79
1988	25.47	39.70	5.55	8.65
1989	27.51	42.87	5.45	8.49
1990	29.71	46.30	5.35	8.33
1991	32.08	50.01	5.26	8.20
1992	34.65	54.01	5.16	8.05
Sum			$118.98	$162.80

Source: Cohen, Zinbarg, and Zeikel, *Investment Analysis and Portfolio Management*, p. 237.

3. The growth and discount rates beyond 1992 are assumed to be those of the average company. These are assumed to be 6 percent and 9 percent, respectively. Therefore, we can capitalize the 1992 dividend by 3 percent (9 percent minus 6 percent) to arrive at hypothetical selling prices of IBM stock in 1992. Dividing $34.65 by 0.03 produces a price of 1155; and dividing $54.01 by 0.03 produces a price of 1800.

4. Discounting these 1992 prices of IBM stock at 10 percent produces present values, in 1972, of $172 and $268 for Path A and Path B, respectively.

5. Summing the present values of future dividends and the present values of the terminal selling price ($119 plus $172, and $163 plus $268), we obtained an indicated value range of IBM stock, in 1972, of approximately $290–$430. Adjusting for the 5-for-4 stock split which became effective in May 1972, we arrive at a value range of $232–$344.

FORECASTING EARNINGS AND PRICE-EARNINGS RATIOS[14]

Most practicing analysts use more down-to-earth techniques than the present value concept. They tend to use varying forms of an eclectic estimate of prospective earnings over a relatively near term and capitalize the resultant earnings forecast, or range, by projecting a probable price-earnings ratio or its reciprocal an earnings-price rate.

Techniques vary from elaborate and exhaustive inquiries into most of the economic, financial, social, and geopolitical factors affecting or likely to affect an industry's and a company's sales and earnings over a time horizon of one to three years, providing a basis for projecting key balance sheet and income account categories and ratios to a relatively simple guesstimate of next year's earnings and next year's p/e ratio. The former may involve elaborate spread sheets or computer printouts, while the latter may rely on the useful Standard & Poor's *Earnings Forecaster* for a consensus opinion. There is a vast and ofttimes confusing literature on estimating earnings and price earnings ratios, and after trying to absorb and evaluate it, the thoughtful analyst may come quietly to agree with the theoretician's conclusion that past earnings and p/e ratios do not provide a useful basis for estimating future earnings or p/e ratios.

A current quixotic illustration, taken from the *New York Times,* is at hand.

> For the last couple of days, two of this nation's mightiest corporations—American Telephone and General Motors—have been trading at virtually the same stock price.
>
> Yesterday, while the snow drifted down on Wall Street and brokers wondered aloud about the fate of the market, Telephone shares wound up unchanged at 49⅞ and G. M. put its stock in the garage at a closing price of 49¾, off ⅛.
>
> Both companies, of course, have vast differences in their product mix, competitive factors and 1974 earnings outlook. At the same time, however, the two corporate giants are selling at nearly identical prices on the Big Board, which means that all expectations have been factored into the stock quotations.
>
> So, on a generally drab day in finance, this question was put to half a dozen brokers: "If you had to recommend either Telephone or G. M. as an investment to clients, which stock would you pick". . . .
>
> In terms of setting the stage a few figures are in order. Ma Bell earned $4.98 a share last year, plus a nonrecurring gain of 8 cents a share from the sale of the company's interest in Comsat. And, unless the sky falls in, profits are expected to climb in 1974.
>
> General Motors showed a net income last year of $8.34 a share and analysts agree that earnings will plummet in 1974.
>
> At a present annual dividend rate totaling $3.08 a share, Telephone

[14] Further discussions may be found in Chapters 33, 38, and 39 of this volume.

common stock yields 6.18 percent. Assuming that General Motors pays out a minimum yearly dividend rate totaling $3.40 without any extras, its current yield is 6.83 percent. In 1973, dividends totaled $5.25 a share but virtually nobody expects such a bonanza this year."[15]

Telephone's p/e was 9: General Motors was 5.

What is the market really saying about these two blue chips? Has all relevant knowledge been factored into the market prices? Do investors have the same expectational outlook on the prospects for the two issues? Is the coincidence purely accidental? Or is it meaningful? Does the market price reflect aspects of intrinsic value or is it merely aberrational? Does it reflect current earnings or prospective earnings? And what about the multiplier? What logic, if any, is there in it?

Intrinsic Value

A whole generation of now elderly security analysts and portfolio managers were educated by Graham and Dodd's epic work and it seems useful to refer briefly to their basic concepts.[16] For common stock analysis, they noted that there were three approaches. The first they called the "anticipations" approach. This involved selecting and recommending stocks that would "out perform" the market over a given span of time, usually the ensuing 12 months. This approach they noted did not involve seeking an answer to the question: "What is the stock worth?" The second concept stands in marked contrast. It attempts to value a stock independently of its current market price. If the value found is substantially above or below the current price, the analyst concludes that the issue should be bought or disposed of. This independent value has a variety of names, the most familiar of which is *intrinsic value*. It may also be called indicated value, central value, normal value, investment value, reasonable value, fair value (in some legal proceedings), and appraised value. Graham, Dodd, and Cottle's third approach is:

> . . . concerned with relative rather than intrinsic value. Instead of accepting the complete independence of intrinsic value from the current level of stock prices, in estimating relative value, the analyst more or less accepts the prevailing market level and seeks to determine the value of a stock in terms of it. . . . His efforts, therefore, are devoted fundamentally to appraising the relative attractiveness of individual issues in terms of the then existing level of stock prices and not to determining the fundamental worth of a stock.

---

[15] Vartanig G. Vartan, "Viewing Virtues of 2 Blue Chips," *The New York Times*, March 30, 1974, p. 38. © 1974 by the New York Times Company. Reprinted by permission.

[16] Benjamin Graham, David L. Dodd, Sidney Cottle, *Security Analysis: Principles and Techniques*, 4th ed. (New York: McGraw-Hill Book Co., 1962). The first edition was published in 1934.

As you can guess, or may know, Graham, Dodd and Cottle favored the intrinsic value approach. They say:

> A general definition of intrinsic value would be "that value which is justified by the facts, e.g., assets, earnings, dividends, definite prospects, including the factor of management." The primary objective in using the adjective *"intrinsic"* is to emphasize the distinction between *value* and *current market price,* but not to invest this "value" wth an aura of permanence . . .
>
> The most important single factor determining a stock's value is now held to be the *indicated future earning power,* i.e., the estimated average earnings for a future span of years. Intrinsic value would then be found by first forecasting this earning power and then multiplying that prediction by an appropriate "capitalization factor."[17]

Graham, Dodd, and Cottle were explicit that their intrinsic value approach could not apply to "inherently speculative issues" such as Polaroid, or to high growth rate stocks, such as IBM and Xerox. They declared:

> "This statement, by its terms, does not apply to inherently speculative issues since these do not admit of a "soundly ascertained value." We consider "growth stocks" at high price earnings ratios basically in this category . . . In other words, a genuine growth stock will typically appear to be selling too high by our evaluation standards, and the true investor may do well to avoid it for this reason. But both the price and the ultimate value may often develop independently of, and contrary to, any given valuation."[18]

The Eclectic Approach

To arrive at a normal or intrinsic value for common stock, Graham, Dodd, and Cottle spelled out an eclectic approach taking all relevant factors that could affect a company's sales and earnings outlook into consideration. Just what is expected of the analyst under an eclectic approach is set forth in a manual of instructions on common stock analysis developed for analysts-in-training by a large institutional investor. Part of this manual reads as follows:

> Institution Z's security analysts are expected to develop and communicate the following information on the companies assigned to them:
>
> 1. Probable earnings per share in the current and following year, the factors affecting earnings, and the potential error range.
> 2. Probable long-term (e.g. 5 years) growth rate of earnings per share, reasons for any change from historic norms, and the potential error range.
> 3. An informed view of investment community opinion regarding

[17] Graham, Dodd, and Cottle, *Security Analysis,* pp. 27–28.

[18] Ibid., p. 29.

(1), (2), and other "qualitative" factors, such as "company image," which affect stock evaluations.

4. A probable range of price-earnings multiples for the next 12–24 months in light of (1) through (3), and taking into account the Department's forecast of "the overall market's" p/e multiples.

5. Recommended buying and selling prices.

Periodic evaluation of the performance of analysts-in-training will focus on:

1. The depth of their understanding of the industry and companies assigned to them.

2. The frequency and quality of their written and oral communication of the above information.

As the analysts gain in technical expertise, the evaluation criteria broaden to include:

1. Their "market feel"—i.e., their ability to predict the relative price action of different stocks.

2. Their understanding of industries and companies other than those assigned specifically.

3. Their leadership potential.

Analysts who are rated highly by these criteria may become Unit Heads. As such, their responsibilities are:

1. To transmit the benefits of their experience to the analysts in their Unit.

2. To motivate the analysts to do thorough, accurate, and creative research; to play the role of "devil's advocate" in critiquing the research; and to be sure that the results of the research are satisfactorily communicated within the Department.

3. To take a broad overview of the industries and companies followed by the Unit and to formulate portfolio recommendations on these stocks within the framework of the Department's then-current strategy. At times, these recommendations may differ from those of particular analysts within the Unit. Such differences should not be interpreted as adverse commentaries on the analysts' work, but rather as alternative points of view in a field in which there are no simple right or wrong answers.

The Decision Process in the Department

1. Strategy is set by the Dep't. Head, Research Director, and Senior Portfolio Manager, with inputs from Unit Heads, analysts, and portfolio managers. Essentially, strategy consists of target percentages of cash, growth stocks, cyclical stocks, and stable stocks for each of two types of accounts, aggressive and conservative.

2. The broad strategy input is translated into industry emphasis by the portfolio managers of the individual accounts. Research Unit Heads are expected to contribute importantly to decisions on industry emphasis.

3. The analysts and Unit Heads have principal responsibility for steering the portfolio managers toward or away from particular companies within the industry framework desired by the portfolio managers. The analysts and Unit Heads bear the major responsibility for security

evaluation and the portfolio managers for the specific buying and selling prices and the proportions held of each stock.

Channels of Communication within the Department

I. The weekly *Research List*.—This publication represents the most comprehensive and up-to-date summary of our analysts' evaluation of their companies. It contains the analysts' estimates of near-term earnings per share and long-term growth, their estimates of probable price-earnings ratios, and their judgments as to appropriate buying and selling prices. Brief commentary on each of these items follows:

1. Near-term earnings estimates. These should reflect: (*a*) the Department's overview of the general economic outlook, (*b*) historical sensitivity (or lack of sensitivity) of particular industries' and companies' sales and profit margins to general economic developments, and (*c*) factors which may make such past relationships inapplicable during the forecast period, such as growth of foreign operations.

2. Long-term earnings growth estimates. These should reflect: (*a*) the probable growth rates of the markets served by the particular industry or company being analyzed, (*b*) the probable penetration of those markets by the industry or company, (*c*) explicit analysis of selling prices as distinct from unit volume, (*d*) explicit analysis of major cost components, and (*e*) analysis of corporate policies regarding leverage, earnings retention rates, and acquisitions.

3. Hi/lo price-earnings ratio estimates for balance of current year. For any given company, these should reflect:

a. The company's actual P/E ranges for the last five or ten years, plus the recent apparent P/E trend. P/E's for years with abnormal earnings should be excluded or given a lesser weight. This analysis should be done both in absolute terms and relative to the P/E of the S & P 500.

b. An upward or downward adjustment to these long-term average ranges, based on:
   (1) The Common Stock Department's hi/lo P/E projection for the S & P 500.
   (2) The company's expected earnings acceleration or deceleration over the next one to three years.
   (3) The expected secular trend of the company's P/E.
   (4) Market interest in the company and its industry group relative to other industry groups.

The selected hi/lo P/Es are not to be considered the absolute maximum and minimum limits for the period, but rather the range which has a reasonable probability of being attained.

4. Next year's "normal" price-earnings ratio. This will be the most probable P/E value for September 30 of next year. Usually it will fall somewhere between the hi/lo P/E range of the current year. In most cases, this normal P/E will be indicative of the company's long-term earnings growth prospects and also will reflect the transition of the

market's attention from the earnings of the year then nearing an end to the following year's expected earnings.

5. Recommended buying and selling prices. The buy price should take into account the expected high and low prices for the current year and also provide an expected rate of return over the next two years that is at least equal to that expected for the S & P 500. A premium above the S & P return should be sought in inverse proportion to the stock's investment quality.

Anytime a current market price is below the buy price and purchase is not being recommended, the buy price should be lowered to reflect this fact to the portfolio manager (or an "X" should be entered to reflect the analyst's reluctance to purchase at any price).

II. Written Reports. Written reports and memos often are viewed as time-consuming chores which serve merely to fill up files "for the record." This is not the view of our Department. While good written reports are, indeed, time-consuming, and while an important purpose of such reports is to create a permanent record of facts and opinions, their usefulness is much greater. As indicated in the appended article "we tend to revise our words and refine our thoughts simultaneously; the improvements we make in our thinking and the improvements we make in our style reinforce each other, and they cannot be divorced." Several types of written reports are used by our analysts to communicate information.

1. Management Contact Reports and Memos for File are brief (one or two pages) outline-type updates on company or industry developments. Their purpose is to provide portfolio managers with a continuous "feel" for the companies being followed by the analysts. They do not necessarily recommend specific buying or selling action, although analysts should take every opportunity to reaffirm their latest evaluations of companies.

2. Major Company Reports (Recommendations for Additions to Approved Lists and Recommendations for Purchase or Sale) are prepared when an analyst thinks that a full-blown review of a company by the Common Stock Committee (all portfolio managers and Research Unit Heads) is in order. A good illustration of a Company Report sets out clearly for the reader the nature of the company, its markets, the critical variables which influence its success, and the basis of the analyst's earnings and p/e estimates.

3. Industry Reports are prepared for the purpose of presenting a broad overview of industry trends, past and projected, and identifying the key factors which will cause a company to do better or worse than its competitors in that industry. Brief descriptions of the leading competitors usually are included in such reports.

The first summary page of a company report prepared in accordance with these guidelines, is shown in the accompanying "Memorandum for Common Stock Committee."

Note the total return calculations, the earnings forecast, the p/e projections, and the risk-reward analysis. The analyst concluded that the

Memorandum for Common Stock Committee: April 7, 1972

In re: THE DASH—DASH COMPANY

Recommendation For Addition To Approved Lists

Current Price (OTC)	43 bid	Earnings Per Share		
Price range 1971–72	46–18	(Fiscal years 9/30):		
Curr. price/1972 Est.	41X	1970	$0.75	
P/E as % of S & P P/E	241%	1971	$0.90	
Dividend	$0.30	12 mos. 12/31/71	$0.96	Street Est.:
Yield	0.7%	1972 Est.	$1.05	$1.00–1.05
		1973 Est.	$1.20	$1.15–1.23

Total Return Calculation:

Earnings Growth:

Historical (1960–71)	16%
1971–1973	16%
Projected "normal" rate (5 yrs.)	14%

P/E Ratios:

Historical (mean of past 5 years)	30 X (176% of S & P at 17)
Current (on 1972 est. E.P.S.)	41 X (241% of S & P at 17)
Estimated range thru 12/31/72	High 47 X
	Low 32 X
9/30/73 Normal	40 X (225% of S & P at 16)

Prices and Returns:

	Estimated risk/reward thru 12/31/72		Projected 1973 normal (9/30)
	High Price	*Low Price*	
	$49	$34	$48
Chg. from curr.	14.0%	(20.9)%	7.6% (1½ yr. basis)
Div. yield	0.7%	0.7%	0.7%
Total Return	14.7%	(20.2)%	8.3%

Capitalization (as of 9/30/71):

	(*MM*)	%	*Current Items:*	
Long-Term Debt	$ 6.0	22	Cash and Marketable Securities	$ 2.5
Common Equity	21.4	78	Debt in Curr. Liab.	0.5
Total	$27.4	100	Net Working Capital	11.9
			Fixed Charge Coverage (1971)	2.8

Common Equivalent Shares Outstanding 4.61MM. (A) Market Value $198MM.
Avg. Monthly Trading Vol. 164,000 shs.

total return calculation based on the then current price resulted in an unsatisfactory risk-reward ratio. He therefore recommended purchase at a lower than then current price, one which would provide a reward-risk ratio of 2.2-to-1 and a total return of 15.6 percent.

The reward-risk ratio is obtained using a proposed purchase price. Over the holding period in question, the analyst first calculates the reward, i.e., the difference between the estimated high price and the proposed purchase price and adds the expected dividend. The latter is then divided by the risk obtained by taking the difference between the proposed purchase price and the estimated low price and subtracting the expected dividend.

Another institutional use of risk-reward analysis is shown in Exhibit

1 and the following pages, reproduced in part, and with the permission of Standard & Poor's InterCapital, Inc., manual entitled "Our Investment Process." The technique is illustrated by an application to Campbell Soup (Exhibit 2)

EXHIBIT 1

Fundamental and Technical Analysis of Risk

The attempt to define absolute risk by estimating earnings and then placing an assumed maximum low p/e multiple on such earnings is open to serious question. For example, the premise that IBM has never traded below 28 times 12 months trailing earnings in its modern market history and therefore, should it decline to that level again, the stock has minimal risk, is not a valid analytical assumption. On the other hand, it is legitimate to observe that the upside on IBM then would appear to be very rewarding, all other things being equal. The point is that a low end p/e target is not a meaningful tool to be used as a way to assess absolute downside risk.

However, forecasting earnings and attempting to assign an upside multiple to these earnings is a legitimate part of fundamental security analysis. Upside multiples have far greater validity than downside multiples for a number of reasons that are readily apparent. On the other hand, there are some basic fallacies in assigning the absolute high end multiple to a certain growth stock, for example, and then postulating that because its EPS are estimated at such and such a level, therefore the stock has an assumed upside potential based on this high end multiple times the expected earnings. This thought process inflates the upside objective without giving adequate consideration to other factors.

Because the upside is analytically measurable, at least to some extent, one can view a series of upside targets within a framework of known factors such as the quality of the company, the predictability of earnings, and historic price/earnings ratios, and assess a possible reward against the unknown of unquantifiable risk. However, upside price targets are not completely legitimate points of analytical measurement without applying some discount factor to this target. After all, the buyer of the stock has to have something working for him commensurate with the risk he is taking and that something is the price target less the discount factor, the latter being some premium over the return available to him in a risk free investment such as a government bond.

Using a discounted present value technique will not automatically trigger a sale but if applied systematically to a portfolio of 35–40 stocks, it will make our investment organization more attuned to the dynamics of price change, and thus will be one of several tools available to initiate a reassessment of the stock's fundamentals in the light of possible portfolio action. In terms of an individual stock, we will view it on the basis of several Risk Levels. To arrive at these various Risk Levels, the following inputs will be used.

A. *"Best guess" EPS estimate.* This is of course a standard technique.

B. *A "normalized" EPS estimate.* This would be more applicable to cyclical stocks than it would be to growth stocks. As an example, Ford's earnings this year will approximate $11.00 whereas cyclically depressed earnings ("normalized") are indicated at $8.00.

C. *Two different upside p/e targets.* The first would be a high end of the p/e range and the second would be a median p/e target. For example, if a particular stock has a long-term history of trading in a 25–17 p/e channel, the high p/e target would be 25 (naturally) and the median p/e target would be 21. Incidentally, while low end p/e's are employed to obtain the median p/e, we are using history, not making a projection. This difference is significant.

D. *Four different sets of discount factors will be used.* For the conservative portion of the Model (Primary Growth and Total Return), a 10 percent and a 12 percent discount factor respectively are appropriate. A 15 percent discount factor (Secondary Growth and Business Cycle) and a 20 percent discount factor (Special Situations) are also mathematically justified. For the two Growth Groups, an 18 months forward earnings will be used to determine the price targets whereas a 12 months forward earnings will be used for the balance of the Groups.

E. By employing the above points, we will then derive three different present value priçe targets using an earnings estimate, a p/e target, a discount factor, and finally, the expected cumulative value of the dividend (if any). These three price targets would be derived as follows and would be assigned Risk Levels.

1. High p/e times "best guess" earnings = Risk Level 4
2. Median p/e times "best guess" earnings = Risk Level 3
3. Median p/e times "normalized" earnings = Risk Level 2

Incidentally, the Risk Levels are listed above in inverse order which is to say, a stock selling above its derived present value using the high p/e (Risk Level 4) is presumably more vulnerable than another stock selling above a present value using the median p/e times "normalized" earnings (Risk Level 2). Risk Level 1 would occur when the price of the stock sells below the most conservatively derived present value target. Parenthetically, a stock selling at a Risk Level 1 could be the most vulnerable security in the portfolio since we must assume that either the analysis and therefore the earnings estimate is wrong and/or the p/e target is inappropriate, otherwise why is the stock so cheap?

What this system would do for us in a portfolio overview sense would be to force priorities in the reassessment of fundamentals on stocks in Risk Levels 1 and 4 with Risk Level 3 probably becoming the second most important priority. We will be able to develop a matrix which will afford us some interesting analysis of our Model Portfolio structure overall.

The example shown is a theoretical abstract of a segment of the Model Portfolio.

By way of some explanation, the Target Price heading indicates the derived discounted present value with Risk 2, the "normalized" EPS times the median p/e, Risk 3, the "best guess" EPS estimate times the median p/e and Risk 4, the "best guess" estimate times the high p/e. The Unit Weighted heading simply takes the percentage minuses and pluses and then multiplies these by the portfolio weighting.

For example, Stock A which is currently selling at $40 per share and has a

Total Return Group

Stock	Current Price	Percent of Portfolio	Current Risk Level	Target Price and Percent Risk −/Reward +			Unit Weighted Percent Risk −/Reward +		
				Risk 2	*Risk 3*	*Risk 4*	*Risk 2*	*Risk 3*	*Risk 4*
A.	$40	6	R–2	$36 − 10	$44 + 10	$53 + 33	− 60	+ 60	+198
B.	21	3	R–3	15 − 29	19 − 10	26 + 23	− 87	− 30	+ 69
C.	73	5	R–4	49 − 33	57 − 22	64 − 12	−165	−110	− 60
D.	50	2	R–1	53 + 6	60 + 20	66 + 33	+ 12	+ 40	+ 66
E.	97	1	R–4	67 − 30	77 − 21	86 − 12	− 30	− 21	− 12
Total		17%					−330	− 61	+261
Averaged		—					− 19	− 4	+ 15

Source: Standard & Poor's/InterCapital, Inc.

Portfolio representation of 6 percent is at a Risk Level of 2 since its price is above $36 (median times "normalized") but is below $44 (median times "best guess"). The figures −10 and +10 indicate the percentage spread between the current price and the two target prices. The Unit Weighted numbers then multiplies these three percentage spreads by 6 (the portfolio representation).

What use would be made of a weekly computer run of this matrix? The order of priority would go as follows:—

A. The Analyst covering Stock C should do an immediate update at the next Investment Group meeting. While both Stock C and Stock E appear mathematically overvalued with each selling at the high multiple less the discount factor (what's left for the buyer), Stock C is a five times more important decision than Stock E because of the portfolio weightings.

B. Something must be wrong in the fundamentals of Stock D. Have the Analyst do an update, and if everything checks out satisfactorily, then the Investment Group should probably consider increasing the portfolio representation above 2 percent. Remember, stocks in the Total Return Group are all top quality companies with most having market values in excess of $1 billion.

C. Stock A, on the other hand, appears to be positioned in the mid part of its trading range and while it is the biggest commitment in this grouping at 6 percent, it does not seem to require immediate analytical attention.

D. What about the fact that the 17 percent portfolio representation in this grouping is a minus variance to the suggested 35 percent representation in the Prototype Model Portfolio? Are we missing opportunities in this important sector of the marketplace? Moreover, with the averaged Unit Weighted Risk Level 3 at a minus percentage (−4 percent), how does this compare with the rest of the portfolio? Why not run two computer sorts, showing the Risk 2 and Risk 3 Unit Weighted percent plus or minus for all portfolio holdings which are 3 percent or greater. One of the sorts would include IBM and the other would not.

Source: Standard & Poor's/InterCapital, Inc.

STANDARD & POOR'S/INTERCAPITAL
FINANCIAL FACT SHEET
SAMPLE

	EPS	*P/E*	*Debt/Equity*	*Ratio*
XYZ Company: ($28)	1972–$1.68	16.6x	Debt	21
Dividend: $1.00	1973– 1.90–E	14.7x	Equity	79
Percent yield: 3.6%	1974– 2.05–E	13.6x		
Shares outstanding: 10,700,000	1974– 1.80–N	15.5x		
Fiscal year ends: December				

E = Best Guess Estimate
N = Normalized

	Revenues ($ million)	*Pre Tax Income ($ million)*	*Net Income ($ million)*	*Return on Equity (%)*	*Return on Total Capital (%)*	*EPS*	*P/E High/Low*
1974 E	$1,010	$114	57			$2.05	
1973 E	950	108	54			1.90	
1972	836	93	48	10.7	12.9	1.68	17–12
1971	801	95	48	11.5	13.9	1.73	18–12
1970	749	98	51	10.1	12.6	1.82	15– 9
1969	703	81	43	9.3	10.2	1.53	18–11
1968	665	77	40	9.4	10.4	1.47	22–13
1967	675	78	40	9.8	11.0	1.49	21–13
1966	590	62	32	8.4	9.0	1.22	18–11
1965	572	51	26	8.0	8.6	1.05	17–10
1964	531	41	20	7.4	8.1	0.88	18–11
1963	483	42	21	8.3	9.8	0.91	19–12
1962	415	38	19	8.9	9.9	0.85	19–12

Compound Growth Rates

	Revenues	*Pre Tax Income*	*Net Income*	*Return on Equity**	*Return on Total Capital**	*EPS*	*Avg. P/E High/Low*
1962–72:	7.5%	9.4%	8.7%	9.4%	9.4%	7.5%	18–11
1967–72:	4.5	3.6	3.6	10.2	12.0	3.9	19–12

Quarterly Earnings Estimates

	1972–A	*1973–E*	*1974–E*
1st	0.42	0.49–A	0.52–E
2nd	0.38	0.40–E	0.43–E
3rd	0.43	0.48–E	0.54–E
4th	0.45	0.53–E	0.56–E
	1.68	1.90–E	2.05–E

A = Actual. E = Estimated. * = Averaged.

STANDARD & POOR'S/INTERCAPITAL RISK ANALYSIS WORK SHEET

I. Risk Level Analysis/Quantitative

Stock__________ Beta__________
Date_____ Current Price_____ Avg. Monthly Trading__________
Risk Level 2__________ # Of Down EPS Since '62__________
Risk Level 3__________ % Maximum EPS Decline Since '62__________
Risk Level 4__________ EPS Predictability 1 (high)—10 (low)*__________
Assigned P/E Range__________

II. Qualitative Consideration/Relate To Check List Below

Check List

---

1. Ease of fundamental coverage
2. Product obsolescence
3. Competition
4. Market saturation/ease of entry
5. Government interference/regulation
6. Patent expiration
7. Price cutting/controls
8. Labor strike
9. Social changes/Naderism
10. Adverse publicity/other
11. Business cycle or other type cycle
12. Overseas exposure and vulnerability
13. Accounting changes/variance to industry
14. Interest rate risk
15. One-man management/depth
16. Dependence on single product, large customer, geographical area
17. Weather conditions
18. Raw materials availability, price
19. Balance sheet leverage
20. Financing requirements
21. Street sponsorship/lack of same
22. Legal
23. Other

III. Historical EPS Deviation* From Trendline_____ Projected 3 Year EPS Growth_____ S&P Quality Rating_____

IV. Subjective Summary

A. Below Average Risk__________
B. Average Risk__________
C. Above Average Risk__________
D. High Risk__________

EXHIBIT 2

Campbell Soup

Campbell Soup is the largest manufacturer in the United States and Canada of canned soups, spaghetti, macaroni, blended vegetable juices and frozen pre-cooked dinners. Principal product brand names include Campbell's, Franco-American, V-8, Swanson, and Pepperidge Farm. Soups, processed in condensed and ready-to-serve forms, represent nearly 50 percent of total sales.

The company is enjoying exceptional unit sales growth as consumers continue to react to inflationary pressure on their slowly rising discretionary income. In addition, profit margins should progressively widen as the expected decline in farm agricultural prices unfolds. Within this framework, Campbell's earnings growth rate is likely to accelerate to a 9–10 percent rate versus a 6½ percent historical growth rate. For 1974, earnings are conservatively estimated at $2.55 per share, up from $2.36 in 1973.

Campbell's financial picture is very sound. The company has no long-term debt and has sufficient cash from operations to finance capital additions. Also, since government controls have restricted dividend payments, we feel dividends will increase at a faster rate once controls are lifted.

In the past, Campbell's stock price has shown a high correlation with profit margins. If, as we anticipate, margins expand from a combination of declining commodity costs and good unit sales growth, an investment in this high quality company should prove very rewarding relative to other investment alternatives.

Source: Standard and Poor's/InterCapital, Inc.

STANDARD & POOR'S/INTERCAPITAL FINANCIAL FACT SHEET *DATE:* 5–7–74

	EPS	*P/E*
CAMPBELL SOUP CO 36⅝		
Dividend: $1.18	1973 –$2.36	14.0 X
Percent yield: 3.2	1974E– 2.55	12.9 X
Shares outstanding: 33,316,626	1974N– 2.50	13.2 X
	1975E– 2.75	12.0 X
	1975N– 2.70	12.2 X

E = Best guess estimate.
N = Normalized.

Debt/Equity Ratio
Debt —0.00
Equity—100.0

Fiscal Year
July

	Revenues ($M)	*Pre Tax Income ($M)*	*Profit Margin (percent)*	*Net Income ($M)*	*Return on Equity (percent)*	*EPS ($)*	*P/E High*	*P/E Low*
1975E	$1,569	$176.0	11.2	$93.5		$2.75		
4E	1,480	160.0	10.8	84.9		2.55		
3	1,233.2	147.3	11.9	78.8	14.1	2.36	15	12
2	1,086.2	113.4	10.4	59.6	11.2	1.78	20	14
1	1,031.5	132.6	12.9	67.2	13.2	2.00	18	13
0	964.8	130.2	13.5	62.7	13.1	1.87	20	13
1969	884.5	107.8	12.2	51.2	11.2	1.54	23	18
8	849.3	116.6	13.7	56.6	12.9	1.70	20	15
7	798.7	93.0	11.6	48.3	11.5	1.45	24	17
6	771.4	99.3	12.9	53.0	13.1	1.59	23	16
5	712.8	101.2	14.2	51.4	13.4	1.54	26	22
4	660.4	100.8	15.3	48.2	13.3	1.44	28	23
3	638.2	96.7	15.2	44.6	13.0	1.34	29	23

COMPOUND GROWTH RATES

Revenues (percent)	*Pre Tax Income (percent)*	*Profit Margin (percent)*	*Net Income (percent)*	*Return on Equity (percent)*	*Return on Inv. Cap.*	*EPS (percent)*	*High/Low*
			1963–1973				
6.8	4.3	13.1	5.9	12.7		5.8	22 17
			1968–1973				
7.7	4.8	12.4	6.8	12.6		6.8	19 14

QUARTERLY EARNINGS ESTIMATE

	1972–A	*1973–A*	*1974–E*	*1975–E*
1st	0.44	0.62	0.66	0.71
2nd	0.51	0.55	0.60	0.65
3rd	0.49	0.55	0.60	0.65
4th	0.70	0.75	0.80	0.86
Total	$2.14	$2.47	$2.66	$2.87

A = Actual.
E = Estimated.
Source: Standard & Poor's/InterCapital, Inc.

STANDARD & POOR'S/INTERCAPITAL RISK ANALYSIS WORK SHEET

I. *Risk Level Analysis/Quantitative*

Stock CAMPBELL SOUP — Beta 0.72

Date 5-7-74 Current Price 36⅝ — Avg. Monthly Trading ______

	EPS	*Price*	*Percent Change*
Risk Level 2–N	2.71	40	+ 9
Risk Level 3–E	2.71	40	+ 9
Risk Level 4–E	2.76	48	+31
Assigned P/E Range	Hi	Low	Med
Historic P/E Range		5 yr	10 yr

Number of Down EPS since '62 3

Percent Maximum EPS Decline since '62 11%

EPS Predictability 1 (high)—10 (low) 3

II. *Qualitative Consideration/Relate to Check List below:*

8. Strikes
10. Contamination Risk

Check List

1. Ease of fundamental coverage
2. Product obsolescence
3. Competition
4. Market saturation/ease of entry
5. Government interference/regulation
6. Patent expiration
7. Price cutting/controls
8. Labor strike
9. Social changes/Naderism
10. Adverse publicity/other
11. Business cycle or other type cycle
12. Overseas exposure and vulnerability
13. Accounting changes/variance to industry
14. Interest rate risk
15. One-man management/depth
16. Dependence on single product, large customer, geographical area
17. Weather conditions
18. Raw materials availability, price
19. Balance sheet leverage
20. Financing requirements
21. Street sponsorship/lack of same
22. Legal
23. Other

III. Historical EPS Deviation From Trendline ______ — Projected 3 Year EPS Growth 8–10% — S&P Quality Rating A

IV. *Subjective Summary*

A. Below Average Risk X — C. Above Average Risk ______

B. Average Risk ______ — D. High Risk ______

ASPECTS OF ANALYSIS

Consider, in general terms, four aspects of any complete and yet concise analysis: (*a*) the sales analysis and forecast, (*b*) the earnings analysis and forecast, (*c*) the multiplier (p/e) analysis and forecast, and (*d*) the analysis of management, a qualitative consideration.[20] Let us turn to a brief consideration of each of these.

Sales Forecasting

Basic to any estimate of earning power is a sales analysis and forecast. Growth of demand for a company's products is essential for common stock appreciation—even so expanding production and sales do not guarantee rising profits. But rising demand, or the introduction of new products, at least, give a company an opportunity to earn a rising profit. In some cases rising demand can even absorb losses from managerial errors that can be expected to occur from time to time. Indeed without the cushion of rising demand, management may be loathe to take risks, and without risk-taking, little can be expected in the way of rising profits.

What the analyst is after is a working forecast of sales in order to determine the profit implications of the sales forecast. But just as a sales forecast is essential to an effective profits forecast, an economic forecast is a preliminary prerequisite to the sales forecast. That is, the starting point of an effective industry and company forecast may be a GNP forecast, with a breakdown of components. For example, a forecast of sales for the automobile industry may be tied to the growth of GNP by using historic figures on the number of cars sold per billion dollar increase in the GNP. Since there has been a relatively stable relationship in the past, over the long run, one can apply the past coefficient to a GNP estimate for the coming year or two years, adjust for expected variations such as cyclical factors or availability of consumer credit. Or, the analyst may use estimates of prospective consumer durable goods expenditures, derived from an econometric model of the composite economy, and use this to forecast automobile sales. Or, the estimate may begin with a forecast of personal disposable income for either the coming year or longer, or both, if a short-run as well as a long-run forecast is desired. Since expenditures on automobiles are a relatively stable percentage of disposable personal income, a reasonable estimate of expenditures for automobiles may be made. Since this will be an estimate for the entire industry, market shares must be allocated to companies. These are all, of

[20] For a detailed discussion of (*a*) and (*b*) see (1) "Sales Forecasting" by Robert S. Schultz, and (2) "Forecasting Corporate Profits" by Edmund A. Mennis, in *Methods and Techniques of Business Forecasting, ed.* William Butler, Robert Kavesh, and Robert Platt (Englewood Cliffs, N.J.: Prentice-Hall, Inc., 1974).

course, rough gross estimates to which appropriate refinements and supplementary techniques may be added. For example, Godfrey Briefs, in exploring demand for automobiles, developed a measure of purchasing power or receipts available to consumers which included gross borrowings plus personal income. This was logical since automobiles represent a consumer investment involving substantial use of borrowed funds.[21]

In our investments text,[22] we suggest a method of forecasting aluminum sales by the use of input-output analysis. It may be summarized as follows:

a. Compile annual historical data in current dollars and in constant dollars, for each GNP sector represented in the latest available input-output tables.

b. Determine by matrix inversion the coefficients applicable to each GNP sector for the industry under analysis.[23] For example, a coefficient will indicate how many dollars of aluminum sales were associated directly and indirectly with a billion dollars of durable personal consumption expenditures in the latest year.

c. Multiply each historical GNP sector amount by the aluminum coefficient for that sector, as derived in (*b*). This will produce two historical series of hypothetical aluminum sales. They show what aluminum sales would have been in the past had the latest input-output coefficients been constant through time. (The series resulting from multiplying current dollar GNP data by the coefficients represent hypothetical *dollar* sales of aluminum, and the series resulting from multiplying *constant* dollar GNP data by the coefficients represent hypothetical *unit* sales of aluminum.)

d. Compile historical *actual* sales of aluminum and calculate the annual differences between actual and hypothetical.

e. Try to explain these differences. Among the possible explanations consider: changes in relative prices (e.g., the use of aluminum in autos may appear different in earlier years in part because the price relationships between aluminum and autos were different); technological changes (e.g., substitution of plastics and aluminum for steel); changes in consumer taste (e.g., small cars do not use materials in the same proportions as large cars); inventory adjustments (this is a key problem in using input-output for analysis of short time spans).

f. Using either a standard forecast of GNP and its major components

---

[21] See Robert J. Eggert and Jane R. Lockshin, "Forecasting the Automobile Market," *Methods and Techniques of Business Forecasting*, ed. Butler, Kavesh, and Platt.

[22] See Cohen, Zinbarg, and Zeikel, *Investment Analysis and Portfolio Management*, chap. 6.

[23] See M. F. Elliott-Jones, *Input-Output Analysis: A Non-Technical Description* (New York: The Conference Board, 1972); See also Clopper Almon, Jr., *Matrix Methods in Economics* (Reading, Mass.: Addison Wesley Publishing Co., 1967).

or the analyst's own forecast, if he or she prefers to undertake one, multiply each forecasted GNP sector amount by the latest aluminum coefficient for that sector, as done in (*c*) with historical GNP sector amounts.

g. Adjust the forecasted aluminum sales to the extent that the explanation derived in (*e*) for historical differences in actual versus hypothetical sales are applicable to the future. This provides the analyst with his or her working forecast of sales and can be the basis of the subsequent effort to determine the profit implications of the sales forecast.[24]

The Earnings Estimate

Having obtained an estimate or range of estimates of prospective sales growth rates, the next step is to proceed to obtain an estimate, or range of estimates, of prospective earnings growth rates. To achieve this an analysis of earnings is necessary.

An immediate caveat is appropriate. As Lorie and Hamilton note:

> The conclusions about prediction are discouraging in that they indicate the great difficulty of the task. Changes in earnings seem to follow a random walk, meaning that the simple extrapolation of historical trends are not likely to be very useful in predicting future changes in earnings. Clearly, however, historical earnings will continue to be useful in predicting future trends.[25]

To elaborate:

> Financial analysts have routinely studied historical changes in earnings in order to guide them in formulating views about earnings in future years. It was with great shock, therefore, that I. M. D. Little's original work, "Higgledy Piggledy Growth,"[26] was received in both the academic and financial communities. Little reported on his study of earnings for British firms and found that changes in earnings, like prices, followed a random walk. This meant that successive changes in earnings per share were statistically independent and that the study of the sequence of historical changes in earnings per share was useless as an aid to predicting future changes. In other terms, historical rates of growth in earnings provide no clue to future rates of growth.[27]

There was a swell of criticism of Little's methods and he redid his study to meet the adverse comments. With corrected methodology the results were much the same. Changes in earnings for British concerns

[24] A prominent forecasting service utilizing this method is Data Resources, Inc., of Lexington, Massachusetts.

[25] Lorie and Hamilton, *The Stock Market*, p. 167.

[26] Ian M. D. Little, "Higgledy Piggledy Growth," *Institute of Statistics*, vol. 24, no. 4 (Oxford, November 1962).

[27] Lorie and Hamilton, *The Stock Market*, p. 158.

followed a random walk.[28] Was the American experience any different? There ensued a number of studies testing this—by Murphy,[29] Lintner and Glauber,[30] and Brealey.[31] In commenting on these studies, Lorie and Hamilton conclude tersely: "In order to relieve the reader's suspense before reviewing these studies, the reader should know that the results for American firms are about the same as for the British firms. Changes in American earnings, like changes in British earnings, follow a random walk.[32]

The aspiring security analyst, however, is offered a faint ray of hope. Lorie and Hamilton hesitate on the brink of the chasm of pessimism and pull back at the every edge. They say:

> None of the foregoing evidence in support of the hypothesis that corporate earnings follow a random walk is meant to imply that it is impossible to forecast corporate earnings. The randomness in corporate earnings merely means that one's ability to forecast changes in earnings will not be significantly enhanced by studying changes in historical rates of growth in earnings. This is generally true, but there may be some kinds of companies—those with the steadiest rates of growth earnings—for which analysis of historical growth rates does have some predicative power. These negative implications are clear; positive implications with respect to promising methods of forecastng are less clear.[33]

Imbued with the zest of youth, the junior security analyst will no doubt scale this pessimistic hurdle and proceed to the task at hand—analyzing and forecasting earnings. There are, of course, a variety of ways of undertaking this task. One approach is to start with the GNP forecast and derive from it a prospective corporate profits trend for all industry. Then factor out a profits trend for the particular industry under review, making such adjustments as special industry characteristics suggest a greater or lesser rate of growth than that of the total corporate profits series. From this develop a company estimate, again making adjustments for special company characteristics which suggest departures from the industry profits series.[34]

---

[28] Ian M. D. Little and A. C. Rayner, *Higgledy Piggledy Growth Again* (Oxford: Basil Blackwell, 1966).

[29] Joseph E. Murphy, Jr., "Relative Growth in Earnings per Share—Past and Future," *Financial Analysts Journal,* November–December 1966.

[30] John Lintner and Robert Glauber, "Higgledy Piggledy Growth in America," and "Further Observations on Higgledy Piggledy Growth," papers presented to the Seminar on the Analysis of Security Prices, University of Chicago, May 1967 and May 1969, respectively.

[31] Richard A. Brealey, "The Character of Earnings Changes," paper presented to the Seminar on Analysis of Security Prices, University of Chicago, May 1967.

[32] Lorie and Hamilton, *The Stock Market,* p. 159.

[33] Ibid., p. 162.

[34] See Edmund A. Mennis, "Forecasting Corporate Profits," *Methods and Techniques of Business Forecasting,* ed. Butler, Kavesh, and Platt; see also Roy E. Moor, "Aggregate Profits vs. Company Profits," *Business Economics,* January 1972; and Gary M. Wenglowski, "Industry-Profit Forecasting," *Business Economics,* January 1972.

Or, one can start with the sales forecast developed earlier and relate this to the company's profit margin, operating income, equity turnover, rate of return on equity, earnings before interest and taxes, net income after interest and taxes, return on total capital, and net earnings per share. By dissecting the anatomical character of a corporation's profitability and measuring the impact of prospective changes on each element, it is possible to derive an estimate of a range of future earnings capacity, one, two, three, or three to five years ahead.[35]

Some Newer Techniques of Earnings Analysis

Some newer analytic techniques for estimating earnings should be mentioned. They include probabilistic forecasting, conditional forecasts, and computer models for forecasting earnings.[36] The concept of probabilistic forecasting is simple; its implementation is complex. In an introductory essay discussing the technique developed or applied in two pioneering studies by the First National City Bank of New York, Peter F. Way wrote:

> The approach used recognizes the analyst's real-life forecasting problems and helps him to do a much better job of grappling with them than does the conventional single-point estimate approach. Every competent analyst recognizes that a wide range of earnings possibilities exists for nearly every company under study. Why then do we typically put our "best" assumptions together, scratch our head and swallow hard, and produce *one* estimate to be revised at a later date?[37]

Forecasting by means of probabilistic models provides a capability of putting together the various relevant factors, which play on a given situation, providing for an outcome of a *range* of expectational forecasts reflecting the analyst's judgment of what is most likely to occur.

The technique is illustrated in detail in an article on the copper industry in the *Financial Analysts Journal,* as well as in two industry studies by First National City Bank.[38]

The uncertainties of the analyst about the variability of the factors in his forecast can be quantified in terms of probabilities. He can start with the factors affecting demand for copper, then consider the factors

---

35 This approach is spelled out in extended detail in Cohen, Zinbarg, and Zeikel, *Investment Analysis and Portfolio Management,* chap. 7.

36 These have been excellently explained by J. Peter Williamson, in *Investments: New Analytic Techniques* (New York: Praeger Publishers, 1970). See especially Chapter V on "Security Analysis," and Chapter VI on "Stock-Selection Techniques."

37 Peter F. Way, "Forecasting by Probabilities," *Financial Analysts Journal,* March–April 1968, p. 35. See also John A. Olsen and Terry A. Blaney, "Forecasting by Probabilities: The Copper Industry," *Financial Analysts Journal,* March–April 1968.

38 See *The Copper Industry* (New York: First National City Bank, Investment Research Department, 1967). See also, *The Steel Industry* (New York: First National City Bank, Investment Research Department, 1969).

affecting supply, and move on to a set of probabilities with respect to price. These suggest the ingredients for an earnings forecast, factoring in costs and in profit margins. See Figure 2. This figure, from the original study, shows 10 principal factors from which earnings per share were estimated. For each of these 10 principal factors, a high,

FIGURE 2

Ingredients for an Earnings Forecast

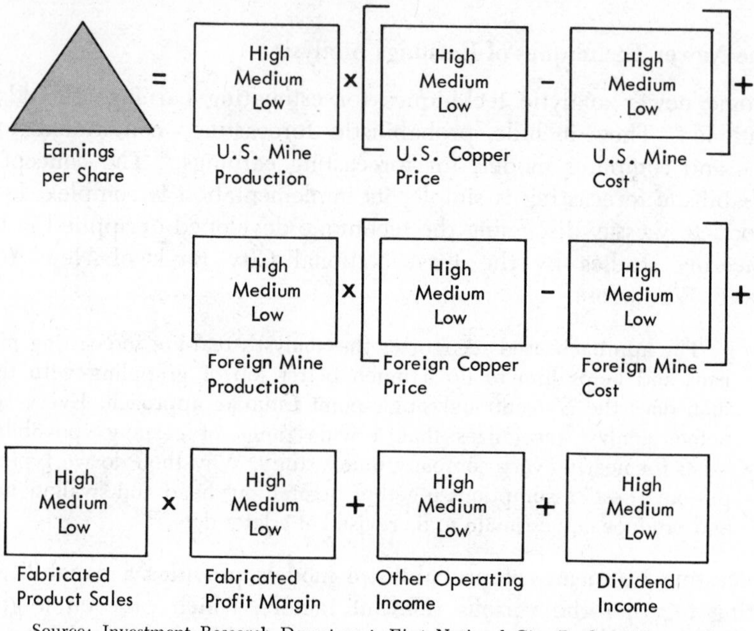

Source: Investment Research Department, First National City Bank of New York.

medium, and low estimate was developed together with probabilities for each. All of these estimates and probabilities were combined to produce an expected value of earnings per share and a range around that expected value. Figure 3, reproduced from the original study, shows the final projection of earnings per share for Anaconda. Olsen and Blaney declare:

> The result, as shown (in Figure 3), is a portrayal of the *earning power* of a company. In the case of Anaconda, Figure 3 shows an earning power of $4.50 to $10.00 a share in 1968. We narrow this wide range by saying that we are 75 percent confident earnings will fall between $5.40 and $8.75 per share. If a single point is required, we will reluctantly suggest $7.75 a share.

Williamson notes: "But the point of this approach should be clear. Instead of asking the analyst to combine in an intuitive way all of the

FIGURE 3

Anaconda Earnings—1959–71

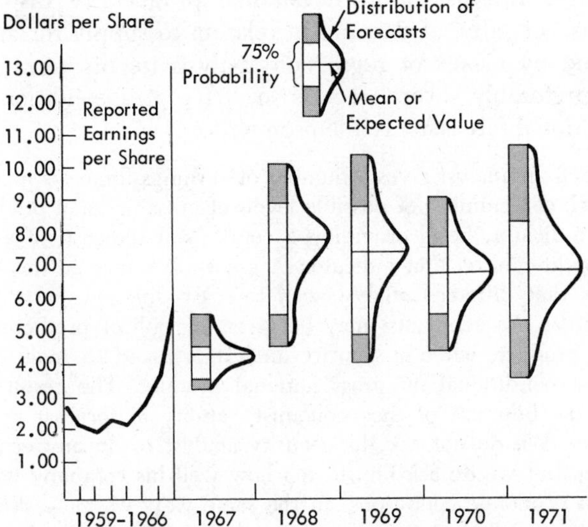

Source: Investment Research Department, First National City Bank of New York.

factors relevant to an earnings forecast, the probabilistic technique insists that he identify each one of these factors, estimate two or three possible values for each factor—generally the high, low, and medium values—and then make his best guess as to the likelihood of each of those values."[39] This requires an analyst to be quite explicit about the factors he considers important in the forecast. He must have a firm basis for his judgment that they are relevant to and play a major role in the forecast. He is better able to do this with circumspection since his final forecast is a range, not a single number.

"But," as Williamson says,

> the probabilistic forecast is still an unconditional forecast. The analyst is, in effect, saying: "My estimates of all future factors and conditions that affect earnings of this company lead me to predict a certain range of earnings for next year." This is very different from a conditional forecast, from an analyst in effect saying: "I don't know what the economy is going to do next year, but if the gross national product is up only 5 percent, then my forecast of earnings is *a;* if gross national product is up 10 percent, then my earnings forecast is *b;* if gross national product is down 5 percent then my earnings forecast is *c,*" and so on.[40]

[39] Williamson, *Investments,* p. 138.

[40] Ibid., p. 138.

The conditional forecast allows the analyst to engage in division of labor. If he thinks the source competent and effective, he can rely on someone else's forecast of gross national product, of disposable personal income, of sales, of demand in relation to supply for an industry's product, and by means of regression analysis tie his earnings forecast to one or preferably several factors to arrive at a conditional forecast.

Of conditional forecasts, Williamson writes:

> When an analyst gives a number of earnings forecasts for a company, for each of a number of possible levels of gross national product or some other indicator, he is providing a conditional forecast, of earnings that are conditional on that indicator. A great advantage in this sort of forecast is that different analysts can forecast different parts of the total prediction. An economist may be given the job of predicting gross national product, while a security analyst is asked to make an earnings forecast conditional on gross national product. The result is that we make the best use of the economist's ability to forecast gross national product. We do not ask the security analyst to do any economic forecasting, but we do ask him to tell how well his company will do under various economic conditions. In the same way, we can ask the security analyst for a forecast of a stock price for different levels of the stock market. And we can turn to someone else for a forecast of the market.[41] What we are really asking the security analyst for in this case, of course, is a "characteristic line" for the stock, just like Treynor's characteristic lines for mutual funds.
>
> Conditional forecasts probably lead to much better use of security analysts' talents. They also make it much easier to determine just what those talents are and where an analyst may be showing good or poor judgment. It is helpful to know whether some poor forecasts of earnings were the result of inability to forecast economic conditions or inability to forecast the response of a particular company to changing economic conditions.[42]

It has probably occurred to you, if you have read this far, that the eclectic approach to earnings forecasting, the probabilistic forecast, and the conditional forecast all involve model building and regression analysis, which are best undertaken on a computer. A model is a set of mathematical formulas, or relationships, which attempt to portray or to abstract from a real life jumble of facts and circumstances the basic

[41] No one, but no one, possesses the ability to consistently forecast the market. Some technical analysts may be right on occasion, but it is just luck, or persistence. For example, if you persist in a prediction that the market will turn up, and you keep issuing such a forecast over a period of time, at some point you will be right, but this is hardly an ability to forecast. For a discussion see Peter F. Bernstein and David Bostian, "How to Forecast the Stock Market," in *Methods and Techniques of Business Forecasting*, ed. Butler, Kavesh, Platt.

[42] Williamson, *Investments*, pp. 138–39. For a description of Treynor's "characteristic" line, see Jack Treynor, "How to Rate Management of Investment Funds," *Harvard Business Review*, January–February 1965, pp. 63–75; also Jack Treynor and Kay K. Mazuy, "Can Mutual Funds Outguess the Market?" *Harvard Business Review* July–August 1966.

relationships between dependent and independent variables impacting on each other.[43] Regression, or correlation, analysis is a statistical technique for estimating the relationship between one variable (dependent variable) and one or more other variables (independent variables). The relationship estimated, usually a least square regression equation, is often used to predict the value of the dependent variable, given the values of the independent variables. Multiple regression is one of the most valuable techniques available to the financial analyst because it permits a number of variables to be used to find a prediction of some unknown variable. For example, the growth rate, debt to equity ratio, and yield of stocks might be used to predict the stock's p/e ratio. Multiple regression is simply an extension of simple regression. In simple regression, the analyst can find an equation of the form $y = a + bx$ which describes (more or less) the relationship between two variables which are being studied. Applications for the two-variable case are often encountered, but quite frequently the analyst has reason to believe that the value of y, in our present usage—earnings per share—is heavily influenced by more than one factor. In this case y is a function of more than one x. Actually, in the extremely complicated financial world, $y = f(x_1,x_2, \ldots, x_n)$ is almost always a model significantly superior to $y = f(x)$.[44]

The computer can be used to test the relationships between the dependent variable (earnings) and the various independent variables affecting earnings. Where seemingly significant relationships have been discerned and refined, a model can be constructed defining the relationship. A program can be written instructing the computer to relate the independent variables fed in, to produce, by means of a multiple regression, the probable value for the dependent variable, the earnings forecast. An analyst who has a number of industries and several score companies to follow and who has a knowledge of economics, statistics, and computer programming can develop and test models, relating inputs of independent variables such as gross national product forecasts, sales, prospective demand and supply, costs, and so on to the desired output, the earnings forecast or forecasts. The output, of course, will be no better than the inputs. Remember "gigo"—"garbage in, garbage out." And the model must be tested and overhauled from time to time as basic relationships change, as they inevitably will over time. But, if skillfully constructed, the earnings forecast model and its computer implementation can be very useful to the security analyst.[45]

---

[43] See Jerome L. Valentine and Edmund A. Mennis, *Quantitative Techniques for Financial Analysis* (Homewood, Ill.: C.F.A. Research Foundation, Richard D. Irwin, Inc., 1971), pp. 8–10.

[44] Ibid., pp. 179–80.

[45] There is now a considerable literature on the subject. See, for example, Cohen, Zinbarg, and Zeikel, *Investment Analysis,* chap. 19; Valentine and Mennis, *Quantitative Techniques,* chaps. 14, 15; J. Peter Williamson and David H. Downes, *Manual*

Price-Earnings Ratios

Once an earnings forecast, or range of forecasts, is derived, it remains to develop and apply a multiplier, the price-earnings ratio. A variety of factors impinge upon and help determine a price-earnings ratio. Among these are the growth rate of earnings, actual and anticipated, the dividend payment, the marketability and volatility of the stock, and the stability or volatility of earnings, and the quality of earnings and of management. Of these, perhaps the growth rate of earnings is the most significant. In general, there seems to be a consensus that the higher the growth rate of earnings, the higher the p/e ratio.

Most analysts begin their attempt to select an appropriate price-earnings ratio for an individual stock with a judgment regarding the appropriate price-earnings ratio for the market as a whole, i.e., for one of the popular stock price indices.[46] In addition, they usually take into consideration the typical p/e ratio of the industry group in which the stock is classified in relation to the p/e ratio of the market averages. Many analysts assume that an appropriate market p/e is the average of actual p/e's of, say, the last 5 or 10 years. During the 1960–72 period, for example, the p/e for the Standard & Poor's industrials averaged 17–18 rather consistently, with a range of about two points either way.

If possible, it is better when dealing with individual stocks, to use normalized earnings. These may be average earnings over a previous normal period (neither boom nor recession). If actual earnings rather than normalized earnings are used as the divisor of a p/e ratio, the ratio may appear to be very high or very low, or can rise or fall sharply, not primarily in reflection of the valuation process, but rather because earnings are abnormally depressed or inflated. For example, in 1970 General Motors earnings plunged to $2.09 per share from $5.95 in 1969 due to the combined impact of the recession and a severe strike. In 1971 earnings rebounded to $6.72 per share. If one were to have calculated GM's price earnings ratio in 1970 by relating the average price of about $70

---

for Computer Programs in Finance and Investments, 2d ed. (Hanover, N.H.: The Amos Tuck School of Business Administration, Dartmouth College, 1971). (See also supplement to 2d ed., 1972). Also Williamson, *Financial Research: Investment Analysis and the Computer* (Hanover, N.H.: Dartmouth College, 1970); Dorothy Bower and Richard S. Bower, "Test of the Stock Evaluation Model," *Journal of Finance,* May 1970; Richard H. Chase, Jr., William C. Gifford, Jr., Richard S. Bower, and J. Peter Williamson, *Computer Applications in Investment Analysis* (Hanover, N.H.: Dartmouth College, 1966); "The Computer as a Research Tool: A Tabulation of Services Available to Institutions," *Institutional Investor,* October 1971. Alan E. Feuerstein and Peter G. Maggi, "Computer Investment Research," *Financial Analysts Journal,* January–February 1968; Heidi A. Fiske, "The Computer: How It Is Changing the Money Manager," *Institutional Investor,* April 1968.

[46] This section is based upon and derived from the latter part—"A More Pragmatic Approach—The Price Earnings Ratio"—of chap. 5 in Cohen, Zinbarg, and Zeikel, *Investment Analysis and Portfolio Management,* pp. 238–51.

to the actual earnings of $2.09, one would arrive at a p/e ratio of over 30. But this was obviously not the market's appraisal of GM's earnings. Presumably, the market was implicitly normalizing earnings. This is evidenced by the fact that in 1971 GM's average price of about $80 was only 15 percent higher than in 1970 while earnings per share tripled. The 1971 p/e of 12 was much more in line with the historical record of GM's p/e ratio.

Of course, actual earnings usually are easier to work with since there is no generally accepted method of normalizing earnings. The concept involves a large element of subjective judgment. One way of at least overcoming this difficulty is to calculate a p/e ratio by relating price to the nearest four-quarter earnings total which is minimally affected by recession or boom conditions in the economy and unaffected by special occurrences such as strikes.

Having developed a p/e range for the market and for the industry group, the security analyst's next step is to make a judgment as to whether the particular stock under study will usually sell at an equivalent, a higher, or a lower p/e than that of the averages and of other companies in its industry group. While this judgment is often an intuitive one, based on an analyst's experience and the historical record on hand, a more analytic approach than a mere extrapolation of past relative p/e is needed.

Over the past 15 years there has developed an extensive literature on the anatomy of the price-earnings ratio and the factors affecting its determination.[47] Several studies of individual company's p/e ratios have

---

[47] See, for example, H. Benishay, "Variability in Earnings-Price Ratios of Corporate Equities," *American Economic Review*, March 1961; V. Whitbeck and M. Kisor, "A New Tool in Investment Decision Making," *Financial Analysts Journal*, May–June 1963; J. D. McWilliams, "Prices, Earnings and P/E Ratios," *Financial Analysts Journal*, May–June 1966; W. Breen, "Low Price Earnings Ratios and Industry Relatives," *Financial Analysts Journal*, July–August 1968; R. S. Bower and D. H. Bower, "Risk and the Valuation of Common Stock," *Journal of Political Economy*, May–June 1969; B. G. Malkiel and J. G. Cragg, "Expectations and the Structure of Share Prices," *American Economic Review*, September 1970; J. E. Hammel and D. Hodes, "Factors Influencing Price-Earnings Multiples," *Financial Analysts Journal*, January–February 1967; J. E. Murphy, Jr. and N. J. Russell, "A Note on the Stability of the Price-Earnings Ratio," *Financial Analysts Journal*, March–April 1969; F. K. Reilly and T. J. Zeller, "An Analysis of Relative Industry Price-Earnings Ratio," *The Financial Review*, Eastern Finance Association, 1973. See also O. Maurice Joy and Charles P. Jones, "Another Look at the Value of P/E Ratios," *Financial Analysts Journal*, September–October 1970; Robert A. Levy and Spero L. Kripatos, "Earnings Growth, P/E's and Relative Price Strength," *Financial Analysts Journal*, November–December 1969; Carl R. Beidleman, "Limitation of Price-Earnings Ratios," *Financial Analysts Journal*, September–October 1971; "The Riddle of the P/E Ratio," *Dun's Review*, September 1972; Earl M. Foster, "Price-Earnings Ratio and Corporate Growth," *Financial Analysts Journal*, January–February 1970; Earl M. Foster, "Price-Earnings Ratio and Corporate Growth—A Revision," *Financial Analysts Journal*, July–August 1970; Nicholas Molodovsky, "Recent Studies of P/E Ratios," *Financial Analysts Journal*, May–June 1967; and Paul F. Miller and Thomas E. Beach, "Recent Studies of P/E Ratios—A Reply," *Financial Analysts Journal*, May–June 1967.

consistently indicated that the p/e ratios are positively related to future earnings growth and negatively related to earnings variability. The most definitive finding of the studies is that the principal reason for p/e differences is the expectation of differences in the future normal trend of growth in earnings per share.

Consider, for example, Figure 4, which is based on data shown in

FIGURE 4

P/E Ratios versus Expected Growth Rates, 1971 Bull Market*

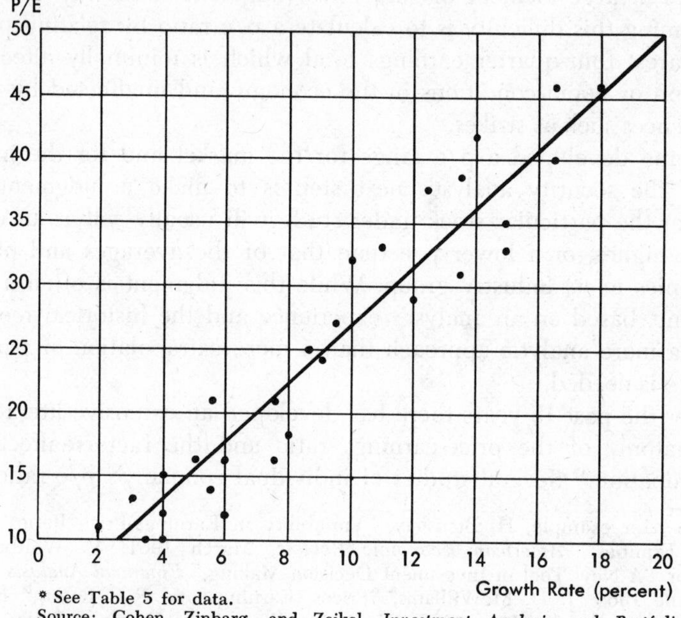

* See Table 5 for data.

Source: Cohen, Zinbarg, and Zeikel, *Investment Analysis and Portfolio Management*, p. 244.

Table 5. The scatter diagram and the line of regression drawn on the diagram illustrate the relationship, at the end of 1971, between the price-earnings ratios and the expected earnings growth rates of 30 well-known companies in a wide variety of industries.

The equation of the line of regression is:

$$p/e = 2.3\ (\text{growth}) + 4$$

This means that on the bull market date represented by the diagram (December 31, 1971), an average growth rate of around 6 percent commanded a p/e of about 18 ($2.3 \times 6 + 4 = 13.8 + 4 = 17.8$). A stock with an expected growth rate of 15 percent commanded a p/e, on the average, of about 38.

TABLE 5

P/E Ratios and Expected Growth Rates (data for Figures 4 and 5)

Company (in Order of Growth Rate)	*Col. 1* Bull Market P/E*	*Col. 2* Bear Market P/E†	*Col. 3* Expected Earnings Growth‡
U.S. Steel	10	8	0
American Metal Climax	11	10	2
Ingersoll Rand	13	8	3
Standard Oil of N.J. (now Exxon)	10	9	3½
General Motors	12	10	4
Johns Manville	15	11	4
American Telephone	10	11	4
Time Inc.	16	10	5
Federated Department Stores	21	13	5½
General Foods	14	15	5½
Clark Equipment	16	8	6
Firestone Tire	12	9	6
Dow Chemical	21	12	7½
Texas Utilities	16	16	7½
Magnavox	18	10	8
Upjohn	25	14	8½
Carrier	24	19	9
Sears Roebuck	27	18	9½
Eastman Kodak	32	23	10
Merck	33	28	11
Emerson Electric	29	20	12
Perkin Elmer	38	18	12½
Anheuser-Busch	31	30	13½
Coca-Cola	39	29	13½
Hewlett Packard	42	27	14
Texas Instruments	35	28	15
International Business Machines	33	29	15
Avon Products	46	44	16½
Xerox	40	34	16½
Johnson and Johnson	46	35	18

* Prices of December 31, 1971 divided by 1972 earnings per share as estimated by analysts.

† Prices of May 26, 1970 divided by 1969 reported earnings per share.

‡ Estimates of basic growth rate (e.g., five years forward) made by "Comparative Values" service of Cowen & Co., New York City. While the estimate for any given company may be subject to argument, conversations with other analysts suggest that there would be general agreement as to the relative magnitudes of the investment community's expectations regarding these companies.

Source: Cohen, Zinbarg, and Zeikel, *Investment Analysis and Portfolio Management*, p. 245.

How was the line of regression derived? We digress for a bit with a statistical explanation (see also Chapter 38). Regression analysis, or correlation, is a statistical technique which can be applied to a comparison of the growth patterns of two series, for example, sales of IBM versus total equipment outlays of American industry, or annual changes in earnings of S & P's industrials versus annual changes in U.S. industrial production. Table 5 showed, in column 1, the price-earnings ratio of 30 stocks on December 31, 1971, and in column 3, the expected earnings growth rates of these stocks. In our regression analysis, the p/e variable would be referred to as Y, the dependent variable (the variable we seek to explain); and the growth rate variable would be referred to as X, the independent variable (the explanatory variable). Figure 4 is a scatter diagram of these data—a series of dots with each dot representing a pair of X and Y values for a specific stock. For example, to plot the IBM data ($X = 15$ percent; $Y = 33$ p/e), run your finger along the horizontal X-axis to 15, then move vertically until you are alongside 33 on the vertical Y-axis. A dot is placed at that point.

If the p/e of any given stock was higher (or lower) by some constant amount, the dots would fall in a straight line. This is known as "perfect linear correlation." If the dots all fell on a smooth curved line, this would be a case of "perfect curvilinear correlation." Perfect correlation is, of course, rare, and our example is no exception. But the line of regression drawn on Figure 4 indicates that the relationship, while not perfect, is fairly close.

How was the line of regression derived and what does it tell us? Although the availability of computer programs eliminates the need for personal calculations, it may help to understand the meaning of the regression analysis if the steps are outlined. The equation form of any straight line is

$$Y = bX + a$$

The b value represents the slope of the line—i.e., how much change in Y is associated, on average, with a change in X. The a value is known as the Y intercept. It sets the *level* as opposed to the *slope* of the line. It is the value of Y when X is equal to zero.[48] From a theory known as "least squares" we can derive a straight line (or a curve) which will pass through the individual observations (the dots) in such a way that the sum of the difference between the Y values of the dots (the p/e's in our case) and the Y values of the line will be zero and that the squares of the differences will be minimized. To do this, two equations (in the case of a straight line) must be constructed from the basic data. The equations are:

$$(\text{Sum } Y) = (\text{Sum } X)\, b + (N)\, a \qquad (1)$$
$$(\text{Sum } XY) = (\text{Sum } X^2)\, b + (\text{Sum } X)\, a \qquad (2)$$

Each of the values in parentheses can be calculated quite easily from the raw data in Table 5. Thus:

---

[48] Modern portfolio theory makes extensive use of the b (beta) and a (alpha) values derived from regressions of individual stock price changes against the corresponding changes of a stock market index such as the S & P's 500 (see chapter 44).

(Sum Y)	is simply the total of the p/e ratios	735
(Sum X)	is the total of the expected growth rates	266
(N)	is the number of pairs of observations	30
(Sum XY)	is the total of the products derived by multiplying each pair of p/e and growth values (e.g., for IBM 15 × 33 = 495; do the same for each other stock and sum the resulting products)	8,097
(Sum X^2)	is the total of the squared values of each growth rate (e.g., for IBM 15 × 15 = 225, etc.)	3,051

Substituting these values, the two equations may be written as follows:

$$(735) = (266)\,b + (30)\,a \quad (1)$$
$$(8{,}097) = (3{,}051)\,b + (266)\,a \quad (2)$$

The equations are solved by multiplying one or the other by a factor which causes either the *a*'s or the *b*'s to be equal. Thus, if equation (1) is multiplied by 8.867, the two equations become:

$$(6{,}510) = (2{,}359)\,b + (266)\,a \quad (1)$$
$$(8{,}097) = (3{,}051)\,b + (266)\,a \quad (2)$$

Equation (1) is then subtracted from equation (2), which gives:

$$1{,}587 = 692b$$

therefore,

$$b = 2.3$$

Substituting 2.3 for *b* in equation (2) gives:

$$(8{,}097) = (3{,}051)\,(2.3) + (266)\,a$$
$$(8{,}097) = (7{,}017) + (266)\,a$$
$$(1{,}080) = (266)\,a$$

therefore,

$$a = 4$$

We now have the *a* and *b* values of the line of regression.

$$\text{p/e} = 2.3\ (\text{growth rate}) + 4$$

To return from our digression, the derivation of our equation of relationship should now be clear. Of course, the relationship is not perfect; all of the points do not fall on the line of regression. For example, both IBM and Texas Instruments have indicated growth rates of 15 percent, yet both carried p/e ratios below the calculated 38 (33 and 35, respectively). On the other hand, Hewlett Packard's estimated growth rate is 14 percent, yet its p/e was 42—well above the 36 indicated by the line of regression. Once the regression equation has been developed, however, the regression values of each stock's price-earnings ratio and the differences between the actual and regression values can be computed readily. See Table 6.

Before considering some of the factors, besides earnings growth expectations, which may help to explain p/e differentials, let us examine the p/e versus growth relationship some 18 months earlier than the previous example—at the depth of the 1970 bear market. This is shown in Figure 5 for the same sample of companies. The equation of this relationship is

$$p/e = 1.8\ (\text{growth}) + 3,$$

and there is a somewhat wider scatter of the individual points around the line of regression. This is in line with the findings of researchers.

TABLE 6

Actual versus Regression Values

Company	X (*Growth Rate*)	*bX (2.3 × Growth Rate)*	*Regression Values of P/E (bX + 4, rounded)*	*Actual P/E*	*Difference, Actual minus Regression*
U.S. Steel	0	0	4	10	6
American Metal Climax	2	4.6	9	11	2
Ingersoll Rand	3	6.9	11	13	2
Standard Oil of N.J.	3.5	8.0	12	10	−2
General Motors	4	9.2	13	12	−1
Johns Manville	4	9.2	13	15	2
American Telephone	4	9.2	13	10	−3
Time Inc.	5	11.5	16	16	0
Federated Department Stores	5.5	12.6	17	21	4
General Foods	5.5	12.6	17	14	−3
Clark Equipment	6	13.8	18	16	−2
Firestone Tire	6	13.8	18	12	−6
Dow Chemical	7.5	17.2	21	21	0
Texas Utilities	7.5	17.2	21	16	−5
Magnavox	8	18.4	22	18	−4
Upjohn	8.5	19.5	24	25	1
Carrier	9	20.7	25	24	−1
Sears Roebuck	9.5	21.8	26	27	1
Eastman Kodak	10	23.0	27	32	5
Merck	11	25.3	29	33	4
Emerson	12	27.6	32	29	−3
Perkin Elmer	12.5	28.7	33	38	5
Anheuser-Busch	13.5	31.0	35	31	−4
Coca-Cola	13.5	31.0	35	39	4
Hewlett Packard	14	32.2	36	42	6
Texas Instruments	15	34.5	38	35	−3
International Business Machines	15	34.5	38	33	−5
Avon	16.5	37.9	42	46	4
Xerox	16.5	37.9	42	40	−2
Johnson & Johnson	18	41.4	45	46	1

Source: Cohen, Zinbarg, and Zeikel, *Investment Analysis and Portfolio Management*, p. 264.

FIGURE 5

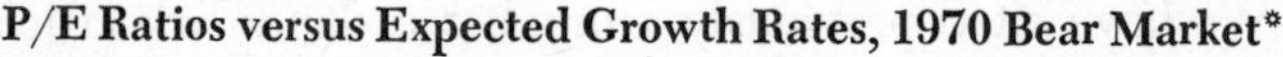

P/E Ratios versus Expected Growth Rates, 1970 Bear Market*

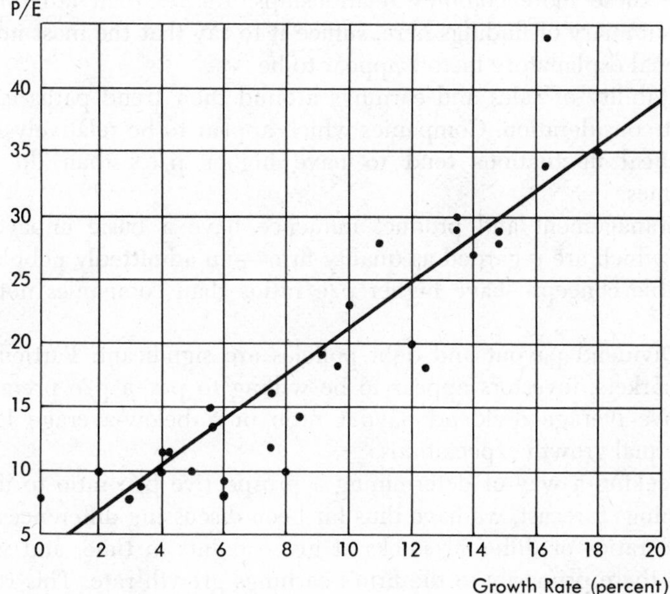

Source: Cohen, Zinbarg, and Zeikel, *Investment Analysis and Portfolio Management,* p. 247.

During bear markets, the growth factor commands a lower premium than during bull markets (in our two illustrations, a growth coefficient of 1.8 as opposed to 2.3), and in addition, growth explains somewhat less of the p/e behavior, while other factors gain in importance. The equation suggests that an average growth rate of around 6 percent commanded a p/e of about 14 on the bear market date represented by the diagram (May 26, 1970).

One may expect numerous additional factors to influence the p/e ratio. For example, it may be that, given equal expected growth rates, companies with higher dividend payout ratios should sell at higher p/e than companies with lower payout ratios. Then there is the quality of management. This may make a difference in p/e ratios. This quality, or image factor, is difficult to express quantitatively, but there is good reason to believe that it influences price-earnings ratios among different companies. Other factors which have been mentioned in the literature are: stability of earnings, financial leverage, stock price volatility, corporate size, and accounting practices (quality of earnings).

Just as a simple regression can be used to analyze the relationship between p/e and a single determining factor, such as expected earnings growth, so multiple regression techniques can be applied when an analyst is considering the more complex relationship between p/e and a number of hypothesized determining factors in addition to earnings growth. We have cited previously a number of landmark articles which explore these more complex relationships. Rather than attempt a detailed summary of findings here, suffice it to say that the most important additional explanatory factors appear to be:

1. Stability of sales and earnings around their trend paths is an important consideration. Companies which appear to be relatively immune to cyclical fluctuations tend to have higher p/e's than do cyclical companies.

2. Management and product influence have a basic impact. Companies which are regarded as quality firms—an admittedly nebulous and intangible concept—have higher p/e ratios than companies not so endowed.

3. Dividend payout and debt policies are significant. Particularly in bear markets, investors appear to be willing to pay a p/e premium for an above-average dividend payout ratio or a below-average leverage, given equal growth expectations.

In seeking a way of determining a prospective p/e ratio to use with an earnings forecast, we have thus far been discussing differences among the p/e ratios of different stocks at given points in time, and we have related these primarily to the firm's earnings growth rate. This is known as cross-section analysis. But what about changes in the relative p/e ratio of a particular stock over time? This is known as time series analysis.

When we look at p/e ratios from this vantage point we do not find a significantly different picture. Obviously, the relative p/e of a stock should be expected to change if the investment community's appraisal of its basic earnings growth potential or stability or quality changes. But what of shorter term fluctuations? Recent studies point toward at least a partial answer,[49] which seems to be that p/e's move up and down in response to acceleration or deceleration of earnings. That is, the basic earnings growth rate is the prime determinant of the normal p/e of a stock. But shorter term movements of earnings around the basic trend seem to cause shorter term movements of the stock's p/e around its own norm. For a given firm, years of rapid earnings acceleration tend to be years of significantly higher p/e's than years of slower growth. It remains, however, to warn that past performance of a stock's p/e ratio, as with past trends of a company's earnings, is not necessarily a good predictor of a company's future p/e ratio.

---

[49] See Volkert S. Whitbeck and Manown Kisor, Jr., "A New Tool in Investment Decision Making," *Financial Analysts Journal,* May–June 1963; Manown Kisor, Jr., "Quantitative Approaches to Common Stock Selection," *Business Economics,* Spring 1966; M. Kisor, Jr. and V. A. Messner, "The Filter Approach and Earnings Forecasts," *Financial Analysts Journal,* January–February 1969; and Richard S. Bower and Dorothy H. Bower, "Risk and the Valuation of Common Stock," *Journal of Political Economy,* May–June 1969.

Management: The Qualitative Factor

Before concluding, we will focus again on a nonquantitative factor, the quality of management. Why do some companies in the same industry have better records than others? Sometimes it is because they possess an unduplicated characteristic such as a unique geographical location or a patented production process. More often, however, it is because they are better managed. The caliber of management is usually not amenable to quantification.[50] To a certain extent it is true that management can be judged by its statistical record—the growth of sales and earnings which it was capable of generating. But frequently it is impossible to separate the causes of the growth record into specific managerial decisions and external factors over which management had little or no control. Moreover, the statistical record does not necessarily reveal management's capacity for coping with change. Contrast S. S. Kresge and J. J. Newberry over the last decade or Burroughs and National Cash Register. If anything is certain about the future it is that changes will occur with increasing rapidity. Thus a thorough analysis of a company's growth prospects must go beyond the quantitative approach which has been discussed. It must take into account the quality of management. To do this the professional security analyst must go beyond the facts and record and attempt, to the extent possible for an outsider, to become acquainted with the officers of a company whose stock is being examined and to attempt to evaluate management at first hand.[51]

Institution Z's instructions to its analysts along these lines, follows:

> *Management Interviews.* Analysts should visit each of their companies at least once a year and should conduct more frequent telephone interviews. The purpose of such interviews is, in part, to fill specific gaps in the analyst's understanding of the company or its industry. Perhaps more importantly, the purpose is to improve the analyst's "feel" for the company's policies and its managerial philosophy. The reason for stressing the latter objective is that the analyst must not ask questions if the response might put him in a position of having obtained "material inside information." This would include any response in the "no comment" category if, on the basis of prior questions or dealings, it conveys meaningful nonpublic information. Institution Z wants to profit from superior analysis of publicly available information and from information which is not generally known but which would be available to any analyst who puts a reasonable amount of effort into ferreting it out. However, this would not include ferreting out such things as reports of earnings before their public release. We do not want to profit by taking advantage of information (as distinct from our analysis of available in-

---

[50] One interesting attempt to quantify the quality factor is found in William P. O'Connor, Jr., *The 14 Point Method for Beating the Market* (Chicago: Henry Regnery Company, 1972).

[51] See also Volume II, chapter 4.

formation) which the other party to a transaction (institutional or individual) does not have and was not in a position to obtain and take into consideration at the time of the transaction.

Although it would be helpful to have a set of precise rules which distinguish with clarity and precision the boundary between permissible inquiry and that which is dangerous and must be avoided, the law is unclear and in flux. As recently as August 1, 1973, the Securities and Exchange Commission publicly sought the comment and views of interested parties on this subject with the objective of developing guidelines. At least until such time as these guidelines are published, in deciding whether any information constitutes "material inside information," analysts should err on the side of conservatism, i.e., discuss it as promptly as possible with the Research Director, Department Head, or Law Department and with no one else without the approval of one of them.

It is the considered opinion of most successful analysts that a management interview is of value almost in direct proportion to the effort spent preparing for the interview. The executive being interviewed is more likely to engage in a frank and thoughtful discussion if he recognizes the analyst's expertise than if he sees that the analyst is simply on a "fishing expedition" and has not done his homework. As an aid in preparing for the interview, a checklist of possible discussion topics is appended. (See Figure 6.)

Note that one of the discussion topics is "social responsibility." Institution Z is committed to the concept that it should be a "good corporate citizen" and that the companies in which it invests should also have a positive attitude toward the need for compliance not only with the letter of the law but with the spirit of the social legislation of our era. Clearly, the common stock analyst is not in a position to investigate or make judgments on highly technical issues. But he is in a position to appraise the attitudes of the company executives with whom he comes in contact, and he should, by appropriate questioning, make it clear to those executives that Institution Z gives consideration to such issues in making its investment evaluations.

Most companies designate a specific official to act as contact man with the investment community. But the analyst should try, if possible, to broaden his contacts within the company, and to observe at first hand the thought processes of the chief executive and the senior operating managers. Meetings with the company's economist may be helpful in understanding the assumptions underlying published company forecasts.

Although some analysts have been known to tape management interviews, most executives tend to be uncomfortable with a microphone in front of them. On the other hand, few people object to an analyst taking notes, and the analyst should be sure to jot down key phrases. As soon as possible after the interview is completed, the analyst should expand his notes while the details of the meeting are fresh in his mind, and should submit a management contact report within 2–3 days thereafter.

FIGURE 6

Checklist of Topics for Pre-interview Investigation and Follow-up at Interview

1. Identification of critical variables for industry and company.
   - *a.* General economy.
   - *b.* Backlogs.
   - *c.* Unit volume versus pricing.
   - *d.* Key customers.
   - *e.* Consumer "tastes," advertising.
   - *f.* New facilities, new products.
   - *g.* Labor costs (including pensions) and productivity.
   - *h.* Raw material, energy, transportation cost, and availability.
2. Company performance relative to its industry.
   - *a.* Market share.
   - *b.* Sales and earnings growth rate.
   - *c.* Return on sales, capital, equity.
   - *d.* Financial and operating leverage.
   - *e.* Unique advantages regarding patents, marketing expertise, natural resources.
3. Foreign operations.
   - *a.* Growth and profitability.
   - *b.* Geographic concentration of production and marketing.
4. Accounting policies and divisional disclosure practices.
5. Management philosophy.
   - *a.* "What business are we in?"
   - *b.* Executive development program (educational and employment background of incumbent senior management).
   - *c.* Decentralization of decision making; internal controls system.
   - *d.* Role of Board of Directors.
   - *e.* Relations with investment community (credibility record).
   - *f.* Mergers and acquisitions; new product development; research and development.
   - *g.* Product pricing.
   - *h.* Labor relations.
   - *i.* Internal versus external financing; concentration of stock ownership; banking relationships.
6. Current and long-term planning and budgeting.
   - *a.* Economic, social, political assumptions.
   - *b.* Contingency plans.
7. Social responsibility issues—any evidence of:
   - *a.* Discrimination in hiring or promotion.
   - *b.* Unsafe working conditions.
   - *c.* Unusual environmental pollution problems.
   - *d.* Misleading advertising.
   - *e.* Unfair trade practices.

CONCLUSION AND SUMMARY

The modern approach to common stock evaluation centers on a two-part question: What is the potential growth of earnings and dividends of a company whose stock is being analyzed? What is a reasonable price to pay for that potential?

Our approach to common stock analysis proceeds from the general to the specific and from the retrospective to the prospective. First, an appraisal of total economic activity (GNP) and of total corporate profits is undertaken. Next, the role of the industry within the economy is examined, and finally, attention is focused on the position of the company within the industry. In each of these steps, an analysis is made of the factors responsible for the past record of growth. This provides some basis for an estimate of probable future developments. The main direction is to appraise in depth the growth of profits in relation to the growth of sales.

The determination of a reasonable stock price, or range of prices, given an estimate of growth prospects, can take several forms. A relatively theoretical—but nonetheless useful—approach is to discount the projected income stream from a stock to a present-value basis, at a discount rate which seems appropriate in relation to the risks involved and in relation to yields available on alternative investments. More eclectic and pragmatic approaches are based on an analysis of earnings past, present, and future and the application thereto of a multiplier, the price-earnings ratio. Methods of analyzing price-earnings ratios may vary from simple calculations of average p/e ratios in recent years to elaborate multiple regression studies. The quantitative approach must be supplemented by a knowledge of the "quality of management." The complete analyst must have a knowledge of accountancy, economics, financial analysis, psychology, statistics, and computer techniques. All this will not produce a certain ability to analyze common stock, but it will help.

6

Bonds and Preferred Stock

JEROME B. COHEN, Ph.D.
Senior Editor, Bankers Magazine
Emeritus Professor of Finance
Baruch College, City University of New York

THE BOND MARKET is primarily an arena for institutional investors, although in the past few years the attractiveness of yields of high-grade bonds, 8 to 9 percent, has commanded the interest of individual investors. A bond is, of course, a creditor instrument, a corporate or governmental obligation to repay the loan at some future maturity date. In contrast to common stock, which represents the equity, or ownership element, bonds are promises to pay. They receive a dubious priority on two occasions: (1) payment of interest due on the bond takes precedence over payment of dividends to common and preferred stockholders, and (2) in the event of failure, liquidation, or reorganization of a company, bondholders as creditors, have a prior claim to assets of the firm, if any. For these prior claims on income and assets ahead of the common stock, bondholders and preferred stockholders sacrifice most of the benefits that may ensue from a company's prospective growth.

Bonds may be either secured or unsecured and may range from first-mortgage bonds on the one hand to subordinated debentures on the other. One point needs to be stressed. The security behind a bond, while important, is not crucial. The earning power, financial condition, and quality of management is vital. Because of this, one company's unsecured bonds may be rated higher than another company's secured obligations. For example, the debentures of A.T.&T. are rated higher than the first mortgage bonds of Indianapolis Power & Light. The debentures of Southwestern Bell Telephone have a higher rating than the first mortgage bonds of Missouri Power and Light.

Types of Bonds

Mortgage bonds are secured by a conditional lien on part or all of a company's property. If the company defaults (fails to pay interest when due, or principal), the bondholders, through the trustee appointed to represent them and look after their rights, may foreclose the mortgage and take over the pledged property. Some corporate mortgages have an *equal-and-ratable security* clause specifying that if a prior lien subsequently is placed on the corporate assets, the bond with the protective clause will have an equal and pro rata share in this lien. Some corporate mortgages have what is known as an *after-acquired property* clause, which provides that all property thereafter acquired will become subject to the mortgage and automatically be pledged to secure the bond issue. This is favorable to the investor-creditor, and where it exists, if the company wishes to float another bond issue secured by a mortgage on its property, this second mortgage will be a *junior lien,* subordinate to the first mortgage or *senior lien* on the property. Usually, when companies float junior issues, secured by junior liens, they do not clearly label them as such. They call them "general" or "consolidated" or some other ambiguous name, and the only way an analyst can determine the security status of the bonds exactly is to read the indenture.

The *indenture* is the formal, and usually lengthy legal contract between the borrowing company and the investor-creditor, spelling out all the detailed terms and conditions of the loan. The indenture will also indicate whether more bonds may be issued with the same security or under the same mortgage. If so, the mortgage is said to be "open-end." Additional issues of bonds under an open-end mortgage will naturally dilute the security available for earlier issues. If the mortgage is "closed-end," no additional bonds may be issued under the same mortgage and the issue therefore has better protection.

A bond secured by a pledge of specific securities is known as a *collateral trust bond.* These are issued mainly by holding companies, closed-end investment companies, and finance companies. They have not been popular in recent years, particularly after the passage of the Public Utility Holding Company Act in 1935. The *equipment trust bond or certificate* is usually used to finance the purchase of rolling stock by railroads. Under the Philadelphia Plan, title to equipment (such as freight cars, locomotives, and passenger cars) being bought by a railroad rests in a trustee who holds it for the benefit of certificate holders. The railroad makes a down payment (perhaps 20 percent), and the trustee issues equipment trust certificates to cover the balance of the purchase price of the equipment. The trustee then leases the equipment to the railroad under an agreement whereby the railroad obtains title to the equipment only when all obligations have been met.

Since the rolling stock can be moved anywhere in the country, should the railroad default, the equipment may be sold or leased to another railroad. Defaults have therefore been very rare in the case of equipment trust certificates.

Debentures are unsecured bonds protected only by the general credit of the borrowing company. They may contain a "covenant of equal coverage" which means that if any mortgage bond is issued in the future, which ordinarily would take precedence over the debentures, the issuer agrees to secure the debentures equally. This is the same as the equal and ratable clause described above. In some states the corporation law requires that this be done. All direct domestic obligations of federal, state, and municipal governments in the United States are debentures. Since this type of security is protected only by the general promise to pay, and in the event of default, the debenture holder is merely a general creditor, debentures can usually be sold only by corporations enjoying high credit standings. The value of a debenture should be judged wholly in terms of the earning power and overall financial status and outlook of the issuer, which is the best basis for evaluating any bond.

Subordinated debentures are junior issues ranking after other unsecured debt, as a result of explicit provisions in the indenture. Finance companies have made extensive use of subordinated debentures. Because of these companies' high liquidity and their need for large sums of capital, they have tended to develop layers of debt of which subordinated debentures are the lowest.

Convertible bonds are debtor instruments of the corporation which may be exchanged at the option of the bondholder for a fixed number of shares of common stock. For example, the Eastern Airlines 5-s of 1992 were convertible into 20 shares of common per $1,000 bond. The conversion price of the common was thus $50 per share. When the common sold above this price, the convertible bond would move up with the common. When the common sold below the conversion parity of $50 per share, the bond would rest upon its investment value as a bond without reference to the conversion feature.[1]

An *income bond* is a debt instrument whose distinguishing characteristic is that interest need be paid only if earned. Originally many income bonds arose out of railroad reorganizations and reflected the effort to reduce the burden of fixed charges to manageable proportions. Most income bonds require sinking funds; interest must be paid if earned, in contrast to preferred stock dividends; and interest is often cumulative, for three years or longer, depending on the terms of the individual bond issue. Income bonds as an alternative to preferred

[1] For a more detailed analysis of convertible bonds, see Jerome B. Cohen, Edward D. Zinbarg, and Arthur Zeikel, *Investment Analysis and Portfolio Management* (Homewood, Ill.: Richard D. Irwin, Inc., 1973), chap. 11.

stock have been taken up and utilized by some industrial companies. Interest payments are, of course, a deductible expense for corporate income tax purposes.

Collateral Provisions

The collateral provisions of bonds used to be heavily stressed in security analysis. There is much less emphasis on this today. For example, only some 40 percent of corporate bond issues during the postwar years have been secured bonds, compared with some 75 percent during the prewar years.[2] The reasons for the deemphasis of collateral are quite clear. Property value is a function of the earnings which the property can produce. Most property, which serves as bond collateral, is in the form of specialized plant and equipment—for example, a turbine generator. When the affairs of the borrowing corporation deteriorate to the point of receivership, reorganization, or bankruptcy, the probability is that the property is incapable of earning an acceptable rate of return and is therefore not worth very much.

In some cases, the property may be convertible into some other use, or may be made more profitable by more efficient managers. Such property can have an intrinsic worth sufficient to meet the claims of secured creditors. But in bankruptcy cases involving truly valuable property, the courts have been extremely reluctant to allow secured creditors to exercise their liens and sell the property to meet their claims. Typically, reorganization proceedings are ordered, the end result of which is to liquidate existing claims by issuing new securities to the claimants. Usually, the more valuable the property, the more strenuously the junior claimants will fight to keep from being left out of the reorganized company.

Under the Supreme Court's "doctrine of absolute priority," each rank of securities must be compensated for the full amount of its claim before anything can be alloted to a junior claim. Determination of the value of the assets of the bankrupt company, however, and of the manner in which the claims are to be satisfied, are subject to debate and interpretation.[3] Court proceedings can last for years. A classic example is that of the Missouri Pacific Railroad. Trustees in bankruptcy were appointed in 1933, and reorganization was not achieved until 1956—23 years later. In the end, even if the senior creditors emerge without a loss of principal, they may well have lost a substantial amount of interest, or they may have been locked into their investment for a long

[2] See T. R. Atkinson, *Trends in Corporate Bond Quality* (New York: National Bureau of Economic Research, 1967), p. 67.

[3] For a further discussion of these problems, see Jerome B. Cohen and Sidney M. Robbins, *The Financial Manager* (New York: Harper & Row, 1966), chap. 26.

period of time, because the market value of even first-mortgage bonds usually is very depressed during reorganization proceedings.

Even in the case of *municipals,* income and/or taxing capacity is more important than asset pledges. The bonds of states, municipalities, and other local subdivisions are usually classified under the broad heading of municipals. This, in turn, may be divided into two categories—*general obligations* (also known as G.O's, or full faith and credit bonds) and *revenue bonds* (or assessment bonds). The general obligation bonds are backed by the total taxing power of the issuer, while revenue bonds are backed only by specific revenues, usually those derived from the facilities which are constructed with the proceeds of the bonds, such as turnpikes, dormitories, and sewers. With municipals even more than with corporates, the bondholder's security lies in the income potential of the community or facility rather than in asset values, for courts are not likely to allow needed public facilities to be seized by creditors.

The modern tendency then in the analysis of fixed-income securities is to stress avoidance of trouble rather than protection in the event of trouble. It is therefore as important to examine the bond contract for the presence of what have been called "rules of good financial practice," as it is to examine the bond for such things as collateral, promises, priorities, and form. For example, a useful provision from the bondholder's point of view is that if the working capital of a debtor corporation falls below a specified level, common stock dividends must be suspended.

Many industrial and utility bond indentures require an annual *sinking-fund* payment by the corporation in order to retire the issue gradually. The specific bonds to be retired at any time may be selected at random and "called" at a specified price, or they may be bought in the open market if a sufficient supply is available at below the call price. In some cases, the annual sinking-fund payments may be left in an escrow account (usually earning interest) for eventual retirement of the entire issue at once. With some types of issues, especially municipals, *serial maturity provisions* are generally used in place of sinking funds. Under this procedure, a portion of the issue actually matures each year, so the bondholder knows precisely when his bonds will be retired. Different maturity dates usually carry different interest rates.

Sinking funds for bonds, like amortization provisions in building mortgages, give the lender greater assurance that the principal amount of the debt will be repaid by the maturity date. Chances of the borrower being embarrassed are greater when a large principal balance suddenly comes due. If the original proceeds of the issue had been used to acquire plant and equipment, as is likely, payments into a sinking fund as the property depreciates help maintain a healthy balance between fixed assets and long-term liabilities. Sinking funds are disadvantageous to the investor in one significant respect, however. After having gone to all the trouble of evaluating and acquiring a bond at what he considers an attractive rate of return, the investor may find the security taken away from him by a sinking-fund call. And at that time interest rates may be lower than when he purchased the issue, so that reinvestment in an equally attractive issue may not be possible.

Callable bonds are those which may be redeemed by the issuing corporation prior to the maturity date. Usually the indenture requires the company to pay a premium over face value when called before maturity. Because bonds are likely to be called when it is advantageous to the issuer and, therefore, disadvantageous to the bondholder, there is usually a premium paid over and above the maturity price if the bond is called. The call price may be 105, for example, if the redemption value at maturity is 100. Frequently, also, the premiums are on a sliding scale, with higher premiums paid for calls in the early life of the bond, when it has a long period to run, and lower premiums if the bond is called later in its existence.

Bond Ratings

The investment services, such as Moody's and Standard & Poor's, provide the investment community with an up-to-date record of their opinions on the quality of most large, publicly held corporate and governmental bond issues. The ratings are usually the result of committee decisions and not of single individuals. The agency ratings are held in such high regard that official regulatory commissions utilize them in evaluating the safety of bonds held by banks and insurance companies. Bond ratings are designed essentially to rank issues in the order of the probability of default—that is, inability to meet interest or sinking-fund payments or repayment of principal. Only issues of the federal government carry no risk of default, because Congress has the power to tax and issue money to pay its debts. However, government bonds entail an interest rate risk—i.e., a risk of capital loss due to rising interest rates. "Triple-A" bonds (Aaa, using Moody's designation; AAA, using Standard & Poor's) are those judged to have a negligible risk of default and therefore to be of the highest quality. "Double-A" bonds are of high quality also but are judged not to be quite as free of default risk as triple-A bonds. Bonds rated A and Baa (BBB is S.&P's designation) are generally referred to as medium-quality obligations, with the latter possessing a higher risk of default than the former. Bonds not falling within the first four rating categories are held to be "speculative."

A strong argument for the use of agency ratings as a guide to bond quality is their excellent record of correlation with actual default experience. An exhaustive study of investor experience with corporate bonds sold during the 1900–43 period was undertaken by the National Bureau of Economic Research.[4]

The study showed the percentage of bonds in each rating category at the time of offering which subsequently defaulted.

Rating Category (composite of ratings of various agencies)	*Default Rates (percent of par value)*
1	6
2	6
3	13
4	19
5–9	42

Thus, during the more than 40 years covered, including the greatest depression in our economic history, only 6 percent of par value of bonds originally rated in the top two categories subsequently defaulted. Twice as high a percentage of third-category bonds defaulted, and three times as high a percentage of fourth-category bonds. Over 40 percent of the bonds classified as "speculative" subsequently defaulted.

Ask members of the agency rating committee what factors go into the makeup of a bond rating, they reply—everything; there is no fixed formula. Nevertheless, certain of the more important yardsticks are well known because they are in general use by all bond analysts. The first is "earnings coverage," or "times fixed charges earned." Then there is the "capitalization ratio" and the "working capital" analysis. Traditional bond analysis places heavy emphasis on the nature of the industry, the size and trade position of the issuer, and the trend as well as the level of earnings available for the payment of fixed charges. For example, bond analysts usually are inclined to favor companies which are in industries that are considered essential. In the same fashion, large corporations which represent a substantial share of their industries' output are believed to involve less risk to creditors than smaller corporations with less entrenched positions. The National Bureau study, discussed earlier, contains clear evidence of an inverse correlation between size and default rates.

Traditional bond analysts also recognize that while earnings coverage, or any other financial ratios, may be adequate in retrospect and on average, it is possible for ratios to conceal incipient weaknesses. Therefore, they pay careful attention to recent trends and to any develop-

[4] See W. Braddock Hickman, *Corporate Bond Quality and Investor Experience* (New York: National Bureau of Economic Research, 1958). See also T. R. Atkinson and E. T. Simpson, *Trends in Corporate Bond Quality* (New York: National Bureau of Economic Research, 1967).

ments which may cause the future earning power of a corporation to deteriorate. To this extent, the bond analyst adopts some of the forward-looking point of view of the common stock analyst. Nonetheless, significant criticism of the traditional approach to bond analysis has developed. The various rule-of-thumb quality ratios provide a reasonable basis for ranking fixed-income securities in order of default probability. They do enable the analyst to identify *relative* risks. On the other hand, they do not provide much, if any, information on *absolute* risks. As Professor Gordon Donaldson noted:

> The basic questions in the appraisal of the magnitude of risk associated with long-term debt can be stated with deceptive simplicity: What are the chances of the business running out of cash in the foreseeable future? How are these chances changed by the addition of X thousands of dollars of annual interest and sinking fund payments? . . .
>
> There are, of course, a variety of possible circumstances under which a company might have its cash reserves drained off. However, considering the problem from the point of view of mature, normally profitable, and reasonably well managed companies, it is fair to say that the primary concern with debt is with what might happen during a general or industry recession when sales and profits are depressed by factors beyond the immediate control of management.[5]

Thus, Donaldson and other critics of traditional ratio analysis say that what is needed, is a thorough-going cash flow analysis. "Cash flow analysis" in this context is more than merely a comparison of fixed charges plus sinking-fund obligations with net income plus depreciation. It is a complete sources and uses of funds network. In Donaldson's words: "it is somewhat artificial to think in terms of the cash available for debt servicing, as the earnings-coverage standard does, as if it were an identifiable hoard where a number of needs equally as urgent are competing for a limited cash reserve." The essence of the cash flow approach to bond analysis is the estimation of the probability of possible recessionary changes in cash flow, the probability attached to each of a range of prospects. This, in turn, provides the basis for an estimate of the probability of exhausting cash during a period of adversity. It provides a measure of the *absolute* risk of default.[6]

Bond Prices, Yields, and Interest Rates

There are a number of risks in bond investment. One is the business risk, that a decline in earning power may impair the corporation's ability to service its debt. The second is the purchasing power risk, the

[5] See Gordon Donaldson, "New Framework for Corporate Debt Policy," *Harvard Business Review*, March–April 1962, pp. 123–24.

[6] For a more detailed exposition of this technique see Cohen, Zinbarg, & Zeikel, *Investment Analysis and Portfolio Management*, chap. 9.

prospect that a severe inflation may impair the buying power of interest on debt as well as of the principal itself. The third is the so-called interest rate risk, which refers to the condition that if the general level of interest rates rises subsequent to the time an investment commitment is made in a fixed-income security, the market price of the security will decline until its yield becomes competitive with new, higher interest rate securities. There is also the counter prospect that if interest rates decline bond prices will rise.

The principal risk, then, in high-grade bonds is not related so much to the course of business activity as it is to the trend of interest rates. If you hold high-grade bonds and interest rates which had been low, start to rise, and for some reason you cannot hold your bonds to maturity but are forced to sell them because you need funds, your portfolio can suffer a capital loss. Why is this and how does it work? If interest rates rise (because the Federal Reserve, for example, pursues a tight money policy), a 3½ percent rate on a bond, bought at par some years back, will no longer look attractive, as it once must have, to holders of the issue who become aware of the new prevailing 8 to 9 percent rates in more recent issues. They may, therefore, sell the old issue. This selling pressure forces the price of the old issue down, and it will move lower until its price in the market yields the new purchaser about the same rate of return as the average new higher level of rates in the market. Thus as a boom progresses and the demand for money grows and interest rates rise, high grade bond prices may fall.

Usually near the peak of the expansion, when the boom seems about to top out, when the central banking authorities are enforcing a tight money policy which has driven interest rates up and bond prices down, shrewd portfolio managers may switch from stocks to high-grade bonds. As a recession develops, tight money will be eased; interest rates may fall; and high-grade bonds rise. In fact the deeper the recession, the higher will go the prices of high-grade bonds, as investment demand switches to them and bids up their prices.

It is not always so clear-cut and simple, however. In the late 1960s and early 1970s, the pressures of inflation drove interest rates up in poor years as well as in good ones, and therefore prices of old bonds with low coupons fell sharply as new bonds were issued with higher and higher coupons. For example, in 1970, General Telephone and Electronics had to offer a coupon of 9¾ percent to sell a debenture maturing in 1995. At the same time another of its debentures issued in 1963 with a coupon of 4½ percent maturing in 1988 sold as low as 58 ($580 for a $1,000 bond) in 1970. Because the 9¾ percent debenture was selling above par in 1971 and the 4½ percent debenture way below par, both had a yield to maturity of over 8 percent. To cite another example, A.T.&T., for AAA-rated debentures, had to provide coupons of 8¾ percent in 1970 for a new issue of debentures due in the year 2,000. In

1946 A.T.&T. had issued debentures with a coupon of only 2⅝ percent (due in 1986). These, in 1970, sold as low as 51. Both debentures provided yields to maturity of over 7 percent in 1971. These examples illustrate the interest rate risk associated with bonds.

The inflation and efforts to control it drove interest rates up. Borrowing corporations and governmental bodies had to pay much higher coupons on new issues and older outstanding bonds with lower coupons fell in price, even in a recession period. The extent to which long-term interest rates reflect an inflation premium may be seen in Figure 1. No one has been able to dissect, with a high degree of precision, the long-term interest rate to quantify the "real" component and that part attributable to long-term expectations of inflation. However, econometric efforts in this area do suggest that in the past seven or eight years, the

FIGURE 1

The Real Rate and the Market Rate

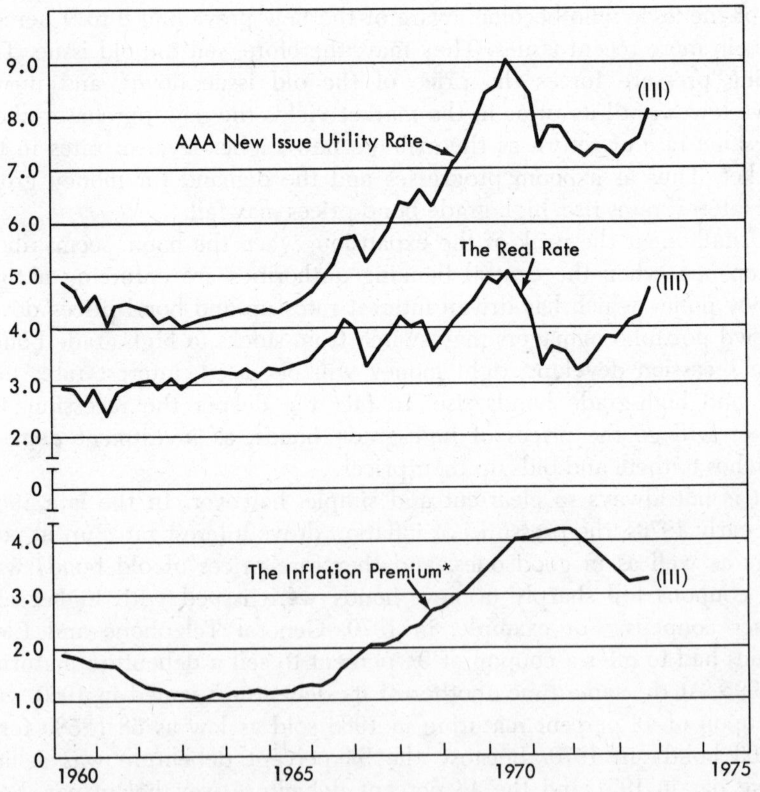

* The "real rate" is derived by subtracting the inflation premium from the new issue market rate. The calculation of the inflation premium is courtesy of Data Resources, Inc., of Lexington, Mass. and is based on a weighted average of past inflation rates.

Source: Board of Governors of the Federal Reserve System, Data Resources, Inc.

FIGURE 2

Long-Term Interest Rates (monthly averages of daily figures)

Ratio Scale of Yields

* FHA 30-year mortgages. Dashed lines indicate data not available.

† Monthly averages of Thursday figures. Latest data plotted: FHA—April 1974; others —May 1974.

Source: Prepared by Federal Reserve Bank of St. Louis.

real rate for AAA utility bonds has fluctuated cyclically but has averaged about 4 percent. See Figure 2.

Calculating Current Yields. To understand the nature of the inverse relationship between price and yield, it is necessary to know something about the methods of yield calculations. The yield of a bond is equal to its coupon rate only when the bond's price is par. At any other price, yield must be calculated according to one of two different concepts. The first, *current yield*, is simply the coupon rate expressed in dollars, divided by the price. Thus, a 4½ percent coupon bond selling at 90 (i.e., $900 per $1,000 bond) has a current yield of 45/900, or 5 percent. This is the same type of calculation used in determining the yield on common stock—dividend divided by price—and is applicable to preferred stock as well.

Current yield, however, is an inadequate measure of a bond's rate of return, for in addition to annual coupon payments, provision must be made for the ultimate appreciation in value of bonds purchased at a discount (below par), or the ultimate depreciation of bonds purchased at a premium (above par), since the bond will ultimately be redeemed, assuming there is no default, at par at maturity. Even if there is no intention of holding the bond to maturity, it ultimately will be sold to some investor who does intend to hold it until maturity.

When an investor buys a bond below par (at a discount) and holds it to maturity, he receives not only the current yield, as described above, but also the difference between the purchase price ($900) and the par value ($1,000) at which the corporation will redeem the bond at maturity. This extra $100 must be added to the interest income from the bond over the period it is held to determine the yield to maturity. On the other hand, if the investor pays more than par for the bond (assume $1,100), and holds it until maturity, he will get back only $1,000 from the corporation. Thus he will lose $100, which must be subtracted from his income from the bond over the period he holds it, in order to arrive at an effective yield to maturity.

If the bond is bought at a discount, the difference between the purchase price and the redemption value is a gain for the investor. If you divide this difference by the number of years remaining in the life of the bond, you may consider the result an average annual gain. If the bonds were bought at a premium, this result would be an average annual loss. Now, if you add this average annual gain to, or subtract the average annual loss from, the total interest payment received in a year, you get the average annual income from the investment.

Yield-to-Maturity Concept. The yield-to-maturity concept meets the need for a common denominator in expressing the yields on different bonds of varying maturity. Obviously, a discount of, say, $100 per $1,000 bond is worth more if the bond is to mature in 5 years than if it matures in 20 years, assuming it is paid in full at maturity.

A simple analogy may make the yield-to-maturity concept clear. Assume a 4½ percent coupon bond, with 10 years remaining to maturity, selling at a price of 90 (90 percent of par, or $900 on a $1,000 bond). The yield to maturity in this situation is equivalent to the rate of interest, compounded semiannually, which a savings institution would have to guarantee to enable you to deposit $900.00 today, withdraw $22.50 every half year (bond interest is usually paid semiannually), and have $1,000 in a passbook 10 years hence. In more technical terms, it is that discount rate which will cause the present values of $1,000.00, 10 years hence, plus a 10-year semiannual annuity of $22.50 to total $900.00.

In practice there are published bond tables which professionals use which can be used to find the answer. When yield tables, however, are not handy, an approximation formula can provide satisfactory results. The formula is:

$$\frac{\text{Annual coupon interest} + (\text{Discount/Number years to maturity})}{(\text{Current price} + \text{Par value})/2}$$

or

$$\frac{\text{Annual coupon interest} - (\text{Premium/Number of years to maturity})}{(\text{Current price} + \text{Par value})/2}$$

The reasoning behind the formula is, the numerator assumes that each year from date of purchase the bondholder will receive: (*a*) $45 of coupon interest, plus (or minus) (*b*) a pro rata portion of the appreciation (or depreciation) attributable to the purchase at a discount (or premium) of a bond which will be paid off at par at maturity. Obviously, the appreciation or depreciation will not be realized until maturity, but an annual amortization of the amount is logical.

The denominator of the formula represents the average true investment during the period to maturity. On an amortized basis, a bond purchased at a discount or premium appreciates or depreciates in value each year. It would therefore be unrealistic to assume that the investor has a constant commitment throughout the life of the bond, equal to his purchase price. What he really has committed is the average of each year's amortized value. This average is approximated by the expression ½ (purchase price + par value). It is, in effect, the amortized value in the middle year of the bond's remaining lifetime.

To illustrate the application of the formula, using the previous example of the bond selling at 90:

$$\frac{45 + 100/10}{(900 + 1{,}000)/2} = \frac{45 + 10}{950} = \frac{55}{950} = 5.79\%$$

Thus the yield to maturity is about 5.79 percent. If the same bond were selling at 110 instead of 90, applying the formula as follows:

$$\frac{45 - 100/10}{(1{,}100 + 1{,}000)/2} = \frac{45 - 10}{1{,}050} = \frac{35}{1{,}050} = 3.33\%$$

giving a yield to maturity of about 3.33 percent.

The relationship between interest rates, bond yields (to maturity), and gains or losses on bond values was interestingly stated by Leonard W. Ascher:

> Bonds rise in price when money eases and interest rates fall, and fall in price as interest rates rise, a phenomenon described in the textbooks as "interest rate risk." For example, suppose that late in 1969 a speculator buys triple AAA rated Union Pacific Railway 2½ percent bonds maturing in 1991 at a price of 47. For that price and time space yield to maturity will be 7.55 percent. Suppose that present tight money conditions ease, bringing a rapid fall in interest rates of one percentage point. Bond prices in the market will rise, and Union Pacific bonds should also rise to a price where their yield to maturity is roughly 6.55

percent. That price for the U.P. bonds should be 53.88, 6.88 points higher than the original price of 47, for a capital gain of 14.6 percent. On the other hand, should interest rates rise in the market by one percentage point, bonds will fall in price and with them U.P. bonds will fall to 41.19, a decline of 12.4 percent, where they will yield 8.55 percent. The interest rate risk here is between +14.6 and −12.4 percent. The spread summarized by these two numbers is an obvious indicator of the capital gain and loss potential of a bond. For convenience, we call it Index of Interest Rate Risk (IIRR).

By picking bonds more carefully an astute speculator may find even more exciting possibilities than Union Pacific bonds and he can use the Index of Interest Rate Risk (IIRR) to find them. A case in point is Southern Pacific Railway 2¾ bonds of 1966, rated A, and priced at 46½ for a yield to maturity of 7.42 percent. Should bond yields in the market fall one percentage point, and should Southern Pacific bonds follow the crowd, our speculator can expect his bond to rise in price to 53.89, a gain of 15.9 percent on his original cost. Conversely, if interest rates rise one percent there will be a capital loss of 12.8 percent. For the bullish speculator S.P. 2¾s offer an IIRR value of +15.9–12.8 percent, in contrast to Union Pacific's +14.6–12.4 percent. Considering capital gains alone the Southern Pacific bonds are clearly a better buy.[7]

It is virtually axiomatic that fluctuations in the general level of interest rates cause long-term bonds to fluctuate more in price than shorter term bonds. When interest rates rise, long-term bonds fall more sharply in price than shorter term bonds; when interest rates fall, long-terms rise faster in price. Looking again at the yield approximation formula will show why this is the case.

Assume the existence of three bonds of identical quality and identical coupon rate—say 6 percent. All are selling at par. The only difference among the bonds is maturity. Bond A has a 1-year maturity, bond B has a 20-year maturity, and bond C has a 40-year maturity. Suppose that a rise in the general level of interest rates causes all three bonds to go to a 7 percent yield basis. To what price will each fall? The following calculations show the approximate answers.

Bond A (1 year):

$$0.07 = \frac{60 + (1{,}000 - x)/1}{(x + 1{,}000)/2}$$

$$0.07 = \frac{60 + 1{,}000 - x}{0.5x + 500}$$

$$0.035x + 35 = 1{,}060 - x$$

$$1.035x = 1{,}025$$

$$x = 990$$

[7] Leonard W. Ascher, "Selecting Bonds for Capital Gains," *Financial Analysts Journal*, March–April 1971, p. 74.

Bond B (20 years):

$$0.07 = \frac{60 + (1{,}000 - x)/20}{(x + 1{,}000)/2}$$

$$0.07 = \frac{60 + 50 - 0.05x}{0.5x + 500}$$

$$0.035x + 35 = 110 - 0.05x$$

$$0.085x = 75$$

$$x = 882$$

Bond C (40 years):

$$0.07 = \frac{60 + (1{,}000 - x)/40}{(x + 1{,}000)/2}$$

$$0.07 = \frac{60 + 25 - 0.025x}{0.5x + 500}$$

$$0.035x + 35 = 85 - 0.25x$$

$$0.06x = 50$$

$$x = 833$$

Thus, with the same 1 percent yield increase, the 1-year issue drops 1 percent in price ($10 per $1,000), the 20-year issue drops 11.8 percent, and the 40-year issue drops 16.7 percent. The reason may be understood from the formula. The additional 1 percent yield to maturity must be derived from the discount since every other value in the formula is identical. But as maturity increases, the discount is being amortized over an increasing number of years. Therefore, in order for the discount to produce an extra 1 percent *per annum,* it must be progressively larger in dollar amount as maturity increases.

Clearly then, bond risk is, in part, a function of maturity. Indeed, long maturity increases risk not only because of the interest rate factor, but also because it increases the time for unexpected occurrences, such as obsolescence of the borrower's product line, general economic dislocations, or severe depreciation in the value of the dollar.

We have assumed identical coupons but varying maturities. Now make a different asumption—the same maturities but varying coupons. Suppose, for example, that three different bonds of equal quality all have 30-year maturities, but that one has a 7½ percent coupon and is selling near par, one has a 4 percent coupon and is selling far below par, and one has a 9 percent coupon and is selling well above par. What is likely to happen to the price of each bond if the general level of interest rates either rises sharply or falls sharply?

The lowest coupon bond will have the greatest price change and the highest coupon bond will have the least, other factors being equal. This is mainly because a large portion of the yield to maturity of the low coupon bond represents capital gain which will not be realized until a distant date, while the yield from the high coupon bond will be realized much earlier in the form of large semiannual interest payments. The distant date for the yield component of the low coupon bond means that a change in the rate at which the final principal is discounted will have a much greater impact on its present value than is the case with the high coupon bond. There are also other considerations which reinforce the tendency of low coupon bonds to fluctuate more in price than high coupon bonds.[8]

One of the most important factors in evaluating the gain or loss potential of a high coupon bond is its callability. Some bonds are fully callable at their issuer's option (usually with 30 days' notice). Others are not callable for any purpose other than sinking-fund requirements. Between these extremes, some bonds are callable for other than refunding purposes—they cannot be called with the intent of replacing them with new bonds at a lower yield, but they may be called to be replaced with stock, or in a debt consolidation move, or because of a merger. Still other bond issues are nonrefundable for a specified number of years, but are refundable thereafter. This is known as a call deferment.

When a bond is callable for refunding purposes, the yield-to-maturity calculation may not be an appropriate measure of the issue's expected rate of return. If there is a significant chance that interest rates may fall to a level which makes refunding attractive to the issuer, the corporation may exercise the call privilege. Then the money manager will be faced with the necessity of reinvesting his portfolio's funds at lower rates if he does not reduce quality. In addition to reinvesting at lower rates, he will incur the annoyance and expense of having to make a new search for an acceptable issue. An offset against this expense will be the "call premium" which the issuer must pay in order to exercise the call privilege. The end result of all these factors may be a realized yield that is substantially different from the originally calculated yield to maturity.[9]

Changes in Yield. The nature of yield changes over time must also be examined in preparing for bond analysis. Bond investors have to concern themselves with three types of changes: (1) changes in the level of yields; (2) changes in the *yield curve*—which refers to the relationship among yields on short-maturity, intermediate-maturity, and long-maturity bonds; and (3) changes in the *yield spreads*—which refer to the rela-

---

[8] For further discussion, see Sidney Homer and Martin L. Leibowitz, *Inside the Yield Book: New Tools for Bond Market Strategy* (New Jersey: Prentice-Hall, Inc., 1972).

[9] For methods of taking the call factor into account when calculating the expected yield from a bond, see A. P. Hess, Jr., and W. J. Winn, *The Value of the Call Privilege* (Philadelphia: University of Pennsylvania Press, 1962); and E. J. Elton and M. J. Gruber, "The Economic Value of the Call Option," *Journal of Finance*, September 1972. See also Frank C. Jen and James E. West, "The Deferred Call Provision and Corporate Bond Yields," *Journal of Financial and Quantitative Analysis*, June 1968; and, same authors, "The Effect of Call Risk on Corporate Bond Yields," *Journal of Finance*, December 1967.

tionships among bonds of different quality, different call features, or different tax status.[10]

Although there has been no overall trend in bond yield during this century, there have been both long and short cycles. Bond yields rose from 1900 to 1920, declined from 1920 to 1946, and climbed steadily back to the level of the 1920s from 1946 to 1965. Thereafter, they moved sharply higher to levels not seen since the Civil War. Recent trends may be seen in the following table:

		Long-Term Bond Yields			*Dividend Yields*	
	Treasury Bill Rate	*U.S. Government*	*Tax-Exempt*	*Corporate*	*Preferred Stocks*	*Common Stocks*
Current*	7.43%	7.05%	5.11%	8.05%	7.82%	3.50%
Year ago	5.15	5.61	5.11	7.35	6.89	2.69
1970 peak	7.96	7.21	7.04	8.95	7.84	4.35
Average:						
1965–69	5.01	5.01	4.29	5.93	5.37	3.18
1955–64	2.78	3.69	3.34	4.03	4.51	3.57
1945–54	1.09	2.46	2.12	2.78	3.96	5.44

* December 28, 1973.

The biggest push behind the rise in bond yields has come from the stepped-up rate of inflation since the mid-1960s. Until then the arithmetic of long-term investing was about as follows:

The Arithmetic of Long-Term Investing, 1871–1967

	Gross Return	Minus *Dollar Shrinkage*	Equals *Return Adjusted for Inflation*
Fixed income assets	4%	2%	2%
Common stocks	8–9*	2	6–7

* Dividends and capital appreciation combined.
Source: David L. Babson & Co., Inc., 1973.

Throughout the long period, the annual return on *all* listed common stocks—the good ones and the losers—averaged 8–9 percent, or twice the 4 percent realized on fixed income investments. And adjusted for the historical 2 percent rate of inflation—equities provided more than three times as much return as bonds and other dollar assets. With rate of inflation rising in the late sixties and the early seventies, corporate bond yields were pushed up to 7½–8½ percent, twice the historic level. In 1973 the corporate bond yield of 8 percent seemed to reflect an inflation rate of 5½ percent and a real return of 2½ percent. This reflected the

[10] For an interesting discussion, see Sidney Homer, *Total Money Management* (New York: Salomon Brothers, 1973).

increasing acceptance, in recent years, of a theory of interest rates which was advanced more than 40 years ago by Professor Irving Fisher. He argued that interest rates contain a premium for inflation expectations. When borrowers and lenders expect a rising rate of inflation, lenders demand higher interest rates to compensate for the expected loss of purchasing power and borrowers are willing to pay higher rates because they expect to be able to pay their debts with cheaper dollars.

When the expected rate of inflation is deducted from observed or "nominal," interest rates, the differences are referred to as "real" interest rates. Fluctuations in real interest rates are most often analyzed in terms of the relative supply and demand for loanable funds. When lenders have more funds and are more anxious to lend than borrowers need or want to borrow, interest rates fall. When the situation is reversed, interest rates rise.

Whatever the causes of changes in interest rate levels, it is apparent that if, at a given point of time, most fixed-income investors expect a substantial rise in rates, they will tend to avoid buying long-term bonds. This is because such bonds will fall substantially in price if the investors are correct and interest rates, in fact, do rise. Investors will prefer to keep funds in shorter term securities, awaiting a more favorable opportunity for switching into long-terms. On the other hand, if investors expect a substantial decline in rates, long-term bonds will appear to be attractive investments from two points of view: (1) they can provide a high level of income for many years; (2) they will rise in prices if rates fall and can be sold at a profit if a holder so chooses.

Therefore a general expectation of rising interest rates will cause lenders (buyers of bonds) to prefer short-maturity issues to longer maturity issues. A general expectation of falling interest rates will lead to a greater relative desire for longer maturities than for shorter maturities. On the borrower side of the market, of course, the relative positions tend to be the opposite. A general expectation of rising interest rates will encourage borrowers to rush their offerings to market in order to minimize the rise in their cost of capital. An expectation of falling rates, however, will encourage them to delay their bond offerings and to do as much financing as possible in the short-term market.

To summarize, expectations regarding future interest rate levels give rise to differing supply and demand pressures in the various maturity sectors of the bond market. These pressures are reflected in differences in the yield movement of bonds of different maturities. If borrowers prefer to sell long-term bonds at the very time lenders prefer to invest in shorter maturity issues, as is the case when interest rates are expected to rise, longer maturity issues will tend to carry higher yields than shorter maturity issues. The "term structure of interest rates," or yield curve, will be upward sloping. If borrowers prefer to sell short-maturity issues at the time lenders prefer to invest in longs, as is the case when interest rates are expected to fall, longer maturity issues will tend to yield less than shorter maturities, and the yield curve will be downward sloping.[11]

Yield Spreads. A yield curve expresses the relationship between yield and one vital characteristic of bonds—maturity. But there are other important relationships between yield and other factors such as quality, call features, and tax status. These relationships are referred to as *yield spreads*. For example, one would naturally expect the yield of Baa bonds to be higher than the yield of Aaa bonds because lower quality gives rise to a "risk premium" in yield.

Changes in expectations also cause changes in the yield relationships among bonds of equal quality but carrying different call provisions. Thus, if interest rates are expected to fall, callable bonds become relatively less attractive to investors than bonds with nonrefunding features. Yields on callable bonds, therefore, other things being equal, will be higher in relation to yields on nonrefundable bonds than would be the case if interest rates were expected to rise. Also, assume two bonds of equal quality, equal maturity, and the same call provisions, but with different coupons. For example, an 8 percent coupon Aa callable bond selling at par, versus a 4 percent coupon Aa callable bond selling at a deep discount. If interest rates fall sharply, the 8 percent coupon bond is more likely to be called. Therefore the 8 percent bond is less attractive if rates are expected to decline. The yield spread between two issues depends in large measure on the market's expectations of future interest rate changes and levels.

There is another reason for the yield spread between the 8 percent coupon bond and the 4 percent coupon bond. The yield on the 8 percent bond, selling at par, is taxed at regular income tax rates. But the yield on the 4 percent discount bond has two components and they are taxed differently. There is a regular income component and a capital gains component. The yield relationship between the two bonds will reflect in part the tax brackets of the investor in the issues. A high-tax-bracket investor may prefer as much capital gain, relative to coupon income, as possible. Another investor may be indifferent to the nature of the return. Yield spreads may change as investors with different tax conditions enter or leave the bond market.

Bond investment can range from a very high grade Aaa well-secured bond, to a speculative, subordinated convertible debenture. The bond market is a huge and complicated arena; interrelationships are not easy to understand. While the bulk of the bond trading is done by institutional investors, in recent years individual investors have become

---

[11] See C. R. Nelson, *The Term Structure of Interest Rates* (New York & London: Basic Books, Inc., 1972); see also B. G. Malkiel, *The Term Structure of Interest Rates: Expectations and Behavior Patterns* (Princeton, N.J.: Princeton University Press, 1966).

bond buyers because of attractive high yields due largely to the inflation induced component in the yield structure. In selecting any bond, the investor should not lose sight of the fact that the value of any bond, indeed of any security, depends on the earning power and financial health of its issuer.*

Preferred Stock

Unlike bonds which are debtor-creditor instruments, preferred stock represents part ownership of a company. Preferred and common stock together represent the equity or ownership of a corporation. As the name implies, however, preferred ranks ahead of the common. A concern must pay the required dividend on the preferred before it may pay anything on the common. Furthermore, if the company liquidates or fails, the preferred shareholders have a claim on the assets, if any, of the company after the bond holders but before the common shareholders.

With respect to dividends the rate to be paid on the preferred stock is usually fixed and stated. If the preferred pays 6 percent a year, the preferred shareholder is entitled to 6 percent of par value, which is usually $100 per share, each year as long as the stock is outstanding. Dividends on preferred stock are, like payments on the common, subject to action of the Board of Directors. They may vote to skip one or more dividends on the preferred and the preferred shareholders have no recourse. Many preferred issues, however, are *cumulative,* which means that if dividends are omitted, the arrears must be paid before any dividends can be paid on the common. The possibility of a dividend omission on the preferred, if not earned, imparts a greater element of risk than that generally present in bonds.

Because of the fixed rate of return and prior claim on assets and earnings, the market action of high-grade preferred tends to be governed by money rates. As in the case of other types of securities, preferred stocks range in quality from sound investments to highly speculative issues. The price action of the more speculative issues may more frequently be affected by the business risk of the issuer than by interest rates.

Preferred stocks do not have the fixed maturities of bonds. They may be subject to call or retirement by the issuing corporation, frequently at some premium over the issue price plus accrued dividends. Preferreds may have sinking-fund provisions, which require the company to allocate funds for the regular retirement of a certain number of shares each year. As in the case of bonds, some preferreds may also be called at a price below current market value. Some preferreds have voting rights, but

* Every junior analyst should read Sidney Homer's, *The Bond Buyer's Primer* (New York: Salomon Bros., 1968).

in most cases preferred holders can vote only if dividends are in arrears for a specified period or if certain provisions of sinking fund requirements are not met. Some preferreds are convertible into a specified number of common shares at a certain price. This privilege gives the preferred holder the opportunity to share in the company's growth and yet lets him or her enjoy the illusory safety and fixed dividend rate of the preferred stock.

Except for public utilities[12] and other companies with a similar need to maintain a certain equity-debt relationship, corporations have not generally desired to issue preferred as a source of new capital because of the tax burden. As you doubtless know, present income tax laws allow corporations to deduct interest payments on debt before computing taxable income. But dividends on preferred stock are not similarly treated. They are paid from income after taxes. This has not only reduced significantly the issuance of new preferreds, but has caused corporations to eliminate preferreds from their capitalizations when possible. The exception to this trend, however, is the practice of issuing preferred stock, usually convertible, to effect mergers and acquisitions. In most cases, an exchange from common to preferred is not taxable, while an exchange from stock to bonds may be subject to a capital gains tax. A convertible preferred issue, which provides a good fixed dividend and the opportunity to share in the growth of the acquiring company, may be an incentive for the shareholders of the company to be acquired.

Even though new preferred issues are not frequent and even though their appeal to the individual investor is questionable when their return and risk are considered, preferreds have a special attraction for any organization that pays taxes as a corporation. Dividends on preferred stock owned by a corporation or by certain institutions are taxable as income only to the extent of 15 percent. The benefits to a corporation of owning a good-quality preferred issue with a high fixed dividend rate are obvious.

In the early 1950s, high-grade preferred stocks yielded (current yield basis) 1 percent—1¼ percent more than highest quality corporate bonds (yield to maturity basis). That spread steadily narrowed, and since the mid-1960s the spread has been negative, with high-grade preferreds yielding less than Aaa corporate bonds. Three main reasons have been responsible for this narrowing:

1. Corporate investors have a tax advantage in buying preferred stocks rather than bonds. Interest income is taxed in full whereas only 15 percent of dividend income is taxed. Consequently, after-tax yields on preferreds have been very attractive relative to bond yields for in-

---

[12] See Ward S. Curran, "Preferred Stock for Public Utilities," *Financial Analysts Journal*, March–April 1972.

stitutional investors such as fire and casualty insurance companies, and the demand for the preferreds has been at a high level.

2. In the face of high investment demand, the supply of new preferreds has been small. Since bond interest is a tax-deductible expense to the issuer, whereas preferred dividends are not, high federal corporate income tax rates have discouraged companies from financing via preferred stock. They have relied heavily on bonds.

3. Not only have corporations refrained from issuing new preferred stock, they have also contracted the amount of outstanding issues by exercising their call privilege and refunding high coupon preferreds with bonds. Moreover, in cases where noncallable preferreds had been issued at high coupons, the issuing corporations have made generous exchange offers to the owners of such issues. This has introduced a capital gains element into the demand for preferred stocks. Buyers of noncallable preferreds have had a chance of benefiting from corporate exchange offers.

7

Analysis of Preferred Stock

DENNIS A. KRAEBEL
Manager of Preferred Stock Trading
Donaldson, Lufkin & Jenrette
New York, New York

TEN YEARS AGO, most published materials relative to preferred stocks likened their existence and proliferation to that of the American buffalo. In 1964 the Securities and Exchange Commission (SEC) reported gross proceeds from issues of preferred stocks of $224 million. Nine years later, a single issuer alone marketed at over four times that amount, i.e., $1 billion of straight preferred stock. Basically, the predictions of 1962–63 were objectively correct. In the period 1962–73, only one industrial corporation has successfully marketed a straight preferred issue. Another went through SEC registration only to "postpone indefinitely" literally hours before it was to be marketed. The soothsayers would have been correct had they confirmed their predictions to the industrials, the rails, and the finance companies. However, utilities proved to be the savior of this hybrid investment vehicle.

Since public utilities constitute virtually all preferred financing in the public sector of recent years, it would follow that analytical procedures relevant to public utility common stocks would similarly apply to preferred issues. Utility analysis is discussed in Chapter 30 Vol. II. Emphasis here will be on familiarizing the analyst with the characteristics and peculiarities associated with preferred stocks as an alternative investment vehicle competing for the investment dollar.

Corporate Charter

As previously mentioned, preferred stock is a hybrid instrument. It is by definition equity, but in terms of behavior acts like corporate debt.

However, the specific characteristics of each issue vary considerably and are stated in the issuer's charter as well as on the preferred certificates themselves. The most common preferences relate to dividend distribution and asset distribution in the event of liquidation. Additional features that may not necessarily be called preferences are sinking-fund provisions, call provisions, and in some cases, voting privileges.

Dividends

The rate set on preferred dividends, with a few exceptions, is either a percentage of the par value, or in the case of a no-par stock, a fixed-dollar amount, whichever is in accordance with the corporate charter. Virtually all charters provide that dividends must be paid to preferred holders before any distribution can be made to common stock holders. However, unlike a bond indenture, where failure to pay interest or principal on specified dates constitutes default, failure to declare and pay a preferred stock dividend does not.

Cumulative Dividends

Dividends may also be cumulative or noncumulative. If the dividend is cumulative and the issuer elects to skip payment over a period or several periods, the arrearages must be paid in full before any distribution can be made to common holders. In the case of a noncumulative dividend, once it is skipped, it is gone forever. This latter situation can exist even if the issuer has earned the preferred dividend but has elected to pass it in lieu of justifiable capital improvements (Barcley vs. Wabash R.R. 1930). Where the corporate charter makes no provision for cumulativity, the courts have held that it is implied that dividends will be cumulative.

Preference to Assets

An *inherent* preference of a preferred stock is in relation to assets upon liquidation. Again, almost all charters provide that upon liquidation preferred stockholders will be satisfied as to par or liquidation value, dividends, and premiums, if any, before any distribution can be made to common or junior securities holders. This preference is weak in that there are usually not enough assets to service the current liabilities, let alone the preferred holders.

Admittedly, all these preferences at best sound weak. Like anything else, a prospective investor in a preferred stock should thoroughly research the charter of the company he has interest in. The preferences previously mentioned are rather basic. However, the following excerpts from a recent Alabama Power Company red herring give a better view of the protection afforded the investor by the issuer:

> The holders of the Preferred Stock of each class are entitled to receive cumulative dividends, payable when and as declared by the Board of Directors, at the rates determined for the respective classes, before any dividends may be declared or paid on the Common Stock. Preferred Stock dividends must have been or be contemporaneously declared and set apart for payment, or paid, on the Preferred Stock of all classes for all dividend periods terminating on the same or an earlier date.
>
> Except as otherwise provided by law or in the charter, the right to vote is vested in the holders of the Common Stock; provided, however, that, if and so long as four quarterly dividends payable on the Preferred Stock of any class shall be in default, the holders of the Preferred Stock of all classes shall have the exclusive right, voting separately and as a single class, to elect the smallest number of directors which shall constitute a majority of the then authorized number of directors, and one vote per share on all other matters. Stockholders are entitled to cumulative voting at elections of directors.
>
> The affirmative vote of 66⅔ of the outstanding shares of Preferred Stock is required for—
>
> *a.* the authorization or creation of any kind of stock preferred as to dividends or assets over the Preferred Stock. . . .
>
> *b.* the issue, sale or other disposition of any shares of Preferred Stock if the total number of shares therof to be outstanding would exceed 300,000, or the issue . . . unless in such case, (*i*) net income available for dividends for a period of 12 consecutive calendar months within the 15 preceding calendar months is at least equal to 2 times the annual dividend requirements on all shares of Preferred Stock. . . . (*ii*) gross income available for interest for a period of 12 consecutive calendar months within the 15 preceding calendar months is at least equal to 1½ times the aggregate of annual interest requirements and annual dividend requirements on all shares of Preferred Stock. . . . (*iii*) the aggregate of Common Stock capital and surplus is not less than the aggregate amount payable upon involuntary liquidation on all shares of Preferred Stock. . . .
>
> The affirmative vote of a majority of the outstanding shares of Preferred Stock is required for
>
> *a.* a disposition of substantially all of ALABAMA'S property, or merger or consolidation, unless. . . .
>
> *b.* the issue or assumption of securities representing unsecured indebtedness in excess of 10% of capital, surplus and secured indebtedness, except. . . .[1]

---

[1] Prospectus, Alabama Power Company, 8.16 percent cumulative preferred stock, issued December 13, 1973.

Obviously, very few of the above statements can be found in a common stock prospectus.

Participating Preferred

In addition to being cumulative or noncumulative, a preferred may be participating. This seldom-found feature provides for *participation* along with the common stockholders in the distribution of earnings, after the preference dividend has been paid. There are numerous variations as to how participation takes place and to what extent. Participating preferreds are scarce, and found only among vintage issues.

Call Provisions

As previously mentioned, preferred stock is legally equity, but behaviorally, debt. Price appreciation as a result of increased earnings capacities will accrue to the common holders, not to the preferred holders. The purchaser of preferred stock has contracted with the issuer for a fixed amount of return. Consequently, preferred stock is interest sensitive, as opposed to earnings sensitive. Increasing interest rates will cause a decline in a preferred stock's value; and conversely, declining rates will reflect increased value.

In order that issuer and buyer be protected from the latter situation, *call provisions* are provided. These provisions basically state at what time, price, and on how much notice, an issuer may force the redemption of any given issue. Once again, call provisions vary greatly from issue to issue. The most common provision is referred to as *standard call.* This generally provides that for the first 5 to 10 years following issuance, the stock may be redeemed by the company at a stated dollar price (usually issue price plus one year's dividend) plus accrued dividends. However, redemption may not be for the purpose or anticipation of refunding through debt or equally or senior ranking stock, unless such issuance would effect a greater interest cost to the company. After five years, the redemption price scales down in 5-year increments for 20 or so years until redemption price approximates issue price. Stated simply, an issuer may not redeem an issue for five years, except through the issuance of common stock at a premium to issue price. After five years, no restriction is placed on the means of redemption, however some premium redemption price usually remains in effect for approximately 20 years.

The second most common provision is referred to as *conventional call* and is considerably easier to define. Conventional call does not restrict the issuer as to how the stock may be redeemed. It merely states that redemption may be forced by the company through any means at specific prices plus accrued dividends from 30- to 60-days notice. Although the issuer is not restricted in means of redemption, the premium which must be paid tends to be considerably higher than the standard call premiums.

Call provisions are extremely important in the purchase and sale of not only new, but seasoned issues. Take as an example, public utility companies A and B. Assume both companies are of equal quality and size. Also assume that both have outstanding preferred stocks; i.e., 100 par, of equal size, pay $8.75 cumulative per annum, and go exdividend on the same dates. Finally, assume that both issues are offered in the open market at a dollar price of $110 per share, to provide a current yield of 7.95 percent (8.75/110) on the invested dollar. A cursory analysis, as above, could lead a potential investor to conclude that purchase of public utility company A preferred stock is equally attractive to the purchaser of public utility company B preferred stock. Such is not necessarily the case.

Further investigation could reveal that both A and B have standard call features, and that neither are redeemable by the company without the restrictions mentioned above for another three years. Assume company A's stock is currently redeemable at $112.50 per share with restrictions; the first drop in redemption price coming in three years to $108.00 per share. However, company B's stock is currently redeemable at $108. Theoretically, if general interest rates remain level, and prudent fiscal management is employed by both companies, company A's stock will remain outstanding for three years and maintain a market price of $110. Assume that after three years company B's stock is redeemed at $108. An investor in company A, assuming the stock is sold at the time of redemption by company B, will have bought and sold at $110 per share. Pretax yield will have been 7.95 percent. An investor in company B will have received equal dividends to that of company A, however the redemption has forced a $2 per share loss. Yield on the investment would be approximately 7.41 percent pretax. The approximate method of computation is:

$$\frac{\text{Annual dividend rate} - \dfrac{\text{Cost price} - \text{Call price}}{\text{Number of years held}}}{\dfrac{\text{Call price} + \text{Call price}}{2}} = 7.41\%$$

Now, assume everything as above, except that both of these stocks are offered currently at $115 per share. Using the approximate yield-to-call method, investing in company A would yield 6.29 percent.

$$\frac{8.75 - \dfrac{115 - 110}{3}}{\dfrac{225}{2}} = 6.29\%$$

Investing in company B would yield 5.76 percent.

$$\frac{8.75 - \dfrac{115 - 108}{3}}{\dfrac{225}{2}} = 5.76\%$$

Company A again appears to be the more attractive selection from a yield base but, in fact, may be a poor one. It is possible that either company in this example may redeem their issues if the issuance of common stock represents a prudent cost reduction to the company. Conceivably, A may redeem the issue one year hence at $112.5 per share, rendering an approximate yield on investment of 5.49 percent.

$$\frac{8.75 - \dfrac{115 - 112.5}{1}}{\dfrac{227.5}{2}} = 5.49\%$$

Voting Rights

General voting rights do not usually accrue to preferred stockholders unless the state in which the company domiciles requires it (Illinois). Most charters provide voting rights to preferred stockholders as a class only when there are dividend arrearages, if the company's financial position is jeopardized by the issuance of additional securities, or for the purpose of disposing of assets. For the majority of cases, voting privileges are the exception, not the rule.

Sinking Funds

Preferred stocks, unlike debt, have no final maturity. They are perpetual securities. The thought of "never getting my money back" has alienated many potential investors from preferred stock. In order to negate this philosophy and increase the market for their issues, many utilities in recent years have issued preferred stocks with sinking-fund provisions.

A sinking fund provides that the issuer will purchase in the open market or make tenders at par for a designated percentage of the greatest number of preferred shares outstanding at any one time. In effect, a debt instrument is created. If a holder maintains a position to the final sink or maturity, substantially all monies invested will be returned.

Straight preferred stock trades on a current-yield basis, whereas sinking fund preferred stock trades on a yield-to-maturity or final-sink basis. The inclusion of a sinking fund brings about a new scenario of terms indicative of the debt market. Such terms as average life, yield to the average life, graduated sink, and squeezing the sinker, are all variations of the basic concept.

Yield to the average life is probably the most misused and dubious term of all. It is not a figure that represents anything concrete to the investor, but rather represents the average amount of time a share of any given issue will remain outstanding.

An example may serve to illustrate this point. Assume East Broken Donut Power & Light Co. has outstanding 100,000 shares of 7 percent preferred, $100 par, that is offered in the open market at $90 per share. The charter states that the company will retire by a graduated sinking fund 2 percent of the initial amount outstanding at any given time for the next 10 years; 3 percent for the following 10 years and 5 percent from then until the issue is retired. What is the current yield, the yield to final sink, and the yield to the average life?

Year ×	*Amount of Sink* =	*Weighted Average*
1	2,000	2,000
2	2,000	4,000
3	2,000	6,000
4	2,000	8,000
5	2,000	10,000
6	2,000	12,000
7	2,000	14,000
8	2,000	16,000
9	2,000	18,000
10	2,000	20,000
11	3,000	33,000
12	3,000	36,000
13	3,000	39,000
14	3,000	42,000
15	3,000	45,000
16	3,000	48,000
17	3,000	51,000
18	3,000	54,000
19	3,000	57,000
20	3,000	60,000
21	5,000	105,000
22	5,000	110,000
23	5,000	115,000
24	5,000	120,000
25	5,000	125,000
26	5,000	130,000
27	5,000	135,000
28	5,000	140,000
29	5,000	145,000
30	5,000	150,000
Total	100,000	1,850,000

This computation reveals that it will take 30 years to retire this issue at the designated rate. Consequently, the final maturity is 30 years hence. The average life is calculated as total weighted average divided by total number of shares redeemed, or 18½ years. With the use of bond tables, it can be found that a $90 investment due in 30 years at $100 par with quarterly payments totaling $7 per annum will yield 7.873 percent (yield to final). The same situation due in 18½ years will yield 8.048 percent (yield to the average life). The current yield is simply 7.00 divided by $90.00, or 7.778 percent. Given that the company remains in business for 30 years, the worst that can be realized is a 7.873 percent return. To assume a return of 8.048 percent (yield to the average life) would be erroneous.

Tax Considerations

In an effort to avoid double taxation, the Internal Revenue Service permits taxable corporations to deduct 85 percent of dividend income derived from investments in taxable corporations. For this reason preferred stock investments may be particularly attractive to corporations.

In the instance of utilities, reference is sometimes made to old and new money preferred stock. Old money preferreds are those issued before October 1, 1942 (or subsequently in a refunding operation) and carry the 60.208 percent dividend exclusion. New money preferreds are those issued subsequent to October 1, 1942 for new money purposes and carry the 85 percent dividend deduction. It should be noted that a new money preferred can exist as a result of refunding, but the issue being refunded would have had to have been issued after the 1942 date. (Example: A preferred issued to refund a bond originally issued August 15, 1942 would classify as old money. A preferred issued to refund a bond originally issued December 1, 1942 would classify as new money.) Greater detail to the provisions mentioned above may be found in the Internal Revenue Code of 1954, sections 244 and 247.

The method of figuring the after-tax yield of any preferred stock investment, given tax bracket, status of preferred (old or new money), dividend rate, and purchase price or cost base is as follows:

$$\frac{\text{Dividend rate} \times [1 - (\text{Tax rate} \times \text{percent of dividend subject to tax})]}{\text{Purchase price or cost base}}$$

Example:

1. Dividend rate, \$8; new money, corporate tax rate, 48%; purchase price, \$103:

$$\frac{8.00 \times [1 - (0.48 \times 0.15)]}{103} = \text{After-tax yield of } 7.20\%$$

2. Assume same as (1), but stock is old money:

$$\frac{8.00 \times [1 - (0.48 \times 0.39792)]}{103} = \text{After-tax yield of } 6.28\%$$

3. Assume same as (1), but corporate tax rate is 25 percent:

$$\frac{8.00 \times [1 - (0.25 \times 0.15)]}{103} = \text{After-tax yield of } 7.47\%$$

4. Assume same as (2), but corporate tax rate is 25 percent:

$$\frac{8.00 \times [1 - (0.25 \times 0.39792)]}{103} = \text{After-tax yield of } 6.99\%$$

8

Analysis and Rating of Corporate Bonds

JACKSON PHILLIPS, Ph.D.
Vice President and Director
Municipal Bonds Research Division
Moody's Investors Service, Inc.
New York, New York

THE ANALYSIS of corporate bonds attempts to determine the investment strengths and weaknesses which are inherent in the conditions of long-term obligations issued by corporations. The conditions of the obligation must first be defined. Then, the relations between the obligation and the economic world in which it exists, particularly in the future, must be established. Finally, the question that must be answered is what the likelihood is that all of the conditions can be discharged successfully in the future world.

A rating is based on the analysis and represents a judgment expressed in shorthand terms of the strengths and weaknesses of the obligation. It is an evaluative assessment of the likelihood that the debtor can successfully meet all of the terms of the obligation. In one sense, the analysis and the rating represent an evaluation of the entrepreneurial function of a company, its ability to combine the inputs of production successfully and, further, to distribute the output in a market at prices that will continue to pay a return on capital required in the business. What the analyst seeks to determine, and the rating to affirm, is the likelihood that the company in pursuit of its ordinary business will produce income to service the debt, any excess being a measure of its strength to withstand the unexpected.

Ratings which are assigned by the national rating agencies attempt to evaluate the credit of the company and to indicate the likelihood that it will meet its debt obligations. These are indicated in the following tabulation. The rating is arrived at through the analysis which asks a series of questions, and the questions cover virtually every area bearing on the future operating ability of the company, much of it based on results of the past. The following discussion outlines broadly the line of inquiry that the analyst may follow, although it should be stressed that every analyst develops his own techniques and methods of obtaining the information needed to answer the basic questions. In following any outline of approach, it should be kept in mind that the greatest danger is in failing to ask questions when a fruitful line of inquiry is developed. Thus, in many cases, the following discussion does not go far enough in some areas, while in other areas the entire inquiry may be dropped as not being particularly relevant.

Symbols Currently Used in Corporate Bond Ratings by the National Rating Agencies

General Description	*Moody's*	*Standard & Poor's**
Best quality grade	Aaa	AAA
High-quality grade	Aa	AA
Upper medium grade	A	A
Medium grade	Baa	BBB
Speculative grade	Ba	BB
Low grade	B	B
Poor grade to default	Caa	CCC
Highly speculative default	Ca	CC
Lowest rated grade	C	C

* Effective June 10, 1974, a plus (+) sign may be added to AA down through BB categories to show relative standing in class; a minus (−) sign shows deterioration. Moody's does not use the subcategories A 1 and Baa 1 in its corporate ratings, as it does in its municipal ratings.

The Industry

The industry within which the creditor operates should be identified and placed within the context of the economy in which it operates. This involves identifying the product or service and the aggregate of producers of the good or service and activities related to them. Aggregate data for the steel industry or distributors of electric power or manufacturers of automobiles, both historical and current, serve to outline the parameters within which a particular company producing a particular good or service will operate. Moreover, when compared with the American economy as a whole and when traced against the historical development of the economy, the behavior of a particular industry may be projected into the future on a total basis with some of the confidence associated with large numbers.

The historical development of the industry and its stage in the economic history of the nation helps to point the direction it is going. In tracing the history of an industry, changes in the rate of output of the industry compared with changes in the rate of growth of gross national product (GNP) over time clearly segregates reasons for change in aggregate demand. Up to about 1920, for example, most indicators of railroad usage in the United States gained at rates as fast as or faster than total GNP; but beginning about that time, the rail indicators grew at a slower rate than GNP, and subsequently indicated absolute decline in the industry. While everyone knows that the automobile and truck eventually absorbed all the growth potential of the railroad industry, and ultimately displaced it in many of its profitable areas of performance, the analyst requires a sharper measure of turning points in secular trends.

Characteristics of the industry should be determined, particularly those which establish its operating trends. Areas of critical importance include the availability of raw materials, necessary labor, and requisite capital machinery to produce the good or services for which the industry exists; in the case of service industries, parallel components of the final output, usually more limited but more highly specialized, will be identified. The market conditions in which a particular industry operates must also be recognized. The American economy is generally characterized as one of mixed enterprise, where prices may be set by the operator of a firm within limitations of the free market but also where prices are set within rules laid down by regulatory governmental bodies. To the extent the industry operates within an identifiable range of the spectrum, this should be clearly recognized. For limitations on the ability of the operator to set prices and to determine levels of output severely circumscribe future operations. Operating under federal controls which were sometimes punitive in nature and rarely aimed at promoting the health of the industry, the railroads were helped into their present state of disrepair by the regulatory climate. Operating largely under widely varying rules set by state regulatory bodies, electric utilities found themselves restricted in their ability to attract capital in widely varying degrees, depending on the state they operated in. Operating with only market controls over prices, the automobile manufacturers became restricted in time only by the conditions of monopoly which evolved in the industry.

It is the operating conditions of the industry and their most likely future course with which the analyst is concerned, not the historical mistakes of governmental policy or ill-advised management decisions. On the other hand, the analyst should have some understanding, clinical even in nature, of the likelihood of the repetition of past mistakes in old industries as applied to new or evolving industries.

Other operating characteristics of the industry that should be isolated are its proneness to cyclical fluctuations, its seasonal characteristics, and random events which may influence its behavior—against aggregate measures of the performance of the economy. Variations in demand for new automobiles over a period of several years usually correlate with other indicators of economic performance, and this particular industry, as opposed to, say, the residential demand for electric energy should be expected to show signs of weakness in aggregate demand in periods of economic slowdown. Seasonal characteristics, which are typical of some industries should be isolated and measured by past industry performance as a guide to the general climate in which the individual company being analyzed operated.

In some industries geographic differentiations must be made to determine the circumstances under which a particular company operates that may differ from any prevailing national average. Any product in which the availability of water is important, for example, will be manufactured under widely varying conditions within the contiguous United States. The attendant effect on costs of abundant versus scarce water supply may make a significant difference for one firm in an industry unless offset by other costs, such as transportation to markets or the availability of other production and delivery costs. In the electric industry, moreover, geography plays a major role in the determination of the availability of energy sources. Cheap hydroelectric power in the Pacific Northwest has produced usage patterns three times as great in size as those in the energy-scarce Northeast. And the abundance of oil and gas in the Southwest has in the past imposed cost patterns on electric energy producers which differ significantly from those of the Southeast which must import energy supplies over varying distances, with the associated additions to costs.

The future of the industry must be assessed and the assessment continuously updated by the analyst as to its place in the totality of the American economy. For the immediate future, such an assessment may have more importance for the owners and the suppliers of short-term credit. For the longer term and for the bondholder, however, technology, tastes and wants, and all of the variables determining an industry's ability to hold its place or to expand require examination.

The Company

In the analysis of the company issuing the particular security in which the analyst is interested, the analyst will determine its historical background for identification purposes and its capabilities within the industry in which it operates. The organization of the company must be suitable for the performance of the job it has undertaken, and its historical performance will indicate the place it currently holds in the industry as well as providing some clue as to where it is heading. In the analysis of the corporate structure, information will be gained as to the company's affiliates and support activities which may contribute to or detract from its main efforts within the industry.

Price Determination. The conditions under which prices in the industry are determined must be isolated and characterized, and their direct applicability to the company involved should be determined. If the market in which the company operates is a truly competitive one, then the likelihood of the continuation of those conditions should be assessed in some manner. But most companies do not operate in competitive markets, at least not under conditions in which the price is truly set by the market, so that the analyst has to determine the elements of monopoly which are present, how those may be continued, and what the chances of their perpetuation are. Sometimes a lack of understanding of the product or service, and the substitutes that exist for it, leads to an incorrect appraisal of the market and its future. In the past, this has been particularly true in the energy and transportation fields. Pricing of electric company services must also take account of technological alternatives such as on-premises facilities to convert natural gas into electric energy. And common carrier truck pricing must take account of costs associated with leased trucking in the short run and the ability of the user to dispense with transportation costs altogether in the long run. The ability of the analyst to make these distinctions and to define their conditions is generally what determines his ability as an analyst.

In the event the company operates in an industry in which prices are regulated and service standards set by government regulatory bodies, the exact application of those standards to the company must be understood. At the present time, an electric utility operating in one state may enjoy a relatively nonrestrictive climate as far as approvals for price increases are concerned, as opposed to another utility operating in another state where the regulatory climate may be highly restrictive. In the latter case, a combination of a management not fully appreciative of its restrictive environment and a dilatory, time-consuming regulating process can put a company in an unfavorable financial position almost inevitably, particularly when changing market or supply conditions emerge. In the electric supply field, the combination of heavy demand pressure; the new, unperfected technology of nuclear power; a shortage of conventional energy supplies; and the political pressure to hold prices down—all as misinterpreted by the management of a company—led in some instances to predictable financial stress.

Plant. Where applicable, the physical plant of the company should be assessed to determine its ability to function reliably at lowest cost levels and to be continued under such conditions into the future. This phase of the analysis has particular application where the security involves a mortgage of the physical assets of the company. But it is of central importance in any event, because only an economic application of borrowed or equity capital can over time return the loaned financial assets to the lender with his payment of interest for the loan.

The conditions of production or supply in many cases involve a number of processes, such as supply of raw materials, production, transmission, distribution, and storage of materials. The degree of success of the company depends in the first instance on the skill with which these processes are combined, without excessive capital investment in any one phase or without shortages in any one. An integrated electric company with rising demand must provide all phases, including distribution on a time schedule that does not tie up borrowed capital in a nonproductive phase while waiting for the others to catch up. Similarly, a well-run company will seize on a new technology, such as was the case of pumped storage a few years ago, in order to meet a particular need which it can forecast.

The analyst's interest in the company's plant extends to its economic concept, its actual physical conditions, and its capacity relative to past, present, and future demand. In some cases, the age of the plant is indicative of the company's ability to meet peak demands only under unfavorable cost conditions. When an electric company must turn frequently to standby capacity which operates under high-cost conditions, meeting its peak loads will predictably lead to high-cost operations. Ancient coal-burning steam capacity or expensive diesel capacity if relied on by some systems can lead to distorted operating expense items, which, if continued, produce serious decays in financial operations. Obviously, the condition of the plant includes its proper maintenance without deferred maintenance that will lead to an even more harmful condition in the future. The analyst's ability to make such an appraisal depends on his knowledge of the industry and its practices, his ability to understand the engineers and the accounting statements, and in many cases his efforts to make his own physical appraisal of the plant condition.

Examples of Usage Ratios

Description	*How Determined*	*Use*	*Illustration*
Load factor	$\frac{\text{Average usage per time period}}{\text{Peak usage per time period}}$ $\frac{\text{Average}}{\text{Peak}} = \frac{600{,}000 \text{ kwh}}{1{,}000{,}000 \text{ kwh}} = 0.60$	Measure of average use related to concept of full capacity for stated or implied time period.	0.50 would indicate that half the seats on a plane were occupied; 0.60 would indicate that 60 percent of peak electric system use was the average use for a 24-hour period.
Loss ratio	$\frac{\text{System input} - \text{loss}}{\text{System input}}$ $= \frac{600{,}000 - 50{,}000}{600{,}000} = 0.91. \quad 1.00 - 0.91 = 0.09$	Measure of loss of energy in system; measure of electric system efficiency.	0.91 indicates 91 percent of system input was delivered, 9 percent having been lost between production and final distribution.

Business. The operations of the company and the demand for its output should be determined over time, past and future, to measure the market in which it operates. The classes of customers which the company serves should be differentiated and the nature of their demand should be traced. Classes are standardized, in some cases, as residential, commercial, industrial or as passengers and freight or as other categories which behave differently under differing circumstances. The history of the demand for each class should be analyzed to determine how the group has responded to cyclical downturns and how it has been influenced by long-term trends. Seasonal and weather influences should be isolated so as to provide explanations for variations in the future. Diversity of load is, of course, highly desirable as a stabilizing factor, while specialized demand which is subject to wide cyclical swings, if characteristic of the industry, should be recognized and accounted for in the company's financing operations and plans. Measurements of the company's demand load by class of customer, as well as cyclical, secular, and other time factors, should be compared with industry averages, and where applicable, with regional averages for the same industry. Variations should be accounted for and explained, particularly as they may account for future trends of operations.

Financial Analysis

Financial analysis of the concern involves examination of its income statements and its balance sheet. An historical record of the trend of both should be compiled to relate financial operating trends to its business trends, as well as to trends of its plant investment and capital structure. Current accounting statements should be examined with a view to projecting past trends into the future.

Income Statements. The income statement is analyzed to determine sources of revenue, categories of expenses, and net revenues which are available for various purposes, including debt service, capital expansion, taxes, and profits. Past trends of these items, particularly as related to the company's past trend of output and sales, are significant in explaining financial capacity.

Revenue sources are to be distinguished as between operating revenues, which are associated with the product, and nonoperating revenues, which arise from functions other than the direct productive one. Nonoperating revenues, investment income, and other such items do not relate directly to the business of the company and hence may be irregular or nonrecurring. Expense analysis involves breaking down total operating expenses among those categories relating to product output, i.e., transmission, distribution, production, and other functional items. Another approach to expense analysis relates to outlays for variable as opposed to fixed expenses and analysis of expenses for operations versus maintenance and for salaries versus material costs. The resultant item, net operating revenues or net operating income, is the measure of performance in any one year and is informative to the lender and bond analyst as well as to the owner and stock analyst.

One of the most useful approaches to income statement analysis is through the derivation of ratios, which relate different items in a manner significant to a judgment of the level of performance. It is useful to compare these ratios with industry experience and with the past in assessing the company's future prospects. Some of the more commonly used ratios are indicated in Table 1.

Balance Sheet. The balance sheet indicates the company's standing at a particular point in time and provides measures of its capitalization, plant account, fund balances, and current account. Past trends of these items are instructive, and intense analysis of present and immediately past showings indicates where the company stands and what its accumulated financial strength is.

The plant account indicates the valuation of investment in plant,

TABLE 1

Examples of Financial Ratios

Description	*How Determined*	*Use*	*Illustration*
Operating ratio (related to capital turnover ratio: low capital turnover ratio = low operating ratio)	Operating & Maintenance Expense + Depreciation + Taxes / Gross operating revenue	Measure of gross revenues expended for expenses (may express maintenance only, if useful). The cost of doing business before compensation of capital; complement is "return margin."	90 percent indicates proportions of annual revenues devoted to cost of doing business; 10 percent is return margin. Company will probably have high capital turnover ratio, indicating relatively low capital requirements.
Interest coverage or debt service coverage ratios	Net revenues or Income available for interest / Total interest due Net revenues or Income available for debt service / Total debt service due	Measure of revenue available for coverage of interest or debt service.	5.5 times indicates relation of annual income available to interest required; total debt service, including principal, will be lower.
Interest or debt service safety margin	Net available after interest / Gross revenues Net available after debt service / Gross revenues	Amount that gross revenues could decline and still cover interest or debt service (assuming operating and maintenance to be constant).	

gross, and after accumulated depreciation, net. Claims on the assets of the company are indicated by capitalization items on the balance sheet. Fund balances will indicate the amounts of cash and investments which have been set aside in compliance with agreements with bondholders and others, while current account items provide a measure of the effectiveness with which the company discharges its current obligations.

As in the case of the income statement, ratios relating different categories of balance sheet items provide the most useful measure of performance, particularly when compared with industry ratios and over the past to indicate trends. Some of the useful ratios in balance sheet analysis are indicated in Table 2.

TABLE 2

Examples of Balance Sheet Ratios

Description	*How Determined*	*Use*	*Illustration*
Plant investment or capital-turnover ratio	Annual gross (or net) revenue / Gross (or net) plant	Amount of capital investment (gross or net) to earn $1 of revenue (gross or net); measure of capital investment requirements.	0.40 indicates a utility must employ $4 of capital to produce $1 of revenues; 2.0 indicates a manufacturing company employs 50¢ in capital to produce $1 of revenues.
Debt ratio	Total bonded debt / Net plant + Net cash and investment assets	Measure of debt related to net asset value, available to support it, expressed as: debt as a percentage of net assets.	50 percent may represent a utility where employment of capital is high; 12 percent may represent an industrial company where it is lower.
Current ratio	Current assets / Current liabilities	Measure of current account, expressed as times current liabilities covered by current assets.	
Surplus ratio	Total surplus / Total assets − Depreciation	Measure of surplus related to net assets.	

Rate Analysis

Perhaps the most significant single area of the analysis of a company relates to its pricing policies, for this is the single relationship within a market that brings together the forces of supply and demand. The nature of the market served is reflected in correct pricing, whether a free or a regulated market. The elements of monopoly which exist in the market must be understood by the company's management and pricing must be established accordingly. Management's strategy within its industry can be understood best by the pricing policies it follows, and management's long-range aims reveal themselves best in the pricing policies that are established. Even where management is severely restricted in setting prices, as in the case of some public utilities operating under some regulatory agencies, its ability to deal with that problem over time is tested. The company's ultimate success depends on the establishment of prices which its consumers are willing to pay, because price is the multiplier that applied to demand which is set by independent factors produces operating revenues. And operating revenues must be at a level sufficient to cover all expenses, including operations and cost of capital and return to the owner.

Prices are analyzable in numerous ways, including comparisons with industry and regional averages as well as their function in equating supply and demand. Rigid, fixed pricing in the local transit industry was a major factor in the ultimate demise of practically all privately-owned traction companies, and the continuation of these pricing policies, with the simple application of raising total charges, under public ownership has accelerated the use of alternatives, the future drying up of demand, and added burdens on the taxpayer. Imaginative pricing based on rather simple economic principles, where the price is related to the cost, including the capital cost, has worked well in such industries as the telephone industry. There, the charge is related to the capital costs, and it would seem reasonable that in a capital-intensive industry that capital costs must be recovered, unless the capital is to be donated by the taxpayer.

Management

The appraisal of management should be an objective judgment of the kinds of policies the company has pursued with what degree of success in the industry. Successful performance in solving the problems presented to the operator of an enterprise are the only true measures, and this appraisal will examine the policies pursued in the solution of these problems. Methods of management, its planning, and the execution of those plans are approaches in the evaluation, but the ultimate measures are found in an evaluative assessment of some of the ratios which have been indicated. One measure of the success of a company's management is, of course, its continued profitability over a period of time, particularly in negotiating through general business downturns and economic setbacks affecting the industry. Comparison of the operating ratio over time and within the industry, particularly when the underlying data are screened to eliminate extraneous factors, indicates the ability of management in reversing cost problems. An examination of pricing policies can prove fruitful in determining management's understanding of its problems of equating supply and demand within the market in which it operates. The financial policy pursued by management, the management of its current accounts, the capital structure it pursues, all are among the indicators reinforcing the central measure, which is maximizing profits over the longest period of time achievable.

Analysis of the Security

The analysis up to this point determines the economic base on which the company's credit rests and the likelihood of the continuation into the future of whatever economic strength it may possess. The analysis of a particular security turns around what is pledged to the payment of a bond that may be sold. An examination of the capitalization of the company is essential to determine what other obligations the company has undertaken and how any particular obligation ranks in claim on the earning power and assets of the company. The final appraisal, summarized in the rating, is then determined on the basis of the future economic strength of the company, as added to or subtracted from by the pledges of management to pursue certain policies with respect to its debt.

A company usually makes certain pledges of a legally enforceable nature to the holders of its bonds. In addition to pledging to pay principal of and interest on the bonds, the company will usually agree to some limitation on issuance of senior debt to prevent dilution of the security afforded that class of claim. The owners of the company will usually agree to follow certain policies in the attempt to assure the bondholder that revenues for debt service will be maximized. Other pledges will be made contractually, particularly regarding business practices and policies, to back up the security which the borrower offers in return for the loan evidenced by the bond which is issued. Protective covenants will include definitions of default, remedies in the event of default, and bankruptcy procedures designed to protect the rights of the holders of the bonds.

How, then, does the analyst reach a conclusion as to the merits of a particular security? The conclusion which is reached is summarized in one final statement, the rating which is assigned. Essentially, a degree of strength is determined based on consideration of all of the factors in the analysis. The weights assigned to the various factors may differ among analysts, but a final conclusion represents the considered judgment of several experienced analysts. The rating represents an assessment of the company's future strength with respect to the obligations considered, and this strength includes the appraisal of all the factors leading to its present position in the economy and its future prospects, as tempered by the company's legally binding pledge to do those things necessary to protect the rights of the bondholder.

9

An Analytic Approach to the Bond Market

MARTIN L. LEIBOWITZ, Ph.D.
Vice President and Director of Investment Systems
Salomon Brothers
New York, New York

INTRODUCTION

THERE ARE many interesting analogies between the investment process in the fixed interest securities market and that in the equity market. However, fixed interest securities have two very distinctive features derived from their basic contractual nature. First, they are readily classified, by and large, into clear-cut groups of securities. Second, there exists a generally accepted yardstick for measuring the value of a given fixed interest security to at least one class of investor—those investors who hold their bonds to maturity. This yardstick is, of course, the conventional yield to maturity (and its variants). This concept of yield is fundamental to the market's operation. The level of the overall market is stated in terms of yield to maturity. The relationship between market sectors is expressed in terms of differences or "spreads," in yields to maturity. The bid and offering market prices of individual securities are quoted as yields to maturity. The relationship between individual securities is also stated as a yield spread.

This general acceptance of yield, together with the clear-cut categorizations of securities, enables relationships within the bond market to be described in rather precise terms.

In the equity market, one does not generally even try to measure relationships so closely. (It is interesting to speculate on how concepts such as Substitution Swaps, Intermarket Spread Swaps, and Rate Anticipation Swaps might apply to the stock market.) This fine resolution of relationships is uniquely characteristic of the fixed interest securities market, and gives it much of its flavor. Most of the options available to the bond portfolio manager are *relationship trades* in one form or another. In practice, the analysis and decision-making associated with such relationship trades are almost invariably expressed in terms of yield spreads. The dependence upon yield spreads as relationship measure can perhaps be seen most dramatically in Substitution Swaps where aberrations of a few 1/100ths of 1 percent often initiate trades. The conventional yield and yield spread measures are used so pervasively in the bond market that they are really taken for granted. In fact, it is all too easy to overlook the very unique role of this yield yardstick in all the different types of relationship trades which are so characteristic of the bond market. The conventional yield is the mechanism of fine tuning within the bond market.

Having said all this, it becomes all the more astounding how few bond market participants could readily give a definition of yield to maturity. If pressed, one might get a definition, but it would probably be only distantly related to any of the several correct ways of looking at the concept of yield. When one observes this same phenomenon with extremely professional and successful participants in the bond market, one perhaps learns a deeper lesson. These professionals recognize that yield alone does not measure investment or trading value. They intuitively go beyond this conventional definition and use market yield values as a numerical language for expressing their more fundamental judgments of relative values. As in all fields, the truly great practice an art, not a science.

This lays a dual burden on anyone who wishes to take an analytic approach to the bond market, either as a financial analyst or as a participant. First of all, he must come to a clear understanding of the conventional yield to maturity. He must learn its different manifestations such as yield to call and cash flow yield, and he must also become familiar with its many direct implications. However, as a second step, the analyst must go beyond the yield-to-maturity surface. He must delve analytically into the more fundamental questions of total prospective return offered by a given debt instrument. He must examine how this prospective return is affected by changing market levels, changing (conventional) yield spread relationships, reinvestment rates over time, changing yield curves, tax effects, price volatilities, and other factors, all over both fixed and sliding time horizons. In short, the analyst will want to methodically explore all the factors constituting prospective total net return. It is the spectrum of probabilities affecting this prospective total net return which the professional bond market participant intuitively knows so well.

In this chapter, we shall try to shed some light on this double burden. However, we will begin with an analytic description of some of the fundamentals of bond investment. The primary focus will be on corporate bonds, but much of the discussion will be largely applicable to all fixed interest securities markets. We will then proceed to a detailed discussion of the conventional yield concept. We will explore the fundamentals of investment analysis in the bond market. This will lead naturally into a classification of different bond swaps and how they can be evaluated.

Our main line of analytic development will concentrate on a new and different characterization of the future value of a bond investment. This approach has two advantages: (1) its construction is more directly descriptive of the investment process, and (2) it provides a convenient and practical method for relating measures of total value to the conventional judgmental variables of the bond market. Moreover, this future value approach, as will be shown, is completely equivalent, mathematically, to both the present value and the realized compound yield methods of investment analysis.

BASIC CHARACTERISTICS OF THE CORPORATE BOND

Issuer

The most useful definition of the *issuer* of a debt instrument would probably be that corporation (or government agency) which has assumed legal responsibility for the provisions of the instrument's indenture, i.e., the coupon, principal, and sinking fund payments. However, in today's financial world, the issuer, under this definition, may not coincide with the original borrower. This original borrower may still have his name attached to the issue, or it might simply be market practice to refer to an issue in terms of its historical origin. Even so, some might argue that the issuer, in the sense of ultimate debtor, should be the corporate entity guaranteeing the debt. This practice is in part followed in some instances, e.g., the GNMA Pass Throughs.

Principal Amount (or Face Value)

This term denominates the level of indebtedness represented by a given holding or in an entire issue. It almost invariably coincides with the redemption value if the bond is held to maturity. Virtually all corporate bonds today are issued in units having a face value of $1,000.

Coupon Rate

This is the annual interest rate, expressed as a percentage of the principal amount, which the bond pays in semiannual installments. Thus, a single bond ($1,000 principal amount) with a 7 percent coupon rate will make semiannual payments of $35 each.

Maturity Date

This is the date on which the corporation must redeem any outstanding holdings of the given issue. It is common market practice to identify a bond issue by stating the issuer, the coupon rate, and the maturity. The maturity date also specifies the timing of the coupon payments, i.e., semiannual cycles coinciding with the maturity date as the last coupon payment.

The time to the maturity date is often referred to as the bond's *remaining life.*

The maturity date is often taken as an absolute measure of the life of the bond issue. However, this view may be misleading in the case of certain bond issues, as a result of the potential impact of calls, refundings, sinking-fund activities, or market repurchases.

Quality[1]

In the narrow sense, the quality of a bond will refer to the rating assigned by one of three standard rating services, Moody's, Standard and Poor, and Fitch. These ratings are based on the services' estimate of the issuer's ability to make the promised payments of interest and principal. In the same narrow sense, the U.S. treasury would be considered to possess the highest level of quality, while the various agency obligations would scale down in order of decreasing directness of the governmental "guarantee."

These explicit and implicit ratings would appear to create distinct quality categories. One might at first presume that such precise categorization means that every issue in a given category has the exact same quality level as any other issue in the same category, e.g., all A-rated bonds are equals. This is not so.

In a larger sense, a bond's quality might be defined, inversely, as the *risk in the prospective total net return* associated with any present or future event bearing on the issuer's ability or willingness to meet its interest and principal obligations. The focus here is on the risk—not of default alone—but on the riskiness of the prospective net return arising out of any distant possibility of default. Clearly, there is a subtle scaling of true quality risk which a classification system can only approximate.

In this larger sense, a weak AAA-rated bond might even have more short-term risk associated with the possibility of being formally downgraded to AA than a solid AA-rated instrument. However, over the longer term the AAA issue subject to categorical downgrading might still possess a much better long-term prospect than the solid AA issue.

This broader definition immediately brings to mind a wide range of factors—beyond the issuer's present financial status and capital structure—which can significantly affect quality risk. For example, the maturity of the bond must itself be one such critical factor. Over a longer period, the possibility grows of unforeseen circumstances which might substantially affect the credit worthiness of any issuer. On the other hand, this growth of uncertainty with maturity affects different issuers

[1] Note: The important subject of credit analysis is discussed in chapter 8.

in different ways. For example, it might be argued that a communications utility would be fairly secure against unpleasant surprises over the years, at least more so than an industrial corporation. Other factors affecting quality risk would include any explicit or implicit guarantees by other corporate entities, sinking-fund provisions; nature, longevity, and transferability of formal or general collateral; coupon rate; and amount of issue and distribution of holdings.

Call and Refunding Features

Any borrower of funds for a stipulated period of time would like the right, if their conditions warranted it, of being able to repay the loan in advance. Corporations are no different from other borrowers in this regard. These early repayment rights take two different forms in the corporate bond market: callability options and refunding options.

A bond issue is said to be callable when the corporation has the option to retire *part or all* of the issue by paying the holders a specified redemption payment. The corporation can exercise its call option for many reasons: availability of cheaper or more desirable financing arrangements; a wish to free or sell the underlying collateral; general recapitalization; or as an investment outlet for excess cash flow. The funds used to repay the called debt issue may come from virtually any source. When an issue is only partially called, the holdings will usually be chosen by lottery or on a pro rata basis.

The call option sounds like a powerful financial weapon granted to the issuing corporation by the lenders or holders of the debt issue. This certainly is true, far more so than is generally recognized. However, the call option invariably carries some important conditions which somewhat moderate the corporation's flexibility.

The most important moderating condition is an initial period of "call protection" during which the bond cannot be called. For example, long-term telephone bonds have five years of call protection. This is commonly expressed by saying that these bonds are *noncallable* (NC) until the fifth year following the issue date. Most other utility and industrial issues lack this period of full call protection and are callable immediately upon issue, although there is usually a restriction that the repayment can only utilize internally generated funds.

When a bond becomes callable, the corporation can exercise its option by paying a specified call price for each bond. At the outset, this call price, quoted as a percentage of principal amount, normally exceeds the redemption price of 100 percent that would be paid at maturity. The difference is referred to as the *call premium* and constitutes a prepayment penalty. For long-term bonds, the beginning call premium often approximates the coupon rate and then scales downward year by year, reaching zero in the last years prior to maturity.

If the call premium were the only safeguard granted to bondholders, then the corporation would almost always win the game of changing interest rate levels. For example, suppose interest rates rose sharply following the issue date. Then the corporation would be very pleased to have borrowed at a bargain rate. The investor, to his dismay, would have a market loss on his bonds. On the other hand, suppose rates dropped sharply, then the corporation could borrow additional funds at the new lower rate and use these funds to call the entire first issue. Through this refunding process, the corporation would immediately and substantially reduce his long-term borrowing rate at the cost of paying the call premium. The investor, however, would lose the higher interest payments. The investor would also be deprived of the full capital gain (i.e., beyond the call premium) that the market forces would have given him in the face of sharply lower rates.

In order to prevent such shabby treatment of the investor, most long-term bonds provide periods of refunding protection. Long-term public utility bonds typically provide five years of protection against refunding. (With telephone bonds, the refunding protection is of course implicit in the five years of call protection.) Long-term industrial bonds ordinarily provide 10 years of refunding protection (although this protection is sometimes subverted by certain types of sinking fund provisions). As with call protection, the marketplace usually describes refunding protection in terms of a bond being *nonrefundable* (NR) for a period of 5 years or 10 years.

The prepayment penalty for a refunding usually corresponds to the call price in effect at the time.

Refunding protection is, of course, a limited form of call protection. However, such protection is not complete. A bond may be nonrefundable, but still subject to call as long as the funds used are not derived from a refunding operation as defined in the indenture. A bond in this situation is often referred to as being "callable except for refunding purposes."

The marketplace focuses much more strongly on the threat of refunding than any other basis for a call. A bond with 10 years of refunding protection will often be quoted as "NR for 10 years," without any reference to the fact that it might be immediately "callable except for refunding purposes." In fact, it is common usage to refer to the expiration date of the refunding protection as the "first call date," and then to refer to the "yield to the first call." This convention would be misleading if a corporation decided to exercise its option for a nonrefunding call, e.g., as an outlet for sizable internal cash accumulations. Recently, a major corporation initiated such a nonrefunding call for a significant percentage of one of its issues.

Here is a brief summary of common call and refunding features:

1. Long-term debt of American Telephone and Telegraph and its subsidiaries is noncallable for five years.

2. Long-term public debt of power utilities is usually immediately callable except for refunding purposes and then becomes refundable after five years. (In the rough markets that developed during 1974, many utilities had to provide ten years of call protection.)
3. Long-term public industrial bonds are usually immediately callable except for refunding purposes and then become refundable after 10 years.
4. Intermediate-term corporate debt (five to eight years) is either completely noncallable or noncallable until the year prior to maturity.
5. Canadian issues often carry 15 years of call protection.
6. U.S. Treasury securities are either completely noncallable or have at least 15 years of full call protection.
7. U.S. agency issues, on the other hand, are either completely noncallable or provide 10 years of full call protection.
8. Municipal issues generally offer full call protection for at least 10 years. Certain issues, e.g., all New York City obligations, are totally noncallable.

Sinking-Fund Provisions

A corporate bond's sinking provision in effect requires the issuer to render a specified schedule of repayments to the trustee in behalf of the bondholders. These repayments may take the form of cash, retired bonds, or additional collateral. The original idea was that such a repayment schedule will match the decreasing value of the collateralized assets as well as provide for a more orderly redemption process.

The Cash Sinking Fund. A cash sinking fund provision will generally state that starting in a given year, the corporation must either make annual deposits of a fixed amount of cash or retire bonds of the same issue having an equivalent *principal value*. This level of annual payments may be maintained for a number of years. At some point, this first phase of the sinking fund may be followed by a second phase in which a new annual payment level is established, and so forth. A strong sinking fund might be designed to retire 90 percent of the original issue prior to maturity.

A typical cash sinking fund will grant important rights to the corporation in connection with its sinking-fund obligations. The first is the right to call bonds—for sinking-fund purposes—at a special call price. For bonds issued at 100, this special price is usually 100. However, when bonds are originally issued at some price other than 100, the special call price usually starts out at this issue level and then scales year by year towards 100 at maturity. Because of this special call price, a corporation will almost always deposit bonds instead of cash to satisfy its sinking-fund requirement. After all, at the time the requirement must be satisfied, the bonds will be selling either at a price above or below the sinking-fund call price. If the market price is above the call price, the corporation will simply call the needed bonds. If the market price is below the call price, the corporation will just buy the bonds in the marketplace. In either case, it will deposit retired bonds, not cash.

This creates an interesting situation from the investor's viewpoint. If rates move up, and the price of a new bond issue drops, then the corporation's requirement to buy bonds for the sinking fund will provide needed price support. In such a case, the investor would be delighted with his foresight in selecting a bond with a strong sinking fund. On the other hand, if rates move down, and the market price of the bonds rises, then the investor stands to lose a portion of his holdings at the sinking-fund call price. In such calls, bonds are usually selected either by lottery or on a pro rata basis. This might entail a sizable loss in the market value of the investor's holdings. In such a case, the investor would perhaps view the sinking-fund provision with its special call price option as something less than an unadulterated blessing.

The Option to Double. The potential investor's loss in this situation is further aggravated by the *doubling option.* This option is actually present in most sinking-fund provisions. It allows the corporation, at the time a sinking-fund payment is due, to call up to twice the normal sinking-fund requirement *at the special call price!* This is an important and powerful option. Since the corporation will only exercise this option when the market price exceeds the special call price, one can see that this can have a serious impact on investor returns.

It can also be seen how a sinking fund with an option to double can infringe upon the bondholder's call protection. Many high coupon industrial bonds have strong doubling sinking funds beginning in the fifth year after issue. The investor in such bonds is protected from refunding for 10 years and may be somewhat protected from a nonrefunding call by a large call premium. However, at the fifth year, if rates remain low, the corporation *must* call the necessary bonds to satisfy his sinking-fund provision. Since this special call for sinking-fund purposes is usually at 100, i.e., entailing no call premium, the corporation with a little extra credit (at the lower rate) would have to give serious consideration to exercising its doubling option. While not a refunding in the strict sense of the indenture, this doubling would be clearly motivated by the availability of lower rates. Consequently, for the bondholder, this process would in effect amount to progressive refunding—without the compensation of a significant call premium. To give an idea of the magnitude of this effect, there is one major industrial bond issue which has a 6 percent annual sinking fund starting in the fifth year. With exercise of the doubling option, this would amount to an annual call on 12 percent of the entire issue at the special sinking fund call price of 100. There would be an opportunity for six such calls between the fifth and the tenth year when the issue becomes refundable. Thus, this sinking fund could, in effect, call 72 percent of the entire issue *without a call premium* prior to the date when the issue becomes formally refundable at a stated call premium!

Other Sinking-Fund Considerations. There are many other different forms of sinking-fund options, each having a definite and sometimes major effect on a bond's investment value. Because of the more complex cash flows associated with certain of these options, an analytic evaluation can prove particularly useful and sometimes even invaluable. Unfortunately, we are unable to pursue this broad and intriguing subject further and still stay within the limits of this article.

CONVENTIONAL MEASURES OF ABSOLUTE AND RELATIVE VALUE

Pricing of Corporate Bonds

At the time when an agreement is reached to trade a given block of bonds, it is highly likely that neither side will know the exact trading price. This remarkable statement is not an indictment. Rather, it is a tribute to the bond market's standardized price and yield measures which allow traders to focus more on the value of a trade instead of a potentially misleading market price.

To understand this somewhat paradoxical statement, let us take a 30-year, 7 percent bond as a concrete example. Assume that this bond has just been issued at a dollar price of 100 percent and that the first coupon will be made in exactly six months. Under these circumstances, the dollar price of 100 percent means that these bonds could be purchased at a cost equal to 100 percent of the bond's face amount, i.e., each $1,000 bond would cost $1,000. Now suppose that the level of interest rates remains absolutely stable for a period of three months. What price would we expect to pay for these same bonds? One might reason that since interest rates had not changed, there would be no market forces leading to a price change, and therefore we can expect to still pay $1,000 for each bond.

This answer would be wrong! The correct answer is that this bond would have a market price of about 101.75 percent, i.e., $1,017.50 per bond. The additional $17.50 arises because the purchaser at this point in time is not only buying a long-term 7 percent instrument in a 7 percent market, he is also buying the right to receive the next $35 coupon payment due in three months' time. By the same token, the seller of the bond is foregoing all rights to any part of this coupon payment. However, the seller has invested for three months in a 7 percent interest-bearing instrument, and he would naturally expect to receive some appropriate interest payment. This incremental payment of $17.50 of accrued interest is a mechanism for settling all these claims.

Under our assumption of absolutely stable interest rates, the actual market price would grow over time as shown in Figure 1. The slight curvature in this curve represents the effect of implicit compounding at that daily rate which provides a 3.5 percent growth every six months. After three months, the exact market price would be $1,017.35. Because of the compounding effect, this value is slightly under the figure of $1,017.0 used above. The market price continues to grow until six months have elapsed. At this point, the market would be exactly equal to $1,035. However, the bond's owner on the beginning of this day is entitled to receive a $35 coupon payment. If the owner were to sell his bond at this six-month point, this coupon payment would fully reim-

FIGURE 1

Market Value over Time at the Same Market Level (30-year, 7 percent bond priced at par to yield 7 percent)

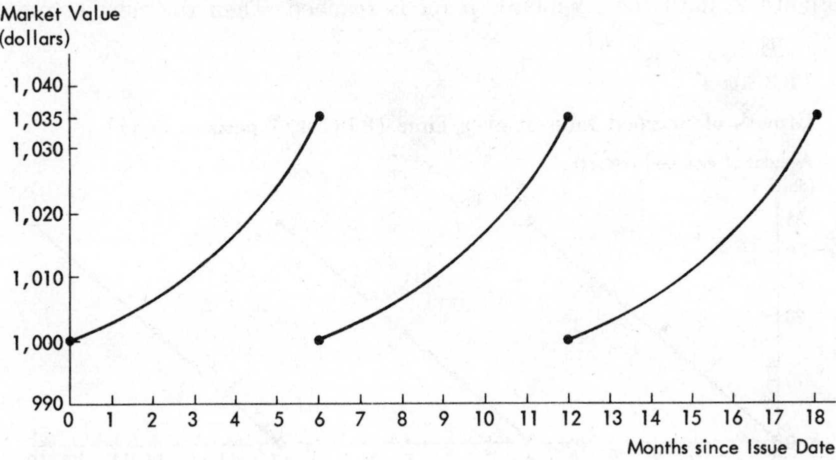

burse him for all interest due. Consequently, the seller would not need to seek additional interest-due compensation from the bond's buyer, i.e., the sale would take place at a market price of $1,000. On the following day, the bondholder would have earned one day's interest, and this would again have to be reflected by an increment in the bond's market price. Over the subsequent six months, we would again see the interest amount being impounded in the bond's market price. This interest cycle is repeated every six months as shown in Figure 1.

This interest cycle effect means that the market price of a par bond changes every day even when there is absolutely no change in interest rate levels. Most market participants would be interested in this bond in terms of its *promised* interest rates and the relationship of this bond to other bonds with similar promised interest rates. They would view this interest cycle effect as essentially irrelevant to these judgments.

They would feel that the daily variation in market price was undesirable, confusing the basic value of the bond as a 7 percent instrument in a 7 percent market.

For these reasons, the bond market has developed the convention of trading on a price figure which excludes this interest build-up cycle. This is done in the following manner. First, the coupon payment is divided by the number of days in the six-month cycle. This gives a value for the amount of interest accrued each day. Whenever the bond is sold, this accrual would have developed over the period from the last coupon payment to the date of sale, i.e., the delivery date. By multiplying the number of days since the last coupon payment by interest accrued per day, we obtain a figure called the accrued interest for that specific trading date. This accrued interest figure is taken as a measure of the holder's fractional interest in the next coupon payment.

The magnitude of the accrued interest grows day by day as shown in Figure 2, until the six-month point is reached. Then the next coupon

FIGURE 2

Growth of Accrued Interest over Time (30-year, 7 percent bond)

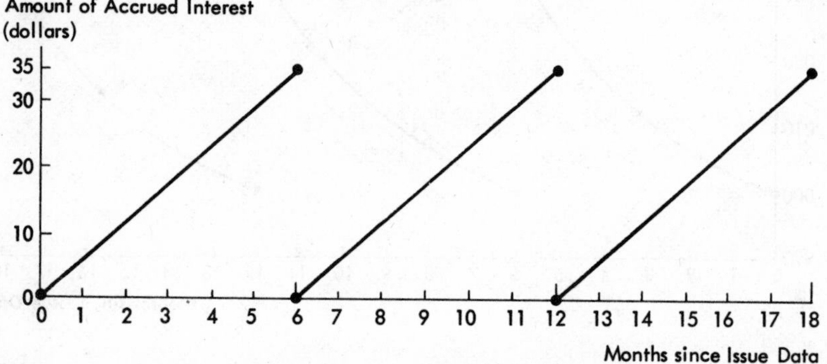

payment is made. Consequently, on that payment day, there are zero days since the last coupon payment, and the accrued interest amount drops to zero. The accrued interest then starts to grow once more day by day until the subsequent coupon payment.

Comparing Figure 2 with Figure 1, we see (not unexpectedly) that the pattern of accrued interest over time closely matches the interest cycle in the bond's market price. This is the basis for the market trading price convention. When the accrued interest for a given day is subtracted from the market price for that day, we obtain a number called the bond's *principal value*. This term indicates that it represents the cost of buying the bond's intrinsic principal as opposed to its incidental interest accrual. As seen from Figure 3, the principal value figure is

FIGURE 3

Principal Value over Time at the Same Market Level (30-year, 7 percent bond priced at par to yield 7 percent)

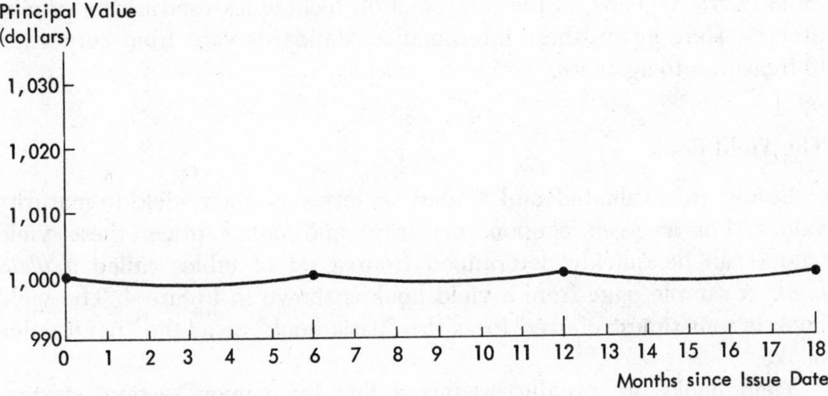

removed from most of the effects of the interest cycle. The principal value is an essentially constant price in a constant market. This is precisely what the marketplace wants. The market can focus on this principal value figure even though it knows that the accrued interest must be added to determine the final trade price. The accrued interest is just a straightforward mechanical computation. Consequently, all the forces of market fluctuation can be viewed as expressed in the principal value figure.

The market has one further convention: the principal value is stated as a percentage of the bond's face value. This percentage figure is referred to as the "dollar price" (a curiously inappropriate choice of terms). Thus, for a 7 percent bond with the usual face value of $1,000 at a time three months past its last coupon payment, a dollar price of 100 would imply a principal value of $1,000 and a market cost of $1,000 plus accrued interest of $17.50, i.e., a market cost of $1,017.50. Similarly, a dollar price of 80 would correspond to a principal value of $800.00 and a market cost of $817.50.

Looking closely at Figure 3, we see that there still remains some slight coupon cycle effect. This arises because the bond's market price has a slight curvature associated with the increasing growth rate achieved through compounding. However, to keep trade computations simple, the accrued interest grows along the straight line curve characteristic of simple interest. This slight inconsistency explains the market paradox of why 7 percent bonds in a 7 percent market do not always have a dollar price of exactly 100.

In the above, we have avoided any discussion of many detailed conventions and standards used in trade computations for different fixed interest securities. For example, there is one method for counting the elapsed time from the last coupon date for corporates, and quite another method for treasury bonds. As another example, Figures 1 and 3 show the market price and principal value as a smooth curve over time. The exact curve depends on the interpolation techniques used in the pricing process. Here again, these interpolation standards vary from corporates to treasuries to agencies.[2]

The Yield Book

Bonds are evaluated and traded in terms of their yield-to-maturity values. For a given coupon, maturity, and dollar price, these yield values can be quickly determined from a set of tables called a *yield book*. A sample page from a yield book is shown in Figure 4. The yield book is sometimes referred to as the "basis book" or as the "bond value book."

Yield books are usually organized first by coupon section, starting with the lowest and proceeding in steps of one eighth of 1 percent to the highest coupons covered. Within each coupon section, each column corresponds to a different remaining life, usually incrementing from one-month steps under five years to six-month steps for longer lifes. (As we shall see, the reason for this higher resolution at the shorter life is that the price/yield relationships are more critically dependent here on the passage of time.) The rows designate different yield values, usually at increments of 0.10 percent within the practically important range of values. The body of the yield table contains dollar prices. For each specific yield value, i.e., a given row, and each specific remaining life, i.e., a given column, there is a corresponding dollar price shown where the row and column intersect.

As an example of how a yield book is used in practice, suppose we have a bond with a 7 percent coupon and a remaining life of 30 years. First we assume that the bond has a yield of 7.5 percent. We then want to find the bond's dollar price. We would first turn to the 7 percent coupon section of the yield book. Then we would find that page in that section containing a column heading of 30 years. Figure 4 represents one such page. We would then find the row (shown in the left-most column) associated with our desired yield value of 7.5 percent.

At the intersection of the 30-year column and the 7.5 percent row, we find our answer—a dollar price of 94.07. This says that a 30-year, 7 percent bond selling to yield 7.50 percent to maturity would have a dollar price of 94.07.

By the same token, we could also turn the above statement around and say that a 30-year, 7 percent bond selling at a dollar price of 94.07

---

[2] For a comprehensive, detailed discussion of the various standard price computation methods, see Bruce Spence, Jacob Y. Graudenz, and John J. Lynch, Jr., *Standard Securities Calculation Methods* (Security Industry Association, 1973).

FIGURE 4

Sample Page from a Yield Book

7%				**YEARS** and MONTHS				
Yield	**26**-6	**27**-0	**27**-6	**28**-0	**28**-6	**29**-0	**29**-6	**30**-0
4.00	148.74	149.26	149.76	150.26	150.74	151.22	151.68	152.14
4.20	144.51	144.96	145.41	145.85	146.28	146.69	147.11	147.51
4.40	140.44	140.84	141.24	141.62	142.00	142.37	142.73	143.08
4.60	136.54	136.89	137.24	137.57	137.90	138.22	138.53	138.84
4.80	132.79	133.10	133.40	133.69	133.97	134.25	134.52	134.79
5.00	129.19	129.46	129.71	129.96	130.21	130.45	130.68	130.91
5.20	125.73	125.96	126.18	126.39	126.60	126.80	127.00	127.19
5.40	122.41	122.60	122.78	122.96	123.14	123.31	123.48	123.64
5.60	119.21	119.37	119.53	119.67	119.82	119.96	120.10	120.23
5.80	116.14	116.27	116.40	116.52	116.63	116.75	116.86	116.97
6.00	113.19	113.29	113.39	113.48	113.58	113.67	113.75	113.84
6.10	111.75	111.84	111.93	112.01	112.09	112.17	112.25	112.32
6.20	110.34	110.42	110.50	110.57	110.64	110.71	110.77	110.84
6.30	108.96	109.03	109.09	109.15	109.21	109.27	109.33	109.38
6.40	107.61	107.66	107.72	107.77	107.82	107.87	107.91	107.96
6.50	106.28	106.32	106.37	106.41	106.45	106.49	106.53	106.56
6.60	104.98	105.01	105.04	105.08	105.11	105.14	105.17	105.20
6.70	103.70	103.72	103.75	103.77	103.79	103.82	103.84	103.86
6.80	102.44	102.46	102.47	102.49	102.50	102.52	102.53	102.55
6.90	101.21	101.22	101.22	101.23	101.24	101.25	101.25	101.26
7.00	100.00	100.00	100.00	100.00	100.00	100.00	100.00	100.00
7.10	98.81	98.81	98.80	98.79	98.78	98.78	98.77	98.77
7.20	97.65	97.63	97.62	97.61	97.59	97.58	97.57	97.55
7.30	96.51	96.48	96.46	96.44	96.42	96.40	96.39	96.37
7.40	95.38	95.35	95.33	95.30	95.28	95.25	95.23	95.21
7.50	94.28	94.25	94.21	94.18	94.15	94.12	94.09	94.07
7.60	93.20	93.16	93.12	93.08	93.05	93.01	92.98	92.95
7.70	92.14	92.09	92.05	92.01	91.96	91.93	91.89	91.85
7.80	91.09	91.04	90.99	90.95	90.90	90.86	90.82	90.78
7.90	90.07	90.01	89.96	89.91	89.86	89.81	89.77	89.72
8.00	89.06	89.00	88.95	88.89	88.84	88.79	88.74	88.69
8.10	88.08	88.01	87.95	87.89	87.83	87.78	87.72	87.67
8.20	87.11	87.04	86.97	86.91	86.85	86.79	86.73	86.68
8.30	86.15	86.08	86.01	85.94	85.88	85.82	85.76	85.70
8.40	85.22	85.14	85.07	85.00	84.93	84.87	84.80	84.75
8.50	84.30	84.22	84.14	84.07	84.00	83.93	83.87	83.81
8.60	83.39	83.31	83.23	83.16	83.08	83.01	82.95	82.88
8.70	82.51	82.42	82.34	82.26	82.19	82.11	82.04	81.98
8.80	81.63	81.55	81.46	81.38	81.30	81.23	81.16	81.09
8.90	80.78	80.69	80.60	80.52	80.44	80.36	80.29	80.22
9.00	79.93	79.84	79.75	79.67	79.59	79.51	79.43	79.36
9.10	79.11	79.01	78.92	78.83	78.75	78.67	78.59	78.52
9.20	78.29	78.20	78.10	78.01	77.93	77.85	77.77	77.70
9.30	77.49	77.39	77.30	77.21	77.12	77.04	76.96	76.89
9.40	76.71	76.61	76.51	76.42	76.33	76.25	76.17	76.09
9.50	75.93	75.83	75.73	75.64	75.55	75.47	75.39	75.31
9.60	75.17	75.07	74.97	74.88	74.79	74.70	74.62	74.54
9.70	74.43	74.32	74.22	74.13	74.04	73.95	73.87	73.79
9.80	73.69	73.59	73.49	73.39	73.30	73.21	73.13	73.05
9.90	72.97	72.86	72.76	72.66	72.57	72.48	72.40	72.32
10.00	72.26	72.15	72.05	71.95	71.86	71.77	71.69	71.61
10.20	70.87	70.77	70.66	70.56	70.47	70.38	70.29	70.21
10.40	69.53	69.42	69.32	69.22	69.13	69.04	68.95	68.87
10.60	68.24	68.13	68.02	67.92	67.83	67.74	67.65	67.57
10.80	66.98	66.87	66.77	66.67	66.57	66.48	66.40	66.31
11.00	65.77	65.65	65.55	65.45	65.36	65.27	65.18	65.10
11.20	64.59	64.48	64.37	64.27	64.18	64.09	64.01	63.93
11.40	63.45	63.34	63.23	63.13	63.04	62.95	62.87	62.79
11.60	62.34	62.23	62.13	62.03	61.94	61.85	61.77	61.69
11.80	61.27	61.16	61.06	60.96	60.87	60.79	60.70	60.63
12.00	60.23	60.13	60.02	59.93	59.84	59.75	59.67	59.60

Source: Reproduced from Expanded Bond Value Tables, desk edition, p. 738, copyright 1970, Financial Publishing Company, Boston, Mass.

provides a yield to maturity of 7.50 percent. The yield book can also be used in this reverse fashion to find the yield value corresponding to a given dollar price. For example, if we had only known that our 30-year, 7 percent bond was selling at a dollar price of 94.07, then we would have searched down the 30-year column until we found the dollar price of 94.07. By tracing across this row to the left, we would find that this corresponds to the yield value of 7.50 percent. As another example of finding the yield value associated from a given price, suppose that our 30-year, 7 percent bond now has a dollar price of 100. Searching down the 30-year column, we find the figure 100 in a certain row. Tracing across that row to the left, we see that this dollar price of 100 corresponds to a yield of exactly 7.00 percent.

Even the thickest yield books only contain a limited representation of different values for lifetimes, coupons, yields, and dollar prices. Fortunately, bonds do trade more often than at six-month intervals and they do move in yield increments of less than 0.10 percent. As with any tabular presentation, the gaps in the yield book are filled by a process of interpolation. Using this interpolation process, one can find the dollar price corresponding to any yield value for any given bond. The process can also be reversed to find the yield value corresponding to any bond's dollar price.[3]

A skilled practitioner with the yield book can perform the table look-up and interpolation process in an amazingly brief span of time. In fact, most professional traders can immediately provide a good estimate of a bond's yield—without any reference at all to a yield book.

In recent years, several compact computer calculators have been developed which have the capability of computing yields from prices or pries from yields. These calculators perform all interpolations and produce exact results. These are rapidly becoming invaluable tools on many trading desks.

The Many Facets of Yield to Maturity

It is relatively easy to learn how to calculate a yield-to-maturity value for a given bond. However, it is quite another matter to understand what this yield value really means.

Most people think of the yield to maturity as an average percentage rate at which coupon income plus principal gain accumulates over the bond's life. This corresponds closely with the main connotation of the word *yield* as a rate of return. It is certainly this interpretation which underlies most yield-related investment decisions.

However, there are a surprising number of different ways of interpret-

---

[3] For a more theoretical explanation of interpolation methodology, the reader is referred to Sidney Homer and Martin L. Leibowitz, *Inside the Yield Book* (New York Institute of Finance and Prentice-Hall, Inc., 1972); or Spence, Graudenz, and Lynch, *Standard Securities Calculation Methods.*

ing the conventional yield to maturity. These interpretations may seem, at first glance, very different from one another. Yet every one of them is consistent with the basic mathematics for computing yield to maturity. Consequently, all of these interpretations are mathematically equivalent with one another.

First of all, one can interpret the yield to maturity as a special discount rate. The cash flow of a bond consists of its coupon payments together with its redemption payment at maturity. The present value of this cash flow depends on the assumed discount rate. As the discount rate increases, the bond's fixed cash flow is discounted more severely, and so its present value *decreases*. If the discount rate is increased, step by step, from a sufficiently low starting level, then the present value will gradually decrease until it just equals the bond's market price. The yield to maturity is that specific discount rate which produces this equality of present value and market price.

Thus, when future cash flows are discounted at the yield rate, then the bond's cost corresponds precisely to its investment worth as measured by its present value.

This interpretation coincides with the definition of the fundamental analytic concept of an internal rate of return (IRR). It is quite proper to say that a yield to maturity is just the internal rate of return over the bond's remaining life. However, it should be recognized that yield to maturity is an internal rate of return expressed in terms of certain special bond market conventions. For example, the yield figure is based upon semiannual compounding and is actually quoted as twice the semiannual rate.

The equality of the bond's market cost with its present value at the yield rate provides the key to a related interpretation. The bond's present value can be expressed as the sum of the present value of its stream of coupon payments and the present value of its redemption payment (see section 8.1). But the present value of the redemption payment less the bond's market cost is just the bond's principal appreciation in terms of present value. Actually, this appreciation is invariably negative, i.e., the investor always incurs a loss of principal value in terms of present value. However, this principal loss in present value is exactly compensated by the present value of the coupon stream. This compensation follows directly from the starting equality of the present value of all future payments with the bond's cost. This "break-even situation" when discounting at the yield rate means that the investor cannot increase his present worth by purchasing the bond: he gets precisely what he pays for and no more. Thus, when he gives up the cost value of the bond, he accepts a future principal repayment having a smaller present value. In return for this principal loss, he receives compensation through the coupon stream. Because of the break-even situation, the principal loss must exactly match the worth of the coupon stream in present value terms.

For example, consider a 30-year, 7 percent bond with a market cost of \$940.65. The yield to maturity is 7.50 percent. Using this value of 7.50 percent as a discount rate, the \$1,000 redemption payment due 30 years from now would have a present value today of \$109.83. Since the principal value of the bond today is \$940.65, the investor would experience a net principal loss of:

$$\$109.83 - \$940.65 = -\$830.82$$

in terms of present value. Again using the 7.50 percent yield value as a discount rate, a stream of 60 semiannual payments of \$35 has a total present value of:

$$23.74 \times \$35.00 = \$830.82.$$

So we see that the buyer of this bond accepts a principal loss worth \$830.82 today and in return receives a future coupon stream having this same present value of \$830.82.

The present value break-even situation provides yet another interesting and somewhat surprising interpretation. Consider a par bond with a coupon rate equal to the yield rate of the given bond and having the same maturity date. This par bond will, by definition, have the same yield to maturity as the given bond. The break-even situation for the par bond will consist of equality between the par cost of \$1,000 and the sum of the present value of the yield-level coupon stream and the present value of the future redemption payment. If we take the difference between the equalities for these two bonds, then the present value of the redemption payment drops out. This says that the difference between par and the given bond's market cost must be equal to the difference between the present values of the two coupon streams. This difference, in turn, is just equal to the present value of the incremental coupon stream of the yield-level par bond over the given bond. Assuming that the investor could theoretically purchase such a yield-level par bond, then by foregoing this par bond in favor of, say, a lower coupon discount bond, he is, in a sense, foregoing this incremental coupon stream. In return, the investor of course pays a reduced price for his discount bond. In fact, he saves the discount and this savings just equals the present value lost through his giving up the incremental coupon stream.

Thus, a bond's discount (or premium) can be viewed as exact compensation in present value terms for the greater (or lesser) coupon flow that would be theoretically available from a par bond having the same yield.

As a numerical illustration, take our earlier example of a 30-year, 7 percent bond priced at 94.065 for a yield to maturity of 7.50 percent. As we saw earlier, the market cost of \$940.65 per bond can be equated to the present value of the semiannual \$35.00 coupons, \$830.82, plus the \$109.83 present value of the final \$1,000.00 redemption payment (\$940.65 = \$830.82 + \$109.83). The corresponding yield-level bond would be a 30-year, 7.50 percent bond selling at 100 for a yield to maturity of 7.50 percent. This bond would provide 60 semiannual coupon payments of $37.50 each. This is $2.50 more per coupon payment than we would get from the 7 percent bond. These 60 semiannual increments of $2.50 each have a combined present value of $59.35. The investor who chooses the 7.00 percent bond over the theoretically available 7.50 percent bond gives up this incremental present value of $59.35. In return, he only pays $940.65 for the 7 percent bond. This is exactly $59.35 ($1000.00 – $940.65 = $59.35) less than he would have paid for the 7.50 percent par bond. This discount of $59.35 precisely matches the $59.35 present value of the incremental coupon flow foregone.

In the interpretations of yield to maturity discussed above, only the original cost price of the bonds has been mentioned. There has been no reference to any interim price values for the bond between the purchase date and maturity. The mathematical calculation of yield to maturity is indeed based upon a bond purchased today at a given price and then held to its maturity date. Consequently, for the computation of yield to maturity, it is not necessary to make any assumptions regarding interim prices.

However, there is one important interpretation of yield which leads to a normative statement about interim prices. The key idea here is that a bond provides a constant uniform yield over every six-month period. To the extent that the coupon payment falls short, the yield deficit is made up by an assumed amortization of the bond's principal value. One can actually define the yield to maturity as that uniform rate which just amortizes the bond to its $1,000 maturity value over its remaining life.

To see how this works, again take the example of our 30-year, 7.00 percent bond priced at 94.065 for a yield to maturity of 7.50 percent. Over the first six-month period, this interpretation would require a return of:

$$7.50\% \div 2 = 3.75\%$$

or

$$0.0375 \times \$940.65 = \$35.27.$$

The first coupon payment would only provide $35.00, so that the additional

$$\$35.27 - \$35.00 = \$.27$$

would have to be achieved through principal amortization. Adding this $.27 to the original $940.65 cost value, the bond's amortized value after six months becomes $940.92. Over the next six months, the return must now be

$$0.0375 \times \$940.92 = \$35.28.$$

The second coupon payment will handle $35.00 of the requirement, leaving $.28 to be obtained through amortization. Consequently, at the end of one year, the bond will have an amortized value of $941.20, or an amortized dollar price of $94.12. If we continued in this fashion for each of the next 58 semiannual periods, we would find that the bond's amortized value just reached $1,000, or a dollar price of 100, at the end of the last period.

This method of price amortization is often referred to as *scientific amortization.*

As mentioned earlier, one can actually define yield to maturity as that constant yield rate which produces a scientific amortization to 100 at maturity. Consequently, the scientifically amortized price value at any given interim point in time must result in the same yield to maturity. For example, we saw that a 30-year, 7 percent bond costing 94.065 would have a scientifically amortized value after the first six months of 94.092, corresponding to the yield rate of 7.50 percent. Now suppose one could purchase a 29.5-year, 7 percent bond for 94.092. Since this bond lies along the same scientific amortization path, we would expect both bonds to have same yield to maturity, i.e., 7.50 percent. Similarly, after one year, our 30-year, 7 percent bond would have scientifically amortized to a value of 94.12, which corresponds to a 7.50 percent yield to maturity for a 29-year, 7 percent bond.

Thus, scientific amortization can be viewed in terms of the sequence of dollar prices that would result if the bond maintained a constant yield to maturity over time. In other words, scientific amortization corresponds to the sequence of prices lying in the same row of the yield book (Figure 4).

This observation leads to another closely related interpretation of yield to maturity. The yield to maturity can be defined as the total return rate over the next six-month period when the bond is then assumed to be priced at the same yield to maturity. While this definition seems somewhat circular, it is worth stressing the assumptions required to turn the yield-to-maturity figure into a rate of return value, even over the first six months.

As a side point, it might be noted that under conditions of generally stable interest rates, the price of a discount bond will move upwards towards par with the passage of time. Of course, the particular orbit of prices which it will follow over time cannot be known precisely, even under the dullest and most stable of real-life markets. However, it is very convenient, both for purposes of accounting as well as for investment analysis, to have some normative method of describing price amortization over time. For such purposes, a bond is often treated as maintaining an absolutely constant book yield to maturity over its entire life. Scientific amortization then becomes the most natural and consistent price amortization technique for use wtih this constant yield convention. The only other amortization scheme in common usage, the straight line method, has the utmost in simplicity as being its only rationale. Whatever amortization scheme may be used, the investor is well advised to keep constantly in mind that it is a highly artificial projection of prices, that amortized price figures need not reflect any market or opportunity value, and that amortization schemes have been designed for convenience and do not represent even the most elementary factors (e.g., yield curves) which are sure to affect future price levels in reality.

The yield to maturity can also be interpreted as a growth rate of total compounded return, but only under some rather restrictive assumptions. First of all, the bond must be held to maturity. Second, all coupon payments must be reinvested and compounded at the yield rate itself. Third, the yield must be accepted as an *equivalent* growth rate over the bond's entire life, with no implication about rates of return over interim periods. If the growth at the yield rate is assumed to be *uniform* over interim periods, then this implies that scientific price amortization is assumed to be occurring in the marketplace. As we shall discuss in some detail later, these rather restrictive conditions cause problems.

All the above interpretations are perfectly valid, and each would equally well serve as the definition of yield to maturity. However, there is little doubt that most practitioners subjectively interpret yield to maturity as a rate of growth from the combined dollar value of interest and principal. This growth rate of total net return is the measure that indeed should be most important to bond investment decisions. Consequently it is reasonable to suspect that most practitioners conveniently presume that the yield-to-maturity value is equivalent to this fully compounded growth rate measure. This presumption can be misleading when yields to maturity, interpreted as growth rates, are used to compare two different bonds with their different maturity dates in the long run, and their different price actions in the short run.

To summarize, all of these interpretations of yield to maturity show a number of important features. They are all measures of *total* cash flow in the sense that they incorporate both income and principal appreciation to maturity. Moreover, the yield to maturity does not distinguish between coupon income and principal repayments as elements of this cash flow, except, of course, in terms of their timing.

Time value means that a dollar received in the future will be measurably less valuable than a dollar available today for use or investment. In all the interpretations of yield to maturity, the entire cash flow is assumed to be time-valued (or reinvestable) at a constant, uniform discount rate throughout the bond's life, and this time-valuing rate is just the yield to maturity itself. This time-value rate may be interpreted as either a discount rate, an opportunity rate, a consumption value rate, or a reinvestment rate. In any case, this time valuing is crucial, and the time-valuing link between different future points is through *full compounding* at the yield rate. Thus, compounded time-valuation is an intrinsic and inescapable ingredient of the yield-to-maturity concept.

The Yield to Call

One can extend the principles used to compute yields to maturity to evaluate a bond where the coupon payments are terminated by an assumed call. When the date of the call and the call premium are specified, then this leads to a *yield-to-call* figure. If there is no definite specification, the yield to call generally represents a computation to the first date of possible refunding.

There are a number of problems in the conventional use of the yield to call (see *Inside the Yield Book* for a discussion of some of these problems). However, a discussion of this important subject would constitute too great a digression for the scope of this chapter.

INVESTMENT ANALYSIS OF BONDS

The Future Value of a Bond Investment

For portfolios where coupon income is always reinvested and compounded, the most important investment measure is the total dollars accumulated over time. Any given investment decision for such portfolios should be evaluated in terms of how it contributes to this total growth of future dollars. Even for portfolios which do not reinvest their coupon income or their capital gains, this approach can prove most fruitful, especially in terms of the somewhat more general concept of *future value* (FV). The generalization from *dollars* to *value* consists in interpreting the time-valuing discount rate, not as a literal process of reinvestment, but as providing weighting factors for equalizing the value of different timings and types of cash flow components. This matter will be discussed in more detail at a later point.

For several reasons, a study of the future value provides a good starting point for any discussion of investment analysis. First of all, one can select a time horizon (or workout time) which matches the expectations and purposes of the portfolio manager. At the outset, this avoids the natural tendency to focus on some overt time characteristic of the instrument, e.g., its maturity, to the exclusion of time frames more appropriate to the investment decision itself. Another benefit of the future value approach is that it requires very clear-cut and explicit assumptions regarding the reinvestment (or time-valuing) rate and price movements over time. These two factors constitute the two major sources of uncertainty in any bond investment. Consequently, while it may be difficult (and sometimes even unpleasant) for the portfolio manager to develop explicit estimate(s) for these two factors, it is also crucial to any reasoned, analytic approach. Any investment decision automatically implies a set of implicit estimates. It would seem that the portfolio manager should always want to assure himself—in advance—that these implicit estimates coincide with his range of market expectations. This can be facilitated by expressing the future value in terms of those market variables which are natural and comfortable for the portfolio manager. For example, by expressing future price levels in terms of moves in various yields-to-maturity and/or yield spreads, the manager can continue to render his judgment in the usual way. At the same time, he can explore the impact of these judgments in terms of a more comprehensive and exact measure of investment value—future value. Another advantage is that, while future value analyses are mathematically equivalent to the corresponding present value and rate of return analyses, they provide a simpler and more readily comprehended framework. This may be because it is more directly descriptive of the investment process. One can quite literally see future value accumulating in most institutional reports. On the other hand, rates of return and especially present values are not as directly visible in such reports. In particular, while many people have an intellectual grasp of the present value concept, it is quite another matter to be intuitively conversant with all its implications and many buried assumptions. For example, an investment providing an immediate improvement in present value does not represent an immediate windfall gain—*until* the assumed future workout time and *unless* the future rate and price assumptions are realized.

For a straight bond investment, i.e., when sinking-fund and refunding considerations can be neglected, the three ingredients of future value are coupon income, reinvestment (or time-value) return from the earlier receipt of this coupon income, and future price level. For the sake of convenience, we will now begin to use a more compact notation. We denote (1) the coupon income flow by COUP-FLOW, (2) the time value (or reinvested value) of this coupon flow as of the workout time by TV (COUP-FLOW), and (3) the bond's assumed market value at the workout time by PR (WORK-OUT) (short for principal). Then the future value at the given workout time, denoted by FV can be written as follows:

$$\text{FV} = \text{TV (COUP-FLOW)} + \text{PR (WORK-OUT)}$$

The General Role of Time Valuation

At this point, it is important to review the many implications of the time-value concept in the future value formula.

From the future value formula as written above, we see that the coupon flow enters the future value equation only through its cumulative time value, TV (COUP-FLOW), while the future market value, PR (WORK-OUT), enters the equation directly. One could therefore interpret future value as being denominated in terms of future principal dollars.

There are, of course, several intrinsic differences between these future dollars of market value and the dollars received as part of the coupon flow. First of all, there is the obvious difference of time of receipt. For the compounding portfolio manager, who reinvests all his coupon receipts and who does not distinguish between the sources of his return, the time-value function would translate each of these coupon payments into their contribution to the future value at the workout time. This translation would be based on the assumption that each coupon payment is invested at some rate of interest for some period of time, and that the returns from this investment are then again reinvested at some (possibly different) rate, and so on. The original coupon payment together with its total accumulation of compound interest through reinvestment will build up to a certain figure by the workout time. This amount represents the coupon payment's future value. When this process is carried out over all the payments in the coupon flow, then the sum of the future value contributions provides the time-value translation of the coupon flow.

In theory, this computation could involve a complex sequence of different reinvestment rates over varying time periods comprising the workout period. However, in practice, a uniform semiannual compounding rate is usually assumed. When the workout period starts and ends on coupon payment dates, then the time value of the coupon flow can be expressed in terms of the standard compound interest function, S_w (this is the same as the function $[F/A, i, n]$ in chapter 36 with R substituted for i and w for n), the future value of \$1 per period (FVPP),

$$\text{TV (COUP-FLOW)} = (5C) \times S_w$$

Using the algebraic expression, this becomes

$$\text{TV (COUP-FLOW)} = (5C) \times \left[\frac{(1+R)^w - 1}{R}\right]$$

where:

C = Coupon rate expressed as an annual percentage.
$5C$ = Dollar value of each coupon payment per \$1,000 bond.
w = Number of semiannual periods in the workout period.
R = Uniform reinvestment rate, expressed as a fraction per semiannual period.

The FVPP can be found in all expanded compound interest tables.

The adoption of a uniform rate, *R,* is a pretty crude assumption in most cases, and any given value *R* will at best be a somewhat tenuous estimate. Consequently, it is common practice to study the future value under a range of alternative reinvestment rate values so as to explore the sensitivity of the analyses to this factor.

The reinvestment approach described above is fine for certain fully compounding investors. However, there are many portfolios which must pay out some portion of their coupon receipts. How can their coupon flow be translated into a future value contribution? This is the point of departure where we must distinguish between future *dollars* literally accumulated over time and the much broader concept of future *value.*

Future value measures the total value provided by an investment's cash flow, expressed in terms of the currency of the principal dollars available as of the workout time. For example, a new bond fund manager may place a heavy emphasis on marginal coupon income, especially over the next six months. Even though all such income would be paid out (i.e., not reinvested), it would provide contribution to investment value. In terms of the fund's future value, say two years hence, these first six months of coupon income might be weighted very heavily in any tradeoff with marginal principal dollars. This would correspond to a high time-value rate for these early payments. In essence, the manager would be quantifying this tradeoff by stating how many dollars he would forego of marginal asset value two years hence in return for each dollar of marginal coupon income over the next six months. A more generalized time-valuing function can readily accommodate this linking of interim cash flows to future value contributions. Apart from these literal differences in time schedule, this generalized time-valuing function can also provide a tradeoff adjustment for different accounting treatments of coupon payments as opposed to principal appreciation, for the greater certainty of coupon flows, and for any other factors required to relate the desirability of a coupon payment at one time to a dollar of incremental principal at the workout time.

It could, of course, become quite difficult to incorporate this preference pattern into the time-valuing function for a given non-compounding portfolio manager. However, it often suffices in practice to assume one time-valuing discount rate throughout the workout period, and then to vary the value assigned to this rate across a wide range. This sensitivity analysis will then quickly identify at what point the time-valuing function begins to have a significant impact upon the investment decision at hand.

Many portfolio managers who do not explicitly reinvest and compound their coupon income will often feel most impatient with the time-value concept, even as generalized above. However, one cannot escape the need to find some method for incorporating all the sources of return into a comprehensive investment measure. Noncompounding managers often rely upon the conventional yield to maturity as being a safe guide. Yet, as we have pointed out above, the yield to maturity, in *all its interpretations,* is based upon an implicit time-value function. In effect, yield to maturity assumes that all coupon flows are time-related to the redemption payment at maturity as if each coupon were reinvested and compounded at the yield rate itself.

Future Value per Opportunity Dollar

Any investment measure, to be useful, must be translated into a mechanism for comparing alternative investments. This is also true for future value.

Suppose an investor holds $1 million of cash which he intends to invest into one of two bonds. For the moment, let us denote these alternative bonds as Bond A or Bond B. To make comparable future value estimates, we must first set a common workout period and then apply the same time-value function to both bonds. We must then make some consistent pricing estimates for the two bonds. Suppose we have done all this and have obtained the future value estimates A-FV and B-FV, respectively. At this point, we encounter a certain problem. These two estimates, A-FV and B-FV, represent the future value *per bond,* i.e., per $1,000 face value. In order to obtain the total future value corresponding to a decision to invest in Bond A or Bond B, we must reflect the number of bonds of each category that can be purchased with the $1 million. Suppose A-PR and B-PR denote market costs of the two bonds, i.e., both priced on the offered side of the market. Then, assuming that one can purchase fractions of a bond, the investor will be able to buy either ($1,000,000) ÷ (A-PR) of Bond A, or ($1,000,000) ÷ (B-PR) of Bond B. The purchase of Bond A would therefore lead to a total estimated future value of

$$\frac{(\$1{,}000{,}000)}{(\text{A-PR})} \times (\text{A-FV}) = (\$1{,}000{,}000) \times \frac{(\text{A-FV})}{(\text{A-PR})}$$
$$= (\$1{,}000{,}000) \times (\text{A-FVPD}),$$

where FVPD is the future value per (invested) dollar. Similarly, the purchase of Bond B would provide a total estimated future value of

$$\frac{(\$1{,}000{,}000)}{(\text{B-PR})} \times (\text{B-FV}) = (\$1{,}000{,}000) \times \frac{(\text{B-FV})}{(\text{B-PR})}$$
$$= (\$1{,}000{,}000) \times (\text{B-FVPD}).$$

Now suppose the investor wished to base his investment decision on these two sets of estimates of total future value. Then clearly the investor would select that bond having the largest future value per dollar (FVPD). (Actually, one should always use more than one set of estimates—there should be a sensitivity analysis using different workout times, pricing asumptions, and time-value functions.)

As we would expect, the actual magnitude of the cash to be invested does not matter—as long as one can purchase fractional bonds.

A similar situation arises when an investor considers swapping an H-Bond (for held bond) in his portfolio for some P-Bond (for proposed purchase). The investor here is bid a net amount H-PR for each of his H-Bonds, and is simultaneously offered the P-Bonds at a market cost of P-PR. It should be noted that the bid H-PR represents dollars of opportunity value for the investor. (This concept of the opportunity value locked up in a portfolio holding proves particularly helpful in dealing with taxable portfolios, where the market bid does not fully reflect the net value realized through sale, for example, when the direct market proceeds must be integrated with the effects of tax liabilities or capital gains distribution.) Let H-FV be the future value per bond resulting from continued holding of the H-Bond, and let P-FV be future value per bond achieved from the purchase of each P-Bond. Then in a dollar-for-dollar swap, the investor would give up H-FV for each H-Bond sold. At the same time, he would realize opportunity dollars in the amount of H-PR for every H-Bond sold. This amount could then purchase, on swap, the following number of P-Bonds,

$$\left(\frac{\text{H-PR}}{\text{P-PR}}\right)$$

for a total future value of

$$\begin{aligned}\left(\frac{\text{H-PR}}{\text{P-PR}}\right) \times \text{P-FV} &= (\text{H-PR}) \times \frac{(\text{P-FV})}{(\text{P-PR})}\\ &= (\text{H-PR}) \times (\text{P-FVPD}).\end{aligned}$$

Here again, we have made the tacit assumption that fractional numbers bonds can be freely purchased. If these future value estimates form the sole basis for the swap decision, then the investor would execute the swap as long as he obtains a greater total future value than he gives up, on *per bond sold* basis. In other words, he would swap as long as

$$(\text{H-PR}) \times (\text{P-FVPD}) > (\text{H-FV}),$$

or

$$(\text{P-FVPD}) > \frac{(\text{H-FV})}{(\text{H-PR})}$$

or

$$(\text{P-FVPD}) > (\text{H-FVPD}).$$

Here again, the future value per (opportunity) dollar is seen to be the key comparative measure.

The idea that any given amount can be fully expended in the purchase of a given bond may be referred to as the assumption of *complete divisibility*. Superficially, this assumption might appear to be resolved by simply rounding to the nearest bond. However, many institutional transactions actually involve specific lot sizes and consequently could lead to a potentially fragmented holding on one side or the other. In such cases, a correct theoretical framework can be established by viewing one side of the transaction as consisting of packages of the specific bond in question together with a cash pay-up or take-out. The contribution of this pay-up or take-out would then have to be incorporated into the future value per dollar computation using some appropriate time-value function.

Using our general equation for a bond's future value, we can now write the future value per dollar as

$$\begin{aligned} \text{FVPD} &= \frac{\text{TV (COUP-FLOW)} + \text{PR (WORKOUT)}}{\text{PR}} \\ &= \frac{\text{TV (COUP-FLOW)}}{\text{PR}} + \frac{\text{PR (WORKOUT)}}{\text{PR}}. \end{aligned}$$

Now if we let PR-CH represent the principal appreciation over the workout period, then we can express the principal value at the end of the workout period as

$$\text{PR (WORKOUT)} = \text{PR} + \text{PR-CH}.$$

Then dividing by the beginning market cost, PR, we get

$$\begin{aligned} \frac{\text{PR (WORKOUT)}}{\text{PR}} &= \frac{\text{PR} + \text{PR-CH}}{\text{PR}} \\ &= 1 + \frac{\text{PR-CH}}{\text{PR}} \\ &= 1 + \text{PR-RET} \end{aligned}$$

where PR-RET is just the principal return expressed as a fraction.

If the time-value function can be represented by some uniform discount rate R, then its contribution to FVPD can be expressed as

$$\begin{aligned} \frac{\text{TV (COUP-FLOW)}}{\text{PR}} &= \frac{(5C) \times S_w}{\text{PR}} \\ &= \left(\frac{10C}{\text{PR}}\right) \times \left(\frac{S_w}{2}\right) \\ &= \text{CURYLD} \times \left(\frac{S_w}{2}\right) \\ &= \text{CURYLD} \times \left[\frac{(1+R)^w - 1}{2R}\right], \end{aligned}$$

where CURYLD is the bond's current yield expressed as a fraction, and

$$S_w = \left[\frac{(1+R)^w - 1}{R}\right]$$

is the standard future value of \$1 per period for w periods at rate R. (Tabulations of values for S_w can readily be found in any standard book of compound interest tables.)

Putting these two contributions together, we get

$$\text{FVPD} = 1 + \left[\text{CURYLD} \times \frac{S_w}{2}\right] + (\text{PR-RET}).$$

This shows clearly how the principal return directly enters the FVPD formula while the current yield must be multiplied by a compounding factor reflecting the cumulative effect of time-valuing.

It is also interesting to see how this expression further simplifies when time value is ignored completely. Under such an extreme (and almost always unrealistic) assumption, $S_w = W$, and we obtain

$$\text{FVPD} = 1 + \left[\text{CURYLD} \times \left(\frac{W}{2}\right)\right] + \text{PR-RET}.$$

It should perhaps be mentioned that W is the number of semiannual periods in the workout period, and so $W/2$ is the number of years in this period. This formulation clearly shows how the contribution of current yield (especially when time-valued) grows over time relative to the contributions from principal return.

The Analysis of Principal Return

The bond's price change can be viewed in terms of two basic factors: the passage of time and movements in future yield level. If the yield to maturity remains absolutely constant throughout the workout period, then we know from the preceding discussion that the bond's price would change in accordance with the so-called scientific amortization method. Any further change in the bond's price could therefore be ascribed to deviations from this constant yield to maturity.

We denote by PR-CH-AMORT the principal appreciation per bond resulting from this constant yield amortization process. We use the symbol YLD-MOVE to designate the change in the bond's yield to maturity over the workout period, and the expression PR-CH (YLD-MOVE) for that portion of the principal appreciation due to this change in yield to maturity. With this symbology, the principal appreciation can be expressed as

$$\text{PR-CH} = \text{PR-CH-AMORT} + \text{PR-CH (YLD-MOVE)}.$$

The principal return can then be resolved into two terms as well,

$$\begin{aligned}\text{PR-RET} &= \frac{\text{PR-CH}}{\text{PR}}\\ &= \frac{\text{PR-CH-AMORT} + \text{PR-CH (YLD-MOVE)}}{\text{PR}}\\ &= \left(\frac{\text{PR-CH-AMORT}}{\text{PR}}\right) + \left[\frac{\text{PR-CH (YLD-MOVE)}}{\text{PR}}\right].\end{aligned}$$

The first term in the above equation represents the principal return component resulting from constant yield amortization. Consequently, we can conveniently represent this term by the shorthand symbol PR-RET-AMORT, i.e.,

$$\text{PR-RET-AMORT} = \frac{\text{PR-CH-AMORT}}{\text{PR}}.$$

The second term in the equation can be rewritten as follows

$$\begin{aligned}
\frac{\text{PR-CH (YLD-MOVE)}}{\text{PR}} &= \left(\frac{\text{PR} + \text{PR-CH-AMORT}}{\text{PR} + \text{PR-CH-AMORT}}\right) \\
&\quad \times \left[\frac{\text{PR-CH (YLD-MOVE)}}{\text{PR}}\right] \\
&= \left(\frac{\text{PR} + \text{PR-CH-AMORT}}{\text{PR}}\right) \\
&\quad \times \left[\frac{\text{PR-CH (YLD-MOVE)}}{\text{PR} + \text{PR-CH-AMORT}}\right] \\
&= \left(\frac{\text{PR}}{\text{PR}} + \frac{\text{PR-CH-AMORT}}{\text{PR}}\right) \\
&\quad \times \left[\frac{\text{PR-CH (YLD-MOVE)}}{\text{PR} + \text{PR-CH-AMORT}}\right] \\
&= (1 + \text{PR-RET-AMORT}) \\
&\quad \times [\text{PR-RET (YLD-MOVE)}],
\end{aligned}$$

where the new symbol PR-RET (YLD-MOVE) is a shorthand symbol for the principal return due to a change in yield. This definition requires some justification. We first observe that the sum, PR + PR-CH-AMORT, is just the bond's principal value at the workout time when the bond's yield to maturity remains constant. The principal appreciation due to a yield move, PR-CH (YLD-MOVE), is measured from the base line of this principal value under constant yield. For purposes of the mathematical analysis, this yield move and the resulting price change can be viewed as all taking place at the end of the workout period. From this viewpoint, at the workout time, the bond is at first priced on a constant yield basis so that its principal value is PR + PR-CH-AMORT. There then occurs an instantaneous change in yield-to-maturity level, YLD-MOVE, which results in an instantaneous change in principal value, PR-CH (YLD-MOVE). Consequently, the ratio.

$$\frac{\text{PR-CH (YLD-MOVE)}}{\text{PR} + \text{PR-CH-AMORT}}$$

represents the fractional change in principal value resulting from an instantaneous change in yield by the amount YLD-MOVE. This provides the justification for referring to this ratio as an instantaneous principal return,

$$\text{PR-RET (YLD-MOVE)} = \frac{\text{PR-CH (YLD-MOVE)}}{\text{PR + PR-CH-AMORT}}$$

It must always be remembered that these instantaneous yield and price movements are assumed to occur at the workout time. Consequently, the price change corresponds to that of a bond whose maturity has been foreshortened by the workout period. The advantage to this definition of PR-RET (YLD-MOVE) lies in the fact that it is closely related to the bond's basic volatility characteristics.

Making use of these new definitions, the principal return contribution to *FVPD* can be written as follows,

$$\begin{aligned}\text{PR-RET} &= \left[\frac{\text{PR-CH-AMORT}}{\text{PR}}\right] + \left[\frac{\text{PR-CH (YLD-MOVE)}}{\text{PR}}\right] \\ &= \text{PR-RET-AMORT} + (1 + \text{PR-RET-AMORT}) \\ &\quad \times \left[\frac{\text{PR-CH (YLD-MOVE)}}{\text{PR + PR-CH-AMORT}}\right] \\ &= \text{PR-RET-AMORT} + (1 + \text{PR-RET-AMORT}) \\ &\quad \times [\text{PR-RET (YLD-MOVE)}].\end{aligned}$$

This analysis thus resolves the total principal return over the workout period into two distinct ingredients, the first resulting solely from the passage of time, and the second one which can be viewed as the result of a sudden yield change at the end of the workout period. As we shall soon see in some detail, these return components can readily be related to the basic judgmental variables of the bond market.

The Volatility Factor

For a given yield move, the instantaneous principal return will correspond exactly to the instantaneous percentage price change. As we observed in *Inside the Yield Book*, a bond's percentage price change depends on (1) the maturity, (2) the coupon rate, (3) the starting yield level, and (4) the direction and magnitude of the yield move. It is worth examining the dependence on these last two factors in some detail.

As a starting point, let us consider the volatility of a 25-year, 7.0 percent bond priced at 94.391 to yield 7.50 percent. This corresponds to our earlier example of a 30-year, 7 percent bond, at the end of a five-year workout period. Table 1 shows the percentage price change of this bond in response to yield moves ranging from −100 basis points to +100 basis points. We see immediately that the percentage price change is not precisely symmetric. A −100 basis point yield move gives rise to a +12.44 percent price increase, while a +100 basis point yield move results in a loss of −10.42 percent. This nonsymmetry has often been discussed in the theoretical literature. However, it is important to also note that this lack of symmetry in the price response is not really all that great, especially for the more modest yield moves.

The last column of Table 1 shows the ratio of the percentage price change to the number of basis points in the corresponding yield move. This "rate of price change per unit yield move" is not constant. For example, in negative yield move direction, this figure grows from −0.1140 percent for a −5 basis point move to 0.1244 percent for a −100 basis point move. In mathematical terminology, this means that the percentage price change is *nonlinear*. In other words, we cannot exactly express the percentage price change, % PR-RET (YLD-MOVE), as some fixed volatility factor times the yield move, YLD-MOVE, i.e., the equation

TABLE 1

Instantaneous Percentage Price Change, 25-Year, 7.0% Bond (priced at 94.391 for yield to maturity of 7.50%)

Instantaneous Yield Move	*New Yield Level*	*Price Following Yield Move*	*Percentage Price Change*	*Ratio of Percentage Price Change to Yield Move in B.P.*
−100B.P.	6.50%	106.138	+12.44%	−0.1244%
− 75	6.75	102.999	+ 9.12	−0.1216
− 50	7.00	100.000	+ 5.94	−0.1188
− 35	7.15	98.264	+ 4.10	−0.1171
− 25	7.25	97.133	+ 2.90	−0.1160
− 20	7.30	96.575	+ 2.31	−0.1155
− 15	7.35	96.022	+ 1.73	−0.1153
− 10	7.40	95.474	+ 1.15	−0.1150
− 5	7.45	94.929	+ 0.57	−0.1140
0	7.50	94.391	0	—
+ 5	7.55	93.858	− 0.57	−0.1140
+ 10	7.60	93.329	− 1.13	−0.1130
+ 15	7.65	92.804	− 1.68	−0.1120
+ 20	7.70	92.284	− 2.23	−0.1116
+ 25	7.75	91.769	− 2.78	−0.1112
+ 35	7.85	90.752	− 3.86	−0.1102
+ 50	8.00	89.259	− 5.44	−0.1088
+ 75	8.25	86.856	− 7.98	−0.1064
+100	8.50	84.555	−10.42	−0.1042

$$\%\ \text{PR-RET (YLD-MOVE)} = (\text{Volatility factor}) \times (\text{YLD-MOVE})$$

could not be true for yield moves of different magnitudes or directions. At the same time, the extent of this nonlinearity is not overwhelming. For example, suppose we try to approximate positive price changes by the formula

$$\%\ \text{PR-RET (YLD-MOVE)} \cong (-0.1160) \times (\text{YLD-MOVE})$$

i.e., using the ratio for a −25 basis point yield move as a constant factor. As shown in Table 2, the approximation slightly overstates the price change for yield moves from −5 to −20 basis points. It of course matches the −25 basis point move exactly, and then begins to increasingly understate the percentage price change for greater yield moves.

TABLE 2

Comparison of Volatility Approximations with Actual Percentage Price Changes

		Percentage Price Change or Percentage Principal Return		
Instantaneous Yield Move	*Actual Value*	*Approximation Using 0.1160*	*Approximation Using 0.1112*	*Approximation Using 0.1136*
−100B.P.	+12.44%	+11.60%		+11.36%
− 75	+ 9.12	+ 8.70		+ 8.52
− 50	+ 5.94	+ 5.80		+ 5.68
− 35	+ 4.10	+ 4.6		+ 3.98
− 25	+ 2.90	+ 2.90		+ 2.84
− 20	+ 2.31	+ 2.32		+ 2.27
− 15	+ 1.73	+ 1.74		+ 1.70
− 10	+ 1.15	+ 1.16		+ 1.14
− 5	+ 0.57	+ 0.58		+ 0.56
0	0	0	0	0
+ 5	− 0.57		− 0.62	− 0.56
+ 10	− 1.13		− 1.11	− 1.14
+ 15	− 1.68		− 1.67	− 1.70
+ 20	− 2.23		− 2.22	− 2.27
+ 25	− 2.78		− 2.78	− 2.84
+ 35	− 3.86		− 3.89	− 3.98
+ 50	− 5.44		− 5.56	− 5.68
+ 75	− 7.98		− 8.34	− 8.52
+100	−10.42		−11.12	−11.36

However, the important thing to note is that the approximation is reasonably good for yield moves under 50 basis points. Similarly, for negative price changes, we can more or less arbitrarily select the ratio for a +25 basis point move, and set up the approximation,

$$\% \text{ PR-RET (YLD-MOVE)} \cong (-0.1112) \times \text{(YLD-MOVE)}.$$

As Table 2 shows, this approximation is also reasonably in line with the actual price changes for yield moves under 50 basis points.

It would of course be desirable to have a common approximating factor which could be used for both positive and negative price changes. Because of the particular form of the mathematical price function, one must sacrifice some further accuracy in order to obtain such a symmetrical approximation. To construct such a factor simply, we can take the average of the two ratios for 25 basis point moves in either direction, i.e.,

$$\tfrac{1}{2}[(-0.1160) + (-0.1112)] = -0.1136$$

so that the symmetric approximation would become

$$\%\ \text{PR-RET (YLD-MOVE)} = (-0.1136) \times \text{(YLD-MOVE)}.$$

Table 2 shows that the results are what might be expected. This symmetric approximation is not too bad for yield moves under 35 basis points. While more accurate fits can of course be obtained, these simple techniques will be sufficient for our purposes here.

If we are able to accept the accuracy limitations of this symmetric fit, then the principal return PR-RET (YLD-MOVE) of any bond can be approximated by an expression of the form,

$$\text{PR-RET (YLD-MOVE)} = (-\text{VOL}/100) \times \text{(YLD-MOVE)}.$$

The symbol VOL denotes the volatility factor selected to fit this bond at the prescribed starting yield level, and the divisor of 100 is needed to translate the percentage price change back into a fractional value. For a given bond, i.e., for a given coupon and maturity, we can construct average volatility factors corresponding to a series of different starting yield levels. Using the same method as above—averaging the percentage price change per basis point for +25 and −25 basis points—we have constructed Table 3 for 7 percent bonds with various maturities.

TABLE 3

Instantaneous Volatility Factors for 7% Bonds

	Maturity in Years						
Starting Yield	*5*	*10*	*15*	*20*	*25*	*30*	*40*
7.00%	.0416	.0711	.0920	.1068	.1173	.1248	.1338
7.25	.0415	.0707	.0912	.1055	.1155	.1224	.1306
7.50	.0414	.0704	.0904	.1042	.1136	.1201	.1274
7.75	.0413	.0700	.0897	.1030	.1119	.1178	.1243
8.00	.0412	.0697	.0889	.1017	.1101	.1155	.1213
8.25	.0411	.0693	.0881	.1004	.1083	.1133	.1184
8.50	.0410	.0690	.0874	.0992	.1066	.1111	.1156
8.75	.0409	.0686	.0866	.0979	.1048	.1090	.1128
9.00	.0408	.0683	.0859	.0967	.1031	.1069	.1102

For purposes of comparison, the corresponding volatility factors for a 4 percent bond are given in Table 4.

Analysis of Yield Relationships

A careful analysis of the components of a yield move is necessary to understand how many bond market participants perceive the variables of

TABLE 4
Instantaneous Volatility Factors for 4% Bonds

Starting Yield	Maturity in Years						
	5	*10*	*15*	*20*	*25*	*30*	*40*
7.00%	.0439	.0781	.1031	.1206	.1320	.1392	.1454
7.25	.0438	.0778	.1024	.1192	.1300	.1364	.1416
7.50	.0438	.0774	.1016	.1178	.1279	.1337	.1378
7.75	.0437	.0771	.1009	.1165	.1259	.1310	.1342
8.00	.0436	.0768	.1001	.1151	.1239	.1284	.1307
8.25	.0435	.0765	.0993	.1137	.1219	.1258	.1273
8.50	.0434	.0762	.0986	.1124	.1199	.1233	.1240
8.75	.0433	.0758	.0978	.1110	.1179	.1208	.1208
9.00	.0433	.0755	.0970	.1096	.1159	.1183	.1177

the marketplace. Since most judgments and decision making are conducted in terms of these perceived variables, such understanding is a prerequisite to gaining an insight into the art of bond swapping.

A bond's yield to maturity at a given point in time can be analyzed in many different ways. The particular analytic breakdown which follows was selected because we feel it provides the greatest insight into motivations and judgments underlying many different types of bond swaps.

First of all, each individual security trades within the broad confines of some "market," and there is usually some readily accepted indicator of the general yield level of this market. For example, most high-grade corporate bonds can usefully be viewed as bearing some relation to a standard index for this market as a whole. The estimated rate for a new issue AA 30-year utility bond is often taken as one such indicator. One usually has a fair degree of leeway in the choice of an assigned market indicator. As we shall see in the ensuing discussion, the best choice can usually be made only in the context of a given swap situation.

Assuming that the market indicator has been selected in some appropriate fashion, we shall denote its yield value by the symbol YLD-MKT. Similarily, we use the symbol YLD-IND to represent the yield level of the individual security. We then turn our attention to the yield spread, (YLD-IND) − (YLD-MKT), which exists between the individual security and the general market level. This yield spread can be further analyzed in terms of three fundamental relationships:

1. The maturity-to-general-market relationship (sometimes called the "yield curve" effect).
2. The sector-to-maturity relationship.
3. The individual-security-to-sector relationship.

Since we have chosen a single point indicator, YLD-MKT, for the general market level, we must compensate for the difference in maturity between this general market issue and the individual security in question. In the corporate bond market, this relationship is usually subsumed under a broader concept of the sector-to-market link. This practice probably arose because of the close association between maturities, dates of issuance, and coupon rates in the long-term corporate market. However, for our analytic purposes, we shall find that it makes good sense to first interpose this additional maturity-to-market relationship.

Specifically, we shall quantify this relationship by envisioning a theoretical yield curve (i.e., a pattern of yield values associated with each possible maturity date) which is consistent with our definition of the general market. For example, if the new issue AA 30-year utility rate were selected as the general market indicator, and if the individual security under study were a 15-year bond, then our maturity adjustment would be the estimated yield spread between a new issue AA 15-year utility and the given general market level. As mentioned above, this yield spread may admittedly be highly theoretical in light of the fact that such 15-year bonds are almost never issued. However, we shall see that this approach ultimately provides much greater clarity and generality, and ends up to be easily handled in practice. We shall refer to this yield curve adjustment by the symbol YLD-SPRD-MAT as shorthand for "yield spread accounting for the maturity difference from the selected general market indicator."

The remaining yield spread, (YLD-IND) – (YLD-MKT) – (YLD-SPRD-MAT), can now be easily related to the two remaining relationships. The particular sector in which the bond lies is usually defined in terms of a combination of several factors:

1. Type of issuer (e.g., utility, industrial, finance).
2. Quality rating (e.g., Aaa, Aa, A, "split-rated" Aaa/AA).
3. Coupon rate (e.g., 4⅛'s to 4⅜'s, 4⅝'s to 4¾'s).
4. Indenture characteristics (e.g., strong sinking fund, weak sinking fund, no sinking fund, early sinking fund, refundability features).
5. Various factors having a major impact on marketability within the secondary market (e.g., "publics" versus "privates," size outstanding, structure of institutional holdings).
6. Maturity structure.

Because of our prior adjustment for maturity, we must now view definition of the relevant sector to be specific to the maturity of the individual security. Theoretically, this sector can then be represented by some benchmark issue or by some average of various issues. The yield level of this sector indicator, however chosen, will then bear some spread relationship to the general market level as adjusted to the corresponding maturity. We shall use the symbol YLD-SPRD-SECT as shorthand for this "yield spread between the sector indicator yield and the yield level of the general market *after* adjustment for maturity." As noted earlier, in the corporate market, it is general practice to subsume the maturity adjustment, YLD-SPRD-MAT, into a less refined sector-to-market spread relationship. This more conventional sector-to-market spread then just corresponds to the sum of our two yield spreads, i.e., (YLD-SPR-MAT) + (YLD-SPRD-SECT).

The final relationship is that between the individual security and sector indicator. The corresponding yield spread reflecting this relationship will be denoted by YLD-SPRD-IND as a shorthand for the "yield spread between the individual security's yield level and the yield level of its sector indicator." This yield spread will generally depend on the individual security's unique characteristics, fine gradations of quality and tradeability, its "color" the name value of the issuer, and recent sinking-fund activity, as well as its relative availability in the marketplace at any particular moment in time.

Bringing all these definitions together, we can now relate the yield level of the individual security to the yield level of the general market and to the yield spread measures of the three fundamental market relationships,

$$(\text{YLD-IND}) = (\text{YLD-MKT}) + (\text{YLD-SPRD-MAT}) + (\text{YLD-SPRD-SECT}) + (\text{YLD-SPRD-IND}).$$

This is a static relationship which holds for any given point in time. We shall shortly see how this breakdown provides the basis for an understanding of dynamic yield movements and the analysis of swap opportunities (see Figure 5).

Analysis of Yield Changes

The yield level of a given security will change over time in response to a variety of market forces. From the analytic point of view, the first step is to relate these changes in the overall yield to changes in the fundamental yield relationships between markets, maturities, and sectors.

Consider a yield change in a given security which takes place over some workout period. (See Figure 6.) At the beginning of the period, the security's yield (YLD-IND) is given by

$$(\text{YLD-IND}) = (\text{YLD-MKT}) + (\text{YLD-SPRD-MAT}) + (\text{YLD-SPRD-SECT}) + (\text{YLD-SPRD-IND}).$$

At the end of the workout period, all yields and yield spreads will have new values which will be denoted by an overhead bar, i.e., the security's yield at the workout time would just be

$$\overline{(\text{YLD-IND})} = \overline{(\text{YLD-MKT})} + \overline{(\text{YLD-SPRD-MAT})} + \overline{(\text{YLD-SPRD-SECT})} + \overline{(\text{YLD-SPRD-IND})}.$$

In earlier sections, we have already denoted the change in yield to maturity over a workout period by YLD-MOVE. Consequently, we can write

FIGURE 5

The Structure of a Bond's Yields at the Start and the End of a Workout Period

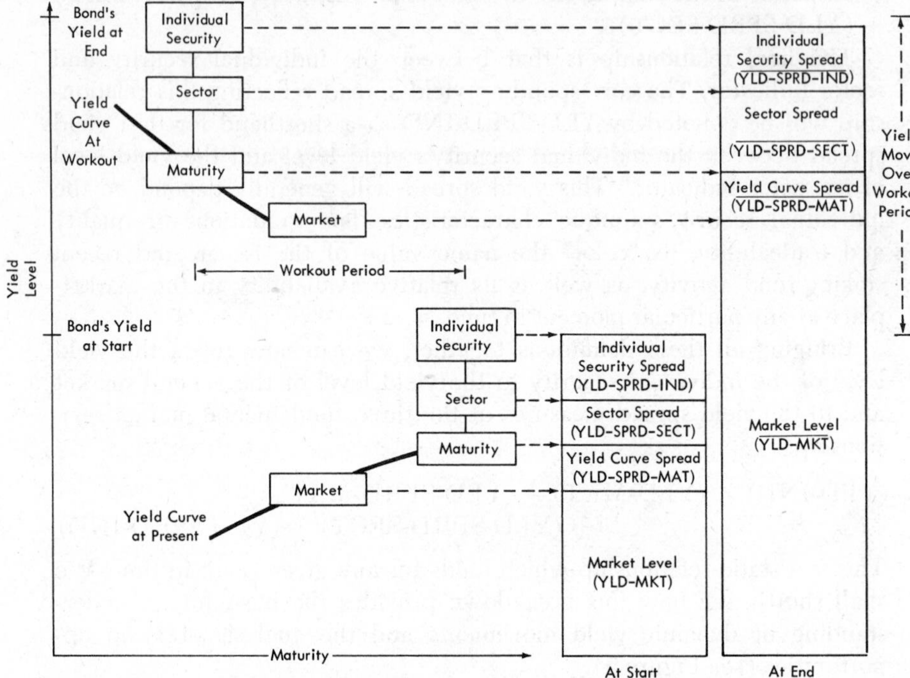

$$
\begin{aligned}
(\text{YLD-MOVE}) &= \overline{(\text{YLD-IND})} - (\text{YLD-IND}) \\
&= [\overline{(\text{YLD-MKT})} - (\text{YLD-MKT})] \\
&\quad + [\overline{(\text{YLD-SPRD-MAT})} - (\text{YLD-SPRD-MAT})] \\
&\quad + [\overline{(\text{YLD-SPRD-SECT})} - (\text{YLD-SPRD-SECT})] \\
&\quad + [\overline{(\text{YLD-SPRD-IND})} - (\text{YLD-SPRD-IND})].
\end{aligned}
$$

We can simplify this equation by using the prefix CH to stand for change over the workout period, so that (CH-YLD-MKT) represents the change in the yield level of the general market over the workout period (see Figure 6), i.e.,

$$(\text{CH-YLD-MKT}) = \overline{(\text{YLD-MKT})} - (\text{YLD-MKT}).$$

Similarly, (CH-YLD-SPRD-MAT) represents the change in the yield spread relating the maturity to general market yield, i.e.,

$$(\text{CH-YLD-SPRD-MAT}) = \overline{(\text{YLD-SPRD-MAT})} - (\text{YLD-SPRD-MAT}).$$

Since the maturity itself (in the sense of remaining life) changes over the workout period, we would expect some change here even in absolutely stable markets. This term would therefore include the effect of "rolling down the yield curve" in stable markets as well as for the im-

FIGURE 6

The Anatomy of a Bond's Yield Move over a Workout Period

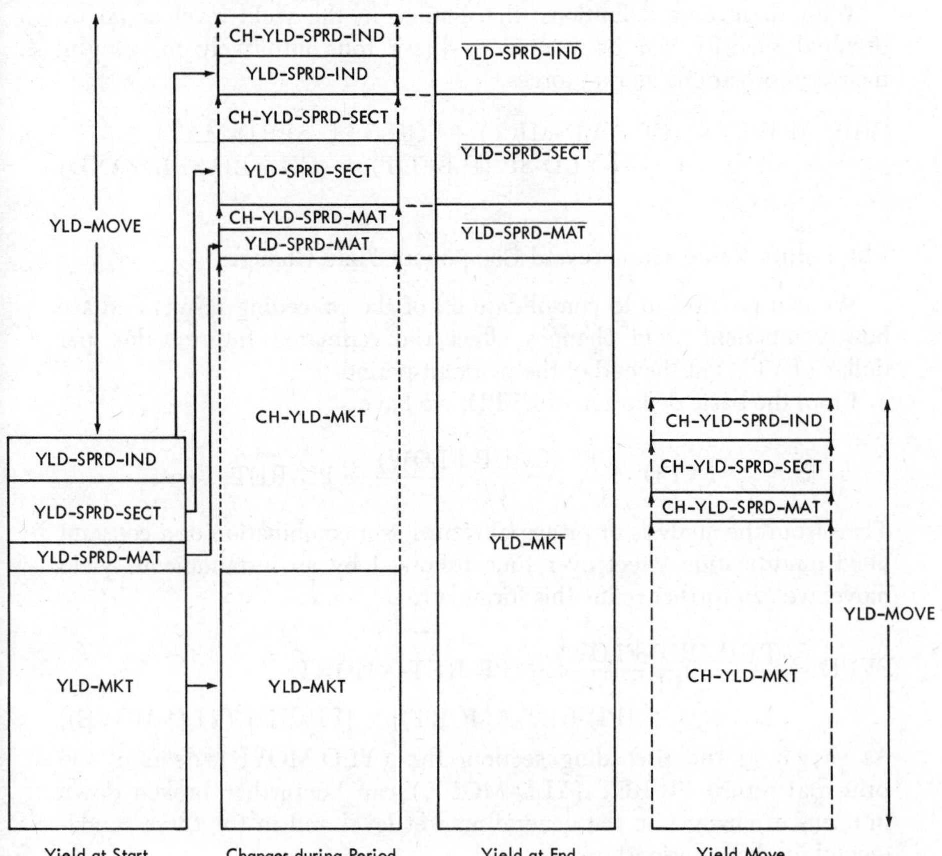

pact of changing overall yield curves in more dynamic markets. In fact, it is this specific capture of these two practically important market effects which motivated our singling out this relationship, even though this departs from the conventional approach in the corporate market.

The change in the yield spread relating the sector to the general yield curve,

$$(\text{CH-YLD-SPRD-SECT}) = (\overline{\text{YLD-SPRD-SECT}}) - (\text{YLD-SPRD-SECT})$$

incorporates the market forces which have specifically affected the sector in question.

Finally, the change in the yield spread, relating the individual security to its sector,

$$(\text{CH-YLD-SPRD-IND}) = (\overline{\text{YLD-SPRD-IND}}) - (\text{YLD-SPRD-IND})$$

should account for the market impact of forces directly related to the specific issue under study.

With these new definitions, the change in the yield level of an individual security can be related to these four intuitively meaningful measures of various market forces,

$$\text{(YLD-MOVE)} = \text{(CH-YLD-MKT)} + \text{(CH-YLD-SPRD-MAT)} + \text{(CH-YLD-SPRD-SECT)} + \text{(CH-YLD-SPRD-IND)}.$$

The Future Value Measure and Component Yield Changes

We can now begin to consolidate all of the preceding results and see how component yield changes affect the estimated future value per dollar (FVPD) at the end of the workout period.

From the basic definition of FVPD, we have

$$\text{FVPD} = \frac{\text{TV (COUP-FLOW)}}{\text{PR}} + \text{PR-RET}.$$

Then from the analysis of principal return as a combination of a constant yield amortization effect over time followed by an instantaneous yield move, we can further refine this formula to

$$\text{FVPD} = \frac{\text{TV (COUP-FLOW)}}{\text{PR}} + \text{PR-RET-AMORT} + [1 + \text{(PR-RET-AMORT)}] \times [\text{PR-RET (YLD-MOVE)}].$$

As shown in the preceding section, the (YLD-MOVE) defining the principal return PR-RET (YLD-MOVE) can be further broken down in terms of changes in the general market level and in the three fundamental market relationships.

This FVPD can be refined further through acceptance of a time value function that can be represented as some constant time-valuing or discount rate *R*. With acceptance of such a uniform time value model, we obtain

$$\frac{\text{TV (COUP-FLOW)}}{\text{PR}} = \tfrac{1}{2} \times \text{(CUR-YLD)} \times S_w = \tfrac{1}{2} \times \text{(CUR-YLD)} \times \left[\frac{(1+R)^w - 1}{R}\right]$$

Then if we can accept the loss of absolute precision, we can approximate the PR-RET (YLD-MOVE) by using the volatility factor as a constant of proportionality,

$$\text{PR-RET (YLD-MOVE)} = -\text{(VOL/100)} \times \text{(YLD-MOVE)}.$$

As we shall see most strikingly in the later discussion of bond swaps, what may be lost in precision through this approximation is more than recovered in terms of clarity, insight, and ease of applicability to practical situations. For starters, the PR-RET (YLD-MOVE) can be directly related to the component yield changes,

$$\text{PR-RET (YLD-MOVE)} = [-\text{VOL}/100] \times [(\text{CH-YLD-MKT}) + (\text{CH-YLD-SPRD-MAT}) + (\text{CH-YLD-SPRD-SECT}) + (\text{CH-YLD-SPRD-IND})].$$

Putting it all together, we obtain the following expression for the future value per dollar,

$$\text{FVPD} = 1 + [\tfrac{1}{2} \times (\text{CUR-YLD}) \times S_w] + [\text{PR-RET-AMORT}] + [1 + (\text{PR-RET-AMORT}] \times [-\text{VOL}/100] [(\text{CH-YLD-MKT}) + (\text{CH-YLD-SPRD-MAT}) + (\text{CH-YLD-SPRD-SECT}) + (\text{CH-YLD-SPRD-IND})].$$

A Numerical Example: Future Value per Dollar

Consider an AAA-rated, 30-year, 7.0 percent bond of a power utility priced at 94.065 to yield 7.50 percent. Over a five-year workout period, an investor wishes to estimate the FVPD under the following assumptions:

1. All coupon income is used to help maintain a short-term liquidity reserve and hence is time-valued at a uniform 6 percent rate.
2. The AA utility new issue rate for 30-year bonds is assumed to improve from its 8.00 percent level today to 7.60 percent by the end of the five-year period.
3. If a new 25-year AA utility were to be issued at the end of the workout period, it would be priced to yield 10 basis points under the 30-year rate, i.e., at 7.50 percent.
4. The bond's sector consists of seasoned, medium-size, AAA-rated utility bonds, ranging from 27 to 30 years in maturity, and with coupon rates of 7.25 percent to 7.50 percent. Right now this sector is selling at 40 basis points under the 30-year AA new issue rate, i.e., at 7.60 percent. At the end of the workout period, in a 7.60 percent market for 30-year AA new utilities and a corresponding 7.50 percent market for the hypothetical 25-year AA new utility, this sector of higher quality, seasoned issues would be expected to yield 15 basis points under the 25-year general market rate, i.e., 7.35 percent.
5. The particular bond now sells at 10 basis points under the sector level of 7.60 percent, but it is felt that this spread will probably narrow to 5 basis points by the end of the workout period. This implies that the bond is assumed to be priced to yield 7.30 percent at the end of the five-year workout period.

Now in terms of the variables in the FVPD formula, the basic description together with the above five assumptions imply, respectively, the following sets of values. From the basic description of the bond and the workout period,

$$C = 7.00\%$$
$$\text{PR} = \$940.65$$
$$\text{CURYLD} = \left(\frac{10 \times 7.00}{940.65}\right) = 0.0744 \text{ (i.e., 7.44\%)}$$
$$W = 10 \text{ (number of semiannual periods in 5 years)}$$
$$\text{PR-RET-AMORT} = \frac{\text{CH-PR-AMORT}}{\text{PR}}$$
$$= \frac{(\text{Principal value of 25-yr., 7.0\% bond @ 7.50}) - (\text{PR})}{\text{PR}}$$
$$= \frac{943.91 - 940.65}{940.65} = 0.0035$$
$$(\text{VOL}) = (0.1136) \text{ (from Table 3 for a 25-year 7.0\% bond with a starting yield of 7.50\%)}$$

1. $R = 0.03$ (fractional time-value rate per semiannual period).

$$S_w = \frac{(1 + R)^w - 1}{R} = 11.464$$ (from compound interest table for future value of $1 per period over 10 periods invested at a rate of 3 percent per period).

2. (CH-YLD-MKT) = −40 (basis points).
3. (CH-YLD-SPRD-MAT) = −10 − 0 = −10 (basis points).
4. (CH-YLD-SPRD-SECT) = −15 − (−40) = −15 + 40 = +25 (basis points).
5. (CH-YLD-SPRD-IND) = −5 − (−10) = −5 + 10 = +5 (basis points).

Plugging these numbers into the formula at the end of the last section, we get

$$\begin{aligned}\text{FVPD} &= 1 + [\tfrac{1}{2} \times (0.0744) \times 11.464] + [0.0035] \\ &\quad + [1 + 0.0035] \times [-0.1136/100] \\ &\quad \times [(-40) + (-10) + (+25) + (+5)] \\ &= 1 + [0.4265] + [0.0035] + [1.0035] \times [-0.001136] \times [-20] \\ &= 1 + [0.4265] + [0.0035] + [-0.001140] \times [-20] \\ &= 1 + [0.4265] + [0.0035] + [0.0228] \\ &= 1.4528\end{aligned}$$

In other words, the total gain over the five-year period, after repayment of the original investment, would amount to 45.28 percent. Of this figure, 42.65 percent would be time-valued coupon flow, 0.35 percent would be price amortization, and 2.28 percent would arise from a 20-

basis-point decline in the bond's yield. (The figure of 2.28 percent is based upon our volatility approximation—the exact number is 2.31 percent.)

Other Investment Measures

While we have developed our argument in terms of the future value approach, it should be noted that there are a number of other investment measures which are used in the bond market.

The realized compound yield (or effective yield) measure can be derived directly from the future value per dollar. Basically, the realized compound yield represents the uniform rate at which an investment would have to be compounded in order to grow to the magnitude of the future value per dollar. Mathematically, if the realized compound yield, as a fractional rate per semiannual period, is denoted by RCY, then

$$[1 + (\mathrm{RCY})]^{w} = \mathrm{FVPD}.$$

This equation can be solved for (RCY) by extracting the wth root,

$$(\mathrm{RCY}) = (\mathrm{FVPD})^{1/w} - 1.$$

The present value is a discounted translation of the future value back to today's dollars. The same time-value function used in future value computation should be used for these discounting purposes. If the time-value function is based upon a uniform semiannual rate R, then one has

$$\mathrm{PV} = \frac{\mathrm{FV}}{(1 + R)^{w}}$$

where PV represents the present value. One can define a present value per (invested) dollar, PVPD, by

$$\begin{aligned} \mathrm{PVPD} &= \frac{\mathrm{PV}}{\mathrm{PR}} \\ &= \left(\frac{1}{\mathrm{PR}}\right) \times \left[\frac{\mathrm{FV}}{(1 + R)^{w}}\right] \\ &= \frac{\mathrm{FVPD}}{(1 + R)^{w}} \end{aligned}$$

The present value per dollar is mathematically completely equivalent to the FVPD, and any P-bond having a greater FVPD than an H-bond will also have a greater PVPD and RCY as well.

The internal rate of return (IRR) is an investment measure which is, of course, frequently used (and, we believe, misused as well). To place the internal rate of return into the context of this discussion, assume a time-value function based upon uniform compounding but at some unspecified discount rate. This discount rate will also be used to make the present value per dollar computations. Suppose a sequence of different discount rates is used, each leading to different values of FVPD and PVPD, until one rate U is found which leads to PVPD = 1. This rate U is then the internal rate of return. In a certain sense, this internal rate of return represents a sort of a "break-even time value rate" for the bond investment *relative to the alternative of cash.*

When the workout period is the bond's maturity, then the internal rate of return is the bond's conventional yield to maturity.

When the workout period extends to a specified call or refunding date, at which time the bond is assumed to be called at the then prevailing call price, the resulting internal rate of return figure is the bond's conventional yield to call.

When the bond has a pro rata sinking fund and the workout period is taken to be the final redemption date, then the resulting internal rate of return figure is often called the bond's "cash flow yield."

BOND SWAPS AND THEIR EVALUATION

Bond Swaps and Net Future Value per Dollar

A swap from a given H-bond into a given P-bond can be evaluated through the resulting net improvement in FVPD over a range of assumed market scenarios. As we shall see, the form of the formula for this net improvement in FVPD provides many valuable insights into the structural dynamics of a bond swap.

While the basic concepts and the manipulations are not difficult in themselves, there are a large number of interrelating factors, and we must be careful to develop a clear notational framework. Generally, we shall use the prefix H for variables related to the H-bond, the prefix P for variables related to the P-bond, and NET for the difference between a P-variable and an H-variable. For example, the net improvement in FVPD will be written as

$$\text{(NET-FVPD)} = \text{(P-FVPD)} - \text{(H-FVPD)}.$$

Apart from 1, which represents the repayment of the original investment and which drops out in the difference equation, the first term in the FVPD expression represents the time-valued coupon flows. The swap improvement here is

$$[\tfrac{1}{2} \times \text{(P-CUR-YLD)} \times S_w] - [\tfrac{1}{2} \times \text{(H-CUR-YLD)} \times S_w] = \tfrac{1}{2} \times \text{(NET-CUR-YLD)} \times S_w.$$

The second term in the FVPD formula deals with the principal return obtained through constant yield amortization over time. The swap improvement here is just the difference,

$$\text{(NET-PR-RET-AMORT)} = \text{(P-PR-RET-AMORT)} - \text{(H-PR-RET-AMORT)}.$$

The third term in the FVPD measures the principal return resulting from a yield move at the end of the workout period. We can shorten this expression greatly by first defining a new variable, the "amortized volatility,"

$$(\text{AMORT-VOL}) = [1 + \text{PR-RET-AMORT}] \times [(\text{VOL}/100)].$$

Essentially, the AMORT-VOL is just the volatility factor VOL, adjusted (slightly in most cases) to reflect the fractional impact, relative to today's investment base, of an instantaneous percentage price change from the future amortized price level. With this definition, the third term can be written as

$$-[(\text{AMORT-VOL})] \times [(\text{YLD-MOVE})],$$

and the swap improvement arising from principal return becomes

$$\{-[(\text{P-AMORT-VOL})] \times [(\text{P-YLD-MOVE})]\} - \{-[(\text{H-AMORT-VOL})] \times [(\text{H-YLD-MOVE})]\}.$$

By making the definition,

$$(\text{NET-YLD-MOVE}) = (\text{P-YLD-MOVE}) - (\text{H-YLD-MOVE}),$$

we can write

$$(\text{P-YLD-MOVE}) = (\text{H-YLD-MOVE}) + (\text{NET-YLD-MOVE}).$$

Substituting this expression for (P-YLD-MOVE) into the third term of the FVPD formula, we get

$$\begin{aligned} &-[(\text{P-AMORT-VOL})] \times [(\text{H-YLD-MOVE}) + (\text{NET-YLD-MOVE})] \\ &\quad + [(\text{H-AMORT-VOL})] \times [(\text{H-YLD-MOVE})] \\ &= -[(\text{P-AMORT-VOL}) - (\text{H-AMORT-VOL})] \times [(\text{H-YLD-MOVE})] \\ &\quad - [\text{P-AMORT-VOL}) \times (\text{NET-YLD-MOVE})] \\ &= -[(\text{NET-AMORT-VOL})] \times [(\text{H-YLD-MOVE})] \\ &\qquad - [(\text{P-AMORT-VOL}) \times (\text{NET-YLD-MOVE})], \end{aligned}$$

where (NET-AMORT-VOL) is defined as the improvement in amortized volatility resulting from the swap, i.e.,

$$(\text{NET-AMORT-VOL}) = (\text{P-AMORT-VOL}) - (\text{H-AMORT-VOL}).$$

Now bringing all these mathematical manipulations and definitions together, we can express the swap improvement in FVPD as the sum of four basic terms,

$$\begin{aligned} \text{NET-FVPD} = {} & [\tfrac{1}{2} \times (\text{NET-CUR-YLD}) \times S_w] \\ & + [(\text{NET-PR-RET-AMORT})] \\ & + [-(\text{NET-AMORT-VOL}) \times (\text{H-YLD-MOVE})] \\ & + [-(\text{P-AMORT-VOL}) \times (\text{NET-YLD-MOVE})]. \end{aligned}$$

This four-term form can help illuminate the elements of good bond swap.

Investment Implications of the Net Future Value per Dollar Expression

The analyses of any bond swap must be reflective of the motivations and market judgments underlying that swap. Since these underlying intentions range across radically different types of investment decisions, it is most critical that the primary purpose of a swap be clearly defined. It is, in a sense, most unfortunate that the one term *swap* can be conveniently stretched to cover a wide spectrum of different tactical and strategic actions. This lack of refinement in the language of investment has often led to many unnecessary problems, both in communication and in thinking.

In an attempt to introduce some organization into this area, we defined four idealized swap categories in *Inside the Yield Book.* In spite of its simplicity and limited refinement, this classification scheme has proven most useful. The four categories in this classification scheme are:

I. Substitution swaps.
II. Intermarket spread swaps.
III. Rate anticipation swaps.
IV. Pure yield pickup swaps.

The *substitution swap* is ideally an exchange of a bond for a perfect substitute or "twin" bond. The motivation here is a temporary price advantage, presumably resulting from a momentary imbalance in the relative supply/demand conditions in the marketplace.

The *intermarket spread swap* is a more general movement out of one market component and into another with the intention of exploiting a currently advantageous yield relationship. The idea here is to trade off of these changing relationships between the two market components. Short-term workout periods are usually anticipated. While such swaps will almost always have some sensitivity to the direction of the overall market, the idealized focus of this type of swap is the spread relationship itself.

On the other hand, the *rate anticipation swap* is frankly geared towards profiting from an anticipated movement in overall market rates.

The *pure yield pickup swap* is oriented towards yield improvement over the long term, with little heed being paid to interim price movements in either the respective market components or the market as a whole.

It should be recognized that this categorization implies much sharper demarcations than are encountered in practice. A real-life swap may incorporate elements of all four swap categories, as well as some considerations well beyond the limits of this simple classification system.

It is interesting to examine this swap classification system as it is reflected in the four-term expression given above for (NET-FVPD).

The first two terms, $[1/2 \times (\text{NET-CUR-YLD}) \times S_w] + [(\text{NET-PR-RET-AMORT})]$, represent the income and principal appreciation components, respectively, of the NET-FVPD, independent of any change in the yield levels of either bond. Consequently, it is tempting to identify these two terms as representing the pure yield pickup component of the NET-FVPD.

The third term, [−(NET-AMORT-VOL) × (H-YLD-MOVE)], accounts for the effects of all yield movements *shared* by the two bonds. Consequently, this term can be viewed as the primary focus of the rate anticipation facets of the swap. This interpretation holds additional interest because the newly defined (NET-AMORT-VOL) variable, i.e., the net pickup in adjusted volatility, is the critical constant of proportionality (see Figure 7).

FIGURE 7

Yield Move Components in a Bond Swap

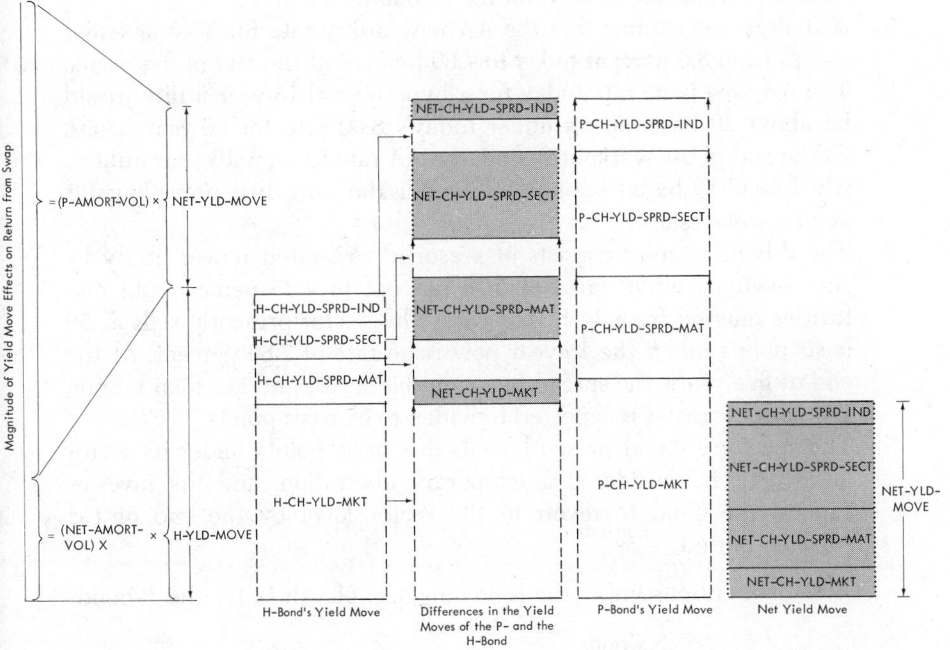

Finally, the fourth term, [−(P-AMORT-VOL) × (NET-YLD-MOVE)], accounts for the principal appreciation arising from any change in the yield spread relationship between the two bonds. (Any change in this yield spread relationship would have to be the result of the two bonds having different yield moves over the workout period. The variable [NET-YLD-MOVE] is precisely the difference between these yield moves.) Therefore, the impact of intermarket spread swaps and substitution swaps would be expected to be concentrated in this fourth term. Differentiation between those two swap categories becomes possible once one delves into the component elements of the (NET-YLD-MOVE).

A Numerical Example of a Bond Swap

Let us evaluate a simple bond swap using the same context as in our earlier numerical example. The investor sells the 30-year, 7.0 percent bond of the previous example and buys an AA-rated, 15-year, 4.0 percent P-bond of a power utility company which is priced at 70.575 to yield 7.25 percent. We retain all the earlier assumptions about the H-bond's behavior over the five-year workout period, and we make the following related assumptions regarding the 4.0 percent P-bond's performance:

1. All coupon income from the P-bond would be time-valued at the same 6 percent rate as used for the H-bond.
2. As before, we assume that the AA new utility rate for 30-year issues moves from 8.0 percent today to 7.60 percent at the end of five years.
3. The AA new issue rate today for a hypothetical 15-year utility would be about 20 basis points under today's 8.00 rate for 30-year issues. At the end of the workout period, the AA rate for new 10-year utilities is assumed to be 50 basis points under the rate then prevailing for 30-year new issues.
4. The P-bond's sector consists of seasoned, AA-rated power utility issues having coupon rates of 3.75 percent to 4.25 percent and maturities ranging from 14 to 16 years. This sector presently sells at 50 basis points under the 15-year new issue rate of 7.80 percent. At the end of five years, the spread between this sector and the then rate on 10-year new issues is expected to widen to 65 basis points.
5. The specific P-bond presently sells five basis points under its sector level. This is considered a temporary aberration, and the investor expects the bond to revert to the sector level by the end of the workout period.

These assumptions imply the following sets of values for the P-bond:

$$C = 4.00\%$$

$$\text{PR} = \$705.75$$

$$\text{CURYLD} = \left(\frac{10 \times 4.00}{505.75}\right) = 0.0567 \qquad \text{(i.e., 5.67\%)}$$

$$W = 10$$

$$\text{PR-RET-AMORT} = \frac{(\text{Principal value of 10-year } 4.00\% \text{ @ } 7.25\%) - (\text{PR})}{\text{PR}}$$

$$= \frac{771.63 - 705.75}{705.75} = \frac{65.88}{705.75} = 0.0933$$

$$\text{VOL} = 0.0778 \text{ (from Table 4 for a 10-year, 4.00\% bond with a starting yield of 7.25\%)}$$

1. $R = 0.03.$
   $S_w = 11.464$
2. (YLD-MKT) = 8.00
   $\overline{\text{(YLD-MKT)}}$ = 7.60%
   (CH-YLD-MKT) = −40 (basis points)
3. (YLD-SPRD-MAT) = −20
   $\overline{\text{(YLD-SPRD-MAT)}}$ = −50
   (CH-YLD-SPRD-MAT) = (−50) − (−20) = −30
4. (YLD-SPRD-SECT) = −50
   $\overline{\text{(YLD-SPRD-SECT)}}$ = −65
   (CH-YLD-SPRD-SECT) = (−65) − (−50) = −15
5. (YLD-SPRD-IND) = −5
   $\overline{\text{(YLD-SPRD-IND)}}$ = 0
   (CH-YLD-SPRD-IND) = 0 − (−5) = +5

Putting all these P-bond yield changes together,

$$\begin{aligned}\text{(P-YLD-MOVE)} &= \text{(CH-YLD-MKT)} + \text{(CH-YLD-SPRD-MAT)} \\ &\quad + \text{(CH-YLD-SECT)} + \text{(CH-YLD-SPRD-IND)} \\ &= (-40) + (-30) + (-15) + (+5) \\ &= -80\end{aligned}$$

From the earlier example worked out for the 30-year, 7 percent H-bond, we have

$$\text{(H-YLD-MOVE)} = -20,$$

so that

$$\begin{aligned}\text{(NET-YLD-MOVE)} &= \text{(P-YLD-MOVE)} - \text{(H-YLD-MOVE)} \\ &= (-80) - (-20) \\ &= -60.\end{aligned}$$

For the amortized volatility factors, we have

$$\begin{aligned}\text{(P-AMORT-VOL)} &= [1 + \text{P-PR-RET-AMORT}] \times [(\text{VOL}/100)] \\ &= [1.0933] \times [0.000778] \\ &= 0.0008505,\end{aligned}$$

while from the numerical example for the 7 percent H-bond,

$$\begin{aligned}\text{(H-AMORT-VOL)} &= [1 + 0.0035] \times [(0.1136/100)] \\ &= 0.001140,\end{aligned}$$

so that the net volatility effect of the swap is

$$\begin{aligned}\text{(NET-AMORT-VOL)} &= \text{(P-AMORT-VOL)} - \text{(H-AMORT-VOL)} \\ &= 0.0008505 - 0.001140 \\ &= 0.0002895.\end{aligned}$$

The difference in principal return due to amortization is

$$\begin{aligned}(\text{NET-PR-RET-AMORT}) &= (\text{P-PR-RET-AMORT}) \\ &\quad - (\text{H-PR-RET-AMORT}) \\ &= (0.0933) - (0.0035) \\ &= +\,0.0898.\end{aligned}$$

This swap actually entails a net give-up of current yield,

$$\begin{aligned}(\text{NET-CURYLD}) &= (\text{P-CURYLD}) - (\text{H-CURYLD}) \\ &= (0.0567) - (0.0744) \\ &= -0.0177\end{aligned}$$

Now all these values can be inserted into the NET-FVPD expression,

$$\begin{aligned}\text{NET-FVPD} &= [\tfrac{1}{2} \times (\text{NET-CURYLD}) \times S_w] \\ &\quad + [(\text{NET-PR-RET-AMORT})] \\ &\quad + [-(\text{NET-AMORT-VOL}) \times (\text{H-YLD-MOVE})] \\ &\quad + [-(\text{P-AMORT-VOL}) \times (\text{NET-YLD-MOVE})] \\ &= [\tfrac{1}{2} \times (-0.0177) \times 11.464] + [0.0898] \\ &\quad + [-(-0.0002895) \times (-20)] \\ &\quad + [-(0.0008505) \times (-60)] \\ &= [-0.1015] + [0.0898] + [-0.0058] + [0.0510] \\ &= 0.0335\end{aligned}$$

In other words, over the five-year workout period, the swap would have provided, under the assumptions given, an incremental improvement of 3.35 percent in future value. It is interesting to see how this improvement is derived relative to the swap classification system discussed in the preceding section. The swap actually gives up 177 basis points of current yield, and this accumulates to a −10.15 percent loss in future value per dollar. This current yield give-up is offset by a 8.98 percent pickup in amortized principal value, so that the net loss in the pure yield pickup component is only −1.17 percent over the five years. The swap leads to a reduced amortized volatility. This lowers the exposure to the risk of rate anticipation effects in general. However, in this particular case, the shared yield move is downward, so that the reduced rate anticipation exposure works against the swap, resulting in a relative loss of 0.58 percent. At the same time, there is a strong net yield *spread* move of 60 basis points. When coupled with the P-bond's effective volatility, this net yield move results in a 5.10 percent improvement in future value.

In all likelihood, this swap would have been undertaken as an intermarket spread swap. As we saw from the foregoing, it is the *net yield spread* move which makes the swap work out favorably in the face of a known yield give-up at the outset and a slightly unfavorable *shared* yield move. Because of the crucial importance of this change in yield spread relationships, it is worthwhile examining how each component spread move affected the swap's overall net yield spread move.

Both the general market for both the P- and H-bond underwent the same 40 basis point decline over the workout period. This market movement affected both bonds equally and consequently had no impact on their yield spread relationship.

With respect to the yield curve yield spread, the 30-year H-bond went from a 0 basis point market-to-maturity spread to a −10 basis point spread at the workout time. The 15-year P-bond, on the other hand, began with −20 basis point spread under the 30-year market rate, and then rolled down the yield curve to a −50 basis point spread as a 10-year bond. This −30 basis point P-bond move exceeded the H-bond's move by −20 basis points. This shows the potentially major impact of such yield curve effects over intermediate length workout periods.

The yield-curve-to-sector spread for the H-bond increased by 25 basis points as the current coupon market moved down towards the H-bond's 7 percent coupon level. For the P-bond, this sector spread was assumed to decrease by −15 basis points over the workout period. This leads to a −40 basis point net change in these spread relationships, thereby accounting for the majority of the swap's net yield spread move.

Both the H-bond and the P-bond were assumed to undergo a +5 basis points as the current coupon market moved down towards the moves would cancel out and hence would have no impact on the net yield move.

GLOSSARY OF SYMBOLS

A-FV	Bond A's estimated future value per $1,000 bond as of the workout time.
A-FVPD	Bond A's future value per (invested) dollar.
A-PR	Present market cost of bond A.
AMORT-VOL	The amortized volatility, i.e., the approximate fractional return per basis point of a yield move over the workout period.
B-FV	Bond B's estimated future value per bond as of the workout time.
B-FVPD	Bond B's future value per (invested) dollar.
B-PR	Present market cost of bond B.
C	Coupon rate expressed as an annual percentage, e.g., $C = 7.00$ percent implies that for each $1,000 bond, the holder receives $70 per year in two semiannual payments of $35 each.
CH-YLD-MKT	Increase in the market yield level (YLD-MKT) over the workout period (in basis points).
CH-YLD-SPRD-IND	Increase in the yield spread relationship (YLD-SPRD-IND) between the individual bond and its appropriate sector indicator over the workout period (in basis points).
CH-YLD-SPRD-MAT	Increase in the maturity-adjustment yield spread (YLD-SPRD-MAT) over the workout period (in basis points).

CH-YLD-SPRD-SECT	Increase in the sector yield spread (YLD-SPRD-SECT) over the workout period.
COUP-FLOW	Cash flow from direct coupon payments.
CURYLD	The bond's current yield, expressed as a fraction.
FV	Bond's total future value as of the workout time.
FVPD	Future value per (invested) dollar.
FVPP	Future value of $1 per period (see S_w).
H	Prefix referring to the H-bond.
H-Bond	The bond presently held in the portfolio.
H-CURYLD	The H-bond's current yield.
H-FV	H-bond's future value per bond as of the workout time.
H-FVPD	H-bond's future value per (invested) dollar.
H-PR	Market (bid) value of the H-bond.
IRR	Internal rate of return.
NET	A prefix generally indicating the swap improvement.
NET-AMORT-VOL	The increase in amortized volatility (AMORT-VOL) resulting from the swap.
NET-CURYLD	The improvement in fractional current yield resulting from a swap out of the H-bond and into the P-bond.
NET-FVPD	The improvement in future value per (invested) dollar resulting from the swap.
NET-PR-RET-AMORT	The improvement in the amortization return resulting from a swap out of the H-bond into the P-bond.
NET-YLD-MOVE	The basis-point difference by which the P-bond's yield move exceeds the H-bond's yield move.
P	A prefix referring to the P-bond.
P-Bond	The bond proposed for purchase.
P-CURYLD	The P-bond's current yield.
P-FV	P-bond's future value per bond as of the workout time.
P-FVPD	P-bond's future value per (invested) dollar.
PR	Present market value per bond.
PR-CH	Increase in market value per bond over the workout period.
PR-CH-AMORT	Increase in market value per bond which is due to constant yield amortization over the workout period.
PR-CH(YLD-MOVE)	Increase in bond's market value per bond resulting from a yield change of magnitude YLD-MOVE over the workout period.
PR-RET	Increase in market value over the workout period, expressed as a fractional return per dollar invested.
PR-RET-AMORT	Increase in bond's market value as a result of constant yield amortization over the workout period, expressed as a fractional return per dollar invested.
PR-RET(YLD-MOVE)	Increase in bond's market value resulting from a yield change of magnitude YLD-MOVE over the workout period, expressed as a fractional return per dollar invested.
%PR-RET(YLD-MOVE)	PR-RET(YLD-MOVE) expressed as percentage.
PR(WORKOUT)	Bond's principal value as of the workout time.
PV	Present value per bond.
PVPD	Present value per (invested) dollar.

R	The reinvestment rate expressed as a fraction per semiannual period, e.g., a 6.00 percent rate corresponds to $R = 0.03$.
RCY	Realized compound yield.
S_w	Future value after w periods of a stream of $1 payments received at the end of each period and then reinvested and compounded at the specified rate.
TV(COUP-FLOW)	The future value of the coupon flow as of the workout time, including interest-on-interest when coupon receipts have been reinvested (or time-valued) at some specified compounding rate.
U	Trial discount rate.
VOL	An approximation for percentage price change per basis point of yield move (always expressed as a positive number regardless of the direction of the price change).
W	Number of semiannual periods in the workout period.
$\frac{W}{2}$	Number of years in the workout period.
YLD-IND	Yield level of an individual security.
YLD-MKT	Yield level of the market indicator appropriate for the individual security in question.
YLD-MOVE	The increase in the bond's yield over the workout period, expressed in basis points.
YLD-SPRD-IND	The basis-point spread by which the bond's yield exceeds the yield level of the appropriate sector indicator.
YLD-SPRD-MAT	The basis-point spread by which the market yield curve point for the particular bond's maturity exceeds the yield level of the general market indicator.
YLD-SPRD-SECT	The basis-point spread by which the yield level of an appropriate indicator for the bond's sector exceeds the maturity-adjusted market yield level.

10

Analysis of Convertible Bonds

MARTIN L. LEIBOWITZ, Ph.D.
Vice President and Director of Investment Systems
Salomon Brothers
New York, New York

The Structure of a Convertible Security

CONVERTIBLE BONDS and convertible preferreds have many common features, and we shall combine much of our discussion by referring to both bonds and preferreds as *convertible securities.*

A convertible bond or preferred stock is simply a bond or a preferred stock, often of junior grade, with a conversion feature. The conversion feature is usually formulated as an option granting the investor the right to exchange, at any time of his choosing, each of his convertible securities for a fixed number of the company's common shares. There are many possible variations upon this simple scheme. The exchange ratio (or *conversion ratio* as it is sometimes called) can change over time, either stepping up or stepping down according to some prescribed schedule. The exchange ratio might be determined in some fashion which is dependent on the price movement of the common. The exchange option need not be continuous throughout time. For example, the right to convert may be restricted to certain dates within the calendar year (a constraint frequently found among British convertibles). The conversion right might terminate after a certain time prior to the security's maturity. Or, the right to convert might be deferred for a certain period. The exchange could require a further pay-up of either cash or fixed interest securities. One could go on and on citing actual and theoretical variations upon the basic conversion concept.

This section will deal primarily with convertible bonds. However, it should be noted that while both types of convertibles have a number of common features, there are significant differences as has been summarized by T. C. Noddings.

Safety. Since bondholder claims to a company's assets are senior to those of preferred stockholders, bonds are inherently safer, all other factors considered to be equal. This distinction may be of little consequence if the company is financially sound. For a speculative company, however, it may be of major importance.

Interest and Dividend Payments. Like common stocks, preferred dividends are paid quarterly and the market price of the preferred will reflect a pending dividend. On the "ex-date," the price of the preferred stock will normally decline by the amount of the dividend.

When a bond is purchased, the buyer pays the seller the interest which has accrued since the last payment date. This expense is recouped at the next semiannual interest payment date. The bondholder, in effect, receives daily interest on his investment regardless of the time period held.

Maturity. Since bonds have a fixed maturity date, they must ultimately be redeemed by the company at par value. An approaching maturity date provides additional protection against broad price swings caused by interest rate changes. It may also protect the convertible bond against a serious price decline by the common stock without limiting its upside potential. Preferred stocks have no fixed maturity date and are therefore more sensitive to changing market conditions.

Continuity of Payments. During adverse times, a company will suspend dividends on its preferred stock before discontinuing bond interest payments—the failure of a company to meet bond interest obligations places it in default, the first step toward bankruptcy.

Even though the dividends paid on preferred stock are usually cumulative (arrearages must be made up before dividends are paid to common shareholders) the holder of preferred stock may have a long wait before receiving his dividends, once suspended. Eventually, he may even have to accept some sort of exchange offer from the company and may, therefore, never see the dividend arrearages paid.

Brokerage Commissions. The buyer of preferred stock pays the same commission rate as for common stocks. The commission charged on bonds is currently only $5 per bond (there is usually a $25 minimum). Bond commissions are, therefore, almost always lower than for preferred stocks and often the difference may be quite substantial.

Margin Buying. Historically, buyers of securities on margin were able to purchase convertible bonds at substantially lower margin rates than common or preferred stocks. The differential, however, has narrowed in recent years and is presently 50 percent for convertible bonds and 65 percent for preferred stocks or common stocks.

Tax Consequences. Dividends paid on preferred stocks (or common stocks) possess unique tax advantages over interest received from bonds. Bond interest is fully taxable as ordinary income whereas the first $100 of annual dividends is excluded on individual tax returns ($200 on joint returns).

The tax advantage to corporations is even greater as they are permitted to exclude 85 percent of the dividends received on most preferreds and common stocks. These tax benefits have historically kept the yields of straight preferreds close to bonds despite the greater safety of the bond.

Bond interest paid is a tax deductible expense to the issuing corporation whereas dividends paid on common or preferred stocks must come from after-tax earnings.

Call Provisions. The call price is the price at which a company may "buy back" a security if it desires to do so. Calls on convertibles are usually made to force conversion into the company's common stock. This occurs when the conversion value and hence the market price of the convertible is above the call price. Holders of the convertible must then convert rather than accept the lower value of the call price upon redemption.[1]

The convertible bond has the character of a fixed interest security. It will provide scheduled fixed payments of interest or dividends. The company is liable for the full amount of these payments whether or not they are earned. Consequently, as long as the company maintains its financial ability to discharge its debt obligations, the convertible will retain a certain investment value as a fixed interest instrument. This investment value can be viewed as the hypothetical price that the convertible would command if it lost its conversion feature and sold as a straight bond. This view forms the basis for the popular concept of the convertible's investment value acting as a sort of rigid "floor," i.e., as setting a lower level for the price of the convertible, regardless of the price action of the underlying common stock.

The Convertible's Response Pattern

Figure 1 illustrates how the market price of a convertible bond might be expected to respond to changing price levels in the underlying common stock. (For the sake of clarity, the remaining discussion will be framed in terms of convertible bonds. The translation of these discussions and formulas to the case of convertible preferreds is quite straightforward.)

As Figure 1 shows, when the common price is very depressed, the value of the conversion feature will be minimal, and the price of the convertible will be essentially that of a straight bond. As the common price level improves, the conversion feature becomes increasingly valuable because of both the direct increased value of the underlying common stock and the enhanced prospects for further growth in the common price.

At higher common price levels, the convertible approaches the value of the common stock into which it is convertible, and there is little extra value accorded to its fixed interest characteristics. These fixed interest characteristics become somewhat diluted at these higher levels. The

[1] Thomas C. Noddings, *Dow Jones-Irwin Guide to Convertible Securities* (Homewood, Ill.: Dow Jones-Irwin, 1973).

convertible's current yield and yield to maturity are now much lower than that available on straight bonds or preferreds. It is now a long way down to the investment value "floor." And the threat of call may loom, which would essentially force the investor to exercise the conversion at current price levels, and thereby lose any premium value associated with the conversion feature.

In a general way, Figure 1 is reasonably descriptive. However, in practice, such neat diagrams can easily prove a little too pat and possibly even lead the analyst into a trap. An investment value is a somewhat intangible concept at the best of times, yet its estimate becomes significant only under the worst of times. Thus, an estimate of investment value is often made when the company and its stock appear to be reasonably attractive—at least attractive enough for the company and its convertible to be considered as viable investment candidates. Suppose that the analyst constructed a response curve based on such an estimate of the investment value as a floor. If the common stock price should then plunge, either through general market deterioration and/or a dimming of the company's prospects and/or the effects of very high interest rates, then these combined adverse circumstances might invalidate the original estimate of the investment value at the very time when a rigid floor would be most needed.

More generally, it could be argued that the convertible's response curve on the way up might be significantly different from its shape on the way down.

The Convertible as a Stock Substitute

The dual structure of the convertible allows many different approaches to evaluating its investment merits. However, most institutional portfolio managers approach convertible securities as a relatively defensive alternative vehicle for taking a commitment in the underlying common stock. The analysis in this article will be focused on this viewpoint as a stock substitute, as opposed to that of the arbitrageur or the bond portfolio manager seeking an equity "kicker."

One often hears portfolio managers say that they cannot (or would not) consider an investment in a given convertible security unless they or their institution were favorably inclined toward the company itself and the underlying common stock. For such investors, the possibility of a convertible purchase exists only as a direct alternative to a pure equity position. Consequently, the convertible's return relative to the equity alternative provides a simple and clear-cut framework for analysis.

The Conversion Premium

The convertible has attraction as a stock substitute for three basic reasons: (1) a generally higher current yield than the underlying common, (2) a higher quality of yield, and (3) the greater resistance to price declines as exemplified in Figure 1.

In order to obtain these incremental benefits, the investor must generally pay a premium above and beyond the market value of the underlying common stock. This *conversion premium* is usually defined as a percentage value, and it is one of the key measures used in the convertible market. Its value at a given time, the relationship of this value to past values, and its estimated response to common stock movements all enter critically into the convertible's investment equation.

To characterize these concepts more precisely, let us define the following symbols:

N = The exchange ratio, i.e., the number of shares of common stock received upon conversion.

S = Common stock price per share.

$SV = N \times S$ = Parity value (sometimes called the stock value or conversion value), i.e., the market value of the common stock that would be obtained if the conversion were to be immediately exercised.

C = The convertible security's cost *per unit* (i.e., the price per share for convertible preferreds or the price of a bond of $1,000 par amount. Note that the conventionally quoted *dollar price* of a bond would then be given by ($C/10$).

The *dollar premium, PD,* can then be defined as the amount by which the convertible's price exceeds its parity value, i.e.,

$$PD = C - SV.$$

The *percentage conversion premium, P,* is then defined as this dollar premium as a percentage of parity,

$$P = 100\% \times (PD/SV).$$

Alternately, one can express the premium as

$$\begin{aligned} P &= 100\%\left[\frac{(C - SV)}{SV}\right] \\ &= 100\%[(C/SV) - 1] \\ &= 100\%\left(\frac{1}{N}\right) \times \left(\frac{C}{S}\right) - 1]. \end{aligned}$$

This last expression shows how the premium depends critically on the ratio of the convertible price to the common price.

The Response Pattern of the Conversion Premium

If the convertible price responds to stock movements in accordance with Figure 1, then the premium would respond as shown in Figure 2. As the stock price rises, at some point the parity value will exceed the

The Response Curve of the Percentage Conversion Premium

FIGURE 1

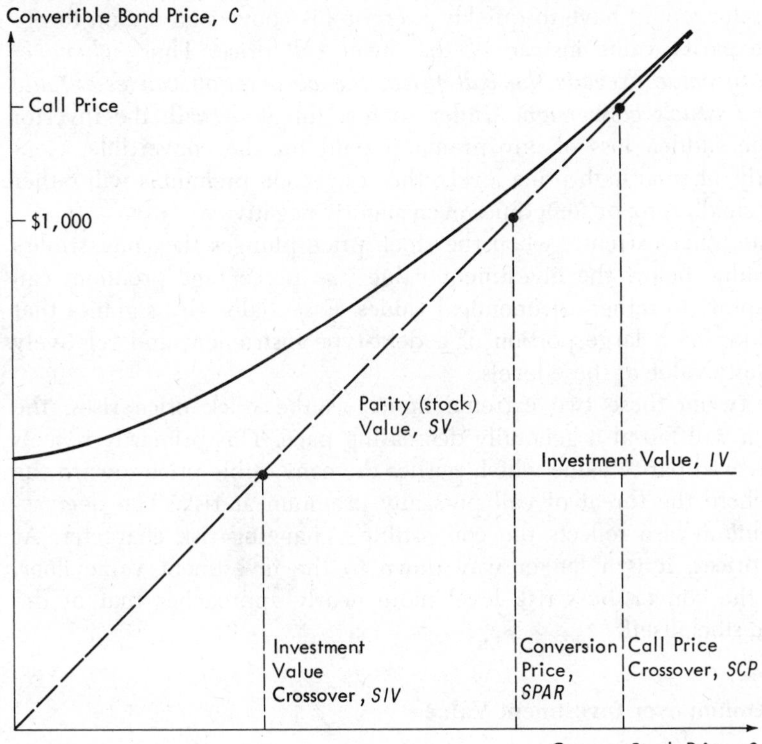

FIGURE 2

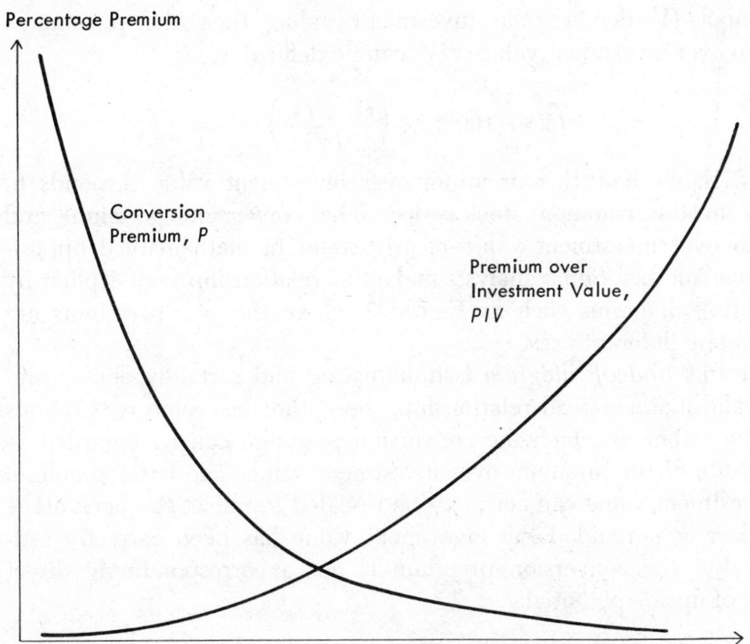

bond's call price. At this point, if the corporation were to call the issue, the investor would have to quickly exercise his conversion option to obtain the parity value instead of the lower call price. Thus, *whenever the parity value exceeds the call price, the corporation can essentially force the issue's conversion.* Under such a threat of call, the investor faces the sudden loss of any premium paid for the convertible. Consequently, at such high price levels, the conversion premiums will either be very small, zero, or sometimes even slightly negative.

At the other extreme, when the stock price plunges the convertible's parity value below the investment value, the percentage premium can grow rapidly to rather astronomical values. Essentially, this signifies that one is burying a large portion of a debt-type instrument and relatively little equity value at these levels.

In between these two extreme limits, as the stock price rises, the premium will fall at a generally decreasing pace. This primarily reflects the increased parity value which pushes the convertible price toward the point where the threat of call puts any premium at risk. The decreasing premium also reflects the convertible's changing risk character. At higher prices, it is a longer way down to the investment value floor, and so the convertible's risk level more nearly approaches that of the common stock itself.

The Premium over Investment Value

The convertible's changing risk characteristics can be further quantified in terms of a "percentage premium over the investment value." If the symbol *IV* denotes the investment value, then the percentage premium over investment value, *PIV*, can be defined as

$$PIV = 100\% \times \left(\frac{C - IV}{IV}\right).$$

Figure 2 shows how this premium over investment value responds to changes in the common stock price. The conversion premium and premium over investment value clearly stand in mathematical opposition to one another. Some analysts make this relationship very explicit by constructing diagrams such as Figure 3 where the two premiums are plotted along different axes.

While this *tradeoff diagram* is illuminating and certainly does represent a valid mathematical relationship, the author has some reservations about the extent to which the conversion premium can be regarded as the opposite of the premium over investment value. The latter premium over investment value can certainly be rescaled to reflect the percentage downside risk (provided the investment value has been correctly estimated), but the conversion premium is not a correspondingly direct measure of upside potential.

FIGURE 3

The Tradeoff between the Premium over Investment Value and the Conversion Premium

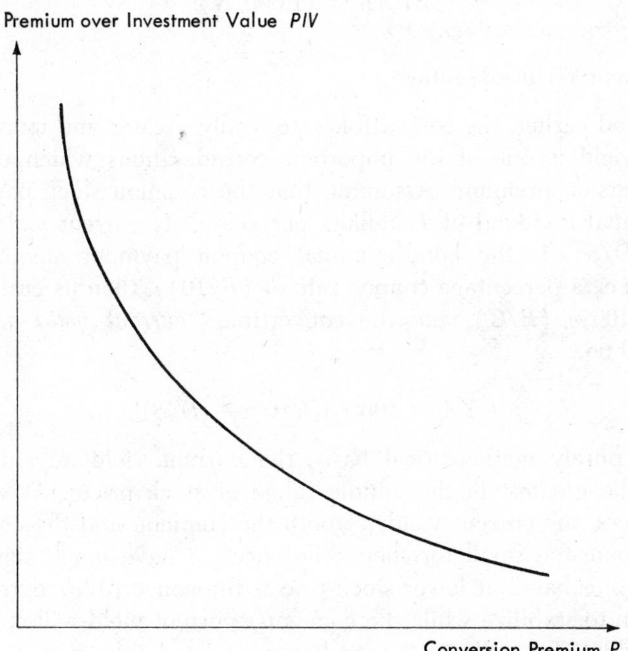

Key Convertible Levels in Terms of the Stock Price

Figures 1 and 2 illustrate how the key equity and debt characteristics of the convertible depend upon the underlying common stock price. One might therefore think that investors would want to see the convertible's *extreme points*, i.e., the investment value and the call price, expressed in terms of the corresponding common stock prices. Curiously, this is rarely done, although these price levels could be defined quite simply. For example, we might define the *investment value cross-over* to be that stock price *SIV*, where the convertible's parity value equals its investment value,

$$SIV = (IV/N).$$

Similarly, the *call price cross-over* could be defined to be that stock price *SCP*, where the convertible's parity value just equals the call price *CP*,

$$SCP = (CP/N).$$

The one figure which is commonly quoted in terms of the stock price is the *conversion price*. For a convertible bond, this is the nominal stock price at which the bond's $1,000 par value can be converted into equity. In other words, if *SPAR* is the conversion price, then

$$SPAR = (1{,}000/N).$$

The Current Yield Advantage

As noted earlier, the convertible's generally greater and more assured current yield is one of the important considerations which determine the conversion premium. Assuming that the common stock pays a constant annual dividend of D dollars per share, its current yield will be 100% (D/S). If the bond's annual coupon payment amounts to R dollars (i.e., a percentage coupon rate of $(R/10)$), then its current yield will be 100% (R/C), and the convertible's *current yield advantage, CYA,* will be

$$CYA = 100\%\,[(R/C) - (D/S)].$$

On a purely mathematical basis, the current yield advantage may actually be greatest in the middle range of stock prices. At very high stock prices, the current yields of both the common and the convertible may become too small for their differences to have much significance. On the other hand, at lower stock prices, the convertible's current yield will begin to stabilize while the common's current yield will continue to rise rapidly. This will result in a lower, and possibly even a negative, current yield advantage. This latter situation is often somewhat hypothetical, since when the stock price plunges into the depths, the assumption that dividend levels will remain constant may be dubious at best.

The current yield advantage bears quite directly upon the magnitude of the conversion premium. Consider a dollar-for-dollar swap from the common into the convertible. For each share of common sold, S dollars are received which can be used to purchase (S/C) units of the convertible. Each convertible unit has a dollar premium over conversion value of

$$PD = (C - N \times S),$$

so that the total premium cost per share of common sold is

$$(S/C) \times PD = (S/C) \times (C - N \times S).$$

In terms of current income, each share of common sold means foregoing an annual dividend of D in return for R dollars of coupon payments from each of the (S/C) bonds purchased. The dollar-for-dollar swap, therefore, increases the current income by the annual amount,

$$\begin{aligned}(S/C) \times R - D &= S \times [R/C - D/S] \\ &= S \times (CYA/100),\end{aligned}$$

which is just the dollar price of the common shares sold times the current yield advantage.

Break-even Times for a Dollar-for-Dollar Swap

Break-even times are perhaps the most common evaluative measures used in dealing with convertible securities. The objective is to try to determine how long it takes for the convertible's current yield advantage to recoup the disadvantage of the conversion premium. A low break-even time is taken as an inducement for the investor to swap from the common into the convertible.

The concept of break-even time is so fundamental and so apparently simple that it seems to have been deemed unworthy of discussion in the literature. Actually, there are at least three different break-even formulas which can be used, each of which may give quite significantly different results!

The first break-even time formula arises from the straightforward dollar-for-dollar swap. For each share of common, the total dollar premium purchased was above shown to be $(S/C) \times PD$. This premium amount would be recouped by the current yield advantage after a period of B years where,

$$B = \frac{(S/C) \times PD}{S \times (CYA/100)}$$

$$= \frac{(PD/C)}{(CYA/100)}$$

The numerator in this ratio is the dollar premium divided by the convertible's price and may, therefore, be viewed as the number of pennies of *premium component* per dollar invested in the convertible. This turns out to be a most useful alternative measure of the conversion premium, so let us formally define the percentage premium component PC to be

$$PC = 100\% \times (PD/C).$$

The preceding break-even time can then be expressed simply as $B = (PC/CYA)$.

If the premium paid is viewed as somehow representing a risk element, then after B years, the convertible's current yield advantage will have recouped this amount at risk. For example, the premium loss resulting from forced conversion would have been covered. Another way of looking at this popular break-even time concept is that the investor could take the accumulated incremental income and purchase a dollar amount of equity equal to his original give-up of equity. If the common stock price remains unchanged over this period, then this purchase would put the investor back into his original common stock position in terms of number of shares held directly and/or indirectly through the convertible. At the same time, he would continue to enjoy the convertible's defensive and higher yielding characteristics. The basic problem with this model is, of course, the presumption that the stock price will wait patiently at the same level throughout the break-even period.

Break-even Times for an Equity Maintenance (Pay-up) Swap

An alternative approach is to consider a pay-up swap which maintains the original equity interest from the outset. Here, the investor adds an amount of cash equal to the dollar premium and uses it to purchase additional common stock. For each share of stock originally sold, the investor would then have a holding consisting of (S/C) convertible units and

$$\frac{[(S/C) \times PD]}{S} = \frac{PD}{C}$$

shares of common stock. His total equity interest would then consist of the number of shares represented by the parity value of his convertible holding, $(S/C) \times N$, plus his outright stock purchases for a total of

$$\begin{aligned}(S/C) \times N + (PD/C) &= (S/C) \times N + \frac{[C - (N \times S)]}{C} \\ &= (1/C)[S \times N + C - N \times S] \\ &= (1/C)[C] \\ &= 1\end{aligned}$$

The investor has thus received a net one share equity interest for every share originally sold, i.e., his equity interest has been maintained. At this point, the incremental income from the swap is often computed to be the convertible income, $(S/C) \times R$, plus the dividends from his additional stock purchase,

$$\left(\frac{PD}{C}\right) \times D$$

less the annual dividend D on the original common share sold, i.e., the incremental income would then be

$$\begin{aligned}\left(\frac{S}{C}\right) \times R + \left(\frac{PD}{C}\right) - D &= \left(\frac{S}{C}\right) \times R + \left(\frac{[C - (N \times S)]}{C}\right) \times D - D \\ &= \left(\frac{S}{C}\right) \times R - \left(\frac{S}{C}\right) \times (N \times D) \\ &= \left(\frac{S}{C}\right) \times [R - (N \times D)].\end{aligned}$$

With this formula for the incremental income, the premium pay-up would be recovered in BPE years,

$$BPE = \frac{(S/C) \times PD}{(S/C) \times [R - (N \times D)]} = \frac{PD}{R - N \times D}.$$

This is an appealingly simple computation, and this may be the reason for its fairly common use. However, it has one rather serious problem in that it fails to accord any alternative opportunity value to the cash pay-up. After all, the cash used to effect the pay-up could have alternatively been invested in some fixed interest instrument having a percentage yield of I per year. The incremental income from the swap would then consist of the convertible coupons, $(S/C) \times R$, plus the dividends from the additional stock purchase,

$$\left(\frac{PD}{C}\right) \times D,$$

less the sum of the original stock dividend D and the alternative interest from the cash payup,

$$(S/C) \times PD \times (I/100),$$

for a net incremental income of

$$\begin{aligned}
&(S/C) \times R + (S/C) \times (PD/S) \times D - D - (S/C) \times PD \times (I/100) \\
&= (S/C) \times [R + (PD/S) \times D - PD \times (I/100)] - D \\
&= (S/C) \times [R + PD(D/S - I/100)] - D \\
&= S/C\,[R + (C - NS) \times (D/S - I/100)] - D \\
&= S/C\,[R - ND - (C - NS) \times (I/100)].
\end{aligned}$$

Consequently, a more reasonable appraisal of the break-even time under a pay-up or equity maintenance swap model would be

$$BP = \frac{(S/C) \times PD}{(S/C)[R - ND - PD \times (I/100)]} = \frac{PD}{R - ND - PD(I/100)}.$$

This formula corresponds to the erroneous pay-up break-even time formula BPE when $I = 0$. It can also be shown to equate to the dollar-for-dollar break-even time formula B when the interest rate I is set equal to the stock's current yield.

The above expression for BP shows how the higher the available interest rate I, the longer will be the break-even time for a given premium. Turning it around, one might say that, for these break-even times to remain reasonably constant, the premiums would have to be smaller during times of higher interest rates. (These interest rates for alternative use of the cash pay-up should perhaps be distinguished from the longer term yield levels which determine the bond's investment value.)

For more complete accuracy, both break-even time models should really incorporate the effects of the compounded reinvestment of the incremental income. However, these models are generally used only when the convertible is selling fairly high in its price range, i.e., well above the investment floor. Under such conditions, the break-even time will be fairly short and hence reinvestment effects are not generally very significant.

The break-even time is a popular concept, and it can be quite useful as a sort of reasonability measure for the premium "per unit of current yield advantage." However, it is essentially a static measure and fails to reflect many of the key dynamic factors involved in using the convertible as a stock substitute.

Total Return over Time

A convertible security's total return can be viewed in terms of three primary factors: (1) coupon income, (2) gain in parity value, and (3) changes in the conversion premium. (This is not a complete list. There are a number of secondary factors which should be considered, such as the direct effects of changing interest rates on the investment value, coupon reinvestment, amortization of the investment value, and possible sinking-fund activity.)

If we let *CRPD* denote the convertible's gain per dollar of original investment over a holding period of T years, then

$$CRPD = \frac{T \times R + (C' - C)}{C}$$

$$= T(R/C) + (C'/C) - 1,$$

where C' represents the convertible's price at the end of the holding period. Now let S' symbolize the stock price at this point. Next, let $P_T(S')$ correspond to the percentage premium response curve (as a function of the stock price S') expected at the time T, i.e., $P_T(S')$ is the future normal premium curve. Then by the definition of the percentage premium,

$$P_T(S') = \frac{100\%(C' - N \times S')}{NS'},$$

and we can write

$$C' = (P_T(S')/100) \times N \times S' + N \times S'.$$

However, the current premium level may be aberrantly high or low relative to today's normal premium curve. If $P_o(S)$ represents today's normal curve, then one can express the actual premium in terms of this curve value plus an aberration from that curve value,

$$P = P_o(S) + [P - P_o(S)],$$

and today's convertible price then becomes

$$C = (P/100) \times N \times S + NS$$
$$= (1/100)\{P_o(S) + [P - P_o(S)]\} \times NS + NS.$$

Over the period T, the convertible's price change then becomes

$$C' - C = (1/100) \times P_T(S') \times N \times S' + N \times S'$$
$$- (1/100) \times \{P_o(S) + [P - P_o(S)]\} \times N \times S - N \times S$$
$$= (1/100) \times [P_T(S') \times N \times S' - P_o(S) \times N \times S]$$
$$+ (1/100) \times [P_o(S) - P] \times N \times S + N[S' - S].$$

In the above equation, the first term represents the change in the normal (dollar) premium due to stock price move and/or a change in the normal premium curve over time. The second term is the return from the presumed unwinding of the current aberrant premium. Finally, the third term reflects the direct change in parity value.

This situation can be represented graphically as shown in Figure 4 where the convertible's return per dollar is plotted against the stock price for holding periods of $T = 1$ year, $T = 2$ years, and so on. The first ele-

FIGURE 4
The Convertible's "Orbits" of Total Return per Dollar Invested

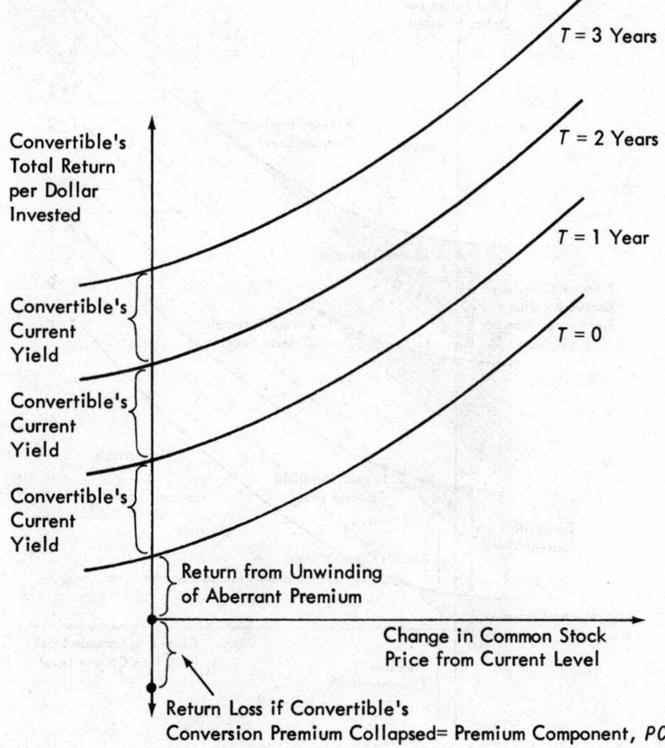

ment of return is the aberrant premium which is shown here as being recouped in fairly short order. Then the return follows a rescaled version of the convertible price response curve depicted in Figure 1. With the passage of time, the curve shifts upward with accumulation of the convertible current yield.

The common stock return has only two primary sources of return: (1) principal appreciation and (2) dividends. Consequently, the equity's return per invested dollar is just

$$SRPD = \frac{T \times D + (S' - S)}{S}$$
$$= T \times (D/S) + (S'/S) - 1.$$

Plotted graphically, the equity's return is just a series of 45-degree straight lines, shifting upward by the magnitude of the annual dividend yield. With proper rescaling, these parallel return lines can be superimposed on the convertible's pattern of return over time (Figure 4). This superimposition is shown in Figure 5. The convertible and stock returns

FIGURE 5

Comparison of Returns from Convertible versus Common Stock

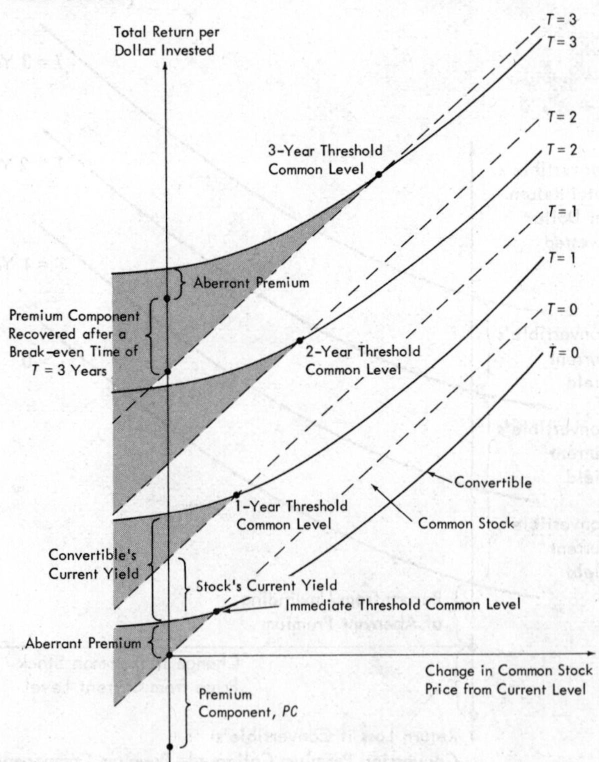

for a given holding period, i.e., for the same T value, are directly comparable in this graph. The shaded portion indicates the stock price region where the convertible provides the greater relative return.

This graphic presentation also affords some insights into the limitations of the dollar-for-dollar break-even time. Suppose the convertible premium collapsed to nothing at the outset. Then the convertible's return per dollar invested would become

$$\begin{aligned} CRPD &= o \times (R/C) + (NS/C) - 1 \\ &= \frac{(NS - C)}{C} \\ &= \frac{-(C - NS)}{C} \\ &= -(PC/100), \end{aligned}$$

i.e., just the negative of the premium component PC. The dollar-for-dollar break-even time B was earlier shown to be

$$B = \frac{(PC)}{(CYA)},$$

or

$$B \times (100\%) \times [(R/C) - (D/S)] = PC.$$

Now assume that the common price and the convertible premium remain unchanged (i.e., $S' = S$ and $C' = C$), then the convertible's relative return advantage over time is derived solely from the accumulating current yield advantage,

$$\begin{aligned} CRPD - SRPD &= [T \times (R/C) + C'/C - 1] - [T \times (D/S) + S'/S - 1] \\ &= T \times [(R/C) - (D/S)]. \end{aligned}$$

Under these highly restricted circumstances, when the current yield advantage accumulating over time T reaches the level PC, then

$$\begin{aligned} PC &= CRPD - SRPD \\ &= T[(R/C) - (D/S)] \end{aligned}$$

and so this time T must be the break-even time B.

In this context of the dynamics of total return as shown in Figure 5, the break-even time is seen to constitute a rather limited view of the overall investment problem.

The Threshold Common Level

As Figure 5 illustrates, for each holding period T, there is always one common price at which the equity's return begins to exceed the return from the convertible. As the stock price falls below the *threshold common level,* the convertible's return becomes increasingly attractive relative to the return on the common. Thus, for a given investment horizon, the one question is the magnitude of the expected stock price move. If the stock is expected to rise above the threshold common level, then the common stock itself would be the better vehicle. On the other hand, if there were considerable doubt as to the stock price reaching the threshold common level by the first time horizon, then the convertible should be considered as a strong alternative route for participating in the equity prospects. In terms of possible adverse stock price moves, both the convertible's de-leveraging and the accumulating current yield advantage, of course, work to reduce the investor's downside risk. In an actual investment situation, the uncertainties regarding future premium curves as well as the stock price projections must be factored into the decision framework.

Figure 5 illustrates the key importance of the interrelationships among the factors of accumulating current yield over time, changing premiums, and stock price movements. Any dollar-for-dollar swap from an equity position into the convertible with a positive premium leads to a certain "de-leveraging." An instantaneous upward movement in stock price will almost always induce a lower percentage move in the convertible. However, with the passage of time, the convertible with a current yield advantage builds up a cushion of accumulated return. This income cushion may be supplemented or reduced by the unwinding of any aberrant premium. The resulting "cushion of return" compensates for this de-leveraging effect, and the stock price must undergo an increasingly larger upward move before reaching the threshold common level. For this reason, the longer the investor's horizon and the more modest his expectations for the growth rate of the common stock price, the stronger becomes the case for using the convertible as an alternative vehicle to a pure equity position.

As Figure 5 shows, the threshold common level will tend to grow over time, provided that the convertible enjoys a positive current yield advantage at the outset. In fact, over longer investment horizons, this growth may become quite rapid. A typical time pattern for the threshold common level is shown in Figure 6. The range of expectations regarding the behavior of the stock price over time can then be superimposed upon this time plot, also as shown in Figure 6. From such analyses, one can see that the same premium curve assumption might lead one investor to stay fully leveraged in an equity position while a second investor, with a somewhat longer term or more conservative view, should de-leverage his position into the convertible.

Short-Term Opportunities

The actual price action of the common stock as well as that of the convertible can provide many short-term opportunities even for the

FIGURE 6

The Threshold Common Level over Time

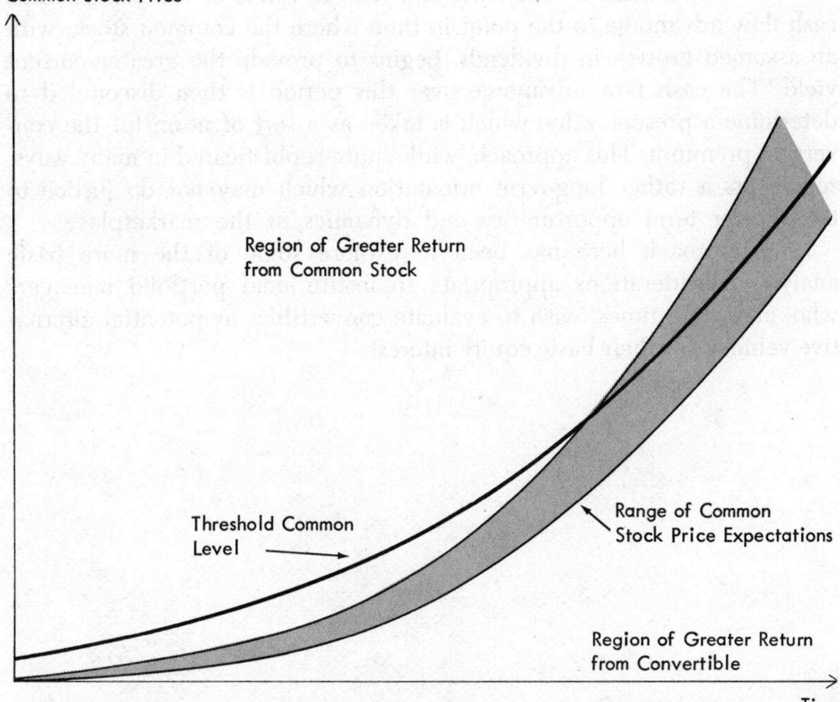

basically long-term equity investor. For the exact same assumptions regarding future premium curves, changes in the common stock price will lead to radical shifts in the threshold common levels. These shifts may provide clear signals for a corresponding shift from the convertibles back into the common, or vice versa. On the other hand, changes in the convertible prices may lead to aberrant conversion premiums whose effects can be either avoided or used to advantage. By astute tracking of such short-term price movements, there may be a whole sequence of profitable interim convertible-to-common-stock moves and reversals, even for an intrinsically long-term investor within the framework of a basically stable equity outlook.

Other Approaches

There are a number of other ways of analyzing convertible securities. For example, a convertible can be decomposed into a bond with attached implicit warrants. This decomposition has the virtue of enabling the theory of option pricing to be brought to bear.

Quite a different tactic is taken in the London market. There, the conversion premium is commonly analyzed in terms of the convertible's cash flow advantage to the point in time where the common stock, with an assumed growth in dividends, begins to provide the greater current yield. The cash flow advantage over this period is then discounted to determine a present value which is taken as a sort of norm for the conversion premium. This approach, while quite sophisticated in many ways, represents a rather long-term orientation which may not do justice to the shorter term opportunities and dynamics of the marketplace.

Our approach here has been to explore some of the more basic analytic considerations appropriate to institutional portfolio managers who, at certain times, wish to evaluate convertibles as potential alternative vehicles for their basic equity interests.

11

U.S. Government Securities, Federal Agencies, and International Obligations

IRA O. SCOTT, JR., Ph.D.
Executive Vice President
Savings Banks Association of New York State
New York, New York

U.S. Government Debt

AT THE APEX of the U.S. capital market stands the market for U.S. government securities; in Great Britain, government bonds are referred to as "gilt-edge." At the end of fiscal 1973, the total debt subject to statutory limitation amounted to $459,958 million (Table 1). Present-day authority to issue direct obligations of the U.S. Treasury was conferred upon the secretary of the treasury by Congress through the enactment of the Second Liberty Bond Act of September 24, 1917, as amended, for the purpose of financing government expenditures in excess of tax revenues.

The gilt-edge quality of government securities stems from the taxing and money-creating powers that reside in the U.S. Congress. Moreover, the proportion of gross public and private debt outstanding accounted for by the debt of the federal government has declined markedly since World War II. In 1945, federal government debt amounted to 62 percent

TABLE 1

Part A. Status under Limitation July 31, 1973* (in millions of dollars)

The statutory debt limit established by the Second Liberty Bond Act, as amended (31 U.S.C. 757b)		465,000
Amounts outstanding subject to statutory debt limitation:		
U.S. government securities issued under the Second Liberty Bond Act, as amended	458,384	
Debt of U.S. government agencies	439	
Participation certificates (12 U.S.C. 1717(c))	1,135	
Total amount outstanding subject to statutory debt limitation		459,958
Balance Issuable under Limitation		5,042

Part B. Application of Statutory Limitation July 31, 1973 (in millions of dollars)

Classification	*Total outstanding*
Public debt:	
Interest-bearing debt:	
Public issues—marketable:	
Treasury bills	99,860
Treasury notes	117,840
Treasury bonds	45,008
Total Public Issues—Marketable	262,708
Public issues—nonmarketable:	
Certificates of indebtedness:	
Foreign series	11,887
Foreign currency series	189
Treasury notes:	
Foreign series	14,533
Foreign currency series	1,556
Treasury bonds	250
Treasury certificates	370
Treasury notes	55
U.S. savings bonds	59,652
U.S. savings notes	516
U.S. retirement plan bonds	64
Depositary bonds	17
Treasury bonds, R.E.A. series	7
Treasury bonds, investment series	2,275
Certificates of indebtedness—state and local government series	3
Treasury notes—state and local government series	60
Treasury bonds—state and local government series	78
Total Public Issues—Nonmarketable	91,513
Special issues to government agencies and trust funds	102,996
Total Interest-bearing Debt	457,217
Matured debt on which interest has ceased	253
Debt bearing no interest:	
Special note of the United States:	
International Monetary Fund series	825
Mortgage Guaranty Insurance Company tax and loss bonds	41
U.S. savings stamps	49
Excess profits tax refund bonds	1
U.S. notes	323
Deposits for retirement of national bank and Federal Reserve bank notes	71
Silver certificates	213
Other debt bearing no interest	10
Total Debt Bearing No Interest	1,533
Total Public Debt	459,003
Debt of U.S. government agencies:	
Interest-bearing debt	439*
Matured debt on which interest has ceased	
Total Debt of U.S. Government Agencies	439
Total Public Debt and Debt of U.S. Government Agencies	459,443
Deduct debt not subject to limitation	620
Add participation certificates	1,135
Total Subject to Limitation	459,958

* The Second Liberty Bond Act (31 U.S.C. 757b), as amended, provides that the face amount of obligations issued under authority of that act, and the face amount of obligations guaranteed as to principal and interest by the United States, shall not exceed in the aggregate $400 billion outstanding at any one time. Public Law 92–599 provides that beginning on November 1, 1972, and ending on November 30, 1973, the public debt limit shall be temporarily increased by $65 billion.

The act of June 30, 1967 (Public Law 90–39) provides that the face amount of beneficial interests and participations issued under section 302 (c) of the Federal National Mortgage Association Charter Act (12 U.S.C. 1717 [c]) during the fiscal year 1968 and outstanding at any time shall be added to the amount otherwise taken into account in determining whether the requirements of the above provisions are met.

Source: *Treasury Bulletin.*

TABLE 2

Gross Public and Private Debt 1945–70 (in billions of dollars)

Year	*Total*	*Federal Government**	*Federal Agencies†*	*State and Local*	*Corporate*	*Individual and Noncorporate*
1945...	$ 449.8	$279.6	—	$ 16.0	$ 99.5	$ 54.7
1950....	555.1	257.8	$ 0.7	25.3	167.0	104.3
1955....	762.5	282.2	2.9	46.3	251.0	180.1
1960....	997.0	296.6	3.5	72.0	361.6	263.3
1965....	1,401.4	330.7	8.9	103.1	543.0	415.7
1970....	2,119.5	401.6	38.8	149.2	954.0	575.9
1945....	100.0%	62.2%	—	3.5%	22.1%	12.2%
1950....	100.0	46.4	0.1%	4.6	30.1	18.8
1955....	100.0	37.0	0.4	6.1	32.9	23.6
1960....	100.0	29.7	0.4	7.2	36.3	26.4
1965....	100.0	23.6	0.6	7.4	38.7	29.7
1970....	100.0	19.0	1.8	7.0	45.0	27.2

* Net federal government and agency debt is the outstanding debt held by the public as defined in the budget of the U.S. government, fiscal year 1969. Gross federal government debt consists of the public debt as defined in the Second Liberty Bond Act of 1917, as amended, plus the obligations to the public of federal agencies in which the federal government has a proprietary interest each year.

† This comprises the debt of federally sponsored agencies, in which there is no longer any federal proprietary interest. The obligations of the Federal Land Banks and the debt of the Federal Home Loan Banks are included in all years shown in this table, and the debts of the Federal National Mortgage Association, Federal Intermediate Credit Banks, and Banks for Cooperatives are included beginning with 1968.

Source: *Survey of Current Business*, May 1969, May 1970, and May 1973.

TABLE 3

Gross and Net Federal Government Debt and Their Relationship to GNP (in billions of dollars)

Year	*Gross Debt*	*Held by Federal Agencies and Trust Funds*	*Held by Federal Reserve Banks*	*Held by Federal Agencies and Trust Funds and Federal Reserve Banks*	*Net Debt*
1945............	$279.6	$27.0	$24.3	$51.3	$228.3
1950............	257.8	39.2	20.8	60.0	197.8
1955............	282.2	51.7	24.8	76.5	205.7
1960............	296.6	55.0	27.4	82.4	214.2
1965............	330.7	59.7	40.8	100.5	230.2
1970............	401.6	97.1	62.1	159.2	242.4

Relationship to GNP

Year	*Gross Debt*	*Net Debt*	*GNP*	*Ratio of Gross Debt to GNP*	*Ratio of Net Debt to GNP*
1945............	$279.6	$228.3	$213.6	1.309	1.069
1950............	257.8	197.8	284.6	0.906	0.695
1955............	282.2	205.7	397.5	0.710	0.517
1960............	296.6	214.2	502.6	0.590	0.426
1965............	330.7	230.2	681.2	0.485	0.338
1970............	401.6	242.4	977.1	0.411	0.248

Source: *Survey of Current Business, Federal Reserve Bulletin.*

of total outstanding debt. Other forms of debt then grew relatively to that of the federal government, and by 1970 the latter accounted for only 19 percent of the total (Table 2).

The capacity of the U.S. economy to carry the government debt has, at the same time, increased substantially. To cite two measures: (1) the ratio of the net debt to the gross national product (GNP) declined from 1.069 in 1945 to 0.248 in 1970. (Table 3); (2) during the same period, interest on the net debt as a percentage of GNP decreased from 1.38 percent to 1.25 percent (Table 4). Moreover, this record was established in

TABLE 4

Interest on the Federal Debt and GNP (in billions of dollars)

Year	*Interest on Net Debt**	*GNP*	*Interest as a Percent of GNP*
1945	$ 2.957	$213.6	1.38%
1950	4.217	284.6	1.48
1955	4.643	397.5	1.17
1960	6.631	502.6	1.32
1965	7.982	681.2	1.17
1970	12.277	977.1	1.25

* Estimated from ratio of net debt to gross debt.
Source: *Treasury Bulletin; Federal Reserve Bulletin.*

spite of the dramatic increase in interest rates that has occurred since the close of World War II.

In the nonmarketable sector of the public debt, of primary interest to the private investor are U.S. savings bonds; the treasury no longer sells U.S. savings notes (Table 1). There are two issues of savings bonds outstanding, Series E and H. Both issues are registered, noncallable, and nontransferable. They mature over a period of five years and ten months for E bonds to ten years for H bonds, but liberal reinvestment programs are maintained. They may also be redeemed on demand after a preliminary waiting period.

Purchase of savings bonds by an individual investor is subject to an annual limitation of $5,000, but they are available on a tap basis.[1] Series E bonds are issued at a discount and provide for a gradual increase in redemption value so that the effective interest rate increases over time. Series H bonds carry coupons which may be cashed semiannually thereby providing current cash incomes. Income taxes on E bond appreciation may be deferred until the bonds are cashed.

A substantial majority of public issues are in marketable form. There are three major types of marketable issues, which are differentiated chiefly according to maturity. These are bills, notes, and bonds (Table 1). Treasury bills have an original maturity of up to one year. Notes

[1] That is, on demand, whatever that may be on the basis of terms announced by the treasury department.

usually mature in one to five years, and bonds in more than five years.

Treasury bills are normally offered in 3-, 6-, 9-, and 12-month maturities. The 3-month, or 91-day, and the 6-month, or 182-day, bills are offered weekly. A 52-week bill is offered every 4 weeks.

The treasury may also offer strips of weekly treasury bills, with each component of a strip increasing the amount outstanding of an existing issue. Finally, there are TABs, or tax-anticipation bills. Though not maturing until several days following the tax date, TABs may be accepted at face value in payment of income taxes due on a quarterly tax date.

Treasury bills are offered for cash, although maturing bills can be used to pay for new offerings, and are available in denominations of $10,000 and above. They are issued in bearer form only. Treasury bills are normally offered at competitive auctions on a discount basis. Limited amounts are offered on a noncompetitive basis. Bills are widely quoted on a bank discount basis, so that the true discount, or bond equivalent yield, is somewhat higher. The amount of the discount at which treasury bills are sold is considered to be interest for taxation purposes.

Treasury notes and bonds are usually offered with longer maturities, in denominations which vary upward from $1,000, in registered or bearer form, and on a coupon basis. Price quotations are in 32nds of a point. These securities may be offered for cash or in exchange for either a maturing or an outstanding issue. Income derived from treasury notes and bonds is fully taxable.

The U.S. marketable debt thus provides a broad range of maturities for the individual or institutional investor (Table 5). This fact, plus the unmatched marketability of U.S. securities, has contributed to their widespread use as an instrument of portfolio policy. (See Table 6.) U.S. government securities may be purchased through brokers, investment banks, commercial banks, savings and loan associations, mutual savings banks, and Federal Reserve banks and branches. Federal Reserve banks and branches serve as fiscal agents for the U.S. Treasury.

FEDERAL AGENCY OBLIGATIONS

Two classes of federal agencies issue marketable obligations of various kinds and maturities (See Tables 5 and 7). These securities emerge from the federal government's lending programs. These programs are designed to influence the flow of credit from private sources to particular sectors of the economy in a manner which reflects various national goals. Thus, obligations of the Banks for Cooperatives (COOP), Federal Land Banks (FLB), and Federal Intermediate Credit Banks (FICB) are issued for the purpose of supporting agriculture; while those of the Federal Home Loan Banks (FHLB), the Federal National Mortgage Association (FNMA), the Federal Housing Administration (FHA), and

TABLE 5

United States Government and Agency Bonds

Tuesday, Ooctober 16, 1973

(Prices in 32d of a point, composite bill yields in basis points.)

BONDS & NOTES

	Bid	Asked	Chg.	Yld.
Nov., '73, 4⅛s	99.22	99.26	...	6.48
Feb., '74, 4⅛s	98.25	98.29	...	7.46
Feb., '74, 7¾s	99.31	100.3	...	7.37
May, '74, 4¼s	98.6	98.10	...	7.26
May, '74, 7¼s	99.27	99.31	—.1	7.31
Aug., '74, 5⅝s	98.17	98.21	—.1	7.33
Sept., '74, 5⅝s	98.17	98.21	—.1	7.33
Sept., '74, 6s	98.24	98.28	—.1	7.24
Nov., '74, 3⅞s	96.17	96.21	—.1	7.15
Nov., '74, 5¾s	98.9	98.13	—.1	7.31
Dec., '74, 5⅞s	98.9	98.13	—.1	7.28
Feb., '75, 5¾s	98.7	98.15	—.1	6.98
Feb., '75, 5⅞s	98.14	98.22	—.1	6.93
May, '75, 5⅞s	98.7	98.15	—.3	6.92
May, '75, 6s	98.14	98.22	—.2	6.89
Aug., '75, 5⅞s	98.6	98.14	—.3	6.80
Sept., '75, 8⅜s	102.10	102.14	—.2	7.03
Nov., '75, 5⅞s	100.0	100.8	—.4	6.87
Feb., '76, 5⅞s	97.26	98.2	—.3	6.79
Feb., '76, 6¼s	98.20	98.28	—.4	6.78
May, '76, 6½s	99.4	99.12	—.4	6.77
Aug., '76, 6½s	99.4	99.12	—.4	6.74
Aug., '76, 7½s	101.27	102.3	—.2	6.68
Nov., '76, 6¼s	98.14	98.22	—.4	6.73
Feb., '77, 8s	103.14	103.22	—.4	6.74
Aug., '77, 7¾s	102.30	103.6	—.3	6.79
Feb., '78, 6¼s	97.30	98.6	—.4	6.74
Nov., '78, 6s	96.20	96.28	—.8	6.74
Aug., '79, 6¼s	97.30	98.6	—.6	6.63
Nov., '79, 6⅝s	99.4	99.12	—.6	6.75
Feb., '80, 4s	86.0	86.16	—.5	6.65
May, '80, 6+s	100.4	100.12	—.5	6.80
Nov. '80, 3½s	92.0	82.16	—.6	6.64
Aug., '81, 7s	101.16	....	—.6	6.67
Feb., '82, 6⅜s	97.12	97.28	—.8	6.71
June, '83-'78, 3¼s	76.24	77.24	—.8	6.37
Aug., '84, 6⅜s	96.14	97.14	—.14	6.71
May, '85, 3¼s	96.22	97.22	—.8	5.94
May, '85-'75, 4¼s	81.12	82.12	—.6	6.43
Nov., '86, 6⅛s	94.18	95.18	—.6	6.64
Feb., '90, 3½s	76.12	77.12	—.8	5.64
Aug., '92-'87, 4¼s	78.28	79.28	—.8	6.06
Feb., '93-'88, 4s	77.8	78.8	—.14	5.90
Feb., '93, 6¾s	95.20	96.20	—.14	7.07
Aug., '93-'88, 7½s	102.16	103.30	—.20	7.21
May, '94-'89, 4⅛s	78.24	79.24	—.10	5.83
Feb., '95, 3s	76.10	77.10	—.8	4.70
May, '98-'93, 7s	97.22	98.22	—.18	7.11
Nov., '98, 3½s	76.12	77.12	—.8	5.11

TREASURY BILLS

Oct. 23	7.72	6.82	...	6.92
Oct. 25	7.56	6.84	...	6.94
Nov. 1	7.31	6.69	—9	6.80
Nov. 8	7.31	6.69	—9	6.81
Nov. 15	7.31	6.69	—9	6.81
Nov. 20	7.31	6.69	—8	6.83
Nov. 23	7.29	6.79	—6	6.93
Nov. 29	7.31	6.79	—4	6.94
Dec. 6	7.24	6.82	—1	6.98
Dec. 13	7.24	6.84	—1	7.01
Dec. 20	7.22	6.90	—1	7.08
Dec. 18	7.24	6.90	—2	7.08
Dec. 27	7.21	6.93	+1	7.12
1974—				
Jan. 3	7.28	7.10	+6	7.31
Jan. 10	7.27	7.13	+8	7.35
Jan. 15	7.29	7.07	+1	7.31
W.I. Jan. 17	7.28	7.22	—1	7.46
Jan. 24	7.35	7.11	+2	7.34
Jan. 31	7.37	7.13	+5	7.38
Feb. 7	7.44	7.20	+2	7.47
Feb. 12	7.44	7.18	+2	7.45
Feb. 14	7.44	7.18	+2	7.46
Feb. 21	7.44	7.20	+2	7.49
Feb. 28	7.45	7.21	...	7.51
Mar. 7	7.43	7.29	+2	7.61
Mar. 12	7.43	7.23	+2	7.55
Mar. 28	7.45	7.27	+4	7.62
Mar. 21	7.44	7.26	+3	7.60
Apr. 4	7.42	7.28	...	7.64
Apr. 9	7.39	7.21	+1	7.57
Apr. 11	7.40	7.28	+4	7.65
W.I. Apr. 18	7.30	7.22	...	7.60
May 7	7.44	7.18	+1	7.56
June 4	7.42	7.18	+1	7.57
July 2	7.43	7.21	+1	7.62
July 30	7.39	7.31	+5	7.76
Aug. 27	7.41	7.25	+1	7.72
Sept. 24	7.30	7.20	+3	7.70

FEDERAL INTERMEDIATE

Millions outstanding					
559	Nov., '73	6.00	99.26	99.30	7.30
544	Dec., '73	6.15	99.21	99.25	7.59
212	Jan., '74	6.85	99.21	99.25	7.76
660	Jan., '74	7.00	99.21	99.25	7.77
695	Feb., '74	6.90	99.17	99.21	7.83
644	Mar., '74	7.00	99.16	99.20	7.81
421	Apr., '74	7.50	99.18	99.22	8.04
523	May, '74	8.65	100.6	100.10	7.90
661	June, '74	9.75	100.31	101.3	7.83
224	July, '74	5.95	98.8	98.24	7.79
669	July '74	9¾	101.6	101.10	7.75
240	Jan., '75	6.05	96.16	98.28	7.03
302	July, '75	5.70	97.8	97.28	7.04
261	Jan., '77	6.65	98.4	98.20	7.33
236	Jan., '77	7.10	99.8	99.24	7.18

INTER-AMERICAN BANK

75	Dec., '82	4¼	79.16	80.16	7.19
54	Apr., '84	4½	79.0	8.00	7.26
100	Nov., '84	4½	77.8	78.8	7.27
50	Jan., '92	5.20	78.16	80.0	7.18
60	Nov, '92	6½	89.0	90.0	7.49
75	Nov., '93	6⅝	90.0	91.0	7.50
700	Oct., '95	8⅝	105.24	107.24	7.87

BANK FOR COOPERATIVES

259	Nov., '73	6¾	99.27	99.31	7.28
656	Dec., '73	6.85	99.24	99.28	7.64
463	Jan., '74	7.55	99.26	99.30	7.69
542	Feb., '74	8.70	100.3	100.7	7.80
306	Mar., '74	9.90	100.19	100.23	7.92
302	Apr., '74	8.95	100.22	100.26	7.97
200	Apr., '77	7.70	101.12	101.20	7.16

INTERNATIONAL BANK BONDS

33	May, '75	3⅜	93.24	94.8	7.29
250	Jan., '76	6½	97.24	98.16	7.23
50	Jan., '77	6⅜	96.24	97.16	7.25
100	Jan, '79	4¼	86.8	86.24	7.34
17	Nov., '80	4¾	85.0	85.24	7.38
108	Oct., '81	3¼	75.0	76.0	7.28
100	Feb., '85	5	80.24	81.24	7.41
75	July, '91	5⅜	79.8	80.8	7.39
—	Apr., '92	5⅜	78.24	79.24	7.41
50	Sept., '93	5⅞	83.0	84.0	7.43
100	Mar., '94	6½	89.0	90.0	7.46
50	Oct., '94	6⅜	87.24	88.24	7.44
100	Aug., '95	8⅝	106.8	107.8	7.92
100	Aug., '96	8⅛	103.24	101.24	7.63

FEDERAL LAND BANK

300	Oct., '73	7.80	99.28	100.0	7.55
462	Oct., '73	5.90	99.27	99.31	7.51
450	Jan., '74	5.55	99.4	99.12	7.89
155	Feb., '74	4½	98.18	98.26	8.01
350	Apr., '74	5.85	98.22	98.30	8.00
354	Apr., '74	7.30	99.14	99.22	7.93
326	July, '74	5.85	98.0	98.8	8.24
300	Oct., '74	5.30	96.16	97.0	8.46
300	Jan., '75	7.15	99.20	100.4	7.03
220	Jan., '75	8⅜	101.0	101.20	6.99
200	Apr., '75	4⅜	95.8	96.8	7.03
300	Apr., '75	7.45	100.0	100.16	7.29
425	July, '75	5.70	97.8	97.24	7.07
300	Oct., '75	7.40	99.28	100.12	7.00
W.I.	Oct., '75	7.40	100.8	100.16	7.13
300	Jan., '76	6.25	87.28	98.16	6.97
123	Feb., '76	5.00	94.24	95.24	6.97
373	Apr., '76	6¼	97.24	98.12	6.97
150	July, '76	5⅜	95.0	96.0	6.99
450	Oct., '76	7.15	99.28	100.12	7.01
550	July, '77	7.50	100.16	101.0	7.19
300	Oct., '77	6.25	96.12	96.28	7.26
148	Feb., '78-'74	4⅛	88.0	89.0	7.11

150	Apr., '78	5⅛	91.16	92.16	7.10
269	July, '78	6.40	95.28	96.28	7.18
W.I.	Oct., '73	7.35	100.14	100.22	7.18
285	Jan., '70	5.00	89.28	90.28	7.11
235	Apr., '79	6.85	97.24	98.24	7.13
400	Oct., '79	6.80	97.12	98.12	7.14
300	Jan., '80	6.70	96.24	97.24	7.15
250	July, '80	7.50	101.0	101.16	7.21
224	Apr., '81	6.70	96.8	97.8	7.18
200	Apr., '82	6.90	97.24	98.24	7.10
239	Oct., '82	7.30	100.8	101.0	7.15
W.I.	Oct., '82	7.30	100.12	100.20	7.21

FEDERAL HOME LOAN BANK

600	Nov., '73	5.55	99.21	99.25	7.38
300	Jan., '74	8.40	99.28	100.4	7.78
500	Jan., '74	9⅜	100.9	100.13	7.80
300	Feb., '74	7.10	99.16	99.24	7.74
205	Feb., '74	8.40	99.30	100.6	7.76
700	Feb., '74	9¾	100.16	100.20	7.84
300	May, '74	6.45	98.20	98.28	8.26
700	May, '74	6.45	98.22	98.30	8.24
201	Aug., '74	7.65	99.16	100.0	7.63
400	Aug., '74	5⅜	97.20	98.4	7.66
800	Aug., '74	9⅝	101.10	101.18	7.6
1000	Nov., '74	7.05	98.16	98.28	8.12
250	Nov., '74	8.00	99.8	100.0	7.99
400	Feb., '75	5⅞	97.28	98.12	7.15
250	Feb., '75	6.10	98.8	98.20	7.17
500	Feb., '75	8.20	101.0	101.8	7.20
265	May, '75	8.05	100.20	101.12	7.12
700	May, '75	7.15	99.16	100.0	7.14
500	Aug., '75	7.15	99.29	100.1	7.12
300	Aug., '75	7⅞	100.16	101.0	7.28
300	Aug., '75	7.95	100.16	101.4	7.28
350	Nov., '75	6½	98.8	98.28	7.08
600	Nov., '75	6½	99.16	100.0	7.04
300	Feb., '76	7⅜	99.24	100.16	7.13
300	Feb., '76	8¾	103.4	103.20	7.05
600	May, '76	7.20	99.12	99.28	7.25
500	Aug., '76	7⅞	100.24	101.8	7.30
W.I.	Feb., '77	7.20	99.30	100.2	7.17
200	May, '77	8.96	98.24	99.4	7.23
300	Aug., '77	7.15	99.0	99.20	7.26
300	Nov., '77	6¾	97.20	98.4	7.28
500	May, '78	7.60	101.10	101.18	7.19
350	Feb., '80	7⅞	102.8	103.8	7.10
700	Oct., '80	7.80	102.16	103.16	7.15
200	Nov., '81	6.60	95.12	96.12	7.20
200	May, '83	7.30	100.0	100.24	7.19
W.I.	Nov., '93	7⅜	99.0	99.16	7.42

FEDERAL NATIONAL MORTGAGE

500	Dec., '73	5¾	99.19	99.23	7.53
500	Dec., '73	7.15	99.25	99.29	7.60
400	Mar., '74	5.45	98.20	99.4	7.66
350	Mar., '74	7.75	99.16	100.0	7.69
350	June, '74	6.80	98.8	98.24	7.70
400	June, '74	7.90	99.24	100.4	7.67
300	Sept., '74	5.65	97.12	97.28	8.14
250	Sept., '74	7.85	99.12	99.28	7.98
250	Dec., '74	6.10	97.0	97.16	8.42
450	Dec., '74	6.45	97.12	97.28	8.42
600	Mar., '75	6.35	98.12	99.4	7.01
300	Mar., '75	7.55	100.0	100.24	6.97
500	June, '75	5¼	96.16	97.8	7.04
650	Sept., '75	6.80	99.4	99.20	7.01
350	Sept., '75	7.50	100.4	100.28	6.99
500	Dec., '75	5.70	96.28	97.12	7.03
300	Dec., '75	8¼	101.30	102.6	7.13
500	Mar., '76	5.65	96.12	97.4	6.97
400	Mar., '76	7⅛	99.24	100.8	7.01
450	June, '76	5.80	96.12	97.0	7.11
250	June, '76	6.80	98.0	99.0	7.12
500	Sept., '76	5.85	96.4	96.20	7.16
300	Sept., '86	6⅛	96.28	97.12	7.14
500	Dec., '76	6¼	96.24	97.8	7.24
00	Dec., '76	7.45	99.20	100.20	7.22
98	Feb., '77	4½	91.4	92.4	7.21
500	Mar., '77	6.30	96.24	97.8	7.22
50	June, '77	6⅜	96.20	97.8	7.24
50	June, '77	6½	96.28	97.16	7.29
00	Sept., '77	6⅞	98.16	99.0	7.17
400	Sept., '77	7.85	102.2	102.10	7.16
500	Dec., '77	7.25	99.24	100.4	7.21
500	Dec., '71	7.35	101.2	101.10	7.17
600	June, '78	7.15	99.0	99.16	7.27
300	Dec., '78	6¾	97.0	98.0	7.22
300	June, '79	7.85	102.20	103.4	7.16
200	Sept., '79	6.40	95.20	96.20	7.14
350	Dec., '79	6.55	96.8	97.8	7.11
250	Mar., '80	6⅞	97.24	98.24	7.12
400	Sept., '80	7½	101.0	101.8	7.20
300	Dec., '80	6.60	96.0	97.0	7.16
350	Mar, '81	7.05	98.16	99.16	7.14
250	June, '81	7¼	99.16	100.16	7.16
250	Sept., '81	7¼	99.16	100.16	7.16
250	June, '82	6.65	96.0	97.0	7.12
200	Sept., '82	6.80	96.24	97.24	7.14
200	June, '83	6¾	96.8	97.8	7.15
300	June, '83	7.30	100.8	101.0	7.15
250	Sept., '83	6¾	96.8	97.8	7.14
200	June, '84	6¼	92.16	93.16	7.13
250	Dec., '84	6.90	96.24	97.24	7.20
200	Mar., '92	7.00	95.0	96.0	7.40
200	June, '82	7.06	95.0	96.0	7.45
200	Dec., '92-'82	7.10	95.0	96.0	7.46

Money

Tuesday, Oct. 16, 1973

DOMESTIC MARKET RATES IN PER CENT

FEDERAL FUNDS

10⅛ 10⅛ 9⅞ 10

Discount Rate 7½
Effective August 31, 1973

Prime Rate 10
Effective Sept. 19, 1973

Dealers Loan Rate (Government) .... N.Q.
3 months Treasury bills (asked) .. 7.06

Dealer's Commercial Paper:
5-270 days 9⅜-10
Effective Oct. 15, 1973

Finance Paper:
3-4 days 8
5-29 days 9½
30-89 days 8½
90-270 days 8
Effective Oct. 16, 1973

Acceptance:
1-90 days 9¼- 9
91-180 days 9⅛- 8⅞

Certificate of Deposit:
30-59 days 9½
60-89 days 9¼- 9⅜
90-119 days .... 9 - 9¼
120-179 days 8¾- 6½
120-360 days 6½- 8½

INTERNATIONAL ARBITRAGE

United Kingdom Treasury Bills:
90 days (hedged in New York) 7.14
Canadian Treasury Bills:
90 days (hedged in New York) .. 6.83
Canadian Finance Paper:
90 days (hedged in New York) .. 9.43

LONDON MONEY MARKET

Demand loans 10½-11
Eurodollars 9½- 9⅜
1 month 10⅛-10
3 months 10⅛-10
6 months 9 5/16- 9 7/16

GOLD

Yesterday	Previous	High	Low
$101.85	$101.25	$127.00	$63.90

SILVER

119.10p	121.70p	121.70p	82.90p

GOLD (N.Y.) H & H Base Price

$102.15	$101.55	$126.30	$64.20

GOLD (N.Y.) Englhd Selling Price

$102.35	$101.75	$126.45	$64.35

N.Q.—Not Quoted.

Source: *New York Times*, October 17, 1973. © 1973 by the New York Times Company. Reprinted by permission.

the Government National Mortgage Association (GNMA) are offered in behalf of our national housing objectives.

The COOPs were organized in 1933. Their function has been to help finance cooperative organizations that engage in marketing farm supplies or in providing farm business services. Typically, COOPs issue short-term debentures in bearer form in denominations of $5,000 or higher. Income derived from the securities, through interest or gain from sale, is subject to federal income taxes but is exempt from state, municipal, and local income taxes. The securities are not guaranteed by the U.S. government.

For over a half century, the FLBs have raised funds for local organizations which extend long-term real estate credits to farmers. The FLBs issue bonds, usually secured by first mortgages on farm properties, in denominations of $1,000 and above. Interest is subject to federal taxation, but the bonds and interest are exempt from state, municipal, and local income taxation. Gains from their sale or transfer by inheritance or gift are subject to federal or state taxes. These issues are not guaranteed by the U.S. government.

FICBs were established in 1923. These banks finance farmers indirectly by discounting notes which represent credits extended to farmers by agricultural credit corporations, livestock loan companies, and commercial banks. FICBs issue short-term debentures in bearer form in denominations of $5,000 and above. The securities and interest are exempt from state, municipal, and local income taxes, but gain from sale or transfer by inheritance and gift are subject to federal and state taxes. The debentures are not guaranteed by the U.S. government.

FHLBs were organized in 1932 for the purpose of reviving the mortgage market, all but totally destroyed by the collapse of real estate values in the Great Depression. The 12 regional FHLBs lend funds to member thrift institutions to enable them to meet credit demands arising out of seasonal factors or cyclical developments such as disintermediation. FHLBs are supervised by the federal government through the Federal Home Loan Bank Board. FHLBs issue notes and bonds with original maturities of less than, and more than, one year, respectively, in denominations of $10,000 and above. They are sold on a coupon basis against collateral of insured and guaranteed mortgages, U.S. securities, and cash assets. Interest income from the obligations is subject to federal taxation but exempt from state, municipal, and local taxes. Gain from sale or transfer by inheritance and gift are subject to federal and state taxation. The U.S. government does not guarantee FHLB securities.

The Federal Home Loan Mortgage Corporation (FHLMC) is owned by the 12 FHLBs and promotes the secondary markets in home mortgages. The FHLMC (Freddie Mae) raises funds through the sale of mortgage-backed bonds guaranteed by GNMA (Ginny Mae). Bonds are issued in coupon form in denominations of $25,000 and up, with maturities ranging from 2 to 25 years. Income derived from the bonds is fully taxable.

FNMA (Fannie Mae) was originally chartered by the federal government in 1938, but in 1963, FNMA was converted to private ownership. Its primary function is to conduct secondary market operations in FHA-insured and VA-guaranteed mortgages. These operations are con-

TABLE 6

Treasury Survey of Ownership, June 30, 1973 (par values—in millions of dollars)

				Held by Private	
Classification	*Total Amount Outstanding**	*U.S. Government Accounts and Federal Reserve Banks*	*Total Private Investors*	*5,614 Commercial Banks†*	*480 Mutual Savings Banks†*
Public debt issues:					
Interest-bearing public debt securities:					
Marketable	262,971	95,102	167,869	45,139	2,351
Nonmarketable‖	91,644	2,056	89,588	39#	3
Special issues	101,738	101,248	490		—
Total interest-bearing public debt securities	456,353	198,406	257,947	45,177	2,355
Matured debt and debt bearing no interest	1,788	—	1,788	—	—
Total Public Debt Securities	458,142	198,406	259,735	45,177	2,355
Government agency issues:					
Regular issues	4,560	227	4,333	755	238
Participation certificates**	5,057	1,737	3,320	593	437
Total government agency securities covered in treasury survey	9,617	1,964	7,653	1,348	675
Nonsurveyed government agency securities	1,492	192	1,300		
Total Government Agency Securities††	11,109	2,156	8,953		
Total Federal Securities	469,251	200,562	268,688		

* Securities issued by treasury and government agencies that are classified as debt under the new unified budget concept. For debt subject to limitation, see Table 1.

† Includes trust departments.

‡ Included with all other investors are those banks, insurance companies, savings and loan associations, corporations, and state and local government funds not reporting in the Treasury Survey. Also included are certain government deposit accounts and government-sponsored agencies.

§ Consists of corporate pension trust funds and profit sharing plans which involve retirement benefits. The data are compiled from quarterly reports by bank trustees who report total number of funds administered and public debt and agency securities held. It is estimated that these funds account for approximately 90 percent of federal securities held by all corporate pension trust funds. Since the data are not available each month, the regular monthly survey includes holdings by these funds under "held by all other private investors." The quarterly data are presented as supplemental information in a memorandum column accompanying the survey for each reporting date, beginning with December 31, 1953.

ducted in a cyclical fashion, supplying funds to the market in periods of high interest rates and supplying mortgages to the market in periods of low interest rates. To raise funds to finance its purchases, FNMA issues both notes and debentures. Short-term notes are offered on a discount basis in much the same way as commerical paper or bankers' acceptances. Secondary market rates on FNMA notes are published for maturities in the 30- to 270-day range. Debentures are usually offered in maturities of two years or over. None are guaranteed by the U.S. government.

Investors Covered in Treasury Survey							
Insurance Companies				*State and Local Governments*			
291 Life	*448 Fire, Casualty and Marine*	*486 Savings and Loan Associations*	*464 Corporations*	*316 General Funds*	*189 Pension and Retirement Funds*	*All Other Private Investors‡*	*Memorandum Held by 49,880 Corporate Pension Trust Funds§*
2,765	2,167	2,674	4,599	8,606	1,800	97,769	2,158
16	26	3	‡‡	12	58	89,431	153
—	—	—	—			490	—
2,781	2,193	2,677	4,599	8,617	1,858	187,690	2,312
—	—	—	—	—	—	1,788	—
2,781	2,193	2,677	4,599	8,617	1,858	189,478	2,312
114	15	177	62	272	216	2,483	64
54	194	85	18	132	604	1,203	76
168	210	262	80	404	820	3,686	140

|| U.S. savings bonds, Series E, are reported to the Treasury Survey at maturity value but have been adjusted to current redemption value for use in this table.
Includes $11 million depositary bonds held by commercial banks not included in the Treasury Survey.
** Includes Export-Import Bank and Government National Mortgage Association participation certificates.
†† Includes matured securities outstanding on which interest has ceased.
‡‡ Less than $500,000.
Note: The monthly Treasury Survey of Ownership covers securities issued by the U.S. Government, federal agencies, and the District of Columbia. The banks and insurance companies included in the survey currently account for about 90 percent of all such securities held by these institutions. The similar proportion for corporations and for savings and loan associations is 50 percent, and for state and local governments, 70 percent.
Source: *Treasury Bulletin.*

Also included in the government-sponsored list is $20 million in bonds issued by the District of Columbia Armory Board to finance a stadium in the nation's capital. These bonds are guaranteed by the U.S. government. Also, the Federal Housing Administration has a modest amount of long-term debentures outstanding which are guaranteed by the U.S. government.

GNMA (Ginny Mae) is a wholly owned subsidiary of the Department of Housing and Urban Development. Funds are raised through direct borrowing from the treasury, the sale of participation certificates, the

TABLE 7

Federal Agency Securities, End of June 1973 (in millions of dollars)

Issuing Agencies	
U.S. government sponsored:	
Banks for Cooperatives (COOP)	2,338
Federal Land Banks (FLB)	9,058
Federal Intermediate Credit Banks (FICB)	6,673
Federal Home Loan Banks (FHLB)	12,149*
Federal National Mortgage Association (FNMA)	21,087
District of Columbia Stadium Fund	20
Total	51,325
U.S. government owned:	
Federal Housing Administration (FHA)	412
Government National Mortgage Association (GNMA)	4,480
Export-Import Bank (Eximbank)	2,221
Tennessee Valley Authority (TVA)	2,255
Total	9,368

*** Includes Federal Home Loan Mortgage Corporation mortgage backed bonds.**
Source: *Treasury Bulletin.*

issuance of mortgage-backed securities, and the sale of pass-through securities. Participation certificates representing beneficial interests in mortgage pools have been issued in bearer or registered form in denominations of $5,000 or above. Mortgage-backed bonds with maturities of from 1 to 25 years are issued in bearer and registered forms in denominations of $10,000 and up. Under the pass-through arrangement, payments of principal and interest on a specified mortgage pool are passed through to Ginny Mae guaranteed certificates after servicing and guaranty fees have been deducted. These securities are issued in denominations of $5,000 and above. Ginny Mae's are guaranteed by the U.S. government and are fully taxable.

The Export-Import Bank (Eximbank), which assists in foreign trade financing, issues discount notes, debentures, and participation certificates of varying maturity and denomination. Eximbank issues are guaranteed by the U.S. government and are fully taxable.

The Tennessee Valley Authority (TVA) issues discount notes and bonds. Four-month discount notes are sold at auction every month with minimum bids at $1 million and in bearer form. TVA bonds are issued in coupon and bearer form in denominations of $5,000 and above. TVA obligations are not guaranteed by the U.S. government, and they are fully taxable at the federal level.

As noted above, the obligations of most government owned agency securities are guaranteed; those of most government sponsored are not. However, it is generally agreed that the federal government would not stand idly by if the agencies it sponsors were threatened with bankruptcy. Moreover, in many cases, the agency has access to direct borrowing from the Treasury.

In addition to their basic soundness, the marketability of agency securities is enchanced by several institutional arrangements. The majority of agency issues may be used as collateral for treasury deposits at commerical banks. They are usually accepted as eligible paper at the Federal Reserve discount window. Finally, the Federal Reserve may conduct open-market operations in agency securities. The fact that they are not gilt-edge results in an interest differential that is hardly supported by political reality. Like treasuries, agencies may be purchased through the usual brokerage and banking channels or directly through specifically identified fiscal agents.

THE GOVERNMENT SECURITIES MARKET

At present, there are 24 primary dealers in government securities. In addition to their crucial role in treasury financing, these dealers handle the buy and sell orders of the Federal Reserve Bank of New York (acting in behalf of the Federal Open Market Committee), as well as those of all major financial institutions. Ordinarily an individual investor's order should be placed with a banker who, in turn, would give the order to a primary dealer.

The primary dealer in U.S. government securities plays a crucial role in the U.S. money and capital markets. The debt-management operations of the U.S. Treasury; the open-market operations of the Federal Open Market Committee (FOMC); and the government securities transactions of the great financial intermediaries, nonfinancial corporations, and individual investors are all centered upon the dealers who make the market in government securities. These dealer houses, some of which are themselves money-market banks, stand with the remaining money-market banks at the apex of the money and capital markets. As, for example, local business activity increases in a particular region and the pressures of loan demand expand, the government securities portfolios of local lending institutions will be reduced. Initially, these securities may be absorbed by the larger correspondent banks in the regional money market center. But eventually the pressure will be felt in New York as these larger banks trim the size of their portfolios through adjusting sales to the government securities dealers. Dealers will find the flow of offers exceeding the flow of bids. They will reduce their bid quotations to prevent an undue expansion in their portfolios. The rising yield structure will stimulate the inward flow of funds from other regions. Thus from a particular region, through the money-market center, a stringency will be spread throughout the rest of the economy. In this manner, a more profitable use of resources locally will attract funds from the economy as a whole, with dealers providing a crucial link.

Alternatively, a credit stringency may originate in the money-market center. Again, the primary dealers, along with the nationwide network of correspondent banks, will transmit the stringency throughout the country as a whole. Credit weaknesses, whatever their origin, follow a similar course.

From the viewpoint of both the execution of stabilization policy and the day-to-day smoothing of money-market pressures, a critical dealer function involves the trading arm of the FOMC, the trading desk of the securities department of the Federal Reserve Bank of New York. If, for example, the trading account wishes to offset some factor which is momentarily pushing bank reserves beyond the current target level, it will solicit dealer bids. Payment by nonbank dealers is made through debits to the reserve account of the money-market bank that serves as their clearing agent. Payment by bank dealers is made by drawing on their reserve accounts directly. In each case, therefore, member bank reserves are reduced.

If the FOMC institutes a policy of restraint, the trading account will follow a similar procedure, with far-reaching effects upon interest rates and the rate of growth in the supply of money and credit. As dealers take on additional securities from the trading account and from the money-market banks, they gradually lower their bid and offer quotations. At the same time, the dealers step up their selling efforts through branch offices and correspondent banking connections all over the country.

These efforts, combined with the rise in yields, lead to widely dispersed sales. As the securities are taken up by banks and local investors, local member bank reserves decline. As member banks find that their reserves are under greater pressure, they will borrow temporarily in the federal funds market or from the Federal Reserve bank of their district. Or they may sell government securities, chiefly to dealers. In this manner—and again with the dealers providing the connecting link—the contraction of bank reserves directly due to the open-market sale is spread throughout the banking system. Ultimately, after a lag, the rate of growth of money and credit will be reduced. As a consequence, borrowing and spending decisions will become more conservative, and inflationary pressures will be ameliorated.

In similar fashion, the dealers participate in the underwriting and distribution of new treasury issues. Accordingly, if the Treasury changes the maturity structure of the debt, the dealers aid in communicating the shift in yield structure to the outstanding government debt and other investment media. The government securities dealers, therefore, provide the channel through which the effects of monetary and debt-management policy are transmitted to the economy, and they supply a constant means of communication for participants in the money and capital markets.

COMPARATIVE YIELD EXPERIENCE

Within the federal sector, yields on agencies are generally higher than yields on U.S. treasuries. Since treasuries are riskless while not all agencies are guaranteed, some of the yield differential may be due to the difference in default risk. However, as has been noted above, agencies are de facto, if not de jure, free from default risk, whether they are guaranteed or not. Hence, a major part of the yield differential must be attributed to the superior marketability of treasury obligations. This superior marketability is based upon the greater size of treasury issues and the greater volume of transactions in the treasury market. Direct obligations of the U.S. treasury, therefore, carry a lower yield not only because they are free from default risk but also because they bear a lower market risk.

It follows that agency issues are a good buy for someone who wants an essentially riskless investment but does not require the liquidity levels provided only by treasury obligations. When compared with securities issued by the private sector, agencies have lower yields because of a combination of default and market risk factors.

In addition to default and market risk, the taxability of alternative investment outlets obviously has an effect upon relative returns. This fact is vividly portrayed by comparing the recent yield experienced by long-term treasuries and 30-year prime municipals (Charts 1 and 2). Clearly, the default and market risk of municipal obligations exceeds that of treasury issues. These risk considerations, however, are offset by the fact that the municipal obligations are not subject to federal income tax. Consequently, prime municipal yields are lower throughout the entire period.

Unfortunately from an analytical point of view, the treasury-municipal yield relationship shows little evidence of cyclical regularity. In the 1960 recession, the yield differential declines. In the recession of 1970, the differential tends to increase. Moreover, during the 1966 tight money period, the differential varied over a relatively narrow range; whereas a marked increase occurred in 1973. The tax-exempt feature of municipals, therefore, remains as the primary tradeoff for both the yield and risk advantages of U.S. treasuries. Changes in the tax structure and the distribution of taxable income, as well as the tax status of municipal securities, will affect this particular yield differential with the passage of time. Barring changes in institutional arrangements, the analyst should, in judging the relative attractiveness of market opportunities, compare the current differentials during, say, the two previous business cycles.

CHART 1

Yield of Long-Term Treasury and High-Grade Municipal Bonds

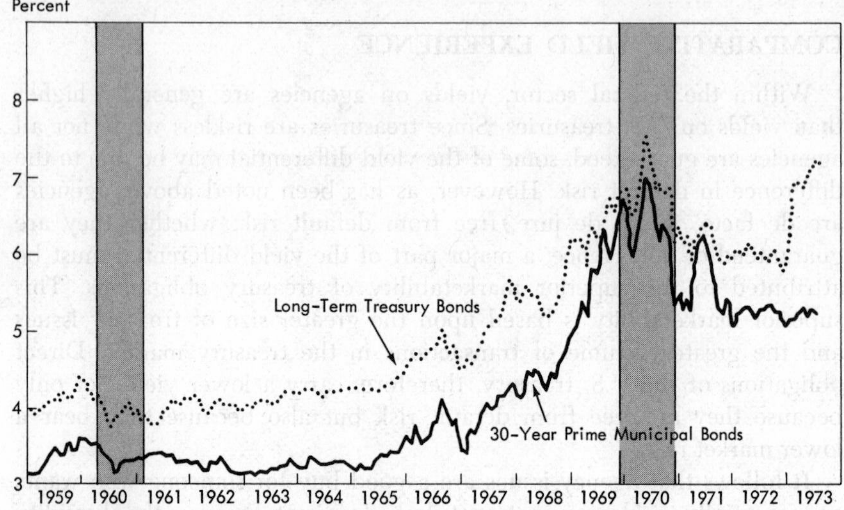

Note: Shaded areas represent periods of recession.
Source: *An Analytical Record of Yields and Spreads*, Salomon Brothers, July 1973.

The role of credit, or default, risk may be seen more clearly by comparing long-term treasuries with corporate securities having a Baa rating (Charts 3 and 4). During the recessions of 1960 and 1970, the yield differential tended to widen. Two factors may be identified as contributing to this pattern. First, in a recessionary environment the prospects for corporate enterprises become less favorable and the quality of their instruments of indebtedness deteriorates. Thus, the risk differential, when a comparison is made with a security that is free from default risk, increases because of the increase in default risk of the inferior instrument. Second, during periods of recesssion, the economic outlook from the point of view of the investor tends to become unfavorable. Prospects for employment and income may be bleak. There is less of a willingness to undergo risk, a stronger preference for safety. Consequently, a new market equilibrium is brought about in which holders of the outstanding government and corporate debt require a higher yield differential.

Opposite and symmetrical considerations presumably govern the yield differential during periods of prosperity. And yield differentials, in fact, did narrow in the early 1960s as well as in the early 1970s. The pattern of the late 1960s is, however, inconsistent. Here, certain institutional factors apparently played a dominant role. First, the treasury labored under a 4¼ percent bond interest ceiling. Contemporary market conditions thus forced treasury officials to restrict their offerings

CHART 2

Yield Differential of Long-Term Treasuries Less 30-Year Prime Municipals

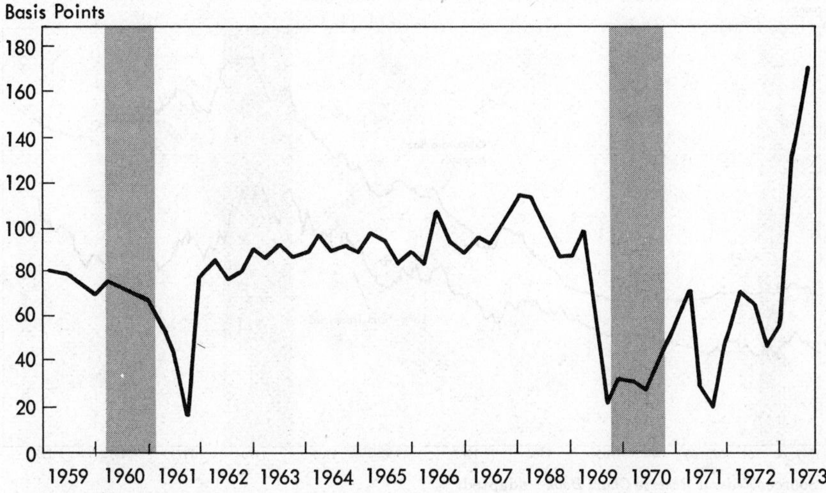

Source: *An Analytical Record of Yields and Spreads*, Salomon Brothers, July 1973.

to the intermediate and short-term areas, and long-term treasuries took on an added scarcity value. At the same time, corporations were stepping up their funding operations as new records were being established in the demand for long-term capital. Corporate securities became relatively plentiful. Hence, developments in both sectors reinforced each other and brought about a widening of the yield differential in spite of prosperous economic conditions. Barring such institutional factors, however, the inherent risk qualities of the two types of securities will undoubtedly interact with the economic environment to produce the cyclical pattern of yield differentials apparent during most of the recent period.

In comparing bond and equity yields, two risk factors must be kept in mind. First, bondholders have a prior claim to the assets of the enterprise in the process of liquidation. The owners are residual claimants. Secondly, bonds have been issued in greater volume than stocks in recent years. This fact enhances the marketability of bonds relatively to stocks. As a consequence, the bond portfolio tends to be more liquid than one composed of equities. For these reasons, equity yields tend to be higher, that is, to compensate for the greater risk.

When making the bond-equity yield comparison, it is, of course, necessary to include an allowance for expected capital appreciation along with the dividend rate in calculating the yield on equities.

If a company's fortunes are favored by an inflationary environment, its shares will provide an effective hedge against inflation. On the other

CHART 3

Yields on Corporate Baa (Moody's) and Long-Term Treasuries

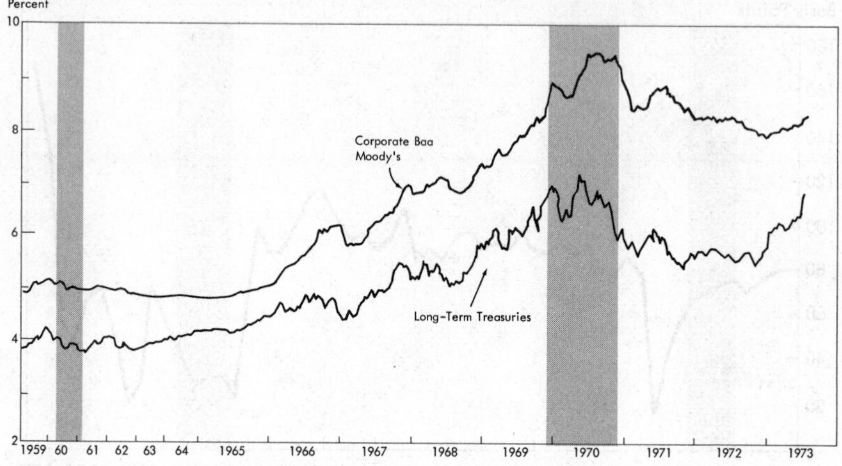

Source: *Federal Reserve Chart Book*—adapted.

hand, the force of competition will tend to introduce a corresponding element into the yields of fixed interest-bearing securities, leaving the underlying risk characteristics as a major determinant of yield relationships.

FORECASTING THE LEVEL OF INTEREST RATES

The crucial decision in money and capital market analysis concerns the specification of future interest rate levels. Since interest rates move sympathetically with—they are an outgrowth of—real economic forces, the first and fundamental step in interest rate forecasting consists of a forecast of economic conditions. Such forecasts are readily available to the market analyst and must form the basis for whatever refinement he may add.

Given the state of the economy, the level of interest rates will depend upon the policy mix; that is the degree to which the federal government relies upon fiscal, as opposed to monetary, policy as a means of achieving its stabilization objectives. If, for example, fiscal, or budget, policy is relatively restrictive, monetary policy may be relatively easy, and interest rates will be relatively low. Contrariwise, if fiscal policy is relatively easy and monetary policy relatively tight, interest rates will be relatively high. Consequently, the tax and expenditure, or budget, policies of the federal government must be carefully gauged along with

CHART 4

Yield Differential of Long-Term Treasuries less Corporate Baa (Moody's) Bonds

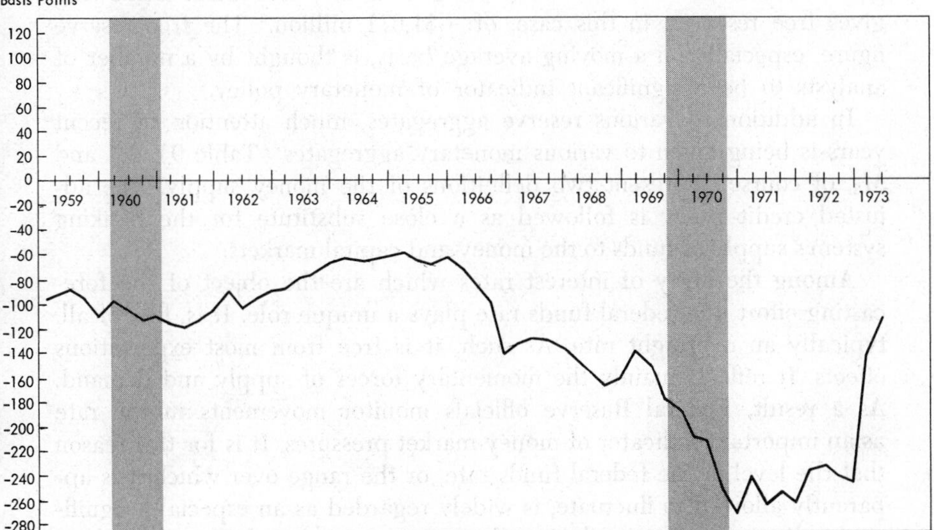

Source: *An Analytical Record of Yields and Spreads,* Salomon Brothers, July 1973; and *Treasury Bulletin.*

indicators of monetary policy as enforced by the Federal Reserve System, the U.S. central bank.

Whatever the conjuncture, the policy mix, and the current status of monetary policy, various monetary indicators may provide signals of turning points in interest rate cycles. They may perform this function for two reasons. First, regardless of underlying cyclical conditions, monetary policy will have, at least, a marginal effect on the level of interest rates. Secondly, Federal Reserve officials have first access to economic data measuring the health of the economy. This fact plus their continuing effort, as a basis for monetary policy formulation, to pierce the veil separating the present from the future increase the probability that Federal Reserve actions will provide valuable insights into the future itself.

The basic Federal Reserve release describes the factors affecting bank reserves (Tables 8a and 8b). Since the level of the money supply depends upon the level of bank reserves, the various determinants of the level of reserves must be followed carefully. Sources of reserves such as U.S. government securities bought outright or held under repurchase agreement may reveal significant changes—or lack thereof—in the direction of Federal Reserve policy and interest rates.

The difference between the sources and uses items gives member bank reserves in the form of deposits with the Federal Reserve banks. Adding vault cash gives total reserves; subtracting required reserves gives excess reserves; and subtracting total member bank borrowing gives free reserves, in this case, of −$1,671 million.[2] The free reserve figure, especially on a moving average basis, is thought by a number of analysts to be a significant indicator of monetary policy.

In addition to various reserve aggregates, much attention in recent years is being given to various monetary aggregates (Table 9). M_1 and M_2, of course, represent two definitions of the money supply. The adjusted credit proxy is followed as a close substitute for the banking system's supply of funds to the money and capital markets.

Among the array of interest rates which are the object of the forecasting effort, the federal funds rate plays a unique role. It is, first of all, typically an overnight rate. As such, it is free from most expectations effects. It reflects mainly the momentary forces of supply and demand. As a result, Federal Reserve officials monitor movements in the rate as an important indicator of money-market pressures. It is for this reason that the level of the federal funds rate, or the range over which it is apparently allowed to fluctuate, is widely regarded as an especially significant indicator of the complexion of current monetary policy.

THE TERM STRUCTURE OF INTEREST RATES

Over the business cycle, the treasury yield pattern shifts in a manner which, by and large, appears to be consistent with the so-called expecta-

TABLE 8a

Federal Reserve Factors Affecting Bank Reserves and Condition Statement of Federal Reserve Banks

H.4.1

For immediate release
October 25, 1973

The average of daily figures for total reserves of member banks increased slightly in the latest statement week to $34,989 million. Required reserves declined while excess reserves and member bank borrowings at Federal Reserve banks increased.

A decline in float and increases in treasury cash holdings, treasury deposits, and other deposits with Federal Reserve banks and other Federal Reserve liabilities and capital were all factors absorbing a significant amount of reserves in the latest statement week. Partially offsetting these reserve drains were increases in gold stock and other Federal Reserve assets and a decline in currency in circulation. In addition, System Open Market Operations provided $351 million reserves net, on a weekly average basis, through outright purchases of treasury bills and repurchase agreements.

[2] When free reserves are negative, they are often referred to as net borrowed reserves.

TABLE 8a (continued)

Member Bank Reserves, Reserve Bank Credit, and Related Items	*Averages of Daily Figures (in millions of dollars)*			
		Change from Week Ended		
	Week Ended Oct. 24, 1973	*Oct. 17, 1973*	*Oct. 25, 1972*	*Wednesday, Oct. 24, 1973*
Sources:				
Reserve bank credit:				
U.S. government securities				
Bought outright—system account	76,525	+ 419	+6,647	76,563*
Held under repurchase agreements	128	− 176	− 53	897
Federal agency obligations				
Bought outright	1,742	+ 156	+ 721	1,739
Held under repurchase agreements	24	− 33	+ 22	172
Acceptances				
Bought outright	49	+ 4	− 23	48
Held under repurchase agreements	7	− 19	− 3	47
Loans				
Total member bank borrowing	1,914	+ 746	+1,149	3,367
Includes seasonal borrowing of:	125	+ 5	+ 125	123
Other borrowing	—	—	—	—
Float	2,988	− 459	−1,491	3,078
Other Federal Reserve assets	1,198	+ 89	− 71	1,215
Total Reserve bank credit	84,575	+ 727	+6,898	87,126
Gold stock	11,567	+1,157	+1,157	11,567
Special drawing rights certificate account	400	—		400
Treasury currency outstanding	8,622	+ 8	+ 383	8,623
	105,165	+1,892	+8,439	107,716
Uses:				
Currency in circulation	68,970	− 186	+5,486	69,077
Treasury cash holdings	1,522	+1,168	+1,156	1,537
Treasury deposits with Federal Reserve banks	1,566	+ 127	+ 104	1,252
Foreign deposits with Federal Reserve banks	254	− 22	+ 33	272
Other deposits with Federal Reserve banks†	950	+ 186	+ 335	673
Other Federal Reserve liabilities and capital	2,904	+ 102	+ 556	2,986
	76,167	+1,375	+7,671	75,797
Member bank reserves:				
With Federal Reserve banks	28,998	+ 516	+ 768	31,919
Currency and coin	5,907	− 507	+ 582	5,907
Total reserves held‡	34,989	+ 9	+1,434	37,910
Required reserves	34,746	− 352	+1,341	34,746
Excess reserves‡	243	+ 361	+ 93	3,164

Note: A net of $100 million of surplus reserves was eligible to be carried forward from the week ended October 17, into the week ending October 24.

On October 24, 1973, marketable U.S. government securities held in custody by the Federal Reserve banks for foreign and international accounts were $27,603 million, an increase of $237 million for the week.

* Includes $53 million securities loaned—fully secured by U.S. government securities pledged with Federal Reserve banks.

† Includes $36 million of certain deposits of domestic nonmember banks and foreign-owned banking institutions held with member banks and redeposited in full with Federal Reserve banks in connection with voluntary participation by nonmember institutions in the Federal Reserve system's program of credit restraint.

‡ Adjusted to include $84 million of certain reserve deficiencies on which penalties can be waived for a transition period in connection with bank adaptation to Regulation J as amended effective November 9, 1972.

TABLE 8b

Consolidated Statement of Condition of All Federal Reserve Banks (in millions of dollars)

		Wednesday Oct. 24, 1973	Change since Oct. 17, 1973	Change since Oct. 25, 1972
ASSETS				
Gold certificate account		10,303	—	—
Special drawing rights certificate accounts		400	—	—
Cash	(1,167)*	311	—	26
Loans		3,367	+1,831	+ 192
Acceptances—bought outright		48	+ 2	— 23
Held under repurchase agreements		47	— 37	— 27
Federal agency obligations—bought outright		1,739	+ 153	+ 719
Held under repurchase agreements		172	+ 6	+ 160
U.S. government securities:				
Bought outright—				
Bills		35,761	+ 300	+5,924
Certificates				
Other		—	—	—
Notes		37,374	—	+ 642
Bonds		3,428	—	— 170
Total bought outright	—†	76,563	+ 300	+6,396
Held under repurchase agreements		897	— 40	— 367
Total U.S. government securities		77,460	+ 260	+6,029
Total loans and securities		82,833	+2,215	+7,050
Cash items in process of collection	(1,601)	9,196	−1,010	−3,613
Bank premises		216	+ 3	+ 49
Other assets‡		999	+ 42	— 285
Total Assets	(2,768)	104,258	+1,250	+3,175
LIABILITIES				
Federal Reserve notes	(1,167)	61,038	— 116	+5,035
Deposits: Member bank-reserves account		31,839	+1,438	+ 130
U.S. treasurer—general account		1,252	+ 128	— 140
Foreign		272	14	+ 75
Other§		673	— 70	+ 105
Total deposits		34,036	+1,482	+ 170
Deferred availability cash items	(1,601)	6,198	— 256	−2,637
Other liabilities and accrued dividends		1,001	+ 39	+ 418
Total Liabilities	(2,768)	102,273	+1,149	+2,986
CAPITAL ACCOUNTS				
Capital paid in		834	+ 3	+ 53
Surplus		793	—	+ 51
Other capital accounts		358	+ 98	+ 85
Contingent liability on acceptances purchased for foreign correspondents		530	— 5	+ 309

* Figures in parentheses are the eliminations made in the consolidating process.

† Includes $53 million securities loaned—fully secured by U.S. government securities pledged with Federal Reserve banks.

‡ Includes assets denominated in foreign currencies.

§ Includes $36 million of certain deposits of domestic nonmember banks and foreign-owned banking institutions held with member banks and redeposited in full with Federal Reserve banks in connection with voluntary participation by nonmember institutions in the Federal Reserve system's program of credit restraint.

TABLE 8b (continued)
Maturities of Federal Reserve Assets

	Loans	Acceptances	U.S. Government Securities: Holdings	U.S. Government Securities: Weekly Changes	Federal Agency Obligations: Holdings	Federal Agency Obligations: Weekly Changes
Within 15 days	3,310	64	6,121	−682	172	+ 2
16 days to 90 days	57	31	18,813	+ 37	116	+ 10
91 days to 1 year	—	—	19,318	+905	300	+ 7
Over 1 year to 5 years	—	—	22,148	—	671	+ 46
Over 5 years to 10 years	—	—	9,358	—	425	+ 78
Over 10 years	—	—	1,702	—	227	+ 16
Total	3,367	95	77,460	+260	1,911	+159

* Acceptances and securities held under repurchase agreements are classified as maturing within 15 days in accordance with maximum maturity of the agreements.

tions theory of the term structure. Institutional constraints which inhibit the free movement of investments over the maturity scale prevent the full applicability of the expectational model. But to the extent that funds do move freely, there will tend to be an adjustment in the yield pattern bringing equality between the expected returns of all possible maturity combinations throughout the maturity of the outstanding security with the longest existing maturity. Such a condition of equality then implies that expectations of declining interest rates during the period of time represented by the yield pattern will result in a negatively sloped pattern. In this case, interest rates decrease as time to maturity increases.

Suppose, for example, that the yield curve is fairly horizontal. Then suppose that lower rates of interest are expected with certainty. Investors having these changed expectations will lengthen their portfolios until the yield pattern has become sufficiently negative to satisfy the aforementioned equilibrium condition. In other words, the shift in loanable funds from shorter to longer term commitments brings about a negatively sloped yield curve. Alternatively, an expected rise in rates of interest will lead to a positively sloped yield pattern.

With uncertain expectations, the term structure will be determined not only by the pattern of those expectations but by the balance of investor preferences for capital-value and income certainty relative to the supply of short- and long-term securities. If an investor is primarily concerned with the preservation of capital value, he will tend to favor shorter term securities. This choice stems from the characteristic behavior of the capital market, wherein the prices of long-term securities fluctuate over a wider range than the prices of short-term securities.[3]

[3] This assumes, also, diminishing marginal utility of wealth and an equal probability of a rise and fall in long-term bond prices. Then the loss in utility due to a fall in bond prices will exceed the gain in utility due to a rise.

TABLE 9

Federal Reserve Statistical Release—Weekly Summary of Banking and Credit Measures (averages of daily figures, October 25, 1973)

	Levels (seasonally adjusted, in billions)				Percent Change (seasonally adjusted annual rates); Average of 4 Weeks Ended Oct. 24, 1973, from 4-Week Averages		
	Week Ended		4 Weeks Ended				
Reserve Aggregates:*	Oct. 24	Oct. 17	Oct. 24	Sept. 26	13 Weeks Previous	26 Weeks Previous	52 Weeks Previous
Total reserves	$ 35.13	$ 34.83	$ 34.85	$ 34.09	5.0%	7.3%	9.0%
Nonborrowed reserves	33.44	33.64	33.41	32.55	2.5	13.4	6.4
Required reserves	34.72	35.03	34.61	33.91	5.1	7.5	9.0
Reserves available to support private nonbank deposits	32.84	32.51	32.69	32.29	8.2	10.6	11.2
	Week Ended		4 Weeks Ended		Average of 4 Weeks Ended Oct. 17, 1973, from 4-Week Averages		
Monetary Aggregates:	Oct. 17	Oct. 10	Oct. 17	Sept. 19	13 Weeks Previous	26 Weeks Previous	52 Weeks Previous
M_1 (currency plus demand deposits)	$ 265.7	$ 263.6	$ 263.9	$ 263.6	−0.5%	5.0%	5.1%
M_2 (M_1 plus time deposits at commercial banks other than large time CD's)	558.3	555.2	554.9	551.7	5.9	7.6	7.8
Adjusted credit proxy†	448.4	446.1	446.8	445.4	9.2	10.3	12.5
Time deposits, all commercial banks	355.7	355.4	355.6	355.5	10.9	12.2	17.1
U.S. government demand deposits, member banks	7.5	6.9	6.4	4.6			
	(not seasonally adjusted, in millions)						
	Week Ended		4 Weeks Ended				
Other Reserve Measures and Interest Rates:	Oct. 24	Oct. 17	Oct. 24	Sept. 26			
Member bank borrowings	$1914.00	$1168.00	$1489.00	$1936.00			
Includes seasonal borrowings of	125.00	120.00	130.00	151.00			
Federal funds rate	9.98	10.07	10.16	10.79			
Three-month treasury bill rate	7.06	7.19	7.19	8.47			
90- to 119-day dealer placed commercial paper rate‡	9.06	9.33	9.39	10.40			
Three-month CD rate (secondary market) §	9.15	9.36	9.46	10.79			
Three-month Euro-dollar rate	9.60	10.06	10.17	11.30			
U.S. government bond rate‖	7.24	7.17	7.16	7.29			

* Includes required reserves against Euro-dollar borrowings and bank-related commercial paper. Reserves available to support private nonbank deposits are required reserves for private demand deposits, total time and savings deposits, nondeposit sources subject to reserve requirements, and excess reserves. Reserve aggregates reflect the change in Regulation D effective November 9, 1972, which reduced required reserves by about $3.2 billion; and effective July 19, 1973, which increased required reserves by about $760 million; and effective October 4, 1973, which increased required reserves $465 million. Effective July 12, 1973, marginal reserve requirements on ineligible acceptances increased required reserves by about $90 million. Percent annual rates of growth for required reserves and other reserve aggregates have been adjusted to remove the effect of these structural changes.

Adjusted to include certain reserve deficiencies on which penalties can be waived for a transition period in connection with bank adaptation to Regulation J as amended effective November 9, 1972. The adjustment amounted to $450 million from November 9 to December 27, 1972; $279 million from December 28, 1972 to March 28, 1973; $172 million from March 29, 1973 to June 27, 1973; $112 million from June 28, 1973 to September 26, 1973; and $84 million thereafter.

† Includes member bank deposits, bank-related commercial paper, Euro-dollar borrowings of U.S. banks, and certain nondeposit items.

‡ On October 17, bank-related commercial paper amounted to $4,729 million.

§ Average of range of offering rates of negotiable certificates of deposit with three-month maturity in second market.

Daily average yield on 20-year bonds.

On the other hand, if the investor emphasizes the preservation of income, he will prefer to invest in long-term obligations.[4] It follows, therefore, that the preponderance of investor preferences with respect to capital and income certainty will add its weight to expectations and noneconomic portfolio constraints in the determination of the term structure of interest rates.

Examples of treasury yield patterns showing peaks and troughs from 1965 to 1973 are depicted in Charts 5 through 12. These patterns represent the structure of yields near cyclical turning points. The balance of investor preferences with regard to capital and income certainty is therefore overlaid in each instance by expectations of interest rate changes. The force of these expectations, however, is apparently not sufficiently strong to offset investor concern for liquidity—hence the hump-shaped curve near the cyclical peak.

The yield pattern as a function of time to maturity can be used as a

CHART 5

Yields of Treasury Securities, Sept. 30, 1965 (based on closing bid quotations)

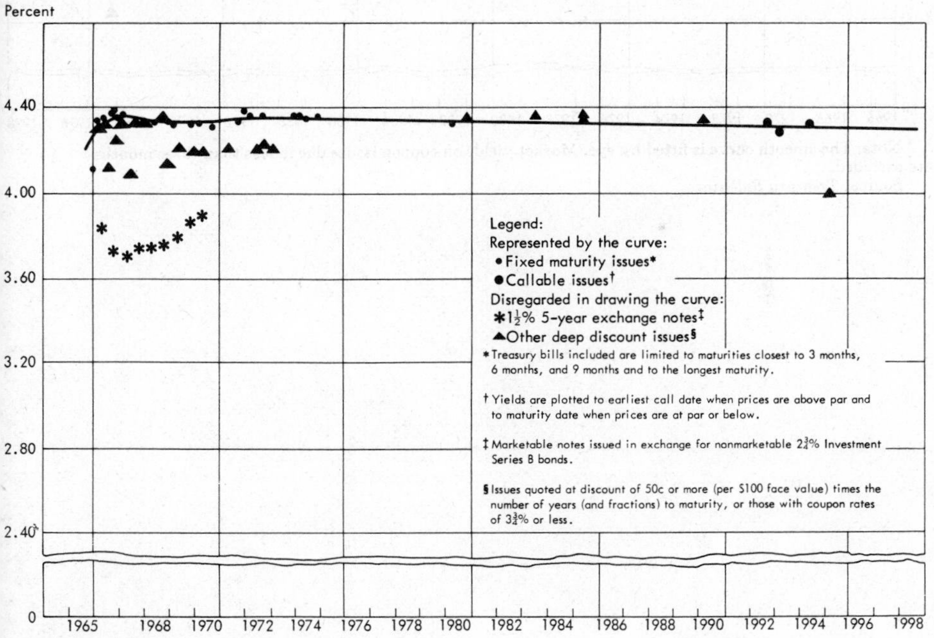
Percent
4.40
4.00
3.60
3.20
2.80
2.40
0
1965
1968
1970
1972
1974
1976
1978
1980
1982
1984
1986
1988
1990
1992
1994
1996
1998
Legend:
Represented by the curve:
• Fixed maturity issues*
● Callable issues†
Disregarded in drawing the curve:
✱ 1½% 5-year exchange notes‡
▲ Other deep discount issues§
* Treasury bills included are limited to maturities closest to 3 months, 6 months, and 9 months and to the longest maturity.
† Yields are plotted to earliest call date when prices are above par and to maturity date when prices are at par or below.
‡ Marketable notes issued in exchange for nonmarketable 2¾% Investment Series B bonds.
§ Issues quoted at discount of 50c or more (per $100 face value) times the number of years (and fractions) to maturity, or those with coupon rates of 3¾% or less.

Note: The smooth curve is fitted by eye. Market yields on coupon issues due in less than three months are excluded.
Source: *Treasury Bulletin.*

[4] Interest rates on long-term securities tend to fluctuate over a more narrow range than those on short-term obligations, and the utility of a possible rise in interest rates will be less than the utility of a possible decline.

CHART 6

Yields of Treasury Securities, Oct. 31, 1966 (based on closing bid quotations)

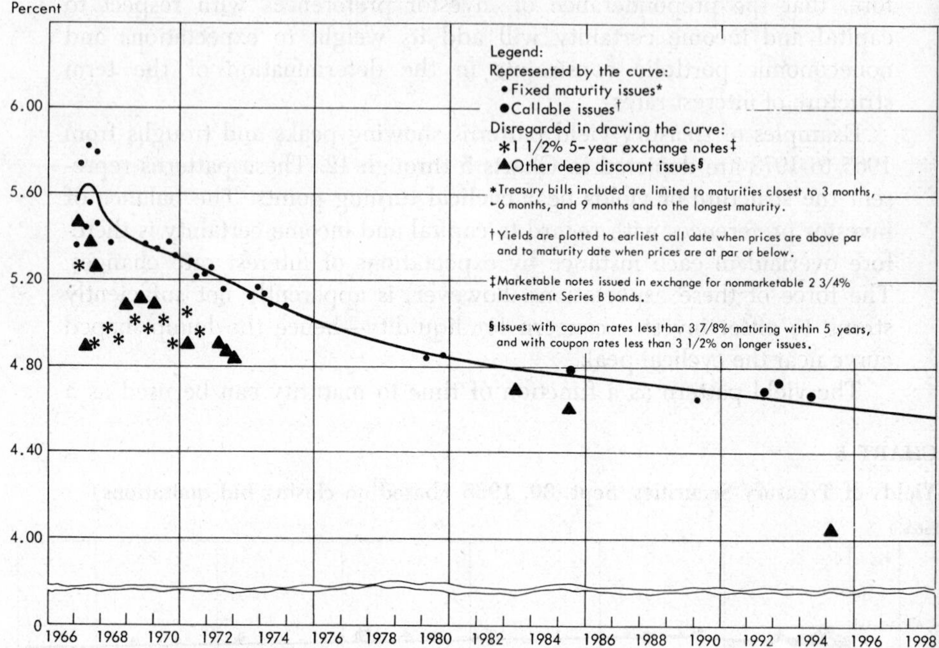

Percent
Legend:
Represented by the curve:
• Fixed maturity issues*
● Callable issues†
Disregarded in drawing the curve:
* 1 1/2% 5-year exchange notes‡
▲ Other deep discount issues§
* Treasury bills included are limited to maturities closest to 3 months, 6 months, and 9 months and to the longest maturity.
† Yields are plotted to earliest call date when prices are above par and to maturity date when prices are at par or below.
‡ Marketable notes issued in exchange for nonmarketable 2 3/4% Investment Series B bonds.
§ Issues with coupon rates less than 3 7/8% maturing within 5 years, and with coupon rates less than 3 1/2% on longer issues.
6.00
5.60
5.20
4.80
4.40
4.00
0
1966
1968
1970
1972
1974
1976
1978
1980
1982
1984
1986
1988
1990
1992
1994
1996
1998

Note: The smooth curve is fitted by eye. Market yields on coupon issues due in less than three months are excluded.

Source: *Treasury Bulletin.*

CHART 7

Yields of Treasury Securities, May 31, 1967 (based on closing bid quotations)

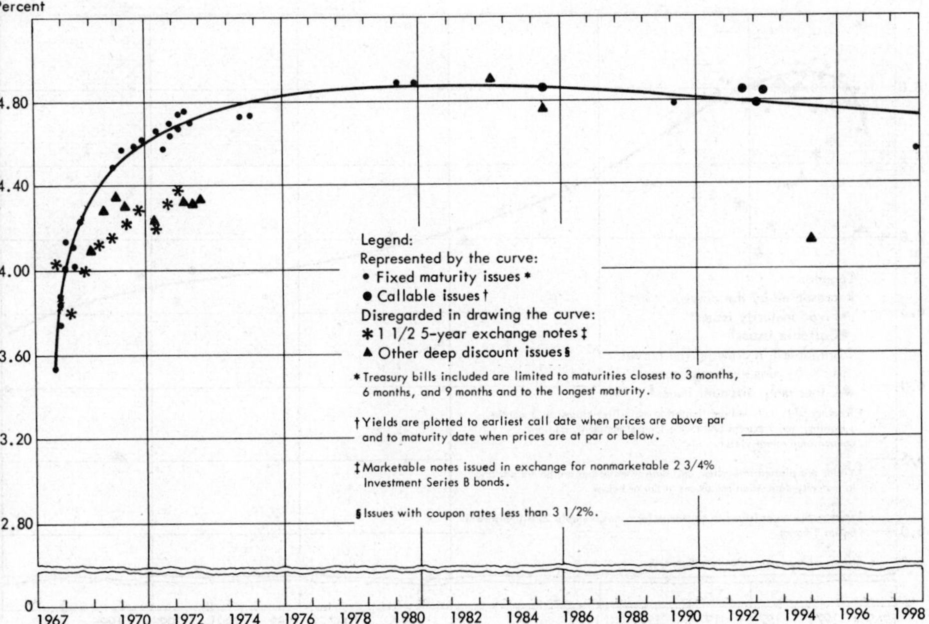
Percent
4.80
4.40
4.00
3.60
3.20
2.80
0
1967
1970
1972
1974
1976
1978
1980
1982
1984
1986
1988
1990
1992
1994
1996
1998
Legend:
Represented by the curve:
● Fixed maturity issues *
● Callable issues †
Disregarded in drawing the curve:
✱ 1 1/2 5-year exchange notes ‡
▲ Other deep discount issues §
* Treasury bills included are limited to maturities closest to 3 months, 6 months, and 9 months and to the longest maturity.
† Yields are plotted to earliest call date when prices are above par and to maturity date when prices are at par or below.
‡ Marketable notes issued in exchange for nonmarketable 2 3/4% Investment Series B bonds.
§ Issues with coupon rates less than 3 1/2%.

Note: The smooth curve is fitted by eye. Market yields on coupon issues due in less than three months are excluded.

Source: *Treasury Bulletin.*

CHART 8

Yields of Treasury Securities, Sept. 30, 1969 (based on closing bid quotations)

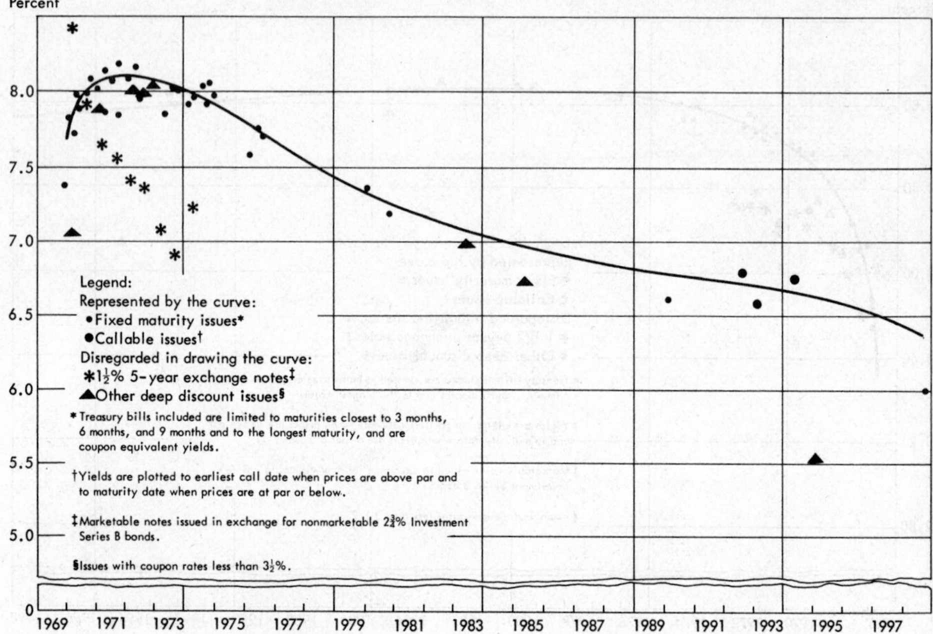
Percent
8.0
7.5
7.0
6.5
6.0
5.5
5.0
0
1969
1971
1973
1975
1977
1979
1981
1983
1985
1987
1989
1991
1993
1995
1997
Legend:
Represented by the curve:
•Fixed maturity issues*
●Callable issues†
Disregarded in drawing the curve:
✱1½% 5-year exchange notes‡
▲Other deep discount issues§
* Treasury bills included are limited to maturities closest to 3 months, 6 months, and 9 months and to the longest maturity, and are coupon equivalent yields.
† Yields are plotted to earliest call date when prices are above par and to maturity date when prices are at par or below.
‡ Marketable notes issued in exchange for nonmarketable 2¾% Investment Series B bonds.
§ Issues with coupon rates less than 3½%.

Note: The smooth curve is fitted by eye. Market yields on coupon issues due in less than three months are excluded.

Source: *Treasury Bulletin.*

CHART 9

Yields of Treasury Securities, February 26, 1971 (based on closing bid quotations)

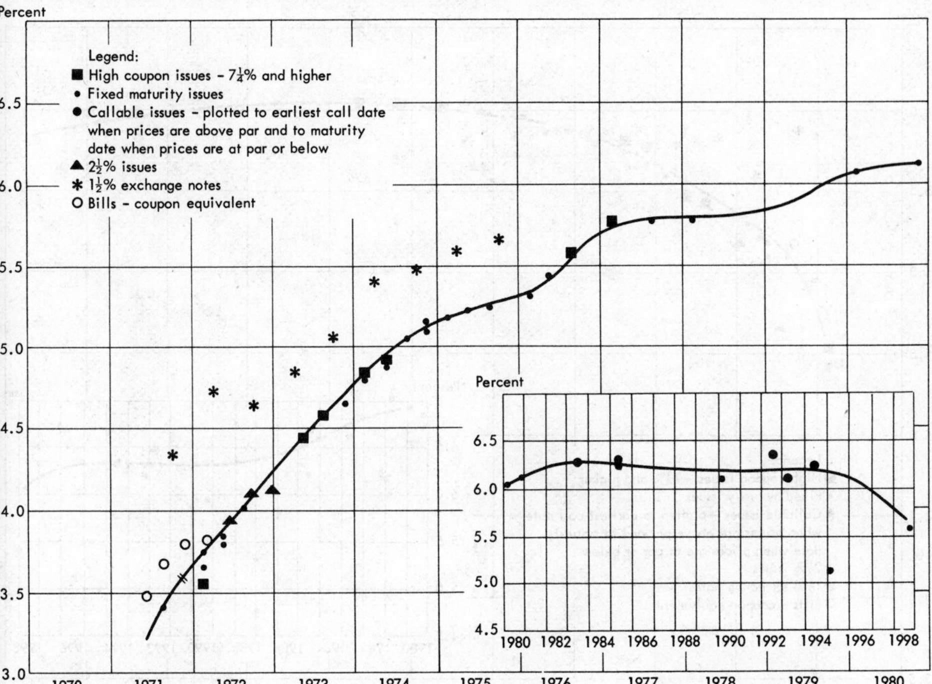

Note: The smooth curve is fitted by eye. Market yields on coupon issues due in less than three months are excluded.

Source: *Treasury Bulletin*.

CHART 10

Yields of Treasury Securities, July 30, 1971 (based on closing bid quotations)

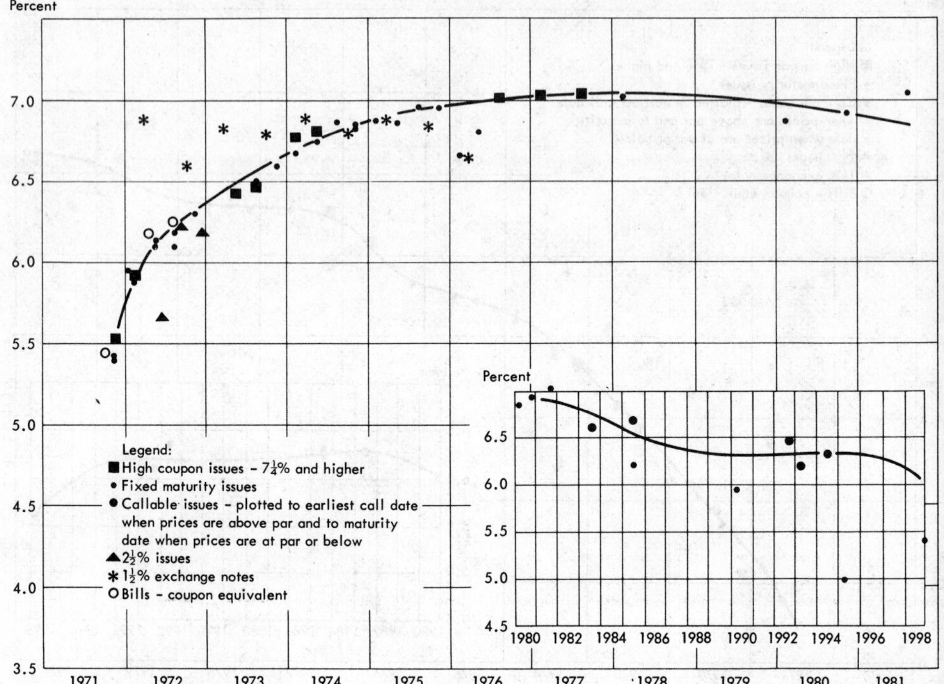

Note: The smooth curve is fitted by eye. Market yields on coupon issues due in less than three months are excluded.

Source: *Treasury Bulletin.*

CHART 11

Yields of Treasury Securities, January 31, 1972 (based on closing bid quotations)

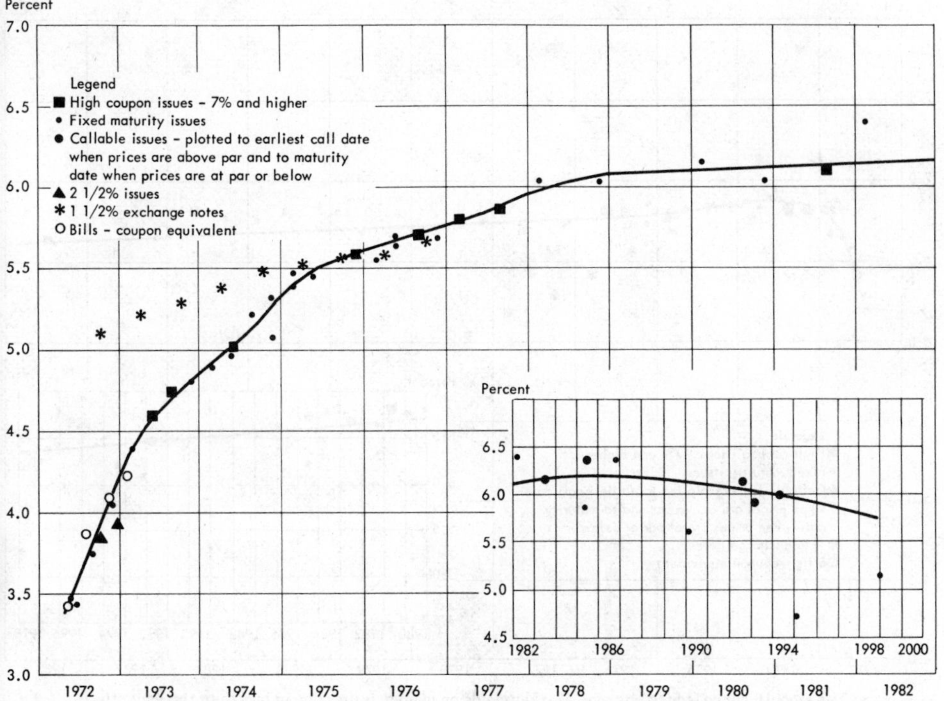

Note: The smooth curve is fitted by eye. Market yields on coupon issues due in less than three months are excluded.

Source: *Treasury Bulletin.*

CHART 12

Yields of Treasury Securities, April 30, 1973 (based on closing bid quotations)

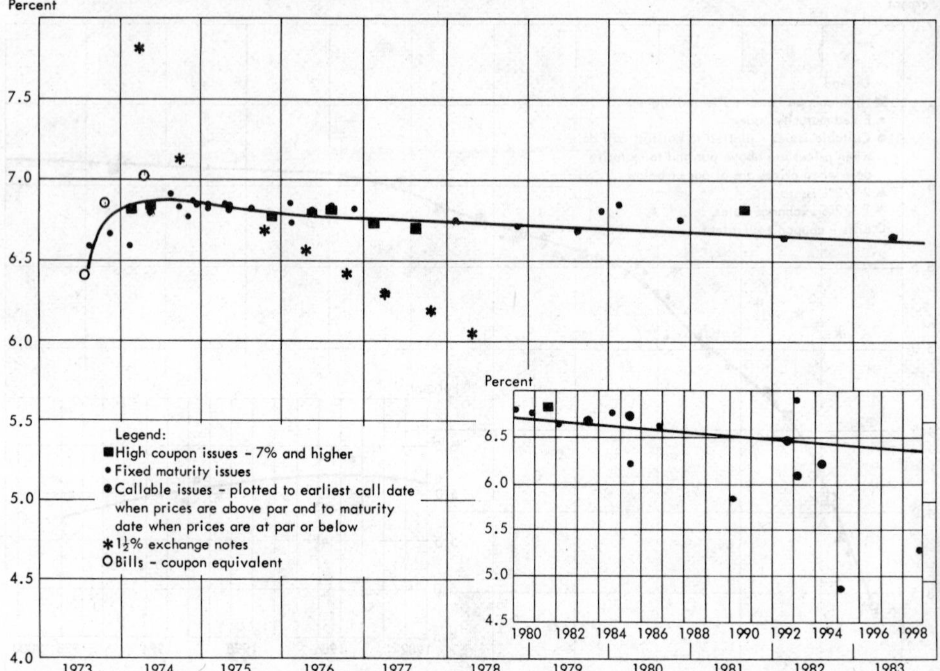

Note: The smooth curve is fitted by eye. Market yields on coupon issues due in less than three months are excluded.
Source: *Treasury Bulletin.*

forecasting device in the sense that it tells the forecaster what the market is forecasting, with some allowance, of course, for risk aversion, whether in the form of liquidity premium or a premium for income certainty. This is not to say, of course, that the market is always right. However, the bond market tends to be dominated by market professionals who have abundant experience and keen insight into economic forces and their implication for money rates. Hence, to say the least, the current yield pattern provides a point of departure for constructing an interest rate forecast.

INTERNATIONAL MONEY AND SECURITIES MARKETS

The heart of the international money market is the so-called Eurodollar market. It is the market for bank deposits which are denominated in foreign currencies. Most of the banks that accept deposits in the form of a foreign currency are located in Europe, and the great preponderance of such deposits is denominated in U.S. dollars. Thus, transactions in the Euro-dollar market consist primarily of purchases and sales by European banks, including the European branches of U.S. banks, of the demand liabilities of banks located in the United States.

Euro-dollar commitments vary from call to seven days, to one month, three months, and longer. Negotiable time certificates of deposit (CD's) are also issued in Euro-dollars, usually for maturities of one month or longer (Tables 10 and 11, and Chart 13). Deposits are received without the pledge of collateral. Trading units are usually in blocks of $1 million or more.

TABLE 10

Representative Rates of London Dollar Certificates of Deposit

	Percent Offer	
	July 31, 1973	*August 31, 1973*
Short		
One month	11¼	11½
Three months	11¼	11½
Six months	11⅛	11½
One year	10⅜	10¾
Medium Term		
Two years	9⅝	9¾
Three years	9⅜	9½
Four years	9⅜	9⅜
Five years	9¼	9¼
	Bid—Offer	
Medium Term Tranche Issues		
6½% Credit Lyonnais, January 1975	94 –95	95 –96
7½% The Fuji Bank, September 1976	93 –94	94 –95
7½% British & French Bank Limited, November 1976	93 –94	94 –95
7⅝% The Sanwa Bank, September 1977	92½–93½	92½–93½
7⅝% The Sumitomo Bank, September 1977	92½–93½	92½–93½
7⅝% The Mitsubishi Bank, September 1977	92½–93½	92½–93½
7¼% The Dai-Ichi Kangyo Bank, January 1978	92 –93	91½–92½
7¼% The Fuji Bank, January 1978	92 –93	91½–92½

Source: *The International Bond Letter*, White, Weld and Co., Ltd., September 3, 1973.

London is the center of the Euro-dollar market, and U.S. dollars may be placed there through U.S. investment and commercial banks by means of their overseas branches or correspondents.

The international capital market is composed of two sectors, those devoted to foreign bonds and those to Euro-bonds. (See Tables 12 and 13.) The foreign bond market is essentially a national market in which a foreign borrower floats an issue denominated in the domestic currency. In these cases, the investor exercises his legal claim in the jurisdiction belonging to the issues.

The Euro-bond is in reality an international security. Securities floated

TABLE 11

Euro-Dollar Deposit Rates (prime banks' bid rates in London, at or near end of month)

		Call	*7-day notice*	*One month*	*Three months*	*Six months*	*Twelve months*
1971	*Dec*	5.13	5.25	5.75	5.75	5.81	6.00
1972	*Mar*	4.00	4.00	5.00	5.44	5.94	6.38
	Jun	4.13	4.13	4.69	5.25	5.69	6.06
	Sep	4.63	4.63	5.00	6.00	6.13	6.38
	Dec	5.00	5.13	5.69	5.88	6.19	6.38
1973	*Mar*	9.75	8.00	8.38	8.63	8.63	8.50
	Apr	7.88	7.94	7.88	8.25	8.50	8.38
	May	7.50	7.63	8.44	8.44	8.56	8.63
	Jun	8.13	8.63	8.75	9.00	9.25	9.00
	Jul	10.13	10.38	10.81	11.38	11.38	10.50
	Aug	10.63	10.88	11.44	11.50	11.50	10.75
	Sep	10.38	10.38	10.88	10.38	10.31	9.69
	Oct	9.38	9.38	8.88	9.13	8.81	8.50
	Nov	9.38	9.50	10.88	10.38	9.81	9.19
	Dec	9.38	9.63	10.06	10.13	10.13	9.56
1974	*Jan*	8.50	8.63	8.94	8.94	8.88	8.69
	Feb	8.38	8.38	8.50	8.50	8.50	8.38

Source: *World Financial Markets*, Morgan Guaranty Trust Company of New York, March 1974.

CHART 13

Term-Structure of Dollar CD Rates in London (secondary market offered)

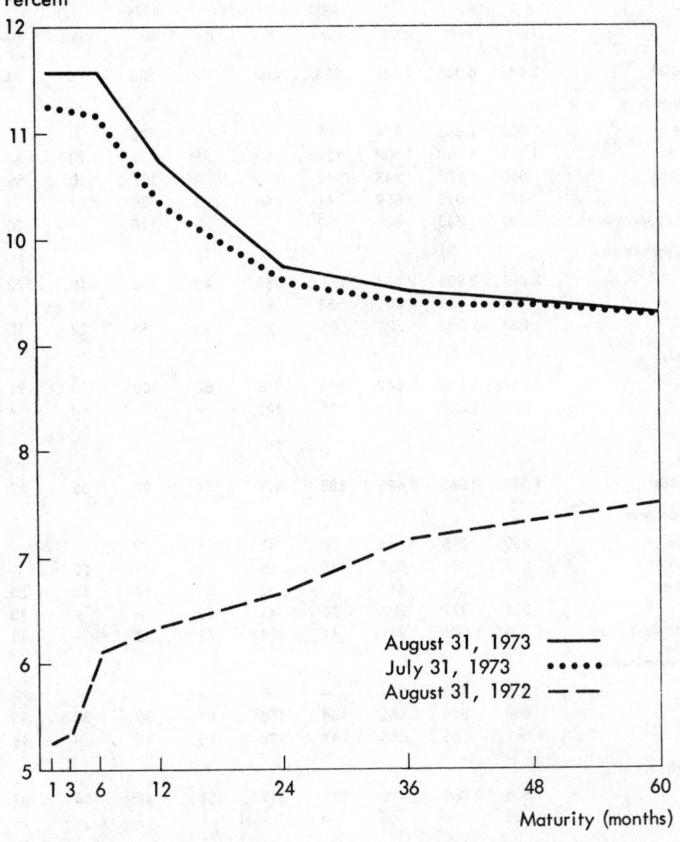

Source: *The International Bond Letter*, White, Weld and Co., Ltd., September 3, 1973.

in this market may be denominated in a currency other than that belonging either to the issuer or to the investor. Moreover, the issuer and investor may be subject to different legal jurisdictions.

Euro-bonds may take on many dimensions in terms of denomination. In terms of financial innovation, the Euro-bond market is a unique area. There are optional currency loans as well as loans expressed in European units of account or European currency units. Bond yields are shown in Table 14.

Borrowers in these markets are well established. They include the great companies of the world, national governments and their subsidiaries, and substantial international financial institutions, such as the International Bank for Reconstruction and Development,[5] the Euro-

[5] The tax status of International Bank issues along with that of U.S. government and federal agency issues is summarized in Table 15. Needless to say, the investor should consult his tax counsel for further details.

TABLE 12

New International Bond Issues (new issues in period, in millions of dollars)

				1973			1974			Jan-Mar	
	1971	1972	1973	Oct	Nov	Dec	Jan	Feb	Mar p	1974 p	1973
Euro-bonds, total	**3 642**	**6 335**	**4 189**	**433**	**403**	**62**	**280**	**179**	**91**	**550**	**1 676**
by category of borrower											
U.S. companies	1 098	1 992	874	68	165	–	25	–	–	25	479
Other companies	1 119	1 759	1 309	122	80	19	–	73	12	85	642
State enterprises	848	1 170	943	142	118	–	107	15	59	181	356
Governments	479	1 019	659	41	40	43	30	91	–	121	79
International organizations	98	395	404	60	–	–	118	–	20	138	120
by currency of denomination											
U.S. dollar	2 221	3 908	2 467	255	285	49	195	119	72	386	1 122
German mark	786	1 129	1 001	83	97	–	–	37	–	37	325
Other	635	1 298	721	95	21	13	85	23	19	127	229
by type of security											
Straight debt	3 347	5 115	3 542	418	278	62	280	129	91	500	1 319
Convertible	295	1 220	647	15	125	–	–	50	–	50	357
Foreign bonds outside U.S., total	**1 538**	**2 060**	**2 485**	**195**	**317**	**157**	**47**	**38**	**87**	**172**	**710**
by category of borrower											
U.S. companies	200	215	484	70	45	25	–	–	–	–	154
Other companies	212	345	365	18	25	–	–	22	–	22	77
State enterprises	163	249	412	–	82	61	17	16	20	53	115
Governments	254	177	283	66	41	29	–	–	19	19	51
International organizations	709	1 074	941	41	124	42	30	–	48	78	313
by currency of denomination											
German mark	308	500	374	–	39	–	–	–	–	–	191
Swiss franc	669	815	1 456	154	156	61	30	38	39	107	281
Other	561	745	655	41	122	96	17	–	48	65	238
by type of security											
Straight debt	1 508	2 060	2 476	195	317	157	47	38	87	172	710
Convertible	30	–	9	–	–	–	–	–	–	–	–
Foreign bonds in U.S., total	**1 106**	**1 361**	**715**	**185**	**40**	**225**	**–**	**140**	**200**	**340**	**40**
by category of borrower											
Other companies	270	199	78	–	–	–	–	25	–	25	–
State enterprises	141	382	347	60	–	100	–	35	50	85	40
Governments	270	530	290	–	40	125	–	80	150	230	–
International organizations	425	250	–	–	–	–	–	–	–	–	–
International bonds, total	**6 286**	**9 756**	**7 389**	**688**	**760**	**444**	**327**	**357**	**378**	**1 062**	**2 426**

p = preliminary.
Source: *World Financial Markets*, Morgan Guaranty Trust Company of New York, March 1974.

TABLE 13

New International Bond Issues

Issuer (Guarantor) (Euro-bond: E; Foreign bond: outside United States—F,O; in United States—F,US)	Country/state of domicile	Amount, millions	Offer date	Coupon rate a	Maturity	Offer price	Yield b
February 1974							
Other companies							
Wedgwood Limited (F,O)	U.K.	SwF 9	4	8 a	1989	100	7.85
N.V. Philip Gloeilampenfabriken (F,O)	Netherlands	SwF 60	12	7 a	1989	101	6.78
Asia Navigation International Ltd. (Eastern Asia Navigation Ltd.) (E) c	Bermuda	$50	14	6½ a	1989	100	6.40
Pechiney-Ugine-Kuhlman-International N.V. (Pechiney-Ugine-Kuhlman S.A.) (E)	Netherlands	EUA 20	15	8¾ a	1989	98	8.80
Canadian Pacific Limited (F,US) d	Canada	$25	n.a.	8½	1989	n.a.	n.a.
State enterprises							
Electricity Supply Commission of South Africa (Republic of South Africa) (E)	S. Africa	$15	15	9¼ a	1989	98½	9.23
Jutland Telefon-Aktieselskab (F,O)	Denmark	SwF 50	20	7¼ a	1989	99½	7.18
Neste Oy (Republic of Finland) (F,US) d	Finland	$10	20	8½	1988	n.a.	n.a.
Banque Française du Commerce Exterieur (F,US) d	France	$25	n.a.	9	n.a.	n.a.	n.a.
Governments							
City of Coventry (E)	U.K.	$20	1	8⅞ a	1981	98¾	8.93
Kingdom of Denmark (E)		DM 100	15	9¼ a	1989	99	9.17
City of Montreal (F,US) d	Canada	$80	20	8.85	1999	100	8.85
City of Bristol (E) d	U.K.	$34	23	8⅞	1980	n.a.	n.a.
March 1974 — preliminary							
Other companies							
Mitsubishi Rayon Conpany Ltd. (Mitsubishi Bank Limited) (E)	Japan	$12	7	9 a	1989	98½	8.99
State enterprises							
Cie. Financiere et Industrielle des Autoroutes (Republic of France) (E)	France	EUA 17	6	9 a	1989	99½	8.87
Oesterreichische Donaukraftwerke (Republic of Austria) (F,O)	Austria	SwF 60	11	7 a	1989	100	6.88
Banque Française du Commerce Exterieur (Republic of France) (E)	France	$20 $20	13 13	8⅜ a 8¾ a	1981 1989		
New Brunswick Electric Power Company (F,US)	Canada	$50	14		2004		
Governments							
City of Saint-Leonard (F,O)	Canada	SwF 9	7	7½ a	1989	97¾	7.61
City of Helsinki (F,US)	Finland	$25	13		1999		
Province of Ontario (F,US)	Canada	$125	13	8.60	2004	100	8.60
Government of Papua New Guinea (Commonwealth of Australia) (F,O)		SwF 50	25	7¼ a	1989		
International organizations							
International Bank for Reconstruction and Development (F,O)		Bv 100	7	7	1981	97	7.56
Inter-American Development Bank (F,O)		Bv 100		7	1981		
European Coal and Steel Community (E)		$20		8¼ a	1978		

a Coupon interest is payable semiannually unless followed by an "a" which indicates an annual coupon.

b Where coupon interest is payable annually, payment is discounted semiannually for comparability in computation of yield.

c Convertible into the common stock of the parent after September 2, 1974. Conversion price premium over closing price of common on day preceding offering was 10.2%.

d Private placement.

Source: *World Financial Markets*, Morgan Guaranty Trust Company of New York, March 1974.

pean Investment Bank, the Asian Development Bank, and the Inter-American Development Bank.

Since the fate of a national currency is involved in these investments, the ordinary terms of interest, maturity, and underlying quality must be interpreted in the ever apparent context of fluctuating exchange rates.

TABLE 14

International Bond Yields (long-term issues, at or near end of month)

		U.S. Companies			European companies		Governments
		U.S. dollar	German mark	Swiss franc	U.S. dollar	German mark	U.S. dollar
1972	*Dec*	7.49	7.01	5.89	7.69	7.19	7.65
1973	*Mar*	7.90	6.83	5.69	8.07	6.91	8.03
	Apr	7.96	6.77	5.72	8.15	6.90	8.07
	May	8.51	6.86	5.63	8.64	6.94	8.55
	Jun	8.53	7.20	5.65	8.72	7.29	8.61
	Jul	8.61	7.51	5.74	8.75	7.64	8.53
	Aug	8.48	7.71	6.17	8.62	7.92	8.66
	Sep	8.36	7.92	6.19	8.61	8.01	8.75
	Oct	8.12	7.76	5.94	8.30	7.93	8.55
	Nov	8.27	8.62	6.53	8.56	8.75	8.48
	Dec	8.26	9.27	6.68	8.56	9.25	8.69
1974	*Jan*	8.13	9.22	6.78	8.62	9.39	8.60
	Feb	8.17	9.28	7.02	8.70	9.42	8.66

Source: *World Financial Markets*, Morgan Guaranty Trust Company of New York, March 1974.

TABLE 15

Taxable Status—Government and Agency Securities

Security	*Federal*	*State*	*Local*	*Inheritance*	*Capital Gains*
U.S. Treasury securities	T	E	E	T	T
Federal Land Banks	T	E	E	T	T
Bank for Cooperatives	T	E	L	T	T
Federal Intermediate Credit Banks	T	E	L	T	T
Federal Home Loan Bank	T	E	E	T	T
Federal National Mortgage Association	T	T	T	T	T
Government National Mortgage Association	T	T	T	T	T
Export-Import Bank	T	E	E	T	T
Tennessee Valley Authority	T	E	E	T	T
Federal Home Loan Mortgage Corporation	T	E	E	T	T
International Bank for Reconstruction & Development	T	T	T	T	T

T = Taxable (unless exempt under the respective acts authorizing the issuance of such obligations).
E = Exempt.
L = Taxable status depends on local laws.

SUGGESTED REFERENCES

BANK FOR INTERNATIONAL SETTLEMENTS. *Forty-fourth Annual Report.* Basle, Switzerland, June 1974.

BARRETT, MARTIN. "Euro-Bonds: An Emerging International Capital Market." *Federal Reserve Bank of New York Monthly Review,* August 1968.

FEDERAL RESERVE BANK OF CLEVELAND. *Money Market Instruments.* September 1971.

FEDERAL RESERVE BANK OF NEW YORK. *Essays in Money and Credit.* December 1964.

FEDERAL RESERVE BANK OF NEW YORK. "Government-Sponsored Credit Agencies." *Federal Reserve Bank of New York Monthly Review,* April 1970.

FEDERAL RESERVE BANK OF RICHMOND. *Instruments of the Money Market.* February 1968.

LITTLE, JANE SNEDDON. "The Euro-dollar Market: Its Nature and Impact." *Federal Reserve Bank of Boston, New England Economic Review,* May/June 1969.

MORGAN GUARANTY TRUST COMPANY OF NEW YORK. *Money-Market Investments; World Financial Markets;* and *World Financial Statistics.*

PIGGOTT, WILLIAM et al. *Financial Institutions and the Economy.* Englewood Cliffs, N.J.: Prentice-Hall, 1974.

POLAKOFF, MURRAY E. et al. *Financial Institutions and Markets.* New York: Houghton Mifflin, 1970.

ROBINSON, ROLAND I. *Money and Capital Markets.* New York: McGraw-Hill, 1964.

SCOTT, IRA O., Jr. *Government Securities Market.* New York: McGraw-Hill, 1965.

———. *European Capital Markets.* Washington, D.C.: U.S. Treasury Department, Office of the Comptroller of the Currency, 1968.

Treasury Bulletin. Washington, D.C.: Superintendent of Documents, U.S. Government Printing Office.

VAN HORNE, JAMES C. *Function and Analysis of Capital Market Rates.* Englewood Cliffs, N.J.: Prentice-Hall, 1970.

WHITE, WELD, AND COMPANY. *The International Bond Letter.* New York.

WOODWORTH, G. WALTER. *The Money Market and Monetary Management.* New York: Harper and Row, 1972.

12

State and Municipal Obligations

GORDON L. CALVERT, J.D.
Vice President and General Counsel (Washington)
The New York Stock Exchange
Washington, D.C.

TYPES OF BONDS

THE TERM *municipal bonds* is generally understood to include all bonds issued by state and local governments and their agencies. This includes bonds issued by a state, territory or possession of the United States or by any municipality, political subdivision (including cities, counties, school districts, and special districts for fire prevention, water, sewer, irrigation, and other purposes), or public agency or instrumentality (such as an authority or commission) of one or more of the foregoing. These bonds all have a common feature in that the Internal Revenue Code exempts interest on such bonds from federal income tax (except for a few classes of bonds which are not issued to finance public facilities, discussed later in the section on tax exemption). State and municipal bonds could be classified according to the purpose for which they are issued (such as construction of schools, water and sewer facilities, and highways). However, they are usually classified in categories based on the sources of funds for their payment, as general obligations, revenue bonds, or special types (housing authority bonds, industrial bonds, pollution control bonds, and arbitrage bonds).

General Obligations

General obligation bonds are secured by the issuer's pledge of its full faith, credit, and taxing power for payment of the bonds. If bonds are secured by the full faith, credit, and taxing power of the issuer, and the issuer's taxing power is limited to a specified maximum tax rate, the bonds are still classified as general obligation bonds; but they are *limited tax bonds* and purchasers should be informed of the limitation on the taxing authority of the issuer.

Revenue Bonds

Revenue bonds are payable from revenues derived from tolls, user charges or rents paid by those who use the facilities acquired or constructed with the proceeds from the bonds (such as toll roads or bridges). Revenues from other facilities owned by the issuer of the bonds also may serve as a source of payment. For example, Port of New York Authority Consolidated Bonds are payable from net revenues of certain facilities owned by the authority and from net revenues—subject to existing liens of prior bonds—of all other existing authority facilities and from general reserve fund. If bonds payable primarily from revenues of a particular facility are also secured by a pledge of the full faith, credit, and taxing power of the issuer, the bonds are general obligations. An example is sewer bonds payable primarily from revenues of the sewer system but also secured by the full faith, credit, and taxing power of a city.

Special tax bonds are payable only from the proceeds from a special tax, such as highway bonds which are payable only from gasoline taxes. For purposes of general classification, special tax bonds are sometimes classed in the general category of revenue bonds because they are payable only from a special fund, as distinguished from general obligation bonds which are secured by the full faith, credit, and taxing power of the issuer. If bonds payable primarily from a special tax are also secured by a pledge of the full faith, credit, and taxing power of the issuer, the bonds are general obligations. This category could also include *special assessment* bonds payable only from assessment against those who benefit from the facilities constructed with the proceeds from the sale of the bonds (such as special improvement bonds for curbs and gutters). However, the great majority of special assessment bonds recently issued have been additionally secured by a pledge of full faith, credit, and taxing power, so that they are general obligations.

Special Types

Most of the bonds included here as special types are usually revenue bonds but they have unique features which merit separate description.

Housing Authority Bonds. These are issued by local public housing authorities and are secured by an annual pledge of the net rental revenues of the local housing authority and by an annual contributions contract with the Public Housing Administration (PHA) of the United States. The PHA is unconditionally obligated to pay annual contributions of amounts which, together with other funds of the local public housing authority available for such purpose, will be sufficient to pay the principal and interest on the bonds when due. The obligation of the PHA to make payment of the annual contribution provided for in the contract is unconditional, and thereby the faith of the United States is solemnly pledged to the payment of such annual contributions.

Industrial Development Bonds. In the early 1960s there was a sudden boom in the number and size of municipal bond issues (mostly by counties and cities) to finance the construction of industrial facilities to be leased to private companies and secured by the rental payments of those companies.[1] This type of financing originated in efforts by southern states with largely agricultural economies to attract industry. Such financing, utilizing tax-exempt bonds to finance industrial facilities to be leased to private companies, usually was secured only by rental payments from the private company; but in some cases was also secured as general obligations of the issuing municipality. These bonds were used to finance plants for tires, textiles, fertilizer, aluminum, and a wide variety of other industrial products.

This use of tax-exempt public credit to finance plants leased to private companies, although sustained by some courts as a proper use of public credit to provide employment and economic growth, was widely criticized as an improper use of tax exemption for the benefit of private companies.

The Internal Revenue Code was amended to provide that the interest on industrial development bonds issued after April 30, 1968, is not tax exempt in an issue in excess of $1 million or, at the election of the issuer, $5 million for all facilities in the same municipality or county for the same principal user. However, the interest is still exempt on issues for specified purposes which are deemed to be a public purpose, even though the facilities are operated by a private company. Thus, bonds issued to finance facilities to be leased for operation by a private company still are tax exempt if the proceeds will be used to provide residential real property for family units, sports facilities, convention or trade show facilities, airports, docks, wharves, mass commuting facilities, parking facilities, sewage or solid waste disposal facilities, facilities for the local furnishing of electric energy, gas or water, or air or water pollution control facilities.[2]

Pollution Control Bonds. The adoption of mandatory requirements for pollution control facilities caused a sudden surge in 1973 in the use of municipal bonds to finance pollution control facilities for utilities and private companies. Two methods are used in such financing (1) using the proceeds from the bonds to construct pollution control facilities

[1] For general discussion of such financing, see *Industrial Development Financing*, Advisory Commission on Intergovernmental Relations (June 1963).

[2] Section 103(c) of the Internal Revenue Code.

to be leased to a private company or (2) loaning proceeds from the bonds to the private company to construct the pollution control facilities, with the loan secured by mortgage bonds of the corporation which are delivered to the municipality. Three large issues of this type sold in 1973 were $87 million, Sweetwater County, Wyoming Pollution Control Bonds for Pacific Power and Light Company and Idaho Power and Light Company; $60 million, Calvert County, Maryland Pollution Control Bonds for Bethlehem Steel Company; and $67 million, Baltimore County, Maryland Bonds for Baltimore Gas and Electric Company.

Arbitrage Bonds. It is possible to issue tax-exempt municipal bonds and invest the proceeds in taxable bonds paying substantially higher interest, thus providing profitable arbitrage to the municipality which is not required to pay tax on the proceeds from the taxable bonds. Some bonds have been issued for this purpose. A clear distinction must be made between situations where municipal bonds are issued for the primary purpose of arbitrage with reinvestment of the proceeds in bonds paying higher interest, as distinguished from regular munipical bonds issued to finance a public facility where some portion of the proceeds are invested for a temporary period until needed or are invested in a required reserve or replacement fund.

The use of tax-exempt municipal bonds for the primary purpose of arbitrage was widely considered to be an improper use of tax-exempt public credit, and the Tax Reform Act of 1969 included a provision that the exemption for interest on municipal bonds does not apply to arbitrage bonds.[3] This provision specifically states that a bond shall not be treated as an arbitrage bond solely by reason of the fact that a part of the proceeds may be invested for a temporary period until needed for the purpose for which the bonds were issued or if part of the proceeds are part of a reasonably required reserve or replacement fund.

GENERAL FORM AND PRICE QUOTATION

Several years ago practically all municipal bonds were issued with a face amount (or denomination) of $1,000, which the issuer promised to pay at a specified date known as the maturity date. In recent years bonds in most large issues have been in $5,000 denominations at the request of the underwriters because many institutions which purchase large amounts of bonds prefer the $5,000 denominations to save storage space and to reduce the number of bonds to be handled. Purchasers of large amounts may obtain denominations greater than $5,000.

Some municipal bonds are *term bonds*, which means that all of the bonds in the issue mature at the same time, i.e., at the end of the specified term of years. It is now more general practice to issue general obliga-

---

[3] Section 103(d) of the Internal Revenue Code.

tion bonds as *serial bonds* which mature serially, i.e., some of the bonds mature each year, beginning after the date of issue on through a maximum period of 10, 20, or 30 years or longer. Some bonds are *callable,* which means that the issuer may pay the bonds before the maturity date. Usually, if the bonds are called before maturity, the issuer will pay to the holder a specified *premium,* which is an amount in excess of the face value of the bond.

Interest Rate. The interest which the issuer agrees to pay on the bonds is shown (1) in coupons attached to the bonds if the bonds are coupon bonds or (2) in the bond itself if the bond is a registered bond. On coupon bonds the holder detaches and presents the coupon for payment of the interest. On registered bonds the interest payment is sent directly to the registered holder by the paying agent.

Form. There are two forms of municipal bonds, coupon and registered. The coupon bond is transferable by delivery to bearer, whereas a registered bond is registered on the books of the municipality and title can only be transferred by endorsement. Therefore, one of the advantages of a registered bond is that in case it is stolen or lost there is a certain protection for the registered owner. On the other hand, the advantage of the coupon bond is that it is more marketable and is easier to use for collateral. Some bonds are interchangeable between registered and coupon form, usually at the expense of the holder.

In many instances, coupon bonds have the privilege of registration, either as to principal only or as to principal and interest. If a bond is registered as to principal only, that means that the coupons are left on the bond and are cashed to collect the interest. At maturity, however, the registered owner is the only person who can be paid the principal of the bond. If it is registered as to principal and interest, it is a fully registered bond, the coupons are detached, the name is recorded on the books of the municipality, and interest payments are sent to the registered owner by check.

Price. Prices of municipal bonds maturing serially are usually stated on a yield basis, plus accrued interest. *Yield Basis* means that the price is stated as the percentage of yield (investment return) which will be obtained if the bond is held to maturity (if the bond is callable, the yield basis stated should be the minimum yield to the purchaser under any of the possible options). Since it requires a complicated mathematical computation (see Chapter 36) to determine the dollar price of a bond at a specified yield basis, there are available basis books which contain tables showing the dollar price for bonds in the usual range of interest coupon rates, maturities, and yields.

From a basis book it could quickly be determined that a bond with 5.0 percent interest coupons, maturing in 25 years, priced to yield 5.25 percent would have a dollar price of $96.54, which for a $1,000.00 bond would be $965.40.

When a bond is priced at its face value, it is priced at *par*. When a bond is priced on a yield basis lower than the rate of interest specified in the coupons, the dollar price of the bond is higher than its face value and the bond is priced at a *premium*. Conversely, when a bond is priced on a yield basis higher than the rate of interest specified in the coupons, the dollar price of the bond is lower than its face value and the bond is priced at a *discount*.

A typical quotation of a bond price would be "City of Chicago, Illinois, 5 of '89 at 5.05%," which would mean that bonds issued by the City of Chicago, Illinois, carrying 5.0 percent interest coupons, maturing in 1989, are offered at a price to yield 5.05 percent.

The price of some municipal bonds is stated as a dollar amount and these bonds are known as *dollar bonds*. Dollar bonds are frequently term bonds which will all mature at one time.

When an investor purchases a municipal bond at a discount, so that the yield is higher than the specified rate of interest, only the interest is exempt from federal income tax and the additional yield is taxable as capital gain when the gain is realized.

Plus Accrued Interest. The person who owns a bond on the interest payment date receives all of the interest on the bond for the period subsequent to the last interest payment date. However, each person who owned the bond for any period between interest payment dates is entitled to the interest for the period during which he owned the bond. Therefore, each purchaser of a tax-exempt bond pays to the seller the accrued interest from the last interest payment date up to the date of delivery and payment.

For example, if the interest coupons on a bond are payable semi-annually on July 1 and January 1, if Mr. A purchased the bond on July 1 and sold it to Mr. B for delivery and payment on August 1, Mr. A would receive from Mr. B, in addition to the purchase price of the bond, the accrued interest due Mr A for the period from July 1 until August 1. Mr. B on January 1 would receive all of the interest for the six-month period from July 1 to January 1 (thereby receiving interest for the five months which he owned the bonds plus interest, which he paid to Mr. A at the time of purchase, for the one month that Mr. A owned the bond).

REGULATION AND PROCEDURE IN SALE

Role of the SEC

Municipal bonds are exempt from the registration requirements of the federal Securities Act of 1933,[4] except that industrial development

[4] Section 3(a)(2) of the Securities Act of 1933 exempts ("except as hereinafter expressly provided") any security issued or guaranteed "by any State of the United States, or by any political subdivision of a State or Territory, or by any public instrumentality of one or more states or territories."

bonds are exempt only if they qualify for tax exemption under section 103(a)(1) of the Internal Revenue Code. However, even securities exempt from registration are subject to the fraud provisions making it unlawful to employ any device scheme or artifice to defraud or to obtain money or property by means of any untrue statement of a material fact or any omission to state a material fact necessary in order to make the statements made not misleading.[5]

Similarly, municipal bonds are exempted from the federal Securities Exchange Act,[6] and dealers selling only municipal bonds are exempt from registration under that act.[7] However, a bill introduced in the United States Senate in September 1973 would require municipal dealers (including the bond departments of banks) to register as "municipal securities dealers" under the Securities Exchange Act.[8]

Procedure in Sale by Issuer[9]

The authority for the issuance of municipal bonds stems from the constitution of the state or statutory authority. In some cases it may be necessary for a municipality to obtain a vote of its electorate in order to issue and sell bonds.

In most states the law requires that issuers sell general obligation bonds by competitive bidding, usually by submission of sealed bids. Even when negotiated sales are permitted, many bonds are sold by competitive bidding. A high percentage of revenue bonds are also sold by competitive bidding, but there are many negotiated sales of revenue bonds because in some situations it is advantageous to the issuer to have the underwriter participate in setting up the issue.

Legal Opinion. Each municipal bond issue must be approved by an attorney whose legal opinions satisfy the market where the bonds are sold. Usually the city attorney or corporation counsel is not a specialist, although he can offer valuable assistance to the bond attorney. It is customary in bidding on municipal bonds for underwriters to bid subject to the bonds being accompanied by an unqualified approving legal opinion of some firm of municipal bond attorneys whose opinions are recognized as marketable. There are a number of firms of bond attorneys in the United States which specialize in municipal law exclusively, or which have a department that does so. It is generally the practice for the issuing municipality to secure, before the bonds are offered for sale,

[5] Section 17, Securities Act of 1933.

[6] Section 3(a)(12), Securities Exchange Act.

[7] Section 15(a)(1), Securities Exchange Act.

[8] S.2474 by Senator Harrison Williams for himself and Senators Brooke and Biden.

[9] For detailed suggestions for issuers marketing municipal bonds and discussion of the function of the bond attorney and procedures in underwriting and distributing municipal bonds, see *Fundamentals of Municipal Bonds,* published by the Securities Industry Association, 1972.

the services of a firm of bond attorneys whose opinion is marketable. The municipality specifies in the advertisement that the unqualified approving legal opinion of that firm will be furnished to the buyer. This may be done at the expense of the issuer or the buyer, but more often it is done at the expense of the issuer because bids will reflect the additional expense when the buyer must pay for the legal opinion.

Any resolutions, ordinances, ballots, or actions taken before the attorney is retained should be submitted to him at once. Prior to the sale the attorney should examine all proceedings so that his preliminary approval can be given in advance.

It is the practice to deliver to each purchaser of municipal bonds a copy of the legal opinion for such bonds. If a copy of the complete final legal opinion is printed on the back of the bond, it eliminates the work and expense involved in delivering a separate copy of the legal opinion to each purchaser of the bonds.

The Prospectus or Official Statement. The municipality which sells bonds must give comprehensive data about the community, its economic background, and its financial situation. This information should be sent to financial papers which circulate among investment bankers and investors. Papers that publish the paid notices about the sale will usually carry a news story about the community.

The prospectus about a municipal bond issue may be divided into three parts: (1) a financial statement of the issuer, (2) complete information about the bond sale in about the same form as the material in the advertisement, and (3) facts about the economic and social life of the community. The prospectus should be sent, without request, to the investment bankers and other financial institutions that are interested in the municipality's securities and to a select list of large investors. Rating and information agencies should also be given this data.

The Bond Sale. All bids should be on a basis which permits a comparison of total costs to the issuer. Officials should insist that all bids comply strictly with the terms of the sale. Usually bids that are qualified or not responsive to the notice of sale will be discarded. The bid requiring the lowest net interest cost should prevail, assuming that all other conditions are comparable, that is, the printing and delivery of the bonds and the cost of the legal opinion must be on the same basis for all bidders.

In bidding on serial bonds at public sale it has become the accepted practice to determine the highest bid, especially where there is more than one interest rate, by what is known as the "IBA" (Investment Bankers Association) or "interest cost per annum" method. In other words, if there are two bids, each with a different combination of interest rates, the problem is to determine which one is a better bid from the standpoint of the issuer.

Under this method, the total amount of dollars which the municipality will pay out on the issue in interest over the life of the loan is computed. Then any premium that is bid is deducted. If bids below par are permitted, the amount of discount is added. Finally, it is necessary to divide the net interest cost by the total bond years (the number of bonds of each maturity multiplied by the number of years of life in that maturity) to obtain the net interest cost in dollars per bond per year which, when divided by 10 (assuming $1,000 denominations), will give the net interest cost rate.

In addition to the generally used IBA method of computing the lowest interest cost to the issuer, there is another method referred to as the "Canadian" or "effective semiannual interest cost" method, which is used occasionally and results in a slightly different interest cost. Under this method the interest cost is defined as the rate, compounded semiannually, necessary to discount the amounts payable on the respective principal and interest maturity dates to the purchase price received for the bonds.[10]

The bidder who purchases the bond reoffers them, usually at basis prices (i.e., on a yield basis). Sometimes the longer maturities may be offered at a dollar price. Other dealers are allowed a concession from the offering price which is known as the dealer's concession. On a new issue this concession may range from no concession at all on the first or the first two maturities to possibly one fourth of a point or one half of a point or more on the longer bonds. In other words, if the syndicate is offering a new issue of municipals and some dealer who is not in the syndicate gets an order for those bonds, he will buy them from a member of the syndicate at the offering price less the concession, and then sell them to his customer at the offering price, his profit being the amount of the concession. A point on a municipal bond, in reference to the dollar price or the take-down or dealer's concession, is $1.00 per $100.00, or $10.00 per $1,000.00 so that one fourth of a point is $2.50 on a $1,000.00 bond. This differs from a basis point, in reference to the percentage of yield, which is 1/100th of a percentage point, so that on a bond yielding 3.05 percent an increase of 3 basis points in yield would provide a yield of 3.08 percent. The reoffering of the bonds is on a "when, as and if issued" basis, because the bonds cannot be delivered until they are printed and executed, which ordinarily takes several weeks.

When the bonds are ready for delivery and the municipal attorneys have signified they are ready to render their final approving opinion, the issuer delivers to the underwriters the executed bonds and usual closing papers (usually including a no-litigation certificate), and the underwriters make payment to the issuer. After the underwriters pay for and receive delivery of the bonds, they then (if they sold the bonds

[10] For detailed explanation of methods of computing net interest cost, see *Fundamentals of Municipal Bonds,* chap. 5.

during the period of time between the award and the time of delivery) redeliver the bonds to the investors to whom they have sold the bonds. A copy of the legal opinion for the bonds is also delivered to each purchaser, either as a separate certified or photo-process copy of the legal opinion or as a copy of the complete final legal opinion printed on the back of the bonds.

TAX EXEMPTION

The interest on municipal bonds is exempt from federal income tax, with the exception of certain industrial development bonds and arbitrage bonds.[11] Therefore, tax-free interest on municipal bonds provides more income *after taxes* than a like amount of taxable interest. Taxable equivalent yield tables are published which show for different income tax brackets the approximate yields on taxable bonds necessary to produce an after-tax yield equivalent to the tax-free interest on municipal bonds. Thus, for a person in the 50 percent tax bracket 5 percent tax-free interest is the equivalent of 10 percent in taxable interest.

The interest on municipal bonds is usually also exempt from state income taxes in the state where the issuer is located. The interest on bonds issued by territories of the United States or by their political subdivisions is exempt from federal income tax and state income tax in all states.

Tax exemption is particularly important because it makes possible the sale of municipal bonds at substantially lower interest rates than are required for taxable bonds, but the lower tax-exempt interest is not attractive to certain types of institutional investors, such as pension funds, which are not required to pay income taxes.

Proposals for Optional Taxable Bond. In recent years there have been several proposals in Congress to authorize state and local governments at their option to issue taxable bonds on which the federal government would pay to the issuer an interest subsidy of a percentage of the interest cost (the subsidy varying in different proposals from 25 percent to 50 percent).[12] It is contended that taxable municipal bonds, paying higher interest than tax-exempt bonds, would broaden the market for municipal bonds by attracting investors who receive little or no benefit

---

[11] The basic exemption is in section 103(a) of the Internal Revenue Code. Section 103(c) allows the exemption to industrial development bonds only if they were issued before May 1, 1968, or are part of an issue not larger than $1 million (or at election of the issuer, not more than $5 million for all facilities in the same municipality or county for the same principal user), or are for specified types of facilities discussed earlier. Section 103(d) denies the exemption to arbitrage bonds.

[12] S.3215 was introduced by Senator Proxmire on February 22, 1972, to authorize optional taxable municipal bonds in a proposed "Municipal Capital Market Expansion Act." See hearings on this and other bills before the Senate Committee on Banking, Housing and Urban Affairs in May 1972.

from the tax exemption of interest, such as individuals in lower tax brackets and pension funds. At the time of this writing in late 1973 none of these proposals have been adopted.

ANALYSIS OF MUNICIPAL CREDIT

Two basic approaches to analysis of municipal credit are reliance on ratings by professional advisory services and independent analysis by securities analysts. There is little question that a rating by a major advisory service, when available, has the greater impact on the interest rate paid by a municipality.

Ratings

The weight which is now given to ratings is illustrated by two specific cases:

The Director of the Fairfax County (Virginia) Department of Budget and Financial Management on September 22, 1973, elatedly announced that action by Moody's raising the Fairfax bond rating from A to Aa should reduce the interest rate on a forthcoming bond issue from about 5.35 percent to about 5.20 percent, saving the county more than $400,000 in interest over the 20-year term of the $32 million issue.[13]

Conversely, the Director of Finance for New York City at hearings before a Congressional Committee in December 1967, after stating that Moody's action on July 19, 1965, of lowering the rating of New York City's tax-secured bonds from A to BAA was triggered by a $250 million borrow-now, pay-later financing undertaken by a prior administration to balance its current expense budget through the flotation of serial bonds, commented:

> At today's interest rates, bond experts have advised me that a BAA bond carries a 5.20 percent net interest cost versus an A-rated bond's 4.70 percent. This is a difference of 50 basis points or one-half of one percent annual interest. Since New York City floats $500 million per year of new debt, the extra interest cost occasioned by the lowering of New York City's rating will be $2.5 million per year on each issue. Since the average life of recent issues has been about eight years, this will mean about $20 million per year total extra cost.[14]

The two major rating services are Moody's and Standard & Poor's. Until a few years ago, Moody's rated bonds of issuers which had $600,000 or more of debt, with the exception of bonds of educational

[13] *The Washington Post*, September 22, 1973, p. D–10.

[14] Hearings on Financing Municipal Facilities before Subcommittee on Economic Progress of the Joint Economic Committee, December 5, 1967, vol. 1, pp. 20–21. For further discussion on this point, see Gerald R. Jantscher, *The Effects of Changes in Credit Rating on Municipal Borrowing Costs* (The Brookings Institution, 1970).

institutions, projects under construction, enterprises without established earnings records, and situations where current financial data were lacking. Standard & Poor's rated all governmental bodies having at least $1 million of debt outstanding, unless adequate information was not available for appraisal. Both services now rate municipal bonds only on a fee basis, Moody's beginning in May 1970 and Standard & Poor's in 1968.

Moody's fee for rating general obligation bonds is based on population of the municipality, ranging from $650 to $2,500. For revenue issues, the exact fee is based on the amount of work involved, from a minimum of $1,000 to a maximum of $3,000. Moody's ratings are as follows:

Aaa Bonds which are rated Aaa are judged to be of the best quality. They carry the smallest degree of investment risk and are generally referred to as "gilt edge." Interest payments are protected by a large or by an exceptionally stable margin and principal is secure. While the various protective elements are likely to change, such changes as can be visualized are most unlikely to impair the fundamentally strong position of such issues.

Aa Bonds which are rated Aa are judged to be of high quality by all standards. Together with the Aaa group they comprise what are generally known as high-grade bonds. They are rated lower than the best bonds because margins of protection may not be as large as in Aaa securities or fluctuation of protective elements may be of greater amplitude or there may be other elements present which make the long-term risks appear somewhat larger than in Aaa securities.

A Bonds which are rated A possess many favorable investment attributes and are to be considered as upper medium grade obligations. Factors giving security to principal and interest are considered adequate, but elements may be present which suggest a susceptibility to impairment sometime in the future.

Baa Bonds which are rated Baa are considered as medium-grade obligations, i.e., they are neither highly protected nor poorly secured. Interest payments and principal security appear adequate for the present but certain protective elements may be lacking or may be characteristically unreliable over any great length of time. Such bonds lack outstanding investment characteristics and in fact have speculative characteristics as well.

Ba Bonds which are rated Ba are judged to have speculative elements; their future cannot be considered as well assured. Often the protection of interest and principal payments may be very moderate, and thereby not well safeguarded during both good and bad times over the future. Uncertainty of position characterizes bonds in this class.

B Bonds which are rated B generally lack characteristics of the desirable investment. Assurance of interest and principal payments or of maintenance of other terms of the contract over any long period of time may be small.

Caa Bonds which are rated Caa are of poor standing. Such issues may be in default or there may be present elements of danger with respect to principal or interest.

Ca Bonds which are rated Ca represent obligations which are speculative in a high degree. Such issues are often in default or have other marked shortcomings.

C Bonds which are rated C are the lowest rated class of bonds, and issues so rated can be regarded as having extremely poor prospects of ever attaining any real investment standing.

Eng. (—) Revenue bonds to be secured by the earnings of projects which are (*a*) under construction or (*b*) unseasoned in terms of operating experience. The parenthetical rating denotes the probable credit stature to be attained upon completion of construction and or refunding and the establishment of an earnings history.

Con. (—) Lease rental obligation wherein rents begin when facilities are completed but insurance coverage minimizes construction risks. Parenthetical rating denotes probable credit stature to be attained upon completion of construction.

Those bonds in the A and Baa groups which Moody's believes possess the strongest investment attributes are designated by the symbols A–1 and Baa–1.

Standard & Poor's fees for rating depend entirely upon the amount of work necessary but range from a few hundred dollars to several thousand dollars in rare situations, usually averaging $400 to $700. Standard & Poor's ratings are:

AAA Prime—These are obligations of the highest quality. They have the lowest probability of default. In a period of economic stress the issuers will suffer the smallest declines in income and will be least susceptible to autonomous decline. Debt burden is not inordinately high. Revenue structure appears adequate to meet future expenditure needs. Quality of management would not appear to endanger repayment of principal and interest.

AA High Grade—The investment characteristics of bonds in this group are only slightly less marked than those of the prime quality issues. Bonds rated AA have the second lowest probability of default.

A Upper Medium Grade—Principal and interest on bonds in this category are regarded as safe. This rating describes the third lowest probability of default. It differs from the two higher ratings because there is some weakness, either in the local economic base, in debt burden, in the balance between revenues and expenditures, or in quality of management. Under certain adverse circumstances, *any one such weakness* might impair the ability of the issuer to meet debt obligations at some future date.

BBB Medium Grade—This is the lowest investment grade security rating. Under certain adverse conditions, several of the above factors could contribute to a higher default probability. The difference between A and BBB ratings is that the latter shows *more than one* fundamental weakness, whereas the former shows only one deficiency among the factors considered.

BB Lower Medium Grade—Bonds in this group have some investment characteristics, but they no longer predominate. For the most part this rating indicates a speculative, noninvestment grade obligation.

B Low Grade—Investment characteristics are virtually nonexistent and default could be imminent.

D Defaults—Interest and/or principal in arrears.

p The letter p following a rating indicates rating is provisional, subject to timely completion of the project.

There are also local organizations in a few states which rate bonds of issues in those states.

Ratings are general and are not absolute standards of quality. There may be substantial variations in interest rates for bonds of the same maturity with the same rating, because ratings are only a general appraisal of quality and there are differences in quality between bonds with the same rating. On the other hand, bonds with different ratings may be of substantially identical quality because there are borderline situations where one bond was considered barely meriting a certain rating, while another bond was considered not quite meriting that rating, and experts might disagree as to which bond merited the higher rating. Consequently, the limitations of ratings must be noted; but ratings are a useful general appraisal of quality and their importance must be recognized.

Three of the principal criticisms of present ratings are that the coverage is too narrow (too many issuers are not rated), the rating bands are too wide (there are wide variations of quality within rating classes), and rating decisions are arbitrary judgments. The coverage should be broadened by the availability of a rating to any municipality for a fee, and efforts are being made to minimize the judgment factor by standardizing the evaluation of data.[15]

Some new rating systems are being developed which would provide more precise numerical ratings on a scale of 0 to 100 and would minimize the judgment factor, but they are not yet widely recognized.[16]

Lastly, the importance of ratings is that they determine the eligibility of bonds for purchase by certain large investors of municipal bonds. Particularly important is that bonds in the top four ratings are generally considered eligible for bank investment. There are also statutory provisions in some states restricting investment by certain classes of institutions to bonds with certain ratings. Eligibility for purchase by banks and other institutions is a major factor in the interest rate on bonds because the market for the bonds is greatly narrowed if they are ineligible for purchase by certain institutions.

Availability of Information

If an investment banking firm or an institutional investor wants an analyst to make an independent analysis of a municipal bond, either because it is unrated or to obtain a more specific evaluation, there are some specific criteria which can be applied. But to apply those criteria it is necessary to have complete current information about the issuing municipality, both financial and general economic information.

When municipalities sell a new issue of bonds to underwriters, they make available current financial and economic information for consideration (1) by underwriters in bidding on bonds offered for competitive bids or in negotiating the price and (2) by major institutions who are prospective investors. The problem has been to obtain current information in years subsequent to the initial sale for periodic analysis of the

---

[15] For discussion of procedures of Moody's and Standard & Poor's in rating bonds, see testimony of Robert C. Riehle and Brenton W. Harries at Hearings on Financing Municipal Facilities, July 16, 1968, vol. II, pp. 191 and 208.

[16] For discussion of proposed new rating system, see testimony of Walter H. Tyler, President, W. H. Tyler & Co., at Hearings on Financing Municipal Facilities, July 11, 1968, vol. II, p. 384.

municipal credit. In several states municipal advisory councils have done excellent jobs in obtaining complete current information from municipalities in their states, including Texas, Ohio, Michigan, North Carolina, and South Carolina. Current information on some issuers is available from the rating services referred to above.

The information which is needed for analysis is suggested in recommendations by the Investment Bankers Association of America in "Report on Finances for Municipal General Obligation Bonds" in Appendix A and in "Report on Finances for Municipal Revenue Bonds" in Appendix B. These recommendations were issued years ago but still are basically sound. Data required by Standard & Poor's for general obligation bond rating and for revenue bond analysis are in Appendix C.

Factors in General Obligation Bonds

Since the full faith and credit of the issuer of general obligation bonds is pledged to secure the payment of principal and interest on those bonds, the object of analysis is to determine whether the projected income of the municipality from taxes (and other sources) will be sufficient to pay the principal and interest of the bonds after payment of other charges including bonds previously issued and bonds likely to be issued thereafter. Historically the real estate tax has been the primary source of tax income for local governments below the state level; the income tax has been the primary source for many states, and the sales tax has become a major source in other states. The principal factors which must be considered in the credit of a municipality are these:

Ratio of Net Debt to Assessed Valuation of Property. This is particularly important where real property taxes are the primary source of tax revenue and is easily computed by the following tabulation:

1. Real value of taxable property (estimated).
2. Assessed valuation for taxation 19__.
3. Total bonded debt.
4. Less self-supporting debt.
5. Less sinking funds (other than for self-supporting debt).
6. Net bonded debt.
7. Floating debt.
8. Net direct debt
   Ratio net direct debt to assessed valuation
   Ratio net direct debt to estimated real valuation.
9. Net overlapping debt.
10. Net overall debt
    Ratio net overall debt to assessed valuation
    Ratio net overall debt to estimated real valuation
        Population 19__ census
        Population 19__ estimated.

When the total of self-supporting debt (item 4) and sinking funds (item 5) is deducted from total bonded debt (item 3), the remainder is net bonded debt (item 6). In deducting sinking funds, of course, include only sinking funds for other than the self-supporting debt included in item 4.

Floating debt (item 7) is added to the net bonded debt (item 6) to determine net direct debt (item 8). In floating debt is included any floating debt which may become a charge against future taxes. Ordinary tax anticipation borrowing, which presumably will be paid off during the current year, is not included since taxes have already been levied to satisfy that obligation. Any items of floating debt payable from special assessments or from any source that is not a charge against taxes would likewise be excluded. Items such as bond anticipation notes or any other items which will be a charge against future years' tax revenues or which will eventually have to be funded should be included.

The ratio of net direct debt to assessed valuation is determined by dividing item 8 by item 2 and is expressed as a percentage. The ratio of net direct debt to estimated real value is determined by dividing item 8 by item 1 and is also expressed as a percentage.

The value of this form of statement lies in the fact that after the above computations have been made, it is possible to go further and determine the net overall debt and the ratios of net overall debt to assessed valuation and to estimated real value. The net direct debt might be relatively small, but a municipality might have a radically heavy burden of overlapping debt in the form of county or district debt of coterminous, underlying, and overlapping units.

In determining the amount of such debt applicable to the municipality being analyzed, it is considered that: (1) in the case of a coterminous or underlying unit, 100 percent of the net debt of such unit or units is applicable; and (2) where there is an overlapping unit, such for instance as a county, the proportionate part of the net debt of such overlapping unit as the assessed valuation of the municipality bears to the assessed valuation of the overlapping unit is also applicable. Thus, the net overlapping debt burden on the property within the municipality being analyzed is determined (item 9) and added to net direct debt (item 8), furnishing the net overall debt (item 10).

The ratio of net overall debt to assessed valuation is computed by dividing item 10 by item 2, and the ratio of net overall debt to estimated real value of taxable property is computed by dividing item 10 by item 1. The latter ratio furnishes a fairly accurate estimate of the overall debt burden.

There is no definite figure which can be considered the dividing line between a conservative and a high overall debt ratio. Conditions and resources in municipalities differ so widely that a percentage of debt which might be an undue burden in one city might cause little difficulty in another. In the average community, however, when the ratio of net overall debt to estimated assessed value passes 9 or 10 percent, it is usually considered as being out of the conservative class.

Debt Trend. The debt trend, indicated by whether the municipality's ratio of debt to valuation has been progressively increasing or progressively decreasing in recent years, furnishes an indication of the fiscal policy of the municipality and what the future may hold for it. If it is clear that the ratio has been progressively increasing for a number of years, even though it is not unduly high at the moment, the circumstances should be closely examined.

If the amount of principal which comes due each year is the same, the total debt service is going to decline because as bonds are paid off the interest requirements will decrease. That is desirable because it enables the municipality to issue new debt for the purpose of meeting future requirements without increasing its debt service beyond desirable levels. If one year has a very large maturity which is much larger than the normal year and for which sinking funds are not being set up, it is pretty certain that the municipality will be forced to give serious consideration to refunding a portion of that maturity in order to prevent raising the tax rate to abnormal proportions.

Relationship of Annual Debt Service Requirements to Total Annual Revenues. If the total debt service requirement begins to run much above 25 percent of the annual budget, it may be considered rather high. Debt service requirements are a fixed charge. If, for example, in an annual budget of $2 million, debt service requires $1 million and operating expenses require $1 million, and the revenue collections in that particular year decline 10 percent, or $200,000, that $200,000 deficit is going to apply against the amount provided for operating expenses since the debt service must be paid. Thus, if there is a 10 percent delinquency where there is a 50 percent debt service requirement, the actual result is a 20 percent delinquency as far as operating expenses are concerned, which may cause serious embarrassment. If the debt service is only 25 percent of the total budget, a 10 percent delinquency would represent only about 13 percent of the operating budget, which would not necessarily be as serious.

Anticipated Additional Financing. If the municipality is planning additional bond issues in the near future which are going to upset the debt service schedule, that additional financing should be taken into consideration.

Amount of Floating Debt. It usually is not considered improper to have a normal amount of debt outstanding for what is known as current tax debt. The amount of such debt usually depends on the manner in which taxes are collected. In some cases a municipality may collect taxes once a year. On that basis the municipality may have to operate for about 10 months of the year on tax anticipation borrowing, which is paid off as taxes are paid in the fall. On the other hand, where taxes are collected quarterly, there is practically no tax anticipation borrowing because funds come in frequently enough so that the municipalities are able to operate on a current basis.

The best procedure in examining floating debt is to compare the current floating debt with various periods in the past. A rising trend, just as with the bonded debt, is an indication that an examination should be made of the reason for such increase. There may be a plausible explanation and there may be nothing serious involved. On the other hand, if the floating debt is continually accumulating and the debt is large enough, eventually the municipality will not be able to pay it in any one year and will have to fund it.

Sinking Funds for Term Bonds Should Be Adequate. The sinking fund should be kept up to actuarial requirements so that when the term bonds, i.e., bonds which have one single maturity to an issue, come due there is sufficient money to pay them and avoid the necessity of refunding.

Limitations on Source of Payment. If the bonds are general obligations payable from a limited tax or are payable from some special source of revenue, the limited tax or source of revenue should be examined carefully to be sure that it is entirely adequate. There may be a constitutional or statutory limit on the amount of tax which may be levied for debt service. If there is a tax limit, the extent to which it is a danger factor depends on the limit of taxing power which remains. If there is a tax limit of $30 per thousand and the municipality is already levying $30 per thousand, it has absolutely no leeway in the event that assessed valuations decline, operating expenses increase, or it wants to issue more bonds. On the other hand, if it had a $30 limit and is only levying $20, it has a $10 per thousand leeway. The amount that represents in dollars can be found by multiplying $10 by the number of thousands of dollars of assessed value. This will indicate just how much margin the municipality has for future needs. Obviously, unlimited tax bonds are always preferable to limited tax bonds because there is nothing, in that case, to prevent the municipality from levying an adequate tax other than the law of diminishing returns, since too high a tax rate may defeat its own purpose.

The purpose of a tax limit is not only to keep the tax rate down but to keep the borrowing of the municipality within reasonable bounds. The latter is a desirable objective, but the best way to control the borrowing power is through a limitation on the incurring of debt rather than a limit on the taxing power.

There usually is no priority of one issue over another with respect to the revenues from which they are payable. General obligation bonds, with rare exceptions, rank equally as to their claim upon ad valorem taxes; but in some cases, there is a priority of claim against tax collections between local taxing units. In some cases, the taxes for both the counties and cities are collected by the cities, which are supposed to turn over to the county in full the county's share of the tax bill. If there is any delinquency, it applies against the city's portion. In other cases, the county collects taxes for cities and school districts, and after the school districts and cities are paid in full, any delinquency has to be borne by the county.

Revenue Collections. A reserve should be provided in the annual budget against anticipated delinquency. The municipality might expect to collect only 90 percent of its tax levy. In effect, therefore, the levy must be padded to provide revenues sufficient for the annual budget over and above all delinquencies. That is done simply by dividing the required amount by the percentage which the municipality expects to collect. In other words, if the municipality required $2 million and expects to collect 90 percent, it must levy taxes in the amount of $2,222,222.

It is also important that the municipality have adequate penalties for nonpayment of taxes when due. Some individuals simply let their real estate taxes go if the tax penalty is not sufficient to more than offset what they would have to pay for money at the bank. In other words, if there was a 5 percent penalty for nonpaid taxes and they had to pay 7 percent at the bank, they might let their real estate taxes go and use that money rather than go to the bank and borrow at 7 percent. Thus, while it is difficult to state definitely what an adequate penalty might be, it would seem desirable that it should be no less than current bank interest rates and should provide for sale of the property if taxes are unpaid for more than a year.

Tax Rate Comparisons. Tax rates vary considerably in different states. To determine a tax rate it is necessary to take into consideration the basis on which property is assessed. If the assessed valuation is only 20 percent of actual value, for example, it is necessary to have an apparently high tax rate in order to raise the needed funds. Also, in reviewing a tax rate it is important to see how it compares with what the municipality has successfully levied in the past. Although a tax rate may be increased in a certain year over what it was the previous year, if it is still considerably below the rate which was being levied a few years ago without any difficulty, there is likely to be little resistance on the part of the taxpayers.

General Character, Economy, and Outlook for the Community. This is a broad but fundamental consideration. If the economy of a prosperous community is based on employment at a single plant, the closing of that plant could drastically affect employment, land values, tax collections, and population in that area. Accordingly, this factor involves a critical comprehensive study of the area.

This historical background of the community in its past attitude toward debt should be noted. The principal criterion is whether the municipality has defaulted at any time in the past. If it has defaulted, the first thing that should be looked into is the cause of the default, because there might or might not have been mitigating circumstances due to factors beyond the municipality's control. For instance, in the last depression communities that had their funds tied up in closed banks had no possible way of getting the money with which to operate or pay their debt service.

Debt-paying ability is indicated by a variety of figures, such as the percentage of population making income tax returns, retail sales per capita, average monthly rental of dwellings, bank deposits, and similar data.

The fact that a municipality is dependent on a single industry does not necessarily mean that it is going to have difficulty in meeting its debt; but if that particular industry is depressed when industry generally is not, that municipality will likely be affected to a greater degree than municipalities in which there is greater diversification. Thus it is logical for the investor to attempt to spread his risk by preferring, other things being equal, a municipality where there is a diversification of industry so that if one type of industry is depressed, another one may be doing nicely and counteract it. Also, there are agricultural towns in areas which are dependent on one crop with the same attendant problems in the event of a crop failure.

In general, the size of the community, from the standpoint of security, does not make any particular difference. It is possible to have a very small community which is a much better credit risk than a large community.

Factors in State Bonds

In the case of state bonds, however, the situation is quite different. The states, on the whole, depend very little on real estate taxes. There are some that do not levy any taxes whatever against real estate. The major sources of income to the states consist of income taxes, sales taxes, gasoline taxes, motor vehicle license fees, tobacco taxes, corporation taxes, beverage taxes, franchise taxes, business license fees, and various other taxes.

There are three general types of state obligations. First, there are general obligations in connection with which there are no pledged revenues, payable from the general funds which come into the state. These funds are not segregated in any particular manner. While the bonds usually have a priority against those funds, there is no pledge of any specific source of revenue.

Second, there is a type of state obligation which, while it is a general obligation of the state, is payable primarily from a special pledged source of revenue.

Third, there are state obligations which, while issued by the state, are not a general obligation of the state but are payable solely from some special source of revenue, such as highway revenues of the state. The state, in such a case, has no legal obligation to raise funds from any other source if the pledged revenues prove inadequate.

Factors in Revenue Bonds

Municipal revenue bonds are payable solely from a specified source of revenue, which may be (1) revenues derived from operating a facility acquired or constructed with proceeds from the bonds or (2) rental payments from a private lessee of facilities acquired or constructed with proceeds from the bonds. Bonds which are payable only from a special tax or a special fund also are customarily included in the general classification of municipal revenue bonds. Revenue bonds are issued to finance many and varied projects such as: water, sewer, electric, and gas systems; hydroelectric power projects; bridges, tunnels, turnpikes, and expressways; airports, parking facilities, rapid transit, dock and harbor facilities, arenas, auditoriums, parks, hospitals, schools, dormitories, student union halls, stadiums, and industrial and pollution control facilities.

The authority or commission, which is a municipal corporation formed for the purpose of operating certain facilities which may or may not be confined within the limits of a given municipality, has grown in popularity as an issuer of municipal revenue bonds.

Since the revenue is the security for the payment of principal and interest on a revenue bond, the primary factor is whether the revenue, judged by past operating results (if any) and by estimates of competent engineers as to future earnings will be sufficient to provide adequate coverage for debt service with a margin for unforeseen contingencies.

Generally, the sources of revenue may be user charges (particularly for water, sewer, electric, and gas systems), tolls, special taxes, rental payments under leases, and legislative appropriations. With the latter type an authority or commission is created to issue bonds to finance a project and the then current legislature appropriates sufficient sums to pay debt service on the outstanding bonds for the fiscal period preceding the next regular legislative session.

Important factors to be considered are these:

Need for or Estimated Use of the Facility. This usually will require comprehensive engineering studies of the probable use of the facility. There have been a few horrible examples where the estimated use of a bridge or toll road did not materialize. Analysis of this critical factor involves not only reliance on the professional ability of the firm or person preparing the estimates, but also on a realistic evaluation of all circumstances by the analyst. The point which must be emphasized is the necessity that (1) earnings provide a margin of coverage in excess of minimum requirements and (2) estimates of revenues, operating expenses, and other matters are on a conservative basis. Also, it is necessary to be sure that there is sufficient margin of safety against unforeseen contingencies.

Where the bond is issued for pollution control facilities or for an industrial plant and is secured only by the rental payments of the lessee, analysis of the security of the bond is primarily based on the credit of the lessee corporation and its prospects, much like any corporate bond. The difference is that the issuing municipality usually retains ownership of the facility in the event of default in payments by the lessee.

Cost Estimates. Again great reliance must be put on engineering firms which prepare cost estimates for the facility to be sure that adequate allowance has been made for any factors which might increase the cost, including inflation and availability of materials.

Application of Revenues. In the trust indenture or bond resolution, which are the basic instruments of security for revenue bonds, there is set forth the manner in which the trustee shall apply revenue to the cost of operation and maintenance, debt service, and other obligatory payments. The order of such application is sometimes referred to as "the flow of funds." There is a broad pattern that has developed with respect to the handling of income and revenues. In most cases the basic fund is known as the *Revenue Fund* and all receipts and income derived from the operation of a project or projects are deposited into such fund and held there by the trustee. Moneys in the Revenue Fund are usually distributed monthly in the following order:

Operation and Maintenance Fund. A prorated amount to meet costs of operation and maintenance as set forth in the annual budget. The most common pattern is for bonds to be payable from net revenues after paying operating and maintenance charges. The theory behind this is that without proper operation and maintenance the facility or project may experience severe loss of revenue. However, there are many issues where principal and interest requirements constitute a first lien on all revenues derived from the project or projects prior to any payment of operating and maintenance charges, and these are known as gross revenue or gross income bonds.

Bond Service Account. An amount which with other such monthly payments will be sufficient to pay the semiannual interest next due as well as the principal next serially maturing.

Debt Service Reserve Fund. Payments into this fund, in the case of serial bonds, are usually accumulated and maintained equivalent to one year's maximum principal and interest requirements. In the case of term bonds, the normal requirement is two years' interest. For some preferred purpose such as water, one year's maximum interest requirements on term bonds may be acceptable.

Reserve Maintenance Fund. Payments to this fund are usually in an amount recommended by the consulting engineer. The purpose of the fund is to meet unusual or extraordinary maintenance charges which have not been budgeted. As a matter of practice, deposits to this fund are sometimes payable prior to deposit in the Debt Service Reserve Fund on the theory that it is essential to keep the facility in good operating condition.

Renewal and Replacement Fund. This is sometimes called a "Replacement Reserve" and deposits by the trustee from the Revenue Fund into this fund are usually in amounts recommended by the consulting engineer. Deposits into this fund are made only if available but may be cumulative. The purpose of the fund is, as the title implies, to replace equipment or provide for repairs that are necessary at irregular intervals.

Surplus Fund. Moneys remaining in the Revenue Fund after the foregoing distribution are paid into the Surplus Fund.

Protective Covenants. In all trust indentures or bond resolutions, certain covenants for the protection of the bondholder are spelled out. These covenants vary, but there are certain basic provisions which bondholders have come to expect, and failure to incorporate these into the basic instrument generally results in higher interest rates. Some of the principal covenants are as follows:

Rate Covenant. One of the more important covenants is that which pledges the issuing body to maintain rates sufficient to meet operating and maintenance charges and annual debt service requirements and to provide for certain reserves. Generally speaking, this covenant requires that rates be maintained sufficient to provide some minimum margin of safety in excess of the foregoing charges. For toll facilities the covenant has generally been about 120 percent of the foregoing charges.

Insurance. In order to assure the bondholder of continuity of operation of the facility, the issuing body attempts to carry insurance on the facility which would correspond in amount and in kind to that which is normally carried under private enterprise operation.

Maintenance. In most cases, the issuing body covenants to maintain the properties in good repair and working order at all times.

Nondiscrimination Covenant. In recent years, the practice has been established whereby no preferential treatment shall be accorded any group or groups in the matter of payment of rates for services. The intent here is to assure the bondholder that no free service shall be rendered and is generally departed from only in the case of certain essential municipal agencies in the performance of their duties such as fire and police protection.

Consulting Engineer. Since the advent of toll road financing, the practice has been to create a covenant by the issuing body whereby they will maintain a consulting engineer of national reputation to perform the duties of a watch dog over the operation of the facility. This practice is now extended into other municipal functions such as water revenue systems and electric systems.

Records and Financial Report. Most issuing bodies covenant that they will keep proper books of records and accounts and that there will be an audit at least annually of the properties by a certified public accountant.

Issuance of Additional Bonds. One of the more important features of a trust indenture or bond resolution is that governing the issuance of additional bonds. Sometimes, when the facility is being constructed, it is not possible to foresee just what the future may hold. It may become necessary to increase the size of the facility. Various improvements may be needed which will require financing. Therefore, there should be sufficient leeway in the indenture or the resolution to permit additional financing. The new issues may rank equally with the outstanding bonds, or they may be second lien bonds ranking junior to those outstanding. If bonds of equal rank are permitted, there should be safeguards set up which would require that earnings (including estimated additions from rate increases and additional customers) should be at a certain figure before additional bonds can be issued.

The provisions governing financing subsequent to the original bond issue are designed as a safeguard against undue dilution of the security of the original bonds. Most indentures permit the issuance of additional bonds to complete the project, but financing of extensions or additional facilities may be permitted only under the most carefully thought out provisions.

Competitive Facilities. Another factor which should be considered in connection with a revenue project, particularly with a river crossing or project of that nature, is that there be protection against competition. This may be done by placing restrictions on the power of the appropriate municipal or state officials to grant permission for a competing facility to be built. It is clear that it is not desirable to purchase bonds for a toll bridge where there is no restriction preventing someone from building a similar bridge nearby which might be harmfully competitive.

APPENDIX A†

Report on Finances for Municipal General Obligation Bonds

Municipality or political subdivision__________
County__________ State__________
Form of government (commission, mayor-council, manager, etc.)__________
Fiscal year begins__________
U.S. Census 19__: ________ State Census 19__: ________ Present estimate: ________
Has this issuer defaulted on any debt obligation since 1930?____
If so, give full particulars in a separate statement.

Part 1. Property Valuation (as of________19__)

	Current Year			Previous Year	
	Assessed	*Actual*	*Ratio of Assessed to Actual Value*	*Assessed*	*Actual*
1. Real estate	$____	$____	____%	$____	$____
2. Personal property	____	____	____	____	____
3. Public utility	____	____	____	____	____
4. Other (specify)____	____	____	____	____	____

Part 2. Bonded Debt and Related Information (as of________19__)

	Amount	*Sinking Funds*
1. General obligations (not listed below)	$____	$____
2. Special assessments secured also by general tax	____	____
3. Utility and public enterprise debt secured also by general tax:		
a. Water	____	____
b. Sewer	____	____
c. Light and power	____	____
d. Other (specify)	____	____
Total General Obligation Bonds	____	____
4. Special assessments only		
5. Utility and public enterprise revenue only:*		
a. Water	____	____
b. Sewer	____	____
c. Light and power	____	____
d. Other (specify)	____	____
Total Other Than General Obligations	____	____

6. Legal debt limit of this issuer?__% of (describe base)____; $____
7. Debt outstanding chargeable to debt limit? $____ Unused borrowing margin? $____
8. Bonds authorized but not issued: Purpose________ Amount $____
9. Are utility and public enterprise bonds reported in item 3 fully supported by earnings of the facilities?____If not, what proportion of general taxes was necessary for debt service on such bonds in the last fiscal year?________
10. Total general obligation bonds outstanding year ago? $____ Two years ago? $____
11. Amount of refunding bonds issued within last two years for the following purposes:
    a. To refund maturing bonds $____ Maturities____
    b. To refund callable bonds $____ Maturities____

Part 3. Overlapping Debt

That part of debt of overlapping entities (school or special districts, counties, etc.) payable by taxes levied in this municipality or political subdivision

*For utility and other public enterprise revenue bonds, please submit separate reports on report form for municipal revenue bonds.

Name of Overlapping Entity	*Debt Limit %*	*Gross Debt Less Sinking Fund*	*This Issuer's Share*
________	________	$________	$________
________	________	________	________
________	________	________	________
________	________	________	________

Part 4. Unfunded Debt Outstanding

	Amount	*Due*
1. Tax anticipation notes	$________	________
2. Delinquent tax notes	$________	________
3. Bond anticipation notes	$________	________
4. Bank loans	$________	________
5. Warrants	$________	________
6. Judgments	$________	________
7. Unpaid bills 60 days past due	$________	________
8. Miscellaneous items	$________	________
Total	$________	________

9. Unfunded debt one year ago $________; Two years ago $________

Part 5. Composition of Sinking Funds

1. Cash on hand or in banks	$________
2. U.S. government securities	$________
3. Bonds of this municipality	$________
4. Bonds of states and other municipalities	$________
5. Other investments (specify nature)	$________
Total	$________
6. Amount of term bonds for which sinking funds are required	$________

Part 6. Debt Service Requirements for Next Five Years (for principal, interest, and sinking-fund installments)

	Fiscal Year Beginning				
Authorized Source of Payment	*19__*	*19__*	*19__*	*19__*	*19__*
1. General taxation	$________	$________	$________	$________	$________
2. Special assessments and general taxation	$________	$________	$________	$________	$________
3. Utility revenues and general taxation	$________	$________	$________	$________	$________
4. Special assessments only	$________	$________	$________	$________	$________
5. Utility revenues only	$________	$________	$________	$________	$________

Part 7. Comparative Statement of Operating Revenues and Expenditures

Do not include municipally operated utilities or public enterprises, unless surplus revenues therefrom are transferred to general fund (in revenues) or debt service on general obligations issued therefor are paid from general fund (in expenditures).

	Fiscal Year Beginning		
	19__	19__	19__
1. Cash balance at beginning of year	$________	$________	$________
2. Revenues:			
a. Proceeds from notes and bonds	$________	$________	$________
b. From ad valorem taxes	$________	$________	$________
c. From other taxes	$________	$________	$________
d. From federal or state aid	$________	$________	$________
e. From other sources	$________	$________	$________
Total Revenues	$________	$________	$________
3. Expenditures:			
a. Government operating expenses	$________	$________	$________
b. Expenditures from bond proceeds	$________	$________	$________

c. Bond principal	$______	$______	$______
d. Bond interest	$______	$______	$______
e. Sinking funds	$______	$______	$______
f. All other purposes	$______	$______	$______
Total Expenditures	$______	$______	$______
4. Cash balance at end of year	$______	$______	$______

Part 8. Tax Data

a. Tax collection report—ad valorem or general property tax for last three years. For tax or fiscal year ending______
Omit levies of other entities and special assessments.

	Amount of Levy by This Issuer	*Uncollected at End of Year*	*Uncollected Latest Available Date*	*Delinquent Taxes from Prior Years Collected during Year*
19__	$______	$______	$______	$______
19__	$______	$______	$______	$______
19__	$______	$______	$______	$______

(*b*) Total current levy

For tax or fiscal year beginning______
Include levies of other entities which are part of general property tax.

		Amount Levied	*Rate per $100 of Assessed Value**
Total general property tax (or ad valorem tax) is composed of:	This issuer	$______	$______
	School	$______	$______
	County	$______	$______
	State	$______	$______
	Other______	$______	$______
	______	$______	$______
	Total	$______	$______

* If any property included in your taxable assessed valuation is taxed at rate different from real estate, specify______

(*c*) General tax information

1. Taxes for fiscal year are due:______ Became delinquent:______
2. If payable in installments give particulars______
3. Discounts for prepayment and when applied?______
4. Specific practice for delinquency?______
5. Explain in detail any modifications of practice during the past two years______
______
6. How are uncollected taxes handled?
   a. Anticipated as revenue in next year's budget?____If yes, what percentage?______
   b. Turned over to other governing bodies?____If yes, when?______
   c. Sale of tax certificates?____If yes, when?______
   d. Other methods______
7. Has tax sale period been extended in last two years?____If yes, explain______
8. Accumulated total of uncollected taxes for fiscal years prior to those reported above $______
9. Are tax title liens included in uncollected tax totals above?______
   How much $______
10. Total tax title liens owned by municipality (years 19__ to 19__ inclusive) $______
11. Is there a tax rate limit?____How much?______Statutory or constitutional?______
12. Do tax rate limits apply to debt service?____If yes, what are the limits?______
13. Do you levy taxes in excess of actual requirements to provide margin against delinquencies?
    Yes____No____
    If yes, what ratio? Current year?____%; Previous year?____%; Two years ago?______

Part 9. Supplementary Information

Please furnish in a separate statement information regarding the location and economic background of the issuer, the general character of industries and transportation facilities in the area- and any other pertinent data or comments. If additional space is needed to report fully the infor, mation requested in this form, please attach separate sheets with appropriate cross-references.

Signed________________________________

Official Title____________________________

Date____________________________________

† Investment Bankers Association of America.

APPENDIX B*

Report on Finances for Municipal Revenue Bonds

Name of issuer________________________
Type of facility________________________

Part I—General Information and Protective Features

1. Population of area served____________(U.S. Census 19__)
2. Amount of bonds authorized $____________Amount issued $____________
3. Date of issue________________
4. Maturities (state below):

Amount	*Rate*	*Date*	*Amount*	*Rate*	*Date*	*Amount*	*Rate*	*Date*
$____	____	____	$____	____	____	$____	____	____
____	____	____	____	____	____	____	____	____
____	____	____	____	____	____	____	____	____
____	____	____	____	____	____	____	____	____
____	____	____	____	____	____	____	____	____
____	____	____	____	____	____	____	____	____
____	____	____	____	____	____	____	____	____
____	____	____	____	____	____	____	____	____

5. Call provisions, if any. If noncallable prior to maturity please so state.
____
____
____
6. What is purpose of issue?________________________
____
7. If purpose is for new construction or development give engineer's estimate of gross and net revenue expected over next five years:

Gross	$____	$____	$____	$____	$____
Net	$____	$____	$____	$____	$____

8. What is peak requirement for interest and principal or sinking fund?____________
What year is peak reached?________
9. Amount of outstanding revenue or other bonds which have a claim on the revenue from this project $________
   a. Are there securities having a claim junior to this issue? Yes___No___If "Yes," show Amount $________Maturity________Peak debt service requirements $________
   b. Are there securities having a claim equal to this issue? Yes___No___If "Yes," show Amount $________Maturity________Peak debt service requirements $________
   c. Are there securities having a claim prior to this issue? Yes___No___If "Yes," show Amount $________Maturity________Peak debt service requirements $________
10. Schedule of rates or charges for services of the facility. Date effective____________
(Give particulars in a separate statement)
11. Controlling covenants of the bond indenture, authorizing resolution, or act. Attach separate statement, if necessary.
   a. In what order are the revenues disposed of (flow of funds)?____________
   ____
   ____
   b. What reserve funds are provided for and what are the requirements of each? What is the amount in each at present?

Name of Reserve Fund	*Requirements*	*Present Amount*
________	________	$________
________	________	________
________	________	________
________	________	________
________	________	________

   How are reserve funds invested?________________________

c. What is the covenant or legal requirement respecting the rates to be charged for the services rendered?________

d. What are the provisions for issuance of additional bonds?________

e. Is the preparation of an annual budget required? Yes____No____
If "Yes," is a public hearing provided for? Yes____No____

f. Is issuer required to make public statement regularly re earnings? Yes____No____
If "Yes," how often?________

g. What insurance is required:
Type________ Amount $____
Type________ Amount $____
Type________ Amount $____

h. Is there a requirement that consulting engineers be retained? Yes____No____ If "Yes," for what purpose and how often?________

i. Do bondholders have the benefit of a mortgage? Yes____No____

12. Name of corporate trustee, if any________
13. Name of consulting engineer(s), if any________
14. Name of the attorney(s) approving the legality of the issue________
15. Has the facility defaulted during the past 20 years for a period of 60 days or more in the payment of either principal or interest of any of its bonds or notes? Yes____No____ If "Yes," give full particulars in a separate statement, including terms of settlement.
16. Is there a competitive system in operation? Yes____No____ If "Yes," give in a separate statement the system's name, location, and extent of its operations.
17. Are any contributions to be made to or received from any political body? Yes____No____ If "Yes," give details________
18. Please furnish in a separate statement information regarding the location and economic background of the issuer, and the general character of industries and transportation facilities in the area served. Attach a statement of any other pertinent data or comments.

Part 2—Current Data on Revenues, Expenditures, and Financial Condition

	Fiscal Year Ended ____	*Same Period One Year Ago*	*Same Period Two Years Ago*
1. Operating revenue	$____	$____	$____
2. Nonoperating revenue			
3. Total gross revenue	$____	$____	$____
4. Expenditures:			
a. For operation	____	____	____
b. For maintenance	____		
5. Other charges, if any, against gross revenue	____	____	____
6. Net Income available for debt service	____	____	____
7. Interest paid on bonded debt	____	____	____
8. Principal paid on bonded debt	____	____	____
a. Matured	____	____	____
b. Called	____	____	____
9. Other charges against Net Income (specify various funds)*			
a. ____	____	____	____
b. ____	____	____	____
c. ____	____	____	____
d.			____
10. Amount available for retirement of debt by call			____
11. Surplus (state to what uses surplus has been or may be put) ____	____	____	____

12. Total amount of bonds issued (original and subsequent) ________
13. Bonded debt at end of period (also show below) ________
    a. Bank loans at end of period ________
    b. Other unfunded debt at end of period ________
14. Principal and interest on bonded debt next fiscal year ________
15. Present book value of plant or facility, equipment, and fixed assets, after depreciation ________
16. Attach copy of latest balance sheet, as of________
    Are there any contingent liabilities not shown in the balance sheet? Yes____No____ If "Yes," explain________
    Name and address of auditor preparing the annual audit________
    Is the auditor an independent auditor? Yes____No____
    *What method of depreciation is used?________
    *What disposition is made of revenue in these funds?________

Part 3—Special Information on Particular Types of Revenue Bonds

(A) For electric revenue bonds only:		*Fiscal Year Ended ____*	*Same Period One Year Ago*	*Same Period Two Years Ago*
(A) 1. KWH's generated		________		
2. KWH's purchased		________		
3. KWH's sold		________		
4. Number of customers at end of period:	Residential	________	________	________
	Industrial	________	________	________
	Commercial	________	________	________
	All others	________	________	________
5. KWH's consumed per customer:	Residential:	________	________	________
	Industrial	________	________	________
	Commercial	________	________	________
	All others	________	________	________

(B) For water or sewer revenue bonds only:		*Fiscal Year Ended ____*	*Same Period One Year Ago*	*Same Period Two Years Ago*
1. Estimated average daily water supply (in gallons)		________	________	________
2. Average daily water consumption (in gallons)		________	________	________
3. Water storage capacity (in gallons)		________	________	________
4. Number of customers at end of period:	Residential	________	________	________
	Commercial	________	________	________
	Industrial	________	________	________
	All others	________	________	________
5. Gallons water consumed per customer:	Residential	________	________	________
	Commercial	________	________	________
	Industrial	________	________	________
	All others	________	________	________

6. Is sewer service charge based on amount of water metered? Yes____No____ If not, what is the base?________
7. Does the sewer charge appear on water bill? Yes____No____
8. May water and sewer charges be paid separately? Yes____No____If "Yes," explain________

9. Does the law provide that past due bills become a lien on the property? ______
10. Does the law provide that water may be cut off if bills are not paid? ______
11. What is the source of water supply? ______

______

______

(C) For toll bridge or highway:

	12 Months Ended		Same Period Last Year		Same Period Two Years Ago	
1. Traffic:	*Vehicles*	*Revenue*	*Vehicles*	*Revenue*	*Vehicles*	*Revenue*
Passenger cars	______	$______	______	$______	______	$______
Trucks and busses	______	______	______	______	______	______
2. Other income (specify)						
______		______		______		______

Signed ______

Official Title ______

Date ______

* Investment Bankers Association of American.

APPENDIX C: Data Required by Standard & Poor's

Data Required for General Obligation Bond Rating

1. Debt statement, including maturities, with bonds segregated as to security, overlapping debt, which is this unit's share (on the basis of proportionate valuations) of the debt of overlapping taxing units.
2. Assessed valuation for the last four years, segregated as to realty and personalty, and as to industrial, commercial, utility, and residential basis of assessment.
3. Tax collection statement for four years including amount of current levy, amount collected on that levy in ensuing year, and amount collected to some recent date. Statement of this unit's tax rate and the overall tax rate for the past four years.
4. Recent population estimate.
5. Copies of the past two annual reports and the latest budget.
6. List of the 10 leading taxpayers with their assessed valuations, including the number of employees for industrial taxpayers.
7. Brief description of the economy of the area, including the character of development, the level of building activity, and the value of homes (for residential areas).
8. School enrollment for the past 10 years (where applicable).
9. Future borrowing plans by this unit and overlapping units.
10. Five-year proposed capital improvement program.

Data Required for Revenue Bond Analysis

I. In addition to the notice of sale and bidding information, the following should be made available on all revenue financings.
   - A. Purpose of issue
     1. Construction cost breakdown.
     2. Starting date of construction.
     3. Completion date of construction.
   - B. Engineering report and/or feasibility study
     1. Need for construction and benefits to be derived.
     2. Complete history of system (if existing).
     3. Competitive systems in area with comparison of all service being rendered.
   - C. Audit reports for three to five years (if existing).
   - D. Bond security
     1. Gross or net pledge of revenues.
     2. Flow of funds.
     3. Special funds.
     4. Parity provisions.
     5. Indenture.

6. Outstanding liens with full explanation.
7. Debt service schedules—outstanding as well as new bonds.

E. Other covenants

1. Insurance coverage.
2. Maintenance and repair responsibility.
3. Compulsory audits, etc.

F. Complete economic information concerning area of project.

II. In addition to the basics above stated, the following will be needed depending on purpose of financing:

A. Electric revenues

1. Power capacities.
2. Power use.
3. Rates and charges (complete breakdown).
4. Customer count (historical and projected).
5. Large commercial and/or industrial users (projected).
6. Power contracts availability.

B. Water revenues

1. Source of supply.
2. Historical and projected usage.
3. Climate conditions which affect revenues.
4. Customer count (historical and projected).
5. Connections (historical and projected).
6. Rates and charges and fees involved.
7. Treatment involved.
8. Comparison of all systems in area.
9. Industrial users, if any, with annual volume used; are these industries cyclical?
10. New development projections.

C. Sewer revenues

1. What type system?
2. Historical and projected system.
3. Rates and charges.
4. Mandatory connection to system?
5. Terrain of area being, or to be, served.
6. Contracts with developers in area?
7. Waste discharges, where and how?
8. Water usage in area.
9. Growth of area.
10. Customer count.
11. Assessments, if any; penalties.
12. State aid and/or federal aid?
13. Responsibility for treatment.

D. Parking revenues

1. Traffic count into area to be served.
2. Transportation facilities available in and out of area.

3. Access routes existing and to be constructed in future.
4. Rates and charges.
5. Master plan of area involved.
6. Availability of free parking.
7. Shopping facilities in area of parking facility.

E. Airport revenues
1. Area being served.
2. Airlines using facility.
3. Traffic count and passenger enplanements.
4. Airline use agreements.

13

Analysis and Rating of Municipal Bonds

JACKSON PHILLIPS, Ph.D.
Vice President and Director
Municipal Bonds Research Division
Moody's Investors Service, Inc.
New York, New York

THE ANALYSIS of municipal bonds seeks to define the investment strengths and weaknesses which inhere in and are attached to a long-term obligation issued by nonfederal governmental units in the United States. The conditions of the obligation must be isolated and defined; to the extent possible, they should be quantified. Then, the interrelations between the conditions of the obligation and between them and the rest of the world have to be established to determine what the analyst is seeking: the likelihood that the obligor will be able to keep all of the promises he has made. With a knowledge of the conditions under which the debtor could not meet the terms of his obligation, the analyst has only to determine the possibility of those conditions arising during the bond's life span.

A rating of a municipal bond is based on the analysis and may be regarded as a shorthand statement of the final judgment which is reached. It is an evaluative assessment of the probability that the debtor can and will do what he says regarding his obligations. The rating must be taken for what it is, a simplified classification of the credit risks associated with a particular obligation. The market finds this simplification to be a useful tool in making comparisons between bonds and in maintaining liquidity of capital funds. Time simply does not permit every trader and every underwriter to gather all of the facts and to perform the analysis involved in each of the great number of situations with which he is confronted daily. Obviously, though, as in all security analysis, when the individual can substitute his own superior analysis for that which is generally accepted, he stands to gain accordingly.

One set of legal ground rules should be borne in mind throughout the process of municipal analysis, a term which itself lacks precision. The market generally includes under the heading of municipal bonds all obligations issued by states, counties, cities, villages, and special districts, although obviously only a limited number of these units constitute legally incorporated units of governments; others are separate administrative

Symbols Currently Used in Municipal Bond Ratings by the National Rating Agencies*

General Description	*Moody's†*	*Standard & Poor's††*
Best quality grade	Aaa	AAA
High-quality grade	Aa	AA
Upper medium grade	A 1, A	A
Medium grade	Baa 1, Baa	BBB
Speculative grade	Ba	BB
Low grade	B	B
Poor grade to default	Caa	CCC
Highly speculative default	Ca	CC
Lowest rated grade	C	C

* In addition, specialized conditions may be denoted by a qualification such as Moody's *Eng.*, for engineering, which preceding a rating indicates a revenue bond where the project is under construction and the rating is that expected to be attached when the project is operating.

† Bonds with strongest investment attributes within a grade are designated by A-1 and Baa-1.

†† Effective June 10, 1974, a plus (+) sign may be added to AA down through BB categories to show relative standing; a minus (−) shows deterioration.

governmental units through which in most cases a state discharges limited functions. Common to all of them, however, is their power to issue bonds which bear interest which is exempt from taxation under the federal income tax laws, a power which historically is associated with the "sovereignty" of each of the states. Under the federal system of government as it has evolved in the United States, each state government is regarded as sovereign within its own boundaries and over those affairs which are purely its own. Municipal and all other governmental units derive their powers from their respective state government and must have specific authorizations for what they do.

The First Question

The analyst must first determine what assets the obligor is pledging to the discharge of the obligation. Because of the public nature of the issuer, true mortgages and the usual physical security associated with other long-term debt instruments will be lacking. Aside from pledges concerning time, amount, and mechanics of payment, the central question is what will the debtor pay the obligation from, or what will be his source of funds? The answer determines the questions which will be asked in the subsequent analysis, and there are several broad categories of pledges. These are as follows:

1. The general obligation pledge in which the borrower pledges his full faith and credit and unlimited taxing power. This is the broadest form of analysis, the most general, the traditional.
2. The limited pledge involving a single tax or a specific governmental revenue. A variant of the special fund doctrine, the unlimited tax pledge nevertheless involves use of a governmental power, the power to tax.
3. The enterprise or quasi-enterprise revenue pledge. Another variant of the special fund doctrine, this produces the true revenue bond, and the analysis leans heavily on long-standing corporate experience.
4. The lease pledge whereby funds derive immediately from resources of the lessee, which are other than those of the lessor-issuer but in which the issuer does something to justify payments which include debt service.
5. A backup pledge of someone else's resources.

There are, of course, combinations of these pledges. They cover the spectrum from an outright pledge to discharge the obligation almost to a denial that a debt even exists. Aside from the general obligation pledge, involving the general taxing power and the general fund, the others, limited and indirect, have been inspired by the legal and constitutional limitations placed on governmental debt usage over the last 130 years.

The General Rule

Generally, the credit aspect of bond security analysis seeks to appraise future performance in terms of future debt service requirements. For these purposes, the debt commitment of a municipal issuer is compared with the pledged resources, and both factors are measured on a current basis and projected into the future. Expressed as a ratio, this measure may be compared as between situations and with empirical evidence from the past. The likelihood of converting pledged wealth into sustainable annual future income must be separately appraised to validate the equation. Protections that may be established against the uncertainties of the future must also be evaluated.

THE GENERAL OBLIGATION

In general obligation bond analysis, a great number of determinants present themselves, but these may be subsumed under four headings for analytical purposes. These are debt, economic, financial, and governmental factors. While the term *general obligation* has a broader application, its most general usage is the one applied here, to a unit of government possessing general powers of taxation and whose revenues flow into a general fund.

Analysis of Debt

The analyst is concerned with the total impact of all debt obligations on the reasonable ability of the taxpayers of the issuing unit to meet them. To this end, his central and first task is to derive a measure of the debt burden. In simplest terms, this is the relationship between the total debt burden on the tax base in the governmental unit and the wealth located there. Total debt includes not only the debt obligations issued by the subject government, which is the gross debt, but also the proportionate share of the debt obligations of overlapping governmental units on the taxpayers of the subject unit. Thus, the *gross* bonded debt of a city is adjusted to *net* by subtracting obligations accounted for by sinking funds or by self-supporting (nontax) utility operations; but to the net figure is added a proportionate share of any county, school district, or other local governmental debt payable from the same tax base. It is this burden which the taxpayers of the city are confronted with and which is generally designated as the *overall net debt.*

The overall net debt is related to the broadest and most generally available measure of the community's wealth, which is the assessed valuation of all taxable property adjusted to reflect market value as nearly as possible. The adjustment is made through application of an equalization ratio, which generally reflects a state government's appraisal of local assessment practices and which is widely necessitated by grants-in-aid which require measures of local wealth. Empirical evidence indicates that there is good reason to expect difficulty in meeting debt obligations when the debt burden exceeds the 12 percent range and when an exogenous factor, such as an economic recession, comes into play.

The analyst also examines the structure of the debt, and how the issuer plans to pay it out. Unnecessary deferral of debt payment raises questions as to reason, and as a general rule, the analyst prefers payment to be reasonably related to the life of the improvement the debt is used to finance. The payment of half the debt of a community over the ensuing 10 years is generally recognized as prudent, accounting theoretically at least for some depreciation as well as maintaining capacity to borrow in the future. Another aspect of debt structure analysis seeks to determine irregularities and any special problems which might be incurred in meeting them.

Further checks in the analyst's appraisal of the debt of a community. The latter factor is of utmost importance, being an extension of has been done to prevent their recurrence; the uses the community makes of debt and how it plans debt incurrence related to both need and resources; and the necessity of future borrowing by the community. The latter factor is of utmost importance, being an extension of the numerator of the fundamental equation of debt burden. It involves an assessment of a city's capital plant relative to its position in history: for a deteriorating, older city or for a rapidly growing, newer city, future borrowing policy dictates particular and careful planning. As he turns to other factors in the analysis, the analyst must bear in mind the possible future debt policies of the borrowing unit.

Commonly Used Debt Measures in Municipal Bond Analysis

The debt burden: $\dfrac{\text{Overall net tax-supported debt}}{\text{Total market value of taxable property}}$

Example: $\dfrac{\text{Debt}}{\text{Valuation}} = \dfrac{\$\ 1{,}500{,}000}{\$17{,}500{,}000} = 8.57\%$

Rule-of-thumb ranges:

5% : Moderate
10% : Heavy
15% : Too heavy

The debt payout: $\dfrac{\text{Scheduled maturities in } x \text{ years}}{\text{Total bonded debt}}$

Example: $\dfrac{\text{Debt maturing in 10 years}}{\text{Total debt}} = \dfrac{\$\ 750{,}000}{\$1{,}500{,}000} = 50\%$

Rule-of-thumb ranges:

5 years : 25%
10 years : 50%
20 years : 100%

Slower rates are questionable.

Economic Analysis

As the debt of the unit measures the problem the analyst is solving regarding any particular governmental unit, the economic background and analysis largely measure the dimensions of the solution to the problem. As in any form of security analysis, the future is of more importance than the past or present, so the analyst is concerned that he properly project what he can measure now against what will happen in the future. Briefly, the economic analysis of a borrowing unit should reveal the characteristics of any time-series analysis: the secular, cyclical, seasonal, and random trends applicable to the unit involved.

The economic geography, the locational advantages, and the land use characteristics of the borrower need to be determined as a matter of identification. The degree to which a particular unit is subject to natural catastrophe may be enough to rule out some bonds as far as some investors are concerned. Earthquakes, for example, are not yet predictable occurrences, although they are more predictable in some areas than others; where they are, the analyst and the investor should at least recognize this factor before, rather than after, the event. The natural setting of the unit may provide clues as to its future development.

As a reinforcement of the knowledge gained through assessed valuations of taxable property, the analyst will seek out other measures of the wealth of the community. These include population characteristics, the level of income of families and individuals, and the market valuation per capita of the unit. Housing characteristics as measured by age of housing, value of owner-occupied homes, rental values, and new construction costs add further insight into the nature of the community. Additional surrogates are available through educational attainments of the adult population and occupational characteristics.

The economic structure of the community is among the most important factors to be examined. The types of employment which the community offers and the industry structure offer one of the best clues as to the economic future, as well as to the cyclical stability. Specifically, the firms which offer employment in the community, and the valuation of their investments there, lend verification, which reinforces theoretical knowledge of employment structures. The relationship of the community to the economic unit of which it is a part, the Standard Metropolitan Statistical Area or the agricultural area, is basic to an understanding of its economic future. Finally, the way the unit is related to the outside world by transportation facilities has been basic in the past to an understanding of its future development.

Financial Analysis

An examination of the financial operations of the community for the latest period available serves to confirm its performance under existing conditions. To relate debt to economic resources only sets the problem; the translation of resources into revenues to pay expenses, including debt service, requires periodic and constant examination of the issuer's audited accounts. A singularly difficult aspect of municipal security analysis, as opposed to corporate analysis, is the general lack of standardization of accounting and reporting procedures, particularly among smaller units.

The analysis of the revenue system involves determination of the reliance on the property tax, the trend of assessed valuation, and tax delinquencies, in addition to the diversification of the revenue structure. Expenditures should be analyzed to ascertain the relationship of debt service payments to total current expenses as well as the vulnerability of the unit to mandated expenditures, which could create financial problems for it. Of particular importance is sensitivity of the revenue and expenditure structures to cyclical fluctuation, and the record of tax delinquencies may be particularly useful as a tool in the determination of local cyclical sensitivity. The issuers' budgets require examination as a forecast, as well as the adequacy of the financial planning and management. Assessment practices, tax collection procedures, and methods of enforcement may require examination, as the analyst attempts to determine the ability of the unit's management to convert resources into tax receipts which are adequate for all its purposes.

The analyst will examine the audited accounts of the unit to determine the year-end relation of current liabilities to available cash. The unit's promptness in disposing of casual deficits, as well as devices to keep deficits from accumulating should be determined, as should the liquidity of current account cash and uncollected taxes relative to demand liabilities outstanding. A prime concern of the analyst is that the current account be maintained soundly, because often in the past, difficulty with debt service has been signaled first by current account difficulties, particularly when steps are not taken immediately to correct such troubles before they spread to longer term obligations.

Government

In this endeavor, the analyst will seek to determine how well organized the governmental unit is to perform its functions and how well staffed and administered it is to carry out those functions. A major concern is that services are provided which will perpetuate a liveable community. Knowledge of the professionalism of government, as well as the traditions of the community in its governmental affairs, will help considerably, although the projection of these factors into the future may be tenuous and the element of subjectivity must be guarded against consciously. Intergovernmental relations constitute an important segment of this analysis in determining the cooperation and competition among and between this and other units, the relations with the state government, particularly in finance, and the actions of other units which may drain off resources of the subject unit. A major aspect of government is the availability of adequate financial documents, annual reports, and meaningful capital planning devices and records.

THE RATING

The question is how these are put together to determine a rating. Simply, it is a question of examining each area of information and their interrelations and making a judgment modified as necessary by evidence and experience. There is no way to cram them all into a single formula, which invariably produces the right answer. The stumbling block is weighting, and most disagreements on ratings spring from different weights attached to the factors in analysis by different analysts. Table

TABLE 1

Representative Data for Two Cities Rated Differently

Identification	*City A*	*City B*
1970 population (percent change/1960)	715,674 (−3.3%)	382,417 (−5.6%)
1970 density (1960), population/square mile	15,904 (16,451)	16,204 (17,170)
Year incorporated	1850	1836
Debt:		
1970 net direct debt (000)	$179,605	$135,616
Percent change 1973/70	−16.4%	4.4%
1973 overall net debt (000)	$408,511	$162,601
1973 debt burden	4.2	9.4
1973 overall net debt per capita	$ 570.81	$ 425.19
Debt payout, 10 years	83.7%	69.0%
Economic:		
1973 assessed value, millions (percent change 1964)	$ 2,434 (+54%)	$ 1,213 (−20%)
1973 full value per capita	$ 13,616	$ 4,603
1970 median family income	$ 10,503	$ 7,735
1970 median values homes	$ 28,100	$ 17,300
1970 median school years	12.4	10.0
Percent employed, principal lines		
Manufacturing	11.7%	36.9%
Wholesale and retail trade	20.4	15.6
Business, professional services	44.5	18.3
Finance:		
Percent revenues from property tax	44.3%	48.9%
Property tax rate per $1,000 a.v., 1973	$112.82	$ 93.90
Tax delinquency rate 1972	1.65%	13.2%
Cash surplus, 1972 (000)	$46,098	$ 277
Comment:	Rich, western service, and port city; moderate and declining debt with excellent payout; expanding tax base; current finances in excellent condition; governmental services numerous and varied.	Poor eastern manufacturing and port city; rising debt burden; declining tax base, below average wealth factors; current finances tenuous; low level of governmental services.
Rating:		
Moody's	Aaa	Baa
S & P's	AAA	BBB

1 lists some of the factors utilized by analysts in arriving at their conclusions about the relative credit risks involved in two well-known American cities.

THE REVENUE BOND

Revenue bond analysis is in many ways less elusive than general obligation bond analysis. Generally, it involves a closed system with a finite number of variables and greater possibilities for quantification. This pledge of security involves an enterprise where the debt is related to an earning asset. The principles of credit analysis are the same, but the analysis shifts from the use of the sovereign power of government to extract a tax to the operation of a user enterprise involving benefit analysis. Generally, there is a measurable benefit for which people either are or are not willing to pay. Thus, we have bonds secured by pledges of electric, water, toll bridge, college dormitory, parking facility, toll road, or airport revenue.

Chief among the factors that must be examined are those pertaining to the revenue-producing enterprise, its demand-creating potential, and the legal protections which are safeguards against the unexpected.

The physical plant involves engineers' appraisals of the soundness of the system and its ability to produce a service that can be sold at a price consumers are willing to pay. This involves system capability, and the ability of management to operate it with financial success. Other factors incude the secular, cyclical, and operating characteristics of the industry and the particular system which is being analyzed.

Legal protections involve detailed examination of the covenants in the trust indenture or bond resolution. Of particular importance are the flow of funds which is established for the enterprise, the additional bond clause, and the rate covenant. There are many examples of difficulties caused by the establishment of an improper flow of funds or an additional bond clause that was too liberal in its permissiveness. And the rate covenant establishes a base by which to measure management and its performance.

Covenants inserted in indentures as protections have a way of gaining currency with the passage of time. A traditional one has been that pertaining to how the indenture itself is amended. Right now, there are prosperous revenue-bond-financed enterprises being watched by the operators of less successful undertakings with a view to how their surpluses can be absorbed by the less financially adroit. The difficult process of amending the indenture may be the chief obstacle standing in the way of some of the changes economic and political pressures dictate.

THE LEASE-RENTAL BOND

The lease-rental type obligation has come increasingly into use in recent years, and its analysis adds an examination of the legal relationships between the lessor, the lessee, and any other party to the arrangement. In this case, of course, the economic base of the lessee and credit factors pertaining to his ability to meet debt service obligations assume central importance. Most of this type of analysis is covered in the general obligation bond discussion previously noted.

THE MORAL OBLIGATION

The newest major force in the market has been the bond referred as a *moral obligation.* Most frequently in this case, the issuer pledges as security the revenues associated with the undertaking. Then, to strengthen the bond, funds from another source, usually the state, are pledged in one way or another. A common way is to establish a reserve fund for the bond, usually out of bond sale proceeds, which the state *may* contribute to and presumably keep filled if necessary, thereby establishing in the beholder's mind a flow of funds from the state treasury to the bondholder. The term *moral obligation* has set down roots in these discussions that may someday prove to be unfortunate. In this regard, dictionary phraseology runs "sanctioned by or operative upon one's conscience or ethical judgment; as to feel a moral obligation. It should be emphasized that on their face, all such obligations deny strongly that the state has any *legal* commitment to the obligation.

There is considerable disagreement among analysts as to how such obligations should be rated and what weight is to be attached to an obligation without legal enforceability. One line of thought is that no state would have the termerity to allow such an obligation to experience difficulty. Another approach says the bond analyst must ask under what set of circumstances, political or economic, would meeting the commitments become a burden? The legislature clearly may or may not elect to appropriate moneys to fill the reserve once it has been drawn upon. If two options are provided, may not either be exercised, particularly under some conceivable circumstances?

It is probably the continuing emergence of difficult analytical problems that gives the field of municipal analysis its vitality. Because municipal finance itself is a vital area of the American financial scene, new ways of financing necessary or desirable (to someone) projects evolve. Hemmed in by restrictive laws borne of suspicion, often justified, those charged with financing seek new methods. The analyst thus faces new and stimulating problems and is armed only with principles and tools which have come out of the past.

14

Mortgage Market: Structure and Characteristics

SAUL B. KLAMAN, Ph.D.
Vice President and Chief Economist
National Association of Mutual Savings Banks
New York, New York

and

JACK RUBINSON
Assistant Director of Research
National Association of Mutual Savings Banks
New York, New York

INTRODUCTION

OF THE major types of debt instruments in the nation's credit structure, mortgage loans have consistently attracted the largest amount of investment funds over the past three decades. From the years immediately following World War II to the mid-1960s, the dominant position of mortgage credit in capital markets largely reflected pent-up mortgage demands built up during the depression and war years and the establishment of a wide variety of federal government programs aimed at stimulating the flow of credit into real estate markets. At the same time, many of these programs—most notably in the areas of mortgage insurance and guaranty—were steadily liberalized by the Congress to enable greater numbers of moderate income borrowers to qualify for real estate loans.

By and large, the massive flow of mortgage funds into both residential and nonresidential properties in the years following World War II represented a remarkable achievement in meeting the nation's housing and other capital needs. In the residential sector, for example, mortgage debt expansion totaled more than $600 billion in the 1945–73 period,[1]

[1] *Flow of Funds Accounts, 1945–1972,* Board of Governors of the Federal Reserve System, August 1973, pp. 4–6; subsequent quarterly issues published in 1973 and 1974.

helping to finance the construction and purchase of nearly 43 million new dwelling units.[2]

During most of this period, the mortgage financing process—notwithstanding a number of improvements—remained essentially unchanged. In general, the individual mortgage contract provided for the conveyance of property as security for the payment of a debt, the major terms of which dealt with the interest rate charged by the lender, the maturity of the loan, prepayment penalties, and the default conditions under which the lender could take possession of, and foreclose, the property. From the point of view of both borrower and lender, however, mortgage financing techniques still left much to be desired. Unlike many other forms of long-term debt, the liquidity and marketability of individual mortgage loans were seriously limited, reflecting in part the unique characteristics of individual parcels of real estate underlying the mortgage instrument and in part the imperfect institutional, regulatory, and geographic framework surrounding mortgage market operations.

Furthermore, significant changes in federal economic and monetary policies introduced in the 1950s revealed serious underlying weaknesses in the ability of the mortgage sector to compete for investors' funds. This was particularly so during recurring periods of credit stringency when rising mortgage rates and reduced availability of mortgage credit—especially in the housing sector—catalyzed private and government efforts in the 1960s and early 1970s to strengthen the structure of mortgage finance. The result has been significant mortgage market changes, many of which, though still in their early stages, are likely to lead to a fundamental restructuring of the real estate financing process.

PROPERTY AND LOAN CATEGORIES

By far the major share of mortgage financing in the United States is secured by residential properties—largely owner-occupied homes. As of year-end 1973, for example, three fourths of the $635 billion of total mortgage debt outstanding covered residential dwelling units.[3] Within the residential mortgage market, loans can be classified into the following broad categories:

FHA-insured Mortgages. Mortgage loans insured by the Federal Housing Administration remain the single most important type of federally assisted mortgage, accounting for about one fifth of total residential mortgage holdings.[4] FHA insurance programs have multiplied rapidly

---

[2] *Housing Construction Statistics, 1889 to 1964,* U.S. Department of Commerce, Bureau of the Census; *Construction Reports, Housing Starts, 1965–1973,* C-20 supplements monthly, U.S. Department of Commerce, Bureau of the Census.

[3] *Federal Reserve Bulletin,* July 1974, Board of Governors of the Federal Reserve System, p. A44.

[4] Ibid.

since the establishment of the Federal Housing Administration in 1934. In 1974, these programs encompassed the following areas:

Regular Home and Apartment House Mortgage Insurance. These programs continue to account for the dominant share of FHA mortgage insurance activity. The basic objectives of regular FHA insurance operations have changed little since their original inception, namely the insuring of private lenders against loss on mortgages carrying more liberal mortgage terms than the home buyer or renter might otherwise be able to obtain. Repeated liberalization of FHA mortgage terms by the Congress has brought the maximum single-family home mortgage amount to $45,000, the minimum down payment to as little as 3 percent of the value of the property and the maturity to as long as 35 years.

The maximum interest rate on FHA-insured mortgages (9½ percent as of early September 1974) is determined by the Secretary of the Department of Housing and Urban Development, and changed periodically according to mortgage market conditions. In recent years, regular FHA program operations have shifted somewhat from the insuring of new to existing housing as nonfederally insured loans have become increasingly competitive in residential mortgage markets.

Major Subsidized Programs. Unlike the regular mortgage insurance programs which are financed by premiums charged to borrowers, FHA-subsidized housing programs involve direct federal outlays to help meet the housing needs of low- and moderate-income groups. FHA-subsidized housing construction grew rapidly, though erratically, during the 1960–72 period, increasing from less than 40,000 units per year at the beginning of the 1960s to 430,000 units in 1971 and 340,000 units in 1972.[5]

This growth reflected primarily the establishment of new mortgage interest assistance programs under Sections 235 (for owner-occupied homes) and 236 (for multifamily properties) of the Housing and Urban Development (HUD) Act of 1968. Under the Section 235 program, mortgage interest rates are lowered significantly—to as little as 1 percent for eligible moderate income home buyers. Federal subsidy payments are equivalent to the difference between market interest rate mortgage payments (including principal, interest, taxes, and insurance) and one fifth of the buyers' income. HUD mortgage assistance under the Section 236 multifamily program is made to the owner, who, in turn, must pass on the benefits of the reduction to eligible moderate income tenants in the form of reduced rents.

Adminstrative problems in the Section 235–236 housing programs led to the suspension of new commitments for this type of housing construction in January 1973. As a result the number of subsidized housing starts dropped sharply in 1973 to less than 200,000 units. The future of these

[5] Data on federally subsidized housing starts were obtained from unpublished data compiled by the U.S. Department of Housing and Urban Development, Division of Research and Statistics.

programs continues uncertain, with the administration actively exploring the possibility of substituting alternative approaches. Under the Housing and Community Development Act of 1974, authority for the Section 235 and 236 programs was extended on a limited basis to June 1976.[6]

Other FHA Programs. The Federal Housing Administration also maintains a wide variety of other mortgage credit programs, some of which are intended to encourage the flow of private mortgage funds, and others, to provide direct federal housing credit assistance.[7] The more significant ones involve insurance for loans covering:

1. Property improvement and rehabilitation.
2. Land development.
3. Low-cost homes in outlying areas and farm homes.
4. Cooperative and condominium housing, and mobile homes.
5. Housing for veterans and military and civilian personnel in defense-related installations.
6. Rental housing for the elderly and handicapped and nursing homes.

VA-guaranteed Loans. The Veterans Administration (VA) Mortgage Guarantee Program aids eligible veterans to obtain home mortgage loans carrying liberal down payment, maturity, and other contract provisions. The maximum VA loan guarantee to lenders is $12,500 or 60 percent of the loan, whichever is less.[8] As in the case of FHA loans, maximum interest rates on VA mortgages are administratively fixed, and have typically matched the FHA contract rate—9½ percent as of early September 1974.

The VA role in mortgage and housing markets was most significant in the mid-1950s when VA-guaranteed housing starts averaged 325,000 units a year or one fifth of total housing starts. Since then, however, housing construction under VA-guaranteed loans has declined in relative importance, as cumulative increases in the total number of veterans utilizing their loan guarantee benefits have reduced the overall mortgage lending potential under the VA program.

Conventional Loans. These loans, which are neither insured by FHA nor guaranteed by VA, make up by far the largest segment of both the residential and nonresidential mortgage markets. In the 1960–73 period, conventional mortgages absorbed 70 percent of the total net gain in residential mortgage debt.[9]

In recent years, the market for conventional mortgage loans has been competitively strengthened by (1) lender liberalization of maturity and

---

[6] See Title III of the Housing and Community Development Act of 1974.

[7] For basic descriptions of these and other FHA mortgage programs, see the annual reports of the Department of Housing and Urban Development, and *Federal Banking Reports,* Commerce Clearing House.

[8] *Federal Banking Reports.*

[9] *Federal Reserve Bulletin,* November 1973 and July 1974, p. A49.

down payment provisions; (2) improved secondary market facilities; and (3) the spreading use of private mortgage insurance. Although these developments have increased the investment appeal of conventional loans relative to federally underwritten mortgages, (Chart 1) the conventional mortgage market (and to a lesser extent FHA and VA markets as well) remains highly fragmented with wide variations in interest rates and other mortgage terms persisting among different areas.

A major reason for this lies in state regulatory and statutory differences concerning maximum allowable interest rates, procedures for trans-

CHART 1

FHA-insured Home Mortgage Yields minus Conventional Home Mortgage Yields, 1965–74

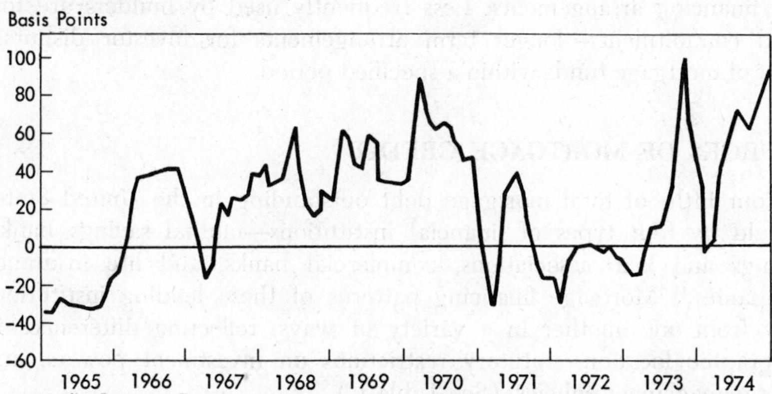

Note: Yield spreads measure the difference between gross mortgage yields (before deduction of mortgage servicing costs) and bond yields, and are based on month-end data for FHA home mortgages and monthly averages for new Aa corporate bond data. FHA mortgage yield data assume a 15-year prepayment and a 30-year original maturity from August 1961 to December 1973, and a mortgage term of 25 years and prepayment at the end of 12 years from January 1960 to July 1971. FHA mortgage yield information is compiled from reports on secondary market transactions.

Sources: Departments of Housing and Urban Development and the U.S. Treasury.

ferring mortgaged property, mortgage investment powers allowed various types of local financial institutions, restrictions on out-of-state lender activity, and foreclosure procedures. State variations in these areas also prevail with respect to nonresidential loans. A major exception here, however, is the absence of statutory interest rate ceilings on these investments—a factor which has helped to maintain the flow of funds into commercial, industrial, and other types of nonresidential mortgages during periods of rising interest rates.

Construction Loans. Construction financing represents a highly specialized segment of the mortgage market with its own unique lending techniques. The flow of construction credits to builders is, nonetheless, closely linked to the availability of permanent mortgage funds, since construction lenders usually require that the builder obtain long-term mortgage financing for the completed property in advance. Construction credits are generally provided on a short-term basis and paid out to builders in installments as work progresses on the structure.

Partly reflecting their greater risk exposure, construction loans generally earn higher interest rates than permanent mortgage loans. Investor practices concerning construction loans vary widely from lender to lender. In some cases, lenders provide mortgage funds for both the construction and final sale of the completed property. In others, only construction credit is supplied.

A variety of commitment techniques are utilized to facilitate the construction financing process.[10] Standby commitments given by the institutional investor to a builder are pledges to purchase the permanent mortgages at below market prices, thereby making possible construction financing arrangements. Less frequently used by builders are forward commitments—longer term arrangements for investor disbursement of mortgage funds within a specified period.

SOURCES OF MORTGAGE CREDIT

Four fifths of total mortgage debt outstanding in the United States is held by four types of financial institutions—mutual savings banks, savings and loan associations, commercial banks, and life insurance companies.[11] Mortgage financing patterns of these lending institutions vary from one another in a variety of ways, reflecting differences in geographic location, statutory restrictions on investment powers, and asset management policies. (See Table 1.)

Mutual savings banks are essentially long-term mortgage lenders, channeling the bulk of their mortgage funds into permanent type loans. Residential loans generally dominate savings bank mortgage lending activity with more than four fifths of total industry portfolios secured by single and multifamily structures. Although savings banks are restricted mainly to the northeastern section of the nation, the industry is an important source of conventional mortgage credit and a leading nationwide source of federally underwritten mortgage funds.

The industry's significance in national FHA and VA markets stems from the passage of legislation in most states in the early 1950s permitting savings banks to invest in federally underwritten mortgage loans secured by properties located beyond their own state boundaries. Since the granting of this authorization, savings banks have expanded their nationwide lending markedly and, by the end of 1973, held nearly $30 billion in federally underwritten mortgage loans or over one fifth of

[10] For an extensive discussion of commitment techniques in construction and interim financing, see Saul B. Klaman, *The Postwar Residential Mortgage Market* (Princeton, N.J.: Princeton University Press, 1961), pp. 182–95.

[11] *Federal Reserve Bulletin,* July 1974, p. A44.

TABLE 1

Percentage Distribution of Mortgage Debt Outstanding by Selected Type of Holder, Property, and Loan, September 30, 1973

	Total Mortgage Debt Outstanding*	*Long-Term Mortgage Debt Outstanding* — Residential Mortgage Loans: Total	FHA-insured	VA-guaranteed	Conventional	Nonresidential Mortgage Loans	Farm Mortgage Loans	Construction Loans	Land Loans
Savings and loan associations	38.9	47.7	17.9	29.1	58.2	16.6	1.6	29.7	21.4
Commercial banks	19.4	14.4	9.4	7.4	16.7	29.4	20.6	41.2	40.6
Life insurance companies	13.0	8.9	12.1	10.2	7.9	33.7	22.4	1.0	3.3
Mutual savings banks	12.2	14.2	20.3	29.4	10.4	11.3	0.2	3.5	2.7
Federal credit agencies†	8.4	8.5	27.4	16.6	2.4	3.4	42.0	0.2	—‡
GNMA pools and FHDA blocks of loans§	2.6	3.0	6.6	4.8	1.8	0.1	10.2	0	0
Mortgage investment trusts	2.5	0.2	0.1	0.1	0.3	2.2	—‡	21.4	31.7
State and local credit agencies	1.4	1.4	1.0	0.1	1.7	0.8	1.7	2.8	—‡
State and local retirement funds	1.2	1.2	4.4	1.8	0.3	1.4	1.1	0.1	—‡
Private noninsured pension funds	0.4	0.3	0.8	0.5	0.2	0.8	—‡	—‡	0.2
Total	100.0	100.0	100.0	100.0	100.0	100.0	100.0	100.0	100.0
Total (billions of dollars)	589.2	416.5	76.9	43.7	295.9	98.2	25.8	39.3	9.3

* Figures for total mortgage debt exclude mortgage companies, individuals, and other lenders accounting for about 5 percent of total mortgage debt outstanding; breakdown of holdings for these groups is not available.

† Included in this category are holdings of the Federal National Mortgage Association, the Federal Home Loan Mortgage Corporation, Federal Land Banks, Government National Mortgage Association, Department of Housing and Urban Development, Farmers Home Administration, Veterans Administration, and relatively small amounts held by a variety of other federal agencies.

‡ Less than one half of 1 percent.

§ This category refers to GNMA-guaranteed mortgage-backed "pass-through" securities and blocks of loans sold by the Farmers Home Administration.

Source: Department of Housing and Urban Development.

total FHA and VA debt outstanding. In more recent years, savings banks have shifted their mortgage investment emphasis to conventional loans in out-of-state markets, following the enactment of expanded legislative authority in major states.

All told, the industry holds about seven tenths of total assets in mortgages—a substantially larger proportion than commercial banks and life insurance companies, but a smaller share than savings and loan associations. Savings bank mortgage lending capacity has been hampered by the industry's confinement to 17 states—largely due to legal restrictions which prevent geographic extension. Savings banks are exclusively state chartered, remaining the only deposit-type institution denied access to federal chartering privileges.[12]

Savings and loan associations[13] are also primarily residential mortgage lenders. However, the composition of their residential lending activity differs somewhat from that of mutual savings banks. Short-term construction loans assume greater importance in the industry's overall mortgage investment programs, while conventional loans dominate long-term mortgage holdings, despite a substantial increase in federally underwritten mortgage activity in recent years. Savings and loan associations hold a larger total amount of residential mortgage debt than other types of financial institutions, although their importance as a source of real estate credit varies widely from area to area.

Unlike mutual savings banks and life insurance companies, savings and loan associations largely limit their mortgage lending activity to local market areas, reflecting, in large part, the relatively modest size of most savings associations. At the end of 1973, for instance, average assets per institution amounted to about 52 million, compared with 221 million for mutual savings banks, $139 million for life insurance companies, and $52 million for commercial banks. Some expansion in nationwide lending activity, however, has been achieved in recent years through expanded purchases of mortgage participations and mortgage-backed securities. Despite broadened investment powers, investment activity of savings and loan associations remains restricted largely to mortgage lending—a fact which largely explains the seven-eighths share of the industry's total resources devoted to mortgage loans.

While continuing to channel the bulk of their mortgage investment funds into loans on owner-occupied homes, savings and loan associations have increased their income-property activity significantly in the past 10 years. Combined holdings of multifamily and nonresidential mortgages have risen from 11 percent to 19 percent of total portfolios from 1963 to 1973.

Commercial banks devote a significantly smaller share of their assets

---

[12] *National Fact Book of Mutual Savings Banking—1974,* National Association of Mutual Saving Banks, pp. 6, 25, and 49.

[13] *1973 Savings and Loan Fact Book,* United States Savings and Loan League.

to mortgage loans than do savings banks, savings and loan associations, and life insurance companies, reflecting their basic orientation toward meeting business credit demands. By virtue of the industry's larger size, however, they represent a major source of mortgage funds.[14] Commercial banks place a significantly greater emphasis on nonresidential lending than do thrift institutions, and they are the nation's leading suppliers of short-term construction loans.

In addition to their role as suppliers of direct permanent and construction mortgage funds, commercial banks are the single most important source of interim financing (warehousing) to other real estate mortgage lenders and, in an increasing number of instances, also carry on a mortgage banking function—originating and servicing mortgage loans for permanent investors.

The relative significance of mortgage loans in the overall investment activity of commercial banks has changed little over the post-World War II period—remaining in the neighborhood of about one tenth of total assets. Significant shifts, however, have developed more recently within existing residential holdings where the conventional loan share has risen from two-thirds to about seven-eighths over the past decade. The commercial bank industry has typically been a relatively unstable source of residential mortgage credit, adjusting its investment activity according to variations in demand and time deposit inflows which have resulted from shifts in Federal Reserve monetary policy and economic and financial changes.

Life insurance companies are major suppliers of nonresidential and multifamily mortgage credit. During the early post-World War II decades, these institutions were also major providers of home mortgage credit. Since the 1960s, however, life insurance companies have cut back sharply their home mortgage lending activity as the competitive yield position of alternative investments, mainly corporate bonds and nonresidential and apartment house mortgages, strengthened significantly. The extent of this shift into income property mortgage loans can be seen in the two-thirds share of total mortgage portfolios accounted for by multifamily and nonresidential loans, compared with only one third at the end of 1960.[15]

Mortgage loans have diminished in relative significance on the asset side of the life insurance industry balance sheet. The ratio of mortgage loans to total assets has declined steadily from nearly four tenths at the end of 1966 to about three tenths at year-end 1973.

Unlike thrift institutions and commercial banks, life insurance com-

---

[14] *The Commercial Banking Industry,* a monograph prepared for the Commission on Money and Credit, American Bankers Association (Englewood Cliffs, N.J.: Prentice Hall, Inc., 1962).

[15] *Life Insurance Fact Book 1973* (New York: Institute of Life Insurance), pp. 80–83.

panies enjoy relatively stable inflows of investment funds from contractual additions to policyholders' reserves. This factor enables life insurance companies to plan their mortgage investment programs on a long-term basis through the forward commitment process. As a result, many life companies—particularly the larger ones—maintain nationwide branch systems and close working relationships with mortgage correspondents who originate and service mortgage loans for their portfolios.

Since the early 1960s, different mortgage market sectors have attracted funds in increasing amounts from a variety of new or heretofore minor private and government sources. Indeed, sources other than the four major types of financial institutions have supplied an increased share of the flow of funds into mortgage markets during this period, especially in periods of credit stringency when the mortgage lending capacity of major types of financial institutions was seriously impaired. Among the major new providers of mortgage credit deserving particular attention are:

Federally Sponsored Credit Agencies. Two of these agencies—the *Federal National Mortgage Association (FNMA) and the Federal Home Loan Bank System*—represent the most important supplementary federal agency sources of credit in residential mortgage markets. FNMA lending operations are the most important in this group, typically exceeding the net flow of residential mortgage funds from other types of federal credit agencies. A mixed federal-private corporation, FNMA buys and sells residential mortgages in secondary markets to help stabilize residential construction and increase the liquidity of mortgage loans.[16]

The Federal Home Loan Bank System provides mortgage credit indirectly by advancing funds to members—almost exclusively savings and loan associations—partly to help sustain the flow of credit into housing markets in periods of mortgage credit scarcity, to mitigate seasonal imbalances between inflows of investment funds and mortgage credit demands, and to promote interregional mobility of mortgage funds from capital surplus to capital deficit areas.

A new and potentially significant source of mortgage funds is the Federal Home Loan Mortgage Corporation—a subsidiary agency of the Federal Home Loan Bank System organized to further improve secondary mortgage market developments (see pages 399–400 for further details).

A variety of other federal agencies are also major participants in the mortgage market. These include: (1) the Government National Mortgage Association—a wholly owned government corporation within the

[16] *Annual Report 1973* and *Mid-Year Report 1974,* Federal National Mortgage Association.

Department of Housing and Urban Development providing special assistance for the financing of selected types of mortgages, the guaranteeing of timely payments of principal and interest on mortgage-backed securities issued by private financial enterprises, and the sales of participations in its own mortgage holdings (see pages 400 and 401); (2) the Farmers Home Administration, which extends direct mortgage credit in rural areas for the purchase of farms or homes by borrowers unable to obtain adequate credit elsewhere and which operates an insured loan program to protect private lenders against default losses in cases where the borrower is able to arrange private mortgage financing; and (3) Federal Land Banks—a government-sponsored agency providing farm mortgage credit to eligible borrowers who purchase stock in associations owning shares in the Federal Land Bank System.

Mortgage Investment Trusts (MIT's). This relatively new type of organization has developed rapidly as a major source of construction and land development loans. Raising funds through the issuance of equity and debt securities, borrowings, and commercial paper, assets of MIT's have grown from less than $13 billion in 1970 to some $16 billion at the end of 1973, including $14.5 billion in mortgage loans. They represent the third largest private holders of construction loans—second only to commercial banks and savings and loan associations.[17] During 1974, however, many firms in the industry encountered serious difficulties when interest rates soared to record levels on short-term loans. Lending by MIT's dropped sharply and an increasing number of firms in the industry failed.

State and Local Government Credit Agencies. Direct financing of housing by state and local government credit programs has proliferated in recent years, and represents a major source of residential mortgage credit in an increasing number of areas.[18]

Nonfinancial Corporations and Real Estate Companies. Although still small in dollar volume, combined mortgage loan holdings of these two lender groups have grown rapidly, more than quadrupling to over $7 billion from 1965 to 1973.[19]

Mortgage Companies. These institutions have been highly significant generators of mortgage credit over the past 30 years. They are not basically holders of mortgage loans. Their primary function is to originate loans for sale to investors and then service these loans on a continuing basis. As such they perform an important economic function of channeling funds from capital surplus to capital deficit areas. Originally concentrating their efforts in the federally underwritten sector, mortgage

---

[17] *Monthly Mortgage Lending Activity,* March 1974, Department of Housing and Urban Development.

[18] Ibid.

[19] Ibid.

companies have allocated an increasing share of their investment funds to conventional residential and nonresidential loans in recent years.[20]

The structure of the mortgage banking industry is undergoing far-reaching changes. An increasing number of these organizations have been acquired by commercial banks in recent years, while numerous mergers within the industry have produced large-size firms operating in mortgage markets on a nationwide basis. This trend, together with the significant narrowing of interregional imbalances in mortgage flows, points to the possibility of fundamental revisions in the mortgage banking function.

ROLE OF MORTGAGE LOANS IN FINANCIAL MARKETS

Mortgage loans represent the single most important type of capital market investment. Over the past 30 years, the growth in mortgage credit has surpassed the expansion in long-term debt incurred by federal, state, and local governments, corporations and other forms of business; and consumers. Mortgage debt on properties of individuals and businesses amounts to about one fourth of total net public and private debt and three eighths of capital market debt.[21]

Notwithstanding this leading position, unique and partially independent supply-demand factors have caused mortgage flows to fluctuate more widely than activity in other types of capital market debt. On the one hand, the availability of mortgage credit depends strongly on short-run cyclical changes in economic and financial market conditions, and on monetary and fiscal policy. Real estate credit demands, on the other, tend to reflect longer run demographic trends, the adequacy of the existing inventory of housing and nonresidential structures, and borrower evaluation of the relationship between incomes—both current and future—and real estate needs.

The more dynamic short-run forces affecting the availability of mortgage credit, together with the unique vulnerability of these investments to financial market shifts, have led to considerable instability in mortgage market conditions. Indeed, drastic reductions in the supply of mortgage credit have developed with increasing frequency during the post-World War II period.

Over the past decade alone, there have been four severe mortgage credit shortages, in 1966, 1969, 1973, and 1974 while during the preceding two decades, there was only one, in 1959. Conversely, in other periods, particularly during 1961–64 and 1971–72, the supply of mortgage credit rose so sharply that overliberalized underwriting standards in some areas led to increased delinquency and foreclosure problems.

---

[20] *Mortgage Banking 1973—Economics and Research Committee Trends Report No. 13*, Mortgage Bankers Association of America.

[21] *Flow of Funds Accounts, 1945–1974.*

Underlying these hypersensitive conditions in mortgage markets are a variety of exogenous and endogenous factors affecting the real estate financing process, the most important of which may be broadly summarized as follows:

Federal Economic and Financial Policies. Since the Federal Reserve–Treasury Accord of 1951—which ended a Federal Reserve commitment to support the market for U.S. government securities—the nation's monetary policy makers have aggressively regulated the flow of credit in response to cyclical changes in the economy. Restrictive credit policies have been pursued during periods of inflation and overly rapid economic growth, in order to bring about a more sustainable rate of business expansion.

By contrast, when business activity turned sluggish or recessionary, the credit reins were loosened to encourage high-level economic activity. In point of fact, monetary policy became the dominant federal tool for promoting noninflationary, full-employment economic conditions, with fiscal and wage-price control policies generally occupying subordinate or relatively ineffective roles. As a result, shifts in both financial market conditions and investor expectations concerning future Federal Reserve actions led to wider, more frequent fluctuations in interest rates.[22] The impact of these developments was, and continues to be, particularly destabilizing for the highly credit-dependent construction industry, with the flow of credit funds into structurally imperfect mortgage markets varying widely with changes in money and capital market conditions.

Sensitivity of Thrift Institutions to Changes in the Financial Climate. Mutual savings banks and savings and loan associations provide about three fifths of the nation's total residential mortgage credit. However, a serious maturity imbalance between the long-term asset and short-term liability structure of these institutions impairs their ability to attract a relatively stable flow of funds for mortgage investment over the business cycle.[23] During periods of rising interest rates, for example, these institutions have experienced large-scale withdrawals of funds from time and savings accounts as individuals shifted into higher-yielding marketable securities. Operating with narrowly restricted investment powers which hamper their ability to compete in short- and intermediate-term markets, savings institutions have been compelled to cut back drastically their mortgage lending activity under such conditions.

Mortgage Interest Rate Ceilings. Federal and state governmental control of interest rates on certain types of residential mortgages have also contributed to the volatility of mortgage flows, tending to attract investor funds into mortgages and away from other types of investments during periods of market ease, and to reduce the flow of mortgage credit

---

[22] *Report of the Commission on Mortgage Interest Rates,* August 1969, chap. 3.

[23] *May 1971 Annual Report of the Executive Vice President,* National Association of Mutual Savings Banks, pp. 16–20.

during periods of credit stringency. As noted earlier, FHA and VA mortgage interest rate ceilings are set by the Secretary of the Department of Housing and Urban Development and the Administrator of the Veterans Administration, respectively.

The development of discount and premium adjustments on FHA and VA contract rates as a means of bringing effective yields on these investments more in line with alternative financial market instruments have proven cumbersome and inefficient because of legal restrictions and equity considerations.[24] At the same time, state-imposed statutory ceilings on conventional home mortgages have influenced mortgage lending activity in many local areas. At the end of 1973, 45 states had "usury" statutes specifying maximum permissible interest rates on nonfederally insured home mortgages. In general, interest rates on mortgages not subject to statutory ceilings—nonresidential loans and most types of multifamily mortgages—have displayed greater flexibility in responding to financial market shifts. As a result, income property mortgage markets have maintained a stronger competitive rate position in financial markets.

Restrictive Liquidity and Marketability Characteristics. Investor attitudes toward the mortgage instrument have always been colored by the lack of a viable secondary market. Although transactions volume in secondary mortgage markets has risen substantially over the years—particularly for federally underwritten loans and, more recently, for conventional loans—the marketability of mortgage loans has remained inferior to that of securities where extensive trading operations have long prevailed. Both variations in nonrate provisions of different mortgage contracts and the uniqueness of the properties underlying each individual mortgage loan have complicated efforts to seek the uniform valuation standards required for an effectively functioning secondary mortgage market. As a result, many lending institutions have tended to view mortgage loans either with disfavor or as a residual investment, channeling excess funds into real estate markets but placing relatively low priority on these instruments during periods of reduced inflows of investment capital.

MORTGAGE RISK AND YIELD CONSIDERATIONS

From the financial analyst's viewpoint, significant changes in the relative yield position of mortgage loans in the nation's capital markets strongly suggest, among other things, that lender evaluation of mortgage risk has undergone fundamental changes. Until the mid-1960s, residential mortgage interest rates typically exceeded yields on competing capital market instruments by a wide margin. High-quality corporate bonds—generally considered the major alternative investment to mortgages—

[24] *Report of the Commission on Mortgage Interest Rates,* August 1969, chap. 7.

commanded yields ranging from 100 to 200 basis points below rates of return on FHA-insured mortgage in secondary markets during the 1945–65 period.

Over the past decade, however, this relationship has changed dramatically with mortgage-bond yield spreads narrowing markedly, even turning in favor of bonds during limited periods of time (Chart 2). This indicates that mortgage markets may have become better integrated into the capital market system as a whole as lenders responded to im-

CHART 2

FHA-insured Home Mortgage Yields Minus New Aa Corporate Bond Yields, 1960–73

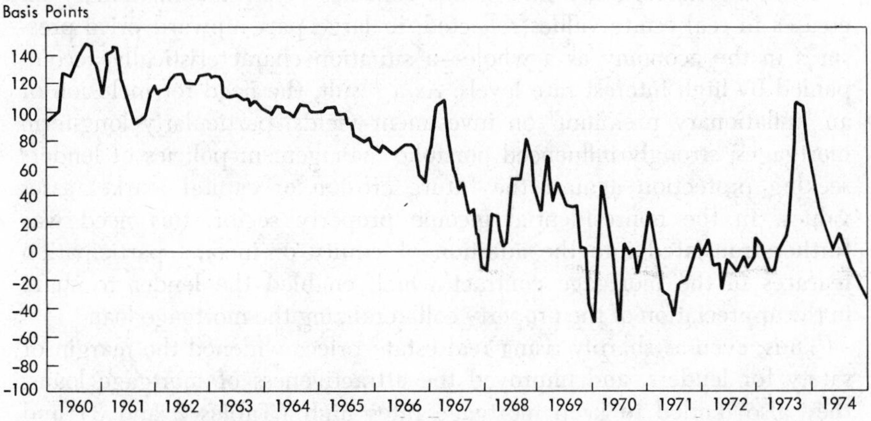

Note: Yield spreads measure the difference between gross FHA and conventional new home mortgage yields (before deduction of servicing costs). Conventional home mortgage yields refer to unweighted averages of monthly contract interest rates charged by major lending institutions, adjusted for fees and charges amortized over a 10-year period. From 1965 to 1972, data refer to loan approvals and, in 1973, to loan closings. See note to Chart 1 for explanation of FHA mortgage yield data.

provements in both the mortgage market structure and the risk characteristics of the mortgage instrument. At the same time, regional variations in mortgage rates have narrowed significantly, accompanying the improved geographic mobility of mortgage funds through expanded secondary mortgage market facilities.

The following changes in the basic underlying elements of mortgage risk—borrower, property, and loan characteristics—have helped to alter lender policies concerning the role of mortgage loans in investment portfolios:

1. Inflation and Property Values. During the highly inflationary 1965–73 period, building cost increases outpaced price advances in most other segments of the economy. This can be seen by comparing the estimated 42 percent increase for all goods and services with the 55 percent rise in construction costs of residential structures.[25] The impact of this inflationary surge has been somewhat paradoxical from the lender's viewpoint. On the one hand, the chances for incurring losses from borrower delinquency or foreclosure were reduced. Frequently, homeowners who foresaw problems in meeting their mortgage payments were able to avoid foreclosure and pay off their outstanding debt by selling the property, probably at a substantial gain. In cases where foreclosure did occur, lender losses were also minimized or eliminated in the strong sellers' market generally prevailing. The fact that mortgage delinquency and foreclosure experience of lending institutions generally improved from the decade of the 1950s and the early 1960s to the 1965–73 period tend to support this view.[26]

By contrast, the other side of this coin has been that inflationary increases in real estate values reflected, in large part, upward price pressures in the economy as a whole—a situation characteristically accompanied by high interest rate levels. As a result, the need for inclusion of an "inflationary premium" on investment yields, particularly long-term mortgages, strongly influenced portfolio management policies of lenders seeking protection against the future erosion of capital market asset values. In the nonresidential income property sector, this need was further translated into the addition of equity or income participation features in the mortgage contract which enabled the lender to share in the appreciation of the property collateralizing the mortgage loan.

Thus, even as sharply rising real estate prices widened the margin of safety for lenders, and improved the attractiveness of mortgage loans, they also tended to keep mortgage rates high (Tables 2 and 3) and the availability of mortgage credit uncertain in an environment of frequent monetary restraint.

Liquidity and Marketability. While many of the basic features of the individual mortgage instrument have remained essentially unchanged, a great deal of progress has been made in facilitating secondary market trading operations and, hence, in reducing the illiquidity of mortgage loans. Major advances have occurred in the following areas:

The Reorganized Federal National Mortgage Association. Holding more than $24 billion in residential mortgages by the end of 1973, the Federal National Mortgage Association has expanded and improved its mortgage trading operations in a variety of ways since its reorganization from a federal mortgage agency to a government-sponsored private corporation in 1968 whose stock is now traded on the New York Stock Ex-

---

[25] U.S. Department of Commerce, *Survey of Current Business,* various monthly issues, 1970–74.

[26] John P. Herzog and James S. Earley, *Home Mortgage Delinquency and Foreclosure,* (Columbia University Press, 1970); quarterly mortgage delinquency and foreclosure statistics compiled by the American Life Insurance Association, National Association of Mutual Savings Banks, Mortgage Bankers Association of America, and United States League of Savings Associations, 1969–73.

TABLE 2

Estimated Secondary Market Yields on FHA-insured Home Mortgages, 1960–1974 (in percent)*

Year	*Jan.*	*Feb.*	*Mar.*	*Apr.*	*May*	*June*	*July*	*Aug.*	*Sept.*	*Oct.*	*Nov.*	*Dec.*
1960	6.25	6.23	6.22	6.21	5.21	6.19	6.18	6.14	6.11	6.09	6.06	6.04
1961	6.01	5.89	5.82	5.77	n.a.	n.a.	5.68	5.68	5.69	5.70	5.70	5.69
1962	5.69	5.68	5.65	5.64	5.60	5.59	5.58	5.57	5.56	5.55	5.54	5.53
1963	5.51	5.48	5.47	5.46	5.45	5.45	5.45	5.45	5.45	5.45	5.45	5.45
1964	5.45	5.45	5.45	5.45	5.45	5.45	5.46	5.46	5.46	5.45	5.45	5.45
1965	5.45	5.45	5.45	5.45	5.45	5.44	5.44	5.45	5.46	5.49	5.51	5.62
1966	5.70	n.a.	6.00	n.a.	6.32	6.45	6.51	6.58	6.63	n.a.	6.81	6.77
1967	6.62	6.46	6.35	6.29	6.44	6.51	6.53	6.60	6.63	6.65	6.77	6.81
1968	6.81	6.78	6.83	6.94	n.a.	7.52	7.42	7.35	7.28	7.29	7.36	7.50
1969	n.a.	7.99	8.05	8.06	8.06	8.35	8.36	8.36	8.40	8.48	8.48	8.62
1970	n.a.	9.29	9.20	9.10	9.11	9.16	9.11	9.07	9.01	8.97	8.90	8.40
1971	n.a.	n.a.	7.32	7.37	7.75	7.89	7.97	7.92	7.84	7.75	7.62	7.77
1972	7.49	7.46	7.45	7.50	7.53	7.54	7.54	7.55	7.56	7.57	7.57	7.56
1973	7.55	7.56	7.63	7.73	7.79	7.89	7.54	n.a.	9.18	8.97	8.86	8.78
1974	n.a.	8.54	8.66	9.17	9.46	9.46	9.85					

* See note to Chart 1.
n.a.—Not available.
Source: U.S. Department of Housing and Urban Development.

TABLE 3

Effective Interest Rates on Conventional New Home Mortgages Monthly, 1965–74 (in percent)*

Year	*Jan.*	*Feb.*	*Mar.*	*Apr.*	*May*	*June*	*July*	*Aug.*	*Sept.*	*Oct.*	*Nov.*	*Dec.*
1965	5.79	5.79	5.72	5.74	5.77	5.76	5.77	5.76	5.75	5.75	5.80	5.78
1966	5.81	5.85	5.90	5.99	6.02	6.07	6.12	6.18	6.22	6.32	6.40	6.49
1967	6.47	6.44	6.41	6.37	6.28	6.29	6.34	6.34	6.37	6.37	6.37	6.41
1968	6.39	6.47	6.50	6.57	6.69	6.88	7.04	7.10	7.10	7.09	7.07	7.23
1969	7.30	7.39	7.47	7.62	7.65	7.76	7.91	8.00	8.05	8.12	8.11	8.25
1970	8.34	8.41	8.47	8.41	8.45	8.48	8.49	8.52	8.48	8.51	8.43	8.37
1971	8.18	7.91	7.66	7.49	7.47	7.50	7.65	7.73	7.82	7.83	7.79	7.77
1972	7.78	7.61	7.52	7.51	7.53	7.55	7.58	7.59	7.56	7.62	7.65	7.66
1973	7.67	7.69	7.69	7.70	7.72	7.79	7.87	7.94	8.17	8.31	8.39	8.49
1974	8.52	8.62	8.64	8.67	8.74	8.85	8.97					

* See note to Chart 2.
Source: Federal Home Loan Bank Board.

change. A major innovation has been the establishment of a free market system under which FNMA commitments are issued on a competitive bid basis, marking the first time that nationwide prices for government-backed mortgages in secondary markets had been set by a competitive pricing system.

In 1972, FNMA further helped to broaden the scope of secondary mortgage markets by extending its free market system to conventional home mortgages. In conjunction with the Federal Home Loan Mortgage Corporation (see below), FNMA developed standardized conventional mortgage documents which it would accept for purchase.[27] In addition to increasing the effectiveness of FNMA mortgage operations, the development of these uniform mortgage documents has served as a model for investors who seek to purchase and sell these investments in the private market.

The Federal Home Loan Mortgage Corporation. The FHLMC—created by Congress in the Emergency Home Finance Act of 1970—is a privately funded corporation, within the Federal Home Loan Bank system, whose objective is "to increase the secondary market volume of sales and purchases of residential mortgages and, thus, to increase the effective supply of mortgage investments."[28] The FHLMC's primary emphasis is to strengthen the secondary market for conventional residential mortgages, although it also deals in federally underwritten loans.

In addition to maintaining a variety of trading programs for home loans, mortgage participations, and participation sale certificates based on the mortgage interests which it has purchased, FHLMC has done pioneering work in the development of computer-based underwriting standards and loan processing procedures. More recently, a nationwide automated mortgage market information network (AMMINET) was established in June 1974, which would make available to participants information on mortgage offerings. The system is expected to include GNMA-guaranteed mortgage-backed securities by 1975 and, subsequently, commercial mortgages and mortgage participations, as well. The AMMINET system should contribute significantly to the development of a centralized information network for secondary mortgage markets and, hence, to further improvements in the liquidity and marketability of mortgage loans.

Private Mortgage Insurance. A key stimulus to the volume of trading in conventional mortgages has been the extraordinary growth of private mortgage insurance companies during the past decade. Growing investor disenchantment with the long processing delays encountered in FHA mortgage insurance applications, continued lender liberalization of maturity and down-payment provisions in conventional mortgage con-

---

[27] *Annual Report 1972,* Federal National Mortgage Association.

[28] *The Federal Home Loan Mortgage Corporation Annual Report 1972.*

tracts, and the below-market maximum loan amounts permitted on FHA-insured mortgages in the face of accelerated increases in housing costs have stimulated new efforts to improve the conventional mortgage market structure. Private mortgage insurance exemplified an important result of these efforts.

By guaranteeing investors protection against loss on the top 10–20 percent of a conventional mortgage loan, private mortgage insurance companies were simultaneously providing competition for the FHA insurance program, offering a degree of standardization to conventional mortgages carrying varying loan and property characteristics, and increasing investor incentives to liberalize loan terms to potential mortgage borrowers. The expansion of private mortgage insurance received new stimulus from the Emergency Home Finance Act of 1970 which provided that conventional mortgage loans purchased by FNMA and FHLMC could carry loan-to-value ratios up to 90 percent if the excess over 75 percent is insured or guaranteed by an acceptable private insurer.

The longer run viability of the private mortgage insurance industry remains an intensively discussed question in terms of the greater safety of federal insurance and uncertainty over its ability to withstand periods of adverse housing and mortgage market conditions. However, there is little question that the continued expansion of financially sound private mortgage insurance companies would contribute strongly to the further development of efficient, nationwide conventional mortgage markets.

Mortgage-backed Securities. A major federal innovation in mortgage financing that has grown with unexpected rapidity is the mortgage-backed security. This new type of security is collateralized by pools of federally underwritten mortgages and is guaranteed as to timely payment of interest and principal by the Government National Mortgage Association. Two basic types of securities are in existence—the *pass-through* and *bond* type. The pass through—by far the more widely used—involves the payment of principal and interest on the underlying pool of mortgages directly to the holders of the securities. Holders of the bond type security receive specified annual rates of interest and principal upon maturity.[29]

Sold largely by private mortgage lenders, mortgage-backed securities have turned out to be a highly successful mortgage financing vehicle. Yields on these investments have compared favorably with rates available on high-quality corporate bonds, while their safety, cash flow, and marketability features have led to the rapid development of an active secondary trading market. (See Table 4.) GNMA-guaranteed pass-through securities are issued in minimum denominations of $25,000.

In 1973, the GNMA guarantee program for mortgage-backed securities

---

[29] Government National Mortgage Association, *Annual Report 1972.*

was broadened to include: (1) FHA-insured mobile home loans; and (2) certificates backed by FHA-insured construction loans for apartment house projects, hospitals, and nursing homes. These certificates can, in turn, be converted to GNMA-guaranteed securities backed by the permanent mortgage upon completion of construction; and (3) the introduction of "serial notes"—a variation of the pass-through security whereby monthly payments of principal and interest are passed through in sequential order to holders of serially numbered securities. Thus, by providing a variety of maturities, serial notes are expected to attract a broader spectrum of investors into the market for mortgage-backed securities.[30]

Although still relatively small in dollar volume—more than $8 billion of the pass-through type had been issued by year-end 1973—mortgage-backed securities are expected to maintain a rapid pace of expansion in the years ahead, a development which promises to bridge the gap between mortgage and securities markets even further.

FUTURE DEVELOPMENTS IN MORTGAGE FINANCING

Numerous studies have been prepared by private and government groups over the years dealing with the problems of strengthening the mortgage financing system so that the housing and other real estate capital needs for the nation could be met more effectively. As a result of these reports, a broad consensus has developed over the approach that should be adopted in this regard. In general, these recommendations has focused on the following areas:

Revision of the Financial Structure. Efforts to bring about significant reforms in the operations of the nation's financial system originate partly from the need to end, or at least, mitigate the boom-bust cycles in mortgage credit and housing activity. This was recognized in the Report of the President's Commission on Financial Structure, which formed the basis for legislative proposals transmitted to the Congress by the President in 1973.[31] Those recommendations regarding improvement of the mortgage credit structure included:

Elimination of interest rate ceilings on FHA and VA ceilings on the grounds that they have been ineffective in holding down mortgage interest rates during periods of financial market stringency, serving only to reduce the supply of federally underwritten mortgage funds, as well as to increase the use of the inefficient discount system.

Provision of a federal chartering system for mutual savings banks and stock savings and loan associations, which together with existing federal

---

[30] Woodward Kingman, "GNMA's Multi-Front Programs Thrust Ahead," *Savings Bank Journal,* October 1973, pp. 23–28.

[31] *Report on the Financial Institutions Act of 1973,* a section by section analysis, U.S. Treasury Department, October 1973.

TABLE 4

Estimated Yields on Mortgage-Backed Securities Guaranteed by the Government National Mortgage Association, Monthly 1972–74 (in percent)

Year	*Jan.*	*Feb.*	*Mar.*	*Apr.*	*May*	*June*	*July*	*Aug.*	*Sept.*	*Oct.*	*Nov.*	*Dec.*
1972	7.02	6.94	7.03	7.13	7.06	7.11	7.15	7.21	7.31	7.29	7.16	7.22
1973	7.29	7.34	7.49	7.59	7.67	7.81	8.46	8.59	7.97	7.89	7.85	7.97
1974	7.97	8.05	8.51	8.78	8.96	9.25						

TABLE 4a

Yields on GNMA-Guaranteed Mortgage-Backed Securities less New Aa Corporate Bond Yields, Monthly, 1972–74 (in percent)

Year	*Jan.*	*Feb.*	*Mar.*	*Apr.*	*May*	*June*	*July*	*Aug.*	*Sept.*	*Oct.*	*Nov.*	*Dec.*
1972	−.34	−.63	−.50	−.64	−.55	−.52	−.55	−.38	−.41	−.37	−.30	−.28
1973	−.32	−.33	−.26	−.02	−.02	.08	.49	.14	−.13	.08	.06	−.12
1974	−.35	−.16	−.09	−.26	−.43	−.25	−.29					

Note: Data in Table 4 are end-of-month yields on mortgage-backed securities carrying 6½ percent coupon rates. Figures assume a 12-year maturity and refer to pass-through securities. See note to Chart 2 for explanation of corporate bond yield data included in Table 4a.

Source: Salomon Brothers and U.S. Department of the Treasury.

thrift institutions, would be endowed with broadened asset and liability powers, including personal loans, checking accounts, credit cards, and negotiable order of withdrawal accounts. The reasoning behind this proposal is that broadened loan, investment, and service powers would enable savings institutions to compete more effectively for individuals' savings funds under different financial market conditions and, hence, supply a more stable volume of mortgage credit over the long run.

Equalization of tax provisions for competing financial institutions and the establishment of a new mortgage interest tax credit for thrift institutions and commercial banks for the purpose of stimulating mortgage lending activity by these institutions.

Achieving Better Balance in Federal Economic and Monetary Policies. Real estate analysts generally agree that overreliance on monetary policy to control inflationary pressures or stimulate lagging economic activity results in serious adverse effects on the efficiency of mortgage and housing markets, and otherwise hampers consistent fulfillment of the nation's housing requirements. Larger roles for fiscal and incomes policies are needed in federal economic stabilization programs to permit a more stable, lower interest rate environment required for more effectively functioning real estate credit markets and expanding housing production.

Effective federal budget control was stressed by President Gerald R. Ford in August 1974 as a major weapon to combat severe upward price and interest rate pressures in the economy, which had drastically reduced the availability of mortgage credit and housing construction during the year. If federal government efforts in this regard prove successful and usher in a new era of fiscal responsibility, real estate market vulnerability to shifts in monetary policy will be significantly lessened.

Variable Mortgage Rates. A more controversial approach to the problem of stabilizing the flow of mortgage credit is the use of mortgage loans which allow for periodic adjustments in the interest rate. These adjustments would be made by tying the mortgage rate to some acceptable measure of financial market conditions or cost of funds to the lender.[32] The most frequently mentioned indicators in this regard are the Federal Reserve discount rate, prime rate, and U.S. government bond yield.

While the use of variable rate mortgages would aid lending institutions, who typically "borrow short and lend long," to reduce the maturity imbalance between their asset and liability structure, a host of serious obstacles strongly argue against the immediate, widespread adoption of this technique. These include: (*a*) the difficulty of selecting an appropriate formula for triggering rate adjustments; (*b*) the doubtful marketability of these instruments stemming from uncertainties over

[32] Robert Moore Fisher, *Variable Rate Mortgages,* Staff Economic Study #30, Board of Governors of the Federal Reserve System, 1967.

future yield changes; and (*c*) the competition from fixed-rate mortgages during periods of low interest rates and investor expectations of rising interest rates in the future. Nonetheless, increasing support for the enactment of necessary legislation and public education programs has developed in the hope that variable rate mortgage contracts will be helpful in averting future mortgage credit crises.

Increasing the Effectiveness of Federal Mortgage Credit Programs. The tremendous increase in the federal government's financing role in mortgage markets has generated a great deal of controversy over the real impact of federal activity on housing output. Some observers have pointed to the fact that increased borrowing by federal credit agencies to finance mortgage market support operations: (*a*) is partly self-defeating since it intensifies upward pressures on interest rates and contributes to incremental disintermediation; (*b*) carries potential dangers of lessening the mortgage financing role of the private sector to such an extent that private financial institutions would become mere conduits for channeling federally induced funds through the mortgage market; and (*c*) could eventually frustrate general economic stabilization policies by unduly insulating housing from the impact of monetary policy, causing adverse side effects on other sectors of the economy.[33]

Contradictory responses to recent federal government interest rate subsidy programs have also been evident with mismanagement problems and the creation of large, long-term fixed obligations by the government with no new production drawing criticism from some quarters. Supporters of this basic approach, on the other hand, endorse its objective of relying on private institutions to provide credit for the construction and rehabilitation of such housing, and encouraging increases in the housing supply for moderate income groups. Adherents of these programs call for more effective administration rather than elimination.

More recently, direct cash assistance programs for families whose incomes are too low to afford privately built housing have been started on an experimental basis by the federal government as a possible substitute for the more traditional approaches to federal housing programs. The relative merits of the *housing allowance* system are still in an early stage of discussion, especially with respect to its alleged cost-saving advantages, and widespread concern that recipients would merely bid up rents and house prices in areas where housing shortages exist. In any event, public pressure for an active federal role in helping the nation meet its mortgage financing and housing requirements is likely to persist indefinitely in view of the growing difficulty large numbers of Americans are encountering in seeking decent shelter for their families.

---

[33] "Institutional Changes in the Mortgage Market: Recent and Prospective," remarks by Dr. Saul B. Klaman, Vice President and Chief Economist, National Association of Mutual Savings Banks, before the Conference of Business Economists, Washington, D.C., February 24, 1972.

Adjusting Real Estate Financing to the Changing Composition of Housing Demands. The rapid growth of nonconventional types of housing such as mobile homes, condominiums, cluster housing developments, and new towns may call for innovations in real estate financing. For example, purchases of mobile homes—which have grown into a major force in the low- and moderate-cost segment of the housing market—are typically financed through short-term personal loans carrying higher interest rates than obtainable in longer term mortgages. In recent years, mortgage-oriented thrift institutions have been given new expanded authority to make mobile home loans, perhaps signaling a broadened financing market for this important housing market sector.

Apartment ownership through the condominium financing route has also attracted growing numbers of people, especially for retirement purposes. Although financed through mortgages, investors must apply somewhat different lending standards to this type of loan than to mortgage loans on owner-occupied homes.

Significant shifts in the geographic composition of housing requirements may also be in the offing, as the United States enters a new era of energy supply constraints. Early readings suggest the possibility of future shifts in residential building activity to areas offering convenient nonauto transportation facilities and adequate supplies of home heating fuels.

In sum, both federal and private sources of real estate credit will be required to explore continually new approaches to fulfill the changing housing and other real estate requirements of the nation in the years ahead. Housing projections indicate that about 2.5 million new units per year will be required over the balance of this decade to accommodate new demands from population growth, losses from the existing housing stock, and the maintenance of normal vacancy rates. The availability of credit funds to support these massive shelter needs will require continued progress in private-public efforts to develop a nationwide network of mortgage finance capable of withstanding short-run cyclical disruptions and providing increasing amounts of funds over the longer run.

BIBLIOGRAPHY

Background and History of the Federal National Mortgage Association. 1963.

"Financing the Nation's Housing Needs." A Statement on National Policy by the Research and Policy Committee of the Committee for Economic Development, April 1973.

GREBLER, LEO. *The Future of Thrift Institutions.* Joint Savings and Loan and Mutual Savings Bank Exchange Groups, 1969.

JONES, OLIVER, and GREBLER, LEO. *The Secondary Mortgage Market, Its Purpose, Performance and Potential.* University of California, 1961.

KENDALL, LEON T. *The Savings and Loan Business.* A monograph prepared for the Commission on Money and Credit for the United States Savings and Loan League. Englewood Cliffs, N.J.: Prentice Hall, Inc., 1962.

KLAMAN, SAUL B. "Public/Private Approaches to Urban Mortgage and Housing Problems." *Law and Contemporary Problems,* Spring 1967 issue, Duke University School of Law.

Life Insurance Companies as Financial Institutions. A monograph prepared for the Commission on Money and Credit by the Life Insurance Association of America. Englewood Cliffs, N.J.: Prentice-Hall, Inc., 1962.

Money and Credit. The Report of the Commission on Money and Credit. Englewood Cliffs, N.J.: Prentice Hall, Inc., 1961.

RAPKIN, CHESTER; FEIRARI, ROBERT J.; BLOOD, ROGER; and MILGRAM, GRACE. *The Private Insurance of Home Mortgages.* A study of Mortgage Guaranty Insurance Corporation. Philadelphia: University of Pennsylvania, 1967.

15

Short-Term Investments

JEROME B. COHEN, Ph.D.
Senior Editor, Bankers Magazine
Emeritus Professor of Finance
Baruch College, City University of New York
New York, New York

THE LAST decade or so has witnessed a marked rise in the level of short-term interest rates. This has led corporations, individuals of means, and institutional investors to place funds in various short-term money-market instruments.

In contrast to the capital market which concentrates on long-term funds, the money market focuses on short-term outlets for funds.[1] It is customary to distinguish between the money and capital markets by saying that the money market is the arena in which claims to funds change hands for from one day up to one year, but not beyond. Money-market instruments include promissory notes and bills of exchange, commercial paper, bankers' acceptances, treasury bills, short-term tax exempts, Euro-dollar claims, dealer paper, and negotiable time certificates of deposit.

Institutions participating in the money market include commercial banks, large and small corporations, the Federal Reserve system, U.S. government securities dealers, and indeed, anyone who lends or borrows on short term, including those who borrow on the collateral of securities to speculate. Activities in the money market range from a one-day loan of several millions by one commercial bank with surplus reserve funds to another which is short of reserves—the federal funds market—to an investor borrowing to buy securities on margin. Corporations with temporarily surplus funds may place them in treasury bills for 91 and 182

[1] For an excellent, comprehensive account, see Wesley Lindow, *Inside the Money Market,* (New York: Random House, 1972).

days or in time certificates of deposit tailored to their financial time requirements. The money market is, of course, the vital arena in which the Federal Reserve influences the reserve position of commercial banks, and therefore their capacity to lend, by engaging in open-market operations in U.S. government securities.[2]

Generally, money-market instruments are issued by borrowers of very high credit ratings and are, therefore, characterized by a high degree of safety of principal. Maturities may be as long as one year but are usually 90 days or less, and indeed can be arranged to span only a few days or even one day. These instruments accordingly involve small risk of loss due to changes in interest rates. Moreover, the market for these instruments is quite broad and on a given day can absorb a large volume of transactions with relatively little effect on yields. The highly efficient money-market machinery allows quick and convenient trading in virtually any volume.

Unlike organized securities or commodities markets, the money market has no specific location. As in the case of other financial markets in the United States, it centers in New York. It is primarily a "telephone" market and is easily accessible. No one is more than a phone call away from the money market.

It consists of approximately 45 "money center banks," including large banks in New York and other important financial centers; the Federal Reserve system and its open-market operations through the open-market money desk at the Federal Reserve Bank of New York; about 20 government securities dealers, some of which are large banks; about a dozen commercial paper dealers; a few bankers' acceptance dealers; and a number of money brokers who specialize in finding short-term funds for money-market borrowers and placing such funds for money-market lenders. Amongst these money brokers are three which will make a market for federal funds.

Besides the groups that provide the basic trading machinery, money-market participants usually enter the market either to raise funds or to convert temporary cash surpluses into highly liquid interest-bearing investments. Most of the time money-market rates are below rates on bank loans, and the ability of large corporations to borrow funds on the open market is therefore advantageous. The U.S. Treasury, many commercial banks, large sales finance companies, and well-known nonfinancial corporations of the highest credit standing borrow regularly in the money market by issuing their own short-term debt obligations, which make up the standard money-market instruments. Short-term loans to govern-

[2] For further information, see *Money Market Instruments*, 3d ed. (Federal Reserve Bank of Cleveland, 1971); *Instruments of the Money Market*, Federal Reserve Bank of Richmond, 1970 2d ed.; or *Money-Market Instruments: The Risk and the Return*, rev. ed. (New York: Morgan Guaranty Trust Co., 1970). William A. Hawk, *The U.S. Government Securities Market*, Harris Trust and Savings Bank, Chicago, 1973.

ment securities dealers, loans of reserves among commercial banks, and Federal Reserve loans to commercial banks are also money-market transactions, but they do not give rise to negotiable paper. The major suppliers on the money market are commercial banks, state and local governments, large nonfinancial business firms, and nonbank financial institutions such as insurance companies and pension funds. Foreign banks and industrial companies also buy money-market instruments or make short-term loans.

The most important participant in the money market is the Federal Reserve system. Through the open market trading desk at the New York Federal Reserve Bank, which executes the directives of the Federal Open Market Committee, the system is in the market on a virtually continuous basis, either as a buyer or as a seller, depending on economic and financial conditions and monetary policy objectives. The system's purpose in entering the market is quite different from that of other participants. The Fed buys and sells not to manage its own cash position more efficently but rather to supply or to withdraw bank reserves. In addition, the Federal Reserve acts as an agent, either as buyer or seller, for the accounts of foreign official institutions and for the U.S. Treasury. Overall, the operations of the Federal Reserve dwarf those of any other money-market participant.

The Fed influences the money market not only through open market operations conducted in New York but also through the discount windows of the 12 Reserve banks. Commercial banks that are members of the Federal Reserve system may borrow temporarily from the Federal Reserve as an alternative to selling money-market securities or borrowing federal funds to cover cash or reserve deficiencies. Similarly, banks with cash or reserve surpluses can repay outstanding borrowings at the Federal Reserve rather than invest surpluses in money-market instruments. Thus, for member banks, the Federal Reserve discount window is an operational part of the money market.

INTEREST RATE CHANGES AND RELATIONSHIPS

While the various money-market instruments have their individual differences (see Table 1), they are close substitutes for each other in many investment portfolios; and for this reason, the rates of return on the various instruments tend to fluctuate closely together. For short periods of time, the rate of return on a particular instrument may diverge from the rest or "get out of line," but this sets in motion forces which tend to pull the rates back together again. (See Chart 1.) For example, particular circumstances in the market for commercial paper may produce a rapid run-up of commercial paper rates, resulting in a relatively large spread between these rates and rates on treasury bills. Experienced traders note the abnormal differential and shift funds from bills into commercial

TABLE 1 Money-Market Investments (United States)

	Obligation	*Denomination*	*Maturities*	*Marketability*	*Basis*
U.S. Treasury bills	U.S. government obligation. U.S. Treasury auctions 3- and 6-month bills weekly, 9-month and 1-year bills monthly. Also offers tax anticipation bills through special auctions.	$10,000 to $1 million	Up to 1 year.	Excellent secondary market.	Discounted. Actual days on a 360-day year.
Prime sales finance paper	Promissory notes of finance companies placed directly with the investor.	$1,000 to $5 million ($25,000 minimum order)	Issued to mature on any day from 3 to 270 days.	No secondary market. Under certain conditions companies will buy back paper prior to maturity. Most companies will adjust rate.	Discounted or interest bearing. Actual days on a 360-day year.
Dealer paper					
1. Finance	Promissory notes of finance companies sold through commercial paper dealers.	$100,000 to $5 million	Issued to mature on any day from 15 to 270 days.	Limited secondary market. Buy-back arrangement usually can be negotiated through the dealer.	Discounted or interest bearing. Actual days on a 360-day year.
2. Industrial	Promissory notes of leading industrial firms sold through commercial paper dealers.	$500,000 to $5 million	Usually available on certain dates between 30 and 180 days.	Limited secondary market.	Discounted. Actual days on a 360-day year.
Prime bankers' acceptances	Time drafts drawn on and accepted by a banking institution, which in effect substitutes its credit for that of the importer or holder of merchandise.	$25,000 to $1 million	Up to 6 months.	Good secondary market. Bid usually ⅛ of 1% higher than offered side of market.	Discounted. Actual days on a 360-day year.
Negotiable time certificates of deposit	Certificates of time deposit at a commercial bank.	$500,000 to $1 million	Unlimited.	Good secondary market.	Yield basis. Actual days on a 360-day year. Interest at maturity.
Short-term tax-exempts					
1. Project notes of local public housing agencies	Notes of local agencies secured by a contract with federal agencies and by pledge of "full faith and credit" of U.S.	$1,000 to $1 million	Up to 1 year.	Good secondary market.	Yield basis. 30-day month on a 360-day year. Interest at maturity.
2. Tax and bond anticipation notes	Notes of states, municipalities, or political subdivisions.	$1,000 to $1 million	Various, usually 3 months to 1 year from issue.	Good secondary market.	Yield basis. Usually 30 days on a 360-day year. Interest at maturity.

Source: Reprinted (with permission) from *Money-Market Investments—The Risk and the Return* published by Morgan Guaranty Trust Company of New York.

CHART 1

Money Rates

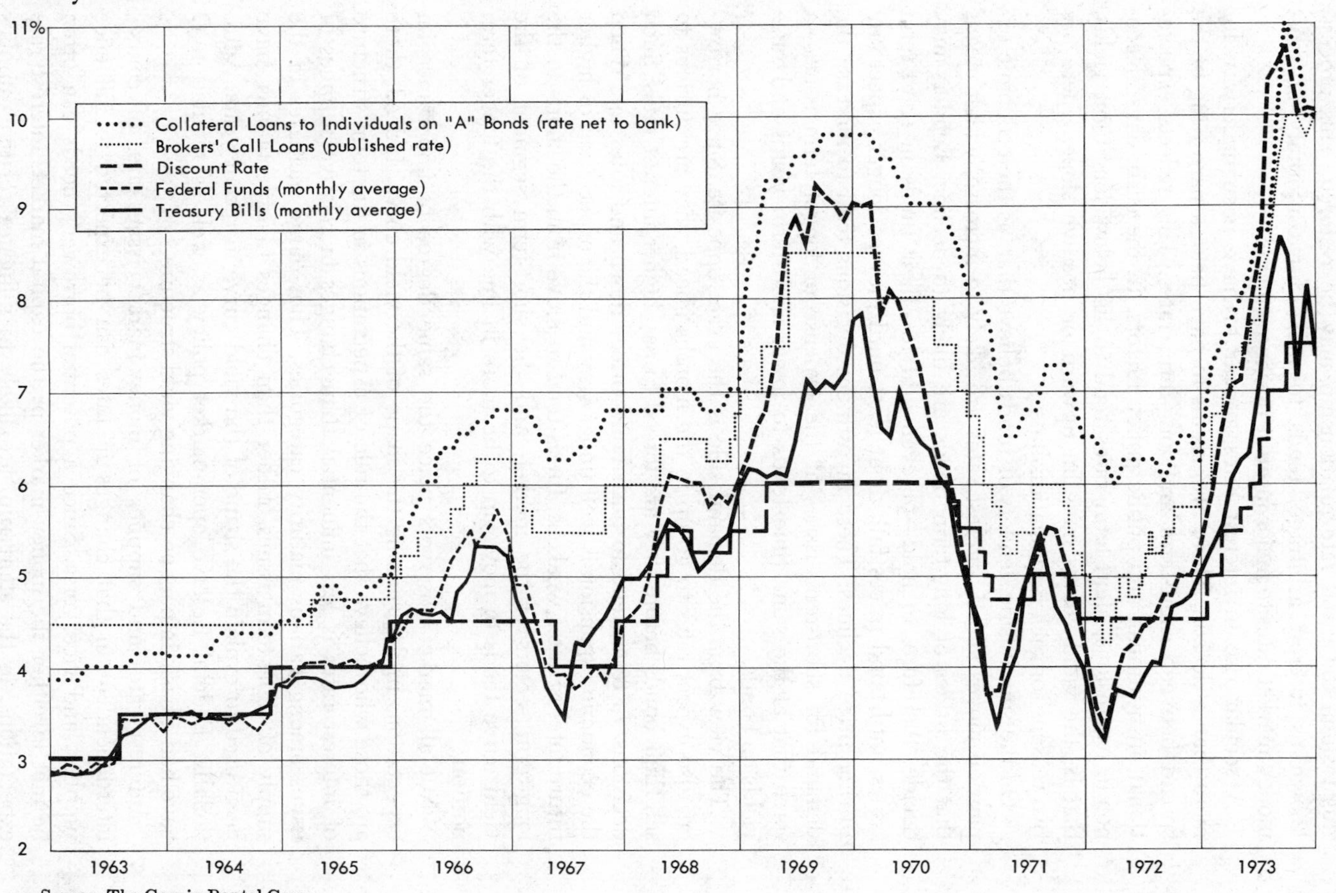

Source: The Garvin Bantel Corp.

paper, causing bill rates to rise and commercial paper rates to fall. In this fashion the usual rate relationship may be restored. This process, known as interest arbitrage, tends to make for conformity of most money-market rates to major interest rate movements.

A secular rise in interest rates appear to have been underway for more than a decade. There also seems to have been a narrowing of the spread between short-term and long-term rates. This reflects expectational, institutional, and public policy factors. In the early days of economic expansions, short-term rates tend to lie below long-term yields, that is, the yield curves have an upward or positive slope. There are two reasons for such rate relationships.

On the supply side, lenders of funds believe that, as the economic expansion moves ahead, interest rates are likely to increase, which means that the prices of long-term bonds are likely to decline. Lenders may decide, therefore, to hold—or even add to—their funds in short-term issues until bond prices fall, or at least until they no longer expect any further price declines. These investment decisions tend to increase the demand for short-term issues at the expense of longer term issues—a force that at the same time tends to lower short-term yields and raise yields on bonds.

The view from the demand side is the exact opposite. Since borrowers also expect rates to go up in the months ahead, they are anxious to sell their bonds before they are forced to pay higher interest rates. Such decisions, in term, tend to push bond prices down and rates up. When the economic expansion is well under way and the expectation of higher future interest rates weakens, funds tend to move from the short- to the long-term sectors of the market, and the short-term segment of the yield curve tends to move up to be more in line with the longer term portion.

Not all market observers place the same degree of importance on expectations in determining the shape of the yield curve. Indeed, there are those who believe that the role of expectations in the term structure of interest rates is less influential than changes in relative supplies of issues among various maturity categories. Thus, large increases in the supply of short-term issues, rather than changes in expectations, have been used to explain the shape of the yield curve in recent years. Additionally, Federal Reserve open-market policy as well as regulation Q have had a basic impact on changing yield structure.

Interest rates and supplies of money-market issues are, of course, interdependent in that changes in rates can be expected to influence supplies, and vice versa. Since a potential borrower's needs can often be met in either the money market or the capital market, interest rate expectations, in the short run, are likely to influence relative supplies of issues in both markets. For example, a corporate treasurer who expects long-term rates to fall in the near future may postpone contemplated capital market financing and attempt to raise the necessary funds in the money market, for example, by issuing more commercial paper.

Because money-market instruments are "temporary" in nature, they have been designed to be sold when short-term funds are needed by borrowers and when such funds are available from investors. This is the basic factor behind seasonal fluctuations in the volume of outstanding money-market instruments. The volume of outstanding treasury bills, for example, tends to decline after corporate tax payment dates, reflecting repayments of tax anticipation bills, while the upswing in the volume of commercial paper in certain months generally coincide with the need to finance inventories in manufacturing and retailing.

Interest rate differentials are seldom explainable by one factor alone, and there are at least two distinct concepts of interest rate differentials: (*a*) interest rate spreads among different maturities of the *same* issue, and (*b*) interest rate spreads among *different* issues of the same maturities. In the money market, the yield differential between three- and six-month maturities is usually considered as the prime indicator of the term structure relationship in the short-term area. On a month-to-month basis, yield spreads between three- and six-month maturities tended to vary more widely for treasury bills and federal agency issues than for the other selected instruments.

A number of factors give rise to yield spreads among different issues with the same maturity. The relative extent of default risk is one consideration. But this risk is minimal, if not nonexistent, for treasury bills. Consequently other factors such as outstanding volume of a particular issue, the minimum denomination in which an issue is available, how widely an issue is held, and the liquidity of an issue are more relevant in explaining yield spreads among money-market instruments. Treasury bills are the best known and most widely used short-term investment instrument, hence yields on treasury bills are generally lower than yields on other money-market instruments of comparable maturity. In any period when there is fear of a "liquidity crisis," Treasury bills are the "safest" instruments.

INVESTMENT MEDIA AND OBJECTIVES

The Morgan Guaranty study of money-market investments notes that:

> A corporation's funds in excess of prudent requirements for working cash and for support of bank borrowings, credit lines, and other even more important banking services and facilities, constitute the basis for a short-term portfolio. These funds are ultimately needed for the regular operations and the capital programs of a corporation but, by virtue of being temporarily of an excess nature, are in a position to earn some return. They may be viewed as reserves to be employed with a minimum

> of risk. Holders of such funds turn to the money market for income-producing investments. Their objectives are quality (of credit), liquidity, safety (from price fluctuations), and income at as high a level as possible.[3]

The various media are shown in Table 1. As for quality of credit, the direct obligations of the U.S. government stand at the top of the list, in the light of the fact that the taxing power of the government is the guaranty of payment. Notes of local U.S. public housing agencies appear to follow since the notes "shall be incontestable in the hands of a bearer, and the full faith and credit of the United States is pledged to the payment of all amounts." Thus the quality of these issues is based on U.S. government standby credit. Of almost equal stature are the various federal agency issues. Then come the issues of state or local bodies rated Aaa or Aa by Moody's and Standard & Poor's, which are considered to rank virtually on a par with federal agency issues. Perhaps next are the obligations of prime banks in the form of bankers' acceptances or negotiable certificates of deposit. Promissory notes of prime finance and industrial companies enjoy a high degree of strength based on the financial credit and earning power of the borrowers.

When ranked with respect to liquidity or marketability, U.S. government obligations again head the list, with treasury bills being the most liquid of all. Short-term obligations of the federal agencies would seem to follow. An active secondary market has developed for the certificates of deposit of major banks, giving such paper a high degree of liquidity. The acceptance market provides a similar liquidity for this type of instrument; however, the day-to-day volume is not so great as that of CDs. Project notes, formerly known as Public Housing Authority (PHA) notes, and other top-grade, tax-exempt issues enjoy a marketability close to that of certificates of deposit. Lower rated tax-exempts have a lesser degree of liquidity, while commercial paper is not really marketable prior to maturity, generally speaking.

With respect to safety from price fluctuation, in general, longer maturities mean greater exposure to price fluctuation. Treasury bills are the least vulnerable, with short-term treasury coupon issues and federal agency issues following in that order. Certificates of deposit probably come next, with project notes and high-grade tax-exempts ranking alongside or close after. Bankers' acceptances, besides being subject to fluctuations in the general interest rate structure, carry a known additional element of price exposure, namely, the yield between "bid" and "asked" prices that is most common in the acceptance market. If commercial paper is redeemed prior to maturity, a rate adjustment may be involved.

The Morgan Guaranty study notes that after World War II, many nonfinancial corporations adopted the practice of investing surplus funds in

[3] *Money-Market Investments,* p. 1.

money-market instruments.[4] The emphasis was at first heavily on short-term U.S. treasury securities. Many corporations followed a policy of keeping a minimum of perhaps 75 percent of their surplus funds in governments. A number of companies have shifted this emphasis, gradually moving to a point where governments prior to the credit constraint of 1973–74 constituted as little as 25 percent or less of their portfolios. Prudent diversification and sophisticated portfolio management offered greater earning potential.

The degree of risk a corporation should take in searching for higher returns on its portfolio funds, Morgan Guaranty notes, is really the major question facing the manager of a short-term investment portfolio. Concerned as he is with obtaining a satisfactory yield, he is engaged in a constant balancing of risk and return.

The projected ultimate purpose of the funds committed largely determines the degree of portfolio diversification. This will dictate the degree of added risk justified by the quest for higher returns. For example, some funds may be earmarked to meet specific future payments, such as dividends, taxes, or debt maturities; others may be intended for use in capital expansion or acquisition programs. Once the purposes of the portfolio funds have been identified, the flexibility to diversify in order to improve yield can be judged. If there is such flexibility, alternative investment media may be viewed as involving incremental degrees of risk in terms of quality, liquidity, and safety. On the basis of a broad classification of portfolio purposes, Morgan Guaranty suggests three purpose segments into which the funds of most portfolios can be divided. The allocation into the segments suggested may be used to integrate the cash forecasts with portfolio management.

Segment I (General Liquidity). The purpose of the funds in this segment is principally to provide for both regular and unexpected operational needs. Flexibility is of prime importance, consequently liquidity and limited price exposure are essential. The characteristics of the individual company—in terms of its cash forecasts and expected needs, together with the extent of estimated deviations in these flows or demands—will determine how large this segment should be. The investment instruments especially suitable for this segment, Morgan Guaranty suggests, include the shorter U.S. treasury and federal agency obligations, project notes, and certificates of deposit of prime money-market banks.

Segment II (Specific Payments). Funds earmarked for such cash outflows as dividends, taxes, or other specific payments lend themselves to investments that can be tailored to provide funds on a specific date. Certificates of deposit and commercial paper have the advantage of allowing the investor to specify his maturity. Various short-term tax-exempt

[4] *Money-Market Investments;* see also *Money Market Handbook for the Short Term Investor,* 3d ed., (New York: Brown Brothers, Harriman & Co., 1970).

securities are often issued to mature around tax dates and thus are available for funds destined to be used for tax payments.

Segment III (More Permanent Reserve). This segment allows the greatest flexibility in varying the standards to improve yield. It includes funds against which longer term commitments have been made under capital expansion programs or those for which no immediately foreseeable need is pending. Historical low points in the size of the portfolio may serve as rough guides to the extent of the need for such funds, but this indicator should be refined to allow for cash requirement deviations that may result from unanticipated developments such as expansion projects, acquisitions, strikes, and recessions. Medium-term U.S. governments and short-term tax-exempt securities are especially suitable for this category. Here the effort to raise yields may face the risk of having to liquidate at inopportune times.

An examination of the important characteristics of each of the several instruments for short-term investment will provide a basis for selection for portfolio management purposes.

TREASURY BILLS

Of all U.S. government debt instruments—bills, certificates, notes, and bonds—treasury bills have the shortest maturity and the greatest liquidity. Out of a total U.S. government debt of approximately $470 billion, treasury bills account for about $142 billion, or roughly 30 percent. For many years treasury bills have been the single most important money-market instrument. In their modern form, U.S. treasury bills were first offered in 1929. A treasury bill is an obligation of the United States government to pay the bearer a fixed sum after a specified number of days from the date of issue.

Bills are sold by the Treasury at a discount through competitive bidding, and the return to the investor is the difference between the purchase price and the face or par value. Treasury bills then are discount issues. Interest is not paid in the form of a coupon as in the case of a bond, but is the difference between the price the bidder pays for the bill and the par amount which he receives at maturity. The rate of return on a treasury bill of a given maturity is calculated by dividing the discount by par and expressing this percentage as an annual rate, using a 360-day year. For example, a price of $98.940 per $100 of face amount for a 91-day bill would produce an annual rate of return equal to

$$\frac{100 - 98.940}{100} \times \frac{360}{91} = 4.193\%.$$

Such a rate of return cannot be compared directly with the yield to maturity of a coupon-bearing issue having 91 days to maturity, since yields to maturity on coupon issues are calculated by using the purchase price instead of par as the divisor and by using a 365-day year instead of a 360-day year.

Wesley Lindow uses the example of a 91-day bill with a buying price of $98.641 per $100, the discount of 1.359 per $100 representing the income to be received at maturity, to be compared with a bond yield, or what is called the bond equivalent yield. His computation, given below, shows how a bill yield of 5.376 percent is derived from a price of 98.641.

1. Derive discount:

$100,000	Par value (receivable at maturity)
−98,641	Issue price (bid)
$ 1,359	Discount

2. Calculate interest

$$\frac{\text{Discount}}{\text{Par value}}\ \frac{1.359}{100{,}000} = 1.359\% \text{ interest for 91 days}$$

3. Calculate yield (*Y*)

$$\frac{\text{Interest}}{\text{Days}}\ \frac{1.359\%}{91} = \frac{Y}{360 \text{ days (not 365)}}$$

$$Y = 5.376\% \text{ yield (annual basis)}$$

To get the bond equivalent yield, the computation must be put on a 365-day basis, the same as used for treasury bonds.

The calculation is as follows:

1. Calculate discount (as above)
2. Calculate interest

$$\frac{\text{Discount}}{\text{Issue price}}\ \frac{1{,}359}{98{,}641} = 1.38\% \text{ interest for 91 days}$$

3. Calculate bond equivalent yield (*Y*)

$$\frac{\text{Interest}}{\text{Days}}\ \frac{1.38\%}{91} = \frac{Y}{365}$$

$$Y = 5.54\% \text{ yield (annual basis).}$$

Thus a 91-day bill yielding 5.38 percent (rounded) would be equivalent to a 91-day coupon bond yielding 5.54 percent.[5]

Treasury bills are issued in a variety of maturities and denominations, tailored to meet the needs of a diverse group of investors, mainly institutional, seeking both liquidity and income in a single instrument. Bills are offered on a regular schedule with maturities of 91 days, 182 days, and 365 days. In addition the treasury has occasional offerings of tax anticipation bills with maturities that have ranged up to nine

[5] Lindow, *Inside the Money Market*, pp. 26–27.

months. The bills are issued in five denominations, from $10,000 to $1 million. All may be exchanged at maturity for new issues (rolled over) or redeemed for cash.

New offerings of three- and six-month bills are made each week by the Treasury. Ordinarily, subscriptions or bids are invited on Thursdays, and the amounts of the offerings set at that time. The auction is usually conducted on the following Monday, with delivery and payment on the following Thursday. Bids or tenders in the weekly auctions must be presented at the Federal Reserve banks or their branches, which act as agents for the Treasury, by 1:30 P.M., New York time, on the day of the auction. Bids may be on a competitive or noncompetitive basis. Competitive bids are usually made by the larger investors who are in close contact with the market. These bids comprise the largest portion of subscriptions on a dollar basis. In this type of tender the investor states the quantity of bills desired and the price he is willing to pay. A subscriber may enter more than one bid indicating the various quantities he is willing to take at different prices. Individuals, and other small investors usually enter noncompetitive bids, which are awarded in full up to $200,000 on both the 91-day and 182-day bills. Noncompetitive awards are sold at the average price of accepted competitive bids.

Subscription books at the various Federal Reserve banks and branches close promptly at 1:30 P.M., and the bids are then opened, tabulated, and submitted to the Treasury for allocation. The Treasury first makes all noncompetitive awards. The remainder is then allocated to those competitive bidders submitting the highest offers, ranging downward from the highest bid until the amount offered is allocated. The "stop-out" price is the lowest price, or highest yield, at which bills are awarded. Usually only a portion of the total bids made at this price is accepted. The average issuing price, which is usually closer to the lowest accepted price than to the highest, is then computed on the basis of the competitive bids accepted. By bidding noncompetitively, smaller investors avoid several risks inherent in competitive bidding. In the first place, they do not risk losing their chance to buy as a result of bidding too low. Nor do they run the risk of bidding too high and paying a price near the top. It is not surprising, therefore, that most bids are noncompetitive, although the dollar amount they represent is relatively small.

Treasury bills are marketed by the Treasury solely through the auction technique. In general the auction method of marketing new bills is simpler and much less time consuming than the more involved technique employed in marketing other securities. In auctions, the market establishes a price for the bills, making it unnecessary for the Treasury to second-guess market conditions. Also auctions eliminate the problems associated with oversubscriptions or undersubscriptions. The Treasury merely sets the amount of the offering and the market does the rest. From the Treasury's point of view, the bill auctions provide a very convenient and flexible means of raising funds. From an investor's standpoint the bills provide a predictable supply of highly liquid assets in a convenient range of short maturities.

Treasury bills perform an important role in the application of monetary policy since the Fed influences the reserve positions of commercial banks primarily through the purchase and sale of bills. The Federal Reserve's purchases supply reserves to the banking system, and their sales have an opposite effect. While the Fed can and does function outside the bill area, as a practical matter, most of its purchases and sales are concentrated in short maturities, principally treasury bills.

The private sector's great demand for bills is attributable chiefly to their high degree of liquidity or "nearness to money." Financial and other institutions find it convenient to park temporarily surplus funds in short-time investments which yield a good going return and which can readily be converted into cash with little or no risk of loss. Treasury bills neatly fill these requirements. The highly organized market for bills insures their easy convertibility into cash and decreases the risk of loss should the investor need cash before the maturity of the bills. The short maturities minimize any risk from price fluctuations resulting from changing market conditions. Available in the secondary market are bills which range in maturity from a week or less to one year, and which therefore are appropriate to a variety of short-term investment needs. Moreover yields on bills are generally relatively competitive with other short-term investment media. For example, they ordinarily constitute an important part of commercial banks' "secondary reserves." Through purchases of bills, banks can quickly convert excess reserves into earning assets with little loss of liquidity. Through sales of bills they can promptly acquire additional funds for lending or for meeting legal reserve requirements. Bank holdings of treasury bills tend to vary seasonally and cyclically; when business is slack and loan demand is shrinking and the Fed is adding to bank reserves, commercial banks may turn to treasury bills as a temporary investment outlet. Conversely, when business is expanding and loan demand is increasing, banks generally liquidate bills in order to expand loans.

Corporations also resort to Treasury bills as a temporary investment and a potential source of ready cash. Rising interest rates lead corporate financial officers to attempt to reduce cash balances and to seek liquidity, where possible, in income-earning assets. In managing their cash flow, many corporate financial officers have become increasingly adept in arranging their prospective cash flows so that the maturities of their short-term investments coincide with future cash requirements. At times, however, unforeseen cash needs arise and it becomes necessary to raise money in a hurry. For such purposes, treasury bills are ideally suited. There is no credit risk and little trading risk. There is virtually instant liquidity.

SECURITIES OF U.S. GOVERNMENT AGENCIES

Issues of short-term securities of federal agencies constitute another important segment of the money market. The outstanding volume of federal agency debt exceeds $50 billion, and it is estimated that about 40 percent is short term. Agriculture and housing have traditionally been the two largest areas of federal credit programs. Among the agencies involved are Federal Home Loan Banks, Federal Land Banks, Federal National Mortgage Association,[6] Government National Mortgage Association, Federal Intermediate Credit Banks, Bank for Cooperatives, Export-Import Bank, the Commodity Credit Corporation, Tennessee Valley Authority, and others.

Federal agency securities differ when compared with other types of securities as well as among themselves. Three categories of agency issues may be distinguished: (1) participation certificates (PC's); (2) certificates of interest; and (3) notes, bonds, and debentures. PC's are securities issued against a pool of assets (usually loans) of the participating agencies. Interest received from the pooled loans is used to pay interest on the PC's. Originally PC's were issued with fairly long maturities. Some issues do not mature until 1988. Therefore most PC's currently outstanding are more of a capital-market instrument than a money-market instrument, but over time, PC's will increase in importance to the money market as their term of maturity declines. The Eximbank has made extensive use of participation certificates which were issued against its outstanding loans.

Certificates of interest are similar in many respects to PC's. Those of the Commodity Credit Corporation, for example, were sold exclusively to eligible financial institutions and were backed by a pool of loans originally made to farmers under price support programs.

The remaining federal agency securities are somewhat more conventional in nature, consisting mainly of notes, bonds, and debentures. To finance its secondary market purchases, FNMA relies on the sale of notes and debentures. The short-term notes are discounted at published rates that are closely aligned to the rates on treasury bills, that is, rates on FNMA notes are set at a certain level above the market rate on treasury bills.

Securities of the Federal Home Loan Banks are issued against collateral of guaranteed mortgages, U.S. government securities, or cash assets. FHLB obligations with original maturities of more than one year are classified as bonds, while those issued with a one year maturity or less are notes. These notes differ from FNMA notes in that the FHLB

[6] The Federal National Mortgage Association was converted to private ownership in 1968, and the responsibility for servicing the outstanding FNMA participation certificates was transferred to the newly formed Government National Mortgage Association.

issues carry a fixed (coupon) rate of interest, while FNMA notes are sold on a discount basis.

With certain exceptions, such as outstanding GNMA and Eximbank PC's, most agency securities are not guaranteed by the U.S. government. Such instruments are often referred to as nonguaranteed agency debt. Some form of federal backing is, however, implicit for the nonguaranteed issues. The high credit standing of agency securities is indicated by the facts that: (1) the Secretary of the Treasury is authorized to buy federal agency obligations, (2) most agency issues can be used as collateral for treasury tax and loan accounts maintained by commercial banks, (3) member banks can use some agency issues as collateral for any advances obtained from their Federal Reserve banks, and (4) in recent years some agency issues have been purchased and sold by the Federal Reserve system's open market account. There is probably little difference in terms of risk between federal agency securities and treasury issues. Thus the difference in interest rates on the two types of securities is probably only remotely associated with relative risk.

There are two other characteristics of agency issues worth noting—call features and tax status. With few exceptions, agency securities presently outstanding cannot be called before maturity. Interest and any capital gains or losses on agency securities are subject to federal income taxes but, with few exceptions, are not subject to state or local levies.

Most agency securities are sold initially through financial specialists known as *fiscal agents*. The agencies maintain their separate fiscal agents under contract. Once sold, however, federal agency issues are traded in the secondary market in much the same way U.S. government securities are. Most dealers in U.S. government issues also make markets in agency issues. In volume of trading, however, the agency issues rank far below regular government issues.

All types of agency issues are not equally important to the money market. Some are clearly capital market instruments; some are of mixed character, depending on the specific maturity. On the other hand, all of the Cooperative Bank and Federal Intermediate Credit Bank debentures are short-term money-market obligations, with original maturities of less than one year. The agencies that are currently most active in the money market are the farm credit agencies and the housing agencies. Outstanding issues of some five of these agencies constitute virtually the entire amount of the nonguaranteed agency debt.

Ownership of federal agency issues is found primarily in commercial banks and other financial institutions such as insurance companies, mutual savings banks, and savings and loan associations. Government trust funds have, at times, made significant purchases of agency instruments. Commercial banks and the other financial institutions have legal limitations on the type of investments that they can make and therefore find these agency issues attractive. They provide many of the advantages of regular treasury issues but have higher yields. Most agency securities are considered legal investments and are accepted as security against deposits of public funds, such as treasury tax and loan accounts at commercial banks. Consequently when banks need additional liquidity and hold both agency and regular treasury issues, they probably choose to sell the latter, lower earning issues.

Over the years corporations have been important buyers of agency issues, although their holdings have varied widely. On the whole, however, the corporate share of the agency issue market has declined due in part, no doubt, to developments in markets for other money-market instruments such as CDs or commercial paper, which as a rule offer better rates of return than agency or treasury issues.

Maturity for maturity, agency yields are higher than yields on regular U.S. treasury issues, but generally below yields on private issues such as commercial paper, bankers' acceptances, or CDs in the secondary market. The difference in yields of agency issues over treasury securities can be attributed only in a small degree to the element of risk and must be accounted for by elements other than risk. One determining factor might be differences in "tradeability." Treasury issues have been in the market for many more years and in larger dollar volume than agency securities. As a result, the investing public is better acquainted with treasury issues. In addition, they comprise a more homogeneous group than agency issues in terms of tax treatment, call features, or marketing methods. Generally, the secondary market for agency issues is not as well developed as that for direct treasury obligations. Furthermore, the dollar volume of individual treasury issues is usually far greater than the dollar volume of single agency issues. Commercial banks and other portfolio managers are less well acquainted with government agency issues.

BANKERS' ACCEPTANCES

With a rise in interest rates there has been a dramatic growth in the volume of two long-standing money-market instruments—bankers' acceptances and commercial paper. Bankers' acceptances are probably as old as commerce itself, and commercial paper's origins are also obscure. In spite of the growth in bankers' acceptances over the last decade, they remain one of the least familiar of all money-market instruments.

Bankers' acceptances represent one type of a broad class of credit instruments known as bills of exchange. Bills of exchange are drafts, or orders to pay specified amounts at a specified time, drawn on individuals, business firms, or financial institutions. When the drawer formally acknowledges his obligation to honor such a draft—usually by writing "accepted" with the appropriate signature across the face of the draft—

it becomes an acceptance. An acceptance which represents the liability of a well-known bank is, obviously, a more desirable credit instrument than one drawn on a little-known firm or individual.

Legally, acceptances are negotiable instruments which the payee or holder in due course may discount in the money market. Both the drawer, who endorses the acceptance when he sells it, and the accepting bank are obligors of the draft. This makes the acceptance, in money-market terminology, "two-name paper," which has a higher degree of safety and is attractive as a short-term investment.

Bankers' acceptances usually arise from letters of credit issued in foreign trade transactions. A U.S. firm, for example, may wish to import goods and may ask its bank to issue a letter of credit on its behalf in favor of the foreign exporter. If the bank finds the customer's credit standing satisfactory, it will issue a letter of credit authorizing the foreign exporter to draw a draft upon it in payment for the goods. Equipped with this authorization, the exporter, on shipping the goods, can discount the draft with his bank, thereby receiving payment immediately. The foreign bank, in turn, forwards the draft, with appropriate shipping documents, to its correspondent bank in the United States with instructions regarding its disposition. Generally, the U.S. correspondent bank will present the draft for acceptance at the drawee bank, which forwards the shipping documents to the importer, who uses them to claim the shipment. The correspondent bank may be requested to hold the acceptance until maturity as an investment for the foreign bank. Or it may be instructed to offer the acceptance for sale in the money market and to credit the account of the foreign bank. Whoever holds the acceptance until maturity finances the transaction.

The accepting bank may, of course, itself buy the acceptance which it originated. In this case it then earns the difference between the purchase price and the face amount which the importer must ultimately pay. When a bank follows this course, it is actually financing the transaction, and its position is much the same as when it extends a loan directly to the customer. On the other hand, if some other bank or party buys and holds the acceptance, the originating bank has tied up no funds. It has substituted its credit for that of the importer and assumed a contingent liability for which it collects a fee.

While individual banks often acquire acceptances drawn on themselves, many prefer to hold instruments drawn on other banks. Such instruments tend to have superior marketability. When sold under endorsement they become three-name paper, the drawer and two banks. Three-name paper is especially attractive to foreign investors, some of whom purchase only this type.

Maturities on bankers' acceptances range from 30 to 180 days, but 90 days is most common. Maturities can often be tailored to cover the entire period needed to ship and dispose of the goods financed. With regard to both liquidity and safety, bankers' acceptances are almost as good as treasury bills. This is reflected in a market yield which generally runs only fractionally higher than treasury bill yields.

Most acceptances in this country have arisen in the financing of U.S. imports and exports. In recent years, however, acceptances have found growing use in the financing of goods stored in or shipped between foreign countries.

Despite its recent growth, the market for bankers' acceptances remain far less extensive than that for treasury bills or commercial paper. The most active institutions in the market are foreign banks and financial institutions, the Federal Reserve banks (especially the New York Fed), a relatively small group of large banks, and a small group of nonbank dealers. Recently, however, private domestic investors have become increasingly interested in bankers' acceptances. There are only about seven dealers, apart from the banks, in the bankers' acceptance market. Most of them deal primarily in U.S. government securities and only incidentally in acceptances. These dealers make a market for acceptances by their willingness to buy or sell on a continuous basis at preannounced rates, which are adjusted frequently in the light of money-market conditions. The dealers earn their profit through the spread between buying and selling rates.

Under authorization from the Federal Open Market Committee, the Federal Reserve Bank of New York buys acceptances outright for its own account and typically holds them to maturity, only occasionally making outright sales in the market. The New York Fed also makes repurchase agreements which are more important to the system from the standpoint of open market operations than changes in outright holdings. Repurchase arrangements are from time to time conducted in large volume, but on the whole, the Fed's operation in bankers' acceptances is dwarfed by its activity in treasury bills.

The rate structure on acceptances is usually indicated by dealers' bid and asked quotations. For example, the dealer rate may be 6⅞ percent bid, 6¾ percent asked, for a 90-day acceptance. The quotations are in terms of a discount rate, rather than in terms of price, but the effect of a higher rate naturally means a lower price. The borrower pays the bid yield, in effect, plus at least the minimum fee of 1½ percent, for prime names to the bank for lending its credit by accepting the draft. In the example above, the total charge to the borrower would be 8⅜ percent (6⅞ percent + 1½ percent). As money gets tighter, banks encourage the use of acceptance financing to save their lending resources. Use of acceptances allows banks' customers to obtain funds without the use of bank funds. That is, from the banks' standpoint, acceptances have an important advantage over direct loans. The bank may be using only its credit, not its funds. Furthermore, bankers' acceptances are a better secondary reserve than customers' loans. Bankers experiencing reserve losses can cover these through the sale of acceptances to dealers, whereas liquidation or rediscounting of customers' loans would probably involve higher costs and poor customer relations. Banks and dealers are the ones, for the most part, involved in the bankers' acceptance corner of the money market; other investors, primarily nonbank corporations, become involved only infrequently. Activity by corporations depends in large part upon the relationship of acceptance yields to those of other short-term investments.

COMMERCIAL PAPER

Over the past decade there has been a surprising growth in the use of commercial paper. As Lindow notes, commercial paper is a very convenient device by which corporations borrow from other corporations for short-term periods. Technically, commercial paper includes all short-term evidences of indebtedness of business firms; however, in the money market, commercial paper is generally defined as unsecured, short-term notes issued in bearer form by large, well-known business firms. Maturities on commercial paper range from a few days to nine months (270 days). Notes with a maturity of more than 270 days are uncommon because such issues, for the most part, must be registered with the SEC.

There are basically two types of commercial paper, direct paper and dealer paper, with the former predominant. Directly placed paper has frequently been called "finance company paper," because the majority of the issuing companies are finance companies that sell their notes to investors without using the services of a dealer. A few industrial corporations also issue direct paper. The smaller sector of the commercial paper market is composed of dealers who purchase notes outright from issuers. The dealers then generally place their paper with institutional investors and with the larger banks, acting as agents for investors.

There is no active trading in a secondary market for commercial paper as there is for other money-market instruments. Consequently, investors in commercial paper generally select a note with a maturity that closely parallels their investment needs. Commercial paper notes do not carry a stipulated rate of interest but instead are sold at a discount, with the difference between the purchase and redemption prices being the interest paid. Usually the effective rates are from ⅜ percent to ½ percent over the yields on treasury bills of corresponding maturities.

In the case of dealer paper, the notes are placed in one of three ways. One method is to sell the notes outright to the dealer, that is, the borrowing firm is immediately paid the face value of the notes less the discount and commission. This method assures the borrower of a specific amount of funds at a definite time. The dealer assumes the risk of being unable to resell the notes at the agreed rate; however, he may benefit by being able to sell the notes at a premium. The outright sale method of placing dealer commercial paper is the most popular. A second method of placement referred to as "bought as sold" allows the dealer to market the borrowing firm's paper at the best available price, transferring the proceeds of the sale less commission to the borrower after the sale is completed. This method of commercial paper placement accounts, however, for less than 10 percent of the dollar volume of dealer-placed notes. Dealer paper is also placed by the "open rate" method. In this technique, the borrowing firm receives a percentage of the face amount of the notes when they are delivered to the dealer. After the notes are sold, the dealer remits the balance less his commission to the borrower. Both the bought as sold and open rate methods shift the market risk from the dealer to the borrower.

Directly placed paper is identical to dealer paper in all characteristics except the manner in which it is sold. For both dealer paper and direct paper, the amount of the discount depends on prevailing interest rates for similar money-market paper with similar maturities. The discount on direct paper, however, is generally less than the discount on comparable dealer paper. This difference reflects the strong financial condition and size of the companies that issue direct paper. Many of the companies that use direct placement are finance companies with such large and continuous borrowing needs that it is worthwhile for them to maintain their own sales force in order to save the commission charged by dealers. It is estimated that when a corporation has at least $100 million of commercial paper outstanding at all times, it is profitable to begin direct placements. The sales procedures used for directly placed commercial paper are different from those used for dealer paper. The company placing paper directly quotes an interest rate at which funds will be accepted, allowing the lender to set the maturity of the note, generally between 3 and 270 days.

Commercial paper has distinct advantages for the issuer, or borrower, over other types of short-term financing. Interest costs are generally lower on commercial paper than on bank loans, which often carry the added costs of compensating balances. Furthermore, in periods of credit stringency, when compensating balances are frequently increased, the differential between rates on commercial and bank loans (with compensating balances) has been as great as 200 basis points.[7]

In recent years, public utilities, bank holding companies, and transportation companies have joined finance companies and other large industrial corporations in borrowing via commercial paper. Historically, banks have been the principal purchasers of commercial paper, but in recent years, the lending side of the market has also expanded and now includes industrial firms, nonbank financial institutions, pension funds,

[7] For instance, the effective interest rate of an 8 percent (prime) bank loan with a 20 percent compensating balance is 10 percent.

mutual funds, and others. Commercial paper has appealed to these institutional investors because of its combination of relative security, attractive yield, and short maturity.

Prime commercial paper is considered to be of high quality. The commercial paper market had historically experienced modest financial losses until the Penn Central debacle. The National Credit Office collects data on virtually all firms issuing commercial paper and issues statements on each commercial paper borrower, including the names of the borrower's principal banks and the amounts of unused lines of credit open to the firm. (These lines of credit are sometimes interpreted as being the collateral behind commercial paper. However, the notes are actually unsecured in the usual sense.) After analysis the National Credit Office rates the new paper issues as "prime," "desirable," or "satisfactory." More than two thirds of the outstanding commercial paper is rated prime, with nearly all of the remaining paper rated desirable. The National Credit Office's rating is reflected in the rate of discount (yield) paid on the notes. Prime paper is generally 25 basis points lower in yield than desirable paper. Most quoted commercial paper yields refer to prime commercial paper.

Yields on commercial paper are closely related to other interest rates prevailing in the money market. Commercial paper rates are most often quoted on a discount basis (360-day year). Thus the bond-yield equivalent is fractionally greater than the interest quoted. Typically, commercial paper notes bear interest at rates that are above yields on short-term treasury bills as well as rates on bankers' acceptances and CDs. With few exceptions, the rates rise and fall together in similar cyclical patterns. The rates tend to move down in times of monetary ease and to increase sharply in periods of monetary restraint. Historically, the prime commercial paper rate was at least 1 percent below the prime loan rate of commercial banks, but in the last few years, the commercial paper rate rose above the prime rate. In recent years, new investors, issuers, and dealers entered the commercial paper market and increased its size and depth.

NEGOTIABLE CERTIFICATES OF DEPOSIT

A negotiable time certificate of deposit is a receipt issued by a bank in exchange for the deposit of funds. The bank agrees to pay the amount deposited, plus interest, to the bearer of the receipt on the date specified on the certificate. Because the certificate is negotiable, it can be traded in the secondary market before maturity.

In February 1961, the First National City Bank of New York announced that it would issue negotiable certificates of deposit in large denominations and that a major government securities' dealer agreed to make a market in them. Other money-market banks and dealers quickly followed suit, thus preparing the way for the spectacular growth of this money-market instrument. Time certificates did not originate in 1961, but prior to that time they represented primarily savings-type deposits, nonnegotiable, with no secondary market. They developed as an effort by banks to buy funds, corporate funds, which otherwise would have been siphoned off into other money-market instruments, such as treasury bills, for example. The negotiable CD was designed specifically to attract corporate deposits and to enable banks to compete more effectively for short-term funds.

There are no legal limitations per se on the size in which negotiable CDs can be issued. The denomination depends primarily on the needs of the original buyer and the size of the issuing bank. Large metropolitan banks dealing with large corporations can and do sell CDs in larger denominations. Although negotiable CDs have been issued for amounts ranging from $25,000 to $10 million or more, in general, denominations in amounts greater than $1 million are unusual. The development of the secondary market for CDs has led to some standardization of sizes, and as a result, most CDs are issued in amounts of $100,000, $500,000, or $1 million. CDs may be in registered or bearer form, although the latter is most convenient for secondary market trading. The CD maturity date is chosen by the purchaser to fit his cash needs and may range from 1 to about 18 months. It has been estimated that slightly over 70 percent of total CDs outstanding at weekly reporting member banks mature within four months. Interest is paid on the certificate's par value and accrues on a 360-day basis. The actual rate is determined by current money-market conditions and is competitive with yields on other short-term instruments. In general, a CD must yield a number of basis points[8] more than treasury bills of comparable maturity to attract investors. Certificates bearing popular maturity dates, such as tax and dividend dates, do not require as large a premium in order to be competitive. The size of the issuing bank and the denomination of the certificate also influence the rate. CDs smaller than $1 million, for instance, will usually carry a higher rate than larger CDs of comparable maturity. The 20 or so largest "prime-name" banks can ordinarily issue CDs bearing lower rates than those of smaller banks which are not widely known. The latter must usually pay one eighth to one half of 1 percent above the prime CD rate to attract funds.

The Federal Reserve's Regulation Q, which sets the maximum rates payable on time and savings deposits, is a fundamental consideration in the market for CDs. When short-term market rates rise above, or even approach, the prescribed ceiling, CDs cease to be competitive. Bankers find it increasingly difficult to replace maturing certificates and are likely to experience large deposit losses as investors turn to higher yielding

[8] A basis point is 1|100 of 1 percent, that is, 100 basis points equal 1 percent; 50 basis points are one half of 1 percent.

instruments. For example, the majority of new CDs issued in early 1973 had initial maturities of under 90 days. Since Regulation Q ceilings on CDs of 90 days to one year initial maturity were substantially below competing money-market rates, the entire maturity structure of outstanding CDs began to shorten rapidly. To prevent the emergence of disorderly money-market conditions and to allow banks to reestablish a more balanced deposit structure, the Federal Reserve suspended Regulation Q ceilings.

Several factors are involved in bank decisions on CDs. Considerations include the profitability of investment outlets for the new funds and also the outlook for renewals at maturity. Most banks establish a flexible limit on total CDs issued. This limit may be expressed in dollars or, more often, as a percent of total deposits.

Although a bank often will negotiate, frequently, with a large and important customer, it usually has a set of "base rates," expressed in eighths, for various maturities. The bank adjusts these rates according to its eagerness for new deposits, and a very small change often results in appreciable increases or decreases in deposits. Most large money-market banks will issue CDs to any corporation or financial institution without having had any previous relationship with the depositor. CDs may indeed afford the bank the opportunity to acquire new depositors. Of course a bank may refuse to issue a CD if the deposit consists of funds which otherwise would constitute a company's normal demand deposit.

The CD appeals to corporate treasurers interested in maximizing returns on their liquid balances to such an extent that nonfinancial corporations dominate the demand side of the CD market. Other depositors (purchasers of CDs) include state and municipalities, central banks, foreign governments, institutional investors, and individuals. Dealers, from time to time, take CDs directly from the issuing banks. Some corporations prefer the certificates of banks with which they have lines of credit. Others, however, seek a more impersonal approach and limit themselves largely to prime CDs. As a rule, corporations use treasury bills to adjust their cash positions, with CDs providing secondary liquidity.

While most original purchasers hold their CDs to maturity, the existence of an organized secondary market is of vital importance to prime-name banks in attracting corporate funds. Participants in this market show a marked perference for prime CDs, chiefly because of their greater marketability. Corporations may enter the market at any time, on the selling side when they wish to raise cash or to realize a profit, or on the buying side when they want maturities shorter than can be acquired in new issues.

The hub of the secondary market is in New York City. Since many of the larger corporations have accounts at New York banks, transactions between dealers and customers can be conducted with ease. CDs of out-of-town banks are frequently issued and redeemed through their New York correspondents. New York's money-market banks will lend funds to dealers against CDs. Although Regulation Q does not permit a bank to purchase its own CDs in the secondary market, for investment, it may as an agent acquire them for customers. A bank may purchase, either for its own account or for the accounts of customers, CDs issued by another bank. A bank is permitted to make a loan secured by its own CD only if it charges an interest rate at least 2 percent above the rate at which the certificate was originally issued.

The relative standing of CDs in the money market, as far as interest rate levels are concerned, lies somewhere above treasury bills and federal agency issues and slightly below commercial paper and bankers' acceptances. CDs emerged from a relatively insignificant position—in terms of volume—in the money market to a position second only to that of treasury bills.

The introduction of negotiable CDs reflected an attempt by some banks to overcome the deterioration of their competitive position vis-à-vis nonbank financial institutions and what had been a steady reduction in the proportion of total deposits accounted for by large banks. Large banks, caught in the dilemma of increasing demands for credit and little prospect for increased deposits, turned to CDs in the hope that they would be able to retain some of the corporate funds that otherwise might have been invested in other money-market instruments, such as treasury bills or commercial paper. In retrospect it appears that they were successful in their innovation. Since owners of short-term funds are responsive to interest rate differentials, banks have been known to acquire millions of dollars of new deposits in a single day by this method.

SHORT-TERM, TAX-EXEMPT SECURITIES

Corporate funds earmarked for liquidity purposes may find liquidity plus a higher return in the short-term segment of the vast array of state and municipal obligations and of the many projects, districts, and local agencies and authorities, such as the public housing authorities, which are local agencies whose securities, in effect, are guaranteed by the federal government. These issues are customarily called *tax-exempts* because interest on them is exempt, under existing regulations, from the federal income tax and from income taxes, if any, of the states in which they are issued.

The Morgan Guaranty Trust Company study of money-market instruments divides the short-term, tax-exempt field into three categories, in order of their relative importance as a source of supply: (1) project notes of local public agencies; (2) notes of states and municipalities; and (3) early maturities of serial bonds. The project notes of the federal agencies (primarily housing) are secured by agreements with an agency of the federal government and are regarded as prime investments, as evidenced, for example, by the fact that national banks may purchase them in unlimited amounts, that they may be used as security for treasury deposits, and that in many states they are regarded as legal investments for savings banks and for trust funds. In effect, project notes are regarded as equal to the obligations of federal agencies in essential security provisions. The second broad category of short-term securities arises out of temporary borrowing by states and municipalities either in anticipation of taxes or other revenue or in anticipation of longer term bond financing. The third group is comprised of early maturities of serial bond issues which in some cases have six-month or one-year series.

The professional market for tax-exempts, both primary and secondary, is principally in New York. It is not a big market as money-market segments go, but it has a number of large banks and dealers who continuously make a market for these issues. The short maturities of serial bond issues are almost always issued in denominations of $5,000. Note issues, on the other hand, whether state, municipal, or federal housing, are frequently supplied in large units ranging from $5,000 to $1 million at the option of the purchaser. The market is now so well developed that large investors may take units of $100,000 to $1 million without loss of marketability. Virtually all of these certificates are in bearer form and are fully negotiable instruments.

SUMMARY AND CONCLUSION

In its annual review of financial markets, a leading financial house, Salomon Brothers, declared:

> For the second time within the last five years, money market investments outperformed the total returns on either bonds or stocks (price change plus dividends or interest payments as a percent of starting values). As shown in the accompanying table (Table 2), the return on 3-month negotiable CDs rolled over quarterly, for a 12-month period, was 8 percent in 1973 as compared with a total return of a negative 15 percent for an average (S & P's 500 composite) of common stocks, and returns ranging from zero to 4 percent for bonds. The last time the money markets similarly outperformed investment securities was in 1969 when 3-month CDs also yielded 8 percent and both stocks and bonds turned in negative total performances. . . . During the past five years, however, both bonds and money market obligations outperformed stocks on average with stocks showing an average annual return of 3 percent as compared with 7 percent for three-month negotiable CDs and 5 to 6 percent for bonds.[9]

[9] *1973 Annual Review of the Bond Market* (New York: Salomon Brothers, 1974), p. 405.

In reviewing trends in short-term rates, Salomon Brothers noted:

In contrast to the moderate net increase in long-term interest rates, short-term rates rose dramatically to new postwar peaks in August and September. . . . From the start of the year to their August–September highs, three-month money market rates rose 535 basis points to 10.95 percent for negotiable CDs, 525 basis points to 10.75 percent for dealer-placed paper, and 393 basis points to 9.05 percent for Treasury bills. . . . From their August highs, money market rates declined quickly

TABLE 2

Total Performance of Selected Market Sectors—1969–73 (price change + dividend income or interest income as percent of starting value)

	U.S. Governments		*Hi-Grade*	*Prime*		*3*
			Corporates Long	*Municipals Long*	*Common Stock**	*Month CDs*
	Long	*Medium*				
1969	− 5%	− 1%	− 8%	−17%	− 8%	+8%
1970	+12	+16	+18	+21	+ 4	+8
1971	+13	+ 9	+11	+13	+14	+5
1972	+ 6	+ 4	+ 7	+ 4	+19	+5
1973	0	+ 4	+ 1	+ 4	−15	+8
1969–73 Annual Average	+ 5%	+ 6%	+ 6%	+ 5%	+ 3%	+7%

Note: Excludes reinvestment.
* Based on Standard & Poor's 500 Common Stock Composite.
Source: Salomon Brothers, New York, 1974.

and steeply (see Chart 2) for two months as the Federal Reserve loosened its grip on the money market in order to rekindle desired growth in the flagging monetary aggregates. . . . Thus, at the close, money rates generally were still very high, around the peak levels reached in the 1969–70 period, but below their 1973 highs.

The substantial demand for short-term credit is partly reflected in Table 3 which shows the increase in the volume of outstanding money market obligations annually from 1966 to 1973. For 1973, the major money market obligations increased a record $36 billion, surpassing by a third the previous record increase registered in 1970. Even with the net liquidation of negotiable CDs in the closing months of the year, the increase of $20 billion in these obligations for the year as a whole was a record. The $7-billion increase in the volume of outstanding commercial paper was second only to the $11.4 billion issued in 1969. The increase in the volume of outstanding Treasury bills was about average. These differences in new volume accounted for much of the difference in the interest rate behavior of key money market rates.[10]

[10] Salomon Brothers, *1973 Annual Review*, p. 7.

CHART 2

Short-Term Interest Rates in 1967–73

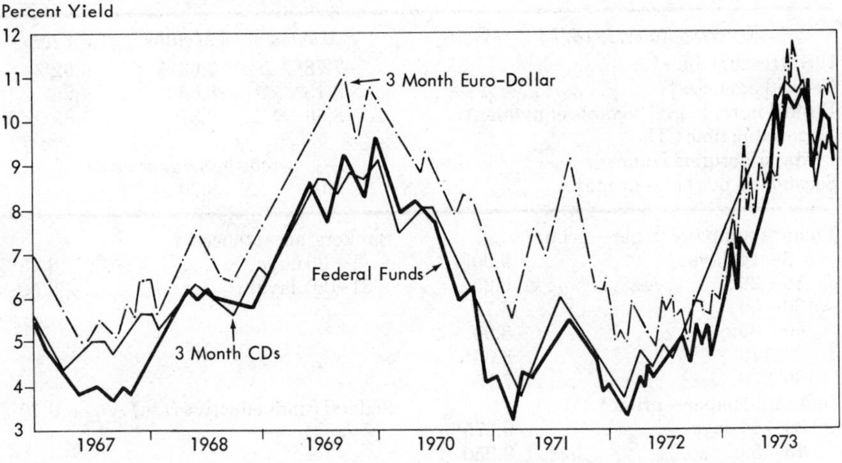

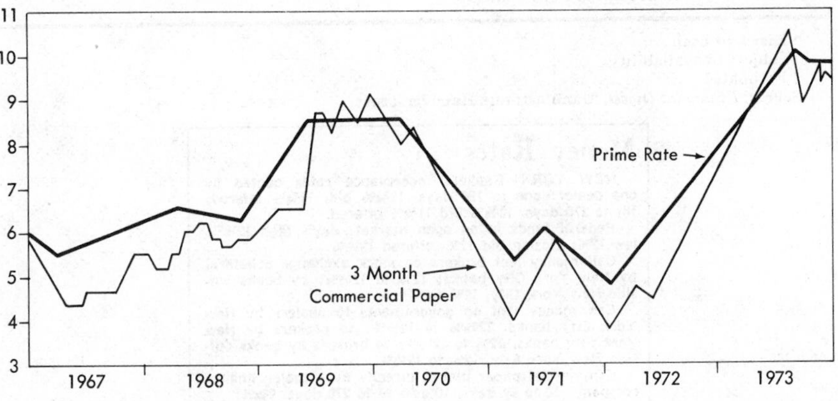

Source: Salomon Brothers, New York, 1974.

TABLE 3

Net Change in Volume of Outstanding Money Market Obligations ($ billions)

	1966	*1967*	*1968*	*1969*	*1970*	*1971*	*1972*	*1973E*
Treasury bills	4.5	5.2	5.1	5.6	7.4	9.6	6.4	6.0
Commercial paper	4.3	3.4	4.1	11.4	0.5	−0.9	2.6	7.3
Negotiable CDs	−0.6	4.7	3.1	−12.5	15.2	8.7	9.8	20.1
Agency paper	0.5	0.5	1.6	0.7	−0.4	−1.2	−0.6	0.9
Bankers' acceptances	0.2	0.7	0.1	1.0	1.6	0.8	−1.0	1.6
Total	8.9	14.5	14.0	6.2	24.3	17.0	17.2	35.9

E—Estimated.
Source: Salomon Brothers, New York, 1974.

APPENDIX

New York Money Market

Offering Rates, 1/18/74	*3 Months*	*6 Months*	*1 Year*
U.S. treasury bills*	7.78%	7.63%	6.92%
Federal agencies†	8.15	8.05	7.25
Project notes† (48% taxable equivalent)	8.56	8.37	7.88
Negotiable time CDs			
Manufacturers Hanover		(*rates by arrangement*)	
Secondary market—prime†	9.05	8.70	

Finance company paper—prime*	
5– 14 days	9.00%
15– 29	9.25
30– 59	8.75
60– 89	8.50
90–179	8.00
180–270	7.75
Industrial paper—prime*	
30– 44 days	9.375%
45– 59	9.250
60– 89	9.125
90	9.000

Bankers' acceptances*†	
1– 30 days	8.25%
31–180 days	8.50
Federal funds effective rate‡	9.70%

* Discount basis.
† Subject to availability.
‡ Estimated.
Source: *Financial Digest*, Manufacturers Hanover Trust

Money Rates

NEW YORK—Bankers' acceptance rates quoted by one dealer: one to 180 days, 12¾% bid, 11¾% offered; 181 to 270 days, 12⅝% bid 11⅝% offered.

Federal funds in an open market: day's high 12⅛%, low 12%; closing bid 12%, offered 12½%.

Call money lent brokers on stock exchange collateral by New York City banks: 12% to 12½%; by banks outside New York City, 12% to 12½%.

Call money lent on governments to dealers by New York City banks, 12⅜% to 12½%; to brokers by New York City banks, 12% to 12½%; to brokers by banks outside New York City, 12% to 12½%.

Commercial paper placed directly by a major finance company: 30 to 89 days, 10⅛%; 90 to 270 days, 9⅜%.

Commercial paper sold through dealers: 30 to 270 days, 12⅛% to 13⅜%.

Certificates of deposit ($100,000 or more): top rates paid by major banks in the newly issued market, one month 12⅛%; two months 12⅜%; three months, 12½%; six months, 12½%; one year, 11%.

Eurodollar rates in London include: one month, 12⅞% to 12¾%; two months, 13½% to 13⅜%; three months, 14 1-16% to 13 15-16%; four months, 13⅞% to 13¾%; five months, 14% to 13⅞%; six months, 14⅛% to 14%.

Rates shown are only a guideline to general trends, and don't necessarily represent actual transactions.

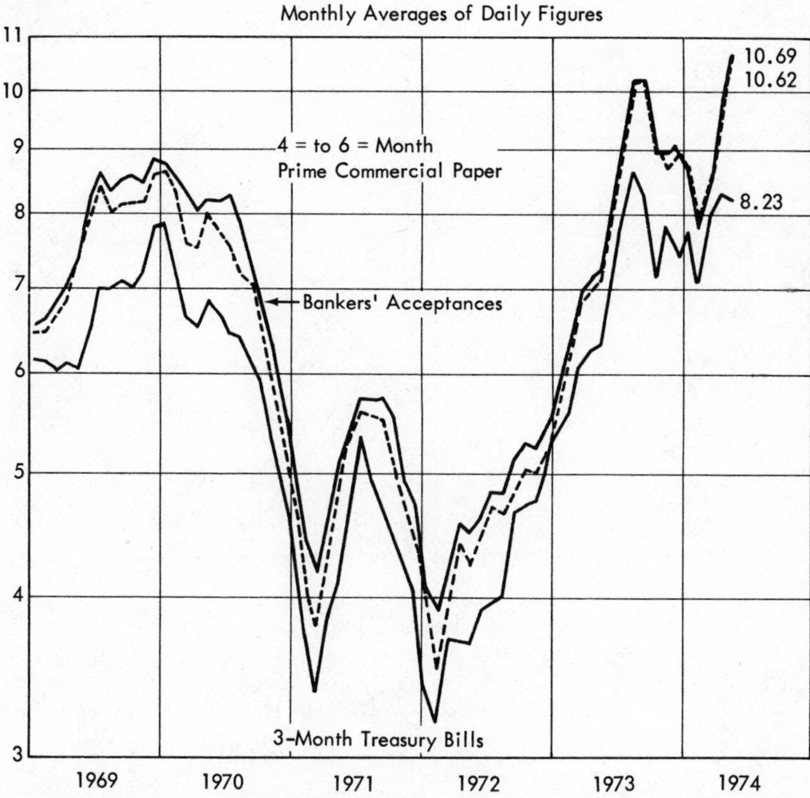

Latest Data Plotted: May

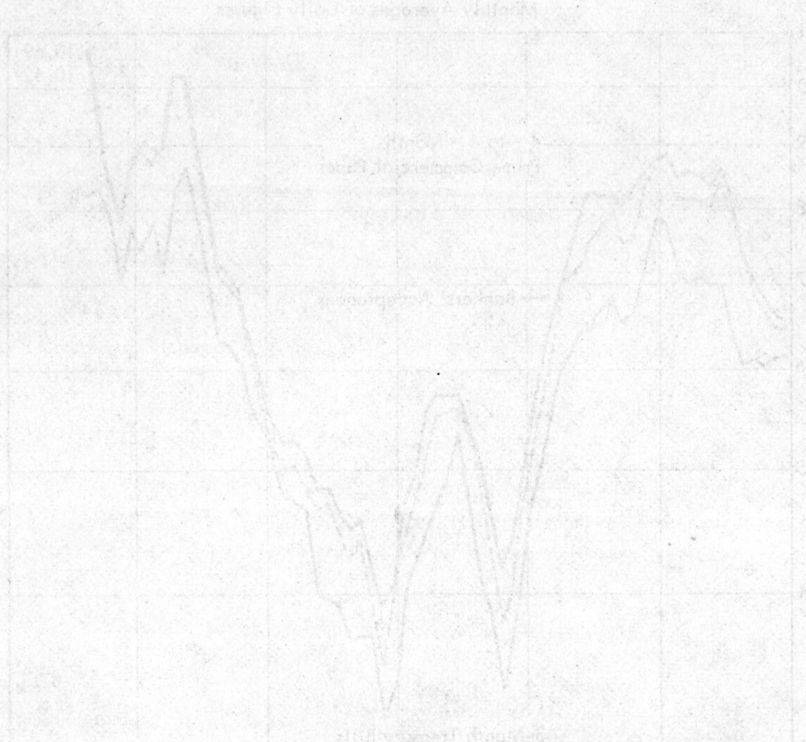

PART III

Special Investment Vehicles

16

Special Situations

MAURECE SCHILLER
Goleta, California
and
MARTIN BENIS, Ph.D., CPA
Baruch College
The City University of New York
New York, New York

Description. The term *special situations,* in the classical sense, refers to opportunities for gains which arise from unique developments of limited duration due to changes in the corporate structure. Once the details of the corporate action which give rise to the special situation are known, it is possible to estimate the expected gains and risks. Barring unusual market conditions, the potential gains are usually insulated from market fluctuations. If the analyst can spot the special situation early enough, substantial gains may be realized at relatively minimal risk. However, timing and judgment are of importance since the expected corporate action may not be consummated or, even if consummated, may require an excessive amount of time resulting in a poor rate of return. On the other hand, too long a delay in taking a position can eliminate the possibility of realizing a gain because of adjustments in the market. Locating an appropriate special situation at the right time is clearly a difficult matter requiring a painstaking analysis of, among other things, the corporate plan, possible sources of delay in closing the deal, and the underlying financial positions of the companies involved.

Classifications of Special Situations. Typical special situations are listed below:

Liquidation occurs when a company, in whole or in part, disposes of its assets and distributes the proceeds. Liquidating companies may issue *stubs* (also called certificates of participation, beneficial interests, liquidation certificates, revisionary certificates) providing for cash payments resulting from residual values.

Tenders are offers by outsiders or by the company to buy shares at a price usually above that of the market.

Mergers and acquisitions refer to the combination of two or more organizations into a single enterprise. Shareholders of the acquired company may receive securities and possibly cash with values in excess of the value of their original investments.

Appraisal of a security is the consequence of a court action taken by dissident shareholders seeking a better price (fair value) for their securities than that offered in a merger, liquidation, reorganization, or other situation. If successful, the investor may realize a gain measured by the favorable differential between the appraised value and the initially indicated purchase price.

Oversubscriptions are privileges extended to shareholders who have already exercised their stock rights (short-term claims to purchase the issuing corporation's stock) to acquire any remaining unsubscribed shares. A profit may be realized when the market price exceeds the subscription price.

Divestiture refers to a disposition by an organization of a subsidiary, an affiliate, or an operating division. The shares in the new company are distributed to the shareholders of the original corporation as a dividend or in exchange for shares of the distributing corporation. The value of the resulting securities may be greater than that of the securities held prior to the divestiture.

Reorganization is an attempt to salvage a failing company by restructuring its debt and equity components and often by changing its management. Gain is possible since the corporation's securities may have been sold by their holders at panic prices but reemerged after reorganization at higher values.

Recapitalization results from an administered change in the capital structure of the company. Holders of the securities may realize profits as a result of the restructured values of such securities.

While the above listing encompasses classical special situations, the term is sometimes employed in a broader sense to include:

1. Turn-around situations in the prospects of a company resulting from new management, infusion of new capital, or changes in business conditions.
2. Companies benefiting from favorable decisions in legal suits.
3. New product companies.

The present discussion is devoted solely to the classical special situations.

DEVELOPMENT OF A SPECIAL SITUATION

Segments. There are many and varied segments in the time spectrum of a special situation. However, it is convenient to refer to a *preliminary* *phase,* often conducted under considerable secrecy, involving the initial planning and negotiating without formal commitments by the interested parties. Although there have been situations where public announcement of an agreement has been made during this stage, it is more common for such announcement to be made at the beginning of the second stage after the prospective action has been approved in principle by management.

Before the agreement is completed there is a *waiting period* associated with obtaining the approval of interested parties such as directors, shareholders, creditors, the Securities and Exchange Commission, and possibly other federal regulatory agencies. For mergers and acquisitions, a proxy statement setting forth the terms of the agreement must be cleared by the SEC and sent to the shareholders in advance of their meeting to vote on such agreement. Time is also required to obtain an Internal Revenue Service ruling on the tax status of the agreement and to obtain the approval of other affected regulatory agencies. During this period, government agencies or dissident shareholders may resort to court action to prevent execution of the agreement. Further delays may be caused by dissenting stockholders demanding the right of appraisal or cash payments for their shares.

After all approvals have been obtained, the *closing period*—consummation—commences. During this final phase, distributions are made and all necessary administrative procedures are completed.

Timing. After recognizing a special situation, the investor confronts the problem of action and the timing of such action. The possibility for the realization of gain in a special situation is dependent upon individual action preceding market adjustment. That is, the special situation investor must have inside information, anticipate information by means of his analysis, or act during the initial and short period of market adjustment to such information in order to profit from the impending corporate action. Studies indicate that "the stock market is efficient in the sense that stock prices adjust very rapidly to new information."[1] Thus, the special situation investor must recognize it, analyze it, and act on it in a short period of time.

CHARACTERISTICS OF SPECIAL SITUATIONS

Corporate Action. The common thread running through all special situations is corporate action—action affecting capital structure such as mergers and acquisitions, divestitures, liquidations, reorganizations, and recapitalizations. Once corporate action is a reality then, the following characteristics are observable.

[1] Eugene F. Fama, Lawrence Fisher, Michael C. Jensen, and Richard Roll, "The Adjustment of Stock Prices to New Information," *International Economic Review* (February 1969), vol. x, no. 1, pp. 1–21.

1. The capital gain is reasonably calculable.
2. All relevant information is available.
3. The capital gain is not dependent upon the general trend of prices in the securities market.
4. Dividends and interest are of minor significance.
5. A semiautomatic out is usually present. The investor need not make the decision to sell; consummation of the corporate action determines the time of sale.
6. Downside risk is minimal.
7. The corporate action usually has a limited life, thereby increasing the per annum rate of return.

Thus, unlike the ordinary investment where the rate of increase in past earnings, the projection of future earnings, the stage in the cycle of economic development, and the trend in market prices are the decision-making factors, the special situation stock is relatively insulated from general market fluctuations and corporate growth. Special situations are viewed in relation to adequacy of capital gain; this is the determining factor in the purchase decision.

RECOGNITION AND ANALYSIS OF SPECIAL SITUATIONS

Indication. Any corporate action not directed toward operations is a signal to the special situation investor. At first evidence of the action, the investor should classify it as outlined above. After recognition and classification, the special situation candidate is studied and analyzed depending on its classification, as follows:

Balance sheet analysis:

1. Determine book value per share of stock.
2. Determine the working capital.
3. Determine the cash position.
4. Determine the status of the inventory.
5. Determine the value of patents, goodwill, and other intangibles.
6. Ascertain the existence and nature of reserves.
7. Ascertain the existence of contingent liabilities.

Going concern analysis:

1. Ascertain earnings per share.
2. Ascertain total dollar sales.
3. Ascertain the dividend record.
4. Determine depreciation, depletion, and other noncash charges to income.
5. Determine the percentage of each class of outstanding securities to the total capitalization.

The first group of procedures would be undertaken in a liquidation situation; whereas, the second group would be utilized in situations where relative values are relevant—mergers and acquisitions, reorganizations, recapitalizations, appraisals, and divestitures. The line of demarcation between the two groups is fluid, that is, part of the balance sheet analysis may prove useful in an overall appraisal analysis. The information necessary for the aforementioned analyses is available in annual reports, interim reports, proxy statements, company publications, the financial press, trade publications, Securities and Exchange Commission and other federal regulatory agency reports. In addition, public relations and stockholder relations departments and corporate officers are sources of information.

With the foregoing as a base, discussion, analysis, and examples of the various classifications of special situations follows.

LIQUIDATIONS

Description. A liquidation is the process of winding up the affairs of a business by converting its assets into cash, discharging all liabilities, and distributing the remaining cash balance to the securities holders. There is a minimal risk involved in such an investment, and depending on the life of the liquidation, the rate of return may be substantial. The opportunity for large gains exists because of the following:

1. The present investors require the cash for other purposes.
2. The current investors are doubtful of the time required for the consummation of the liquidation. It is this level of doubt which creates the potential for gain. As the liquidation moves toward completion, this potential is reduced.
3. The present investors are unwilling to cope with the technicalities of a liquidation.

Liquidation Classfications. Corporate liquidations are either mandatory or voluntary. Mandatory liquidations are generally the result of bankruptcy proceedings and usually do not offer capital gain prospects. However, in some situations, the underlying asset value of corporate property is greater than its going-concern value. An example of this is the 4 percent, 2007 bonds of the New York, New Haven & Hartford Railroad. While the company was struggling to maintain its status as a going concern, the bonds were priced at approximately 20; however, with the inevitability of bankruptcy, the price of the bonds advanced to over 40. Another example is the liquidation of the Boston & Providence Railroad. Prior to the first payment of $110, the stock could have been purchased at prices between $160 and $220. A subsequent payment of $277 per share was made, and additional payments are anticipated. Another railroad liquidation—that of the Hudson & Manhattan Railroad

Corporation—is discussed in the section on reorganizations. Bankrupt railroads in liquidation offer potential gains to its securities holders.

Voluntary liquidations generally occur for economic reasons—declining sales and earnings. In this situation, a company, on a piecemeal and orderly basis, may sell its assets and ultimately distribute the cash in liquidation. Here again, if the underlying value of the assets exceeds the market value of the company, the alert investor can realize capital gain.

Liquidations may be either complete or partial. The more common is complete in which all assets of the company are distributed to the securities holders and the company ceases to exist. In a partial liquidation, a company disposes of a segment of its business using the funds so obtained to redeem a portion of its outstanding stock. In essence, the company is contracting its business horizons.

Analysis of Prospective Liquidations. Liquidation situations should be analyzed from both its financial and its corporate action aspects. The financial analysis is directed toward locating unrecorded and/or undervalued assets. Most companies expense the costs of obtaining intangibles; therefore, valuable patents, trade names, secret processes, and similar items will not appear on most corporate balance sheets. Under generally accepted accounting principles, assets are recorded at historical costs; therefore, because of inflation, demographic changes, or other environmental changes, certain assets may have market values in excess of book values.

In addition to realistically valuing assets, the financial analysis must ascertain the existence of reserves and contingent liabilities which may have been necessary for a going concern but are no longer appropriate for a business in liquidation. Finally, in accordance with the plan of analysis outlined earlier, working capital must be determined and adjusted book value per share computed in order to ascertain that the indicated liquidation price is commensurate with the values so computed.

In addition to the financial analysis, the corporate action must be analyzed to determine if management has sufficient control to ensure shareholder approval of the plan of liquidation. Generally, if management holds 20 percent to 25 percent of the outstanding stock, it is sufficient to assure approval; however, even with this control, liquidation may be slowed by a stockholder suit.

The tax status of the action should be known. A liquidation under the provisions of section 337 of the Internal Revenue Code requires a capital gains tax at the shareholder level and no tax at the corporate level; whereas, liquidation under the provisions of other sections of the code are subject to different tax consequences. Since the tax status will affect the net proceeds of the investment and therefore the percentage return on such investment, it is essential to know the tax results of such actions.

Existing and potential litigation should be reviewed. Litigation usually benefiting stockholders includes condemnation suits, tax adjustment suits, claims against company officials for insider gains, and the usual commercial suits. Litigation usually detrimental to stockholders includes damage suits, commercial suits, government suits, and union and other suits arising out of the liquidation.

Stubs. Stubs are infrequently used negotiable instruments representing the residual interest of companies in the process of liquidation. Liquidations designed for cash payments lend themselves to the creation of a stub—an instrument offering participation in any future distributions. The objective of this approach is to purchase the security prior to the first distribution at a price below, equal to, or not much above the estimated amount of the first payment in liquidation. Not only will this approach ensure the quick return of the investment, or most of it, it will also make the investor eligible for subsequent distributions. Subsequent distributions will include the proceeds of unrecorded and undervalued assets and funds released because liability reserves have been found excessive. Essentially then, a stub represents unfinished business. In addition to being named stubs, they are also called certificates of participation, certificates of beneficial interest, certificates of contingent interest, liquidation certificates, and revisionary certificates. These are negotiable instruments and are traded in securities markets.

TENDERS

Description. In general terms, a tender offer is a cash or stock bid for a percentage of the outstanding stock of a company on the open market. Tender offers may be classified as follows:

1. A cash offer by the company for its own shares. Its purpose is to acquire stock which will be available for stock options and other general corporate purposes such as acquistions. A not unforeseen result of a successful offer is the increase in earnings per share.
2. An exchange offer whereby one company seeks a minority position or control in another company by means of a stock exchange.
3. A cash take-over bid whereby a group seeking a controlling position in a corporation offers to acquire a percentage of the corporation's outstanding stock for cash at a premium above the current market price.

In recent years, the total value of cash tender offers have increased at a rate in excess of that of stock tenders and presently exceeds the total value of stock tenders.

Characteristics. The tender offer is of limited duration and usually contingent upon the rendering of a specified minimum number of shares. Where this minimum is exceeded, the offerer may either accept or reject such excess, or accept shares tendered on a pro rata basis or on a first-come, first-served basis.

In order to ensure the success of a tender, the offer is made at a premium over the existing market price. Generally speaking, a premium of 20 percent is offered. However, where there is evidence of incumbent management resistance, the premium is higher.

Anticipating a Tender. Since the investor has no opportunity to earn profits subsequent to the public announcement of the offer, he must anticipate such offers. The characteristics of a potential target company usually include some or all of the following:

1. Low price-earnings ratio.
2. A lower or declining rate of earnings as compared to its industry.
3. Excess liquid funds which may ultimately be used to finance the tender.
4. Concentrated share ownership.
5. Asset size. Generally speaking, larger corporations are less vulnerable than small and moderate sized corporations to the tender offer.
6. Minimal stock ownership by management.
7. Substantial cash flows.
8. Undervalued tangible and/or intangible assets.
9. Low debt.
10. Declining dividends.
11. Poor market performance of target corporation's stock.
12. Absence of strong management leadership.

Advantages and Disadvantages. Generally, tenders provide the following advantages:

1. The investor, as a seller, obtains a better price for his securities.
2. The tender contributes to market stability since large blocks of stock may change hands without depressing the market.
3. The trader obtains the potential of a quick trade.
4. There is stability for the one offering the tender and protection against an unwanted stock position since the offer usually specifies a number of shares before it becomes operative.

The disadvantages are:

1. When the securities are deposited in response to a tender, the investor is locked in until expiration date.
2. If none of his tendered stock is accepted, the investor may incur a substantial loss. If part of the tendered stock is accepted, a loss may be incurred on the residual.
3. The principal discloses his objectives.

4. The principal may have to increase the premium—an advantage to the investor, but a disadvantage to the principal.
5. A tender offer may arouse opposition, create a reaction, and generate a costly fight.

Analysis of the Tender. The analysis of a tender offer should provide the investor with the following information.

1. Reason for the tender.
2. Prospective increase in the tender price.
3. Ultimate possibilities of merger.
4. Effect on future earnings per share.
5. Opposition to the tender.
6. The percentage of outstanding securities that will be accepted.
7. Terms of acceptance of tendered shares—on a first-come, first-served basis or on a pro rata basis.

Information to aid the above analysis may be obtained from the proxy statements filed with the Securities and Exchange Commission and the various financial newspapers.

Risks and Rewards. The risks faced by one who invests in stocks to be tendered is twofold.

1. The tender will not be consummated, or he may be late in tendering his shares and none will be accepted.
2. Only a part of his shares will be accepted.

From the time the investor tenders his shares until some time after the expiration date of the tender, the investor is locked in to those shares not accepted. No matter what the course of the market, he cannot sell.

Recently, Cavenham Ltd., London, proposed a tender offer of $19 per share for 51 percent of the outstanding shares of Grand Union Company. Apparently, rumors circulated about the impending offer; trading in Grand Union stock was halted the day prior to the offer after it had gone up to $1.875 a share, closing at $13.125. A day after the tender offer, trading resumed at $15.625 and a few days later went to $16.00 a share. The dilemma facing the investor is the purchase decision at $16 a share; if all tendered shares are not accepted, he might experience a loss on the residual. The investor who had inside information and purchased at $13.125 or less has an easier decision—to sell at $16 or hold until the expiration date, realize $19 on a portion of his shares, and hope the market price after the expiration date will not fall below his purchase price. On the expiration date of the tender, Grand Union closed at $11.375; Cavenham announced acceptance of 61.4 percent of the tendered shares and stated that the shares not accepted will be returned *as soon as possible.* Thus, during this as-soon-as-possible period, the investor was subject to losses he could not minimize. Grand Union, however, hovered at around $12 a share; thus, the investor experienced no additional loss. An investor who acquired Grand Union stock at $16 to participate in the tender suffered an overall loss if he subsequently disposed of his residual shares at $12 per share.

A tender offer which proved profitable to the stockholders was that made for the stock of Gimbel Brothers initially by Loews Corporation and subsequently by Brown & Williamson Corporation. The day before the tender offer by Loews, Gimbel stock reached its low for the year of $12.50 per share and closed for the day at $12.875. The following day Loews proposed a tender offer for 2,650,000 shares at $16 per share. The stock closed at $15.125 and remained at that level for a week, after which Brown & Williamson proposed a 100 percent tender at $23 a share. Under the terms of the tender, Brown & Williamson would not accept or pay for stock until 51 percent of the shares were tendered. Loews accepted the tender offer and permitted those who tendered to them at $16 to back out. Thus, the investor who bought Gimbels one week prior to the Loews' tender doubled his investment in less than two months; an investor who bought after the Loews' tender but before the Brown & Williamson offer realized a 50 percent return on his investment in less than two months.

It should be noted that in both the Grand Union and Gimbel tender offers, management did not contest the offers. Nonetheless, in both cases, the premium was substantial. Finally, the adjustment of the market to the news was too rapid for the investor to gain unless he had anticipated the events, because of analysis or inside information, and therefore acquired stock prior to the public announcement of the offer.

MERGERS AND ACQUISITIONS

Description. In recent years, corporations have pursued growth through internal and external means. External growth is accomplished through corporate mergers and acquisitions. Since the mid 1950's, the United States has been undergoing its third period of mergers—the first occurred between 1898 and 1906, and the second during the 1920's.

An acquisition gives rise to a parent-subsidiary relationship when the acquired company retains its corporate identity subject to the control of the acquiring corporation. In an acquisition of this nature, the parent must merely acquire more than 50 percent of the subsidiary's outstanding stock; however, in order to conform to the consolidated income tax provisions of the Internal Revenue Code, the parent must own at least 80 percent of the subsidiary's outstanding stock.

In a merger, a combination of two corporations is effected by one losing its corporate existence. The surviving company directly or indirectly acquires the assets and assumes the liabilities of the merged company.

Merger Effects. Studies have been conducted to determine the overall effects of mergers and acquisitions. The general conclusions may be summarized by quoting the results of tests conducted by Gort and Hogarty.[2]

1. Mergers, on the average, have an approximately neutral effect on the aggregate worth of firms that participate in them.
2. The owners of acquiring firms lose on the average.
3. The owners of acquired firms gain on the average.

The conclusions of Block's 1968 study of completed mergers relating to gains in the prices of acquired companies' stocks over various time segments may be summarized as follows:[3]

Price Increase	*Acquired Companies*	*Control Group*
9 months to 6 months before announcement	4.34%	3.66%
6 months to 3 months before announcement	1.17	5.06
3 months to 1 month before announcement	3.05	(1.87)
1 month before announcement	17.01	3.08
Announcement to consummation	9.69	0.51

The above results indicate inception of the merger effect on stock prices to be one to three months prior to the merger announcement with the major effect occuring during the month prior to announcement. It would appear, therefore, that either the acquiring corporation is making substantial purchases or that some investors are the beneficiaries of inside information.

An important finding of the study is that the investor can make profits during the period following the announcement; however, during this period there is the possibility of cancellation, in which case there will be a decline in the price of the prospective acquired company's stock comparable to its previous gain.

Procedures for Effecting Mergers. The following are the usual procedures by which a merger or an acquisition is executed.

1. Cash acquisition.
2. Direct offer to exchange securities.
3. Offer by a current holder to existing shareholders for the balance of outstanding stock.

---

[2] Michael Gort and Thomas F. Hogarty, "New Evidence on Mergers," *The Journal of Law and Economics* (April 1970), vol. xiii, no. 2, pp. 167–84.

[3] Stanley B. Block, "The Effect of Mergers and Acquisitions on the Market Value of Common Stock," *The Journal of Finance* (December 1968), vol. xxiii, no. 5, pp. 889–90.

4. Acquisition of a substantial block of stock from insiders combined with an offer on similar terms for the balance from the other shareholders.

It is customary for the managements of the companies involved to agree on an exchange ratio, make the announcement, and then seek approval from the boards of directors and the stockholders at a specified date. Studies indicate that the cash offer or exchange ratio is of such a relationship that on the average a premium is offered of approximately 25 percent above the value three months prior to the announcement.

Analysis. In determining whether to take a position in the stock of the prospective acquired company after the merger announcement or to maintain a position taken prior to such announcement, the investor must consider certain factors.

Impediments to Consummation. Minority shareholders may contest the value attributed to their stock. In order to eliminate such dissent and prevent delay in consummation, the acquiring corporation may increase its offer.

Other corporations desirous of making the same acquisition may present a higher bid. In order to eliminate this competition, the prospective acquirer will have to increase its offer. Thus, certain impediments to consummation may prove beneficial to existing shareholders.

Consummation. Certain impediments may delay or prevent consummation. The investor must determine the chances of these possibilities since such events may substantially reduce or eliminate his gains. Where insiders have in excess of 25 percent of the voting stock of the prospective acquired corporation and they are in favor of the merger, it is not unreasonable to assume successful consummation. Absence of opposition and fairness of offering price are additional indications of successful consummation.

The investor must learn the positions of the Justice Department, Securities and Exchange Commission, Federal Trade Commission, and other regulatory agencies. An unfavorable reaction by such agencies may delay or halt the impending merger; thereby causing a decline in the price of the stock of the acquiree corporation.

The investor must also determine his downside risk. Where he purchased stock of the acquiree prior to the merger announcement, his downside losses are minimal, and where the prospective acquiree has a dividends paying record or a high book value relative to market value, the downside risks are minimal. However, purchase of the acquiree's stock subsequent to announcement creates a situation of considerable downside risk.

Time Spectrum. As was indicated earlier, the anatomy of a merger or acquisition covers the period from three months prior to announcement to consummation. At most points along this spectrum, profits are available with the potential diminishing the closer one moves toward consummation date. Once an investor has taken a position in the stock of the acquiree, he may protect such position by creating a hedge, that is, by selling short the stock of the acquirer. This is demonstrated in a subsequent section.

Anatomy of an Acquisition. One week prior to the announcement by the managements of both companies of the agreed-upon acquisition of Scientific Data Systems, Inc., by Xerox Corporation, the stock of Scientific Data was selling on the New York Stock Exchange for $86.75 per share. During the week, Scientific Data's stock rose $15.25, and at the close of the week, its stock was selling at $100.25 a share. The stock of Xerox Corporation was selling at $268.75 a share. The announcement of agreement in principle indicated the terms of exchange would be one share of Xerox for each two of Scientific Data. Thus, on the day of the announcement, based on prevailing values, the shareholders of Scientific Data were offered a premium of approximately 35 percent. One month later, the boards of directors of both companies approved the plan; the following day Xerox stock sold for $254.375 per share and Scientific Data stock sold for $111 per share. Thus, immediately subsequent to board approval but two months prior to shareholder approval, the purchaser of Scientific Data stock would obtain a premium of approximately 15 percent. As the day of the stockholders' meetings moved closer, the premium narrowed; and two weeks prior to the meetings, Scientific Data stock was selling for $124.50 a share and Xerox stock was selling for $266.25 a share for a premium of approximately 7 percent.

During the early stages of the above acquisition, the Justice Department examined the proposal, and there was, as always, the possibility of disapproval by the directors or by the shareholders. This could have proved harmful to the investor in Scientific Data. As events transpired however, an investor who bought Scientific Data one week before the announcement and sold it the day of approval—15 weeks later—would have realized a gain of approximately 60 percent. At any point during this period the gain could have been protected by means of a hedge—the purchase of 200 shares of Scientific Data and the concurrent short sale of 100 shares of Xerox.

The investor able to identify merger candidates prior to public announcements will do well. Even after the announcement, the opportunity for gain exists; however, in any merger or acquisition situation, there is the possibility of cancellation, in which case, the market price of the stock of the prospective acquired corporation will usually decline.

APPRAISALS

Description. Appraisal situations arise from the rights of stockholders. Generally, the rights are exercised when corporate action is present. The objective of an appraisal is to obtain a better price for a security than that indicated by the pending corporate action. The request for an appraisal provides the dissenter with a vehicle for the exercise of his rights. Thus, when a merger or acquisition is being considered, a stockholder, who believes his shares are worth more than the value placed on them in the merger agreement, may request from the company whose stock he holds "a fair value" for his shares. To obtain a fair value for one's security, it may be necessary to resort to litigation or arbitration.

A request for an appraisal of fair value is the sole area of corporate action initiated by the stockholder. The rights of stockholders are enumerated in corporate charters and laws of the state of incorporation. Procedures for instituting an appraisal of fair value are noted in prospectuses, in security indentures, and in notices of meetings.

Applicable Situations. A request for an appraisal of fair value is made when a corporate change may create a stockholder loss. The following are situations where such a request should be considered.

1. A merger, acquisition, reorganization, or recapitalization in which an exchange of securities reduces the stockholder's voting strength.
2. Loss of convertibility of a security.
3. Elimination of cumulative voting.
4. Elimination of dividend rights.

Risks. In requesting an appraisal of fair value, the stockholder is subject to certain risks.

1. Courts are inclined to accept the market value of the stock at the date of the corporate action or the average market value over a period of time as an indication of fair value. This may be less than the company's appraisal.
2. Loss of control of securities since they cannot be sold until the claim has been settled unless the defending company agrees to a withdrawal of the appraisal request.
3. A slow court procedure aided by delaying tactics of the company will create a locked-in securities position, thereby exposing one to potential losses.
4. The cost of litigation may be high; however, it may be possible to combine forces with other dissenters thereby reducing ones litigation cost and strengthening the overall negotiating position. Generally, requests for appraisal of fair value are resolved by means of an out-of-court settlement.

Estimation of Fair Value. In view of the risks involved and the fact that agreement may be negotiated, the one requesting the appraisal should first estimate the fair value of the security in order to determine if the possible gain from such action is worth the enumerated risks. In estimating fair value, the stockholder should consider:

1. The long-term earnings record.
2. The quality of such earnings.
3. The status of the company in the industry and the status of the industry in the economy.
4. The book value of the security.
5. The possibility of unrecorded assets.
6. The comparative voting rights under existing and proposed conditions.
7. The relative position in the capital structure of the old and the new securities.

When a security holder requests an appraisal of fair value, he is obligated to sell his security at the appraised price; therefore, it is essential that the holder undertake an extensive analysis of the company prior to submitting such request.

OVERSUBSCRIPTIONS

Description. An oversubscription is a unique trading special situation which may exist in current portfolios. It is a bonus privilege extended to stockholders who have already participated in a rights offering. Rights exist in three distinct stages in the following order:

1. The shareholder is offered the privilege of purchasing additional shares of stock in the company. The privilege is represented by rights wherein each share of stock receives one right representing a pro rata interest in the additional shares.
2. The stockholder is permitted to subscribe to a sufficient additional number of fractional shares to round out his holdings to one full share.
3. The stockholders who exercised their rights are offered the opportunity to purchase on a pro rata basis any unsubscribed remaining shares at the subscription price.

The third stage, the additional privilege, represents the oversubscription right.

Situation. Most rights offerings are underwritten by an investment syndicate, thereby eliminating the possibility of the oversubscription privilege. Some companies, however, bypass the underwriter and offer the rights directly to their shareholders. In a situation of this nature, the oversubscription privilege arises. Recently, American Electric Power Company announced plans for a rights offering of 7 million shares of its common stock. Under the terms of the plan, each stockholder will receive the right to purchase 1 new share for every 10 shares held. Any unsubscribed shares may be purchased by those shareholders who initially exercise their rights. This right to purchase the unsubscribed shares is the oversubscription privilege.

Reward. Profits in an oversubscription are created by means of the spread between the market price of the security and the subscription price. Rights generally afford the holder the opportunity to subscribe to shares of stock at a price below the market; the oversubscription privilege merely expands this opportunity.

The opportunity for gain in an oversubscription privilege is illustrated by the following example.

A company having 100,000 shares outstanding at a market price of $20 a share plans to sell an additional 10,000 shares at $18 a share by means of a rights offering; therefore, each share is entitled to receive a right to subscribe to one tenth of a share of stock. Each right therefore has a value of $.20 ($20 − $18 ÷ 10). If, by the expiration of the offering period, only 9,000 shares have been subscribed for, there will be a residual of 1,000 shares. The 1,000 shares are subject to the oversubscription privilege, and it is with these 1,000 shares that profits may be generated.

An investor who had purchased, in the open market, 1,000 rights would have paid $.20 a right, or $200. If, at the same time, the investor sold 100 shares at the market price, he would realize no gain or loss when he exercised his 1,000 rights and delivered the previously sold 100 shares. Since the investor exercised the rights, he would then be able to subscribe, pro rata, to the 1,000 unsubscribed shares, and since this right would carry no cost, his gain would be the difference between the market price of the stock—$20—and the subscription price of $18.

Analysis of an Oversubscription. In addition to the normal financial analysis, the investor must determine the price stability of the stock in an oversubscription situation. Since the opportunity for gain lies in the oversubscription period and in the spread between market and subscription prices, it is essential that the market price remain above the subscription price. Where the underlying stock has had a substantial price rise prior to the rights offering and the company's earnings are of doubtful quality, the spread between market and subscription prices may not hold. An additional consideration is the marketability of such shares. Since, in an ideal oversubscription situation there is a simultaneous purchase of rights and sale of stock followed by a subsequent and immediate sale of the shares making up the oversubscription, easy marketability must exist. With marketability and price stability, the oversubscription is a situation creating an opportunity for short-term trading gains.

DIVESTITURES

Description. The merger wave of the late fifties and the sixties, as discussed previously, created the environment for corporate divestitures which developed during the late sixties. A divestment is the process of eliminating a portion of the enterprise; it takes place when there is a disposal of company assets and discontinuance of the activity associated with those assets.

Classification. Divestments may be either voluntary or involuntary. An involuntary divestiture results from a court decision involving anti-trust legislation. Procter & Gamble's divestment of Clorox was an example of a court ordered divestiture. The divestment may be agreed upon prior to court action as was the case with International Telephone & Telegraph (ITT) and certain of its subsidiaries.

A divestiture is voluntary when the decision and control are in the hands of management. Divestitures of this nature occur as part of the evolutionary development of the corporation or to eliminate divisions generating losses or minimum profits. General Electric divests itself of small, potentially profitable divisions as part of its corporate strategy. In the early seventies, Ling-Temco-Vought (LTV) and other conglomerates divested themselves of some unsatisfactory acquisitions of the sixties.

Rewards. Capital gain potential exists because the investment in the subsidiary may be undervalued on the books of the parent and favorable future earnings growth is projected. An example of how a divestiture operates was the tax-free distribution by J. Ray McDermott Company of one of its subsidiaries—Transocean Oil.

When J. Ray McDermott distributed 0.88 shares of Transocean for each share of J. Ray McDermott, its stock was selling at $32 per share. Nine months later, J. Ray McDermott stock was selling at $36 per share and Transocean Oil stock was selling at $16 per share. Thus, in a period of nine months, the investment increased in excess of 60 percent —a full year's return exceeding 75 percent.

Analysis of Divestitures. There are four areas for capital gain potential. They are:

1. Shares of the parent prior to divestiture.
2. Shares of the subsidiary when such shares are traded on a when-issued basis.
3. Shares of the subsidiary subsequent to the divestiture.
4. Shares of the parent subsequent to the divestiture.

Any analysis must be made from these four reference points. For example, when Procter & Gamble divested itself of Clorox, it was accomplished by an exchange of stock whereby an alert investor could have realized substantial gains by acquiring the stock of the parent. Pursuant to a Supreme Court decision, Procter & Gamble divested itself of Clorox in two steps. As a first step, it sold 15 percent of its investment to the public; five months later its president indicated to shareholders that sometime within the ensuing seven months they would be given the opportunity to exchange their Procter & Gamble stock for shares of Clorox. He further stated, "Exchange offers of this kind usually carry with them a premium which makes them attractive." On the date of the announcement, Procter & Gamble shares were selling for $89.375 per share and Clorox shares were selling for $28.625 a share. Less than two months later, Procter & Gamble announced it would exchange its 6.8 million shares of Clorox for its own outstanding stock at a rate of 3.95 to 1. Based on the previous day's closing prices, this exchange rate represented a premium of 18 percent. Three days after the announcement, Procter and Gamble stock was selling at $98.25 per share, up almost $9 a share from its price nine weeks earlier when the president initially announced the divestment plans. Thus, a purchase on the announcement would have generated substantial profits. After the exchange ratio was announced, it would have been advisable to sell the Procter and Gamble stock. By the expiration date, 5.9 million shares of Procter & Gamble were tendered rather than the 1.7 million shares required; therefore, on a pro rata basis 29 percent of the Procter & Gamble shares tendered were exchanged for Clorox stock and the balance ultimately returned. Within one week after the expiration date, the stock of Procter & Gamble was selling at a price below that prevailing on the day of the initial announcement ten weeks earlier.

In analyzing the potential results of a divestiture, the segregation of prior years' earnings of the subsidiary is of prime importance. In this way, future earnings of the subsidiary and the parent can be projected. In recent years, with the development of segmented reporting, this information is reasonably attainable. In addition, the unit to be spun off must be analyzed from the point of working capital adequacy and capital structure with specific attention to the extent and nature of the long-term debt. An analysis of the subsidiary's management is advisable. If the management is transferred in tact, there will be no loss of income or time in pursuing a similar or a new corporate direction. As with all special situations, the tax status of the divestiture should be known since this will be one factor in determining the extent of one's investment and ultimate gain. The attractiveness of the Clorox divestiture was that the exchange was tax free, and the prior management team remained and took an equity position in the company.

REORGANIZATIONS

Description. Most special situations involve companies considered to be going concerns, that is, it is assumed that they are and will continue to be viable business entities. However, during times of general economic stress, or at other times, a corporation may experience adverse conditions whereby it becomes increasingly difficult for it to meet obligations as they mature. In order to ease the pressure of financial stress and prevent its liquidation, the corporation may undertake a reorganization. A reorganization involves efforts to maintain the viability of the corporation by means of adjusting its capital structure, reducing or eliminating its fixed charges, and extending the time and reducing the amount of its matured obligations.

Bankruptcy Act. Reorganizations of industrial companies are governed by the provisions of Chapters X and XI of the Federal Bankruptcy Act. Under Chapter X, a court-appointed trustee operates the business during reorganization, whereas under Chapter XI, the current company management, under court supervision, guides the corporation through its reorganization. Railroad reorganizations are governed by Section 77 of the Bankruptcy Act and the Mahaffie Act of 1948, with an active role being played by the Interstate Commerce Commission.

Effects. The effect of a reorganization is to reduce existing financial pressures; the method is a capital restructuring which involves:

1. An extension of maturities.
2. An exchange of junior debt for stock.
3. An exchange of senior debt for junior debt and/or stock.

Reorganization brings new shares to the market representing a company unburdened of oppressive debt and the accompanying fixed charges.

Since a reorganization represents a fresh start for a corporation, investors view the future differently than they did prior to reorganization. However, many investors of the old corporation either do not wish to continue their investment or wish to establish capital losses for income tax purposes. Thus, those who wish to get out are prepared to dispose of their interests at a substantial loss, and it is at this point that the potential for gain is established.

Analysis. Investing in a reorganization may be initiated prior to the proposal of a plan or while the plan is pending approval. Investing prior to the submission of a proposed plan should be analyzed from the viewpoint of underlying asset values. The theory behind this analysis is that a company may not be a viable business entity and may therefore be of greater value dead than as a going concern. Companies of this nature usually have senior securities that will fare better if the company is liquidated than if it survives. An example of this is the Hudson & Manhattan Corporation—a combination real estate and commuter railroad company. During its reorganization period its adjustment bonds could have been acquired for around 20—$200 per $1,000 bond. Each bond was subsequently exchanged for 3½ shares of class B stock. The reorganization developed into a liquidation when the corporation's properties were seized by a quasi-public agency—the New York Port Authority—in condemnation proceedings. Ten years later, each class B shareholder received $372.50 as the initial liquidation distribution. Thus, a $200 investment realized $1,303 ten years later. Subsequent liquidation distributions amounted to $28.12 per share, or $98.00 per original bond. Hence, a $200 investment returned $1,400 in liquidation. If the investor had retained his investment over the long liquidation period, his return was substantial.

Procedure. In seeking out and analyzing a reorganization situation, the following procedures are recommended.

1. Seek out possible reorganizations.
   a. Is there a default in interest and/or preferred dividend accruals?
   b. Are there continuous losses from operations?
   c. Is there an erosion of working capital?
2. Determine the prospects of undervalued assets and unrecorded tax refunds.
3. Prepare earnings projections of the reorganized company giving effect to the relief from heavy interest expenses.
4. Ascertain which of the old securities have a current value. In a reorganization there is a distinct possibility that former common shareholders will receive very little or nothing.
5. Ascertain the discount between the old and the new securities.
6. Estimate the consummation period of the plan of reorganization.
7. Determine the existence of opposition to the proposed plan either from regulatory authorities or from current creditors.

Although difficult to ascertain candiates for bankruptcy reorganizations, recent studies indicate a relationship between deteriorating financial ratios and ultimate bankruptcy. The trend of certain liquidity ratios and rates of return serve to alert the investor to bankruptcy possibilities up to five years prior to the event.[4]

Merger. At times, a company will attempt to avoid bankruptcy by means of a merger. For the acquiring company, the benefits of a potentially bankrupt company come from tax loss carry-forwards, sales diversification by both product and customer, trained work force, and efficient and valuable assets. An example of this was the Douglas Aircraft Company-McDonnell merger. In order to avoid impending disaster, Douglas sought the merger. Under the terms of the agreement, Douglas stockholders received 1¾ shares of McDonnell for each of their shares. On the date prior to the merger approval, Douglas shares were selling for $45.25 per share and McDonnell for $32.00 per share—a premium of approximately 25 percent for Douglas stockholders. On the day of approval the premium was approximately 30 percent. Not only did the merger prevent the bankruptcy of Douglas, it also provided gains to its shareholders.

---

[4] Edward I. Altman, "Financial Ratios, Discriminant Analysis and the Prediction of Bankruptcy," *The Journal of Finance* (September 1968), vol. xxiii, no. 4, pp. 589–609; William Beaver, "Financial Ratios as Predictors of Failure," *Empirical Research in Accounting: Selected Studies, 1966,* supplement to *Journal of Accounting Research,* 1966, pp. 71–111.

Opportunities exist for realizing gains from the securities of insolvent companies undergoing reorganization or attempting to avoid reorganization. The investor must estimate the time involved in completing the reorganization, the intrinsic value of the underlying assets, and the projected future earnings after relief has been granted from the heavy burden of debt.

RECAPITALIZATIONS

Description. A recapitalization is a corporate action taking place within the corporate structure. A recapitalization is used to eliminate conflicts between different classes of stock, remove impediments to dividends, and generally correct unbalanced capital structures.

Conditions indicating the possibility of a recapitalization are:

1. The accumulation of preferred dividends and/or certain bond interest.
2. Outstanding securities carrying high dividend or interest rates.
3. Capital structures burdened by excessive securities of a single issue.

Some of the benefits sought by recapitalization are:

1. Avoidance of bankruptcy and the emergence from financial problems.
2. Rearrangement of capital structure, possibly in anticipation of prospective mergers and acquisitions.
3. Improvement of corporate credit.
4. Attainment of a tax advantage by the substitution of debt for preferred stock, since interest is a tax deductible expense whereas preferred dividends are not.

There is a conflict between (3) and (4), since improving corporate credit by the issuance of preferred stock for debt will replace the tax deductible interest payment with the nontax deductible dividend payment.

Procedure. A recapitalization is initiated by the board of directors and is subject to the approval of the stockholders. Recapitalizations take the following forms:

1. The issuance of a new class of securities in exchange for an old class.
2. The issuance of new securities and cash in exchange for old securities.
3. Issuance of a new class of securities in payment of accumulated interest and dividends.

Analysis. In an analysis of the proposed recapitalization, the investor should consider the following:

1. Prospective corporate earnings after the recapitalization.
2. Effect on credit and the ability to meet fixed charges after the recapitalization.
3. The dilution and loss of priority status of the old securities.
4. The rights and privileges of the new securities.

In analyzing a recapitalization, the investor should also be cognizant of the reasons for such action. This may be indicative of subsequent long-run complications. Some recapitalizations serve to forestall but not prevent ultimate bankruptcy; whereas others serve to eliminate genuine conflicts between different classes of securities holders. An example of the latter was the recapitalization of the Missouri Pacific Railroad Corporation. In order to eliminate a long-standing conflict between the company's different classes of stock, the shareholders approved a plan of recapitalization under the terms of which each share of class B stock would be converted into 16 shares of new common stock and $850 in cash. Each share of class A stock would be exchanged for one share of new $5 cumulative preferred stock with conversion privileges. Six months later, the ICC approved the plan of recapitalization. At the close of the month of shareholder approval, the class A stock had a market price of $71.75; six months later, after execution of the exchange, the new preferred stock was selling for $85.00 per share.

The holders of the class B stock, although few in number, encountered an even more fortuitous situation. At the time of shareholder approval of the recapitalization, class B stock was selling for approximately $1,800 a share; six months later, the Mississippi River Corporation, a major corporate shareholder of Missouri Pacific, made a cash tender offer for 400,000 shares of the new common stock at $100 per share. Thus, an investment of $1,800 immediately after stockholder approval would have been converted into $2,450—16 shares at $100 a share plus $850—six months later.

Recapitalizations are executed through exchange of securities, cash payments, or package offers; therefore, capital gain opportunities are found in both old and new issues. Comparative analysis of old and new capitalizations reveals estimated values for new securities upon which capital gain potentials are based. Since recapitalizations may influence more than one security in a corporate structure, participating by purchasing a package deal is a procedure to be considered.

CONCLUSION

As previously noted, the stock market adjusts rapidly to new information. Where the investor can anticipate this new information in a special situation, the potential for gain is substantial. On the other hand, where anticipation is not possible, speed of action is essential, since an entry into the situation early in the market adjustment process provides the investor with the opportunity for moderate gains. Locating an appropriate special situation has been demonstrated to be a difficult matter requiring painstaking and thorough analysis; profiting from such a situation requires early action. There are risks involved in special situations; however, the potential gain is sufficient to justify undertaking such risks.

17

Warrants and Options

DANIEL TUROV
Warrant and Convertible Securities Analyst
Thomson & McKinnon Auchincloss Kohlmeyer, Inc.
New York, New York

The core of the equity market is common stock, and as time has passed, a greater variety of options to obtain that common stock have evolved.

TYPES OF STOCK OPTIONS

There are essentially four such types of options. *Executive compensation options* are an ever-expanding field and include numerous different ways of rewarding executives for helping the corporation to prosper. In theory, at least, if the executives perform well, the company will flourish, and the stock will advance giving the executive a bonus for his work. These options are essentially nontraded warrants which are given by the company to the employee rather than purchased by him. A great deal of analysis can and has been done on these vehicles, but since they have no trading market, they will not be discussed here.

The second type of important option is the *call option.* A call is an option written by a broker or investor granting the buyer the right to purchase a specified number of shares at a specific price for a given time. In actuality, the seller of a call option need not own the stock on which he is selling the call, but can sell it "naked"; if the stock is called from him, he will have to purchase or borrow the stock for delivery. Calls and kindred artificial options will be discussed in greater detail later in this chapter.

Rights (also called preemptive rights) are short-term options to acquire a new issue granted to existing stockholders by the corporation. They also will be dealt with later.

The most important type of option, in that it offers the greatest investment and speculative opportunities, is the *warrant.* A full understanding of warrants can not only be beneficial in its own right, but the mode of their analysis can be used in studying other types of options.

By definition, a warrant is an option, issued by a corporation, granting the buyer the right to purchase a number of shares (usually one) of its common stock at a given exercise price for a given period of time. Occasionally, a company will issue warrants to purchase shares of stock which it owns in a different corporation. For example, Northern Natural Gas issued warrants for the purchase of its Mobil Oil shares, and Cities Service offered warrants for the purchase of its Atlantic Richfield holdings. Note that a *warrant* is written by a corporation, usually on its own stock, whereas a *call* is written by a broker or investor.

Warrants have gotten a bad reputation twice in this century, once in the 1930s when they were issued in an attempt to placate irate shareholders of companies which went bankrupt when the market collapsed, and again in the late 1960s when they were extensively issued by conglomerates. Despite these abuses, their strong basic appeal have kept warrants very much alive. Within the last several years such respected companies as B. F. Goodrich, Chrysler, and American Telephone and Telegraph, among others, have issued warrants.

Warrants' greatest usage in the 1960s were as so-called sweeteners to mergers and acquisitions. In the 1970s they have been issued more frequently attached to an underwritten bond or stock issue to make the deal more saleable. Giving a warrant along with a bond permits the investor to participate in the growth of a company. In rare cases, such as with Ward Foods and UV Industries, they were given to shareholders as a dividend. In equally rare cases, such as Ryder Systems, they were underwritten as an entity unto itself. In a related vein, warrants have also been issued via a rights offering to shareholders, as with the Gulf and Western-Atlantic Richfield warrants.

There are two advantages to a corporation in issuing warrants. The first is obvious, i.e., as an aid in a merger or financing. The second is less appreciated. In hard times, when a company is in great need of funds, the market for secondary financings is usually quite tight and a public financing may be next to impossible. However, if the company has a warrant outstanding it may be able to force a financing. For example, say that as the expiration date approaches, the stock is selling at $22 a share and the warrant has an exercise price of $20. Clearly, at any fractional price of the common above $20 sufficient to cover commissions, the warrants will be exercised. The company would obtain a large amount of cash without the expense of an underwriting. But even if the stock is below the exercise price, at say $15, the company has an alternative to letting the warrant expire worthless. It could, for example, lower the exercise price to $10 for a short period of time to encourage a large amount of the warrants to be exercised. True, the $10 is only two thirds of the market price, but if the secondary market is tight, it is an alternative which may be better than no new funding at all.

In an effort to protect short sellers, the American and New York Stock Exchanges have a policy of forbidding the reduction of the exercise price of listed warrants. However, this can be circumvented by a desperate company either by requesting the delisting of its warrant there or by making a tender to shareholders offering to exchange a $10 exercise price warrant for the outstanding $20 exercise price ones. The mere threat of doing this might force the exchange to change its stand; the American Stock Exchange has already backed down from its position against allowing the extension of warrants' life spans. The most important point of the preceding, and the reason it was belabored despite its limited importance in actual practice, is to demonstrate that warrants can offer great flexibility from several vantage points including the investor's, and the company's at the time of public offering, as well as to the company at a later date.

A major disadvantage to a company with warrants outstanding is that they dilute earnings per share. Though this may affect the stock price, it only affects the company in a secondary way, i.e., a lower price/earnings multiple at the time of the next public financing. A more important disadvantage to the company is that if the corporation does well, with the stock advancing from say $20 to $80, the warrants will be exercised for only $20 when a secondary distribution could have yielded a price of $75 to $80. In truth though, an ingenuitive board of directors could somewhat temper the effects of this by offering to exchange a longer lived warrant with a higher exercise price in exchange for the existing one. This would allow the warrant holders to continue to participate in the growth of the company for several additional years without having to come up with the cash necessary to exercise at the present.

Of what importance is this to the practicing analyst? Mainly, it has been presented to demonstrate the tremendous flexibility that warrants can offer. But now let us examine warrants from the warrant holders' point of view.

Investors buy warrants because of leverage; the expectation that the warrant will show a greater precentage appreciation than the common. If, for instance, XYZ is selling at $20 and there is an outstanding warrant which allows the purchase of one share over a five-year period at an exercise price of $10, theoretically the warrant should sell for $10. However, if the stock doubled to $40, the warrant would now be worth (have an intrinsic value of) $30, or triple its former price. An investment of $10 in the warrant would yield as much of a profit as an investment of $20 in the stock (ignoring dividends). Since this leverage is desirable in a rising stock, the warrant has added appeal and investors willingly bid for it, paying $11, $12, and perhaps as high as $15 for it. Even paying

$15 for the warrant, a 50 percent premium over its intrinsic worth, would fare the speculator no worse than purchase of the stock at $20, and he would do better than the common shareholder if the stock advanced above $40.

What about the warrant with no intrinsic value? Assume an exercise price of $20 on the warrant, a stock price of $15, and a warrant price of $5. Clearly, the warrant has no current intrinsic worth. In fact, even if the stock rose 5 points, the warrant would have no intrinsic value, and a 10-point move on the stock would for the first time make the warrant worth its $5 price tag. But what if the stock tripled to $45 a share. The warrants would then have an intrinsic worth of $25 (45–20) or five times their current worth. So, clearly, a premium on a warrant is very much in order and is readily paid by investors who are bullish on the stock. Furthermore, in both cases, we have assumed that when the stock advanced, the warrant only rose to its new intrinsic value. In actuality, its price might well be two or three points higher, and it still would demonstrate leverage over the common if the latter continued to rise.

Of course, leverage is a two-edged sword. In our second example the stock tripled from $15 to $45, and the warrant advanced fivefold from $5 to $25. Negative leverage can be seen three ways from the following example. If the stock price stayed constant as the warrant reached expiration, the warrant would show a 100 percent loss and expire worthless. Even if the common had advanced from $15 to $20 during this period of time, the warrant would show a 100 percent loss! Looking at the matter from the other point of view, if the warrant were purchased at its intrinsic value when the stock was $45, and the stock then declined 67 percent to $15, the warrant would decline 80 percent to $5. It might even fall below $5 since now it has less time before expiration.

WARRANT LEVERAGE RATIO

There are several different ways of measuring leverage. The first is by estimating a future price for the common and then determining what the warrant's intrinsic value will be at that point. This is essentially what we have done in the previous examples. From this, we can next arrive at the concept of a leverage ratio. There are two concepts of how to arrive at a correct measurement of the leverage ratio. This writer prefers the constant leverage ratio concept which asks in essence, "If the stock doubles, what will the warrant do?" To answer the question, an estimate is made (as discussed later) of the future price of the warrant (at a not too distant time period) including both the intrinsic value and the estimated premium. If this warrant price is triple the current warrant price, then the leverage ratio would be two to one (representing a 200 percent advance for the warrant on a 100 percent move for the common).

The second method of measuring leverage ratios employs the concept of a variable ratio. If the warrant advances 30 percent for a 10 percent move in the stock then the leverage ratio is 3 to 1. But if the warrant advances 50 percent on a 20 percent move in the stock, the leverage ratio is 2.5 to 1. In essence, with a variable leverage ratio, the same warrant can have a different ratio for each different percentage move anticipated for the common. Some analysts refer to the variable leverage ratio as the leverage indicator, but we would prefer to reserve that name for another ratio to be discussed shortly.

Occasionally, as a variation on the preceding, an analyst will calculate a constant ratio based on a warrant gain or decline of either 25 percent or 50 percent and derive the ratio from relative performance to these numbers. It should furthermore be clear that since warrants normally decline further than their underlying common in bear markets, that there is negative leverage on the downside. It then becomes possible to establish a leverage index. For example, if a warrant has a positive leverage ratio of 2:1 and a downside leverage ratio of 1.5:1, then the warrant has a leverage index of 4:3 or 1.33:1, making for a favorable risk/reward ratio, all other things being equal.

The leverage ratio, *L*, in general is given by the formula

$$L = \left(\frac{W_2 - W_1}{W_1}\right) \Big/ \left(\frac{S_2 - S_1}{S_1}\right),$$

where: S_1 is the current price of the stock.
W_1 is the current price of the warrant.
S_2 is the expected price of the stock.
W_2 is the expected price of the warrant when the stock sells at S_2.

The *constant leverage ratio* is obtained from the above by assuming that the stock price doubles so that $S_2 = 2S_1$, hence,

$$L = \frac{W_2 - W_1}{W_1},$$

where W_2 is now the expected price of the warrant when the common has doubled in value.

If the stock pays a dividend, *D*, during the time the warrant is held, then the leverage ratio (which is a measure of the return to be expected from holding the warrant as compared to that of holding the common) is in general:

$$L = \left(\frac{W_2 - W_1}{W_1}\right) \Big/ \left[\left(\frac{S_2 - S_1}{S_1}\right) + \frac{D}{S_1}\right],$$

or for the *constant leverage case:*

$$L = \left(\frac{W_2 - W_1}{W_1}\right) \Big/ (1 + Y),$$

where $Y = \frac{D}{S_1}$, the dividend yield during the holding period. It is evident that other things being equal, the dividend will decrease the leverage.

Example. The common stock of XYZ corporation is selling for $10 (at the exercise price) and the warrant, at $4. If the stock doubles over a period of one year so that it sells at $20, and if it is assumed that the warrant then trades at $12, the constant leverage ratio would be (neglecting the dividends)

$$L = \frac{12.00 - 4.00}{4.00} = 2.00.$$

If the stock pays a 5 percent dividend during the year, the constant leverage ratio would be

$$L = \frac{2.00}{1.05} = 1.90.$$

It is important to note from the above formula that the constant leverage ratio decreases as the stock price ratio (S/E) increases. Thus, when (S/E) is 0.5, from Table 1 (page 471) below we see that W/E is 0.414. If the stock price doubles so that S/E is 1.00, then normal (W/E) is 1.24. Hence,

$$L = \frac{(W_2/E) - (W_1/E)}{(W_1/E)} = \frac{1.24 - 0.414}{0.414} = 2.02$$

However, if the stock is selling above the exercise price, say at $(S/E) = 1.2$, so that the normal (W/E) is 0.562, when the stock doubles, (S/E) is 2.40 and the normal (W/E) is 1.60. The leverage ratio would then be reduced to 1.85.

When a warrant is convertible into other than one share, it is convenient to adjust both the price of the warrant and the exercise price by dividing these quantities by the number of shares which would be obtained on converting the warrant, so that all the values are on a single share basis.

Another way of measuring leverage is via the leverage indicator. This is a simple and greatly overused device. It represents the number of warrants that could be purchased with the same common stock dollar. For example, if a stock is at $40 and the warrant at $1, then the leverage indicator is 40 to 1. The fact that the warrant may be expiring tomorrow or that the exercise price is $500 a share does not matter; it is a simple ratio between the common price and the warrant price. Unfortunately, this is the only ratio that many unsophisticated speculators look at. On the other hand, warrants with very high leverage indicators, but not so attractive constant leverage ratios, have put in some of the truly spectacular performances in the history of the warrant market. But a good deal more has undoubtedly been lost by placing too much importance on this figure.

Perhaps because so many warrant analysts studied convertible bonds (where percentage premiums are the most important measurement), they feel that calculating percentage premiums for warrants is also important. Warrant premiums can be calculated in several ways. Assume an exercise price of $25, a stock price of $30, and a warrant price of $15. The most accepted method of calculating the percentage premium would say the intrinsic value is $5 and therefore the premium is $10, or 33 percent (10/30). The premium is expressed as a percentage of the stock's price. The greatest controversy in calculating percentage premiums arises when the warrant has a negative intrinsic value. For example, assume an exercise price of $25, a stock price of $20, and a warrant price of $10. The warrant has an intrinsic value of minus $5. What is the premium? It is the entire warrant price, $10. Ten dollars as a percentage of the stock price of $20 equals a 50 percent premium. Other analysts say, no, the premium is $15, which includes both the $10 actual warrant price and the minus $5 intrinsic worth. Fifteen dollars as a percentage of $20 yields a percentage premium figure of 75 percent. Which calculation is correct?

It is a question which presents a philosophical dichotomy. The first type of calculation correctly takes the position that an intrinsic value can be negative but a premium cannot be. This is so since the intrinsic value is a theoretic calculative number, but a premium is what an investor actually pays, in cash, for the warrant over and above not the intrinsic value, but the intrinsic value subject to a minimum of zero (known as the conversion value). Unfortunately, the number arrived at using this method is totally unsatisfactory since proper calculation of a percentage premium should give us a number which represents the percentage amount that the stock has to rise to be at a level at which the warrant, at its current price, would be selling without premium. Illustrating with previous example, the stock would have to rise 75 percent (not 50 percent) from $20 to $35 for the warrant to have an intrinsic value of $10, its now current price. So despite the fact that it is perhaps less theoretically correct, the second method of calculation is far superior in results and, as such, should be the one used.

Even so, of what great value is it to know that if the stock advances 75 percent that the warrant would be selling at intrinsic value if it did not advance—for surely, unless the warrant was to expire the next day, it would certainly have a premium? More helpful is the use of an appreciation factor, which can represent the number of times the stock must appreciate for the warrant to have a value on expiration (i.e., without premium) representing the same percentage amount of appreciation. Such a factor is equal to the exercise price of the warrant divided by the current price of the stock, minus the current price of the warrant. In letters, this is: $f = e/(s - w)$. It should be noted that when the number of shares a warrant can purchase is not one, both the exercise and the warrant prices must be divided by the number of shares which the warrant buys.[1] This is not only true with this formula, but with the calculation of all warrant ratios.

[1] Daniel Turov, "Stock or Warrant?" *Barron's*, March 9, 1970.

Let us see how this formula works, using as an example a hypothetical warrant which allows the purchase of two shares of common for a total of $100 for the next five years. Let us further assume the stock is selling at $45 a share and each warrant is trading at $10. The adjusted warrant price would be $5 and the adjusted exercise price, $50. The formula is: $f = 50/(45 - 5) = 1.25$. This means that if the stock advances by 25 percent over current levels by expiration, the warrant must perform at least as well. If by less than 25 percent, the warrant on expiration will have advanced less than that amount, although if the 25 percent level was reached prior to expiration (i.e., when the warrant would still be expected to trade at a premium), the warrant could still have outperformed the equity. If, on expiration, the common advances by more than 25 percent, the warrant *must* outperform the stock (since not to would mean the warrant would be below intrinsic value or parity, and arbitragers would not allow that to happen for long).

Does this prove out with actual prices? First, 1.25 times the current price of $45 translates into $56.25. At $56.25 for the common, each adjusted warrant would have an intrinsic worth of $6.25 (i.e., $56.25 – $50.00), and hence each actual warrant would be worth twice that, or $12.50—which is exactly 1.25 times its current price of $10!

One criticism of the formula is that it does not consider the effect of dividends the common pays. The previous formula can be adjusted to consider the effect of dividends, however.[2] The dividend adjusted appreciation factor is $(e + d/s - w) - (d/s)$, where d equals the total expected amount (in dollars) that the common will pay by expiration. In actuality, the dividend effect is quite small and the adjusted factor need only be used in the case of very high dividend paying stocks where the warrant has many years before expiration. Further adjustments in the formula can be made for rising dividends, reinvestment of dividends, and so on, but they really add nothing to the analyst's ability to evaluate the warrant. Probably the greatest use of the appreciation factor is that it enables an analyst to evaluate a warrant quickly. If, for example, the factor is 1.2, the warrant is reasonably priced if it has two years to run; if it is 6.0, it is overpriced regardless of the terms. Familiarity with the formula's use will give the analyst a feel for the factors quickly.

WARRANT VERSUS STOCK PRICES

So far we have discussed at length the different ways of measuring leverage, but we have not answered the crucial question, "If the stock advances x percent what will the warrant do?"

Before we can answer this question however, a judgment must be made as to the relative current price reasonableness. In other words, how close to a statistical norm is the warrant currently trading. This is

[2] Daniel Turov, "Dividend Paying Stocks and Their Warrants," *Financial Analysts Journal,* March–April 1973.

important because, generally speaking, overvalued warrants tend to stay overvalued, and undervalued warrants tend to stay undervalued over the short term, except in the case of major price moves.

One of the most accurate normal value formula to date is that developed by Sheen Kassouf and is the following:[3]

$$y = (X^z + 1)^{1/z} - 1,$$

where:

$z = 1.307 + 5.355/T + 14.257R + 0.298D + 1.015 \log(X/\bar{X}) + 0.405x.$
$y =$ Predicted price of adjusted warrant/adjusted exercise price.
$X =$ Price of common stock.
$x = X/$adjusted exercise price.
$\bar{X} =$ Mean of previous 11-month high-low average.
$T =$ Months remaining before expiration.
$R =$ Annual stock dividend$/X$.
$D =$ (Number of new shares if all options are exercised) $\div$ (Number of outstanding common shares).
$\log =$ Natural logarithm.

While Kassouf's formula will give a relatively accurate normal value for any warrant regardless of life span, its complexity is an obvious drawback. Fortunately, he has also provided us with another, simpler formula which works fairly well with long-lived (more than three years), speculative warrants.[4]

The formula is

$$W = \sqrt{E^2 + S^2} - E$$

where:

$W =$ The price of the warrant.
$E =$ The exercise price.
$S =$ The stock price.

Both W and E should be adjusted to a single share basis if necessary. This is done by dividing actual values by the number of shares which each warrant purchases. The above may also be written as

$$W/E = \sqrt{(S/E)^2 + 1} - 1$$

so that only two values (W/E) and (S/E) need be specified.

This formula can be utilized in two ways. First is the obvious; for any warrant of which purchase is contemplated, calculate the formula and determine how far from the norm the warrant does trade. The second is via establishing normal price curves in the following manner: It

[3] Edward O. Thorp and Sheen T. Kassouf, *Beat the Market* (New York: Random House, 1967).

[4] S. T. Kassouf, *Evaluation of Convertible Securities* (New York: Analytical Publishers Co., 1966).

is very simple to establish a basic axis chart, with the warrant price being the vertical axis and the stock price as the horizontal axis. The problem with this is that it omits the warrant's exercise price, a major consideration. This can be overcome if we let the vertical axis be the warrant price divided by the exercise price (W/E) and the horizontal axis represent the stock price divided by the exercise price (S/E). By using adjusted warrant and adjusted exercise prices, the entire universe of warrants can be plotted on a single chart. Furthermore, using Kassouf's formula, a normal price curve for a typical long-lived speculative warrant can be drawn using the following data:

TABLE 1

S/E	W/E	S/E	W/E
0.1	0.005	2.1	1.326
0.2	0.020	2.2	1.417
0.3	0.044	2.3	1.508
0.4	0.077	2.4	1.600
0.5	0.118	2.5	1.693
0.6	0.166	2.6	1.786
0.7	0.221	2.7	1.879
0.8	0.281	2.8	1.973
0.9	0.345	2.9	2.068
1.0	0.414	3.0	2.162
1.1	0.487	3.1	2.258
1.2	0.562	3.2	2.354
1.3	0.640	3.3	2.448
1.4	0.720	3.4	2.544
1.5	0.803	3.5	2.641
1.6	0.887	3.6	2.736
1.7	0.972	3.7	2.832
1.8	1.059	3.8	2.930
1.9	1.147	3.9	3.026
2.0	1.236	4.0	3.123

Even without plotting the numbers, they can be helpful. For example, we see that when the stock is selling at the warrant's exercise price ($S/E = 1.0$) we would expect the long-term speculative warrant to trade at about 41 percent of the exercise price (e.g., with the stock at 40 and an exercise price of 40, the warrant's normal price would be about 16). With the stock double the exercise price, we would expect the warrant to trade at about 1.24 times the exercise price, and with the stock at half the exercise price, a warrant price of about 12 percent of the exercise price would be the norm.

Thomas Noddings has refined this a little further by first establishing a normal curve for speculative warrants based on the Kassouf formula and then lowering the normal curve based on yield and volatility.[5] In

[5] Thomas C. Noddings, *The Dow Jones-Irwin Guide to Convertible Securities* (Homewood, Ill.: Dow Jones-Irwin, 1973).

addition to the yield adjustments explained on the chart, he would reduce the band rating by one in the case of relatively stable stocks like Carrier, Goodrich, and Louisiana Land, and by two ratings for more stable stocks such as AT&T, Commonwealth Edison, and Tenneco. While this certainly is an aid, Noddings has informed this writer that the bands were established on intuitive experience rather than by an alteration to the formula. This is unfortunate in that an analyst without tremendous experience in evaluating warrants would not know how to construct the

FIGURE 1

Normal Value Curves for Long-Term Warrants Based on Stock Yield

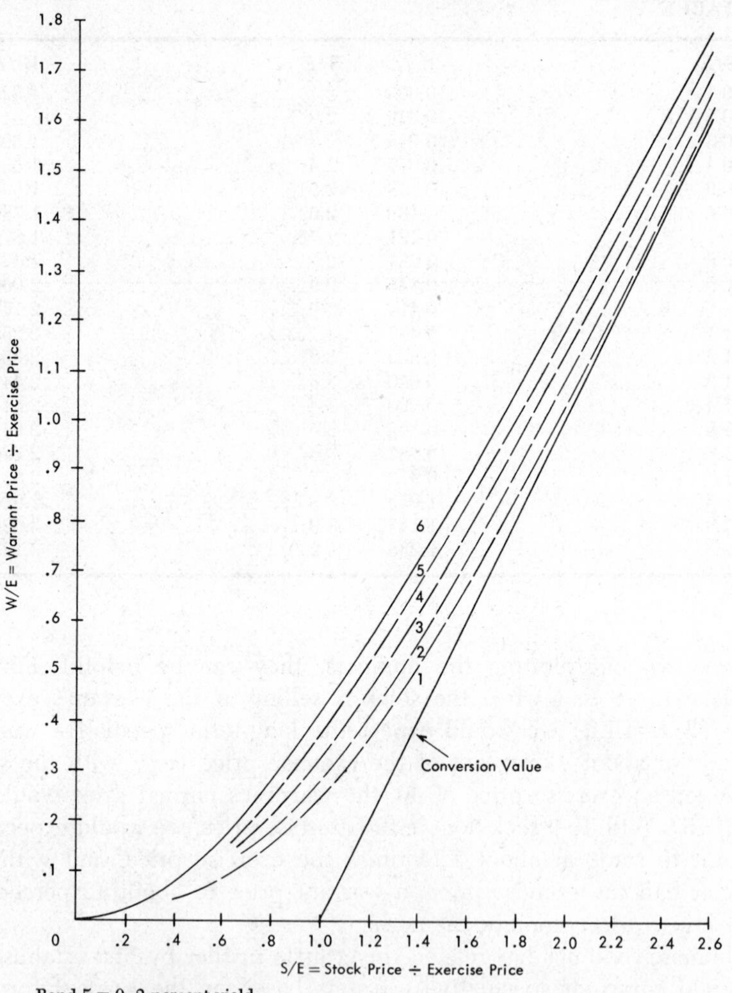

Band 5 = 0–2 percent yield.
4 = 2–4 percent.
3 = 4–6 percent.
2 = 6–8 percent.
1 = above 8 percent.

Note: Area 6 represents all warrants above band 5.

band for the warrant he wished to analyze. There must be some way to adjust the formula itself in terms of yield and beta to enable more simplified analysis of low volatility warrants whose underlying common pay high dividends. It has not yet been done, and we leave it as an open challenge to fellow analysts.

What about short-term warrants? Of course the lengthy Kassouf formula could be used, but once again, without the aid of a computer it is impractical. Unfortunately, a shortened approximate formula is not possible since warrant premiums' rapid dissipation in their last two years of life would call for a constantly changing variable. Thorp and Kassouf, in the previously mentioned book *Beat the Market* (which specializes in the analysis of short-term warrants) presents a normal curve on S/E, W/E axes, but it is only for warrants of 0 to 24 months' lifetime. A quick rule for warrants with less than three years of life is: Don't buy them unless they are selling at virtually no premium at all and you are bullish enough on the company to exercise them if necessary. Short-term warrants will be discussed further along in this chapter as they relate to reverse warrant hedging.

FACTORS INFLUENCING WARRANT PURCHASE

So far we have discussed how to evaluate the warrant. Which ones should be bought? This writer asks eight questions before purchasing any warrant; the first five are mandatory, the last three a little less so.

1. Is the underlying common stock attractive? It is highly unlikely that the warrant will advance while the stock is declining. This is the most crucial question. Never ask, "Which warrants are attractive to buy now?" Make the evaluation of the underlying common first and then evaluate the warrant relative to that common.

2. Does the warrant have a reasonable life span? Don't buy the warrant unless it has at least three, preferably four, years before expiration. If you must buy a short-term warrant, make sure that the premium is especially low since on expiration none of that premium will still exist.

3. Is the warrant protected against dilution? Will the warrant terms be adjusted in case of stock splits, stock dividends, or issuance of additional stock below the warrant's exercise price? Do not reject the warrant simply because it does not have complete protection, but substantial protection should be demanded.

4. Is the warrant protected against call? Some warrants can be called by the company at will at \$.25 or \$1.00. In the case where the common is selling at \$15 and the \$13 exercise price warrant is trading at \$7, a call would cause the warrant to fall to its \$2 intrinsic worth immediately. These warrants should be avoided. However, other warrants have provisions that they can be called at prices significantly above current prices. This type of call should not preclude warrant purchase.

5. Is the premium sufficiently low so that if the stock advances the warrant will increase by a greater percentage amount? In other words, is the leverage ratio favorable? This question could be alerted to ask, "Is the leverage index favorable?" thereby also considering the risk factor.

6. Is the premium reasonable not only in terms of normal values but also in light of the expected volatility of the underlying common? Don't forget that the normal values presented before for long-lived speculative warrants do not hold for less speculative ones.

7. Is the premium reasonable in light of the normal trading pattern for this particular warrant? Even warrants of equal volatility will sometimes trade at different normal levels, for example, because of differing levels of institutional sponsorship. This is rather difficult to judge for someone not engaged full time in the monitoring of warrant trading.

8. Is the premium reasonable in light of aberrations which may be occurring to warrant premiums in general during a specific market period? For example, during roaring bull markets, newly issued warrants tend to trade at above average premiums since price expectations for the underlying common are inflated. Strangely enough, at the bottom of bear markets, premiums increase as speculators buy the warrants at $.50 or $1.00 because they are cheap in absolute terms, even though they might have a normal value of $.10 or $.20. Recently, in early 1973, warrant premiums retreated to very low levels in light of what this writer refers to as the swindle factor.[6] The swindle factor must now be considered every bit as much if not more than all the other factors heretofore discussed.

Swindle Factor

Since this swindle factor is now one of the most important considerations and it is virtually impossible for the casual analyst to deal with, an article dealing with this now crucial factor is reprinted in full:[7]

> One day in early December, an investor telephoned his stockbroker, told him he was interested in Far West Financial Corp., which happened to have publicly traded warrants; would he please check on their terms and report back to him? Diligently following instructions, the broker learned that the terms permit purchase of one share of common stock at $24 until November 1974, and then at $26.50 until November 1979, at which time the warrants expire.
>
> As a double check, the broker looked into the very comprehensive Standard & Poor's Corporation Records, where the identical terms were indicated followed by a statement that the warrants are "protected

[6] It may or may not be a swindle in the criminal sense of the word (since at this writing it is still in the courts) but certainly is in the dictionary definition of it as a trick or deception.

[7] Daniel Turov, "Trampled Rights," *Barron's*, March 19, 1973.

against dilution, as defined, with no adjustment made of less than $0.50 a share, but such fraction shall be retained for the purpose of computing any further changes; terms and trading basis should be checked with brokers." The broker then queried his trading department and found that one warrant served as a call on one share of common. Armed with the information from this thorough investigation, his customer proceeded to purchase a number of warrants at the market price of 3¼.

Several days later, Leasco Corp. announced that it had agreed in principle to acquire the assets of Far West Financial for about $18 in cash per common share. At the same time, Leasco and Far West both announced that if the proposed sale were consummated, the Far West warrants would expire worthless upon the transaction's closing. In that single day, the warrants plunged 77 percent to $0.75 each. They have subsequently recovered to about $1.50, on speculative hopes that the merger will fall through.

While the broker-customer conversation cited above is fictitious, it could have happened. Incredulous at the newspaper story, I called Far West and requested a copy of the Warrant Agreement. A Warrant Agreement, for those not familiar with it, is a formal, legalistic statement of the warrant's terms and how those terms may be altered under various contingencies. Warrant Agreements generally run 15 pages or more, are virtually impossible for the layman to understand, and are not distributed to the investing public. In most cases, a securities analyst who wants a copy will receive one if he asks for it.

Far West sent me such a photocopy, the text of which is worth quoting. Under the heading "Other Provisions for Protection (sic) of Warrant-holders," the Agreement states that "in the event of the liquidation, dissolution or winding up of the Company . . . a notice thereof shall be filed by the Company with the Warrant Agent . . . at least thirty days before the record date . . . for determining holders of the Capital Stock entitled to receive any distribution upon such liquidation, dissolution, or winding up. Such notice shall also specify the date on which the right to exercise Warrants shall expire, as provided in Section 2.01."

The latter states: "Warrants may be exercised at any time on and after November 1, 1964, and on or before November 1, 1979, except that if notice has been given as provided in Section 4.01 in connection with the liquidation, dissolution or winding up of the company, the right to exercise Warrants shall expire at the close of business on the third full business day before the date specified in such notice as the record date for determining holders entitled to receive any distribution upon such liquidation, dissolution or winding up. Any Warrant not so exercised shall become void, and all rights thereunder and under this Agreement shall cease."

The Far West case raises the question of whether an ordinary investor, contemplating buying a warrant, can make such a purchase without first consulting an attorney. For example, in the unlikely event that an individual investor could obtain a copy of a Warrant Agreement, how would he interpret a phrase such as "liquidation, dissolution or winding up"? As a poll of the popular interpretation of such a phrase, I questioned at random one day the first 10 clients who called me. Each one thought that the phrase meant "bankruptcy"; not one felt that it could be interpreted to mean an acquisition, which, of course, is what is proposed between Leasco and Far West.

In essence, then, the ordinary investor faced a situation where no immediately available information even hinted at the possibility of these warrants expiring before 1979. Picture then the investor, paying a reasonable premium for the Far West warrant and the right to participate in the underlying growth of the common stock for another 6½ years, being told that because of an acquisition, on which he cannot even vote, his property is suddenly worthless.

Far West has indicated that it can do nothing for its warrant-holders, since it could do so only at the expense of stockholders; apparently it is Leasco's responsibility to provide for the Far West warrant-holders if it sees fit. Leasco, in turn, says that it can not make an offer since it can not expect its stockholders to pay for something which Leasco doesn't need. More recently, Leasco observed that since a warrant-holders' class action suit has been filed, it would be more difficult to do anything at all. The class action suit against Far West urges that the two companies be enjoined from completing the sale. The company's defense is that the warrant certificate states that "upon liquidation of the company, this warrant shall expire as provided in the Warrant Agreement." It is obvious by now that the word "liquidate" is ambiguous, that the Warrant Agreement is both difficult to obtain and to understand, and that many investors keep their certificates in Street name and hence never see it.

While the Far West case in principle is more damaging, the recently proposed acquisition of National General Corp. by American Financial is quite similar. National General new warrants authorize the purchase of one share of NGC common at $40 until September 1978. With the stock at 33, the warrants until recently traded with a very reasonable premium at 6¾. (The premium is considered reasonable in that if the common had doubled to 66, the warrants would sell for 26, quadruple their then current price.)

American Financial (which had only recently stated that it had no plans to merge with National General) and National General (which had stated categorically that it did not wish to be merged) announced in early January that they had agreed to a consolidation. Under its provisions, National General stockholders would be offered a package of securities consisting of slightly more than 50 percent equity in American Financial, with the remainder comprising a combination of cash and notes.

The deal was not a bad one for NGC stockholders, since the package has an estimated value of about $41; however, it created countless headaches for the warrant-holders. For one thing, American Financial had not made up its mind whether the acquisition was to be made by formal merger or via tender offer. If by a merger, the NGC warrants would become a call on this heavily non-equity package at $40 until 1978. If

> there were to be a tender offer for NGC common, the warrants could continue to call NGC stock at $40 until expiration.
>
> The warrant-holders' problem in evaluating the offer was that they had no way of knowing how successful a tender for the common would be. If, for extreme example, all or nearly all of NGC common were tendered, the warrants would become a call on a stock with limited or no marketability. Furthermore, at that point, American Financial could vote its NGC shares for a formal merger and squeeze out the warrant-holders with no compensation at all, a la Leasco-Far West. Not surprisingly, the warrants plummeted 30 percent in value to 4¾ in less than an hour's trading, at which point trading was halted.
>
> Subsequently, American Financial announced that the consolidation would be made via tender; then, because of a combination of adverse publicity and a warrant-holders' class action suit, it announced a separate tender for all the NGC warrants at $6.75, the closing price at the time the consolidation intent was announced. While this may assuage some warrant-holders, it remains grossly inadequate.
>
> An investor who purchases a call on equity should be safeguarded in the case of merger or acquisition from having that call on equity become either a call on non-equity or a call on nothing. Security regulations should stipulate that in the event of consolidation, a warrant-holder must be guaranteed that his warrants become a call on the equivalent amount of equity in the acquiring or merged company.
>
> The mathematics of implementing such a rule are really quite simple. For example, at the time Leasco announced its proposed $18 offer for Far West, Leasco itself was trading near 18. What could be simpler than for the Far West warrant to become a warrant to buy one share of Leasco at the same $24/$26.50 exercise price until 1979?
>
> National General warrants, at the time the offer was announced, had an intrinsic negative value of $7 ($40–$33), and American Financial was trading at 19½. What could be simpler and more equitable than having each NGC warrant become a warrant to purchase two shares of American Financial at $23 until 1978? The warrant would still have an intrinsic negative value of $7 ($23.00–19.50 × 2).
>
> The publicity surrounding these transactions, coming as it were back-to-back, has cast a pall over all warrants. Investors have reacted by dumping them en masse. In the first two months of 1973, only five of the American Stock Exchange's 79 warrants have advanced, four are unchanged, and an incredible 70 have declined.

To date, nothing has come from the NGC class action suit, and since the Leasco-Far West merger has been called off, the question of the Far West warrants has not yet been resolved. As a practical means of protecting themselves, analysts and prospective warrant purchasers should carefully read the warrant agreement of any warrant whose underlying common stock might be the object of a tender offer or merger. In the longer run, it is hoped that the Securities and Exchange Commission will take affirmative action to protect warrant-holders' rights.

WARRANTS WITH SPECIAL FEATURES

We have left to the end the matter of unusual warrants, not that they are unimportant (quite to the contrary) but because it would have been confusing to discuss them before a full understanding of warrant analysis had been gleaned. There are basically six different types of warrant variations.

Warrants That Purchase Securities Other than Common Stock. For example, the now expired Hilton Hotels warrants were a call on 2 Hilton common, 0.144375 Trans World Airlines common, and 0.2625 TWA preferred stock, for a total of $50. Because of the difficulty of their analysis, they were purchased almost exclusively by professionals and in their later years traded at no premium. Frequently, they traded below parity and provided arbitrage opportunities for member firms not having to pay the high commissions of four separate securities transactions. Such warrants can come into being because of a merger or acquisition, as in the case just discussed, or they can be a willful creation. For example, suppose that company A has a large position in company B convertible preferred stock and, either by choice or by governmental antitrust action, wishes to dispose of it. The company could issue warrants for the purchase of the convertible preferred, thereby receiving more than if it had sold the preferred alone.

Warrants That Purchase More or Less than One Share of Common. This is a particularly frequent occurrence. Although companies do occasionally issue warrants to purchase only one-half share of their common stock as part of an offering, most frequently these multiple or fractional purchase warrants come into being as a result of adjustments under the warrant agreement's antidilution terms. For example, a 10 percent stock dividend would cause the warrant to become a call on 1.1 common. An additional 15 percent stock dividend would adjust the terms so as to call 1.265 common. A subsequent 2½-for-1 stock split makes the warrant a call on 3.1625 shares, and years later in hard times, a 5-for-1 reverse split would make the warrant a call for 0.6325 common. When corporate successes and rising prices cause frequent stock splits, it is possible for the warrant to sell at a higher absolute price than the common even though the adjusted price would have to be lower. (This is only theoretically correct; in 1971 the Okonite warrants sold at a higher adjusted price than the Ling-Temco-Voight common shares on which they were a call; this can be attributed only to extreme investor ignorance as to the pricing of warrants.) Conversely, when a stock has performed very poorly and reverse splits, ridiculous terms can result. For example, in 1973, the 1974 expiring Nytronics warrants were a call on 0.1 Nytronics common at $16.50 ($165 per full share). Even selling at five cents, they were extraordinarily overvalued having an appreciation factor of 330. The common would have to rise from $1 to $330 in one year for the warrant to just do as well as the common. Cheapness does not make value.

Warrants with Usable Bonds. The third type of warrant quirk arises from those that have usable senior securities. Instead of paying the exercise price in cash, the investor may submit a bond the company has indicated is usable in lieu of cash at face value. This has the effect of reducing the exercise price. For example, a warrant is exercisable at $20, but there is a usable bond trading at 80. The bond adjusted exercise price would be $16, since instead of submitting $2,000 to exercise 100 warrants, the investor could submit $2,000 face amount of the bonds which only cost him $1,600. There are several caveats to this, however. The investor buying these bonds has an additional cash outlay and this severely cuts down on leverage. In addition, he now has the additional risk that because of rises in interest rates that the bond may decline in price. An important consideration is the percentage amount of the bond issue that is necessary to retire the warrant. For example, let us imagine a warrant with a $20 exercise price with 1 million outstanding. Total exercise would require $20 million cash or, if there is a usable bond, $20 million face value. If there are $300 million face value of the bonds outstanding, bond purchases for the exercise of the warrants will probably not have much impact on the bond's price. However, if there are only $15 million of bonds outstanding and the warrants are exercisable (i.e., selling above their actual exercise price), the bonds could be bid up from a deep discount level up to the high 90's. This could reward the early bond buyer with additional profits or, conversely, throw a monkey wrench into the calculations of the investor who bought the warrants calculating a much reduced bond adjusted exercise price, but who found that instead of a 20 percent or 30 percent reduction, his failure to purchase the bonds early meant only a 1 percent or 2 percent reduction. Consequently, except in cases where the bond issue is substantially in excess of the amount needed for exercise, it is generally best to ignore the bond in making price estimates.

Those analysts familiar with *convertible bonds* probably have already noted that joint purchase of a warrant and a usable bond is, in effect, an artificial (or synthetic) convertible. Purchase for $5 each of a warrant with a $20 exercise price, and the simultaneous purchase for $800 each of $2,000 face amount of a usable bond has the same investment effect as the purchase of two $1,000 bonds for $1,050 when each $1,000 bond is convertible into 50 shares. In both cases $2,100 has been invested and the securities obtained are convertible into 100 common shares.

In a somewhat reverse manner, it is possible to look at a convertible bond and break it down into its straight bond and warrant components. For example, say that a bond, convertible into 50 shares, is selling for $1,000 and that it has an investment value of $700. (Investment value refers to the price at which it is estimated the bond would be trading if it were not convertible. It is obtained by observing at what price non-convertible bonds with a similar credit rating in the same industry are trading.) Hence the warrant value of the convertible is $300, and the number of warrants that $300 represents is 50, the number of shares into which the bond is convertible. The exercise price of the latent warrants is $14 (the investment worth of the bond divided by the number of shares obtainable by conversion). The price per warrant would be $6 (the amount paid for the convertible part of the entire bond divided by the number of shares obtainable on conversion).

Warrants with Step-Ups in Exercise Price. Many warrants have step-ups in the exercise price, i.e., the exercise price increases every two or three or five years. The reason for this is to encourage warrant holders to exercise their warrants early, thereby bringing the corporation funds early. In addition, the company knows that some warrant holders will exercise early to take advantage of the lower price, while others will not exercise but rather keep the warrants for the leverage which their remaining lifetime gives them. This tends to spread out the receipt of funds by the corporation and avoids having a huge inflow of funds at one time. For analytical purposes, the following (somewhat oversimplified) guidelines are used: Consider the lifetime of the warrant as the period until final expiration. If the warrant has three years or more to run before a step-up, consider only the current terms. If the warrant has two or three years of life remaining, add one third of the step-up amount to the current exercise price. If the warrant has one to two years remaining, use the mean between the current and future exercise prices; and if the warrant has less than one year before a step-up, add two thirds of the step-up amount to the current exercise price. In all cases, of course, the warrant will not sell below its intrinsic value based on its current exercise price.

Convertible Warrants. A relatively recent and not too frequently used feature is the convertible warrant, i.e., a warrant that can be either exercised in the traditional manner or alternatively converted into common without the use of additional cash. For example, the Commonwealth Edison warrants (the series A and B warrants are essentially identical) are exercisable into one common share upon payment of $30 through 1981, or alternatively are convertible into one-third Commonwealth Edison common perpetually without any cash payment. This effectively places a floor on the warrant's price of one third of the level of the common at any given time. In theory, it would be expected that a warrant with this important advantage would trade at a higher premium than would otherwise be anticipated; in actuality, the low volatility of the common has precluded this from occurring.

Dividend Paying Warrants. The last current type of warrant quirk is the dividend paying warrant. They could alternatively be described as warrant-like preferreds. The best known of these is the Warner Communications series C preferred stock. Each preferred pays only a token dividend of five cents per year and is convertible into one common with the payment of $37. Clearly, this is nothing more than a warrant with a $37 exercise price. The preferred's call date is tantamount to an expiration date, although if the preferred is not called at that time (1979) it will probably trade at its intrinsic value (if any) or at a very low level (if there is no intrinsic value) from the call date on. Alternatively, each preferred is convertible into one-sixteenth common share, an option which is of very little value. A more true convertible preferred–warrant mixture can be seen in the case of the R. J. Reynolds $2.25 convertible preferred. Each preferred is convertible into 1.5 common shares with the payment of $22 cash. Excepting the sizable dividend and added stature of a preferred, this preferred is in no way different from a warrant allowing the purchase of 1.5 common for a total exercise price of $22 ($14.67 per share).

In the years ahead, there will probably evolve new and different types of warrants—step-down exercise priced warrants convertible at expiration if not exercised, warrants with delayed convertibility features, and so on—all designed to meet specific needs of the companies issuing them and to appeal to investors seeking new opportunities.

WARRANT HEDGING

Because warrants fluctuate in price at different rates than their underlying common, there frequently arise opportunities to hedge common against warrant. It should be emphasized that hedging is not the same as arbitrage. Arbitrage (in the sense that it is confused with hedging) entails the purchase of a convertible trading below parity and the simultaneous short sale of the common into which it is convertible, coupled with the issuance of conversion instructions for the convertible, and the common thus received delivered against the common previously shorted. In hedging, conversion is not called for, but rather the long and short positions are kept for a period of time to take advantage of unequal movements in the direction of the two securities. In order to understand hedging it is necessary to comprehend short selling.

Short Selling

The short sale concept is not really difficult, although the investing public as a whole tends to regard it as esoteric. An investor selling short borrows a security from another investor (a process handled by the brokerage house) and sells the stock on the exchange or (infrequently) over the counter. If he buys it back lower, a profit has been made; if it is repurchased at a higher price, there is a loss. In order to prevent rampant short selling from decimating a stock's price when it is already under pressure, it is required that a short sale be effected on an up-tick (a trade at a higher price than the previous one) or on a zero up-tick (a trade at the same price as the last one but where the last trade was at a price higher than the last previous different price). Hence, a short seller can sell only into strength. It should be pointed out that the short sale must constitute the up-tick; the short seller does not wait for an up-tick and then sell the stock. There is an exception to the up-tick rule; on regional exchanges, short sales can be made on down-ticks so long as they are at a higher price than the last trade on the principal exchange. In addition, most regional exchanges allow the short sales of odd lots without up-ticks.

Brokers gladly lend stocks to other brokers since the borrowing broker gives the lender a check for the stock borrowed in the amount of its market value. This represents in essence on interest-free loan to the lender. On rare occasions the lender needs his stock back; if the borrower is unable to reborrow it from another source, the short seller will be forced to repurchase the short stock immediately. Despite this being a well-publicized risk of short selling, it is actually quite a rare occurrence.

Margin requirements for a short sale are similar to the margin requirements for the purchase of stock (or warrants). If margin requirements are say 65 percent, a buyer of $10,000 of stock will have to deposit $6,500 to secure his position. The short seller of $10,000 worth of securities would have the same requirement but with one big difference: The buyer, by not paying for $3,500 of his purchase, has created a debit balance on which interest will be charged. The short seller will have the short part of his margin account credited with the $10,000 proceeds of the short sale (which is not really his and which cannot be withdrawn), and his long account will show a credit of $6,500, representing the amount he has deposited as security. There is no debit balance created and hence no interest charges, even though he has only put up 65 percent (or whatever the Federal Reserve requirements happen to be at the time).

When it comes to convertible securities, there is a strange quirk in the rules. Only the long side of the transaction must be paid for. Section 220.3(d)(3) of Regulation T reads in part: "(the) amount as the Board shall prescribe from time to time . . . as the margin required for short sales, except that such amount so prescribed . . . need not be included when there are held in the account securities exchangeable or convertible within 90 calendar days, without restrictions other than the payment of money, into such securities sold short." This means that if an investor owns a security, convertible into common stock within 90 days, the stock may be sold short without depositing any additional funds. Furthermore, as we have seen, that short sale not only requires no additional funds but creates no debit balance. The only possible margin costs result from marks to the market (moving funds from the long account to the short account to keep the funds there equal to the current market value of the short position), but this could just as easily work to the investor's benefit if the securities were declining.

How are hedges constructed? Picture a reasonably speculative stock which is trading at $20 at a time when its warrant, with an exercise price of $40 and a five-year remaining life time, is selling at $2. We can see from Table 1 that when S/E equals 0.5 (40/20), W/E should equal approximately 0.118, equivalent in this example to a warrant price of $4.72 (0.118 × 40). The warrant is clearly undervalued. However, purchase of the warrant by itself entails the same risks of stock purchase, for despite its being undervalued, if the stock declines the warrant will follow suit. What if an investor bought one warrant and shorted one common. On the downside he would fare well as the common would almost certainly fall more than the warrant in absolute terms. Assuming the warrant returned to its normal value as the stock regained speculative favor, we would expect a warrant price of $16.56 with the common at $40.00, say two years hence. The investor would have an $11.84 profit on the one warrant long, but a $20.00 loss on the short stock—not too satisfactory.

But suppose an investor did not want to subject himself to the risks of unhedged ownership. He could purchase 400 warrants at $2 each and sell short 100 common at $20. If the stock fell to $10, the warrants probably would not fall below $1 (normal price would be about $1.35) for a resultant loss of $400 on the warrants and a profit of $1,000 on the stock. Even if the company went bankrupt and all securities were worthless, the investor would lose $800 on the warrants and gain $2,000 on the common. On the other hand, if the stock advanced to $40 and the warrant traded at $12 (a 17.5 percent discount from its normal value of $16.56), the investor would show a warrant profit of $4,000 and a common loss of $2,000. In other words, merely by making some reasonable assumptions about the future prices of the warrants vis-à-vis the common, a conservative investor using short sales of common and warrant purchases can profit either if the stock advances or if it declines!

Now, in all fairness, this was a very exaggerated example for the purpose of explanation. Such neutral hedges (profitable regardless of stock direction) are rare. It is unlikely that the warrant would have traded at $2 in the first place. More common situations, however, frequently find similarly termed warrants trading at $3. If an investor were to set up a four to one hedge as before (and making the same assumptions), he would have a warrant profit of $3,600 and a $2,000 loss on the stock, with an upside stock move to 40. On the downside, the warrant loss would be $800 and the stock profit $1,000 if the stock fell to $10. If the company went bankrupt and all securities fell to zero, the warrant loss would be $1,200 and the stock profit $2,000. Hence, we see the basic elements of a bullish hedge: a profit if the stock acts as expected and advances, and an approximate break-even if the stock falls even by 50 percent. If the investor is right he profits; if he is wrong he doesn't lose.

A bearish hedge is somewhat different, and there are two distinctly different types. The first is where the mix is adjusted heavily on the short side to take advantage of an expected stock decline. Using the same example as above (with a $3 current warrant price), a bearish hedger could buy 500 warrants and sell short 200 common. At $10, the warrant loss would probably be about $1,000 ($3 – $1) and the stock profit, $2,000. If he had misjudged the stock's direction, with the stock at $40, he would show a loss of $4,000 on the common but a profit of $4,500 on the warrants. So we see that the bearish hedge searches for a profit if the stock expectedly declines but provides an approximate break-even on the upside.

The second type of bearish hedge is of a different nature and involves high-price warrants selling for little or no premium. For instance, assume that $S = 60$, $E = 40$, and $W = 20$. The simultaneous purchase of 100 warrants and short sale of 100 common will probably show a profit if the stock does in fact decline, for as it does the warrant will begin to obtain a higher premium. For example, if the stock fell to $30, the warrant would likely sell at about $7. The profit on the common short would be $3,000 and the loss on the warrant long, $1,300. If the stock had in fact kept rising, the warrant would have to keep in tune since it was trading at no premium and could always be exercised. In fact, even if there had been a two- or three-point premium on the warrant, it still would have been an attractive hedge.

There could of course be countless variations of the three previous types of hedges, adjusting mixes, altering expected values. To the analyst considering hedges for the first time the advice should be, first, identify a severely undervalued warrant making sure to consider life span and volatility, and then play with the numbers based upon future price assumptions. Remember always to consider the calculations on the opposite side of the expected move. Remember, in addition, that undervalued warrants tend to remain undervalued and haircuts should be given to future otherwise normal price estimations.

What Can Go Wrong

What can go wrong with warrant hedging? There are several risks. First and least important is that of commissions; they cost money and any time money is expended its cost should be considered. This is especially true in the case of the second type of bearish hedging.

Secondly, and the most serious possible error is that of misevaluating the future warrant price at various levels for the stock. The numbers we used worked beautifully; in the real world, predictions do not come true simply because we think they will. Even though we said the warrant should sell at $12.00, and thought that was trimmed enough from its expected value of $16.56, Congress has not yet passed any laws that says it could not trade at $6.00—and that would certainly put a crimp into the calculations. Of course, the better an analyst is the less will be the number of miscalculations.

The third risk is that of common stock dividends. When a short position is held in the common stock at the time of the dvidend record date, the short seller is required to pay the dividend, and it is deducted from his account on the payable date.

Fourth is the risk of sterile money; if neither the stock nor the warrant move over a period of time, the money used to carry that position is not earning any return. Furthermore, if the stock does not move substantially for many year, the warrant will slowly but surely depreciate in price as its premium evaporates as expiration approaches. Such complete price stability is virtually unheard of, fortunately.

The fifth and most pernicious factor to be reckoned with is the previously mentioned swindle factor. Previous to the announcement of acquisition of National General by American Financial, purchase of the NGC $40 warrants and sale of 100 common for each 250 to 350 warrants bought would have provided an excellent hedge profile. In fact, many knowledgeable investors had indeed entered into such a hedge. They lost both in the warrants if they panicked and sold them when they were dumped in heavy American Stock Exchange trading and on the common which advanced in price. A word to the wise: Until the SEC acts decisively in this matter, avoid warrant hedges in companies where management has questionable ethics or where the likelihood of takeover is great.

There is another side of hedging, reverse hedging. Reverse hedging involves the short sale of an overvalued warrant and the purchase of the underlying stock, in equal or unequal quantities. While it could be accomplished in a fashion opposite to the hedging procedure just described, i.e., merely locating severely overvalued warrants and shorting them while buying the stock, the tremendous upside leverage of even overvalued warrants when the common takes off is too much to contend with in most instances. It is significantly less risky and more profitable when the previous techniques can be combined with the gravitational forces of expiring warrants. Once a warrant has but two years of life remaining, its premium starts to decline dramatically. A rule of thumb is that the expected normal price should be reduced by 4 percent per month, not compounded, starting 24 months prior to expiration. By shorting even a normally valued warrant two years before expiration, profits can generally be expected. When coupled with the purchase of common, the expected return can be increased. Generally speaking, the lower the *S/E* the better the profit potential since the common then has to rise substantially just to get up to the point where the warrant is worthless. At *S/E*'s above about 1.2, reverse hedging loses a good part of its appeal unless the warrant is particularly overvalued.

There are two negatives which cut into reverse hedging profit potential, but not nearly by enough to make it prohibitive. First is that there is a standard Regulation T margin requirement on both the long and short sides of the transaction, unlike with hedging. In addition, New York Stock Exchange maintenance requirements for short positions are higher than initial Regulation T requirements in certain cases. Secondly, because of recent widespread interest in reverse hedging, it is sometimes necessary to sell short two and a half or three years before expiration since waiting may mean that there are few warrants available for shorting. This additional waiting period cuts into per annum expected profits.

How does an analyst pick reverse hedge candidates? First, segregate those listed warrants with a life span of less than three years, a market price of at least $1, an outstanding size of 200,000, and an *S/E* of 2.0 or less. Then eliminate those with an S/E of between 1.2 and 2.0 unless they have a W/E of at least 10 percent in excess of expected values for long-term warrants. Then make sure the warrants can be borrowed for shorting. The simplest way of evaluating the warrant's hedge potential is by constructing a reverse hedge analysis chart.

Assume that a warrant has an exercise price of $34 with an expiration date 32 months in the future. Assume the stock is trading at 26 and the warrant at 9. (These are the actual calculations by this writer in September 1973 evaluating the Chrysler warrant reverse hedge.)

The mix of the reverse should be determined by both how overvalued the warrant is and also by the expected stock price at the time of the warrant's expiration. An additional consideration is the degree of risk which the hedger wishes to assume in the hopes of greater profits. Furthermore, as expectations for the stock change, the mix can (and should) be altered to maximize profits.

Several weeks before the warrants are scheduled to expire they will be delisted from exchange trading. After that point they will trade over the counter where their market may be less than ideal. It is always advised that the position be covered prior to delisting.

One problem in any kind of hedging is that of the short squeeze, i.e., lending brokers demanding their stock back. While this is a rare occurrence, the reverse hedger is more likely to encounter it than other short sellers, primarily because it is easier to corner the market on a low-priced issue such as warrants which will have to be covered in a relatively short period of time. In addition, a corporate tender offer to purchase its own warrants can drive the price up quickly, and although it could decline after the culmination of the tender, many shorts would be forced to cover. This happened in late 1973 with the Gould Inc. warrants.

This brings up another difficulty in entering into reverse hedges. It is frequently difficult to borrow the needed warrants. Furthermore, when the short interest reaches about 25 percent of the total outstanding issue, the exchange will ban future short sales. Thus it is imperative that the position taken is large enough so that if the hedge is to be increased on the short side after a period of time it can be done by selling off part of the long position rather than by shorting additional warrants, since the latter may not be available.

There is another obstacle to reverse hedging, and it has come from the Internal Revenue Service. This IRS has ruled that if a company issued warrants in, say, 1969, and if they expire worthless in 1975, the money the company received in 1969 is taxable income in 1975. Aside from putting an additional burden on the company, it places real estate investment trusts (REIT) in a totally untenable position. Under the conduit rule, if an REIT pays out 90 percent or more of its income to shareholders in the form of dividends, it does not have to pay any income taxes. However, if an REIT warrant expires worthless, the trust must, under the IRS ruling, consider it ordinary income. It then must either liquidate mortgage or construction loans and disburse the supposed income out of capital or alternatively pay taxes on the money and lose its tax-free status. The net result of this is that no REIT warrants will expire worthless, since if they have no value as expiration approaches, the REIT merely extends the warrant's life. For some unknown reason, the American Stock Exchange allows this but not the reduction of warrant exercise prices.

In the opinion of many warrant analysts, both practices should be disallowed for the protection of short sellers. The net effect of the current situation has been to eliminate all REIT warrants from consideration as reverse hedge candidates. Furthermore, many other companies will face the same problem in the years ahead unless the courts reverse the IRS's decision. While they would not be faced with the tax status question, they would nonetheless be reluctant to pay taxes on a substantial amount of extraordinary income. Warrants of these companies should be avoided also.

The crucial question is what value was assigned to the warrants at the time of issuance. For example, when American Telephone and Telegraph issued debentures with warrants attached to shareholders by rights offering in 1970, the company valued the debentures at 100 and the warrants at zero. They were able to do this since the debentures did indeed begin trading at that level. In essence, the warrants assumed the value of the rights which were necessary to purchase the units. The initial value of the warrants can be obtained from the company's secretary, and it is a factor which should be investigated prior to entering a

Warrants Ratio to Stocks (a)	*Downside Break-Even* (b)	*Percent* (c)	*Upside Break-Even* (d)	*Percent* (e)	*Maximum Percent Return* (f)	*Unchanged Price Percent Return* *Actual* (g)	*Annual* (h)
1:1	$ 15	− 42%	infinite	—	53.3%	28.3%	10.6%
2:1	6	− 76	$60	+130%	69.0	47.7	17.9
3:1	− 3 (*i*)	−100	51.50	+ 98	80.4	62.0	23.3
4:1	−12 (*i*)	−100	48.67	+ 87	89.1	72.9	27.3

(*a*) This is the number of warrants sold short for each common purchased.

(*b*) This indicates to what price the common could fall before the hedge would begin to show a loss. The figures ignore commissions and dividends. It is calculated in the following manner: Downside break-even $= S - RW$, where S equals the current stock price; W, the current adjusted warrant price; and R, the ratio of the number of shares called by the shorted warrants to the number of shares purchased, in fractional form.

(*c*) This figure represents how much from the current stock price the price in column *b* represents.

(*d*) This indicates to what price the common would have to rise before the hedge would begin to show a loss. The figures ignore commissions and dividends. It is calculated in the following manner: Upside break-even $= \frac{R(W + E) - S}{R - 1}$, where E represents the adjusted exercise price of the warrant at scheduled expiration.

(*e*) This represents how much from the current stock price the price in column *d* represents.

(*f*) The maximum profit on a reverse hedge arises when the common stock is selling at the warrant's exercise price on the day of expiration. It is assumed that the warrant will be at zero (in actuality it will trade at some level between $.01 and $.50, more likely near the lower level). The figures ignore commissions and dividends and assume that the original investment was 100 percent of the cost of the common and 65 percent of the receipts of the warrants shorted. No provisions were made for any interest charges that might have occurred because of marks to the market if the warrants advanced in price before beginning their decline.

(*g*) This is the actual percentage return on the hedge if the common is at the same price at expiration as it is "now." The same assumptions as were made in column *f* are made again.

(*h*) The annual percentage return is determined by dividing the amount in column *g* by the number of months before expiration and then multiplying by 12.

(*i*) The downside break-even price will not actually fall below zero. This is a theoretic value.

reverse hedge. Generally speaking, warrants which were issued as a result of a rights offering to shareholders, or which were issued by another company to purchase common shares which it owns in the company, are less likely to be faced with this problem.

An additional comment should be made about the art of hedging. Most properly conceived hedges work out well and provide a rate of return in excess of the return on other, unhedged stock investments. But, as has been illustrated, things can go wrong. Hedging is a numbers game and the more the risk can be spread around by diversification, the better will be the consistent results.

Finally, what are the tax consequences of hedging? All profits and losses on short sales, regardless of whether they are held for 10 minutes or 10 years are short-term capital gains or short-term capital losses. Long positions are more open to interpretation. The crucial words are "substantially identical securities." To date, the IRS has (correctly) held that warrants and common stock are not substantially identical and hence long positions would be either long-term or short-term depending on the length of the holding period. However, should the IRS, in the future, decide that they are substantially identical securities any period of time during which the investor is long a warrant and short the common, or vice versa, would have to be deducted from the long position's holding period for determining the capital gains status. In this writer's opinion, it would be hard to justify calling them substantially identical, but then again everyone was substantially surprised when the IRS issued its ruling regarding expiring warrants.

Warrants are undoubtedly most interesting and potentially profitable securities. However, the analyst should be most certain that he understands them before venturing into the arena.

OPTIONS

The basic type of stock option, the call, is an artificially created warrant. An investor, who may or may not own the stock in question, agrees to sell his stock (or go short the stock) to another investor for a specified period of time in return for a certain premium. Outside of some minor ramifications, which will be discussed, a call option is truly an artificially created warrant.

Some definitions are different in option lexicon. First difference is that the *premium* means either the amount over intrinsic value (as with warrants) or the entire amount received for selling the call. The latter is technically inaccurate, but it is the more common usage. In addition, the exercise price of the call is usually referred to as the striking price. A call with a negative intrinsic value is said to be "out of the money" and a call with some intrinsic value is "in the money."

Until 1973, all calls were traded over the counter (OTC) by specialized put and call dealers, whose task is to match up buyers and sellers. Their profit is the spread which they take between the buying and selling prices. An additional cost in trading options is the endorsement fee paid to a member of the New York Stock Exchange who must guarantee deliverance of the called stock. Furthermore, the exercise of any option, unlike the exercise of a warrant, involves regular NYSE commission charges. These costs are not inconsiderable.

Most calls are written for short periods of time, generally 35, 65, 95 days, and 6 months 10 days, although of late there has been a larger number of 7- and 13-month paper traded. The longer the life of the option, the higher will be the cost. Volatility and a thin market for the stock will also yield higher premiums for the call. Prices for calls, as for all other securities, are determined by supply and demand. There are percentage guidelines for determining normal prices for call options, but it is worthwhile for comparison to use the Kassouf formula on page 470 and subtract 4 percent (not compounded) for each month less than 24 months remaining on the call. This would tend to disagree with the accepted theory that a one-month call should sell for more than one third that of a three-month call. In most cases the normal price, using the formula method, is lower under the percentage method. For example, assuming a strike price of 40 and an identical stock price, S/E is 1.0 and $W/E = 0.41$. A two-year call would have a normal value of \$16.40. For a one-year call, subtract 48 percent of that value (4 percent times 12) and a normal price would be \$8.53. A six-month call would be \$5.90; a three-month call, \$2.62; and a one-month call, .65. (Since calls are quoted in terms of 100 shares, the prices would be quoted \$590, \$262, and \$65.)

If the analyst is familiar with calls, it is obvious that we have a difference in normal expected values. That is partially so because under traditional percentage analysis call options are overpriced. For example, it is generally accepted that a normal six-month call price when the stock and the striking price are both 40 would be about 15 percent of that amount, or \$600—no significant disagreement here. Under the percentage method, a normal price on a 95-day call would be \$400, as opposed to \$262 with the warrant formula method. On a one-month call, the discrepancy is even greater—\$250 versus \$65. The great disparity with the short-term call is that the premium has to be high enough to encourage a seller to write and cover his expected commission and carrying (interest) costs. This should be less of a consideration on the Chicago Board Options Exchange since calls sold there can be covered at lower commission costs. Other reasons for the disparity are (1) the margin costs of selling a naked option are much higher than selling a warrant short and (2) S/E is always very close to 1.0, giving the call great percentage leverage potential albeit at the risk of high percentage loss. But the discrepancy does point out one thing: if short-term warrants are overpriced even when they sell at normal values (and the section on warrant hedging should have proved that) then short-term calls are certainly overvalued, since investors would expect to pay $400 for a 95-day and $250 for a 35-day call.

Despite all the encouragements from put and call brokers for buying calls, they should not be bought except in exceptional cases. The only time that short-term calls should be purchased is if the investor has specific and strong reasons for believing the stock will advance quickly and sharply. In essence then, sell calls; don't buy them, except in special instances.

In addition to the disadvantages of calls as described above, a major problem with them is that OTC calls (that is calls for listed or unlisted stocks which are not exchange traded) are almost impossible to resell at a reasonable price. They are very illiquid, and the call speculator is in a locked-in position if he cannot exercise the call. Advertisements in the financial press for options are generally the only way to resell. This is the major reason for the success of the Chicago Board Options Exchange (CBOE) which will be discussed shortly.

OTC calls have full dilution protection and then some. Even cash dividends are deducted from the striking price if the call is exercised. When pricing calls, this factor should be considered, especially with calls for high dividend paying stocks.

The problems with OTC calls are many: they are illiquid and the spread between bid and asked quotations is frequently too large. In addition, terms of calls have to be fixed separately for each contract. Not only is the cost of the option a variable, but so are the expiration date and striking price. The CBOE has put an end to this for those options traded there. All striking prices and expiration dates are set in advance and the option has liquidity. Furthermore, dividend reductions do not result in a reduction of the strike price, so this factor does not have to be calculated. This factor has resulted in lower premiums for calls on conservative stocks. Another factor in reducing the premiums for CBOE options has been their marketability, thereby avoiding for both buyer and seller the high costs of commissions when exercising the option; commissions for the options are significantly lower than for the underlying common. In sum, it appears that fixed exercise priced, exchange listed options are the wave of the future, and OTC options will have limited use. As the American Stock Exchange and PBW exchanges try to get into the act in competition with the CBOE, it seems inevitable that options will become more warrant-like.

If calls are so overvalued, why do people buy them? First is the obvious—speculators get a hot tip on a stock and don't have the money to buy it. A call is cheaper in actual dollars. Second is the investor who wants to buy a stock but is afraid that it will decline in value; buying a call rather than the stock will reduce his profit by the amount of the premium if he is correct and the stock advances, but it will limit his loss to the amount of the premium if it declines sharply. Other investors want to take profits in a stock which they have held for a long time—either for tax purposes or simple profit-taking desires—but cannot separate from their love affair with the stock that has made them so much money. A call can be bought with a percentage of the profits although this is emotional not intelligent investing. A call can be bought for protection: A speculator has sold a stock short but wants to limit his loss should the stock advance. He could enter a stop order but he then runs the risk of being whipsawed. A call would prevent that at least until expiration and the maximum loss can be easily identified. Lastly, the reason for the tremendous call buying on the CBOE is rank speculation. There is nothing wrong with speculation, but those who buy there should know precisely what they are doing.

There are other more esoteric reasons for buying calls, but these are the basic ones, and the others are merely variations of these. It should be pointed out that while all of the preceding are valid reasons for speculating in calls, it does not negate the fact that their prices are generally too high for sensible investing.

Put Options

A put option is the opposite of a call in that it allows the holder to sell a stock at the striking price until expiration. Generally speaking, they trade at premiums 80 percent to 90 percent those of calls although at bear market bottoms they may even sell at higher prices than calls.

Investors and speculators buy puts for several reasons: to profit from a rapid decline in the stock, to control stock on the short side without unlimited risk, to short stock with less of a dollar commitment, to protect a long position against a precipitous decline, and as a substitute for a stop order either to prevent great loss or to lock in a profit. These reasons are pretty much the opposites of those given for buying calls. In addition, there are tax reasons for buying puts. A short sale is always a short-term capital gain or loss; a put option which is resold six months and a day later qualifies for long-term status.

There are also variations of puts and calls. A *straddle* is a combination of one call and one put. A straddle should be bought only if it is obtainable at reasonable prices (it is generally cheaper than buying the two components separately), and if the buyer is convinced the stock will show extreme volatility, but he does not know in which direction. They can be bought, for example, after a merger has been announced but not finalized. Completion would cause the stock to advance sharply, incompletion to decline sharply. It is theoretically possible to exercise both sides of a straddle if the stock moves in one direction quickly and in the other subsequently.

Other combinations of options which are very infrequently used are spreads (a put and a call with different striking prices for the components—generally both are out of the money so as to buy the spread at a lower premium), straps (two calls and a put), and strips (two puts and a call).

Who sells calls? Most calls are sold by conservative investors who want additional income. An investor may own a stock for which he paid $30 and is now $40. He does not want to sell it at this level, but if he could get five points more he would be willing to part with it. He can get these five points by selling a call, but his gain is limited to those five points. On the other hand, if the stock price declines, he has the $500 premium and still owns the stock which he would have kept anyway (although if the stock rises quickly to $45, the buyer might not exercise, waiting for higher prices, and then watch the price decline; this would prevent the seller from taking his profits). If a writer is particularly bullish on the stock he can sell a straddle, thereby getting additional premium money for the put side which he does not expect to be exercised. However, he is committing himself to buy stock only if that stock is declining in price, a practice that can be quite dangerous. Needless to say, it is also possible to write puts on short positions. This writer would venture an opinion that an option writing program is less profitable on a consistent basis than is warrant (and convertible bond) hedging, but much easier to explain to prospective clients, as well as simpler to manage. Many writers of options write them naked, i.e., without either owning or being short the underlying stock. This is dangerous if done for one or two stocks, but if an investor utilizes substantial amounts of capital and writes puts and calls on a largely diversified group of securities, the percentage gains work out well since, as we have already seen, most short-term options are significantly overvalued. It should be pointed out that writing naked options well requires nerves of steel and substantial capital.

What about margin requirements? On the long side all options have to be paid for in full since the SEC has stated that they may have no loan value. The situation with selling options is confused and getting worse. At this writing, covered writers (those who own the underlying common) may sell calls without any additional requirements. In fact, the monies received on the sale of OTC calls are credited to the Special Miscellaneous Account (SMA) as cash. Those who sell puts on covered short positions are in the same position. The CBOE margin situation is in a state of flux, and changes are expected.

Naked sellers are dealt with harshly in sharp contrast with the requirements for the short sale of a warrant. For the short sale of a warrant, only normal margin requirements are required. However, for the short sale of a call the NYSE requires 30 percent of the *stock's* market price and some brokers increase that to 40 percent or 50 percent in addition to a $15,000 to $30,000 equity requirement. To this writer, it seems somewhat excessive to have a $2,500 requirement for the sale of a $2 option on American Telephone and Telegraph at $50, when a similar warrant can be shorted for $390. This is a carryover from the days when all options were traded over the counter and high percentage and equity requirements were necessary to protect an illiquid position. They still seem reasonable for OTC options. But for CBOE options they make no sense at all.

> Already the CBOE has proved itself a liquid exchange where an under-margined speculator could be bought in if he failed to meet marks to the market. Some who realize this counter that the CBOE is still a very new exchange and there is no guarantee that continued liquidity can be assured. While this has a modicum of validity, it can also be argued with a fair degree of certainty that any price aberrations caused by a mad rush to buy option contracts would be met by a significant amount of selling on the part of traditional covered option writers wanting to take advantage of the temporary advances. . . .
>
> Another argument is made for the high (margin) requirement—that a call can be exercised from a naked seller but a warrant only from the issuing company. To this the solution is deceptively simple: a rule that any naked seller being called stock immediately bring his new short position up to full initial margin requirements unless it is (bought in) by 10:30 the following morning. Actually, options will rarely be exercised until expiration, since exercise rather than resale is tantamount to throwing out part of the premium.[8] [Furthermore, naked sellers could be required to buy in two weeks prior to expiration to simplify the situation.]

The net effect of current margin regulations is to make it expensive to sell naked calls. Forcing sellers out of the market keeps prices higher to the disadvantage of call buyers—who are already at enough of a disadvantage. In addition, it excludes the use of CBOE calls from reverse hedging tactics, except in one-to-one mixes.

It would be expected that as the exchange market for calls (and puts) matures, changes will be made in regulations so as to make the market both more equitable and more liquid.

One of the more interesting features of OTC option trading is the conversion. A call buyer, through the aid of a put and call dealer, may get his call because another investor is willing to sell a put, and an intermediary (the NYSE member firm) can convert the put into a call. This occurs frequently as many investors prefer writing straddles to calls, but since there are more call buyers than put buyers, it is necessary to convert the put into a call. This is how it is done:

Assume a stock and striking price of $30. An investor is willing to

[8] Daniel Turov, "New Look in Calls," *Barron's*, August 6, 1973.

sell a put for $350, and a speculator is willing to buy a call for $500. The converter (broker) buys the put for $350, buys 100 shares of the stock in the open market for $3,000, and writes a call on it for $500. If the stock advances to $45, the call will be exercised; the broker will deliver the stock he bought at $30 to the caller for $30 and let the put expire. The broker's profit is the $500 he received for the call's sale minus the $350 cost of the put, or +$150 on an investment of $2,850 (3,000 − 500 + 350). The percentage profit depends on how long the call's life span was. On the other hand, if the stock had declined to $15, the broker would exercise the put option, selling its $30-cost-basis stock for $30. The broker's profit is once again $150, representing the proceeds of the call minus the cost of the input. Commissions are negligible for brokers who are members of the New York Stock Exchange, although they are prohibitively high for individual investors who would be converters. Most conversions are done by converting straddles into two calls. In such cases, the broker will charge a flat fee for the conversion, although the preceding explains how his profit is calculated; the fee will rise or fall with changing interest rate costs for carrying the stock.

It is also possible to convert a call into a put in the same fashion, although it is much less common. The major value of conversion to a trader is that if he has, for example, purchased a six-month call at $30 and three months later the stock is $50, and if he feels the stock will now decline rapidly, he can have his broker convert his call into a put. He has not wasted the remaining three months of the option, and the costs of conversion will be substantially less than those of purchasing a new three-month put option. This "reverse conversion" is generally called a reversal.

Another interesting technique with over-the-counter options is the down-and-out or up-and-out option. At the same time, the down- (or up-) and-out option has both vastly more speculative potential and risk. The option has an expiration price as well as an expiration date. Generally speaking, the expiration price is 10 percent below the striking price for a call or 10 percent above for a put. If that price is reached, the call or put is cancelled and "you're out." The advantage to the buyer is that if he exercised the call before the expiration date, he gets a prorated premium return. If, for example, a six-month call is exercised after only 30 days, the buyer gets back five sixths of his premium. The big disadvantage is that if the stop point is reached, the remaining time on the option is immediately cancelled. Some brokers' out options even raise the expiration price every month which increases the risk even further, although slightly lowering the cost. The advantage to the seller is that the writer does not have to hold on to a plummeting issue because, in effect, the out option will act as a stop loss order without the possibility of a whipsaw. The disadvantages are only from the buyer's side, although there are potential advantages to both buyer and seller.

This type of option seems to be losing popularity with the advent of the CBOE.

Taxes are of major consequence to many option traders, especially to sellers, since writers are frequently wealthy individuals in high tax brackets. There are three basic rules: (1) If an option expires worthless, the premium paid is a capital loss to the buyer and is long or short term depending on whether the option was held for more or less than six months. Most brokers will, as a service, repurchase an option for $1 just prior to the six-month expiration to enable the buyer to get the more favorable short-term tax treatment on the loss. Profits on expired worthless options are ordinary income to the seller, and the gain is taxed in the year the option expires. (2) If a call is exercised, the premium paid is added to the price of the called stock. If a put is exercised, the price paid is subtracted from the price of the called stock. (3) If a put or call is resold, the profit or loss is the difference between the two prices, and it is long or short term depending on how long the position was held. Although the preceding will cover most cases, investors who intend to do a substantial amount of option trading should refer to an option manual specializing in tax consequences, such as *Maximum Leverage from Puts and Calls* by John Cunnion, chief editor of the Lasser Tax Report.

As previously mentioned, the wave of the future seems to be exchange traded options such as those traded on the CBOE. The main analytical difference between those options and warrants will revolve around margin requirements which are currently quite different. It is quite probable that as pressure builds up against the NYSE's and FRB's excessively rigid requirements that adjustment will be made. At this time, however, it seems pointless to discuss it in depth since comments might well be out of date by publication date, and again outdated six months later. The analyst is advised to keep appraised of the margin requirements through his margin department. New developments may also be found in updated copies of the CBOE prospectus, which must be distributed to every CBOE trader. It is anticipated that put trading will begin in the near future on the CBOE, and analysis for these options should be the same as for calls, except in reverse.

RIGHTS

Of the four types of securities options, rights are the least profitable from an investment point of view, yet they are extremely important from the vantage point of the issuing corporation. Also called preemptive rights, they evidence the right of shareholders to purchase new stock in a company in proportion to their current holdings so as to retain their proportionate corporate ownership. This preemptive right does not exist in the bylaws of all companies, and where it does not, which is the majority of cases, the corporation can sell new stock directly to the public without first offering it to present shareholders. Companies without preemptive rights in their bylaws can still use a rights offering as a means of raising new capital, though. The mechanics are as follows: Each shareholder of record as of a given day is issued one right, frequently, and misleadingly, called a subscription warrant. A given number of these rights can then be surrendered, along with a stipulated amount of cash, to purchase more shares of the company's common stock.

The difference between rights and warrants are: (1) warrants are longer term, rights generally having a life span of between 2 and 10 weeks; (2) rights are issued to effect current financing and warrants are sold partially to facilitate future financing; (3) the exercise price of warrants is usually above the current market, while the exercise price of a right is below the market price of the stock so as to encourage immediate exercise; and (4) one warrant generally buys one common, whereas many rights are required to buy one common share. Rights furthermore generally sell at several cents apiece since the exercise price is only slightly below the market price for the common, and several rights are needed for one common. If rights have a life span of 60 or 90 days, they can be treated as short-term call options, but it is unusual for a stock to have a marked advance during a financing, thereby taking a good deal of the leverage out of the rights.

Rights go "ex" the same way that dividends do. Their value is determined by the difference between the current common price and the rights' exercise price, divided by the number of rights needed to buy one share of stock, or in letter terms, $R = (S - E)/N$. However, many times the rights will trade on a when-issued basis, i.e., there is a market for the rights before the stock has gone ex-rights. Since the value of S before the ex-date is higher than it will be after going ex-rights, all other things being equal, the formula for determining the value of the rights prior to the ex-rights date has to be adjusted to $R = (S - E)/(N + 1)$. The number 1 merely represents the one right which is still attached to the common. Since rights will sell at their intrinsic value, there being no reason to place a premium on a security with only weeks to live, it is obvious that it makes no difference whether the rights are exercised or if they are sold on the open market and the identical number of common purchased on the market, except for higher commission costs with the latter. In theory it would be possible to arbitrage rights if they fell below intrinsic value, but don't hold your breath.

Probably the most important investment advantage of rights is that their exercise enables the investor to purchase the underlying common on very low margin in a "special subscription account," as described in Regulation T, 220.4(h).

In recent years, rights have been issued to purchase securities other than common stock. For example, in 1970, American Telephone and Telegraph issued rights for the purchase of a unit consisting of bonds and warrants, and in 1973, Gulf and Western Industries issued rights for the purchase of warrants to buy shares it owned in Atlantic Richfield Corporation.

CONCLUSION

The general theme of this chapter has been that options are all basically alike, and that all options can be analyzed as warrants with modifications as needed for specific differences. A great deal of work has been done in mathematical analyses of warrants and options. The simpler algebraic formulas have been presented earlier in the chapter. For those analysts with a knowledge of calculus and higher mathematics, and the desire to encounter a great deal of eyestrain, the following papers, all published by the Massachusetts Institute of Technology, are extraordinarily thorough: *Capital Market Equilibrium and the Pricing of Corporate Liabilities* by Fischer Black and Myron Scholes (1971), *The Theory of Rational Option Pricing* by Robert Merton (1971), and *A Complete Model of Warrant Pricing that Maximizes Utility* by Paul Samuelson and Robert Merton (1969). And, as Mr. Samuelson says, "Good luck."

18

Venture Capital Investments

STANLEY M. RUBEL
President
S.M. Rubel and Company
The Vencap Fund
Chicago, Illinois

Introduction

SECURITY ANALYSTS and investment advisors are sometimes asked by clients to screen and make recommendations on investments in companies that are privately held. Broadly categorized into what is called *venture capital,* this type of investing can encompass many different types of projects:

Start-ups (also called seed deals) involve either companies in the process of being organized or those that have been in business a short time (one year or less) but have not yet completed a prototype or taken orders for a product. Generally such firms would have selected the key officers, prepared a business plan, made market studies, and so on. Capital for start-ups is generally provided by informal sources, such as relatives, friends, customers, clients, wealthy individuals, and so forth.

First-stage financing involves companies that have expanded their initial capital on the prototype, developed some evidence of commercial interest in the product, evolved a going organization, perhaps acquired some pilot production equipment, and even obtained a small line of bank credit. It is generally at this stage of financing that the first outside capital flows in from organized venture capital sources, although about 50-70 venture firms regularly make start-up investments also.

Second-stage financing describes an investment in a company that is producing and shipping, whose accounts receivable and inventories are building up, and whose marketing expenses begin to mount. The company needs working capital and expansion capital. Although it has clearly made progress, it is probably still operating at a loss.

Third-stage financing involves companies in which sales volume has increased to where they are breaking even or making a profit. Funds are needed for further plant expansion, marketing, working capital, or perhaps acquisitions.

Bridge financing describes the situation where a company is expecting to go public within six months a year. Often bridge financing is structured so that it can be repaid from proceeds of the public underwriting.

Buy-out, or acquisition, financing (or special-situation investing) refers to situations where new or existing management purchases an undermanaged business. These situations also include asset plays or investments in loss companies that are expected to show profits shortly. In terms of risk, such situations tend to fall within the range of first- or second-stage financing.

Obviously, each of these types of situations have their own special characteristics and the analytical requirements, terms, pricing and monitoring for each can differ quite drastically.

In this short chapter on the subject of venture capital it is not possible to cover the differing complexities in each type of transaction. However, the key elements is the venture transactions will be described with some reference made to differences between the various aspects of venture capital financings.

DESCRIPTION OF VENTURE CAPITAL INDUSTRY

As a reference point, it is important to understand the structure and makeup of the present venture capital industry. The industry presently consists of about 600 companies and identifiable individuals in the United States who have established a pattern of professional and continuous investment interest in private transactions. Obviously, there are many more people in the country who will invest in a given transaction, but generally they are not regular investors who have concentrated in this field. They might take an occasional flyer, depending on the level of the stock market or their own personal preferences. Most start-up ventures are financed by friends, relatives, suppliers, customers, and others who have special relationships with the entrepreneur. They are not included as part of the professional venture community, but certainly play a significant role in the creation and financing of new and young companies. The total capital of the industry is estimated at about

$3 billion, and American venture capital companies invest about $500 to $700 million in an average year.

There is also an active venturing community in Canada, consisting of about 60 companies. A number of active venture capitalists also operate in London, Paris, Brussels, Geneva, Tokyo, and other cities throughout the world. Although venture capital has been largely an American activity, at least in organized form, there does seem to be an increasing international interest in the field. In the third edition of *Guide to Venture Capital Sources,* published in mid-1974 by Capital Publishing Corporation, Chicago, about 600 American sources were identified and fully described, plus another 100 international sources. The guide is a unique way to learn how the venture capitalists operate as it contains 19 presentations by active members of the venturing community on all facets of the business. The directory section provides detailed descriptions of these firms, both in America and abroad.

The American venturing community consists of a number of rather different types of entities and includes the following:

Venture Capital Corporation or Partnership with Institutional Ownership. This type of venture structure was first organized in 1968 when the Heizer Corporation was formed in Chicago with $81 million. Since then some 40 such firms have been formed with capital provided largely by bank trust departments, insurance companies, pension and profit sharing trusts, wealthy families, and corporations. While the Heizer Corporation is still the largest, two others (New Court Private Equity Fund and EMW Associates) have been formed in the $30–$50 million range, and most of the others are capitalized between $10 and $20 million.

Family Venture Capital Partnerships. The original form of organized venturing was conducted by such families as Rockefeller, Whitney, Payson, Phipps, Rosenwald, Hale, and some others. The traditional form was a family partnership, directed by professional managers. While many of these groups remain active, the advent of other forms of organized venturing has reduced their relative importance in the industry.

Small Business Investment Companies. SBICs were first created through congressional legislation in 1958, and this segment of the venturing industry has gone through a trying initiation period. The basic concept is that government-type funding will enable the venture-type SBIC to borrow three times its capital on a long-term basis. At the present time, such funding is handled by public underwritings similar to other federal agency paper, and is fully guaranteed by the treasury department. Three or four times a year, the Small Business Administration (the federal agency responsible for administration of the program) organizes such underwritings, which are managed by the major investment banking firms. Goldman Sachs, Salomon Brothers, Merrill Lynch, Kidder

Peabody, and others have been major underwriters for SBIC paper; and in 1973 alone, over $100 million was raised for the SBICs.

Although the industry experienced many traumatic moments in its early history, due to indiscriminate licensing, unseasoned SBIC managers, undue SBA regulation, and intermittent funding, these problems seem to have been satisfactorily resolved in the last few years. The present SBA administrators are competent, and the rules have been amended to conform to the needs of the venturing industry. As described, the funding problems seem to have been resolved, and in 1973 the average cost of 10-year money (no amortization required) was about 7½ percent per year. The quality of the remaining 100 or so venture-type SBICs is quite high, and the new companies being licensed are being carefully screened by the SBA. (It should be noted that there are another 150 SBICs primarily engaged in secured lending and real estate development.) In early 1974, there seemed to be a trend for venture capitalists to obtain SBIC licenses as an alternative means of raising capital. Many of the nation's leading banks such as First National City Bank, Chase Manhattan, Bank of America, Security Pacific, First National Bank of Boston, First National Bank of Chicago, Continental Illinois, First National Bank of Dallas, and many others have excellent SBIC operations, but publicly held SBICs no longer represent a major part of the industry.

Corporate Venture Divisions. Another trend that seems to have started in the late 1960s is for large corporations to form venture capital subsidiaries. Such firms have been formed by General Electric, Exxon, Dow Chemical, Singer, Johnson & Johnson, Eastman Kodak, GTE, Control Data, Sun Oil, Eaton Corporation, and others. The reasons for this action are varied, but generally, venture capital can provide a different type of research input at potentially a far lower cost than the regular research operation. Some corporations are in the business strictly to make money, and some have concluded that the venture department can utilize internal research developments where the markets are insufficient to be of interest to the parent company. Through venture capital, the corporation could recover the research cost and perhaps make a profit. However, most corporate venture operations are primarily interested in funding projects that in time could become divisions of the corporation. These types of venture situations usually are structured so that the parent company can acquire a majority or 80 percent interest in the business either at the outset or upon the achievement of specified goals.

Venture Capital Affiliates of Investment Banking Firms. There are a dozen or more venture partnerships and corporations that have been organized by investment banking firms and are operated through their auspices. Such firms as A. G. Becker & Company, Donaldson Lufkin & Jenrette, Hambrecht & Quist, Lehman Brothers, Oppenheimer & Company, Paine Webber Jackson & Curtis, Smith Barney & Company, Tucker Anthony & R. L. Day, and some others manage such funds.

Other Type of Venture Operations. Certain of the nation's most successful venture operations have been investment sections of large insurance companies. Allstate Insurance Company conducts one of the largest venture operations in the country. Some pension and profit-sharing trusts engage directly in venturing, as do certain bank trust departments. Many of these types of investors recognized certain inherent limitations when they attempted to engage directly in venturing and decided to back the venture corporation instead. A number of successful individual venture capitalists are active in the field, and there are a number of offshore funds also in the business. Various large bank holding companies have organized venture capital operations to supplement their SBIC activities, and some investment advisory firms and mutual fund managers also manage venture capital operations.

Mesbics. Since 1970, there has been a government-sponsored move to create special firms to make equity investments in businesses owned by minority groups such as blacks, Puerto Ricans, Mexican Americans, American Indians, and Eskimos. A special type of SBIC, called a minority enterprise SBIC (MESBIC), has been created for this purpose. The MESBIC operates under rules that are similar to, but more liberal than, the rules for SBICs, but they must channel all their capital to businesses owned by these minority groups. MESBICs have been established by commercial banks, community groups, large corporations, and private investors, and the program is still in an experimental stage. MESBICs often will invest funds in conjunction with bank loans made to minority-owned small companies that have been 90 percent guaranteed by the Small Business Administration.

There are about 70 MESBICs in operation throughout the country, but whether this program will be successful or not and whether or not these firms will survive as permanent institutions is not yet clear. While most MESBIC managements are highly motivated and conscientious, they are also inexperienced in high-risk investing. If the SBIC industry offers any criteria, it will take at least 10 years to evaluate this program.

Types of Investments Completed by Venture Industry

In terms of the different stages of investments described earlier, probably no more than 10 percent to 20 percent of the industry's capital is employed in any given year in start-up deals, although some firms specialize in such deals. This would be particularly true in years like 1973 and 1974 when terms for second- and third-round financings were exceedingly attractive. The bulk of the industry's capital normally is employed in first- and second-round deals and in buy-out transactions, perhaps in equal proportions. During such periods as occurred in 1968 and

1969, the incidence of the start-up type transactions is much higher, since competition from the public marketplace drives up the price of second stage and subsequent rounds of financings, whereas the structure of the start-up is not affected nearly to the same extent.

Industry Preferences

The venture capitalist seeks the highest return on his investment. To do this, he must find the fastest growing types of businesses or those that will carry the highest price earnings multiple once they become successful. In the past decade, technological-based companies have been better able to achieve these objectives than other types of businesses. Venture capitalists, therefore, have tended to prefer technology-oriented businesses such as in computer-related fields, data communications, telephone-related equipment, development of new materials, semiconductor manufacturing, instrumentation, electronics, and others. Perhaps the greatest concentration has been in computer-related businesses (mainframes, minis, software, time sharing, peripherals, terminals) over the past half-dozen years, but even so, no more than about 15 percent or so of the industry's investments have been concentrated in any single category. Venture capitalists were responsible for the formation of the nation's two leading minicomputer companies and many of the leading peripheral and terminal companies, MOS semiconductor makers, time sharing companies, and specialized computer applications in a variety of areas have been started or backed by venture firms. However notable successes have also occurred in a wide variety of businesses such as specialty publishing, franchised hamburger outlets, CATV, medical products, and many others.

General Investment Objectives

Venture capitalists tend to speak of their investment goals in rather imprecise terms. They say they would like to "double their money in three years," "make a triple in five years," "make ten times their money in five years," and so on. Generally, on start-ups the venture capitalists would expect to make about 10 times or more on their money, while in a third-round financing, a profit of 3 times the amount invested for five years or longer might be anticipated. Actually, the experienced venture capitalist knows it is impossible to pinpoint how long it will take to achieve investment targets. Gains are subject to so many variables and unknowns that it is considered a sign of immaturity to attempt too much precision in expecting investment goals to be achieved as indicated. Results usually lag behind expectations during periods of weak stock markets, while forging ahead much faster than anticipated during good markets.

In terms of how the generally described investment targets can be translated to actual return percentages, the following simple chart has been prepared.

Profit Targets of Venture Capitalists	*Compounded Annual Rates of Return (pretax)*
Triple their money in three years	44%
Triple their money in five years	32
Four times their money in four years	41
Five times their money in three years	71
Five times their money in five years	38
Seven times their money in three years	91
Seven times their money in five years	48
Ten times their money in three years	115
Ten times their money in five years	58

As a general rule, if venture capitalists are financing start-ups or first-stage projects, they will look for a return at the high end of the scale, such as seven to ten times their money in five years. Thus, these investors would be looking for a 48 percent to 58 percent compounded return on their investment. On the other hand, investors in second-stage financing tend to be looking for a 35 percent to 40 percent return per year and those making third-stage deals generally seek 25 percent per year.

What Kind of People Make Good Venture Capitalists?

There is simply no answer to this question. A track record is the only identifiable way to prejudge the venture capitalist. While this does not necessarily mean that lightning will strike twice, it does take years to develop the skills and business judgment necessary to make the right decisions at critical points in the development of a business. A man can be trained in manufacturing, marketing, finance, investment banking, or publishing for that matter, but he must experience the multitude of problems that can arise in this business and demonstrate the energy, aggression, and strength to resolve such problems if he is to be a successful venture capitalist.

The successful venture capitalists are highly intelligent, and resourceful and have a very strong sense of individual ego. At times they must bet their judgment against those of the world, and this requires great inner confidence. They do not tend to be plungers or speculators, and most are fairly conservative, despite the fact they are playing in the highest risk part of the investment field. They tend to work exceedingly long hours, engage in extensive travel, and while they enjoy money and prestige, it is not clear that these are principal motives for their daily activities. They like to feel they are accomplishing something—

backing companies that can add some value to daily life. Yet they are also adopting the portfolio manager's approach of diversification in order to spread the risk.

Venture capitalists must be patient, both with the entrepreneurs they are backing and with all the problems they know will arise before the business will emerge successfully. Yet they must have killer instincts in order to negotiate effective purchase terms and to avoid the lurking trap of fraud which is amazingly easy to fall into. Venture capitalists must also be effective salesmen. They must keep their investors happy and be able to raise additional capital from time to time for their own operation. They must have a close rapport with commercial and investment bankers in order to help raise capital for their portfolio companies. While maintaining a somewhat low profile, they must find ways to make their presence known in the business and financial communities so they will see the best new investment prospects. They must have great fortitude so as not to panic during moments of great stress.

In all, it takes a very unique person to be a successful venture capitalist over a prolonged period of time. The venture capitalist must have youthful energies, but older maturity and judgment. He must have the entrepreneur's instinct as to business opportunities and involvements, yet not to the extent of being involved in the daily operation of the business. He must relish the high-risk elements of the business, yet he must also be conservative for purposes of self-preservation and have a strong desire to win.

HOW DOES VENTURE CAPITAL DIFFER FROM OPEN MARKET INVESTMENT OPERATIONS?

When venture capital deals work out, the business looks very simple. Investors make huge profits and are generally considered the smartest of operators. What does not show is the fact that it has taken years of specialized training and focus to be in a position to achieve such success, and in many ways, the venture capitalist plays a direct role in achieving his own success.

Often cited as the most outstanding venture investment by the industry, American Research & Development Corporation (ARD) invested about $70,000 in Digital Equipment Corporation in 1958 and saw the equity rise to a value of $500–$600 million in 1969. However, what is generally overlooked is that it took ARD from 1946 to 1958 to develop the skills to identify Digital and to help the company in its meteoric rise; and for most of that period, the Dow Jones industrials greatly outperformed ARD.

Alan Patricof, President of Alan Patricof Associates, Inc., put it most succinctly in an address before the New York Society of Security Analysts in January 1973. In his opinion, the fundamental difference between a venture capitalist (VC) and a security analyst (SA) is that of attitude. The SA *invests* in companies and a VC *becomes a partner*. An SA purchases shares of stock, whereas a VC buys a percentage interest.

Expressed in other terms, the SA has the opportunity to take advantage of the inherent human instinct of changing his mind. However, once a VC has committed an investment, he is locked in for an indefinite period of time. This alone is enough to separate the two activities. Furthermore, the SA may be basing a great part of his decision on the psychological factors of general market conditions at the time an investment is made. The VC who is influenced by transient stock market enthusiasm for a particular industry is asking for trouble. In 1969 and 1970, most venture capitalists avoided the nursing homes and computer leasing companies, and in 1971, the industrial building system and double knit equipment companies were hot market plays, but poor venture investments and generally ignored by venture capitalists. Yet it has been exceedingly difficult to avoid paying too much for solid business opportunities in the computer-related fields, medical instrument companies, and others that are financed through the venture process during periods of a strong stock market. Overpaying for a venture is one of the major hazards of the business particularly if the investment vehicle is common stock. The problem is that it can take years before securities purchased in a private, nonregistered transaction can be cleared for public sale. This makes it impossible to be protected from shifts in market sentiment as to industries, prices, and so on by selling the securities. As a result venture capitalists must rely on basics; fads, temporary trends, or other short-term plays must be avoided.

There are many other interesting differences between the two types of investing. The venture capitalist begins his investigation after receiving a detailed proposal from the company. All the factors that the security analyst must spend hours, days, and weeks to compile have been supplied to the venture capitalist at the initial meeting. While the security analyst's skills are partly dependent on how well he can ferret out such information from management, the venture capitalist has the entire report dropped at his feet.

However, since the venture capitalist is making an irrevocable decision (at least for two to five years or more), he must engage in a far more detailed investigation of the business. Any significant weakness could cause its downfall. Even more important is the analysis of the management team and of the president of the company. It takes a different type of person to build a small company to the point where it becomes a viable growth company than it does to run a successful publicly held growth company. Many successful entrepreneurs never make the transition to becoming successful managers of growth companies. The style of leadership is different, organizing and planning methods differ, and motivations differ, and these often spell major problems for the highly successful venture backed company that is reaching the next size level.

The partnership concept between the venture capitalist and entrepreneur carries a marked difference to that of security analyst and management. The venture capitalist is probably a director of the company, who spends days or weeks each month working on problems of the business or helping make critical business decisions. Although financials are reviewed, the venture capitalist often plays a role in setting internal budgets and financial planning procedures, often represents the company with banks and insurance companies to obtain loans, and helps arrange for the initial public offering. It is quite easy for the venture capitalist to lose his perspective since he becomes so close to the business. While venture capitalists have been fairly successful buyers, their success as sellers has been far less notable.

It may be belaboring the point, but the security analyst must be aware of the traps awaiting him if he attempts to engage in venture capital investing directly. Part-time venture capital investing has proven to be particularly treacherous. The business is far too demanding and time consuming to be conducted successfully on a part-time basis. It is far too easy to make poor investment decisions without the intimate knowledge of the business that comes from total immersion, often at the early stages of development. The venture capitalist often must decide whether to cut bait and lose all or most of his investment or to continue to fish along with more bait—in the form of dollars.

At the same time, the security analyst has certain critical skills and perspective often not shared by the venture capitalist. He should be in a far better position to know when it is time to sell a maturing investment and when the market for the company's shares is far too overpriced to offer an effective gamble, and he can provide interesting value judgments as to the relative merits of the venture backed company compared to other companies in the same field.

While the purpose of this chapter is to describe in detail how the venture process works, rather than attempt to put this information to use and engage directly in venture activities, the security analyst or investment advisor might explore the idea of forming a relationship with an established venture capitalist. The analyst or advisor could turn over a portion of client money to the venture capitalist for management purposes and then retain a more passive interest in the fund. This could combine the best of both skills—the venture capitalist's ability to spot and negotiate a solid opportunity and then work to make sure it succeeds as anticipated, and the security analyst's ability to sense market conditions and security values in terms of when to sell. Another alternative would be to participate with venture capitalists as part of their investment syndicates, usually for second- and third-stage projects.

In any event, the venture capital business does not work on a short-term basis. Making investments and then trying to hedge bets, selling short or selling on brief market strength just will not work. A venture capital investment entails locking money up for a minimum of three and more likely five or seven years. The venture capitalist cannot simply walk away from his investment particularly during the early stages without greatly increasing the odds of disaster occurring. He cannot sell when he is discouraged, if he thinks the economic climate might be changing, or if the market is overbought. He is locked into the business, for better or for worse, and if it is for the worst, the loss exposure can easily approach 100 percent.

THE VARIOUS PROCESSES THROUGH WHICH VENTURE CAPITAL INVESTMENTS ARE MADE, DEVELOPED, AND SOLD

Initial Screening

The most active venture capital firm probably sees as many as 500 to 1,000 proposals for financing each year. The average active firm might see 200–300 such proposals. Deals come from a wide variety of sources, such as other venture firms, investment bankers, consultants, attorneys, accountants, references from business acquaintances, cold solicitation, and others. By far the most productive are referrals from knowledgeable sources, such as executives of companies with prior dealings with venture sources, certain key professionals, bankers, and other venture capitalists. While investment bankers create the majority of the deals, they tend to be overpriced and underinvestigated. Often intermediaries' fees are too high relative to the amount of services they perform. However certain types of more advanced second- and third-round situations during good market conditions can be handled quite effectively by investment bankers. In the weak 1973–74 markets, a number of venture capitalists themselves were syndicating financings for companies in which they already had investments.

Venture firms find it exceedingly difficult to establish specific standards by which to accept or reject proposals. While the ridiculous proposal from the wild-investor type is easily rejected and the firm may have instituted a rule to go easy on start-ups during a given period, a critical aspect of the business is to decide which of various attractive proposals warrant the extensive investigation needed before any deal can be completed.

Usually the venture firm will reject deals out of hand that appear impossibly risky or unfeasible. Those that seem to have appeal and where the pricing appears reasonable will receive fairly early attention.

Often venture firms will respond to proposals by saying that the pricing is too high and that the deal will receive consideration only if the pricing, or structuring, could be altered.

Generally venture firms look for unique products, protected markets, or areas where exceedingly high sales and profit growth are possible—50 to 100 percent per year or more in some cases. They are seeking exceedingly competent management usually with an identifiable track record or an employment level that provided management experience at a divisional or financial level. Usually the venture firm will have some preferred industries, but most are interested in a wide variety of fields. However, the business must have the potential of carrying some reasonably healthy PE multiple at time of sale. The risk level of the deal must also comply with the venture firm's policies.

Approaching a venture firm is an important maneuver. Strong references from successful businessmen whom the venture firm has backed or with whom the firm has a close relationship is best, followed by commercial bankers, lawyers, accountants, investment bankers, consultants, and finders. Unless an exceedingly strong personal introduction is arranged, most venture firms prefer to receive a written proposal before meeting with management or the entrepreneur.

If the deal has sufficient interest to warrant a meeting, the venture firm is likely to make a few phone calls to verify the capability and reputation of the key man, or to double-check the attractiveness of the industry. Most venture capitalists have a wide circle of acquaintances throughout the business and financial world. Often it is possible to verify these characteristics with a few telephone calls.

As a guide to the type of information venture firms like to see in financing proposals, the enclosed is a sample of a proposal outline used by Continental Illinois Venture Corporation.

A. Summary (very brief).
B. The proposed financing.
   1. Amount.
   2. Terms (including type of security and price).
   3. Agents and fees (cash and other fees).
C. Use of proceeds of the financing.
D. History and business.
   1. Nature of business (historical, current, planned). (Include: patent or similar protection, renegotiation obligations, description of physical assets, leases, encumbrances, casualty insurance, product and other liability insurance, key man life insurance, material contracts, franchises, licenses.)
   2. Marketing (methods, sales, competition, seasonal factors, cyclical factors, any outside consultant, concentration of customers, aging of receivables, bad debt experience).

3. Production (methods, materials, sources of supply, aging of payables).
4. Employees (number, function, labor relations, collective bargaining agreements, availability of manpower, fringe benefits including insurance, pension, and profit-sharing plans).
5. Corporate history (formation, mergers, acquisitions, purchases or sales of assets, reorganizations, prior offerings of securities).
6. Affiliates (controlled, controlling, under common control).

E. Control.
1. Founders, management, directors, major stockholders (name, address, principal occupation, etc.), detailed resumes for executive officers.
2. Voting trust or similar arrangements (including any pledge of stock).
3. Remuneration, current and planned.
4. Transactions between any principals or their associates and the company.

F. Financial.
1. Capitalization (current and contemplated, including paid-in capital, dilution from options, warrants, conversion, and other rights; treasury shares).
2. Five-year history (income, balance sheet, cash flow; audited if available).
3. Five-year forecast (income, balance sheet, cash flow). (Specify assumptions, correlate with physical volume and price, and indicate in notes physical volume and price during past periods.)

D. History and business.

G. Miscellaneous (past, pending, or threatened legal administrative proceedings; accountants; attorneys; management studies; banks and other sources of financing).

There is no industry standard for such presentations. Some venture firms prefer simpler presentations, while others like to see proposals that are prepared in great detail.

If the project entails a start-up or early stage proposal, it is essential that the venture firm also reviews the business plan, including the strategy by which the firm expects to enter the marketplace. This often entails a detailed analysis of each step to be achieved and how it will be implemented.

Generally venture firms look for two types of opportunities. The first involves companies that have the potential to become major corporations. Under current economic conditions, such projects usually require large sums, in the millions of dollars, provided through participation among a number of venture firms. Recent examples of such projects include a new air carrier to provide overnight small package delivery service, a company attempting to exploit a breakthrough technology in high-speed computer printing and xeroxing fields, a company building main frame computers using fourth generation technology, a firm attempting to build a marine motor using aluminum engine blocks and others.

INVESTIGATING AND INITIAL STRUCTURING

Hard work and sound business instincts are the key words to investigating a new venture proposal. Venture capitalists generally spend a great deal of time with management or the entrepreneur trying to take their measure in terms of both personal characteristics and business skills. The Institute for New Enterprise Development (INED) in Belmont, Massachusetts, has done a great deal of work in identifying the key characteristics of successful entrepreneurs—from the point of venture capital investment—and also the necessary skills required to be successful. For example, INED has identified the following as the key character requirements for the entrepreneur:

Drive and Energy Level. Success as an entrepreneur demands the ability to work actively for long hours with less than the normal amount of sleep.

Self-confidence. You need self-confidence—a belief in yourself and your ability to achieve goals and a sense that events in your life are self-determined.

Long-Term Involvement. You have to be able to commit yourself to projects that will see completion in five to seven years and to work toward goals that may be quite distant in the future. This ability implies a total immersion and concentration on the attainment of distant goals.

Using Money as a Performance Measure. Money, in the form of salary, profits, or capital gains, should be viewed as a measure of what you are doing and have done, not as an end in itself.

Persistence Problem Solving. You must have an intense and determined desire to complete a task or solve a problem.

Setting Challenging but Realistic Goals. You need the ability to set clear goals and objectives that are challenging, yet realistic and attainable.

Taking Moderate Risks. Entrepreneurial success implies a preference for taking moderate, calculated risks, where the chances of winning are not so small as to make the effort a gamble, nor so large as to make it a sure thing, but which provide a reasonable and challenging chance of success.

Learning from Failure. You have to use failures as learning experiences, and you need to understand your role in causing the failures so that you can avoid similar problems in the future. You should be disappointed but not discouraged by failures.

Using Criticism. You need the demonstrated capacity to seek and use criticism of your performance so that you can take corrective action and do better next time.

Taking Initiative and Seeking Personal Responsibility. You need the desire to seek and take initiative and to put yourself in situations where you are personally responsible for the success or failure of the operation. You should be able to take the initiative to solve problems or fill leadership vacuums, and you should enjoy situations where your impact on a problem can be measured.

Making Good Use of Resources. Can you identify and use expertise and assistance that are relevant to the accomplishment of your goals? You cannot be so involved in the achievement of your goals and in independent accomplishment that you will not let anyone help you.

Competing Against Self-imposed Standards. Do you tend to establish your own standard of performance, which is high yet realistic, and then compete with yourself?

INED has also developed a list of 43 key management skills broken down by such key areas as marketing, engineering and research, operations, financial administration, management skills, personnel, and legal and tax areas. The institute conducts three weekend sessions for budding entrepreneurs to test and measure their skills and characteristics, using a variety of techniques.

There is no standard way venture capitalists test for these characteristics. Some use stress interview techniques, constantly probing for weak points. Some spend months with management observing how the variety of responsibilities in building a major enterprise are handled. Some use industrial psychologists to test entrepreneurs. All extensively check backgrounds, prior working conditions, and performance records. As in other areas of security analysis, evaluation of management is critical for a successful investment, but in the case of venture capital, wrong decisions are far more difficult to remedy.

Most venture capitalists are looking for a team approach to business management and thus are interested in determining if the team complements each other's skills and characteristics. The team must have a clearly determined leader, though, who must demonstrate the needed ability to act as the catalyst.

While the management factors are being appraised, venture capitalists also review other key areas: marketing, research and development, manufacturing, and financial considerations. Marketing is becoming an increasingly more critical factor in the success of small companies, and venture capitalists spend considerable time evaluating marketing strategies, testing product acceptance, studying market potential for the product, and speed with which markets can be expanded, both domestically and internationally. Interviews are conducted with customers, potential customers, competitors, salesmen, and distributors in order to decide the true potential of the business. Key questions are related to how fast the product will gain consumer acceptance, how well protected the product is from competition, how fast additional products can be introduced once the initial product is successful, and other matters.

In essence the venture capitalist must satisfy himself with regards to three major issues: Will it work? Can it be made at about the indicated cost and in the indicated quantity? Can it be sold?

It may take outside experts to answer the question of whether or not a new technology-type product will really work as indicated. This in turn entails a special knowledge of how to evaluate the report of an outside expert, who might either be too enthusiastic about the product without considering commercial problems (since he has no money at risk) or too negative due to a prior bias with the state of the art. The bill of materials must be reviewed by experienced manufacturing people to ascertain feasibility under production conditions. Availability of materials is a critical issue and one, for example, that kept venture capitalists out of the Viatron debacle. When venture capitalists checked the bill of materials, they found it would have been impossible to obtain the needed semiconductors for Viatron's proposed machines at the indicated prices for many years. Costs would also have been much too high, relative to indicated selling price of Viatron's equipment due to the state of the art of the semiconductor industry at that time. Other issues include availability of a work force if the plant must be rapidly expanded, and capability for rapid acceleration or deceleration of production must be considered.

For most early-stage ventures, the company will be dealing in what Stanley Golder, President of First Chicago Capital Corporation (wholly SBIC-venture capital subsidiary of First National Bank of Chicago) calls the "single sell or double sell" market. The single sell market entails a product being introduced into an existing market, which will be cheaper, work more effectively, or have some other reason for capturing the market from competitors. These types of situations are relatively simpler to investigate as there are identifiable buyers and products against which the new product can be compared. The problems in evaluating the double sell product are much greater. This would entail a totally new product for which there is no established market. In such cases, it is usually extremely difficult to pinpoint the extent of the potential market; and considerable imagination, tempered by business judgment, must be used to conceptualize how the business will evolve. Such a product must be considerably more cost effective than in a single sell situation, because customers will often have to change basic buying or manufacturing habits in order to acquire the product. First Chicago Capital Corporation has various investments of this nature, for example, involving a totally new type of plastic packaging and in ferrofluidics, and the investigation involved various innovative approaches to deciding whether or not the product really would be purchased by the market and if it could be produced in the manner indicated. Often these types of products have by far the greatest growth potential; and Digital Equipment, Raychem, Spectra Physics and Coherent Radiation, and many others illustrate this type of potential.

The extent of research and development needed to maintain product leadership is often a highly critical issue. Also, in many of the technological areas, change occurs rapidly and spin-offs of highly creative new groups can have a major impact on competition. The proliferation of minicomputer companies, MOS semiconductor manufacturers, and peripheral companies have had a major impact on the attractiveness of projects in these fields. Ease of entry into a new market is a critical consideration in evaluating venture projects.

Patent protection is one way to overcome such problems, but probably less than half the projects financed by venture capitalists involve meaningful patent protection. A lead time in the state of the art, unique marketing strategies, or product applications that will give the business sufficient time to establish leadership are usually the only protection provided to venture capitalists, plus the knowledge that management is hungrier and more aggressive than the competition.

Investigating a buy-out transaction is a far easier exercise and probably falls closer to the role played by most security analysts. Such projects entail on-going companies, that are usually profitable, where a new management is brought in to revitalize the business. The stability of the company in the marketplace, product acceptance, influence of competition, and plant capacity are far easier to ascertain. In such cases the quality of management is not quite as critical, and the continuity of the business should provide time in which to measure a man's skills and capabilities. Also, it is often easier to structure a buy-out with low-cost equity and heavy debt, combined with bank leverage. Leveraged buyouts are a major profit area for the venture industry.

Financial analysis is an important part of venture analysis. Most venture firms require profit and loss (P & L) statements for the past two to five years, plus P & L and cash flow projections on a monthly basis for the coming year and quarterly for the following year or two. The items included in the profit and cash flow forecasts are carefully checked against the information turned up in the investigation to see whether or not projections are feasible. In turn, this gives the venture firm a measure of the true financial needs of the business which often differ dramatically from those estimated by management. Changes in the time it takes to complete product development, testing, manufacturing, distribution, and customer acceptance all have a major bearing on cash flow forecasts, and thus on the key financial aspects of the business. The venture capitalist must also know when bank financing can be obtained, estimate dilution caused by subsequent rounds of equity financing, and evaluate other aspects of the company's financial plan. The following is a check list used by Federal Street Capital Corporation, a successful SBIC in the Boston area. The check list is used to be sure all critical areas of evaluation were covered in the investigation.

A. Product and market.
   1. Can any company succeed in this area? If not, kill it.
   2. Should market approach or product definition be changed to assure success? How implement the proposed change?

B. Product analysis.
   1. Proprietary aspects of product.
   2. State of the art.
   3. Product direct costs now and with volume production.
   4. Product life cycle.
   5. Follow on products.
   6. Service problems.

C. Market.
   1. Define end-user market-size.
   2. Does product fill an end-user need?
   3. Is this need recognized or must customer be educated?
   4. Can need be filled in any other way—other products?
   5. How does competition fill this need—size and number of competitors.
   6. Is there or will there be price competition—severity?
   7. Will selling price produce gross margins sufficient to justify direct costs?
   8. Are there buy/lease factors?
   9. Are there long lead purchase considerations?
   10. Is R.O.I. critical to buyer?
   11. Is company dependent on one or two large customers?

D. Management.
   1. Are all management positions filled with good, experienced people? Backgrounds.
   2. Deficiencies in management—correctable?
   3. Is management hungry—disciplined?
   4. Is management financially committed?
   5. Has management defined possible problem areas—solutions?
   6. Management attitude toward directors—is present board strong?
   7. Management attitude toward financial reporting.
   8. Can we live with management for long term—chemistry?
   9. Will management be able to delegate on time?
   10. Is management aware of various critical volume levels?

E. Financial plan.
   1. Are sales forecasts realistic (relate to market analysis)?
   2. Are expenses realistic—relate to revenues?

3. Is there a margin for slippage?
4. Start-up costs—prototype costs—new product development.
5. Cash flow—relate to income/expense projections.
6. Is other financing provided for—bank—leasing?
7. Alternate plans for 25 percent less sales—50 percent less sales.
8. Implementation of alternate plans.
9. Use of funds—maximum utilization—timing.
10. Controls—adequate?

F. Investment structure.

1. Is sufficient capital being invested to reach objectives?
2. Is risk/reward ratio adequate?
3. What is down-side exposure?
4. Are we on equal or better basis than prior investors?
5. Is valuation of company realistic?
6. Does purchase agreement provide adequate protection and default clauses?
7. Does stockholder agreement cover board control if needed?
8. Equity versus debt relationship.

This detailed examination of the business serves a number of major benefits in the future relationship between venture capitalist and entrepreneur:

1. It enables the venture capitalist to function more effectively as an advisor to the company, being better able to evaluate management decisions.

2. It gives the venture firm a much better knowledge as to its ability to work closely with the management, or entrepreneur. The best venture firms like to work as partners in the business in ways discussed under the section on services provided by venture capitalists. Extensive investigations work to this relationship.

3. There will always be critical decisions to be made for the business—should the venture firm put in more money or decide against putting good money after bad? Should management be allowed to remain in power, or be removed? Should the management team be supplemented and, if so, by what kinds of executives? These and a myriad of other important issues that constantly arise necessitate that the venture firm be as well schooled as possible in the business and maintain this knowledge as the business progresses. But despite all these studies and analysis, the entrepreneur is still the key factor in the ultimate success of the business.

All venture capitalists like to cite Murphy's Law which states "if something can go wrong . . . it will go wrong." Nothing progresses along the initially indicated pathway. A company that has a monopoly on a new material suddenly finds that the mines in Bolivia are being shut down due to a national emergency. A competitor unexpectedly introduces a new product not anticipated to be on the market for another year or two. Consumers create a boycott unexpectedly due to a Ralph Nader inspired revolt. At early stages, small companies are highly vulnerable to both errors and unexpected developments of this nature.

The energy crisis is already crippling entire industries. Recreational and leisure time companies that have been of considerable interest to venture capitalists for some time may well be hard hit by the gas shortage. Yet some aggressive, imaginative businessmen will find ways to turn the sow's ear into a silk purse—and these are the types of people venture capitalists are trying to identify and work with. These are the men who will work against the odds to establish viable, fast growing companies.

NEGOTIATING, STRUCTURING, AND PRICING

In the period of 1972–74, many venture capitalists have been turning away from straight equity and investing in interest or divided bearing securities (such as notes with warrants, convertible debentures, convertible preferred stock, or a combination of such instruments). The advantage is that of obtaining immediate yield (although this might also entail a somewhat lower equity position) and also of being able to renegotiate conversion terms if the company defaults. A variety of protections can often be built into the instrument—working capital requirements, performance and cost standards, antidilution controls, registration rights, and others. These provisions have been included not because the venture capitalist wants to take control of the business, but merely because he wants to have a strong voice in how certain key decisions are made. If management proves to be inept, he wants to be able to make changes.

Working capital is a critical commodity in all early stage companies and must be conserved to whatever degree possible. If it becomes necessary to cut back expenses to save working capital, the venture capitalist wants to be able to so dictate. If certain product lines are not working well, the venture capitalist wants to be in a position to help resolve the dilemma by dropping certain products and concentrating on others. Many young companies fall into the trap of trying to develop too many products and not concentrating on those most likely to impact their market. Such instruments also enable the venture capitalist to specify various other measures of protection—controls on capital expansion, mergers and acquisitions, equity financings, and many others.

The question of equity control is often a problem in venture situations involving early stage companies where the entrepreneurs have limited means. Often venture firms will take control initially, but will offer the management an "earn-out" contract, by which a formula is set so that management can increase their equity position if operating standards are met. In some cases, if the venture capitalists have a minority position, they will insist that the entrepreneur pledge his control stock position as security to the note, and a voting trust controlled by the investors will vote the stock if defaults occur.

In recent years, increasing numbers of venture capitalists have noted that although entrepreneurs have been quite successful in starting companies, they have not been able to cope with the complexities of managing the next stage in the company's development. The venture capitalists want to have a strong voice in seeing that management changes can be made at an appropriate time, so the progress of the business will not be affected.

The demise of the new issue market in 1973–74 along with increased problems in selling nonregistered stock due to the SEC rules on what is called #144 stock have encouraged many venture firms to enter into "side agreements" with their portfolio companies. These provide legal assurances that under certain situations the management will agree to sell the business or will buy out the venture capitalists at the same prices that are paid by an acquiring company. There are a wide variety of agreements to cover the fact that in 1973 and early 1974 it was almost impossible for a small company to go public, much less for venture capitalists to have a secondary offering of shares they held in such companies.

Side agreements and the use of notes with warrants, convertible debentures, or convertible preferred stock provide a great deal more flexibility in negotiating equity percentages and the cost of equities. These provisions give venture capitalists greater assurances that they can get their investment back, and perhaps some gains, regardless of the condition of the public market, or perhaps even though the business does not become a major success. Particularly in the case of third-stage financings, such businesses have sufficient substance so that creativity in the structure of the financing can solve many of the problems of the locked-in investor.

SERVICES PROVIDED BY VENTURE CAPITALISTS

A venture capitalist who can function as an effective partner is indeed a uniquely valuable addition to the business. Most entrepreneurs suffer from the loneliness of command. They simply have no constructive people with whom they can discuss their problems without fear of having bank loans called, answers that are much too conservative to be practical, large fees incurred, and so forth. Venture capitalists generally do not charge for the time they spend with their portfolio companies unless some major project is involved. They can help the entrepreneur decide business strategies, personnel problems, and marketing problems. While the venture capitalist is not likely to engage in the day-to-day aspect of the business, for the businessman, he can serve as an effective sounding board or devil's advocate. Since both have nearly the same objectives, the results can be highly beneficial, provided both are compatible. This compatibility which enables the venture capitalist to participate effectively in the business is a critical element in the initial investigation. Venture people seek those entrepreneurs who are sufficiently strong, aggressive, and ambitious to be able to found and build large companies, yet who are sufficiently flexible and receptive to listen to varying points of view and remain open-minded.

Most venture capitalists review financial results weekly or monthly until projects begin to reach maturity. They watch for negative trends, hoping they can catch problems before they become major drains on the business. They can assist in the budgeting and cost control side of the business and in financial management. They insist on cash flow statements integrated with the business plan and progress of the business.

Naturally, the venture capitalists are deeply engaged in the financial planning of the business, because if it runs short of money, they will have to make up the difference or jeopardize their initial position. They generally introduce the company to commercial and investment brokers, insurance companies, and others when additional funds are needed.

Many venture capitalists can also assist the company by finding key consultants to solve specific types of business problems, successful businessmen with whom the entrepreneur can consult on certain problems, top level managers in the companies that could represent potential customers, and others. Venture capitalists often have contacts with the management of the larger companies in the country.

Venture firms often assist the smaller company in finding personnel in key areas of management, marketing, manufacturing, and financial administration. The most successful venture capitalists are those who take an active role in the development of their portfolio companies and who have proven to be effective in this role themselves. They tend to invest at an earlier stage and at lower prices and attempt to continuously monitor the progress of the business. When they identify signs that the business is beginning to mature, they will start to reduce their position. The more passive investors tend to pay higher prices when they invest and must rely more on open-market analytical skills in timing their sales.

LEGAL ASPECTS OF VENTURE CAPITAL INVESTING

There are a wide variety of legal considerations involved in venturing. Developing effective loan agreements in a science all to itself, but of course there are a number of highly experienced attorneys in the large cities who are knowledgeable on this subject. Usually the venture capitalists review each loan agreement to be that certain areas of concern areas are protected.

The Securities Act of 1933 states that all financings must be registered with SEC unless certain exemptions are met. Rule #146, adopted in 1974, defines those private placements as are exempt from registration.

1. There must be direct communication between the issuer and persons contemplating acquiring securities.
2. There must be an opportunity for the offeree or his representatives to ask questions and receive answers from the issuer.
3. The offeree must have access to all information that would normally be required pursuant to full registration.
4. General advertising would be prohibited.
5. There would have to be a showing that the offeree or his representative have such knowledge and experience in financial and business matters that they are capable of utilizing the information necessary to evaluate the risks of the investment.
6. There must be a showing that the offeree is able to bear the economic risks of the investment.
7. In any consecutive 12-month period there shall be no more than 35 persons who purchase securities of the issuer pursuant to the rule, but persons who purchase for cash in an amount of not less than $150,000 and directors or executive officers of the issuer would be excluded in determining the number of purchasers.
8. The usual limitations on transfers of "restricted securities" would be imposed.
9. Persons relying on the proposed Rule 146 would be required to file reports of sales.

If a financing does not qualify for the private offering exception under Rule 146, the financing must be registered under the Securities Act of 1933. The Securities Act of 1933 also specifies that securities issued pursuant to the private offering exemption will be "restricted" in the sense that they cannot thereafter be sold or transferred unless they satisfy the conditions of the Act. This section has been the subject of extensive litigation over the years, but in 1972 the SEC adopted specific rules to govern such transactions. Called Rule 144, the SEC now specifies the following essential elements if investors wish to sell restricted securities:

1. There must be adequate current information available with respect to the issuer of the securities. This provision is deemed satisfied if an issuer has been subject to the reporting requirements of Section 13 or 15(d) of the Securities Exchange Act of 1934 for a period of at least 90 days immediately preceding the sale of securities and has filed all reports required by that act.

2. The securities must have been beneficially owned and fully paid for by the seller for a holding period of at least two years prior to his sale.
3. Not more than 1 percent of the class of the securities outstanding may be sold in any six-month period. If the securities are traded on an exchange, then the amount which may be sold in any six-month period shall not exceed the lesser of 1 percent of the amount of the class outstanding or the average weekly reported volume of trading on all exchanges over the four-week period preceding the sale.
4. Securities shall be sold only in brokers' transactions, and the person selling the securities shall not solicit or arrange for the solicitation of buy orders or make any payment in connection with the sale other than to the broker who executes the sell order.
5. The person desiring to sell securities must file a notice to that effect with the SEC. The notice must be transmitted to the commission concurrently with the placing of an order with a broker for the sale of the securities. A notice is not required with respect to transactions during any period of six months involving not more than 500 shares or other units, or $10,000, whichever is less.

Note that restricted securities can be registered, but registration must follow time-consuming and costly procedures and must comply with regulations of the Securities Act of 1933.

Some venture firms are subject to the Investment Company Act of 1940, which can impose limitations that need prior approval from SEC for certain types of transactions. Investors in the same company as the 1940 Act venture firm and who own 5 percent or more of the securities of the company may find themselves subjected to similar rules if they attempt to invest with the same venture firm again or make another investment in the same business. NASD members who also are venture capitalists are subject to various rules that could affect the terms under which a company in which they have an investment can go public. This would obviously affect the non-NASD investors in the same company.

The Internal Revenue Service has recently been looking more closely at various areas that can affect venture investments. Valuations placed on warrants are being subjected to greater scrutiny. The IRS is also looking more closely at thin capitalization of a company under which a debt instrument might be considered as equity, thus disallowing interest expense paid by the business and affecting the capital gains treatment of the transaction. Under certain circumstances venture capitalists can be held liable for federal taxes that have been withheld but not paid to the government. There are a variety of complexities that could occur if the venture capitalist is to adequately protect a prior position in a company that becomes bankrupt. Obviously these problems are too complex to be more than merely mentioned in this section. They do require attention by an attorney experienced in such matters.

GETTING OUT OF THE INVESTMENT

Essentially, there are three ways in which to realize gains or losses on investments. The public route is well known, and during periods of strong markets of sufficiently long duration, venture capitalists can sell shares in companies that have become publicly held. Rule 144 sales can be made if the shares have been held two years or longer and other qualifications are met. The shares can be registered with the SEC and sold through an underwriting or "dribbled into the market" through a shelf registration. Registration is time consuming and costly and will only be effective if done with the cooperation of the company. Often secondary registrations have a depressing effect on market prices, thus it is unlikely that the venture capitalist will be able to sell out at the top market price using this approach. Rule 144 sales are also somewhat depressing on market prices.

An effective way to realize gains is through merger with a larger company. A significant part of the gains realized by venture capitalists over the years have come from this channel. In such transactions sellers often receive registered shares. The limitations of Rule 144 do not pose a problem in selling shares of a large corporation where the venture capitalist is not likely to own more than a small percentage of the outstanding shares.

The third method is through repurchase by the management or the company. Usually this transaction is used only if the venture has not worked out as anticipated and the venture firm exercises a "put" to the company or management. This approach usually entails lower price earnings multiples and is generally considered a poor alternative.

FINAL RESULTS

After this long difficult process, how much money do venture capitalists really make as a return on their capital. This is a rather mystical number and cannot be fully answered, due to the private nature of the venturing community. Based on studies that appear in *Venture Capital*, (Capital Publishing Corp., Chicago), the professional journal of the venturing community, the top venture firms may earn 15 percent to 20 percent per year compounded on their money, net after taxes. To do this it usually takes a strong bull market and a skilled venture group. While some have averaged 25 percent to 30 percent or more, many venture firms operate in the 5 percent to 10 percent range, and of course, this is also an easy business in which to lose a significant amount of capital. If anything, the increasing regulation of venture transactions, plus increased capital gains taxes, and the spotty nature of the OTC and new issue market have reduced the returns possible through venturing.

But despite all its complexities, the venture capital business is exciting, constructive, and highly rewarding to the professionals in the industry. Venture capital has made major contributions to the present economic and technical strength of the United States. Virtually every major corporation in the country either was started with venture capital or received a major infusion of high-risk capital at some crucial point in its history. In the past decade, a surprisingly high number of NYSE companies were founded with venture capital.

Perhaps Charles Lea, Executive Vice President of New Court Securities, said it best in 1969 when the financial community thought venture capital was the next best thing to sliced bread, "This business consists of six years of blood, sweat, and tears," he said, "followed by six months of glorious excitement and heady profits."

There is plenty of opportunity in the field for dedicated, full-time, well-capitalized professionals. It is no game for the light hearted, the inexperienced, or the part-timer.

19

Tax Shelter Concept

JAMES E. WHEELER, Ph.D.
Graduate School of Business Administration
University of Michigan
Ann Arbor, Michigan

THIS CHAPTER discusses the operating aspects of tax shelters in enough detail to enable the reader to begin to evaluate the risks and merits of some tax shelter programs. However, it is not the purpose of this chapter to impart enough knowledge of the detail of these programs to enable a financial analyst to become a tax adviser for himself or anyone else.

The First Step

To understand the workings of a tax shelter program for federal income tax, it is necessary first to have or obtain knowledge of the rate structure. The graph in Figure 1 reflects the marginal federal tax rates at different taxable income levels for individuals filing joint returns. The other three regular rate tables, for married persons filing separately, single persons, and heads of households, follow the same general pattern but are even more progressive at the same income levels. The ability-to-pay concept, the theoretical justification for progressive tax rates, cannot justify the curve shown in this graph. If anything, the ability-to-pay concept would justify a concave rather than a convex curve.[1] Thus, at certain income levels we have an almost geometrically progressive rate

[1] This would require the largest rate increases in the upper income tax brackets rather than in the lower brackets. However, in an analysis of the economic burden of this tax it would also be necessary to have data on the transfer payments, e.g., the federal payments to individuals such as social security and aid to dependent children.

FIGURE 1

Marginal Tax Rate Graph for Joint Tax Returns

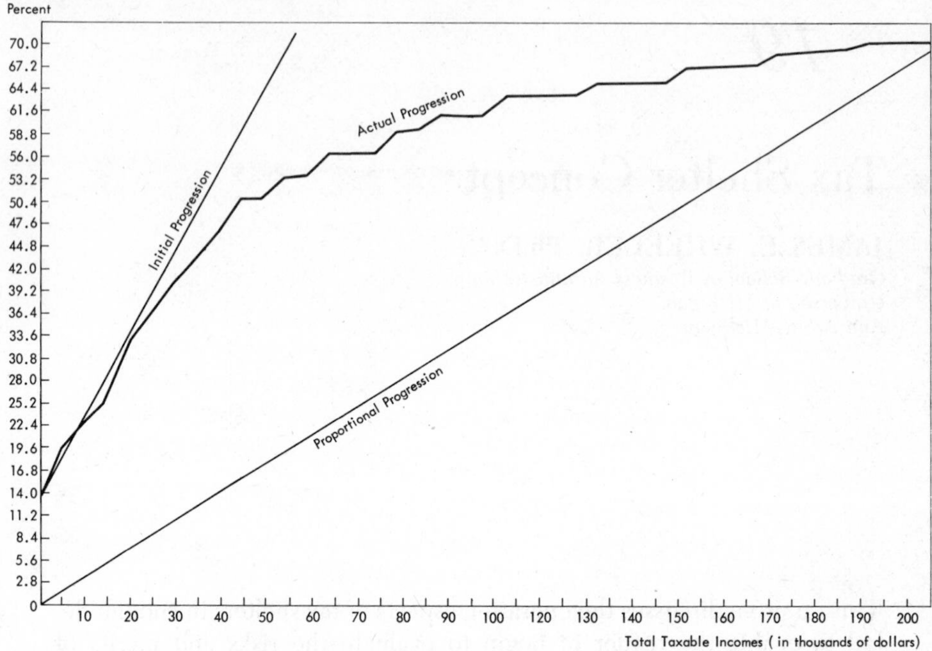

structure which means that tax sheltering activities can be important to persons in fairly modest taxable income brackets.

The conditions reflected in Figure 1 are caused by very small brackets at the lower ends of the tax rate tables, e.g., the four brackets between zero and $4,000 of taxable income are only $1,000 each with a 14 percent rate applied to the first bracket and with a 1 percent rate increase at each new bracket;[2] the five brackets between $4,000 and $20,000 are $4,000 each, but there is a 3 percent rate increase at each bracket; the two brackets between $20,000 and $28,000 are still $4,000 each, but there is a 4 percent rate increase at each bracket; the four brackets between $28,000 and $44,000 are still $3,000 each, but the tax rate increase is now back to 3 percent; from $44,000 to $52,000 there is only one $8,000 bracket, and the rate increase drops to 2 percent; from $52,000 to $76,000 there are two brackets of $12,000 each, and the rate increase remains at 2 percent for each bracket; for the one $12,000 bracket between $76,000 and $88,000, there is a 3 percent rate increase; for the one $12,000 bracket between $88,000 and $100,000, there is a 2 percent rate increase; from $100,000 to $180,000 there are four brackets of $20,000

[2] If this rate after starting at 14 percent were continued, the 70 percent bracket would be reached at $56,001 rather than at the present $200,001 on a joint return.

each, and the rate increase is 2 percent for each bracket; from $180,000 to $200,000 is one bracket with a 1 percent rate increase, and there is a final 1 percent rate increase after the $200,000 taxable income level is crossed which makes the top rate 70 percent.[3]

With more than half the progression in rates ($\frac{1}{2} \times 70$ percent = 35 percent) coming before or within the $28,000 to $32,000 taxable income bracket and more than 30 percent of the progression within the $12,000 to $16,000 bracket, there is ample reason to minimize federal income tax at almost every significant taxable income level.

The Second Step

The definition of a tax shelter is the next necessary piece of information. A broad definition would include (1) all forms of economic income that receive preferential treatment and (2) many deductions, granted by Congress in legislation, the Treasury Department in interpretation and enforcement, and the courts in judicial interpretation and resolution of conflicts.

Viewed in this light, every individual regardless of his tax bracket has some tax sheltered income. The 16th amendment to the Constitution gives Congress the power to tax gross income (i.e., sales less cost of goods sold). Thus all business operating expenses, itemized deductions, personal exemptions, tax credits, tax-free federal transfer payments, and so on represent forms of tax shelters.

While such a broad definition is perfectly valid, a more limited definition is perhaps more useful for tax planning. Thus, tax sheltering activity can be defined as *investment activity* undertaken at least partially because of the related tax consequences. This is still a very broad definition and could include decisions such as whether to buy or rent a home. Without designating an area of activity, such as real estate, it is difficult to further reduce the definition. In fact, income tax sheltering activity is only one part of total tax planning which to really be effective must consider, in addition to the federal income tax, the impact of various state, local, and perhaps foreign taxes as well as the federal estate and gift taxes.

THE PHILOSOPHY OF TAX SHELTERS

Sheltering income from taxation can be a worthwhile activity; but total income, need for cash, age of the taxpayer, and many other factors

[3] But there are also other rates which can and do affect tax planning, e.g., the alternative net long-term capital gain rate of 25 percent (on the first $50,000 of such gain), the 50 percent maximum tax on earned income, and the 10 percent minimum tax on tax preferences. There is also a possible advantage in income averaging.

should influence this effort. The idea of paying the minimum legal amount of tax seems to have universal appeal. However, due to the appeal of this concept, some persons may end up oversheltering their income and others may be using illegal means of obtaining the desired result. Contrary to popular belief, the most desirable result is seldom a zero tax although this seems to be a rather universal goal. Even congressmen and presidents of late have been participators in the activity of tax "avoidance,"[4] and the extent of legality in the latest case is even under question. Fortunately, for the good of our country not everyone achieves that rather universal goal of a zero tax.

The general philosophy of a tax shelter is to enter into an investment arrangement which will be producing real economic income or gain but which due to tax accounting measurements will provide tax losses or deductions so as to reduce or offset recognized income from other sources. This, of course, requires some personal wealth to invest and/or the ability to borrow investment funds.

However, the need for tax shelter losses should never induce an investor to invest in something that he believes will produce an economic loss. The first requirement is for economic success; tax considerations are second. If it were not for this constraint, tax attorneys and CPA's could provide tax shelter deductions for their clients by merely increasing their billings to the taxpayers for tax advice or services rendered.

The typical shelter, if there is such a thing, involves losses for tax purposes in the early years of activity with a period of increasing income for tax purposes in the later years. Because of this, a period of reckoning is sometimes unavoidable; thus, certain tax shelter programs have characteristics similar to a treadmill. Once on, continued investment in similar activities is necessary in order not to lose the advantage created with the initial venture into the program. Indeed, failure to continue investing could, due to progressive tax rates and bunching of income, produce a higher total tax result than not investing in tax shelters originally.[5] However, for some investments the postponement of income recognition through tax-free exchanges makes it possible to escape taxation and pass the property on at death at its fair market value. Other tax shelters have been created by congressional action to stimulate a particular activity. Some of these incentives, such as percentage depletion, do not bring forth a later day of reckoning. For other investments, income received during the period of reckoning may be taxed at least partially at capital gains tax rates. But recent tax reform legislation has converted some of this type of gain into ordinary income taxed at full regular rates.[6]

---

[4] What is a tax shelter to a tax planner is frequently tax avoidance to a tax reformer. However, neither term is to be confused with tax evasion which is the reduction of tax through illegal means.

[5] This can be true even with the possibility of some income averaging.

[6] This process is often termed *recapture*.

The deferral of the day of reckoning in addition to the advantage of later payment, an advantage inherent in the time value of money, can be important if the taxpayer can expect a future decrease in recognized income, e.g., through retirement. But a warning on deferral is perhaps important—inflation frequently results in rises in dollar income without increases in real income and this can affect the tax rate eventually applied to the currently deferred income. This could completely negate the deferral advantage of paying later. In other words, having more dollars (with perhaps even less purchasing power) can put you into a higher tax bracket. The tax laws do not recognize the real effects of changes in the value of the dollar.

In summary, tax shelters can be classified as (1) those which produce nontaxable income or tax deductions which do not reverse at a later date, (2) those which produce current deductions with capital gain taxation at a later date, and (3) those which produce current deductions with ordinary income at a later date—the advantage here is in deferral. It should also be noted that tax shelters are generally available to corporations as well as to individuals and that incorporation may itself be a form of tax sheltering in a complex tax planning situation (e.g., professional corporations).

A REVIEW OF THE IMPACTS OF THE 1969 TAX REFORM ACT[7]

In General. This legislative enactment reduced the advantages of most tax shelters. It introduced the concepts of the "minimum tax on tax preferences," and "maximum tax on earned income." It also repealed the investment tax credit (later reinstated in the Revenue Act of 1971), limited investment interest deductions, and reduced depreciation deductions for most real estate investments. However, certain investments were given special five-year amortization write-offs (but with the advent of the asset depreciation range [ADR] and the resurrected investment credit under the Revenue Act of 1971, these have generally become less desirable than the regular treatment and, thus, presently constitute tax traps for the unwary).

The 1969 Act also reduced the percentage depletion rate for oil and gas ventures (and for most of the other extractive industries) but made percentage depletion available to oil extracted from oil shale. It did not affect the immediate write-off of intangible drilling and development costs (IDC).

In addition, there were many other changes including provisions which altered capital gain taxation. This was done by changing the rates and by recapturing more depreciation and other items such as recovery of farm losses as ordinary income.

---

[7] Staff of the Joint Committee on Internal Revenue Taxation, *General Explanation of the Tax Reform Act of 1969 H.R. 13270, 91st Congress, Public Law 91–172* (Washington, D.C.: U.S. Government Printing Office, December 3, 1970).

The Minimum Tax on Tax Preferences

The concept involved is to tax that tax shelter activity which exceeds a stated or minimum amount. Thus, the sum of the *values* of these preferences is determined, and a 10 percent rate is applied to the excess over $30,000 and over the amount of regular income tax paid (with carryovers of excess regular tax for seven years). The exclusions from the minimum tax are often large enough and the tax rate small enough so as not to deter an investment in a viable tax shelter.

The items of preferences for individuals include among other items:

1. The excess of accelerated depreciation over straight line on *real* property.
2. The excess of accelerated depreciation over straight line on personal property *subject to a net lease.*
3. The excess of certain five-year amortization write-off provisions over straight line depreciation deductions.
4. Certain benefits of particular stock options.
5. The capital gain deduction.
6. Percentage depletion in excess of the *basis* of the property.

Noticeably absent from the above list is tax-exempt state and local bond interest and the intangible drilling and development costs of the oil and gas industry. Thus, future tax reform could expand the list, reduce the amount of exemptions, and/or increase the 10 percent tax rate.

The Maximum Tax on Earned Income

This concept could be called the antitax shelter incentive. It is designed to discourage persons with large earned incomes (as opposed to investment incomes) from sheltering this income from taxation. The effect is to tax earned taxable income at no more than a 50 percent rate. However, there are relatively few persons who benefit from this provision; but for some executives, it is important and has caused shifts from qualified stock option plans to taxable stock options.

Investment Interest Deductions

This limitation restricts the deduction of interest paid or incurred to carry particular investments. Investment interest does not include interest on loans on a personal residence, on rental property (unless subject to a net lease), on business property during the construction period, or on obligations incurred prior to December 17, 1969. The deduction is limited to the sum of (1) $25,000, (2) interest and dividend income, (3) net long-term capital gain, and (4) 50 percent of the excess of the interest expense over the sum of the first three items. The remaining

50 percent is carried forward. Where interest has offset capital gain the gain is taxed as ordinary income for purposes of the capital gain deduction, the alternative tax, and the minimum tax on tax preferences. To tax reformers there is obviously slack to be taken up in this limitation of interest deduction area.

Depreciation

The use of accelerated depreciation on real estate has been significantly reduced, and the amount of depreciation subject to recapture has been increased. However, the Revenue Act of 1971 has greatly increased depreciation on many assets (primarily personal property) by shortening the useful lives and by eliminating the *reserve ratio test.* The specific rules will be covered in the real estate section.

Hobby Losses

The 1969 Tax Reform Act also established an objective test for individuals to determine whether or not a particular activity is a hobby. In general, any activity must be profit motivated before its related operating expenses in excess of gross profit are deductible. In other words, losses associated with activities not engaged in for profit (e.g., hobbies) are not deductible against income from other sources, and this, of course, is the essence of many tax shelters. The objective test requires profits in two or more years in a five-year consecutive period (a seven-year consecutive period for race horses) ending with the current taxable year. The rules may, for example, eliminate some of the tax deductions of gentlemen farmers. However, even where an activity is not engaged in for profit, interest, state and local property taxes, and capital gain deductions would still be allowed.

The Future of Tax Shelters

While no one would predict the total demise of tax shelter programs, there is some pressure to limit the tax reduction possible to any one individual. For example, the House-passed version of the 1969 Tax Reform Act contained an "allocation of deductions" concept; and while this concept was removed by the Senate, it could reappear in future tax legislation. Its major effect would be to reduce itemized deductions of individuals by the ratio of tax-exempt income to total income. The concept being that if the income is not taxed the spending of it should not be deductible. While this concept has not as yet been adopted, the Treasury has proposed a minimum taxable income concept which would achieve almost the same result.[8]

[8] Testimony of George P. Shultz before the House Ways and Means Committee, *Proposals for Tax Change,* Department of the Treasury, April 30, 1973, p. 83.

Another concept which would strike at the heart of some tax shelters would be to limit net losses from certain types of investments to future gains from these or similar investments. This would require new loss carryover provisions. A modification of this concept, "limitation on artificial accounting losses," has been proposed by the Treasury and would eliminate the deferral advantages present in many tax shelter programs where tax losses are artifically created.[9] The concept here would be to place the tax effect in line with the economic effect.

There have been and will continue to be advanced many ideas for ways to prevent the wealthy from escaping virtually all income tax. The realization that some persons with huge wealth accumulations and hundreds of thousands of dollars of annual income are frequently paying little if any income tax will continue to put pressure on Congress for removal or limitation on the use of tax shelters.

THE INTERWORKINGS OF SOME TAX SHELTER PROGRAMS

Bonds

With Tax-Free Yields. Perhaps the most ideal shelter is to have income but not have it taxed. This is, of course, the concept inherent in the tax-free status of interest on most state and local bond issues. This tax-free status is not universal. Many states and local governments tax this interest the same as other interest income. In addition, gain on sale or exchange of these securities is taxable, and loss is deductible at the federal as well as at many state and local levels.[10]

The federal tax advantage is shared with the particular state or local governmental unit that issued the bonds through lower interest rates. The tax advantage of this shelter depends on the marginal income tax bracket of the investor. If a particular city bond issue is yielding a 6 percent tax-free interest rate while a corporate bond of comparable risk is yielding 10 percent taxable interest rate, a person in the 40 percent marginal tax bracket breaks even on these two alternative investments. Thus, a person in the top 70 percent tax bracket needs a yield on the comparable risk corporate bond of 20 percent to equate these yields on an after-tax basis (20 percent − 70 percent × 20 percent = 6 percent). With a corporate tax rate of 48 percent, there is some incentive toward corporate ownership of this type of investment. When this is the major or perhaps the only source of income for individuals, there is the possibility of switching to taxable yields every third year or so to obtain the higher yields and the advantage of income averaging.

[9] Ibid., p. 94.

[10] Because of this, premium on acquisition must be amortized for federal purposes. This amortization will increase the gains or decrease the losses.

Because of the tax-free nature of this interest income, the Internal Revenue Code does not permit a deduction for any interest cost (or other expenses) incurred in carrying these issues. Indeed, a person owning these bonds is running a risk of having interest disallowed on borrowing to carry other taxable investments on the theory that the tax exempts could have been sold to obtain these funds. However, the Internal Revenue Service continues to allow the deduction of state and local income tax incurred on this tax-free interest income. Indeed, this deduction may fully offset income otherwise taxed at the federal level.

If recent tax reform proposals are adopted, tax exempts may be a vanishing species. Most recommendations would make new issues fully taxable, with the federal government subsidizing the state or local governments by, in effect, picking up part of the resulting increase in interest rates.

With Taxable Yields. During periods of increasing interest rates, older bond issues at lower coupon rates become *deep-discount* issues. For persons financially secure and in high tax brackets, this offers the opportunity to convert what would otherwise constitute ordinary interest income into capital gain. By holding these deep-discount issues to maturity, the excess maturity value over the adjusted basis (usually cost) becomes capital gain. It may also be advantageous to leverage these deep-discount issues as long as they are not tax exempts. Of course, the potential minimum tax on the capital gain at maturity and limitation on investment interest must be considered. In addition, if interest rates fall then these bonds will rise in value and can be sold to realize capital gain before maturity.

There is an additional problem if the deep-discount issue was involved in *original issue discount*. This problem can be eliminated, however, by simply avoiding original discount issues.

There is also an important tax advantage for corporations that can buy up their own debt issues after effects of the inflation have driven down the market value. The gain on this debt retirement is the excess of the amount received upon issue (less any amortization of premiums or plus any amortization of discount) over the amount paid to retire the debt. This gain can then be deferred by adjusting downward the basis of selected assets.

Stocks

The advantages to individuals are the $100 dividend exclusion on the yield, capital gain taxation on the net long-term gain resulting from sales of these investments, and the fact that these investments can be purchased on the margin (leveraged). Net losses on sales of capital assets are carried forward (indefinitely) and can offset future capital gains plus up to $1,000 of ordinary income. In the case of long-term losses,

$2 of long-term loss is required for each $1 deducted from ordinary income, i.e., to deduct $1,000 from ordinary income, the long-term loss must be at least $2,000.

For corporations the biggest advantage is in the yield; generally only 15 percent of it is taxed (i.e., there is an 85 percent dividend received deduction—for dividends from affiliated domestic corporations the deduction is 100 percent; however, this simply is another entity in the same chain and, thus, not an investment as such). If there is dividend income from a nonaffiliated domestic company, the effective corporate tax rate is only 7.2 percent on this source (100 percent − 85 percent × 48 percent), while net long-term gain on sale of these securities (whether affiliated or not) is taxed at 30 percent. Capital losses of corporation are carried back three years and forward five years but may offset only capital gain income during that nine-year span.

Leasing Personal Property

Many railroads, airlines, and other companies have in recent years fulfilled their needs for rolling stock, aircraft, computers, and so on, by leasing these assets. This is particularly attractive to companies that have tax losses and tax credits carried forward. These companies may not be able to use the increased depreciation and investment credits and are willing to pass these along for more favorable lease terms. In addition, the off balance sheet financing (depending on the accounting method employed in reflecting the lease arrangements) can improve almost any company's working capital position. However, accounting for lease commitments is currently under review by the Financial Accounting Standards Board.

For the owner lessor, these arrangements often generate a positive cash flow while resulting in tax losses in the initial years which increase this cash flow. The lessor can also leverage his investment, often with up to 80 percent financing.

With the introduction in 1971 of ADR and the "job development credit," the five-year write-off provisions are now generally not the best route for tax purposes. In addition, the excess of the five-year amortization deduction over straight line depreciation is a tax perference item, whereas the excess of the accelerated depreciation deduction over straight line is not a tax preference item (unless the arrangements constitute a "net lease").

Railroad rolling stock (not including engines) can serve as an example of this rapid write-off procedure. Many useful life studies show that this equipment has a useful life of 30 to 35 years. Under the 1962 guideline procedure, this equipment was assigned a guideline life of 14 years. ADR then reduced this by 20 percent (rounded to the nearest full or half year) to 11 years. ADR also permits use of DDB with a switch to SYD at anytime without approval of the Commissioner of the IRS. In addition, ADR removed the reserve ratio test (a part of the original 1962 guideline procedure and a testing procedure which would have forced the use of longer lives). In addition to ADR, the 1971 Revenue Act also resurrected the 7 percent investment tax credit (and termed it the "job development credit"). However, this credit is not available if the five-year amortization provisions (introduced by the 1969 Tax Reform Act) are used instead of regular depreciation. The combination of the present value of the investment credit and the tax effects of accelerated depreciation using shortened ADR lives is greater than the present value of the tax effects of a straight 5 year write-off for any lower range ADR life up to 16 years using an 8 percent discount rate for the present value computation.

There are some very limiting rules on the rights of certain noncorporate lessors to avail themselves of this credit. Thus, when considering such lease investments, a good tax adviser is an absolute necessity.

If the investment credit is available and if the taxpayer were continuously in a 50 percent marginal income tax bracket, the following would reflect the cash flow effects of the tax aspects of depreciation and the investment credit on a nondiscounted basis on railroad rolling stock during the 11-year ADR life, assuming the equipment cost $400,000 with DDB depreciation in year 1 and a switch to SYD in year 2.[11]

	Year 1	*Year 2*	*Year 3*	*Years 4–11*	*11-Year Total*
Investment credit = 0.07 × 400,000......	$28,000				$ 28,000
Tax benefit of DDB depreciation					
= 0.05 × 72,727......................	36,364				36,364
Tax benefit of SYD depreciation					
0.50 (10/55 × 327,273)					
= 0.50 × 59,504..................		$29,752			29,752
0.50 × 53,554 for year 3..............			$26,777		26,777
0.50 × 214,215 for years 4–11........				$107,107	107,107
	$64,364	$29,752	$26,777	$107,107	$228,000

The gain or loss from this lease in the early years would depend on the annual lease rentals and other costs such as administration and interest on any financing. The interest rate and amount of leverage employed in this venture and the pay-back terms of the loan will affect the actual cash flow as will any residual value received from the leased asset. Since there are many factors to consider, these arrangements must be thoroughly explored by competent advisers.

[11] The tax benefit of the five-year amortization would be $40,000 (0.5 × 400,000 ÷ 5) in each of the first five years.

Farming Ventures

Most farming tax shelters involve obtaining deductions on a cash basis which would normally be capitalized on an accrual basis. This is the essence of the cattle feeder operations where current deductions are taken for cost of feeding cattle which will be sold in the following year with ordinary income being recognized. In an unusually high income year or in the year before retirement, this timing of the deductions, due to the progressive tax rates, can be worth substantially more than the mere one year deferral of income tax. In addition, continuing the feeding process with a new herd each year will sustain the tax deferral; this is the treadmill effect. These operations are often heavily leveraged and even on a nonrecourse basis. Some cattle feeders prepay feed costs (acquire feed inventory) before year-end to increase the tax loss; however, the IRS has challenged the deduction of these prepaid costs. This also appears to fit the definition of an "artifical accounting loss," which the Treasury has asked Congress to eliminate.

A cattle breeder operation has all the tax deferral advantages of a cattle feeder operation plus some capital gain taxation on the sale of animals. After the initial purchase of breeding stock, almost all costs are currently deductible and the original investment is depreciable. Once again, the original investment and expenses may be leveraged.

The operating concept is to increase the herd by selling off only the steers and culls (other undesirable animals). When one of the original animals is sold, there is depreciation to recapture as ordinary income. But as the second generation on is sold, there is capital gain (cattle and horses are subject to a two-year holding period in order to qualify for capital gain treatment) because no depreciation has been taken on these animals. In fact, the capitalizable costs of producing and raising these animals were expensed in the years incurred. This is even better than capitalization followed by depreciation, and these write-offs are not subject to depreciation recapture. For any large operation, there is the possibility of some recapture due to the excess deductions account (EDA) rules which are discussed later.

Because of the tax advantages, cattle farming has been a popular tax shelter. There are professional managers offering various tax shelter cattle programs, many of which are limited partnerships. One IRS official several years ago remarked that there were more schedule F farming schedules filed by persons living in Manhattan than in the state of Kansas. Whether this was said in jest is unknown, but farming has been a popular tax shelter.

There are many tax shelters in farming other than those in the cattle operations. Farm land located near growing metropolitan areas often appreciates in value far out of proportion to its ability to produce food crops while losses incurred in crop production are deductible. In addition, certain costs for clearing land and for soil and water conservation can be expenses, but are subject to full recapture as ordinary income if the property is sold within five years. The recapture rules apply to those costs incurred after December 31, 1969, and there is partial recapture for sales after 5 years and no recapture after 10 years.

A chicken flock is another example of a farming tax shelter. Unlike cattle the cost of chickens can be immediately expensed. Thus, if a chicken and egg farmer has had a good year, due to the high price of eggs, he can buy more chickens at the end of December and immediately expense this cost so as to offset his operating income.

In order to reduce the emphasis on farming tax shelters, the Tax Reform Act of 1969, in addition to establishing stronger rules on hobby losses, introduced the concept of the excess deductions account (EDA). This does not in any way reduce current deductions attributable to farm losses, but it does introduce the possibility that later capital gains may be taxed at least partially as ordinary income. However, capital gain on sale of farm land is not subject to recapture under the EDA rules, but the gain on the sale of cattle from breeding herds, for example, would be covered. The EDA accounts must be kept only by those persons with nonfarm adjusted gross income of over $50,000 and who have farm losses that exceed $25,000 in that year. Only the excess over $25,000 in these cases is added to the EDA account, and future farm net income reduces the EDA accumulation. The EDA account establishes the upper limit on recapture of prior farm loss deductions when future farm property other than land is sold. Thus, there is no EDA limitation on the current deduction of farm losses which would reduce the benefits of tax deferral.

Oil and Gas

This tax shelter area has probably received more publicity and, yet, less tax reform changes than most of the other shelters. The principle advantages are the right to percentage depletion on the sale of crude product; the write-off of intangible drilling costs (IDC) of successful wells, which often constitute 70 percent of the cost of a producing well; and the write-off of the entire cost of unsuccessful or dry wells. Not only has this area escaped significant tax reform, the Treasury Department has recently proposed a 7 percent exploratory drilling investment credit and an additional 5 percent supplementary credit allowed on the IDC of new productive exploratory wells.[12]

The 1969 tax reform changes in this area reduced the percentage depletion from 27½ percent to 22 percent (which just happened to approximate the effective depletion rate the large oil companies were receiving after the application of the 50 percent of predepletion net in-

[12] Testimony of George P. Shultz, *Proposals for Tax Change,* p. 135.

come limitation). Percentage depletion in excess of the basis of the property was also made a tax preference item. However, the more important IDC deductions were not reduced nor made subject to the tax preference rules, and while depreciation is limited to the basis of the asset, no such limitation has been placed on the amount of percentage depletion which can be taken during the life of a well.

Due to the high cost and risk in these ventures, many are run in the form of limited partnerships. Through nonrecourse loans, some limited partners have been taking deductions in excess of their actual investment in these ventures because they are able to add to their basis a portion of the non-recourse loans. Deductions for loss are limited to the partner's basis, which in these cases included nonrecourse loans. However, the IRS has been trying to attack this element of the drilling ventures.

Since World War II, the Treasury Department has allowed oil royalties paid to foreign governments to be credited (a reduction \$1 for \$1 in the tax liability rather than a deduction in determining taxable income) against the U.S. tax on foreign source income. This treatment was given by the Treasury, and not by Congress, and is currently under attack by many tax reform groups.

Because of the high risk involved, most promoters and tax advisers limit their recommendations on oil ventures to persons in marginal tax brackets of 50 percent or more.

Real Estate

This classification of tax shelter activity encompasses many diverse programs. This can include owning your own home in lieu of renting, owning a second or vacation home, owning other forms of residential rental property, owning commercial rental property, or speculating in land or land development. Real estate tax shelters (excluding personal residences) have probably been the most popular of all shelter programs. Its popularity can be attributed to the diversity of programs; opportunity for leverage, usually on favorable terms; the existence of a positive cash flow in most cases; and the fact that it has been an excellent hedge against inflation. Among the disadvantages are the lack of a readily determinable market value and the fact that this value and marketability are often affected by changes in interest rates. Many real estate projects, due to their size, require a fairly large investment. Thus, many ventures are owned by syndicates or partnerships. Some of these group ventures involve very high management and other load charges which can materially reduce the desirability of the project.

The Effects of Tax Reform.[13] The minimum tax on tax preferences, the limitation on the deduction of investment interest, and to a lesser

[13] See the Appendix for an example of the type of changes currently being recommended.

extent, the changes in capital gain taxation have already been discussed, but the discussion of changes in depreciation rules were left for this section. The changes were primarily a reduction in the rate of depreciation write-off on most depreciable real properties and an increase in the amount of depreciation subject to recapture.

Prior to 1969, most depreciable real estate was eligible for accelerated depreciation if new and 150 percent declining balance is used. However, the Tax Reform Act now classifies depreciable real estate into (1) residential rental property new and used, (2) nonresidential rental property new and used, and (3) depreciable real estate acquired new or used before July 24, 1969. For this last classification, the former rules on accelerated depreciation still apply, and new residential rental property is still eligible for accelerated depreciation. But the used property in this class is limited to the 125 percent declining balance method as the upper limit on the depreciation rate, and the property must have a 20-year or longer useful life. New nonresidential rental property (such as commercial property and factory buildings) is now limited to the 150 percent declining balance method as the most rapid depreciation method available, and the used property of this category can only be depreciated under the straight line method.

Prior to the 1969 changes, depreciation in excess of straight line was subject to recapture upon the sale of the real estate, based on a decreasing rate depending on how long the property had been held. Now, for excess depreciation taken over straight line after January 1, 1970, on the second or third classification of depreciable real estate, there is complete recapture which is measured by the smaller of the gain or the excess depreciation. Depreciation recapture on residential rental property is subject to a decreasing rate of recapture which reaches zero after the property has been held 16⅔ years. The old recapture rules still apply to certain property such as that insured under certain sections of the National Housing Act. These rules reach a zero recapture rate after 10 years.

Since the sale of depreciable real property usually involves the sale of the related land, it is important that the sale be treated as the sale of separate assets with the net sales price properly allocated to each separate asset involved. The gain on the land is not subject to the recapture rules.

It should be noted that, unlike depreciation on personal depreciable assets such as machinery and equipment, there is no recapture of straight line depreciation. It should also be noted that depreciation deductions are taken even though the real estate may be appreciating in value. However, unlike percentage depletion, depreciation taken cannot exceed the basis of the asset.

Some tax reform advocates have recommended that depreciation be limited to the taxpayer's equity interest in depreciable real property.

Thus, if an apartment building cost $1 million and the owner borrowed $900,000 and put up $100,000 of his own funds, his depreciation deductions while calculated from the $1 million basis could not exceed $100,000 until and to the extent that he repays the loan. Thus, if real property is continuously financed (and perhaps is appreciating in value), depreciation would stop when the owner's equity investment is recovered. This would remove much of the cash flow incentive in depreciable real estate tax shelters.

Land Speculation. The real advantages of this tax shelter depend on how long the land must be held before it significantly appreciates in value. The tax advantages are that the interest costs on loans to purchase the property and the related property taxes are deductible even though there may be no revenue from the land. The interest, however, may be subject to the limitation on the investment interest deduction. In addition, unlike some rental properties, there is normally a net cash outflow associated with this investment.

If the investor avoids the pitfalls of being classified as a dealer—such as by subdividing the property or advertising it for sale shortly after acquisition—gain on sale will qualify as capital gain; and if sold in an installment sale, more of the gain will probably be taxed at the 25 percent alternative capital gain rate. This will also help to reduce any minimum tax on the capital gain preference. The capital gain tax can be avoided if this property is exchanged for other like kind investment property in a tax-free exchange. The old basis carries over to the new property; thus, both the gain recognition and the related income tax will have been postponed.

Depreciable Real Estate. In addition to the write-off of interest, taxes, maintenance, insurance, and so on, this property may be depreciated. If the property is being properly maintained, the real depreciation due to physical deterioration may be far less than the actual depreciation allowed, and some properties may actually be increasing in value. Participation in the construction phase of real estate has tax advantages because the interest and taxes during construction can be written off or capitalized at the option of the taxpayer. If written off, they are not subject to recapture on a later sale. Depreciable real estate is also subject to the tax-free exchange rules under which tax on the unrecognized gain may be postponed or even avoided if the exchanged property is held at death.

Low-Income Housing. Congress has adopted provisions aimed at improving the quality of low-income rental units and at increasing the number of such units. The provisions for improving the quality allow amortization of the cost of rehabilitation to be written off over a 60-month period up to a maximum of $15,000 per unit.

For new low-income housing—that financed by a mortgage guaranteed be FHA under Section 221(d)(3) or Section 236 of the National

Housing Act or similar local statutes—accelerated depreciation is permitted; excess depreciation over straight line is recaptured under the former rules where there is no recapture after 10 years. If the units are sold to tenants and the sales proceeds are reinvested within the prescribed period, the tax on the sale is deferred.

Because this is considered a trade or business, the interest on the mortgage is not subject to the investment interest limitation. However, the depreciation in excess of straight line is a tax preference item for purposes of computing the minimum tax on tax preferences.

Even though there are substantial tax advantages in low-income housing, the overall economic aspects may not be good. The rental on an FHA project is controlled; thus, an owner cannot receive more than a 6 percent cash flow on his investment. There is also a management fee of 6 percent to 7 percent allowed, but this is often absorbed by the professional manager who might also be the builder. The builder's construction profit is limited to 10 percent. The control, regulation, and red tape plus the economics of low-income housing may keep many investors and builders away from this area even though the after-tax yields can be substantial.

IN CONCLUSION

Only a few of the many tax shelter areas have been discussed. Some major shelter areas, such as timber and mine investment, have not even been mentioned. To adequately introduce all tax shelters would require a complete text, and it would take a multivolume service to present the operating details of each.

Since the purpose of this chapter has been to provide an understanding of the tax shelter concept, some of the more important shelters have been presented, and the past and prospective tax reform changes have also been discussed.

As was stated in the beginning of this chapter, the ideal tax is not zero at least for those with significant adjusted gross incomes. The returns with $200,000 or more of adjusted gross income (AGI) and a zero tax (approximately 110 of these in 1970) are often examined by staff of the Joint Committee on Internal Revenue Taxation in preparing tax data for the House Ways and Means Committee in addition to the Treasury Department examinations. To avoid this classification, these taxpayers should arrange to pay at least $1. Of the approximately 110 returns with $200,000 or more AGI and no tax in 1970, 3 had AGI's over $1 million, 17 had AGI's between $500,000 and $1 million, and about 90 had AGI between $200,000 and $500,000. Obviously, tax shelters were involved in some of these returns, if not most of them, but these generally are returns of taxpayers who have deductions often far in excess of their AGI's. Thus, these persons lost the value of their personal exemptions as well as of any excess itemized deductions, and these deductions are not usually available for net operating loss calculations. Therefore, there is usually no carryover benefit. Since these returns normally represent horror stories rather than smart tax planning, one must wonder why Congress does not select a better sample to review.

There is obviously pressure on Congress for more tax reform as indicated by the testimony of many persons before the House Ways and Means Committee in April 1973. As soon as Congress settles the impeachment issue and returns to its more normal routine, tax reform bills will begin to make their way through the legislative process. Thus, perhaps there is no better time than the present to begin a tax shelter program. Legislative changes are seldom retroactive. Therefore, existing shelter programs may produce better tax results than they would after another round of tax reform.

Since tax sheltering is only one aspect of total family tax planning, the selection of the proper shelters, which blend with both a person's financial status and investment philosophy, is not an easy task. However, the economics of the shelter should always be considered before looking at the tax results of the program. If a project is not economically viable before tax, there is almost no chance of it being acceptable on an after-tax basis. Perhaps the best way to compare alternative ventures is on a rate of return on investment, although cash flow, risk, and other factors must also be considered. Since the advent of the 1969 Tax Reform Act, a combination of various shelters often produces the best result.

Because of the complexity in tax planning and the volume of brokers and promoters (of varying reputations) selling deals, any individual wealthy enough to consider tax shelters must obtain professional investment advice.

APPENDIX

The testimony of Adrian W. DeWind before the House Ways and Means Committee on February 8, 1973.

Mr. ULLMAN. Thank you, Mr. Aronsohn.

We will now be glad to hear from Mr. Adrian DeWind, who, I would say to the committee, was formerly with the Treasury Department and has had a lot of experience with this committee in connection with the King subcommittee in the old days. We are happy to have you back, Mr. DeWind.

STATEMENT OF ADRIAN W. DeWIND

Mr. DEWIND. Thank you, Mr. Ullman.

I guess it has been 20 years since I appeared before this committee. It has been a long time, and there are a lot of new faces, but I am glad to have the opportunity to be here again. I think my friend Alan Aronsohn and I are not going to agree very much on whether or not there are very large tax incentives to rental real estate, and perhaps what should be done about them.

I think perhaps it might be helpful to try to state at the outset just how a so-called tax shelter in conventional real estate works. I don't think there will be too much disagreement on the facts. Perhaps it would be helpful to give some indication how one of these transactions goes, and then we can discuss it and maybe reach a conclusion whether or not there are unjustified tax shelters, tax incentives.

In a typical rental housing apartment project, let us take some sample figures which are too small, but they will be illustrative.

Supppose you have a project that is going to cost a million dollars. Normally, the construction on that project will be financed to a very substantial degree by a construction mortgage loan that will be replaced, on completion, by a long-term mortgage loan. Perhaps $850,000 will be advanced in the construction loan and $150,000 will be produced through equity investment, so you start out with the equity investor in the rental project putting up about 15 percent of the total cost.

During the construction period, as this equity investment is made, the tax law permits the investor to deduct from his other taxable income, as it goes along, various costs—real estate taxes, interest on the loan, some portion of the builder's fees, points that are paid to the lender above the interest rate—so that, while construction is going on, the financing costs of the $850,000 borrowed, part of the builder's fees, and the real estate taxes are all deducted.

Normally in the couple of years, let us say, that it takes to complete these projects, the deductions are very likely to be equal to or perhaps in excess of that $150,000 equity investment. So that, by the time construction is completed, the investor has deducted substantially his entire equity investment of $150,000.

If he is in the 60-percent bracket—if you live in New York City, your tax bracket can reach 75 percent with city, State, and Federal taxes—by the time construction is completed, tax benefits given to the investor would be $90,000, so that his remaining outlay net to him is $60,000.

Then, when construction is completed, he is now considered by the tax law to have an $850,000 investment for tax depreciation purposes—that is, the $850,000 permanent loan is part of his basis available for depreciation.

If he takes 200 percent declining balance depreciation, that means his depreciation in this case is going to run something like $40,000 a year at the outset so that, in less than three years after the project gets going, he has had over $100,000 of depreciation deductions. At this point, it is clear that he has recovered in tax benefits his entire investment and more.

The tax savings have returned to him his total investment. Depending, of course, on interest rates and the size of the mortgage loan and real estate tax rates and so forth, normally the investor will have received in tax savings the entire amount he had laid out, within two or three years after completion.

From then on in he is regarded as continuing to be the complete owner of the investment, and he continues to depreciate that debt, depreciate the cost of the property, despite the fact that, say, 14 or 15 years down the line—there will not be much disagreement—that project is very likely to sell for at least a million dollars.

Upon the completion of construction, it is probably worth more than a million dollars. That is, the whole input of production produced more than a million in value. Studies have shown after 14 or 15 years such projects are likely to sell at about original cost.

So the effect of the tax treatment has been to defer taxes by giving deductions for depreciation and expenses which have not been reflected in any diminution of the value of the investment. That is what is known as tax shelter. Whether it is good or bad, that is tax shelter.

If you receive tax deductions, which are said to be operating losses or to represent depreciation, which do not reflect diminution of the dollar amount of your investment that can be said to be equivalent to an interest-free Government loan which may go on for a period of 15 years. So, you have the use of the tax money for that period based on excessive allowances, in excess of any loss of dollar value and that is the tax shelter. It is the use of the money at no cost for long periods of years.

Then something else happens. At the end of, say, the 15-year period, if the project is then sold, obviously, at that time, all of these prior deductions have to be accounted for, so there will be a gain equal to the difference between the depreciation and deductions taken and the value of the property, so that the taxpayer does have to, in effect, repay his loan to the Government at the end of 15 years. At that time, instead of paying it based on 60 percent tax, he repays it on a capital gain basis, which may be at rates from 25 to 40 percent.

He has converted the deductions he took on construction expenses from a 60 percent deduction or a 70 or 75 percent deduction, to a capital gain rate which, true, in some States, such as New York, may come to 40 percent capital gain tax—State, city, and Federal—but the differential of a maximum rate of 60 to 75 percent over 25 to 40 percent means only about a one-half repayment of the money the Government has advanced to him without interest through tax deferrals.

After 10 years or so from construction, the mortgage terms will generally permit the investor to refinance his mortgage. At this point he may very well be able to restore the mortgage to the original $850,000, or even more. So, generally on a nonrecourse, no-liability basis, the investor is able to take out of the investment the money representing the then value in that investment. He gets it in cash, free and clear, and pays no tax at all; so, in effect, he has borrowed again from the Government by deferring his tax on the gain until he gets rid of his project.

In 1969 the Congress to some extent began to cut down on the capital gain treatment, but for all rental housing there is still no recapture on gains attributable to straight-line depreciation—no ordinary income recapture—and for low-income housing the recapture of accelerated depreciation at ordinary rates is phased out after 10 years and all of the recovery is capital gain. In the case of other housing it phases out in 8⅓ to 16⅔ years. There is not very much recapture at ordinary rates. Most of it is converted into capital gain.

That is tax shelter and the thing to observe about how it operates is that the higher the income of the investor and the higher his tax bracket, the greater his returns are, so the investment return depends not on the risk of the property, not on the nature of the investment, but on the other income and the tax rate of the taxpayer. The higher the tax bracket, the greater the return after taxes is just the opposite of the usual rule.

This seems a peculiar system. To say that certain people should get a higher return on the same risk investment because of the extraneous fact they have other income is paradoxical. People with less income get lower return and you get a distortion because of unwarranted tax allowances.

The result of this has been that in certain areas of housing, particularly low-income housing, which Mr. Kurtz will talk about in greater detail, there is generally nothing but tax benefits. The investor puts his money in and he gets nothing back but tax benefits.

In middle-income housing, such as garden apartments, almost the sole source of equity investment has become the high-bracket investor. There is also tax shelter in luxury apartments, in shopping centers, in office buildings, and commercial buildings that are constructed for rent. But there the rents are more elastic, so the profit tends to be greater. The professional builders and operators tend to retain a far greater share of those investments so that the individual nonprofessional investor gets less of that and you find the tax shelter being used in the major part by the builders and operators. Only when their tax benefits are at a level that is in excess of what they can use to offset taxable income are they likely to turn and, in effect, "sell" those tax benefits to the private investor, who will get part of the benefit.

That is the picture now.

I don't know of any other form of investment where that kind of tax treatment occurs, where you are able to write off the whole of your investment for which you have any personal involvement or liability very, very rapidly and continue to get tax deferral through depreciation of debt capital for a period of years and pay a capital gain tax at the end of it, because you have converted the whole thing to capital gain.

It seems to me the tax incentives operate in an accidental and capricious manner. The same amount of money the Government is giving away in tax deferrals and capital gain rates could be directed more specifically and effectively toward the particular object. Where luxury apartments and office buildings and shopping centers which don't need tax incentives to attract capital are given these benefits as part of a plan assuring low-income housing, we seem to be directing the money in the wrong direction, benefiting the wrong people, whether builders, operators, or tenants.

Thank you.

20

Foreign Securities

RUBEN SHOHET, C.F.A.
First Vice President and Director
Drexel Burnham and Co., Incorporated
New York, New York

SUMMARY

A global approach to the investment process appears to be developing. This is largely due to the success of the U.S. multinational companies. Foreign securities offer opportunities for substantial capital appreciation.

The research and analysis of foreign securities is, in most ways, similar to that of U.S. common stocks. The key differences involve the need:

1. To monitor political developments abroad;
2. To follow the external (foreign trade and foreign exchange) influences on economic development, on competitive position, and/or on the outlook for particular industries; and
3. To identify corporate and management objectives.

While the differences in accounting standards and securities regulation are an important area for analysis, a trend is developing for major companies abroad to present their accounts on a basis consistent with U.S. and/or U.K. standards. Attracted by the size and the competitiveness of the U.S. capital market, it appears reasonable to assume that many foreign enterprises will list their securities on U.S. stock exchanges and adhere to SEC regulations.

It is possible to identify many investment opportunities abroad that involve companies that can benefit from the special nature of the markets they serve, the economies they operate within, or the natural resources available to them. Another area of opportunity is the development of competitive advantages for certain industries in the United States or abroad based on comparisons of unit labor costs.

INTRODUCTION

THE OBJECTIVE of this section is to provide background information to identify some of the key variables involved with foreign investments. Indeed, the rapid development of the U.S. multinational companies in the past decade may make a global approach crucial to the portfolio investment process.

FOREIGN INVESTMENTS

Investment abroad can be made directly through the purchase of foreign securities or through investment in U.S. multinational companies.

THE U.S. BASED MULTINATIONALS

The American-based multinational companies have built up large operations abroad, which in many cases account for a sizeable portion of earnings. Some 49 selected multinational companies, listed in Table 1, generate a large percentage of their earnings abroad and their market value as of March 25, 1974, amounted to $166.4 billion, or 24 percent of the dollar market value of all securities listed on the New York Stock Exchange (NYSE) as of March 31, 1974.

The Rationale for Foreign Securities

Investments abroad through direct participation in foreign companies can provide attractive opportunities, based on:

1. The generalization that saturation rates for many products abroad are lower than in the United States. The "catching up" process is expected to generate opportunities for sizeable gains in corporate profits and, hence, opportunities for capital appreciation.

2. Economic cycles in different countries, and hence their effects on corporate profits and stock market prices, often do not coincide. This generates opportunities for the truly international investor.

3. The broader choice of potential investments made possible by the larger universe. This is particularly valuable where companies can be identified that have a unique advantage, such as access to natural re-

TABLE 1

Selected Multinationals—Impact of Foreign Operations 1972–73 (millions)

	Total Company				*Foreign*				
	Sales		*Net Income**		*Sales*		*Net Income**		*Market Value as of 3/25/74*
	1973	*1972*	*1973*	*1972*	*1973*	*1972*	*1973*	*1972*	
AMF, Inc.	$ 962.1	$ 928.9	$ 57.8	$ 55.6	$ 141.1	$ 135.2	$ 18.3	$ 21.8	$ 377.8
AMP, Inc.	418.0	302.1	45.5	33.2	232.0E	143.0E	26.0	16.0	1,640.1
Addressograph-Multigraph Corp. (7/31)	498.5	450.3	3.2	16.6	161.9	141.5	9.2	8.6	79.4
Beatrice Foods Co. (2/28)	2,787.0	2,384.4	90.4	77.7	440.0	345.0	18.3	14.7	1,594.0
Black and Decker Mfg. Co. (9/30)	427.0	345.7	33.3	26.6	191.3	147.1	18.0	12.7	1,460.3
Borden, Inc.	2,554.0	2,249.0	73.0	67.5	424.1	360.9	14.0E	12.0E	703.2
Burroughs Corp.	1,284.2	1,052.8	115.9	87.5	454.0	380.3	45.0E	38.0E	4,174.1
CPC International, Inc.	1,889.7	1,559.7	75.5	66.4	1,018.0	848.0	46.0	39.0	792.7
Caterpillar Tractor Co.	3,182.4	2,602.2	246.8	206.4	1,581.7	1,251.0	134.0E	106.0E	3,437.5
Chesebrough-Pond's, Inc.	466.7	416.9	37.4	33.1	146.6	124.8	10.5	7.6	932.6
Coca-Cola Co.	2,145.0	1,876.2	215.0	190.2	943.8	769.2	126.9	104.6	7,068.5
Colgate-Palmolive Co.	2,195.3	1,905.9	88.8	62.3	1,213.0	1,007.6	61.0E	40.0E	1,833.6
E. I. duPont de Nemours & Co.	5,367.6	4,427.1	585.6	414.5	1,616.0	1,141.0	194.0E	131.0E	8,133.6
Eastman Kodak Co.	4,355.2	3,477.8	653.5	546.3	1,472.6	1,177.5	162.8	116.1	18,985.8
Firestone Tire & Rubber Co. (10/31)	3,154.9	2,691.0	164.9	135.8	946.5	807.3	59.0	42.7	1,023.4
First National City Corp.	3,091.6	1,954.8	254.8	201.8	1,793.1	1,153.3	137.6	121.1	1,010.2
General Mills, Inc. (5/73)	1,593.2	1,316.3	65.6	52.2	253.5	209.3	9.0E	7.5E	1,610.9
Gillette Co.	1,064.4	870.5	86.7	75.0	519.9	381.5	53.1	38.5	913.3
Goodyear Tire & Rubber Co.	4,703.3	4,095.9	184.8	193.2	1,433.0E	1,073.0E	64.5	59.0	1,293.1
W. R. Grace & Co.	2,833.0	2,362.8	84.6	65.6	973.0	762.0	38.2	26.2	781.4
Halliburton Co.	2,131.0	1,422.3	90.4	66.0	581.0	310.0	35.0	17.0	2,958.9
H. J. Heinz Co. (4/30)	1,205.9	1,098.9	46.6	42.3	501.3	471.7	23.5	20.6	741.9
Honeywell, Inc.	2,408.4	2,133.7	97.3	76.6	964.9	819.8	48.2	30.8	1,516.9
Hoover Co.	550.3	467.0	33.0	29.5	277.0E	254.0E	19.4	17.8	275.1
IBM Corp.	10,993.2	9,532.6	1,575.5	1,279.3	5,142.5	4,152.4	852.5	686.6	36,311.5
Int'l Flavors & Fragrances, Inc.	174.1	137.8	27.1	21.5	110.3	81.7	15.2	11.2	1,401.5

TABLE 1 (*Continued*)

	Total Company				Foreign				
	Sales		Net Income*		Sales		Net Income*		Market Value as
	1973	1972	1973	1972	1973	1972	1973	1972	of 3/25/74
Int'l Harvester Co.	$ 4,208.9	$ 3,525.6	$ 106.9	$ 86.6	$ 1,170.2	$ 861.7	$ 85.8	$ 34.0	$ 788.7
Int'l Telephone & Telegraph Corp.	10,183.0	8,569.3	527.8	484.0	5,295.2	4,027.6	279.7	217.8	2,331.9
Eli Lilly & Co.	998.3	838.1	155.5	126.3	353.4	269.1	61.4	40.0	5,029.2
Merck & Co., Inc.	1,137.8	971.5	178.4	147.6	512.0	408.0	79.9	62.0	6,317.6
Minnesota Mining & Manufacturing Co.	2,579.9	2,144.9	295.5	244.4	1,005.0	800.0	131.0E	104.0E	1,007.6
Monsanto Co.	2,647.7	2,225.4	238.3	122.0	770.0	551.5	43.4	17.2	2,041.9
Pfizer, Inc.	1,306.6	1,110.7	120.7	103.2	667.0	538.0	72.0	58.4	2,708.9
Philip Morris, Inc.	2,602.5	2,131.2	148.6	124.5	710.1	521.2	28.8	25.0	2,810.1
Procter and Gamble Co. (6/30)	3,937.2	3,541.6	302.1	276.3	1,042.0E	900.0E	88.6	76.5	7,647.5
Raytheon Co.	1,590.5	1,465.0	46.2	37.9	238.9	283.2	7.2	7.8	544.5
Richardson-Merrell, Inc.	509.2	449.6	41.4	36.7	228.0	194.0	21.0E	17.0E	631.4
Schering-Plough Corp.	632.3	517.4	106.0	77.3	259.2	186.3	44.0E	28.0E	3,865.4
Schlumberger Ltd.	945.8	812.1	92.4	70.2	690.4	568.5	72.0E	57.0E	3,893.2
Sterling Drug, Inc.	800.0	721.0	76.0	69.0	266.4	230.0	25.3	26.7	1,655.8
Sunbeam Corp. (3/31)	581.2	495.4	26.0	21.8	202.0	162.8	9.8	7.4	282.2
Tektronix, Inc.	198.2	164.3	15.7	11.2	80.5	65.9	7.0E	5.0E	3,879.9
Texas Instruments, Inc.	1,287.3	943.7	83.2	48.0	450.6	283.1	32.0E	17.0E	2,345.0
Union Carbide Corp.	3,938.8	3,261.3	290.9	207.4	1,339.7	990.8	99.5	75.0	2,341.3
Uniroyal, Inc.	2,090.0	1,809.9	47.1	46.7	626.2	522.1	27.0	25.0	251.9
Upjohn Co.	647.5	511.3	68.6	46.5	248.4	182.9	26.0E	17.0E	2,172.5
Warner-Lambert Co.	1,703.5	1,509.3	138.6	122.7	696.7	572.2	63.0E	51.0E	2,959.3
F. W. Woolworth Co.	3,722.1	3,119.2	93.5	79.2	n.a.	n.a.	n.a.	n.a.	508.5
Xerox Corp.	2,989.7	2,419.1	300.5	249.5	1,194.0	890.0	147.0	114.0	9,364.2
Total	$113,674.0	$95,319.5	$8,532.9	$6,961.7	$41,579.0	$32,457.0	$3,640.2	$2,829.9	$166,429.8

* Before extraordinary items.
E—Estimated by Drexel Burnham & Co., Inc., assuming slightly higher margins abroad.
n.a.—Not available.

sources or to markets with special characteristics, a technological advantage, or other similar factors.

Foreign securities can therefore be a valuable means of diversification, particularly as one or more of these factors come into play.

THE MECHANICS OF FOREIGN SECURITIES INVESTMENT

The principal market for individual foreign securities is generally in their home countries. Exceptions occur from time to time. Examples: London has been an active market for South African gold mining stocks and a number of Australian securities; New York for the shares of The Rank Organisation, Philips N. V., Royal Dutch, KLM Royal Dutch Airlines, Sony Corporation, and some South African gold mining stocks.

Listed Securities

A small number of foreign enterprises have listed their securities on the New York Stock Exchange or the American Stock Exchange. See Figure 1. Listings are believed to have been limited because of:

1. The imposition in 1963 of a U.S. tax on purchases of foreign securities (see Appendix A for a brief description of the interest equalization tax).
2. Voluntary restraints on purchases of foreign securities by institutions in the United States, imposed by the Federal Reserve Board.
3. The NYSE listing requirements required audited and consolidated statements and a minimum level of disclosure which in the early sixties involved substantially more information than many foreign enterprises were willing to disclose.

In recent years, many of Europe's major enterprises have, on a voluntary basis, adopted international accounting standards while others, including Japanese enterprises which have raised funds on the international capital market, have conformed to such standards.

The gap between acceptable NYSE and SEC standards of accounting and disclosure and those acceptable to major multinational enterprises has narrowed meaningfully. This, combined with the elimination of the U.S. restrictions to investment in foreign securities, may encourage many foreign enterprises to list their securities and gain access to the U.S. capital market.

Other Securities

Specialized firms make over-the-counter markets in a number of foreign securities that are not listed and in which there is an active in-

FIGURE 1

Some Foreign Stocks Traded on the New York Stock Exchange

Alcan Aluminium Limited (Canada)
ASA Ltd. (South Africa)
Benguet Consolidated, Inc. (Philippines)
British Petroleum Company Ltd.
Campbell Red Lake Mines, Ltd. (Canada)
Canadian Southern Railway Co.
Canadian Breweries, Ltd.
Canadian Pacific Limited
Deltec International Limited (Canada)
Distillers Corp.-Seagrams Ltd. (Canada)
Dome Mines, Limited (Canada)
EMI Limited (United Kingdom)
Genstar Limited (Canada)
Granby Mining Co., Ltd. (Canada)
Hudson's Bay Mining and Smelting Co. (Canada)
International Nickel Co. of Canada Ltd.
KLM Royal Dutch Airlines
Massey-Ferguson, Ltd. (Canada)
Matsushita Electric Industrial Co., Ltd. (Japan)
Norlin Corporation (Panama)
Northern & Central Gas Corp. Ltd. (Canada)
Northgate Exploration Limited (Canada)
Pacific Petroleums Ltd. (Canada)
Plessey Company Ltd. (United Kingdom)
Roan Selection Trust Ltd. (Zambia)
Royal Dutch Petroleum Co.
Schlumberger, N.V. (the Netherlands)
"Shell" Transport and Trading Co., Ltd. (United Kingdom)
Sony Corporation (Japan)
Unilever Ltd. (United Kingdom)
Unilever, N.V. (the Netherlands)
Walker (Hiram)-Gooderham & Worts, Ltd. (Canada)

American Stock Exchange—Canadian Stocks Traded

Aquitaine Company of Canada Ltd.
Asamera Oil Corporation Ltd.
Ashland Oil Canada Ltd.
Bow Valley Industries, Ltd.
Brascan Ltd.
Campbell Chibougamau Mines Ltd.
Canadian Export Gas & Oil Ltd.
Canadian Homestead Oils Ltd.
Canadian Hydrocarbons Limited
Canadian International Power Co. Ltd.
Canadian Javelin Limited
Canadian Marconi Company
Canadian Merrill Ltd.
Canadian Occidental Petroleum, Ltd.
Canadian Superior Oil Co. Ltd.
Cominco Ltd.
Dome Petroleum Ltd.
Domtar Limited
Ford Motor Co. of Canada Ltd.
Giant Yellowknife Mines Ltd.
Gulf Oil Canada, Limited
Home Oil Co. Ltd.

FIGURE 1 (continued)

Hudson's Bay Oil & Gas Co. Ltd.
Husky Oil Ltd.
Imperial Oil Ltd.
Kilembe Copper Cobalt Ltd.
Lake Shore Mines Ltd.
Neonex International Ltd.
North Canadian Oils Ltd.
Numac Oil & Gas Ltd.
Pato Consolidated Gold Dredging Ltd.
Peel-Elder Limited
Placer Development Company Limited
Prairie Oil Royalties Co. Ltd.
Preston Mines Ltd.
Quebecor Inc.
Ranger Oil (Canada) Limited
Revenue Properties Co. Ltd.
Scurry-Rainbow Oil Ltd.
Supercrete Ltd.
Total Petroleum (North America) Ltd.
Union Gas Co. of Canada, Ltd.
United Asbestos Corp. Ltd.
Wainoco Oil Ltd.
Western Decalta Petroleum Ltd.
Wright-Hargreaves Mines, Ltd.

American Stock Exchange—Some Foreign Stocks Other than Canadian Traded

Alliance Tire and Rubber Company Limited (Israel)
American Israel Paper Mills Limited (Israel)
Anglo Company Limited (Bahama Islands)
Atlas Consolidated Mining and Development Corp. (Philippines)
British-American Tobacco Company Ltd. (United Kingdom)
Courtaulds Ltd. (United Kingdom)
Dunlop Holdings Ltd. (United Kingdom)
Etz Lavud Limited (Israel)
Imperial Chemical Industries, Ltd. (United Kingdom)
Imperial Tobacco Group Ltd. (United Kingdom)
Kesko Oy (Finland)
Marinduque Mining & Industrial Corp.(Philippines)
Mortgage Bank and Financial Agency of the Kingdom of Denmark
O'okiep Copper Co. Ltd. (South Africa)
Philippine Long Distance Telephone Co.
Sumitomo Chemical Company Ltd. (Japan)
Syntex Corporation (Panama)
Tubos de Acero de Mexico, S.A.
Woolworth (F. W.) & Company Ltd. (United Kingdom)

terest. In many foreign securities, there is often more than two or three competing market makers.

While the market makers take positions, long or short, in the securities they trade, they can purchase or sell the securities abroad to satisfy the needs of the U.S. market. The process of simultaneous purchase and sale of securities in two different markets is known as *arbitrage*. The arbitrage specialists, many of whom are also market makers, concentrate on identifying spreads in prices between two markets, in the United States and abroad, and through arbitrage contribute toward a narrowing of price spreads.

Investors can buy or sell securities abroad directly; this involves the purchase or sale of the securities in the foreign currency, purchase or sale of the necessary foreign exchange, and physical transfer of the securities. The transaction tends to involve a number of steps which may require specialized knowledge of the markets, which are often done more efficiently through the market makers in the United States.

American Shares and Depositary Receipts

Securities traded in the United States are generally handled in the form of American shares or American depositary receipts (ADR's). *American shares* are securities certificates issued in the United States by a transfer agent acting on behalf of the foreign issuer. *American depositary receipts* are certificates of ownership issued by a U.S. bank, as a convenience to the investors in lieu of the underlying shares which it holds in custody. The principal differences between American shares and American depositary receipts is that the former are issued on behalf and under the sponsorship of the foreign issuer who may absorb part of the handling expenses involved, while ADR's are issued by U.S. banks at their sole initiative. The shareholders absorb the handling costs through higher transfer expenses and a handling charge deducted from corporate dividend payments.

The New York and American stock exchanges publish lists of all ADR's as well as other foreign certificates traded on the exchanges. In addition, the National Association of Security Dealers located in Washington publishes lists of all ADR's and foreign shares traded over the counter.

U.S. Investment in Foreign Securities

Investments in foreign securities by those living in the United States have not been substantial, and in fact, the process has often involved a net divestiture, as shown in Table 2.

Foreign Bonds

Foreign bonds account for an important part of the purchases and sales as shown in Table 2. Interest rates abroad have often been higher than in the United States. Foreign issuers are attracted to the U.S. market when they can raise the needed capital at cheaper rates than they could in their home market. Conversely, U.S. institutional investors would be attracted to foreign bond issues that provide higher yields than the corresponding domestic issues. The differences in the net interest cost,

TABLE 2

Foreign Securities Investment by U.S. Persons, 1958–73 (in millions)

	Foreign Bonds			*Foreign Stocks*		
	Gross Sales	*Gross Purchases*	*Net Purchases*	*Gross Sales*	*Gross Purchases*	*Net Purchases*
1958	$ 889	$1,915	$ 1,026	$ 467	$ 804	$337
1959	946	1,458	512	566	804	238
1960	883	1,445	562	509	592	83
1961	802	1,262	460	596	966	370
1962	1,093	2,037	944	702	806	104
1963	991	2,086	1,095	696	644	− 51
1964	915	1,843	928	748	548	−200
1965	1,198	2,440	1,242	906	617	−289
1966	1,778	2,692	914	960	731	229
1967	2,024	3,187	1,163	880	1,037	157
1968	2,306	3,686	1,380	1,252	1,566	314
1969	1,552	2,581	1,029	1,519	2,037	518
1970	1,490	2,441	951	1,033	998	− 35
1971	1,687	2,621	934	1,385	1,434	49
1972	1,901	2,961	1,060	2,532	2,123	−409
1973P	1,468	2,449	981	1,729	1,554	−175
1974—January	71	364	292	209	207	− 2

P—Preliminary.
Source: *Treasury Bulletin*, U.S. Treasury Department, Office of the Secretary.

which takes into account the underwriting expenses, to the foreign issuer is such that the expenses related to registration and listing of the securities are not a meaningful factor.

In the analysis of foreign bond issues, the criteria as to interest coverage and debt equity ratios are similar to those used for domestic issues. In addition, the economic environment and other external factors may affect the borrower.

THE FRAMEWORK FOR INTERNATIONAL INVESTMENT

Investment in foreign securities involves a number of factors which affect the underlying business. The principal stock exchanges are those of the leading industrialized nations. This text attempts to provide a framework of the key factors as they affect some of the leading economies or stock markets.

The Economies in Perspective

To place the economies in perspective, relative to the United States and to one another, they are compared in Tables 3 and 4. The size of the U.S. economy dwarfs that of the countries. In addition, they are much more dependent on foreign trade than the United States.

While the combined Common Market countries approach the United States in terms of population, they are outdistanced in terms of GNP. The Common Market is composed of nine countries with different languages, cultures, and entirely different national identities. The process of integration, begun in 1958, may take another 10 years and possibly longer. For practical investment purposes, therefore, it seems appropriate to consider the European countries as separate entities.

From an investment standpoint, the principal differences between the various countries lie in the relative importance of government spending, capital formation, and private consumption, as shown in Table 5.

Unit Labor Costs—A Measure of Competitive Position

Foreign trade is an important factor for the leading industrial economies abroad. Until August 15, 1971, when the United States adopted its New Economic Program, the relationship between currencies was fixed (except for the DM floated since April 1971 and revalued). When the floating of international currencies was adopted in December 1971, currencies could fluctuate freely relative to one another and readjust the international price of a nation's industrial output available for export.

A broad guide to relative competitive position on a national basis is provided by a comparison of unit labor costs internationally, in the same currency. Unit labor costs are computed by dividing the output per man-hour related into the level of hourly compensation. Fluctuations in exchange parities affect the relative level of unit labor costs. A brief summary of the analysis follows:

1. Productivity. Output per man-hour has increased at a much faster rate for Japan and Germany than for the United Kingdom or the United States. The key to this achievement was a high level of capital expenditures.

Table 6 compares output per man-hour for selected countries over the period 1960–73:

2. Money Wages. In every country, hourly compensation in national currency terms shows very steep increases. For Japan, the increases amounted to 532 percent for the 1960–73 period, as compared to a 96 percent increase for the United States.

The trends in hourly compensation in the 1960–73 period are summarized in Table 7.

3. Unit Labor Costs. When unit labor costs are computed in national currency, they show only a small advantage for U.S. manufacturing. Our costs rose by 23 percent in the 1966–73 period as compared to a 35 percent increase for Japan and a 39 percent increase for Germany. The trends in unit labor costs in the 1960–73 period—in national currency—are summarized in Table 8. As noted above, these numbers leave out of account the effect of the devaluations.

4. Impact of Parity Changes. In contrast to the relatively slight advantage afforded the U.S. dollar by productivity and money-wage trends, the parity changes have had a major impact. This impact is easily seen when unit labor costs are translated from the national currency into U.S. dollars (See Table 9). Table 10 demonstrates the advantage accruing to the United States from the changes in parities between December 31, 1972, and December 31, 1973.

The exchange rate of the U.S. dollar relative to major foreign currencies had been constant for most of the postwar period until the spring of 1971, when the German mark was permitted to float. A comparison of the exchange parities as of March 31, 1971, and December 31, 1973, is shown in Table 11.

5. U.S. Economic Growth in Perspective. The danger of relying too heavily on recent price trends in interpreting money-wage, hence unit-labor-cost, trends is shown in Table 12, which illustrates real GNP growth and rates of price increases for some of the key countries involved in this analysis. (Persistent differences in the general levels of countries' growth rates are nevertheless apparent, and remind us that minimizing unit labor cost increases is not the only objective of long-run economic policy.)

The need to limit the high rates of inflation prevailing worldwide and to bring them under control has caused governments to take drastic action in some cases, particularly in Germany. These actions have trig-

TABLE 3

Selected Industrialized Nations' GNP, Exports and Imports as Percentage of GNP (in billions of current dollars)*

	1967	*1968*	*1969*	*1970*	*1971*	*1972*
Belgium						
GNP	19.8	20.8	23.4	26.1	31.7	35.9
Exports	7.1	8.2	10.1	11.6	12.7	16.2
As percentage of GNP	35.4%	39.4%	43.8%	44.4%	40.1%	45.1%
Imports	7.3	8.4	10.9	11.4	12.9	15.5
As percentage of GNP	36.9%	40.4%	42.7%	43.7%	40.7%	43.2%
France						
GNP	117.1	127.3	130.2	146.6	172.2	195.5
Exports	11.6	12.9	15.3	18.1	20.7	26.4
As percentage of GNP	9.9%	10.1%	11.8%	12.3%	12.0%	13.5%
Imports	12.4	14.0	17.5	19.1	21.3	27.0
As percentage of GNP	10.6%	11.0%	13.4%	13.0%	12.4%	13.8%
Germany						
GNP	123.7	134.7	164.0	187.9	232.2	258.9
Exports	21.7	24.8	29.1	34.2	38.9	46.7
As percentage of GNP	17.5%	18.4%	17.7%	18.2%	16.8%	18.0%
Imports	17.4	20.2	24.9	29.8	34.3	40.2
As percentage of GNP	14.1%	15.0%	15.2%	15.9%	14.8%	15.5%
Italy						
GNP	70.2	75.8	83.3	93.4	106.3	118.4
Exports	8.7	10.2	11.7	13.2	15.1	18.5
As percentage of GNP	12.4%	13.5%	14.0%	14.1%	14.2%	15.6%
Imports	9.8	10.3	12.5	15.0	16.0	19.3
As percentage of GNP	14.0%	13.6%	15.0%	16.1%	15.1%	16.3%
Netherlands						
GNP	22.8	25.1	28.4	32.0	39.8	45.7
Exports	7.3	8.4	10.0	11.8	13.9	16.8
As percentage of GNP	32.0%	33.5%	35.2%	36.9%	34.9%	36.8%
Imports	8.4	9.3	11.0	13.4	15.4	17.5
As percentage of GNP	36.8%	36.0%	38.7%	41.9%	38.7%	38.3%
United Kingdom						
GNP	97.2	103.7	111.9	121.8	143.1	145.8
Exports	14.5	15.4	17.6	19.4	22.3	24.4
As percentage of GNP	14.9%	14.9%	15.7%	15.9%	15.6%	16.7%
Imports	17.8	19.0	20.0	21.7	23.9	27.9
As percentage of GNP	18.3%	18.3%	17.9%	17.8%	16.7%	19.1%
Nine EEC Countries						
GNP	464.5	502.0	559.8	628.5	748.2	826.2
Exports	74.2	83.4	97.8	113.0	128.6	155.0
As percentage of GNP	16.0%	16.6%	17.5%	18.0%	17.2%	18.8%
Imports	77.4	85.6	101.2	116.4	130.2	154.6
As percentage of GNP	16.7%	17.1%	18.1%	18.5%	17.4%	18.7%
Japan						
GNP	120.4	144.5	168.5	198.6	251.9	300.1
Exports	10.5	13.0	16.0	19.3	24.0	28.6
As percentage of GNP	8.7%	9.0%	9.5%	9.7%	9.5%	9.5%
Imports	11.7	13.0	15.0	18.9	19.7	23.5
As percentage of GNP	9.7%	9.0%	8.9%	9.5%	7.8%	7.8%
United States						
GNP	793.9	865.0	930.3	977.1	1,055.5	1,155.2
Exports	31.6	34.6	38.0	43.2	44.1	49.8
As percentage of GNP	4.0%	4.0%	4.1%	4.4%	4.2%	4.3%
Imports	28.7	35.3	38.3	42.4	48.3	58.9
As percentage of GNP	3.6%	4.1%	4.1%	4.3%	4.6%	5.1%

* Converted at historically prevailing exchange rates.

Source: *International Financial Statistics* published by the International Monetary Fund.

TABLE 4

Population (in millions)

Year	*Belgium and Luxembourg*	*France*	*Germany*	*Italy*	*Netherlands*	*United Kingdom*	*Canada*	*Japan*	*United States*	*Total EEC Countries*	*Total Major Industrial Countries*
1960	9.5	45.7	55.4	49.6	11.5	52.4	17.9	93.0	180.7	229.3	520.9
1961	9.5	46.2	56.2	49.9	11.6	52.8	18.3	94.1	183.8	231.2	527.4
1962	9.5	47.0	56.9	50.2	11.8	53.3	18.6	94.9	186.7	234.0	534.2
1963	9.6	47.9	57.6	50.6	12.0	53.7	18.9	95.9	189.4	236.7	540.9
1964	9.7	48.3	58.3	51.1	12.1	54.0	19.3	97.8†	192.1	241.5	550.7
1965	9.8	48.8	59.0	51.9	12.3	54.4	19.7	98.9	194.3	243.7	556.6
1966	9.9	49.1	59.7	52.6	12.5	54.7	20.1	99.8	196.6	245.7	562.2
1967	9.9	49.6	59.9	52.6	12.6	55.0	20.4	100.8	198.7	247.5	567.4
1968	10.0	49.9	60.2	52.9	12.7	55.3	20.7	102.0	200.7	248.6	572.0
1969	10.0	50.3	60.9	53.2	12.9	55.6	21.0	103.2	202.7	250.3	577.2
1970	10.0	50.8	61.6	53.6	13.0	55.7	21.3	104.3	204.9	251.4	581.9
1971	10.0	51.3	61.3	53.9	13.2	55.6*	21.6	105.6	207.1	253.2	587.5
1972	10.1	51.7	61.7	54.4	13.3	55.8	21.9	107.0	208.8	255.0	592.7
1973	10.2	52.1	62.0	54.9	13.4	55.9	22.1	108.4	210.4	256.5	597.4
Percentage change:											
1960–73	7.4%	14.0%	11.9%	10.7%	16.5%	6.7%	23.5%	16.6%	16.4%	11.9%	13.3%
1960–66	3.3	7.4	7.8	6.0	8.7	4.4	12.3	6.1	8.8	7.2	6.6
1966–73	3.0	6.1	3.9	4.4	7.2	2.2	10.0	8.6	7.0	4.4	6.3
Compound annual percentage change											
1960–73	0.5%	1.0%	0.8%	0.8%	1.2%	0.5%	1.6%	1.2%	1.2%	0.8%	1.0%
1960–66	0.5	1.2	1.3	1.0	1.4	0.7	1.9	1.2	1.4	1.2	1.1
1966–73	0.5	0.9	0.5	0.6	1.0	0.3	1.4	1.2	1.0	0.6	0.9

* Series break (data not comparable with previous years).
† Including Ryukyu Islands, previously shown separately.
Source: *U.N. Monthly Bulletin of Statistics.*

TABLE 5

Selected Industrial Nations' Government Spending, Private Consumption, and Capital Formation (in billions of current $)*

	1968	*1969*	*1970*	*1971*	*1972*
Canada					
GNP	67.7	74.4	84.7	93.2	103.9
Government spending	11.8	13.3	16.4	18.4	20.6
As percentage of GNP	17.4%	17.9%	19.4%	19.7%	19.8%
Private consumption	40.7	44.3	49.6	53.9	60.5
As percentage of GNP	60.1%	59.5%	58.6%	57.8%	58.2%
Capital formation	14.7	16.1	17.9	20.5	22.4
As percentage of GNP	21.7%	21.6%	21.1%	22.0%	21.6%
Japan					
GNP	144.5	168.5	198.6	251.9	300.1
Government spending	12.0	13.8	16.3	21.8	27.2
As percentage of GNP	8.3%	8.2%	8.2%	8.7%	9.1%
Private consumption	76.2	87.7	101.6	131.0	156.1
As percentage of GNP	52.7%	52.0%	51.2%	52.0%	52.0%
Capital formation	48.4	58.5	69.5	86.4	103.4
As percentage of GNP	33.5%	34.7%	35.0%	34.3%	34.5%
Germany					
GNP	134.7	164.0	187.9	232.2	258.9
Government spending	20.3	22.8	26.1	33.4	40.8
As percentage of GNP	15.1%	13.9%	13.9%	14.4%	15.8%
Private consumption	75.5	90.5	101.2	125.2	140.1
As percentage of GNP	56.1%	55.2%	53.9%	53.9%	54.1%
Capital formation	31.2	39.6	49.6	62.1	67.3
As percentage of GNP	23.2%	24.1%	26.4%	26.7%	26.0%
United Kingdom					
GNP	103.7	111.9	121.8	143.1	145.8
Government spending	17.3	18.6	19.2	23.2	24.3
As percentage of GNP	16.7%	16.6%	15.6%	16.2%	16.7%
Private consumption	65.2	69.5	75.2	88.9	92.2
As percentage of GNP	62.9%	62.1%	61.7%	62.1%	63.2%
Capital formation	19.2	20.3	22.1	25.8	26.3
As percentage of GNP	18.5%	18.1%	18.1%	18.0%	18.0%
France					
GNP	127.3	130.2	146.6	172.2	195.5
Government spending	16.1	16.2	18.1	21.3	24.1
As percentage of GNP	12.6%	12.4%	12.3%	12.4%	12.3%
Private consumption	77.0	78.1	86.7	102.5	116.7
As percentage of GNP	60.5%	60.0%	59.1%	59.5%	59.7%
Capital formation	31.6	33.1	37.9	46.1	50.7
As percentage of GNP	24.8%	25.4%	25.9%	26.8%	25.9%
Netherlands					
GNP	25.1	28.4	32.0	39.8	45.7
Government spending	4.0	4.5	5.2	6.7	7.6
As percentage of GNP	15.9%	15.8%	16.3%	16.8%	16.6%
Private consumption	14.4	16.1	18.2	22.5	25.4
As percentage of GNP	57.4%	56.7%	56.9%	56.5%	55.6%
Capital formation	6.7	8.1	8.2	10.2	10.9
As percentage of GNP	26.7%	28.5%	25.6%	25.6%	23.9%
Italy					
GNP	75.8	83.3	93.4	106.3	118.4
Government spending	10.2	11.0	11.9	15.1	17.4
As percentage of GNP	13.5%	13.2%	12.7%	14.2%	14.7%
Private consumption	48.2	52.5	59.9	68.0	76.1
As percentage of GNP	63.6%	63.0%	64.1%	64.0%	64.3%

TABLE 5 (*Continued*)

	1968	*1969*	*1970*	*1971*	*1972*
Capital formation	15.0	17.1	19.7	21.3	22.9
As percentage of GNP	19.8%	20.5%	21.1%	20.0%	19.3%
South Africa					
GNP	13.5	15.2	16.6	17.3	18.9
Government spending	1.6	1.8	2.1	2.4	2.4
As percentage of GNP	11.9%	11.8%	12.7%	13.9%	12.7%
Private consumption	8.7	9.6	10.7	11.1	12.0
As percentage of GNP	64.4%	63.2%	64.4%	64.2%	63.5%
Capital formation	3.2	3.7	4.3	4.8	5.2
As percentage of GNP	23.7%	24.3%	25.9%	27.7%	27.5%
United States					
GNP	865.0	930.3	977.1	1,055.5	1,155.2
Government spending	200.2	210.0	219.5	234.3	255.0
As percentage of GNP	23.1%	22.6%	22.5%	22.2%	22.1%
Private consumption	535.8	579.5	617.6	667.2	726.5
As percentage of GNP	61.9%	62.2%	63.2%	63.2%	62.9%
Capital formation	118.9	131.1	131.7	147.1	172.3
As percentage of GNP	13.7%	14.1%	13.5%	13.9%	14.9%

* Converted at historically prevailing exchange rates.
Source: *International Financial Statistics*, published by the International Monetary Fund.

gered independent measures by other countries, including Japan and the United States.

Inflation

Inflation, or the rate of price increases, has tended to be higher in many foreign countries than in the United States. Inasmuch as it affects a nation's competitive position, many countries may be expected to make serious attempts to control the resulting wage spiral.

TABLE 6

Output per Man-Hour (1960 = 100)

Year	*France*	*Germany*	*United Kingdom*	*Canada*	*Japan*	*United States*
1960	100.0	100.0	100.0	100.0	100.0	100.0
1966	136.2	141.7	124.1	128.2	165.9	124.1
1970	173.7	175.8	140.3	151.3	278.5	134.2
1971	182.0	184.2	148.0	160.0	288.4	143.7
1972	193.5	196.5	157.0	167.0	319.6	151.3
1973P	207.2	209.2	171.0	173.8	377.9	158.4
Percentage change						
1960–73	107.2%	109.2%	71.0%	73.8%	277.9%	58.4%
1960–66	36.2	41.7	24.1	28.2	65.9	24.1
1966–73	52.1	47.6	37.8	35.6	127.8	27.6
Compound annual percentage change						
1960–73	5.7%	5.8%	4.2%	4.3%	10.8%	3.6%

P—Preliminary.
Source: U.S. Bureau of Labor Statistics, Washington, D.C.

TABLE 7

Hourly Compensation in National Currency (1960 = 100)

Year	France	Germany	United Kingdom	Canada	Japan	United States
1960	100.0	100.0	100.0	100.0	100.0	100.0
1966	163.4	174.4	152.5	130.9	205.3	124.4
1970	246.6	245.4	205.8	175.1	377.4	159.7
1971	277.3	279.7	232.0	189.2	436.5	170.8
1972	311.9	316.8	265.5	203.2	507.9	181.5
1973P	360.1	357.9	313.1	220.8	632.3	195.8
Percentage change						
1960–73	260.1%	257.9%	213.1%	120.8%	532.3%	95.8%
1960–66	63.4	74.4	52.5	30.9	105.3	24.4
1966–73	120.4	105.2	105.3	68.7	208.0	57.4
Compound annual percentage change						
1960–73	10.4%	10.3%	9.2%	6.2%	15.2%	5.3%

P—Preliminary.
Source: U.S. Bureau of Labor Statistics, Washington, D.C.

The implications of *accelerating* rates of price inflation in the major industrial countries could have a serious effect on equity investments if left unchecked.

The developed world's inflationary spiral has been worsened by the oil-producing countries' decision to raise prices. The higher oil prices could impact negatively the balance of payments of the major European countries and Japan. Inflation and higher oil prices are to some extent related, because the inflationary pressures and the devaluation of the dollar of recent years eroded the real value of the oil producers' revenues and, in their eyes, justified the need to adjust prices upward and protect the value of their product. In turn, the higher oil prices implemented

TABLE 8

Unit Labor Cost in National Currency (1960 = 100)

Year	France	Germany	United Kingdom	Canada	Japan	United States
1960	100.0	100.0	100.0	100.0	100.0	100.0
1966	119.9	122.9	123.0	102.1	123.8	100.2
1970	141.9	139.5	146.9	115.6	135.5	118.9
1971	152.2	151.7	156.8	118.2	151.4	118.7
1972	161.0	161.1	169.1	121.6	158.9	119.9
1973P	173.7	170.9	183.1	127.0	167.3	123.5
Percentage change						
1960–73	73.7%	70.9%	83.1%	27.0%	67.3%	23.5%
1960–66	19.9	22.9	23.0	2.1	23.8	0.2
1966–73	44.9	39.1	48.9	24.4	35.1	23.3
Compound annual percentage change						
1960–73	4.4%	4.2%	4.8%	1.9%	4.0%	1.6%

P—Preliminary.
Source: U.S. Bureau of Labor Statistics, Washington, D.C.

TABLE 9

Unit Labor Cost in U.S. Dollars (1960 = 100)

Year	*France*	*Germany*	*United Kingdom*	*Canada*	*Japan*	*United States*
1960	100.0	100.0	100.0	100.0	100.0	100.0
1966	119.5	128.2	122.4	91.9	122.9	100.2
1970	125.8	159.5	125.3	107.5	136.1	118.9
1971	135.4	181.9	136.6	113.5	156.9	118.7
1972	156.5	210.8	150.8	119.1	188.8	119.9
1973P	191.9	269.0	160.0	123.2	222.2	123.5
Percentage change						
1960–73	91.9%	169.0%	60.0%	23.2%	122.2%	23.5%
1960–66	19.5	28.2	22.4	−8.1	22.9	0.2
1966–73	60.6	109.8	30.7	34.1	80.8	23.3
Compound annual percentage change						
1960–73	5.2%	7.9%	3.7%	1.6%	6.3%	1.6%

P—Preliminary.
Source: U.S. Bureau of Labor Statistics, Washington, D.C.

late in 1973 are causing an acceleration in price increases in 1974. The economies of Europe, Japan, and the United States have been affected by inflation, as shown below in Table 13.

Wage Increases

The rate of increases in prices has been accelerated by parallel gains in wages as shown in Table 14.

Inflation and Common Stocks

Inflation rates abroad tend to be higher than in the United States. Common stocks may be a good hedge against inflation *over time* and as a final store of value. In the interim, the value of common stocks can be affected by reduced liquidity and by comparison with alternative investments.

An important by-product of inflation is the change in value of fixed

TABLE 10

Changes in Unit Labor Cost between December 31, 1972, and December 31, 1973

	France	*Germany*	*United Kingdom*	*Canada*	*Japan*	*United States*
1972	156.5	210.8	150.8	119.1	188.8	119.9
1973P	191.9	269.0	160.0	123.2	222.2	123.5
Percentage change	+22.6%	+27.6%	+6.1%	+3.4%	+17.7%	+3.0%

P—*Preliminary.*

TABLE 11

Effective Parity Change since March 1971

	Currency Unit	Per U.S. $ March 31, 1971	Per U.S. $ December 31, 1973	Percentage Decrease
France	F	5.514	4.708	14.6%
Germany	DM	3.630	2.703	25.5
United Kingdom	£	0.414	0.430	3.9
Canada	Can. $	1.0081	0.9958	1.2
Japan	Yen	357.4	280.0	21.7

assets and plant-in-place—assuming no technological change or plant obsolescence. Companies that would particularly benefit, assuming that economic and corporate policies are undertaken that ensure their survival during the period of overall economic readjustment, are those which have large asset bases. Such companies would emerge from the period of contraction with the monetary value of their assets enhanced and the burden of their debt reduced; consequently, they stand to benefit from increases both in their real net worth in terms of the replacement value of the assets and, therefore, from higher return on their capital.

Major Risks

Careful research is necessary to identify major risks which can be summarized as follows:

Political. These are the risks of government intervention, nationalization, changes in taxation rates, and related factors that are a function of government policies.

Exchange Controls. A possible risk in this area would be that the host government not permit the free repatriation of funds when securities are sold.

Foreign Exchange. A change in foreign exchange rates could affect the *dollar value* of a company's assets, its earnings, and the market price for its securities.

FOREIGN EXCHANGE

Changes in exchange rates affect investments in foreign securities because of the following reasons:

1. The price of the securities in their home market is in local currency denominations.
2. This also is the case for corporate sales, earnings, and dividend payments.

TABLE 12

GNP Growth and Price Incrcase (in percentages)

	Real GNP Growth					Rate of Price Increase				
	1969	*1970*	*1971*	*1972*	*1973E*	*1969*	*1970*	*1971*	*1972*	*1973E*
France	7.7	6.0	5.0	5.5	6.0	7.9	5.6	5.0	6.5	8.5
Germany	8.0	5.4	2.7	2.9	5.5	3.5	7.2	7.8	6.1	7.5
United Kingdom	1.6	2.0	1.5	2.8	5.0	5.1	7.3	8.9	8.7	9.0
Japan	11.9	10.5	6.2	9.2	8.0	4.1	6.7	4.8	4.9	11.5
United States	2.5	−0.6	2.7	6.4	6.0	4.9	5.5	4.8	3.0	6.0

E—Estimated.

TABLE 13

Selected Countries—Rate of Price Increase (GNP Deflator)

Countries	*1964*	*1965*	*1966*	*1967*	*1968*	*1969*	*1970*	*1971*	*1972*	*1973*	*1974E*
Belgium	4.7	5.1	4.5	3.0	2.7	3.9	5.2	5.8	7.0	7.0	11.0
Denmark	4.9	7.2	7.1	5.3	5.5	5.1	7.2	6.1	9.0	9.0	14.5
France	4.0	2.5	2.9	2.8	4.7	7.9	5.6	5.0	6.5	8.5	11.0
Italy	6.3	3.9	2.1	3.0	1.5	4.1	6.2	6.6	5.8	11.0	14.5
Netherlands	8.0	5.9	6.0	4.1	3.6	5.6	4.7	7.8	9.5	8.5	14.0
United Kingdom	2.9	4.9	4.4	3.1	3.8	5.1	7.3	8.9	8.7	9.0	14.0
Western Germany	2.8	3.6	3.5	1.2	1.6	3.5	7.2	7.8	6.1	7.5	9.5
EEC, old	4.2	3.5	3.3	2.4	2.8	5.0	6.1	6.6	6.3	7.5	—
EEC, new								(7.0)	6.6	9.0	13.0
Austria	3.2	5.3	3.0	3.7	1.4	3.6	4.6	5.7	7.7	7.5	11.0
Norway	5.5	4.8	4.4	4.1	3.3	3.5	11.6	7.0	7.0	7.5	10.0
Sweden	4.4	5.9	6.2	4.5	2.2	3.4	6.2	7.3	7.8	7.0	11.0
Switzerland	4.9	3.5	4.7	4.6	3.5	2.9	3.6	8.9	9.5	9.0	12.0
Japan	4.0	5.5	4.6	4.3	3.8	4.1	6.7	4.8	4.9	11.5	20.0
United States	1.7	1.9	2.8	3.1	3.7	4.9	5.5	4.8	3.0	6.0	8.0

E—Estimated.

TABLE 14

Selected Countries—Increase in Hourly Wages and Social Cost in Manufacturing (in national currency)

Year	*Netherlands*	*Belgium*	*France*	*Western Germany*	*United Kingdom*	*Italy*	*United States*
October—							
1966	100	100	100	100	100	100	100
1968	119	116	124	110	111	108	112
1969	132	127	132	122	123	118	118
1970	149	143	148	145	141	142	125
1971	170	163	166	162	160	160	134
1972	191	189	188	179	183	180	146
1973	219	219	218	202	205	219	159
1974E	247	250	246	232	232	261	174
Percentage change							
1966–74E	147.0	150.0	146.0	132.0	132.0	161.0	74.0
1966–70	49.0	43.0	48.0	45.0	41.0	42.0	25.0
1970–74E	65.8	74.8	66.2	60.0	64.5	83.8	39.2
Compound annual percentage change							
1966–74E	13.8	14.0	13.7	12.8	12.8	14.6	8.3

E—Estimated.

3. The cost structure of the foreign company is often in its home currency while export sales have to be competitive on an international basis.
4. When raw materials are imported by a nation or a company, a change in parities could affect costs and therefore corporate profits.

The foreign exchange factor also influences the international competitive position of the companies and countries involved. (See discussion of competitive position.)

Exchange rates have been fixed since 1944, and except for minor changes, they have been relatively stable until August 1971 when the New Economic Program was introduced by the United States. In December 1971, the Smithsonian agreement reached among major developed nations resulted in floating exchange rates. Floating exchange rates that can freely fluctuate have added an important variable to investments abroad.

The changes in the exchange rate for selected foreign currencies relative to the U.S. dollar in the December 31, 1971–December 31, 1973 period is shown in Table 15.

The International Monetary Fund, Washington, D.C., publishes an *Annual Report of Exchange Restrictions,* which provides useful data as to national foreign exchange regulations.

TABLE 15

Change in Exchange Parities for Selected Currencies Relative to the U.S. Dollar December 31, 1971, to July 27, 1973, and to December 31, 1973

	Change to July 27, 1973	*Change to December 31, 1973*
Belgium	+19.9%	+ 7.7%
France	+21.0	+ 9.9
Germany	+28.0	+17.3
Italy	+ 1.5	− 2.3
Netherlands	+20.1	+13.2
United Kingdom	− 1.5	− 9.0
Sweden	+16.2	+ 5.7
Switzerland	+26.8	+17.1
Canada	n.m.	+ 0.6
Japan	+16.3	+11.1

n.m.—Not meaningful.

STOCK MARKETS ABROAD

The market value of securities listed on the New York Stock Exchange as of December 31, 1973 amounted to $721 billion, or 60% more than the principal foreign stock markets listed below in Table 16. The NYSE market capitalization includes investment companies and foreign-based companies that are excluded from the data from the markets abroad.

Stock markets play a much less important role abroad than in the United States, as illustrated by Table 17.

TABLE 16
Market Value of Selected Foreign Markets (December 31, 1973)

	Market Capitalization ($ billion)
Europe	
United Kingdom	$ 90.0
Germany	43.8
France	34.6
Spain	27.6
Switzerland	16.7
Netherlands	14.5
Italy	15.7
Belgium/Luxembourg	10.5
Sweden	7.6
Denmark	2.4
Norway	2.7
Austria	1.3
Europe	$267.4
Far East	
Japan	$128.6
Hong Kong	10.3
Singapore	5.8
	$144.7
Australia	$ 27.3
Total Europe, Far East, and Australia	$439.4
United States (NYSE)	$721.0

Source: *Capital International Perspective.*

The more modest ratios abroad do not convey the full story. In Belgium, a number of holding companies have sizeable participations in financial institutions and industrial companies whose securities are also listed. In France, the government has large interests in the listed natural resource enterprises, the nationalized banks, and insurance companies; in turn the financial institutions own large interests in other listed companies. In Germany, the banks and other financial institutions have sizeable equity interests in one another and in other business enterprises. In Italy, the holding company concept is important, and the government, through the Instituto Ricostruzione Industriale (IRI), has large interests in Italian industry.

TABLE 17

Comparison of the Market Value of Listed Securities to Gross National Product (in billions)

	GNP—1972	*Market Capitalization as of 12/31/72*	*Market Capitalization as Percentage of GNP*
Belgium/Luxembourg	$ 35.9	$ 9.2	25.6%
France	195.5	30.7	15.7
Germany	258.9	43.3	16.7
Italy	118.4	14.2	12.0
Netherlands	45.7	14.7	32.2
United Kingdom	145.8	122.6	84.1
Japan	300.1	152.3	50.7
United States	1,155.2	871.5	75.4

In the Netherlands, the figures are not representative because the Dutch Internationals, which include Royal Dutch, Unilever, and Philips, operate on a truly worldwide basis; and a large part of their equity capital is held by investors outside The Netherlands.

In Japan, business enterprises tend to own substantial common stock participations in the capital of one another. The common stock cross-holdings may take many forms including the close relationships resulting from the pre-World War II existence of financial industrial groups, known as "zaibatsu." Some of these relationships have been replaced by a new form of cooperation which involves, among others, large cross-holdings of common stock among the enterprises of the group. Such cross-holdings prevail between customer and supplier and between borrower and lender. The financial institutions, banks, and insurance companies also have sizeable participations in "friendly" enterprises.

The United Kingdom has the highest ratio of market capitalization to GNP among the foreign economies. This appears to be a proper reflection of the role of the London Stock Exchange, traditionally an important source of capital for business in Britain and in many other countries.

The large ownership of common stock by other enterprises, banks, insurance or holding companies affects the liquidity of the markets involved. This, when combined with the lower percentage represented by the market value of listed securities to GNP, compared to the United States (NYSE market capitalization), explains an important difference in the methods used to finance business abroad and those in the United States; namely, equity capital abroad cannot be raised as easily publicly. Debt financing, therefore tends to play a greater role than in the United

TABLE 18

Comparison of Volatility of International Stock Markets

	Stock Market Percentage Change 1961–72	*Performance*	*Performance as A Multiple of Stock Market Appreciation*	*Number of Advances*	*Average Advance*	*Number of Declines*	*Average Decline*
United States	+ 70.8%	+ 634%	9.0x	6	41%	6	24%
Japan	+297.0	+3,464	11.7x	10	50	10	21
United Kingdom	+ 66.5	+1,115	16.8x	11	29	10	21
Netherlands	+ 72.0	+ 890	12.4x	8	35	8	21
France	+ 19.4	+1,634	84.2x	16	21	15	17
Germany	− 3.0	+ 743	—	9	29	8	23

United States—Dow Jones Industrial Average.
Japan—Tokyo Stock Exchange Dow Jones Average.
United Kingdom—Financial Times Industrial Ordinary Index.
Netherlands—ANP/CBS Index.
France—I.N.S.E.E. Index.
Germany—Herstatt Index.

States. This increases the financial leverage and accounts for the high volatility of certain foreign markets.

New enterprises are emerging, particularly in France and Japan, with ambitious expansion plans. They have been able to raise large amounts publicly based on their earnings performance. Active markets have developed in their securities. Some major international companies are now reporting their earnings on a consolidated basis and, in some cases, with a certificate from a major U.S. auditing firm. This may result in a substantial broadening of markets over time.

Volatility of Markets Abroad

The volatility of stock markets abroad creates opportunities for investment. The volatility of some of the key international markets is illustrated in Table 18.

The performance figures are based on the assumption that it would have been possible to sell the investment in the index before a decline of 10 percent or more and to reinvest the proceeds at the new low. In practical terms, there are three problems with this approach: (1) It can only be realized with the benefit of hindsight; (2) it involves purchasing the overall index; and (3) it requires an adequate market liquidity. Even if (1) and (2) could have been realized, it is unlikely that substantial funds could have been invested at the peaks or bottoms of the market.

The volatility of international markets and the much larger potential appreciation available by optimizing on major swings in the markets illustrate in principle the investment opportunities available in foreign securities.

Valuation of Securities

A comparison of the principal markets, in terms of dividend yield, price to earnings multiple (P/E), and price to cash flow ratio (CE) is shown in Table 19. Price/earnings ratios are lower abroad than they are

TABLE 19

Selected Markets—Relative Value of Securities as of March 29, 1974

	Yield	*P/E*	*P/CE*
France	4.8	11.4	3.9
Germany	4.6	10.7	3.5
United Kingdom	6.0	6.4	4.2
Canada	3.7	11.4	n.a.
Japan	2.6	15.0	5.6
United States	3.8	11.6	7.2

n.a. = Not available.
Source: *Capital International Perspective*, April 1974.

in the United States, while the difference in yields is not very large. The spread in the price to cash flow ratio is indicative of the higher foreign depreciation relative to earnings.

CORPORATE ACCOUNTING ABROAD

The standards of accounting and auditing abroad differ substantially from country to country, particularly relative to those used in the United States. Some major international corporations in Europe and Japan have decided to present their accounts based on U.S. and/or U.K. standards. This is often an independent management decision, or one related to an international financing or the international listing of the company's securities.

The development of international capital markets in the past 10 years, accelerated by the growth of the Euro-dollar market and, more recently, by the elimination of the Interest Equalization Tax and the U.S. guidelines, is providing a major impetus to the larger international enterprises to publish their results on a basis comparable to that prevailing in the United States and the United Kingdom. A large number of foreign companies have already adopted such standards, while similar efforts are underway in others.

Accounting standards in Canada and the United Kingdom are close to those used in the United States. Generally, in Continental Europe and Japan: (1) the accounts are presented on a parent company basis rather than on a consolidated basis and (2) large allocations to and from reserves are made in some cases. The principal reserve accounts are in the form of visible reserve accounts or understatement of assets via accelerated depreciation, write-offs, or reserves against assets; the latter three are not always visible and can be hidden. This is based on the principle that corporate assets are to be presented in a conservative manner.

In Germany, the accounts are often on a parent company basis with large allocations to reserves, some of which are hidden. Techniques have been developed to estimate real earnings, based on published tax payments. Because some reserves are not taxable and because the published tax payments apply to the parent company, these techniques present some problems.

In France, parent company accounting and allocations to reserves prevail.

In the Netherlands, some of the major companies report their results on a basis comparable with U.S. and U.K. accounting standards. However, other companies do not always consolidate the accounts of subsidiaries and are permitted to make allocations to reserves.

In Sweden, accounting standards are relatively strict. Companies are allowed, under Swedish tax regulations, to make allocations to inventory and investment reserves which can generally be added back to earnings by the security analyst after deducting applicable taxes.

In Belgium, parent company reporting and allocations to reserves are used broadly. Consolidation of subsidiaries and international accounting standards appear to be the exception rather than the rule.

In Italy, accounts are presented on a parent company basis, often with sizeable allocations to hidden reserves or transfers from such reserves. It is difficult with Italian accounts at present to determine whether reported earnings and their development have any bearing on actual business developments.

In Japan, parent company accounting and allocations to reserves are generally used. Proposed legislation to make consolidated statements mandatory is pending.

Accounting for inflation, which has tended to advance at a high rate, presents a major problem in many foreign countries. Philips N.V., in the Netherlands, has for many years presented its accounts on the basis of the replacement value of assets. In the United Kingdom, a proposal to adopt "inflation accounting" has been defeated. Considering the current rates of inflation, it is possible that such accounting techniques will be adopted in the United States and abroad.

SECURITY ANALYSIS ABROAD

The differences in language, culture, social, and political environment render a careful assessment of these and other factors necessary. Some of these factors are identified below:

The *corporate objective* for the individual companies has to be determined early in the analysis process, preferably in an interview with senior management. The prime objective of companies is not always to achieve growth or to show higher earnings or earnings per share each calendar quarter or each year.

Abroad, managements operate in a different environment than in the United States, particularly in terms of access to capital markets, social legislation, and dependence on their smaller domestic markets, which are open to foreign competition. For them, expansion and growth are not always as important as they have been in the United States since the early sixties.

Labor and social conditions are different; it is difficult to lay off personnel or close plants in many European countries or Japan. This affects the decision to expand and build new facilities and must be made with a much longer time horizon than the 5- to 10-year "discounted cash flow" or similar rate of return valuation which could be based on a 5- to 10-year time horizon.

In Germany, under proposed legislation, personnel will be entitled to 10 percent of corporate profits. In Italy, severance payments are particularly onerous. In Japan, personnel is practically considered to be employed for life; the employer is under the moral and sometimes legal obligation to keep employees on the payroll.

Unions are well organized in the United Kingdom. Labor leaders in France, Germany, the Netherlands, and Japan have tended to take a long-term view in their negotiations with managements. Overall, in Europe and Japan, wage settlements have been relatively high because of the rates of price increases.

Corporate management abroad, to an increasing degree, is using advanced techniques; the level of sophistication varies widely in different companies, industries, or countries. Younger executives, in some instances trained by major multinational business, compare favorably with their U.S. counterparts.

Stock options or direct financial remuneration are not the principal incentive of the foreign executive. An important part of the compensation package consists of special fringe benefits. Employer and government retirement plans are liberal and provide a certain level of financial security.

Corporate ownership influences both corporate objectives and management actions. It is understandable that when business is controlled by family, banking, or industrial interests, they may have different corporate objectives than enterprises whose shares, broadly held, are valued on growth and earnings performance.

Government's role in business tends to be more important abroad than in the United States. It ranges from sizeable participation in industry through holding companies in Italy to a considerable degree of corporate independence in the Netherlands, the home country for some large international enterprises—Royal Dutch, Unilever, and Philips N.V. In Japan, the cooperation of business and government is close. In some other countries, laissez-faire prevails in many areas, while the government plays an active role in the key industries and owns or controls telephone operating companies, railroads, airlines, and public utilities. Utilities are publicly owned in Japan and Germany. There is some public participation in airlines in Switzerland, the Netherlands, Germany, France, and Japan.

In France, the major commercial banks and insurance companies are government owned; in the United Kingdom, the British coal mines and the steel industry are government owned. The health care industry is increasingly under government control and scrutiny.

In high technology areas, governments have actively intervened in the market process, sometimes through subsidies, particularly in the computer industry and in aircraft manufacturing.

In natural resources, governments are taking a more active role by: (1) increasing taxation, (2) limiting foreign control, (3) taking direct participations in the exploiting enterprises, and (4) controlling selling prices.

SECURITIES REGULATION ABROAD

The standards of securities regulation abroad vary widely from country to country. Generally, rules and regulations regarding *disclosure, inside information,* and *insider trading* are not as strict abroad as they are in the United States.

The frequency of financial reports also varies. Some of the large enterprises, which have adopted accounting standards similar to those in the United States, publish quarterly statements; some companies, in the United Kingdom and Japan, publish financial statements semiannually and others publish annually.

DIVIDEND WITHHOLDING TAXES

In most foreign countries, taxes are withheld at the source on dividend payments. The taxes withheld can be claimed, under certain conditions, as a credit against U.S. tax liabilities.

Foreign issuers pay their dividends in their national currencies. For American shares, the dividend is paid by the company's agent in the United States in dollars representing the conversion of the foreign currency at the then current rates of exchange. For ADR's, the dividends are paid by the company to the bank, the holder of record of the underlying shares. The ADR issuer converts the dividend received into U.S. dollars and distributes the proceeds to the ADR holders after deducting handling charges; such handling charges amount to $0.01 per share per dividend payment.

Dividend withholding taxes vary from country to country. The rates prevailing as of December 31, 1973, are shown in Table 20. The rates at which taxes are withheld from dividend payments to U.S. persons are influenced by the bilateral tax agreements between the foreign country involved and the United States.

TABLE 20

Dividend Withholding Taxes

Shareholder's domicile \ Company's domicile		Australia	Austria	Belgium 1	Canada 2	Denmark	France 3	Germany	Hong-Kong	Italy 4	Japan	Luxemburg 5	Netherlands	Norway	Singapore 6	Spain	Sweden	Switzerland	UK 11	US
Australia	I		20	20	15	30	25	28.25	0	30	15	15	25	25	0	15	30	30	0	15
	II		C	C	C	C	C	C	–	C	C	C	C	C	–	C	C	C	–	C
Austria	I	30		15	15	10	15[3]	28.25	0	30	20	15	15	15	0	15	10	0	0	15
	II	D		C	D	C	C	C	–	D	C	C	C	C	–	C	C	–	–	C
Belgium[9]	I	30	15		15	15	15[3]	15	0	15	15	15	15	15	0	15	15	30	0	15
	II	D,C	D,C		D.C	D,C	D,C	D,C	–	D,C	D,C	D,C	D,C	D,C	–	D,C	D,C	D,C	–	D,C
Canada	I	15	20	20		15	25	28.25	0	30	15	15	15	15	0	15	15	30	0	15
	II	C	C	C		C	C	C	–	C	C	C	C	C	–	C	C	C	–	C
Denmark	I	30	10	15	15		0	15	0	15	15	15	15	15	0	15	15	0	15[11]	15
	II	C	C	C	C		–	C	–	C	C	C	C	C	–	C	C	–	C	C
France	I	30	15	15	15	0		15	0	15	15	15	15	10	0	15	0	5	15[11]	15
	II	D	C	C	C	–		C	–	C	C	C	C	Cter 5[7]	–	C	–	C	C	C
Germany	I	30	20	15	15	15	0[3]		0	30	15	15	15	15	0	15	15	15	0	15
	II	C	C	C	C	C	–		–	C	C	C	C	C	–	C	C	C	–	C
Hong-Kong[10]	I	30	20	20	15	30	25	28.25		30	20	15	25	25	0	15	30	30	0	30
	II	–	–	–	–	–	–	–		–	–	–	–	–	–	–	–	–	–	–
Italy	I	30	20	15	15	15	15	28.25	0		15	15	0	25	0	15	15	30	0	15
	II	D	D	D	D	D	D	D	–		C	D	–	C	–	D	D	D	–	Cter 8[7]
Japan	I	15	20	15	15	15	15	15	0	15		15	15	15	0	15	15	15	0	15
	II	C	C	C	C	C	C	C	–	C		C	C	C	–	C	C	C	–	C
Luxemburg	I	30	15	15	15	30	15[3]	15	0	30	20		15	25	0	15	30	30	0	15
	II	D	C	C	D	D	C	C	–	D	D		C	D	–	D	D	D	–	C
Netherlands	I	30	15	15	15	15	15[3]	15	0	30	15	15		15	0	15	15	15	0	15
	II	D	C	C	C	C	C	D	–	D	C	C		C	–	C	C	C	–	C
Norway	I	30	15	15	15	15	10	15	0	30	15	15	15		0	15	15	5	0	15
	II	D	C	C	C	C	Cter 5[7]	C	–	C	C	D	C			C	C	D	–	C
Singapore	I	15	20	20	15	15	25	28.25	0	30	15	15	15	0		15	15	30	0	30
	II	C	D	D	D	C	D	D	–	D	C	D	C	–		D	C	D	–	D
Spain	I	30	15	15	15	15	15	15	0	30	20	15	15	15	0		15	15	0	30
	II	C	C	C	C	C	C	C	–	C	C	C	C	C	–		C	C	–	C
Sweden	I	30	10	15	15	15	15[3]	15	0	15	15	15	15	15	0	15		5	0	15
	II	C[8]	C	C	C	C	C	C	–	C	C	C[8]	C	C	–	C		C	–	C
Switzerland	I	30	0	20	15	0	15[3]	15	0	30	15	15	15	5	0	15	5		0	15
	II	D	–	D	D	–	C	C	–	D	C	D	C	D	–	C	C		–	D
UK	I	15	15	15	15	15	15[3]	15	0	15	15	15	15	15	0	15	15	15		15
	II	C	C	C	C	C	C	C	–	C	C	C	C	C	–	C	C	C		C
US	I	15	10	15	15	15	15[3]	15	0	15	15	7.5	15	15	0	15	15	15	0	
	II	C	C	C	C	C	C	C	–	C	C	C	C	C	–	C	C	C	–	

I. Indicates the effective rate of dividend withholding tax.

II. Describes the treatment of the foreign withholding tax in the shareholder's country of residence:

D = Deduction for foreign tax paid, i.e., the shareholder's country of residence imposes its tax on net foreign dividends.

C = Credit for foreign tax paid, i.e., the shareholder's country of residence imposes its tax on gross foreign dividends, but the amount of this tax is reduced by the amount of the foreign dividend withholding tax.

Note: The data table in Table 20 has been compiled especially for Capital International Perspective by the International Bureau of Fiscal Documentation, Sarphatistraat 124, Amsterdam. More information on taxation of investment income may be found in: "The Taxation of Private Investment Income," published by the same bureau.

1. Dividends of Belgian companies generally include the "credit d'impot" which is applicable exclusively to Belgian residents. To calculate the net dividend received by nonresident shareholders 15/85 or 17.6 percent should first be deducted from these reported dividends before applying the withholding tax indicated in this column.

2. The normal 15 percent rate of the Canadian withholding tax is reduced to 10 percent if the distributing Canadian company has a "degree of Canadian ownership" as defined in Sec. 139A of the Canadian Income Tax Act.

3. Dividends of French Companies generally include the "avoir fiscal" which is applicable to residents of Austria, Belgium, France, Germany, Luxembourg, Netherlands, Sweden, Switzer-

TABLE 20 (*Continued*)

land, the United Kingdom, and the United States. In the case of German shareholders, the avoir fiscal may be credited against German income tax. If a French company distributes a dividend to an Austrian, Belgian, Dutch, Luxembourg, Swedish, Swiss, U.K. or U.S. resident, the avoir fiscal is paid directly by the French government. To calculate the net dividend received by other shareholders, one third or 33.3 percent should first be deducted from these reported dividends before applying the withholding tax indicated in this column.

4. The Italian withholding tax (normally 30 percent) may be reduced by the amount of foreign income tax imposed on the dividends in the shareholder's country of residence. However, the Italian withholding tax cannot be reduced below a minimum of 10 percent.

5. Dividends distributed by Luxembourg holding companies are exempt from the Luxembourg withholding tax. The rates indicated apply to nonholding companies only.

6. Dividends payable by Singapore companies are not subject to dividend withholding tax. However, the companies may deduct for their own benefit the income tax due by them on their distributed profits.

7. The foreign withholding tax is only partially creditable in the shareholder's country of residence. The remaining foreign tax is deductible.

8. Unless otherwise provided for by treaty, foreign withholding tax is deductible in Sweden. In addition, a credit may be granted toward Swedish national income taxes.

9. In Belgium, net foreign dividends are included in taxable income. In addition, a credit equal to 15 percent of the net dividend is granted irrespective of the rate of the foreign withholding tax on gross dividends.

10. Due to the territorial basis of the Hong Kong income tax, foreign dividends received are normally exempt from tax in Hong Kong.

11. In the United Kingdom, resident shareholders are entitled to a special tax credit (three sevenths of the dividend received) credited against their income tax liability on the dividend plus the credit. Upon renegotiations of treaties, this credit may also apply to nonresidents in the form of an additional payment, but in that case a 15 percent withholding tax will normally be imposed. This currently applies to residents of Denmark and France.

Source: *Capital International Perspective,* April 1974. Published by Capital International S.A., Geneva, Switzerland.

SOURCES OF INFORMATION

Large amounts of information can be gathered on the economic, corporate, and financial fronts in the individual countries. The quality of the underlying information varies widely depending on the country and the source. Some of the sources of information are listed below and are meant to serve only as a broad guide.

In each country, a substantial amount of information, economic data, and industrial statistics are published by: (1) the government and its agencies, (2) the central bank, (3) the manufacturers' association or industry groups, (4) the commercial banks, and (5) the brokerage firms. In addition, a number of research-oriented firms publish material on a large number of international securities. Capital International S.A. in Geneva covers a large number of international markets, with charts for indvidual securities and summary statistics.

Corporate profiles are published by: (1) the Financial Post Corporation in Canada; (2) DAFSA in France; (3) Hoppenstedt in Germany; (4) Vas Oss' in the Netherlands; (5) Memento des Valeurs in Belgium; (6) Svenska Aktiebolag in Sweden (in Swedish and in condensed form in English); (7) Nihon Kenzai (in Japanese) for Japan; and (8) the Extel Statistical Services, Ltd. in London, which publishes profiles for the companies listed on the London Stock Exchange as well as for the major European international, Australian, and Japanese companies. The names and addresses of the publishers are listed under (C), Financial Publications, in the following outline.

Sources of Information

A. General Economic

1. *International Financial Statistics*
   The Secretary
   International Monetary Fund
   Washington, D.C. 20431
2. *Monthly Bulletin of Statistics*
   United Nations
   Sales Section
   New York, New York 10017
3. *OECD Economic Surveys*
   OECD Publications Center, Suite 1207
   1750 Pennsylvania Avenue NW
   Washington, D.C. 20006
   OECD members: Australia, Austria, Belgium, Canada, Denmark, Finland, France, Germany, Greece, Iceland, Ireland, Italy, Japan, Luxembourg, the Netherlands, New Zealand, Norway, Portugal, Spain, Sweden, Switzerland, Turkey, United Kingdom, and the United States
4. *International Monetary Fund Annual Report*
   The Secretary
   International Monetary Fund
   Washington, D.C. 20431
5. Bank for International Settlements
   Annual reports published by Boehm & Co.
   Buchdruckerei, Basel
   Switzerland
6. Esslen, Rainer, *How to Buy Foreign Securities.* Frenchtown, N.J.: Columbia Publishing Co., Inc., 1974.
7. *European Stock Exchange Handbook.* Park Ridge, N.J.: Noyes Data Corporation, 1973.
8. Federal Bank of St. Louis—*The Review*
   P.O. Box 442
   St. Louis, Missouri 63166
9. Morgan Guaranty Trust Co.—*World Financial Market*
   23 Wall Street
   New York, New York 10006
10. *International Stock Reports*
    Standard & Poor's
    345 Hudson Street
    New York, New York 10014

B. Individual Country Publications

1. *Canada*
   Financial Post Corporation Service
   10 Arundel-Place Bonaventure
   Montreal, Quebec, Canada

2. *France*
   DAFSA
   Societé de Documentation & d'Analyses Financiéres
   125 rue Montmartre
   Paris, 2 France
3. *Belgium*
   Agence Economique & Financiére
   5–7 Quai au Bois-à Bruler
   Brussels, Belgium
4. *The Netherlands*
   Financial Dagblad
   Postbus 216
   Amsterdam, The Netherlands
5. *Germany*
   Handelsblatt GmbH
   Zeitungs-und Zeitschriftenverlag
   D-4000 Dusseldorf 1 Germany
   Postfach 1102
6. *United Kingdom*
   The Economist
   54 St. James Street
   London SW 1A 1JT, England

   The Investors Chronicle
   30 Finsbury Square
   London EC 2A 1PJ, England

   The Financial Times
   Bracken House
   Cannon Street
   London EC 4P 4B4, England
7. *South Africa*
   Financial Mail
   P.O. Box 10493
   Johannesburg, South Africa
8. *Switzerland*
   Agence Economique & Financiére
   4 rue Montblanc
   Geneva, Switzerland

C. Financial Publications
1. *Belgium*
   Memento des Valeurs
   (Available through Belgian banks and stockbrokers)
2. *Canada*
   Financial Post
   Maclean Hunter, Ltd.
   481 University Avenue
   Toronto, Canada

Financial Times of Canada
10 Arundel-Place Bonaventure
Montreal 114, Quebec, Canada

3. *France*
   AGEFI
   108 Rue de Richelieu
   Paris, France 75002

   L'Opinion Vie Francaise
   67 Avenue Franklin D. Roosevelt
   75381 Paris-Cedex 08, France
4. *Germany*
   Verlag Hoppenstedt & Co.
   Postfach 4006
   Havelstrasse 9
   D 6100
   Darmstadt, Germany
5. *Japan*
   Diamond Japan Business Directory
   Diamond Lead Co.
   4–2 Kasumigaseki 1-chome
   Chiyoda-ku, Tokyo, Japan (or available from OCS America, Inc., 27–08 42d Road, Long Island City, N.Y. 11101)

   Japan Company Directory
   Oriental Economist
   Nihonbashi, Tokyo, Japan

   Japan Economic Journal
   Nihon Kenzai Shimbun
   Tokyo International
   P.O. Box 5004
   Tokyo, Japan
6. *The Netherlands*
   Van Oss' Effectenboek
   J. H. DeBussy
   Amsterdam, The Netherlands
7. *Sweden*
   Svenska Aktiebolag
   Kungl. Boktryckeriet P.A.
   Norstedt & Soner
   Box 2030 S103–12
   Stockholm, Sweden
8. *Switzerland*
   Handbuch der Schweizerischen Anlagewerte
   Editions Cosmos SA
   Bern, Switzerland

9. *United Kingdom*
Extel Statistical Services, Ltd.
37/45 Paul Street
London EC 2A 4PB, England (Extel's other services include: Australian Company Service, European Company Service, Monthly New Issues and Placings Service, Registrar's Service)

Moodies Services Ltd.
6–8 Bonhill Street
London EC 2A 4BU, England

APPENDIX A: INTEREST EQUALIZATION TAX

The Interest Equalization Tax (IET) was imposed in July 1963, and was initially established at 15 percent. The purpose of the tax was to help stem the capital outflow on the U.S. balance of payments. It was intended that the differential between foreign borrowing costs and their U.S. counterparts via bond floatations be equalized through imposition of the tax, thereby discouraging foreigners from floating bond issues in the U.S. capital market. In order to prevent their circumventing the intention of the tax through equity issues, the provisions of the IET was extended to equity issues also. The IET rate was altered several times during the course of its life, until it was finally eliminated on January 29, 1974.

The following table traces the evolution of the tax:

From–To	*Percentage*
7/19/63–1/25/67	15.00
8/26/67–8/29/67	22.50
8/30/67–4/4/69	18.75
4/5/69–12/31/73	11.25
1/1/74–1/28/74	3.75
1/29/74*	

* Eliminated.

APPENDIX B: FEDERAL RESERVE GUIDELINES LIMITING PURCHASE OF FOREIGN SECURITIES

Starting in February 1965, U.S. nonbank financial institutions, with a number of exceptions, were restricted in their purchase of securities of developed countries by Federal Reserve Board guidelines, except to the extent that such securities were purchased from other U.S. investors or to a percentage of the amount they owned.

The guidelines were abolished together with the Interest Equalization Tax on January 29, 1974.

PART IV

Analysis of Financial Reports

21

Analysis of Financial Statements

ERICH A. HELFERT, D.B.A.
Assistant to the President
Crown Zellerbach
San Francisco, California

PURPOSE OF FINANCIAL STATEMENTS

SINCE ONE PURPOSE of this handbook is to deal with the analysis of externally published financial statements, the discussion will focus on *financial accounting statements* as contrasted to the many forms of analyses, reports, and statements prepared for *internal* use in business organizations, often referred to as *management accounting*.

The purpose of financial statements published by business for the outside world, i.e., balance sheets, income statements, funds flow analyses, and special subsidiary statements is basically to inform various parties of the financial condition and past operating performance of the business entity. Also, they are prepared to provide a basis for future projection of operations. Periodic reports provide snapshots in time of the status of assets, liabilities, and ownership equity and represent a period-by-period determination of profitability and funds movements. Thus they serve as an accounting of the stewardship of management over the assets entrusted to it, a determination of the increase or decrease in economic wealth during the period, and a measurement of the movement of funds caused by management decisions. The statements are directed to the public, the shareholders and employees, labor representatives, bankers and other financial parties and creditors, the various levels of government, industry associations, and the financial analysts employed by one of these groups or independently.

The construction of statements presented to these publics involves a variety of measurements and choices by the preparer—basically management through their accountants and auditors—which rest on a wide group of principles and conventions but leave room for interpretation and variation. Thus the statement's purpose to inform is limited by the nature of the data presented and the conventions employed in calculating and displaying conditions and results. Accounting has often been called the language of management, but like any language it has idiosyncrasies, accents, and regional idioms difficult to understand for the uninitiated.

Characteristics

The keystone of financial statement preparation is the system of financial accounting employed, which is governed for all publicly held or traded companies by "generally accepted accounting principles." These cover areas of comparability, historical value, conservatism, the matching of revenues and expenses, and others, elements which shall be discussed later in this section. While the specific elements vary, the general observation is possible that there is a tendency toward conservative evaluation and accounting in past terms—with little attempt to reflect current economic conditions or future values. Thus financial statements are historical and current records, oriented toward disclosure of material events of the past, and colored by the caution not to mislead or speculate. Moreover, regulatory conditions in various industries tend to influence the methodology.

As shown by Figure 1, the basic financial statements are quite interrelated. Any one operating period for a business is flanked by two balance sheets, which are linked through the funds flow statement (statement of change in financial position), reflecting changes in each of the balance sheet accounts. The statements are further linked by a more detailed accounting of the changes in ownership equity, the most important of which is the income statement which reflects profitable or unprofitable operations in an income sense. They are further related by additional detailed analyses of changes in other equity accounts to inform the owner of the transactions affecting their residual claims on the business.

BALANCE SHEETS

As momentary snapshots of financial condition at a given point in time, balance sheets represent a basic listing of assets held by the business, liabilities owed to outsiders, and equity claims by the owners.

FIGURE 1

Interrelationship of Financial Statements

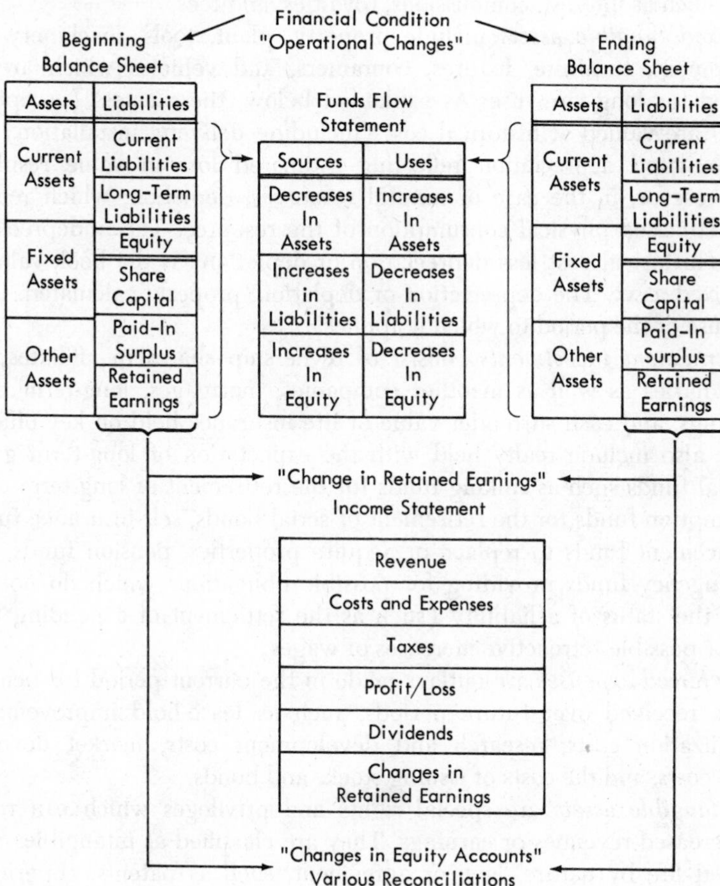

Assets

Assets are tangible and intangible properties and/or claims upon others, and they generally are stated conservatively at the cost of acquisition. They are usually categorized into the following:

Current assets include cash, or assets intended to be converted into cash one year from the indicated balance sheet date, or more during a longer operating cycle. Examples include short-term investments in government and other securities; notes; accounts receivable, which includes the entire amount of installment receivables collectible over several years; inventories of all types; prepaid expenses (current expenditures for goods or services to be received in the following period, such as magazine subscriptions); and certain accrued assets resulting from income still accumulating at the end of the year but due in the following year, such as interest, commissions, royalties, and fees.

Fixed tangible assets include property, plant, tools, machinery and equipment, furniture, fixtures, containers, and vehicles which are required for long-term use. As explained below, these assets (except for land) are valued at historical cost (including delivery, installation) less accumulated depreciation reflecting estimated loss in value resulting from use or, in the case of natural resources, depletion, which reflects the estimated physical consumption of the resource. The undepreciated cost (historical cost less depreciation or depletion) is the book value of the fixed asset. The depreciation or depletion, properly calculated, is an expense of the period to which it applies.

Permanent investments consist of ownership shares in affiliates and subsidiaries as well as in other companies, mortgages, long-term bond holdings, and cash surrender value of life insurance held on key officers. They also include realty held with the expectation of long-term gains, special funds such as sinking funds for the retirement of long-term debt, redemption funds for the retirement of serial bonds, self-insurance funds, replacement funds to replace or acquire properties, pension funds, and contingency funds providing for possible obligations which do not yet have the status of a liability (such as the settlement of a pending lawsuit or possible retroactive increases of wages).

Deferred expenses are outlays made in the current period for benefits to be received over future periods, such as lease-hold improvements, organization costs, research and development costs, market development costs, and the costs of issuing stocks and bonds.

Intangible assets are special rights and privileges which can result in increased revenues or earnings. They are classified as intangibles with limited life by nature, law, or agreement, such as patents, copyrights, limited life franchises, research and development costs, and leasehold improvements, or they are classified as intangibles of indeterminate life, such as trademarks, trade names, goodwill, and secret processes.

By those definitions, deferred expenses are a form of intangible asset. The cost of intangible assets is normally amortized (converted into an expense with a corresponding reduction in book value) on the basis of the estimated life of the asset (not to exceed 40 years) as prescribed in APB Opinion 17. The straight line method (see Appendix A) is generally required.

Goodwill is the cost paid for a business in excess of the fair market value of the business, and this asset arises only as the result of a purchase. Write-off of goodwill which is often practiced is not deductible for tax purposes, in contrast to amortization of deferred expenses.

Total assets at any time, therefore, is a list of all elements of value controlled (but not necessarily owned, such as leases), valued at the historical cost or current market value, whichever is less. Rarely, if ever, are assets valued upward if current value exceeds historical cost, as this would defeat the principle of conservatism. Only in the case of major reorganizations or combinations of businesses will recorded asset values change upward.

Liabilities

Liabilities are claims of a nonownership character against the business, that is, claims of creditors on the business. APB Statement No. 4 also includes as a liability deferred credits against income, and its definition is as follows:

> Liabilities—economic obligations of an enterprise that are recognized and measured in conformity with generally accepted accounting principles. Liabilities also include certain deferred credits that are not obligations but that are recognized and measured in conformity with generally accepted accounting principles.

Examples of deferred credits not representing a creditor claim are the investment credit (see below) and the profit recognized from the sale of property which is subsequently leased back.

Current liabilities are obligations due within one year from the balance sheet date or over the normal operating cycle if greater than one year. Examples are accounts and notes payable, accrued taxes, wages and salaries, commissions, and dividends payable in the following year. Also generally included are deferred income (liability from advanced payments received for services or goods to be provided in the following period).

Fixed or *long-term liabilities* are obligations of a nonrecurring nature and of duration greater than one year. Examples are long-term notes and bonds due beyond the next fiscal year and certain deferred incomes of duration longer than one year and not related to the operating cycle. *Contingent* (potential) *liabilities* may be shown as liabilities on the balance sheet but are most often indicated as footnotes. Bonds payable are shown on the balance sheet at par (face value). Any excess of the proceeds from the bonds over their face value is shown as a premium and a deficit is shown as a discount. Generally, all issuing costs (underwriting, taxes, legal, printing) are deducted from the proceeds of the sale in determining the premium or discount. Premiums are often shown as deferred income (liability), while discounts are shown as deferred expense (asset) and are amortized by straight line method over the life of the issue.

Equity

Equity is in effect the residual value, the difference between stated assets and liabilities. It consists of the following:

1. *Ownership shares* in various forms, which in the corporate structure consist of preferred and common stock in many variations.

2. *Paid-in and set-aside surplus* elements to allow recognition of value received over stated share values or to show potential claims.

3. *Retained earnings,* which is the cumulative amount of profit and/or loss left in the business after paying dividends and making other adjustments. Past earnings and dividend payments, as well as downward adjustments of assets, and the goodwill impact of acquisitions all reflect themselves in the equity balance. Since the details of the change in equity are often of considerable interest, the reconciliation of earned surplus alone or ownership equity as a whole are provided for the stockholder and analyst and will be discussed later.

Forms of Balance Sheets

The most commonly used balance sheet presentations are the *account form* with total assets on the left hand of the statement equal to liability and equity on the right side; the *report form* with assets listed on top, under which are listed liabilities followed by stockholder equity; and the less common *modified report form* with current assets listed first, followed by current liabilities which are subtracted to result in working capital. To working capital are added fixed assets, long-term investments, and deferred expenses, and from this total are deducted fixed liabilities to result in owner's equity.

INCOME AND RETAINED EARNINGS STATEMENT

The income statement provides a periodic assessment of operating conditions to determine, for a specified period of time, the matching of revenues, expenses, and costs in order to determine the profit or loss for the period. The process involves calculating the following:

Revenues for the period from the *sale of goods and services* must be determined, whether they be in the form of cash and receivables, installment payments, lease agreements, and so forth. This calls for decisions as to when to count transactions as having resulted in revenue and into which time slot of operating conditions to fit these. The choice is not always automatic, and judgments based on general accounting principles are required.

The definition of revenues given in APB Statement No. 4 is:

> . . . gross increases in assets or gross decreases in liabilities recognized and measured in conformity with generally accepted accounting principles that result from those types of profit-directed activities of an enterprise that can change owners' equity. . . . Revenue does not, however, include all recognized increases in assets or decreases in liabilities. Revenue results only from those types of profit-directed ac-

> tivities that can change owners' equity under generally accepted accounting principles. Receipt of the proceeds of a cash sale is revenue under present generally accepted accounting principles, for example, because the net result of the sale is a change in owners' equity. On the other hand, receipt of the proceeds of a loan or receipt of an asset purchased for cash, for example, is not revenue under present generally accepted accounting principles because owners' equity cannot change at the time of the loan or purchase.[1]

Expenses reflect the *apportionment of current outlays* for wages, supplies, merchandise, utilities, and so forth, which are subject to some interpretation and which may result in accrual of deferred items to be moved into different time slots.

The APB definition of expenses is:

> . . . gross decreases in assets or gross increases in liabilities recognized and measured in conformity with generally accepted accounting principles that result from those types of profit-directed activities of an enterprise that can change owners' equity. . . . Expenses, like revenue, result only from those types of profit-directed activities that can change owners' equity under generally accepted accounting principles. Delivery of product in a sale is an expense under present generally accepted accounting principles, for example, because the net result of the sale is a change in owners' equity. On the other hand, incurring a liability for the purchase of an asset is not an expense under present generally accepted accounting principles because owners' equity cannot change at the time of the purchase.[2]

Costs represent the expiration of asset values in the form of the price paid, which is subject to the write-off process converting such assets into periodic expenses charged to the operation. This process is based on a variety of judgments as to the timing and nature of amortization as permitted by accounting practice.

Net income is the *difference between revenue and all expenses and costs* attributable to the period, including financing charges, administrative expenses, and other items. In view of the nature of the accounting process, profit is only an approximation of the change in economic value of the business. It is a mixture of conservatively recognized revenues and variously determined applicable expenses and costs, all of which have left some latitude to the judgment of management and the accountant.

The major items of the income statement are as follows:

Net sales is defined as gross sales less the sum of sales returns, allowances, and trade and cash discounts.

Other incomes are derived from sources other than the sale of goods and services representing the major business activity.

Cost of sales (cost of goods sold) is the cost of the goods or services sold. In the case of a manufacturing enterprise the cost of finished goods for sale includes direct labor, direct materials, and indirect costs (such as depreciation of plant and equipment, and plant supervision).

The cost of goods sold (I_s) is determined from the recorded cost of the initial inventories (I_i), the cost of the additions to inventories during the period (I_a) and the cost of the inventories at the end of the period (I_f):

$$I_s = I_i + I_a - I_f$$

The cost of the final inventory (I_f) may be estimated on the asumption that the first items added to inventory are the first sold (Fifo), that the last items added are the first sold (Lifo), or on the basis of various averaging methods.

Selling expenses include all of the costs resulting from advertising and promotion, obtaining orders, and storing finished goods as well as packing and shipping the goods or transmitting services to the customer.

Administrative and general expenses include expenses of administering the overall activities of the company and other expenses of a broad corporate character.

Financial expenses include interest on short- and long-term debt as well as on factored receivables.

Extraordinary items are not related to the primary operating activity of the firm and are generally nonrecurrent. Under *APB Opinion No. 9* such items must be segregated from other items in the income statement. Examples are sale or abandonment of a plant, sale of an investment not acquired for resale, condemnation or expropriation of property, a major devaluation of foreign currency, and the write-off of goodwill under certain circumstances. The nature of extraordinary items is usually disclosed in the footnotes to the financial statements.

Income tax appears as the last item of expense and usually represents an anticipation of taxes due. When operating losses have been incurred the tax impact may be carried back up to three prior years. Any tax refund so obtained is applicable to the year of the loss. The tax law also provides for a carry-forward of losses for a period up to five years. However, the carry forward benefits are generally not recognized until realized.

Problems associated with the proper allocation of income taxes arise because of differences in reporting procedures used for income tax filing purposes and those used for *financial statements.* For example, revenue may be reported for an installment sale on an installment basis (which recognizes revenue as paid) for income tax purposes and on an accrual basis (which recognizes revenue at the time of the sale) for financial reporting purposes. Another example is the use of accelerated depreciation for income tax purposes and straight line depreciation for financial reporting. As a result the tax actually paid and that reported in the financial statements are different; most commonly, tax payments are thereby delayed. APB Opinion No. 11 requires that such deferred taxes be recognized as a liability on the balance sheet until a change in methods or company growth eventually extinguishes the liability by charging the account with future higher tax payments.

Dividends, when paid in cash or in shares, are an allocation of profits to the stockholders, and a reduction in the income retained for the future.

The income statement is tied to the balance sheet, since it is an expansion of the elements which, over time, result in an increase or reduction of the retained earnings section of owners' equity. Less obviously, the income statement reflects the change in assets and liabilities between the beginning and the end of the accounting period, insofar as these fall within the principle of revenue and expense recognition.

FUNDS FLOW STATEMENTS

The funds flow statement is an expanded analysis of the changes in the balance sheet accounts of a company over time. Not limited to the recognition of revenue, expenses, and costs, the funds flow statement uses the wider concept of funds. Funds are not only the cash results of transactions, but rather the full set of commitments and releases of value caused by management decisions over time. Funds movements are the result of, for example, repayment of debt, when cash is used to reduce a liability. This funds use would not be reflected as an element of expense, and thus would not show up as part of an income statement.

Normally, the funds flow statement is a collection of changes in balance sheet accounts, separated into sources and uses of funds. The sources represent releases of funds as assets decrease, or additional funds availability as liabilities and equity accounts increase, including profits from operations. The *uses* represent further commitments of funds toward increasing assets or decreasing liabilities through repayment or refinancing. Losses from operations similarly are funds uses. Corrections are made in the process for nonfunds adjustments, such as depreciation, depletion, and revaluations, which as accounting transactions reflect only judgments of value expiration and not fresh movements of funds. Thus depreciation is usually added back to net income to arrive at cash flow or funds flow from operations, and similar corrections are made for other adjustment entries reflected in the balance sheet.

The funds flow statement can be displayed in a great variety of ways, from a simple listing of sources and uses to summing selected elements into categories such as funds from operations, funds affected by financing, funds affected by discretionary outlays, and so on. The statement can also be developed to focus on changes in such elements as working capital.

Wider in scope than the income statement, the funds flow statement is an attempt to visualize management decisions in terms of the impact on the total balance sheet and the funds under the control of the enterprise. Answers to such questions as the nature of financing supporting new investment commitments, the relative buildup of working capital versus short-term loans, and the coverage of dividends with cash flow become quite visible in this analysis.

Reconciliations of Surplus and Other Accounts

As stated before, there are a variety of statements which have become common (and required) in published financial data to provide additional insight into the details behind ownership equity. The most common of these is a reconciliation of earned surplus or retained earnings, which shows the beginning balance adjusted for any increases or decreases, such as profits, dividends, and a multitude of other adjustments which are possible as financing arrangements, stock options, and value adjustments take place during an accounting period. The form of these statements varies widely, since they are tailored in each case to provide additional disclosure of data that could be of importance to the financial analyst or the owners.

Other statements are broader reconciliations of the ownership equity, providing some details on the stated value of the shares outstanding, both preferred and common, providing additional insight into the movements in paid-in surplus, if any, and also providing for information on the establishment of contingency reserves and other amounts set aside for future needs. The connection of these statements with the balance sheets bordering the accounting period and the income statement should be clear, since they are simply expansions of the information behind the changes in the balance sheets.

REGULATION OF FINANCIAL STATEMENTS

As stated before, the development of financial statements is governed by a variety of forces and interests. Paramount among these are the so-called generally accepted accounting principles, set down by the accounting profession as a guideline to their members in preparing financial statements for publication. Increasingly important are the influences of government regulations through bodies such as the Securities and Exchange Commission, the Federal Trade Commission, the Internal Revenue Service, and various regulatory agencies governing the affairs of members of particular industries, such as airlines, railroads, public utilities, and banks. Finally, there are the regulations required by the regional and national stock exchanges themselves to provide minimum standards of disclosure and consistency for companies allowed to be listed on these various boards.

Key Accounting Principles

The roots of today's generally accepted accounting principles lie in the legislation of the early 1930s, when the Securities Act of 1933 set the stage for the Securities and Exchange Commission to regulate the degree of disclosure for new offerings as well as to require reports from companies trading in the public securities markets. The move to standardization of reports for publicly traded companies brought about a parallel development in the accounting profession, where the American Institute of Public Accountants established the Committee on Accounting Procedure to develop accounting research bulletins (51 in total), which were designed as background documents to help narrow differences and inconsistencies in accounting practices. There was no legal enforcement, but the principles rested upon their general acceptability. Beginning in 1959, the institute created the *Accounting Principles Board* (now the Financial Accounting Standards Board) which issued research studies (11 in total) and so-called opinions (31 in total), which helped to evolve the standards and generally accepted practices of the profession throughout the years.

While the accounting research studies and opinions deal with special problems, such as accounting for the cost of pension plans, and some sweeping issues, such as the development of earnings per share, they are all expansions upon a series of accounting principles which over time had been recognized by the accounting profession, even though they were often interpreted differently. They can be categorized into the following three broad areas:

Institutional Concepts	*Measurement Concepts*	*Attitudinal Concepts*
Business entity	Historical costs	Conservatism
Going concern	Monetary value	Materiality
Property rights	Consistency	Disclosure
Accounting period	Matching	Reliability of evidence
Duality principle	Realization	Enforcement

The highlights of these principles can be defined as follows:

Business Entity. This accounting concept assumes that financial statements are prepared for the business entity as distinct from its owners.

Going Concern. Accounting is done under the assumption that the business will continue to operate into the foreseeable future.

Property Rights. Accounting for assets assumes that property rights are legally enforceable.

Accounting Period. Accounting is based on the recognized need to report periodically on the activities of a going business. The basic period is 12 months in length, unless operations dictate a different cycle. Many companies issue interim reports referring to quarterly or semiannual periods, while monthly or weekly periods are common for internal use.

Duality Principle. Accounting is based on the recognition that all assets (resources owned or held by the business) are claimed either by creditors or by owners. The creditors' claims are referred to as liabilities and the claims of the owners, as stockholders' equity. Consequently, the total assets can be expressed as an inviolate equation

$$\text{Assets} = \text{Liabilities} + \text{Stockholders' equity}$$

Accordingly, all accounting events are recorded through simultaneous debits and credits in terms of their effect on this equation.

Historical Costs. Accounting transactions are measured in terms of costs at the time the transaction is consummated, to avoid unsubstantiated judgmental values; and no updating to higher values is permitted, only reductions (write-downs) when significant.

Monetary Value. Accounting deals only with events which can be measured in terms of money equivalents.

Consistency. Accounting requires that similar transactions be treated in a consistent manner from period to period for a given company. However, modifications of accounting procedures are allowed when justified.

Matching. Accounting requires that in determining profit over a given period the applicable cost must be related to the revenues recorded for that period. The matching concept implies an important conceptual distinction between the flow of cash and an expense, which may be considerably out of phase. The accrual concept permits the accounting recognition through appropriate balance sheet accounts.

Realization. Revenue from the sales of goods or services is regarded as realized (recognized) when there is a high probability of receipt of payment when the conditions of the sales are fulfilled, and it is distinguished from the actual receipt of the cash payment. Four categories of realization are recognized:

1. Recognition at the time of shipping and invoicing when the credit status of the customer leaves little doubt as to payment. This is the most commonly used method in industry.

2. Recognition at the time of payment of the sales price, the so-called installment method. This method is often used by firms which sell to customers whose ability to pay may be in doubt.

3. Recognition when production is complete but sales have not yet been made, the so-called production method. This method of recognition implies that there are ready and able buyers (immediate marketability), and it is sometimes used in the mining industry.

4. Recognition with long-term contracts either under the percentage of completion method, with income reflected proportionately as the work progresses, or under the completed contract method, with revenue reflected on completion of the contract.

Conservatism. Accounting requires that among alternative treatments preference will be given to that which understates current income and asset values.

Materiality. Accounting is so oriented that attention will be given only to significant items.

Disclosure. Accounting statements must disclose sufficient information so that they are not misleading. There has been increasing pressure by analysts and the SEC for more complete disclosure of information, particularly by lines of business. In 1969 the SEC adopted a regulation specifying disclosure by principal lines of business, i.e., those that contribute 10 percent or more to revenues.

Reliability of Evidence; Enforcement. Accountants are expected to utilize objective and verifiable evidence, and the onus in the profession is to enforce its principles.

The various efforts of the accounting profession as assisted and reinforced, but also at times countermanded, by government regulations have not yet resulted in a fully comparable approach to accounting. The most recent attempt to narrow differences and to bring about a closer correspondence between the interests of government agencies and the accounting profession, not to speak of business enterprises, is the establishment of the Financial Accounting Standards Board. Formed in early 1973, the seven-member, full-time board has taken over from the much criticized Accounting Principles Board as the private sector's top authority on the rules that companies must follow in reporting earnings. Fully staffed and funded, the board is beginning to tackle issues such as consolidation of international operations, treatment of leases, and inflation accounting. It is unlikely that the new board, like its predecessors, will succeed in narrowing differences in interpretation down to legal precision, since the nature of the problems and the judgments required cannot be oversimplified.

The wide range of subjects dealt with by the earlier Accounting Principles Board is demonstrated in a listing of the 31 opinions as of December 1973:

1. "New Depreciation Guidelines and Rules."
2. "Accounting for the 'Investment Credit'."[3]
3. "The Statement of Source and Application of Funds."
4. "Accounting for the 'Investment Credit.' (Amendment of no. 2)"
5. "Reporting of Leases in Financial Statements of Lessee."
6. "Status of Accounting Research Bulletins."

[3] This opinion was the basis of disagreement with the SEC.

7. "Accounting for Leases in Financial Statements of Lessors."
8. "Accounting for the Cost of Pension Plans."
9. "Reporting the Results of Operations (Net Income; Earnings per Share)."
10. "Omnibus Opinion—1966 (Consolidation; Pooling; Tax Allocation; Offset against Taxes Payable; Convertible Debt; Liquidation Preference of Preferred; Installment Method."
11. "Accounting for Income Taxes."
12. "Omnibus Opinion—1967 (Classification and Disclosure of Allowances; Disclosure of Depreciable Assets; Deferred Compensation; Capital Changes; Convertible Debt; Amortization of Debt Discount, Expense, Premium)."
13. "Amending Paragraph 6 of *APB Opinion No.* 9, Application to Commercial Banks."
14. "Accounting for Convertible Debt and Debt Issued with Stock Purchase Warrants."
15. "Earnings per Share."
16. "Business Combinations."
17. "Intangible Assets."
18. "The Equity Method of Accounting for Investment in Common Stock."
19. "Reporting Changes in Financial Position."
20. "Account Changes."
21. "Interest on Receivables and Payables."
22. "Disclosure of Accounting Policies."
23. "Accounting for Income Taxes—Special Areas."
24. "Accounting for Income Taxes—Investments in Common Stock Accounted for by the Equity Method (Other than Subsidiaries and Corporate Joint Ventures)."
25. "Accounting for Stock Issued to Employees."
26. "Early Extinguishment of Debt."
27. "Accounting for Lease Transactions by Manufacturer or Dealer Lessors."
28. "Interim Financial Reporting."
29. "Accounting for Nonmonetary Transactions."
30. "Reporting the Results of Operations—Reporting the Effects of Disposal of a Segment of a Business, and Extraordinary, Unusual and Infrequently Occurring Events and Transactions."
31. "Disclosure of Lease Commitments by Lessees."

Government Regulations

The basic tenet of guidelines and regulations of the SEC, FTC, and various other regulatory agencies is the attempt to provide consistent disclosure of sufficient relevant details in financial reports to permit informed judgments by the investing public about the financial condition and operating performance of the companies under their jurisdiction. Generally the requirements of the SEC have increased disclosure and detail supplied in financial statements and in prospectuses for new stock offerings. Form 10-K, the annual information report to the SEC, has over the years brought about the inclusion of funds flow statements and quite recently the reporting of sales and profits by major lines of business, for example. Appendix C summarizes the contents of the 10-K form.

The rules and regulations of the Internal Revenue Code have an indirect influence on published statements. Usually, there are deliberate differences in statements submitted to the Internal Revenue Service compared to published statements, in the legal and proper endeavor to minimize taxes under currently applicable rules. Differences in income recognition, depreciation methods, expense deferrals, and others items will reflect themselves in the recorded tax liability on published statements through accounts such as deferred taxes. It must be remembered that the objectives of tax accounting and public accounting differ—one is designed to conform to the government's need to raise revenue, while the other is designed to inform the various publics of the success or failure of the enterprise.

Requirements of the Financial Community

The most important requirements of the financial community are embodied in the listing requirements of the national and regional stock exchanges. Companies wishing to trade their securities on these exchanges must conform to the information requirements which are generally quite closely patterned after SEC requirements. Again, the purpose is to ensure sufficient disclosure and detail for informed judgment by the investors.

Key Problem Areas

Although most areas of accounting and reporting are subject to some interpretation and even controversy, there are four specific categories of reporting which are still considered problem areas. They cover the accounting for and reporting of mergers and consolidations, the accounting for and reporting of leases and other financial devices, the whole area of international accounting, and the problems of how to deal with inflation and valuation in general.

1. *Mergers and consolidations* can usually be recorded under two methods of accounting—the purchase method and the pooling of interest method. In the former, usually a cash transaction, the assets of the acquired business are recorded at their fair market value at the time of acquisition, thus causing a revaluation at this point. Goodwill is shown for the difference between historic and new values. In the latter, usually a stock transaction, the assets of the entities are combined at the previous

stated values, on the assumption that no new business entity has been created and no goodwill is recognized. It is obvious that the revaluation under the purchase method is problematic as a valuation process itself and by its subsequent impact of high depreciation charges against income. The pooling method is problematic because of the nonrecognition of the actual value paid for by the acquiring company, which is nowhere recorded as such.

Further problems arise in providing continuity of past trends, i.e., backward adjustments of financial statements preceding the acquisition date. In the case of partially owned subsidiaries and joint ventures, various choices exist in depicting the investment and the share of earnings due the investor company, depending on the percent of ownership. The equity method is a means of showing the investor company's changing claim with less detail than in full consolidation, which is generally required when ownership reaches 50 percent or more. There is still enough leeway in these choices to cause some problems of interpretation and continuity.

2. *Leasing*, as a special case of financing, involves particular disclosure problems. So-called financial leases with a duration of over two or three years represent specific liabilities which under current accounting practice are not shown in the financial statements, unless the lease in effect is an installment purchase. While footnotes on material lease commitments are required, the full extent of the liabilities created is not reflected along with more traditional financing forms. Significant differences exist among companies' use of leasing, and making balance sheet analyses can become difficult. Similar issues arise on the part of lessor companies, which face the problem of income recognition and recording of future claims.

3. *International accounting* by multinational companies dealing with subsidiaries stated in different currencies has given rise to knotty problems. Fluctuating exchange rates, devaluations and revaluations of currencies, and exchange gains and losses contribute to great uncertainties in the interpretation of such statements. A common practice is the use of the so-called financial method, which states monetary assets and liabilities at current rates of exchange and physical assets at the historical exchange rate. While convenient, the method does not solve all issues, and modifications of the approach are in use, none of which have been able to overcome all difficulties.

4. *Inflation* and other valuation problems have become more current as the United States has undergone increasing inflationary tendencies. Price level accounting is an attempt to deal with these issues and is an exact parallel to the process applied to international exchange rate fluctuations. While not yet widespread in the United States, there is increasing interest in such adjustments, and the measurement process will be affected accordingly.

APPENDIX A: SAMPLE FINANCIAL STATEMENTS

Financial Review, Income Statements, Balance Sheets, Statement of Changes in Financial Position, Notes to Financial Statements, Five-Year Review*

Financial Review

Consolidated sales and earnings established new records by a considerable margin in 1973. In round figures, sales were $1,364 million, up 21 percent from the prior year. Net income was $103 million, an increase of 126 percent over the $45 million earned before an extraordinary charge of $9 million in 1972. On a per share basis, earnings were $4.26 vs. $1.87.

These results were achieved on strong domestic and world demand in all our major lines of business—pulp and paper, containers and packaging, distribution, timber and wood products. The contribution of timber and wood products was particularly significant in 1973 due to exceptionally strong demand during the early part of the year.

	1973*		1972*		% Improvement	
	Sales	Operating Income	Sales	Operating Income	Sales	Operating Income
Pulp and Paper	$ 522	$ 61	$ 452	$ 39	15%	56%
Containers and Packaging	267	25	226	12	18	108
Distribution	279	7	236	5	18	40
Wood Products	296	108	211	51	40	112
Share in Affiliates	–	6	–	–	–	–
	$1,364	207	$1,125	107	21%	93%
Unallocated general expense		(50)		(36)		(39)
Taxes on income		(54)		(26)		(107)
Net income before extraordinary item		$103		$ 45		126%

Distribution sales and related earnings on products transferred within the Corporation reflect only incremental sales and earnings. Wholesale and retail distribution are characteristically low sales margin businesses with a satisfactory return on capital employed.

Unallocated general expense includes certain general and administrative expenses, interest on debt, interest income and certain non-operating revenue and expense items. The greatest single portion of the increase of $14 million in unallocated general expense in 1973 resulted from the write-off of the unamortized portion of research and development and computer software expenses which had previously been capitalized.

Working capital rose to $318 million, up $49 million from $269 million at the end of 1972. Current assets were 2.7 times current liabilities, in contrast with 3.1 at the close of the previous year.

December 31,	1973*	1972*	% Change
Current Assets:			
Cash and short-term investments	$152	$ 71	+114
Accounts receivable	131	132	− 1
Inventories	207	177	+ 17
Prepaid expenses	14	15	− 7
	504	395	+ 28
Less current liabilities	186	126	+ 48
Working Capital	$318	$269	+ 18

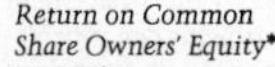

Return on Common
Share Owners' Equity*
(as a percent)

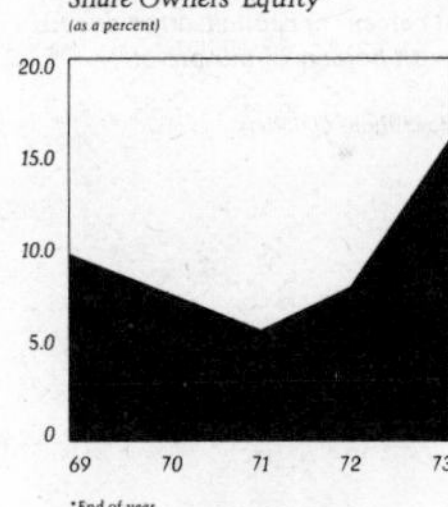

*End of year.

---

* From the 1973 Annual Report of Crown Zellerbach and Subsidiaries.

Appendix A (continued)

Capital expenditures for the year totaled $90 million, up $29 million from the $61 million spent in 1972, mainly going for improvements to existing facilities. Additions to environmental control facilities are forecasted at approximately $20 million per year in 1974 and 1975.

	1973*	1972*	% Change
Environmental control	$ 7	$ 8	− 12
Improvements to existing facilities	55	37	+ 49
New plant capacity	12	5	+140
Land and timberlands	16	11	+ 45
	$ 90	$ 61	+ 48

Total capitalization excluding deferred income taxes and minority interest reached $975 million, compared with $893 million at the end of 1972. Most of the $82 million increase was in earnings retained to finance future growth in the business.

December 31,	1973*	1972*	% Change
Long-term debt, after deducting installments due within one year	$318	$305	+ 4
Share owners' equity:			
Preferred stock	16	20	− 20
Common stock	641	568	+ 13
Total share owners' equity	657	588	+ 12
Total Capitalization	$975	$893	+ 9

During 1973, the Corporation had a successful 80 million Swiss franc ($24.6 million) 15-year bond issue at an interest rate of 6-1/2 percent. The funds are to be used for international and general corporate purposes. Financing was managed by a group of Swiss banks headed by the Swiss Credit Bank. The Corporation's borrowing capacity is currently set at 50 percent of capitalization due to past agreements with holders of our privately placed notes. On this basis we have additional borrowing power of over $300 million. We anticipate further borrowing from time to time to finance capital requirements, remaining well within overall debt capacity. The ratio of debt to capitalization was 33 percent at year-end.

The number of authorized common shares was increased from 30 million to 40 million by share owners at the 1973 Annual Meeting. During the year, 288,333 shares were issued for acquisition purposes, and 1,350 shares were issued under stock options exercised during the year. 40,840 preferred shares were purchased during the year at a cost of $2.8 million, which covers redemption requirements through July 31, 1984.

Dividend declarations in 1973 were $31.5 million, or 31 percent of net income. In November, the Board of Directors raised the quarterly dividend from 30 to 40 cents a share, an indicated annual rate of $1.60. At year-end, 23,913,778 common shares were outstanding, and the number of common share owners was 32,014.

Sales and income per quarter for 1973 and 1972 were:

	1973[1]	1972[1]
Net Sales		
First Quarter	$ 324,075,000	$ 261,858,000
Second Quarter	342,720,000	282,335,000
Third Quarter	355,515,000	285,101,000
Fourth Quarter	341,312,000	295,609,000
Years Ended December 31	$1,363,622,000	$1,124,903,000
Income (before extraordinary item)		
First Quarter	$ 23,298,000	$ 7,819,000
Second Quarter	28,311,000	12,652,000
Third Quarter	29,192,000	12,423,000
Fourth Quarter	21,796,000	12,568,000
Years Ended December 31	$ 102,597,000	$ 45,462,000[2]
Income Per Share (before extraordinary item)		
First Quarter	$ .97	$ .32
Second Quarter	1.18	.52
Third Quarter	1.21	.51
Fourth Quarter	.90	.52
Years Ended December 31	$ 4.26	$ 1.87[2]

[1]Restated to include effect of company added through pooling of interests in 1973.

[2]Excludes extraordinary charge of $9,113,000, net of related taxes, or 38¢ per share.

*All figures rounded to millions of dollars

Appendix A (continued)

Crown Zellerbach and Subsidiaries

Statement of Income

Years Ended December 31,	1973	1972
Income:		
Net sales	$1,363,622,000	$1,124,903,000
Other income:		
From operations	5,100,000	5,545,000
Miscellaneous, net	18,687,000	2,040,000
	1,387,409,000	1,132,488,000
Expenses:		
Cost of goods sold excluding various taxes ($35,325,000 in 1973; $29,683,000 in 1972)	1,027,512,000	907,259,000
Selling and administrative costs	133,685,000	97,985,000
Interest on debt	21,705,000	18,706,000
Real and personal property, social security, state income and franchise, use and occupational taxes	47,262,000	36,682,000
United States and foreign income taxes	54,648,000	26,394,000
	1,284,812,000	1,087,026,000
Income before extraordinary item	102,597,000	45,462,000
Net book value of certain facilities retired during the year, net of related taxes ($7,821,000)	—	(9,113,000)
Net Income	$ 102,597,000	$ 36,349,000
Income per share of common stock before extraordinary item	$ 4.26	$ 1.87
Extraordinary item, net of related taxes	—	(.38)
Net income per share of common stock	$ 4.26	$ 1.49

The accompanying notes are an integral part of these financial statements.

Appendix A (continued)

Statement of Share Owners' Equity

	Preferred Stock	*Common Stock*	*Other Capital*	*Income Retained in the Business*
Balances, January 1, 1972, as previously reported	$20,053,000	$118,120,000	$64,988,000	$374,098,000
Issuance of 288,333 shares for acquisition accounted for as pooling of interests	—	1,442,000	(1,347,000)	3,654,000
Balances, January 1, 1972, as restated	20,053,000	119,562,000	63,641,000	377,752,000
Sale of shares by a subsidiary	—	—	90,000	—
Retirement of 4,200 shares of preferred stock	(420,000)	—	149,000	—
Net income	—	—	—	36,349,000
Cash dividends:				
On $4.20 cumulative preferred stock	—	—	—	(838,000)
On common stock, $1.20 per share	—	—	—	(28,349,000)
Balances, December 31, 1972	19,633,000	119,562,000	63,880,000	384,914,000
Proceeds from sale of 1,350 shares of common stock under option plan	—	7,000	40,000	—
Sale of shares by a subsidiary	—	—	158,000	—
Retirement of 40,840 shares of preferred stock	(4,084,000)	—	1,325,000	—
Net income	—	—	—	102,597,000
Cash dividends:				
On $4.20 cumulative preferred stock	—	—	—	(717,000)
On common stock, $1.30 per share	—	—	—	(30,827,000)
Balances, December 31, 1973	$15,549,000	$119,569,000	$65,403,000	$455,967,000

Appendix A (continued)

Crown Zellerbach and Subsidiaries

Balance Sheet

December 31,	1973	1972
Current Assets:		
Cash	$ 3,238,000	$ 5,677,000
Short-term investments, at cost (approximates market)	149,099,000	65,362,000
Accounts receivable, net of allowances for losses ($4,377,000 in 1973; $3,594,000 in 1972)	130,881,000	132,149,000
Inventories	206,529,000	176,555,000
Prepaid expenses	14,061,000	14,757,000
Total current assets	503,808,000	394,500,000
Properties, at cost:		
Buildings, machinery and equipment	1,095,902,000	1,071,197,000
Less allowances for depreciation	525,951,000	512,942,000
	569,951,000	558,255,000
Land, timberlands, pulp leases and logging facilities, net of amortization and cost of timber harvested	111,784,000	105,408,000
Intangibles, principally licenses, net of amortization	205,000	348,000
	681,940,000	664,011,000
Other Assets:		
Investments in affiliated companies	27,599,000	19,680,000
Other investments (at cost) and receivables	9,058,000	4,654,000
Deferred charges	6,067,000	13,976,000
Deposit	10,000,000	—
	52,724,000	38,310,000
	$1,238,472,000	$1,096,821,000

The accompanying notes are an integral part of these financial statements.

Appendix A (continued)

Balance Sheet

December 31,	*1973*	*1972*
Current Liabilities:		
Dividends payable	$ 9,566,000	$ 7,084,000
Trade accounts payable and other liabilities	127,794,000	95,902,000
Notes payable	2,400,000	1,400,000
Long-term debt, installments due within one year	14,457,000	12,647,000
Accrued United States and foreign income taxes	31,702,000	8,579,000
Total current liabilities	185,919,000	125,612,000
Other Liabilities and Reserves:		
Long-term debt, net of installments due within one year	318,362,000	304,797,000
Deferred income taxes	56,763,000	60,193,000
Reserve for self-insurance	5,184,000	5,131,000
Total liabilities and reserves	566,228,000	495,733,000
Minority Interest:		
Canadian subsidiaries	15,756,000	13,099,000
Share Owners' Equity:		
Cumulative preferred stock— No par value, $100 liquidation and stated value. Authorized 402,386 in 1973 and 443,226 in 1972, issuable in series. Initial series $4.20 stock, issued and outstanding 155,489 shares in 1973 and 196,329 shares in 1972	15,549,000	19,633,000
Common stock— $5 par value. Authorized 40,000,000 shares in 1973 and 30,000,000 in 1972, issued and outstanding 23,913,778 shares in 1973 and 23,912,428 in 1972	119,569,000	119,562,000
Other capital	65,403,000	63,880,000
Income retained in the business	455,967,000	384,914,000
Total share owners' equity	656,488,000	587,989,000
	$1,238,472,000	$1,096,821,000

Appendix A (continued)

Crown Zellerbach and Subsidiaries

Statement of Changes in Financial Position

Years Ended December 31,	1973	1972
Financial resources were provided by:		
Income before extraordinary item	$102,597,000	$ 45,462,000
Charges (credits) to income which did not affect working capital:		
Depreciation, amortization and cost of timber harvested	63,332,000	58,521,000
Write-off of unamortized research and development and computer software development costs	7,902,000	—
Share in undistributed earnings of affiliates	(6,537,000)	(225,000)
Provision for deferred income taxes	(3,429,000)	349,000
Net loss on disposition of properties	1,199,000	3,444,000
Total from operations, excluding extraordinary item	165,064,000	107,551,000
Net use of funds related to extraordinary item	—	(2,950,000)
Internal funds generated	165,064,000	104,601,000
Net source of funds from purchase of St. Francisville Paper Company	—	7,252,000
Increase in long-term debt	31,507,000	34,980,000
Proceeds from sale of common stock under option plan	47,000	—
Proceeds from sale of properties	7,545,000	3,736,000
	$204,163,000	$150,569,000
Financial resources were used for:		
Long-term debt paid or currently maturing	$ 15,987,000	$ 8,857,000
Deposit	10,000,000	—
Additions to properties	90,006,000	60,987,000
Dividends declared	31,544,000	29,187,000
Retirement of preferred stock	2,759,000	271,000
Investments in affiliated companies	1,382,000	4,216,000
Miscellaneous—net	3,484,000	(738,000)
Net increase in working capital	49,001,000	47,789,000
	$204,163,000	$150,569,000
Analysis of changes in working capital:		
Increase (decrease) in current assets—		
Cash and short-term investments	$ 81,298,000	$ 45,879,000
Accounts receivable	(1,268,000)	13,548,000
Inventories	29,974,000	852,000
Prepaid expenses	(696,000)	(3,295,000)
	109,308,000	56,984,000
(Increase) decrease in current liabilities—		
Dividends and accounts payable	(34,374,000)	(9,541,000)
Notes payable and current maturities of long-term debt	(2,810,000)	(464,000)
Accrued income taxes	(23,123,000)	810,000
	(60,307,000)	(9,195,000)
Net increase in working capital	$ 49,001,000	$ 47,789,000

The accompanying notes are an integral part of these financial statements.

Appendix A (continued)

Crown Zellerbach and Subsidiaries *Year ended December 31, 1973*

Notes to Financial Statements

Summary of Significant Accounting Policies

Consolidation
The consolidated financial statements include the accounts of Crown Zellerbach Corporation and majority-owned subsidiaries.

Foreign Currency Translation
Current assets and liabilities and long-term debt are translated from foreign currency into U.S. dollars based on the exchange rates existing at year-end. All other assets, liabilities and capital accounts are translated at the rates of exchange in effect when acquired. Income and expense accounts are translated at a weighted average of exchange rates in effect during the year, except for depreciation, amortization and cost of timber harvested, which are translated at the rates of exchange in effect when the respective assets were acquired. Translation adjustments are charged or credited to income.

Inventories
Inventories are valued at the lower of cost or market. Cost has been determined by the moving average method for all items except purchased finished products determined by the first-in, first-out method.

Depreciation, Amortization and Cost of Timber Harvested
Depreciation is provided on a straight-line basis over the useful lives of all depreciable assets. Cost of timber harvested is based generally on the book value of specific tracts from which the timber is removed. Amortization of rail, truck roads and other logging facility costs is based on the estimated recoverable timber to be removed over the facilities. Amortization of leases, licenses and patents is based on their respective legal lives.

Investments
Investments in 50% owned affiliated companies are accounted for on the equity method.

Research and Development
Research and experimental and computer software development costs are expensed during the year incurred.

Taxes
Deferred taxes are provided to reflect the tax effect that results from timing differences between book and tax reporting of certain items, principally depreciation, research and development and log inventories. Investment tax credits are reflected in income on the flow-through method.

Pension Plans
Pension plan costs include amortization of prior service costs which are being written off over periods ranging from 17 to 30 years. The Corporation's policy is to fund pension costs accrued.

Earnings Per Share
Earnings per share are computed on the average number of common shares outstanding during each period, adjusted to include, retroactively, shares issued in acquisitions accounted for as pooling of interests.

Appendix A (continued)

Acquisitions

In November, 1973, the Corporation and The Southern Timber Trust jointly made a successful bid of $185,100,000 for the purchase of certain assets of Tremont Lumber Company, including 215,000 acres of Louisiana timberlands, two sawmills, a plywood plant and interests in producing oil properties. The parties are jointly negotiating a definitive contract under which the Corporation will purchase certain Tremont assets, and The Southern Timber Trust will purchase the remainder. Under the terms of a letter of intent between the Corporation and The Southern Timber Trust, a jointly owned company will be organized to operate the mills and timberlands. The Corporation will provide operating management to the jointly owned company and will purchase all of the output of the Trust's properties on terms to be negotiated between the parties. At December 31, 1973, a $10,000,000 deposit had been made by the Corporation.

The Corporation acquired, as of November 30, 1973, Rainier Manufacturing Co. for 288,333 shares of the Corporation's common stock. The acquisition was accounted for as a pooling of interests. Accordingly, the consolidated financial statements for 1972 have been restated to include the effect of this company. Net sales were increased by $17,327,000 and net income by $1,355,000.

Foreign Currency Translation

Translation gains, net of provision for income taxes, totaled $1,238,000 in 1973 and $627,000 in 1972 and are included in miscellaneous other income.

Inventories

Inventories are as follows:

December 31,	1973	1972
Finished products	$115,578,000	$104,669,000
In process	13,318,000	14,705,000
Raw materials	59,252,000	42,333,000
Supplies	18,381,000	14,848,000
	$206,529,000	$176,555,000

Properties

The major classes of property, plant and equipment are as follows:

December 31,	1973	1972
Buildings, machinery and equipment:		
Buildings, improvements, docks and wharves	$ 219,001,000	$ 218,320,000
Machinery and equipment	851,541,000	827,002,000
Construction in progress	25,360,000	25,875,000
	$1,095,902,000	$1,071,197,000
Other properties, net of amortization and cost of timber harvested:		
Land	$ 16,960,000	$ 17,029,000
Timberlands, pulp leases and cutting rights	73,621,000	69,349,000
Logging facilities	21,203,000	19,030,000
	$ 111,784,000	$ 105,408,000

Lease Commitments

Premises and equipment are leased under agreements which provide in some instances for renewal privileges at reduced annual rentals or for purchase at option prices established in the lease agreements. Certain of these agreements are financing leases.

Annual rental expense under lease agreements was as follows:

	1973	1972
Financing leases	$10,620,000	$ 9,763,000
Other leases	4,548,000	3,710,000
	15,168,000	13,473,000
Less subleases	847,000	766,000
	$14,321,000	$12,707,000

Appendix A (continued)

At December 31, 1973, minimum rental commitments, net of subleases, for the periods indicated are as follows:

	Financing leases	Other leases
Year ending December 31		
1974	$ 9,473,000	$4,137,000
1975	8,388,000	3,563,000
1976	6,803,000	3,016,000
1977	6,212,000	2,526,000
1978	5,357,000	2,199,000
Five years ending December 31		
1983	24,116,000	8,601,000
1988	15,865,000	5,213,000
1993	10,802,000	3,335,000
Remainder of payments under lease commitments expiring 1994-2019	5,584,000	1,729,000

Aggregate annual rentals under sale-and-leaseback agreements are restricted by certain long-term debt agreements.

The present value of commitments under financing leases and subleases at December 31, 1973, discounted at interest rates ranging from 3.4% to 11.0% and averaging 5.7% was as follows:

Buildings	$41,316,000
Machinery and equipment	24,620,000
Land	1,464,000
	67,400,000
Less building subleases	3,057,000
	$64,343,000

The difference in net income between capitalizing all financing leases, with the resulting amortization and interest expense, and expensing lease rentals was not material.

Taxes

Annual provisions for United States and foreign income taxes consist of:

	1973	1972
Current		
U. S. Federal	$34,517,000	$14,830,000
Foreign	25,811,000	12,940,000
Investment tax credits	(2,251,000)	(1,725,000)
	58,077,000	26,045,000
Deferred		
U. S. Federal	(8,329,000)	(1,316,000)
Foreign	4,900,000	1,665,000
	(3,429,000)	349,000
	$54,648,000	$26,394,000

The provision for federal income taxes gives effect to the capital gains treatment for timber harvested.

Due to reinvestment policies and available tax credits, no additional tax liability is necessary on $129,000,000 of undistributed earnings of subsidiaries and 50% owned affiliated companies.

Investments in Affiliated Companies

The Corporation holds 50% equity in the following companies:
Crown Simpson Corporation
Crown Simpson Pulp Company (a partnership)
Crown Simpson Manufacturing Company (a partnership)
Laja Crown S.A. Papeles Especiales
Mitsui Zellerbach K. K.
Nippon Zellerbach Kakohshi K. K.
Papierfabrieken Van Gelder Zonen N. V.

The investments are reflected in the Corporation's balance sheet as follows:

Equity investments	$15,576,000
Undistributed earnings	8,754,000
Long-term advances	3,269,000
	$27,599,000

At December 31, 1973, the Corporation's share of the underlying equity in Van Gelder exceeded the carrying value of the investment by $33,878,000. This excess was applied against the depreciable assets and results in a reduction of depreciation charges over the remaining life of the related properties.

Appendix A (continued)

The combined assets, liabilities and net worth of these affiliated companies as of December 31, 1973, were:

Assets	$294,746,000
Liabilities	180,793,000
Net worth	$113,953,000

The Corporation's share of the earnings of affiliated companies, $6,537,000 in 1973 and $225,000 in 1972, is included in miscellaneous other income.

Long-Term Debt

Long-term debt due after one year at December 31, 1973, consists of:

Unsecured sinking fund debentures, 8-7/8%, due 1978-2000	$125,000,000
Unsecured notes, 3-1/2% to 4-4/5%, due through 1990	111,400,000
Canadian term bank loan, 3/4% above prime rates, due through 1979	33,500,000
Swiss bond issue, 6-1/2%, due 1984-1988	24,608,000
Mortgage bonds, 5%, due through 1983	19,595,000
Timber severance taxes, non-interest bearing	1,346,000
Other	2,913,000
	$318,362,000

Retirements of long-term debt during the next five years will be as follows:

1974 $14,500,000
1975 $13,500,000
1976 $12,400,000
1977 $12,700,000
1978 $19,300,000

Beginning in 1978, the Corporation is required to retire $5,000,000 principal amount of the sinking fund debentures annually and may, at its option, provide for the redemption of up to an additional $5,000,000 principal in each year. With certain restrictions, the debentures may be redeemed at any time, in whole or in part, at 108.030% of the principal amount to March 15, 1974, and at declining premiums to 1995.

Certain properties of St. Francisville Paper Company are collateral for the mortgage bonds.

Dividends which can be declared from income retained in the business are restricted by agreements related to long-term debt and the Corporation's Articles of Incorporation. There was $220,283,000 available for dividends over the most stringent of these restrictions at December 31, 1973.

Pension Plans

The Corporation and its subsidiaries contributed to several pension plans covering substantially all of their eligible employees, including certain employees in foreign countries. In general, officers and employees are eligible to participate in the company plans after five years service, and normal retirement is at age 65. Annual pension expenses, including amortization of prior service costs for 1973 and 1972 were, respectively, $19,935,000 and $12,516,000. During 1973, benefits under some plans were improved, and company contributions increased in relation to prior and current service factors, as well as higher payroll coverage.

Incentive Compensation and Stock Option Plans

Under two incentive compensation programs approved by the share owners in 1973, key employees of the Corporation and its subsidiaries may become eligible for awards in cash or performance units (each of which is equivalent in value to a share of the Corporation's common stock as of the date of the award). Awards under the programs are subject to certain limitations and will not be made unless a prescribed minimum Corporation earnings performance is achieved. The charge to earnings under the programs was $1,899,000 in 1973.

On April 26, 1973, the share owners approved a Nonqualified Stock Option Plan which replaces the Incentive Stock Option Plan. Options under the Nonqualified Plan are granted for periods not exceeding ten years, and are fully exercisable after a two year waiting period. Options under the Incentive Plan were granted for periods not exceeding five years and are fully exercisable after a one-year waiting period.

Appendix A (continued)

Common shares under option at December 31, 1973, and activity during the year then ended were as follows:

	Dec. 31, 1972	Granted or (Cancelled)	Exercised	Dec. 31, 1973	Price Per Share
Incentive Stock Option Plan:					
10/23/69	44,400	(1,650)	(1,350)	41,400	$35.00
4/23/70	7,200	—	—	7,200	33.82
11/24/70	6,000	—	—	6,000	28.82
6/22/72	2,000	—	—	2,000	29.82
10/26/72	22,400	—	—	22,400	27.88
2/22/73	—	4,500	—	4,500	26.07
	82,000	2,850	(1,350)	83,500	
Nonqualified Stock Option Plan:					
5/24/73	—	115,000	—	115,000	28.00
6/5/73	—	3,000	—	3,000	28.50
10/25/73	—	6,100	—	6,100	41.88
	—	124,100	—	124,100	

There were 375,900 additional shares of authorized and unissued common stock reserved for options which may be granted in the future.

Cumulative Preferred Stock

The Articles of Incorporation require an annual retirement fund deposit of $530,000 or, in lieu thereof, the application of purchased shares against such requirements at the rate of $102.50 a share. Total purchases of preferred stock have provided for this requirement through July 31, 1984.

Report of Certified Public Accountants

To the Board of Directors
Crown Zellerbach
San Francisco, California

We have examined the consolidated balance sheet of Crown Zellerbach and Subsidiaries as of December 31, 1973, and the related consolidated statements of income, share owners' equity and changes in financial position for the year then ended. Our examination was made in accordance with generally accepted auditing standards and accordingly included such tests of the accounting records and such other auditing procedures as we considered necessary in the circumstances. We previously examined and reported upon the consolidated financial statements of the company and its subsidiaries for the year ended December 31, 1972. We did not examine financial statements of Crown Zellerbach Canada Limited and Subsidiaries, which statements reflect total assets and revenues constituting 21% and 16%, respectively in 1973, and 20% and 15%, respectively in 1972, of the related consolidated totals. These statements were examined by Canadian chartered accountants whose reports thereon have been furnished to us, and our opinion expressed herein, insofar as it relates to amounts included for Canadian companies, is based solely on such reports.

In our opinion, based upon our examinations and the reports of other auditors, the above mentioned financial statements present fairly the consolidated financial position of Crown Zellerbach and Subsidiaries at December 31, 1973 and 1972, and the consolidated results of their operations and changes in financial position for the years then ended, in conformity with generally accepted accounting principles applied on a consistent basis.

Coopers & Lybrand
Certified Public Accountants
San Francisco, California
January 21, 1974

Appendix A (continued)

Crown Zellerbach and Subsidiaries

Five Year Review[1]

	1973	1972	1971	1970	1969
Earnings and Dividends (thousands of dollars):					
Net sales	$1,363,622	$1,124,903	$986,544	$955,288	$919,282
Depreciation, amortization and cost of timber harvested	63,332	58,521	53,786	51,935	48,377
Employment costs, excluding social security taxes	365,073	320,802	284,707	273,240	256,205
All taxes	101,910	63,076	56,473	58,212	58,995
Other operating and production costs, net	730,710	637,042	559,782	529,996	501,742
Income before extraordinary items	102,597	45,462	31,796	41,905	53,963
Extraordinary items, net of related taxes	–	(9,113)[2]	(1,007)[3]	–	–
Net income	102,597	36,349	30,789	41,905	53,963
Dividends declared	31,544	29,187	28,841	35,721	37,210
Net income retained	71,053	7,162	1,948	6,184	15,970[4]
Dollars Per Share of Common Stock[5]					
Income before extraordinary items	4.26	1.87	1.31	1.77	2.29
Extraordinary items, net of related taxes	–	(.38)[2]	(.04)[3]	–	–
Net income	4.26	1.49	1.27	1.77	2.29
Common dividends declared	1.30	1.20	1.20	1.50	1.56⅔
Percent of Income Before Extraordinary Items:					
Distributed to share owners	30.7	64.2	90.7	85.2	69.0
To total capitalization	9.8	4.7	3.5	4.6	6.3
To common stock equity	16.0	8.0	5.7	7.6	9.9

Note 1: 1972 has been restated for Rainier Manufacturing Co. which was added through a pooling of interests. Prior years have not been restated as the effect is not significant.

Note 2: All costs, net of related taxes, associated with the disposition of an uneconomic pulp and paper mill in British Columbia.

Appendix A (concluded)

Five Year Review[1]

	1973	1972	1971	1970	1969
Financial Position (thousands of dollars):					
Working capital and other assets:					
Current assets	$503,808	$394,500	$332,763	$322,293	$314,522
Current liabilities	185,919	125,612	114,044	111,002	148,098
Working capital	317,889	268,888	218,719	211,291	166,424
Properties, net	681,940	664,011	655,908	664,528	650,896
Other assets, net	47,540	33,179	39,587	39,570	38,893
Total working capital and other assets	$1,047,369	$966,078	$914,214	$915,389	$856,213
Financed by (thousands of dollars):					
Long-term debt	$318,362	$304,797	$256,596	$266,626	$220,211
% of total	30	32	28	29	26
Deferred income taxes	56,763	60,193	67,567	66,978	61,887
% of total	5	6	8	8	7
Minority interest	15,756	13,099	12,792	12,058	10,958
% of total	2	1	1	1	1
Preferred stock	15,549	19,633	20,053	20,053	20,053
% of total	2	2	2	2	2
Common stock equity	640,939	568,356	557,206	549,674	543,104
% of total	61	59	61	60	64
Total capitalization	$1,047,369	$966,078	$914,214	$915,389	$856,213
Ratio of current assets to current liabilities	2.7 to 1	3.1 to 1	2.9 to 1	2.9 to 1	2.1 to 1
Equity per common share—in dollars	$ 26.80	$ 23.77	$ 23.59	$ 23.64	$ 23.37
Additions to properties—in thousands of dollars	$ 90,006	$ 60,987	$ 50,570	$ 68,351	$ 82,739

Note 3: Net book value of certain facilities in British Columbia retired during the year, net of related taxes.

Note 4: Net of adjustment related to pooling of interests.

Note 5: Per share figures for 1969 reflect the 3 for 2 stock split in 1969.

APPENDIX B

Depreciation

Depreciation is an accountancy procedure for recognizing the limited useful life of a fixed asset and for charging accounting periods with an appropriate portion of the expiring asset's cost. The process systematically decreases the book value of an asset and allocates such charges to expenses in accordance with the matching principle. Depreciation as such does not create a fund for the replacement of an asset, since it is simply the allocation of a past cost.

Calculation of depreciation charges requires estimates of the service life (N) and the salvage value on disposal of the asset (L). Given the cost of the asset (P), then the annual depreciation (D_t) and the book value (B_t) at the end of the year (t) are calculated by the following methods:

Straight line:

$$D_t = \left(\frac{P - L}{N}\right)$$

$$B_t = P - \left(\frac{P - L}{N}\right) t$$

Double declining balance:

$$R = 2/\mathrm{N}$$
$$D_t = R(1 - R)^{t-1}P$$
$$B_t = (1 - R)^t P$$

Sum-of-the-years' digits:

$$S = \frac{N(N + 1)}{2}$$

$$D_t = \frac{(N - t + 1)(P - L)}{S}$$

$$B_t = \frac{(N - t)(N - t + 1)(P - L)}{2S} + L$$

Example. A fixed asset is purchased at a price of \$6,000 (P) and has an estimated life (N) of five years and an expected salvage value (L) of \$1,000. In this case,

$$R = 2/5 = 0.4$$
$$S = \frac{5 \times 6}{2} = 15$$

The calculations for each of the above methods are shown below:

Annual Depreciation

End of Year	(a) Straight Line	(b) Double Declining Balance	(c) Sum-of-the-Years' Digits
1	$1,000.00	$2,400.00	$1,666.67
2	1,000.00	1,400.00	1,333.33
3	1,000.00	864.00	1,000.00
4	1,000.00	518.40	666.67
5	1,000.00	311.04	333.33
Total	$5,000.00	$5,493.44	$5,000.00*

* Rounded.

The accelerated depreciation methods (b) and (c) result in an initially higher write-off compared to the straight line method (a), but subsequently the magnitudes reverse. Also, since double declining balance depreciation always leaves a remaining book balance (a straight percentage is applied to the decreasing book value), no salvage value is recognized.

Depletion

The systematic expensing of the cost of investment in natural resources (minerals, forest, gas, and oil) which are exhausted is referred to as depletion. Two methods are used, the production method and the percentage method. Although both methods are acceptable for tax purposes, only the production method is acceptable for accounting purposes.

Production Method. Given the cost of the investment (C), and if U_t represents the units produced in year t and the estimated total production units U; the depletion charge $(DE)_t$ to income at the end of the year t will depend on the units sold during the year (U_{ts}), according to the matching principle:

$$(DE)_t = \left(\frac{C}{U}\right) U_{ts}.$$

Example. An iron mine containing an estimated profitable output of 20 million tons of ore is developed at a cost of $2 million. During the first year of operation 100,000 tons of ore are mined and 50,000 sold. The depletion allocated to each ton will be

$$\frac{C}{U} = \frac{\$2 \text{ million}}{20 \text{ million tons}} = \$0.1 \text{ per ton.}$$

The depletion charged to income during the first operating year (DE) will then be:

$$(DE) = 0.1 \times 50{,}000 = \$5{,}000,$$

and the depletion charged to inventory will be $0.1 × 50,000, or $5,000.

Percentage Method. The percentage method applies a fixed percentage (R_d) to the gross income from the property. The percentage R_d for a given resource is specified by the Internal Revenue Code and Regulations and varies, at this time, from 5 percent to 22 percent. However, the depletion charge is limited to 50 percent of the net income from the property before depletion charges.

Example. An oil well annually produces 100,000 barrels which are sold at $3 gross income per barrel. The oil depletion rate (r) is 22 percent. Production costs before depletion are $150,000 and the tax rate is 50 percent. Determine the depletion allowance.

Gross income		$300,000
Production costs		150,000
Net Income		$150,000
Depletion calculation:		
@ 50 percent of net income	$75,000	
@ 22 percent of gross income	66,000	
Depletion allowance		66,000
Taxable Income		$ 84,000

Investment Tax Credit

The Internal Revenue Acts of 1962 and 1964, with a view toward encouraging investment, allowed a taxpayer credits against income taxes of up to 7 percent of the acquisition costs of eligible tangible personal property used in business. The investment credit (V_t) is a direct reduction of income taxes which would otherwise be payable. Two methods of computing the credit are used.

Flow through Method. This method applies the full credit in the year in which the credit is granted.

Deferred Method. The deferred method distributes the credit over the estimated life of the asset.

Example. Equipment is purchased, in 1974, costing $100,000, which is eligible for the full credit of 7 percent. The estimated life of the equipment is 10 years. There is no estimated salvage value and straight line depreciation is used for tax purposes. The flow through calculations are:

Profit before depreciation and taxes	$500,000
Less depreciation ($100,000 × 0.1)	10,000
Taxable income	490,000
Income taxes before credit (50%)	245,000
Less investment credit ($100,000 × 0.07)	7,000
Taxes Payable in 1974	$238,000

The deferred method distributes the $7,000 credit over 10 years so that the annual deduction from the income taxes before the investment credit is $700. The tax payment for 1974 would be $244,300.

General Relationship

The general formula for earnings after taxes which explicitly takes into account depletion, depreciation, and the tax credit for any year t is given below:

$$\text{Income tax in year } t = [I_t - [E_t + D_t + (DE)_t]]\, T - V_t$$

$$\text{Net income after taxes} = [I_t - [E_t + D_t + (DE)_t]]\,(1 - T) + V_t$$

where:

I_t = Net revenues in year t.
E_t = Deductible expenses before depreciation and depletion.
D_t = Depreciation expense in year t.
$(DE)_t$ = Depletion allowance in year t.
T = Tax rate.
V_t = Investment tax credit.

The cash flow in year t is obtained by adding back allocated costs (depreciation, depletion, amortization) to after-tax income:

$$\text{Cash flow} = (I_t - E_t)(1 - T) + D_tT + (DE)_tT + V_t$$

APPENDIX C
Summary of Contents of SEC Form 10-K*

Name of corporation.
Securities registered, by class.
Business.
Products; including sales and profits by major line of business.
Consolidated income statement.
Properties in detail.
Parents and subsidiaries.
Legal proceedings.
Increases and decreases in outstanding equity securities.
Shareholders.
Executive officers.
Indentification of directors and officers.
Financial statements and exhibits (includes detailed schedules of subsidiaries, properties, depreciation).

---

* See Chapter 26.

22

Evaluation of Financial Statements

ERICH A. HELFERT, D.B.A.
Assistant to the President
Crown Zellerbach
San Francisco, California

Financial Statements and the Analyst

THE PURPOSE of financial statements, as discussed in the previous chapter, is to inform, to disclose, to account for past and present conditions, and to provide a basis for projecting future performance. There are many limitations affecting the ability to fulfill this purpose, the most important of which include leeway on accounting principles, comparability, industry characteristics, valuation problems, changes in accounting practices, and changes in the nature of the business itself. The approach to financial statement analysis and evaluation thus must be taken with an open mind and with a fair grounding in the principles of statement preparation. Moreover, rarely can financial statements satisfy all the potential viewpoints with which analysis can be undertaken.

Elementary as it may seem, the suggestion to define clearly the objective of any analysis is an important discipline which will help overcome some of the questionable areas in financial statements as they relate to the points of inquiry. Assumptions and adjustments can be made more clearly, and the most useful tools can be selected for the purpose. Also, it is usually necessary to analyze operating performance and financial viability over a period of time rather than at a selected point in order to establish trends and to avoid conclusions from random or unusual fluctuations. Finally, the choice of analytical tools should be made both with the objective in mind and with an eye toward likely distortions in the results which may be brought about by known industry and company conditions and practices. Before any projections can be made about future conditions, it is most necessary to understand as fully as possible the past and present conditions and practices.

Shown below are typical elements of balance sheets and income statements as presented by publicly held companies:

Typical Balance Sheet
Key Elements
Date

ASSETS	LIABILITIES
Current assets	Current liabilities
Cash and securities	Trade obligations
Accounts receivable	Accrued items
Inventories	Accrued taxes
Other assets	Current debt due
Fixed assets	Other liabilities
Land and improvements	Deferred taxes
Buildings and equipment	Contingencies
Less: Accumulated depreciation	
Net fixed assets	Long-term liabilities
	Mortgages, other contracts
Other assets	Bonds and similar obligations
Accrued items	
Goodwill	Net worth
Prepaid items	Preferred stock
	Common stock
	Paid-in surplus
	Retained earnings

Typical Income Statement
Key Elements
Period

Revenue (net of adjustments)
Cost of goods, services
Gross profit (margin)
Operating expenses (salaries, general and administrative, etc.)
Operating income
Nonoperating income, expenses
Interest income, expense
Income before taxes
Income taxes
Net income

Measures of Profitability

The analysis of profitability is the most direct approach to judging a business's operating success, both short term and long term. Commonly, profitability is measured in two basic ways—(1) in terms of the income statement, by measuring the excess of revenue over expense as an indicator of efficiency, and (2) in terms of the balance sheet and the effectiveness with which capital has been employed, by relating profit to capital investment. Clearly the quality of the profit calculation and of the measurement of investment is critical to meaningful analysis.

Profit Margins. A quick analysis based on data published in ready-made form is the calculation of *gross margin* from income statements. Normally this refers to the difference between sales revenue (adjusted for returns and allowances) and the full costs of the goods or services provided. The relationship is a simple one indeed:

$$\text{Revenue} - \text{Cost of goods, services} = \text{Gross margin}$$

$$\frac{\text{Gross margin}}{\text{Net revenue}} = \text{Gross margin percentage}$$

This ratio indicates the margin available to cover operating expenses, financial and other expenses, taxes, and profit. Usually it is a direct reflection of the pricing and costing policies of the enterprise, and the typical margin percentage will be a reflection of the nature of the business and the industry. Comparisons can be made to industry averages, usually by size of company. Care must be taken to understand the nature of the accounting conventions employed by the company regarding the recognition of income (particularly if installment sales or leases are employed) and the costing policies as they relate to inventories, depreciation method, write-off of development costs, and so forth. All of these are variables which influence final results observed.

Another common profitability measure is the calculation of *operating profit* as a percentage of net revenue. Here the attempt is to derive a profit margin after deduction from revenue of all appropriate and directly applicable expenses of operations beyond the cost of goods and services themselves. Judgment is applied to the adequacy of margin left over for financial charges (interest), other expense and income items not associated with primary operations, income taxes, and profit. Again, comparisons of industry data and trends for the company can be made, with due regard to the particular company's practices on revenue and expense recognition.

The most frequent comparison is the ratio of net income after taxes to net revenue. This represents the cents of profit contribution from every dollar of revenue after taxes and after all directly and indirectly associated expenses for the period are deducted. It is noteworthy that extraordinary items, such as major gains or losses, acquisition or disposition of assets, and investments, are separated out; and net profit before such elements is normally the more meaningful number for analysis.

Another item of some interest is the ratio of the effective tax rate applied to net income. Industries with special tax considerations such as depletion allowances or rapid depreciation write-offs will show characteristic tax rate patterns against which individual company performance can be held. Again, the particular accounting elections chosen by the company under analysis must be considered, to the extent that they are publicly known.

Return on Investment Ratios. The next step of gauging management effectiveness is the attempt to relate net income (before extraordinary items) to a measure of the investment entrusted to the management. Several approaches are possible. An overall measurement is the relationship of total assets (at the end of the period or the average during the period) to net income generated:

$$\frac{\text{Net income}}{\text{Total assets}} = \text{Return on investment}$$

Total assets as reflected on the balance sheet are a mixture of current values and past costs, adjusted for depreciation charges. The ratio thus is not necessarily an expression of the economic return obtained on the stated investment. Moreover, the degree of financial leverage obtained through use of debt will distort this picture, since interest charges on such debts have been deducted from income, and comparability between companies using different financial policies is disturbed.

A modification of this measure is the relationship of capitalization (total assets less current liabilities) to net income, on the argument that current liabilities represent operating capital largely available without economic obligation. Thus, net income is related to the permanent capital used in its generation. Arguments about the true stated value apply again, and it is good practice to increase net income by the interest charges (adjusted for taxes) originally deducted to arrive at the return on stated capital free from distortion by different debt policies:

$$\frac{\text{Net income} + (1 - \text{Tax rate})\ \text{Interest}}{\text{Capitalization}} = \text{Return on investment}$$

A more refined measure, and by many considered to be the best ratio, is *return on stockholders' equity.* The ratio relates the residual ownership investment to the net income for the period. In theory this is the most useful comparison since the relationship is calculated after all legal claims by outsiders have been taken care of, including interest to lenders. In practice, the residual ownership balance takes the brunt of all accounting principles and adjustments and, as the book value of the company, rarely reflects or resembles the economic value of the shareholders' claim. Nevertheless, the ratio is frequently followed and cited as the indication of management's ability to further the stockholder's interest:

$$\frac{\text{Net income}}{\text{Equity (net worth)}} = \text{Return on equity}$$

Stockholder Position. A logical step from return on shareholders' equity is the calculation of per share results for the period under analysis.

It is common practice to derive earnings per share (before and after extraordinary items) based on the average number of shares outstanding during the period. It is also frequent practice to calculate earnings per share based on the number of shares outstanding at the end of the period, particularly if sizeable change in the number of shares has taken place. If such changes for new stock issues or mergers and acquisitions occurred, it is also common to recalculate the past earnings per share on a consolidated basis to obtain a comparable view reaching back into several years of history.

Earnings per share analysis is an attempt to relate corporate earnings performance to the market price performance of the various classes of stock. Earnings per share for common stocks are calculated after preferred dividends have been paid. Common dividends are then stated on a per share basis and are often related as a ratio to earnings per share before extraordinary items to judge the degree of payout of earnings to the stockholders.

Further per share comparisons are made of cash flow per share (net income per share plus depreciation and other noncash charges per share) to indicate the ability to pay cash dividends. At times other variations, such as interest per share, or extraordinary gains or losses per share are developed, all in an attempt to gauge the impact on market performance of such aspects. Again, all cautions regarding earnings recognition and expense allocation apply to this measure, as they did in the previous items.

Earnings Fluctuations. Operational analysis cannot be performed in a static manner, nor can individual period performance be used as a reliable clue for future expectations. In calculating margins, profit rates, per share data, and so on, it is extremely important that the pattern of conditions, either seasonal or cyclical or both can be determined and weighed, particularly if predictions are to be made about future earnings performance. Some indication of the likely patterns of fluctuations can be gained from industry background studies, and the analyst will find it helpful to determine if the same pattern holds for the company under analysis. It is generally useful to derive a range of likely values of earnings patterns, return ratios, and per share fluctuations to gauge the risk involved in future repayments of debt or the general viability of the operation. Earnings patterns, growth trends, or declining conditions have a great deal of influence on future cash flows and will thus figure prominently in any lending arrangements under consideration. They also have a bearing on the timing of potential new securities issued, particularly if the cycle of operations should be different from the general economic cycle or the industry pattern.

Industry Comparisons. As mentioned before, there is a great deal of information available about various classifications of industries and service groupings, which can become a background for the analysis of financial statements. Such financial services as Dun & Bradstreet,

Moody's, Standard & Poor's, and others, as well as selected analysts and other authors, have published and continue to update selected ratios and other guidelines about industry performance of which samples are listed in the bibliography. It should be pointed out, however, that usually a particular company is not quite like any other and may cover several industries. Thus the development of industry classifications with the best fit of the company's conditions is often difficult. Moreover, government statistics in the form of standard industrial classification codes and trade association data are not often in the exact form or detail desired. Nevertheless, if the analyst is aware that industry data can provide a very broad background, it is usually worthwhile to check out this information.

Measures of Financial Viability

Financial viability usually has the implication of ability to meet debt payments as a matter of normal operations, or in a more drastic sense the ability to service all claims in the case of liquidation. While under normal circumstances the operational view is best, many of the measures employed in analysis tend to have overtones of the finality of liquidation. In contrast to the profitability measures discussed earlier, the viewpoint in this group of analytical tools is that of the lender, the claimant who is concerned about obtaining his debt service (interest and principal on schedule) and having the security of a sound position in the case of disastrous liquidation.

Liquidity Measures. The two most common liquidity measures applied in financial analysis are the so-called acid test ratio and the current ratio. Both ratios pretend to be operational tests of the ability to meet current obligations, but in fact imply coverage of current debt in case of liquidation. The acid test ratio is a relationship of cash assets, such as cash and market securities, and accounts receivable to all current liabilities on the balance sheet. Generally a 1:1 coverage is considered desirable, although in fact very sound companies have ranged far from this generalized test. A more inclusive measure is the current ratio, which relates total current assets to total current liabilities, with the general notion that a 2:1 ratio is considered desirable. Again, the measure implies liquidation, since normally operating debt obligations will be met from cash flows of the ongoing business, rather than from a liquidation of the balance sheet amounts as stated at any one point in time.

$$\frac{\text{Cash assets}}{\text{Current liabilities}} = \text{Acid test}$$

$$\frac{\text{Current assets}}{\text{Current liabilities}} = \text{Current ratio}$$

A variety of other analyses are possible to determine the relative liquidity of the assets shown on the balance sheet and to relate them with the various contractual debt obligations. As observed before, these analyses are really only important when the business runs some risk of liquidation.

Cash Flow Analysis. A more useful and operational concept is cash flow analysis, which in its simplest term is a determination of net income after taxes, adjusted for noncash items which have been deducted in arriving at the net income figure. Most prominent among these are depreciation, depletion, and other similar adjustments, which, when added back to net income, yield a number that closely represents the cash obtained from operations. The reader will recall the nature of funds flow statements and how they are constructed to reflect cash movements. In fact, funds flow statements can usually be examined for a fair indication of cash flow. Once total operating cash flow and cash flow per share of stock outstanding have been calculated, these magnitudes can be related to contractual obligations coming due in the ensuing period in the hope of judging the degree by which liquid funds generated by the business will cover such ongoing arrangements. A more involved but useful device is the detailed development of a funds flow statement which segregates the various cash flow elements over a period of time into operational cash flows, financial cash flows, discretionary cash flows, and others to see the relative proportions of cash in and out movements over time, with an eye to judging what the future might hold.

Debt Ratios. The concept of a debt ratio is an attempt to compare relative magnitudes of debt to ownership claims in order to assess the relative risk exposure of a business operation. The most common ratio in this area is the so-called debt to equity ratio, which relates total long-term debt to the total stockholders' equity in a simple proportion as follows:

$$\frac{\text{Long-term debt}}{\text{Equity (Net worth)}} = \text{Debt to equity ratio}$$

Again industry characteristics are considered as a guide in this ratio, which serves to point out extreme riskiness or conservatism rather than providing a fine gradation of financial viability. Another way of showing this relationship is to calculate the percentage of long-term debt and of ownership equity in total capitalization, which is, of course, total assets minus current liabilities. Thus a capital structure showing a 2:1 debt/equity proportion in its capitalization is likely to be considered much more risky than one showing a 0.5:1 proportion. No hard and fast rules exist; only the relative exposure can be judged.

There are many variations on this theme, all of which serve the purpose of showing the debt obligations in the balance sheet at one point in time and of developing the proportionality of relevant items. The same criticism voice as before holds: Usually exposure is not a question of proportion but of ability to pay, and for this purpose the concept of debt coverage discussed below is much more useful.

Coverage of Obligations. A more operational concept of risk exposure through debt, dividend obligations, and sinking-fund payments is the relationship of such fixed periodic payments to net income or, better yet, cash flow from operations. A commonly used ratio is the relationship of interest to net income earned, either before or after taxes, to show the relative safety of the interest payment of the lenders. The ratio used is the number of times interest has been covered by pretax income.

$$\frac{\text{Net income before interest and taxes}}{\text{Interest charges}} = \text{Coverage of interest charges}$$

A more stringent test uses principal repayment requirements per period added to the interest amount, tax adjusted, and relates the total to aftertax income or cash flow from operations. An even more telling analysis is the addition of preferred dividends and normally paid common dividends to the other obligations named, and relating the total to operating cash flow.

Asset Management. A variety of ratios are often developed to indicate the proportionality of assets and liabilities in a particular company as it relates to industry averages or norms. Again, this concept is fraught with difficulty, particularly in companies with widely different operating histories. The simplest form of analysis is to develop a proportion analysis of the balance sheet by simply calculating the percentages of total assets and of total liabilities represented by individual key elements. More detailed inquiries are made into particular accounts, such as inventories, accounts receivable, and accounts payable, to see if those amounts are within accepted industry practice or if there is an indication of slipping management attention.

Inventories are often related either to the sales of the period or more appropriately to the cost of goods sold for a given period. So-called inventory turnover is the number of times the ending inventory (or often the average inventory) will fit into the annual cost of goods sold. This ratio can be further translated by indicating how many months or weeks of inventories are outstanding at any one point in time, given the operating level preceding the balance sheet date. Again, it is useful to look at trends to see if management is increasing or decreasing inventory levels and to ascertain if this is necessary or merely an oversight. Accounts receivable are often related to the number of days' sales they represent, and this result is then compared to normal trade terms and to industry averages. It is an indication of the collection effectiveness of the business or, conversely, the quality of accounts to which the company is selling. The ratios take this form:

$$\frac{\text{Periodic cost of goods sold}}{\text{Ending inventory}} = \text{Inventory turnover}$$

$$\frac{\text{Periodic sales}}{\text{Number of days}} = \text{Days' sales;}$$

$$\frac{\text{Accounts receivable}}{\text{Days' sales}} = \text{Days' accounts receivable outstanding}$$

A similar process can be applied to accounts payable although no immediately useful indicator can be found, in contrast to inventories and receivables. Trade accounts payable usually impact only on part of total cost of goods sold or cost of services, and only crude approximations can be drawn (without access to the books) by using the number of days' cost of sales outstanding in the form of accounts payable.

A variety of other ratios, such as total asset turnover or fixed asset turnover, in relation to sales for the period can be developed, indicating broadly the effectiveness with which assets are managed in relation to the volume of sales they support. None of these indicators are final; rather, when viewed over time they can give some clues as to the direction of management decisions toward greater or lesser capital intensity and as to how the company ranks with industry counterparts.

Projections of Performance

One of the more critical elements of financial statement analysis is the highly judgmental area of earnings and performance projections based on past conditions. Since most decisions deal with the present and the future, much past analysis can be useful only as a guide to future decisions. Consequently, performance projection is one of the most useful and most difficult parts of the analyst's job. Such projections must rest on a number of well-thought-out assumptions and past trends, which must be judged in terms of future expected conditions.

Earnings Projections. These can range from a mere extrapolation of past trends of variables such as earnings per share or net profit after taxes to the building of a detailed projected income statement with specific assumptions about volume, margin ratios, expense ratios, and specific revenue forecasts based on detailed product line analyses. This latter process in effect is a line-by-line questioning of a company's income statement, applying known or expected future conditions to it. Earnings are the net result of a great number of management decisions and actions during any one period of time, which are apart from the method of recording. The degree of precision desired in earnings forecasts governs the number of assumptions and judgments necessary. Considerable effort can be spent to derive all possible income statement ratios, making specific corrections for known future changes and then projecting potential results based on the framework of the income statement and modified by known balance sheet changes, such as inventories flowing into the production process. At the other extreme is the process of trend analysis which will allow for economic cycles, seasonal conditions, and industry prospects to arrive at an outright earnings figure over time, without detailed adjustments. The whole range of measures of profitability will become useful for these purposes.

Cash Flow Projections. Since an effort is being made to analyze the major cash movements over time, cash flow projections are somewhat more detailed than pure earnings projections. The interested parties in this process will be bankers and other lenders concerned with the ability of the business to repay, or security analysts wondering about dividend and future investment rates. The process can range from a simple adjustment of earnings projections for known depreciation and depletion to a full-fledged funds flow analysis based on a projected balance sheet at the end of the projection period, in which major funds movements are analyzed and the cash effect is detailed. Again it will be useful to put upper and lower bounds on the projections if a range of conditions is expected.

Financial Condition Projection. Similar to income statement analysis, the process of balance sheet projection is basically an exercise in selecting appropriate ratios and making the best informed judgments about their future range at a given point in time. As in the case of projected income statements, a line-by-line questioning of the balance sheet takes place and a projected statement is assembled. Usually such ratios as accounts receivable periods, inventory turnovers, payable periods, fixed and current asset proportions, and likely operating liabilities can be projected specifically and related to an expected operating level in the future. Often the process results in a forced "plug" figure which represents the borrowing requirements or repayment possible if all other conditions implied in the projections hold. The process is simply the reverse of the statement analysis practiced on past conditions—taking advantage of the results of that analysis and projecting to a future point what appears to be reasonable. Industry ratios and similar data on background conditions can be helpful.

Performance Models. The prior discussion dealt essentially with a handmade process of selecting particular ratios and conditions on which to project future conditions. Performance models are an automated method of achieving the same if not more exact and quicker results. Increasingly, both analysts within corporations as well as those analyzing business from outside have resorted to computerized models of an operation specifically or to generalized industry models. With the help of models, detailed income statements, balance sheets, funds flow analyses, and other data can be prepared. The process is a logical step forward from individual rule-of-thumb analysis. The computerized model incorporates into the computer's memory the basic relationships in the form of simple mathematical formulas and lets the machine make the appropriate calculations. The result will be a set of possible financial statements and, given different assumptions, a whole series of potential outcomes. Of course, the results will be only as good as the assumptions put forth, and modeling can do no more than run complicated calculations more quickly and display the results in a familiar fashion.

Key Cautions. Since earnings, performance, and financial projections deal with expected future conditions, it is critical to remember that the process involves a series of judgments, usually by outsiders looking in and trying to predict the operating conditions and the decision-making processes of management. The results of the analysis will resemble actual conditions only if these judgments were reasonably near the target. There are many variables which can go awry, from the general economic conditions to industry problems and the specific environment of the corporation itself. Nevertheless, there is considerable value in projecting conditions, both for inside management and for a company being viewed from the outside in order to lay contingency plans for lending decisions, stock market options, and financing decisions. In fact, it will be the rare banker or other lender that will not require a fairly well worked out set of financial statements and cash flow projections from the potential borrower in order to gauge the desirability of the investment.

Changes in Capitalization

The constant movement and change in corporate capital structures arising from expansions, normal growth, acquisitions, recapitalization, stock splits, dividends, and options cause changes in the bases of per share analysis and at times in the nature of the equity base itself. The analyst should carefully study the notes to financial statements provided by companies publishing such statements and make certain that adjustments have been made in the number of shares outstanding, allowance for preferred dividends, and so on. A few of the major elements influencing the analytical picture are discussed below.

Stocks Splits and Dividends. Stock splits are basically significant increases in the number of shares participating in the same equity value through issuance of common shares to current common stockholders without consideration. These splits are most often carried out to enhance the marketability of the shares by bringing the averages price down. Since the proportion of a given stockholder's participation is unchanged, the total investment remains the same. Yet from the company's standpoint there are more shares outstanding, both with a lower market value and lower earnings per share each. To insure comparability of past data, the number of shares outstanding must be adjusted backward in time to restate per share values on the new basis. Generally this is done by the reporting company, since it is required by current accounting principles.

Stock dividends are, in effect, stocks splits in smaller proportions and similarly result merely in a change in the number of shares outstanding on the same value base. Earnings per share are affected as before and must be adjusted backward as is true of other per share data. The analyst must be careful to allow for this fact if it has not been clearly stated. Also, if the stock dividend is of significant size, an amount representing the fair market value of the new shares issued is transferred from earned surplus to the capital accounts.

Dilution from Conversion of Securities. This dilution results from exercise of the conversion privilege built into special issues of preferred stock, debentures, and other special classes of stock, as well as through the conversion of purchase warrants and options. Recent accounting practice and SEC requirements have made mandatory the disclosure of the effect of potential conversion by stating earnings per share based on currently outstanding shares and also by restating earnings per share as if all conversion had taken place. The overhang from conversion can often have a dampening effect on market performance of the stock as the price approaches the area where conversion could become profitable to the holders. Thus potential dilution is a significant factor in the analytical package of the financial analyst interested in stock price movements.

Acquisitions, Mergers. The effect of acquisitions or mergers is that of immediate dilution or strengthening of earnings per share, especially if the transaction involved the issuance of existing or newly created classes of stock. The analysis of merger and acquisition impact adds another dimension of performance projection, since the analyst commonly is interested in projecting the synergistic performance of the combined enterprise. The analysis thus involves an earnings projection of the combined entities and a gauging of the per share performance as well as other performance ratios for the combined enterprise, taking due account of the new capital structures. The most straightforward analysis takes place when consolidation is achieved on the balance sheet, since the total combined enterprise will be visible; analysis is more difficult when one deals with partial acquisitions shown only under the investment section of the balance sheets.

Other effects of changes in capitalization come about in case of serious reorganization of a company. These are rather infrequent events in the life of selected companies, and the analyst must usually develop a great deal of background information, much of it readily available from company pronouncements or public analysis, in order to judge the future performance of the enterprise under the new capital structure. Often major reorganizations are achieved to remove barriers or difficulty from outdated obligations or to free a company from unprofitable or difficult operations. No hard and fast rules can be established for this purpose, but most ratios and comparisons based on past performance become naturally obsolete under such circumstances.

Limitations

All of the foregoing discussion of financial analysis had to be couched in terms of careful consideration of any announced or implied changes in operations as well as financial and accounting policies. It will be useful to restate here the need to be particularly aware of periodic or one-time changes in accounting policy which a company's management may choose to take. Among examples for this are changes in depreciation methods both for financial accounting and tax accounting, each having a significant impact on reported profits for the period under analysis. Other elements are the treatment of the investment tax credit, where applicable, the policy regarding capitalization of research and development and similar expenses, and, as pointed out, the treatment of mergers and acquisitions under the several options possible. Two companies in the same industry can have rather widely different performance depending on the choice of such options.

Another, more fundamental change is implied in the changing conditions an industry may be undergoing over time. The impact of technological progress, changes in basic processing methods, or competitive inroads by entirely different ways of serving the market needs can have a serious impact on the operating performance of members of that industry. Such changes are particularly frequent in highly technology based industries, such as computer oriented manufacturers and service organizations, but they can happen in more basic industries as well. The analyst will be wise to be quite familiar with past and current industry conditions for this purpose.

A common and difficult-to-deal-with phenomenon is the increasing trend towards multi-industry participation by major corporations in the United States and overseas. No longer is it possible to think of companies neatly fitting the industry classifications that are being used for statistical and analytical purposes by the U.S. government, trade associations, and others. Over the past 25 years a rapid diversification of corporate efforts has taken place, with the result that it is a rare case where a company can be fitted precisely into one or two of the basic industries of which it is a part. More commonly, the analyst has the problem of trying to separate the relative participation in various industries both by investment and profit contribution in order to better understand both current conditions and likely future performance. Such diversification tends to defeat the purpose of broad industry statistics as one of the background measures against which to judge corporate performance.

ACCESS TO FINANCIAL STATEMENT INFORMATION

The common problem for the financial analyst dealing with publicly held corporations is one of abundance of data, but not necessarily an abundance of the specific information that will help him with his analytical purpose. While there are a great number of sources to which one is able to turn for standardized financial data—mostly patterned after published financial statements—specific details to allow incisive analysis into a company's operations is usually not readily available. Over the last several years there has been a trend toward earlier and earlier reporting after the close of the accounting period, with information being made available both through company releases to the financial press and through line computer storage provided by a number of service firms that have sprung up to offer quick accessibility to basic financial information. The three basic reference areas making such information available are company information, published manuals, and computerized data services.

Company Information

Publicly held corporations provide, as a matter of legal disclosure and for public relations purposes, at least annually fairly detailed accounts of the company's operations in the form of an annual report. The specific formats used by individual companies vary widely, and they range from cryptic publications of financial statements to color-illustrated booklets covering in detail the products and services, facilities, resources, management, and even comments on current company, industry, and national issues. Some historical perspective is commonly provided on operating and financial statistics of the company, going as far back as 10 or 15 years in time. SEC and stock exchange requirements have over the years brought about more and more disclosure of details, including sales and profit contribution by major product line.

Annual reports are, therefore, generally quite useful as a direct source of financial information, and the analyst can count on reasonable consistency of the data presented therein, due to the combined influence of the public accountants and the various governmental agencies.

Data in somewhat greater detail are provided in the 10-K reports on file with the SEC, which are open for public inspection either through the SEC offices or more currently through computerized data services.

Quarterly reports issued by companies are generally limited to comparative, abbreviated financial statements and comments on major developments affecting the corporation.

An additional source of company information is found in the fairly common practice by management of making formal presentations to gatherings of security analysts. While little new in the way of specific financial details is usually given on such occasions, these forums help analysts to ascertain management plans, objectives, and likely future direction. Transcripts of such formal gatherings, including some major question-and-answer exchanges, are found in the weekly *Wall Street Transcript*.

Published Manuals

The most widely used and best-known set of services both in the form of current news and bound manuals is provided by Moody's and by Standard and Poor's. The Moody's services are issued in five volumes (1) Industrials; (2) Banks, Insurance, Real Estate, and Investment Funds; (3) Public Utilities; (4) Railroads; and (5) Government and Municipals. The manuals, which appear annually, contain financial statements, key historical data on company products, services, mergers, acquisitions, security price ranges, dividend records, and so on of a large number of companies, including practically all publicly held companies. The center sections of the manuals, (blue section) contain useful summary statistics and industry data. The information in the annual manuals is updated through semiweekly supplements, cross-referenced in great detail.

Another service of Moody's is the *Quarterly Handbook*, which contains one-page summaries of publicly held corporations, covering stock price ranges, key financial statistics, ratings, and company developments. Other, more specialized services include Moody's semiweekly *Dividend Record* and the semimonthly *Bond Record*, with current prices, ratings, and earnings of the most important bonds traded in the United States.

Publications of Standard & Poor's include the *Standard Corporation Records*, which provide in loose-leaf form financial information about a large number of individual companies which is updated through daily supplements. *The Analyst's Handbook* compiles individual company and industry data in handy reference form. Other, more specialized services include weekly forecasts of the security markets, securities statistics, information services on the bond market, and a monthly earnings and stock rating guide.

Among the other services covering company financial data, Dun & Bradstreet fills a somewhat unique position. Upon request clients can receive financial statements and other key company data on a large number of smaller companies not normally covered by the major services, which concentrate on the publicly held and traded corporations. The preoccupation of the Dun & Bradstreet service is with credit worthiness, which rests, of course, to a large extent upon financial performance.

Additional information services include *Fitch's Corporation Manuals, Walker's Manual of Pacific Securities,* and the many individual company analyses provided by the major brokerage houses through their research departments. Services concentrating on rating stock investments for their clients, through critical evaluation of financial performance, include *The Value Line, United Business Service,* and *Babson's,* to name only the more important ones.

Computerized Data Services

The latest development for providing ready access to financial information is the enlistment of the computer and its storage and retrieval capabilities. This process has evolved over the past decade to the point that today it is possible through the services of one of the nationwide time share computer networks, such as Rapidata, General Electric, Interactive Data, or Online Decisions, to obtain almost instantly the latest financial information, reports, and data on the corporations listed on the major stock exchanges.

The pioneering work in this area was done by Standard & Poor's, which through its subsidiary, Investors Management Sciences, Inc., developed computer storage of key financial data normally collected and presented in the Standard & Poor's manuals and handbooks. The initial storage was in the form of rentable computer tapes, but as technology developed, on-line storage became available. The "Compustat" primary, supplementary, and tertiary file system now provides, on tape or through time sharing, as well as in hard copy reports, coverage of the financial data of Standard & Poor's 425 industrial and 75 other companies listed on the major stock exchanges. More recently it began providing full coverage for all listed industrials on the New York and American Stock Exchanges, as well as on many banks, utilities, REIT's, railroads, and insurance companies.

In a similar vein, the *Value Line Analytical Data Base–1* was developed and is maintained by Arnold Bernhard and Company, Inc. It contains annual and quarterly data on about 1,300 companies, including necessary and significant industry data. The annual data begin in 1954, with quarterly data extending back to 1967.

A more recent development is that of a computerized file of complete full-text SEC reports on all publicly held companies registered with the SEC in Washington, D.C. These include annual forms 10-K, quarterly forms 10-Q, significant developments 8-K, registration forms S-1, transportation forms 14-K, prospectuses, proxies, and annual reports. This file, continuously updated, is made available through *Financial Information Services.* In addition, this service provides for its clients company profiles and rankings against industry averages.

Time share service companies such as Rapidata and Interactive Data Corporation will market some or all of the financial data bases to users. In addition, these service companies will provide statistical analysis packages and routines, as well as financial report writing capabilities which the analyst can use to analyze and describe the information made available to him. Furthermore, economic background statistics and projections can be found in readily accessible form directly from econometric modeling services, such as Chase Econometrics, Data Resources, Lionel D. Edie, General Electric Mapcast, and Wharton EFA, or through time share services marketing their output.

Other data bases are constantly being developed. They include securities price data bases, bond price data bases, and others which have some common appeal.

In summary, the key advantage of computerized data bases are ready availability, some editing for consistency, and ability to manipulate data through powerful analytical routines in the computer. It should be observed, however, that the data bases themselves have not added any new insights into data that historically have been available to the analyst, if only with greater effort. All the cautions about accounting decisions, disclosure, and comparability inherent in financial statements still exist—only the task of assembly and calculation has been eased.

SELECTED REFERENCES

ANTHONY, ROBERT N. *Management Accounting, Text and Cases.* 4th ed. Homewood, Ill.; Richard D. Irwin, Inc., 1970. Chaps. 10–12, 16.

BONBRIGHT, J. C. *The Valuation of Property.* 2 vols. New York: McGraw-Hill Book Co., 1937.

DONALDSON, GORDON. *Strategy of Financial Mobility.* Boston: Division of Research, Graduate School of Business Administration, Harvard University, 1969.

FOULKE, ROY A. *Practical Financial Statement Analysis.* 6th ed. New York: McGraw-Hill Book Co., 1968.

GRAHAM, B.; DODD, D. L.; and COTTLE, S. *Security Analysis.* 4th ed. New York: McGraw-Hill Book Co., 1962. Pts. II, IV.

GUTHMANN, H. G., and DOUGALL, H. E. *Corporate Financial Policy.* 4th ed. Englewood Cliffs, N.J.: Prentice-Hall, 1962. Chaps. 5, 6.

HAWKINS, DAVID F. *Financial Reporting Practices of Corporations.* Homewood, Ill.: Dow Jones-Irwin, 1972.

HELFERT, ERICH A. *Techniques of Financial Analysis.* 3d ed. Homewood, Ill.: Dow Jones-Irwin, 1972. Chaps. 1–3.

Hunt, Pearson; Williams, Charles M.; and Donaldson, Gordon. *Basic Business Finance.* 3d ed. Homewood, Ill.: Richard D. Irwin, Inc., 1966. Pt. I, chaps. 7, 8.

Jaedicke, Robert K., and Sprouse, Robert T. *Accounting Flows: Income, Funds and Cash.* Englewood Cliffs, N.J.: Prentice-Hall, 1965.

Troy, Leo. *Almanac of Business and Industrial Financial Ratios.* Englewood Cliffs, N.J.: Prentice-Hall, 1968.

Vancil, Richard F., ed. *Financial Executive's Handbook.* Homewood, Ill.: Dow Jones-Irwin, 1970.

Van Horne, James C. *Financial Management and Policy.* Englewood Cliffs, N.J.,: Prentice-Hall, 1968. Chaps. 6–8, 24, 25.

Wasserman, Paul, ed. *Encyclopedia of Business Information Sources.* Detroit: Gale Research Co., 1970.

23

Effect of Taxes on Earnings and Earnings Estimates

JOSEPH A. MAURIELLO, Ph.D., C.P.A.
Graduate School of Business Administration
New York University
New York, New York

Nature of Federal and State Taxes on Income

FEDERAL AND state taxes on income, as well as any city income taxes imposed, such as in New York City, are construed by business as expenses of doing business. Whether such taxes are transferable to customers in the sales price of product or services is irrelevant. Corporate budgets translate aftertax income amounts into pretax rates of return so that the effect in most instances is to recover in product price the amounts of taxes being paid. The substantial increases in federal income tax rates as a result of World War II, and the gradual increases in state income tax rates and in the number of states adopting state income taxes as a source of revenue have caused the composite of federal, state, and city income taxes to consume more than 50 percent of the pretax income dollar. The prevailing federal income tax rates are 22 percent on the first $25,000 of taxable income and 48 percent on the income in excess of $25,000. For a corporation domiciled in New York City, the current combined New York State and New York City income tax rates approximate 15 percent, both of which are deductible in computing the federal income tax. Accordingly, the effective New York State and city rates combined, net of the 48 percent federal tax savings is 7.8 percent (15 percent − 48 percent × 15 percent); the sum of the federal, state, and city tax rates in therefore 55.8 percent.

Many states levy a tax on corporate capital, as well as on income, usually employing the same tax form, but the income tax component normally accounts for at least 90 percent of the total tax.

Generalizing, state and city income taxes are computed, with minor exceptions which vary among taxing jurisdictions, with reference to the same composition of items and formula used for federal tax purposes. Accordingly, subsequent discussion focusing on specific items and situations will center on the federal income tax treatment under the Internal Revenue Code and related supporting interpretive regulations.

Accounting View of Federal and State Income Taxes

The Accounting Principles Board, in *Opinion No. 11,* issued December 1967, stated in succinct terms, in paragraph 14, its position that taxes on income are unequivocally an expense of doing business, as follows: "Income taxes are an expense of business enterprises earning income subject to tax."

The foregoing viewpoint was reiterated in the restatement and revision of the accounting research bulletins previously issued by the Committee on Accounting Procedure. Such codification issued as of June 1953, and known as Accounting Research Bulletin No. 43, contains the following statement in Chapter 10, "Taxes," Section B on income taxes, paragraph 4: "Income taxes are an expense that should be allocated as other expenses are allocated." This statement recognizes that income taxes are an expense, and hence their treatment is governed by applications of the matching principle, i.e., that the expense be matched against the income that created the expense, or to which the expense is related. This required matching of accounting income tax was also expressed in APB *Opinion No. 11,* in paragraph 14:

> Accounting for income tax expense requires measurement and identification with the appropriate time period and therefore involves annual deferral and estimation concepts in the same manner as these concepts are applied in the measurement and time period identification of other expenses.

The income tax provision on quarterly interim statements is dictated by the pretax income or the loss for the particular quarter. However, to prevent misleading results, the provision also takes into account factors which bear on the taxable income for the entire year.

Characteristics of Tax Structure Affecting Reporting

The determinations of taxable income and of financial income are similar in that both computations are concerned with financial data for a specific entity compiled under the accounting concepts of (1) ignoring of the changing purchasing power of the dollar; (2) adherence to historical cost as being objective and measurable with reasonable accuracy; and (3) necessity for sales and exchanges as a basis for reflecting gains and, in most cases, for reflecting losses.

The two determinations, despite their similarities, may differ considerably. Tax accounting is statutory in character, whereas financial reporting is based on generally accepted accounting principles which are applied independent of tax rules. Financial reporting follows tax precepts only in those cases in which the differences in reported results are immaterial.

Differences in Tax Accounting and Financial Accounting

The types of differences in tax accounting and financial accounting for a particular fiscal year, and examples of each type, are as follows:

1. Income items excluded from taxable income and included in financial income:
    a. Interest on state, county, and municipal bonds which are exempt from tax.
    b. Proceeds on "key-man" life insurance policies of officers, collected by the corporation as beneficiary.
    c. Earnings of subsidiary companies and other companies whose common stocks are owned 20 percent or more. These earnings are reflected under the equity method for the fiscal years in which earned by the companies owned, before legal transmission in the form of dividends, at which time the dividends are taxed.
    d. Gains from involuntary conversions of property not subject to tax in the year of realization under elective provisions of the Code.

       (If such gains are not taxed, the effect is to reduce the tax basis for purposes of future depreciation and for determining gain or loss on a later disposal of the property.)
    e. Income from rents and other services reflected as financial income in the current period in which the services are rendered, but for tax purposes included in taxable income in a prior period of collection under the "claim-of-right" doctrine of the Code.
    f. Capital gains in the current year offset by carryover of a net capital loss of a prior year and which was nondeductible in such year and the possible tax benefit of which was not set up as an asset because realization was not assured beyond a reasonable doubt.

       (The tax treatment of capital losses is explained under the next topical caption.)
2. Income items included in taxable income and excluded from financial income:
    a. Current-year capital gains absorbed by capital loss carryovers from prior years.
    b. Income from rents and other services reflected in taxable income in the current year of collection, but not included in financial

income since the collected amounts are to be earned in a subsequent period.

c. Dividends from subsidiaries and other corporations more than 20 percent and less than 80 percent owned, included in taxable income to the extent of 15 percent of the dividends, but treated for financial accounting purposes as a conversion of the investment account into cash under the equity method.

d. Income from adjustments of prior-year state income taxes or of contract prices subject to renegotiation, currently taxable, but treated for financial accounting purposes as correcting the beginning-of-the-year balance of Retained Earnings.

3. Expenses and losses not deducted in determining taxable income but deducted in determining financial net income:

a. An excess of capital losses over capital gains of the three preceding years and of the subsequent five years.

b. The provision for the federal income tax item itself.

c. Depreciation and depletion deducted in lesser amount than used in determining financial income.

d. Insurance premiums on lives of officers, where the corporation is the beneficiary.

e. Penalties and fines.

f. Additions for estimated expenses to liability accounts for product warranties and to asset valuation accounts for estimated sales returns, sales allowances, and cash discounts greater in total than the actual amounts for these items deductible for tax purposes.

(Although these items are estimated and reflected in the year of sale for purposes of financial reporting, the estimates are ignored and the actual data are used for income tax purposes.)

g. Additions for estimated losses to accrued liabilities for self-insurance and for employee pensions greater in amount than the actual casualty losses and cash contributions into the pension fund deductible for tax purposes.

(These items are ignored for income tax purposes until the losses are sustained and the pension fund contributions are made.)

h. Write-down of inventory at Lifo cost to lower market value for financial reporting purposes, not allowable for tax purposes until sale of the inventory.

i. Amortization of goodwill, not deductible for tax purposes but for financial accounting purposes required to be amortized as an expense over a period of not more than 40 years if acquired after October 31, 1970.

4. Expense and loss elements deducted in determining taxable income but not deducted in determining financial net income:

a. Depreciation and depletion deducted for tax purposes in an amount greater than that used in determining financial income.

b. Deductible disbursements against liability accounts for product warranties in excess of nondeductible estimated amounts added to the liability account for financial accounting purposes.

c. Deductible casualty losses and contributions into pension fund charged to liability accounts for self-insurance and pensions in excess of nondeductible estimated amounts added to the respective liability accounts for financial accounting purposes.

d. Preoperating costs and research and experimentation costs capitalized for financial accounting purposes and amortized over specified future periods, but expended in larger amount as incurred each year and deducted for income tax purposes.

e. Sales returns, allowances, and discounts deductible for tax purposes in the current year of occurrence and charged to asset valuation accounts set up in the prior year on the basis of estimates serving to reduce financial income at that time.

f. Net operating loss carryover to the current year from a prior year.

In addition to the foregoing, the cumulative effect of a change in accounting principle, additive or subtractive, shown in the determination of current-year financial net income either will be entirely excluded in the determination of taxable income or will be included therein at an unlike amount. Such cumulative effect represents the impact on the financial net income of prior periods reflected in whole in the current period.

(The tax treatment of net operating losses is explained under the next topical caption.)

Carry-back or Carry-forward Provisions of Internal Revenue Code

Annual net losses are treated for tax purposes over a period of years so as to provide tax benefit through offset against income of years other than those in which the unfavorable elements or items originated. The effects of these items, except when they create a net loss in the year of origin, are to prevent a correspondence between the tax payable for a particular year and the tax expense based on pretax financial income for such year.

The first type of item is a net loss for the current year. Such net loss, after statutory adjustments, is termed a *net operating loss,* which functions as a *carry-back* to offset taxable income of the third, second, and first preceding years in that sequence. Any amount still unutilized after carry-back to the three years is carried forward as a net operating loss carry-over against the following five future years in sequence. Such net operating losses therefore serve to (1) to produce federal income tax refunds with respect to taxes paid in prior years and (2) to reduce the taxable income of future years, and therefore the income taxes payable for such years.

A second type of item is a net capital loss measuring the excess of capital losses over capital gains for the year. Capital losses and capital gains are classified as short term, where the holding period of the asset is not more than six months, and long term, where the holding period exceeds six months. The short-term capital gains and losses are combined to create a net short-term capital gain or a net short-term capital loss, and the long-term capital gains and losses are likewise combined to produce a net long-term capital gain or a net long-term capital loss. A net capital loss consists of an excess of net long-term capital loss over net short-term capital gain, a converse excess of net short-term loss over net long-term capital gain, or a combination of net long-term capital loss and net short-term capital loss.

Such net capital loss is not deductible in any degree for the year of origin, but serves as a carry-back to offset capital gains whether net short term or net long term, for the third, second, and first preceding years in sequence. The balance of net capital loss not utilized constitutes a capital loss carry-over against capital gains, net short term or long term, over the five future years in sequence.

A third type of carry-over is the "recovery exclusion," provided in Internal Revenue Code Section 111. This section provides that if certain types of tax deductions fail to produce tax benefit measured by the amount of reduction in the corporation's taxable income, taking into account carry-overs and carry-backs, recovery of the items in a subsequent year is not taxable to the extent of the amount corresponding to the lack of benefit. The types of deductions covered by this rule include bad debts, state income and franchise taxes, real estate taxes, excise taxes, and payroll taxes; capital losses; and interest on tax delinquency amounts.

Credits against the Income Tax

The Internal Revenue Code provides for deductions directly against the tax payable, termed *tax credits.* A tax credit reduces the tax otherwise payable in an amount equal to 100 percent of the credit. In contrast, a deduction and an income exclusion reduce the tax by the amount involved, multiplied by the tax rate at the corporation's top tax bracket, i.e., 50 percent to 55 percent for federal and state income taxes combined.

The major types of tax credits are the following:

1. The investment tax credit.
2. The foreign income tax credit.
3. The Work Incentive Program tax credit.

The Investment Tax Credit. The investment credit is measured at 7 percent of the cost of personal property having a life of at least three years and weighted for the length of life. The weights are 33⅓ percent for property having a life of at least three years and less than five years; 66⅔ percent for a life of at least five years and less than seven years; and 100 percent for a life of at least seven years. Alternatively stated, the investment credit rate weighted for life is 2⅓ percent, 4⅔ percent, and 7 percent for the respective life ranges of three to under five years, of five to under seven years, and of seven years and more. The investment credit is restricted to the first $50,000 cost of used property, but otherwise is not limited as to total cost subject to the credit. There are limitations on the benefit flowing from the credit, namely, 100 percent benefit on the first $25,000 of federal income tax, and 50 percent benefit with respect to the tax in excess of $25,000, with a three-year carry-back and seven-year carry-forward of any unused amount.

For financial accounting purposes, the investment credit is treated under the alternative methods permitted in the Accounting Principles Board's Opinion No. 4, issued in March 1964, as follows:

1. As a reduction of the federal income tax expense and corresponding liability in the year in which the credit arises, i.e., the period in which the asset is acquired and put to use. This method is termed the "flow-through" method.
2. As a reduction of the federal income tax expense over the period of the productive life of the asset. This method is termed the "deferral method."

The first method is by far the more commonly employed, in the ratio of 6 or 7 to 1 of the second method. Under the latter method, the tax liability for the year in which the credit arises is reduced and a deferred investment credit account is created; over the life of the related asset, the deferred investment credit and the income tax expense of each year embraced in such life are reduced.

The Foreign Income Tax Credit. The foreign tax credit is intended to remove from the computed U.S. income tax, the tax imposed by foreign countries and U.S. possessions on income from these foreign sources included in the taxable gross income. The tax credit is restricted to foreign income, war profits, and excess-profits taxes or, in lieu thereof, of sales tax, gross income tax, or other similar type of tax on income. These forms of income tax may alternatively be treated as tax deductions, which normally would only be employed in a tax year of loss, so that the foreign tax will thus add to the net operating loss for the year and thereby reduce, through carry-back, the income of a prior taxable year.

The foreign tax credit may not reduce the U.S. tax in greater amount than the foreign income contributes to the total tax. The tax credit is accordingly the smaller of (1) the actual foreign income tax incurred or paid or (2) a limitation amount based on formula intended to measure the U.S. tax resulting from the foreign income. Under the formula, the tax credit is limited to the U.S. tax multiplied by the ratio of the taxable income from the foreign country to the total taxable income on the federal tax return. If the foreign income is derived from more than one foreign country, the taxpayer makes two sets of computations and uses that computation which produces the higher tax credit. The first computation is mandatory; it considers each foreign country individually and is therefore termed the *per country* limitation. The second computation is elective; it treats all foreign countries combined and is therefore termed the *overall* limitation. Under the per country limitation, the tax credit is based on the foreign tax rate if lower than the U.S. tax rate, and on the U.S. tax rate if the foreign tax rate is higher. Under the overall limitation, the foreign tax rates in excess of the U.S. tax rates are used to increase the lower foreign tax rates to a higher average rate overall and thereby to increase the foreign tax rate credit. If the foreign tax rates of the various foreign countries are all lower than the U.S. tax rate, the tax credits for the individual countries will be limited to the actual foreign tax amounts incurred and paid.

In these times of political flux and of scarce natural resources, foreign countries enjoying new positions of power may raise their tax rates closer to or equal to higher U.S. tax rates in recognition of the fact that the total of domestic and foreign income taxes paid by the corporation will remain unaltered. The only effect of the increase in the foreign tax rate is to cause the foreign country to obtain a larger portion, and the United States a correspondingly lower portion, of an unchanged amount of total tax paid by the American corporation.

A U.S. corporation owning at least 10 percent of the voting stock of a foreign corporation is entitled to a tax credit for foreign taxes on dividends which it receives from *accumulated profits* of foreign corporations. The measurement of the dividends and of the accumulated profits serving as the source of the dividends depends on whether the foreign corporation is a "less developed corporation" or not.

A less developed country corporation has its situs in those countries in Asia, Africa, Central America, and South America which are designated as less developed countries by the President of the United States. Such less developed country corporation must derive at least 80 percent of its gross income from the less developed country and must utilize at least 80 percent of its assets in the conduct of a business in such a country. Dividends received from a corporation which is not a less developed country corporation consist of the dividend itself and of a *dividend gross-up* for the related foreign tax paid by the foreign corporation. The accumulated profits are measured by gains, profits, and income for a corporation which is not a less developed country corporation; and by such gains, profits and income diminished by related income taxes for a corporation which is a less developed country corporation. The tax paid and profits distributed as dividends are measured by the total tax paid by the foreign corporation scaled down by the proportions that the dividends received bear to the accumulated profits of the foreign corporation. The two sets of definitions of dividends and of accumulated profits result in a higher proportion for a corporation which is a less developed country corporation than for a corporation which is not so classified, and accordingly, other things equal, the foreign tax credit will be higher for the former class of corporation.

The foreign tax credit is usually operative at the time that dividends are received and included in taxable gross income on the U.S. tax returns. The tax credit, on the other hand, is derived from the tax paid in the foreign country for the year in which the income subject to foreign tax was earned. Typically, a lag occurs as between (1) the period in which the foreign income is earned and included in the income statement but omitted from the U.S. tax return and (2) the later period in which the foreign income is received as a dividend and included in U.S. taxable income. This lag requires recognition in the financial reporting, as explained in this section.

An excess of the foreign tax over the limitation amount is carried back and taken as a credit in the second and first preceding years in that order, and then carried forward for use in each of the subsequent five years. The carry-back and carry-forward amounts are usable only to the extent of the excess of the limitation amount over the actual tax for the particular year of carry-back or carry-forward. The unused foreign tax credit can be carried back or forward only to a year in which the computation of credit was consistent in method, as between the "per country" basis or the "overall" basis. The two-year carry-back and five-year carry-forward periods, nevertheless, expire even though non-utilization of the credit is attributable to the dissimilarity in computation.

The Work Incentive Program Tax Credit. Employers are granted a work incentive tax credit equal to 20 percent of cash wages or salaries paid or accrued during the first 12 months of U.S. employment of a 24-month period with respect to new employees, other than replacement personnel, training under a work incentive program authorized by Section 432 (b) of the Social Security Act certified by the Secretary of Labor.

The work incentive tax credit is like the investment tax credit in that (1) it is allowed 100 percent on the first $25,000 of tax and 50 percent on the excess of tax above $25,000, and (2) any unused credit is carried back three years and forward seven years.

The work incentive tax credit is subject to recapture to the extent that wages and salaries paid are less than the amounts paid to other employees for comparable services and in the event that the employee is retired prior to his being employed 12 months or within 12 calendar months following 12 months of employment. There is no recapture in the case of voluntary severance of employees or discharge because of misconduct or disability.

One of the prime purposes of the work incentive credit is to afford employment opportunities for welfare recipients. Despite the increased social responsibility being assumed by business enterprise, for the typical corporation the credit is not significant.

Differences in Methods of Tax Reporting and Financial Accounting

Tax reporting is governed by objectives of shifting deductions and income as between two years or of deferring tax indefinitely. For a public corporation of relatively permanent existence, an indefinite deferment of tax is tantamount to an interest-free loan without maturity. The present value of the deferred obligation is nominal.

Tax is deferred by reference to overall methods of reporting and to methods of accounting for specific items. Overall methods which defer tax are (1) the installment method used by installment dealers, (2) the completed contract method used by contractors for contracts of more than one year's duration, and (3) the cash method, used to some extent in the construction field, but more commonly in accounting for income from farming and from schools.

The installment method reports gross profit, i.e., net sales less cost of goods sold, in the proportion that sales are collected. Assume that the sales for an installment department for a particular year are $10 million, the gross profit ratio is 30 percent, and the collections on sales are $2,500,000. The gross profit of $3 million is reported 25 percent as earned in the current year ($2,500,000 ÷ $10,000,000) and 75 percent to be earned in later years as the remaining $7,500,000 of installment receivables are collected. Accordingly, $750,000 gross profit is reported as realized in the current year and $2,250,000 as deferred and to be realized each year in the degree that the receivables are collected. The total gross profit realized for a given current year is measured by applying the gross profit ratios of sales of the prior and current years to the collections on sales of the years involved. Income taxes are deferred in the amount of deferred gross profit on the sales uncollected, multiplied by the combined federal and state income tax rates.

The installment method is also available for use on casual sales of personalty and realty so long as not more than 30 percent of the gross selling price is collected in cash or in marketable securities in the year of sale. The profit on the casual sale is reported for each year of the credit period in the degree that the total amount to be collected by the seller is received in each such year.

The completed contract method reports the gross profit or gross loss on long-term contracts of more than one year's duration in the year of contract completion. The method is to be contrasted with the percentage of completion method which reports gross profit as earned each year in the degree that work on the contract is completed during the year. Completion is measured by taking into account costs incurred to date and estimated costs to complete, with reference to all cost elements or selected cost elements, whichever approach produces the more accurate measure of contract price earned. The percentage of completion for the fiscal period is applied to the total contract price to arrive at the amount of contract price earned assignable to the period.

The completed contract method is preferable to the percentage of completion method from an income tax standpoint, in that the former method defers tax applicable to gross profit on contracts in process as at the end of a particular year. Since contracts will always be in progress, and assuming profitability, the deferred tax at the end of each fiscal year will be the gross profit on all contracts multiplied by the combined federal and state income tax rates. Also, the taxpayer is often capable on a bona fide basis of controlling the year in which a specific contract is to be completed, and thereby preestablish the taxable gross profit for the year.

The cash method serves to defer tax on unreported pretax net income measured largely by uncollected receivables in excess of unpaid accounts payable creative of expenses.

From a financial accounting point of view, installment dealers are required to use the accrual method on the financial statements, despite the fact that the installment method is used for federal and state income tax purposes. In *Opinion No. 10—Omnibus Opinion, 1966,* the Accounting Principles Board stated that in the absence of exceptional costs and conditions under which there is no reasonable basis for estimating the degree of collectibility of receivables, the installment method of recognizing revenue is not acceptable. Also, from a financial accounting standpoint, and as expressed in *Accounting Research Bulletin* No. 45 issued by the Committee on Accounting Procedure, the percentage of completion method is preferable to the completed contract method when reasonably dependable estimates of costs to complete and extent of completion are available. The percentage of completion method avoids the irregular recognition of income resulting from reporting accumulations of contract gross profit in entirety in the year of completion. The completed contract method is preferable to the percentage of completion method only when forecasts are doubtful due to undependable estimates or inherent hazards of the contract. The cash method is unacceptable for purposes of financial reporting because it violates the principle of matching expense with income and omits from the balance sheet (1) assets in the form of accounts receivable, certain types of inventories, and prepaid expenses and (2) liabilities in the form of accounts payable and accrued expenses.

Deferment of tax accomplished by the selected treatment of specific items is exemplified in the Lifo method of costing materials and merchandise and the use of accelerated depreciation methods. Regarding the Lifo method, assuming that the method is adopted at a low point in an inflationary period, Lifo costing serves to assess sales revenues with more recent and higher costs. Taxes are deferred on the excess of the inventory value at current cost, determined under the contrasting Fifo method, over the Lifo cost amount. Regarding depreciation, accelerated methods are employed for tax purposes in order to maximize depreciation in the early years of life of the property being depreciated. Assuming new replacements of property in at least the same rate of retirements, there is an indefinite deferment of tax even though depreciation on the earlier acquisitions of property may be less than the uniform annual depreciation determined under the straight line method.

Classification of Federal Income Tax Charges and Credits on Income Statement and Retained Earnings Statement

The income statement, whether single step or multistep, contains several sections, as follows:

1. An operating section, which includes the results of current operating performance and of unusual items which do not qualify as extraordinary items.

2. An extraordinary items section, expected to be relatively sparse in the future, inasmuch as APB Opinion No. 30, issued in June 1973, reclassified as unusual items includable in the operating section most of the items previously presented as extraordinary items. One item still to be shown as an extraordinary item is the reduction in current year's tax attributable to the carryover of a net operating loss not set up as an asset in the earlier year of loss, in accordance with paragraphs 46 and 47 of the APB Opinion No. 11, discussed in ensuing paragraphs.

3. A section to reflect the cumulative effect of a change in accounting principle.

The retained earnings statement reconciles the retained earnings balance as at the end of the prior fiscal period to the balance as at the end of the current period. The change is accounted for by the items of (1) prior-period adjustments to the opening balance, (2) the net income or net loss for the period, (3) cash dividends or stock dividends, and (4) premiums on stock redemptions and treasury stock purchases.

The principle of matching expense against income or, stated in a broader sense, of matching or associating negative elements and related benefits requires that the income tax increase in the case of income and the income tax decrease in the case of loss be identified with the related income or loss. Assuming for the moment that taxable income and pretax financial income are the same, the single tax per tax return must be allocated to each section in the income statement contributing, positively or negatively, to the tax amount. Also, if a prior-period adjustment shown in the retained earnings statement served to offset the tax of the current year or prior years, the adjustment is reflected net of the related tax increase or decrease. Accordingly, a tax of $5 million may be expressed componentially as (1) a tax charge of $6 million in the operating section showing pretax income of $12 million, (2) a tax credit of $1,500,000 in the extraordinary items section because of an extraordinary loss of $3 million, and (3) a tax charge of $500,000 applicable to a favorable prior-period adjustment shown in the retained earnings statement.

The matching principle requires that a net operating loss or a net capital loss for the current year be reduced directly by the refundable tax resulting from the carry-back of the losses to the three preceding years. In the event that such losses are not fully utilized through carry-back, they are further reduced by the expected tax-benefit amount from their carry-forward over the next five years if realization of the benefit is realizable beyond any reasonable doubt. This reduction of loss is permitted in paragraphs 46 and 47 of *APB Opinion No. 11,* issued December 1967. In determining whether realization is beyond any reasonable doubt, factors to be considered are the cause of the current loss, company experience as to past losses and profits, and the elements expected in the next five-year carry-forward period, projected in the light of past experience which support the position that income will be earned to absorb the current-period loss.

The matching principle and the identification of taxes with related items affect the entire fabric of financial accounting. Thus, the cumulative effect of a change in accounting principles is shown net of tax effect in the current-period income statement. Restatements of income of prior years required in exceptional cases are also net of tax effect. Pro forma computations showing the impact on earnings per share are also net of related tax amounts.

Principles of Financial Accounting Relating to Differences in Tax Reporting

Financial accounting principles are independent of, and therefore not governed by, statutory rules for determining taxable income. Furthermore, financial accounting does not adopt tax precepts or otherwise subserve itself to tax accounting. The position of the accounting profession was expressed in *ARB No. 43,* Chapter, 9, "Depreciation," in paragraph 4, as follows:

> Sound financial procedures do not necessarily coincide with the rules as to what shall be included in "gross income," or allowed as a deduc-

tion therefrom, in arriving at taxable net income. It is well recognized that such rules should not be followed for financial accounting purposes if they do not conform to generally accepted accounting principles. However, where the results obtained from following income-tax procedures do not materially differ from those obtained where generally accepted accounting principles are followed, there are practical advantages in keeping the accounts in agreement with the income-tax returns.

Permanent and Timing Differences as between Financial and Taxable Income

By reason of the separateness of financial accounting and tax accounting, annual financial income will differ from taxable income by reason of differences in overall methods of reporting and in treatments of specific items and situations or events.

On further analysis, it is seen that the differences in overall methods of accounting eventually equalize over time, due to variations in activity and possible ultimate cessation of activity. Thus, the deferred profit and deferred tax resulting from use of the installment method for tax purposes decline, and the tax is paid when the volume of installment sales declines or if the company changes its operating policy and discontinues the installment sales department. In the latter case of termination, outstanding accounts receivable are collected, gross profit previously reported as deferred is earned, and the commensurate tax previously deferred becomes payable. There are no new installment sales, no new accounts receivable containing gross profit on which to defer taxes. These conclusions apply also to the great number of contractors which use the completed contract method for tax purposes and the percentage of completion method in financial reporting.

Regarding differences in treatment of specific items or events, such differences either are absolute and final with respect to the fiscal period of origin or equalize over time. The equalization may be complete within a short time or only partially in the near future with postponement of ultimate equalization until the item ceases to exist, either because the particular operation or activity creating the item is altered or discontinued or because the corporate entity is liquidated.

Differences which are absolute or final for the fiscal period and therefore never equalize over time are termed *permanent differences*. Differences which equalize over time are termed *timing differences* even though the greater portion of the equalization may be postponed indefinitely in the case of large public corporations which, for all practical purposes, have perpetual life.

Examples of permanent differences taken from the list of differences presented early in the chapter are as follows:

1-*a*. Tax-exempt interest on state, county, and municipal bonds.
1-*b*. Proceeds on life insurance policies, collected by the corporation as beneficiary.
1-*f*. Capital gains in the current year offset by a capital loss carry-over from a prior year.
3-*d*. Insurance premiums on life insurance policies on officers, the corporation being the beneficiary.
3-*e*. Penalties and fines.
3-*i*. Amortization of good will.
4-*a*. Depletion under percentage depletion, creating a tax deduction even after the cost of the natural resources is recovered.

Carry-forward loss elements utilized in reducing current taxable income automatically create a permanent difference. An example is a capital loss of a prior year, the potential tax benefit of which had not been seen set up as an asset, and which is used for tax purposes in the current year to offset capital gains included in financial income.

A permanent difference also occurs in the case of a recovery in the current year included in financial income but not in taxable income because of a recovery exclusion derived from a prior year.

Treatment of Permanent Differences in Financial Reporting

Permanent differences do not occasion a reporting problem. The tax expense identified with financial income is the actual tax, which, of course, has either been reduced or increased by the impact of the permanent differences. Thus, if pretax financial net income of $1,300,000 includes $100,000 of tax-exempt income, the actual tax at 50 percent on $1,200,000 is $600,000, and such amount is reflected as the tax expense applicable to the net income of $1,300,000. Similarly, if the $1,300,000 pretax financial net income were net of an unfavorable permanent difference of $100,000, a tax expense of $700,000 ($1,400,000 × 50 percent) would offset the net income of $1,300,000.

Treatment of Timing Differences in Financial Reporting

Timing differences are far more common than permanent differences. The numerous examples of differences in tax accounting and financial accounting listed early in the chapter are largely timing differences. These differences represent either (1) current tax savings to be paid for later or (2) current tax payments to be saved later. The first category of differences is predominant in that corporate taxpayers employ those tax reporting methods which will defer tax and thereby provide liquidity to the corporation. The installment and completed contract methods and accelerated depreciation are prime examples of this category.

The second category is relatively rare and arises only if (*a*) the situation is beyond the control of the taxpayer or (*b*) the current tax payable is invoked by the taxpayer for the reason that it is less than the present value of the future tax benefit expected. An example of the first circumstance is a write-down of a Lifo inventory close-out from cost to lower market for financial accounting purposes, which is not recognized for tax purposes until the following fiscal year of sale of the merchandise. An example of the second circumstance is the current reporting of a full capital gain taxable at 30 percent on an involuntary conversion of property with a commensurate additional amount of future depreciation providing tax benefit at 48 percent of the taxable gain included in the basis. The alternative, through election, is to avoid reporting the gain and utilizing a corresponding smaller tax basis for future depreciation.

Timing differences which save tax in the current year require inclusion of the deferred tax in current tax expense. The savings in tax is in recognition of the fact that current taxable income is less than pretax financial income. On the income statement, the tax expense which is offset against the higher pretax financial income is the sum of the current tax per return plus the deferred tax. The current tax per return contributes to the current liability federal income tax payable, and the deferred tax is shown on the balance sheet under liabilities as a deferred tax credit. The entry involved (1) achieves a matching of tax expense in relation to the financial income shown on the income statement and (2) establishes a deferred tax credit for the amount of tax to be equalized over time. In the future time period that the current tax savings becomes payable either in part or in whole, the deferred tax credit is converted into a current liability.

The item of accelerated depreciation is an excellent example of a deferred tax credit. Assuming pretax financial income of $1 million and taxable income to be the same, except for a $40,000 excess of accelerated depreciation for tax purpose over straight line depreciation for financial accounting purposes, the analysis is as follows:

	Tax Reporting	*Financial Reporting*
Pretax Income	$960,000	$1,000,000
Tax at 50 percent	480,000	500,000
Tax expense (expense increase) offset by:		500,000
Tax payable—current (liability increase)		480,000
Deferred tax credit (liability increase)		20,000

Timing differences exemplified by a payment of tax currently and a commensurate tax savings later require exclusion of the prepaid tax from current tax expense. The prepaid tax payment, termed a *deferred tax charge*, results from the fact that current taxable income is greater than current pretax financial income. The income statement matches against the lower pretax financial income a tax expense amount which is the current tax per return shown as an expense less the prepaid tax shown as an asset. The current tax per return plus the prepaid tax measure the current liability federal income tax payable. This treatment, like that for deferred tax credits, reflects a tax expense commensurate with the financial income shown on the income statement and sets up a deferred tax charge as an asset for the amount to be equalized in the future. At the future time that the current tax payment is saved, either in part or in whole, the deferred tax charge serves to reduce the tax otherwise payable.

As an example of a deferred tax charge, assume prefinancial income of $800,000 after a $50,000 reduction of inventory from Lifo cost to a lower market value in recognition of a current year's decision for the sale of discontinued merchandise in the early part of the next period at a $50,000 loss. Assume a taxable income of $850,000, or the same amount as the financial income except for the inventory loss of $50,000, which is recognized for tax purposes in the following year of sale. The analysis is as follows:

	Tax Reporting	*Financial Reporting*
Pretax Income	$850,000	$800,000
Tax at 50 percent	425,000	400,000
Tax expense (expense increase)		400,000
Deferred tax charge (asset increase)		25,000
offset by:		
Tax payable—current (liability increase)		425,000

Assuming in the next period the same pretax financial income of $850,000 (before the inventory loss) and taxable income of $800,000 after reduction for the inventory loss, the following analysis applies:

	Tax Reporting	*Financial Reporting*
Pretax Income	$800,000	$850,000
Tax at 50 percent	400,000	425,000
Tax expense (expense increase)		425,000
offset by:		
Deferred tax charge (asset decrease)		25,000
Tax payable—current (liability increase)		400,000

The process of setting up deferred tax charges and deferred tax credits in order to normalize or equalize the tax expense due to timing differences is referred to as *interperiod tax allocation.* The taking into account of these timing differences, irrespective of how soon or how distant in time equalization is effected, is known as *comprehensive allocation.* An alternative procedure of restricting the recognition of timing differences to situations in which equalization is definite to occur in a relatively few future fiscal periods is known as *partial allocation.* This second approach is not acceptable. The proponents of the accepted practice of interperiod tax allocation argue that equalization does take place within a relatively short time, but new elements arise which result in new deferments in the same or larger degree to offset the equalization with respect to older elements. Thus, collections of earlier installment sales cause new deferred tax credits to replace the old. Similarly, as tax depreciation under an accelerated method declines below financial depreciation under the straight line method and the deferred tax credit previously set up becomes payable, new property continually being acquired entails new accelerated depreciation for tax purposes which may prove higher than the corresponding straight line amount used in financial accounting, so that a new deferred tax credit takes the place of the old maturing amount. This recurring process of new amounts taking the place of the old, so that in a sense the old still persists, is known as *rollover.*

Timing differences occur under the equity method used by an investor corporation to carry investments in the voting stock of other corporations owned (*a*) 20 percent to 49 percent (minority investee company), (*b*) 50 percent (associated company), and (*c*) 51 percent or more (subsidiary company). Under the equity method, earnings and losses of the investee company are reflected by the investor corporation to the extent of the percentage of stock owned in the company. Inasmuch as the investor and the investee corporations are separate legal entities, the earnings and losses recorded do not occasion a tax impact until dividends are declared or the stock of the investee company is sold. Accordingly, deferred tax charges and credits are set up currently for the estimated future tax on dividends or on capital gains. Thus, for a subsidiary less than 80 percent owned, a federal dividend tax of 7.2 percent applies to dividends remitted from earnings. As another example, if an investor corporation plans to sell the stock of a minority investee company, recorded current earnings signify a future capital gain tax at the time of stock sale. Policies and plans of both the investor and investee corporations must be studied, and if supported by the evidence, provision must be made currently for deferred taxes. In certain cases, there will be no future taxes. For example, there is no dividend tax in the case of a subsidiary at least 80 percent owned with respect to dividends received in taxable years after 1974. Also, no future tax will be incurred if the intent is to merge the subsidiary into the parent company, for the reason that Section 332 of the Internal Revenue Code provides for a nonrecognition of gain or loss on the complete liquidation of a subsidiary.

Measurement of Deferred Taxes Attributable to Timing Differences

The rate of tax employed for the purpose of measuring deferred tax credits and charges is the rate at the top tax bracket for the current period in which the timing difference originates. Such rate is the 48 percent federal tax rate plus the applicable state tax rates, with the latter rates being adjusted for the federal tax savings resulting from the deduction of the state taxes for federal income tax purposes. APB Opinion No. 11, "Accounting for Income Taxes," terms this approach of using current tax rates as the *deferred method.* The current rates used remain unadjusted for subsequent changes in tax rates or for the imposition of new taxes. At the future date of equalization, any difference between the rate then prevailing and the prior rates employed is taken into income in the period in which realized and is not treated as a prior-period adjustment.

The amounts resulting from the use of current tax rates are not adjusted to a present value basis, despite the time lapse between the periods of origin and equalization of the deferred tax amounts. The deferred taxes are unlike contractual debts in that maturity dates are unknown and the tax amounts eventually payable or saved are vague estimates affected by future tax rates and uncertain economic factors. Rejection of present value theory avoids the problems inherent in the selection of a discount rate or series of discount rates for the long periods of equalization involved. In the case of tax deferment of indefinite duration, a present value amount would be nominal, and would tend to nullify the entire procedure of tax allocation. Thus, a deferred tax credit of $10 million due 40 years hence and discounted at 8 percent has a present value of only five cents per dollar, or $500,000.

Classification of Deferred Tax Credits and Charges on Statement of Financial Position

The position of deferred tax credits and charges on the balance sheet is determined by the classification of the related asset or liability item creating the deferred tax. This dictum is based on the precept of comparability of elements on financial statements generally. As an example, installment accounts receivable are a current asset. Since the receivable includes the gross profit not yet reported for tax purposes under the installment method, the deferred tax credit applicable to the gross profit included in the receivable is a current liability. As a second example, the

TABLE 1

Timing Differences

	1972	*1971*	*1970*	*1969*
Reasons for:				
Depreciation	439	381	366	335
Installment sales	68	59	54	54
Deferred expenses	56	54	57	101
Unremitted earnings	56	11	N/C	N/C
Deferred income	36	29	38	31
Pensions	30	27	27	26
Other employee benefits	44	32	32	N/C
Discontinued operations	30	12	N/C	N/C
Research and development	20	21	19	N/C
Long-term contracts	16	15	N/C	N/C
Inventory pricing	15	9	7	12
Warranties and guaranties	12	10	N/C	N/C
Preoperating expenses	11	13	N/C	N/C
Other estimated expenses	47	45	60	57
Total Disclosures	880	718	660	616
Number of companies:				
Reasons disclosed	461	428	410	385
Reasons not disclosed	92	102	111	135
No timing differences disclosed	47	70	79	80
Total	600	600	600	600
Tax effects:				
Disclosed within income statement	188	192	197	200
Disclosed in notes to financial statements	269	242	204	193
Disclosed elsewhere	44	54	51	25
Subtotal	501	488	452	418
Not disclosed	52	42	69	102
No indication of timing differences	47	70	79	80
Total Companies	600	600	600	600

N/C—Not compiled.

deferred tax credit resulting from the use of accelerated depreciation is a noncurrent liability because it relates to real estate or equipment classified as a noncurrent asset. Similarly, the deferred tax credit arising by reason of the use of the equity method of recording stock investments in corporations at least 20 percent owned is a noncurrent liability because the investment is a noncurrent asset. As a final example, the deferred tax charge occasioned by a write-down of Lifo inventory not recognized for tax purposes is a current asset because the inventory item creating the deferred tax charge is a current asset.

The classification of the deferred tax is controlled by the facts peculiar to the situation. Thus, if a deferred tax through logical association should be classified as a noncurrent liability or noncurrent asset, but the expectation and evidence points to an equalization in the next fiscal year or over the prevailing operating cycle, the deferred tax is shown in the current section of the balance sheet.

Disclosures of Current and Deferred Taxes in Stockholders' Reports

The American Institute of Certified Public Accountants' seventh annual cumulative survey of the annual reports of 600 industrial and commercial corporations, summarized in the publication *Accounting Trends and Techniques,* discloses that most corporations furnish both the amount and reason for major timing differences. Table 1 (given above) from the Survey summarizes the findings with respect to timing differences.

Examples of Income Tax Reporting

Comprehensive disclosures of the various aspects of income tax reporting are seen in the annual reports of Admiral Corporation, Anheuser-Busch, Incorporated, Foote Mineral Company, and Curtiss-Wright Corporation. The tabular presentations of Maryland Cup Corporation, Marcor Inc. and Broadway Glass Company, Inc. are also informative. The pertinent excerpts from such reports are given below.

*****

ADMIRAL CORPORATION (DEC)

Income before items show below	$22,421,000
Provision for inome taxes:	
Currently payable, principally foreign	6,682,000
Provision in lieu of U.S. taxes	4,183,000
Deferred—U.S. and foreign	(241,000)
	10,624,000
Income before minority interests and extraordinary items	$11,797,000

Summary of Accounting Policies

Income Taxes charged to operations are provided at appropriate rates for the countries in which the income is earned. In addition, commencing in 1972, provision has been made for the incremental U.S. income taxes which would be payable upon distribution of those earnings of the subsidiary in Taiwan which the Company does not intend to continue to invest in less developed foreign country operations. The incremental U.S. income taxes which would be payable upon distribution of the unremitted earnings of all other foreign subsidiaries would be substantially offset by foreign tax credits; accordingly no additional provision is made. Utilizations of U.S. net operating loss carryovers are reflected as extraordinary credits to income.

Income Taxes Allocable to Future Years arise principally from timing differences related to provisions for product and service warranties recorded in the financial statements, but not yet deductible for income tax purposes, partially reduced, in years prior to 1971, by an excess of depreciation claimed for tax purposes over depreciation recorded in the financial statements.

Investment Tax Credits which the Company is able to apply against its current income tax liability are recorded as a reduction of the current provision for income taxes under the flow-through method of accounting.

Financial Review

U.S. Income Taxes are not payable, principally because of utilization of a net operating loss carryover from 1970. The total loss carryover available for U.S. income tax purposes was utilized in 1972, including $4,400,000 of foreign taxes paid or deemed paid in 1969 which the Company presently intends to claim as reductions of taxable income by amending its U.S. tax return for that year. A final decision on whether to so amend the 1969 return does not have to be made before 1974.

At December 31, 1972, there are loss carryovers of approximately $11,100,000 arising from timing differences for which the related tax benefits have not been recognized in the financial statements. These timing differences relate principally to estimated losses on disposition of properties, accrued pension costs and depreciation recorded in the financial statements, but not yet deducted for tax purposes.

There are, at December 31, 1972, foreign tax credit carryovers of approximately $1,240,000 (reflecting the proposed amendment to the 1969 federal income tax return) and investment tax credit carryovers of approximately $140,000. The foreign tax credits expire as to $580,000 in 1975 and $660,000 in 1976; investment tax credits expire as to $33,000 in 1976, $42,000 in 1978 and $65,000 in 1979.

U.S. income taxes have not been provided on $36,525,000 of undistributed earnings of foreign subsidiaries included in consolidated retained earnings at December 31, 1972. If such undistributed earnings, other than $5,710,000 of the subsidiary in Taiwan, were to be distributed or otherwise become subject to U.S. income taxes for reasons not presently contemplated, available credits would substantially reduce the taxes otherwise payable.

The subsidiary in Taiwan has received certain exemptions from normal Taiwan income taxes on its operations, which expire at varying dates to 1975. Without these exemptions, provisions for income taxes would have been greater by approximately $334,000 ($.06 per share) in 1972 and $375,000 ($.07 per share) in 1971.

*****

ANHEUSER-BUSH, INCORPORATED (DEC)

	($ thousands)	
	1972	*1971*
Income before Income Taxes and Extraordinary Item	$146,887	$136,050
Provision for Income Taxes (Note 8):		
Current	62,305	56,870
Deferred	8,182	7,542
	70,487	64,412

Summary of Accounting Principles and Policies

Income Taxes. The provision for income taxes is based on elements of income and expense as reported in the Statement of Income. The Company has elected to utilize certain provisions of federal income tax laws and regulations to reduce current taxes payable, the primary item being the calculation of depreciation for tax purposes on the basis of shorter lives permitted by the Treasury Department. The resulting tax benefit has been deferred and will be recognized in the provision for income taxes at such time as depreciation reported in the Statement of Income exceeds that taken for income tax purposes.

The Company follows the practice of adding the investment tax credit to income over the productive lives of the assets generating such credit, rather than in the year in which the assets are placed in service. Accordingly, benefits realized from the investment tax credit have been deferred and will be recognized as reductions in the provisions for income taxes in the appropriate years.

Notes to Consolidated Financial Statements

Note 8: Income Taxes. The provision for income taxes on income before income taxes and extraordinary item for the years ended December 31, 1972 and 1971, includes the following:

	(*$ thousands*)	
	1972	*1971*
Current Tax Provision:		
Federal income taxes	$57,547	$53,289
Other income taxes	4,758	3,581
	62,305	56,870
Deferred Tax Provision:		
Investment tax credit		
Reduction in current taxes payable	1,869	2,377
Less amortization of deferred investment tax credit	(1,775)	(1,644)
Charge equivalent to reduction in taxes due to investment tax credit	94	713
Deferred income taxes, primarily from the calculation of depreciation for tax purposes on the basis of guideline and class life rates permitted by the Treasury Department	8,088	6,829
	8,182	7,542
	$70,487	$64,412

The $70,487,000 provision for income taxes in 1972 is before giving effect to the income tax reduction of $4,006,000 ($3,271,000 current; $735,000 deferred) resulting from the loss on the discontinued Houston Busch Gardens operation.

The Internal Revenue Service has examined and substantially cleared federal income tax returns of the Company for years through 1969.

* * * * *

FOOTE MINERAL COMPANY (DEC)

Consolidated Balance Sheets	1972	1971
Assets:		
Total current assets	$50,597,588	$54,956,370
Deferred income taxes (notes 1 and 5)	1,229,466	—
Liabilities and Stockholders Equity		
Total current liabilities	$19,221,896	$20,897,366
Deferred income taxes (notes 1 and 5)	—	5,714,711
Statements of Consolidated Operations		
Federal and State Income Tax Provision (Recovery) (Notes 1 and 5):		
Current	$ (252,000)	$ 1,484,000
Deferred	(75,000)	249,000
Investment credit	(49,000)	(49,000)
	$ (376,000)	$ 1,684,000

Notes to Financial Statements

Note 1 (in part): Income taxes. The Company has deferred to future periods the income tax effect resulting from timing differences between financial statement pretax income and taxable income. The deferred tax pertains principally to depreciable plant and equipment, start-up costs of new plant and extended vacation benefits not currently tax deductible. The investment tax credit, to the extent allowable, is applied as a reduction of the provision for income taxes. The Company is amortizing credits deferred prior to 1967 over the estimated lives of the related assets.

Note (5): Income Taxes. Recovery of Federal Income taxes consists of the following:

	1972	1971
Carryback of net operating loss to 1969	$465,000	—
Overpayment of estimated income taxes	140,000	230,000
Utilization of investment credit carryover	—	445,000
	$605,000	675,000

The tax effect of noncurrent timing differences is included in deferred income taxes on the balance sheet as shown below:

	1972	1971
Deferred taxes payable in future years relating principally to accelerated depreciation and capitalized start-up costs	$ 5,639,711	5,714,711
Tax effect of costs and losses relating to discontinuance of operations recorded in the financial statements not yet deductible for tax purposes	(4,492,000)	—
Elimination of deferred taxes no longer required—provided in prior years on facilities to be discontinued	(1,777,000)	—
Reclassification of certain Federal income tax benefits	(600,177)	—
	$(1,229,466)	5,714,711

The provision for (recovery of) Federal and State income taxes does not bear the customary relationship to earnings before income taxes because of a permanent difference between book and tax income representing percentage depletion allowances.

Deferred investment credits relating to periods prior to 1967 are being amortized in annual amounts of $49,000. The unamortized portion of the deferred investment credit at December 31, 1972 will be amortized during 1973 and 1974.

*****

CURTIS-WRIGHT CORPORATION (DEC)

	($ thousands)	
	1972	*1971*
Earnings from continuing operations before federal and foreign income taxes	$7,546	$7,524
Provision for federal and foreign income taxes (see Note 4)	3,149	4,150
Earnings from continuing operations	$4,397	$3,374

Note 4: Federal and Foreign Income Taxes. The components of the provisions for federal and foreign income taxes applicable to continuing operations are as follows:

	($ thousands)	
	1972	*1971*
Provision (credit) for current federal income taxes	$1,343	$ (479)
Investment tax credit recapture (credit)	276	(188)
Federal income taxes currently payable (recoverabe)	1,619	(667)
Provision (credit) for deferred federal income taxes	(861)	2,000
Provision for foreign income taxes	3,602	2,817
Reversal of provision for federal income taxes no longer required	(1,211)	—
Total provision for federal and foreign income taxes	$3,149	$4,150

Deferred federal income taxes have been provided (credited) in recognition of timing differences in reporting various items of income and expense in the Corporation's financial statements as compared to the Corporation's tax returns.

The net tax effects of these timing differences have been reflected in the accompanying balance sheets as deferred taxes of $807,000 included in federal and foreign income taxes at December 31, 1972 and $507,000 included in federal income taxes recoverable at December 31, 1971 and noncurrent deferred taxes in both years.

In prior years, the Corporation's liability for federal income taxes included a provision estimated on the basis of applicable statutes and government regulations then in effect. As a result of a recent Internal Revenue Service examination, a portion of such provision is no longer required and accordingly $1,211,000 has been credited to income in 1972. Federal income tax returns of the Corporation have been examined by the Internal Revenue Service through 1971.

The consolidated tax provision does not include additional income taxes that might result from receipt of dividends paid out of undistributed earnings of Dorr-Oliver's foreign subsidiaries and a Domestic International Sales Corporation to the extent that it is intended to reinvest such earnings. Undistributed earnings upon which income taxes have not been accrued amounted to approximately $4,000,000 at December 31, 1972.

The rate used in computing the provision for federal income tax varies from the statutory tax rate (48%) principally due to the reversal of provision for income taxes no longer required, favorable tax treatment afforded Domestic International Sales Corportions and capital gains, investment credits, tax exempt interest and equity in net loss of an affiliated company (which has no tax effect).

*****

MARYLAND CUP CORPORATION (SEP)

Consolidated Statement of Financial Position

	1972	*1971*
Long-term liabilities	$46,169,543	$57,262,980
Deferred income taxes (Note 5)	9,292,000	9,171,028
Consolidated Statement of Operations		
Provision for federal and state taxes on income (Note 5)	8,323,654	5,932,867

Note 5: Income Taxes.

	(*$ thousands*)	
	1972	*1971*
Provision for federal and state income taxes:		
Currently payable	$8,202	$5,562
Deferred	12	370
	$8,323	$5,932

A summary of income taxes deferred to future years follows:

	Balance October 1, 1971	*Provision*	*Balance Sept 30, 1972*
Tax effect of excess of tax over book depreciation	$6,956	$250	$7,206
Tax effect of unfunded pension costs	(173)	(198)	(371)
Tax effect of gain on repurchase of 5.8% sinking fund debentures		52	52
Investment credit	2,388	17	2,405
	$9,171	$121	$9,292

The provision for deferred investment credit represents 1972 investment credit of $515,364 less $498,361 amortization of prior years.

*****

MARCOR INC. (JAN)

	1973	*1972*
Earnings before taxes on income	$132,052,000	$101,035,000
Provision for taxes on income	59,380,000	43,523,000
Net Earnings	$ 72,672,000	$ 57,512,000

Financial Information

Reconciliation of Effective Rates to Statutory Federal (48%) Rate	*1972 Amount (thousands)*	*1972 Effective Rate (%)*	*1971 Amount (thousands)*	*1971 Effective Rate (%)*
At statutory (48%) rate	$63,385	48.0	$48,497	48.0
Investment tax credit	(4,741)	(3.6)	(4,772)	(4.7)
Lower tax rates on foreign operations	(931)	(.7)	(831)	(.8)
State taxes on income less applicable federal taxes	2,256	1.7	909	.9
All other—net	(589)	(.4)	(280)	(.3)
Provision for Taxes on Income	$59,380	45.0	$43,523	43.1

Provision for Taxes on Income	*1972 (thousands)*	*1971 (thousands)*	*Percent Increase*
Current and Deferred Taxes			
Federal and overseas taxes on income:			
Currently payable	$13,510	$12,679	6.6
Deferred	41,530	29,095	42.7
	$55,040	$41,774	31.8
State income taxes (principally current)	4,340	1,749	148.1
Total	$59,380	$43,523	36.4

*****

BROCKWAY GLASS COMPANY, INC. (DEC)

Consolidated Balance Sheet

	1972	*1971*
Long-term debt, less current maturities	$28,818,500	$22,131,500
Deferred income taxes—net (Note 4)	6,767,244	5,935,040
Consolidated Statement of Income		
Income before income taxes	$27,983,876	$26,726,308
Provision for income taxes (Note 2)	13,407,400	13,385,530
Net Income	$14,576,476	$13,340,778

Note 2: Income Taxes. The provision for income taxes shown on the consolidated statement of income is as follows:

	1972	*1971*
Computed tax	$14,209,100	$13,555,100
Less: Investment tax credit	801,700	169,570
Tax provision	13,407,400	13,385,530
Tax effect of current timing differences reflected in deferred income taxes	832,204	1,009,402
Portion estimated payable	$12,575,196	$12,376,128

No provision is made for additional taxes which might be payable if undistributed earnings of the consolidated subsidiaries were paid as dividends to the parent company inasmuch as such earnings have been and will be reinvested in the businesses. At December 31, 1972, undistributed earnings of consolidated subsidiaries totaled $2,524,000.

Note 4: Deferred Income Taxes—Net. The Company uses deferred tax accounting for all material areas of divergence between book and tax income. The deferred income taxes shown on the consolidated balance sheet consist of the following:

	1972	*1971*
Deferred income taxes which will be payable in future years when annual depreciation for tax purposes is less than the straight-line depreciation provided in the financial statements	$7,782,616	$6,621,676
Tax effect of costs and losses recorded in the financial statements not yet deductible for tax purposes	(1,015,372)	(686,636)
Totals	$6,767,244	$5,935,040

Effect of Method of Accounting for Taxes on Reported Earnings

The reconciling of taxable income with financial income for timing differences and the setting up of related deferred tax credits and deferred charges, serve to smooth the reporting of aftertax net income. The deferred tax amounts serve to create a tax expense or tax savings commensurable with and proportional to the related taxable income or loss for the year.

As an example, the Dow Chemical Company shows a provision for income taxes for the years 1972 and 1971, explained by footnote as follows:

	($ millions)	
	1972	*1971*
Current provision	$130.5	90.3
Investment credits	11.3	5.0
Taxes currently payable	$119.2	85.3
Tax effects of timing differences	7.9	5.7
Taxes on Income	$127.1	91.0

The investment credits are treated above under the flow-through method.

As another example, the Bendix Corporation, which amortizes the investment credit over the estimated useful lives of the related assets, summarizes its provision for taxes in the following footnote:

	($ millions)	
	1972	*1971*
Provision:		
Current	$56.3	$30.7
Deferred	(3.7)	2.9
Deferred investment credit	0.7	(0.8)
Total	53.3	32.8
Deferred Investment Credit:		
Balance at beginning of year	4.1	4.9
Investment credit:		
Earned	1.7	
Amortized	(1.0)	(0.8)
Total	0.7	(0.8)
Balance at end of year	$ 4.8	$ 4.1

The foregoing tabulation reveals the following:

1. The deferred tax credit declined in 1972 by $3.7 million indicating that amounts previously deferred have matured and are currently payable.

2. The investment credits originating in the year exceeded by $0.7 million the amount treated as a reduction of the income tax for the year through amortization of prior and current investment credits. The relative amounts are $1.7 million of credits originating in the year and $1.0 million amortized and credited to the year.

That permanent differences distort the usual relationship of the income tax provision to financial income is seen in a portion of the note to the 1972 and 1971 financial statements of Foote Mineral Company, cited previously: "The provision for (recovery of) Federal and State income taxes does not bear the customary relationship to earnings before income taxes because of a permanent difference between book and tax income representing percentage depletion allowances."

The treatment of the investment tax credit under the flow-through method may upset the normal relationship of income taxes to financial income. The method requires a reduction in income tax expense for the year that the asset is placed into service, and therefore automatically serves to reduce the percentage of income tax to pretax financial income. In a year of inordinately high purchases of personal property, the income tax percentage may prove to be unusually low. Thus, if pretax income is $1 million, entailing a combined federal and state tax of $500,000, and purchases of new personal property placed into service are $3 million, the investment credit based on a life of seven years at 7 percent is tentatively $210,000 which then becomes limited by statute to 100 percent of the first $25,000 portion of tax plus 50 percent of the remaining balance of $185,000 or a total usable credit for the year of $117,500. The net tax under the flow-through method is therefore $382,500, or 38.25 percent of pretax financial income. If the purchases of personal property had been only $1 million, the tentative investment tax credit of $70,000 would be adjusted to $47,500 and the net tax would be $452,500, or 45.25 percent of the pretax financial income. The credits unusable for the year would be available, of course, for carry-back three years and for carry-forward five years.

Treatment of the investment credit under the deferral method, whereby the credit is spread over the life of the asset, reduces the impact of irregular or fluctuating annual amounts of investment credit on the provision for income tax, and therefore results in a smoother, more stable relationship of income tax and aftertax financial income to pretax financial income. Such treatment, however, while satisfactory for purposes of analysis of a particular company over time, destroys the comparability of data among companies, since the lives creating the tax credit and employed for purposes of amortization are unknown.

Modification of Financial Statement Practices for Purposes of Financial Analysis

The typical income tax disclosures in annual stockholders' reports must be further probed into, dissected, expanded, and rearranged for more effective association with related data.

Financial analysis requires uniform treatment and methodology of data among companies under comparison. Comparability between companies and consistency in approach and treatment over time are essential. Toward this end, two items should be modified for meaningful analysis: (1) the investment credit and (2) Lifo inventories.

Conversion of Deferral Method to Flow-Through Method—Investment Credit

Regarding the investment credit, it is recommended that the deferral method be converted to the flow-through method. In this way the effect of the investment credit on the income tax provision for the year can be established and the income tax item adjusted for meaningful correlation with other elements.

To illustrate, companies using the deferral method with respect to the investment tax credit show in their annual reports the entire content of the deferred investment credit account for the year. In short, shown are the opening balance, the investment credit originating for the year, the amortization amount reducing the tax expense for the year, and the ending balance. To convert the income tax expense to the flow-through method, the amortization should be superseded by, and therefore adjusted to, the credit originating in the year. Also, from a balance sheet standpoint, the opening balance in the deferred investment credit should be treated as additional Retained Earnings. After these adjustments are made, the modified income tax provision can be increased by the investment credit for the year to arrive at an income tax expense before investment credit to compare with the comparable tax provisions (before investment credits) of other companies under study and comparison.

To illustrate the procedure, the data of Maryland Cup Corporation will be used. The income tax provision for 1972 of $8,323,000 is after reduction of $498,000 for amortization of the investment credit under the deferral method. Using the investment credit originating in 1972 of $515,000 as the measure of reduction of federal income tax expense under the flow-through method, the revised tax expense is $8,306,000, and the tax provision before investment credit and before other possible adjustments is $8,821,000 ($8,306,000 + $515,000). Simultaneously, the Deferred Income Taxes balances at December 31, 1971, and December 31, 1972, are eliminated, and the Retained Earnings at December 31, 1971, will be increased $2,388,000.

Modification of Data for Inventories at Lifo Cost

Companies using the Lifo cost method of valuing inventories generally disclose, by footnote, the related current cost value (invariably higher) measured by Fifo cost, average cost, or current replacement. The disclosures are deficient in that they fail to state the deferred income tax on the excess of the higher alternative current cost over Lifo cost. To adjust financial net income from Lifo to the alternative cost method, the procedure involves four steps:

1. Modify the cost of goods sold by the differences in the alternative amounts of inventories in relation to Lifo cost as at the beginning and end of the current period. Assuming the alternative amounts are higher for each of the two dates, the excess as at the earlier date is offset against the excess as at the later date, and the difference will measure the effect on the cost of goods sold; if the second excess is the greater, the difference decreases the cost of goods sold. These effects are mandated by the fact that beginning inventories increase, and ending inventories decrease, the cost of goods sold.

2. Modify the income tax provision commensurably by multiplying the change in cost of goods sold by the prevailing tax rate, say 50 percent.

3. Introduce into the balance sheet deferred tax amounts as at the beginning and end of the period equal to 50 percent of the excess of each alternative amount over Lifo cost.

4. Increase Retained Earnings as at the beginning and as at the end of the period by the excess of the inventory amount at the alternative amount over Lifo cost reduced by the related tax of, say, 50 percent as at each date.

The annual report of Koehring Company as at November 30, 1972, is an exception to the general indictment of inadequate disclosure. Its presentation on inventories appears below.

KOEHRING COMPANY (NOV)

	($ *thousands*)
Current Assets:	
Inventories: at current cost (approximates first-in, first-out method)	$120,295
Less allowance to reduce domestic inventories to cost on the last-in, first-out method	(28,052)
	92,243

Notes to Financial Statements

Note (5): *Lifo Inventories and Cost of Products Sold.* As explained in "Statement of Accounting Practices," the Company uses the last-in, first-out (LIFO) method for determining the cost of domestic inventories.

If the Lifo method had not been adopted:

(a) The reported net earnings for 1972 and 1971 would have been higher by approximately $925,000 ($.32 a share) and $2,060,000 ($.71 a share), respectively;

(b) Domestic inventories as of November 30, 1972, would have been $93,496,000 instead of $65,444,000, or $28,052,000 greater;

(c) Earnings retained in the business at November 30, 1972, would have been increased by approximately $14,025,000; and

(d) Additional Federal income taxes of approximately $14,000,000 would have been paid or accrued from 1957 to 1972, inclusive.

Statement of Accounting Practices

Inventories. Domestic inventories are stated on the basis of the last-in, first-out (Lifo) method of inventory accounting adopted in 1956. Under the Lifo method the procedure has been to charge higher costs to cost of products sold than would be the case under the first-in, first-out (Fifo) method while deferring relatively lower costs in inventory, thereby reducing earnings and inventories both for financial reporting and income tax purposes. International inventories are stated at costs which approximate the first-in, first-out (Fifo) basis.

The presentation is complete except for nondisclosure of the inventory amounts at November 30, 1971. The missing inventory amounts as of November 30, 1971, would be obtained, of course, from the annual report of that date. The difference between the November 30, 1971, and November 30, 1972, inventories can be established by reference to the fact that the reported net earnings, i.e., aftertax financial income, for 1972 would have been $925,000 higher. The data would therefore appear as follows (in thousands):

	November 30, 1972	*November 30, 1971*	*Effect on 1972 Net Earnings*
Inventories:			
At current cost	$120,295	?	?
At Lifo cost	92,243	?	?
Excess of current cost over Lifo cost	$ 28,052	$26,200	$1,852
Related cumulative tax at 50 percent	14,027	13,100	927
Net Increase in Cumulative Earnings	$ 14,025	$13,100	$ 925

Since the excess of current cost over Lifo cost at November 30, 1972, exceeds that as at November 30, 1971, cost of goods sold for the year ended November 30, 1972, is reduced $1,852 thereby increasing pre-tax income correspondingly and increasing the income tax provision at 50 percent or $927, so that net earnings for the year would have been $925 higher. The excess of current cost over Lifo cost of the inventories as at November 30, 1972, entails a deferred tax of $14,027 (rounded out in the report to $14,000) or 50 percent of the excess. Retained Earnings would be $14,025 higher because of the increase in the inventories asset of $28,052, reduced by the related deferred tax of $14,027. If the balance sheet were to be adjusted to reflect the current cost of inventories, the inventories would be stated at $120,295, current liabilities would include a deferred tax credit of $14,027, current-year net earnings would be $925 higher, and retained earnings at November 30, 1971, would be $13,100 higher and at November 30, 1972, $14,025 higher. The classification of the deferred tax credit as a current liability follows from the fact that the related item causally responsible for the credit is a current asset, i.e., inventory.

Analysis of Operating Section of Income Statement

Under generally accepted accounting principles, the income tax provision applicable to the operating section of the income statement is stated as a single amount, with the exception of the tax relating to the operations of a discontinued major segment of the business. The Accounting Principles Board is Opinion No. 30, issued June 1973, is epochal in that it includes in the operating section the following items occurring after September 30, 1973, previously presented in the extraordinary items section of the income statement:

1. Write-down or write-off of receivables, inventories, equipment leased to others, deferred research and development costs, or other intangible assets.
2. Gains or losses from exchange or translation of foreign currencies, including those relating to major devaluations and revaluations.

3. Gains or losses on disposal of a segment of a business.
4. Other gains or losses from sale or abandonment of property, plant, or equipment used in the business.
5. Effects of a strike, including those against competitors and major suppliers.
6. Adjustment of accruals on long-term contracts.

Most of the foregoing items are unusal. For purposes of financial analysis income tax expense or savings should therefore be imputed to each category, despite the fact that generally accepted accounting principles require that the related tax effect be shown only for the third item listed.

It will be helpful if corporate reports beginning with the year 1973 will disclose, by footnote, the effect of each item on the tax expense for the period. In the absence of such disclosure, the analyst will assign tax expense or tax savings the approximate rate of 50 percent to items constituting ordinary income or deductions and the capital gain tax rate of 30 percent to net long-term capital gain. The residue of tax remaining after assignments of taxes to the unusual items will then be assumed to apply to the income or loss from usual, customary, or continuing business operations.

If the operating section of the income statement contains a permanent difference between book and taxable income, the analyst may take either of two approaches:

1. Isolate the permanent-difference item and adjust it to a gross level and assign to it the deferred tax amount that would apply if it had not been a permanent difference.

2. Isolate the permanent-difference item and treat the amount thereof as both gross and net, without imputation of tax.

Either procedure will insure a proper assignment of tax expense or tax savings to the other elements on the income statement, without adulteration by the fact that the permanent-difference item does not occasion a tax. If the permanent-difference item is an extraordinary item, only the second approach applies, since separate classification of the item as extraordinary will not becloud the assignment of tax charges and credits to the related items or item-groups.

The position of items on the income statement may have to be modified to permit proper correlation of the tax item with related income or loss. As an example, the minority interest share in subsidiary earnings is an aftertax income amount. If, as is occasionally the case, such share is deducted from pretax income on the consolidated income statement, it must be added back to pretax income so as not to distort the relationships between the income tax item separately shown and the pretax income. Thus, assuming a pretax income of $80 million, a minority interest share in subsidiary aftertax income of $10 million, and a 50 percent tax rate, the first presentation below must be revised to the second for purposes of analysis:

Presentation 1:

Pretax income (majority and minority interests)	$80,000,000
Minority interest share of subsidiary aftertax income	10,000,000
Pretax income, as adjusted	$70,000,000
Income tax	40,000,000
Aftertax income (consolidated)	$30,000,000

Presentation 2:

Pretax income (majority and minority interests)	$80,000,000
Income tax (on pretax income above)	40,000,000
Aftertax income (majority and minority interests)	$40,000,000
Minority interest share of subsidiary aftertax income	10,000,000
Aftertax income (consolidated)	$30,000,000

Where a subsidiary is not consolidated because of dissimilarity of operations or other reason, and the subsidiary's aftertax income is shown as a single amount (known as "one-line consolidation") under total income before reduction for expenses, the subsidiary aftertax income should be eliminated in correlating the remaining operations and the related income tax. As an example, assume that revenues exclusive of Subsidiary X diverse income are $100 million, related expenses are $70 million, and the resulting pretax income of $30 million entails a tax of $15 million. Subsidiary X pretax income is $20 million and aftertax income is $10 million. A common presentation of the above data follows:

Revenues other than of Subsidiary X	$100,000,000
Subsidiary X aftertax income	10,000,000
Total	$110,000,000
Expenses	70,000,000
Pretax income	$ 40,000,000
Income tax	15,000,000
Aftertax Income	$ 25,000,000

The modified presentation to satisfy the analyst's requirements follows:

	Other than Subsidiary X	*Subsidiary X*
Revenues	$100,000,000	
Expenses	70,000,000	
Pretax income	$ 30,000,000	$20,000,000
Income tax	15,000,000	10,000,000
Aftertax income	$ 15,000,000	$10,000,000

Relating of Taxes to Business Line Reporting

The disclosure in corporate reports of business line activity is becoming increasingly common and will probably be made mandatory by the Financial Accounting Standards Board, successor to the Accounting Principles Board. Business segment data are required to be included in Form 10K filed with the Securities and Exchange Commission.

TABLE 2

Presentation of Revenue Information

	1972	*1971*	*1970*	*1969*
Information presented:				
By product line	218	176	162	152
By division or subsidiary	140	144	139	117
Total foreign sales	115	139	116	103
Sales to government	33	44	53	61
Sales to particular industry or type of customer	45	29	54	58
By geographic areas	30	20	17	19
Total Presentations	581	552	541	510
Number of companies:				
Revenue information presented	382	358	335	319
Revenue information not presented	218	242	265	281
Total	600	600	600	600

The types of classification of revenue and income information by business lines contained in the 1972 reports of the 600 corporations embraced in *Accounting Trends and Techniques* are summarized in Tables 2 and 3 of the American Institute.

Illustrative presentations are shown here for Boise Cascade Corporation, American Standard, Inc., and The Williams Companies. As can be seen, the income tax provision is shown overall for the company and therefore for all business lines as a whole. The analyst may find it useful to impute the combined federal and state tax rate of 50 percent to 55 percent to the income or loss for the product line or other divisional classification and impute the same rate to interest and general corporate expenses in order to establish the tax reduction effected by these items.

TABLE 3

Presentation of Income Information

	1972	*1971*	*1970*	*1969*
Information presented:				
By product line	114	83	59	30
By division or subsidiary	98	88	70	53
Total foreign income	71	97	96	87
Income attributable to business with government, particular industry, or type of customer	19	13	17	12
By geographical areas	16	12	16	12
Subtotal	318	293	258	194
Separate financial statements or summaries for subsidiaries or groups of subsidiaries	68	65	79	65
Segment of reporting entity operating at a loss	28	14	55	50
Total Presentations	414	372	392	309
Number of companies:				
Income information presented	281	280	270	225
Income information not presented	319	320	330	375
Total	600	600	600	600

BOISE CASCADE CORPORATION (DEC)

Statement of Income by Businesses (expressed in thousands)

	Income by Businesses					Boise Cascade Corporation and Subsidiaries Consolidated	
	Wood Products Manufacturing and Sales	*Other Operations*	*Unconsolidated Joint Ventures*	*Total*	*Corporate Finance and Administration*	*Eliminations*	*Year Ended December 31, 1972*
Revenues							
Sales	$438,858	32,098	$ —	$1,370,474	$ —	$(219,574)*	$1,150,900
Interest and other income	2,175	376	(42)	16,207	63	—	16,270
	441,033	**32,474**	**(42)**	**1,386,681**	**63**	**(219,574***	**1,167,170**
Costs and expenses							
Cost of sales	347,473	22,827	—	1,088,697	1,044	(219,574)*	870,167
Depreciation and depletion	15,271	299	—	40,878	1,802	—	42,680
Selling and administrative expenses	16,128	15,001	—	121,049	22,430	—	143,479
Interest expense	—	—	—	—	36,244	—	36,244
	378,872	**38,127**	**—**	**1,250,624**	**61,520**	**(219,574)***	**1,092,570**
Operating income (loss)	$ 62,161	(5,653)	$(42)	$136,057	$(61,457)		74,600
Percentage of operating income	45.7%	(4.1)%	—	100%			
Income taxes							
Current							39,519
Deferred							(3,699)
Investment tax credit							(1,600)
							34,250
Income from continuing operations before extraordinary items							40,350
Loss from operations discontinued or to be discontinued							(15,960)
Income (loss) before extraordinary items							**24,390**
Extraordinary items							(195,000)
Net loss							**$ (170,610)**

Note: For presentation purposes Income by Businesses columns for building materials, paper manufacturing, packaging and office products, and Latin American operations have been omitted.

* Elimination of intercompany sales to cost of sales. Transfers between business are primarily at market price.

AMERICAN STANDARD INC. (DEC)

	Sales		*Income*	
	Amount	*Percent*	*Amount*	*Percent*
Building products	$ 649.1	49	$42.8	51
Transportation systems	264.2	20	18.2	21
Industrial and construction products	216.0	17	9.2	11
Security and graphic arts	189.7	14	15.9	19
Miscellaneous	1.6	—	(1.6)	(2)
Sales and product income	**$1,320.6**	**100**	**84.5**	**100**
Other income			8.0	
Interest expense			(27.6)	
Corporate			(9.7)	
Taxes on income			(27.6)	
Equity in net income (loss before extraordinary charge) of:				
Real estate subsidiary			(3.4)	
Finance subsidiary			1.0	
Income before extraordinary charges			**$25.2**	

Notes to Consolidated Financial Statements:

Distribution of sales and product income (1971 omitted for presentation purposes).

Sales and income may be distributed as follows (dollars in millions):

THE WILLIAMS COMPANIES (DEC)

Profit Center Earnings. In keeping with the trend toward more informative financial reports, the following summary of profit center operating data is presented. Such data is particularly appropriate and

	($ millions)			
	1972		*1971*	
	Revenues	*Operating Earnings*	*Revenues*	*Operating Earnings*
Agrico Chemical Company	$205.4	17.7	$ 50.5	$ 3.7
Williams Brothers Pipe Line Company	61.3	29.0	57.3	27.1
Williams International Group	82.1	12.0	72.7	10.7
Williams Energy Company	46.9	6.7	41.4	6.4
Edgcomb Steel Company	100.7	7.8	86.4	6.8
Valley Distributing Company	47.2	4.8	27.8	2.4
Pacific Merchandising Group	34.3	1.7	33.9	1.8
Colonial Insurance Company		2.4		2.0
The Resource Sciences Corporation (sold in 1971)			42.4	1.5
Investment Income		10.9		9.3
Totals	**$577.9**	**93.0**	**$412.4**	**71.7**
Corporate headquarters expense not assigned and other income and expenses, net		(1.9)		(1.5)
Interest and debt expense		(33.0)		(24.7)
Income taxes		(20.1)		(15.7)
Income before extraordinary Items		**$38.0**		**$29.8**

meaningful for a company as diversified as The Williams Companies.

Operating earnings by profit center are based upon directly identifiable revenues, operating costs and general and administrative expense and certain general and administrative expenses of corporate headquarters representing charges for services performed. In 1972, the method of allocating and charging corporate general and administrative expenses was modified to give more specific effect to revenue and earnings levels of individual profit centers resulting in generally higher allocations. Amounts for 1971 have been restated on a comparable basis with the method employed in 1972.

Profit Center Assets

Total assets of individual profit centers exclude funds used for short, interim and long-term investment purposes; such funds are included in investment income assets.

The results (percentages omitted) for American Standard, Inc., would be as follows:

	Sales	Product and Other Income (Pretax)	Tax	Product Income (Aftertax)
Sales and Product Income:				
Building products	649.1	42.80	21.40	21.40
Transportation systems	264.2	18.20	9.10	9.10
Industrial construction products	216.0	9.20	4.60	4.60
Security and graphic arts	189.7	15.90	7.95	7.95
Miscellaneous	1.6	(1.60)	(.80)	(.80)
Total	1,320.6	84.50	42.25	42.25
Other income		8.00	4.00	4.00
Total		92.50	46.25	46.25
Expenses:				
Interest		27.60	13.80	13.80
Other corporate expense		9.70	4.85	4.85
Total		37.30	18.65	18.65
Income, before extraordinary charges exclusive of real estate and finance subsidiary operations		55.20	27.60	27.60
Net loss—real estate subsidiary				(3.40)
Net income—finance subsidiary				1.00
Income before Extraordinary Charges				25.20

The process of tax imputation to foreign income presented as a separate divisional activity must take into account the possibility of a lack of tax on such income; and the tax, where it applies, is net of foreign tax credits.

Effects of Deferred Tax Credits and Charges on Financial Analysis

Deferred tax credits and charges have maturity dates which may fall serially or on a single date within (1) a short period of, say, five years or (2) a long period measured in decades and half centuries.

The first possibility is illustrated by a casual sale of realty or personalty in which the contract price, plus interest, is collected within a relatively short period, and the transaction is accounted for under the installment method for tax purposes and under the accrual method for financial accounting purposes. Under the tax method, the profit is taxed in the degree that the contract price is collected, whereas under the accrual method the full profit is reported in the year of sale.

The second possibility is by far the more common. Discussion earlier in the chapter pointed out that through rollover, new initiating events—whether they be product sales reported on the tax return under the installment method or purchases of equipment depreciated for tax purposes under an accelerated method—create deferred taxes with new future maturities offsetting the maturities falling due in the current year from earlier events.

In analyzing deferred taxes, therefore, the significant consideration is the extent to which the total deferment increases or decreases by individual time periods embraced in the future time span of significance to the analysis being made. In short, if the financial analysis stresses the next five years, the present magnitude of the deferred tax credit or tax charge is appreciably less important than the changes in such magnitude by individual years for a five-year period. If, for example, in an analysis of cash flow and working capital, the deferred tax credits are expected to increase annually, such increases constitute sources of cash, and also of working capital unless the deferred tax credit is of such a nature that it is classified as a current liability. Expected decreases in the deferred tax credits, on the other hand, signify required payments for maturing taxes, serving to reduce cash and also working capital if the deferred tax credit does not qualify as a current liability.

Where the deferred elements are of indefinite maturity, there is a basis from the standpoint of practical financial analysis of treating a deferred tax charge as a reduction of, and a deferred tax credit as an increase in, stockholders' equity, to the extent of amounts maturing outside the time span embraced in the analysis. As an example, in the construction field, bonding companies usually issue performance bonds up to 10 times the net quick assets, i.e., quick assets less current liabilities. Assuming that the financial statements are prepared on the percentage of completion method and the tax returns on the completed contract method, current liabilities include deferred tax credits applicable to the profits on uncompleted contracts. If projections indicate no significant reduction in the deferred tax credits over the next several years, the deferred tax credits can logically be either omitted from current liabilities or, alternatively, included therein at a substantially reduced amount. In this connection, it must be borne in mind that deferred tax amounts may, for purposes of financial analysis, be scaled down to present values, even though this procedure is not acceptable in preparing the financial statements. It may be pointed out, however, that the present value approach conforms to generally accepted accounting principles applicable to long-term receivables and payables and to acquisitions of property through installment financing in the legal guise of a lease.

Adjustment of stockholders' equity for deferred tax credits or charges will, of course, affect the ratios of debt and of net income to stockholders' equity. Generalizing any modification in amount or in classification of financial income—income tax provisions, deferred tax credits, and deferred tax charges—will affect analyses which focus on (1) changes in financial position generally and on working capital, net quick assets, quick assets, and cash in particular; (2) proportions of assets and liabilities to one another and to stockholders' equity; and (3) correlation of intermediate and net financial income amounts to assets and to stockholders' equity.

Disclosure Requirements of SEC Accounting Series Release No. 149

Financial analysis is aided considerably by greater disclosure of all data relevant to taxes. Toward this end, and in conformance with the views previously expressed in this section, SEC Accounting Series Release No. 149, issued in 1973, requires that the annual 10-K report filed with the Securities and Exchange Commission contains the following types of information:

1. The difference between the tax provision on the income statement and a tax computed by applying the statutory tax rate of 48 percent to the financial income. Such differences must be explained in detail for each item accountable for more than 5 percent of the 48 percent amount.
2. The composition of deferred taxes, with a specific description for items exceeding 15 percent of the deferred amount.
3. The expected excess amounts of actual income taxes payable over the income tax provision in any one of the succeeding three years.

The first requirement will disclose permanent differences as well as the timing differences for which deferred tax amounts are set up. Thus, if a permanent difference in the form of $100,000 nontaxable income is superimposed on taxable income of $1 million, the tax provision is shown as $480,000, or 48 percent of taxable income of $1 million. The annual filing with the SEC will require in this case a disclosure of the permanent difference, and the fact that a $48,000 tax would have been incurred had the $100,000 tax-exempt income item been taxable. The disclosure is required, since the $48,000 tax on the permanent difference item is greater than $26,400, or 5 percent of the $528,000 tax that would be expected at the statutory tax rate of 48 percent on the financial income of $1,100,000.

The second requirement has been complied with in the past in very general terms by footnote disclosures in annual stockholders' reports. Such disclosures will probably be more detailed in the future.

The third requirement recognizes the point previously expressed in the chapter, to the effect that the significant portions of the deferred tax amount are the expected changes therein in the relatively near future. Such changes measure the impact on the Cash account; a decrease in a deferred tax credit and an increase in a deferred tax charge signify a reduction in cash, whereas opposite changes indicate an increase in cash.

24

An Evaluation of Current Financial Reporting of the Financial Analysts Federation Corporate Information Subcommittee

ARTHUR K. CARLSON, Chairman
GLENELG P. CATERER, C.F.A., Coordinating Member
WILLIAM C. NORBY, C.F.A., Executive Director

THERE IS no rigid schedule of the components of a good reporting program. Nevertheless, 25 years of work of the Corporate Information Committee, branching in the later years into 23 industry subcommittees; cross-fertilized by the work of the Financial Accounting Policy Committee, the Financial Executives Institute, the accounting profession, and the SEC; and innumerable conferences with the reporting companies themselves have produced a body of criteria that can be assembled into a useful checklist.

Here is the outline of elements, reflecting the present stage of development in the committee's studies, which has been made available for the guidance of the individual subcommittees.

I. Annual Report.
   A. Letters to the stockholders.
      1. Review of year.
      2. Operating rates.
      3. Unit production, where applicable.
      4. Indexes of sales prices.
      5. Acquisitions and divestments; importance.
      6. Government business.
      7. Capital expenditures; program, start-up expenses.
      8. Research and development effort.
      9. Employment, costs, labor relations.
      10. Backlog, if appropriate.

11. New products.
12. Pollution abatement program; estimated cost.
13. Visual aids.
14. Outlook.

B. Officers and directors.
1. Age, background, responsibilities of officers; current photos of directors and principal officers.
2. Outside connections of directors.
3. Principal changes.

C. Financial.
1. Statement of accounting principles, including explanation of changes and their effects.
2. Divisional operations, including earnings.
3. Adjustment to EPS for dilution.
4. Foreign operations—revenues, earnings, markets.
5. Unconsolidated subsidiaries and affiliates.
6. Sources and applications of funds, comparative.
7. Tax accounting, including handling of ITC (Investment Tax Credit).
8. Treatment of nonrecurring items.
9. Year-end adjustments.
10. Restatement of quarterly reports to year-end accounting basis.
11. Property accounts—gross, net, major components.
12. Investments, market or appraised value.
13. Inventory valuation basis.
14. Leases, rentals.
15. Debt repayment schedules.
16. Pension program; funding.
17. Contingent liabilities.
18. Warrants, options, shares reserved for conversion.
19. Ten-year summary, including physical data, where applicable; employment data; capital expenditures.

II. Other published material.

A. Interim reports including depreciation, pretax earnings, interest, current assets and liabilities; comment on operations.
B. Proxy statements.
C. Annual meeting report.
D. Statistical supplements, where indicated.
E. Stockholder news.
F. 10-K reports (should conform to annual reports to stockholders); availability to shareholders.
G. Copies of addresses to analysts groups.
H. House magazine.
I. Press releases.

III. Other aspects.
   A. Interviews, including Access to policy makers, cooperativeness, access to operating management.
   B. Presentations to analysts groups.
   C. Plant tours.
   D. Annual meetings.
      1. Worthwhile to analysts?
      2. Accessible?

The outline is better adapted to manufacturing and to merchandising companies than to the financial services, transportation, and utility industries. Subcommittees serving these industries have developed specialized sets of standards.

In a general way, the subcommittees attach the following weightings to the three main categories of corporate reporting: the annual report, 50–65%; other published material, 20–30%; and other aspects, 20–30%. Here again, the relative importance of these three divisions may differ materially in the transportation, utility, and financial industries from that appropriate for manufacturing and trade.

WHERE FURTHER PROGRESS IS NEEDED

A rundown of the guidelines to a proper corporate reporting program reminds us that there are subject headings treated routinely now that were given little attention only a few years ago, and none when this committee began its work 25-years ago. Notable are information on funding of pension past-service liability, adjustments to earnings per share for indicated dilution, and statements of sources and disposition of funds. We set forth in this section recommendations for strengthening of reporting.

Statement of Accounting Principles

Such statements are uniformly presented now as notes to the income statement and balance sheet, but they are not uniformly comprehensive. The Corporate Information Committee, with the particular support of the Financial Accounting Policy Committee, continues to press for fuller disclosure of depreciation policy, basis of inventory valuation, accounting for the Investment Tax Credit, and rental and debt repayment schedules. The quantitative effect on net income of alternative accounting policies would be welcome additional information.

Divisional Earnings

The SEC now requires reporting of revenues and earnings of the separate segments of diversified companies on Form 10-K. While this information is also becoming more generally available in annual reports, there remain recalcitrants who do not report fully to shareholders. Since the 10-K is on the public record, we do not understand why these companies are unwilling to take stockholders into their confidence.

The proliferation of widely diversified companies in the last decade has made such information vitally necessary to the financial analyst. Earlier this year the federation made an opinion survey of directors of research which elicited the following information.

1. Substantially all (92 percent) respondents use divisional segment information in their analytical work.

2. Two thirds indicated that this data improved their earnings projections in at least some cases.

3. More than two thirds said that this data changed their appraisal of a company to a significant degree in at least some cases.

4. Slightly more than half indicated a need for more segment data.

5. Almost three fourths thought that the data should be *required* in annual reports. (The SEC is trying to get at this indirectly by its proposed requirement that companies list items reported in the 10-K that are omitted in the annual report).

6. Three fourths indicated either that present definitions adopted by reporting companies were unsatisfactory or that more segments were needed.

7. About half desired better definition of segments and an explanation of the accounting procedures.

Reporting for diversified companies is now before the APB (replaced by the Financial Accounting Standards Board in 1973), and it would appear that audit and certification of segment data would give an added dimension to corporate financial statements. The great diversity of American industry precludes an all-encompassing definition of segments that will fit all cases. Financial analysts have been content to leave the determination of a company's segments to management. The accounting for joint and overhead costs also requires some flexibility for company managements in view of differences in organization structure. Most companies showing segment results in annual reports are allocating all or substantially all costs to segments, and the results appear to be satisfactory from the standpoint of investment analysis. The analyst is content to work with reasonable approximations in segment accounting so long as the accounting method is understood and the total company figures are accurate.

Effective presentation of divisional segment data is of great importance also. Graphic summary alone, particularly in pie charts, is inadequate. It is not a substitute for specific accounting data. A useful format for the presentation of this data is exemplified by the Dresser Industries 1971 report. (This report was rated highly by the Services Group of the Oil Industry Subcommittee.)

A two-page statistical review contains a section on sales and profit contribution by principal segments with an explanation of the accounting method used. In the narrative section, there is an explanation of the financial and operating results for each segment. These are supplemented by graphics showing five-year trends of sales and earnings contribution by segment and a breakdown of sales by product group, by type of product, by market, and by geographic area. The method of presenting divisional data will vary according to circumstances, but the Dresser report is typical of the best practice in this aspect of corporate reporting at the present time.

Adjustments for Pooling of Interests

The present accounting standards for mergers and acquisitions were established by the APB several years ago, but the presentation of historical financial data reflecting pooling of interests is not yet satisfactory in all cases. Historical earnings as originally reported do not give a true indication of the likely performance of the present entity, but they are a record of management's actual accomplishments in those years. Pro forma retroactively adjusted data reflecting all acquisitions and mergers are only theoretical and do not relate to actual market prices recorded in earlier years. Usually the adjusted data will moderate the growth rates presented in actual data, but sometimes the reverse will be true where the merger causes a dilution of earnings.

The truth lies somewhere in between these sets of figures, and the investor should be given both actual and retroactively adjusted data in order to draw his own conclusions. Some companies are now presenting both historical and pro forma sales and earnings, and we urge all to do so.

Interim Reports

There is room for improvement here. Few interim reports include all the information suggested under this heading in our previous outline. Corporate reporting has become a continuous process which should be independent of an arbitrary 12-month period. Expansion of the quarterly report to include full financial statements and interpretation of corporate developments is the easiest and most satisfactory method of adapting to this continuous reporting concept.

In this context the annual report would become a review of management's stewardship for a full year and would provide a bench mark for measuring financial progress over several years.

One company that has adopted this concept is Continental Illinois Corporation (Continental Illinois National Bank in Chicago). Each quarterly report is in the annual report format, with financial statements in complete detail and a management letter commenting on current trends. Each quarterly report also selects some aspect of the business for more extensive comment. The annual report has become, in effect, the fourth quarterly report for the year.

In the aforementioned opinion survey of directors of research, the responses strongly supported improvement in interim reports. To summarize:

1. More than a majority consider interim data of equal or greater importance than annual data.

2. More than 80 percent believe the same level of detail in the interim income account as in the annual report would add significant information for their analytical work; two thirds would like an interim balance sheet; and almost half believe an interim statement of funds would be useful.

3. A substantial majority of respondents indicated they had encountered all of the listed problems in the use of interim reports: unexplained changes in accounting methods; retroactive adjustments during the year; and inconsistent treatment of extraordinary items.

We recommend that companies adopt the continuous reporting, expanded quarterly concept and present the following information in interim statements:

1. Income account in same detail as the annual report, including in particular depreciation and income taxes, for the current period and year to date as compared with the previous year.
2. Full balance sheet for current period and year ago.
3. Funds statement for current period and year to date.
4. Surplus reconciliation.
5. Adequate discussion of current developments in the business.
6. Publication of fourth quarter results in the annual report or in a separate fourth quarter report if the annual report is unduly delayed.
7. Explanation of unusual charges, changes in accounting methods, or retroactive adjustments during the year. Statements for year ago quarters should be revised where necessary to reflect these changes and also pooling of interest adjustments.

Respondents have mixed views on the usefulness of reporting in each quarter the latest 12 months' data, as some utility companies now do. This presentation is especially useful for companies with a large seasonal variation. With increased acceptance of the continuous reporting concept, the latest 12 months' data is likely to become more useful to investors.

Not only should quarterly reports be more comprehensive but they should be more timely. Frequently there is a considerable time lag between the press release and the mailing to stockholders. Sometimes the mailing date is keyed to a dividend payment to save postage, but this is a false economy. Reports should be distributed to shareholders with utmost promptness.

All recommendations for improvements in corporate reporting should be subjected to a cost-benefit analysis. In this case, the cost increment should be minimal. The data is available internally, and the proposed format and content is consistent with the annual report. Printing and mailing costs might be higher, but perhaps these can be offset by economies in annual report costs in the new pattern. This redistribution of reporting emphasis should contribute to improved investor understanding of the company and is desirable on grounds of fairness to all shareholders.

Social Costs

Cost, particularly for preventing or reducing air and water pollution, should be separated out as a portion of capital expenditures. The overall program should be described, as well as the time required to accomplish it.

Financial Forecasts

"Corporate earnings forecasts are an idea whose time has come," in the words of George S. Bissell, former president of the Federation. Many managements already include approximate or generalized forecasts in their annual reports or in stockholders' or analysts' meetings. In fact, analysts say they already receive some kind of forecast information, in one way or another, from most companies. The real issue, then, is not whether forecasts will be made by management but when made, how they can best be disclosed to investors.

Pension Liability

Pension programs and obligations are rapidly assuming material significance in the corporate financial outlook. Yet the amount of data given in almost all company annual reports to stockholders is far from sufficient to allow the outside analyst to project these obligations ahead. The following suggested checklist of information required for adequate disclosure of pension liability is based largely upon the November 1966 *Opinion* of the Accounting Principles Board:

1. Approximate percentages of employees covered.
2. Accounting and funding policies including (1) interest assumption in use and whether it includes recognition of unrealized appreciation and (2) period over which unfunded past service costs are being amortized.

3. The year's provision for pension cost including, separately, normal cost and amortization of past service cost.
4. Difference between actuarially computed value of vested benefits and total value of the pension fund.
5. Nature and effect of significant changes in accounting methods, actuarial assumptions, amendment to plan, and other matters affecting year-to-year comparability of the statement.

Fixed and Variable Expenses

The process of forecasting earnings involves forecasting sales and, just as importantly, profit margins. The mix of fixed expenses (interpreting this term more broadly than as rent, interest, general taxes, and depreciation) and of variable expenses is known to a satisfactory degree by most large companies and would constitute extremely useful information to the investment analyst.

IN CONCLUSION

The FAF Financial Accounting Policy Committee has contributed to the effort to render financial statements more representative of the transactions they report. The Corporate Information Committee is part of this effort but pushes in addition for that information of a non-accounting nature that helps determine what the accounts will look like in the future. Thus more specific information on management personnel; more on the age, location, and condition of properties; more on share of market and marketing systems; more on labor conditions and relations; and other of the items listed in the checklist of elements of a company reporting program aid the investor in evaluating increasingly complex business organizations.

25

Calculations of Earnings per Share (APB Opinion No. 15)

EARNINGS PER SHARE

AICPA Accounting Principles Board

CONTENTS

INTRODUCTION

1. Earnings per share data are used in evaluating the past operating performance of a business, in forming an opinion as to its potential and in making investment decisions. They are commonly presented in prospectuses, proxy material and reports to stockholders. They are used in the compilation of business earnings data for the press, statistical services and other publications. When presented with formal financial statements, they assist the investor in weighing the significance of a corporation's current net income and of changes in its net income from period to period in relation to the shares he holds or may acquire.

2. In view of the widespread use of earnings per share data, it is important that such data be computed on a consistent basis and presented in the most meaningful manner. The Board and its predecessor committee have previously expressed their views on general standards designed to achieve these objectives, most recently in Part II of APB Opinion No. 9, *Reporting the Results of Operations.*

3. In this Opinion the Board expresses its views on some of the more specific aspects of the subject, including the guidelines that should be applied uniformly in the computation and presentation of earnings per share data in financial statements. Accordingly, this Opinion supersedes Part II (paragraphs 30-51) and Exhibit E of APB Opinion No. 9. In some respects, practice under APB Opinion No. 9 will be changed by this Opinion.

4. Computational guidelines for the implementation of this Opinion are contained in Appendix A. Certain views differing from those adopted in this Opinion are summarized in Appendix B. Illustrations of the presentations described in this Opinion are included in the Exhibits contained in Appendix C. Definitions of certain terms as used in this Opinion are contained in Appendix D.

APPLICABILITY

5. This Opinion applies to financial presentations which purport to present results of operations of corporations in conformity with generally accepted accounting principles and to summaries of those presentations, except as excluded in paragraph 6. Thus, it applies to corporations whose capital structures include only common stock or common stock and senior securities and to those whose capital structures also include securities that should be considered the equivalent of common stock[1] in computing earnings per share data.

6. This Opinion does not apply to mutual companies that do not have outstanding common stock or common stock equivalents (for example, mutual savings banks, cooperatives, credit unions, and similar entities); to registered investment companies; to government-owned corporations; or to nonprofit corporations. This Opinion also does not apply to parent company statements accompanied by consolidated financial statements, to statements of wholly owned subsidiaries, or to special purpose statements.

HISTORICAL BACKGROUND

7. Prior to the issuance of APB Opinion No. 9, earnings per share were generally computed by dividing net income (after deducting preferred stock dividends, if any) by the number of common shares outstanding. The divisor used in the computation usually was a weighted average of the number of common shares outstanding during the period, but sometimes was simply the number of common shares outstanding at the end of the period.

8. ARB No. 49, *Earnings per Share,* referred to "common stock or other residual security;" however, the concept that a security other than a common stock could be the substantial equivalent of common stock and should, therefore, enter into

1 APB Opinion No. 9 referred to certain securities as *residual* securities, the determination of which was generally based upon the market value of the security as it related to investment value. In this Opinion, the Board now uses the term *common stock equivalents* as being more descriptive of those securities other than common stock that should be dealt with as common stock in the determination of earnings per share.

the computation of earnings per share was seldom followed prior to the issuance of APB Opinion No. 9. Paragraph 33 of APB Opinion No. 9 stated that earnings per share should be computed by reference to common stock and other residual securities and defined a residual security as follows:

> "When more than one class of common stock is outstanding, or when an outstanding security has participating dividend rights with the common stock, or when an outstanding security clearly derives a major portion of its value from its conversion rights or its common stock characteristics, such securities should be considered 'residual securities' and not 'senior securities' for purposes of computing earnings per share."

9. APB Opinion No. 9 also stated in part (paragraph 43) that:

> "Under certain circumstances, earnings per share may be subject to dilution in the future if existing contingencies permitting issuance of common shares eventuate. Such circumstances include contingent changes resulting from the existence of (a) outstanding senior stock or debt which is convertible into common shares, (b) outstanding stock options, warrants or similar agreements and (c) agreements for the issuance of common shares for little or no consideration upon the satisfaction of certain conditions (e.g., the attainment of specified levels of earnings following a business combination). If such potential dilution is material, supplementary pro forma computations of earnings per share should be furnished, showing what the earnings would be if the conversions or contingent issuances took place."

Before the issuance of APB Opinion No. 9 corporations had rarely presented pro forma earnings per share data of this type except in prospectuses and proxy statements.

10. Under the definition of a residual security contained in paragraph 33 of APB Opinion No. 9, residual status of convertible securities has been determined using the "major-portion-of-value" test at the time of the issuance of the security and from time to time thereafter whenever earnings per share

data were presented. In practice this test has been applied by comparing a convertible security's market value with its investment value, and the security has been considered to be residual whenever more than half its market value was attributable to its common stock characteristics at time of issuance. Practice has varied in applying this test subsequent to issuance with a higher measure used in many cases. Thus, a convertible security's status as a residual security has been affected by equity and debt market conditions at and after the security's issuance.

11. Application of the residual security concept as set forth in paragraph 33 of APB Opinion No. 9 has raised questions as to the validity of the concept and as to the guidelines developed for its application in practice. The Board has reviewed the concept of residual securities as it relates to earnings per share and, as a result of its own study and the constructive comments on the matter received from interested parties, has concluded that modification of the residual concept is desirable. The Board has also considered the disclosure and presentation requirements of earnings per share data contained in APB Opinion No. 9 and has concluded that these should be revised.

OPINION

Presentation on Face of Income Statement

12. The Board believes that the significance attached by investors and others to earnings per share data, together with the importance of evaluating the data in conjunction with the financial statements, requires that such data be presented prominently in the financial statements. The Board has therefore concluded that earnings per share or net loss per share data should be shown on the face of the income statement. The extent of the data to be presented and the captions used will vary with the complexity of the company's capital structure, as discussed in the following paragraphs.

13. The reporting of earnings per share data should be consistent with the income statement presentation called for by paragraph 20 of APB Opinion No. 9. Earnings per share amounts should therefore be presented for (a) income before extraordinary items and (b) net income. It may also be desir-

able to present earnings per share amounts for extraordinary items, if any.

Simple Capital Structures

14. The capital structures of many corporations are relatively simple—that is, they either consist of only common stock or include no potentially dilutive convertible securities, options, warrants or other rights that upon conversion or exercise could in the aggregate dilute[2] earnings per common share. In these cases, a single presentation expressed in terms such as *Earnings per common share* on the face of the income statement (based on common shares outstanding and computed in accordance with the provisions of paragraphs 47-50 of Appendix A) is the appropriate presentation of earnings per share data.

Complex Capital Structures

15. Corporations with capital structures other than those described in the preceding paragraph should present two types of earnings per share data (dual presentation) with equal prominence on the face of the income statement. The first presentation is based on the outstanding common shares and those securities that are in substance equivalent to common shares and have a dilutive[2] effect. The second is a pro-forma presentation which reflects the dilution[2] of earnings per share that would have occurred if *all* contingent issuances of common stock that would individually reduce earnings per share had taken place at the beginning of the period (or time of issuance of the convertible security, etc., if later). For convenience in this Opinion, these two presentations are referred to as "primary earnings per share" and "fully diluted earnings per share,"[3] respectively, and would in certain circumstances

2 Any reduction of less than 3% in the aggregate need not be considered as dilution in the computation and presentation of earnings per share data as discussed throughout this Opinion. In applying this test only issues which reduce earnings per share should be considered. In establishing this guideline the Board does not imply that a similar measure should be applied in any circumstances other than the computation and presentation of earnings per share data under this Opinion.

3 APB Opinion No. 9 referred to the latter presentation as "supplementary pro forma earnings per share."

discussed elsewhere in this Opinion be supplemented by other disclosures and other earnings per share data. (See paragraphs 19-23.)

Dual Presentation

16. When dual presentation of earnings per share data is required, the primary and fully diluted earnings per share amounts should be presented with equal prominence on the face of the income statement. The difference between the primary and fully diluted earnings per share amounts shows the maximum extent of potential dilution of current earnings which conversions of securities that are not common stock equivalents could create. If the capital structure contains no common stock equivalents, the first may be designated *Earnings per common share—assuming no dilution* and the second *Earnings per common share—assuming full dilution*. When common stock equivalents are present and dilutive, the primary amount may be designated *Earnings per common and common equivalent share*. The Board recognizes that precise designations should not be prescribed; corporations should be free to designate these dual presentations in a manner which best fits the circumstances provided they are in accord with the substance of this Opinion. The term *Earnings per common share* should not be used without appropriate qualification except under the conditions discussed in paragraph 14.

Periods Presented

17. Earnings per share data should be presented for all periods covered by the statement of income or summary of earnings. If potential dilution exists in any of the periods presented, the dual presentation of primary earnings per share and fully diluted earnings per share data should be made for all periods presented. This information together with other disclosures required (see paragraphs 19-23) will give the reader an understanding of the extent and trend of the potential dilution.

18. When results of operations of a prior period included in the statement of income or summary of earnings have been

restated as a result of a prior period adjustment, earnings per share data given for the prior period should be restated. The effect of the restatement, expressed in per share terms, should be disclosed in the year of restatement.

Additional Disclosures

Capital Structure

19. The use of complex securities complicates earnings per share computations and makes additional disclosures necessary. The Board has concluded that financial statements should include a description, in summary form, sufficient to explain the pertinent rights and privileges of the various securities outstanding. Examples of information which should be disclosed are dividend and liquidation preferences, participation rights, call prices and dates, conversion or exercise prices or rates and pertinent dates, sinking fund requirements, unusual voting rights, etc.

Dual Earnings per Share Data

20. A schedule or note relating to the earnings per share data should explain the bases upon which both primary and fully diluted earnings per share are calculated. This information should include identification of any issues regarded as common stock equivalents in the computation of primary earnings per share and the securities included in the computation of fully diluted earnings per share. It should describe all assumptions and any resulting adjustments used in deriving the earnings per share data.[4] There should also be disclosed the number of shares issued upon conversion, exercise or satisfaction of required conditions, etc., during at least the most recent annual fiscal period and any subsequent interim period presented.[5]

21. Computations and/or reconciliations may sometimes be desirable to provide a clear understanding of the manner in

4 These computations should give effect to all adjustments which would result from conversion: for example, dividends paid on convertible preferred stocks should not be deducted from net income; interest and related expenses on convertible debt, less applicable income tax, should be added to net income, and any other adjustments affecting net income because of these assumptions should also be made. (See paragraph 51.)

5 See also paragraphs 9 and 10 of APB Opinion No. 12.

which the earnings per share amounts were obtained. This information may include data on each issue of securities entering into the computation of the primary and fully diluted earnings per share. It should not, however, be shown on the face of the income statement or otherwise furnished in a manner implying that an earnings per share amount which ignores the effect of common stock equivalents (that is, earnings per share based on outstanding common shares only) constitutes an acceptable presentation of primary earnings per share.

Supplementary Earnings per Share Data

22. Primary earnings per share should be related to the capital structures existing during each of the various periods presented.[6] Although conversions ordinarily do not alter substantially the amount of capital employed in the business, they can significantly affect the trend in earnings per share data. Therefore, if conversions during the current period would have affected (either dilutively or incrementally) primary earnings per share if they had taken place at the beginning of the period, supplementary information should be furnished (preferably in a note) for the latest period showing what primary earnings per share would have been if such conversions had taken place at the beginning of that period (or date of issuance of the security, if within the period). Similar supplementary per share earnings should be furnished if conversions occur after the close of the period but before completion of the financial report. It may also be desirable to furnish supplementary per share data for each period presented, giving the cumulative retroactive effect of all such conversions or changes. However, primary earnings per share data should not be adjusted retroactively for conversions.

23. Occasionally a sale of common stock or common stock equivalents for cash occurs during the latest period presented or shortly after its close but before completion of the financial report. When a portion or all of the proceeds of such a sale has been used to retire preferred stock or debt, or is to be used for that purpose, supplementary earnings per share data should be

[6] See paragraphs 48-49 and 62-64 for exceptions to this general rule.

furnished (preferably in a note) to show what the earnings would have been for the latest fiscal year and any subsequent interim period presented if the retirement had taken place at the beginning of the respective period (or date of issuance of the retired security, if later). The number of shares of common stock whose proceeds are to be used to retire the preferred stock or debt should be included in this computation. The bases of these supplementary computations should be disclosed.[7]

Primary Earnings Per Share

24. If a corporation's capital structure is complex and either does not include common stock equivalents or includes common stock equivalents which do not have a dilutive effect, the primary earnings per share figures should be based on the weighted average number of shares of common stock outstanding during the period. In such cases, potential dilutive effects of contingent issuances would be reflected in the fully diluted earnings per share amounts. Certain securities, however, are considered to be the equivalent of outstanding common stock and should be recognized in the computation of primary earnings per share if they have a dilutive effect.

Nature of Common Stock Equivalents

25. The concept that a security may be the equivalent of common stock has evolved to meet the reporting needs of investors in corporations that have issued certain types of convertible and other complex securities. A common stock equivalent is a security which is not, in form, a common stock but which usually contains provisions to enable its holder to become a common stockholder and which, because of its terms and the circumstances under which it was issued, is in substance equivalent to a common stock. The holders of these securities can expect to participate in the appreciation of the value of the common stock resulting principally from the earnings and earnings potential of the issuing corporation. This participation is essentially the same as that of a common stock-

7 There may be other forms of recapitalization which should be reflected in a similar manner.

holder except that the security may carry a specified dividend or interest rate yielding a return different from that received by a common stockholder. The attractiveness of this type of security to investors is often based principally on this potential right to share in increases in the earnings potential of the issuing corporation rather than on its fixed return or other senior security characteristics. With respect to a convertible security, any difference in yield between it and the underlying common stock as well as any other senior characteristics of the convertible security become secondary. The value of a common stock equivalent is derived in large part from the value of the common stock to which it is related, and changes in its value tend to reflect changes in the value of the common stock. Neither conversion nor the imminence of conversion is necessary to cause a security to be a common stock equivalent.

26. The Board has concluded that outstanding convertible securities which have the foregoing characteristics and which meet the criteria set forth in this Opinion for the determination of common stock equivalents at the time they are issued should be considered the equivalent of common stock in computing primary earnings per share if the effect is dilutive. The recognition of common stock equivalents in the computation of primary earnings per share avoids the misleading implication which would otherwise result from the use of common stock only; use of the latter basis would place form over substance.

27. In addition to convertible debt and convertible preferred stocks, the following types of securities are or may be considered as common stock equivalents:

Stock options and warrants (and their equivalents) and stock purchase contracts—should always be considered common stock equivalents (see paragraphs 35-38).

Participating securities and two-class common stocks—if their participation features enable their holders to share in the earnings potential of the issuing corporation on substantially the same basis as common stock even though the securities may not give the holder the right to exchange his shares for common stock (see paragraphs 59 and 60).

Contingent shares—if shares are to be issued in the future upon the mere passage of time (or are held in escrow pending the satisfaction of conditions unrelated to earnings or market value) they should be considered as outstanding for the computation of earnings per share. If additional shares of stock are issuable for little or no consideration upon the satisfaction of certain conditions they should be considered as outstanding when the conditions are met (see paragraphs 61-64).

Determination of Common Stock Equivalents at Issuance

28. The Board has concluded that determination of whether a convertible security is a common stock equivalent should be made only at the time of issuance and should not be changed thereafter so long as the security remains outstanding. However, convertible securities outstanding or subsequently issued with the same terms as those of a common stock equivalent also should be classified as common stock equivalents. After full consideration of whether a convertible security may change its status as a common stock equivalent subsequent to issuance, including the differing views which are set forth in Appendix B hereto, the Board has concluded that the dilutive effect of any convertible securities that were not common stock equivalents at time of their issuance should be included only in the fully diluted earnings per share amount. This conclusion is based upon the belief (a) that only the conditions which existed at the time of issuance of the convertible security should govern the determination of status as a common stock equivalent, and (b) that the presentation of fully diluted earnings per share data adequately discloses the potential dilution which may exist because of changes in conditions subsequent to time of issuance.

29. Various factors should be considered in determining the appropriate "time of issuance" in evaluating whether a security is substantially equivalent to a common stock. The time of issuance generally is the date when agreement as to terms has been reached and announced, even though subject to certain further actions, such as directors' or stockholders' approval.

No Anti-Dilution

30. Computations of primary earnings per share should not give effect to common stock equivalents or other contingent issuance for any period in which their inclusion would have the effect of increasing the earnings per share amount or decreasing the loss per share amount otherwise computed.[8] Consequently, while a security once determined to be a common stock equivalent retains that status, it may enter into the computation of primary earnings per share in one period and not in another.

Test of Common Stock Equivalent Status

31. *Convertible securities.* A convertible security which at the time of issuance has terms that make it for all practical purposes substantially equivalent to a common stock should be regarded as a common stock equivalent. The complexity of convertible securities makes it impractical to establish definitive guidelines to encompass all the varying terms which might bear on this determination. Consideration has been given, however, to various characteristics of a convertible security which might affect its status as a common stock equivalent, such as cash yield at issuance, increasing or decreasing conversion rates, liquidation and redemption amounts, and the conversion price in relation to the market price of the common stock. In addition, consideration has been given to the pattern of various nonconvertible security yields in recent years, during which period most of the existing convertible securities have been issued, as well as over a longer period of time. Many of the characteristics noted above, which in various degrees may indicate status as a common stock equivalent, are also closely related to the interest or dividend rate of the security and to its market price at the time of issuance.

32. The Board has also studied the use of market price in relation to investment value (value of a convertible security without the conversion option) and market parity (relationship

---

8 The presence of a common stock equivalent together with extraordinary items may result in diluting income before extraordinary items on a per share basis while increasing net income per share, or vice versa. If an extraordinary item is present and a common stock equivalent results in dilution of either income before extraordinary items or net income on a per share basis, the common stock equivalent should be recognized for all computations even though it has an anti-dilutive effect on one of the per share amounts.

of conversion value of a convertible security to its market price) as means of determining if a convertible security is equivalent to a common stock. (See discussion of investment value and market parity tests in Appendix B.) It has concluded, however, that these tests are too subjective or not sufficiently practicable.

33. The Board believes that convertible securities should be considered common stock equivalents if the cash yield to the holder at time of issuance is significantly below what would be a comparable rate for a similar security of the issuer without the conversion option. Recognizing that it may frequently be difficult or impossible to ascertain such comparable rates, and in the interest of simplicity and objectivity, the Board has concluded that a convertible security should be considered as a common stock equivalent at the time of issuance if, based on its market price[9], it has a cash yield of less than 66⅔% of the then current bank prime interest rate.[10] For any convertible security which has a change in its cash interest rate or cash dividend rate scheduled within the first five years after issuance, the lowest scheduled rate during such five years should be used in determining the cash yield of the security at issuance.

34. The Board believes that the current bank prime interest rate in general use for short-term loans represents a practical, simple and readily available basis on which to establish the criteria for determining a common stock equivalent, as set forth in the preceding paragraph. The Board recognizes that there are other rates and averages of interest rates relating to various grades of long-term debt securities and preferred stocks which might be appropriate or that a more complex approach could be adopted. However, after giving consideration to various approaches and interest rates in this regard, the Board has concluded that since there is a high degree of correlation between such indices and the bank prime interest rate, the latter is the most practical rate available for this particular purpose.

---

9 If no market price is available, this test should be based on the fair value of the security.

10 If convertible securities are sold or issued outside the United States, the most comparable interest rate in the foreign country should be used for this test.

35. *Options and warrants (and their equivalents).* Options, warrants and similar arrangements usually have no cash yield and derive their value from their right to obtain common stock at specified prices for an extended period. Therefore, these securities should be regarded as common stock equivalents at all times. Other securities, usually having a low cash yield (see definition of "cash yield", Appendix D), require the payment of cash upon conversion and should be considered the equivalents of warrants for the purposes of this Opinion. Accordingly, they should also be regarded as common stock equivalents at all times. Primary earnings per share should reflect the dilution that would result from exercise or conversion of these securities and use of the funds, if any, obtained. Options and warrants (and their equivalents) should, therefore, be treated as if they had been exercised and earnings per share data should be computed as described in the following paragraphs. The computation of earnings per share should not, however, reflect exercise or conversion of any such security[11] if its effect on earnings per share is anti-dilutive (see paragraph 30) except as indicated in paragraph 38.

36. Except as indicated in this paragraph and in paragraphs 37 and 38, the amount of dilution to be reflected in earnings per share data should be computed by application of the "treasury stock" method. Under this method, earnings per share data are computed as if the options and warrants were exercised at the beginning of the period (or at time of issuance, if later) and as if the funds obtained thereby were used to purchase common stock at the average market price during the period.[12] As a practical matter, the Board recommends that assumption of exercise not be reflected in earnings per share data until the market price of the common stock obtainable has been in excess of the exercise price for substantially all of three consecutive months ending with the last month of the

11 Reasonable grouping of like securities may be appropriate.

12 For example, if a corporation has 10,000 warrants outstanding, exercisable at $54 and the average market price of the common stock during the reporting period is $60, the $540,000 which would be realized from exercise of the warrants and issuance of 10,000 shares would be an amount sufficient to acquire 9,000 shares; thus 1,000 shares would be added to the outstanding common shares in computing primary earnings per share for the period.

period to which earnings per share data relate. Under the treasury stock method, options and warrants have a dilutive effect (and are, therefore, reflected in earnings per share computations) only when the average market price of the common stock obtainable upon exercise during the period exceeds the exercise price of the options or warrants. Previously reported earnings per share amounts should not be retroactively adjusted, in the case of options and warrants, as a result of changes in market prices of common stock. The Board recognizes that the funds obtained by issuers from the exercise of options and warrants are used in many ways with a wide variety of results that cannot be anticipated. Application of the treasury stock method in earnings per share computations is not based on an assumption that the funds will or could actually be used in that manner. In the usual case, it represents a practical approach to reflecting the dilutive effect that would result from the issuance of common stock under option and warrant agreements at an effective price below the current market price. The Board has concluded, however, that the treasury stock method is inappropriate, or should be modified, in certain cases described in paragraphs 37 and 38.

37. Some warrants contain provisions which permit, or require, the tendering of debt (usually at face amount) or other securities of the issuer in payment for all or a portion of the exercise price. The terms of some debt securities issued with warrants require that the proceeds of the exercise of the related warrants be applied toward retirement of the debt. As indicated in paragraph 35, some convertible securities require cash payments upon conversion and are, therefore, considered to be the equivalent of warrants. In all of these cases, the "if converted" method (see paragraph 51) should be applied as if retirement or conversion of the securities had occurred and as if the excess proceeds, if any, had been applied to the purchase of common stock under the treasury stock method. However, exercise of the options and warrants should not be reflected in the computation unless for the period specified in paragraph 36 either (a) the market price of the related common stock exceeds the exercise price or (b) the security which may be (or

must be) tendered is selling at a price below that at which it may be tendered under the option or warrant agreement and the resulting discount is sufficient to establish an effective exercise price below the market price of the common stock that can be obtained upon exercise. Similar treatment should be followed for preferred stock bearing similar provisions or other securities having conversion options permitting payment of cash for a more favorable conversion rate from the standpoint of the investor.

38. The treasury stock method of reflecting use of proceeds from options and warrants may not adequately reflect potential dilution when options or warrants to acquire a substantial number of common shares are outstanding. Accordingly, the Board has concluded that, if the number of shares of common stock obtainable upon exercise of outstanding options and warrants in the aggregate exceeds 20% of the number of common shares outstanding at the end of the period for which the computation is being made, the treasury stock method should be modified in determining the dilutive effect of the options and warrants upon earnings per share data. In these circumstances all the options and warrants should be assumed to have been exercised and the aggregate proceeds therefrom to have been applied in two steps:

a. As if the funds obtained were first applied to the repurchase of outstanding common shares at the average market price during the period (treasury stock method) but not to exceed 20% of the outstanding shares; and then

b. As if the balance of the funds were applied first to reduce any short-term or long-term borrowings and any remaining funds were invested in U.S. government securities or commercial paper, with appropriate recognition of any income tax effect.

The results of steps (a) and (b) of the computation (whether dilutive or anti-dilutive) should be aggregated and, if the net effect is dilutive, should enter into the earnings per share computation.[13]

Non-Recognition of Common Stock Equivalents in Financial Statements

39. The designation of securities as common stock equivalents in this Opinion is solely for the purpose of determining primary earnings per share. No changes from present practices are recommended in the accounting for such securities, in their presentation within the financial statements or in the manner of determining net assets per common share. Information is available in the financial statements and elsewhere for readers to make judgments as to the present and potential status of the various securities outstanding.

---

13 The following are examples of the application of Paragraph 38:

Assumptions:	*Case 1*	*Case 2*
Net income for year	$ 4,000,000	$ 2,000,000
Common shares outstanding	3,000,000	3,000,000
Options and warrants outstanding to purchase equivalent shares	1,000,000	1,000,000
20% limitation on assumed repurchase	600,000	600,000
Exercise price per share	$15	$15
Average and year-end market value per common share to be used (see paragraph 42)	$20	$12
Computations:		
Application of assumed proceeds ($15,000,000):		
Toward repurchase of outstanding common shares at applicable market value	$12,000,000	$ 7,200,000
Reduction of debt	3,000,000	7,800,000
	$15,000,000	$15,000,000
Adjustment of net income:		
Actual net income	$ 4,000,000	$ 2,000,000
Interest reduction (6%) less 50% tax effect	90,000	234,000
Adjusted net income (A)	$ 4,090,000	$ 2,234,000
Adjustment of shares outstanding:		
Actual outstanding	3,000,000	3,000,000
Net additional shares issuable (1,000,000 – 600,000)	400,000	400,000
Adjusted shares outstanding (B)	3,400,000	3,400,000
Earnings per share:		
Before adjustment	$1.33	$ .67
After adjustment (A ÷ B)	$1.20	$ .66

Fully Diluted Earnings Per Share

No Anti-Dilution

40. The purpose of the fully diluted earnings per share presentation is to show the maximum potential dilution of current earnings per share on a prospective basis. Consequently, computations of fully diluted earnings per share for each period should exclude those securities whose conversion, exercise or other contingent issuance would have the effect of increasing the earnings per share amount or decreasing the loss per share amount[14] for such period.

When Required

41. Fully diluted earnings per share data should be presented on the face of the statement of income for each period presented if shares of common stock (a) were issued during the period on conversions, exercise, etc., or (b) were contingently issuable at the close of any period presented and if primary earnings per share for such period would have been affected (either dilutively or incrementally) had such actual issuances taken place at the beginning of the period or would have been reduced had such contingent issuances taken place at the beginning of the period. The above contingencies may result from the existence of (a) senior stock or debt which is convertible into common shares but is not a common stock equivalent, (b) options or warrants, or (c) agreements for the issuance of common shares upon the satisfaction of certain conditions (for example, the attainment of specified higher levels of earnings following a business combination). The computation should be based on the assumption that all such issued and issuable shares were outstanding from the beginning of the period (or from the time the contingency arose, if after the beginning of the period). Previously reported fully diluted earnings per share amounts should not be retroactively adjusted for subsequent conversions or subsequent changes in the market prices of the common stock.

42. The methods described in paragraphs 36-38 should be used to compute fully diluted earnings per share if dilution results from outstanding options and warrants; however, in

---

[14] See footnote 8.

order to reflect maximum potential dilution, the market price at the close of the period reported upon should be used to determine the number of shares which would be assumed to be repurchased (under the treasury stock method) if such market price is higher than the average price used in computing primary earnings per share (see paragraph 30). Common shares issued on exercise of options or warrants during each period should be included in fully diluted earnings per share from the beginning of the period or date of issuance of the options or warrants if later; the computation for the portion of the period prior to the date of exercise should be based on market prices of the common stock when exercised.

Situations Not Covered in Opinion

43. The Board recognizes that it is impracticable to cover all possible conditions and circumstances that may be encountered in computing earnings per share. When situations not expressly covered in this Opinion occur, however, they should be dealt with in accordance with their substance, giving cognizance to the guidelines and criteria outlined herein.

Computational Guidelines

44. The determination of earnings per share data required under this Opinion reflects the complexities of the capital structures of some businesses. The calculations should give effect to matters such as stock dividends and splits, business combinations, changes in conversion rates, etc. Guidelines which should be used in dealing with some of the more common computational matters are set forth in Appendix A hereto.

EFFECTIVE DATE

45. This Opinion shall be effective for fiscal periods beginning after December 31, 1968 for all earnings per share data (primary, fully diluted and supplementary) regardless of when the securities entering into computations of earnings per share were issued, except as described in paragraph 46 as it relates to primary earnings per share. The Board recommends that (a) computations for periods beginning before January 1, 1969 be made for all securities in conformity with the provisions of this Opinion and (b) in comparative statements in which the data for some periods are subject to this Opinion and others are not,

the provisions of the Opinion be applied to all periods—in either case based on the conditions existing in the prior periods.

46. In the case of securities whose time of issuance is prior to June 1, 1969 the following election should be made as of May 31, 1969 (and not subsequently changed) with respect to all such securities for the purpose of computing primary earnings per share:

a. determine the classifications of all such securities under the provisions of this Opinion, or
b. classify as common stock equivalents only those securities which are classified as residual securities under APB Opinion No. 9 regardless of how they would be classified under this Opinion.

If the former election is made, the provisions of this Opinion should be applied in the computation of both primary and fully diluted earnings per share data for all periods presented.

The Opinion entitled "Earnings per Share" was adopted by the assenting votes of fifteen members of the Board, of whom five, Messrs. Axelson, Davidson, Harrington, Hellerson and Watt, assented with qualification. Messrs. Halvorson, Seidman and Weston dissented.

Messrs. Axelson and Watt dissent to the requirement in paragraphs 35 and 36 that options and warrants whose exercise price is at or above the market price of related common stock at time of issuance be taken into account in the computation of *primary* earnings per share. They believe that this destroys the usefulness of the dual presentation of primary and fully diluted earnings per share by failing to disclose the magnitude of the contingency arising from the outstanding warrants and options and is inconsistent with the determination of the status of convertible securities at time of issuance only. Therefore, they concur with the comments in paragraph 86. They also dissent to the 20 percent limitation in paragraph 38 on use of the treasury stock method of applying proceeds from the assumed exercise of options and warrants because such limitation is arbitrary and unsupported and because of the inconsistency between this limitation and the Board's conclusion expressed in paragraph 36 that use of the treasury stock method "is not based on an assumption that the funds will or could actually be used in that manner." Further, they dissent to the requirement in paragraphs 63 and 64 that the computation of *primary* earnings per share take into account shares of stock issuable in connection with business combinations on a purely contingent basis, wholly dependent upon the movement of market prices in the future.

Mr. Davidson assents to the issuance of this Opinion because he believes that practice under Part II of APB Opinion No. 9 has been so varied that clarification of APB Opinion No. 9 is necessary. He agrees with the concept of common stock equivalents, but dissents to the conclusion that convertible securities can be classified as common stock equivalents only by consideration of conditions prevailing at the time of their issuance (paragraph 28). He believes that in determining common stock equivalency, current conditions reflected in the market place are the significant criterion (paragraphs 74-77). The use of the investment value method (paragraphs 79-81) adequately reflects these current conditions.

Mr. Davidson also dissents to the use of the bank prime rate for the cash-yield test (paragraphs 33-34). It does not differentiate among types of securities issued nor the standing of the issuers.

Mr. Harrington assents to the issuance of the Opinion; however, he dissents from paragraphs 36, 37 and 38. He believes it is inconsistent in computing fully diluted earnings per share to measure potential dilution by the treasury stock method in the case of most warrants and to assume conversion in the case of convertible securities. This inconsistency, in his view, results in required recognition of potential dilution attributable to all convertible securities; and, at the same time through the use of the treasury stock method, permits understatement or no recognition of potential dilution attributable to warrants. He further believes that the potential dilution inherent in warrants should be recognized in fully diluted earning per share, but need not be recognized in primary earnings per share, when the exercise price exceeds the market price of the stock.

Mr. Hellerson assents to the issuance of this Opinion because he believes the Board has an obligation to resolve without further delay the implementation problems raised by Part II of APB Opinion No. 9 which have been greatly extended by the characteristics of a number of the securities issued since the release of that Opinion. However, he dissents from the mandatory requirement that earnings per share be shown on the face of the income statement as prescribed in paragraphs 12 through 16 and paragraph 41. The accounting profession has taken the position, and in his view rightly so, that fair presentation of financial position and results of operations requires the presentation of certain basic financial statements supplemented by disclosure of additional information in the form of separate statements or notes to the basic financial statements. Fair presentation is achieved by the whole presentation, not by the specific location of any item. This principle was most recently restated by the Board in paragraph 10 of APB Opinion No. 12 on capital changes as follows: "Disclosure of such changes may take the form of separate statements or may be made in the basic financial statements or notes thereto." Accordingly, it is his view that, although the Opinion should require dual presentation of earnings per share, it should not specify that the presentation must be made on the face of the income statement and thereby dignify one figure above all others.

Mr. Halvorson dissents to the Opinion because he believes the subject matter is one of financial analysis, not accounting principles, and that any expression by the Accounting Principles Board on the subject should not go beyond requiring such disclosure of the respective rights and priorities of the several issues of securities which may be represented in the capital structure of a reporting corporation as will permit an investor to make his own analysis of the effects of such rights and priorities on earnings per common share. Mr. Halvorson agrees that certain nominally senior securities are the equivalent of common shares under certain circumstances, but believes that the determination of common-stock equivalence is a subjective one which cannot be accommodated within prescribed formulae or arithmetical rules, although it can be facilitated by disclosure of information which does fall within the bounds of fair presentation in conformity with generally accepted accounting principles. Mr. Halvorson believes that a corporation should not be denied the right to report factually determined earnings per weighted average outstanding common share on the face of the income statement as a basis against which to measure the potential dilutive effects on earnings per share of senior issues, and that from such basis the investor may make such pro forma calculations of common-stock equivalence as he believes best serve his purpose.

Mr. Seidman dissents for the reasons set forth in paragraphs 72, 73, 92 and 93, dealing with the invalidity and inconsistent application of the concept of common stock equivalents. He adds: (1) It is unsound for the determination of earnings per share to depend on the fluctuations of security prices. It is even more unsound when an increase in security prices can result in a decrease in earnings per share, and vice versa. These matters arise under this Opinion since it calls for earnings per share based on cash yield of convertibles, comparison of stock and exercise prices of options and warrants, and no anti-dilution. (2) It is erroneous to attribute earnings to securities that do not currently and may never share in those earnings, particularly when part or all of those earnings may have already been distributed to others as dividends. (3) It does not serve the interests of meaningful disclosure when, as in paragraph 21, the Opinion bans showing on the face of the income statement any reference to the amount of earnings per share in relation to the one factual base, namely the number of shares actually outstanding, and instead fashions from various surmises what it calls "primary earnings per share". (4) It is baffling to say, as does this Opinion, that convertible debt is debt in the statement of earnings but is common stock equivalent in the statement of earnings per share; and that dividends per share are based on the actual number of shares outstanding, while earnings per share are based on a different and larger number of shares.

Mr. Weston dissents to the issuance of this Opinion because he believes it represents a significant retrogression in terms of the purpose of the Accounting Principles Board. The residual security concept, which has been successfully and appropriately applied to convertible securities during the period since issuance of APB Opinion No. 9, has, in this Opinion, been so restricted as to be meaningless for all practical purposes with respect to such securities. Accordingly, computations of primary earnings per share data under the provisions of this Opinion (paragraph 28 in particular) will not properly reflect the characteristics of those convertible securities which are currently the substantial equivalent of common stock—and are so recognized in the marketplace—which did not qualify for residual status at their date of issuance—possibly years previously. Such disregard of basic principles is a disservice to investors, who have a right to view the primary earnings per share data computed under this Opinion as a realistic attribution of the earnings of the issuer to the various complex elements of its capital structure based on the economic realities of today—not those existing years ago.

Mr. Weston also disagrees with the conclusions contained in paragraphs 33, 36, 39 and 51.

NOTES

Opinions present the considered opinion of at least two-thirds of the members of the Accounting Principles Board, reached on a formal vote after examination of the subject matter.

Except as indicated in the succeeding paragraph, the authority of the Opinions rests upon their general acceptability. While it is recognized that general rules may be subject to exception, the burden of justifying departures from Board Opinions must be assumed by those who adopt other practices.

Action of Council of the Institute (Special Bulletin, Disclosure of Departures from Opinions of the Accounting Principles Board, *October, 1964) provides that:*

a. "Generally accepted accounting principles" are those principles which have substantial authoritative support.

b. Opinions of the Accounting Principles Board constitute "substantial authoritative support."

c. "Substantial authoritative support" can exist for accounting principles that differ from Opinions of the Accounting Principles Board.

The Council action also requires that departures from Board Opinions be disclosed in footnotes to the financial statements or in independent auditors' reports when the effect of the departure on the financial statements is material.

Unless otherwise stated, Opinions of the Board are not intended to be retroactive. They are not intended to be applicable to immaterial items.

APPENDIX A

COMPUTATIONAL GUIDELINES

CONTENTS

APPENDIX A

COMPUTATIONAL GUIDELINES

The Board has adopted the following general guidelines which should be used in the computation of earnings per share data.

47. *Weighted average.* Computations of earnings per share data should be based on the weighted average number of common shares and common share equivalents outstanding during each period presented. Use of a weighted average is necessary so that the effect of increases or decreases in outstanding shares on earnings per share data is related to the portion of the period during which the related consideration affected operations. Reacquired shares should be excluded from date of their acquisition. (See definition in Appendix D.)

48. *Stock dividends or splits.* If the number of common shares outstanding increases as a result of a stock dividend or stock split[15] or decreases as a result of a reverse split, the computations should give retroactive recognition to an appropriate equivalent change in capital structure for all periods presented. If changes in common stock resulting from stock dividends or stock splits or reverse splits have been consummated after the close of the period but before completion of the financial report, the per share computations should be based on the new number of shares because the readers' primary interest is presumed to be related to the current capitalization. When per share computations reflect such changes in the number of shares after the close of the period, this fact should be disclosed.

49. *Business combinations and reorganizations.* When shares are issued to acquire a business in a transaction accounted for as a purchase, the computation of earnings per share should give recognition to the existence of the new shares only from the date the acquisition took place. When a business combination is accounted for as a pooling of interests, the computation should be based on the aggregate of the

---

[15] See ARB No. 43, Chapter 7B, *Capital Accounts–Stock Dividends and Stock Split Ups.*

weighted average outstanding shares of the constituent businesses, adjusted to equivalent shares of the surviving business for all periods presented. This difference in treatment reflects the fact that in a purchase the results of operations of the acquired business are included in the statement of income only from the date of acquisition, whereas in a pooling of interests the results of operations are combined for all periods presented. In reorganizations, the computations should be based on analysis of the particular transaction according to the criteria contained in this Opinion.

50. *Claims of senior securities.* The claims of senior securities on earnings of a period should be deducted from net income (and also from income before extraordinary items if an amount therefor appears in the statement) before computing earnings per share. Dividends on cumulative preferred senior securities, whether or not earned, should be deducted from net income.[16] If there is a net loss, the amount of the loss should be increased by any cumulative dividends for the period on these preferred stocks. If interest or preferred dividends are cumulative only if earned, no adjustment of this type is required, except to the extent of income available therefor. If interest or preferred dividends are not cumulative, only the interest accruable or dividends declared should be deducted. In all cases, the effect that has been given to rights of senior securities in arriving at the earnings per share should be disclosed.

51. *Use of "if converted" method of computation.* If convertible securities are deemed to be common stock equivalents for the purpose of computing primary earnings per share, or are assumed to have been converted for the purpose of computing fully diluted earnings per share, the securities should be assumed to have been converted at the beginning of the earliest period reported (or at time of issuance, if later). Interest charges applicable to convertible securities and non-discretionary adjustments that would have been made to items based on net income or income before taxes—such as profit sharing ex-

[16] The per share and aggregate amounts of cumulative preferred dividends in arrears should be disclosed.

pense, certain royalties, and investment credit—or preferred dividends applicable to the convertible securities should be taken into account in determining the balance of income applicable to common stock. As to primary earnings per share this amount should be divided by the total of the average outstanding common shares and the number of shares which would have been issued on conversion or exercise of common stock equivalents.[17] As to fully diluted earnings per share this amount should be divided by the total of the average outstanding common shares plus the number of shares applicable to conversions during the period from the beginning of the period to the date of conversion and the number of shares which would have been issued upon conversion or exercise of any other security which might dilute earnings.

52. The if converted method recognizes the fact that the holders of convertible securities cannot share in distributions of earnings applicable to the common stock unless they relinquish their right to senior distributions. Conversion is assumed and earnings applicable to common stock and common stock equivalents are determined before distributions to holders of these securities.

53. The if converted method also recognizes the fact that a convertible issue can participate in earnings, through dividends or interest, either as a senior security or as a common stock, but not both. The two-class method (see paragraph 55) does not recognize this limitation and may attribute to common stock an amount of earnings per share less than if the convertible security had actually been converted. The amount of earnings per share on common stock as computed under the two-class method is affected by the amount of dividends declared on the common stock.

54. *Use of "two-class" method of computation.* Although the two-class method is considered inappropriate with respect to the securities described in paragraph 51, its use may be necessary in the case of participating securities and two-class common stock. (See paragraphs 59-60 for discussion of these

[17] Determined as to options and warrants by application of the method described in paragraphs 36-38 of this Opinion.

securities.) This is the case, for example, when these securities are not convertible into common stock.

55. Under the two-class method, common stock equivalents are treated as common stock with a dividend rate different from the dividend rate on the common stock and, therefore, conversion of convertible securities is not assumed. No use of proceeds is assumed. Distributions to holders of senior securities, common stock equivalents and common stock are first deducted from net income. The remaining amount (the undistributed earnings) is divided by the total of common shares and common share equivalents. Per share distributions to the common stockholders are added to this per share amount to arrive at primary earnings per share.

56. *Delayed effectiveness and changing conversion rates or exercise prices.* In some cases, a conversion option does not become effective until a future date; in others conversion becomes more (or less) advantageous to the security holder at some later date as the conversion rate increases (or decreases), generally over an extended period. For example, an issue may be convertible into one share of common stock in the first year, 1.10 shares in the second year, 1.20 shares in the third year, etc. Frequently, these securities receive little or no cash dividends. Hence, under these circumstances, their value is derived principally from their conversion or exercise option and they would be deemed to be common stock equivalents under the yield test previously described. (See paragraph 33 of this Opinion.)[18] Similarly, the right to exercise options or warrants may be deferred or the exercise price may increase or decrease.

57. *Conversion rate or exercise price to be used – primary earnings per share.* The conversion rate or exercise price of a common stock equivalent in effect during each period presented should be used in computing primary earnings per share, with the exceptions stated hereinafter in this paragraph. Prior period primary earnings per share should not be restated for changes in the conversion ratio or exercise price. If options, warrants or other common stock equivalents are not immedi-

[18] An increasing conversion rate should not be accounted for as a stock dividend.

ately exercisable or convertible, the earliest effective exercise price or conversion rate if any during the succeeding five years should be used. If a convertible security having an increasing conversion rate is issued in exchange for another class of security of the issuing company and is convertible back into the same or a similar security, and if a conversion rate equal to or greater than the original exchange rate becomes effective during the period of convertibility, the conversion rate used in the computation should not result in a reduction in the number of common shares (or common share equivalents) existing before the original exchange took place until a greater rate becomes effective.

58. *Conversion rate or exercise price to be used — fully diluted earnings per share.* Fully diluted earnings per share computations should be based on the most advantageous (from the standpoint of the security holder) conversion or exercise rights that become effective within ten years following the closing date of the period being reported upon.[19] Conversion or exercise options that are not effective until after ten or more years may be expected to be of limited significance because (a) investors' decisions are not likely to be influenced substantially by events beyond ten years, and (b) it is questionable whether they are relevant to current operating results.

59. *Participating securities and two-class common.* The capital structures of some companies include:

a. Securities which may participate in dividends with common stocks according to a predetermined formula (for example, two for one) with, at times, an upper limit on the extent of participation (for example, up to but not beyond a specified amount per share).

b. A class of common stock with different dividend rates or voting rights from those of another class of common stock, but without prior or senior rights.

Additionally, some of these securities are convertible into

[19] The conversion rate should also reflect the cumulative effect of any stock dividends on the preferred stock which the company has contracted or otherwise committed itself to issue within the next ten years.

common stock. Earnings per share computations relating to certain types of participating securities may require the use of the two-class method. (See paragraphs 54-55.)

60. Because of the variety of features which these securities possess, frequently representing combinations of the features referred to above, it is not practicable to set out specific guidelines as to when they should be considered common stock equivalents. Dividend participation does not *per se* make a security a common stock equivalent. A determination of the status of one of these securities should be based on an analysis of all the characteristics of the security, including the ability to share in the earnings potential of the issuing corporation on substantially the same basis as the common stock.

61. *Issuance contingent on certain conditions.* At times, agreements call for the issuance of additional shares contingent upon certain conditions being met. Frequently these conditions are either:

a. the maintenance of current earnings levels, or

b. the attainment of specified increased earnings.

Alternatively, agreements sometimes provide for immediate issuance of the maximum number of shares issuable in the transaction with some to be placed in escrow and later returned to the issuer if specified conditions are not met. For purposes of computing earnings per share, contingently returnable shares placed in escrow should be treated in the same manner as contingently issuable shares.

62. If attainment or maintenance of a level of earnings is the condition, and if that level is currently being attained, the additional shares should be considered as outstanding for the purpose of computing both primary and fully diluted earnings per share. If attainment of increased earnings reasonably above the present level or maintenance of increased earnings above the present level over a period of years is the condition, the additional shares should be considered as outstanding only for the purpose of computing fully diluted earnings per share (but only if dilution is the result); for this computation, earnings

should be adjusted to give effect to the increase in earnings specified by the particular agreements (if different levels of earnings are specified, the level that would result in the largest potential dilution should be used). Previously reported earnings per share data should not be restated to give retroactive effect to shares subsequently issued as a result of attainment of specified increased earnings levels. If upon expiration of the term of the agreement providing for contingent issuance of additional shares the conditions have not been met, the shares should not be considered outstanding in that year. Previously reported earnings per share data should then be restated to give retroactive effect to the removal of the contingency.

63. The number of shares contingently issuable may depend on the market price of the stock at a future date. In such a case, computations of earnings per share should reflect the number of shares which would be issuable based on the market price at the close of the period being reported on. Prior period earnings per share should be restated if the number of shares issued or contingently issuable subsequently changes because the market price changes.

64. In some cases, the number of shares contingently issuable may depend on both future earnings and future prices of the shares. In that case, the number of shares which would be issuable should be based on both conditions, that is, market prices and earnings to date as they exist at the end of each period being reported on. (For example, if (a) a certain number of shares will be issued at the end of three years following an acquisition if earnings of the acquired company increase during those three years by a specified amount and (b) a stipulated number of additional shares will be issued if the value of the shares issued in the acquisition is not at least a designated amount at the end of the three-year period, the number of shares to be included in the earnings per share for each period should be determined by reference to the cumulative earnings of the acquired company and the value of the shares at the end of the latest period.) Prior-period earnings per share should be restated if the number of shares issued or contingently issuable subsequently changes from the number of

shares previously included in the earnings per share computation.

65. *Securities of subsidiaries.* At times subsidiaries issue securities which should be considered common stock equivalents from the standpoint of consolidated and parent company financial statements for the purpose of computing earnings per share. This could occur when convertible securities, options, warrants or common stock issued by the subsidiary are in the hands of the public and the subsidiary's results of operations are either consolidated or reflected on the equity method. Circumstances in which conversion or exercise of a subsidiary's securities should be assumed for the purpose of computing the consolidated and parent company earnings per share, or which would otherwise require recognition in the computation of earnings per share data, include those where:

As to the Subsidiary

a. Certain of the subsidiary's securities are common stock equivalents in relation to its own common stock.
b. Other of the subsidiary's convertible securities, although not common stock equivalents in relation to its own common stock, would enter into the computation of its fully diluted earnings per share.

As to the Parent

a. The subsidiary's securities are convertible into the parent company's common stock.
b. The subsidiary issues options and warrants to purchase the parent company's common stock.

The treatment of these securities for the purpose of consolidated and parent company reporting of earnings per share is discussed in the following four paragraphs.

66. If a subsidiary has dilutive warrants or options outstanding or dilutive convertible securities which are common stock equivalents from the standpoint of the subsidiary, consolidated and parent company primary earnings per share should include the portion of the subsidiary's income that would be applicable to the consolidated group based on its

holdings and the subsidiary's primary earnings per share. (See paragraph 39 of this Opinion.)

67. If a subsidiary's convertible securities are not common stock equivalents from the standpoint of the subsidiary, only the portion of the subsidiary's income that would be applicable to the consolidated group based on its holdings and the fully diluted earnings per share of the subsidiary should be included in consolidated and parent company fully diluted earnings per share. (See paragraph 40 of this Opinion.)

68. If a subsidiary's securities are convertible into its parent company's stock, they should be considered among the common stock equivalents of the parent company for the purpose of computing consolidated and parent company primary and fully diluted earnings per share if the conditions set forth in paragraph 33 of this Opinion exist. If these conditions do not exist, the subsidiary's convertible securities should be included in the computation of the consolidated and parent company fully diluted earnings per share only.

69. If a subsidiary issues options or warrants to purchase stock of the parent company, they should be considered common stock equivalents by the parent in computing consolidated and parent company primary and fully diluted earnings per share.

70. *Dividends per share.* Dividends constitute historical facts and usually are so reported. However, in certain cases, such as those affected by stock dividends or splits or reverse splits, the presentation of dividends per share should be made in terms of the current equivalent of the number of common shares outstanding at the time of the dividend. A disclosure problem exists in presenting data as to dividends per share following a pooling of interests. In such cases, it is usually preferable to disclose the dividends declared per share by the principal constituent and to disclose, in addition, either the amount per equivalent share or the total amount for each period for the other constituent, with appropriate explanation of the circumstances. When dividends per share are presented on other than an historical basis, the basis of presentation should be disclosed.

APPENDIX B

SUMMARY OF DIFFERING VIEWPOINTS

CONTENTS

APPENDIX B

SUMMARY OF DIFFERING VIEWPOINTS

This Appendix contains a summary of various viewpoints on a number of matters relating to the computation of earnings per share data, which viewpoints differ from the conclusions of the Board as stated in this Opinion. The views in this Appendix therefore do not represent the views of the Board as a whole.

Common Stock Equivalent or Residual Concept

71. This Opinion concludes (paragraph 26) that, for purposes of computing primary earnings per share, certain securities should be considered the equivalent of common stock. The Opinion further concludes (paragraph 28) that such treatment – as to convertible securities – should be based on a determination of status made at the time of issuance of each security, based on conditions existing at that date and not subsequently changed. Viewpoints which differ from those conclusions are based on a number of positions, which are summarized below.

Concept Has No Validity

72. Some believe there should be no such category as "common stock equivalent" or "residual" security, and hence no such classification as "primary" earnings per share including such securities. They contend that the common stock equivalent or residual security concept involves assumptions and arbitrary, intricate determinations which result in figures of questionable meaning which are more likely to confuse than enlighten readers. They advocate that earnings per share data be presented in a tabulation – as part of the financial statements – which first discloses the relationship of net income and the number of common shares actually outstanding and then moves through adjustments to determine adjusted net income and the number of common shares which would be outstanding if all conversions, exercises and contingent issuances took place. Under this approach, all the figures involved would be

readily determinable, understandable and significant. Such information, together with the other disclosures required in this Opinion regarding the terms of securities, would place the reader in a position to make his own judgment regarding prospects of conversion or exercise and the resulting impact on per share earnings. Accounting should not make or pre-empt that judgment.

73. Until convertible securities, etc., are in fact converted, the actual common stockholders are in control, and the entire earnings could often be distributed as dividends. The conversions, exercises and contingent issuances may, in fact, never take place. Hence, the reporting as "primary" earnings per share of an amount which results from treating as common stock securities which are not common stock is, in the view of some, improper.

Concept Has Validity Both At Issuance and Subsequently

74. Some who believe in the validity of the common stock equivalent or residual concept feel that the status of a security should be determined not only at the time of its issuance but from time to time thereafter. Securities having the characteristics associated with residual securities – among other things the ability to participate in the economic benefits resulting from the underlying earnings and earnings potential of the common stock through the right of their holders to become common stockholders – do change their nature with increases and decreases in the market value of the common stock after issuance. These securities are designed for this purpose, and therefore, in certain circumstances, they react to changes in the earnings or earnings potential of the issuer just as does the common stock. Furthermore, although many such securities are issued under market and yield conditions which do not place major emphasis at the time of issuance on their common stock characteristics, both the issuer and the holder recognize the possibility that these characteristics may become of increasing significance if, and when, the value of the underlying common stock increases. The limitation of the residual concept for convertible securities to "at issuance only" disregards these

significant factors. (For example, a convertible security with a cash yield of 4% at time of issuance [assumed to be in excess of the yield test for common stock equivalent status in this Opinion] may well appreciate in value subsequent to issuance, due to its common stock characteristics, to such an extent that its cash yield will drop to 2% or less. It seems unsound to consider such a security a "senior security" for earnings per share purposes at such later dates merely because its yield at date of issuance – possibly years previously – was 4%. This seems particularly unwise when the investment community evaluates such a security currently as the substantial equivalent of the common stock into which it is convertible.) Thus, the "at issuance only" application of the residual security concept is, in the opinion of some, illogical and arbitrary. In connection with the computation of earnings per share data, this approach disregards current conditions in reporting a financial statistic whose very purpose is a reflection of the *current* substantive relationship between the earnings of the issuer and its complex capital structure.

75. Furthermore, the adoption of the treasury stock method to determine the number of shares to be considered as common stock equivalents under outstanding options and warrants (see paragraphs 36-38) is apparent recognition of the fact that market conditions subsequent to issuance should influence the determination of the status of a security. Thus, the conclusions of the Opinion in these matters are inconsistent.

76. As for the contention that use of the residual concept subsequent to issuance has a "circular" effect – in that reported earnings per share influences the market, which, in turn, influences the classification status of a security, which, in turn, influences the computation of earnings per share, which, in turn, influences the market – analysts give appropriate recognition to the increasing importance of the common stock characteristics of convertible securities as the market rises or falls. It seems only appropriate that a computation purporting to attribute the earnings of a corporation to the various components of its capital structure should also give adequate recognition to the changing substance of these securities. Thus, the

movement of securities in and out of residual status subsequent to their issuance is a logical and integral part of the entire concept.

77. As for the contention that the dual presentation of earnings per share data required by this Opinion appropriately reflects the dilutive effect of any convertible securities which were not residual at time of issuance but which might subsequently be considered as residual, the disclosure of "fully-diluted" earnings per share data is aimed at *potential* (i.e., possible future) dilution; for issuers with securities having extremely low yields of the levels described in the preceding paragraph, the dilution has already taken place – these common stock equivalents are being so traded in the market, and any method which does not reflect these conditions results in an amount for "primary earnings per share" which may be misleading. Furthermore, whenever an issuer has more than one convertible security outstanding, the effect of even the "potential" dilution of such "residual" securities is not appropriately reflected in any meaningful manner in the fully-diluted earnings per share amount, since its impact is combined with that of other convertible securities of the issuer which may not currently be "residual".

Criteria and Methods for Determination of Residual Status

78. This Opinion concludes (paragraph 33) that a cash yield test – based on a specified percentage of the bank prime interest rate – should be used to determine the residual status of convertible securities, and that options and warrants should be considered residual securities at all times. Viewpoints differing from those conclusions and supporting other criteria or methods are summarized below.

Convertible Securities

79. *Investment value method.* As explained in paragraphs 8-11 of this Opinion, a previous Opinion specified a relative value method for the determination of the residual status of a security. In practice the method has been applied by comparing the market value of a convertible security with its "invest-

ment value", and by classifying a security as residual at time of issuance if such market value were 200% or more of investment value, with certain practical modifications of this test subsequent to time of issuance to assure the substance of an apparent change in status and to prevent frequent changes of status for possible temporary fluctuations in the market.

80. The establishment of investment values for convertible securities involves considerable estimation, and frequently requires the use of experts. Published financial services report estimates of investment value for many, but not all, convertible securities. Most convertible securities are issued under conditions which permit a reasonable estimate of their investment values. In addition, reference to the movements of long-term borrowing rates for groups of issuers with similar credit and risk circumstances — or even reference to general long-term borrowing rates — can furnish effective evidence for an appropriate determination of the investment value of a convertible security subsequent to its issuance. As in many determinations made for accounting purposes, estimates of this nature are often necessary. The necessity of establishing some percentage or level as the line of demarcation between residual and nonresidual status is common to all methods under consideration — including the market parity test and various yield tests — and appears justifiable in the interest of reasonable consistency of treatment, both for a single issuer and among issuers.

81. The investment value method is somewhat similar to the cash yield method specified in paragraph 33 of this Opinion. However, the latter method has two apparent weaknesses, in the view of those who support the investment value method. In the first place, it does not differentiate between issuers — that is, it is based on the same borrowing rate for all issuers, without regard for their credit ratings or other risks inherent in their activities. Second, it is based on the current bank prime interest rate, which is essentially a short-term borrowing rate. The relationship between this rate — assuming that it is constant in all sections of the country at any given time — and the long-term corporate borrowing rate may fluctuate to such an extent that the claimed ease of determination may be offset by

a lack of correlation. The investment value method, based on the terms of each issue and the status of each issuer, is thus considered by some to be a more satisfactory method.

82. *Market parity method.* This method compares a convertible security's market value with its conversion value. In general, if the two values are substantially equivalent and in excess of redemption price, the convertible security is considered to be "residual".

83. The market parity method has the advantage, as compared to the investment value method, of using amounts that usually are readily available or ascertainable, and of avoiding estimates of investment value. More importantly, in the view of some, the equivalence of values is clearly an indication of the equivalence of the securities, while a comparison of relative values of the characteristics of a security is an indication of its status only if arbitrary rules, such as the "major portion of value" test, are used. In similar vein, the yield test also requires the establishment of a point at which to determine residuality. On the other hand, a practical application of the market parity test would also require the establishment of a percentage relationship at which to determine residual status, due to the many variables involved and the need for consistent application. Also, the call or redemption price of a convertible security has an effect on the point at which market parity is achieved.

84. *Yield methods.* There are various other methods of determining the residual nature of a convertible security based on yield relationships. Each of these is based on a comparison of the cash yield on the convertible security (based on its market value) and some predetermined rate of yield (based on other values, conditions or ratings). The discussion of the various methods contained in this Opinion comprehends the advantages and disadvantages of these other methods.

Options and Warrants

85. As explained in paragraphs 35-38 of this Opinion, options and warrants should be regarded as common stock equivalents

at all times; the "treasury stock method" should be used in most cases to determine the number of common shares to be considered the equivalent of the options and warrants; and the number of common shares so computed should be included in the computation of both the "primary" and "fully-diluted" earnings per share (assuming a dilutive effect). Viewpoints which differ from those conclusions and support other treatments or other methods of measurement are summarized below.

86. *Exclusion from computation of primary earnings per share.* In this Opinion the Board has for the first time considered options and warrants to be common stock equivalents at all times and, because of the treasury stock method of computation established, the primary earnings per share will in some cases be affected by the market price of the stock obtainable on exercise, rather than solely by the economics of the transaction entered into. Some believe that this produces a circular effect in that the reporting of earnings per share may then influence the market which, in turn, influences earnings per share. They believe that earnings per share should affect the market and not vice versa. They point out that the classification of convertible debentures and convertible preferred stocks is determined at time of issuance only and consequently subsequent fluctuations in the market prices of these securities do not affect primary earnings per share. Therefore, they believe that the dual, equally prominent presentation of primary and fully diluted earnings per share is most informative when the effect of options and warrants, other than those whose exercise price is substantially lower than market price at time of issuance, is included only in the fully diluted earnings per share which would be lower than primary earnings per share and thus would emphasize the potential dilution.

87. *Determination of equivalent common shares.* Some believe that the "treasury stock method" described in paragraph 36 of the Opinion is unsatisfactory and that other methods are preferable. Under one such method the number of equivalent shares is computed by reference to the relationship between the market value of the option or warrant and the market value of the related common stock. In general, it reflects the impact

of options and warrants on earnings per share whenever the option or warrant has a market value, and not only when the market price of the related common stock exceeds the exercise price (as does the treasury stock method).

88. *Measurement of effect of options and warrants.* Some believe that the effect of outstanding options and warrants on earnings per share should be computed by assuming exercise as of the beginning of the period and assuming some use of the funds so attributed to the issuer. The uses which have been suggested include application of such assumed proceeds to (a) reduce outstanding short or long term borrowings, (b) invest in government obligations or commercial paper, (c) invest in operations of the issuer or (d) fulfill other corporate objectives of the issuer. Each of these methods is felt by some to be the preferable approach. Many who support one of these methods feel that the "treasury stock method" is improper since (a) it fails to reflect any dilution unless the market price of the common stock exceeds the exercise price, (b) it assumes a hypothetical purchase of treasury stock which in many cases – due to the significant number of common shares involved – would either not be possible or be possible only at a considerably increased price per share, and (c) it may be considered to be the attribution of earnings assumed on the funds received – in which case the earnings rate for each issuer is a function of the price-earnings ratio of its common stock and is thus similar in result to an arbitrary assumption of a possibly inappropriate earnings rate.

89. Some believe that no increment in earnings should be attributed to the funds assumed to be received upon the exercise of options and warrants, particularly if such instruments are to be reflected in the computation of primary earnings per share, since the funds were not available to the issuer during the period.

Computational Methods—Convertible Securities

90. This Opinion concludes (paragraph 51) that the "if converted" method of computation should be used for primary earnings per share when convertible securities are considered

the equivalent of common stock. Some believe that this method does not properly reflect the actual circumstances existing during the period, and favor, instead, the so-called "two-class" method of computation. (See paragraphs 54-55.) Under the latter method, securities considered common stock equivalents are treated as common shares with a different dividend rate from that of the regular common shares. The residual security concept is based on common stock equivalence without the necessity of actual conversion; therefore, this method properly recognizes the fact that these securities receive a preferential distribution before the common stock – and also share in the potential benefits of the undistributed earnings through their substantial common stock characteristics in the same way as do the common shares. These securities are designed to achieve these two goals. Those who favor this method believe that the "if converted" method disregards the realities of what occurred during the period. Thus, in their view, the "if converted" method is a "pro-forma" method which assumes conversion and the elimination of preferential distributions to these securities; as such, it is not suitable for use in the computation of *primary earnings per share data*, since the assumed conversions did not take place and the preferential distributions did take place.

91. Those who favor the "two-class" method point out that it is considered appropriate in the case of certain participating and two-class common situations. In their view, the circumstances existing when common stock equivalents are outstanding are similar; therefore, use of this method is appropriate.

Recognition of Common Stock Equivalents in the Finanical Statements

92. This Opinion concludes (paragraph 39) that the designation of securities as common stock equivalents is solely for the purpose of determining primary earnings per share; no changes from present practice are recommended in the presentation of such securities in the financial statements. Some believe, however, that the financial statements should reflect a treatment of such securities which is consistent with the method used to determine earnings per share in the financial

statements. Accordingly, convertible debt considered to be a common stock equivalent would be classified in the balance sheet in association with stockholders' equity – either under a separate caption immediately preceding stockholders' equity, or in a combined section with a caption such as "Equity of common stockholders and holders of common stock equivalents". In the statement of income and retained earnings, interest paid on convertible debt considered a common stock equivalent would be shown as a "distribution to holders of common stock equivalents", either following the caption of "net income" in the statement of income or grouped with other distributions in the statement of retained earnings.

93. Some believe that the inconsistency of the positions taken on this matter in this Opinion is clearly evident in the requirement (paragraph 66) that, when a subsidiary has convertible securities which are common stock equivalents, the portion of the income of the subsidiary to be included in the consolidated statement of income of the parent and its subsidiaries should be computed disregarding the effect of the common stock equivalents, but that the computation of the primary earnings per share of the parent should reflect the effect of these common stock equivalents in attributing the income of the subsidiary to its various outstanding securities. This inconsistent treatment is, in the opinion of some, not only illogical but misleading.

APPENDIX C

ILLUSTRATIVE STATEMENTS

The following exhibits illustrate the disclosure of earnings per share data on the assumption that this Opinion was effective for all periods covered. The format of the disclosure is illustrative only, and does not necessarily reflect a preference by the Accounting Principles Board.

Exhibit A. This exhibit illustrates the disclosure of earnings per share data for a company with a simple capital structure (see paragraph 14 of this Opinion). The facts assumed for Exhibit A are as follows:

	Number of Shares	
	1968	*1967*
Common stock outstanding:		
Beginning of year	3,300,000	3,300,000
End of year	3,300,000	3,300,000
Issued or acquired during year	None	None
Common stock reserved under employee stock options granted	7,200	7,200
Weighted average number of shares	3,300,000	3,300,000

NOTE: Shares issuable under employee stock options are excluded from the weighted average number of shares on the assumption that their effect is not dilutive (see paragraph 14 of this Opinion).

EXHIBIT A

EXAMPLE OF DISCLOSURE OF EARNINGS PER SHARE
Simple Capital Structure

(Bottom of Income Statement)	*Thousands Except per share data*	
	1968	*1967*
Income before extraordinary item	$ 9,150	$7,650
Extraordinary item – gain on sale of property less applicable income taxes	900	–
Net Income	$10,050	$7,650
Earnings per common share:		
Income before extraordinary item	$ 2.77	$ 2.32
Extraordinary item	.28	–
Net Income	$ 3.05	$ 2.32

Exhibit B. This exhibit illustrates the disclosure of earnings per share data for a company with a complex capital structure (see paragraph 15 of this Opinion). The facts assumed for Exhibit B are as follows:

Market price of common stock. The market price of the common stock was as follows:

Average Price:	*1968*	*1967*	*1966*
First quarter	50	45	40
Second quarter	60	52	41
Third quarter	70	50	40
Fourth quarter	70	50	45
December 31 closing price	72	51	44

Cash dividends. Cash dividends of $0.125 per common share were declared and paid for each quarter of 1966 and 1967. Cash dividends of $0.25 per common share were declared and paid for each quarter of 1968.

Convertible debentures. 4% convertible debentures with a principal amount of $10,000,000 due 1986 were sold for cash at a price of 100 in the last quarter of 1966. Each $100 debenture was convertible into two shares of common stock. No debentures were converted during 1966 or 1967. The entire issue was converted at the beginning of the third quarter of 1968 because the issue was called by the company.

These convertible debentures were not common stock equivalents under the terms of this Opinion. The bank prime rate at the time the debentures were sold in the last quarter of 1966 was 6%. The debentures carried a coupon interest rate of 4% and had a market value of $100 at issuance. The cash yield of 4% was not less than 66⅔% of the bank prime rate (see paragraph 33 of this Opinion). Cash yield is the same as the coupon interest rate in this case only because the market value at issuance was $100.

Convertible preferred stock. 600,000 shares of convertible preferred stock were issued for assets in a purchase transaction at the beginning of the second quarter of 1967. The annual dividend on each share of this convertible preferred stock is $0.20.

Each share is convertible into one share of common stock. This convertible stock had a market value of $53 at the time of issuance and was therefore a common stock equivalent under the terms of this Opinion at the time of its issuance because the cash yield on market value was only 0.4% and the bank prime rate was 5.5% (see paragraph 33 of this Opinion).

Holders of 500,000 shares of this convertible preferred stock converted their preferred stock into common stock during 1968 because the cash dividend on the common stock exceeded the cash dividend on the preferred stock.

Warrants. Warrants to buy 500,000 shares of common stock at $60 per share for a period of five years were issued along with the convertible preferred stock mentioned above. No warrants have been exercised. (Note that the number of shares issuable upon exercise of the warrants is less than 20% of outstanding common shares; hence paragraph 38 is not applicable.)

The number of common shares represented by the warrants (see paragraph 36 of this Opinion) was 71,428 for each of the third and fourth quarters of 1968 ($60 exercise price × 500,000 warrants = $30,000,000; $30,000,000 ÷ $70 share market price = 428,572 shares; 500,000 shares — 428,572 shares = 71,428 shares). No shares were deemed to be represented by the warrants for the second quarter of 1968 or for any preceding quarter (see paragraph 36 of this Opinion) because the market price of the stock did not exceed the exercise price for substantially all of three consecutive months until the third quarter of 1968.

Common stock. The number of shares of common stock outstanding were as follows:

	1968	*1967*
Beginning of year	3,300,000	3,300,000
Conversion of preferred stock	500,000	—
Conversion of debentures	200,000	—
End of year	4,000,000	3,300,000

Weighted average number of shares. The weighted average number of shares of common stock and common stock equivalents was determined as follows:

	1968	*1967*
Common stock:		
Shares outstanding from beginning of period	3,300,000	3,300,000
500,000 shares issued on conversion of preferred stock; assume issuance evenly during year	250,000	–
200,000 shares issued on conversion of convertible debentures at beginning of third quarter of 1968 ..	100,000	–
	3,650,000	3,300,000
Common stock equivalents:		
600,000 shares convertible preferred stock issued at the beginning of the second quarter of 1967, excluding 250,000 shares included under common stock in 1968	350,000	450,000
Warrants: 71,428 common share equivalents outstanding for third and fourth quarters of 1968, i.e., one-half year	35,714	–
	385,714	450,000
Weighted average number of shares	4,035,714	3,750,000

The weighted average number of shares would be adjusted to calculate fully diluted earnings per share as follows:

	1968	*1967*
Weighted average number of shares	4.035,714	3,750,000
Shares applicable to convertible debentures converted at the beginning of the third quarter of 1968, excluding 100,000 shares included under common stock for 1968	100,000	200,000
Shares applicable to warrants included above	(35,714)	–
Shares applicable to warrants based on year-end price of $72 (see paragraph 42 of this Opinion)	83,333	–
	4,183,333	3,950,000

Income before extraordinary item and net income would be adjusted for interest expense on the debentures in calculating fully diluted earnings per share as follows:

	Thousands		
	Before Adjustment	*Interest, net of tax effect*	*After Adjustment*
1967: Net income	$10,300	$208	$10,508
1968:			
Income before extraordinary item	12,900	94	12,994
Net income	13,800	94	13,894

NOTES: (a) Taxes in 1967 were 48%; in 1968 they were 52.8%.
(b) Net income is before dividends on preferred stock.

EXHIBIT B

EXAMPLE OF DISCLOSURE OF EARNINGS PER SHARE

Complex Capital Structure

(Bottom of Income Statement)	*Thousands Except per share data*	
	1968	*1967*
Income before extraordinary item	$12,900	$10,300
Extraordinary item – gain on sale of property less applicable income taxes ..	900	–
Net Income	$13,800	$10,300
Earnings per common share and common equivalent share (note x):		
Income before extraordinary item..	$ 3.20	$ 2.75
Extraordinary item	.22	–
Net Income	$ 3.42	$ 2.75
Earnings per common share – assuming full dilution (note x):		
Income before extraordinary item..	$ 3.11	$ 2.66
Extraordinary item	.21	–
Net Income	$ 3.32	$ 2.66

EXHIBIT C

EXAMPLE OF NOTE X* TO EXHIBIT B

The $0.20 convertible preferred stock is callable by the company after March 31, 1972 at $53 per share. Each share is convertible into one share of common stock.

During 1968, 700,000 shares of common stock were issued on conversions: 500,000 shares on conversion of preferred stock and 200,000 on conversion of all the 4% convertible debentures.

Warrants to acquire 500,000 shares of the company's stock at $60 per share were outstanding at the end of 1968 and 1967. These warrants expire March 31, 1972.

Earnings per common share and common equivalent share were computed by dividing net income by the weighted average number of shares of common stock and common stock equivalents outstanding during the year. The convertible preferred stock has been considered to be the equivalent of common stock from the time of its issuance in 1967. The number of shares issuable on conversion of preferred stock was added to the number

* The following disclosure in the December 31, 1968 balance sheet is assumed for this note:

	1968	*1967*
Long-term debt:		
4% convertible debentures, due 1986	–	$10,000,000
Stockholders' equity (note x):		
Convertible voting preferred stock of $1 par value, $0.20 cumulative dividend. Authorized 600,000 shares; issued and outstanding 100,000 shares (600,000 in 1967) ...	$ 100,000	$ 600,000
(Liquidation value $22 per share, aggregating $2,200,000 in 1968 and $13,200,000 in 1967)		
Common stock of $1 par value per share. Authorized 5,000,000 shares; issued and outstanding 4,000,000 shares (3,300,000 in 1967)	4,000,000	3,300,000
Additional paid-in capital	xxx	xxx
Retained earnings	xxx	xxx
	$ xxx	$ xxx

of common shares. The number of common shares was also increased by the number of shares issuable on the exercise of warrants when the market price of the common stock exceeds the exercise price of the warrants. This increase in the number of common shares was reduced by the number of common shares which are assumed to have been purchased with the proceeds from the exercise of the warrants; these purchases were assumed to have been made at the average price of the common stock during that part of the year when the market price of the common stock exceeded the exercise price of the warrants.

Earnings per common share and common equivalent share for 1968 would have been $3.36 for net income and $3.14 for income before extraordinary item had the 4% convertible debentures due 1986 been converted on January 1, 1968. (These debentures were called for redemption as of July 1, 1968 and all were converted into common shares.)

Earnings per common share—assuming full dilution for 1968 were determined on the assumptions that the convertible debentures were converted and the warrants were exercised on January 1, 1968. As to the debentures, net earnings were adjusted for the interest net of its tax effect. As to the warrants, outstanding shares were increased as described above except that purchases of common stock are assumed to have been made at the year-end price of $72.

Earnings per common share—assuming full dilution for 1967 were determined on the assumption that the convertible debentures were converted on January 1, 1967. The outstanding warrants had no effect on the earnings per share data for 1967, as the exercise price was in excess of the market price of the common stock.

APPENDIX D

DEFINITIONS OF TERMS

There are a number of terms used in discussion of earnings per share which have special meanings in that context. When used in this Opinion they are intended to have the meaning given in the following definitions. Some of the terms are not used in the Opinion but are provided as information pertinent to the subject of earnings per share.

Call price. The amount at which a security may be redeemed by the issuer at the issuer's option.

Cash yield. The cash received by the holder of a security as a distribution of accumulated or current earnings or as a contractual payment for return on the amount invested, without regard to the par or face amount of the security. As used in this Opinion the term "cash yield" refers to the relationship or ratio of such cash to be received annually to the market value of the related security at the specified date. For example, a security with a coupon rate of 4% (on par of $100) and a market value of $80 would have a cash yield of 5%.

Common stock. A stock which is subordinate to all other stocks of the issuer.

Common stock equivalent. A security which, because of its terms or the circumstances under which it was issued, is in substance equivalent to common stock.

Contingent issuance. A possible issuance of shares of common stock that is dependent upon the exercise of conversion rights, options or warrants, the satisfaction of certain conditions, or similar arrangements.

Conversion price. The price that determines the number of shares of common stock into which a security is convertible. For example, $100 face value of debt convertible into 5 shares of common stock would be stated to have a conversion price of $20.

Conversion rate. The ratio of (a) the number of common shares issuable upon conversion to (b) a unit of a convertible security. For example, a preferred stock may be convertible at the rate of 3 shares of common stock for each share of preferred stock.

Conversion value. The current market value of the common shares obtainable upon conversion of a convertible security, after deducting any cash payment required upon conversion.

Dilution (Dilutive). A reduction in earnings per share resulting from the assumption that convertible securities have been converted or that options and warrants have been exercised or other shares have been issued upon the fulfillment of certain conditions. (See footnote 2.)

Dual presentation. The presentation with equal prominence of two types of earnings per share amounts on the face of the income statement – one is primary earnings per share; the other is fully diluted earnings per share.

Earnings per share. The amount of earnings attributable to each share of common stock. For convenience, the term is used in this Opinion to refer to either net income (earnings) per share or to net loss per share. It should be used without qualifying language only when no potentially dilutive convertible securities, options, warrants or other agreements providing for contingent issuances of common stock are outstanding.

Exercise price. The amount that must be paid for a share of common stock upon exercise of a stock option or warrant.

Fully diluted earnings per share. The amount of current earnings per share reflecting the maximum dilution that would have resulted from conversions, exercises and other contingent issuances that individually would have decreased earnings per share and in the aggregate would have had a dilutive effect. All such issuances are assumed to have taken place at the beginning of the period (or at the time the contingency arose, if later).

"If converted" method. A method of computing earnings per share data that assumes conversion of convertible securities as of the beginning of the earliest period reported (or at time of issuance, if later).

Investment value. The price at which it is estimated a convertible security would sell if it were not convertible, based upon its stipulated preferred dividend or interest rate and its other senior security characteristics.

Market parity. A market price relationship in which the market price of a convertible security and its conversion value are approximately equal.

Option. The right to purchase shares of common stock in accordance with an agreement, upon payment of a specified amount. As used in this Opinion, options include but are not limited to options granted to and stock purchase agreements entered into with employees. Options are considered "securities" in this Opinion.

Primary earnings per share. The amount of earnings attributable to each share of common stock outstanding, including common stock equivalents.

Redemption price. The amount at which a security is required to be redeemed at maturity or under a sinking fund arrangement.

Security. The evidence of a debt or ownership or related right. For purposes of this Opinion it includes stock options and warrants, as well as debt and stock.

Senior security. A security having preferential rights and which is not a common stock or common stock equivalent, for example, nonconvertible preferred stock.

Supplementary earnings per share. A computation of earnings per share, other than primary or fully diluted earnings per share, which gives effect to conversions, etc., which took place during the period or shortly thereafter as though they had occurred at the beginning of the period (or date of issuance, if later).

Time of issuance. The time of issuance generally is the date when agreement as to terms has been reached and announced, even though such agreement is subject to certain further actions, such as directors' or stockholders' approval.

Treasury stock method. A method of recognizing the use of proceeds that would be obtained upon exercise of options and warrants in computing earnings per share. It assumes that any proceeds would be used to purchase common stock at current market prices. (See paragraphs 36-38).

"Two-class" method. A method of computing primary earnings per share that treats common stock equivalents as though they were common stocks with different dividend rates from that of the common stock.

Warrant. A security giving the holder the right to purchase shares of common stock in accordance with the terms of the instrument, usually upon payment of a specified amount.

Weighted average number of shares. The number of shares determined by relating (a) the portion of time within a reporting period that a particular number of shares of a certain security has been outstanding to (b) the total time in that period. Thus, for example, if 100 shares of a certain security were outstanding during the first quarter of a fiscal year and 300 shares were outstanding during the balance of the year, the weighted average number of outstanding shares would be 250.

26

Form 10-K

Form 10-K (filed annually by companies registered under the Securities and Exchange Act) is a major source of information for the analyst. All analysts should have a fairly good understanding of the kinds of information contained therein and where in the form desired information can be located. For convenience of reference a copy of Form 10-K (as revised, effective August, 1973) is included here. This and other SEC reporting forms are subject to revision from time to time and analysts should attempt to keep abreast of such matters by obtaining copies of releases from the local SEC office.

A 12-K report, similar in form to the 10-K, is filed annally with the SEC by certain companies that are regulated by the Federal Power Commission, Interstate Commerce Commission and the Federal Communications Commission.

Item 1. Business

a. Identify the principal products produced and services rendered by the registrant and its subsidiaries, and the principal markets for, and methods of distribution of, such products and services. Briefly describe any significant changes in the kinds of products produced or services rendered, or in the markets or methods of distribution, since the beginning of the fiscal year.

b. Describe any material changes and developments since the beginning of the fiscal year in the business done and intended to be done by the registrant and its subsidiaries. The description shall include information as to matters such as the following:

1. Competitive conditions in the industry or industries involved and the competitive position of the registrant if known or reasonably available to the registrant. If several products or services are involved, separate consideration shall be given to the principal products or services or classes of products or services. (Formerly paragraph (*b*)(1) of Item 1.)

2. If a material part of the business is dependent upon a single customer or a few customers, the loss of any one or more of whom would have a materially adverse effect on the business of the registrant, the name of the customer or customers, their relationship, if any, to the registrant and material facts regarding their importance to the business of the registrant.

3. To the extent that information concerning backlog is material to an understanding of the business of the registrant, the dollar amount of backlog of orders believed to be firm, as of the end of the registrant's fiscal year, and as of the end of the preceding fiscal year, together with an indication of the portion thereof not reasonably expected to be filled within the current fiscal year and seasonal or other material aspects of the backlog.

4. The sources and availability of raw materials essential to the business.

5. The importance to the business and the duration and effect of all material patents, trademarks, licenses, franchises and concessions held.

6.(*a*) The estimated dollar amount spent during each of the last two fiscal years on material research activities relating to the developments of new products or services or the improvement of existing products or services, indicating those activities which were company-sponsored and/or those which were customer-sponsored.

(*b*) If there has been a public announcement of, or if information otherwise has become public about, a new product or line of business requiring the investment of a material amount of total assets, a description of the status of such product or line (e.g., whether in the planning stage, whether prototypes exist, the degree to which product design has progressed or whether further engineering is necessary).

(*c*) Where material, state the approximate number of employees engaged full time in each of the activities described in (*a*) above during each fiscal year and in (*b*).

Note: Item 1 6(*b*) is not intended to require disclosure of otherwise nonpublic corporate information the disclosure of which would adversely affect the registrant's competitive position. Subparagraph (*a*) requires disclosure of financial information relating to research and development activities. Subparagraph (*b*) is intended to elicit additional specific information only where there has been a public announcement or where information has otherwise become public about a new product or line of business requiring the investment of a material amount of total assets.

7. The material effects that compliance with federal, state and local provisions which have been enacted or adopted regulating the discharge of materials into the environment, or otherwise relating to the protection of the environment, may have upon the capital expenditures, earnings and competitive position of the registrant.

8. The number of persons employed by the registrant.

9. The extent to which the business of the registrant or a material portion thereof is or may be seasonal.

Instructions. 1. If the registrant proposes to enter, or has recently entered or introduced a new line of business or product requiring the investment of a material amount of its total assets, provide as supplemental information, but not as a part of the report, a copy of any market studies conducted or performed by or for the registrant relating to such business or product and a statement as to the actual or proposed use of such study. Where material, disclosure in the report of the absence of such a study is required.

2. The principal methods of competition (e.g., price, service, warranty, or product performance,) should be identified and positive and negative factors pertaining to the competitive position of the registrant, to the extent that they exist, should be explained, if known or reasonably available to the registrant. An estimate of the number of competitors should be included, and, where material, the particular markets in which the registrant competes should be identified. Where one or a small number of competitors are dominant, they should be identified.

3. Where material to understanding the registrant's business, the registrant's and industry practices and conditions as they relate to working capital items should be explained (e.g., where the registrant's business is highly seasonal; where the registrant is required to carry significant amounts of inventory to meet rapid delivery requirements of customers or to assure itself of a continuous allotment of goods from suppliers; or where the registrant has to provide extended payment terms to customers).

4. The description shall not relate to the powers and objects specified in the charter, but to the actual business done and intended to be done. Include the business of subsidiaries and affiliates of the registrant insofar as is necessary to understand the character and development of the business conducted by the total enterprise.

5. In describing developments, information shall be given as to matters such as the following: the nature and results of any bankruptcy, receivership or similar proceedings with respect to the registrant or any of its significant subsidiaries; the nature and results of any other material reorganization, readjustment or succession of the registrant or any of its significant subsidiaries; the acquisition or disposition of any material amount of assets otherwise than in the ordinary course of business; and any material changes in the mode of conducting the business.

6. The business of a predecessor or predecessors shall be deemed to be the business of the registrant for the purpose of this item.

7. Appropriate disclosure shall be made with respect to any material portion of the business which may be subject to renegotiation of profits or termination of contracts or subcontracts at the election of the government.

c. 1. *Information as to lines of business.* If the registrant and its subsidiaries are engaged in more than one line of business, state, for each of the registrant's last five fiscal years, or for each fiscal year ending after December 31, 1966, or for each fiscal year the registrant has been engaged in business, whichever period is less, the approximate amount or percentage of (i) total sales and revenues, and (ii) income (or loss) before income taxes and extraordinary items, attributable to each line of business which during either of the last two fiscal years accounted for—

(*a*) 10 percent or more of the total of sales and revenues,
(*b*) 10 percent or more of income before income taxes and extraordinary items computed without deduction of loss resulting from operations of any line of business, or
(*c*) a loss which equaled or exceeded 10 percent of the amount of income specified in (b) above;

provided, that if total sales and revenues did not exceed $50,000,000 during either of the last two fiscal years, the percentages specified in (*a*), (*b*) and (*c*) above shall be 15 percent, instead of 10 percent.

If it is impracticable to state the contribution to income (or loss) before income taxes and extraordinary items for any line of business, state the contribution thereof to the results of operations most closely approaching such income, together with a brief explanation of the reasons why it is not practicable to state the contribution to such income or loss.

Instructions. 1. If the number of lines of business for which information is required exceeds ten, the registrant may, at its option, furnish the required information only for the ten lines of business deemed most important to an understanding of the business. In such event, a statement to that effect shall be set forth.

2. In grouping products or services as lines of business, appropriate consideration shall be given to all relevant factors, including rates of profitability of operations, degrees of risk and opportunity for growth. The basis for grouping such products or services and any material changes between periods in such groupings shall be briefly described.

3. Where material amounts of products or services are transferred from one line of business to another, the receiving and transferring lines may be considered a single line of business for the purpose of reporting the operating results thereof.

4. If the method of pricing intra-company transfers of products or services or the method of allocation of common or corporate costs materially affects the reported contribution to income of a line of business, such methods and any material changes between periods in such methods and the effect thereof shall be described briefly.

5. Information regarding sales or revenues or income (or loss) from different classes of products or services in operations regulated by federal, state or municipal authorities may be limited to those classes of products or

services required by any uniform system of accounts prescribed by such authorities.

c. 2. *Information as to classes of similar products or services.* State for each fiscal year specified in (1) above the amount or percentage of total sales and revenues contributed by each class of similar products or services which contributed 10 percent or more to total sales and revenues in either of the last two fiscal years, or 15 percent or more of total sales and revenues if total sales and revenues did not exceed $50,000,000 during either of the last two fiscal years.

Instructions. 1. Paragraph (2) calls for information with respect to classes of similar products or services regardless of whether the registrant is engaged in more than one line of business as referred to in paragraph (1) above. However, this information may be combined, where appropriate, with the response to paragraph (1).

2. Instruction 5 to paragraph (1) above shall also apply to paragraph (2).

d. If the registrant and its subsidiaries engage in material operations in foreign countries, or if a material portion of sales or revenues is derived from customers in foreign countries, appropriate disclosure shall be made with respect to the importance of that part of the business to the registrant and the risks attendant thereto. Insofar as practicable, furnish information with respect to volume and relative profitability of such operations.

e. The Commission may, upon written request of the registrant and where consistent with the protection of investors, permit the omission of any of the information herein required or the furnishing in substitution therefor of appropriate information of comparable character. The Commission may also require the furnishing of other information in addition to, or in substitution for, the information herein required in any case where such information is necessary or appropriate for an adequate description of the business done or intended to be done.

Item 2. Summary of Operations

Furnish in comparative columnar form a summary of operations for the registrant, or for the registrant and its subsidiaries consolidated, or both, as appropriate, for (*a*) each of the last five fiscal years of the registrant (or for the life of the registrant and its predecessors, if less), and (*b*) any additional fiscal years necessary to keep the summary from being misleading. Where necessary, include information or explanation of material significance to investors in appraising the results shown, or refer to such information or explanation set forth elsewhere in the report. An analysis of retained earnings and other additional capital accounts shall be furnished for each fiscal year covered by the summary.

Instructions. 1. Subject to appropriate variation to conform to the nature of the business, the following items shall be included: net sales or operating revenues; cost of goods sold or operating expenses (or gross profit); interest charges; income taxes; income before extraordinary items; extraordinary items; and net income. If either the profit and loss or retained earnings statements required by the Instructions as to Financial Statements are included in their entirety in the summary of operations, the statements so included need not be included elsewhere in the report.

2. If a period or periods reported on include operations of a business prior to the date of acquisition or for other causes differ from reports previously issued for any period, the summary shall be reconciled as to sales or revenues and net income in the summary or by footnote with the amounts previously reported.

3. If appropriate, the summary shall be prepared to show earnings applicable to common stock. Per share earnings and dividends declared for each period of the summary shall be included and the basis of the computation stated together with the number of shares used in the computation. The registrant shall file as an exhibit a statement setting forth in reasonable detail the computation of per share earnings, unless the computation is clearly set forth in answer to this item.

4. *a.* If debt securities are registered under Section 12 of the Act, the registrant may, at its option, show in tabular form for each fiscal year the ratio of earnings to fixed charges.

b. Earnings shall be computed after all operating and income deductions except fixed charges and taxes based on income or profits and after eliminating undistributed income of unconsolidated persons. In the case of utilities, interest credits charged to construction shall be added to gross income and not deducted from interest.

c. The term "fixed charges" shall mean (i) interest and amortization of debt discount and expense and premium on all indebtedness; (ii) one-third of all rentals reported in the schedule prepared in accordance with Rule 12–16 of Regulation S-X, or such portion as can be demonstrated to be representative of the interest factor in the particular case; and (iii) in case consolidated figures are used, preferred stock dividend requirements of consolidated subsidiaries, excluding in all cases items eliminated in consolidation.

d. Any registrant electing to show the ratio of earnings to fixed charges, in accordance with this instruction, shall file as an exhibit a statement setting forth in reasonable detail the computations of the ratio shown.

5. Describe any change in accounting principles or practices followed by the registrant, or any change in the method of applying any such accounting principles or practices, which will materially affect the financial statements filed or to be filed for the current year with the Commission and which had not been previously reported hereunder. State the date of the change and the reasons therefor. A letter from the registrant's independent accountants, approving or otherwise commenting on the change, shall be filed as an exhibit.

6. For any event subsequent to January 31, 1973, which was required to be reported pursuant to Item 10(*a*) of Form 8-K in which an amount of cost was estimated to be incurred in the fiscal year being reported on or

the prior fiscal year, summarize such transaction and state the amounts of such estimated cost and the amounts of the actual cost incurred in such periods, the reasons for differences between estimated and actual amounts, if any, and provide a detailed reconciliation showing all charges and credits to any reserve provided.

Item 3. Properties

State briefly the location and general character of the principal plants, mines and other materially important physical properties of the registrant and its subsidiaries, whether held in fee or leased, and if leased, the expiration dates of material leases.

Instruction. What is required is such information as will reasonably inform investors as to the suitability, adequacy, productive capacity and extent of utilization of the facilities used in the enterprise. Detailed descriptions of the physical characteristics of individual properties or legal descriptions by metes and bounds are not required and should not be given.

Item 4. Parents and Subsidiaries

a. Furnish a list or diagram of all parents and subsidiaries of the registrant and as to each person named indicate the percentage of voting securities owned, or other basis of control, by its immediate parent, if any.

Instructions. 1. The list or diagram shall include the registrant and shall be so prepared as to show clearly the relationship of each person named to the registrant and to the other persons named. If any person is controlled by means of the direct ownership of its securities by two or more persons, so indicate by appropriate cross-reference.

2. Designate by appropriate symbols (*a*) subsidiaries for which separate financial statements are filed; (*b*) subsidiaries included in consolidated financial statements; (*c*) subsidiaries included in group financial statements filed for unconsolidated subsidiaries; and (*d*) other subsidiaries, indicating briefly why financial statements of such subsidiaries are not filed.

3. Include the name of the state or other jurisdiction in which each subsidiary was incorporated or organized.

4. The names of particular subsidiaries may be omitted if the unnamed subsidiaries, considered in the aggregate as a single subsidiary, would not constitute a significant subsidiary.

5. The names of consolidated wholly-owned multiple subsidiaries carrying on the same line of business, such as chain stores or small loan companies, may be omitted, provided the name of the immediate parent, the line of business, the number of omitted subsidiaries operating in the United States and the number operating in foreign countries are given. This instruction shall not apply, however, to banks, insurance companies, savings and loan associations or to any subsidiary subject to regulation by another federal agency.

6. If the registrant owns directly or indirectly approximately 50 percent of the voting securities of any person and approximately 50 percent of the voting securities of such person is owned directly or indirectly by another single interest, or if the registrant takes up the equity in undistributed earnings of any other unconsolidated person, such person shall be deemed to be a subsidiary for the purpose of this item.

Item 5. Pending Legal Proceedings

Briefly describe any material pending legal proceedings, other than ordinary routine litigation incidental to the business, to which the registrant or any of its subsidiaries is a party or of which any of their property is the subject. Include the name of the court or agency in which the proceedings were instituted, the date instituted and the principal parties thereto.

Instructions. 1. If the business ordinarily results in actions for negligence or other claims, no such action or claim need be described unless it departs from the normal kind of such actions.

2. No information need be given with respect to any proceeding which involves primarily a claim for damages if the amount involved, exclusive of interest and costs, does not exceed 10 percent of the current assets of the registrant and its subsidiaries on a consolidated basis. However, if any proceedings presents in large degree the same issues as other proceedings pending or known to be contemplated, the amount involved in such other proceedings shall be included in computing such percentage.

3. Notwithstanding Instruction 1 and 2, any material bankruptcy, receivership, or similar proceeding with respect to the registrant or any of its significant subsidiaries shall be described. Any material proceedings to which any director, officer or affiliate of the registrant, any security holder named in answer to Item 11(*a*), or any associate of any such director, officer or security holder, in a party, or has a material interest, adverse to the registrant or any of its subsidiaries shall also be described.

4. Notwithstanding the foregoing, administrative or judicial proceedings arising under any federal, state or local provisions which have been enacted or adopted regulating the discharge of materials into the environment or otherwise relating to the protection of the environment, shall not be deemed "ordinary routine litigation incidental to the business" and shall be described if such proceeding is material to the business or financial condition of the registrant or if it involves primarily a claim for damages and the amount involved, exclusive of interest and costs, exceeds 10 percent of the current assets of the registrant and its subsidiaries on a consolidated basis. Any such proceedings by governmental authorities shall be deemed material and shall be described whether or not the amount of any claim for damages involved exceeds 10 percent of current assets on a consolidated basis and whether or not such proceedings are considered "ordinary routine litigation incidental to the business"; provided, however, that such proceedings which are similar in nature may be grouped and described generically stating: the number of

such proceedings in each group; a generic description of such proceedings; the issues generally involved; and, if such proceedings in the aggregate are material to the business or financial condition of the registrant, the effect of such proceedings on the business or financial condition of the registrant.

Item 6. Increases and Decreases in Outstanding Securities

General Instruction. The information called for herein shall be given as to each "security" as defined in Section 2(1) of the Securities Act of 1933. If the information called for has been previously reported on Form 10-Q or some other form, it may be incorporated by a specific reference to the previous filing.

a. Give the following information as to all increases and decreases during the fiscal year in the amount of equity securities of the registrant outstanding:

1. The title of the class of securities involved;
2. The date of the transaction;
3. The amount of securities involved and whether an increase or a decrease;
4. A brief description of the transaction in which the increase or decrease occurred. If previously reported, the description may be incorporated by a specific reference to the previous filing.

Instruction. The information shall be prepared in the form of a reconciliation between the amounts shown to be outstanding on the balance sheet to be filed with this report and the amounts shown on the registrant's balance sheet for the previous year. The exercise of outstanding options or warrants (separately by class or type of option or warrant), conversions of previously issued convertible securities (separately by class of security) and the issuance of options may be grouped together showing the dates between which all such transactions occurred.

b. Give the following information as to all securities of the registrant sold by the registrant during the fiscal year, which were not registered under the Securities Act of 1933, in reliance upon an exemption from registration. Include sales of the registrant's reacquired securities as well as new issues, securities issued in exchange for property, services or other securities, and new securities resulting from the modification of outstanding securities:

1. Give the date of sale, and the title and amount of the registrant's securities sold;
2. Give the market price on the date of sale, if applicable;
3. Give the names of the brokers, underwriters or finders, if any. As to any securities sold but which were not the subject of a public offering, name the persons or identify the class of persons to whom the securities were sold;
4. As to securities sold for cash, state the aggregate offering price and

the aggregate underwriting discounts, brokerage commissions, or finder's fees. As to any securities sold otherwise than for cash, state the nature of the transaction and the nature and aggregate amount of consideration received by the registrant;

5. Indicate the Section of the Act or Rule of the Commission under which exemption from registration was claimed and state briefly the facts relied upon to make the exemption available; and

6. State whether the securities have been legended and stop-transfer instructions given in connection therewith, and if not, state the reasons why not.

Item 7. Approximate Number of Equity Security Holders

State in the tabular form indicated below the approximate number of holders of record of each class of equity securities of the registrant as of the end of the fiscal year:

(1) *Title of class*	(2) *Number of Record Holders*

Instructions. 1. Attention is directed to the definition of the term "equity security" in Section 3(*a*)(11) of the Act and Rule 3*a*11–1 thereunder and the definition of the term "held of record" in Rule 12*g*5–1.

2. The information shall be given as of the end of the last fiscal year or as of any subsequent date, except that if the latest determination of the number of record holders of any class of equity securities was made for some other purpose within 90 days prior to the end of the last fiscal year, the information may be given as of the date of such determination.

3. Information need not be given with respect to the number of holders of outstanding nontransferable options to purchase securities of the registrant.

Item 8. Executive Officers of the Registrant

a. List the names and ages of all executive officers of the registrant and all persons chosen to become executive officers; state the nature of any family relationship between them; indicate all positions and offices with the registrant held by each such person; state his term of office as officer and the period during which he has served as such and briefly describe any arrangement or understanding between him and any other person pursuant to which he was selected as an officer.

Instructions. 1. Do not include arrangements or understandings with directors or officers of the registrant acting solely in their capacities as such.

2. The term "executive officer" means the president, secretary, treasurer, any vice president in charge of a principal business function (such as sales, administration or finance) and any other person who performs similar policy making functions for the registrant.

3. The term "family relationship" means any relationship by blood, marriage or adoption, not more remote than first cousin.

b. Give a brief account of the business experience during the past five years of each executive officer, including his principal occupations and employment during that period and the name and principal business of any corporation or other organization in which such occupations and employment were carried on. Where an executive officer has been employed by the registrant or a subsidiary of the registrant for less than five years, a brief explanation should be included as to the nature of the responsibilities undertaken by the individual in prior positions to provide adequate disclosure of his prior business experience. What is required is information relating to the level of his professional competence, which may include, depending upon the circumstances, such specific information as the size of the operation supervised.

Item 9. Indemnification of Directors and Officers

State the general effect of any charter provision, bylaw, contract, arrangement or statute under which any director or officer of the registrant is insured or indemnified in any manner against any liability which he may incur in his capacity as such.

Item 10. Financial Statements and Exhibits Filed

List all of the following documents filed as a part of the report:

a. All financial statements.

b. All exhibits, including those incorporated by reference.

Instruction. Where any financial statement or exhibit is incorporated by reference, the incorporation by reference shall be set forth in the last required by this item. See Rule 12*b*–23.

PART II

Item 11. Principal Security Holders and Security Holdings of Management

a. Furnish the following information, in substantially the tabular form indicated, as to the voting securities of the registrant owned of record or beneficially by each person who owns of record, or is known by the registrant to own beneficially, more than 10 percent of any class of such securities. Show in Column (3) whether the securities are owned both of record and beneficially, of record only, or beneficially only, and show in Columns (4) and (5) the respective amounts and percentages owned in each such manner.

Name and Address	*Title of Class*	*Type of Ownership*	*Amount Owned*	*Percent of Class*

b. Furnish the following information in substantially the tabular form indicated as to each class of equity securities of the registrant or any of its parents or subsidiaries, other than directors' qualifying shares, beneficially owned directly or indirectly by all directors and officers of the registrant, as a group, without naming them.

(1) *Title of Class*	*(2)* *Amount Beneficially Owned*	*(3)* *Percent of Class*

Instructions. 1. The percentages are to be calculated on the basis of the amount of outstanding securities, excluding securities held by or for the account of the issuer. In any case where the amount owned by directors and officers as a group is less than 1 percent of the class, the percent of the class owned by them may be omitted.

2. For the purpose of this item a person shall be deemed to be the beneficial owner of securities which he has the right to acquire through the exercise of presently exercisable options, warrants or rights or through the conversion of presently convertible securities. In computing the percentage of the class owned, securities which such person has a right to acquire shall be deemed to be outstanding.

3. If, to the knowledge of the registrant, more than 10 percent of any class of voting securities of the registrant is held or to be held subject to any voting trust or other similar agreement, state the title of such securities, the amount held or to be held and the duration of the agreement. Give the names and addresses of the voting trustees and outline briefly their voting rights and other powers under the agreement.

c. Describe any contractual arrangements, known to the registrant including any pledge of securities of the registrant or any of its parents the operation of the terms which may at a subsequent date result in a change in control of the registrant.

Instruction. This paragraph does not require a description of ordinary default provisions contained in the charter, trust indentures or other governing instruments relating to securities of the registrant.

Item 12. Directors of the Registrants

Note: Paragraph (*c*) of Item 12 also applies to executive officers of the registrant.

a. List the name and age of each director of the registrant, the date on which his present term of office will expire and the nature of all other positions and offices with the registrant presently held by him. The same information shall be provided with respect to each person chosen to become a director.

b. If not previously reported, state the nature of any family relationship between each such director and any other director or any executive officer of the registrant and give a brief account of his business experience during the past five years, including his principal occupations and employment during that period and the name and principal business of any corporation or other organization in which such occupation or employment was carried on. Where a person has been on the registrant's board for less than five years, a brief explanation should be included as to the nature of the responsibilities undertaken by the individual in prior positions to provide adequate disclosure of his prior business experience. What is required is information relating to the level of his professional competence and experience.

c. Describe any of the following events which have occurred during the past 10 years and which are material to an evaluation of the ability and integrity of any director of the registrant:

1. A petition under the Bankruptcy Act or any state insolvency law was filed by or against, or a receiver, fiscal agent or similar officer was appointed by a court for business or property of, such person, or any partnership in which he was a general partner at or within two years before the time of such filing, or any corporation or business association of which he was an executive officer at or within two years before the time of such filing.

2. Such person was convicted in a criminal proceeding (excluding traffic violations and other minor offenses) or is the subject of a criminal proceeding which is presently pending; or

3. Such person was the subject of any order, judgment or decree of any court of competent jurisdiction permanently or temporarily enjoining him from acting as an investment adviser, underwriter, broker or dealer in securities, or as an affiliated person, director or employee of any investment company, bank, savings and loan association or insurance company, or from engaging in or continuing any conduct or practice in connection with any such activity or in connection with the purchase or sale of any security, or was the subject of any order of a federal or state authority barring or suspending for more than 60 days the right of such person to be engaged in any such activity or to be associated with persons engaged in any such activity, which order has not been reversed or suspended.

Instruction. 1. The instruction to Item 8 shall also apply to this item. 2. If any event specified in paragraph (*c*) has occurred but information in regard thereto is omitted on the ground that it is not material, the registrant shall furnish, as supplemental information and not as a part of this report, a description of the event, and a statement of the reasons for the omission of information in regard thereto.

Item 13. Remuneration of Directors and Officers

a. Furnish the following information in substantially the tabular form indicated below as to all direct remuneration paid by the registrant and its subsidiaries during the registrant's last fiscal year to the following persons for services in all capacities:

1. Each director of the registrant whose aggregate direct remuneration exceeded $40,000, and each of the three highest paid officers of the registrant whose aggregate direct remuneration exceeded that amount, naming each such director and officer.

2. All directors and officers of the registrant as a group, stating the number of persons in the group without naming them.

(A) Name of Individual or Number of Persons in Group	*(B)* Capacities in Which Remuneration Was Received	*(C)* Aggregate Direct Remuneration

Instructions. 1. Except as provided in Instruction 2, paragraph (*a*) of this item applies to any person who was a director or officer of the registrant at any time during the period specified. However, information need not be given for any portion of the period during which such person was not a director or officer of the registrant.

2. Paragraph (*a*)(1) of this item does not apply to any person who was not named as a director or officer of the registrant in the first registration statement filed on Form 10 for the registration of a class of securities pursuant to Section 12 of the Act, provided (i) such person has not been a director or officer of the registrant since the filing of such statement and (ii) the same information is not otherwise required to be disclosed in any other material filed with the Commission.

3. The information is to be given on an accrual basis if practicable. The tables required by this paragraph and paragraph (*b*) may be combined if the registrant so desires.

4. Do not include remuneration paid to a partnership in which any director or officer was a partner, but see Item 15.

5. If any part of the remuneration shown in response to this item was paid pursuant to a material bonus or profit-sharing plan, briefly describe the plan and the basis upon which directors or officers participate therein. See Instruction 1 to paragraph (*b*) for the meaning of the term "plan."

b. Furnish the following information in substantially the tabular form indicated as to all annuity, pension or retirement benefits proposed to be paid to the following persons in the event of retirement at normal retirement date pursuant to any existing plan provided or contributed to by the registrant or any of its subsidiaries:

1. Each director or officer named in answer to paragraph (*a*)(1), naming each such person.

2. All directors and officers of the registrant who are eligible for such benefits, as a group, stating the number of persons in the group without naming them.

(A) Name of Individual or Number of Persons in Group	*(B)* Amount Set Aside or Accured during Registrant's Last Fiscal Year	*(C)* Estimated Annual Benefits upon Retirement

Instructions. 1. The term "plan" in this paragraph and in paragraph (*c*) includes all plans, contracts, authorizations or arrangements, whether or not set forth in any formal document.

2. Column (B) need not be answered with respect to payments computed on an actuarial basis under any plan which provides for fixed benefits in the event of retirement at a specified age or after a specified number of years of service. In such case, Columns (A) and (C) need not be answered with respect to directors or officers as a group.

3. The information called for by Column (C) may be given in the form of a table showing the annual benefits payable upon retirement to persons in specified salary classifications.

4. In the case of any plan (other than those specified in Instruction 2) where the amount set aside each year depends upon the amount of earnings of the registrant or its subsidiaries for such year or a prior year, or where it is otherwise impracticable to state the estimated benefits upon retirement, there shall be set forth, in lieu of the information called for by Column (C), the aggregate amount set aside or accrued to date, unless it is impracticable to do so, in which case there shall be stated the method of computing such benefits.

c. Describe briefly all remuneration payments (other than accrued payments reported under paragraph (*a*) or (*b*) of this item) proposed to be made in the future, directly or indirectly, by the registrant or any of its subsidiaries pursuant to any existing plan or arrangement to (i) each director or officer named in answer to paragraph (*a*)(1), naming each such person, and (ii) all directors and officers of the registrant as a group, without naming them.

Instruction. Information need not be included as to payments to be made for, or benefits to be received from, group life or accident insurance, group hospitalization or similar group payments or benefits. If it is impracticable to state the amount of remuneration payments proposed to be made, the aggregate amount set aside or accrued to date in respect of such payments shall be stated, together with an explanation of the basis for future payments.

Item 14. Options Granted to Management to Purchase Securities

Furnish the following information, in substantially the tabular form indicated, as to all options to purchase any securities from the registrant or any of its subsidiaries which were granted to or exercised by the following persons since the beginning of the fiscal year, and as to all options held by such persons as of the latest practicable date regardless of when such options were granted: (i) each director and officer named in answer to Item 13(*a*)(1), naming each such person; and (ii) all directors and officers of the registrant as a group, without naming them:

	(Insert Name)	(Insert Name)	(Insert Name)	All Directors and Officers as a Group
Options granted:				
Number of shares..........	______	______	______	______
Average option price per share....................	$______	______	______	______
Options exercised:				
Number of shares..........	______	______	______	______
Aggregate option price of shares purchased.........	$______	______	______	______
Aggregate market value of shares on date options were exercised...........	$______	______	______	______
Unexercised options held at (insert date):				
Number of shares..........	______	______	______	______
Average option price per share....................	$______	______	______	______

Instructions. 1. The term "options" as used in this item includes all options, warrants or rights, other than those issued to security holders as such on a pro rate basis. Where the average option price per share is called for, the weighted average price per share shall be given.

2. The extension, regranting or material amendment of options shall be deemed the granting of options within the meaning of this item.

3. (i) Where the total market value on the granting dates of the securities called for by all options granted during the period specified does not exceed $10,000 for any officer or director named in answer to Item 13(*a*)(1) or $40,000 for all officers and directors as a group, this item need not be answered with respect to options granted to such person or group. (ii) Where the total market value on the dates of purchase of all securities purchased through the exercise of options during the period specified does not exceed $10,000 for any such person or $40,000 for such group, this item need not be answered with respect to options exercised by such person or group. (iii) Where the total market value as of the latest practicable date of the securities called for by all options held at such time does not exceed $10,000 for any such person or $40,000 for such group, this item need not be answered with respect to options held as of the specified date by such person or group.

4. If the options relate to more than one class of securities, the information shall be given separately for each such class.

Item 15. Interest of Management and Others in Certain Transactions

a. Describe briefly any transactions since the beginning of the last fiscal year or any presently propsed transactions, to which the registrant or any of its subsidiaries was or is to be a party, in which any of the following persons had or is to have a direct or indirect material interest, naming such person and stating his relationship to the registrant, the nature of his interest in the transaction and, where practicable, the amount of such interest:

1. Any director or officer of the registrant;
2. Any security holder named in answer to Item 11(*a*);
3. Any relative or spouse of any of the foregoing persons, or any relative of such spouse, who has the same home as such person or who is a director or officer of any parent or subsidiary of the registrant.

Instructions. 1. This item applies to any person who held any of the positions or relationships specified at any time during the period specified. However, information need not be given for any portion of the period during which such person did not hold any such position or relationship.

2. No information need be given in response to this item as to any remuneration or other transaction reported in response to Items 13 or 14, or as to any transaction with respect to which information may be omitted pursuant to Instruction 2 to Item 13(*b*), the instruction to Item 13(*c*), or Instruction 2 or 3 to paragraph (*b*) of this item.

3. No information need be given in answer to this item as to any transaction where—

(a) the rates or charges involved in the transaction are determined by competitive bids, or the transaction involves the rendering of services as a common or contract carrier, or public utility, at rates or charges fixed in conformity with law or governmental authority;

(*b*) the transaction involves services as a bank depositary of funds, transfer agent, registrar, trustee under a trust indenture, or similar services;

(*c*) the amount involved in the transaction or a series of similar transactions, including all periodic installments in the case of any lease or other agreement providing for periodic payments or installments, does not exceed $40,000; or

(*d*) the interest of the specified person arises solely from the ownership of securities of the registrant and the specified person receives no extra or special benefit not shared on a pro rata basis by all holders of securities of the class.

4. It should be noted that this item calls for disclosures of indirect, as well as direct, material interests in transactions. A person who has a position or relationship with a firm, corporation, or other entity, which engages in a transaction with the registrant or its subsidiaries may have an indirect interest in such transaction by reason of such position or relationship. However, a person shall be deemed not to have a material indirect interest in a transaction within the meaning of this item where—

(*a*) the interest arises only (i) from such person's position as a director of another corporation or organization (other than a partnership) which is a party to the transaction, or (ii) from the direct or indirect ownership by such person and all other persons specified in subparagraphs (1) through (3) above, in the aggregate, of less than a 10 percent equity interest in another person (other than a partnership) which is a party to the transaction, or (iii) from both such position and ownership;

(b) the interest arises only from such person's position as a limited partner in a partnership in which he and all other persons specified in (1) through (3) above had an interest of less than 10 percent; or

(*c*) the interest of such person arises solely from the holding of an equity interest (including a limited partnership interest, but excluding a general partnership interest) or a creditor interest in another person which is a party to the transaction with the issuer or any of its subsidiaries and the transaction is not material to such other person.

5. The amount of the interest of any specified person shall be computed without regard to the amount of the profit or loss involved in the transaction. Where it is not practicable to state the approximate amount of the interest, the approximate amount involved in the transaction shall be indicated.

6. In describing any transaction involving the purchase or sale of assets by or to the registrant or any of its subsidiaries, otherwise than in the ordinary course of business, state the cost of the assets to the purchaser and, if acquired by the seller within two years prior to the transaction, the cost thereof to the seller.

7. The foregoing instructions specify certain transactions and interests as to which information may be omitted in answering this item. There may be situations where, although the foregoing instructions do not expressly authorize non-disclosure, the interest of a specified person in the particular transaction or series of transactions is not a material interest. In that case, information regarding such interest and transaction is not required to be disclosed in response to this item.

b. State as to each of the following persons who was indebted to the registrant or its subsidiaries at any time since the beginning of the last fiscal year of the registrant, (i) the largest aggregate amount of indebtedness outstanding at any time during such period, (ii) the nature of the indebtedness and of the transaction in which it was incurred, (iii) the amount thereof oustanding as of the latest practicable date, and (iv) the rate of interest paid or charged thereon:

1. Each director or officer of the registrant; and
2. Each associate of any such director or officer.

Instructions. 1. Include the name of each person whose indebtedness is described and the nature of the relationship by reason of which the information is required to be given.

2. This paragraph does not apply to any person whose aggregate indebtedness did not exceed $10,000 or 1 percent of the registrant's total assets, whichever is less, at any time during the period specified. Exclude in the determination of the amount of indebtedness all amounts due from the particular person for purchases subject to usual trade terms, for ordinary travel and expense advances and for other transactions in the ordinary course of business.

3. Notwithstanding Instruction 2, if the registrant or any of its subsidiaries

are engaged primarily in the business of making loans and loan to any of the specified persons in excess of $10,000 or 1 percent of its total assets, whichever is less, were outstanding at any time during the period specified, such loans shall be disclosed. However, if the lender is a bank, such disclosure may consist of a statement, if such is the case, that the loans to such persons (i) were made in the ordinary course of business, (ii) were made on substantially the same terms, including interest rates and collateral, at those prevailing at the time for comparable transactions with other persons, and (iii) did not involve more than normal risk of collectibility or present other unfavorable features.

4. If to the knowledge of the registrant any indebtedness required to be described arose under Section 16 (*b*) of the Act and has not been discharged by payment, state the amount of the profit realized, that such profit will inure to the benefit of the registrant or its subsidiaries and whether suit will be brought or other steps taken to recover such profit. If in the opinion of counsel a question reasonably exists as to the recoverability of such profit, it will suffice to state all facts necessary to describe the transaction, including the prices and number of shares involved.

c. Describe briefly any transactions since the beginning of the registrant's last fiscal year or any presently proposed transaction, to which any pension, retirement, savings or similar plan provided by the registrant or any of its parents or subsidiaries, was or is to be a party, in which any of the following persons had or is to have a direct or indirect material interest, naming such person and stating his relationship to the registrant, the nature of his interest in the transaction and, where practicable, the amount of such interest:

1. Any director or officer of the registrant;
2. Any security holder named in answer to Item 11(*a*);
3. Any relative or spouse of any of the foregoing persons, or any relative of such spouse, who has the same home as such person or who is a director or officer of any parent or subsidiary of the registrant; or
4. The registrant or any of its subsidiaries.

Instructions. 1. Instruction 2, 3, 4 and 5 to paragraph (*a*) of this item shall apply to paragraph (*c*) of this item.

2. Without limiting the general meaning of the term "transaction" there shall be included in answer to this item any remuneration received or any loans received or outstanding during the period, or proposed to be received.

3. No information need be given in answer to paragraph (*c*) with respect to—

(*a*) payments to the plan, or payments to beneficiaries, pursuant to the terms of the plan;

(*b*) payment of remuneration for services not in excess of 5 percent of the aggregate remuneration received by the specified person during the registrant's last fiscal year from the registrant and its subsidiaries; or

(*c*) any interest of the registrant or any of its subsidiaries which arises solely from its general interest in the success of the plan.

SIGNATURES

Pursuant to the requirements of Section 13 or 15(*d*) of the Securities Exchange Act of 1934, the registrant has duly caused this report to be signed on its behalf by the undersigned, thereunto duly authorized.

____

(Registrant)

Date____________________ By____________________________

(Signature)*

* Print the name and title of the signing officer under his signature.

PART V

Economic Analysis and Timing

27

Security Markets and Business Cycles

GEOFFREY H. MOORE, Ph.D.
Vice President-Research
National Bureau of Economic Research, Inc.
New York, New York
and
Senior Research Fellow
Hoover Institution
Stanford University
Stanford, California

SUMMARY

Since 1873 the U.S. economy has experienced 23 recessions or contractions in business activity and 23 expansions. With rare exceptions, the recessions have been accompanied by a decline in stock prices. Moreover, there have been few sustained or substantial swings in stock prices that have not been closely associated with swings in the business cycle. An understanding of this association, therefore, is clearly of concern to anyone interested in the stock market.

The bond market also is closely attuned to the business cycle. Yields on corporate, municipal, and U.S. government bonds—as well as other interest rates—have nearly always risen during the later stages of upswings in business and fallen during downswings. Bond prices, of course, have moved in the opposite direction. As a rule, prosperity is good for stock prices but bad for bond prices, while depression is bad for stock prices and good for bond prices.

This does not mean, however, that a turn for the worse in business and in stock prices always occurs at the same time. Typically, the turn in stock prices occurs prior to the turn in business activity. Hence stock prices are said to lead the swing in the business cycle, and stock price indexes are "leading indicators." At the peak of the business cycle, it is characteristic that stock prices have already been declining for some months, and at the trough of the business cycle, stock prices usually have already started to rise. Bond yields, on the other hand, frequently continue to decline for some months after a business upswing has begun, and occasionally continue to rise after a business recession has begun. Bond yields and other interest rates are generally classified as coincident or lagging indicators.

Business cycles also have marked influences on the volume of new issues of stocks and bonds and on the repayment and refunding of bonds. Rising stock prices and falling bond prices tend to encourage the issuance of common stock and discourage bond financing, so a shift toward stock and away from bonds tends to occur during a business upswing. The opposite movements characterize the contraction phase of the business cycle.

A wide variety of factors, summed up in the term *business cycle,* bring about or are related to the regularities in the behavior of the securities markets just described. Among the factors associated with the regularities in the behavior of stock prices during business cycles, probably the most significant are profits and interest rates. Declines in the level or rate of growth of profits or in factors portending such declines—e.g., declines in profit margins or in new orders—during the later stage of a business cycle expansion alter appraisals of common stock values and hence tend to produce a decline in stock prices before the downturn in business. At this stage also, a restricted supply of money and credit and the accompanying higher interest rates tend to lower capital values, may cause postponement of plans to exploit potentially profitable investment opportunities, make common stocks a less attractive security to hold, and diminish incentives to borrow for that purpose. Hence, these changes as well as those in profits depress stock prices in the later stages of business expansions. Both sets of factors operate to produce the "lead" in stock prices. Opposite changes occur during business contractions and help to explain the tendency for stock prices to begin to rise while business activity as a whole is still depressed.

But a wide variety of other factors play upon the market—shifts in investor confidence, fears of inflation, prospects for higher taxes or stiffer government regulation, changes in margin requirements, the flow of funds from abroad, a strike in a major industry, the failure of a large enterprise—and these make the underlying regularities more difficult to observe and to predict. Moreover, developments in the securities markets have repercussions of their own. A rise in capital values can lift the propensity of consumers to spend and encourage enterpreneurs to embark on new ventures; a collapse in capital values can do the opposite. Hence there is a feedback from the markets to business.

DEFINITION AND CHARACTERISTICS OF BUSINESS CYCLES

Business cycles, according to a definition formulated in 1946 by Wesley C. Mitchell and Arthur F. Burns, are

> a type of fluctuation found in the aggregate economic activity of nations that organize their work mainly in business enterprises; a cycle consists of expansions occurring at about the same time in many economic activities, followed by similarly general recessions, contractions, and revivals which merge into the expansion phase of the next cycle; this sequence of changes is recurrent but not periodic; in duration business cycles may last from more than one year to ten or twelve years; they are not divisible into shorter cycles of similar character with amplitudes approximating their own.[1]

This definition resulted from extensive observation of economic data for a number of countries over periods ranging back to the late 18th century and up to the 1930s. Studies of more recent data have, for the most part, confirmed the continued existence of business cycles conforming to the definition, and the chronology of cycles has been extended down to date. However, secular shifts in the character of economic activity, such as the shift toward greater employment in service industries, including government; the creation of new institutions such as bank deposit insurance and unemployment insurance; and the attention given by government to the use of fiscal and monetary policy to modify the business cycle, particularly to offset any tendency toward recession, have led to long-term changes in the character of the cycle. In general, cyclical fluctuations in recent decades, both in the United States and abroad, have been milder, with the contraction phase often characterized by a reduced rate of growth in aggregate economic activity rather than an absolute decline. Hence the term *growth cycle* has come to be applied to these milder fluctuations. This shift has generally been accompanied by a higher rate of inflation during the expansion phase of the cycle, often extending into the contraction phase.

Chronologies of business cycles have been constructed for a number of countries. The one in common use for the United States was developed by the National Bureau of Economic Research, Inc. On an annual basis, it extends from 1834 to 1970 and covers 32 expansions and 32 contractions. The monthly and quarterly chronology begins in 1854 and covers 27 cycles (see Table 1). The latest contraction extended from November 1969 to November 1970.

Table 2 gives a record of the chief characteristics of the 11 business cycle contractions (recessions) in the United States during the past 50 years. Most of the contractions have lasted about a year or less. Only two were substantially longer, the 18-month contraction during 1920–21 and the 43-month contraction during 1929–33. These intervals (the top line of the table) represent the consensus among a number of different measures of economic activity, some of which are also shown in the table.

Business contractions vary in length and depth. In the Great Depression after 1929, gross national product fell by nearly half, and even after

[1] Wesley C. Mitchell and Arthur F. Burns, *Measuring Business Cycles* (New York: National Bureau of Economic Research, 1946).

TABLE 1

Business Cycle Expansions and Contractions in the United States: 1854 to 1970

Business Cycle		Duration in Months			
		Contraction (Trough from Previous Peak)	Expansion (Trough to Peak)	Cycle	
Trough	Peak			Trough from Previous Trough	Peak from Previous Peak
Dec. 1854	June 1857	(X)	30	(X)	(X)
Dec. 1858	Oct. 1960	18	22	48	40
June 1861	Apr. 1865	8	46	30	54
Dec. 1867	June 1869	32	18	78	50
Dec. 1870	Oct. 1873	18	34	36	52
Mar. 1879	Mar. 1882	65	36	99	101
May 1885	Mar. 1887	38	22	74	60
Apr. 1888	July 1890	13	27	35	40
May 1891	Jan. 1893	10	20	37	30
June 1894	Dec. 1895	17	18	37	35
June 1897	June 1899	18	24	36	42
Dec. 1900	Sept. 1902	18	21	42	39
Aug. 1904	May 1907	23	33	44	56
June 1908	Jan. 1910	13	19	46	32
Jan. 1912	Jan. 1913	24	12	43	36
Dec. 1914	Aug. 1918	23	44	35	67
Mar. 1919	Jan. 1920	7	10	51	17
July 1921	May 1923	18	22	28	40
July 1924	Oct. 1926	14	27	36	41
Nov. 1927	Aug. 1929	13	21	40	34
Mar. 1933	May 1937	43	50	64	93
June 1938	Feb. 1945	13	80	63	93
Oct. 1945	Nov. 1948	8	37	88	45
Oct. 1949	July 1953	11	45	48	56
Aug. 1954	July 1957	13	35	58	48
Apr. 1958	May 1960	9	25	44	34
Feb. 1961	Nov. 1969	9	105	34	114
Nov. 1970		12	(X)	117	(X)
Average, all cycles:					
27 cycles, 1854–1970		19	33	52	52*
11 cycles, 1919–1970		15	42	56	60†
5 cycles, 1945–1970		11	49	60	59‡
Average, peacetime cycles:					
22 cycles, 1854–1961		20	26	45	46§
8 cycles, 1919–1961		16	28	45	48‖
3 cycles, 1945–1961		10	32	42	42#

Note: Underscored figures are the wartime expansions (Civil War, World Wars I and II, Korean War, and Vietnam War), the postwar contractions, and the full cycles that include the wartime expansions.

* 26 cycles, 1857–1969.
† 10 cycles, 1920–1969.
‡5 cycles, 1945–1969.
§ 21 cycles, 1857–1960.
‖ 7 cycles, 1920–1960.
3 cycles, 1945–1960.

Source: National Bureau of Economic Research, Inc.

For a quarterly chronology covering the period 1854–1958 and an annual chronology back to 1834, see Geoffrey H. Moore, ed., *Business Cycle Indicators*, National Bureau of Economic Research, Inc., 1961, p. 670.

TABLE 2

Selected Measures of Duration, Depth, and Diffusion of Business Cycle Contractions

	Business Cycle Contraction, from Peak (top line) to Trough (next line)										
	Jan. 1920 *July 1921*	*May 1923* *July 1924*	*Oct. 1926* *Nov. 1927*	*Aug. 1929* *Mar. 1933*	*May 1937* *June 1938*	*Feb. 1945* *Oct. 1945*	*Nov. 1948* *Oct. 1949*	*July 1953* *Aug. 1954*	*July 1957* *Apr. 1958*	*May 1960* *Feb. 1961*	*Nov. 1969* *Nov. 1970*
					(number of months)						
Duration											
Business cycle chronology	18	14	13	43	13	8	11	13	9	9	12
GNP, current dollars	n.a.	6	12	42	9	6	12	12	6	6	—‡
GNP, constant dollars	n.a.	3	3	36	6	n.a.	6	12	6	12	15
Industrial production	14	14	8	36	12	27	15	8	14	13	14
Nonfarm employment	n.a.	n.a.	n.a.	43	11	22	13	16	14	10	8
					(percent)						
Depth*											
GNP, current dollars	n.a.	− 4.9	− 3.0	−49.6	−16.2	−11.9	− 3.4	− 1.9	− 2.6	− 0.3	−‡
GNP, constant dollars	n.a.	− 4.1	− 2.0	−32.6	−13.2	n.a.	− 1.9	− 3.4	− 3.9	− 1.6	− 1.5
Industrial production	−32.4	−17.9	− 7.0	−53.4	−32.4	−38.3	− 9.9	−10.0	−14.3	− 7.2	− 8.1
Nonfarm employment	n.a.	n.a.	n.a.	−31.6	−10.8	−10.1	− 5.2	− 3.4	− 4.3	− 2.2	− 1.6
Unemployment rate											
Maximum	11.9§	5.5§	4.4§	25.2§	20.0	4.3	7.9	6.1	7.5	7.1	6.1
Increase	+10.3§	+ 2.6§	+ 2.4§	+22.0§	+ 9.0	+ 3.4	+ 4.5	+ 3.6	+ 3.8	+ 2.3	+ 2.7
					(percent)						
Diffusion											
Nonfarm industries, maximum percentage with declining employment†	97 Sept. 1920	95 Apr. 1924	71 Nov. 1927	100 June 1933	97 Dec. 1937	n.a.	90 Feb. 1949	87 Mar. 1954	88 Sept. 1957	82 Aug. 1960	83 June 1970

n.a.—Not available.

* Percentage change from the peak month or quarter in the series to the trough month or quarter, over the intervals shown above. For the unemployment rate, the maximum figure is the highest for any month during the contraction and the increases are from the lowest month to the highest, in percentage points.

† Since 1948, based on changes in employment over six-month spans in 30 nonagricultural industries, centered on the fourth month of the span. Prior to 1948 based on cyclical changes in employment in 41 industries.

‡ No decline.

§ The maximum figures are annual averages (monthly data not available) for 1921, 1924, 1928; increases, in percentage points, are for 1919–21, 1923–24, and 1926–28.

Source: U.S. Department of Commerce, U.S. Department of Labor, Board of Governors of the Federal Reserve System, National Bureau of Economic Research. For a fuller version of this table, see Solomon Fabricant, "The Recession of 1969–70," in *The Business Cycle Today*, V. Zarnowitz, ed. (New York: National Bureau of Economic Research, Inc., 1972), pp. 100–10.

allowance for the accompanying fall in the price level, the drop was nearly one third. None of the contractions since then, or for that matter few before then, have approached this magnitude. The declines in real GNP have ranged from 1 to 4 percent. Similarly, the unemployment rate, which by 1933 had climbed to about 25 percent, has not gone higher than 6 to 8 percent in subsequent recessions.

Severe business contractions have wide repercussions throughout the economy, affecting not only production and employment, but also commodity prices, profits, interest rates, wages, stock prices, and many other aspects of economic life. Mild contractions are more scattered in their effects. This phenomenon of diffusion is illustrated in the bottom line of the table, in terms of the percentage of industries, out of 30 that cover the entire nonfarm sector, in which employment declined. Even in the milder contractions, like those of 1926–27, 1960–61, and 1969–70, the percentage of industries registering declines ranged from 71 to 83. In the severe contractions of 1920–21, 1929–33, and 1937–38, the percentage reached as high as 97 to 100, virtually encompassing all industries. These pervasive movements naturally have a vital bearing on conditions in security markets.

The growth cycle concept referred to above has not yet come into wide use in the United States, but it may do so if recessions continue to become milder and if concern about even the mildest continues to mount. Recent research has identified eight growth cycles during 1948–70. Five of the periods of slowdown overlap the business cycle recessions of 1949, 1954, 1958, 1961, and 1970, beginning one or two quarters earlier but ending at about the same time. These five, of course, were the more serious episodes. The other three milder slowdowns occurred in 1951–52, 1962–63, and 1966–67, interrupting the business cycle expansions of 1949–53 and 1961–69. A ninth slowdown appears to have begun in the spring of 1973.

During the five slowdowns that overlapped business cycle recessions, gross national product in constant dollars declined, though not in every quarter, at average rates of decline ranging from a minus one half of 1 percent per year in the mildest to minus 2½ percent per year in the sharpest. In the other three slowdowns real GNP continued to grow, in most quarters, at rates that averaged about 2½ percent per year in 1951–52, 3½ percent in 1962–63, and 3 percent in 1966–67. During the eight intervening upswings, on the other hand, growth rates ranged from 4 to nearly 12 percent and averaged 6 percent per year.

As will be seen, even the milder slowdowns in economic growth have had significant effects on security markets.

STOCK PRICES AND BUSINESS CYCLES

The chronology of business cycles in Table 1 makes it easy to answer the question whether stock prices are higher at the top of a boom than at the bottom of a recession. The answer, surprisingly, is "most of the time but not always." (Table 3). On a few occasions, most recently in 1953–54 and 1960–61, Standard & Poor's index of 500 common stock prices was higher at the bottom of the business cycle contraction than it was when the recession began. The same was true of the Dow-Jones Industrials Index. In most cases, as Table 3 shows, the general level of stock prices has been much higher at the top of a boom than at the botton of a recession. The average of 22 periods of business expansion, 1873–1970, shows the index rising 35 percent, or at an annual rate of 12 percent. The average of 23 periods of business contraction shows the index falling 8 percent or at 2 percent annual rate.

Clearly it is of importance from the investor's point of view to know when the turns in the business cycle occur. Since 1948 the four periods of business cycle expansion witnessed increases of 54, 54, 52, and 34 percent in the Standard & Poor's index. By contrast, during the five periods of business contraction the index never rose as much and on two occasions dropped around 10 percent. The average rate of appreciation during the expansions was 12 percent per year; during the contractions, only 4 percent.

The general correspondence between stock prices and business cycles does not mean that knowledge of the business cycle turns would enable one to pick out all the significant declines in stock prices. For example, substantial declines occurred in 1962 and 1966, when no business cycle contraction is identified (see Chart 1). In both cases, however, slowdowns in economic growth did occur. The sharp decline in the market during 1973 also corresponds with a slowdown in growth. The only instance since 1948 of an economic slowdown where there was no substantial decline in stock prices was in 1951–52.

In short, with this one exception, the market has reflected all the slowdowns in the economy since 1948, and sustained declines in the market have not occurred at other times.

The reason for most of the exceptions to the rule of higher stock prices at the peak than at the trough of the business cycle is not that stocks were not depressed by the business recession, but rather that they began to decline sooner and to recover earlier than business activity as a whole. For example, in 1953–54, the Standard & Poor's index reached its highest monthly average (26) in January 1953, six months before the business cycle peak in July, by which time the index had dropped to 24. The decline in the index continued for only two more months, reaching bottom in September 1953 at 23. From then on it rose vigorously, so that by the time the August 1954 trough in the business cycle had arrived the index was 31, nearly 30 percent higher than its level at the previous business cycle peak. The January–September 1953 decline in the index was evidently associated with the business recession but occurred much earlier (see Chart 1).

TABLE 3

Changes in Standard and Poor's Index of Common Stock Prices During Business Cycles, 1873–1970

Business Cycle		*Index Standing* (1941–43 = 10) at*		*Percentage Change during*		*Length (in months) of*		*Annual Rate (in percent) of Change during*	
Trough	*Peak*	*Trough*	*Peak*	*Contraction†*	*Expansion‡*	*Contraction†*	*Expansion‡*	*Contraction†*	*Expansion‡*
Dec. 1870	Oct. 1873		4.4						
Mar. 1879	Mar. 1882	3.8	6.0	−14	58	65	36	− 3	16
May 1885	Mar. 1887	4.5	5.9	−25	31	38	22	− 9	16
Apr. 1888	July 1890	5.3	5.7	−10	8	13	27	− 9	3
May 1891	Jan. 1893	5.1	5.8	−11	14	10	20	−13	8
June 1894	Dec. 1895	4.5	4.6	−22	2	17	18	−16	1
June 1897	June 1899	4.4	6.4	− 4	45	18	24	− 3	20
Dec. 1900	Sept. 1902	7.1	9.1	11	28	18	21	7	15
Aug. 1904	May 1907	7.5	8.4	−18	12	23	33	−10	4
June 1908	Jan. 1910	8.0	10.4	− 5	30	13	19	− 5	18
Jan. 1912	Jan. 1913	9.5	9.6	− 9	1	24	12	− 5	1
Dec. 1914	Aug. 1918	7.6	8.0	−21	5	23	44	−12	1
Mar. 1919	Jan. 1920	8.6	9.1	8	6	7	10	14	7
July 1921	May 1923	6.9	9.2	−24	33	18	22	17	17
July 1924	Oct. 1926	9.5	13.5	3	42	14	27	3	17
Nov. 1927	Aug. 1929	17.0	28.5	26	68	13	21	24	35
Mar. 1933	May 1937	5.9	15.4	−79	161	43	50	−35	26
June 1938	Feb. 1945	10.4	13.8	−32	33	13	80	−30	4
Oct. 1945	Nov. 1948	16.4	15.6	19	−5	8	37	30	−2
Oct. 1949	July 1953	15.8	24.3	1	54	11	45	1	12
Aug. 1954	July 1957	30.8	47.3	27	54	13	35	25	16
Apr. 1958	May 1960	42.7	56.1	−10	31	9	25	−13	14
Feb. 1961	Nov. 1969	62.0	94.3	11	52	9	105	15	5
Nov. 1970		86.3		− 8		12		− 8	
Average, 1873–1970				− 8	35	19	33	− 2	12
Average, 1873–1948				−12	32	21	29	− 3	12
Average, 1948–1970				4	48	11	52	4	12

* Three-month average centered on business cycle peak or trough month.
† From peak on preceding line to trough.
‡ From trough to peak.
Source: National Bureau of Economic Research, Inc.

CHART 1

Stock Prices, Profits, and Bond Yields, 1952–73

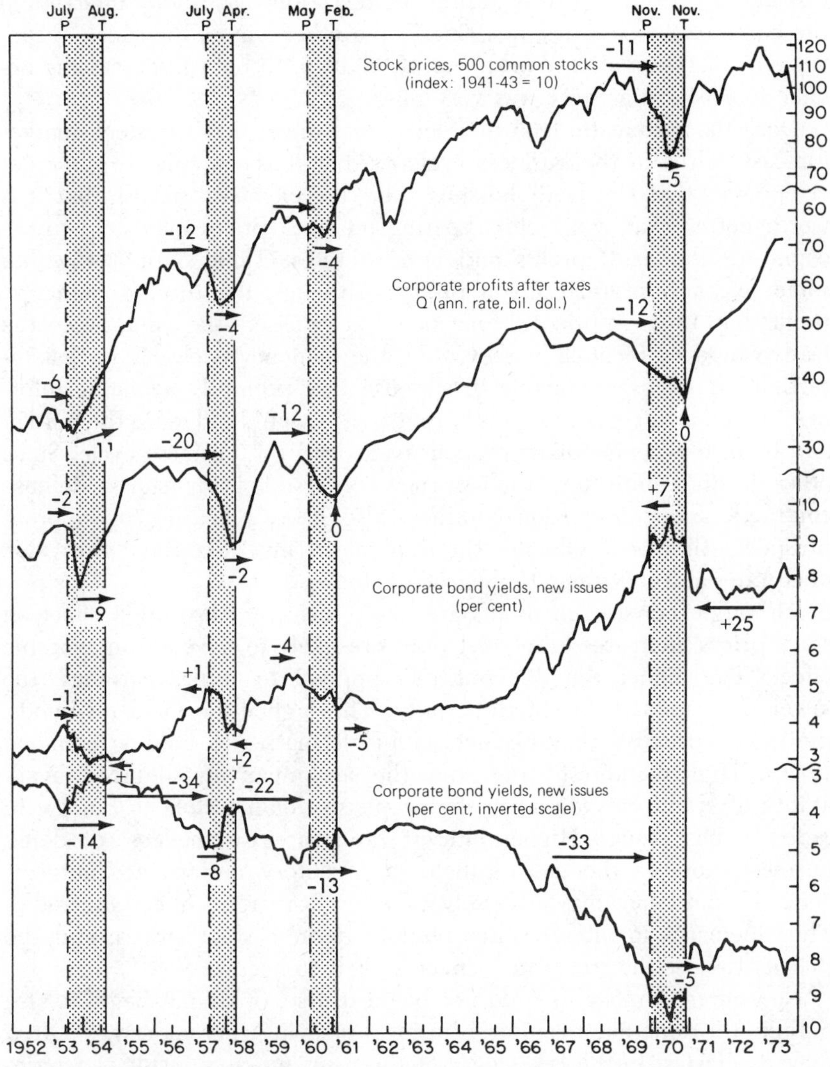

Note: Shaded areas are business recessions. Numbers and arrows indicate length of leads (−) and lags (+) in months from business cycle peaks and troughs.

Source: Standard & Poor's Corporation; U.S. Department of Commerce; First National City Bank of New York; and U.S. Treaury Department.

Table 4 shows that this tendency for stock prices to lead the business cycle is quite characteristic. Since 1873, it has happened at 18 of the 23 business cycle peaks and at 17 of the 23 troughs. Since 1948 there has been no exception to the rule. The average lead is around five or six months, but there have been wide variations around the average. Table

4 also shows that there have been only two occasions since 1873 when a business recession occurred but no cyclical decline in stock prices was associated with it. One was during the recession that briefly interrupted the boom of the twenties, in 1926–27; the other was in the short "reconversion" recession after World War II, in 1945. In both instances the decline in business activity was very mild.

Does the systematic lead in stock prices mean that the stock market forecasts turns in the business cycle or that it is reacting to other developments that also lead? Possibly there are elements of both, but it is worth noting that two factors bearing on stock prices may help to account for the lead: profits and interest rates. Table 5 pulls together some relevant information on profits. Although the turning points in profits and in stock prices do not occur at precisely the same time (the leads would be identical if they did), the tendency is clearly in that direction.[2] It seems reasonable to suppose that promptly available information and astute guesses about profit trends would influence the market and help to account for its propensity to lead the business cycle. Since other leading indicators such as new orders, housing starts, defense contracts, and construction contracts also have a bearing upon profit prospects, they also influence the thinking of investors about the value of equities and contribute to the lead of stock prices.

Although increases in profits are likely to have a favorable effect on stock prices, increases in interest rates are likely to have an unfavorable effect. The higher the discount rate applied to future earnings, the lower the capital value of the equity. The higher the yield on bonds, the more attractive they become as an alternative to holding common stocks. Higher interest rates and the accompanying reduced availability of credit may diminish the propensity of investors to borrow in order to buy stocks. Higher interest rates increase the cost of doing business, notably the cost of holding inventory and of accounts receivable, and hence may adversely affect profit margins in certain trades. Thus increases in interest rates tend to depress stock prices, and the sharper the rise the greater this effect is likely to be.

Now interest rates often do not begin to rise, or do not begin to rise rapidly, for some months after a business upswing gets underway. Often they rise fastest in the late stages of the upswing, as a result of restrictions on the supply of money and credit. Such a development can depress the market even though business activity itself is still expanding. If this surge in interest rates is coupled with a profit squeeze that also antedates

---

[2] The correlation between the length of lead in stock prices and in profits, based on the figures in Table 5, is +0.7. This means that about half the variation in the length of leads in stock prices is accounted for by corresponding variations in the length of leads in profits.

TABLE 4

Leads and Lags of Common Stock Price Index at Business Cycle Peaks and Troughs, 1873–1970

Business Cycle		*Lead(−) or Lag(+) (in months) at*		*Business Cycle*		*Lead(−) or Lag(+) (in months) at*	
Peak	*Trough*	*Peak*	*Trough*	*Peak*	*Trough*	*Peak*	*Trough*
Oct. 1873	Mar. 1879	−17	−21	Jan. 1920	July 1921	− 6	+ 1
Mar. 1882	May 1885	− 9	− 4	May 1923	July 1924	− 2	− 9
Mar. 1887	Apr. 1888	+ 2	+ 2	Oct. 1926	Nov. 1927	n.s.	n.s.
July 1890	May 1891	− 2	− 5	Aug. 1929	Mar. 1933	+ 1	− 9
Jan. 1893	June 1894	− 5	+ 9	May 1937	June 1938	− 3	− 2
Dec. 1895	June 1897	− 3	−10	Feb. 1945	Oct. 1945	n.s.	n.s.
June 1899	Dec. 1900	− 2	− 3	Nov. 1948	Oct. 1949	− 5	− 4
Sept. 1902	Aug. 1904	0	−10	July 1953	Aug. 1954	− 6	−11
May 1907	June 1908	− 8	− 7	July 1957	Apr. 1958	−12	− 4
Jan. 1910	Jan. 1912	− 1	−18	May 1960	Feb. 1961	−10	− 4
Jan. 1913	Dec. 1914	− 4	0	Nov. 1969	Nov. 1970	−11	− 5
Aug. 1918	Mar 1919	−21	−15				

Summary

	1873–1970		*1873–1945*		*1948–1970*	
	Peaks	*Troughs*	*Peaks*	*Troughs*	*Peaks*	*Troughs*
Median lead, in months	− 5	− 5	− 3	− 6	−10	− 4
Average lead, in months	− 6	− 6	− 5	− 6	− 9	− 6
Longest lead, in months	−21	−21	−21	−21	−12	−11
Shortest lead (or longest lag), in months	+ 2	+ 9	+ 2	+ 9	− 5	− 4
Number of						
Leads six months or longer	9	9	5	8	4	1
Leads five months or shorter	9	8	8	4	1	4
Exact coincidences	1	1	1	1	0	0
Lags	2	3	2	3	0	0

n.s.—No specific cycle.

Source: Standard & Poor's index of 500 common stocks, industrials, rails, and utilities. For 1873–1958, leads and lags are from *Business Cycle Indicators*, ed., G. H. Moore, 1961, pp. 674, 677. For 1948–70, *Business Conditions Digest*, June 1973, p. 115.

the business downturn, as frequently happens, stock prices can drop sharply even while business is good and getting better.

A similar sequence of events can be described during a business cycle contraction to account for upturns in stock prices prior to the upturn in business. The fall in interest rates helps the market for stocks, and if the customary early upturn in profits also occurs, optimism among investors in common stocks is doubly justified even though business activity is still depressed and sliding downward.

TABLE 5

Leads and Lags of Corporate Profits and Stock Prices at Business Cycle Peaks and Troughs, 1921–70

Business Cycle		*Lead(−) or Lag(+), in Months, at Business Cycle Peaks and Troughs*			
		Corporate Profits after Taxes		*Stock Price Index, Standard & Poor's 500*	
Peak	*Trough*	*Peak*	*Trough*	*Peak*	*Trough*
	July 1921		−2		+ 1
May 1923	July 1924	0	+1	− 2	− 9
Oct. 1926	Nov. 1927	− 2	0	n.s.	n.s.
Aug. 1929	Mar. 1933	0	−7	+ 1	− 9
May 1937	June 1938	− 6	−1	− 3	− 2
Feb. 1945	Oct. 1945	−12	+1	n.s.	n.s.
Nov. 1948	Oct. 1949	− 6	−5	− 5	− 4
July 1953	Aug. 1954	− 2	−9	− 6	−11
July 1957	Apr. 1958	−20	−2	−12	− 4
May 1960	Feb. 1961	−12	0	−10	− 4
Nov. 1969	Nov. 1970	−12	0	−11	− 5

Summary

	1921–70		*1921–45*		*1948–70*	
	Corporate Profits	*Stock Prices*	*Corporate Profits*	*Stock Prices*	*Corporate Profits*	*Stock Prices*
Median lead, in months	− 2	− 5	− 1	−2	− 6	− 6
Average lead, in months	− 5	− 6	− 3	−3	− 7	− 7
Longest lead, in months	−20	−12	−12	−9	−20	−12
Shortest lead (or longest lag) in months	+ 1	+ 1	+ 1	+1	0	− 4
Number of						
Leads six months or longer	8	7	3	2	5	5
Leads five months or shorter	6	8	3	3	3	5
Exact coincidences	5	0	3	0	2	0
Lags	2	2	2	2	0	0

n.s. No specific cycle

Source: Standard & Poor's index of 500 common stocks, industrials, rails, and utilities. For 1873–1958, leads and lags are from *Business Cycle Indicators*, ed. G. H. Moore, pp. 674, 677. For 1948–70, *Business Conditions Digest*, June 1973, p. 115.

BOND PRICES, INTEREST RATES, AND BUSINESS CYCLES

Among the interrelated factors that pull interest rates and bond yields upward during a business expansion are (1) the rising demand for business credit, both for operating purposes and for capital investment, (2) the rising demand for mortgage credit, both residential and nonresidential, (3) the rising demand for consumer credit, (4) the widening expectation of an increase in the rate of inflation, which makes lenders reluctant to lend at the same interest rate and borrowers more willing to pay a higher rate, and (5) the sluggish response of the supply of lendable funds to these pressures. During a business cycle contraction, all or most of these factors operate in reverse and bring interest rates down.

Certain types of interest rates reflect these forces more promptly and in larger degree than other types. Short-term rates on marketable securities are the most sensitive: treasury bills, federal funds, and commercial paper. New issue yields on corporate bonds are more sensitive than yields on outstanding issues. Bank rates on business loans, mortgage rates, and rates on consumer loans are relatively sluggish. Not only do they typically move in a narrower range, they usually begin their moves later. As a rule, returns on securities traded in the open market move earlier, more frequently, and by larger amounts than rates on sparsely traded debt instruments.

Table 6 illustrates some of these differences for treasury bills and corporate bond yields. Bill yields have usually turned a month or two before or after the business cycle peak or trough, while yields on outstanding bonds (high grade) have usually turned later, especially at troughs. Yields on new issues of corporate bonds (not shown in Table 6) usually turn earlier than those on outstanding issues, and hence at about the same time as bill rates. The basis point change from the peak to the trough of the business cycle has generally been much larger for bills than for bonds, as the table shows.

Although it is customary to look upon interest rates as being pulled up by a rising demand for funds operating against a sluggish supply during a cyclical expansion and as being pushed down by a declining demand during a contraction, it is also possible to look at them in a different way. Interest payments are a part of the cost of doing business, and an increase in rates can act as a deterrent to new investment. The cost of holding inventories and of accounts receivable is particularly sensitive to interest changes. High rates may make an industrial or commercial buliding project look less profitable and cause plans to be cut back or cancelled. Tight money and the accompanying high mortgage rates have a particularly prompt and substantial depressing effect on

TABLE 6

Leads and Lags and Rates of Change in Treasury Bill Rates and Corporate Bond Yields during Business Cycles, 1920–70

Business Cycle		*Lead (−) or Lag (+), in Months, at Business Cycle*				*Lead (−) or Lag (+), in Months, of Bond Yields vs. Bill Rates at*		*Change in Bill Rates and Bond Yields, in Basis Points per Month, during Business Cycle*			
		Trough		*Peak*				*Contraction*		*Expansion*	
Trough (1)	*Peak* (2)	*Treasury Bill Rate* (3)	*Corporate Bond Yield, Moody's Aaa* (4)	*Treasury Bill Rate* (5)	*Corporate Bond Yield, Moody's Aaa* (6)	*Trough* (7)	*Peak* (8)	*Bills* (9)	*Bonds* (10)	*Bills* (11)	*Bonds* (12)
Mar. 1919	Jan. 1920		− 1	+ 5	+ 5		0				3.9*
July 1921	May 1923	+13	+14	− 2	− 1	+ 1	+1	2.4	1.8	−4.8	−4.2
July 1924	Oct. 1926	+ 1		−11				−16.4	−1.5	5.9	−1.0
Nov. 1927	Aug. 1929	− 2	+ 5	− 3	+ 1	+ 7	+4	− 3.4	−1.7	9.3	1.4
Mar. 1933	May 1937	+35*	+46*	− 1*	− 1*	+11*	0*	−10.7	−0.3	−1.0	−2.6
June 1938	Feb. 1945	+31*	+30*		−35*	−1*		− 4.6	−0.8	0.4	−0.7
Oct. 1945	Nov. 1948		+ 6		− 9			0.0	−0.4	2.1	0.6
Oct. 1949	July 1953		+ 8	− 1	− 1		0	− 0.6	−1.9	2.4	1.5
Aug. 1954	July 1957	− 2	+ 1	− 1	+ 1	+ 3	+2	− 9.9	−3.3	7.8	3.2
Apr. 1958	May 1960	+ 2	+ 2	− 5	− 4	0	+1	−26.4	−3.7	8.0	3.3
Feb. 1961	Nov. 1969	− 2	+25†	+ 2	+ 7	+27	+5	− 9.8	−2.4	4.7	3.0
Nov. 1970		+15	+25			+10		−16.3	3.7		
Average, 1920–70		+ 4	+ 9	− 2	0	+ 8	+2	− 8.7	−1.0	3.5	0.4

* Excluded from average.

† This comparison ignores the minor rise in the series from September 1960 to September 1961.

Source: Phillip Cagan, "Changes in the Cyclical Behavior of Interest Rates," in *Essays on Interest Rates*, vol. II, ed. Jack M. Guttentag, National Bureau of Economic Research, pp. 23–32. Bill rates are seasonally adjusted except 1931–47; bond yields are seasonally adjusted 1948–61 only. Updated 1969–73 on basis of unadjusted data. The lag of bond yields at March 1933 trough (46 months) is included here because the turn is comparable with that in bill rates.

new housing starts. Although high yields on bonds enchance their attractiveness as far as investors are concerned, they have the opposite effect on borrowers, and new issues of bonds may be postponed in the belief that yields will go lower.

From this point of view, i.e., looking at the cyclical *effects* of changes in interest rates rather than their *causes,* it is useful to compare upturns in rates with subsequent downturns in business, and downturns in rates with subsequent upturns in business.

TABLE 7

Leads and Lags of Corporate Bond Prices and Stock Prices during Business Cycles, 1920–70

Business Cycle		*Lead (−) or Lag (+), in Months, at Business Cycle*				*Lead (−) or Lag (+) in Months, of Bond Prices vs. Stock Prices at*	
		Trough		*Peak*			
Business Cycle Trough (1)	*Peak* (2)	*Corporate Bond Prices* (3)	*Stock Prices* (4)	*Corporate Bond Prices* (5)	*Stock Prices* (6)	*Trough* (7)	*Peak* (8)
Mar. 1919	Jan. 1920......			−11	− 6		− 5
July 1921	May 1923......	−13	+ 1	− 8	− 2	−14	− 6
July 1924	Oct. 1926......	−15	− 9			− 6	
Nov. 1927	Aug. 1929......			−16	+ 1		−17
Mar. 1933	May 1937......	− 9	− 9	− 4	− 3	0	− 1
June 1938	Feb. 1945......	−14	− 2			−12	
Oct. 1945	Nov. 1948......				− 5		
Oct. 1949	July 1953......		− 4	−37	− 6		−31
Aug. 1954	July 1957......	−14	−11	−34	−12	− 3	−22
Apr. 1958	May 1960......	− 8	− 4	−23	−10	− 4	−13
Feb. 1961	Nov. 1969......	−13	− 4	−33	−11	− 9	−22
Nov. 1970		− 5	− 5			0	
Average, 1920–70...........		−11	− 5	−21	− 6	− 6	−15

Source: Based on Tables 4 and 6. The peaks and troughs in bond prices correspond to the troughs and peaks in bond yields, respectively.

For example, the peak in corporate bond yields in June 1970, which is treated in Table 6 as a lag of seven months behind the November 1969 business cycle peak, can also be looked on as a lead of five months before the November 1970 business cycle trough. Since bond prices move inversely to bond yields, this is equivalent to comparing the trough in bond prices with the trough in business. From some points of view this is a simpler way to put it, and Table 7 is drawn up on this basis. It shows not only that bond prices lead the business cycle but also that their leads are substantially longer than those of stock prices. Hence bond prices also lead stock prices. The leads vary greatly in length, averaging around a year at peaks and a half year at troughs.[3]

[3] The correlation between the length of lead in stock prices and in bond prices, based on the figures in Table 7, is +0.4. The relationship is not so close as that between the leads in stock prices and profits (see footnote 2).

The average sequence during 1920–70 that emerges from the records presented in Tables 6 and 7 is as follows:

	Months
From business cycle trough to bond yield trough (bond price peak)—Table 6, col. 4	9
From bond yield trough to stock price peak—Table 7, col. 8	15
From stock price peak to business cycle peak—Table 7, col. 6	6
From business cycle peak to bond yield peak—Table 6, col. 6	0
From bond yield peak to stock price trough—Table 7, col. 7	6
From stock price trough to business cycle trough—Table 7, col. 4	5

Although the *order* in which these turning points in financial markets and in business activity have occurred has been followed with considerable fidelity, the length of the intervals has varied enormously. Hence the average intervals are of little or no value in pinpointing a future turning point. Moreover, as the blank spaces in the tables indicate, turning points in bond yields, stock prices, and business cycles do not always match, in which case the sequence cannot even be recorded. This means, of course, that many other factors play a part in the financial markets. Nevertheless, the sequence has occurred often enough over a long period—it can be traced back to the 1870s—and has survived severe disturbances like the Great Depression of the 1930s and the economic controls of World War II—so that one can be reasonably confident that it reflects persistent tendencies in the adjustment of financial markets to economic conditions.

THE VOLUME OF STOCK AND BOND FINANCING DURING BUSINESS CYCLES

The most comprehensive study of corporate bond financing during business cycles was conducted during the late 1940s and early 1950s by W. Braddock Hickman for the National Bureau of Economic Research. He covered the period 1900 to 1938 and drew the following conclusions regarding the relationships of bond to stock financing over the various stages of the business cycle:

> While bond extinguishments (repayments plus refundings) usually rise through the expansion phase of the cycle and fall through the contraction phase, bond offerings are usually inverted, rising during most of the contraction phase and falling during most of the expansion. The net change in outstandings—the difference between offerings and extinguishments—consequently shows an inverse relationship to the rise and fall of general business activity. . . .
>
> The conclusion that, on balance, corporations obtain an increasing volume of funds through the bond market during periods of contraction and a decreasing volume during periods of expansion leads to the ques-

> tion, Where, then do corporations obtain funds to meet the increasing monetary requirements of expansion phases? Among the alternative sources of capital funds employed by corporations, a principal one during the period studied was the stock market. The behavior of stock offerings shows that corporations typically obtain an increasing volume of funds in the stock market during expansion stages, when net bond financing declines, and a decreasing amount during contraction stages, when net bond financing expands. Stock and bond financing thus appear to complement each other over the various stages of the cycle. . . .
>
> From analysis of the cyclical movements in the net-change series and its components in relation to bond and stock prices, it appears that both the new-money component and total offerings tend to be directly associated with bond prices, while both repayments and total extinguishments are associated with stock prices (and stock offerings). Since the relation between bond and stock prices during business cycles is complex, and since the price factors do not play with equal strength on the components of net change in bond financing, no simple formula in terms of bond or stock prices seems adequate to explain the behavior of the net change. In general, however, when the ratio of stock to bond prices turns downward during the contraction stages of the business cycle, corporations tend to shift their financing from the stock to the bond market; and conversely, when the ratio of stock to bond prices turns upward during expansion stages, corporations shift from the bond to the stock market.[4]

Since 1938 there has been a vast growth in the volume of stock and bond financing, a sharply rising trend in stock prices and bond yields and a fall in bond prices. To some extent these trends obscure the cyclical movements, especially because the business cycle contractions have been short. Nevertheless, Table 8 suggests that many of Hickman's conclusions regarding the behavior of the markets before 1938 have remained valid.

Common stock offerings rose during each of the five business expansions from 1946 to 1970 and fell in two of the contractions (1957–58 and 1969–70). Offerings of preferred stock (which Hickman did not distinguish) have behaved in the manner he described for bonds. They declined in three of the expansions and rose in four of the contractions, thus conforming inversely to the business cycle. The shift toward common and away from preferred stock financing during the business upswing and the reversal during the downswing appears to reflect cyclical shifts in investor confidence, with prosperity favoring the riskier security and recession favoring the safer.

Bond offerings, on the whole, have not shown as much inverse conformity to the cycle since 1946 as Hickman found for the earlier period. Nevertheless the average volume of offerings at the six business troughs

---

[4] W. Braddock Hickman, *The Volume of Corporate Bond Financing since 1900* (New York: National Bureau of Economic Research, 1953), pp. 132–34.

TABLE 8

Stock and Bond Prices and the Volume of Offerings during Business Cycles, 1946–70

Business Cycle		Corporate Securities Offered for Cash ($ millions): Common Stock at		Preferred Stock at		Bonds and Notes at		Common Stock Price Index, S&P's 500 1941–43 = 10 at		Corporate Bond Yield, Moody's Aaa (%) at		Corporate Bond Price S&P's AAA, ($) at	
Trough	*Peak*	*Trough*	*Peak*	*Trough*	*Peak*	*Trough*	*Peak*	*Trough*	*Peak*	*Trough*	*Peak*	*Trough*	*Peak*
1946	1948	891	614	1127	492	4882	5973	17	16	2.53	2.82	123	118
1949	1953	736	1326	425	489	4890	7083	15	25	2.66	3.20	121	112
1954	1957	1213	2516	816	411	7488	9957	30	44	2.90	3.89	117	101
1958	1960	1334	1664	571	409	9653	8081	46	56	3.79	4.41	103	95
1961	1969	3294	7714	450	682	9420	18348	66	98	4.35	7.03	95	69
1970		7240		1390		30315		83		8.04		62	
Average, 1946–70		2451	2767	796	497	11108	9888	43	48	4.04	4.27	104	99
Conformity Index*		+40		−40		+20		+20		+80		−70	

Business Cycle		Ratio, Common to Preferred Stock Offerings at		Ratio, Common Stock to Bond Offerings at		Ratio, Preferred Stock to Bond Offerings at		Ratio, Common Stock Price Index to Bond Price at	
Trough	*Peak*	*Trough*	*Peak*	*Trough*	*Peak*	*Trough*	*Peak*	*Trough*	*Peak*
1946	1948	0.79	1.25	0.18	0.10	0.23	0.08	0.14	0.14
1949	1953	1.73	2.71	0.15	0.19	0.09	0.07	0.12	0.22
1954	1957	1.49	6.12	0.16	0.25	0.11	0.04	0.26	0.44
1958	1960	2.34	4.07	0.14	0.21	0.06	0.05	0.45	0.58
1961	1969	7.32	11.31	0.35	0.42	0.05	0.04	0.69	1.42
1970		5.21		0.24		0.05		1.34	
Average, 1946–70		3.15	5.09	0.20	0.23	0.10	0.06	0.50	0.56
Conformity Index*		+60		+40		−90		+30	

* Number of positively conforming movements minus number of inversely conforming movements divided by the total (10). Positively conforming movements are increases from business cycle trough to following business cycle peak and decreases from peak to following trough. Inversely conforming movements are the opposite. If all movements conform positively the index is +100; if all conform inversely, −100.

Source: Securities and Exchange Commission, Standard & Poor's Corporation, and Moody's Investors Service.

was higher than the average at the five peaks. This was also true of preferred stock offerings, and from this point of view they belong with bonds. The ratio of common stock to bond offerings, therefore, usually rose during business expansions and fell during contractions.

In terms of the annual average figures used in Table 8, common stock prices declined in only two of the five business contractions. Corporate bond yields declined in all but one contraction, so bond prices rose in all but one. The ratio of stock to bond prices, dominated by the larger movements in stock prices, conformed positively to the business cycle as a rule.

We end up, then, with a picture resembling Hickman's description, of corporate financing shifting from stocks toward bonds as the price ratio of stocks to bonds becomes less favorable for stocks during the contraction phase of the business cycle, and back toward stocks as the price ratio becomes more favorable for stocks during the expansion phase of the cycle. A similar and even more decisive cyclical shift occurs in the relative volume of offerings of common and preferred stock, with preferred stock taking on the character of bonds in this context. It seems fair to say, therefore, that the record of past experience in security markets during business cycles can serve broadly to illuminate current developments and prospects and contribute to a better understanding of the factors that have a significant bearing on the outcome of security investments.

REFERENCES

Burns, Arthur F. *Stock Market Cycle Research.* New York: Twentieth Century Fund, Inc., 1930.

Cagan, Phillip. "The Recent Cyclical Movements of Interest Rates in Historical Perspective." *Business Economics,* January 1972.

Conard, Joseph W. *The Behavior of Interest Rates: A Progress Report.* New York: National Bureau of Economic Research, Inc (NBER), 1966.

Friedman, Milton, and Schwartz, Anna Jacobson. *A Monetary History of the United States, 1867–1960.* New York: NBER, 1963.

Guttentag, Jack M., and Cagan, Phillip, ed. *Essays on Interest Rates.* Vol. I. New York: NBER, 1969.

———. *Essays on Interest Rates.* Vol. II. New York: NBER, 1971.

Hamburger, Michael J., and Kochin, Levis A. "Money and Stock Prices: The Channels of Influence." *Journal of Finance,* May 1972, pp. 231–49, and "Discussion" by Merton H. Miller, pp. 294–98.

Hickman, W. Braddock. *The Volume of Corporate Bond Financing.* New York: NBER, 1953.

———. *Corporate Bond Quality and Investor Experience.* New York: NBER, 1958.

KERAN, MICHAEL W. "Expectations, Money and the Stock Market." Federal Reserve Bank of St. Louis *Review,* January 1971.

MACAULAY, FREDERICK R. *The Movements of Interest Rates, Bond Yields and Stock Prices in the United States since 1856.* New York: NBER, 1938.

MENNIS, EDMUND A. "Security Prices and Business Cycles." *Analysts Journal,* February 1955.

MITCHELL, WESLEY C. *Business Cycles and their Causes.* Berkeley, Calif.: University of California Press, 1941.

———. *What Happens during Business Cycles: A Progress Report.* New York: NBER, 1951.

MOORE, GEOFFREY H., ed. *Business Cycle Indicators.* New York: NBER, 1961.

MORGENSTERN, OSCAR. *International Financial Transactions and Business Cycles.* New York: NBER, 1959.

SELDEN, RICHARD T. *Trends and Cycles in the Commercial Paper Market.* New York: NBER, 1963.

SPRINKEL, BERYL W. *Money and Stock Prices.* Homewood, Ill.: Richard D. Irwin, Inc., 1964.

———. *Money and Markets: A Monetarist View.* Homewood, Ill.: Richard D. Irwin, Inc., 1971.

28

Economic Indicators

NATHAN BELFER, Ph.D., C.F.A.
Vice President
Wood, Struthers & Winthrop, Inc.
New York, New York

THE ANALYST is basically concerned with forecasting the prospects of the companies he is interested in. Most, if not all, companies are subject to the vagaries of the business cycle. It is, therefore, important for the security analyst to be acquainted with the details of economic forecasting.

Many indicators of cyclical movements have been developed by the National Bureau of Economic Research, the Federal Reserve Board, and the Department of Commerce, among others. These are in such areas as money and credit, production, capital spending, employment and unemployment, consumption, income, prices, profits, and costs.

As a result, a vast amount of statistical data relating to the performance of the economy is available. The basic purpose of all these data is to determine where the economy has been, where it is now, and where it is going in the future. In order to simplify the analysis of all this material, economic forecasters have singled out 26 of the most important of the statistical series. These key indicators include 12 leading indicators, 8 coincident indicators, and 6 lagging indicators.

The remainder of this section will be devoted to a discussion of the leading, lagging, and coincident economic indicators. There will be a brief discussion of each, and an attempt will be made to indicate which are the most useful for the security analyst.

Two monthly publications can give the analyst considerable current data on these key economic indicators. These are *Economic Indicators,* published monthly by the Council of Economic Advisers, and *Business Conditions Digest,* a monthly publication of the U.S. Department of Commerce. The charts shown at the end of this section come from *Business Conditions Digest.*

Leading Indicators

The leading indicators are supposed to have forecasting value and should highlight what may happen in the economy in the future. They are as follows:

Average Workweek, Production Workers, Manufacturing. This leading indicator points out the length of the average number of hours worked per week in manufacturing. An increase obviously indicates heightened economic activity in production. Conversely, a downturn is a forecast of declining activity in manufacturing. The workweek changes first because it is a more flexible way to adjust labor input to demand. Some work done at the National Bureau of Economic Research indicates that this index precedes business cycle turning points by about four months. However, the lead period is somewhat longer at peaks than at troughs. It is a useful indicator for the analyst.

Average Weekly Initial Claims, State Unemployment Insurance. This indicator indicates the number of new claims being made each week for unemployment insurance. Its significance lies in the fact that turning points in this index have preceded those in total unemployment. An increase is obviously an unfavorable sign. A decline is an indication that fewer people are being thrown out of work and can be interpreted favorably.

New Orders, Durable Goods Industries. This is a very significant indicator. An increase is quite bullish, as it shows that manufacturers and retailers are increasing orders in anticipation of favorable business conditions in the future. An increase in activity in the durable goods sector of the economy has a multiplier effect on the total economy. Conversely, a decline can be interpreted bearishly for the future of the economy. A study made by the National Bureau of Economic Research indicates that this index leads general business conditions by about five months.

Contracts and Orders for Plant and Equipment. This, also, is a significant indicator. An increase in plant and equipment ordering indicates optimism concerning the future. In addition, increased orders in plant and equipment could have a multiplier effect on other sectors of the economy.

Please note that this is not the same as expenditures on plant and equipment. Current expenditures on plant and equipment reflect contracts and orders from the past. The index of contracts and orders for plant and equipment has far better forecasting value than the index of current expenditures on plant and equipment, which is a lagging indicator (see below).

Index of Net Business Formation. This is a measure of the net number of new businesses formed each month. An increase obviously is a symptom of improved profit opportunities and an indication of heightened business activity in the future. Conversely, a decline is a possible harbinger of lower activity in the future.

Corporate Profits, after Taxes, Current Dollars. This is a closely watched indicator, and its significance is quite obvious. Corporate profits increase during business upswings and fall in the downward phase of the business cycle. Increased corporate profits create an atmosphere in which business has both the means and desire to finance further expansion in the future. A decline in corporate profits can create a more pessimistic outlook.

Ratio, Price to Unit Labor Cost, Manufacturing. This is an indicator of profit margins. It is determined by dividing the index of wholesale prices of industrial commodities by an index of labor cost in manufacturing. In periods of rising economic activity it should increase, as prices will tend to rise faster than unit labor costs. This will result in higher profit margins. On the other hand, in a period of declining economic activity, prices will tend to rise less rapidly than wages. As a result, the indicator will decline. It should be noted that this indicator may not function properly in periods of price and wage controls. The free movement of prices and wages is restricted at such times.

Stock Prices, 500 Common Stocks. While this index is an obvious one, it can be a controversial one. The key question is whether or not the stock market anticipates economic activity or is a reflection of the past. It is generally felt today that the stock market does anticipate future economic activity. It is strongly influenced by the outlook for profits and interest rates.

A study by Edward A. Mennis found that common stock prices anticipated business cycle movements 80 percent of the time. Unfortunately, however, timing is not so certain. There is no precise figure on the number of months by which stock price movements anticipate business cycle peaks and troughs.

Industrial Materials Prices. In a period of rising economic activity, the index of industrial materials prices should rise because of increased demand. The reverse is true in a period of declining business activity. Material prices are especially sensitive to these changes and to the building up or depletion of inventories of materials.

The usefulness of this index may be limited by the existence of permanent inflation in the economy. In the period since 1940, prices have declined slightly or not at all during recession periods. In addition, shortage problems in many areas will cause prices to advance. Thus, this index may have only limited prediction value presently.

New Building Permits, Private Housing. This index measures the number of new private housing units authorized in local communities. An increase in building permits today should result in increased building activity in the future. A decline in permits is an indicator of declining housing activity in the future.

The lag between new building permits and new housing starts is generally several months. However, the lag may be distorted by seasonal weather factors and shortages of building materials and labor.

The figure on new building permits does not include mobile homes. This may diminish somewhat the significance of the index because of the increased importance of mobile home production.

Change, Manufacturing and Trade Inventories, Book Value. This index measures the month-to-month change in manufacturing and trade inventories. In a period of rising economic activity, inventories should be increasing. In a period of declining economic expectations, businesses will tend to allow their inventories to decline.

While this has been a fairly reliable leading indicator, it has not behaved normally in the 1973 business boom. In 1973, sharp increases occurred in consumer purchasing and in spending on plant and equipment. Inventories have grown proportionately much less. This has raised some questions as to whether businessmen are changing their attitudes on the ratio of inventories they hold to sales of their products. If there is such a long-run change, the significance of the inventory index may have to be reconsidered.

Change in Consumer Installment Debt. This is a closely watched indicator as it highlights purchases by consumers of durable goods such as automobiles, refrigerators, washing machines, and other heavy appliances. Increased purchases by the consumer obviously will result in heightened economic activity. Conversely, a decline in consumer installment debt will be translated ultimately into lower manufacturing activity. The lag between changes in consumer installment debt and manufacturing activity should generally be several months. Increases in debt add to purchasing power and are more sensitive to changes in economic conditions than are changes in income.

Coincident Indicators

The eight coincident indicators are of interest but have only limited forecasting value. They should move directly with the business cycle and show what is happening currently in the economy. They are as follows:

Employees on Nonagricultural Payrolls. This is simply a measure of the total number of persons employed in the nonagricultural sectors of the economy. An increase goes along with an improvement of business conditions and a reverse in a downturn period. While it is a good measure of short-term current movements in the economy, it has little forecasting significance for the analyst.

Unemployment Rate. This is a measure of the percentage of the work force out of work and is a closely watched indicator. It obviously will move up and down with movements of the business cycle. While it has political and social significance, its value as a tool for stock market forecasting can be overrated.

Gross National Product in Current Dollars. This well-known statistic (GNP) simply measures the total market value of goods and services produced in the economy. It is a valuable measure of current conditions in the economy, as it directly reflects movements in output and employment. This indicator gets considerable publicity but only reflects current conditions in business.

Gross National Product in 1958 Dollars. This is a measure of GNP in constant dollars. It is calculated by dividing current GNP by appropriate price indexes. It is thus a measure of what GNP would be if the dollar had constant purchasing power and prices were unchanged. Changes in GNP in 1958 dollars reflect only changes in the real physical volume of output. It will generally move in the same direction as GNP in current dollars, but not by the same amount because of price movements, which are generally upward. As it measures the real physical volume of output, it is perhaps a better measure of changing standards of living in the economy than GNP in current dollars.

Industrial Production. The Federal Reserve index of industrial production is published monthly and is given wide publicity. It is exactly what it states—a measure of industrial production. It is quite useful as a measure of what is going on in the economy currently. However, it is not a gauge of the future.

Personal Income. This simply measures the amount of income received by persons in the country. It is obviously directly related to employment, production, and wage rates. It is thus a useful measure of current conditions in business.

Manufacturing and Trade Sales. This measures the monthly volume (in dollars) of sales by manufacturing and wholesale and trade businesses. It simply reflects current events in the economy. Obviously, total sales in manufacturing and trade will move up and down with the business cycle.

Retail Sales. This measures the monthly volume of merchandise sold and receipts for repairs and similar services. It obviously reflects the consumer's current spending and will coincide with general business movements.

Lagging Indicators

Lagging indicators are only of limited value to the analyst in forecasting the future, but they do reflect imbalances that may build up during a period of prosperity or be corrected during recession. For this reason, the analyst should be acquainted with the following six lagging indicators:

Unemployment Rate, 15 Weeks and Over. This indicates the percentage of the work force that has been unemployed for 15 weeks or more. It differs from the total unemployment rate, which is a coincident indicator, and from average weekly claims for unemployment insurance, which is a leading indicator. Its main significance is as a measure of long-term unemployment. When it reaches low levels, it is a sign of shortages developing in the labor market.

Business Expenditures, New Plant and Equipment. This indicates the amount of actual expenditures on plant and equipment. It differs from contracts and orders for plant and equipment, which is a leading indicator discussed earlier. The series on contracts and orders indicate what will happen in the future and are thus more significant for the analyst. However, the government issues regular forecasts of plant and equipment expenditures and these should be watched.

Labor Cost per Unit of Output, Manufacturing. This simply measures the cost of labor involved in manufacturing production. It is a significant component of the ratio of price to unit labor cost, a leading indicator discussed previously. Changes in unit labor cost are one of the dominant factors influencing profit margins.

Bank Rates on Short-Term Business Loans. This is basically the prime rate, which should be familiar to the analyst. While it is considered a lagging indicator, sharply rising short-term interest rates may lead to a slowdown in borrowing. This in turn could result in a business turndown in the future. Thus, it has some forecasting potential. Rising interest rates generally have a bearish influence on stock prices.

Manufacturing and Trade Inventories, Book Value. This simply measures the stocks on hand at the end of the month in manufacturing and wholesale and retail establishments. The change in manufacturing and trade inventories, which is a leading indicator discussed earlier, is derived from it. The level of inventories, particularly in relation to sales, indicates whether imbalances may be developing or are being adjusted.

Commercial and Industrial Loans Outstanding. This is simply a measure of borrowing by business and commercial enterprises. The actual level of such loans lags the business cycle. A measure of the rate of change would be more significant for forecasting purposes.

Composite Indicators

The U.S. Department of Commerce summarizes the various indicators into what are known as Composite Indexes. The 12 leading indicators are lumped together into one series. The same is done for five of the eight coincident indicators and the six lagging indicators. This is a convenient means for the analyst to get a quick summary of the average performance of the indicators. The accompanying charts show the composite indexes.

CHART 1

Composite Indexes

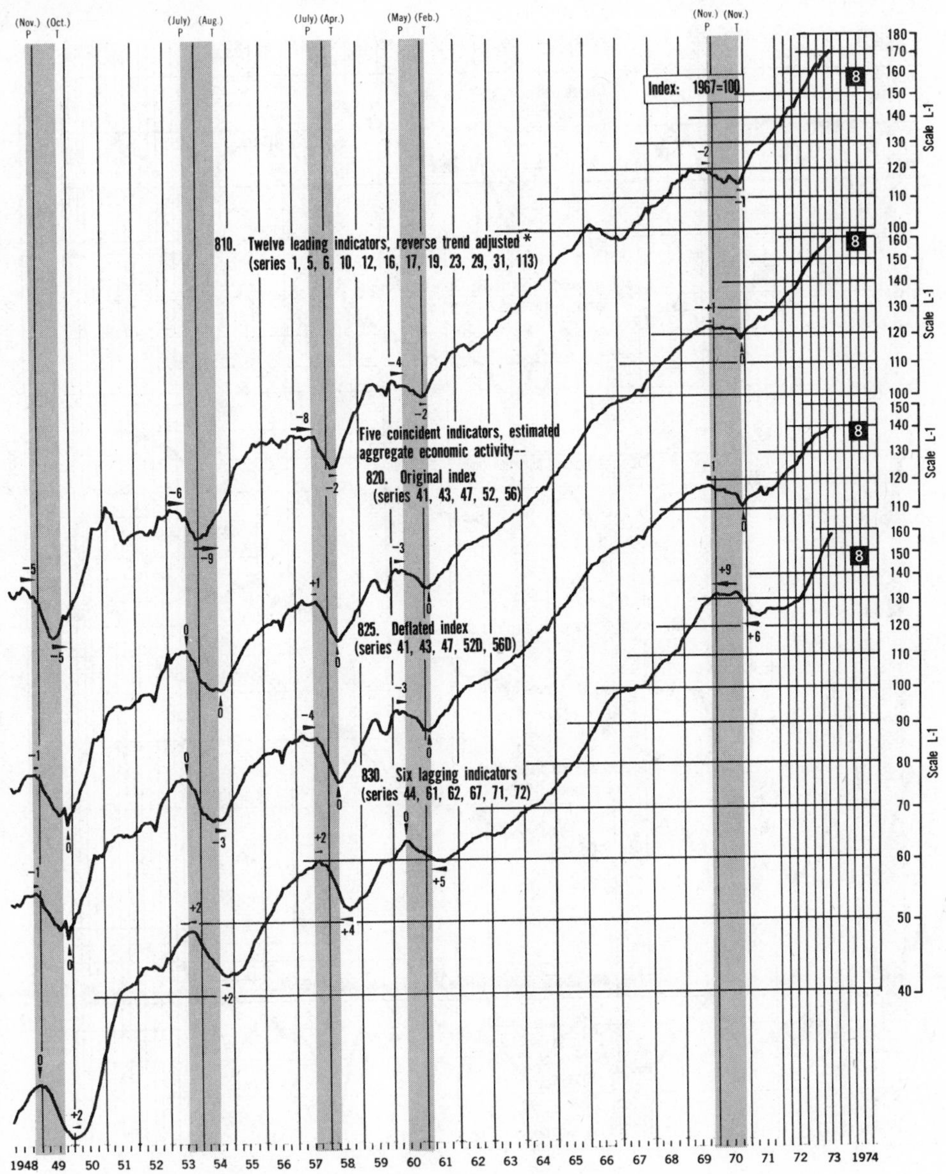

Source: *Business Conditions Digest,* U.S. Department of Commerce, September 1973.

CHART 2

NBER Leading Indicators

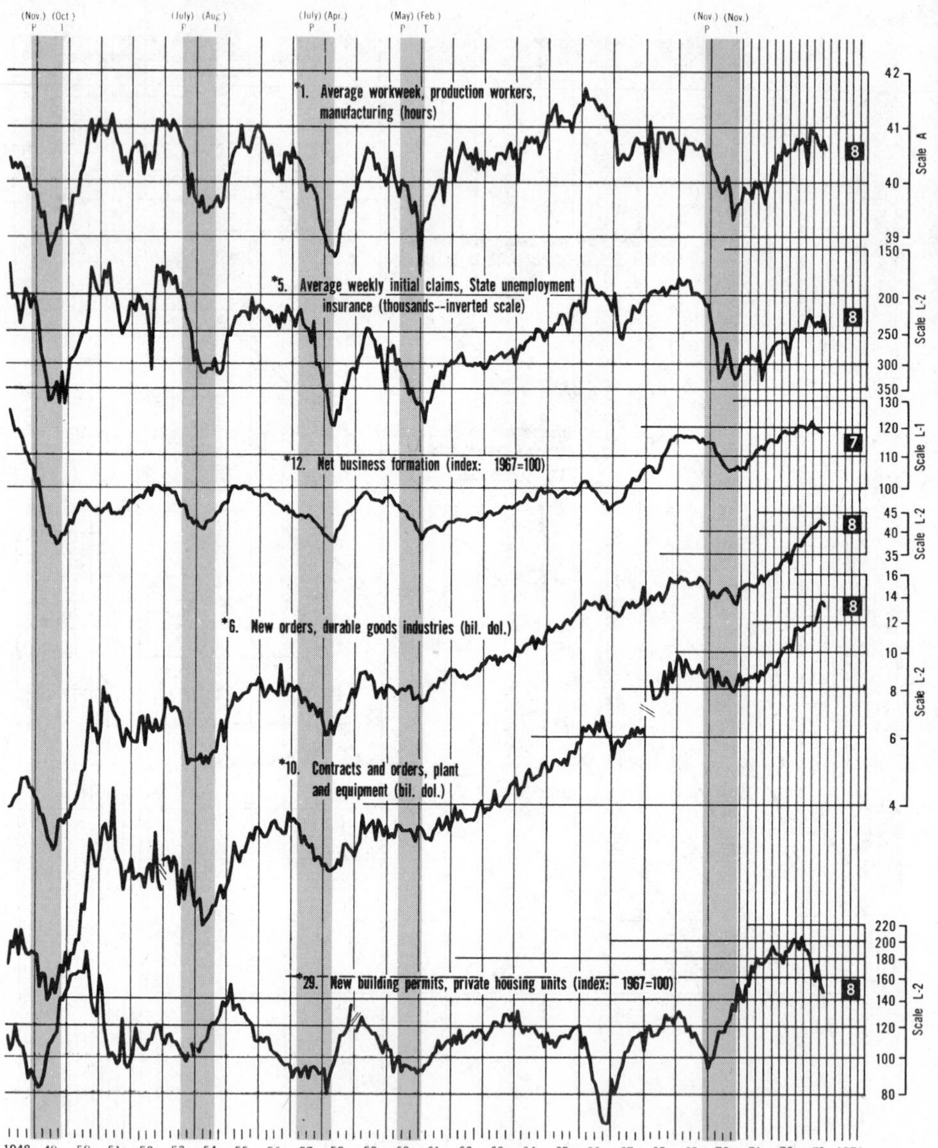

CHART 2 (continued)

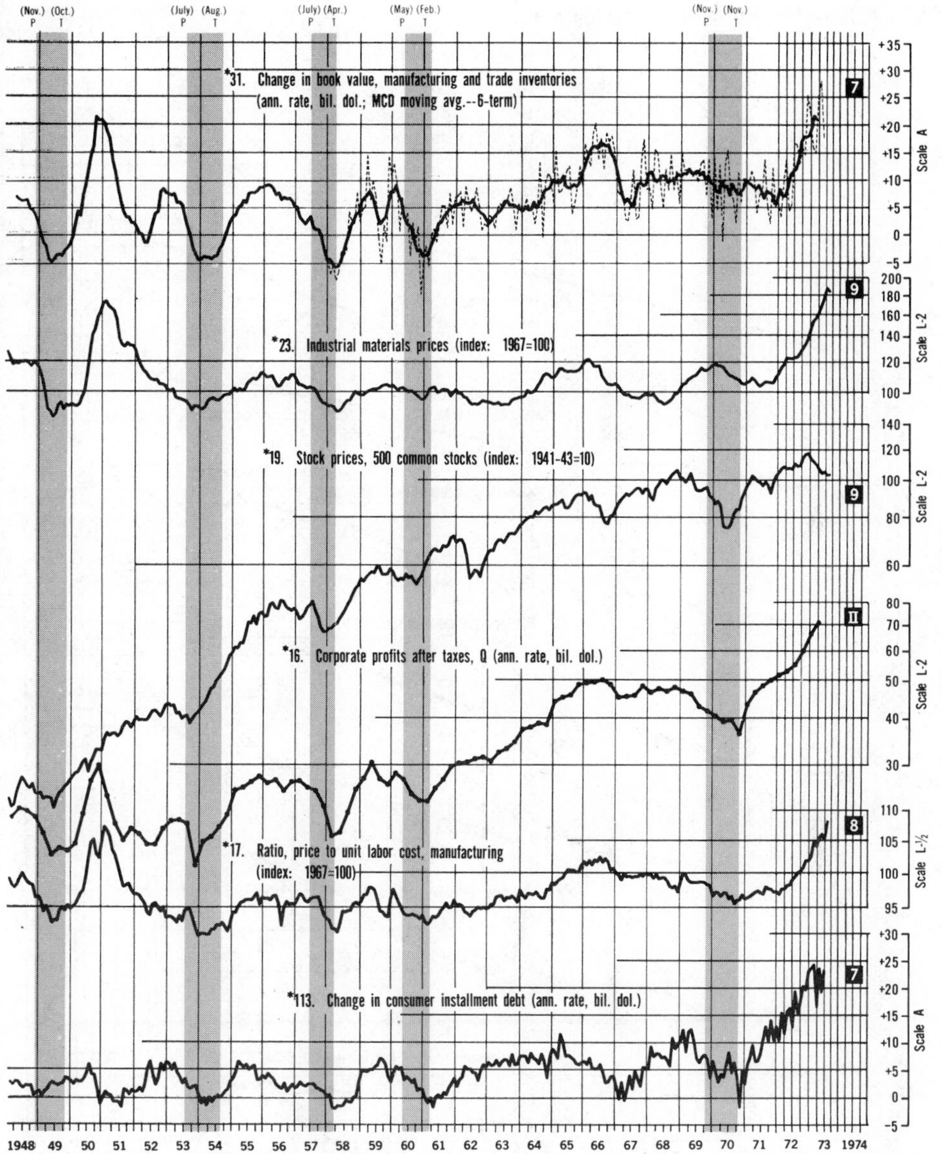

Source: *Business Conditions Digest,* U.S. Department of Commerce, September 1973.

CHART 3

NBER Roughly Coincident Indicators

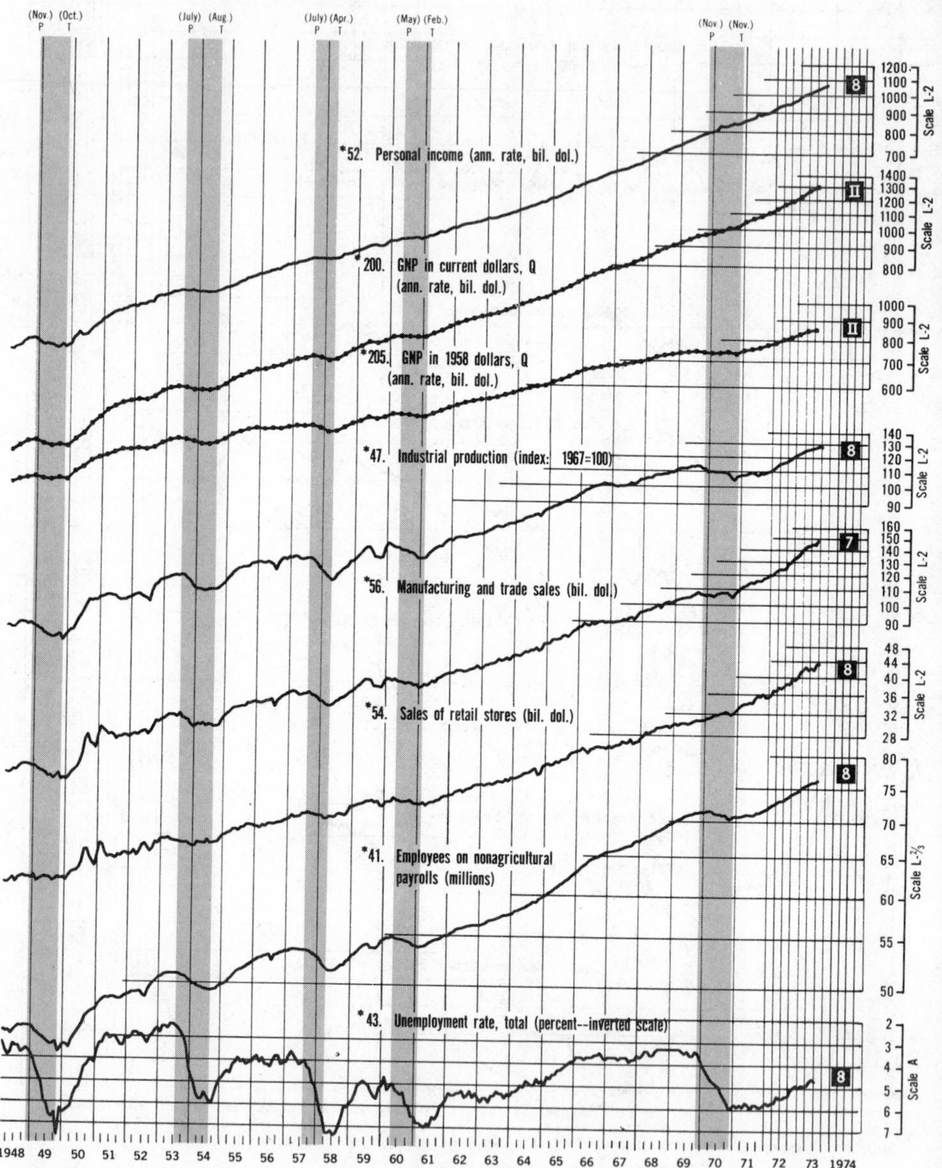

Source: *Business Conditions Digest,* U.S. Department of Commerce, September 1973.

CHART 4

NBER Lagging Indicators

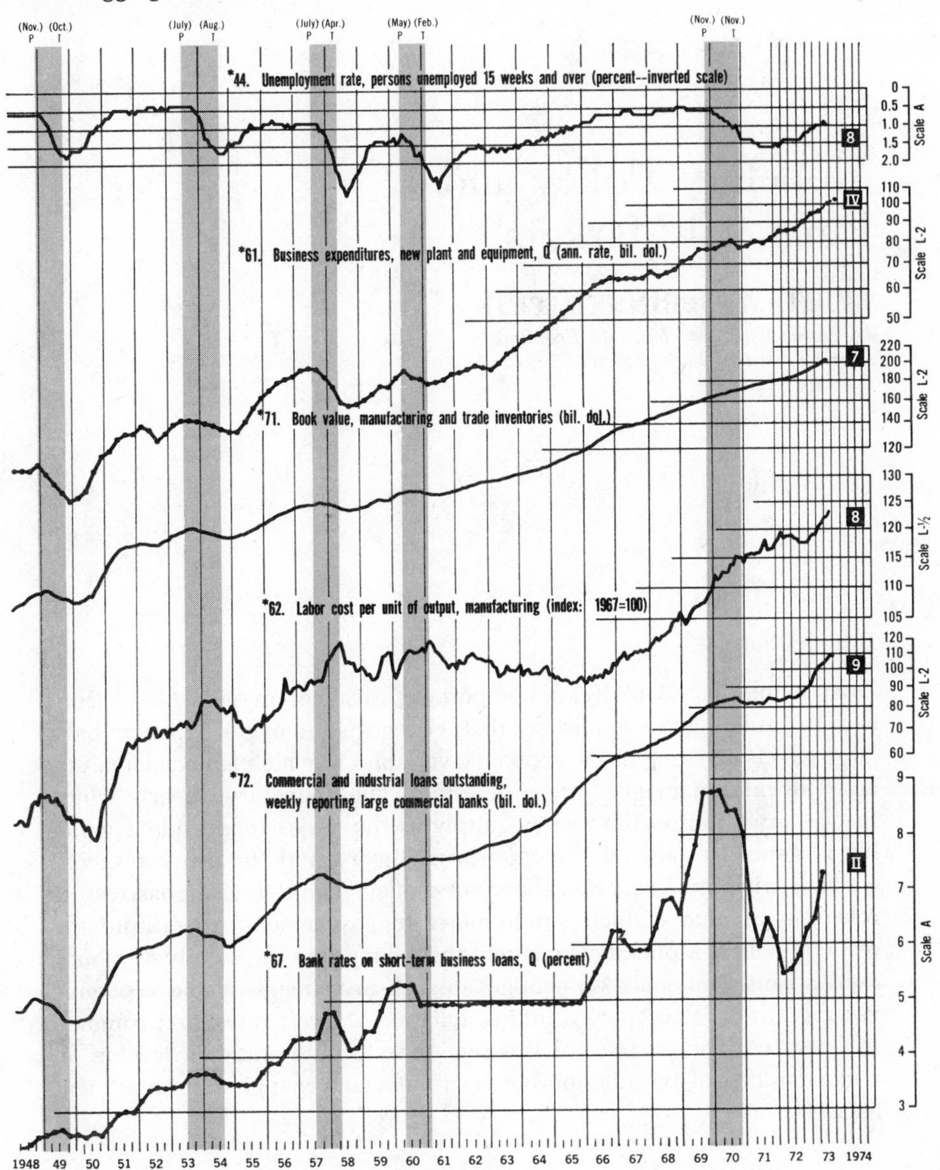

Source: *Business Conditions Digest,* U.S. Department of Commerce, September 1973.

29

Monetary Policy and Financial Markets[1]

BERYL W. SPRINKEL, Ph.D.
Executive Vice President and Economist
Harris Trust and Savings Bank
Chicago, Illinois

Introduction

DURING the past two decades important advances in monetary theory and research have established that changes in monetary policy have large effects on many of the economic variables in which financial analysts and portfolio managers are interested. The monetary theory which focuses attention on the money supply as the major independent variable is generally labeled the *monetarist* theory and, in many respects, conflicts with the *Keynesian* theory of money. The latter emphasizes the role of fiscal factors which is determined by government expenditure and revenue policy. Monetarists contend that changes in the supply of money exert a causal influence on changes in such investment-related economic variables as GNP, corporate profits, inflation, interest rates, and common stock prices. The purpose of this section is to help analysts develop an understanding of the relation between monetary change and investment markets.

MONEY SUPPLY

The term *money supply* cannot be uniquely specified on an a priori basis. Money serves the role of the financial medium by which goods and services can be conveniently exchanged. It also functions as a

[1] The ideas summarized in this section are developed in more detail in B. W. Sprinkel, *Money and Markets: A Monetarist View* (Homewood, Ill.: Dow Jones-Irwin, 1971).

means for storing value, as do other forms of assets. Clearly, cash in circulation, outside banks, is money. Demand deposits in banks also qualify as money. Time deposits in commercial banks serve the liquidity role of money along with shares in savings and loan associations, deposits in mutual savings banks, U.S. government savings bonds, and short-term U.S. government securities. Indeed the whole spectrum of assets ranging from cash to real estate possesses varying degrees of liquidity. The selection of a meaningful definition of money must be based on empirical evidence, i.e., which series is most closely associated with economic and financial data in which the observer is most interested. The three most common definitions of the money supply or money stock are (1) currency outside banks and demand deposits at commercial banks (M_1); (2) M_1 plus net time deposits at commercial banks (M_2); and (3) M_2 plus deposits of mutual savings banks plus savings capital of savings and loan associations. In the following essay the money supply will refer to M_1. This definition is chosen because it is simple, the data is readily available, and it is at least as closely related to economic and financial series as other definitions.

MONEY, VELOCITY, AND INCOME

The monetarist theory argues that an increase in the money supply leads to a subsequent increase in GNP. Perhaps the easiest way to understand this relation is by viewing the quantity equation $MV = PX = GNP$, where M is the average quantity of money for a given time period; P represents the price index of currently produced goods and services for the same period; X represents the real GNP during the period; and V is velocity, the average turnover of money spent on finally produced goods and services for the period. Therefore, MV represents the amount of money spent on current production during a given period, and PX represents the amount of money received from the sale of current production during the same period. To convert the quantity equation into a theory of income determination, monetarists argue that M, the money supply, is the independent causal variable determined by the Federal Reserve system and that changes in M result in changes in GNP, i.e., it will not be offset by compensating changes in V. They contend that the demand for money is relatively stable, thereby resulting in a relatively stable velocity. It is not essential to assume that V is constant in order to derive a useful theory. It is only necessary to establish that changes in V do not consistently offset changes in M, so that changes in the money stock do affect total spending in the same direction.

Monetarists contend that economic units, including individuals and businesses, diversify their asset holdings between money and non-monetary assets such as real estate, stocks, and bonds. Their willingness to hold money depends on its cost, i.e., the sacrificed return from not holding other assets and the demand for money for exchange purposes.

At any point in time, economic units are striving to achieve an optimum distribution of nonmonetary to monetary assets within the context of projected income. If the money supply is rapidly increased by the Federal Reserve system, economic units find they have excess money. They, therefore, spend more on goods, services, and assets. This action has the effect of bidding up prices if the economy is at or near full employment since output cannot be increased, but primarily raises output if economic slack exists. Purchase of assets puts upward pressure on asset prices as well. This increased spending continues until incomes are raised to such a level that the increased value of assets and expected income balances the higher stock of money. Conversely, if the money stock is sharply decreased relative to nonmonetary assets and income, economic units attempt to restore liquidity by rearranging assets and conserving cash. Therefore, total spending on goods, services, and assets declines and exerts downward pressure on prices and production to the point where the lower money stock is in balance with the reduced flow of income and asset values. Although economic units cannot actually increase or decrease the money stock, which is controlled by the Federal Reserve Board, they can bring about changes in asset prices and incomes and, hence, changes in employment and the general price level as well as changes in stock and bond prices.

Financial analysts and portfolio managers therefore should be interested in monetary policy changes because of the effect on such investment-related series as changes in GNP, corporate profits, inflation, and stock and bond prices. This essay will present some of the evidence bearing on the above monetarist view of the world and will elaborate on the brief explanation just presented.

MONEY AND THE BUSINESS CYCLE

An enormous amount of recent economic research substantiates the monetarist view that changes in demand for goods and services are primarily determined by prior changes in the supply of money. Fortunately, from a forecasting point of view, monetary change works with a lag.

Charts 1 and 2 relate monetary changes to business fluctuations in the United States since 1920. These conclusions are evident:

1. Monetary contraction preceded each business recession or depression.
2. Acceleration in monetary growth preceded each recovery including the most recent one.
3. The severity of monetary contraction was closely related to the severity of the following economic contraction with 1920–21, 1929–33, and 1937–38 being the greatest.

CHART 1
Federal Surpluses and Deficits

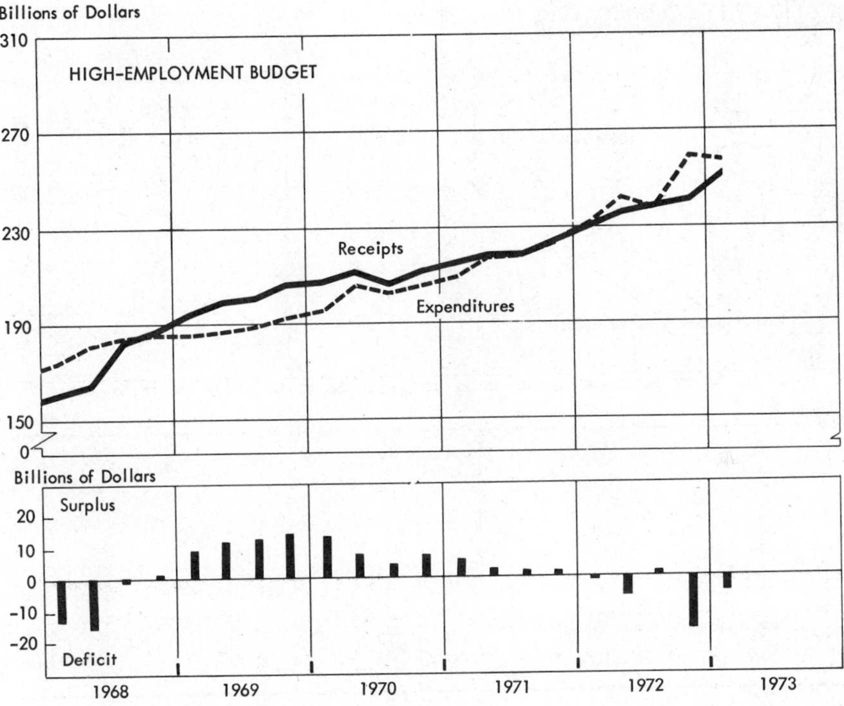

° Seasonally adjusted annual rate.
Source: Federal Reserve Bank of St. Louis

4. Changes in monetary growth affected final demands or income creation with a lag. Most evidence suggests the major impact on income change occurs six to nine months after the prior monetary move.

CASE STUDY OF MONETARY VERSUS FISCAL POLICY

Sometimes monetary and fiscal indicators point in the same direction, but frequently they do not. Two recent examples of disparate indications are particularly instructive. A satisfactory test of the monetarist versus Keynesian, or fiscal, views requires that changes in monetary growth and changes in the full-employment budget predict opposite patterns of economic activity. In other words, monetarists contend that changes in money exert the major causal influence, while Keynesians emphasize changes in the full-employment budget and investment as the major independent variables.

In January 1967, after long deliberation within the administration,

CHART 2
Monetary Velocity and Business

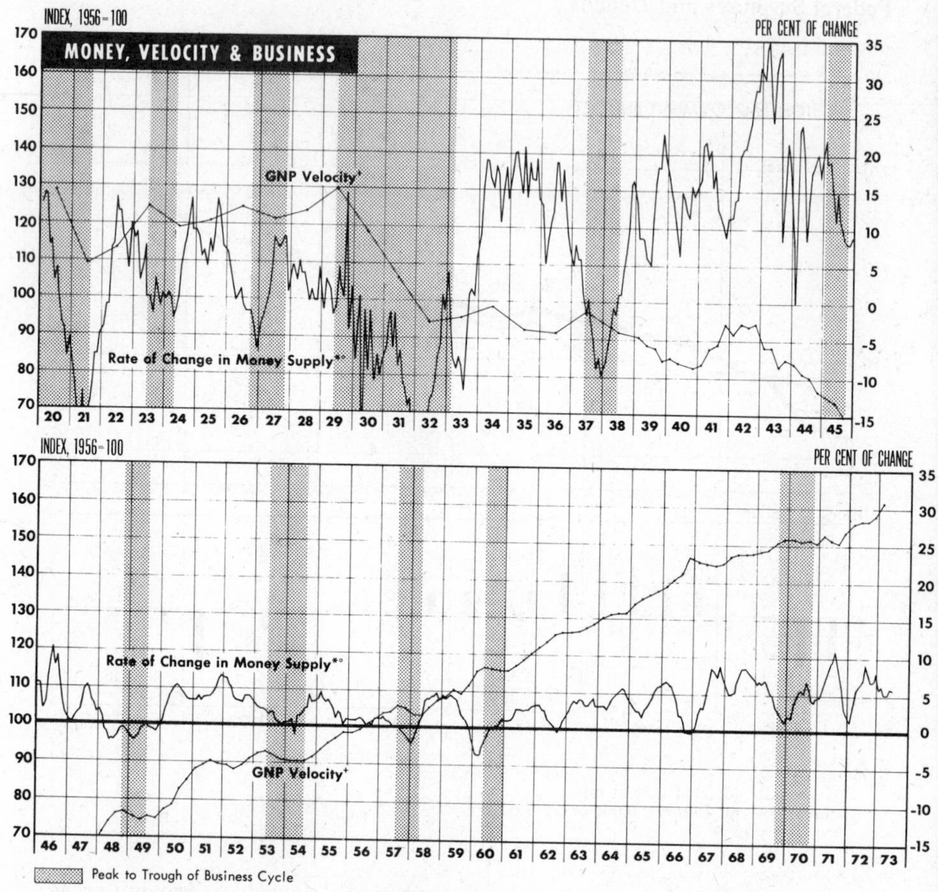

* All commercial banks demand deposits adjusted + currency (seasonally adjusted).
° Annual rate of monthly change, six-month moving average.
† Annual data before 1939; quarterly since 1939.
Source: Department of Commerce, Federal Reserve Board, National Bureau of Economic Research, Inc.

President Johnson requested a large tax increase whose stated objectives were to slow the rate of rise in the economy, reduce inflation, and lower interest rates. Congress debated the request for 17 months, but finally, in June 1968, enacted the surtax requested by the President. President Johnson signed the bill and everyone sat back and waited for the widely advertised economic benefits to arrive. Unfortunately, it was a long wait, even though there was ample reason to expect an imminent slowdown if the budget really did exert an important independent effect on economic conditions. The full-employment-budget (Chart 1) moved from a deficit at the annual rate of $15.0 billion in the second quarter of 1968 to a $10.7 billion surplus by the second quarter of 1969—a $25.7 billion restraining swing. Consequently, fiscalists almost uniformly predicted a significant slowing in the economy, reduced inflation, and lower interest rates.

Monetarists had a different view. They contended that despite the dramatic shift in fiscal "stimulus," monetary evidence pointed to full steam ahead. Monetary policy had turned highly expansive throughout 1967 and through the first half of 1968, with the annual rate of growth in the money supply averaging 6 percent in the last half of 1967 and slightly more in the first half of 1968 (see Chart 2). The Federal Reserve Board feared "overkill" resulting from the dramatic fiscal change. Accordingly, in August 1968, the discount rate was reduced and monetary growth accelerated further. The August 1968 action of the Federal Reserve Board made the monetary-fiscal confrontation more decisive, but the action increased the overheating of the economy and greatly accelerated inflationary pressures, as monetarists expected. Interest rates rose, after a brief respite, and the annual rate of GNP rose only $3.7 billion per quarter less in the last half than in the first half of the year.

Monetarists explained the lack of significant economic slowing in the last half of 1968 by the prior and continued rapid growth in the money supply. They also argued that there was no a priori reason why a large tax increase with unchanged (or increased) monetary growth should deter spending. It is true, as fiscalists argue, that a tax increase reduces disposable income. That follows from the rules of arithmetic, not economics. Will a sharp decrease in disposable income lead to a reduction in consumer spending? That all depends—sometimes it does and sometimes it doesn't. Consumer spending is usually believed to be determined by expected permanent income. If a tax increase is billed as a temporary affair, as was the 1968 tax bill, then there is little reason to expect a dramatic reduction in consumer spending. Reducing one's standard of living is a painful affair and is to be avoided at nearly all costs, especially if the income reduction is likely to be temporary. Why not continue spending and finance that outlay by increased borrowing, reduced saving, and conversion of assets into spendable form? The continued rapid growth in consumer outlays in 1968, accompanied by a decreased savings rate and stepped-up consumer borrowing, suggests that is what happened.

It is necessary to trace the impact of the tax increase somewhat further. Again, arithmetical reasoning suggests that after a tax increase the federal government will have a smaller deficit to finance. This means that investors who would have bought the increased supply of government bonds now have funds available for other purposes, including purchasing other debt instruments such as corporate bonds, assuming that monetary policy remains unchanged. The freeing of additional funds for other purposes will offset, in dollar amounts, the tax increase or the reduction in the deficit. To a first approximation, will not the one offset the other? The monetarist answer is yes. Any possible restraining effect of the tax increase has to be sought at a much deeper level, in terms of its effects on interest rates and on rates of spending. But these effects are likely to be minimal. Therefore, in the judgment of the writer, there is no presumption that a temporary tax increase will restrain spending significantly if monetary policy remains unchanged. Of course, if monetary growth is also reduced at the time that taxes are increased, there is reason to expect spending to be restrained. However, much the same effect would follow from reduced monetary growth even if taxes were not increased. The monetarist regards the disposition of a surplus and the method of financing a deficit as critical in determining their impact on spending. But these matters reflect monetary, not fiscal, policy.

A more recent test developed in late 1969 and early 1970. Keynesian economists, relying on a projected reduction in the full-employment surplus due especially to two scheduled tax cuts and a sharp projected rise in autonomous plant and equipment expenditures, predicted a strong economy in 1970 with only a modest slowing in the rate of rise in GNP and a slight increase in unemployment. Monetarists, however, impressed with the considerable monetary restraint dating primarily from the spring of 1969 and, to a lesser extent, as far back as the third quarter of 1968, flatly predicted a recession with declining real output, sharply rising unemployment, reduced corporate profits, and with an appropriate lag, a lessening of inflationary pressure. The 1969–70 recession has now been duly designated for the archives by the National Bureau of Economic Research, and the inflation rate peaked in the first half of 1970 and trended downward for about two years until excessive monetary growth again accelerated inflation. Even so, most observers, including the monetarists, were unduly optimistic about the extent of the inflationary decline.

Although monetarists contend that fiscal change per se exerts only a nominal impact on future income creation, they *do not* argue that fiscal policy is inconsequential. Clearly, fiscal policies exert an enormous economic impact on the allocation of resources:

1. Between the public and private sectors of the economy,
2. Between consumption and investment decisions within the private sector, and
3. Between various government programs within the government sector.

These influences are of critical import. However, the evidence supports the view that the change in the budget deficit has only a nominal impact on final demands, but the method of financing the deficit, by money creation of the Central Bank or alternative means, frequently plays a decisive role.

MONEY AND INFLATION

Few economic relations are so firmly supported by the evidence as the relation between the rate of monetary growth and the consequent rate of inflation. Since World War II, most governments have concentrated on fiscal change as the major governmental regulator with monetary policy playing an accommodating role at best. In other words, most governments adopted Keynesian policies. We are all now paying the price of inflation for the excessive monetary growth that has occurred.

Monetarists believe that a rise in the money supply per unit of real GNP induces inflation, i.e., the greater the rise, the greater the inflation. Table 1 presents confirming evidence for many countries from 1955–68.

TABLE 1

Money and GNP Growth—1955–68 (compound annual rates of change)

	Money Supply	*Gross National Product*
Brazil	38.9%	42.6%
Chile	34.7	33.2
South Korea	30.0	26.2
Argentina	24.9	28.9
Colombia	16.5	14.8
Japan	14.7	14.0
Peru	12.5	13.8
Mexico	12.4	11.2
France	10.4	10.4
Italy	9.2	12.0
West Germany	8.9	8.7
Ecuador	8.0	6.5
Switzerland	6.7	7.6
Canada	5.9	8.0
United Kingdom	3.9	6.4

Unfortunately, monetary growth in many developed countries, including the United States, accelerated in the latter sixties with attendant rising inflationary pressures as indicated in Table 2.

The major cause of increased monetary growth abroad in recent years was weakness in the U.S. dollar combined, until recently, with a fixed exchange rate system. As the dollar weakened, foreign central banks bought dollars by creating domestic currency. Consequently, monetary growth rose and inflation became more serious. U.S. monetary growth also accelerated from 1971 to the present primarily in an attempt to stimulate economic recovery from the 1969–70 recession. Because of the inevitable lags in the policy-making process, the 1972 stimulus was excessive as evidenced by more serious inflationary pressures. The

TABLE 2

Compound Annual Rates of Change

	4th Quarter 1968–4th Quarter 1972		*1972*		*1st Quarter 1973*	
	Money	*Consumer Prices*	*Money*	*Consumer Prices*	*Money*	*Consumer Prices*
Canada	12.7	4.0	20.3	5.2	15.0	7.7
France	8.2	6.0	14.5	6.8	– 1.7	3.5
Germany	10.8	4.8	13.4	6.4	10.2	9.4
Italy	20.3	5.3	21.6	7.2	n.a.	11.4
Japan	22.5	6.2	23.1	4.6	32.3	11.5
Switzerland	11.8	5.2	5.9	7.0	n.a.	10.4
United Kingdom	9.6	7.4	14.5	7.7	n.a.	7.0
United States	6.1	4.6	7.4	3.4	4.7	5.8

n.a.—Not available.

recent move to a floating exchange rate system, obviating the necessity to support the dollar, creates some hope that inflation may not continue to accelerate abroad.

Since most governments are unwilling to restore price stability by inducing monetary restraint and recession, there has been a persistent tendency to resort to income policies, either mild or severe. Such an approach seems like the logical and easy way out of a serious inflation, but controls have never worked and have eventually been abandoned in most countries. Unfortunately, there appears to be no painless means of restoring price stability once serious inflation begins. The longer the persistence of inflation, the more costly is eventual success. No inflation to date has been conquered without the sacrifice of reduced production and employment. Perhaps we will some day find a way, but it is not now evident.

Arguments that there is a permanent tradeoff between unemployment and inflation a la the Philips curve have also proven to be illusive in practice. In the short run, acceptance of a higher inflation rate will yield lower unemployment so long as participants are misled concerning future inflation rates. But once inflationary expectations become ingrained, the Philips curve shifts and unemployment does not decline. It is significant that in prior postwar periods, inflation did not accelerate until unemployment reached the 4–4½ percent range. During this period when inflationary expectations were higher, inflation acceleration began with unemployment in the 5–5½ percent range.

Therefore, it is critically important that once the sacrifice of lower production and employment is made and price pressures begin to yield, policy decisions must not repeat the go-stop mistakes of the past. Short-run policy decisions should always be consistent with promotion of longer run economic objectives. Otherwise, the inevitable lag in policy impact will generate undesirable oscillations in subsequent economic performance. Fine tuning of economic policies based on the latest wiggle of the indicators is a sure road to the instability we endured in the past ten years. Patience and tenacious pursuit of stable economic policies promise superior results but, unfortunately, governments seldom can endure the short-run political costs.

The Nixon Administration provided a most recent example of a democratic government opting for incomes policies due to their apparent irresistible political appeal, despite clear evidence that wage and price controls would not work. We have now been subjected to Freeze 1, Phase 2, Phase 3, Freeze 2, Phase 4, and Phase Out, and inflation was much worse than at the beginning. Until recently, the defenders of free markets were largely mute while a massive campaign for controls was mounted in the press as well as in the board rooms. Businessmen wanted direct controls placed on wages, not prices, while labor unions wanted the opposite. Regrettably, we had both. Only recently was the public made aware of the dangers of controls as production incentives were dulled and consumption was encouraged. Suppressing prices and wage attacks symptoms, not the root cause. If long continued, it leads to serious misallocation of resources, reduced real growth, shortages, rationing, and ultimately black markets. The first two stages of recent controls did little to control inflation but caused little serious damage to the economy since idle resources existed and inflationary pressures were receding following the 1969–70 recession. However, as usual, controls continued until a state of excess demand developed and serious distortions resulted. The only hope for bringing the U.S. inflation under better control rests on less monetary growth and a balanced budget which removes the incentive for financing a deficit with additional new money. Now that controls have been abandoned and a new Ford Administration is attacking the inflation problem, perhaps there is reason for hoping some progress will be forthcoming.

BONDS

Liquidity Effect

The conventional Keynesian analysis of the effect of an increase in the money supply on interest rates argues that to induce money holders to hold an increased supply of money, interest rates must decline. This effect may be referred to as the *liquidity effect*. Until recently, most economists would have used only the above version in explaining the impact of a changing money supply on interest rates. Some would have argued that the very process by which the money supply increases in our economy, i.e., mainly open market purchases of Treasury bills, leads to higher prices for Treasury bills and ultimately to lower rates on other assets as portfolios are adjusted to the lower Treasury bill rate. This analysis is correct so far as it goes, but it stops much too soon and, in fact, misses the major effect of a changing money supply on interest rates.

The liquidity analysis does not fit even a casual reference to empirical relations between money supply and interest rates. For example, it is well known that in many of the South American countries we previously surveyed, such as Chile and Brazil, interest rates are very high. But we know that monetary expansion in those countries has been very high, not low as the liquidity theory would imply. Or if we search the modern history of the United States, we find that interest rates dropped drastically during the period from 1929 to the mid 1930s. Yet, the money supply declined 29 percent from 1929 to 1932. During the first half of the 1960s, when monetary growth was moderate at about 3 percent, interest rates were much lower than they have been since mid-1965, when monetary growth averaged much more. It appears that high interest rates are typical of countries with high rates of monetary growth and serious inflation and not vice versa.

Many years ago, Gibson, an English financial writer, published several articles drawing attention to the close correlation between the level of interest rates and commodity prices. Keynes was impressed by these data and named the relation "the Gibson Paradox," after the author who first indicated a price-interest rate relation. Since it was known that countries with serious inflation also had rapid monetary growth, it appeared paradoxical that more money caused higher, not lower, interest rates. The facts just do not fit the theory that more money causes lower rates. Since the facts cannot be changed, we must go back to the drawing board to uncover some missing elements in a viable theory of interest rates.

Income and Price Effects

Monetarists argue that an increase in the money supply does indeed tend, in the first instance, to raise asset prices and lower interest rates. However, they also contend that more money leads, with an appropriate lag, to more spending. More spending occurs on both consumer goods and services as well as investment goods. If sufficient idle resources are available to accommodate increased spending with increased real production, then real incomes rise with little significant short-run effect upon prices. Since incomes are higher, resulting from higher sales, production, and employment, there is an increase in the demand for loanable funds. The higher income effect resulting from more money in the economy tends to raise the demand for funds and place upward pressure on interest rates. Therefore, the income effect of higher monetary growth raises interest rates, reversing the initial liquidity effect.

Suppose more rapid monetary growth continues and practical full employment of labor and capital resources is achieved. Additional increases in total spending are reflected in higher prices. The income effect tended to reverse the liquidity effect which lowered interest rates, and now the price effect serves to drive interest rates even higher.

Participants in the credit markets become aware of the fact that prices are rising and probably begin to expect that further increases will be forthcoming, since reversal of an inflationary trend can be achieved only gradually. The borrower recognizes that if he borrows now and pays back later, the value of the money, i.e., purchasing power, will be less at the time the loan is repaid. Presumably it will be less difficult to pay back a loan with inflated dollars than with stable dollars. Therefore, he is interested in increasing his demand for loanable funds. Lenders are aware of the inflationary phenomena as well and insist on receiving the basic real rate of interest plus more to compensate for reduced purchasing power of the money to be repaid at a subsequent date. These demand and supply pressures result in higher rates of interest as well as a proliferation of other devices, such as equity participations and indexed bonds, designed to maintain the purchasing power of the money loaned.

We may now conclude, on the basis of the above argument, that an increase in the quantity of money leads in the first instance to somewhat lower interest rates, but that once income and prices are stimulated, interest rates go up, not down. The greater the amount of money pumped into the economy, the larger the rise in incomes, prices, and, consequently, interest rates. Hence, more money leads to higher, not lower, interest rates. We should expect to find that countries experiencing the highest rate of monetary growth relative to output, and hence the highest rate of inflation, also have the highest interest rates. And indeed that is the case.

Chart 3 published by the St. Louis Federal Reserve Bank presents the yields on highest grade corporate bonds on both a nominal or market rate of return as well as on a real rate basis. As can be noted at a glance, the great bulk of the enormous rise in interest rates since 1964 can be explained by the increased rate of inflation expectation. High interest rates are usually associated with serious inflation. And, of course, the relation works in reverse. As inflation receded in 1970–71, interest rates dropped sharply followed later by higher rates as inflation again accelerated. In a stable, moderate monetary growth environment, the populist objective of lower interest rates is achievable, but attempts to suppress interest rates during inflationary times by open-market purchases of securities which increase the money supply and merely make interest rates higher.

STOCKS

All cyclically related stock price movements since at least 1918, as well as most intermediate movements, have been closely associated with

CHART 3

Yields on Highest-Grade Seasoned Corporate Bonds

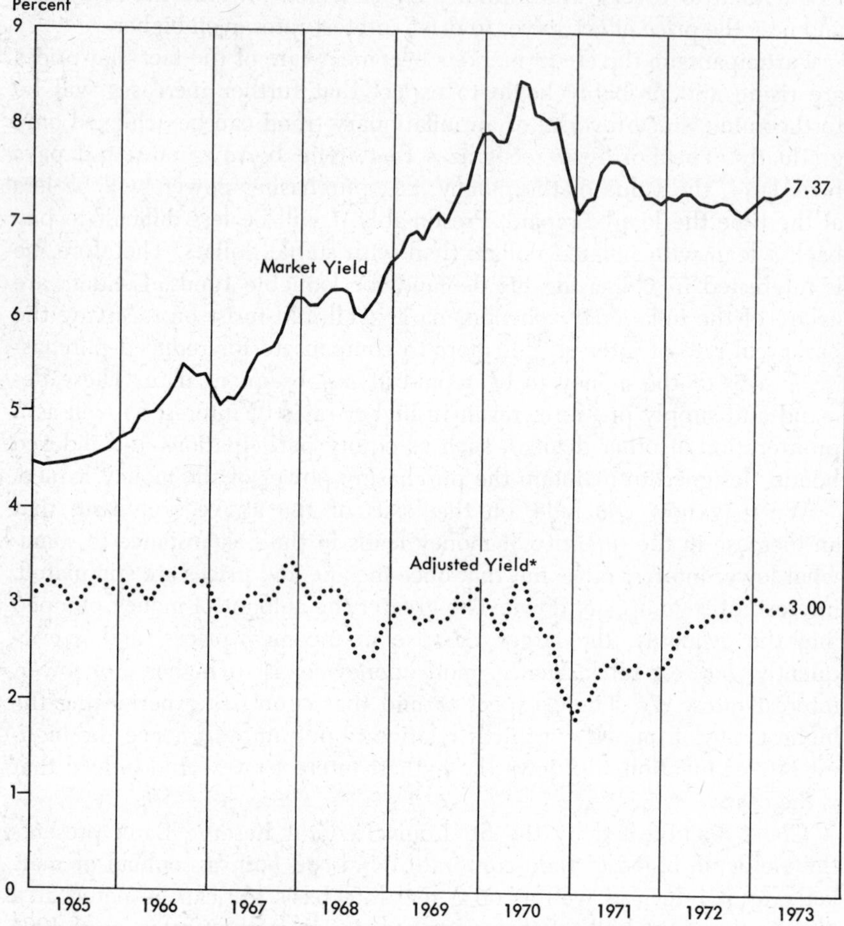

* Market yield less average annual rate of change in consumer prices over three previous years.
Latest data plotted: Market yield–June; adjusted yield–June estimated.
Source: Prepared by Federal Reserve Bank of St. Louis.

monetary change (Chart 4). Similarly, changes in monetary growth are associated with changes in the rate of change in corporate profits before taxes, with the money supply usually shortly in the lead (Chart 5). As previously explained, monetary change is also related to interest rates. Monetarist theory offers some insights into these relationships. Corporate profits are a function of sales volume and profit margins. Reduced monetary growth affects total spending and sales volume over a period of many months, with the initial impact mild but nearly immediate, and with the total or entire effect distributed over a considerable period of time approximating a year. Reduced sales growth emanating from re-

CHART 4

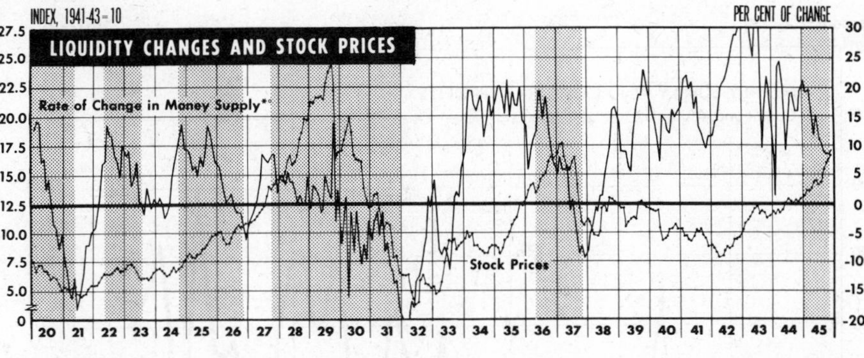

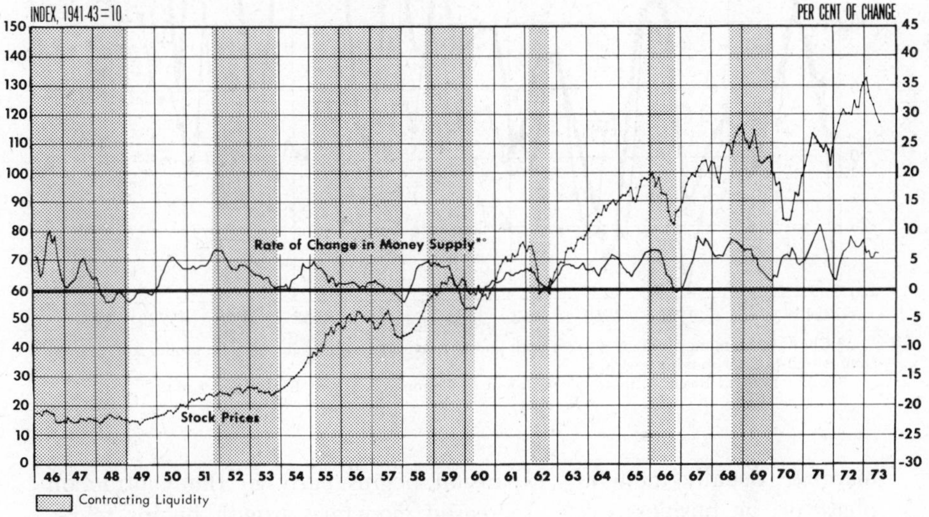

* All commercial banks demand deposits adjusted + currency (seasonally adjusted).
° Annual rate of monthly change, six-month moving average.
Price index scale different on upper and lower charts.
Source: Standard & Poor's Industrial, National Bureau of Economic Research, Inc., Federal Reserve Board.

duced monetary growth results in reduced profit growth almost immediately. As the monetary squeeze continues, profit growth continues to decline, until eventually profits actually decrease.

During the later part of a business expansion, corporate profits actually recede, as do other leading indicators. Since costs continue to rise even after industrial prices weaken, reduced margins add to the declining volume and profits drop sharply. These phenomena are usually compounded by the fact that improvement in productivity weakens or actually declines during the late phase of a business expansion and in the early period of economic contraction. Increased attention to cost control during the recession period eventually relieves the pressure on profit

CHART 5

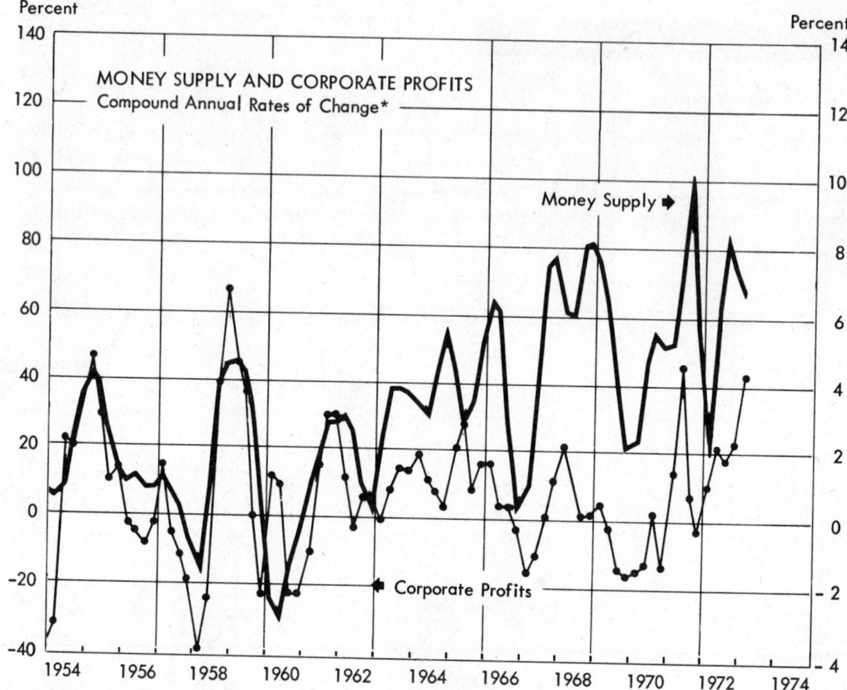

* Changes in money reflect a six-month moving average, while changes in profits are derived from a two-quarter moving average.

Source: Federal Reserve Board, Department of Commerce, Harris Bank (Chicago).

margins. Usually monetary expansion begins early in the contraction phase of the business cycle. Increased monetary growth begins to reduce the downward pressure on total spending and sales and, eventually, leads to an actual increase in sales and output. Improving profit margins reverse the profit trend even before volume improves, and as volume increases, profits expand for both volume and margin reasons. Not only is monetary change closely related to subsequent changes in corporate profit and stock price changes, but also a monetarist explanation is consistent with the standard (present value) theory of stock price determination.

It has long been argued that the price of a stock is equal to the discounted value of expected earnings. The major factors thus determining the value of a stock are expected earnings and the interest rate. Michael W. Keran demonstrated that during the past 15 years the major factors determining stock prices were expected corporate earnings and current interest rates, which in turn were influenced by the money supply.[2] He concluded that, "According to this analysis, changes in the

[2] Michael W. Keran, "Expectations, Money and the Stock Market," Federal Reserve Bank of St. Louis *Review*, January 1971, p. 16.

nominal money stock have little direct impact on the stock price, but a major indirect influence on stock prices through their effect on inflation and corporate earnings expectations." In a later article, Hamburger and Kochin confirmed that there is evidence that stock prices are affected by long-term bond rates and corporate earnings, but that there is also a direct portfolio effect in the short run.[3] They further argue that there exists a risk premium in the level of stock market prices related to the changing variability of the economy. They conclude that instability in the growth rate of money increases economic instability, raises the risk premium in stock ownership and hence depresses stock prices.

In this broader context, changes in the money supply can be viewed as a proxy for the factors that both directly and indirectly influence stock prices. Changes in money directly influence the willingness of asset holders to buy or sell common stocks as they react to changing liquidity pressures, i.e., higher monetary growth raises liquidity and hence the demand for stocks. But the indirect effects are also important. As previously argued, changes in money influence the rate of income creation or business activity. Since corporate profits are a residual, change in the rate of growth in national income exerts a magnified influence on the trend in corporate profits. A mere slowing in the rate of rise in the economy, for example, often causes an absolute decline in corporate profits.

Theory tells us that expected corporate profits are a major variable influencing stock prices. Profit expectations are formed by past trends in corporate profits. If profits have been flat for some time, a current downtrend in profits could result in a significant downward revision in corporate profit expectations, since most recent earnings trends heavily influence current views.

If prior monetary growth were highly expansive, inflation could result in high and rising interest rates as market participants came to expect serious inflation in the future. Furthermore, the short-run impact of a tighter monetary policy would raise interest rates. An inflationary environment, responding to a prior expansive monetary policy, followed in turn by a tighter policy which tended to slow the economy, would exert serious downward pressure on common stock prices due to liquidity, profits, and interest rate influences. Conversely, a period of expanding economic growth in response to stable and moderate monetary growth occurring at a time characterized by waning inflationary pressures would be highly beneficial to equity prices. Expanding money would create liquidity pressures toward common stock acquisition and rising corporate profits would raise profit expectations, whereas reduced inflationary expectations would result in lower interest rates.

According to the present value approach, the value of stocks should increase directly with the expected rate of earnings growth and decrease

[3] Michael J. Hamburger and Levis A. Kochin, "Money and Stock Prices: The Channels of Influence," *Journal of Finance*, May 1972, pp. 231–49.

with interest rates of competing investments such as bonds. The latter follow from the fact that interest rate (opportunity costs) occurs in the denominator of the present value terms so that as the interest rate increases, the magnitude of the terms decreases. It is possible that inflation expectations may raise interest rates more than expected earnings. If inflation leads to expectations of cost increases in excess of price increases, real earnings expectations are lowered relative to real interest rates. The latter possibility appears especially plausible when it is recognized that sensitive wholesale prices respond much more readily to demand changes than labor rates which make up a sizable proportion of most production costs. Hence, in the early phase of a developing inflation, stock prices may respond favorably as expected earnings rise more than interest rates. But later, perhaps after monetary restraint is applied and interest rates continue to rise, it becomes more difficult to raise prices, and costs continue their upward movement. Thus, rising inflation expectations depress stock prices because of rising interest rates along with flat or declining real earnings. Conversely, declining inflation expectations have a favorable impact on stock prices through both lower interest rates and a more favorable cost pattern as costs eventually rise less rapidly, in line with the more stable price trend.

In summary, the observed positive relation between changes in stock prices and monetary growth can be at least partly explained by monetarist theory. Let us begin near the depths of a bear market after the economy has started into a recession. Monetary policy usually turns expansive in order to slow the economic decline. Therefore, actual liquidity rises relative to desired liquidity. Attempts by market participants to dispose of excess liquidity lead to higher expenditures on goods and services as well as assets like common stocks. The short-run liquidity effect tends to raise stock prices. As expenditures on goods and services increase, aftertax corporate income also increases because of both volume and margin improvement. An upward trend in aftertax corporate income also tends to buoy the equity market.

In the early phase of a business recovery, longer term interest rates show little tendency to rise and, in some cases, actually decline. But as the expansion continues in response to high monetary growth, long-term interest rates begin to reflect first the income effect and subsequently the inflation effect, especially as the economy approaches full employment of resources. The rise in interest rates tends to limit the rise in stock prices. As inflation builds, monetary authorities frequently become concerned about excessive price rises and eventually begin to restrain monetary growth. In the meantime, aftertax corporate profit gains become increasingly difficult for reasons explained and, after monetary growth declines, may actually decline. At that point of decreasing liquidity, flat to declining aftertax corporate profits and rising interest rates all exert a depressing effect upon stock prices. This process continues until the economy again enters an economic slowdown and monetary policy is again eased.

Admittedly, the above scenario is an idealized case rarely duplicated precisely in the real world. Outside disruptive forces, such as war, the Cambodian invasion, and the bankruptcy of the Penn Central also impact the level of equity prices. But as a first approximation of reality, the above explanation captures much of the essence of repeated bear and bull markets. Understanding these relationships frequently aids in making critical timing decisions that all portfolio managers and financial analysts must make.

CONCLUSIONS

In conclusion, monetarists argue that causation runs from changes in money to changes in spending on assets, consumer and producers' goods, to inflation, and to interest rates. Therefore, monetarists contend that more money ultimately causes higher interest rates. Not only does the monetarist theory offer a plausible and statistically verifiable explanation of the business cycle, inflation, and interest rate changes, but also it makes a significant contribution to explaning major swings in equity prices. Therefore, understanding the basic aspects of monetarist theory and Federal Reserve policy should enable financial analysts and portfolio managers to adjust profitably to the ever-changing economic environment.

30

The Federal Reserve at Work[1]

B. U. RATCHFORD, Ph.D.
ROBERT P. BLACK, Ph.D.
AUBREY N. SNELLINGS, Ph.D.
First Reserve Bank of Richmond
Richmond, Virginia

SYSTEM POLICY OBJECTIVES

THE FEDERAL RESERVE SYSTEM is the nation's central bank. Like other central banks throughout the world, its chief responsibility is to regulate the flow of money and credit in order to promote economic stability and growth. It also performs many service functions for commercial banks, the Treasury, and the public.

Its policy is aimed at providing monetary conditions favorable to the realization of four objectives: a high level of employment, stability in the overall price level, a growing economy, and a sound international balance of payments. System policy alone cannot, of course, achieve these objectives since many other factors also play important roles. Nevertheless, all System actions are made in an attempt to facilitate the attainment of these goals. As economic conditions shift, the System at times must change the emphasis placed on each of the four objectives, but all four are ever in mind. Policies of restraint and ease are but two phases of System efforts to achieve these ends.

The four goals are closely interdependent. Without high employment, an economy can neither remain prosperous nor grow. With persistent inflation, business practices become wasteful; speculation replaces productive activity; excesses leading to economic collapse may develop; and balance of payments problems are apt to arise. Chronic deficits in

[1] Reprinted with the permission of the Federal Reserve Bank of Richmond.

the balance of payments can so tie the hands of fiscal and monetary authorities that they cannot pursue, as actively as they would like, policies designed to stimulate employment or facilitate economic progress. Achievement of high employment, a stable price level, and a sound international balance of payments, however, promotes the kind of savings, incentives, and enterprise needed in a growing economy. Hence, System policies contributing to these three objectives also produce a monetary environment conducive to long-term growth.

STRUCTURE OF THE FEDERAL RESERVE SYSTEM

The System has several important parts: member banks, the Federal Reserve banks, the Board of Governors, the Federal Open Market Committee, and the Federal Advisory Council.

Member Banks. At the base of the Federal Reserve pyramid are the System's approximately 5,750 member banks. All national banks must be members, and state banks may elect to join if they meet certain requirements. Member banks hold about 77 percent of all commercial bank assets and deposits, although less than half the nation's commercial banks belong to the System.

There are two classes of member banks. Most banks, located in 46 centers designated by the Board of Governors as reserve cities, are classified as reserve city banks, and all other banks are called country banks. Until July 28, 1962, the larger New York and Chicago banks were called central reserve city banks, but now they are classed simply as reserve city banks.

Membership conveys many privileges but also involves obligations. Obligations include: holding specified reserves against deposits; subscribing to capital stock of the district Federal Reserve bank; complying with various requirements of federal banking law; paying at par customers' checks presented through the mail; completing necessary System reports; and in the case of state member banks, being examined and supervised by the Federal Reserve banks.

Among the more important advantages a bank receives from System membership are the prestige of being a member bank and the privileges of borrowing under certain conditions from its district Federal Reserve bank, using System check collection and wire transfer facilities, obtaining currency and coin free of transportation costs, receiving an annual cumulative 6 percent dividend on its Federal Reserve bank stock, participating in the System's functional cost analysis program, using the facilities of the Reserve banks for safekeeping securities, and requesting information and receiving aid on various problems from the Federal Reserve staff.

Federal Reserve Banks. The country is divided into 12 Federal Reserve districts—each with a Federal Reserve bank. There are also 24

Federal Reserve bank branches serving particular areas within the districts. Cities with Federal Reserve head offices are: Boston, New York, Philadelphia, Cleveland, Richmond, Atlanta, Chicago, St. Louis, Minneapolis, Kansas City, Dallas, and San Francisco. These 36 Reserve bank offices comprise the second level of the pyramid.

The corporate structure of Federal Reserve banks resembles that of commercial banks. All issue capital stock, have boards of directors who elect their officers, have many similar official titles and departments, and obtain their earnings largely from interest on loans and investments.

There are three main differences, however, stemming from the Reserve banks' responsibilities to the public. First, Federal Reserve stockholders do not have the full privileges and powers that stockholders of privately managed corporations usually have. Second, Reserve banks are not profit-motivated, although they do earn large profits. Expenses and member bank dividends absorb some earnings, but most are turned over to the U.S. Treasury as "interest" on Federal Reserve notes. In 1970 dividends totaled $41 million, and payments to the Treasury ran almost $3.5 billion. Third, if the Reserve banks should ever be liquidated, the federal government would receive any assets remaining after the stock was paid off at par.

Each Reserve bank has three Class A directors, three Class B directors, and three Class C directors. Member banks elect both Class A and Class B directors by ballot. Those in Class A must be representatives of the member bank stockholders and usually are commercial bankers. Class B directors must be actively engaged in agriculture, industry, or commerce and may not be either bank officers, directors, or employees. Class C directors—one of whom is designated as chairman and one as deputy chairman of the board—are appointed by the Board of Governors. A Class C director may be neither a director, officer, employee, nor stockholder of any bank.

In addition to their regular duties in overseeing the operations of the Reserve banks, the boards of directors also have certain duties in the field of monetary policy. First, they establish, subject to the approval of the Board of Governors, the discount rates Federal Reserve banks charge on short-term loans to member banks. Second, they elect five of the presidents of the Federal Reserve banks to serve as members of the Federal Open Market Committee. Third, they provide the Reserve bank presidents and the Board of Governors with an invaluable source of "grass roots" information on business conditions.

Board of Governors. At the peak of the pyramid is the Board of Governors in Washington. It consists of seven members appointed by the President of the United States with the advice and consent of the Senate. Board members are appointed for 14-year terms and are ineligible for reappointment after having served a full term. No two board members may come from the same Federal Reserve district. The chairman and vice chairman of the board are named by the president of the United States from among the board members for a four-year term and can be redesignated.

One of the board's important duties is supervision. The board approves the salaries of all Reserve bank officers, the appointment of Reserve bank presidents and first vice presidents, and the budgets of Reserve banks. The board also examines Reserve banks and branches each year to ensure compliance with regulations and proper control of expenditures. In addition, it coordinates System economic research and data collection and reviews all System publications. It must also approve acquisitions by bank holding companies, some bank mergers, and certain other commercial bank actions.

The board's prime function, however, is the formulation of monetary policy. In addition to approving proposed changes in the discount rate, it has authority to change member bank reserve requirements within specified limits, to set margin requirements for the financing of securities traded on national security exchanges, and to set maximum interest rates payable on member banks' time and savings deposits. Even more important, members of the Board of Governors are also members of the Federal Open Market Committee and participate in the formulation and administration of open market policy.

Federal Open Market Committee. The Federal Open Market Committee—the System's most important policy-making body—is composed of the seven members of the board plus the president of the New York Federal Reserve bank and four other Reserve bank presidents. Its main responsibility is to establish System open market policy—the extent to which the System buys and sells government and other securities. It also oversees the System's operations in foreign exchange markets. It ordinarily meets every three or four weeks but sometimes more often.

The "Trading Desk" of the New York Reserve bank serves as the committee's agent in making actual purchases and sales. Government securities bought outright are then prorated among the 12 Reserve banks according to a formula based upon the reserve ratios of the various Reserve banks.

Similarly, the foreign department of the New York Reserve bank acts as the committee's agent in foreign exchange transactions. Foreign currencies purchased in these operations are also prorated among the Reserve banks.

Other Committees. Several other committees also play significant roles in System operations. One is the 12-man Federal Advisory Council composed of bankers, one from each of the Federal Reserve districts. Members are elected by the boards of directors of the Reserve banks of their districts. The council meets in Washington four times a year and advises the board on important current developments. The Conference of Presidents and the Conference of Chairmen of the Reserve banks also meet periodically to discuss System problems. In addition, several other System committees continuously review System operations and policy problems.

SYSTEM SERVICE FUNCTIONS

Like most other central banks, the Federal Reserve performs many service functions for the public, the Treasury, and commercial banks.

Fiscal Agency Functions. The 12 Federal Reserve banks act as the government's principal fiscal agents. They hold the Treasury's checking accounts, receive applications from the public for the purchase of securities being sold by the Treasury, allot securities among bidders, deliver securities, collect from security buyers, redeem securities, wire-transfer securities to other cities, make denominational exchanges of securities, pay interest coupons, and assist the Treasury and other government agencies in many other ways. The Reserve banks receive no compensation for handling the Treasury's checking accounts and redeeming its coupons, but they are reimbursed for most of the other fiscal agency work they perform. During 1970 the System handled for the Treasury about 276 million government securities valued at more than $1.4 trillion.

Collection of Checks and Noncash Items. Federal Reserve banks also collect for the public vast quantities of bank checks and substantial amounts of noncash items such as drafts, promissory notes, and bond coupons. During 1970 the System processed almost 8 billion checks, totaling more than $3.5 trillion, and 41.5 million noncash items, valued at over $26.7 billion.

Wire Transfer of Funds. The System also facilitates payments by making available to member banks a wire service that can be used to transfer funds quickly from one part of the country to another. For example, a Richmond buyer wishing to pay a New York seller the same day can have a member bank request the Richmond Reserve bank to transfer the funds to the seller's bank. The Richmond Federal Reserve bank deducts the funds from its member's reserve account, and the New York Federal Reserve bank credits the reserve account of the New York member bank so that it in turn can credit the seller's bank account. The two Reserve banks then settle by wire at the end of the day through the System clearing agency—the Interdistrict Settlement Fund in Washington. During 1970 the System made over 7 million wire transfers totaling about $12.3 trillion.

Handling of Currency and Coin. The Federal Reserve banks are the channels through which practically all cash moves into and out of circulation. When the public withdraws cash from commercial banks, the banks replenish their supply by obtaining shipments from the Reserve banks. As the public's need for cash tapers off, banks return their surplus money and receive credits to their reserve accounts. During 1970 the System received and counted over 19 billion bills and coins valued at over $47 billion.

Note Issue. Nearly 90 percent of the nation's "pocket money" is issued by the Federal Reserve banks in the form of Federal Reserve notes. All Federal Reserve notes must be fully collateralized by government securities, gold certificates, or certain other types of assets. When a Reserve bank needs more currency to meet the demands of commercial banks, it can easily obtain additional Federal Reserve notes by pledging the proper collateral. Conversely, Reserve banks can return the notes and recover their pledged collateral when the demand for currency declines.

Other Service Functions. The Reserve banks and the Board of Governors also provide many other service functions such as answering requests; distributing monthly business reviews and other publications; providing speakers for various occasions; and, upon request, assisting banks in solving problems.

SYSTEM INFLUENCE ON ECONOMIC ACTIVITY

System policy operates primarily through affecting the availability of bank credit and the money supply and thereby the volume of spending. While the initial impact is felt by the commercial banking system, effects of monetary policy spread throughout the nation's entire financial mechanism because of the central role played by commercial banks in major loan and securities markets.

Why Commercial Banks Are Different. Commercial banks play a key role in monetary policy because they alone among financial institutions can "create" new money. Other financial institutions merely transfer existing money to borrowers when they make loans or investments. The commercial banking system, however, can increase the money supply by paying out cash or setting up new demand deposits when it expands its earning assets. Demand deposits are by far the more important of the two, constituting nearly 80 percent of the total and accounting for an estimated 90 percent of all payments.

Of course, not every increase in commercial bank earning assets results in an equal rise in the privately held money supply—that portion of demand deposits and cash held by the public. Sometimes other types of deposits such as time, government, or interbank rise instead. Generally, however, an expansion in bank earning assets increases the privately held money supply.

Here's how the process of money creation works. Assume that the Federal Reserve buys government securities from a dealer, crediting the reserve account of the dealer's bank in payment. Since commercial banks are profit-motivated, that bank will then probably use its new reserve funds to expand earning assets. Whether it makes loans or investments, deposits or cash outside banks will increase. If the bank makes loans, it will probably create the new money by crediting its borrowers' demand deposits. If it purchases securities, deposits will rise when the security dealer deposits the funds received from the bank.

If these new deposits are checked out to other banks, reserves of these banks will increase and those of the dealer's bank will decrease. The banks holding these new deposits must then set aside part of their new reserves to meet reserve requirements against their additional deposits but will be able to lend or invest approximately the remaining amount. As they expand earning assets, deposits and possibly public cash holdings will rise still further. Another part of the new reserves will be used to meet reserve requirements against these additional deposits, but some excess reserves will still be available for further loan or investment expansion. Eventually, the process ends when deposits rise to the point that banks must use all the new reserves in meeting reserve requirements. By this time, however, deposits will have increased by several times the original addition to bank reserves.

The Key Role of Money. Money is unique in that nothing else is generally acceptable in payment for goods and services. Other assets such as savings deposits, short-term treasury securities, and savings and loan shares so closely resemble money that they often perform some of the functions of money. Nevertheless, such assets cannot be spent directly. They must first be converted into cash or demand deposits if a holder is to buy something in place of them.

Rising economic activity involves increasing expenditures, and rising expenditures require either additional money or a higher monetary velocity—the rate at which money is spent on goods and services. If expenditures, financed with either new money or rising velocity, increase faster than the flow of goods and services, inflation results. If expenditures do not keep pace with the flow, demand is insufficient to prevent recession. Thus, a sound economy requires the "right" amount of spending. Since money plays such a key role in the spending process, it is essential that the banking system create neither too much nor too little new money.

The Importance of Bank Reserves. To a large extent, changes in the volume of bank reserves determine the amount of money banks can create. When reserves increase, banks have an incentive to acquire additional earning assets, which expands deposits or cash outside banks. Conversely, a reduction in reserves usually forces banks to cut back loans and/or investments, thereby reducing deposits and cash outside banks.

The extent to which banks can expand the privately held money supply on the basis of new reserves varies according to a number of factors. Normally, the lower the reserve requirements, the larger the expansion since less reserves are required for each dollar of deposits. The more pocket money expands the smaller the increase, since banks must draw down reserves to obtain cash for their customers. Changes in the volume of deposits that are not part of the private money supply—interbank, government, and time deposits—can also have important effects by either absorbing or releasing reserves. In addition, shifts of reserves between country and reserve city banks affect credit creation since the two groups hold varying percentages of reserves against deposits. Finally, variations in the volume of excess reserves that banks choose to maintain can increase or decrease expansion limits.

Despite all these variations an increase in the volume of reserves generally results in the creation of additional money, and a decline in reserves usually leads to a reduction in the money supply. Consequently, the Federal Reserve can affect interest rates, the money supply, and the availability of bank credit through its control over the volume of bank reserves. Because the banking system plays such a vital role in the credit mechanism, such effects generally spread throughout all credit markets.

THE IMPACT OF MONETARY POLICY

Effects on the Domestic Economy. Monetary policy affects domestic expenditures by influencing the behavior of three different groups: lenders, borrowers, and nonborrowing spenders.

Probably the most important effect is its influence on the availability of lenders' funds. During some periods, for instance, the System may observe inflationary pressures developing as the public's demand for goods and services exceeds the available supply. Since part of this demand is always financed by credit, the System at these times adopts a policy of restraint to try to prevent the volume of loanable funds from increasing as fast as the demands for credit rise.

During these periods, lenders may take two types of action to balance credit demands with their available supply of loanable funds. First, they may increase their prices—the interest rates they charge. In many cases, however, interest rates do not rise enough to prevent borrowers' demands from outrunning available funds. Thus, lenders, in addition, often "ration" credit among borrowers by various means—raising their standards of credit worthiness, requiring larger down payments or larger compensating balances in order to limit their available funds to the best credit risks. Marginal borrowers consequently cannot expand their spending since they are unable to obtain as much credit as they want even though they are willing to pay existing interest rates.

On the other hand, the System at times may consider it appropriate to increase the availability of credit to give a boost to total expenditures. This "easy money" policy provides lenders with funds to accommodate marginal borrowers, previously part of the "unsatisfied fringe of borrowers," and also encourages lenders to reduce interest rates to attract still more borrowers.

Borrowers' credit demands are affected in several ways. When money tightens, some demands—nobody knows exactly how many—are undoubtedly cut back because higher interest rates discourage some marginal projects. The expected difficulty of obtaining the desired credit accommodation also may deter borrowers who have doubts about being able to obtain sufficient funds to complete their projects even though initial financing is available. Legal interest rate ceilings on GI loans and some state and local bond issues also cut borrowers' demands by removing potential home buyers and governments from the market when prevailing rates exceed the amounts they can legally pay. Portfolio losses, such as declines in bond prices resulting from higher rates, may likewise discourage potential borrowers from undertaking projects. Conversely, easy money can stimulate borrowers' demands by lowering rates, by fostering expectations that funds will be more readily available, and by creating "paper" portfolio profits.

Tight and easy money can also influence the attitudes of spenders who neither borrow nor lend. An effective tight money policy may, for instance, dampen inflation psychology and cause the postponement of some outlays that might otherwise have been made in anticipation of price increases. In addition, it may cause certain spenders to reduce expenditures by causing portfolio losses in their security holdings. Conversely, easy money can stimulate outlays by fostering a "things-will-get-better" atmosphere and by creating paper profits in spenders' portfolios.

Effects on the Balance of Payments. Monetary policy affects not only domestic expenditures but also, directly and indirectly, international trade and international capital movements. Tight or easy money may have direct effects on the availability of credit to foreign borrowers from U.S. banks and other U.S. lenders and investors. Indirect effects may be complex and varied. Generally speaking, however, actions that encourage noninflationary growth of the domestic economy contribute also in the long run to a healthy balance of international payments.

The Tools of Credit Policy. The Federal Reserve has two types of tools with which it can affect the level of domestic economic activity and the basic balance of international payments: quantitative or general credit controls and qualitative or selective controls. Quantitative controls influence the money supply, interest rates, and the overall availability of credit. Qualitative controls, however, are directed at a particular kind of credit. The System's principal quantitative tools are: changes in the discount rate, changes in reserve requirements, and open market operations. At present the System's only strictly qualitative controls are changes in margin requirements on securities listed on national securities exchanges. The System also has two other tools that are partly quantitative and partly qualitative. One is the setting of maximum interest rates payable on time and savings deposits at member banks. The other is the buying and selling of foreign currencies in the foreign exchange market.

The Discount Rate. Perhaps the best known of the quantitative tools is the discount rate—the interest rate charged member banks on loans from Federal Reserve banks. Member banks can borrow in two ways: by giving their own secured notes or by rediscounting drafts, bills of exchange, or notes from their portfolios. In practice, borrowing banks usually use their own notes secured by government obligations.

Changes in the discount rate must be made separately by each Federal Reserve bank since the bank's directors initiate the change. Generally, all Reserve banks act at about the same time, however, since all make their decisions on the basis of the same sort of evidence. Differences in timing result mainly from variations in the meeting dates of the 12 boards of directors. The initial change is the important one, however, since buyers and sellers in the market generally expect that other Reserve banks will soon take similar actions.

Certain vital effects of changes in the discount rate are psychological. Such effects are particularly important when observers feel the discount rate is being used by the System to signal a shift in the direction of policy. In such cases, the financial markets react immediately—sometimes even in advance of System actions—when the move is anticipated. If the rate is increased, interest rates—particularly those on short-term securities—generally rise, and credit markets tighten. Conversely, a cut in the discount rate that clearly signals on easing of policy is ordinarily followed by easier conditions in the money and capital markets. At times, however, the System nudges credit markets first with its open market operations and changes discount rates only to bring them into line with other money rates. Such changes are often "discounted" in advance and thus have little immediate effect on the money market.

Changes in the discount rate also have some direct effects on short-term interest rates by making borrowings from the central bank either more or less costly. When the discount rate is increased, banks are more inclined to adjust their reserve positions by selling short-term government securities rather than through expanding their borrowings at the Federal Reserve. The increased sale of securities tends to lower security prices and raise their yields. These higher market yields in turn tend to push up longer-term interest rates.

On the other hand, if the discount rate is lowered during an easy money period, banks are likely to maintain borrowings at the Federal Reserve's discount window at a higher level than would otherwise be the case. This tends to push rates lower by encouraging banks to hold larger quantities of government securities.

Open Market Operations. Open market operations are the System's most important credit tool. Operations are conducted primarily in government securities, but the System also buys and sells bankers' acceptances. Both kinds of securities may be purchased either outright or under repurchase agreements requiring the dealers to buy back the securities within a few days.

Security purchases and sales directly affect the volume of member bank reserves and, consequently, the overall cost and availability of credit. When the System buys securities, it credits the reserve account of the seller's bank, and the bank in turn credits the seller's bank account. As a result of the increase in reserves, the banking system can expand credit by a multiple amount. Conversely, System sales reduce reserves and, if ever conducted in large volume, would force banks to contract credit.

Open market operations are either defensive or dynamic. Defensive operations are those taken to offset other factors that change the volume of member bank reserves. If, for example, gold outflows or increases in treasury deposits at the Reserve banks are tending to reduce member bank reserves, the System may make offsetting government security purchases even though it is not trying to ease credit policy. Conversely, when it wishes reserves to drop during a slack season, it may buy securities if other factors are tending to reduce reserves too fast. Thus, it is impossible to tell from a sale or a purchase whether the System is tightening or easing unless one knows how other factors are affecting reserves.

Dynamic operations consist of either causing or permitting changes in banks' reserve positions in order to stimulate economic activity or prevent inflation. Even when the System conducts dynamic operations, it often must take defensive measures as well so that the dynamic policy can proceed smoothly.

Reserve Requirements. The tool with the most immediate and widespread impact is the board's power to vary member bank reserve requirements within specified limits. On time deposits, the limits are 3 percent to 10 percent for all member banks. On demand deposits, they are 10 percent to 22 percent for reserve city banks and 7 percent to 14 percent for country banks.

Changes in reserve requirements affect member bank actions in two ways. First, they either destroy or create excess reserves by changing the amount of reserves required against existing deposits. Reductions in reserve requirements release reserves and generally bring about an expansion in bank credit and the privately held money supply. Increases in requirements have the opposite effect. Second, changes in requirements alter the amount of deposits a given volume of reserves can support. If reserve requirements are 10 percent, \$1 million in additional reserves can support up to \$10 million of new deposits. If requirements are 20 percent, however, the additional reserves cannot support more than $5 million of new deposits.

Margin Requirements. The Federal Reserve Board also has the right to set margin requirements—the percentage down payment required when borrowing to finance purchases or holdings of securities listed on national exchanges. There are three separate regulations—Regulations T, U, and G. Regulation T covers brokers' or dealers' loans to customers. Regulation U regulates commercial bank loans to brokers, dealers, or other customers. Regulation G governs loans of other lenders.

Margin requirements are directed at only one type of credit—that used to finance security purchases and holdings. If expansion of security loans appears to be a factor in undue increases in security prices, requirements can be raised. At other times, when there seems to be little danger of speculation, the System cuts requirements since it prefers not to interfere with the allocation of credit among different sectors of the economy.

Interest Ceilings on Time and Savings Deposits. The board also can use its ability to set interest ceilings on member bank time and savings deposits to influence the overall level of economic activity. The rates are specified in the board's Regulation Q. Rates must be set in consultation with the Federal Deposit Insurance Corporation, which sets ceilings on rates paid at nonmember insured banks, and the Federal Home Loan Bank Board, which sets ceilings on dividend rates payable by its member and other insured savings and loan associations.

Since the board has the freedom to set many combinations of ceilings, there are numerous ways in which the control can be used. If, for example, the board wishes to slow down the rate of growth in bank credit, it can refuse to raise the ceilings payable on certificates of deposit when competitive rates are moving up and thus restrict the ability of banks to compete for time money. If it wishes to lower long-term rates at the expense of short-term rates, it can raise such ceilings and enhance the ability of banks to channel funds into the long-term market.

Foreign Exchange Operations. Since early 1962 the System has also been conducting foreign exchange operations. Foreign exchange balances can be acquired either by purchases in the market or through "swap agreements" with foreign central banks under which the foreign central banks credit the System's account on their books in terms of their own currency in return for like dollar credits on the books of the Federal Reserve.

The System can use such foreign balances to buy from foreigners temporary holdings of surplus dollars that might otherwise result in unnecessary gold outflows, to prevent disorderly speculative capital movements from undermining confidence in the dollar, and to assist foreign monetary authorities in fighting inflation resulting from an inflow of funds. Such measures cannot cure a basic balance of payments problem, but they can provide a temporary respite during which a permanent solution can be sought. System actions to promote a healthy domestic economy can, however, contribute to a permanent solution: (1) by enabling us to compete more successfully in foreign markets and (2) by discouraging excessive outflows of capital resulting from international differences in financial market conditions.

Since System exchange operations have important impacts upon foreign countries as well as upon the United States, they are conducted in close cooperation with foreign monetary authorities. There is also close coordination with treasury officials since the Treasury also operates in foreign exchange markets. Such cooperation is facilitated by the New York Reserve bank's role as agent for the Treasury in its foreign exchange operations.

Coordination among Credit Controls. Except in the case of defensive open market operations, the Federal Reserve's credit control tools are seldom employed independently of each other. To the contrary, all are coordinated toward the same end—the System's current policy objectives. Thus, it is usually not meaningful to speak of "open market policy," or "discount rate policy," or "reserve requirement policy." Instead, it is more correct to view monetary policy as a broad program embracing the three quantitative controls, margin requirements, and any System foreign exchange operations. Action with respect to any single control is always taken in the light of prior or planned action concerning the others.

In selecting various combinations of policy actions, the Federal Reserve considers both psychological and direct effects of its decisions. If it is felt that a psychological effect is needed to reinforce the direct effects, policy measures may well include changes in reserve requirements or the discount rate since these actions are specifically announced whereas open market operations are not. Such changes, of course, cannot be made too frequently without prejudicing their usefulness. This is especially true of changes in reserve requirements because of their large direct effects on bank reserve positions. These limitations on the use of discount rate and reserve requirement changes place a greater burden on open market operations as a tool for attaining policy goals.

The right combination of policy moves necessary to achieve a given end depends on many factors. Policy makers must consider not only domestic economic developments but also the direction and strength of the last policy actions, the length of time since the last moves, the differential impact of alternative policy measures on the structure of domestic interest rates, the country's balance of payments position, and the relationships between domestic and foreign interest rates. These factors are constantly changing, and consequently, the optimum policy combination for achieving a given end varies from one period to the next. Thus, monetary authorities must have considerable latitude in the extent to which they use the various tools. While the choice between alternative paths to a given policy goal is secondary to the problem of setting goals, it is an important aspect of monetary policy because of the interdependence of the various policy tools.

THE POLICY-MAKING PROCESS

The Policy Forum. The meetings of the Federal Open Market Committee are the System's main policy forum. There both board and bank representatives meet regularly to discuss economic developments and reach a policy decision for the weeks immediately ahead. In addition to members of the board and the five presidents currently serving on the committee, the remaining Reserve bank presidents, the manager of the open market account and one of his principal assistants, the special manager of the open market account who handles foreign exchange operations, several board senior staff members, and the senior economist from each of the Reserve banks ordinarily attend. In this manner, not only committee members, but also those presidents who will soon serve on the committee, the chief advisers to the board and the presidents, and those who implement the committee's day-to-day open market policies are always well informed on current policy actions. Cumbersome as this may seem, it nevertheless constitutes probably the smoothest and most efficient way of utilizing the unique contributions of diverse parts of the System to reach the best-informed policy judgments.

Preparation for the Meeting. Prior to the meeting, each participant arms himself with the best available data on domestic and international business conditions and the effects of current Federal Reserve policy. Board members and the presidents receive a steady flow of information and analyses from the research departments of the banks and board and their personal contacts with business, academic, government, and other sources.

Typical of the information sifted and analyzed are statistics on new orders, business incorporations, construction contract awards, retail sales, unemployment, employment, industrial production, personal income, business failures, foreign exchange rates, international reserves, foreign and domestic interest rates, the international balance of payments, the money supply, foreign and domestic prices, Government receipts and expenditures, member bank reserves, inventories, state and local government borrowings, bank loans and investments, business and consumer spending intentions, the turnover of demand deposits, and numerous other indicators. In short, by the time the committee meets, every participant is well prepared to contribute to intelligent policy decisions.

The Interchange of Opinion. Committee meetings generally fall into two parts—a discussion of recent developments and the formulation of policy for the period ahead. The special manager in charge of the System's foreign exchange operations leads off, reviewing important developments in foreign exchange markets and summarizing the System's foreign exchange operations. Next, the manager of the open market account reviews the Trading Desk's experience in implementing open market policy since the last meeting. Senior members of the board's staff then summarize important domestic and international business and financial developments, stressing particularly any new developments that might not yet have come to the attention of committee members.

After the presentation of the board's staff members, each board member and president gives his interpretation of business conditions and makes policy recommendations for the period ahead. Presidents also contribute any significant "grass roots" information they have concerning regional developments.

Between Meetings. Between meetings board members and presidents keep in daily touch with the Trading Desk at the New York bank. One important means is a detailed phone call around 11 A.M. on business days between senior members of the board's staff; sometimes the governors themselves; the officers managing the open market account; and on a rotating basis, one of the president-members of the committee. Among the factors discussed are developments in markets for government and other securities, the tone of the money market, the reserve positions of member banks, inventories of government security dealers, and the probable course of action to be taken by the Trading Desk. Shortly after the conversation, a senior member of the board's staff summarizes the content of the conversation in a memorandum for board members and a telegram for presidents. Thus, any member of the Open Market Committee has ample opportunity to raise with the manager of the account and other committee members any questions he may have concerning the contemplated action.

In addition, the desk prepares daily wires summarizing conditions at the opening and closing of the securities markets and numerous written memoranda describing the desk's operations. Some of these written reports are daily, some weekly, and some less frequent.

Committee members also keep close tab on System foreign exchange operations. A senior board staff member prepares a daily memorandum for board members and a daily telegram for each president describing exchange market conditions, exchange rates, and recent System and Stabilization Fund operations. In addition, the special manager prepares for board members and presidents weekly, tri-weekly, and other periodic memoranda describing similar developments.

BACKGROUND: ECONOMIC DEVELOPMENTS IN THE EARLY 1960s

Background. The decade of the sixties entered on a note of strong confidence and optimism. The economy had rebounded vigorously from the 1959 steel strike, and both consumer and business demands were strong. Prices were stable, and forecasts were glowingly optimistic. Early in 1960, however, the pace of the advance began to falter. The peak of activity was reached in May 1960, and the economy slid into a recession that lasted until February 1961.

It was a very short and mild recession. The decline in GNP was barely measurable, and personal income actually rose slightly. Industrial production fell by about 6 percent, and business expenditures for new plant and equipment dropped somewhat more. Housing starts held up well, and new construction expenditures rose significantly.

In spite of the relative mildness of the recession, however, two developments were important and troublesome. First, total employment fell by about a half million, the number of unemployed rose by a million and a quarter, and the rate of unemployment rose from 5.1 to 6.9 percent. Second, the deficit in our balance of payments, which had been large for some time, rose further. In October 1960 wild speculation drove up the London gold price. Over the whole period our gold stock declined about $2 billion.

The period of recovery, following the trough in February 1961, can be divided into two main periods. The first period, running through July 1963, was one of slow but smooth and well-balanced recovery. There was a distinct lull in the second half of 1962, but the upward movement regained impetus early in 1963. The growth in GNP was a low 3.3 percent in 1961 but rose to 7.7 percent in 1962 before dropping back to 5.4 percent in 1963. Wage increases generally did not exceed productivity gains, and prices were stable except for a slow upcreep of consumer prices. Employment rose slowly during the first year of recovery, and unemployment fell to a level of about four million, or 5.6 percent of the labor force. Thereafter, increases in employment nearly matched additions to the labor force, and over the next two years there was little change in the level or rate of unemployment.

From July 1963 to November 1964 the economy moved ahead at a strong pace. GNP, personal income, and retail sales all showed healthy growth. Paced by a record production of automobiles, industrial production expanded at an increasing rate. Business investment expenditures had lagged throughout the first two years of recovery, but in early 1963 these outlays began to rise sharply. Employment continued its steady growth, and in the last half of 1964 unemployment moved down from its plateau, with the rate touching 5 percent at year-end. Prices showed no significant movements. The deficit in the balance of payments, which continued to be a major source of concern, rose very sharply in the fourth quarter of 1964.

Monetary Policy

Background. Even before the peak was reached in 1960 the System detected signs of the slowdown and began to ease credit. This policy of ease continued through November 1964, although toward the end of the period the System began to move gradually toward less ease. The policy of ease, however, was carried out in a very difficult environment. Gold was flowing out of the country, and interest rates in Europe were high relative to those in the United States. To avoid stimulating the outflow of liquid funds, and thus enlarging the outflow of gold, easing would have to be accomplished without pushing interest rates in the United States to excessively low levels. Open market operations were used throughout this period to provide reserves to the banking system, but these operations exerted direct downward pressure on short-term interest rates. Thus, the System made an effort to supply reserves by means other than open market operations and tried in other ways to minimize downward pressures on short-term interest rates.

Reserve Requirements. One method used involved a change in the legal reserve requirements of member banks. The first change, carried

FIGURE 1

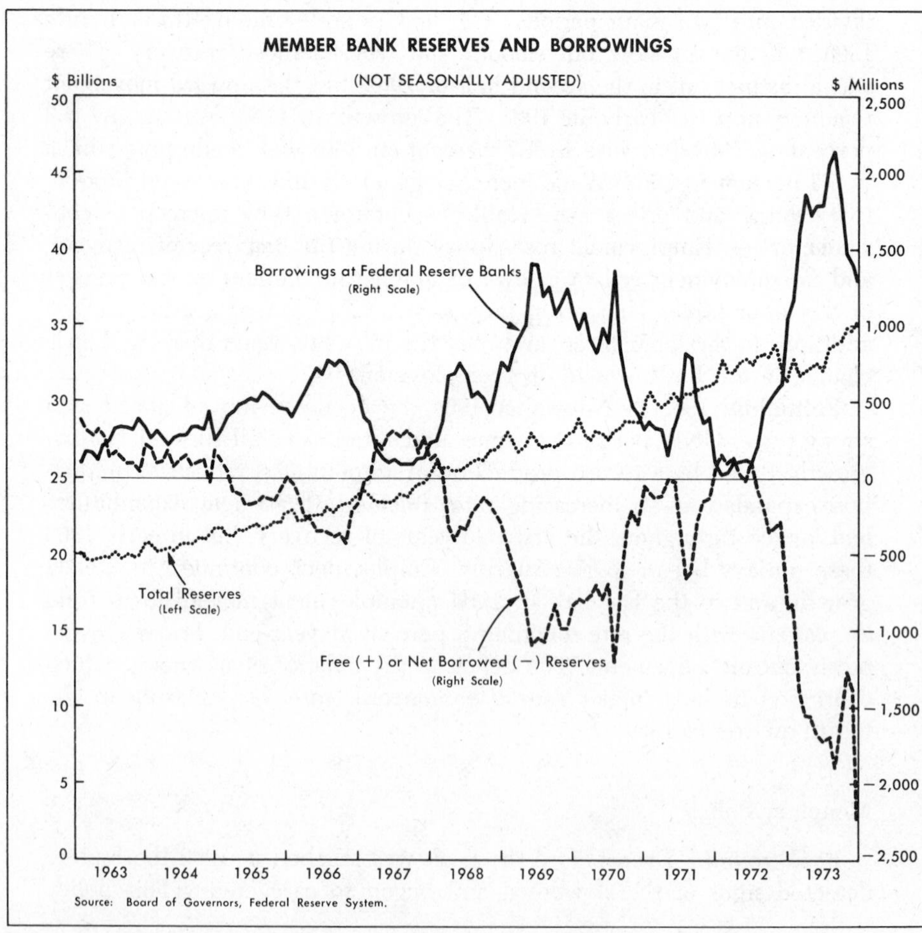

Source: Board of Governors, Federal Reserve System.

out between December 1959 and November 1960, allowed banks to count vault cash toward meeting reserve requirements. The second move was to reduce the reserve requirements of central reserve city banks against demand deposits from 18 to 16½ percent. The 16½ percent requirement was the same as that applied to reserve city banks, and in 1962 the two categories were merged. Since country banks had gained most from the vault cash change, their reserve requirements were raised from 11 to 12 percent. In late 1962 the reserve requirement against time deposits was reduced from 5 to 4 percent.

Open Market Operations. "Operation Twist," as it was called, was another technique devised during this period to avoid downward pressures on short-term rates resulting from open market operations. This involved engaging in open market operations in the intermediate- and long-term maturity ranges. For some time open market purchases had been limited, except in unusual circumstances, to short-term bills. In 1960 purchases were made of securities with maturities up to 15 months, and over the next several years the System extended its practice of buying securities with longer maturities, some running beyond five years. During 1961 and 1962 purchases of securities with maturities in excess of one year amounted to nearly $4.5 billion. It was hoped that this would help to hold up short rates, thus reducing the outflow of liquid funds, and to restrain the rise in long rates, thereby contributing to the domestic economic recovery.

Regulation Q. The policy of holding up or encouraging a rise in short rates was reflected in System policy actions with respect to both Regulation Q and the discount rate. Early in 1961 New York banks had taken the lead in developing a new kind of financial instrument—the large-denomination, negotiable certificate of deposit. It was, at the same time, a money market instrument and evidence of a time deposit in a bank. Development of this instrument represented a large step toward the evolving practice of commercial banks, especially the large money market banks, managing their money positions from the liability rather than the asset side of the balance sheet. Development of the CD was to have far-reaching effects on the flow of funds and on the implementation of monetary policy.

As short-term interest rates rose, the rates banks had to pay on CD's and other time deposits approached the ceiling rates under Regulation Q. To avoid putting undesirable pressure on bank reserve positions through a run-off in time deposits, those ceiling rates were raised in January 1962, July 1963, and November 1964. One consideration involved in these changes was the ability of banks to attract foreign deposits. In 1962 time deposits of foreign governments and financial institutions were exempted from the regulation.

The Discount Rate. The discount rate was reduced twice in the early recession months of 1960, but later on changes in the rate were related to other policy measures designed to slow the outflow of short-term capital. By the second quarter of 1963, for example, it became apparent that action was urgently needed to curb the rapidly rising outflow of funds. Action was taken on several fronts. Parts of the "package deal" were the raising of Regulation Q ceilings and the imposition of what was called an "interest equalization" tax. A third and important part of the package was an increase from 3 to 3½ percent in the discount rate in July 1963. But by November 1964 short-term market rates were near to or above the discount rate, interest rates in Europe were high and rising, and the deficit in our balance of payments and the gold outflow were increasing rapidly. So in November 1964 the discount rate was raised from 3½ to 4 percent. The immediate cause of this move, however, was the sterling crisis and the sharp increase in the English Bank Rate.

A New Tool. The gold speculation of 1960, the large outflows of gold, and continuing threats to the orderly operation of foreign exchange markets led to the development of a new tool of monetary policy. After long deliberations the Federal Open Market Committee, in February 1962, authorized an arrangement whereby the System might engage in foreign currency operations. The purposes were several: (1) to offset or compensate destabilizing fluctuations in the flow of international payments, especially if caused by temporary or speculative factors; (2) to temper and smooth out sharp changes in foreign exchange rates; (3) to supplement international exchange arrangements; and (4) to provide for reciprocal holdings of foreign currencies which might contribute to international liquidity. The arrangement is a means whereby central banks of several countries may, in cooperation, provide for the international area some of the services that a central bank provides for its own country. In time of crisis or great stress large resources can quickly be assembled to meet a threat to monetary stability. The arrangement cannot correct any basic maladjustment in the balance of payments, but it may prevent gold losses or large payment flows due to temporary or speculative movements.

Under the administration of a special manager at the Federal Reserve Bank of New York, reciprocal currency or "swap" agreements were arranged with the central banks of the leading countries of the world. Under these agreements either the System or the other central bank involved in a particular situation may draw on the other up to the amount of the established line. This means, in effect, that the bank with a balance to settle can borrow to get the funds rather than paying gold or using existing funds, if any. If the cause of the payments imbalance is temporary and is soon reversed, the transaction can easily be liquidated. If the imbalance persists, it is expected that the drawing will be funded in some other form and the proceeds used to repay the drawing or, if necessary, that the amount will be paid in gold.

The network of swap agreements proved to be very useful during the latter part of this period, with total drawings of $2 billion during the year 1964. Most of this was initiated by foreign central banks, especially the Bank of England. The System made fewer drawings than in earlier years and at one time in early 1964 it had repaid all drawings. In addition, the network served as a nucleus around which a "credit package" of $3 billion was quickly organized in November 1964 to provide emergency assistance to the pound sterling.

Fiscal Action. Three tax changes were proposed to stimulate employ-

FIGURE 2

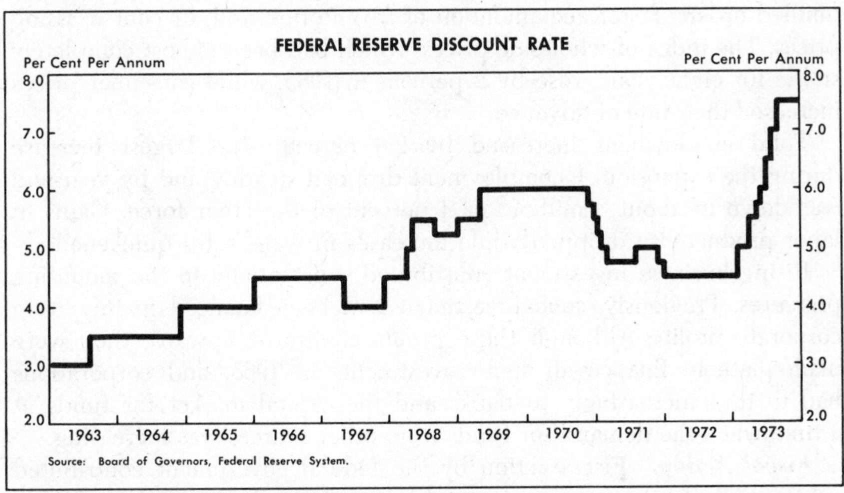

ment. One granted more liberal depreciation allowances, a second allowed a tax credit for new investments, and a third reduced substantially corporate and individual income taxes. The first two became effective in 1962, but the third was not enacted until 1964. With these aids, corporate profits rose rapidly and stimulated business investment. Spending for new plant and equipment, early in 1963, started a long and steep rise.

To stem the outflow of private funds the President, in July 1963, proposed a substantial tax on foreign investments, known as the interest equalization tax. The tax was not levied until the following year but was retroactive to the date it was proposed and was effective immediately in reducing sharply the outflow of funds. This helped to prevent a rise in the deficit but did little to reduce it.

In addition to these steps, the federal budget provided stimulation in the form of a substantial cash deficit each year.

INFLATION APPEARS NOVEMBER 1964–DECEMBER 1965

The Economy

During this period the tempo of activity stepped up considerably in almost every sector of the economy. In employment, industrial production, GNP, personal income, retail sales, and construction, rates of growth exceeded the high levels of 1964 and set new records.

Thus, the economy operated under forced draft for much of 1965. As inflationary pressures mounted, the usual earmarks of inflation began to appear—a longer workweek in manufacturing, a rising level of unfilled orders, faster accumulation of inventories, and, of course, rising prices. The index of wholesale prices, which had been almost completely stable for eight years, rose by 2 percent in 1965, while consumer prices increased their rate of advance.

Total employment increased by 2.6 percent—the largest increase during the expansion. Unemployment dropped steadily and by year-end was down to about 3 million, or 4 percent of the labor force. Gains in labor productivity dropped while increases in wage rates quickened.

Rising business investment contributed substantially to the mounting pressures. Previously, such investment had been financed mainly from corporate profits. Although those profits continued upward, they were inadequate to finance all such investments in 1965, and corporations had to turn increasingly to banks and the capital market for funds at a time when the demand for funds from other sources was increasing.

Fiscal Action. Fiscal action by the federal government contributed substantially to the increase in total demand. At the beginning of 1965 the second step of the 1964 tax reduction became effective. In addition, Congress enacted a substantial reduction in excise taxes. In July our commitment in Vietnam was greatly increased, but no increase in revenues was provided to cover it. In September a substantial increase in social security benefits, including a large retroactive payment, became effective. An increase in payroll taxes to cover the added expenditures was delayed until January 1966. Finally, military and civil service pay scales were increased in October. These extra demands of the federal government were superimposed on an economy already operating at or, in some cases, beyond its optimum rate of utilization.

Monetary Policy

Background. The demand for credit was intense during this period. Although the System moved slowly toward a policy of restraint, member bank reserves, bank credit, and the money supply increased at faster rates than before. Interest rates rose substantially, with the exception of those on bank loans and mortgages, which changed little. Money market banks continued to attract large amounts of funds by the sale of negotiable CD's. Bank borrowing from the System rose sharply to over $500 million, and free reserves gave way to net borrowed reserves. Money in circulation continued to grow.

Open Market Operations. Again in this period monetary policy was implemented mainly through open market operations. Despite the policy of restraint and the increased bank borrowing, purchases were made at a faster rate than in any previous period of the expansion. In large part, this was necessary to offset larger gold outflows and the constantly rising volume of currency outstanding. System holdings of U.S. government securities increased by $4 billion in 13 months to reach $40.8 billion.

Regulation Q Ceilings. As credit conditions tightened and interest rates rose, the rates paid on negotiable CD's moved up steadily and by late 1965 were pushing hard against their ceilings. In early December, in conjunction with the increase in the discount rate, the network of ceilings was again raised.

The Discount Rate. By November 1965 inflation was clearly gaining momentum, and most market rates were well above the discount rate. What fiscal action the federal government might propose in the budget to be presented in January was uncertain. Further, treasury financing in that month would interfere with decisive action by the System. These and other considerations led to the increase in the discount rate from 4 to 4½ percent early in December.

Foreign Currency Operations. The System used and extended its network of swap agreements with foreign central banks in 1965. The principal reason for its use was recurrent speculative attacks on the pound sterling. The interest equalization tax, as proposed in 1963 and adopted in 1964, did not apply to bank loans. Late in 1964 and early in 1965 bank loans to foreigners increased tremendously, and it was suspected that they were being used largely as a substitute for security issues. In February 1965 President Johnson extended the tax to bank loans and at the same time inaugurated the Voluntary Foreign Credit Restraint Program. Under this program, which was administered by the System, banks and other financial institutions were asked to keep outstanding credits to foreigners in 1965 to a level not more than 5 percent above amounts outstanding at the end of 1964. The System issued guidelines for both groups of institutions. Influenced by the tax, the voluntary program, and higher interest rates in this country, the deficit in our balance of payments fell sharply in 1965 to the lowest level since 1957. Despite this, however, the outflow of gold rose substantially. Holdings of gold certificates by the System were drifting down uncomfortably close to the legal minimum, and in March 1965 Congress repealed the 25 percent reserve requirement against deposits in Federal Reserve Banks.

INFLATION CONTAINED DECEMBER 1965–DECEMBER 1966

The year 1966 was one of the most turbulent and eventful in the history of the Federal Reserve System. To deal with fast-changing conditions and unprecedented circumstances, some new monetary tools were forged and put to use.

The Economy

In the early part of the year activity continued at a high and rising rate in nearly all sectors of the economy. As the year progressed, however, activity peaked or slowed in most sectors of the private economy. By year-end, inflationary forces were on the wane, and signs of a slowdown were widespread.

After several record years, automobile sales turned down in April. This was followed closely by a long and steep decline in housing starts. Industrial production leveled off and showed little change after August. Employment and business investment showed distinctly lower rates of growth in the second half. Retail sales registered a small absolute decline in the second half, in sharp contrast to personal income which continued upward. Inventories accumulated at an accelerating rate and reached very large proportions in the fourth quarter. Prices of industrial raw materials dropped rather sharply after midyear, and in the fall the earlier sharp advance in agricultural prices was reversed.

Fiscal Action. Federal expenditures increased rapidly but irregularly, and the cash budget fluctuated sharply from deficit to surplus and back again. Defense expenditures ran far above estimates, but revised estimates and projections were not made public until late in the year, and then it soon became apparent that the deficit for fiscal 1967 would be much larger than was originally anticipated.

An increase in payroll taxes became effective at the beginning of the year. Shortly afterward Congress postponed two reductions in excise taxes enacted the previous year, moved up payment dates for the corporate income tax, and instituted graduated withholding for individual income taxes. One result of this was a very large increase in tax collections in the second quarter when there was a surplus (unadjusted) of $10 billion in the cash budget for the quarter. This helped to hold down the cash deficit for the year ended June 30 to $3.3 billion. Despite much discussion and many proposals, there was no general tax increase during the year. In September the President, in an effort to moderate investment demand, initiated a program to reduce nondefense spending and asked Congress to suspend for a time the 7 percent investment tax credit and the provision for accelerated depreciation on buildings.

Monetary Policy

Background. Activity in the area of monetary policy was intense throughout the year. In an effort to ease the transition to the higher discount rate, the System for a time supplied reserves more liberally. As a result total reserves, bank credit, and the money supply increased faster than before. Business loans in particular grew very rapidly. At the same time, interest rates, bank lending rates, and rates paid on CD's rose rapidly. The higher market and bank rates quickly diverted funds from thrift institutions, causing an acute shortage of mortgage funds and a sharp decline in residential construction. A little later, banks, under pressure to make business loans, began to liquidate investments, especially municipal securities, which threatened the stability of security markets. Much of what the System did during the year represented attempts to: (1) slow down the expansion of credit; (2) provide some relief to the mortgage market; and (3) avoid the development of additional pressures in the capital market.

Regulation Q Ceilings. The ceilings on time deposits under Regulation Q were in this period developed into a complex and rudimentary tool of monetary policy. Banks, especially large money market banks, responded to the pressure to make business loans by pushing up the rates they paid on negotiable CD's. This had the dual effect of draining funds from smaller banks and thrift institutions and shielding the larger banks from the effects of monetary restraint. The funds thus obtained went mainly into business loans, which were used largely to finance fixed investment and increases in inventory, both of which were expanding very rapidly and thereby contributing to the inflationary buildup. In the meantime many smaller banks were competing for funds by issuing various kinds of small CD's, savings certificates, and other instruments bearing rates higher than the rate on savings deposits.

As CD rates approached the 5½ percent ceiling, the large banks continued to issue more and more CD's, the amount outstanding reaching a peak of $18.6 billion in August. The banks apparently were confident that, as in the past, the ceiling would be raised when going rates approached it. But this time it was different. In July the Board of Governors reduced the ceiling on "multiple-maturity" CD's from 5½ to 5 percent. In September, under newly enacted legislation, the board differentiated among CD's by size and reduced from 5½ percent to 5 percent the ceiling on time deposits under $100,000. By this time is was clear that the ceiling on large CD's would not be raised. Secondary market rates on most treasury bills and other short-term market instruments including outstanding CD's had gone far beyond 5½ percent, and many banks were able to roll over only parts of maturing CD's. The amount outstanding started down and by the end of November stood at $15.5 billion. Thus the authority to set maximum rates on time deposits became an auxiliary tool of monetary policy through its ability to influence the flows of funds.

Reserve Requirements. The board also used its power to set reserve requirements in its efforts to cool the competition for time deposits and related liabilities and to restrain the expansion of bank credit generally. In June it raised from 4 to 5 percent and in August to 6 percent reserve requirements against time deposits, other than savings deposits, in excess of $5 million at each member bank. The two increases added an estimated $870 million to member bank reserve requirements. A number of banks had begun to issue short-term promissory notes that had many characteristics of time deposits. In June the board ruled that such notes and similar instruments were subject to the same reserve requirements and interest ceilings as time deposits.

Moral Suasion and Discount Administration. By the spring of 1966 interest rates were rising rapidly, and most short-term rates were above the discount rate. Business loans by member banks were rising at an unprecedented rate. For several reasons the System did not wish to raise the discount rate, but instead used moral suasion to hold down bank borrowing. First, the president of each Reserve bank conferred with a small number of leading bankers in his district and solicited their cooperation in keeping discounting to a minimum.

But pressure for business loans was intense, and those loans continued to expand very rapidly. By August many banks began to lose funds through their inability to roll over CD's. They ceased buying municipal bonds, and some began to sell investments. The investment market was threatened with a crisis. On September 1 each Reserve bank sent a letter to all its member banks asking them to curtail the expansion of business loans and to avoid further substantial reductions of investments.

FIGURE 3

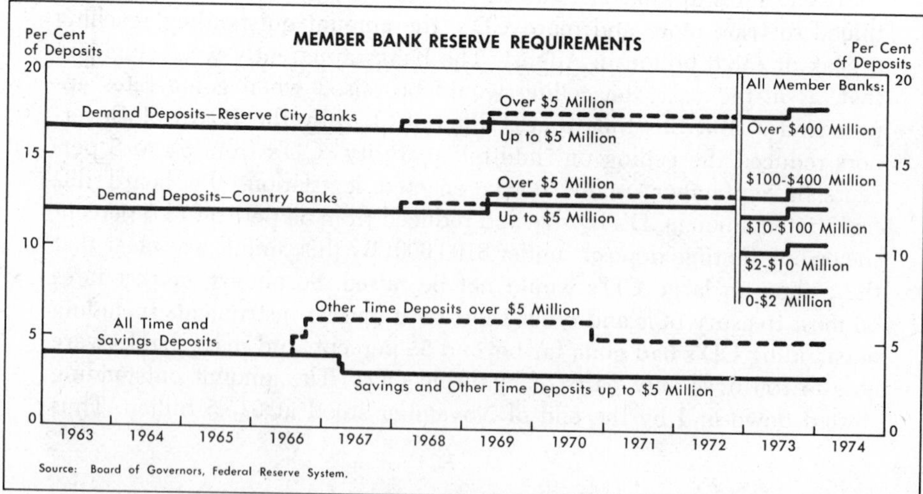

Source: Board of Governors, Federal Reserve System.

In return, it was noted that banks which followed such a program might at times need discount accommodations for longer periods than usual. This admonition, plus the decline of CD's because of the operation of the interest rate ceiling, contributed to a sharp slowing in the growth rate of business loans, and the expansion of bank credit was halted. The September 1 letter was rescinded in late December.

The Discount Rate. As interest rates rose ever higher, there was considerable sentiment for a further increase in the discount rate. During the summer of 1966 five Reserve banks proposed such an increase. The board recognized that several factors suggested such a move but decided that on balance it was not warranted and disapproved the proposals.

Open Market Operations. Despite the several tools fashioned to implement monetary policy, open market operations remained a major instrument. As noted earlier, reserves were supplied liberally to facilitate the transition to higher interest rates after the discount rate was raised in December 1965. From June to November 1965, nonborrowed reserves rose at an annual rate of 2.8 percent. From November 1965 through January 1966 the rate was 10.1 percent. After that, however, reserves were supplied much more sparingly, and for the January–June period the rate fell to 1.7 percent. In the following months reserve availability was reduced even further, and the annual rate registered a decline of 2.1 percent from June through November. Over the whole period holdings of U.S. securities (unadjusted) rose by $3.1 billion to a total of $43.9 billion.

ECONOMIC ACTIVITY EASES DECEMBER 1966–JUNE 1967

The Economy

Economic activity eased in most sectors of the economy beginning in late 1966 and extending through the first half of 1967. A sharp slowdown in inventory accumulation was a major cause. The growth rate of GNP in current dollars was reduced by more than two thirds in the first quarter of 1967, while in constant dollars there was a slight absolute decline. In the second quarter both growth rates increased significantly but remained well below the rates of 1965 and 1966. Total employment declined steadily from January through May for a drop of almost 1 million before rebounding in June. Unemployment increased little because the labor force was also declining until May. The rate of unemployment varied between 3.6 and 3.8 percent before rising to 4.0 percent in June. The workweek in manufacturing was shortened substantially, holding down unemployment; but even so, factory employment declined by some 325,000. Industrial production fell by 2.3 percent from December to June, and the rate of utilization of manufacturing capacity dropped from 89.8 percent in the fourth quarter of 1966 to 84.7 percent in the second quarter of 1967. Wholesale prices showed a small net decline between December and April and then rose rather sharply in May and June. Consumer prices advanced at a slower pace until May when they moved up more rapidly.

Fiscal Action. In view of the large current and prospective federal deficits it was generally agreed that some fiscal restraint would be needed during the year. In the budget for fiscal 1968 the President recommended substantial increases in defense and other expenses and, specifically, increases of $6.2 billion in social security and related benefits and $1 billion in civilian and military pay. On the revenue side he recommended a 6 percent surcharge on individual and corporate income tax liabilities and other minor tax charges to make a total tax increase of $5.8 billion. Proposed also were increases in postal rates to produce some $700 million, which would cut the postal deficit about in half. None of these proposals had been acted on by the end of June.

Monetary Policy

Background. This period featured one of the most massive creations of reserves in the history of the System. As soon as signs of easing appeared, the System, in November, switched to a policy of moderate ease. That became aggressive ease in the first quarter and then tapered off somewhat in the second. All interest rates fell sharply in January, rose in February, and declined irregularly in most of March. From late March, short-term rates continued downward, while intermediate-term and long-term rates started a long rise that, pushed by very large new security offerings in the capital market, took most of them to near their 1966 peaks. Bill rates jumped sharply at the end of June, but most other short rates remained relatively low. Bank borrowing of over $600 million in November dropped to less than $100 million in June, while net borrowed reserves of more than $200 million gave way to free reserves of over $250 million.

Open Market Operations. The major vehicle of monetary policy in this period was open market operations, which were conducted on a very large scale. Nonborrowed reserves declined moderately from May through October 1966. After rising a little in November and December, they soared upward at the phenomenal annual rate of 26.9 percent in the first quarter of 1967. This was nearly four times the growth rate that prevailed during the recession of 1960–61. In the second quarter the growth rate dropped by almost half to 14.4 percent. System holdings of U.S. securities increased by $2.9 billion to a total of $46.2 billion. From May 1960 to June 1967 these holdings rose by a little more than $20 billion.

Reserve Requirements. In March 1967 reserve requirements against savings deposits and the first $5 million of other time deposits in any member bank were lowered from 4 to 3 percent. It was estimated that this reduced total required reserves by about $850 million, mostly at country banks. One reason for the move was to make more mortgage funds available.

The Discount Rate. Early in April all Reserve banks reduced their discount rate from 4½ to 4 percent.

INFLATION REAPPEARS JUNE 1967–DECEMBER 1968

This was a turbulent period, both in the domestic economy and in international financial markets. In the second half of 1967 the economy began to recover from the first half doldrums, and the rapid pace of expansion continued through 1968. Inflationary pressures reappeared, and by mid-1968 some prices were rising at rates not seen since the Korean War. There were three major international financial crises during this period.

The Economy

The entire period from mid-1967 through 1968 was one of strong expansion, with GNP in current dollars increasing at an annual rate of about 9 percent. This upsurge in activity was accompanied by substantial price rises, however, and growth in real GNP was just under 5 percent per year. Inventory rebuilding contributed much of the strength in the second half of 1967, with final sales growing at a slower pace than in the first half. Residential construction was also an important source of strength as the housing industry staged a strong recovery from the depressed levels of early 1967. The expansion became more broadly based in 1968, however, although the strength of particular sectors varied from time to time. Residential construction leveled off after the first quarter and showed little growth until late in the year. Federal government spending on goods and services rose strongly through the first half, tapered off sharply in the third quarter, and increased very little in the fourth quarter. Consumer spending grew enormously through the first three quarters, but increased at a considerably slower pace in the fourth quarter.

The economy was operating at a high level at the beginning of this period of expansion. The unemployment rate for civilian workers stood at 3.9 percent in June 1967, and over the next year and a half it rose above 4 percent in only two months. It was below 4 percent throughout 1968 and at the end of that year stood at 3.3 percent, a 15-year low. It is not surprising, therefore, that inflation became a serious problem. From December 1967 to December 1968, the consumer price index rose 4.7 percent, while wholesale prices rose about 2.8 percent.

The economy expanded strongly throughout 1968, but in the fourth quarter the broadly based expansion of earlier months was changed into one based primarily on business spending. Consumer spending, which had grown at an average annual rate of about 10 percent in the first three quarters, increased only 4.2 percent, and spending on durable consumer goods did not increase at all. The increase in federal government expenditures was far below the gains of earlier quarters. Business fixed investment, on the other hand, increased at an annual rate of more than 18 percent, while inventory accumulation rose from $7.5 billion to $10 billion.

International developments had an important bearing on policy during this period. In November 1967, the parity of the British pound was reduced from $2.80 to $2.40. This was followed by a run on gold, and over the next four months the U.S. gold stock fell more than $2¼ billion. As a result, the gold policies of the major countries were changed by creating a two-tiered market for gold. The French franc was greatly weakened in the summer of 1968 by social unrest in France, and by late fall the weakness of the franc and the pound led to a belief that the German mark would be revalued upward. A massive speculative movement of funds began, and in the next few weeks the German central bank gained billions of dollars in reserves. The governments of France, Germany, and the United Kingdom made a number of policy changes to meet this situation but there were no changes in exchange parities.

Fiscal Action. The federal budget moved into heavy deficit in the first half of calendar 1967 as receipts leveled off and expenditures rose sharply. In early 1967, the President had asked for a 6 percent surcharge on income taxes to become effective in July, but because of the slowing in economic activity this request was not pressed. In fact, the Administration requested, and Congress granted, a restoration of the investment tax credit. Shortly after midyear, however, with the economy again showing signs of overheating and the budget deficit promising to reach massive proportions, the President urgently repeated his request for a surtax. This met strong opposition in Congress, and eventually a major deadlock developed over demands by Congressional leaders that any tax increase be accompanied by a reduction in spending. This deadlock was not resolved until June 1968, at which time the Revenue and Expenditure Control Act of 1968 was enacted. This act imposed a 10 percent surcharge on income taxes and set a ceiling on certain federal spending for fiscal year 1969. Several changes were made in social security taxes and benefits during this period. In January 1968 the maximum income subject to the tax was raised from $6,600 to $7,800, and in March the scale of benefits was substantially increased. The deficit in the federal budget declined sharply in the second half of calendar 1968.

Monetary Policy

Background. By mid-1967 the rapid improvement in the economy suggested the need for moderate restraint in place of the policy of aggressive ease that had been followed in the first half. Exceptionally heavy demands on credit markets and uncertainties as to the course of fiscal action caused interest rates to rise throughout the second half. In the absence of any additional fiscal restraint, and with the devaluation of sterling, the Federal Reserve System moved toward monetary restraint in late 1967. In the early months of 1968, however, it became obvious that further restraint was needed. The international financial system was experiencing a crisis, domestic financial markets were marked by a high degree of tension, while inflationary pressures gathered momentum. Monetary policy bore the entire burden of economic stabilization in the first five months of 1968 and the Federal Reserve used all three traditional monetary controls to restrain the booming economy. Agreement on a fiscal package in May led to expectations of reduced credit demands and a relaxation of monetary policy. This brought an easing in credit markets and a downward movement in interest rates, which the Federal Reserve accommodated. The impact of the fiscal restraint was much slower than had been expected, however, and economic activity continued to advance at a rapid pace. Credit demands pressed against the available supply, and interest rates rose to new highs. In the face of sharp upward price movements and evidence of a growing inflationary psychology, the Federal Reserve System moved in late 1968 to a tighter policy stance.

Open-Market Operations. From July through mid-November 1967, open-market operations supplied reserves at a fairly rapid pace to meet growing credit demands. Following the November devaluation of sterling and the ensuing increase in the Federal Reserve discount rate, however, open-market operations were used first to facilitate orderly market adjustment to these developments and then to bring about firmer conditions in money markets. As a result, nonborrowed reserves, which had risen sharply from July to mid-November, declined in December. Through the first five months of 1968, open-market operations were used in conjunction with other policy tools to maintain pressure on bank reserve positions, and at the end of May 1968 nonborrowed reserves were below the end-November 1967 figure. Following passage of the fiscal package, and in the face of heavy demands on credit markets, open-market operations supplied reserves at a rapid pace in the third quarter, with nonborrowed reserves increasing at an annual rate of more than 13 percent from June to September. Open-market operations became increasingly restrictive in the fourth quarter and although total reserves increased at about the third quarter pace, member banks were forced to obtain more of these reserves through the discount window. Borrowings rose from an average of less than $500 million in September to about $750 million in December, while nonborrowed reserves rose at a 3 percent annual rate over the same period.

The Discount Rate. Frequent use was made of discount rate changes during this period. In November 1967 the rate was raised from 4 to 4½ percent, mainly in response to international developments, but the increased pace of domestic economic activity and the rising level of interest rates also made this move desirable. The speculative run on gold markets reached the crisis stage in March, and as part of the response to this situation, the discount rate was raised to 5 percent. In spite of changes in the international monetary system, however, foreign exchange markets remained tense and domestic inflationary pressures gathered strength. These conditions, together with the deadlock over fiscal policy, contributed to a high degree of uncertainty in domestic financial markets. In mid-April the discount rate was raised to 5½ percent, the highest it had been since 1929. Following enactment of the fiscal legislation and the subsequent easing in interest rates, the rate was reduced to 5¼ percent. This was mainly a technical adjustment, however, and in the face of continued strong inflationary pressures the rate was moved back up to 5½ percent in December.

Reserve Requirements. An increase of one-half percentage point in the reserve requirement against demand deposits in excess of $5 million was announced in late December 1967, to become effective in January 1968.

Regulation Q. At the time of the discount rate increase in April 1968, Regulation Q ceilings were raised on all but the shortest term negotiable time certificates of deposit in denominations of $100,000 or more. This action was taken to preclude a large runoff of CD's at commercial banks as yields on market instruments rose. When the Federal Reserve System returned to a tighter monetary policy late in the year, however, the Regulation Q ceilings were not raised. The resulting decline in CD's added to pressures on reserve positions of commercial banks.

THE BATTLE AGAINST INFLATION DECEMBER 1968–DECEMBER 1969

By the end of 1968 inflation had become the most urgent problem facing economic policy makers. To meet this threat, restrictive monetary and fiscal policies were followed throughout 1969. By the end of 1969, real economic growth had come to a halt, but inflationary pressures remained strong. The disequilibrium in the balance of payments continued to be a major unresolved problem for the United States.

The Economy

Through the first three quarters of 1969 growth in current dollar GNP continued at about the same rate that had been recorded in the second half of 1968, but as the year progressed price increases accounted for an ever larger part of the GNP gains. Growth in real GNP, therefore, fell from an annual rate of 2.4 percent in fourth quarter 1968 to 2.0 percent in third quarter 1969. The effects of the restrictive economic policies became even more evident in the fourth quarter, however, with nominal GNP rising only at a 3.3 percent rate and real GNP declining slightly. Business spending on fixed investment was a major factor in the 1969 expansion, with the increase for the year about double that for 1968. Growth in personal consumption expenditures remained fairly strong throughout the year, but spending on durable consumer goods leveled off in the second half. Residential construction was strong in the first quarter, but housing starts, after peaking at an annual rate of 1.7 million units in January, moved substantially downward to 1.4 million units in the fourth quarter. Industrial production peaked in September, then declined through the end of the year. Employment rose throughout the year, absorbing most of a very large increase in the labor force, and the unemployment rate rose from about 3.4 percent in the first quarter to about 3.6 percent in the final three months of the year. Prices rose at the fastest pace since the Korean War, with all of the major indices recording sharp gains.

Speculative pressures on exchange rates and record-high interest rates in the United States led to massive flows of funds across the international exchanges in 1969. The German mark was the object of heavy speculative buying until the exchange rate for the mark was allowed to float at the end of September. The rate was stabilized at a higher par value in October, after which there was a very heavy reverse flow of funds out of the mark into other European currencies and the dollar. The French franc, subjected to heavy speculative selling in the spring and early summer, was devalued in August. Tight monetary policy and strong demands for credit in the United States led to heavy borrowing in the Euro-dollar market by U.S. banks. Liquid liabilities of U.S. banks to foreign commercial banks and to other private foreigners increased $8.8 billion in 1969, about $7 billion of which was in the form of an increase in liabilities of U.S. banks to their foreign branches.

Fiscal Action. The fiscal policy stance in 1969 was largely determined by the Revenue and Expenditure Control Act of 1968, which imposed a 10 percent surtax on corporate and individual income taxes and provided for restraints on certain types of federal expenditures. Originally, the act was to be in effect until mid-1969. However, during 1969 the surcharge was extended at the 10 percent rate through the end of 1969 and at a 5 percent rate for the first six months of 1970. Social security tax rates were increased on January 1, and the 7 percent investment credit was eliminated effective April 21. These tax measures were accompanied by a determined effort to slow the growth of federal expenditures. Consequently, the federal budget, as measured in the National Income Accounts, shifted from a large deficit in early 1968 to a large surplus in 1969.

Monetary Policy

Background. In 1969 the System continued the course of monetary policy restraint initiated in late 1968. A variety of policy measures were used to subject the reserve position of the banking system to intense pressure. As a result the growth in total member bank reserves, which had been very rapid in 1968, came to a halt.

The narrowly defined money stock rose at an annual rate of about 5 percent in the first half, but in the second half the rate of increase was only slightly in excess of 1 percent. Total member bank deposits declined over the course of the year as certificates of deposit at large commercial banks fell more than $12 billion.

Pressure on the reserve position of the banking system combined with a very strong demand for credit to push interest rates to extremely high levels. The prime lending rate was raised three times during the year, reaching a level of 8½ percent in June, and both short- and long-term market rates rose sharply. Since the maximum rates banks were permitted to pay on time and savings deposits were not raised, funds were withdrawn from banks (and thrift institutions) for investment in market instruments offering more attractive yields. Commercial banks, attempting to satisfy a very strong loan demand in the face of a net deposit outflow, employed a number of techniques (some new and quite innovative) for raising funds. Liquid assets were sharply reduced, member banks borrowed heavily at Federal Reserve banks, and some banks engaged in outright sales of existing loans. Banks also sold earning assets with an agreement for subsequent repurchase. Borrowings by U.S. banks in the Euro-dollar market doubled in the first half of 1969 and by the end of June had reached $14.3 billion. Faced with sharply higher interest rates in the Euro-dollar market and the prospect of a reserve requirement on at least part of such borrowings, banks sought increasingly to raise funds through the sale of commercial paper by bank holding companies, affiliates, and subsidiaries. The proceeds of such sales were transferred to the banks by the purchase of loans from them. Some of the actions of commercial banks, in attempting to acquire liquidity, created both regulatory and policy problems for the System.

Open-Market Operations. Throughout 1969 open-market operations were used in combination with other policy tools to exert sustained pressure on the reserve position of the banking system. As a result, total member bank reserves increased at an annual rate of only 1 percent in the first half, as compared to an 11 percent rate in the second half of 1968, and then declined at a rate of 4 percent in the last six months of the year. Nonborrowed reserves fell even more sharply, and by mid-year net borrowed reserves exceeded $1 billion. The System injected net $4.2 billion of reserves into the banking system during the year. This large expansion in the System's holdings of securities, during a period of very tight money, was necessary primarily to offset the effects of increases in reserve requirements against member banks' demand deposits and the imposition of marginal reserve requirements against liabilities to their foreign branches.

Reserve Requirements. In the face of a continued strong expansion in economic activity and few signs of easing of inflationary pressures, the Board of Governors announced on April 3 a package of measures designed to underline the System's determination to resist inflationary pressures. An increase of 0.5 percent in the reserve requirement against demand deposits at member banks was one part of this package. This action increased required reserves by about $650 million. In July, Regulation D was amended to assure that certain officers' checks issued in connection with transactions with foreign branches were included as deposits for purposes of computing reserve requirements. At the same time Regulations D and Q were amended to narrow the scope of a member bank's liabilities under repurchase agreements that are exempt from those regulations. The amendments provided that a bank liability on a repurchase agreement entered into with a person other than a bank became a deposit liability subject to Regulations D and Q if it involved: (1) assets other than direct obligations of the United States or its agencies or obligations fully guaranteed by them, or (2) a part interest in any obligation. This action was believed to be necessary because it was thought that some banks were using repurchase agreements to avoid reserve requirements and the rules governing payment of interest on deposits. In August the Board of Governors amended Regulation D and Regulation M (Foreign Activities of National Banks) in an effort to moderate the flow of foreign funds between U.S. banks and their foreign branches and also between U.S. banks and foreign banks. The board removed a special advantage to member banks who had used Euro-dollars, which were not subject to reserve requirements, to adjust to domestic credit restraint. The amendments to Regulation M established a 10 percent reserve requirement on net borrowings of member banks from their

FIGURE 4

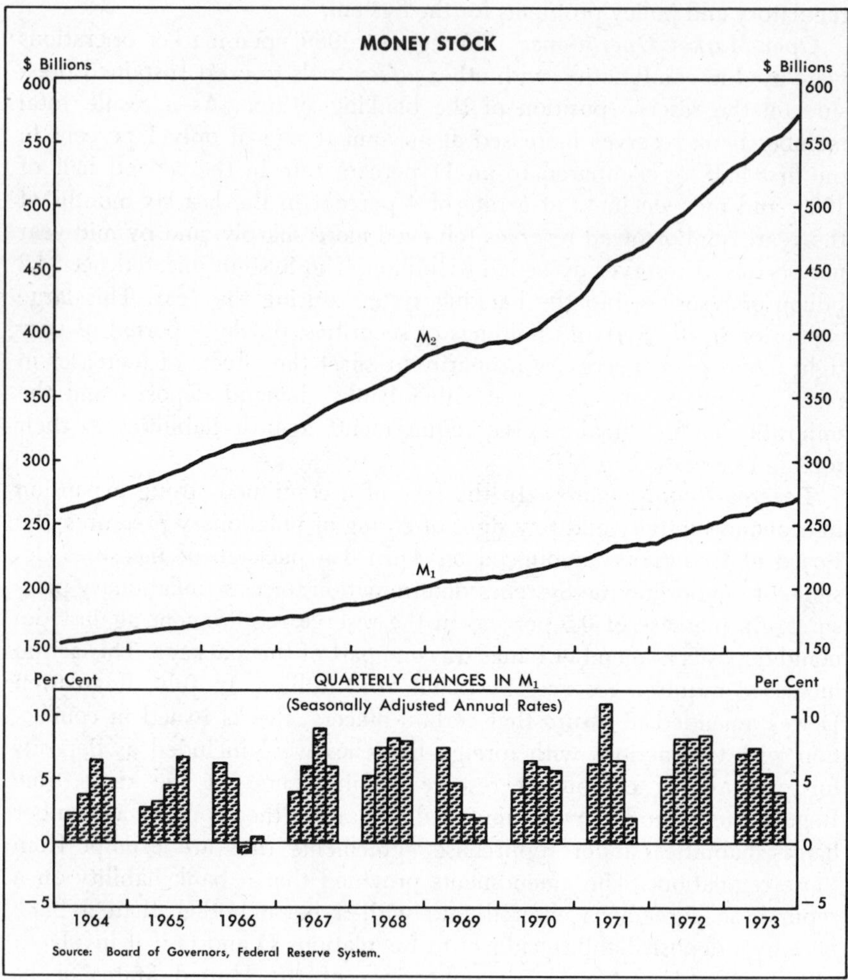

foreign branches to the extent that these borrowings exceeded the amount outstanding in a base period. A similar requirement applied to assets sold by domestic offices to foreign branches and to loans by branches to U.S. residents. The amendment to Regulation D established a 3 percent reserve requirement on borrowings by member banks from foreign banks, up to an amount equal to 4 percent of the member banks' deposits subject to reserve requirements. A 10 percent reserve requirement was imposed on borrowings in excess of that amount.

The Discount Rate. In April the Board of Governors announced approval of an increase of 0.5 percent in the discount rate. This action, which supplemented restrictive action in other policy areas, brought the discount rate to 6 percent, the highest level in 40 years.

ANOTHER DIFFICULT PERIOD JANUARY 1970–AUGUST 1971

The Economy

This was another turbulent period, both in the domestic economy and in the international exchanges. Throughout 1970, the pace of economic activity was slowed by the tight antiinflationary monetary and fiscal policies that had been pursed in 1969. At the same time, the economy was buffeted by the reorganization of one of the country's largest corporations and by a long strike in the automobile industry late in the year. Real output declined slightly in 1970, unemployment rose sharply, while prices continued upward under strong cost pressures. Industrial output fell about 4.8 percent during the year, with declines centered in defense products, consumer durable goods, and business equipment. The reduction in defense production was especially sharp, more than matching the decline in real GNP. Production rebounded sharply in the first quarter of 1971, with real GNP rising at an 8.0 percent annual rate. In the second quarter, however, the growth in real GNP fell to less than half the first quarter gain. Unemployment remained high, and there were few signs of moderation in the inflation rate.

The economy followed a somewhat erratic course over the entire period. In the first quarter of 1970 the level of activity continued the decline that had marked the fourth quarter of 1969, with real output falling some 3.0 percent. Real output rose slightly in the second quarter, however, and this was followed by a slightly larger gain in the third quarter. These gains were realized in spite of the reorganization of the Penn Central Railroad in the second quarter, a development that almost precipitated a liquidity crisis and severely damaged business confidence. Indeed, by the third quarter there was reason to believe that the economy was beginning to recover from the mild downturn that had marked the last quarter of 1969 and the first quarter of 1970. The two small consecutive quarterly increases in real output, combined with favorable movements in a number of economic indicators, led many economists to conclude that a recovery was in progress. These hopes were dashed in the fourth quarter, however, by the depressing impact of the two-month strike against General Motors Corporation. Current dollar GNP rose less than $5 billion in the fourth quarter, compared with a $15 billion gain in the third, and real GNP declined at a 4 percent annual rate. It is difficult to estimate precisely the extent to which total output was reduced by the strike, but the Council of Economic Advisers estimates that the strike's total impact was about $14 billion. The end of the strike in late 1970 was followed by a strong upsurge in production in the first quarter of 1971, with real GNP rising at an 8.0 percent annual rate. This strong gain was largely the result of the rebound in auto production and sales following the end of the strike, and the growth of production soon fell to a more moderate pace. The increase in real GNP in the second quarter was less than half the first quarter gain, despite a strong rise in residential construction and the stockpiling of steel inventories in anticipation of a possible strike later in the year.

Weakness was broadly distributed throughout the economy for much of this period. A rapid increase in disposable income in 1970 was accompanied by a sharp rise in the savings rate and a slowing in the growth of consumer spending, with most of the weakness centered in the durable goods sector. Spending on consumer durables was fairly weak through the first three quarters of 1970 and declined sharply in the fourth quarter as a result of the GM strike. In the first quarter of 1971 disposable personal income rose sharply as a result of tax reductions, a federal pay raise, and the increase in wages and salaries resulting from the resumption of auto production. Although the savings rate remained high, personal consumption outlays rose by more than a $20 billion rate, over twice the average quarterly increase in 1970. Disposable income registered another strong gain in the second quarter, but the savings rate rose sharply and the growth in consumer spending tapered off. The long business fixed investment boom came to an end in 1970 as spending on new fixed capital rose only about 3½ percent. Measured in dollars of constant purchasing power, fixed investment outlays actually declined in 1970. In the first half of 1971, business fixed investment outlays strengthened, but in real terms the improvement was small. Residential construction expenditures continued to fall through the first three quarters of 1970, but as funds became increasingly available in mortgage markets, residential construction turned up in the fourth quarter. The expansion in housing expenditures continued in 1971 at a vigorous pace as mortgage funds were in ample supply and interest rates declining. Federal government purchases of goods and services declined in 1970 as a $3 billion cut in defense spending more than offset a small rise in other expenditures. The decline in defense spending continued through the first half of 1971 almost exactly offsetting a modest rise in other types of spending.

The weakening of demand for goods and services was reflected in the degree of utilization of productive resources. Employment declined by 274,000 between the end of 1969 and the end of 1970, while the civilian labor force increased by 2 million. As a result, the unempolyment rate, which had remained at a very low level throughout 1969, rose sharply from 3.6 percent to 6.2 percent. The rise in employment resumed in early 1971, but through the first eight months of that year, the growth in the labor force almost exactly matched the growth in employment, and the unemployment rate hovered around 6.0 percent throughout that period. Capacity utilization in manufacturing fell from 84.3 percent in the fourth quarter of 1969 to 74.0 percent in the final quarter of 1970. Although the utilization rate improved slightly in the first half of 1971, it only reached 75.1 percent in the second quarter and dropped back to 73.2 percent in the third.

The increase in idle capacity and unemployment did little to halt the rise in wages and prices however. Although employment declined throughout much of 1970, upward pressures on wages continued strong. A large number of union contracts came up for renewal during the year and workers generally attempted to make up for past cost of living increases and to anticipate future increases. As a result, the rise in compensation per man-hour in the private nonfarm sector averaged about 7.0 percent in 1970. The rise in labor costs continued at a rapid pace in the first half of 1971. Average hourly compensation rose at an annual rate of 7.2 percent, even higher than the 1970 pace. Large wage gains were widespread, with workers in construction, transportation, and public utilities chalking up especially large increases.

During the period from January 1970 through August 1971 only modest progress was made toward slowing the pace of inflation. The Consumer Price Index rose 5.5 percent from December 1969 to December 1970, compared to a 6.1 percent rise in the comparable period in 1969. The rate of increase in consumer prices fell to a 3.8 percent annual rate through the first eight months of 1971, but this improvement largely reflected a sharp decline in home mortgage rates. Wholesale prices rose 2.3 percent over the course of 1970, following a rise of 4.7 percent in 1969. Between December 1970 and August 1971, however, the wholesale price index rose at a 5.1 percent annual rate.

The U.S. balance of payments deteriorated sharply over the period. In 1970, the balance of payments picture was dominated by a tremendous volume of short-term capital movements. The move toward an easier monetary policy in the United States brought about a large decline in short-term interest rates. As these rates fell relative to rates abroad and as funds became readily available in domestic markets, U.S. banks repaid part of their borrowings in the Euro-dollar markets. A large part of these dollar repayments flowed through the Euro-dollar market into foreign central banks, causing the U.S. deficit on the official settlements basis to exceed $10 billion. The situation worsened in the first half of 1971 as the outflow of capital increased and the trade account slipped into deficit. During this period funds flowed into Germany in huge amounts as that country continued to pursue a relatively tight monetary policy. By the second quarter the market was speculating on another revaluation of the mark, and on May 10 the mark was allowed to float. This action was followed by a brief period during which pressures on the dollar were relaxed, but as evidence of the serious weakness in the U.S. balance of payments mounted, another and even more massive flow of funds began. In the first seven months of 1971, U.S. liabilities to foreigners soared some $13 billion to reach a total of $37 billion at the end of July.

Fiscal Action. In response to the sluggish performance of the economy, the federal government maintained a substantially easier fiscal policy stance between January 1970 and August 1971. The net budget position as measured in the National Income Accounts shifted from a surplus of about $7 billion in 1969 to a deficit of more than $13 billion in 1970. Purchases of goods and services by the federal government declined for the first time in 10 years, but federal expenditures other than purchases rose a record $17.6 billion. This increase was partly accounted for by a 20 percent increase in grants-in-aid to state and local governments, a 15 percent increase in social security payments, higher disbursements for the Medicare program, and a substantial increase in unemployment compensation. On the other side of the ledger, the income tax surcharge was phased out in two steps in the first half of 1970. Largely because of this action, tax receipts fell some $5 billion in 1970, although receipts were also affected by the unusually small growth in taxable personal and corporate income. Federal outlays on goods and services showed little change in the first half of 1971 as further declines in defense expenditures were about offset by increased purchases of nondefense items. Grants-in-aid to state and local governments, higher social security payments, and increases in other transfer payments resulted in a rapid rise in other expenditures in the first half. At the same time, the increase in revenues was slowed by the sluggish pace of economic activity.

Monetary Policy

Background. By the end of 1969 it was apparent that economic activity had turned downward. Throughout 1970 and the first half of 1971, therefore, monetary policy was concerned with the problem of cushioning the downturn while continuing the fight against inflation. Although inflation was a continuing concern, policy was generally expansive over most of the period. However, there was some slight firming around mid-1971. The unusual turmoil in financial markets in the second quarter of 1970 and the repercussions of the long General Motors strike in the fourth quarter made the achievement of policy objectives much more difficult.

Changes in interest rates during this period were striking, with short-term market rates plunging sharply downward through 1970 and into the first quarter of 1971. They then reversed direction and moved briskly upward through mid-year. During the period of rapid decline, short-term rates generally fell about 5 percentage points with the commercial paper rate, for example, plunging from about 9 percent at the beginning of 1970 to about 4 percent in early 1971. Long-term rates also moved downward over the period, but the reductions were much smaller than those for short rates. The pattern of rate movements was not smooth over the period. Rates declined sharply in the first quarter of 1970 on evidence of the economic slowdown and a move toward monetary ease by the System, a development that was encouraged by a cut in the prime rate from 8½ to 8 percent. The direction of movement was reversed in the second quarter, as a result of growing uncertainties concerning the course of the economy and of monetary policy, repercussions from the Cambodian incursions and the accompanying domestic turmoil, and finally the disarray in financial markets following disclosure of the financial problems of the Penn Central Railroad. After mid-year, tensions in financial markets relaxed and the decline in interest rates continued through the year-end and into the early months of 1971. From mid-September 1970 to the end of December, the commercial bank prime rate was reduced four times, from 8 percent to 6¾ percent. Between the end of 1970 and March 19, 1971, the prime was changed six times, with the rate falling in small steps to 5¼ percent. Toward the end of the first quarter, concern over inflation and the rapid growth in the money supply caused a modest shift in the stance of monetary policy. In view of the continuing slack in the economy the System continued to supply reserves at a substantial rate, but it did so less readily than earlier in the year. This modest firming of monetary policy contributed to a rise in short-term rates that developed in the second quarter and continued into August. Most short-term market rates rose about 2 percentage points, and the prime rate moved back up to 6 percent on July 7.

A New Emphasis. At its regular meetings the Federal Open Market Committee (FOMC) considers and evaluates a broad range of data bearing on the current and prospective course of economic activity. On the basis of this evaluation, the committee makes a decision respecting the appropriate posture of monetary policy for the weeks immediately ahead. It then becomes necessary for the committee to instruct the manager of the System Open Market Account, who acts as the agent of the FOMC in buying and selling securities in the open market, concerning the day-to-day operations necessary to achieve the committee's policy goals. These instructions are embodied in a document known as the Directive.

The operating variable on which these instructions have focused has changed from time to time. For many years the manager was instructed to maintain or to achieve certain specified money-market conditions, but even then the specific money-market variable used as an indicator of money-market conditions varied from one time to another. This term has been defined to include such things as the federal funds rate, the three-month treasury bill rate, and the net reserve position of member banks. At one time, in carrying out instructions to maintain currently prevailing conditions in the money market, the manager might place primary emphasis on the net reserve position of member banks; at another time the three-month treasury bill rate might receive primary attention; and at still another time, the focal point might be the federal funds rate.

In 1966 the FOMC altered the Directive by adding a proviso clause stated in terms of the rate of growth of a selected aggregate, usually the bank credit proxy. That is, the manager would be instructed to maintain or to achieve certain money-market conditions provided the growth in bank credit did not deviate significantly from current projections. If the growth in bank credit did exceed or fall short of projections to a significant degree, the manager was expected to make appropriate changes in money-market conditions. Hence, the addition of the proviso clause to the Directive explicitly recognized the current behavior of a monetary aggregate as an important intermediate target variable in the implementation of monetary policy.

In 1970 the form of the Directive was again changed to place even greater emphasis on the aggregates as a target variable. In the new Directive the FOMC instructed the manager to conduct open-market operations with a view to maintaining money-market conditions consistent with achieving a desired growth in money and bank credit over the months ahead. While the Directive itself specified the desired growth rate in general terms (e.g., a "moderate" or "modest" growth in money and bank credit), the discussion preceding its adoption always made clear to the manager the specific growth rates desired.

The 1970 action on the Directive represented a change in emphasis rather than a sharp break with the past. The FOMC had been concerned with such aggregates as total reserves, bank credit, and the money supply long before the 1970 change; and it continued to be concerned with interest rates, net reserve positions, and other indicators of money-market conditions after the change. Indeed, the Desk continued to use money-market conditions as operating guides in attempting to achieve aggregate targets. Moreover, the committee has at times relegated the aggregates to a subordinate position when conditions in financial markets seemed to warrant it. The Directives issued during the period of turbulence in financial markets in May and June 1970, for example, emphasized the importance of moderate pressures on financial markets. At the same time, however, the manager was directed to continue to pursue the longer run objectives of moderate growth in money and bank credit, to the extent that this was compatible with the goal of moderating pressures on financial markets.

Turbulence in Financial Markets. In May and June of 1970, financial markets were shaken by a series of developments that threatened to precipitate a liquidity crisis. Underlying the instability in financial markets were the heavy corporate demands for long-term funds, uncertainties as to the effectiveness of antiinflation policies, and growing doubts concerning the financial positions of some important corporations. In early May the Cambodian incursion and the accompanying unrest in the United States served to aggravate the already uneasy situation in financial markets. Interest rates rose sharply, especially long-term rates, and the success of the Treasury's May financing was threatened. Because of these developments, the System gave primary emphasis to moderating the pressures on financial markets. Conditions in the financial markets calmed somewhat in early June, and yields on long-term securities moved down from the peaks they had reached in May. In late June, however, the Penn Central Corporation indicated it would be unable to pay off its maturing commercial paper. This brought immediate and intense pressure on the commercial paper market. Over the next three weeks the volume of commercial paper outstanding declined by some $3 billion, setting off fears that many borrowers would be unable to roll over maturing paper and that a sharp credit stringency might ensue. Many corporations were trying to obtain funds in other markets to pay off maturing commercial paper, and much of this demand was centered on commercial banks.

The System moved promptly and effectively to prevent the development of a liquidity crisis by making it possible for banks to provide loans to creditworthy corporations. The Board of Governors suspended Regulation Q ceilings on large-denomination CD's with maturities of 30–89 days. This enabled banks to acquire funds that investors were reluctant to invest in money-market obligations and to channel them to borrowers who needed them to pay off maturing commercial paper. At the same time, open-market operations were used to assist the banking system to meet the overall increase in credit demands, and the Federal Reserve banks informed member banks that accommodation would be available at the discount window in support of loans to creditworthy borrowers who were unable to roll over maturing commercial paper. Following these actions, the scramble for liquidity subsided, and financial markets calmed.

Open Market Operations. The System relied heavily on open-market operations in moving toward an easier monetary policy stance in 1970 and in early 1971, but began to supply reserves more reluctantly in the second quarter of 1971. Between December 1969 and August 1971, total reserves increased by more than $2.4 billion, with almost all of the growth occurring between June 1970 and May 1971. System holdings of U.S. government securities rose almost $9 billion over the entire period. Through the first 16 months of this period, nonborrowed reserves grew more rapidly than total reserves as member banks reduced their borrowing from the Federal Reserve from about $1 billion at the end of 1969 to $148 million in April 1971. Because of concern over the rapid growth of monetary aggregates in the face of strong inflation and a dramatic deterioration in the balance of payments, the System in the second quarter of 1971 began to supply reserves with somewhat greater reluctance. As a result, total reserves grew very little between May and August, while borrowings at the Federal Reserve banks rose strongly to the $800 million level.

Discount Rate. In mid-November 1970 the discount rate was reduced from 6 to 5¾ percent, the first of five one-quarter point reductions designed to keep the rate in better alignment with rapidly falling short-term market rates. Other reductions occurred in December; two, in January 1971; and one, in February. The reduction in February brought the rate to 4¾ percent. Then in July 1971 the rate was raised to 5 percent, a reflection of the moderate firming of monetary policy and the sharp run-up in market rates that had begun earlier in the year.

Reserve Requirements. In June 1970 the Board of Governors amended Regulation D to prescribe the conditions that must be met in order for subordinated notes or debentures issued by member banks to be exempt from reserve requirements. Among other things, the amendment provided that in order to be exempt a subordinated note must have an original maturity of seven years or more and be in an amount of at least $500. Formerly the exemption had applied if the maturity exceeded two years. The change was considered necessary because of evidence that member banks had used such obligations to acquire deposit-type funds.

Effective in the reserve computation period beginning October 1, 1970, the reserve requirement against time deposits in excess of $5 million at each member bank was reduced from 6 to 5 percent. At the same time, a 5 percent reserve requirement was imposed on funds obtained by member banks through the issuance of commercial paper by their affiliates. The purpose of the latter action was to put bank-related commercial paper on the same footing with respect to reserve requirements as large, negotiable CD's. The combined effect of these two actions was to reduce required reserves for the banking system by about $400 million. In November the marginal reserve requirement applicable to Euro-dollar borrowings of member banks was raised from 10 to 20 percent, with the increase to become effective January 7, 1971. Also in January, Regulation M was amended to permit a member bank to include within its reserve-free base the amount of purchases by its foreign branches of certain Export-Import Bank obligations. In April, Regulation M was again amended to include within such reserve-free bases the amount of purchases of certain U.S. treasury obligations by a bank's foreign branches. The purpose of both of these changes was to encourage U.S. banks to retain their Euro-dollar liabilities and thus avoid the deleterious effect on the U.S. balance of payments of a rapid repayment of these borrowings.

Regulation Q. In January 1970 the Board of Governors announced an increase in the maximum interest rates payable by member banks on time and savings deposits. Maximum rates payable on savings deposits were raised from 4 to 4½ percent, the first increase in this ceiling since 1964. In addition, there was a general realignment of ceilings on certificates of deposits, resulting in a scaling upward of ceilings on both large-denomination negotiable CD's and consumer-type certificates. This action was part of a coordinated move by the Federal Reserve System, the Federal Deposit Insurance Corporation, and the Federal Home Loan Bank Board that resulted in increases in ceiling rates on deposits at both bank and nonbank thrift institutions. Its purpose was to make rates payable by these institutions more competitive with market rates and to enlarge the flow of savings into financial institutions. In June 1970 the Board of Governors suspended the rate ceilings on large-denomination CD's with maturities of 30–89 days. This was one of a package of actions taken by the System to deal with the unsettled financial markets that followed the filing of the Penn Central bankruptcy petition. Also in June, the Board of Governors amended Regulation Q to prescribe the conditions that must be met in order for subordinated notes or debentures issued by member banks to be exempt from interest rate ceilings. The provisions of this amendment were the same as those of the amendment to Regulation D, which was made at the same time and for the same purpose.

Margin Requirements. In May 1970 the Board of Governors lowered from 80 to 65 percent the margin requirement for credit extended by brokers, dealers, banks, and other lenders to finance the purchase or carrying of stocks and from 60 to 50 percent for credit extended by such lenders to finance the purchase or carrying of convertible bonds.

A NEW APPROACH AUGUST 1971–DECEMBER 1972

At mid-1971 the U.S. economy was beset by a combination of seemingly intractable economic problems. The economy was growing, but not fast enough to eat into a substantial cushion of unused resources. The unemployment rate remained near 6 percent throughout the first half of the year and only about 75 percent of manufacturing capacity was being utilized. Nevertheless, prices continued to rise at an unacceptable rate, accompanied by substantial increases in wages. At the same time, the U.S. balance of payments position was deteriorating rapidly. The trade balance fell sharply in the spring, and a decline in interest rates relative to rates abroad encouraged a rapid outflow of short-term funds from the United States. By the second quarter these developments gave rise to speculative activities that greatly magnified the outflow of funds.

This combination of problems created something of a dilemma for economic policy makers. The use of traditional monetary and fiscal policies to speed up the rate of growth and reduce the margin of unemployed resources might well exacerbate the problem of inflation and cause further deterioration of the balance of payments. On the other hand, the use of these policies to slow the rate of inflation by reducing aggregate demand might only increase the slack in the economy and raise the already high unemployment rate even higher. Indeed, in view of the large amounts of unemployed resources and evidence of a substantial element of cost-push inflation in the economy, there was some question as to whether the inflation problem was amenable to the traditional monetary-fiscal policy treatment.

The apparent conflict in achieving the nation's economic objectives led to a decisive change of policy. On August 15, 1971, the President announced a new economic policy. The most important elements of the new program were a 90-day freeze on prices, wages, and rents, to be followed by a more flexible system of controls in the second phase; suspension of convertibility of the dollar into gold or other reserve assets; imposition of a temporary surtax of up to 10 percent on dutiable imports; proposal of a package of tax reductions designed to stimulate economic expansion.

The temporary freeze on wages and prices provided the time needed to set up the machinery to carry out the Phase II program that was to succeed the freeze. On October 7 the President announced the outlines of the Phase II program. The goal of the program was to reduce the rate of inflation to the 2 to 3 percent range by the end of 1972. The controls were to cover the economy broadly, were to be mandatory, and were to be removed when, in the President's judgment, reasonable price stability had been restored. An Executive Order established the administrative machinery to develop guidelines and to make the decisions on wages and prices necessary to achieve this goal. A Cost of Living Council, consisting of high government officials, was assigned the responsibility of establishing broad goals, determining the coverage of the control program, overseeing enforcement, and coordinating the anti-inflationary effort in line with overall goals. A Price Commission and a Pay Board were created to develop standards and make decisions on changes in prices and compensation.

The Economy

The new economic program brought about an improved outlook for economic activity. The strong measures to control inflation appeared to raise the level of business and consumer confidence. Prospects for consumer spending were favorably affected by such fiscal measures as the proposal to remove the excise tax on autos and to advance the date of certain personal tax reductions. The proposed investment tax credit provided encouragement for increased business investment spending.

The overall effect of the new economic program and related monetary and fiscal policy measures was quite stimulative. The effect on the economy was not immediate, mainly because economic activity in the third quarter of 1971 was dominated by the liquidation of inventories, particularly excess steel stocks that had been accumulated earlier in the year in anticipation of a strike. Final sales rose somewhat more rapidly than in the second quarter, largely because of a sharp increase in purchases of domestically produced autos after announcement of the new economic program. Overall economic activity accelerated in the fourth quarter as inventory accumulation resumed, as outlays for residential construction continued to rise, and as the rate of business capital spending picked up. Real GNP grew at a 5.8 percent annual rate in the fourth quarter while the implicit price deflator rose only 1.7 percent.

The strong surge in economic activity that began in late 1971 continued through 1972. Measured in current prices, GNP grew almost 10 percent for the year as a whole. The rise in the implicit price deflator was only 3 percent, but real GNP recorded a hefty 6.4 percent advance. This expansion was more than twice that for 1971 and the largest since 1966. Growth in real output was rapid in every quarter of 1972, with quarterly advances ranging from 6.3 percent to 9.4 percent annual rates. Moreover, the expansion in 1972 was broadly distributed, with all major sectors of demand except net exports contributing to the rise in GNP. A very large increase in gross private domestic investment, a step-up in federal purchases, and a substantial expansion in consumer spending were the principal stimulative forces in the economy.

The surge in economic activity between August 1971 and December 1972 resulted in a significant improvement in the utilization of productive resources. The most marked improvement did not occur, though, until the final three quarters of 1972. More than three quarters of a million additional workers found employment between August and December 1971, but the civilian labor force increased by almost exactly the same number, and the unemployment rate remained virtually unchanged at around 6.0 percent. The labor force continued to grow rapidly throughout 1972, but employment grew even more rapidly. As a result, the unemployment rate fell to 5.1 percent by the end of 1972. The index of capacity utilization in manufacturing rose from 74.7 percent at the time of the inauguration of the new economic program to 81.5 percent at the end of 1972.

The performance of prices and wages during the period was somewhat mixed. There was a temporary bulge in the first few months following the termination of the wage-price freeze in November 1971, but after that there was some moderation in the rise of both prices and wages. Employee compensation increased 6.9 percent over the course of 1972, compared with a rate of 8.1 percent in the first half of 1971. Moreover, output per man-hour was sharply higher in 1972, and the rate of advance of unit labor costs was reduced substantially by year end. The average quarterly increase in the GNP implicit price deflator was 2.3 percent (annual rate) over the final three quarters of 1972, compared with an average of 4.8 percent for the first two quarters of 1971. Consumer prices rose 3.4 percent over 1972, compared with an annual rate of 3.8 percent in the precontrol period of 1971. Wholesale prices, on the other hand, advanced rapidly in 1972, propelled by an explosion of farm prices in the final three quarters.

The new economic program recognized the need for a substantial realignment of exchange rates between the dollar and other major currencies in order to restore the competitiveness of U.S.-produced goods in world markets. The first steps toward this goal were taken on August 15 with the suspension of convertibility of the dollar into gold or other reserve assets, imposition of a temporary surtax of up to 10 percent on dutiable imports, and limitation of tax relief for capital expenditures to domestically produced capital goods. Following these actions, all major countries allowed the prices of their currencies to rise relative to the dollar, although there continued to be substantial intervention by foreign central banks. In mid-December, representatives of the major trading countries met in Washington and agreed to a significant adjustment of exchange rates. The agreement also provided for a widening of the intervention band to 2.25 percent on either side of the new parities (it had been 1.00 percent), and U.S. representatives agreed to ask Congress to raise the dollar price of gold from $35 to $38 per ounce. The 10 percent surtax on imports was removed.

Despite the dramatic nature of these actions, they brought little immediate improvement in the U.S. balance of payments. The trade balance worsened as the deficit in 1972 totaled $6.9 billion, more than $4 billion larger than the one in 1971. The strong expansion in the U.S. economy in 1972 led to a strong expansion in the volume of imports. At the same time, prices of U.S. imports rose sharply, both because of the devaluation and because of a general increase in world prices, while export prices expressed in dollars increased much less. Thus, while merchandise exports rose 14 percent in 1972, imports increased even faster. The enormous flows of speculative funds that caused so much havoc in 1971 were largely absent in 1972, and there was a modest reflow of private capital into the United States. As a result, the overall balance of payments deficit on the official settlements basis dropped from almost $30 billion in 1971 to just over $10 billion in 1972.

Fiscal Action. In the period between the announcement of the new economic program and the end of 1972, both fiscal policy and monetary policy were designed to achieve a more vigorous expansion of the economy and to bring about a more complete utilization of the nation's productive resources. As part of the new program, the federal excise tax on automobiles was removed, the investment tax credit was reinstated at 7 percent, and a reduction in the personal income tax that had been scheduled for later was advanced to January 1, 1972. In addition, programmed federal expenditures were stepped up, mainly in the form of transfer payments and grants to state and local governments. As a result, federal expenditures rose some $26 billion in the calendar year 1972. Tax revenues soared as a result of the upsurge in economic activity and because a change in tax-withholding schedules resulted in substantial overpayments on individuals' taxes in 1972. Consequently, the federal deficit on a National Income Accounts basis declined to $18.5 billion in 1972 from $21.7 billion in the previous year.

Monetary Policy

Background. The Federal Reserve adopted a generally accommodative policy stance following the announcement of the wage-price freeze, and bank reserves were supplied somewhat more freely than earlier in the year. Apparently because of a shift in inflationary expectations, the demand for money balances declined. Consequently, growth of the monetary aggregates was quite moderate in the final months of 1971 and interest rates declined. By year end longer term rates were about 1 percentage point below their mid-August levels, and short-term rates were down by about 1½ percentage points over the same period. The commercial bank prime rate dropped from 6 percent in July to 5¼ percent at year end. This moderately stimulative monetary policy was continued through most of 1972. In the first half, System open-market operations provided for a rapid growth of nonborrowed reserves, but in the third quarter nonborrowed reserves declined slightly. Total reserves grew at a 10.6 percent annual rate for the year as a whole, but most of the expansion in the second half came from an increase of more than $1 billion in borrowing at the discount window. Reflecting the rapid economic expansion and the strong demand for credit in 1972, short-term interest rates rose throughout most of the year. Long-term rates remained fairly stable. The commercial bank prime rate continued to move downward in early 1972, but in early March it began to drift upward and through a number of small increases reached a high of 6 percent in late December.

Open-Market Operations. System open-market operations provided reserves at a rapid pace in the second half of 1971 and the first half of 1972. Federal Reserve holdings of U.S. government securities rose more than $6 billion between July 1971 and July 1972, and nonborrowed reserves rose about $3 billion over the same period. Between July and year-end 1972, open-market operations provided reserves much more reluctantly. In late 1972, open-market operations were used to offset some of the impact on bank reserves of changes in Regulations D and J (discussed below).

Reserve Requirements. In November 1972 the System announced a change in Regulation D that had the effect of restructuring the reserve requirements of member banks. A related change in Regulation J was designed to improve the nation's check-clearing system. Both of these changes had a significant impact on the reserve position of the banking system. Prior to the change in Regulation D, member banks were divided into two groups (reserve city banks and country banks) for reserve purposes. Most banks in major financial centers were classified as reserve city banks and all others were classified in the country bank category. The change in Regulation D eliminated the geographically based classification of banks for reserve purposes and substituted a new system of graduated reserve requirements for net demand deposits. The new system, applicable to all member banks wherever located, is based solely on the size of a bank's deposits. Applicable reserve requirements ranged from 8 percent on the first $2 million of net demand deposits to 17½ percent on deposits in excess of $400 million (see chart).

Before the November 1972 change in Regulation J, most banks located outside Federal Reserve bank or branch cities were required to remit funds one or more business days after checks were presented for payment by the Federal Reserve. Most banks located in such cities, on the other hand, were required to remit on the same business day the checks were presented. The November 1972 change in Regulation J requires all banks to remit payment for checks presented by the Federal Reserve on the same day the checks are presented.

Most member banks experienced some reduction in required reserves as a result of the restructuring of reserve requirements against demand deposits. In the aggregate, required reserves were reduced about $3.2 billion. The change in Regulation J, on the other hand, resulted in a net reduction in member bank reserves of about $2.1 billion. Implementation of these two changes came at a time of regular seasonal reserve needs, and open-market operations were employed to smooth the transition. Consequently, the net reserve provision of about $1.1 billion had only a minimal impact on the reserve position of the banking system.

Discount Rate. Changes in the discount rate were rather infrequent during this period. In November 1971 the rate was reduced from 5 percent to 4¾ percent, and in December it was reduced to 4½ percent. In both instances the changes were for the purpose of bringing the rate into better alignment with falling market rates.

Margin Requirements. In December 1971 the margin requirement for purchasing or carrying stocks and the required deposit on short sales were both reduced from 65 percent to 55 percent. In late 1972 it appeared that stock market credit might contribute to inflationary pressures and this action was reversed. The margin requirement on stocks and the deposit on short sales were returned to 65 percent.

LIMITATIONS AND ADVANTAGES OF MONETARY POLICY

Limitations of Monetary Policy

What then are the limitations of monetary policy? Partly, they are the effects of powerful forces working in opposite directions. To some extent they result from the limited influence that monetary policy has over financial markets. In part, they are due to imperfect knowledge and to errors of human judgment.

Price-Cost Inflation. The more competitive the economy, the more effective monetary policy can be. This is particularly true when business activity is running at near-capacity levels, and the System is trying to combat inflationary pressures. At such times, monopolistic pricing practices on the part of labor or business can push prices up from the supply rather than from the demand side. Sufficiently strong monetary policy can undoubtedly prevent some increases of this kind by dampening inflation psychology, but it is doubtful if it can completely cure the problem in a prosperous economy with strong monopolistic pressures. Conversely, continued monopolistic increases in wages and prices during recession tend to hinder the adjustments that lead to business recovery. To combat such pricing problems effectively, there must be additional measures designed to encourage competition.

Differing Fiscal Policy Aims. If the aims of fiscal policy—the manner in which the federal government spends, taxes, and manages its debt—run counter to those of monetary policy, the two can to some extent offset each other. This is almost inevitable at times since the aims of monetary policy are largely economic, whereas those of fiscal policy are often political or social rather than economic. In a democracy it could not be otherwise, but nevertheless the net result may be an expansionary budget deficit when monetary policy—rightly or wrongly—is moving in the opposite direction. Or it may mean a lengthening of treasury debt when the Federal Reserve is combating recession. In such cases, monetary and fiscal policy will partly offset each other.

Slippages in the Financial Mechanism. Even under the best conditions, monetary policy must contend with two types of "slippages" in the financial mechanism. First, commercial banks may not immediately expand or contract earning assets in response to changes in the availability of reserves. Second, even though banks act promptly, shifts in monetary velocity may partly offset changes in the money supply. Both kinds of slippages complicate the task of monetary policy, but their importance is overrated.

Incomplete use of additional bank reserves clearly calls for larger changes in reserves than would otherwise be necessary. This kind of special action is taken quite frequently. During 1960, for example, the System had to supply more reserves than would have been needed had country banks responded more quickly to the release of vault cash. Only if banks did not respond at all would effective System policy be impossible.

A more common difficulty is the increase in the velocity of money ordinarily accompanying a restrictive monetary policy. Perhaps the most important cause is the liquidation by banks of short-term government securities to meet rising loan demands. This leaves the money supply virtually unchanged since the banks merely substitute one form of earning assets for another, but it does tend to increase velocity by transferring bank balances from those who probably would not spend them as quickly—the purchasers of the securities—to those who spend them almost immediately—the new borrowers. Financial intermediaries, such as savings and loan associations or mutual savings banks, also can contribute to increases in velocity by raising interest or dividend rates to attract new funds for lending that might otherwise not have been spent as quickly and by lending the proceeds of government security sales to borrowers who spend them immediately. Finally, velocity can be increased through security sales by nonfinancial institutions and through the adoption of various ways of economizing on business and personal cash needs.

Such increases in velocity mean that monetary policy must permit the money supply to expand more slowly, and at times to contract, in order to prevent spending from rising at an inflationary clip. It is sometimes argued that the money supply cannot undergo such restraint without unduly interfering with treasury financing operations or upsetting securities markets through sharp increases in interest rates.

In practice, however, these fears have not yet been realized. System actions have been delayed at times by treasury financing operations, but the System has not had to alter appreciably the direction and intensity of policy. Nor have securities markets been disrupted by the System's tightening actions. Increases in interest rates have actually been rather moderate—to no small degree because policy affects the availability as well as the cost of credit.

In fact, increases in velocity induced by a tightening policy perform several useful functions. First, by providing a means for financing outlays they act as a safety valve to prevent an inadvertent overtightening of the money supply from becoming serious. Second, security sales resulting in increased velocity help transmit changes in the cost and availability of credit quickly throughout the entire credit mechanism. Finally, shifts in velocity make credit policy more equitable by enabling spenders to maintain those expenditures with the highest priorities by transmitting the effects of the policy to the more marginal outlays.

The Forecasting Problem. Monetary policy—like any discretionary stabilizing policy—necessarily involves judgments based upon incomplete evidence. Errors can occur for two reasons. First, delays in the availability of important business indicators make it impossible to know exactly how the economy is behaving at the moment. Second, policy making involves judgments regarding the course of business activity in the absence of central bank intervention and the probable effects of various policy combinations. Errors of judgment can be minimized through experience and careful analysis, but they can never be eliminated completely.

Advantages of Monetary Policy

Despite its imperfections, monetary policy has several advantages over the alternative methods of stabilizing the economy—fiscal policy and direct controls, such as rationing and price control.

Monetary Policy Is Impersonal. In our market economy, most production decisions are made indirectly by spenders through their demand for goods and services. Only those things that spenders want will continue to be produced, only the cheapest methods of production will last, and only efficient producers can remain in business. Consequently, except for certain interferences, our limited supplies of land, labor, and capital goods are used to produce most efficiently those things spenders want most.

Direct controls obviously change all this. They, in effect, dictate what consumers can and cannot do. Therefore, production decisions are made by the authorities, not by the market.

Fiscal policy is quite impersonal compared with direct controls, but variations in the direction and volume of taxation and spending alter the composition as well as the overall level of production. Those things the government buys will be produced in larger quantities than otherwise would have been the case, and those goods and services taxpayers would have bought will be produced in smaller quantities.

In contrast, general monetary controls are never used to influence particular types of expenditures. A policy of restraint, for example, is designed merely to prevent *total* spending from increasing too fast. It leaves it to the market to decide which *particular* activities will be curtailed. These are generally those things that consumers and other spenders want least. They continue to buy the things they want most. Similarly, when easy money encourages spending, the additional outlays take whatever forms spenders prefer.

Monetary Policy Is Flexible. Monetary policy is more flexible than most stabilizers. There are, of course, lags between policy decisions and the time the actions become effective, just as in the case of any stabilizing policy. There are other lags resulting from the lack of current information—lags affecting all types of discretionary stabilizers. But when it comes to reaching a quick decision, System policy-making machinery is admirable. Every three or four weeks—and sometimes more often—the Open Market Committee reaches some definite policy decision at its meeting. It may decide to stand pat; it may decide to act; but in any event it decides and initiates immediately the necessary implementing steps.

Discretionary fiscal policy actions involving changes in spending and taxation depend to a large degree upon Congressional action. Such decisions in a democracy like ours deserve and receive wide study and debate. Proper consideration thus requires time, and flexibility inevitably suffers. The so-called fiscal *automatic stabilizers*—primarily federal income taxes and unemployment compensation payments—that tend to create budget surpluses during boom and budget deficits during recession do, however, act more quickly. These clearly constitute a valuable, practical adjunct to monetary policy.

Monetary Policy Is Free from Day-to-Day Political Pressures. In establishing the Federal Reserve System, Congress wisely gave it such independence as to enable it to act freely in the best interests of the economy. It spread the policy-making role throughout the System to avoid undue concentration of power; it provided for 14-year terms of office for appointed board members, made them ineligible for reappointment after a full term, and staggered their terms of office; and it provided for the election of Reserve bank presidents by their own boards of directors, subject to the approval of the Federal Reserve Board. The net result is a unique institution, able to base its day-to-day policy on economic nonpolitical grounds.

The System, of course, must answer to Congress and has only such powers as federal laws give it. Within the limits of its broad powers, however, the System is free to use only economic considerations as guides to policy. Such can never be entirely the case with fiscal policy or direct controls, which are always significantly influenced by politics in our type of democracy.

The Net Result

When all its advantages are weighed against its limitations, where does monetary policy stand? What can it do, and what is it unable to do? Perhaps the best summary is the following testimony given by Chairman Martin of the Board of Governors before the Joint Economic Committee on February 2, 1960:

> . . . It [monetary policy] cannot prevent monopoly. It cannot assure that the financial needs of all socially desirable activities are met without intervention by Government. It cannot be relied upon to cover Federal deficits. Alone, it certainly cannot assure either stability or growth.
>
> What a correct monetary policy can do is to foster confidence in the dollar, so that our people can and will save and invest in the future with reasonable assurance that their plans will not be frustrated by irresponsible changes in the value of money.

31

National Income and Balance of Payment Accounts*

THE NATIONAL INCOME and Product Accounts provide a detailed statistical description of the U.S. economy. They depict in dollar terms the volume, composition, and use of the nation's output and, therefore, make it possible to trace long-term trends and current fluctuations in economic activity.

The data that measure the nation's total output are estimated from two principal points of view:

1. The value of the goods and services produced by the economy—referred to as the product side of the account;
2. The costs incurred and types of income earned in producing those goods and services—referred to as the income side.

Because the National Income and Product Accounts offer a total picture, these accounts are basic tools used in analyzing past and current performance of the economy and also in forecasting future economic developments. Furthermore, this quantitative framework makes these accounts of great importance in the formulation of national economic policies.

The product side of the National Income and Product Accounts is divided into the major markets for the output of the economy: consumer purchases, business investment, exports, and government purchases.

* Source: *Dictionary of Economic and Statistical Terms*, U.S. Department of Commerce.

TABLE 1

Summary National Income and Product Accounts, 1971 (billions of dollars)

Line			*Line*		
1	Compensation of employees	644.1	24	Personal consumption expenditures	664.9
2	Wages and salaries	573.5	25	Durable goods	103.5
3	Disbursements	572.9	26	Nondurable goods	278.1
4	Wage accruals less disbursements	.6	27	Services	283.3
5	Supplements to wages and salaries	70.7	28	Gross private domestic investment	152.0
6	Employer contributions for social insurance	34.1	29	Fixed investment	148.3
7	Other labor income	36.5	30	Nonresidential	105.8
8	Proprietors' income	70.0	31	Structures	38.4
9	Rental income of persons	24.5	32	Producers' durable equipment	67.4
10	Corporate profits and inventory valuation		33	Residential structures	42.6
	adjustment	78.6	34	Change in business inventories	3.6
11	Profits before tax	83.3	35	Net exports of goods and services	.7
12	Profits tax liability	37.3	36	Exports	66.1
13	Profits after tax	45.9	37	Imports	65.4
14	Dividends	25.4	38	Government purchases of goods and services	232.8
15	Undistributed profits	20.5	39	Federal	97.8
16	Inventory valuation adjustment	—4.7	40	National defense	71.4
17	Net interest	38.5	41	Other	26.3
18	National Income	855.7	42	State and local	135.0
19	Business transfer payments	4.6			
20	Indirect business tax and nontax liability	101.9			
21	Less: Subsidies less current surplus of government				
	enterprises	.9			
22	Capital consumption allowances	93.8			
23	Statistical discrepancy	—4.8			
	Charges Against Gross National Product	1,050.4	43	Gross National Product	1,050.4

More detailed breakdowns are published in supporting tables in the *Survey of Current Business,* particularly in the July issue. The survey is published monthly by the Bureau of Economic Analysis.

The income side of the National Income and Product Accounts summarizes the wages and salaries and other forms of income, indirect taxes, and capital consumption allowances generated in the production process. These income categories are further broken down by industry and legal form of organization in the July and other issues of the *Survey of Current Business.*

The terms defined in this chapter are organized in the order of the line numbers in the basic summary table reproduced from the *Survey of Current Business,* as indicated in Table 1.

Compensation of Employees (Line 1). Compensation of employees is income received as remuneration for work. It includes not only line 2, Wage and salary disbursements, but also line 5, Supplements to wages and salaries.

Compensation of employees has, historically, accounted for about 70 to 75 percent of national income, with wages and salaries being by far the largest component.

Wage and Salary Disbursements (Lines 2 and 3). Wage and salary disbursements are the wages and salaries paid to employees in a given period of time, irrespective of when these are earned. They cover all employee earnings, including executive salaries and bonuses, commissions, payments in kind, incentive payments, and tips.

Note that this estimate is made on a cash receipts basis—following the usual thinking and practice of households. Other entries in the National Income and Products Accounts are made on an accrual basis—in accord with predominant business practice.

See also wage accruals less disbursements, below.

Wage Accruals less Disbursements (Line 4). Wage accruals less disbursements is an adjustment item occasionally made in the National Income and Product Accounts to take account of the fact that wages and salaries are not always received at the same time as they are earned. Income in the national accounts is typically recorded in the period when earned, rather than when received—i.e., an accrual basis of accounting, but an exception is made in the wage and salary component of personal income. It is regularly estimated on a cash receipts basis—following the usual thinking and practice of households.

Ordinarily, wage and salary payments disbursed in one quarter but earned in the preceding quarter are approximately offset by those earned in the current quarter but not received until the following quarter, making the wage accruals less disbursements adjustment small or negligible.

Supplements to Wages and Salaries (Lines 5, 6, and 7). Supplements to wages and salaries are employer contributions for social insurance and other labor income. The latter includes items such as employer payments

CHART 1

The National Income and Product Accounts-1971

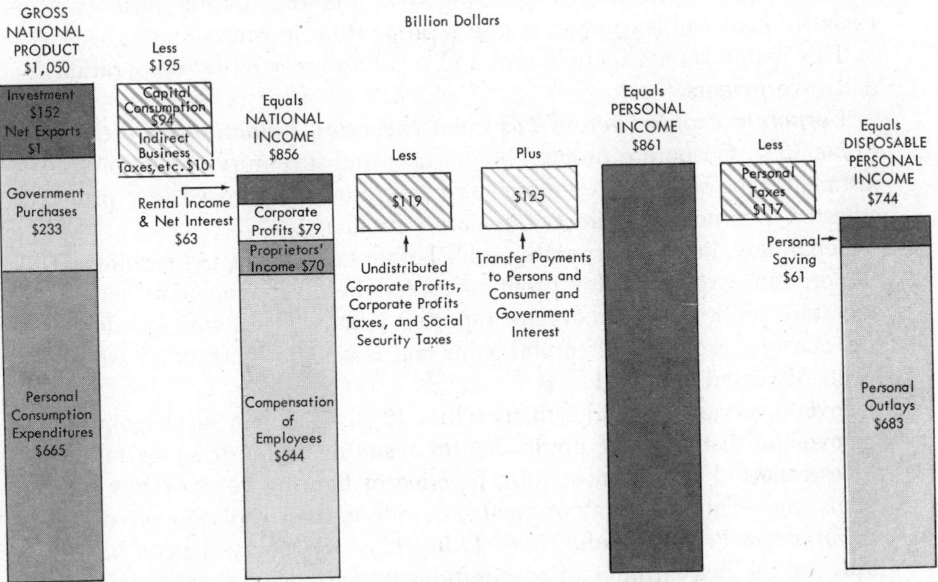

Relation of the Four Major Measures of Production and Income Flows

1. *Gross national product* is the market value of the output of goods and services produced by the nation's economy.
2. *National income* is the total earnings of labor and property from the production of goods and services.
3. *Personal income* is the total income received by persons from all sources.
4. *Disposable personal income* is the income remaining to persons after payment of personal taxes.

Source: U.S. Department of Commerce, Bureau of Economic Analysis.

for private pension, health and welfare funds, compensation for injuries, directors' fees, and pay of the military reserves.

These supplements constituted about 11 percent of total compensation of employees in 1971.

***Proprietors' Income* (*Line 8*).** Proprietors' income measures the earnings of unincorporated businesses—proprietorships, partnerships, and producers' cooperatives—from their current business operations. It does not, however, include supplementary income of individuals derived from renting property. Capital gains and losses are excluded, and no deduction is made for depletion.

See also rental income of persons, below.

***Rental Income of Persons* (*Line 9*).** Rental income of persons consists of money earned by persons from the use of their real property, such as a house, store, or farm. This category also includes imputed net rent of owner-occupants of nonfarm dwellings, and royalties received by persons from patents, copyrights, and rights to natural resources. Income received by persons primarily engaged in the real estate business is excluded here, but is counted in line 8, proprietors' income.

This item does not include rent and royalties received by corporations and governments.

Corporate Profits (before Tax) and Inventory Valuation Adjustment (Line 10). Corporate profits (before tax) and inventory; valuation adjustment represent the earnings of corporations organized for profit, adjusted to remove the effect of inventory profits.

Separately, line 11, corporate profits before taxes, is the net earnings of corporations organized for profit measured before payment of federal and state profit taxes. Profits are reported without deduction for depletion charges, exclusive of capital gains and losses, but with other adjustments discussed in line 11.

Inventory valuation adjustment (line 16) is made in an attempt to remove the distortion of profits figures resulting from rising or falling prices reflected in the accounting practice of figuring costs of raw materials and components at original cost rather than replacement costs.

Corporate Profits before Taxes (Line 11). Corporate profits before taxes are the net earnings of corporations organized for profit measured before payment of federal and state profit taxes. They are, however, net of indirect business taxes (line 20). They are reported without deduction for depletion charges and exclusive of capital gains and losses and intercorporate dividends.

Estimates of corporate profits before taxes for the National Income and Product Accounts are based on the annual tabulations of corporate income tax returns compiled by the Internal Revenue Service (IRS) with several adjustments. Depletion allowances are included. Estimates are made of profits not reported to the IRS, but disclosable by audit. Intercorporate dividends and capital gains are deducted. Bad debt expenses are measured by actual losses, not additions to reserves. And the profit or loss of bankrupt firms includes the gain from unsatisfied debt. Oil-well drilling costs are capitalized, state income taxes are added, as are the profits of federally-sponsored lending agencies. And the costs of trading or issuing corporate securities are deducted. Income earned abroad is adjusted to equal the amount reported in the balance-of-payments statement. This procedure produces estimates of corporate profits in the business sector consistent with the other components of the income and product accounts.

Corporate profits before taxes published in the National Income and Product Accounts are different conceptually from those reported by business firms to their shareholders. Profits reported to shareholders reflect accounting practices which vary from those in the National Income and Product Accounts—particularly in the treatment of depreciation charges, the use of reserve methods of accounting, and the recognition of earnings on foreign investments.

***Corporate Profits Tax Liability* (*Line 12*).** Corporate profits tax liability reflects federal and state taxes levied on corporate earnings.

In the national accounts, taxes on corporate profits are recorded on an accrual basis. In other words, they are assigned to the period when the profits are earned, rather than the period when the taxes are actually paid to the Internal Revenue Service or state governments.

***Corporate Profits after Taxes* (*Line 13*).** Corporate profits after taxes are the earnings of U.S. corporations organized for profit after liability for federal and state taxes has been deducted.

***Dividends* (*Line 14*).** Dividends are cash payments made by corporations organized for profit to stockholders who are U.S. citizens. Capital gains distributions by mutual funds are not included here.

Dividends normally account for 40 to 60 percent of aftertax profits each year. Dividends in the form of additional shares of stock—for instance noncash payments such as a stock split—are excluded.

***Undistributed Profits* (*Line 15*).** Undistributed profits are the portion of a corporation's profit remaining after taxes and dividends have been paid. It is one of the two main components of the corporate cash flow (gross retained earnings of business); the second is capital consumption allowances.

***Inventory Valuation Adjustment* (*Line 16*).** The inventory valuation adjustment is applied to book profits—profits before taxes—in order to exclude the gains or losses due to differences between the replacement cost of goods taken out of inventory and their recorded acquisition cost. Such an adjustment is necessary because many business firms do not keep their books in terms of current market prices, but rather at original cost or some other basis.

This adjustment is required to prevent overstatement or understatement of earned profits in periods of changing prices. Generally, this item carries a minus sign during periods when prices of goods carried in inventory are rising, and a plus sign when inventory prices are falling.

***Net Interest* (*Line 17*).** Net interest measures the excess of interest payments made by the domestic business sector over its interest receipts, plus net interest received from abroad.

Interest paid by one business firm to another business firm is a transaction within the business sector and has no effect on the net interest payments or receipts of the sector. The same is true of interest payments within other sectors—as from one individual to another, or one government agency to another.

***National Income* (*Line 18*).** National income represents aggregate earnings which arise from the current production of goods and services. Earnings are recorded in the forms in which they are received, inclusive of taxes on those earnings. These earnings consist of compensation of employees, the profits of corporate and unincorporated enterprises, net interest, and the rental income of persons.

Because of the manner in which the National Income and Product Accounts are organized, national income is restricted to the earnings of the private sector of the economy plus wages and salaries earned by government employees. The profits of government enterprises are not included in national income, but instead are treated as charges against the value of output not attributable to any particular factor of production.

***Business Transfer Payments* (*Line 19*).** Business transfer payments represent money paid by the business sector to persons for which no goods or services are received in return. Thus, there is no offsetting contribution to the economy's productive process. Major items included in this line are corporate gifts to nonprofit institutions, consumer bad debts, and personal injury payments by business to persons other than employees. Estimates of unrecovered thefts of cash and capital assets and cash prizes are also included.

***Indirect Business Tax and Nontax Liability* (*Line 20*).** Indirect busines tax and nontax liability consists of those tax liabilities paid by business, other than employer contributions for social insurance (line 6) and corporate income taxes (line 12). Sales taxes, excise taxes, and real property taxes paid by businesses are the principal types of indirect taxes. Although these taxes are paid by a business firm, it is presumed that they can be shifted to the firm's customers by adding the tax to the selling prices of products.

Nontax liability consists of those amounts of money paid by business that are for such things as fines, copyrights, royalty payments, and penalties.

***Subsidies less Current Surplus of Government Enterprises* (*Line 21*).** Subsidies are monetary grants provided by government to private business.

The current surplus of government enterprises represents the excess of sales receipts over current operating costs of such enterprises as the U.S. Postal Service, the Commodity Credit Corporation, and the Tennessee Valley Authority. Government enterprises are distinguished from other government activities by the fact that their operations are financed primarily by sale of a product or service rather than through general taxes. In calculating the current surplus, no deduction is made for depreciation, and interest is not included in either receipts or costs.

***Capital Consumption Allowances* (*Line 22*).** Capital consumption allowances are accounting charges which reflect estimates of wear and tear, obsolescence, destruction, and accidental losses of physical capital. The three components which make up the capital consumption allowances figure in the National Income and Product Accounts are depreciation charges by businesses and nonprofit institutions, depreciation of owner-occupied dwellings, and accidental damage to fixed business capital. Allowances for depletion of natural resources are not included in capital consumption allowances.

Gross national product minus capital consumption allowances is referred to as net national product (NNP).

***Statistical Discrepancy* (*Line* 23).** The nation's total output is calculated from two principal points of view: the income approach (lines 1–22) and the product approach (lines 24–42). Both methods yield estimates of gross national product. Statistical discrepancy is the amount by which these two separately made estimates differ. It has no economic significance.

***Personal Consumption Expenditures* (*Line* 24).** Personal consumption expenditures reflect the market value of goods and services purchased by individuals and nonprofit institutions or acquired by them as income in kind. The rental value of owner-occupied dwellings is included, but not the purchases of dwellings (line 33). Purchases are recorded at cost to consumers, including excise or sales taxes, and in full at the time of purchase whether made with cash or on credit. The nonprofit institutions included are those rendering services principally to individuals.

***Durable Goods* (*Line* 25).** Durable goods are items with a normal life expectancy of three years or more. Automobiles, furniture, household appliances, and mobile homes are common examples.

Because of their nature, durable goods expenditures are generally postponable. As a consequence, durable goods sales are the most volatile component of consumer expenditures.

Automobiles and parts, and furniture and household goods account for approximately 80 to 90 percent of expenditures on durable goods.

***Nondurable Goods* (*Line* 26)** Nondurable goods are items which generally last for only a short time (three years or less). Food, beverages, clothing, shoes, and gasoline are common examples.

Because of the nature of nondurable goods, these are generally purchased when needed, and expenditures grow approximately in line with population growth.

Personal consumption expenditures for food and beverages comprise about one half of the expenditures on nondurable goods, while clothing and shoes account for one fifth.

***Services* (*Line* 27).** Services are intangible commodities such as medical care, haircuts, and other personal care; railway, bus, and air transportation; and the use of housing.

***Gross Private Domestic Investment* (*Line* 28).** Gross private domestic investment is composed of line 29, Fixed investment, and line 34, Change in business inventories.

Separately, fixed investment—new additions and replacements—is the change in private capital brought about through purchases of durable equipment and construction by business and nonprofit institutions. The basic purpose of fixed investment is to increase the capacity to produce goods and services for future consumption.

The change in business inventories represents the value of the increase or decrease in physical stock of goods held by business. Included in these inventories are raw materials, semifinished goods, and finished goods ready for sale or shipment.

***Fixed Investment* (*Line 29*).** Fixed investment measures additions to and replacements of private capital brought about through net acquisitions by businesses and nonprofit institutions of durable equipment and structures for business and residential purposes.

Fixed investment expenditures are reflected in GNP in two ways. First, capital investment increases GNP by the value of the asset in the period in which the investment is made. Second, the effects of previous years' fixed investment show up in the products produced with the help of the capital. These products are of all types: consumer goods and services, additional capital goods, exports, and government purchases.

***Nonresidential Fixed Investment* (*Line 30*).** Nonresidential fixed investment includes capital expenditures by the business sector and nonprofit institutions for (1) new and replacement construction (e.g., buildings, stores, and warehouses) and (2) producers' durable equipment (e.g., machinery, office equipment, and motor vehicles).

Estimates for nonresidential fixed investment are based on the Bureau of Economic Analysis (BEA) surveys of plant and equipment expenditures by the business sector and on other information such as the sales of producers' durable goods and the value of construction. Adjustments must be made on the basis of other estimates to include investment in agriculture and other businesses not covered by the BEA surveys.

***Nonresidential Structures* (*Line 31*).** Fixed investment in nonresidential structures includes all new and replacement business expenditures on such buildings as factories, warehouses, and retail stores; expenditures on farm structures; all private, nonprofit institution expenditures on churches, schools, and hospitals; and all public utility expenditures on such items as railroad tracks, stations, telephone, electric and gas distribution systems. It also includes petroleum and gas well drilling and exploration expenditures. Nonresidential structures generally are buildings which are largely assembled on site rather than manufactured in a factory and shipped to the site.

These estimates differ conceptually from those of the Census Bureau by including the cost of petroleum and natural gas well drilling, brokers' commissions on the sale of structures and net purchases of used structures from government, and by excluding farm dwellings.

***Producers' Durable Equipment* (*Line 32*).** Fixed investment expenditures on producers' durable equipment include the new and replacement purchase of automobiles, trucks, various types of machinery, and other equipment used by the private sector in the production of goods and services.

In a given year, expenditures on producers' durables represent approximately two thirds of total fixed investment by the business sector for capital goods.

The three largest components within this category are electrical machinery expenditures; trucks, buses, and truck trailers; and passenger cars. In combination, these three components account for about one third of total investment expenditures on producers' durable equipment.

***Residential Structures* (*Line* 33).** Private investment expenditures on residential structures reflect construction put-in-place on new single-family houses, apartments, or other space in which people can maintain separate households. In addition to housing units, this category includes nonhousekeeping quarters such as hotels, dormitories, and nurses' homes. These expenditures include farm as well as nonfarm dwelling units. Also included are expenditures for additions and alterations made to these structures.

Mobile homes are not in this category. Instead they are included in personal consumption expenditures on durable goods (line 25) if occupied by the owner and in producers' durable equipment (line 32) if rented.

These estimates differ from the residential construction figures published by the Census Bureau by including brokers' commissions on the sale of structures and net purchases of used structures from government, and by the inclusion of farm residences.

***Change in Business Inventories* (*Line* 34).** Change in business inventories, often referred to as inventory investment, represents the value of the increase or decrease in the physical stock of goods held by the business sector valued in current period prices. These inventories are in three stages of production: raw materials, semifinished goods, and finished goods ready for sale or shipment.

An inventory increase is regarded as investment because it represents production not matched by current consumption; an inventory decrease is regarded as "negative investment" because it reflects consumption in excess of current production.

***Net Exports of Goods and Services* (*Line* 35).** Net exports of goods and services is the balance on goods and services, excluding transfers under military grants, as reported in the U.S. balance-of-payments statistics.

Total exports of goods and services are a part of the gross national product, because they are produced by the nation's economy. At the same time, imports of foreign goods and services are included in the purchases of the various market groups (consumers, governments, business) distinguished in the GNP breakdown. These imports must thus be deducted from the sum of purchases. Adding net exports (exports minus imports) has the same effect on GNP as would the addition of total exports and the subtraction of total imports. When this figure is added to the other categories of purchases (lines 24, 28, and 38), the result is a measure of output attributable to the nation's economy alone.

Exports of Goods and Services (Line 36). Exports of goods, often referred to as merchandise exports, are valued at their f.a.s. (free alongside ship) price. As such, they include all costs incurred up to the point of loading the goods on the vessel at the domestic port.

Exports of services include items such as ocean and air fares paid to U.S. carriers, insurance, profits earned by U.S. business firms operating abroad, and earnings received from other U.S. owned public and private assets located abroad.

The export figure included in the National Income and Product Accounts is identical to the export figure contained in line 1, Table 2, in the U.S. balance of payments. Both figures exclude military grant shipments and reflect balance-of-payments adjustments to the Census Bureau merchandise export figure as shown on page 887.

Imports of Goods and Services (Line 37). Imports of goods are valued at their f.o.b. (free on board) foreign port market price and, as such, exclude United States import duties, ocean freight, and marine insurance.

Import services include items such as military expenditures by U.S. servicemen abroad, travel expenses, ocean freight and marine insurance paid to foreign carriers and firms, and earnings of foreigners on their investments in the United States.

The import figure included in the National Income and Product Accounts is identical to the import figure contained in line 15, Table 2, in the U.S. balance of payments. Both figures reflect balance-of-payments adjustments to the Census Bureau merchandise import figures.

Government Purchases of Goods and Services (Line 38). Government purchases of goods and services are made up of the net expenditures on goods and services by the three levels of government—federal, state, and local—and the gross investment of government enterprises. Among the items included in government purchases of goods and services are: compensation of government employees, construction expenditures on highways, bridges, and schools, and net purchases of equipment, supplies and services from business and abroad.

Government purchases of goods and services are one component of government expenditures, other components are transfer payments to persons, net interest paid, subsidies less current surplus of government enterprises and wage accruals less disbursements.

Federal Government Purchases of Goods and Services (Lines 39, 40, and 41). Federal government purchases of goods and services consist of total federal purchases for national defense (line 40) and other purchases (nondefense) (line 41).

National defense purchases include those for Department of Defense military functions, military assistance to other nations, development and control of atomic energy, and stockpiling of strategic materials. Department of Defense purchases for military functions and foreign military assistance typically account for over 95 percent of the total national defense expenditures.

Nondefense purchases include outlays for space research and technology, the purchase of agricultural commodities under price support programs, and investment of government enterprises such as the Tennessee Valley Authority and the U.S. Postal Service.

***State and Local Government Purchases of Goods and Services* (*Line 42*).** State and local government purchases of goods and services are credited to these levels of government in GNP, regardless of who pays for them. For example, federal grants-in-aid for education are counted as purchases of goods and services when spent by state and local governments.

Although education accounts for the major portion of state and local government purchases, substantial expenditures are also made for roads and highways, hospitals, and other public functions.

***Gross National Product* (*GNP*) (*Line 43*).** Gross national product expresses in dollars the market value of goods and services produced by the nation's economy within a specified period of time. It is almost always estimated for a calendar or fiscal year, or for a quarter of a year expressed at an annual rate.

Raw materials, components, and intermediate products are not counted separately in GNP. However, their value is included in the value of finished goods sold to consumers and governments, in investment goods sold to business, or in inventory accumulation.

GNP is a "gross" measure because no deduction is made to reflect the wearing out of machinery and other capital assets used in production. Net national product (NNP) is estimated by subtracting line 22, Capital consumption allowances from GNP.

GNP is generally considered the most comprehensive single measure of economic activity.

BALANCE OF PAYMENTS ACCOUNTS

The balance of international payments accounts is a statistical record of economic transactions between residents of the United States and residents of the rest of the world. The measurement is in terms of dollars and in terms of fixed time periods during which the transactions take place. The transactions involve:

1. Merchandise—movable goods such as wheat, machines, or automobiles.
2. Services—intangible output that is regarded as being transferred at the instant of performance, such as transportation, insurance, and

by convention, the yields on international investments which are considered as fees for the use of capital.

3. Private and governmental capital including financial claims and ownership of property.
4. Monetary gold, which is a physical commodity, but is treated in the balance of payments in the same manner as a financial asset.

An international transaction may involve the exchange of one asset (commodity, service, or capital) for another, or it may involve a gift of an asset. By recording the offsetting figures for exchange and creating a special category of unilateral transfers as the offset for gifts, the balance of payments is presented as a double-entry record, similar in many ways to ordinary business accounts.

The credit items represent the transfer to nonresidents of real or financial assets or services. The debit items represent the acquisition from nonresidents of these same types of assets or services.

Examples of this classification in practice are as follows:

A U.S. export of merchandise is a credit item, and a U.S. import of merchandise is a debit item.

A service performed by U.S. residents for foreigners (such as the sale of services to foreign travelers in the United States) is a credit item, and a service performed by foreigners for U.S. residents (such as for U.S. residents traveling abroad) is a debit item.

A U.S. unilateral transfer to a foreigner is a debit item matching the credit item of the physical asset, service given, or financial asset.

The acquisition by a U.S. resident of an asset abroad, including property and claims on a foreign person, company, bank, or government is a debit item.

The acquisition of an asset in the United States by foreigners, in contrast, is a credit item.

Repayment of a debt is treated as the reacquisition of the debt instrument. So repayment of debt by a foreigner is a credit item, while U.S. repayment of debt to a foreigner is a debit item.

The process of settlement varies from case to case. For example, a U.S. commodity export, which is a credit, gives rise to an equal claim of the United States on foreigners, which is entered as an associated debit. The means of settling the claim will vary. Possibilities include:

1. An increase in the U.S. holdings of financial assets—liabilities or IOU's of foreigners to U.S. residents. This is the same as an increase in U.S. investment abroad.
2. A decrease in foreign holdings of assets in the United States (for example, payment out of a foreign deposit in a U.S. bank). Since these assets are liabilities of U.S. residents, their decrease is a decrease in foreign investment in the United States.

The use of the double entry principle of bookkeeping means that the total of debits equals the total of credits, if the records are perfect. In this sense, the balance-of-payments data must always balance. The actual collection of statistical data, however, is from a wide variety of sources, and it is necessary to make estimates of some figures. Consequently, debit and credit entries are not exactly offsetting and a balancing item—errors and omissions—is required.

Credits are counted as positive, and debits as negative. If, then, the balancing item required to make the algebraic sum of credits and debits equal to zero is positive, it indicates that total credits have been underestimated, total debits have been overestimated, or some combination of these effects has occurred.

The entries in the quarterly report of the U.S. balance of payments published in the *Survey of Current Business* are shown in Table 3. The terms defined in this chapter are organized in the order of the line numbers in the table.

Relation of Balance of Payments and National Income and Product Accounts

The classifications of the U.S. Balance of Payments Accounts have been made in such a way as to make it possible to integrate their results with the National Income and Product Accounts. In the income and product accounts the four major transacting groups are households, business, government, and the rest of the world. The balance of payments records transactions with the last named sector.

The sum of the purchases of these four groups must equal the national output of goods and services plus imports of goods and services.

Gross National Product, however, is defined as the market value of the output of goods and services produced by labor and property supplied by the nation's residents. Therefore, the GNP figure includes exports of goods and services, but excludes imports of goods and services.

Net foreign investment equals the balance of recorded transactions in goods, services, and unilateral transfers plus allocations of special drawing rights (SDR)—designated in the national income and product accounts as "capital grants received by the United States." This is equal to the acquisition of foreign assets by U.S. residents less the acquisition of U.S. assets by foreign residents plus the balance on unrecorded transactions (errors and omissions).

Balances of Payments

It is not possible to define a single balance which can adequately represent the underlying balance-of-payments position of the United States. It follows that equilibrium in the external position of the United

States cannot be equated with zero in any one of the possible balances, in either the short run or the long run. Rather, it appears that presentation of a spectrum of balances permits a more accurate description of the evolving pressures on the dollar and of developments in the U.S. payments position, and that, for analytical purposes, the trends in the balances are often more significant than their levels.

It might also be noted that a complete analysis of external developments should take into account our investment position as well as balance-of-payment flows. The balance of payments records the flows of goods, services, transfers, and capital during a given period; the investment position gives the net excess of external assets over liabilities at the end of the period, as well as the structure of assets and liabilities by type. Data on the investment position are now available only annually but BEA is developing quarterly data.

Regularly computed balances of payments are as follows (line numbers refer to Table 2):

The *balance on goods and services* measures net exports of goods and services from the United States and is a component of the U.S. Gross National Product (line 11).

The *balance on goods, services, and remittances* also takes into account unilateral transfers other than U.S. government grants (line 13).

The *balance on current account* is the net export of goods and services and all unilateral transfers to foreigners (line 15). In combination with the allocations of SDR (line 31), it measures net foreign investment.

The *balance on current account and long-term capital* is the sum of the current account—net exports of goods and services minus all unilateral transfers to foreigners—plus net flows of private long-term capital and of U.S. and foreign government capital other than changes in U.S. official reserve holdings and foreign official reserve holdings in the United States (line 26).

The *net liquidity balance* is the sum of the balance on current account and long-term capital plus net flows of short-term nonliquid private capital, allocations of SDR, and errors and omissions (line 33), Alternatively, one can focus on the "below the line" items that finance the net liquidity balance. From this perspective, it is measured by net flows of U.S. and foreign private liquid funds plus changes in U.S. reserves and in foreign reserves held in the United States.

The net liquidity balance differs in two ways from the "liquidity balance" used for a number of years. For one thing, an increase in liquid claims (to the extent they are recorded) accompanied by a simultaneous increase in liquid liabilities has no effect on the net liquidity balance but increases the deficit on the liquidity balance. A second difference is that changes in nonliquid liabilities to foreign official agencies distort the liquidity balance but do not distort the net liquidity balance. As a result of these two differences, the net liquidity balance serves the purpose intended better than the liquidity balance.

TABLE 2

U.S. Balance-of-Payments Summary (millions of dollars)

Line	(Credits +; debits −)	Reference lines (table 3)	1971
1	Merchandise trade balance [1]		−2,689
2	Exports	2	42,770
3	Imports	16	−45,459
4	Military transactions, net	3, 17	−2,894
5	Travel and transportation, net	4, 5, 6, 18, 19, 20.	−2,432
6	Investment income, net [2]		7,995
7	U.S. direct investments abroad	10, 11	9,455
8	Other U.S. investments abroad	12, 13	3,443
9	Foreign investments in the United States	24, 25, 26, 27,	−4,903
10	Other services, net	7, 8, 9, 21, 22, 23.	748
11	**Balance on goods and services** [3]		727
12	Remittances, pensions and other transfers	31, 32	−1,529
13	**Balance on goods, services and remittances**		−802
14	U.S. Government grants (excluding military)	30	−2,045
15	**Balance on current account** [4]		−2,847
16	U.S. Government capital flows excluding nonscheduled repayments, net.[5]	34, 35, 36.	−2,117
17	Nonscheduled repayments of U.S. Government assets	37	225
18	U.S. Government nonliquid liabilities to other than foreign official reserve agencies	55	−486
19	Long-term private capital flows, net		−4,149
20	U.S. direct investments abroad	39	−4,765
21	Foreign direct investments in the United States	48	−67
22	Foreign securities	40	−909
23	U.S. securities other than Treasury issues	49	2,282
24	Other, reported by U.S. banks	41, 52	−814
25	Other, reported by U.S. nonbanking concerns	44, 50	124
26	**Balance on current account and long-term capital** [5]		−9,374
27	Nonliquid short-term private capital flows, net		−2,420
28	Claims reported by U.S. banks	42	−1,807
29	Claims reported by U.S. nonbank concerns	45	−555
30	Liabilities reported by U.S. nonbanking concerns	51	−58
31	Allocations of special drawing rights (SDR) [4]	63	717
32	Errors and omissions, net	64	−10,927
33	**Net liquidity balance**		−22,002
34	Liquid private capital flows, net		−7,763
35	Liquid claims		−1,072
36	Reported by U.S. banks	43	−566
37	Reported by U.S. nonbanking concerns	46	−506
38	Liquid liabilities	56	−6,691
39	To foreign commercial banks		−6,908
40	To international and regional organizations		682
41	To other foreigners		−465
42	**Official reserve transactions balance**		−29,765
	Financed by changes in:		
43	Nonliquid liabilities to foreign official reserve agencies reported by U.S. Government	54	341
44	Nonliquid liabilities to foreign official agencies reported by U.S. banks	53	−539
45	Liquid liabilities to foreign official agencies	57	27,615
46	U.S. official reserve assets, net	58	2,348
47	Gold	59	866
48	SDR	60	−249
49	Convertible currencies	61	381
50	Gold tranche position in IMF	62	1,350
	Memoranda:		
51	Transfers under military grant programs (excluded from lines 2, 4, and 14)	14, 28	3,153
52	Reinvested earnings of foreign incorporated affiliates of U.S. firms (excluded from lines 7 and 20)		NA
53	Reinvested earnings of U.S. incorporated affiliates of foreign firms (excluded from lines 9 and 21)		NA
54	Liquidity Balance, excluding allocations of SDR	56, 57, 58, 63	−23,989

1. Adjusted to balance of payments basis; excludes exports under U.S. military agency sales contracts and imports of U.S. military agencies.
2. Includes fees and royalties from U.S. direct investments abroad or from foreign direct investments in the United States.
3. Equal to net exports of goods and services in national income and product accounts of the United States.
4. The sum of lines 15 and 31 is equal to "net foreign investment" in the national income and product accounts of the United States.
5. Includes some short-term U.S. Government assets.

NOTE.—Details may not add to totals because of rounding.

SOURCE:—U.S. Department of Commerce, Bureau of Economic Analysis.

Both the balance on current account and long-term capital and the net liquidity balance attempt to focus on more fundamental, longer term trends in the external position of the United States. Neither is quite successful. Both are affected not only by the limitations of the statistical reporting system and other technical difficulties, but also by the complications resulting from the dollar's role as an international currency.

That role results in considerable ambiguity as to what measure, if any, and what level of the measure would indicate fundamental long-term equilibrium in the external accounts of the United States. For instance, a deficit on the net liquidity balance does not necessarily imply disequilibrium in the external position, for a net buildup in liquid dollar holdings by private foreigners may simply reflect the use of the dollar as an international medium of exchange. Because of the difficulties involved, there was some question as to whether either balance should be calculated. Nevertheless, given the need for indicators of underlying trends, it appears that the two balances in combination, particularly when they move together, are the best available, although neither is of a theoretical or statistical quality sufficient to carry the weight of being the balance of payments, nor is there a presumption that either should be zero.

The net liquidity balance plus net flows of U.S. and foreign private liquid capital sum to the *official reserve transactions balance* (line 42). It is financed by changes in U.S. official reserve assets plus changes in liquid and nonliquid liabilities to foreign official agencies. The balance is intended to indicate the net exchange market pressure, assuming relatively fixed exchange rates, on the dollar during the reporting period resulting from international transactions of the United States. (Exchange market pressure, in this sense, reflects the net influence of all transactions "above the line" in the calculation of the official reserve transactions balance.) Of course, foreign central banks themselves may wish to increase or decrease their dollar holdings, and to that extent a deficit or surplus does not necessarily indicate disequilibrium in the U.S. position.

It should be noted, however, that certain types of transactions between foreigners in the Euro-dollar market can have the effect of increasing dollar liabilities. Thus, the dollar could have come under pressure in the exchange market even though transactions of U.S. residents with foreigners and the official reserve transactions balance were in equilibrium.

Major international transactions and the balances are presented in Table 2 which is arranged so that each balance is the sum of the items above it.

Explanatory Notes for Table 3

These notes are intended to provide a brief explanation of the content and sources of data for each account shown in Table 3. These descriptions are not comprehensive nor are they intended to take the place of a precise methodology of the balance-of-payments compilations.

***Exports of Goods and Services—Merchandise, Adjusted, Excluding Military* (*Line* 2).** This account measures, in concept, all movable goods which are sold, given away, or otherwise transferred from United States

TABLE 3

U.S. International Transactions (millions of dollars)

Line	(Credits +, debits —)[1]	1971
1	**Exports of goods and services** [2]	66,133
2	Merchandise, adjusted, excluding military [3]	42,770
3	Transfers under U.S. military agency sales contracts	1,922
4	Travel	2,457
5	Passenger fares	615
6	Other transportation	3,093
7	Fees and royalties from unaffiliated foreigners	621
8	Other private services	1,353
9	U.S. Government miscellaneous services	404
	Receipts for income on U.S. investments abroad:	
10	Direct investment fees and royalties	2,169
11	Direct investment interest, dividends and branch earnings [4]	7,286
12	Other private assets	2,556
13	U.S. Government assets	887
14	**Transfers of goods and services under U.S. military grant programs, net**	3,153
15	**Imports of goods and services**	−65,406
16	Merchandise, adjusted, excluding military [3]	−45,459
17	Direct defense expenditures	−4,816
18	Travel	−4,294
19	Passenger fares	−1,264
20	Other transportation	−3,039
21	Fees and royalties to unaffiliated foreigners	−126
22	Private payments for other services	−743
23	U.S. Government payments for miscellaneous services	−761
	Payments of income on foreign investments in the United States:	
24	Direct investment fees and royalties	−94
25	Direct investment interest, dividends and branch earnings [4]	−621
26	Other private liabilities	−2,344
27	U.S. Government liabilities	−1,844
28	**U.S. military grants of goods and services, net**	−3,153
29	**Unilateral transfers (excluding military grants), net**	−3,574
30	U.S. Government grants (excluding military)	−2,045
31	U.S. Government pensions and other transfers	−541
32	Private remittances and other transfers	−988
33	**U.S. Government capital flows, net**	−1,892
34	Loans and other long-term assets	−4,178
35	Foreign currencies and other short-term assets, net	182
	Repayments on credits:	
36	Scheduled	1,879
37	Nonscheduled [5]	225
38	**U.S. private capital flows, net**	−9,781
39	Direct investments abroad [4]	−4,765
40	Foreign securities	−909
	Claims reported by U.S. banks:	
41	Long-term	−565
42	Short-term, nonliquid	−1,807
43	Short-term, liquid	−566
	Claims reported by U.S. nonbanking concerns:	
44	Long-term	−109
45	Short-term, nonliquid	−555
46	Short-term, liquid	−506
47	**Foreign capital flows, net**	22,381
48	Direct investment in the United States [4]	−67
49	U.S. securities other than Treasury issues	2,282
	Other U.S. nonliquid liabilities to private foreigners:	
50	Long-term, reported by U.S. nonbanking concerns	233
51	Short-term reported by U.S. nonbanking concerns	−58
52	Long-term, reported by U.S. banks	−249
53	Long-term liabilities to foreign official agencies reported by U.S. banks	−539
	Nonliquid liabilities reported by U.S. Government:	
54	To foreign official reserve agencies	341
55	To other official and private foreigners	−486
	U.S. liquid liabilities:	
56	To private foreigners	−6,691
57	To foreign official agencies	27,615
58	**Transactions in U.S. official reserve assets, net**	2,348
59	Gold	866
60	SDR	−249
61	Convertible currencies	381
62	Gold tranche position in IMF	1,350
63	**Allocations of special drawing rights (SDR)**	717
64	**Errors and omissions, net**	−10,927

1. Credits, +: Exports of goods and services; unilateral transfers to the United States; capital inflows (increase in U.S. liabilities or decrease in U.S. assets); decrease in U.S. official reserve assets.

Debits, — : Imports of goods and services; unilateral transfers to foreigners; capital outflows (decrease in U.S. liabilities or increase in U.S. assets); increase in U.S. official reserve assets.

2. Excludes transfers of goods and services under U.S. military grant programs.

3. Excludes exports of goods under U.S. military agency sales contracts identified in Census export documents, and imports of goods included under direct defense expenditures identified in Census import documents, and reflects various other balance-of-payments adjustments (for valuation, coverage, and timing) to Census statistics.

4. Excludes reinvested earnings of foreign incorporated affiliates of U.S. firms or of U.S. incorporated affiliates of foreign firms.

5. Includes sales of foreign obligations to foreigners.

NOTE.—Details may not add to total because of rounding.

SOURCE: U.S. Department of Commerce, Bureau of Economic Analysis.

to foreign ownership, except (1) transfers of goods under U.S. military grant programs (part of line 14), (2) transfers of goods under U.S. military agency sales contracts (part of line 3) whether physically exported from the United States or sold from U.S. installations abroad, and (3) transfers of goods by U.S. nonmilitary agencies from U.S. installations abroad (part of line 9).

In practice, reliance on Census Bureau trade statistics, which are based on the physical movement of goods into and out of the United States rather than change of ownership, and which in various other aspects are not oriented to balance-of-payments concepts, leads to some additional departures from the conceptual definition stated above. Census Bureau export statistics are, in general, valued f.a.s. (free alongside ship) U.S. port of exit, and reflect selling price, f.o.b. (free on board) interior point of shipment—or cost if not sold—plus packaging costs, inland freight, and insurance to place of export. Various adjustments to the Census statistics are made for timing coverage, and valuation in order to bring them into closer conformity with balance-of-payments concepts.

Transfers Under U.S. Military Agency Sales Contracts (Line 3). This account measures delivery of goods and transfer of services by military agencies to foreign governments under sales contracts. Delivery of goods refers to transfer of goods either from the United States or from U.S. installations abroad to foreign governments. Also included, of relatively smaller magnitudes, are sales of excess property of military installations abroad, and logistical support provided to U.S. allies and to United Nations emergency forces in various areas. Excluded, however, is military equipment sold directly to foreigners by U.S. private firms. Estimates are based primarily on Department of Defense reports.

Travel (Line 4). This account measures expenditures in the United States by foreign travelers (excluding foreign government personnel and their dependents and foreign citizens residing in the United States) for lodging, food, transportation within the United States, entertainment, personal purchases, gifts, and other outlays incidental to a trip to the United States. Transocean passenger fares are excluded. Included are passenger fares received by U.S. carriers from Canadian and Mexican travelers visiting the United States. Travel receipts from each major area of the world are estimated by multiplying the average expenditures per traveler, derived from sample surveys of BEA, by the corresponding number of travelers, derived from statistics of U.S. Immigration and Naturalization Service.

Passenger Fares (Line 5). This account measures passenger fares received by U.S. ocean and air carriers from foreign residents traveling between the United States and foreign countries and between two foreign points. Excluded are passenger fares for travel between the United States and Canada, and between the United States and Mexico (part of line 4). For each major area of the world, an estimate is made by multiplying the average round-trip fare derived from travel questionnaires, by the corresponding number of travelers derived from data provided by the U.S. Immigration and Naturalization Service.

***Other Transportation* (*Line 6*).** This account measures the following: freight revenues of U.S.-operated ocean, air, and other carriers (including rail, pipeline, and Great Lakes shipping) for the international transportation of U.S. exports; freight revenues of U.S.-operated carriers for the transportation of foreign freight from one foreign point to another foreign point; port expenditure receipts, representing payments for goods and services purchased in the United States by foreign operators and transportation companies; and receipts of U.S. owners from foreign operators for the charter of vessels and the rental of freight cars. For the major components—freight revenues and port expenditure receipts—value estimates are made by multiplying the average rates, based on reports from a limited number of shipping companies and airlines to BEA, by the corresponding tonnage data, derived essentially from statistics of the Census Bureau. For the other components, estimates are based on reports to BEA and on various other sources of information.

***Fees and Royalties from Unaffiliated Foreigners* (*Line 7*).** This account measures U.S. receipts from foreign residents not affiliated with the U.S. organizations to whom payment is made for the use of intangible property or rights (patents, techniques, processes, formulas, designs, trademarks, copyrights, franchises, manufacturing rights, etc.). Estimates are made on the basis of data obtained from BEA questionnaires circularized among U.S. individuals and firms directly involved in such transactions.

***Other Private Services* (*Line 8*).** This account measures all receipts by U.S. private residents from foreign residents who are not affiliated with the U.S. recipient and from foreign governments and international organizations, for various miscellaneous services rendered domestically or abroad. Such services include international reinsurance operations of U.S. insurance companies; international cable, radio, and telephone operations provided by U.S. communications companies; and foreign contract operations of U.S. construction, engineering, consulting and other technical services firms. Also included in this account are expenditures for services in the United States by foreign embassies, consulates, and registered agents of foreign governments; administrative expenditures by international organizations such as the International Monetary Fund (IMF), World Bank, United Nations, etc.; and various other minor service receipts. Estimates are based on reports filed with BEA by U.S. individuals and firms, statistics provided by U.S. and foreign government agencies, and other information obtained from various publications of foreign governments and international organizations.

***U.S. Government Miscellaneous Services* (*Line 9*).** This account measures receipts of the nonmilitary agencies of the U.S. government for services provided to foreigners and for deliveries of goods to foreigners from U.S. installations abroad. Also included are administrative expenses of AID in the United States and abroad, and similar expenses of other assistance programs. Estimates are based primarily on reports submitted by nonmilitary agencies of the U.S. government.

***Direct Investment Fees and Royalties* (*Line 10*).** This account measures receipts by U.S. parent organizations from their foreign affiliates of fees and royalties (after withheld foreign taxes, if any) for the use of intangible property or rights (patents, techniques, trademarks, copyrights, manufacturing rights, etc.), for rentals of tangible property, motion picture films and TV tapes, and for the use of professional, administrative and management services. Receipts include not only actual transfers but also other amounts due in the reporting period that are not actually transferred. In the latter instances, the amounts are offset by contra-entries in line 39. Data are collected regularly by the BEA from over 1,100 respondents with more than 13,000 foreign affiliates. The data are used to derive estimates for total receipts on the basis of the relation of the reporting sample to benchmark data (based on periodic surveys of U.S. direct investments abroad), with adjustments made for new investments and liquidations. (See line 39 for definition of direct investments.)

***Direct Investment Interest, Dividends, and Branch Earnings* (*Line 11*).** This account measures receipt by U.S. parent organizations from their foreign affiliates of interest and dividends (after withheld foreign taxes, if any) and branch earnings (after foreign income taxes). Receipts include not only actual transfers but also other amounts due in reporting period that are not actually transferred. In the latter instances, the amounts are offset by contra-entries in line 39. Sources of data and estimating procedures are the same as for line 10. (See line 39 for definition of direct investments.)

***Income Receipts on Other U.S. Private Assets Abroad* (*Line 12*).** This account measures (1) interest received by U.S. residents on their holdings of foreign debt securities, short- and long-term bank and commercial loans, deposits and other claims, and (2) dividends received by U.S. residents on their holdings of foreign equities. Excluded are income receipts from U.S. direct investments abroad. Estimates are based on applicable U.S. money market rates and foreign dividend yields applied to amounts outstanding in the appropriate period, with lags when relevant.

***Income Receipts on U.S. Government Assets Abroad* (*Line 13*).** This account measures primarily interest realized on the long- and short-term credits outstanding to the U.S. government from the rest of the world. Also included are interest earned on U.S. government disbursing officers' deposits in commercial banks abroad; interest received on the holdings of official reserve assets by U.S. monetary authorities; interest on advances under other Exchange Stabilization Fund agreements; collections of commitment fees for foreign loans extended by U.S. government agencies; service charges and other earnings from the U.S. investment in the International Monetary Fund; and net income of U.S. monetary authorities from day-to-day transactions in foreign currency exchanges. Excluded are gains or losses on official reserve assets when they result from formal exchange rate revaluation and all gains or losses on foreign currency balances held by disbursing officers.

With the exception of capitalized interest, receipts are based on data reported by the government operating agencies on a collection basis (in both U.S. dollars and foreign currencies).

Net Transfers of Goods and Services Under U.S. Military Grant Programs (Line 14). This account measures net transfers of goods delivered and services rendered by U.S. military services to foreign countries under legislation enacted by the Congress authorizing provision of military assistance for which no repayment is expected or for which repayment terms are indeterminate.

Gross transfers include goods and services purchased from dollar funds appropriated, or foreign currencies owned, by the U.S. government whose use has been authorized by legislation (valued on the basis of the U.S. government financial records reflecting the expenditure of authorized funds); and transfers of goods under authorizations to deliver to foreign nations equipment and material, deemed excess to U.S. requirements (valued according to the legislative authorization under which the transfer is made).

Transactions netted against the gross transfers—reverse grants—include returns of equipment previously transferred; supplies and services provided the U.S. government as part of a mutual assistance program (such as reverse lend-lease); and foreign currency funds provided by foreign nations as offsets for U.S. local expenditures under international agreements to provide U.S. foreign assistance.

This account excludes military goods and services provided on credit with established repayment terms. For transactions which occurred prior to July 1964, the estimates were made by BEA on the basis of information furnished for this purpose by the operating agencies, supplemented by other government records; subsequent estimates are based upon incomplete reports from the operating agencies.

An identical offsetting entry is made in line 28.

Imports of Goods and Services—Merchandise, Adjusted, Excluding Military (Line 16). This account measures, in concept, all movable goods which are sold, given away, or otherwise transferred from foreign to U.S. ownership, except (1) goods purchased abroad by U.S. government defense agencies, whether used or stockpiled abroad or physically imported into the United States directly by such agencies (part of line

17) and (2) goods purchased abroad by other U.S. government agencies, whether used or stockpiled abroad (part of line 23).

In practice, reliance on Census Bureau trade statistics, which are based on the physical movement of goods into and out of the United States rather than change of ownership, and which in various other aspects are not oriented to ideal balance-of-payments concepts, leads to some additional departures from the conceptual definition stated above. Census Bureau import statistics are, in general, valued at the wholesale market price, f.o.b. foreign country of export. This valuation, which is required under U.S. customs legislation, excludes U.S. import duties and freight and insurance charges from the foreign country to the U.S. port of entry. The use of f.o.b. foreign country as the basis for import valuation is in accord with balance-of-payments concepts. However, the Customs requirement for a general "market value at which the goods are freely offered for sale" may not necessarily coincide with the actual purchase-sale contract price, f.o.b. foreign country, agreed to between buyer and seller—the transactions value. In such cases, a valuation adjustment is made to accord with the transactions value, if appropriate information is available. Adjustments for timing and coverage are also made to Census import statistics to bring them into closer conformity with balance-of-payments requirements.

***Direct Defense Expenditures* (*Line 17*).** This account measures direct defense expenditures for foreign goods and services by U.S. government military agencies and similar defense transactions of the Atomic Energy Commission and the Coast Guard which meet the NATO definition of defense expenditures. Also included are the personal expenditures of U.S. military and civilian personnel and their dependents abroad, together with the foreign purchases of the military exchanges and similar agencies which sell to personnel (e.g., post exchanges, commissaries). Other disbursements include foreign expenditures of U.S. contractors employed to construct and operate U.S. foreign military installations and to furnish other services abroad, expenditures for NATO infrastructure, the offshore procurement of military equipment to be transferred as aid to foreign countries, contributions to international military headquarters expenses, and other outlays abroad for administration of military assistance programs. Excluded are foreign products purchased in the United States by U.S. military agencies. Estimates are based primarily on Department of Defense reports.

***Travel* (*Line 18*).** This account measures expenditures in foreign countries by U.S. travelers (excluding U.S. government personnel and their dependents and U.S. citizens residing abroad) for lodging, food, transportation within foreign areas, entertainment, personal purchases, gifts, and other outlays incidental to a trip abroad. Transocean passenger fares are excluded. Included are passenger fares paid to Canadian and Mexican carriers by U.S. residents visiting Canada and Mexico. Travel payments to each major area of the world are estimated by multiplying the average expenditure per traveler derived from sample surveys of BEA, by the corresponding number of travelers derived from statistics of U.S. Immigration and Naturalization Service.

***Passenger Fares* (*Line 19*).** This account measures passenger fares paid to foreign ocean and air carriers by U.S. residents for transocean transportation. Excluded are passenger fares for travel between the United States and Canada, and between the United States and Mexico (part of line 18). For each major area of the world, an estimate is made by multiplying the average roundtrip fare derived from travel questionnaires, by the corresponding number of travelers derived from data provided by the U.S. Immigration and Naturalization Service. The estimate for total passenger fares is the sum of estimates for all areas. Additional adjustments for inter-airline transfers are made on the basis of official reports of U.S. international air carriers.

***Other Transportation* (*Line 20*).** This account measures the following: freight payments to foreign-operated ocean, air and other carriers (including rail and Great Lakes shipping) for the international transportation of U.S. imports; port expenditure payments representing purchases of goods and services in foreign countries by U.S. operators and transportation companies; and payments made to foreign owners by U.S. operators for the charter of vessels and the rental of freight cars. For the major components—freight and port expenditure payments—value estimates are made by multiplying the average rates based on reports of shipping companies and airlines to BEA, by the corresponding tonnage data derived essentially from statistics of the Census Bureau. For the other components, estimates are made on the basis of reports to BEA and various other sources of information.

***Fees and Royalties to unaffiliated Foreigners* (*Line 21*).** This account measures payments by U.S. residents to foreign residents not affiliated with the U.S. payer for the use of intangible property or rights (patents, techniques, processes, formulas, designs, trademarks, copyrights, franchises, manufacturing rights, etc.). Estimates are made on the basis of data obtained from BEA questionnaires circularized among U.S. individuals and firms directly involved in such transactions.

***Private Payments for Other Services* (*Line 22*).** This account measures payments by U.S. private residents to foreign residents not affiliated with the U.S. payer and to foreign governments for various miscellaneous services rendered domestically or abroad. Such outlays include payments of international reinsurance operations of U.S. insurance companies; net payments for direct writing of insurance abroad; payments of U.S. communication companies for foreign cable, radio, and telephone operations; net earnings of Canadian commuters employed in the United States; payments of consular fees for export privileges; and various other minor service payments. Estimates are based on reports filed with BEA by U.S. individuals and firms, statistics provided by foreign government agencies, and other information obtained from various domestic publications.

U.S. Government Payments for Miscellaneous Services (Line 23). This account measures expenditures of the nonmilitary agencies of the U.S. government for foreign services and for foreign goods which are purchased abroad and used or stockpiled abroad. Also included are net payments by such nonmilitary agencies to U.S. nationals employed abroad and their dependents and payments to international organizations for membership assessments. Estimates are based primarily on reports submitted by nonmilitary agencies of the U.S. government.

Direct Investment Fees and Royalties (Line 24). This account measures payments by U.S. companies to their foreign parent organizations of fees and royalties (after withheld taxes) for the use of intangible property or rights (patents, techniques, trademarks, copyrights, manufacturing rights, etc.) and for professional, administrative and management services. Payments include not only actual transfers but also other amounts due in the reporting period that are not actually transferred. In the latter instances, the amounts are offset by contra-entries in line 48. Data are based on quarterly reports filed by approximately 350 U.S. companies with BEA. (See line 48 for definition of direct investments.)

Direct Investment Interest, Dividends, and Branch Earnings (Line 25). This account measures payments by U.S. companies to their foreign parent organizations of interest and dividends (after withheld taxes) and branch earnings (after income taxes). Payments include not only actual transfers but also other amounts due in the reporting period that are not actually transferred. In the latter instances, the amounts are offset by contra-entries in line 48. Data are collected by BEA from approximately 350 U.S. companies. The data are used to derive estimates for total payments on the basis of the relation of the reporting sample to benchmark data (based on the 1959 survey of foreign direct investments in the United States), with adjustments made for new investments and liquidations. (See line 48 for definition of direct investments.)

Income Payments on Other Private Liabilities (Line 26). This account measures (1) interest paid by U.S. residents to foreign holders of U.S. debt obligations and to foreign owners of U.S. bank deposits, and (2) dividends paid by U.S. residents to foreign holders of U.S. equities.

Excluded are income payments on foreign direct investments in the United States (recorded in line 25). Estimates are based on applicable Euro-dollar rates, U.S. money market rates, and U.S. dividend yields applied to amounts outstanding in the appropriate period, with lags when relevant.

***Income Payments on U.S. Government Liabilities* (*Line 27*).** This account measures (1) interest paid to foreign residents on their holdings of U.S. government securities, based on applicable rates, (2) interest paid to foreign official agencies on advance payments for military equipment and on other special deposits with the Treasury Department, (3) interest paid on Export-Import Bank participations, and (4) IMF service charges.

***U.S. Military Grants of Goods and Services, Net* (*Line 28*).** This account measures transfers by U.S. military services to foreign countries under legislation enacted by the Congress authorizing provision of foreign military assistance for which no repayment is expected or for which repayment terms are indeterminate. Excluded are transfers of cash and of nonmilitary items, even when under military aid legislation, and military assistance provided on established credit repayment terms.

An identical offsetting entry is made in line 14. (For details of gross transfers, transactions netted against gross transfers, and the basis of BEA estimates, see note for line 14.)

***Unilateral Transfers* (*Excluding Military Grants*), *Net—U.S. Government Grants* (*Excluding Military*) (*Line 30*).** This account measures utilization of U.S. government financing to transfer resources to foreign governments or other foreign entities under legislation enacted by the Congress for the provision of foreign assistance—other than the goods and services included as military grants in line 28—for which no repayment is expected or for which repayment terms are indeterminate.

Gross transfers represent the dollar equivalent of goods delivered and services rendered by the U.S. government and disbursements by the U.S. government to or for the account of a foreign government or other foreign entity (including payments into acounts from which use may be restricted by agreements). Some of these transactions are financed with dollar funds established, or foreign currencies owned, by the U.S. government, whose use has been authorized by legislation and whose value is based on U.S. government financial records reflecting the expenditure of authorized funds. Other transfers of goods, under authorizations to deliver agricultural commodities to foreign nations, are valued on the basis of the export offering price for such commodities at the time of delivery.

Netted against the gross transfers are reverse grants. These include cash settlements for previously provided grants; foreign currency funds provided by foreign nations as offsets for U.S. local expenditures under international agreements to provide U.S. foreign assistance; supplies, services, and foreign currencies provided the U.S. government as part of a mutual assistance program (such as reverse lend-lease); and returns of equipment previously transferred.

Data are compiled from reports furnished by the operating agencies for inclusion in this table, and from published statements and financial and operating records of government agencies. Prior to the availability of reports from operating agencies, estimates are made by BEA.

U.S. Government Pensions and Other Transfers (Line 31). This account measures (1) payments of annuities and other benefits, to Americans residing abroad or to foreigners entitled to such payments, under social security and allied programs; (2) similar payments under retirement and compensation programs for former government employees, military personnel, and veterans, including costs of providing medical services abroad under Veterans Administration programs; (3) payments abroad under U.S. educational and cultural exchange programs, primarily administered by the Department of State; (4) payments of grants supporting individual and institutional research abroad; and (5) payments and receipts of indemnity claims and of claims settled by intergovernmental agreements, including collections of funds for distribution to private claimants as a result of nationalization of property by foreign governments (when such claims involve receipts in installments over a period of years, the collections are not included in this entry but are recorded in line 36).

Data are reported by U.S. government operating agencies based upon their financial records, generally of checks issued and collections made.

Private Remittances and Other Transfers (Line 32). This account measures net private unilateral transfers of goods, services, cash and other financial claims between U.S. residents and residents or governments of foreign countries. Receipts include transfers to U.S. private residents through postal service money orders; German government indemnification payments; Canadian government pension payments, inheritance and migrants transfers; and various other inflows. Payments include personal remittances of U.S. private residents to foreign residents through banks, communication companies, and the U.S. Postal Service; private parcel post shipments; cash and goods donated abroad by religious, charitable, educational, scientific, and similar nonprofit organizations; and inheritance and migrants transfers. Estimates are made on the basis of data received directly from U.S. banks, nonprofit organizations and other private agencies, from U.S. and foreign government agencies, and on the basis of other statistics obtained from various publications of foreign governments.

U.S. Government Capital Flows, Net—Loans and Other Long-Term Assets (Line 34). This account measures utilization of U.S. government financing to transfer resources under legislation enacted by the Congress for the provision of foreign assistance, or for credits to foreign governments or foreign entities, under agreements which give rise to specific obligations to repay, over a period of years, usually with interest. U.S. government loans to U.S. private entities specifically for projects abroad are included as foreign credits, identified with the country in which the project is located.

Transfers of resources include cash transfers from, or goods and services purchased with, dollar funds established, or foreign currencies owned, by the U.S. government whose use has been authorized by legislation. Such transfers are valued on the basis of the agreed obligation assumed by the debtor under the contractual agreement for repayments. Also included are capital investments in, or contributions to, the international financial institutions; capital flows abroad reflecting the government's direct investment in productive facilities and installations; and equity holdings of "public enterprise" accounts of government agencies.

Data are compiled from reports furnished by the operating agencies for inclusion in this table, and from published statements and financial and operating records of government agencies. Prior to the availability of their records, estimates are made by BEA, particularly for preliminary data. Adjustments are also made to report transactions at time of occurrence, rather than at time of record on books of the operating agencies.

***Foreign Currencies and Other Short-Term Assets** (**Line 35**).* This account measures, in significant part, the financing of exports of U.S. farm products in exchange for foreign currencies under the Agricultural Trade Development and Assistance Act (Public Law 83–480) *less* the government's disbursements of the currencies as grants, credits, or for purchases. Also included are changes in U.S. government deposits abroad from acquisition of foreign currency collected as interest, principal, or reverse grants; accounts receivable of government agencies that report their current transactions on an accrual basis; foreign currencies held by U.S. disbursing officers; and advances of the Exchange Stabilization Fund that are not part of reserve assets.

Excluded are changes in official reserve assets held by U.S. monetary authorites and discernible gains or losses on foreign currency balances. Data sources are the same as for line 34.

***Scheduled Repayments on Credits** (**Line 36**).* This account measures collections of principal on the loans and other credits recorded in line 34 Also included are principal collections in liquidation of outstanding indebtedness formalized by intergovernmental agreement in settlement of assistance originally furnished under indeterminate terms and reported in line 30 and in settlement of claims of the U.S. government or its nationals, when funds are collected by the government for distribution to the claimants; collections on World War I debts; and recoveries of the government's direct investment in productive facilities and installations abroad or on the equity holding of "public enterprise" accounts of government agencies.

Excluded from this account are principal charged off as uncollectible; gains or losses on indebtedness denominated in foreign currency; sales of Export-Import Bank Portfolio Participation Certificates; and extraordinary amortizations that are included in line 37.

Data sources are the same as for line 34.

***Nonscheduled Repayments on Credits* (*Line 37*).** This account measures extraordinary amortizations, which include principal collections identified as occurring more than three months ahead of amortization schedule date stipulated in the repayment agreement and sales of the promissory note (or other evidences of indebtedness) to a third-party foreign participant, either in the country of the borrower or in a third country. Sales are recorded at the book value of the indebtedness liquidated. In many instances, Export-Import Bank has the contingent liability to repurchase such obligations previously sold. Beginning with 1967, collections from promissory notes sold to third countries are recorded in the geographical area of the third country; for earlier periods, such collections are recorded in the geographical area of the debtor.

Excluded from this account are accelerated collections of foreign currency on credits repayable in foreign currency and sales of Export-Import Bank Portfolio Participation Certificates.

Data sources are the same as for line 34.

***U.S. Private Capital Flows, Net–Direct Investments Abroad* (*Line 39*).** This account measures capital transactions by U.S. residents with foreign enterprises in which the U.S. residents by themselves or in affiliation with other U.S. residents own 10 percent or more of the voting securities or of other ownership interests. The account also includes transactions of single or affiliated U.S. residents with foreign residents as the result of the acquisition of at least 10 percent or any additional ownership interest in foreign enterprises or the sale, total or partial, of a direct investment enterprise to a foreigner.

Included in capital transactions are net increases in capital stocks (voting and nonvoting) and capital contributions, in intercompany accounts, and in owners' home office account of foreign branches; excluded is the U.S. parents' share of the reinvested earnings of foreign incorporated affiliates. Funds used for U.S. direct investments abroad include, in addition to those originating in the United States from U.S. parents and their domestic subsidiaries, (1) funds utilized for direct investments that are borrowed abroad by U.S. parents and their domestic subsidiaries, (2) funds utilized for direct investment that are obtained from security issues sold abroad by Netherlands Antilles finance subsidiaries that are initially transferred to U.S. parents, and also (3) funds obtained through long-term debt issues placed by foreign affiliates with public and nonbanking institutional investors in the United States.

Data are based on reports (covering approximately 13,000 foreign affiliates) filed quarterly with BEA by over 1,100 U.S. respondents whose aggregate foreign direct investment (net worth and intercompany account) is $2 million or more. To these data are added verified transactions of nonreporters.

***Foreign Securities* (*Line 40*).** This account measures net transactions (sales less purchases) between U.S. private residents and foreign residents in foreign equities and debt securities with no contractual maturity or with maturities of more than one year (net U.S. purchases are debit entries). Data for foreign securities are based on reports collected by the Federal Reserve System for the Treasury Department, with adjustments made for transactions that are included in other balance-of-payments accounts. On the basis of public market information and other data, BEA prepares estimates for two components of the total, sales of new foreign issues in the U.S. market to U.S. residents and redemptions of U.S. holdings of foreign securities.

Long-Term Claims Reported by U.S. Banks (Line 41). This account measures changes in loans and other long-term claims on foreigners (with a contractual maturity of more than one year) which are reported by U.S. banks, including both the claims of the banks themselves and the claims held in custody for their domestic customers. Unutilized lines of credit and permanent capital invested abroad are excluded. The data are collected monthly by the Federal Reserve System for the Treasury Department.

Short-Term Nonliquid Claims Reported by U.S. Banks (Line 42). This account measures changes in noliquid claims on foreigners (with a contractual maturity of one year or less) which are reported by U.S. banks, including both the claims of the banks themselves and the claims held in custody for their domestic customers. The data are collected monthly by the Federal Reserve System for the Treasury Department. The following categories on the monthly reporting form for short-term claims are considered to be nonliquid: loans, collections outstanding (items in process of collection from foreigners), and acceptance credits (acceptances made for account of foreigners), all payable in dollars; plus short-term claims other than deposits, foreign government obligations, and commercial and finance paper, payable in foreign currencies.

Short-Term Liquid Claims Reported by U.S. Banks (Line 43). This account measures changes in liquid claims on foreigners (with a contractual maturity of one year or less), which are reported by U.S. banks, including both the claims of the banks themselves and the claims held in custody for their domestic customers. The data are collected monthly by the Federal Reserve System for the Treasury Department. The following categories on the monthly reporting form for short-term claims are considered to be liquid: deposits, foreign government obligations, and commercial and finance paper, all payable in foreign currencies; plus short-term claims other than loans, collections outstanding, and acceptance credits, payable in dollars.

Long-Term Claims Reported by U.S. Nonbanking Concerns (Line 44). This account measures changes in loans and other long-term claims of U.S. nonbanking concerns on foreigners other than their foreign affiliates, which have a contractual maturity of more than one year. Such claims originate from long-term supplier's credits and other loans extended to foreigners. Data are obtained from quarterly reports collected by the Federal Reserve System for the Treasury Department on amounts outstanding at the end of the quarter.

Short-Term Nonliquid Claims Reported by U.S. Nonbanking Concerns (Line 45). This account measures changes in claims of U.S. nonbanking concerns on foreigners (other than claims on their foreign affiliates) that have a contractual maturity of one year or less from the date on which the obligation was incurred but are not repayable on demand nor readily marketable or transferable. Such claims include credits extended to foreigners by U.S. brokers to finance security transactions, and by U.S. corporations or other nonbanking concerns to finance exports and other transactions. Data are obtained from quarterly reports collected by the Federal Reserve System for the Treasury Department on amounts outstanding at the end of the quarter.

Short-Term Liquid Claims Reported by U.S. Nonbanking Concerns (Line 46). This account measures changes in short-term liquid claims mainly of major U.S. corporations on foreigners other than their foreign affiliates. Short-term liquid claims, denominated in dollars and in foreign currencies, consist of (1) demand and time deposits held abroad, and (2) negotiable and other readily transferable foreign obligations payable on demand or having a contractual maturity of not more than one year from the date on which the obligation was incurred by the foreigner, including obligations of foreign governments. Loans which are repayable on demand are also included. Data are obtained from reports collected by the Federal Reserve System for the Treasury Department on amounts outstanding at the end of the period.

Foreign Capital Flows, Net–Direct Investments in the United States (Line 48). This account measures capital transactions of U.S. enterprises with foreign owners who control 25 percent or more of the voting securities or other ownership interests. The account also includes transactions of single or affiliated foreign residents with U.S. residents resulting from the acquisition of at least 25 percent ownership interest in U.S. enterprises or from total or partial sales. Included are net increases in capital stock (voting and nonvoting) and capital contributions, in intercompany accounts, and in owners' home office accounts of U.S. branches; excluded is the foreign parents' share of the reinvested earnings of their U.S. corporate affiliates.

Data are based on reports (covering approximately 350 U.S. affiliates) filed by U.S. companies in which the aggregate investment (net worth and intercompany account) by the foreign owner is $2 million or more. To these data are added verified transactions of nonreporters.

U.S. Securities Other Than Treasury Issues (Line 49). This account measures net transactions (purchases less sales) between U.S. and foreign residents in U.S. equities and debt securities with no contractual maturity or with maturities of more than one year. Estimates for transactions are based on data collected by the Treasury Department, with adjustments made for transactions included in other balance-of-payments accounts. Major components are (1) U.S. corporate placements of debt securities in foreign markets, including proceeds transferred to U.S. parents from similar placements by their Netherland Antilles finance subsidiaries (estimated on the basis of BEA reports and other information); and (2) foreign net trading in U.S. equities and other long-term debt securities issued by corporations and local governments, and in nonguaranteed U.S. government agency securities.

U.S. Long-Term Nonliquid Liabilities to Private Foreigners Reported by U.S. Nonbanking Concerns (Line 50). This account measures changes in liabilities of U.S. nonbanking concerns to foreigners (excluding liabilities to affiliated foreigners recorded as direct investments) that have a contractual maturity of more than one year after the date on which the obligation was incurred. Included are direct borrowing from foreign banks by U.S. companies and other loans and advances, whether payable in dollars or in foreign currencies. Estimates, based on reports collected by the Federal Reserve System for the Treasury Department, represent the change in amounts outstanding between the beginning and end of the period. Adjustments to Treasury Department data are made when necessary to account for proceeds of foreign long-term bank loans obtained by U.S. parent companies through their Netherland Antilles finance subsidiaries as reported to BEA.

U.S. Short-Term Nonliquid Liabilities to Private Foreigners Reported by U.S. Nonbanking Concerns (Line 51). This account measures changes in liabilities of U.S. nonbanking concerns to foreigners—other than liabilities to affiliated foreigners recorded as direct investments—that become payable one year or less from the date the obligation was incurred. Such liabilities, payable in dollars or in foreign currencies, are (1) direct borrowing from foreign banks by U.S. companies; (2) accounts, notes, bills, and drafts payable to foreigners; and (3) advance payments received from foreigners for future delivery of goods or services even if such transactions are not completed until after one year. Estimates, based on reports collected by the Federal Reserve System for the Treasury Department, represent the change in amounts outstanding between the beginning and end of the period. Adjustments are made when necessary to account for proceeds of foreign short-term bank loans obtained by U.S. parent companies through their Netherland Antilles finance subsidiaries as reported to BEA.

U.S. Long-Term Liabilities to Private Foreigners Reported by U.S. Banks (Line 52). This account measures changes in obligations to private foreigners reported by U.S. banks, for their own account and for others' accounts under their custody, with a contractual maturity of more than one year. Private foreigners include official international and regional organizations other than the International Monetary Fund (even if located in the United States), foreign branches of U.S. banks, other foreign commercial banks, and other private residents. The data are collected monthly by the Federal Reserve System for the Treasury Department.

Long-Term Liabilities to Foreign Official Agencies Reported by U.S. Banks (Line 53). This account measures changes in obligations to foreign official agencies of reporting U.S. banks, for their own account and for others' accounts under their custody, with a contractual maturity of more than one year. Foreign official agencies include, in addition to reserve agencies (treasuries or finance ministries of central governments and recognized central banks), diplomatic and consular establishments, and other agencies of national governments. Separate data for reserve agencies are not available. The data are collected monthly by the Federal Reserve System for the Treasury Department.

Nonliquid Liabilities Reported by U.S. Government to Foreign Official Reserve Agencies (Line 54). This account measures net transactions representing collections for, and repayments against, deposit and security obligations of U.S. government agencies to foreign official reserve agencies, when such deposits or obligations, bearing original maturities of more than one year, are payable prior to maturity only under special conditions. Some of the deposits represent funds placed in restricted accounts with the U.S. government to be used only to liquidate U.S. claims as these claims reach maturity. Also included are changes in the outstanding amount of nonmarketable treasury securities which are issued subject to redemption prior to maturity for the purpose of paying or prepaying for military purchases in the United States, and the obligations to the government of Canada under the Columbia River basin agreements of 1964.

The bulk of the obligations entering into this entry represents nonmarketable securities issued by the government through arrangements to improve the U.S. liquid liability position with other countries or to obtain convertible currencies for inclusion in the U.S. official reserve assets.

Transactions may be in U.S. dollars or in foreign currencies. Repayments of obligations are recorded at book value, with the exception that an estimated book value is calculated by BEA to reflect any formal exchange rate revaluation which may have affected the U.S. dollar equipment value of an obligation denominated and/or repayable in foreign currencies. Data are compiled from reports furnished by operating agencies and from published statements and financial and operating records of government agencies.

Nonliquid Liabilities Reported by U.S. Government to Other Official and Private Foreigners (Line 55). This account measures net transactions representing collections for, and "repayments" against, deposit and security obligations of U.S. government agencies to other than foreign official reserve agencies. "Repayments" include deliveries of goods or rendering of services by U.S. government agencies; the bulk of the deposits is in prepayment for such purchases (mainly of military equipment) by foreign governments.

Liabilities include deposits associated with military sales contracts; deposit and trust funds with the U.S. government under prepayment sales operations of nonmilitary agencies; funds provided as grants or loans under assistance programs, but held in a restricted account with the U.S. government under arrangements to insure their expenditure for purchases from the United States; accounts payable of government agencies that report their current transactions on an accrual basis; noninterest-bearing treasury securities which were issued as part of U.S. government contributions to international institutions, but are subject to redemption prior to maturity to obtain U.S. dollars for the immediate operating needs of the institutions; and nonmarketable securities issued by the government to other than foreign official reserve agencies through arrangements to improve the U.S. liquid liability position with other countries.

Transactions may be in U.S. dollars or in foreign currencies. Repayments of obligations are recorded at book value, with the exception that an estimated book value is calculated by BEA to reflect any formal exchange rate revaluation which may have affected the U.S. dollar equivalent value of an obligation denominated and/or repayable in foreign currencies. Data are compiled from reports furnished by operating agencies, and from published statements and financial and operating records of government agencies. The entries for the several categories of transactions related to military sales contracts are partially estimated by BEA from incomplete data.

U.S. Liquid Liabilities to Private Foreigners (Line 56). This account measures changes in short-term liabilities (with an original maturity of one year or less) to private foreigners reported by U.S. banks, for their own account and for others' accounts under their custody, and changes in private foreign holdings of U.S. treasury marketable bonds and notes. Liquid liabilities reported by U.S. banks include mainly demand and time deposits, U.S. treasury bills and certificates, negotiable time certificates of deposit, and nonguaranteed U.S. government agency securities. Private foreigners include official international and regional organizations other than IMF even if located in the United States, foreign branches of U.S. banks, other foreign commercial banks, and other private foreign residents. These data are collected monthly by the Federal Reserve System for the Treasury Department from banks and securities brokers and dealers.

U.S. Liquid Liabilities to Foreign Official Agencies (Line 57). This account measures changes in short-term liabilities (with an original maturity of one year or less) to foreign official agencies reported by U.S. banks for their own account and for others' accounts under their custody, changes in foreign official agencies' holdings of U.S. treasury marketable and nonmarketable convertible bonds and notes and changes in liabilities to the IMF arising from gold transactions. Short-term liabilities reported by U.S. banks include mainly demand and time deposits, negotiable time certificates of deposit, nonguaranteed U.S. government agency securities, and U.S. treasury bills and certificates. Foreign official agencies include, in addition to reserve agencies (treasuries or finance ministries of central governments and recognized central banks), diplomatic and consular establishments, and other agencies of national governments. Separate data for reserve agencies are not available. The liability data are collected primarily by the Federal Reserve System for the Treasury Department on a monthly basis.

Transactions in U.S. Official Reserve Assets, Net–Gold (Line 59). This account measures changes in the U.S. gold stock, including changes in gold in the Exchange Stabilization Fund.

This account also includes gold sold to the United States by the International Monetary Fund (IMF) with the right to repurchase, and gold deposited by the IMF to mitigate the impact on the U.S. gold stock of foreign purchases for the purpose of making gold subscriptions to the fund under quota increases. The corresponding changes in liabilities to the IMF arising from the gold transactions are in line 57.

SDR (Line 60). This account measures net changes in U.S. holdings of special drawing rights in the Special Drawing Account in the International Monetary Fund, reflecting allocations, acquisitions, and use.

Convertible Currencies (Line 61). This account measures changes in Treasury and Federal Reserve System holdings of convertible foreign currencies in U.S. dollar equivalents.

Gold Tranche Position in IMF (Line 62). This account measures changes in the U.S. gold tranche position in the International Monetary Fund—the U.S. quota in the IMF minus the fund's holdings of U.S. dollars—which is the amount that the United States could purchase in foreign currencies automatically if needed. Under appropriate conditions, the United States could purchase additional amounts equal to the U.S. quota.

Allocations of Special Drawing Rights (SDR) (Line 63). This account measures the allocations of special drawing rights to the United States by the International Monetary Fund. The initial allocation occurred January 1, 1970; the second, January 1, 1971; and the third, January 1, 1972.

Errors and Omissions, Net (Line 64). This entry is a residual item in Table 2. The sum of this entry and all other accounts in Table 3 equals zero. The residual item includes errors and omissions that may have occurred in any of the lines 1–63 due to such factors as statistical errors, reporting deficiencies, and differences in timing in the recording of the two sides (debit and credit) of a single transaction. It is entered to fulfill the principle of double-entry bookkeeping used in balance-of-payments accounting that credits and debits should exactly balance.

32

Corporate Forecasting

SAMUEL S. STEWART, JR., PhD.
College of Business
The University of Utah
Salt Lake City, Utah

INTRODUCTION

THE TOPIC OF CORPORATE FORECASTING, the issuance of forecasts by corporations of their own future operating performance, has received much attention in recent years. Security analysts generally favor some form of public disclosure of forecasts by corporations of their own future performance. On the other hand, corporate executives tend to be wary of such public disclosure due to the fear of either revealing information of value to competitors or fomenting stockholder unrest as a result of unmet forecasts. Implicit in the desire of analysts to receive forecasts is the belief that such forecasts will be of assistance in predicting future stock prices. *The purpose of this chapter will be to consider the validity of the proposition that forecasts of corporate performance can be used to predict corporate stock prices.*

In order to investigate thoroughly the value of corporate forecasts as an aid to predicting stock prices, we must first turn to a much more fundamental issue, the process by which stock prices are determined. We must explore the possible links between corporate operations and stock market performance. Only after we understand how corporate performance influences stock market performance can we effectively pursue the question of the value of forecasts of these performance parameters in predicting stock prices. A continuing theme of this discussion will be that forecasts as a mere proliferation of data are of little worth. In order to be useful information, *forecasts must serve as a component of a systematic, analytical procedure* designed to weave all relevant information into a coherent, consistent framework for predicting stock prices.

Within the investment community, some disagreement exists over the process of stock price determination. One school of thought, often referred to as technical analysis, views stock prices as primarily a psychological phenomenon. That is, the major determinants of stock prices are the intertwined hopes and fears of investors. This school feels that while underlying corporate performance may ultimately influence the market price, during the relevant short-run time frame, corporate performance is a comparatively unimportant influence on stock prices. Such analysts feel that if investor psychology can be forecast at all, it may be best forecast by observing the history of investor behavior as reflected in past market prices. If such a view of the world is correct, then corporate forecasts, unless they have some influence on investor psychology, are probably of little use as an aid in predicting future stock prices.

The other school of thought, often referred to as fundamental analysis, believes that the primary determinant of stock prices is the performance of the underlying corporation. While investor psychology may cause short-lived bubbles and bursts in stock prices, the dominating influence is that of the firm itself. If this hypothesis is correct, corporate forecasts of the firm's operating results may prove to be an important guide to predicting stock prices. In such a case, it is worth asking an additional question concerning the degree of relative superiority of corporate forecasts to similar forecasts made by outside analysts.

This discussion will first examine the process of stock price determination. We will consider the available evidence supporting the psychological determination of stock prices (technical analysis) and the evidence supporting the determination of stock prices by corporate operating performance (fundamental analysis). Since the evidence tends to indicate that corporate performance does have an impact on stock prices, the investigation of the value of forecasts of corporate operations is worth pursuing. Thus, we next turn to a consideration of the accuracy of forecasts made solely on the basis of past corporate performance in order to establish a benchmark with which to compare the accuracy of corporate forecasts. An additional benchmark is established through examination of the accuracy of external analysts' forecasts. Finally, the groundwork is complete and a consideration of the value of corporate forecasts as an aid in predicting stock prices is examined.

THE DETERMINATION OF STOCK PRICES

Technical Analysis

Although most analysts would agree that both investor psychology and corporate operations have a role in determining stock prices, sharp disagreement exists as to the relative importance of each influence. Those arguing that investor psychology is of paramount importance look to past investor behavior as revealed in the history of stock price movements to seek a key to predicting future stock prices. On the other hand, analysts believing that corporate performance is the prime determinant of stock prices search information about corporate performance to find a clue to future stock prices. Because the question of stock price determination is of such importance, a massive amount of literature has been written proposing answers. The scope of this chapter is obviously sufficiently limited that we can do no more than examine the results of several of the more important studies undertaken to answer this question.

The studies examining the influence of investor psychology as revealed in historical price movements on future stock prices are often referred to as *random walk* studies.[1] Most of these studies have been authored by academicians seeking to prove that the best prediction of future price movements available from an examination of historical prices is that future prices will move in a random walk around a price trend reflecting normal growth. That is, that the information provided by technical analysis is of no value in predicting future stock prices in such a way as to obtain above-normal profits. The evidence examined in these studies often consists of the distribution of stock price changes for a number of stocks for a period of time. Statistical analysis of these stock price change distributions generally produces results consistent with results expected if the distribution were created by random stock price changes.

Technical analysts and other opponents of random walkers claim that such evidence about the distribution of stock price changes is irrelevant to their methods of analysis which are designed to detect relationships more complex than those revealed by distributions of price changes. Indeed, while the distribution evidence is consistent with the random walk theory, much of it is also consistent with persistent trends in stock prices providing above-normal profits. For example, consider a *runs* test which discloses an apparently random up, down, up, down, and so on pattern. If the magnitude of the up movements were much greater than the magnitude of the down movements, the stock price would exhibit a substantial upward trend while the runs test would be indicating a random pattern of up and down movements. Thus, the results of such a test may be ambigiuous since an apparently random pattern of up and down fluctuations could be consistent with either truly random or essentially nonrandom stock price movements.

Further, tests are sometimes conducted to discover whether the

---

[1] Such studies date at least to the turn of the century and several of the most important studies are reprinted in Cootner (1964). Perhaps the most important recent study is that of Fama (1965). (Complete references are given in the bibliography at the end of this chapter.)

distribution of price changes is of a certain variety such as "normal" or "stable paretian" (i.e. without going into statistical detail, distributions which would be consistent with random stock price changes). Although the sample distribution may prove to be normal or stable paretian, no evidence is provided as to how the distribution was created. That is, it is possible to "fill" a distribution with a series of observations above the mean followed by a series of observations below the mean and so forth, in a manner entirely consistent with nonrandom stock price fluctuations. The basic problem with the statistical tests used to examine the stock price change distributions is their lack of ability to simultaneously measure both the direction and the magnitude of stock price changes. For this reason, the available evidence gleaned from distribution tests seems unable to clearly resolve the issue.

Another approach to testing the validity of technical analysis has been to devise certain trading rules based on popular theories of technical trading.[2] The general finding of such studies is that the strategies examined fail to provide profits in excess of those available from a *buy-and-hold* strategy. The technician's answer to such results is again that the type of strategies tested are simplistic in comparison to their own complex trading rules. It is interesting to note that two academic studies claim to provide positive evidence of links between past and future stock market performance. Levy (1968) used a relative strength criterion, which ranked stocks according to their past price movements, to predict future price movements. Levy's tests indicated that this strategy outperformed a buy-and-hold strategy. Also Ying (1966) discovered statistically significant relationships between trading volume and price movements. Although Ying did not attempt to estimate the profitability of using these relationships as a guide to trading activity, his work is of interest since many technical theories are based upon the association between price and volume.

In summary, the case against technical analysis—the psychological determination of stock prices—seems quite broad but not very deep. The sizeable amount of evidence available is reasonably uniform in assigning investor psychology to a relatively minor role in determining stock prices, yet each of the studies taken individually is not overly powerful. Although investor psychology appears to influence stock prices, currently available empirical studies probably do not permit the conclusion that investor psychology determines stock prices. If stock prices could be predicted by using technical analysis, corporate forecasts would be of little value, as there is slight reason to believe that a

---

[2] Numerous tests of technical trading rules have been conducted. Among those finding evidence tending to discredit such rules are Fama and Blume (1966), Jensen and Bennington (1970), Levy (1971), and Van Horne and Parker (1967). Supportive evidence was discovered by Alexander (1961, 1964), Levy (1967*a*, 1967*b*), and Ying (1966).

corporation has any comparative advantages in examining its own stock price history.

The analyst attempting to predict stock prices via technical analysis should certainly acquaint himself with some of the studies discrediting certain technical strategies. Further, the analyst may find it a valuable exercise to formulate his own technical trading strategies with sufficient precision that they may be tested against the computerized data bases so abundantly available. Finally, it should be recognized that in the long run technical strategies which ignore corporate performance data are destined to fail since ultimately market performance and corporate performance converge. For this reason, predictions of stock prices based upon information about corporate performance may be a more fruitful area for analytical research. To this subject we now turn.

Fundamental Analysis

Just as many studies have been undertaken in the attempt to discredit technical analysis, many other studies have been performed to demonstrate the relationship between some particular aspect of corporate operating performance and stock market prices. In order to organize this vast amount of material, we need first to establish a simple, yet plausible, model which explains the relationship between corporate performance and market performance. Perhaps the simplest model is based on the earnings capitalization concept. That is, the price of a firm's stock may be thought of as the product of the earnings (EPS) of the firm and a capitalization rate or multiplier, the price-earnings (P/E) ratio. The concept underlying this model is that the earnings are a *quantitative* measure of the value which the firm is providing its stockholders while the multiplier is a *qualitative* measure dependent upon the growth, stability, and longevity of the earnings. This earnings capitalization model is a familiar tool on Wall Street and is closely related to the constant growth version of the dividend model commonly used in academia. Figure 1 demonstrates how this model may be further subdivided into basic components similar to those which the familiar duPont chart uses to analyze operating performance. The earnings (EPS) of the firm may be regarded as the product of the rate of return on equity (ROE) and the level of equity investment (book value) per share. The rate of return on equity (ROE) may be regarded as the product of the rate of return on the firm's assets (ROA) and the degree of leverage (Total assets/Equity) it employs, and so forth. At this point we make no distinction between the accounting measurement of these variables and their underlying economic value; however, it is important to note that such a model may product confusing results when accounting measurements and economic values diverge.

The purpose of such a model is to demonstrate the precise manner

FIGURE 1

How Is Share Price Determined?

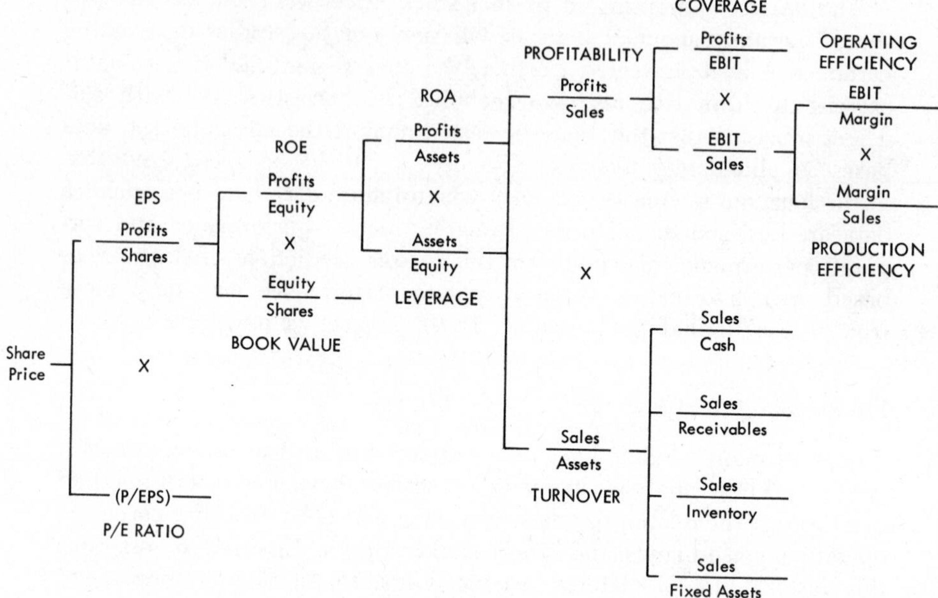

in which corporate operating performance may influence stock price. For example, in order for an increase in the earnings of the firm to have a favorable impact upon its stock price, the P/E ratio of the firm must not decline in such a way as to offset the earnings increase. That is, a forecast of rising earnings is insufficient in and of itself to imply a rising stock price; the earnings forecast must be coupled with a forecast about the behavior of the P/E ratio in order to obtain a stock price prediction.

This section of the chapter will examine the relationship between stock prices and the various measures of corporate performance indicated by the earnings capitalization model to exert an influence on stock prices. It is important to realize that in applying such a model, relationships between operating performance and stock prices are indirect. As mentioned, in order for the relationship between earnings and stock prices to be useful in predicting stock prices, the nature of the relationship between P/E ratios and stock prices must also be known.

Earnings and Stock Prices

At the heart of fundamental models of stock price determination in general and the model introduced in this chapter in particular lies the corporate earnings (EPS) figure. Due to its summarizing, "bottom line" nature, the EPS figure is frequently regarded as the single most revealing indicator of corporate performance. Casual empiricism readily demonstrates the long-run association between earnings and stock prices. Whether considering the historical record of an individual firm or the record of an aggregate index such as the Dow-Jones Industrial Average, visual inspection reveals the close correlation between earnings and stock prices. While historical inspection also shows the existence of short-lived fluctuations in stock prices due to bubbles and bursts of investor psychology as reflected in the P/E multiple, it also reveals that such fluctuations are not sustainable for periods greater than a few years without the support of corporate earnings. For any long period of time an obvious, direct association between earnings and stock prices exists.

Several formal studies have detailed the close association between earnings and stock prices.[3] The general procedure of these studies is to record earnings changes and stock price movements for a particular group of companies during a specified time period. The companies are then ranked by the degree of change in earnings (positive or negative) and the degree of change in stock prices. The two sets of rankings are then compared with the aid of statistical techniques. The consistent finding of such studies is that a strong, direct association between earnings and stock prices exists.

Price-Earnings Ratios and Stock Prices

In addition to the relationship between earnings and stock prices, relationships between other measures of corporate performance and stock prices have been discovered. Perhaps the most important indicator of corporate performance other than the earnings figure is the price-earnings (P/E) multiplier. This earnings capitalization factor may be considered to be jointly determined by corporate performance and investor's perceptions of that performance in relationship to the performance of other corporations and alternative investment media. Thus, while not as directly reflective of corporate performance as earnings, the P/E ratio serves as an important indicator of the perceived quality of corporate earnings.

As previously mentioned, in the long run almost no association between P/E ratios and stock prices exists, since P/E ratios tend to fluctuate within somewhat well-defined ranges. However, investigators have discovered short-run relationships between P/E ratios and stock prices.[4] The observed relationships tend to indicate the wrong-headed-

---

[3] Among these studies are Ball and Brown (1968), Murphy (1968), and Niederhoffer and Regan (1972).

[4] Among these studies are those of Breen (1968), Joy (1972), Levy and Kripotos (1969), Litzenberger, Joy, and Jones (1971), McWilliams (1966), and Nicholson (1968).

ness of investors. That is, low P/E ratios, rather than indicating bad corporate performance, are more often associated with excessive investor pessimism. High P/E ratios, rather than indicating superb corporate performance, are more often associated with excessive investor optimism.

The general procedure of these studies is to group a number of stocks according to the magnitude of their P/E ratios and then to examine the relative performance of each group over some specified time period. The studies' general finding is that the performance of each group varies inversely with the level of the P/E ratios of the stocks in the group. Such studies have been criticized on several grounds. One is that the P/E ratios are frequently computed on year-end prices and earnings although, in reality, the earnings figures are not available until several months following the end of the year. Another criticism is that the variance of the market performance of the stocks within each group makes the conclusions of these studies statistically unreliable when applied to individual stocks. A final criticism is directed at the nature of the P/E ratio itself. While the P/E is most likely *determined* on the basis of normalized earnings, it is *calculated* on the basis of reported earnings. Thus, many of the firms falling in the high P/E groups are not the traditional high-growth firms. Instead they are marginal firms which have reported abnormally low earnings. It is not too surprising that the subsequent performance of such firms is below average. In spite of such criticisms, the uniformity of the findings is impressive. Some consistent, inverse relationship between P/E ratios and stock prices seems to exist.

Other Performance Measures and Stock Prices

Other studies have examined the relationship between additional measures of corporate performance and stock prices. The rationale for such studies often stems from the unreliability of the EPS figure. It has become increasingly apparent that the raw EPS figure is subject to several types of manipulation. During the late 1960s the conglomerate craze demonstrated the possibility of producing growth in reported EPS via acquisition which was not reflective of true economic growth. The growth in reported EPS arose from a bootstrapping-type operation in which a firm would acquire for stock another whose P/E multiple was lower than its own, thereby increasing its earnings per share even though the total net income of the two firms might remain constant. Such growth tended to increase the P/E ratio of the company, allowing it even greater possibilities of future growth.

Another type of manipulation of the reported EPS figure stems from the positive effects of adding leverage. It is possible for a firm to produce a consistent pattern of growth in EPS by merely replacing equity with debt financing even though its operations may remain at some constant, profitable level. This same growth may also be produced by expanding the scale of operations via debt financing without any essential improvement in the quality of operations. That such growth is more apparent than real and inevitably brings as a companion added risk is abundantly revealed in the recent history of the REIT industry where many firms have experienced negative EPS growth just as rapidly as they formerly experienced positive growth.

Finally, EPS manipulation has resulted from the excessive flexibility of accounting principles which have permitted some companies (land development firms are one example) to boost current earnings by borrowing from future earnings. Growth created by liberal accounting practices is inherently limited and often places a firm near a precipice where the slightest adverse operating development pushes the firm into dramatic reversals of their former growth patterns.

Unfortunately, since most measures of corporate performance are accounting based, they are subject to the same flexible accounting as the EPS figure. Certainly, nearly all studies testing the relationship between performance and stock prices not relying directly on the EPS figure or indirectly on the EPS via the P/E ratio still are forced to rely on some type of accounting-based measure of corporate performance and are not free from possible bias due to accounting flexibility. However, studies based upon such performance measures as return on asset investment do avoid possible biases due to acquisitions and added leverage.

Although a number of studies examining the relationship between stock prices and corporate performance measures other than earnings have been conducted, it is virtually impossible to generalize either about the methodology or the findings of these studies.[5] Perhaps the most effective way to indicate the nature of these studies is to describe two representative studies. Beaver (1968) examined a matched sample of bankrupt and nonbankrupt firms in the attempt to discover significant differences between the financial ratios of the two sets of firms. Beaver discovered that such differences did exist and further questioned whether or not the information of impending bankruptcy revealed in the financial ratios was also reflected in the stock market. The conclusion of the study was that three ratios, cash generation to debt, profit to assets, and debt to assets, were good predictors of bankruptcy, and that, for the bankrupt firms, deterioration in these measures of corporate performance was reflected in deteriorating stock prices.

Benishay (1961) examined the relationship between stock market performance and several measures of corporate performance including growth, stability, size, payout, and leverage using regression analysis on

---

[5] Among these studies are those of Beaver (1968) and Benishay (1961) which are described in the text. Additional studies are those of Altman (1968), McKibben (1972), and Nerlove (1968). Several studies have examined the relationship between dividends and stock prices, including Friend and Puckett (1964) and Watts (1973), often finding a less certain relationship than the studies relating earnings and stock prices.

cross-section data for several years for a sample group of firms. Among Benishay's conclusions were that size was negatively correlated with market performance while growth and leverage were positively correlated.

Recently numerous attempts have been made to relate a measure of risk to stock market performance.[6] The risk measure used is often referred to as a *beta factor*. The extent to which this market-based risk measure is reflective of actual corporate risk is somewhat unclear. The general finding of these studies is that while betas can be used to predict the performance of groups of stocks with reasonable accuracy, they are unreliable in predicting the behavior of individual securities due to the extreme instability of the risk measure.

Summary

The overall conclusion of the studies linking operating performance to market performance appears stronger and more uniform than that of the technical analysis studies. Little doubt exists that there is a strong, persistent, consistent relationship between corporate operations and stock prices. The only matter for real dispute would appear to be over what is the shortness of one's investment horizon before this link may be safely ignored. Certainly, day-traders may feel free to ignore corporate performance and to concentrate on market psychology. Maybe week-traders and perhaps even month-traders may also ignore corporate performance. However, anyone who would class himself as an investor (as opposed to a speculator) would do well to note the abundant evidence linking corporate performance and market performance.

THE ACCURACY OF FORECASTS

Unfortunately, the close correlation between measures of corporate performances and stock prices documented in the previous section may not provide any direct assistance in forecasting stock prices. The link between corporate performance and stock prices gives us information about stock price *determination*, not about stock price *prediction*. In order to use measures of corporate performance to predict stock prices, the existence of a relationship between historical performance and future price movements needs to be established. The purpose of this section is to investigate the evidence concerning the possibility of the relationship between corporate performance measures and stock prices requisite for successful stock price forecasting. The section first examines the

---

[6] Many of these studies are proprietary and several beta services are currently being marketed. Among the academic studies are those of Hamada (1972), Levy (1971), and Sharpe and Cooper (1972).

studies attempting to explore the predictive ability of corporate performance measures, that is, studies questioning whether future stock prices can be predicted from past corporate performance. The section then turns to the fundamental topic of this chapter: an examination of the accuracy of stock price predictions based on forecasts of corporate performance. Finally, the accuracy of forecasts originating from external analysts is compared to the accuracy of corporate forecasts generated by internal executives.

Forecasts Based on Past Performance

Numerous studies have explored the predictive ability of corporate operating data.[7] Although some studies have discovered the existence of predictive ability, the general finding of these studies is that information about past corporate performance cannot be used to successfully predict future stock prices. Some of the studies previously cited as supporting the relationship between corporate performance and stock prices can be further used to document the fact that in spite of the existence of such a relationship, data on past corporate performance cannot be used to predict future stock prices. Among these studies are those of Ball and Brown (1968), Beaver (1968), and Watts (1973). These studies indicate that although a close association between corporate performance measures and stock prices exists, this association cannot be used to predict stock prices due to the closeness of the association itself. That is, changes in corporate performance are so quickly reflected in stock prices that by the time an investor becomes aware of the performance change, the stock price will already reflect that change. In other words, studies have demonstrated that the stock market is an efficient medium for the reflection of new information.

Other studies have confirmed the rapid information processing ability of the stock market. Much of the analysis of the predictive content of past earnings information has centered on the question of the durability of growth rates. Several studies have tested the ability of historic growth rates to predict future earnings growth.[8] The general methodology of such studies is to calculate earnings growth during some time period for a sample of stocks, to rank the stocks according to past growth, to calculate the growth during some future time period, to rerank the stocks according to future growth, and then to compare

---

[7] Many of these studies have already been cited including those of Ball and Brown (1968), Beaver (1968), and Watts (1973). Additional studies directed specifically to the predictive content of earnings data are those by Ball and Brown (undated), Brown and Kennelly (1972), Brown and Niederhoffer (1968), Fama, Fisher, Jensen, and Roll (1969), Green and Segall (1966, 1967), and Niederhoffer (1970).

[8] These studies include the works of Leven (1972), Lintner and Glauber (1967), Little (1962), (1966), and Murphy (1966).

the two rankings. The near unanimous finding of such studies is that the correlation between past earnings growth and future growth is quite low. Perhaps one of the reasons for this somewhat surprising finding is that growth rates have been computed on the basis of changes in reported earnings per share. Since the EPS figure, particularly in recent years, has been subjected to much manipulation within the relatively permissive confines of accounting convention, it is possible that past growth in reported earnings does not reflect true economic growth, and, thus, when the accounting growth is exhausted, the firm is left to return to its natural, slow growth state. Nevertheless, whether the lack of association between past earnings growth and future market performance is due to the nonsustainability of growth rates or to their discounted reflection in current stock prices, these findings are again consistent with a stock market which reflects new information quickly and completely.

The only substantial, published body of evidence indicating that measures of past corporate performance possess predictive ability are the previously cited price-earnings ratio studies. The general conclusion of these studies is that low P/E ratios are associated with above-normal future rates of return; high P/E ratios are associated with below-normal future rates of return. Again as previously discussed, such studies are subject to criticism due to the divergence between the *determination* (based on normalized earnings) of the price-earnings ratio and the *calculation* (based on reported earnings) of the price-earnings ratio. Since these studies are the only published evidence indicating that future stock prices may be predicted from past performance data, analysts attempting to predict stock prices would do well to acquaint themselves with the methodology and results of these studies.

Forecasts Based on Forecasts of Corporate Performance

Since the available evidence (with the possible exception of that provided by the price-earnings ratio studies) is consistent with a market which quickly reflects past operating performance in stock prices, thus limiting the predictive content of such information, we now turn to an examination of the evidence concerning the predictive ability of forecasts of future performance. The evidence deals with two dependent aspects of forecasts. One aspect concerns the accuracy of the forecasts themselves; the other concerns the possibility of using forecasts of operating performance to predict stock prices.

Forecasts of corporate performance may be separated into two general categories: forecasts emanating from external analysts and those emanating from corporate executives. Unfortunately, the unsystematic manner in which corporations reveal their own forecasts of earnings and other performance data (if such forecasts are revealed at all) has prevented rigorous study of the accuracy of such forecasts.[9] On the other hand, several studies have examined the accuracy of the forecasts of external analysts.[10] These studies all suffer from the sporadic manner in which forecasts are issued and collected. That is, after an analyst has issued a forecast in a sufficiently formal manner that it is recorded, he may subsequently (the next day even) informally revise that forecast based on new information without updating the formal recorded forecast. In many cases, the published forecast of an analyst does not represent his most current opinion; yet, it is these published forecasts upon which the studies of forecasting accuracy must be based.

Further, the erratic timing of forecast issuance limits the rigor of forecasting studies. Different analysts issue forecasts of the same earnings figure at different times. Since information may change markedly between the two issuance dates, it is difficult to compare the accuracy of the two forecasts. This timing problem is greatly magnified in attempting to compare forecast accuracy for different years. Even though forecasts are issued at the same time during each year, the flow of events is sufficiently uneven over time that the inherent difficulty of making a forecast for different years may vary widely although the futurity of the forecast remains constant.

Such difficulties with the basic input data of studies of forecast accuracy obviously limit the generality of the conclusions of such studies. Nevertheless, with the few exceptions which shall be discussed below, the findings of such studies are surprisingly uniform. The studies all tend to confirm that (1) analysts' forecasts are no more accurate than the forecasts of "naive" models and that (2) analysts' forecasts can not be used as an aid in earning above-normal rates of return in the stock market.[11] For example, Cowles (1944) examined the forecasts published

---

[9] A few studies including Copeland and Marioni (1972) and Green and Segall (1966, 1967) have attempted to assess the accuracy of corporate forecasts. The rigor of such studies is severely limited by the factors mentioned in the text below.

In recent years, several financial services have been introduced which do attempt to systematize the presentation of earnings forecasts. Among these services are Standard and Poor's Earnings Forecaster, Institutional Brokers Estimate System, and Catallactics. Hopefully, these and other similar efforts will provide the data base required for a systematic study of the accuracy of corporate forecasts.

[10] The classic study of the accuracy of analysts' forecasts is that of Cowles (1933, 1944). More recently Cragg and Malkiel (1968) Diefenbach (1972), and Cragg Malkiel (1970), and Niederhoffer and Regan (1972) have investigated this same issue. The author of this chapter has also been permitted access to several proprietary studies conducted by large institutional firms. The conclusions of these studies confirm the findings of the published academic studies.

[11] The naive models used vary from study to study. They are usually based upon some technique of trend extrapolation, with the no-growth trend—i.e., next year's results predicted to be the same as last year's results—as a special case. These naive models may be directly compared to the previously discussed models attempting to predict future stock prices from past corporate performance. Available evidence indicates that predictions generated by such models will not lead investors to above-normal rates of return.

FIGURE 2

Improvements in Forecast Accuracy over Time: Catallactics Casper—Broker Forecasts, Abbott Labs (Calendar 1971 EPS Analysis from 1/01/71 to 12/31/71)

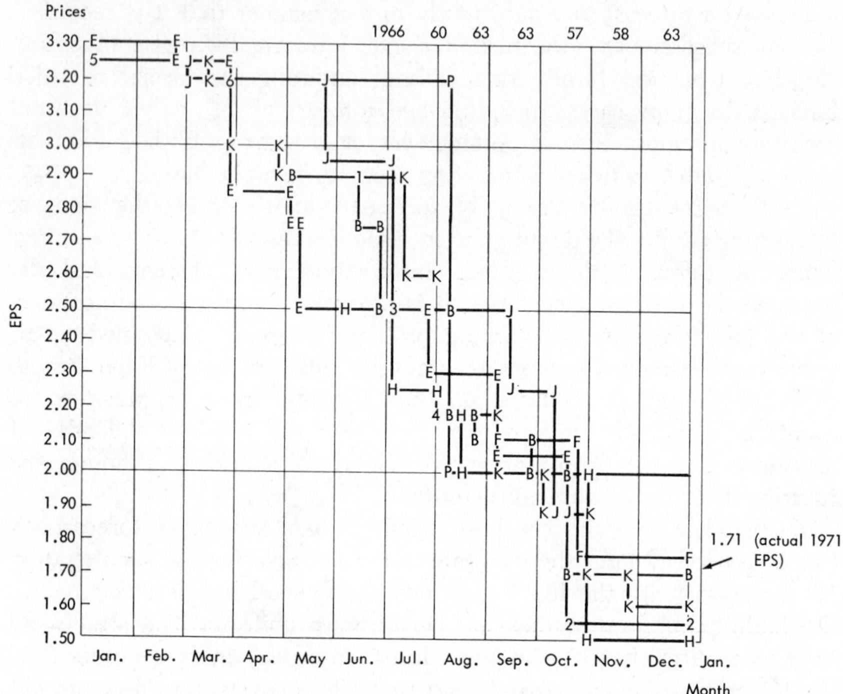

Note: Letters indicate issue date and value forecasts of Abbot Laboratories 1971 EPS for different analysts.

by 11 leading financial periodicals for the period 1927–42. He concluded that, in general, the accuracy of the forecasts was no better than that of random forecasts. He also detected a persistent bullishness in the forecasts (80 percent were classified as bullish) in spite of the fact that the market fell by 33 percent between 1927 and 1942. In a more recent study, Cragg and Malkiel examined the ability of analysts in five investment firms to predict the growth rates of 185 corporations. They concluded that little difference existed between the accuracy of the analysts' forecasts and that of extrapolation of past growth rates. Neither proved very accurate. Similar conclusions have been reached both by other published academic studies and by private proprietary studies.

Occasionally, these studies have discovered certain analysts possessing the ability to achieve above-normal returns in the stock market due to their forecasting accuracy. Cowles (1944) discovered that one analyst consistently outperformed the Dow Jones Industrial Average by an average of 3.3 percent a year. Diefenbach (1972) found evidence the *sell* recommendations out-performed the market on the downside. In evaluating the results of these analysts and others claiming to out-perform the market, the importance of consistency should be remembered. The averaging nature of the market scoreboard guarantees that some analysts will out-perform the market every year, just as some will under-perform every year. The important question to ask is whether or not the identity of the above-average performers remains the same year after year. While not denying the existence of such analysts, the weight of the available evidence suggests that such consistent above-average performance is unlikely.

Two other findings of these studies should be mentioned, both of which are consistent with common-sense expectation. One finding is that the accuracy of analysts' forecasts varies inversely with their futurity. The more distant the time period being forecast, the less accurate the forecast. Figure 2, which is a sample from the Catallactics service, illustrates this increase in forecast accuracy as the forecast futurity declines. The second finding is that forecast accuracy is closely associated with the nature of the firm whose results are being forecasted. Figure 3, which compares the forecast accuracy of four analytical groups and one naive model, demonstrates the dependence of forecast accuracy on the type of business operation. For example, firms in industries with reasonably stable demand such as drugs, food products, and oil are relatively easy to forecast in comparison to firms in industries with fluctuating demand such as aerospace, automobiles, and steel. However, it

FIGURE 3

Mean Percent Error of the Analytical Groups by Industry

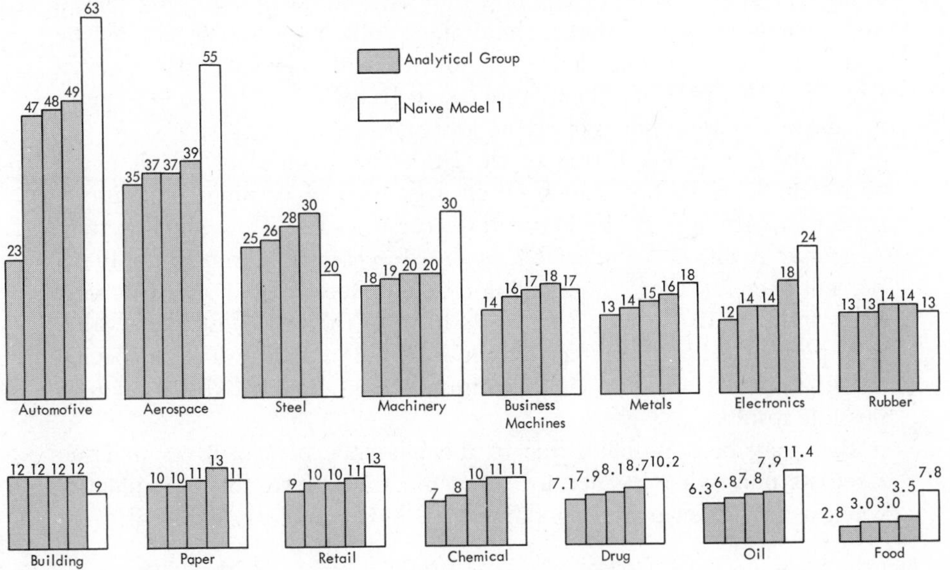

should be noted that in spite of improved analyst accuracy in near-term forecasts of stable demand industries, the accuracy of such forecasts is not markedly different from those generated by a naive model. In fact, there is some evidence indicating that analysts enjoy the greatest superiority in forecasting long-term results of firms in variable demand industries. This finding should not be surprising due to the importance of nonquantifiable, judgment-type factors in such situations.

Summary

The bulk of the evidence indicates that analysts' forecasts offer little in the way of improved accuracy over simple extrapolations in forecasting the operating results or market performance of many firms. Since analysts enjoy the greatest relative superiority in making difficult forecasts, analysts might be advised to rely on computer-based models incorporating extrapolation methods to make easy forecasts, thus freeing their time to concentrate on making the difficult forecasts for those firms and industries where their relative superiority to naive models has proved to be greatest.

Analysts' Forecasts versus Corporate Forecasts

As previously mentioned, no rigorous studies of the accuracy of corporate forecasts has yet been conducted due to the relatively erratic manner in which such forecasts have been issued and recorded. Even if such forecasts as published in *The Wall Street Journal* or other financial publication were systematically collected, the data base required for a study of the accuracy of corporate forecasts would probably be biased and incomplete. In addition to the timing problem (forecasts may not be issued at the same time each year, and even if they were, the uneven flow of events prevents them from being based upon the same amount of information), problems of clarity and bias exist.

Clarity is a problem due to the imprecise manner in which many corporate forecasts are issued. Often a forecast of earnings will simply state that earnings will be better this year than last. How much better? A penny? A dime? A dollar? Or, even a forecast of "earnings up 10–15 percent over last year" contains imprecision. Does it mean that the most likely value is 12.5 percent? Or, does it mean that the most likely value is 15 percent, with 10 percent thrown in for conservatism. Even a specific dollar "most likely" figure yields no information about the distribution of possible results.

Bias may be a problem due to the tendency of executives to issue forecasts only when results are predicted to be favorable. Frequently, when a firm is encountering difficulties, it is reluctant to reveal them publicly for fear of revealing competitive information, initiating possible takeover bids, and, in general, creating shareholder unrest.

In the absence of formal studies, we are left to conjecture as to the relative accuracy of analysts' forecasts and corporate forecasts. It might be tempting to jump to the conclusion that corporate forecasts ought to be more accurate due to the better information access enjoyed by corporate executives. However, several counterarguments can be made against accepting such a conclusion. One counterargument is that much of the information relevant to an earnings forecast is not firm—or industry-specific. That is, factors which are economy-wide or at least industry-wide may exert a more important influence on the earnings of a firm than do its own actions. The external analyst may well have better information about and a better understanding of these economy and industry factors than the corporate executive and, hence, be in a position to render a more accurate forecast. Secondly, the corporate executives may not be able to see the forest for all the trees. The external analyst may gain a better understanding of where a firm fits within a competitive industry and what particular opportunities and difficulties it will face than the understanding possessed by the firm's own executives. If this is true, the analyst may provide a better forecast. Finally, the process by which analysts and executives generate their forecasts is not mutually independent. In many cases, by a process of trial and error, the executive will lead the analyst to a forecast which he already has in mind. Or else the executive may glean information from the analyst about the economy and competitors which will help him formulate a forecast consistent with the analyst's thinking. In either case, the result is that a strong similarity emerges between the forecast of the analyst and that of the executive.

How strong are these countereffects in offsetting the natural advantage the corporate executive has in access to information about his own firm? Who is the better forecaster, the analyst or the executive? A mail survey of research directors, analysts, and portfolio managers discloses that, in the opinion of the respondents (biased though it may be), little difference existed in the accuracy of earnings forecasts of analysts and corporate executives.[12] If such an opinion does, in fact, reflect the truth and if the studies concerning the accuracy of analyst's forecasts also reflect the truth, then it would seem that corporate earnings forecasts are of little value in predicting stock prices. That is, in spite of the strong association between earnings and stock prices, naive predictions of future earnings (and, thus, future stock prices) based on simple linear extrapolation of historic trends may be just as accurate as the

[12] The study, sponsored by the Financial Analysts Federation, was directed by Stewart (1973). A related study sponsored by the Financial Executives Research Foundation (1972) produced essentially similar results.

forecasts of corporate executives. Since the predictions of naive models do not appear to lead investors to above-normal profits, the available evidence indicates that *corporate forecasts are also unable to enable investors to earn above-normal profits.*

While this conclusion may seem somewhat surprising, it is consistent with the many studies documenting the efficiency of the financial markets, of which several have been previously cited in this chapter. That is, many researchers have demonstrated the ability of the stock market to process rapidly new information and reflect its significance in stock prices. If the market operates at least as rapidly as the corporate executive in processing new information, then corporate forecasts will tend to be of little value. Although such forecasts may be news to a particular group of individuals, they may be old news to the market. Thus, the negative evidence as to the value of corporate forecasts may be regarded as positive evidence as to the efficient functioning of the financial markets.

Possible Uses of Corporate Forecasts

Where do our conclusions leave the individual analyst wishing to evaluate a corporate forecast which he has just received? The focus of his attention should certainly be directed toward the news worthiness of the forecast. If the forecast does not contain new news, its information content has probably already been reflected in the market, and the analyst may as well crumple the forecast and throw it into the wastebasket. If the forecast does contain new news not generally available to the public, the analyst has received something of value. Unfortunately, the analyst may also do well to discard this forecast, since news of this type appears by definition to qualify as insider information and the use of such information may qualify the analyst for a severe penalty.[13]

In a certain sense, the evidence of the studies presented in this chapter paints the analyst into a rather gloomy corner. However, a positive directive to the analyst also emerges. That directive is that the *analyst should concentrate his own time upon a small number of firms, hoping to uncover news that is not also insider information* (i.e., nonpublic news which will affect the stock price). If he is additionally required to keep up-to-date on a large number of firms, he may rely on the computer or a financial service for this function. Certainly, the analyst who spreads himself too thin virtually guarantees himself mediocre performance. Further, the evidence in the chapter does direct the

[13] John Gillis discusses this point in "The Metamorphosis of Inside Information," *Financial Analysts Journal,* November–December 1972. Inside information appears to be "material, nonpublic information," which Gillis concludes is information not generally available emanating from the corporation which would influence the stock price.

analyst to fundamental information of the type contained in a corporate forecast as his most likely news source rather than to technical information based on historical price movements.

If systematic corporate forecasts are required, they are not likely to provide much help in predicting stock prices, and the performance of the analyst who believes so is likely to suffer. The analyst who will benefit from such a requirement is one who uses forecasts as one component in his own systematic analytical procedure. Such an analyst may discover that the greatest information value is provided by those corporate forecasts which are inaccurate or fail to conform to his personal forecast. In any case, that analyst who uses a corporate forecast as one component in a systematic analytical process for generating stock price predictions will be in a better position to use effectively whatever information corporate forecasts may contain than the analyst who unquestioningly accepts corporate forecasts as windows to the future.

BIBLIOGRAPHY

ALEXANDER, SIDNEY S. "Price Movements in Speculative Markets: Trends or Random Walks." *Industrial Management Review*, May 1961, pp. 7–26.

———. "Price Movements in Speculative Markets: Trends or Random Walks, Number 2." *Industrial Management* Review, Spring 1964, pp. 25–46.

ALTMAN, E. "Financial Ratios, Discriminant Analysis and the Prediction of Corporate Bankruptcy." *Journal of Finance*, September 1968, pp. 589–609.

BALL, RAY, and BROWN, PHILIP. "An Empirical Evaluation of Accounting Income Numbers." *Journal of Accounting Research*, Autumn 1968, pp. 159–78.

———. "The Information Value of the Annual Earnings Report." Unpublished manuscript, no date.

BEAVER, W. H. "Market Prices, Financial Ratios, and the Prediction of Failure." *Journal of Accounting Research*, Autumn, 1968, pp. 179–92.

BENISHAY, HASKEL. "Variability in Earnings—Price Ratios of Corporate Equities." *American Economic Review*, March 1961, pp. 81–94.

BREEN, WILLIAM. "Low Price-Earnings Ratios and Industry Relatives." *Financial Analysts Journal*, July–August 1968, pp. 125–27.

BROWN, P., and KENNELLY, J. "The Information Content of Quarterly Earnings." *Journal of Business*, July 1972, pp. 403–15.

BROWN, PHILIP, and NIEDERHOFFER, VICTOR. "The Predictive Content of Quarterly Earnings." *Journal of Business*, January 1970, pp. 60–62.

COOTNER, PAUL H., ed. *The Random Character of Stock Market Prices* Cambridge: MIT Press, 1964.

COPELAND, R. M., and MARIONI, R. J. "Executives' Forecasts of Earnings per Share versus Forecasts of Naive Models." *The Journal of Business*, October 1972.

Cowles, A. "Can Stock Market Forecasters Forecast?" *Econometrica* (1933), pp. 309–24.

———. "Stock Market Forecasting." *Econometrica* (1944), pp. 206–16.

Cragg, J. G., and Malkiel, B. G. "The Consensus and Accuracy of Some Predictions of the Growth of Corporate Earnings." *Journal of Finance*, March 1968, pp. 67–84.

———. "Expectations and the Structure of Share Prices." *American Economic Review*, September 1970, pp. 601–17.

Diefenbach, R. E. How Good Is Institutional Brokerage Research?" *Financial Analysts Journal*, January–February 1972, pp. 54–60.

Fama Eugene F. "The Behavior of Stock Market Prices." *Journal of Business*, January 1965, pp. 34–105.

Fama, Eugene F., and Blume, Marshall. "Filter Rules and Stock-Market Trading." *Journal of Business*, January 1966, pp. 226–41.

Fama, Eugene F.; Fisher, Lawrence; Jensen, Michael C.; and Roll, Richard. "The Adjustment of Stock Prices to New Information." *International Economic Review*, February 1969, pp. 1–21.

Financial Research Executives Foundation. *Public Disclosure of Business Forecasts.* New York: Financial Executives Research Foundation, 1972.

Friend, Irwin, and Puckett, Marshall. "Dividends and Stock Prices." *American Economic Review*, September 1964, pp. 656–82.

Green, David, and Segall, Joel. "The Predictive Power of First-Quarter Earnings Reports: A Replication." *Journal of Accounting Research* 4, suppl., 1966, pp. 21–36.

———. "The Predictive Power of First-Quarter Earnings Reports." *Journal of Business*, January 1967, pp. 44–55.

Hamada, R. "The Effect of the Firm's Capital Structure on the Septematic Risk of Common Stocks." *Journal of Finance*, May 1972, pp. 435.

Jensen, Michael C., and Bennington, George A. "Random Walks and Technical Theories: Some Additional Evidence." *Journal of Finance*, May 1970, pp. 469–82.

Joy, O. M. "Industry Security Analysis and Quarterly Earnings." *Southern Economic Journal*, October 1972, pp. 303–06.

Leven, J. "Growth Rates—The Bigger They Are the Harder They Fall." *Financial Analysts Journal*, November–December 1972, pp. 71–72.

Levy, Robert A. "Random Walks: Reality or Myth." *Financial Analysts Journal*, November–December 1967*a*.

———. "Relative Strength as a Criterion for Investment Selection." *Journal of Finance*, December 1967*b*, pp. 595–610.

———. "The Predictive Significance of Five-Point Chart Patterns." *Journal of Business*, July 1971, pp. 316–23.

———. "On the Short-Term Stationarity of Beta Coefficients." *Financial Analysts Journal*, November–December 1971, pp. 55–62.

Levy, Robert A., and Kripotos, S. "Earnings Growth, P/E's and Relative Strength." *Financial Analysts Journal*, November–December 1969, pp. 60–67.

LINTER, JOHN, and GLAUBER, ROBERT. "Higgledy Piggledy Growth in America." Paper presented May 1967, Seminar on the Analysis of Security Prices, University of Chicago.

LITTLE, I. M. D. "Higgledy Piggledy Growth." *Oxford University Institute of Statistics,* November 1962, pp. 387–412.

LITTLE, I. M. D., and RAYNER, A. C. *Higgledy Piggledy Growth Again.* Oxford: Basil Blackwey, 1966.

LITZENBERGER, R., JOY, O. M., and JONES, C. P. "Ordinal Predictions and the Selection of Common Stocks." *Journal of Financial Quantitative Analysis,* September 1971, pp. 1059–68.

MCKIBBEN, W. "Econometric Forecasting of Common Stock Investment Returns: A New Methodology Using Fundamental Operating Data." *Journal of Finance,* May 1972, pp. 371–80.

MCWILLIAMS, J. D. "Prices, Earnings and P/E Ratios." *Financial Analysts Journal,* May–June 1966, pp. 137–42.

MURPHY, J. E. "Relative Growth of Earnings per Share—Past and Future." *Financial Analysts Journal,* November–December 1966, pp. 73–76.

———. "Earnings Growth and Price Change in the Same Time Period." *Financial Analysts Journal,* January–February 1968, pp. 97–99.

NERLOVE, M. "Factors Affecting Differences among Rates of Return on Investments in Individual Common Stocks." *Review of Economics and Statistics,* August 1968, pp. 312–31.

NICHOLSON, S. F. "Price Ratios in Relation to Investment Results." *Financial Analysts Journal,* January–February, 1968, pp. 105–9.

NIEDERHOFFER, VICTOR, and REGAN, PATRICK J. "Earnings Changes Analysts' Forecasts and Stock Price." *Financial Analysts Journal,* May–June 1972, pp. 65–71.

STEWART, SAMUEL S., Jr. "Research Report on Corporate Forecasts." In *Disclosure of Corporate Forecasts to the Investor.* New York: Financial Analysts Federation, 1973, pp. 75–193.

SHARPE, W. and COOPER, G. "Risk-Return Classes of New York Stock Exchange Common Stocks." *Financial Analysts Journal,* March–April 1972, pp. 46–54.

VANHORNE, JAMES C., and PARKER, GEORGE G. C. "The Random Walk Theory: An Empirical Test." *Financial Analysts Journal,* November–December 1967, pp. 87–92.

WATTS, ROSS. "The Information Content of Dividends." *Journal of Business,* April 1973, pp. 191–211.

YING, CHARLES C. "Stock Market Prices and Volumes of Sales." *Econometrica,* July 1966, pp. 676–85.

33

Economic Forecasting

ROBERT A. KAVESH, Ph.D.
Graduate School of Business Administration
New York University
New York, New York
and
ROBERT B. PLATT, Ph.D.
Economist
Delafield Childs, Inc.
New York, New York

INTRODUCTION

What Is Forecasting?

IT HAS BECOME COMMON to use the terms forecasting and prediction synonymously, i.e., to foretell (hopefully accurately) the future. As a tool of decision making (whether selection of a stock or planning a new plant), the term *forecasting* implies more. It implies that buried in the uncertainties which govern the future there are recognizable systematic patterns—patterns which were also present in past occurrences. The *science* of forecasting is analyzing, measuring, and projecting these systematic patterns for the purpose of foretelling the future, or at least to reduce measurably the uncertainties of future events. The *art* of forecasting is that intuitive spark which tells you when and how these systematic patterns have undergone change.

Statistical versus Economic Forecasting

The title of this chapter is "Economic Forecasting," or what used to be called in the early literature on the subject, "Business Cycle Forecasting." The purpose is to describe how one goes about forecasting the broad range of aggregate economic data which are of use to the financial analyst, such as production, sales, costs, and profits. Since the goal of forecasting economic data is no different from that of any other type of forecasting (the reduction of uncertainty), the approaches to the task are virtually endless: hunches, tying economic events to cycle of sunspots, determining rhythmic patterns of behavior in economic events; these approaches and more have been tried by the business forecaster. If we discard some of these extreme forms, however, the approaches to forecasting economic data which are generally described in the literature can be grouped into two broad categories: *statistical* forecasting and *economic* forecasting.

Statistical forecasting is a term which encompasses mathematical methods which attempt to measure and project the systematic patterns that occur in economic data *without concern for what caused them.* Included in this category of forecasting are the analysis of trends in data (fitting curves of "best fit" to previous observations on economic data, calculating moving averages, and so on) and seasonal adjustment techniques. Some of the applications of these statistical methods using data which are relevant to the securities analyst are described elsewhere in this volume in the chapters on time series analysis, statistical methods, and regression analysis. In this chapter, we will limit our concern only to a more constricted definition of economic forecasting which excludes these purely statistical approaches.

For our purposes, the term *Economic Forecasting* will mean applied macroeconomic theory. The systematic patterns which we attempt to recognize and measure in economic forecasting are those which macroeconomic theory (in its simplified and highly stylized way) commonly represents as the behavior and interactions of major classes of economic units: households, business firms, and governments.

When considering the diversities and complexities of economic forecasting in practice, it is often difficult to find the unifying thread of theory. This is because macroeconomic theory is only a model of reality, and like most models it lacks a considerable amount of sometimes important detail. In purely analytical applications, the very simplified structure of macroeconomic theory is an advantage since it permits theoreticians to reach many important policy conclusions and to discuss many important implications of the economic structure, by focusing on only a few key relationships, unencumbered by "messy" institutional considerations or by purely empirical problems such as the lack of data or the problems of operationally defining important but ambiguous concepts. But it is rare when these complicating factors can, or at least should, be ignored by the business forecaster. As a result, the tool of macroeconomic theory is seldom entirely adequate for his purpose. All of the institutional complexities which are swept under the rug in purely analytical treatments of macroeconomic theory must be added back by the forecaster to the macroeconomic model in order to make it a practical business tool. It is this wealth of institutional detail which becomes such an important part of the practical problem of business forecasting that tends to obscure the ultimate reliance of economic forecasting on the basic core of macroeconomic theory.

Why Economic Forecasting Is Important to the Financial Analyst

Clearly, the fortunes of a particular company, and the securities of that company, cannot be treated as isolated phenomena. A firm exists within an industry environment—an industry within the environment of the total economy of the nation and the world. More and more, portfolio managers of major financial institutions have become aware of the dangers and pitfalls in securities analysis done in isolation without the rigorous discipline of an overall economic outlook consistently carried down to forecasts of industry and company prospects. This recognition accounts in part for the increasing number of economists and/or portfolio strategy groups (taking a so-called top-down approach to investment decision making) within the Wall Street community.

The difficulties and problems of securities analysis are taxing enough by themselves, and surely we cannot expect an analyst to always be a fully competent economic forecaster. In order to obtain a macroeconomic overview, the analyst will have to rely, at least in part, on the inputs of others. But these inputs are so often conflicting in their conclusions and implications that some knowledge of economics and the methods and tools of economic forecasting become essential ingredients of the process of weeding out the bad from the good. In the next section, we describe briefly some of the major methods and tools of economic forecasting.

SCIENTIFIC METHODS OF ECONOMIC FORECASTING

Methodological Issues

Forecasting is a most practical endeavor, and forecasters will ultimately use anything that works. As a result, it is rare to find anyone using a single identifiable forecasting method. However, economists have an almost unlimited capacity to categorize, and it has become fashionable in the literature of forecasting to distinguish between what is often called scientfiic and judgmental (or intuitive) forecasting methods.

There are several ways that the term *scientific forecasting* can be defined, but in the end all of them lead to the same conclusion. The most distinguishing characteristic of scientific forecasting is *replicability*. For a forecasting method to be scientific, it must use a clear, precise, logical, and explicitly laid out set of steps leading from the assumptions used in generating the forecast to the actual forecast itself. In other words, the method must be so explicit that *any* forecaster using the techniques with the same set of assumptions will produce the same forecast.

To obtain this degree of explicitness almost invariably requires the representation of the forecasting process in a precise set of formulas or mathematical expressions. Since we are concerned in this chapter only with what we have called economic forecasting, i.e., forecasting which depends ultimately on economic theory, we can redefine scientific forecasting as the use of mathematical equations which represent some aspect or aspects of economic behavior. In this chapter, scientific forecasting is represented by two methods: econometric models and input-output models.

Econometric Models

An econometric model is sometimes defined as an explicit mathematical representation of the economy or some portion of it, and thus in a sense, virtually all forecasting which is both economic and scientific can be called econometric. However, the expression *econometric model* is most often used in a more restrictive way. It usually implies a mathematical representation of the process of aggregate income determination and the interaction between the product and the financial sectors of the economy. It is, therefore, an explicit mathematical representation of those aspects of economic behavior usually described by macroeconomic theory.

Keynesian Economic Models. When most people think of measures of overall economic activity, they usually do so in terms of the major expenditure components of the gross national product accounts (see Chapter 31). There are many ways to subdivide the GNP, but generally we describe the gross national product by the familiar accounting identity:

GNP = Personal consumption expenditures + Nonresidential fixed investment (plant and equipment) + Residential construction + Inventory investment + Federal government expenditures + Expenditures by state and local governments + Net exports (exports minus imports)

Most econometric models are ultimately designed to describe and/or forecast one or more of these major expenditure components of the GNP. The models will vary in size depending on the degree of disaggregation of the expenditure components, the extent to which equations must be added to explain and forecast variables introduced as "explanatory" variables in the basic expenditure equations, and the extent to which the analyst is also interested in forecasting the income side of the GNP accounts (i.e., wages, salaries, and profits generated in producing the gross national product). An econometric model can thus be a single equation or an aggregation of equations which can number a hundred or more.

The theoretical structure which underlies the construction of the GNP accounts and most econometric models is Keynesian macroeconomics as it has evolved over the years since it was first introduced into the economic literature. Keynesian macroeconomic theory is basically a set of propositions (or hypotheses) which state how broad classes of economic units, such as consumers, business firms, and governments, determine their spending. These propositions usually provide the first basis upon which an econometrician will seek those key variables which he can use in his model to explain and forecast the expenditure components.

Some of the key propositions which provide the structure of Keynesian econometric models are the following:

1. Personal consumption expenditures vary positively with total income available to consumers to spend ("disposable personal income").
2. Fixed nonresidential business investment varies positively with the rate of capacity utilization and the availability of funds (cash flow and external finance) and inversely with the cost of funds.
3. Residential construction expenditures is mostly a positive function of the availability of mortgage financing.
4. Inventory investment is primarily determined by the desire of business firms to maintain a normal relationship between the stock of inventories on hand and expected business sales (a normal inventory-sales ratio).
5. Net exports and spending by governments are not determined by any purely (domestic) economic factors. In the drab terminology of the economist, these expenditures are exogenous, i.e., determined outside the economic system.

These propositions seem straightforward enough. Putting them into practice is another matter altogether. How do you measure expected sales, the availability of financing, and capacity utilization? How do you handle changes in tax laws—such as an investment tax credit—when accounting for the effects of the cost of credit on business investment? How long does it take before changes in income affect consumption expenditures or how long before changes in the cost of funds affect business investment? These and many other practical statistical problems and institutional details combine to bedevil the practicing econometric forecaster. When he is finished, he has often so compromised his original theory for the sake of getting something that works that it is often difficult to even find the core of theory that remains. To illustrate how some of these problems are handled in practice, the following is an equation which was estimated for nonresidential fixed investment expenditures in conjunction with the "Brookings—SSRC Quarterly Econometric Model of the United States"—the largest econometric model existing for the U.S. economy (over 300 equations):[1]

$$I_t = -0.86 + 0.0868\, X_{t-1} + 0.104\, X_{t-5} - 0.145\, K_{t-1} - 1.116\, R_{t-5}.$$

Notation:

I = Gross nonresidential fixed business investment in the manufacturing sector.
K = Stock of capital goods in the manufacturing sector.
R = Average corporate bond yield, percent.
t = Subscript representing time: t = current quarter, $t-1$ = previous quarter, $t-5$ = six quarters ago.
X = Gross National Product.

The constants in the equation, which measure the relationship between business investment and the explanatory variables, were estimated by regression analysis (see the chapter on regression analysis in this volume) from historical data.

Note that the equation does, to some extent, include variables representing the various aspects of the Keynesian propositions concerning the determinants of nonresidential fixed investment. Capacity utilization is represented by the variables X and K. As output (X) rises and the stock of capital goods (K) remains constant, the rate of capacity utilization is rising and we would expect investment expenditures to rise, hence the positive sign on the coefficients of X. Similarly, if output stays constant while the stock of capital rises, the rate of capacity utilization is falling, hence the negative sign on the coefficient of K. The rate of interest is the cost of external financing, and its coefficient has the expected negative sign. Missing from the equation (for a reason not explained by the authors) is a variable measuring the availability of internally generated funds. Notice that the estimated equation indicates that it takes six quarters for the maximum impact of interest rates and output to be exerted on actual investment spending.

Monetarist Models. The euphoria in the economics profession which developed soon after the initial publication of Keynes' treatise on macroeconomics has largely disappeared in recent years as a result of the failure of the "New Economics" to provide ready and workable answers to the two most pressing problems of a modern and highly industrialized economy, namely providing for a steady and a high rate of economic growth and reasonable price stability. The result has been in recent years a thorough rethinking of the basic theoretical postulates of economics, and a marked increase in the willingness of the profession to

---

[1] This equation is discussed in G. Froman and L. R. Klein, "The Brookings—S.S.R.C. Quarterly Econometric Model of the United States: Model Properties," *American Economic Review* 55, no. 2 (May 1965): 348–61

discard old beliefs, which now appear to be of limited use, and to opt for new and hopefully more successful formulas for guiding economic policy.

One result has been the emergence of a group of economists (led by Milton Friedman) who hope to discard the developed set of Keynesian propositions and to replace them with the single guiding principle, simply that it is money that matters most of all in determining economic activity. Economic forecasters have not been unaffected by these developments, and an increasing number of them have come to rely on money as the principal, if not the sole, inputs into their forecasts of aggregate demand (and in some instances even in forecasts of major stock price indexes). Chapter 29 provides a discussion of the monetarists' position.

An important stimulus to monetarist forecasting was the success of some followers of this approach in forecasting the minirecession of 1967 and the failure of the tax surcharge of 1968 to moderate aggregate demand significantly. These successes were in sharp contrast to the failures of their colleagues who relied on Keynesian models to successfully predict either occurrence. More recently, the ratio of success has swung more in favor of Keynesian models. There are many complex issues which still separate the Keynesians and the Monetarists. These issues are still the lively topic of many learned journal articles, and it is too early to say what the final synthesis will be. However, one trend is quite clear: economic forecasters have developed a new awareness of the importance of money in determining aggregate economic activity.

Input-Output Models

The second scientific forecasting method to be mentioned in this chapter is the input-output model. This model can be defined as a system of simultaneous mathematical equations which link the output of specific industries (or companies) to the amount of inputs used in production. It is, in other words, a mathematical representation for a group of industries of the familiar concept, the production function. The importance of the input-output model to economic forecasters is that it can be used to analyze and predict all the production transactions by industry categories that go into the determination of the gross national product. Thus, it provides a means by which the economic forecaster can convert his estimates of aggregate final demand (GNP) into estimates of total industry output and resource use.

In order to illustrate input-output, a very simple economy is assumed, in which there are three industry sectors: agriculture, manufacturing, and services. Some of the output over some specified period of time (in practice it is usually one year) of each of these industries may be sold to any industry or industries as raw materials or semifinished goods to be used by them as inputs in their production. The balance of the output not sold as intermediate demand is sold to final users of the product. These final users may be individuals buying consumer goods; business firms buying investment goods, such as plant equipment or additions to inventories; or federal, state, or local governmental units.

To produce its output, each industry requires some intermediate good purchased from other industries—and perhaps uses some of its own product as well—and pays out to the *primary* factors of production—in the form of wages, interest, rents, and profits—their contribution to the industry's total output. In dollar value, each industry's total output

TABLE 1

Interindustry Transactions, 1963 (in billions of dollars at producer's prices)

Sales to / *Purchases from*	*Intermediate Demand*				*Final Demand*				*Total of Rows*
	Agriculture	*Manufacturing*	*Services*	*Sub-Total*	*Consumer*	*Investment*	*Government*	*Sub-Total*	
Agriculture	15	50	5	70	20	0	0	20	90
Manufacturing	20	215	55	290	130	80	80	290	580
Services	10	100	100	210	230	0	60	290	500
Sub-total (intermediate inputs)	45	365	160						
Primary inputs (value added)	45	215	340						600
Totals of columns	90	580	500	570	380	80	140	600	

equals its total inputs. This equality can be visualized by analogy with the familiar accounting profit and loss statement. From the P & L statement, the value of a firm's sales, plus additions to inventories of its finished product, i.e., its total output, is equal to the sum of the costs of production (including the value of any goods used in production) and profits. Profits are the residual and balancing item in the P & L statement and likewise they are the balancing item in the input-output accounts.

The input-output flows in our highly simplified economy are illustrated in Table 1.

Input-output flows, such as those shown in Table 1, provide much interesting information, but they are, by themselves, of little direct use to the forecaster. What makes an input-output table a useful forecasting device is the application of a bold assumption with regard to how an industry's production is related to its use of various inputs. Specifically, as the level of an industry's output changes, the levels of all the inputs it uses are assumed to change proportionately. This implies, of course, that there is no substitution in production among the various inputs available to each of the industry sectors.

The assumption of fixed proportions of inputs can be used to convert a forecast of aggregate final demand—the gross national product—into a forecast of total demand for each industry's product and a forecast of each of the inputs required by that industry to produce its total output. The first step in this procedure is to calculate the fixed proportions of input requirements. These are known in the jargon of input-output analysis as the technical input-output coefficients, or more simply as the technical coefficients. To calculate these, you take the first three columns of Table 1, which represent the inputs required by each of the three industries to produce its total product, and divide each element in that column by the total output for the industry. The results of these calculations are shown in Table 2, under the heading "Direct Requirements"

TABLE 2

Direct Requirements

Sales to / *Purchases from*	*Agriculture*	*Manufacturing*	*Services*
Agriculture	0.17	0.09	0.01
Manufacturing	0.22	0.37	0.11
Services	0.11	0.17	0.20
Primary inputs	0.50	0.37	0.68
Total	1.00	1.00	1.00

since the table gives the direct inputs needed from each industry to produce one unit of output.

Considering the information in the rows of Table 2, it is possible, to represent the output of the three industries in the form of three simple linear equations. There are shown below:

Agriculture: $0.17 \times 90 + 0.90 \times 580 + 0.01 \times 500 + 20 = 90$
Manufacturing: $0.22 \times 90 + 0.37 \times 580 + 0.11 \times 500 + 290 = 580$
Services: $0.11 \times 90 + 0.17 \times 580 + 0.20 \times 500 + 290 = 500$

To see more clearly the implications of these output equations for forecasting, they can be put in somewhat more general form. Let the symbol Y_1 represent the total output of agricultural products; Y_2, the total output of the manufacturing industry; and Y_3, the total output of services. The demand for the products of each of these industries by final users is represented by the symbols, D_1, D_2, and D_3. Using this notation, the three output equations can be written in the form:

Agriculture: $0.17Y_1 + 0.09Y_2 + 0.01Y_3 + D_1 = Y_1$
Manufacturing: $0.22Y_1 + 0.37Y_2 + 0.11Y_3 + D_2 = Y_2$
Services: $0.11Y_1 + 0.17Y_2 + 0.20Y_3 + D_3 = Y_3$

These equations can be rearranged into a form which is more convenient for analysis by moving to the right-hand side of the equations all of the terms in Y that appear on the left. This rearrangement gives us the following equations:

$$\begin{array}{lll} \text{Agriculture:} & D_1 = (1 - 0.17)Y_1 - 0.09Y_2 & - 0.01Y_3 \\ \text{Manufacturing:} & D_2 = \quad -0.22Y_1 + (1 - 0.37)Y_2 & - 0.11Y_3 \\ \text{Services:} & D_3 = \quad -0.11Y_1 - 0.17Y_2 - & (1 - 0.80)Y_3 \end{array}$$

These are three simultaneous equations for the total output of the three industries (Y_1, Y_1, and Y_3) in terms of the demand for each industry's product by the final users (D_1, D_2, and D_3). We have now reached an important step in the conversion of an input-output table to a forecasting device. If we had a forecast of final demand (gross national product), and if we could estimate the portions of this final demand relating to each of the three industries, we could then use these three output equations as a basis for estimating the total demand (both intermediate and final demand) for each industry's product. This could be done by solving the three output equations for the three unknowns (Y_1, Y_2, and Y_3) in terms of the three (estimated) knowns (D_1, D_2, and D_3). This can be done by using any of the standard mathematical techniques for solving a system of simultaneous linear equations. The result of this mathematical exercise for our sample problem gives us the following three equations:

$$\begin{array}{ll} \text{Agriculture:} & 1.26D_1 + 0.185D_2 + 0.04D_3 = Y_1 \\ \text{Manufacturing:} & 0.49D_1 + 1.725D_2 + 0.24D_3 = Y_2 \\ \text{Services:} & 0.08D_1 + 0.40\ D_2 + 1.32D_3 = Y_3 \end{array}$$

The coefficients in these three equations play an important role in the input-output analysis, and they are often presented in tabular form, under the heading: "Direct and Indirect Requirements per Unit of Final Demand." These coefficients are shown in Table 3.

TABLE 3

Direct and Indirect Requirements per Unit of Final Demand

	Agriculture	*Manufacturing*	*Services*
Agriculture	1.26	0.185	0.04
Manufacturing	0.49	1.725	0.24
Services	0.08	0.40	1.32

Tables 2 and 3 are the basic tools of the input-output forecaster. Armed with these tools and an estimate of final demand by industry sector (D_1, D_2, and D_3), he can forecast total demand for each sector's output (Y_1, Y_2, and Y_3), as well as all of the inputs required by each industry to produce that value of total output. In short, he can calculate the amounts in each cell of Table 1. He would do this first by multiplying each column of Table 3 by his estimate of final demand for the appropriate industry. The total of each row, once this multiplication has been carried out, gives the total demand (both intermediate and final) for one of the industry sectors. Once total output of an industry is known, this amount can be multiplied by the technical coefficients in the appropriate column of Table 2. This will give the total dollar inputs from each industry needed to produce the amount of total demand. The difference between the value of total output and the sum of these intermediate product inputs is the total value added by the industry. This is, of course, the same amount that appears in the primary input row of Table 1. This calculation can be continued until each of the first four rows and three columns of Table 1 are completed. While we have gone through these calculations step by step in order to illustrate how a forecast would be produced using input-output tables, in practice the preparation of the forecast can be produced almost instantaneously through the use of high-speed digital computers.

JUDGMENTAL (OR INTUITIVE) FORECASTING

Methodological Issues

The use of the term *scientific forecasting*, although becoming increasingly common among economic forecasters, is somewhat unfortunate. Its use implies a value judgment: scientific forecasting is good and all others are bad. This is not true at all. Indeed, the use of the terms good and bad to describe forecasting methods has little meaning.

To be sure, we would expect good forecasting methods to produce relatively accurate forecasts as judged by usual statistical standards. But there are other dimensions of good and bad in forecasting which depend crucially on the uses to be made on the forecasts. For example, the cost of deriving a forecast with a particular degree of precision is certainly a relevant factor. Other considerations which may be important in the decision include the degree of sectoral detail provided by the forecasting method or the ability or inability of the forecaster to interact with the forecasting system, i.e., to alter easily the assumptions underlying the forecast and thus provide alternative forecasts. Finally, there is an element of the decision which is often ignored in discussions of the use of alternative forecasting methods, but one which is quite important, specifically the human factor. Forecasts are not prepared as idle academic exercises, but as inputs into specific managerial decisions. To be used by management, the forecasts must be trusted by them, and this often depends directly on their understanding and acceptance of the method used in generating the forecasts.

Scientific forecasting methods in general are particularly useful where considerable sectoral detail, all derived within a consistent framework, and a large degree of interaction with the forecasting system are required. However, these advantages are not always those which are of the most importance to business organizations. Moreover, the scientific methods are typically costly to construct and to operate since they require a staff of high-priced experts in such fields as economics, statistics, and computer science. For these reasons, and also because in general there does not appear to be any clear advantage yet for the scientific methods in terms of forecast accuracy, the most commonly used methods of forecasting are the judgmental or, as they are sometimes called, the intuitive methods.

Judgmental methods differ widely from one another. At their best, they are fairly systematic and use the same underlying theoretical framework of macroeconomics that is used in the scientific approaches. The difference between the two approaches is that the theoretical model used by the judgmental forecaster is implicit, while the scientific methods use an explicit, usually mathematical, representation of the same basic theoretical model. As a result, the predictions of each judgmental forecaster are determined by his subjective, and often changing, evaluation of the weights to be given each of the causal factors. Thus, it is rare when the forecasts derived from a judgmental approach can be replicated by any other forecaster. Nevertheless, these methods have been successful in practice. In large part this success has resulted from the great diversity of factors which influence economic activity. No cycle of business activity ever conforms precisely in structure and causal influences to any other. Therefore, any static set of mathematical relations with precise parameter values determined from historical data has an inherent disadvantage in forecasting future events. Judgmental forecasters using their intuition and feel for the numbers can adjust to these changing circumstances. And this flexibility has undoubtedly contributed much to the continued good success of judgmental forecasters.

Judgmental Forecasting in Practice

To illustrate how judgmental forecasting is actually done, let us describe its use in estimating GNP for a year or so ahead.[2]

While the actual procedure will vary according to the skills, habits, and experience of the economists, in general the similarities outweigh the differences. The process involves moving from the known to the unknown or less known, sector by sector. That is, the forecaster will set up the structure of the GNP accounting framework (see the section in this chapter on Keynesian economic models) and will attempt to fill in the

[2] For details on this and related approaches, see W. F. Butler, R. A. Kavesh, and R. B. Platt, *Methods and Techniques of Business Forecasting* (Englewood Cliffs, N.J.: Prentice-Hall, 1974).

empty boxes with his own estimates. Some of the figures will be fairly easy to approximate to a high order of accuracy; others will involve careful weighting and appraisal of a myriad of quantitative and qualitative forces.

Like any craftsman assembling a product, he will try to make sure that each piece fits together in a unified, consistent whole. And if the total seems unrealistic or somehow wrong, he will adjust and adapt the parts until the artist in him is satisfied.

In doing his job he will use tools: economic theory and analysis, elements of statistics and knowledge of history. Most importantly, he should have a deep understanding of how the economy and its sectors operate and interact in practice. This latter quality is the most elusive and generally serves to set apart the superior forecaster from his inferiors. Experience and study may help acquire this understanding, but in many cases they do not. And perhaps it is because the ultimate tool—the one that combines and synthesizes all the others—is that indefinable one of judgment. Without it, the forecaster may become mired in a swamp of statistics; with it he may be able to create order and form.

But let us move on to the actual forecasting process itself—the integration of the relatively known information with what is less well known.

First and foremost, before setting down any figures, the economist must state his basic, underlying assumptions. That is, he must describe in broad terms the overall environment in which business activity will be taking place. Since many external forces may have a substantial bearing upon the economy, the forecaster should cite some of the political, diplomatic, and sociological assumptions under which he is operating. These would include views on the prospects for war or peace, an overview of fiscal prospects, an appraisal of the future of controls—among others. In a sense these represent the counterpart to the exogenous factors incorporated into econometric models.

Once the assumptions have been stated, the judgmental forecaster can then turn to the numerical estimates themselves. Some economists prefer to begin by predicting total GNP and then working backward to supply the details. This technique is a handy one, in that it is much easier to estimate GNP within a small range of error than it is to do as well on each (or even on most) of the sectors. Compensating errors have frequently given the lie to the old saw that the total is merely the sum of the parts. However, this "working from the top down" approach merely delays the detailed effort required to supply the sector accounts. In practice, many forecasters work with a rough overall total in mind as a kind of index to the business environment they anticipate. This total figure, however, is not a constant; if the sum of the sectors is higher or lower, the forecaster will analyze and reappraise all of his estimates.

This brief description of the top-down method serves to highlight a frequently voiced criticism of the entire intuitive school. It is claimed that forecasts of the various sectors are not independently derived because in the process of making these estimates the forecaster is working within a framework of the overall level of business activity and is merely adapting each sector to the predetermined total pattern. Thus, it is averred, the component estimates are simply tailored to fit the cloth and should not be taken seriously.

This claim misses the point. Forecasting total GNP without analyzing the sectors is merely a guessing game, for it overlooks the interactions and stresses that only a more detailed study would furnish. Similarly, it would be absurd to fix rigidly a total for GNP and then mechanically or unimaginatively juggle the sectors until the parts equaled the whole. Rather, the process that is generally followed consists of a series of successive approximations in which the parts add up to a whole that has been roughly approximated in advance. Flexibility provides the key, as the sectors and the totals evolve into a final shape

After all, this is really what should be expected. The forecaster is not operating in a vacuum. He generally has a pretty good idea of what is happening in the economy at the moment; he knows much more about developments of the past few months. He has studied the cyclical behavior of GNP and its parts. Thus, he has a feel for what he anticipates will happen, and that feel extends to both the overall level of the economy and to many of its sectors. In practice, he will usually balance totals and parts until he reaches what he considers to be a unified forecast. This is what is meant by an intuitive approach.

But intuitive does not mean nonanalytical. What specific techniques will the forecaster utilize in deriving his GNP forecast? In brief, he will employ the whole range of statistical and analytical sources at his command. Leading, lagging, and coincident indicators will be studied to help provide the expected tone of the economy. Surveys of various types will be examined to provide insight into probable patterns of expenditures for capital goods, inventories, and consumer durables. Modified extrapolation techniques will be used in attempts to bridge gaps in data. Past cycles will be scrutinized to seek out parallels or comparisons. Ideas, notions, and hunches will comprise the glue for the whole operation. And, ultimately, a series of sectoral totals for the year ahead will evolve. The forecast may then appear complete, except for adding up the several sectors to derive total GNP. In practice, however, it is far from finished and must be regarded merely as a first approximation.

For now the real difficulties begin—the seesaw process of making the parts consistent with a more carefully considered whole. Here is where the talents, insights, and judgment of the forecaster are truly tested. Rare is the economist who simply aggregates and stops at that. Generally, a considerable amount of time is spent on balancing, weighing, and appraising in order to derive a set of estimates the forecaster is willing to accept as a final verdict. And he must always remember that a change here means a change there—in the matrix of interrelationships.

Several procedures can be followed in refining a forecast. One involves working through the income side of the national accounts by estimating the flow of wages, salaries, profits, interest, rent, and taxes which would result from the projected GNP. From the income side, the forecaster can run a series of important checks: Will profits suffice to call forth the investment in new plant and equipment in the GNP estimates? Is the savings rate reasonable? Will government fiscal results stimulate or retard the private economy? In general, is the supply of funds and the probable rate of interest consistent with the demand patterns in the economy? These tests frequently lead the forecaster to modify his estimates of consumption or investment.

Thus, the final step consists of refining the tentative estimates and seeking a set of GNP components that square with the total as the forecaster sees it. This process of successive approximations gives the ultimate stamp to the forecast.

When it is all done, the forecaster will have a detailed picture of the course of business activity as he sees it during the year ahead. It should be clearly noted, however, that there may be a difference between what the economist predicts and what he would like to see happen. A forecast of a recession means simply that the forces are shaping up in that direction—not that the forecaster wishes it to happen, as some corporate officials believe.

And after all is said and done, the forecast may turn out to be wrong! If this happens, the practitioner has no recourse but to analyze what went wrong and to revise his estimates. When to change a forecast—when to abandon a given line of reasoning—and reshape the entire framework is truly one of the forecaster's nightmares. Econometricians have it easy; they simply plug in new values for the exogenous variables and generate new forecasts. Judgmentalists, however, must reconsider the entire range of variables. In deciding upon the need for a revised forecast the judgmentalist will seek out sudden or unanticipated developments: an imposition of wage and price controls, a long strike, a major shift in monetary policy.

Scientific and Judgmental Forecasting in Retrospect

As has been demonstrated, there are strong and cogent arguments to be advanced for the use of both econometric (scientific) and judgmental (intuitive) approaches to forecasting. It would be wrong, however, to regard these methods as separate and distinct. The econometrician uses judgment throughout the entire process of describing and working with his model; the judgmentalist, conversely, will often study details of econometric models as an aid in decision making.

But despite this degree of overlap and complementarity, there has been a notable increase in the emphasis upon econometric models and methods by business forecasters. This trend will undoubtedly continue into the future. The reason is clear: the use of the mathematical approaches is the only way that economic forecasting can advance as a science. Only when we have made explicit the way our sectors interact and have defined precisely the causal variables and the magnitude and timing of their impact can we systematically isolate the causes of forecast errors and improve our forecasting model. Judgmental forecasting is not truly a method at all. The model used exists only in the brain of the forecaster; there is no way that he can pass it on to others so that they can build upon his experiences.

This does not mean, however, that judgment and intuition will in the future no longer play an important role in business forecasting. In the actual application of the scientific approaches, judgment plays, and undoubtedly will always play, an important role. In the early days of econometric forecasting, it was possible to find forecasters who thought that their models could capture all of the relevant systematic economic influences. Econometric forecasting has matured since then, however, and increasingly the users of econometric models have come to realize that their models can only be relied upon to provide a first approximation—a set of consistent forecasts which then must be massaged with intuition and good judgment to take into account those influences on economic activity for which history is a poor guide.

34

Technical Analysis

ALAN R. SHAW
Vice President and a Director of Research
Harris, Upham & Co., Incorporated
New York, New York

THE HISTORY AND EVOLUTION OF TECHNICAL SECURITY ANALYSIS

OF ALL the approaches to analyzing the stock market, technical analysis is perhaps the most misunderstood. And it is the approach most often criticized no doubt because of the lack of understanding. Perhaps part of the mystique lies with the absence of credible text material. But a handful of true works of in-depth discourse compare with volumes of elementary and advanced books concerning economics, accounting, financial statement analysis, and management evaluation methods.

But, it should be pointed out that, in fact, technical analysis is the *oldest* form of security analysis known to man. The approach has been traced back close to 100 years when financial statements were not readily available for any type of quantitative analysis. Or, stated another way, in the late 1800s and early 1900s, if a "researcher" visited the corporate offices of a major concern and asked, "How's the business?" he was no doubt politely told, "It is none of yours!"

Herewith the author shall try to overcome some of the void, as it is earnestly thought that the technical approach deserves its due recognition within the investment community as a valid tool in the decision-making process. Success in the stock market comes about by minimizing risk. But, unfortunately, many look at the market from the viewpoint of reward only, taking unnecessary risks to achieve it. Buying a stock with apparent strong fundamentals and little regard for the stock's technical position can easily result in a quick loss. Many stocks can "top-out" when, as the saying goes, "business couldn't be better." On the other hand, undue risk is also taken when making a commitment strictly on technical grounds. Many good-looking stocks have fallen out of so-called base formations due to an unexpected poor earnings report. Therefore it seems logical that a combination of both types of securities analysis should result in better decision making and the results that follow. The use of both approaches has to maximize profit potential as risk is being lessened. Since technical analysis is primarily a timing tool, it could be said that fundamental analysis represents the "what" input, while technical analysis is the "when." Let us explore some of the different approaches.

BASIC TECHNICAL ASSUMPTIONS—NECESSARY LOGICAL THOUGHTS SUPPORTING THE APPROACH

Before embarking into any area of study there is usually a set of rules or assumptions that first must be explored and/or recognized in order to make the study not only meaningful, but as lucid and clear as possible. Technical analysis is based upon the study of supply and demand or the price movements within the general stock market framework. It is what the movements themselves mean over the short to longer term, that the technician is concerned with. A well-rounded security analyst who utilizes all inputs available must be a very inquisitive person; he will always be anxious to know why a stock is moving up or down. And, in this regard, it has often been said that a good technician has to be an even better fundamentalist.

It is known that the stock market is one of a number of leading economic indicators as compiled by different sources. Although the market is, of course, concerned with day-to-day business developments and worldwide news events, it is primarily concerned with future expectations. In this regard, the market is therefore looked at as more of a barometer rather than a thermometer. Specifically, it has not been uncommon to witness a stock rising in a viable uptrend when current news concerning the company is at its worst. By the same token, one can witness a stock in a major downtrend while earnings are most favorable. To carry our thesis a step further, it would be most uncommon to witness a stock begin a major upside trend just before earnings start to deteriorate. The reverse oddity would occur if a stock commenced a major downtrend just before earnings began to show substantial recovery.

Let us review what we consider to be the three basic and necessary assumptions regarding technical analysis before we embark on the actual methods themselves.

Assumption 1. The market and/or an individual stock acts like a barometer rather than a thermometer. Events are usually discounted in advance with movements likely the result of informed buyers and sellers at work. We should never forget, as we explore the technical implications of market analysis, that the price formations or patterns (as they are called by some) that evolve due to supply/demand behavior are, for the most part, the result of fundamentalists or speculators putting their money to work based upon their established convictions.

Assumption 2. This assumption should not be too difficult to understand or accept as it deals with basic stock market dynamics or the law of supply and demand. First, we should define the terms that are used.

There is a buyer for every seller of stock. But, one of these forces is usually stronger or more influential—especially in the long run. For instance, if 50,000 shares of stock were to change hands on a downtick trade, especially a concession representing a large spread from the last sale, we would consider that the seller was a stronger influence than the buyer. For, if a buyer (or buyers) were all that anxious to purchase the stock, it would be logical to expect that the trade would have taken place with little or no concession of price at all. And, in periods of a more vibrant market atmosphere, the trade could, in fact, occur on an uptick. Usually, a major concession in price on a large block trade is looked upon as evidence of *distribution,* it would most likely be a sign of the stock moving from strong to weak hands.

Accumulation by definition occurs when a stock moves from weak to strong hands or, more importantly, when supply is *eliminated* from the marketplace. Such a trade could take place on an uptick in price. On the other hand, distribution by definition occurs when a stock moves from strong to weak hands or supply is created in the marketplace. Such a trade could occur on a downtick in price.

Assumption 2 therefore reads as follows: Before a stock experiences a markup phase, whether it be minor or major, a period of accumulation usually will take place. Conversely, before a stock enters into a major or minor downtrend, a period of distribution usually will be the preliminary occurrence. Accumulation or distribution activity can occur within neutral trading trends. Obviously an uptrend in prices denotes on-balance buying, while a downtrend is indicative of extreme supply. The ability to analyze accumulation or distribution within neutral price patterns will be discussed herein. Such analysis is the technician's main challenge. He should anticipate, not react.

Assumption 3. This third assumption is actually basically tied into the first two already discussed. It is an observation that can be readily made by any student willing to expend the time and effort. It deals with the scope and extent of market movements in relation to each other. As an example, in most cases, a small phase of stock price consolidation —which is really a phase of backing and filling—will be followed by a relative short-term movement, up or down, in the stock's price. On the other hand, a larger consolidation phase can lead to a greater potential stock price move. Figure 1 should aid in the understanding of this assumption.

In Example A, the minor downward movement in price was followed by a short-term consolidation phase before the stock began to move up once again. In Example B, however, the downside adjustment was somewhat more severe than in the former case and thus the consolidation pattern was slightly longer in perspective. Example C is an extreme, reflecting a major downward trend. Simply stated, when the bulldozer, crane, and steel ball visited this scene, it took longer for the carpenters, electricians, and masons to accomplish their rebuilding procedure; the consolidation pattern was of longer duration.

Assumption 3 therefore states: *Usually,* most movements in the market have a relationship to each other.

FIGURE 1

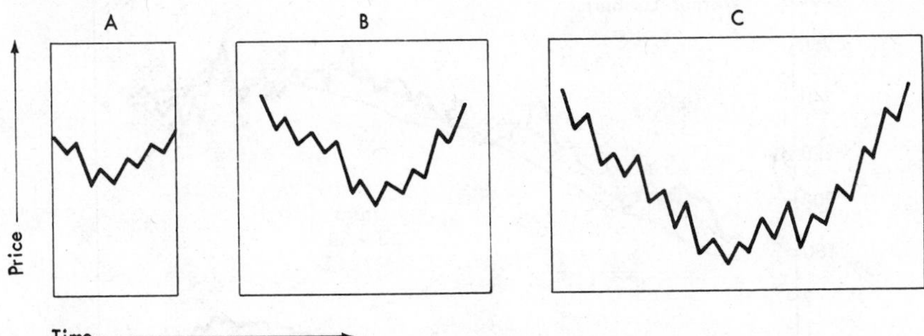

These are the three basic assumptions. They are simple and we hope logical to understand. But, they are often overlooked, even by more astute market students when attempting to understand technical stock market analysis. These assumptions, we hope, provide the framework for a clearer understanding of the methods that follow.

BASIC TECHNICAL METHODS—CHART UTILIZATION, TYPES, THEIR CONSTRUCTION, AND SERVICES AVAILABLE

Despite the growth of a number of mechanical and/or automated stock market techniques, the basic tool of most technically oriented market students is still their chart. Through the years, three basic types of charting techniques have been developed with perhaps one enjoying greater popularity.

Basic Chart Types

The three basic types of charts are the line, bar, and point and figure. In each case the type of chart chosen to record price activity is determined by the amount of information available.

A line chart, as illustrated in Figure 2, is used to denote the trend of a *single* statistic. As an example, the daily closing price of a stock; a weekly group statistic; or a monthly economic figure would most often be plotted on a line chart basis. Figure 2 illustrates a group statistic plotted weekly. In addition, the illustration also contains moving averages (running through the price curve), as well as a relative strength line denoted at the graph's bottom.

The bar chart is the most commonly used technical tool. It is simple to construct as it portrays the high, low, and closing prices of a particular stock or stock market average, for a particular time period chosen. In the latter regard, bar charts are kept either on a daily, weekly, or monthly basis. The type of bar chart will, of course, be predicated upon the time horizon of the investor. The short-term trader would most likely find the daily bar chart of help while the longer term investor would most likely utilize the weekly or monthly bar chart. In addition to price action, a bar chart also contains a volume curve (see Figure 3), especially the daily and weekly varieties. Most often the monthly bar chart simply reveals price action.

FIGURE 2

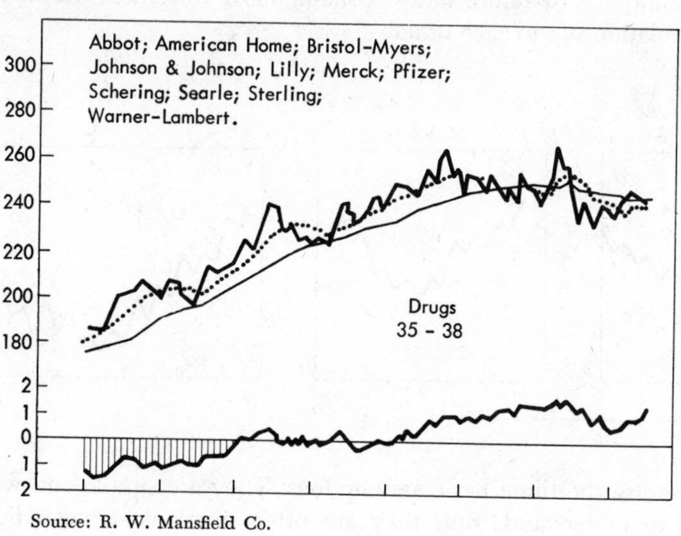

Source: R. W. Mansfield Co.

The two types of charting techniques reviewed above can be portrayed on graph paper utilizing one of two types of scales—the arithmetic or the semilog delineation. Again, the utilization of the type of scale depends greatly upon the desires of the chartist. There are those

FIGURE 3

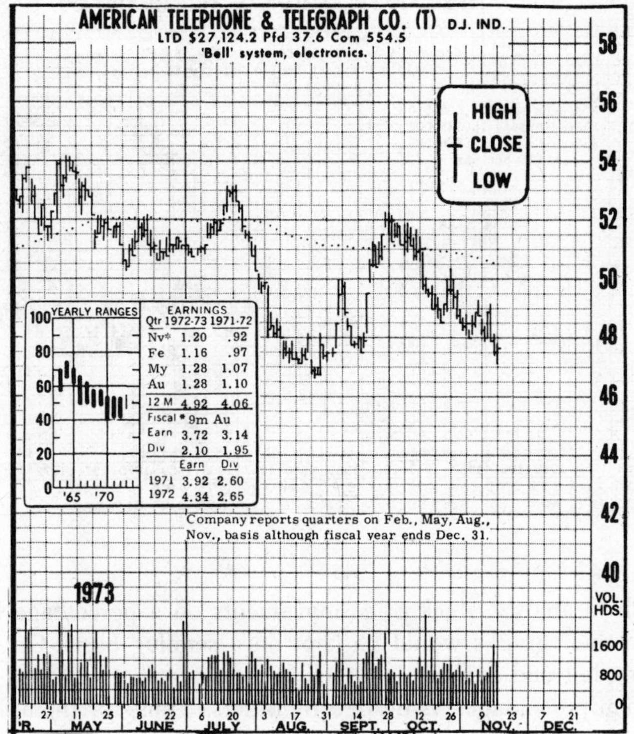

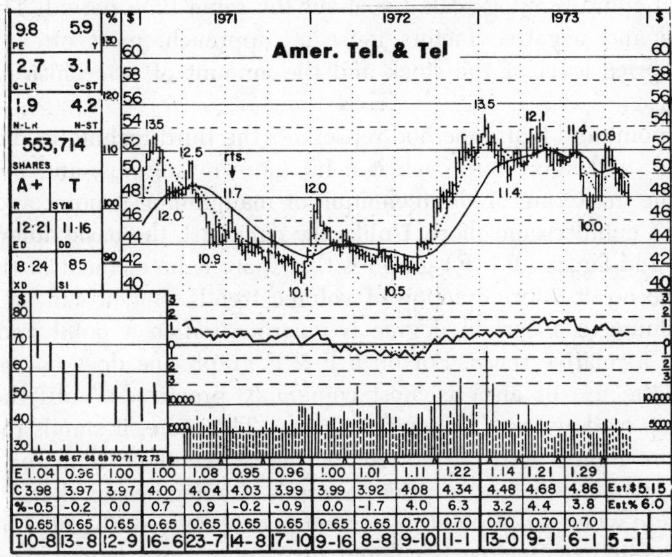

Sources: Chart A, courtesy of Trendline, A Division of Standard & Poor's Corp.; Chart B, R. W. Mansfield Co.; Chart C, courtesy of M. C. Horsey & Co., Inc., Salisbury Maryland 21801

FIGURE 3 (continued)

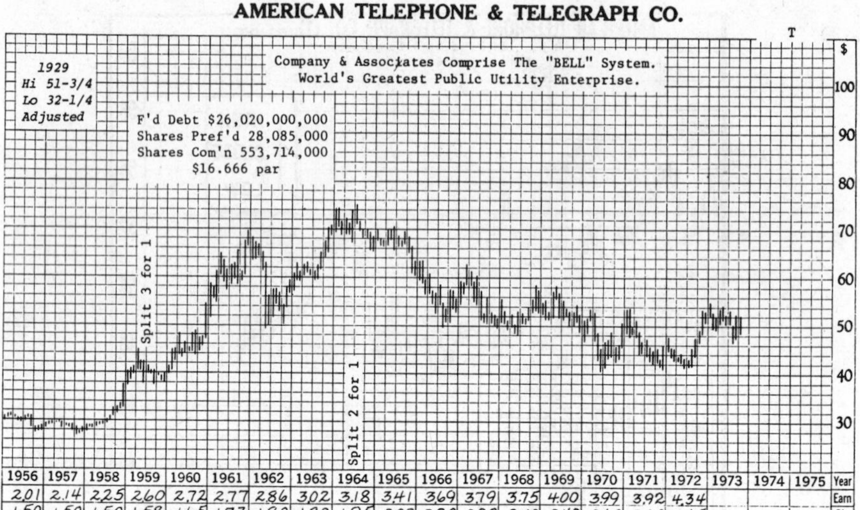

who wish to analyze stock price movements on a percentage basis and therefore their graphs would be kept on a semilog basis. On the other hand, simple trend analysis, or stock price movement in terms of points rather than percentages, is desired by others. Thus, for them, a straight arithmetic scale suffices. Figure 4 illustrates a stock plotted with an arithmetic and semilog scale for about the same time period. There are positive and negative factors for each approach, most often hinging on the price level of the stock and the amount of price history under study.

The point and figure method represents the third technique. To many, the point and figure approach is a bit more mysterious, and indeed to some, the mastering of the technique of maintaining a point and figure chart is a cumbersome chore. Unlike the bar chart, the basic difference in a point and figure (P & F) graph is that there is no element of time and therefore no distinct depiction of volume trends. But, it can be argued that volume to a certain degree is incorporated in a point and figure chart in a relative sense. For on a P & F graph one does not put in a figure (the use of an *x* is most commonly practiced) until the stock moves up or down one full point or more. Therefore, it stands to reason that more figures will be plotted for the active stock than for the inactive; volume will create price reversals. Remembering that a plot is only made when a full point movement is experienced, the next factor to keep in mind is that each column on a point and figure chart must represent a trend or direction of price. Remembering these two inputs should add greatly in the understanding of point and figure chart construction.

Like the bar chart, there are a number of different types of point and figure graphs utilized—again, depending upon the investor's time horizon or investment philosophy. The one-point reversal, which as mentioned, illustrates movements of one point or more in each direction, is the most popular point and figure approach. But, if a more intermediate to longer term trend analysis of a particular equity is desired, no doubt a three-point or five-point reversal chart will be utilized. In the latter two cases, each column on the graph illustrates movements of a minimum of three or five points in each direction respectively. In some cases, to further facilitate longer term stock price movement analysis, point and figure charts are kept on a *unit* basis. Put simply, a reversal chart of more than one point, like a three- or five-point reversal, condenses the horizontal axis of the graph, while the use of a unit scale reduces the vertical axis. A chart on a company like IBM would, no doubt, be kept on a three- or five-point reversal as well as on a unit basis. In fact, a combination of both can be utilized. Versatility is a great asset of the P & F approach.

Let us be more specific regarding the construction technique for a point and figure graph. Whereas a bar chart depicts a daily, weekly, or monthly specific price range, a point and figure chart illustrates trades only as they occur, *and in their sequence*. Figure 5 provides an illustration of a week's price movement in a particular stock. The first set of statistics indicates the initial day's opening (O), high (H), low (L), and close (C), with an accompanying illustration showing how these statistics would be produced on a daily bar chart. Volume is added below. The second set of statistics, however, actually shows the sequence of trades with the fractions eliminated from each day's stock price movement. Or, put another way, the second set of statistics outlines each day's high and low differential but with a sense of the intra-day trend.

To construct a point and figure chart, a starting point must be realized. This is illustrated by the darkened square at a price of 47. Monday's trading reveals that the first full one-point move occurred as a decline to 46, before an intra-day move up to 47. Remembering that each column on a point and figure chart must represent a "trend," it is therefore mandatory that Column 1 cannot contain one "fill-in" by itself. Thus, to start our chart, the first *x* is placed at the 46 line representing Monday's first full point move. Because the column now contains a movement in sequence to 46 from 47, it can be classified as a "down" column (see arrow). This means that from this point on, if there were never to be an up move of one point or more over a period of one week, two weeks, and so on, we would continuously plot the down moves of this stock in the first column of the grid. However, we note that following the initial 46

FIGURE 4

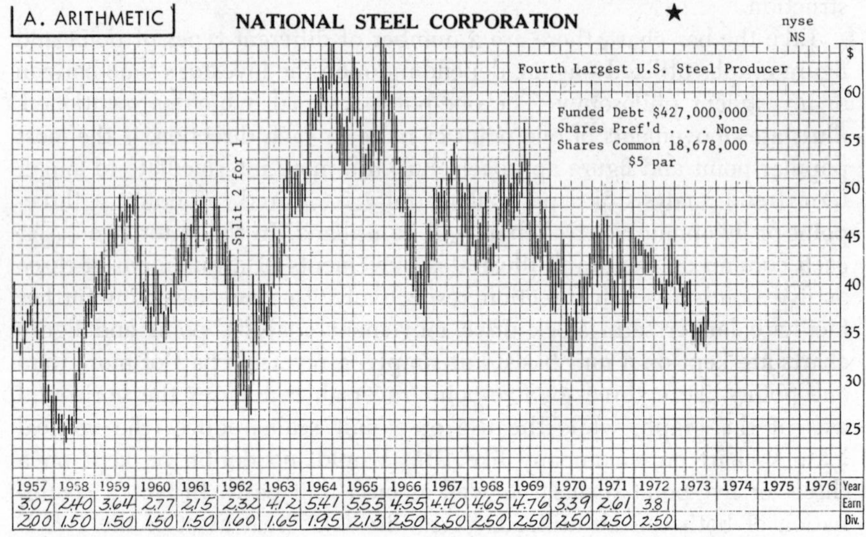

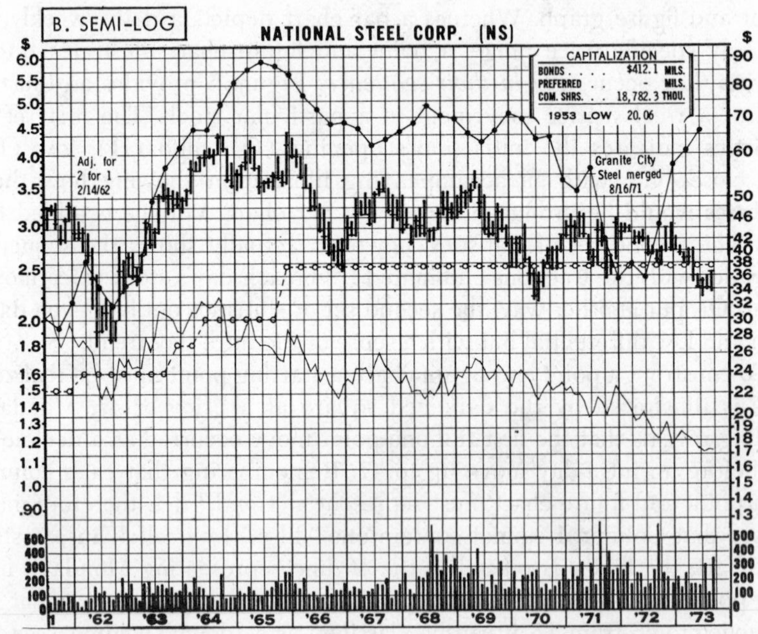

Sources: Chart A, Courtesy of M. C. Horsey & Co., Inc., Salisbury, Maryland 21801; Chart B, Courtesy of Securities Research Company, 208 Newbury St., Boston, Mass. 02116.

FIGURE 5

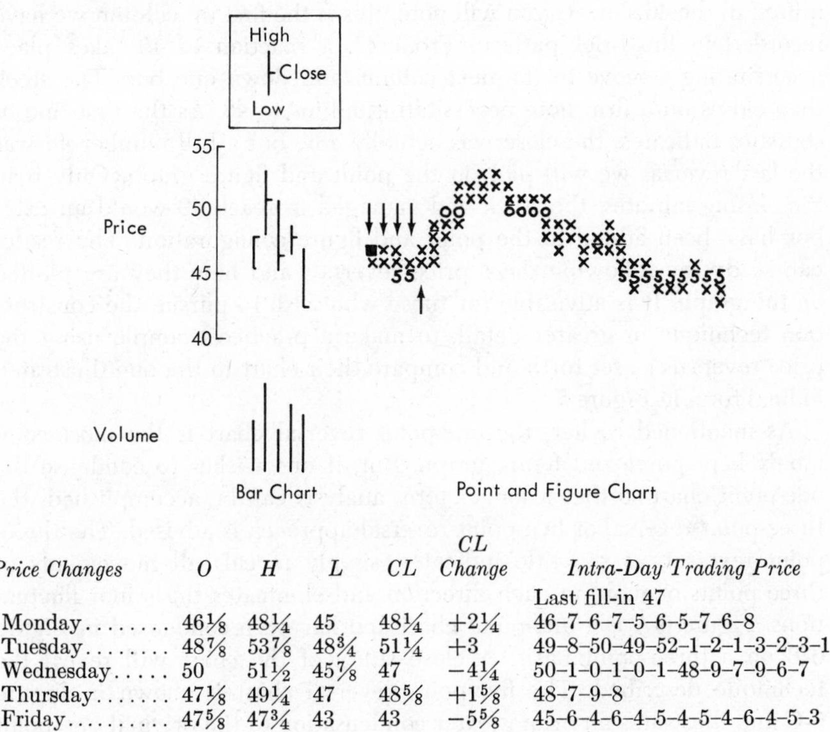

Price Changes	*O*	*H*	*L*	*CL*	*CL Change*	*Intra-Day Trading Price*
						Last fill-in 47
Monday........	46⅛	48¼	45	48¼	+2¼	46-7-6-7-5-6-5-7-6-8
Tuesday........	48⅞	53⅞	48¾	51¼	+3	49-8-50-49-52-1-2-1-3-2-3-1
Wednesday.....	50	51½	45⅞	47	−4¼	50-1-0-1-0-1-48-9-7-9-6-7
Thursday.......	47⅛	49¼	47	48⅝	+1⅝	48-7-9-8
Friday..........	47⅝	47¾	43	43	−5⅝	45-6-4-6-4-5-4-5-4-6-4-5-3

entry, the stock does move up to 47. Therefore, to record the 47 price, we must move one column to the right, up one box, and place an *x* in the 47 slot. The next intra-day move is back down to a full number price of 46, thus we move a box below the last 47 fill-in as, once again, we cannot have a trendless column. Completing this maneuver, we would now have two down columns in succession. According to the statistics, we note that the next reversal is back up to 47. Thus, we move a column to the right and repeat the procedure to record the 47 move. The next illustrated trade again reveals some intra-day pressure taking the stock to the low of the day or a price of 45. To record this movement and to reach the 45 level, an *x* must be placed in the 46 box and then a fill-in is made at 45. (Note: On the 45 line, instead of an *x*, the digit 5 is used. Similarly, with prices ending in a zero, a 0 is used. The use of fives and zeros simply helps to break up the monotony of a concentrated group of *x*'s.)

From 45, the stock rallies briefly to 46 before once again reacting to 45. This sequence of reversals is plotted next. Then a strong rally to 47 occurs. In order to move to 47, from the last fill-in at 45, a fill-in is required in the 46 slot. As you will note, this is the first up column we have recorded in the brief pattern. From 47, a reaction to 46 takes place necessitating a move to the next column and down one box. The stock then closes on a firm note necessitating fill-ins to 48. As the first line of statistics indicates, the close was actually 48¼, but a full number 48 was the last reversal we will plot on the point and figure graph. Only if in the closing minutes, the stock had managed to reach 49 would an extra box have been added to the point and figure configuration. The reader can study the following days' price reversals and how they are plotted on the graph. It is advisable for those who wish to pursue the construction technique in greater detail, to make a practice example using the price reversals as set forth and compare their chart to the one illustrated in final form in Figure 5.

As mentioned earlier, the one-point reversal chart is the most commonly kept point and figure graph. But, if one wishes to condense the one-point chart so that a longer term analysis can be accomplished, the three-point reversal or five-point reversal approach is advised. The three-point reversal, as the title indicates, simply reveals all movements of three points or more in each direction and eliminates the minor fluctuations. Figure 6-A is a one-point chart and has been condensed in Figure 6-B on a three-point basis. A close study of the chart will reveal the technique described. The five-point reversal chart is shown in Figure 6-C and illustrates an even greater condensation of the original one-point chart. It is obvious, that a three- or five-point reversal chart will only be necessary if many columns of price reversals on a one-point graph are to be condensed. Some astute short-term traders oftentimes maintain their point and figure charts on a half-point basis. This necessitates a lot more work and is probably only useful for stocks selling at very low quotations.

Because it is necessary to maintain a point and figure chart with accurate statistics, and because the point and figure chart does reveal intra-day movements in their sequence of trading, a newspaper will not suffice as a source of data. This is especially true regarding higher priced stocks where intra-day price reversals can be quite numerous. Some point and figure chartists maintain their P & F graphs by utilizing the "Fitch Sheets," a service published by Francis Emery Fitch and most often found in the back office section of brokerage firms. It is an expensive service, but it does include the daily price movements in their sequence for all listed stocks from the opening to the close. We advise, however, that interested students secure a service published by Morgan, Rogers and Roberts.[1] This outfit publishes a price change service designed

---

[1] 150 Broadway, New York, New York 10005.

FIGURE 6

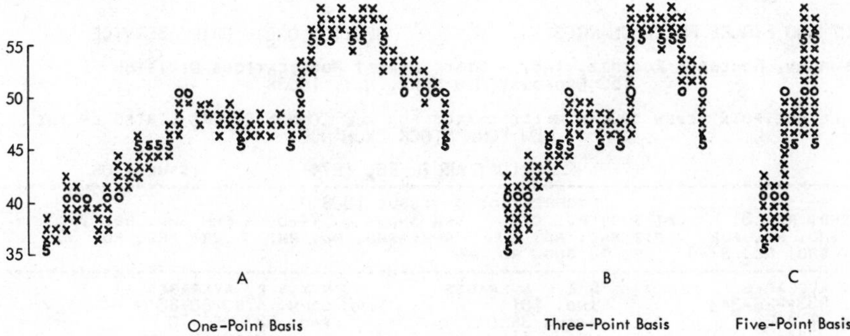

specifically for point and figure chartists. They maintain a staff that eliminates the fractions from the Fitch sheet tabulations and, in an alphabetical order, supply the daily price reversals, as shown in Figure 7.

A common query is, "Well, what type of chart should I maintain?". Or, "Why a bar chart instead of a point and figure chart?" or, "vice versa?". These are questions difficult to answer because the investment objectives of the different practitioners must first be understood. Bar charts have certain advantages over point and figure charts, albeit, primarily on a short-term basis. On the other hand, point and figure charts have a certain advantage over bar charts—in this regard, more on an intermediate to longer term basis. Ideally, both approaches should be used hand in hand when analyzing any particular stock. In the discussion that follows, perhaps the reader can distinguish the advantages most pertinent to his needs. Figure 8 lists a number of the more popular commercial technical chart services that may be purchased for both the bar and point and figure approaches.

BASIC TECHNICAL METHODS (CONTINUED)—ANALYSIS OF SUPPORT AND SUPPLY LEVELS

One of the most important aspects of technical analysis, the type of chart technique notwithstanding, involves the judgment of so-called support and resistance (supply) levels as shown in Figure 9. Often one reads about a stock that is selling, let us say, at 36, having support at 28–30 with potential overhead resistance at 43–45. Just what is the writer talking about?

Let us assume that you have been following the price movement of a certain stock that has been trading for a period of time in a neutral fashion—or fluctuating between the levels of 26 and 30. Obviously, during this neutral price movement the forces of supply and demand

FIGURE 7

POINT AND FIGURE PRICE CHANGES SECTION ONE - DAILY SERVICE

MORGAN, ROGERS & ROBERTS, INC. - STOCK MARKET PUBLICATIONS DIVISION
150 BROADWAY NEW YORK, N.Y. 10038

ALL ONE POINT EVEN DOLLAR PRICE CHANGS FOR ALL COMMON STOCKS LISTED ON THE NEW YORK STOCK EXCHANGE

FRIDAY AFR IL 26, 1974 ISSUE 1309

CORRECTION ON ISSUE 1308

BK SHD. RD. 31 CBT SHD. RC. CFT CRK SHD. RD. 74-5 FNM SHD. RD. 16
BUR SHD. RD. FUR PIZ SHD. RD. 20 RMMI SHD. RD. RMI SRT SHD. RD. 30
SLB SHD. RD. 97-8 TU 12 SHD. RD. WU

D.J. AVERAGES	S & P AVERAGES	N.Y.S.E. AVERAGES
IND. 833½-26-34½	IND. 10140	COMM. 4780-60-80
TRAN. 174-2½	RAILS 3850	IND. 5270-40-70
UTIL. 78½	UTIL. 4110	TRAN. 3440-10
COMP. 256½-4-5½	COMP. 9010	UTIL. 3110-00
		FINC. 5650-20-40

ABT 55
ACF 45
AET 55
AET WI 29
AL 35
ALB 25
AMV 17
AHC 27
ABA 5
AMB 35
ABC 24
ACT 5
AHP 39
AHS 36
ANG 35
ABG 13
AMA 18
AMP 38
AFX 16
ARA 91
AZP 16
ABZ 9
ACK 27
ARM 18
ASA 79-82
DG 24
ARC 87-6
AUD 41
AVY 39
AVP 44-3
BAW 26
BNC 20
BKV 22
BAI 8
BOL 28-7-8
BAX 39-8
BRY 20
BDX 35
BKI 22
BX 21
BIG 54
BDK 35
BMY 46
BWN 10
BGH 195-3-6
CBT 26
CRK 78
CCL 62-0
CPL 17
CRS 24
CAT 59
CNC 11
CTX 13
CEA 13
CHR 31
CMR 26
CBM 59-8

CO 46
CSN 20
CMZ 31
FNC 41
CS 46
CZS 17
CLF 72
KO 106-4
CF 6
CSP 75
CWO 13
CGM 16
CIC 34
CIE 10-1
CLL 37
CPX 31
CUZ 12
CR 22
CCK 21
ZB 36
CUM 31
CW-A 22
DMN 30
DAL 48
DEC 107-6-7
DMG 9
DM 155-4-7
DOW 61
DNB 27
DD 171-69
EFU 24
EK 105-4-
106-5
ECK 22
EQ 14
ESM 28
ESL 4
EY 27-6
FCI 51-0-2-1
FSS 7
FOE 19
FWB 24
FIS 39
FHR 14
FLY 15
FMC 18
FOX 35
FM 17
FTR 22

GSK 31
GDC 27
GMT 44
GE 51
GFC 12
GLE 12
GDW 11
GR 24
GAA 10
GNN 44
GMR 12
GRE 12
HAL 142
HL 25
HP 28
HWP 81-0
HWC 15
HM 79-8-9-
78-80-79
HON 76
HW 15
HT 60
IDA 27
ITW 23
INA 31
IIS 17
IR 75
IBM 224-3-4
222-6
IFF 35-4
IGL 36
IWG 15
JP 25
JWC 20
JHI 22
JNJ 107
JL 19
KYR .17
KWD 13
KN 38
KMG 66-5
KES 19
KOP 51-0
KRA 45
KG 31
LLY 72
LCE 17
LDG 60
LLX 33
LPX 22
LZ 33-4
MDA 20
MHS 19
MF 18
MMA 18
MAS 39

MCA 24
MS 15
MCD 53-2
MP 47
MKE 25
MRK 80-79
MSA 21-0
MSB 7
MGI 29-8
MAI 16
MIL 27
MLY 22
JPM 64
MRN 23
MT 8
MNP 20
MOT 53
MFS 66
MUR 65
NAL 18
NCH 43
NBD 41
NHX 3
NUM 26
NOM 46
NEM 31
NGE 24
NAM 14
NU 9
NGX 7

PLT 18
PP 27
PAY 10
PBD 23
JCP 70
PEP 60
PFE 35
MO 96
PVH 7
PIK 15
PNA 19
PIZ 21
PNI 11
PRD 58-6-7
PON 31-2
PG 91
PU 55-4
PPD 26
PLM 24
ROF 15
RAH 21
RTC 12-3
ROK 26
ROH 89
ROS 30
RDR 20
FN 29
SRT 29
SJR 10
SAF 26
SLB 99-8-
100
SDV 6
SVE 6
S 82-1
SED 44
SUO 48
SST 15
SNE 27
STB 31
NRG 48
SR 42
SUG 25
SWF 8
SMI 13
SQD 31
STA 31
SN 87
SOH 54
SWK 24
SW 59
SUN 42
SSC 17
SOC 191-4
SYB 22
TLC 7

TAL 6
TSO 22
TET 31
TG 27
TXN 100-99-100-
99
THI 15
TNB 45
JWT 9
TKA 14
TRA 30
TA 8
UK 39
UCL 39
UNP 78-7
UNI 8
UA 27
FG 33
UFG 16
UVV 27
UPJ 68-7-8
UC 35
UV 37-6
VET 22
HIR 46
WLA 34
WMX 14
WAL 11
WBC 22
WMB 50
WY 45
WIN 40
XRX 108-10-09

FIGURE 8

Chart Services

Service	*Publisher and Location*	*Type*	*Markets*	*Averages, a; Groups, b; Indicators, c*
Andrews	Parlin Publishers Sterling, N.J.	P & F x1, x3	AMEX & NYSE	a
Chartcraft	Chartcraft, Inc. Larchmont, N.Y.	P & F x3	AMEX & NYSE	a
Crosschart	Dines Chart Corp. New York, N.Y.	P & F x3	AMEX & NYSE	a,c
Cycli-Graphs	Securities Research Boston, Mass.	Bar-monthly	AMEX & NYSE	a,c
Security Charts		Bar-weekly		a,b,c
Daily Graphs	Daily Graphics Los Angeles, Cal.	Bar-daily	AMEX & NYSE	a,b,c
Horsey—The Stock Picture	M. C. Horsey & Co. Salisbury, Md.	Bar-monthly	NYSE, AMEX, Toronto, Mid-west, PBW, OTC (1,700 stocks total)	a,b
25-Year Picture		Bar-monthly		a,b
Mansfield	R. W. Mansfield Jersey City, N.J.	Bar-weekly	AMEX, NYSE, OTC	a,b,c
Paflibe	Dines Chart Corp. New York, N.Y.	P & F x1	NYSE & AMEX	a,b,c
Trendline	Trendline Div. New York, N.Y. Standard & Poor's	Bar-daily	NYSE & AMEX (Total-672 stocks)	a,c

have been fairly equal. Ultimately the stock will break out of this consolidation pattern in either an upward or downward direction. If the direction is upward, thus indicating a surge of demand, a distinctive clue would be given that the on-balance activity that most likely occurred during the consolidation phase was accumulation, rather than distribution (review Assumption 2). Let us assume you made a commitment in the stock in the 26–30 zone prior to the upside breakout.

Oftentimes, an investment story is not bought by all on the first go round. Some extra convincing is necessary. Such convincing can be accomplished by the mere price performance of the stock itself. In our case at hand, the stock has just moved up in price as profiled by the breakout from the consolidation phase. Let us assume that some adverse external news comes to the fore (e.g., political-military), and the stock experiences some minor selling pressure, falling back to the area of the original price consolidation. Chances are quite good that those who purchased shares initially would not now be sellers of stock. In fact, they may even be inclined to buy more. And, of added importance, investors who did not purchase the shares initially may now seize upon this second opportunity to make a commitment. The motivations just discussed are primarily predicated upon (1) the recent price activity in the stock, whereby it was just selling at a higher price after breaking out of its consolidation trend, and (2) a feeling of confidence, to a degree based on this price action, that the stock will eventually resume its upward trend. It is mainly because of these psychological factors that market analysts would anticipate that the stock in question should find support between 26 and 30. At least initially, there is a good chance of the stock bouncing back up.

Thus, by definition, a support level is a phase of price consolidation —or congestion—below the current quotation of a stock. Utilizing Assumption 3 for a minute, the extent of the lateral consolidation oftentimes

FIGURE 9

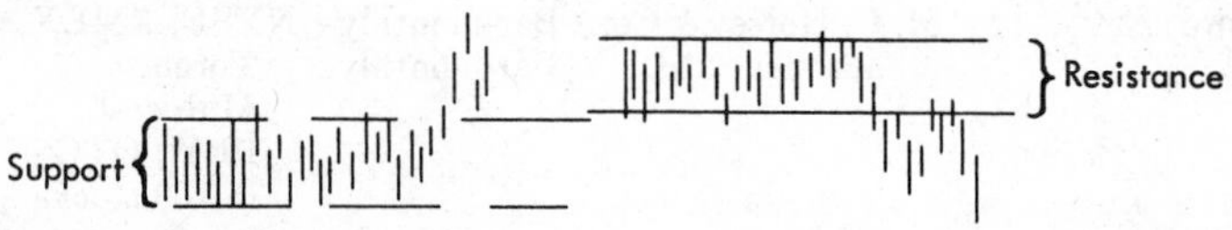

has a bearing on the validity of the support. Minor consolidation infers a minor support level where a more elongated congestion zone infers major support.

It will now be simple to explain resistance. Let us say your investment made between 26–30 turns out to be unwise. For instead of the stock moving up, it breaks down out of the congestion pattern, reaching a level of 20. Mass psychology now begins to work quite differently. For instead of taking the opportunity to buy more shares at the current cheaper price, many investors will simply bemoan their mistake and hope for a chance to break even. This psychological behavior by the masses infers that on any strength back into the overhead consolidation area, the stock will meet supply or sellers will dominate. Whereas in the first example you did not buy the stock to break even, in the latter case you are hoping that a break-even position can be attained. Thus, by definition, a resistance zone is an area of price activity above a stock's current quotation. The validity of the resistance may well depend upon the duration of the consolidation in the pattern.

Support and supply levels in individual stocks are real, as people are actively buying and selling the specific equities. But, it is important to recognize that when talking about support and supply levels for market averages, they are more psychological than real; one does not buy and sell the averages directly.

Knowing the type of security being analyzed also aids in deciding the extent of support or supply validity. A stock like Natomas certainly possesses quite different market characteristics than American Telephone. Where one issue primarily may attract hot trading money, the other enjoys a greater investment stature. Thus, if we were analyzing a supply area of three years previous for both stocks, our respect for the Telephone configuration would be much greater than that for Natomas.

Trend Analysis

Many users of technical analysis do not wish to get too involved in all the possible applications. In fact, they may use their market studies as nothing more than a road map is used to travel upstate. Trend analysis of stock price movements, as an example, does aid the investor to at least examine where on the route he will be making his commitment. The simple observation of a stock's chart can reveal to the portfolio manager the precise point whereby a particular issue is currently being recommended. The stock may have already moved up in price from $30 to $55 per share. He can therefore ask the analyst making the presentation, "Where have you been with your story before visiting me?" And perhaps, more importantly, he may add, "Where do you still have to go when you leave here?" The portfolio manager's observation of the chart pattern reveals the stock's price performance and certainly indicates that he is not the first to hear the bullish tale and, more importantly, he had better not be the last.

A trend to a stock is really nothing more than a navigator is to a pilot. It is not all that important to know—by using a chart—that a stock is in an uptrend or a downtrend, or is moving laterally in price. What is important is to be alerted to the possibility of a *trend reversal* or a shift in the slope of the stock's price movement.

Most chart followers and technically oriented students will maintain trend lines with the simple use of a ruler and a pencil. Other more sophisticated technicians may utilize computer strategy by mathematically calculating trends either by degree of slope and/or rate-of-change analysis. Simply speaking, the use of a hand-drawn trendline can most often suffice.

The violation of a trend is the same as the navigator shifting in his seat and informing the captain that the course of the aircraft is now changing. The shifting of a trend should offer impetus for the security analyst to more fully investigate the issue under review. Why are market forces indicating a change in attitude toward the stock? It could simply be that the stock is about to embark upon a consolidation pattern in preparation for another markup phase later on. Or, it could be an early signal that, in fact, a reversal phase will shortly occur shifting the overall trend on a major basis. The discounting movement of stocks in relationship to future expectations is one reason why a good market technician has got to be an even better fundamentalist.

Moving Averages

In addition to the above stated approach to trend analysis, market students also separately follow *moving averages* of a stock's price trend. A moving average is a *mathematical* trendline. It is also used as a measurement of stock momentum. Moving averages are often calculated for different time periods such as a 10-day moving average for the short term, a 25-day moving average for the intermediate term, and a 200-day moving average for longer term trend analysis. The simple moving average is calculated merely by adding the closing prices of the number of days under question and dividing by the number of days. A 200-day moving average would be the sum of the closes for the previous 200 market days divided by 200.

Because of its computation, a moving average will always lag stock price movement. As Figure 10 shows, in a downtrend, the 200-day moving average is above the stock price but below it once an uptrend

FIGURE 10

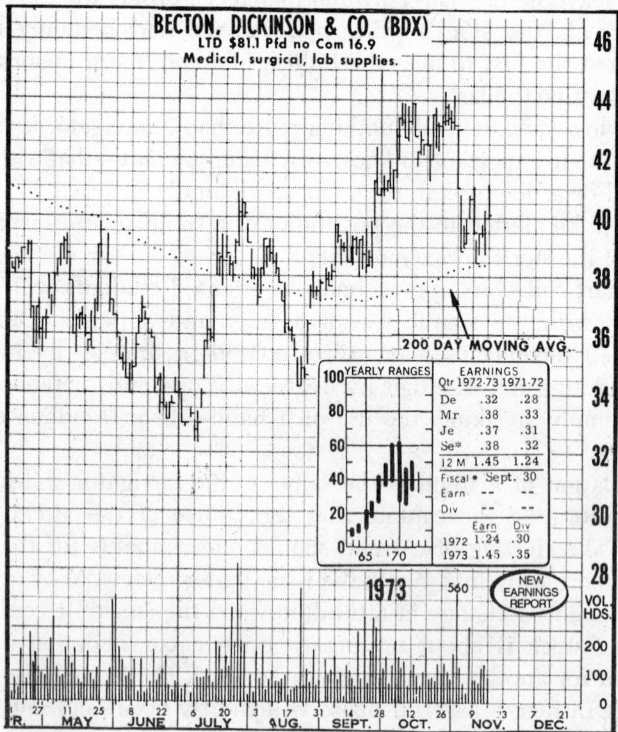

Source: Chart courtesy of Trendline, A Division of Standard & Poor's Corp.

commences. The movement of a stock below an uptrending moving average is considered by many to be a sign of impending weakness. More important is that as the moving average itself flattens out and begins to trend down, it many times will confirm that a shift in the basic trend in the stock has occurred.

Many market technicians keep more than one set of moving averages for a stock under review. For instance, the maintenance of a 25-day and 200-day moving average may be desired so that the analysis of both the intermediate and longer term trends can be judged. Some short-term market traders have been known to keep up 5- and 10-day moving averages for their "in and out" trading purposes. Some technicians utilize weighted moving averages rather than simple straight mathematical computations. The weighted moving average places more emphasis on the more recent price activity.

Relative Strength

One of the oldest approaches of technical analysis and still one of the most widely adopted is the approach of relative strength. As the term signifies, action of a stock or a group of stocks is often compared to the market as a whole, so that it can be determined whether or not the stock is acting better than or worse than the market. Many different mathematical computations are used, but the simplest is whereby the daily close of a stock is divided by the S & P 500 close to arrive at a *ratio*. If this ratio moves up or down over a period of time, it will indicate whether or not the stock is acting better or worse than the general market trend. A stock that is moving laterally while the market is trending lower will possess a strong relative strength curve. On the other hand, a stock that is moving laterally as the market moves laterally will possess flat relative strength, indicating that the issue is acting in line with the general market trend.

Relative strength is an important technical tool but must be used properly. As an example, it should be remembered that, without utilizing any other technical parameter, an investor could be "whipsawed." It is a known fact that a stock can top out while maintaining a strong relative strength curve and that it could bottom out while relative strength appears poor. Thus, it is sometimes inadvisable to utilize relative strength solely as a technical tool.

TECHNICAL ANALYSIS OF INDIVIDUAL STOCKS

Bar Chart Analysis

At this stage we will briefly explain some of the basic tenets of technical analysis, now that the construction of charts and some of the routine technical methodology have been reviewed. In particular, the ability to distinguish major trend reversals in a stock's performance is important. It is in this regard that a great deal of the mystery regarding technical analysis comes to the fore. Perhaps the terminology itself is at fault. Our purpose is to be brief and not to get too deeply involved in semantics or esoteric technical wording.

One of the common reversal patterns that occurs on the different charts of stock price movement is called a *head and shoulders* configuration. We suppose that some observer came up with this descriptive name many decades ago simply because the pattern does profile that part of the human anatomy for which it is named. The head and shoulders reversal pattern is really nothing more than the indication of a stock moving from an uptrend to a downtrend or vice versa. (See Figure 11.)

While observing such a reversal phase, it is important to note volume trends. As an example, if a head and shoulders top is being formed, volume on each of the rally phases within the top formation usually decreases. On the other hand, if it is a head and shoulders bottom that is being observed, volume should show an increase on each of the rally phases within the reversal pattern. The completion of a head and shoulders top or bottom is not considered final until the penetration of a so-called neckline is apparent. In a top formation, this neckline is really nothing more than a support line. (See Figure 11.) Put another way, the penetration of such a support line usually coincides with the initiation of the new trend; it will represent a new reaction low.

Variations of the above-mentioned reversal formations are great in number. The so-called double and triple top and bottom classifications are but two. (See Figure 12.)

Oftentimes, stocks may also display very unusual price and/or volume activity while coming to a peak or a trough in their major trends. Such action may be followed by consolidation at either a lower (in the case of a top) or higher (in the case of a bottom) trading range than where the extreme high or low level was first registered. Many times, such unusual price and/or volume action is caused by external news coming to the fore, and the trend in force is accentuated and an extreme level in stock prices is at least temporarily reached. The stock market bottoms of 1962 and 1970 are two that come quickly to mind whereby an extreme market reaction to external news preceded the registering of an important low. In 1962 it was the pressure by President Kennedy for the steel industry to roll back announced price increases while the 1970 downside plummet (on the heels of a 15-month decline) was caused in part by the Cambodian invasion, the Kent State turbulence, the I.O.S. revelations, and the Penn Central bankruptcy.

While talking about reversal formations in particular, there are some

FIGURE 11

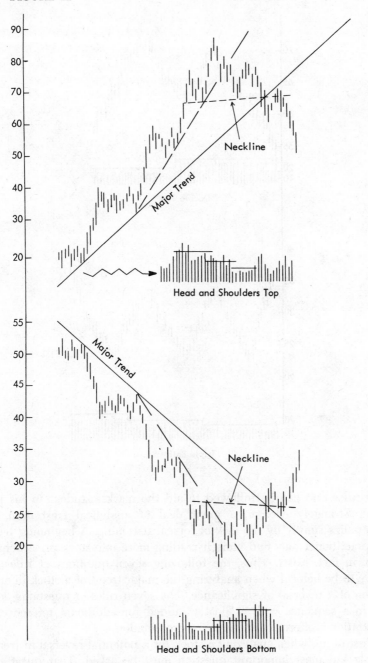

Neckline

Major Trend

Head and Shoulders Top

Major Trend

Neckline

Head and Shoulders Bottom

FIGURE 12

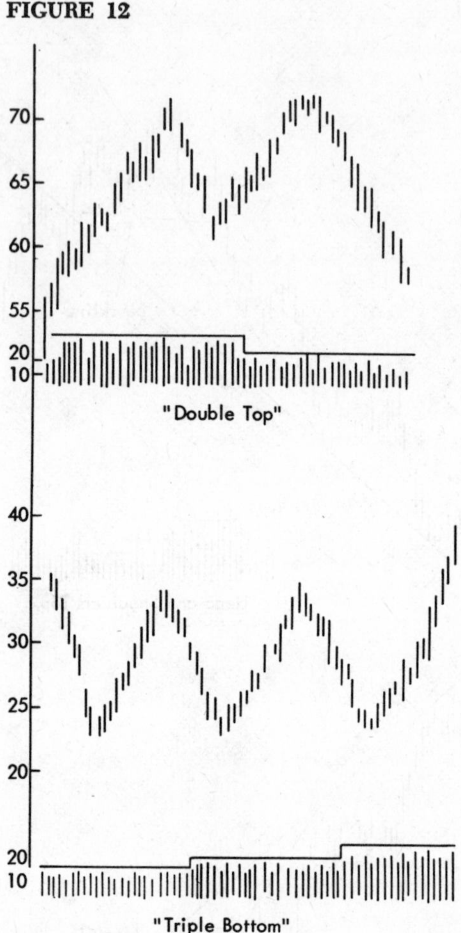

easy rules that can be followed to aid the market student in his judgment. Strangely enough, a great deal of analytical frustration does materialize simply by the lack of logical reasoning. A beginning technical practitioner may find himself reading more into stock price behavior than, in fact, exists. Thus, the following seven questions or rules may prove to be helpful when analyzing the major trend of a stock in anticipation of a reversal of significance. The seven rules or questions do occur in a sequence with a "floater" added for additional reference. An illustration is offered to enhance the presentation.

First of all, when analyzing a stock for a potential reversal in trend, a simple but most important question must be asked. That question is, "*Does the stock have a move of substance to reverse?*" A major reversal formation certainly would not be looked for in a stock that has only moved from 20 to 26, but if a move from 20 to 45 had been experienced, any reversal in trend could be major.

If the first question is answered yes, we then ask, "*Has the stock fulfilled readable price objectives?*" As mentioned earlier, technical analysis does afford the occasional opportunity to calculate price objectives. Various methods can be employed, and we shall be more explicit in the discussion regarding point and figure charting.

If the answer to question 2 is yes, we can then move to question 3, "*Has the stock violated its trends?*" If a trend violation does occur, it could be the forerunner or an early warning for a reversal in the major direction of the stock's price movement.

Question 4 then asks, "*Are there signs of distribution (or accumulation) evident?*" Evidence of distribution can take on many forms. Bar charts display certain patterns (head and shoulders, as an example), and point and figure charts display others. This question does pivot off our second basic assumption as reviewed earlier.

"*If distribution (or accumulation) is evident, is it significant enough to imply that a more than minor movement in price could be in the offing?*" is the fifth query. This question is in reference to our basic assumption number three.

If we have moved through the first five questions in an affirmative manner, Question 6, asks, "*Has the stock violated a readable support (or resistance) level?*" A yes answer here takes us to the last question (7) in the sequence, which the market technician of experience should not have to reach, and that is, "*Has the stock initiated a downward (or an upward) trend?*"

The floater question, which can be inserted in between any of the above seven, asks, "*Is there any evidence of unusual price and/or volume action?*" Sharp upward or downward runs following a major move can often be an indication of a "climactic" phase of market action, especially if accompanied by a bulge in turnover.

All securities analysis should be practiced with the thought in mind of anticipating and not reacting. A good fundamental analyst will always be anticipating trends of earnings, product development, and so on; a good technician should be anticipating stock price trends. Thus, the astute technician should be turning bearish during a stock's top formation rather than afterward, or turning bullish during a bottom pattern rather than during the following uptrend.

Although the head and shoulders reversal pattern, as well as the double and the triple tops, can be observed on both bar charts and point and figure charts, there are certain price configurations more easily identified on bar charts; point and figure charts have a number of peculiar patterns of their own.

Although primarily continuation patterns, the *triangles* are an ex-

FIGURE 13

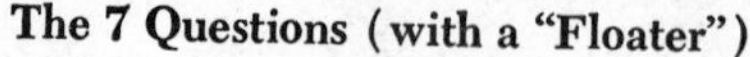

The 7 Questions (with a "Floater")

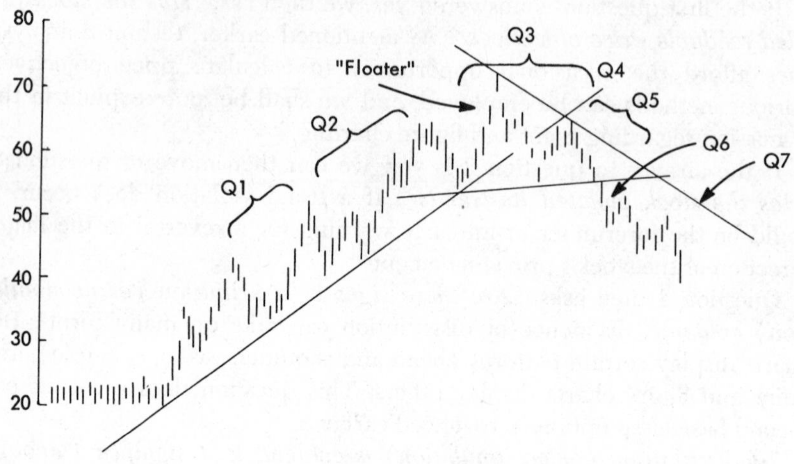

ample of a formation more readily apparent on a bar chart than on a point and figure variety. The three types of triangles that are most often found are the "symmetrical," the "ascending," and the "descending." Figure 14 illustrates these three types of triangular formations.

Two of the triangle patterns do have some predictive value, namely, the ascending and the descending varieties. These two configurations reveal a positive force of market action versus a neutral force. An ascending triangle, as an example, illustrates a positive force of buying (higher lows) versus the neutral force of selling (the flat top). In most cases, the positive force will eventually win out, indicating that the ascending triangle is a consolidation phase most often found in a stock's upward trend. Conversely, the descending triangle has the same qualifications; a positive force of selling (the descending highs) against a neutral force

FIGURE 14

Triangles

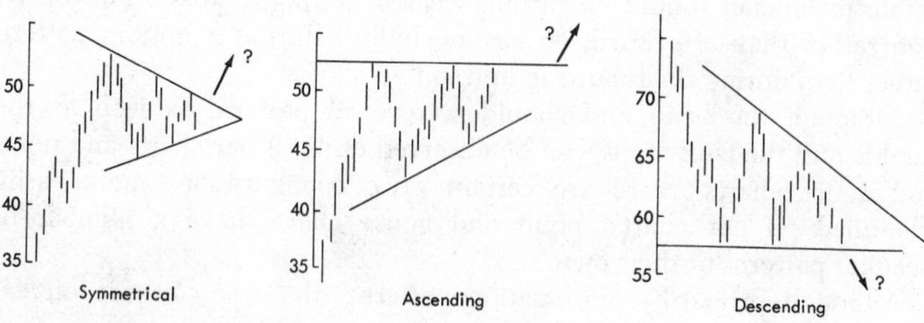

of buying (the flat bottoms). The descending version is, therefore, most often found within the confines of a stock's major downtrend.

The symmetrical triangle, as illustrated, is made up of two positive forces—the buying side (the ascending bottoms) and the selling side (the descending tops). Although such a triangle is oftentimes completed with a move in the direction from which the stock came, we caution that there have been times when a symmetrical triangle has also been a reversal pattern. By using trendlines and following closely a stock's movement within the neutral trend, a hint is often given as to the possible direction of the impending movement. Volume trends and relative strength analysis can often be additional aids toward determining the eventual direction of the *breakout*.

FIGURE 15

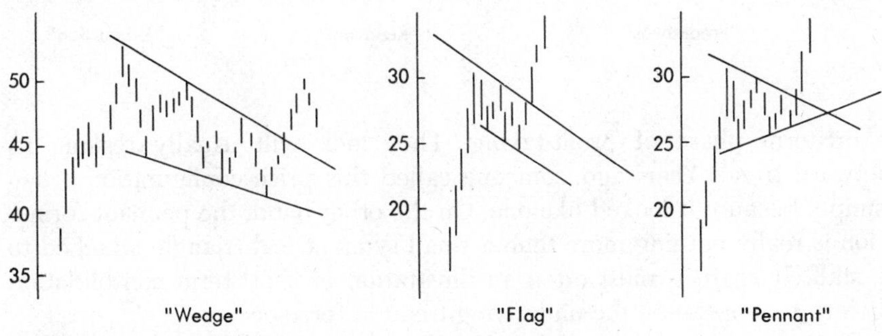

Aside from the triangles, there are a number of other technical configurations that qualify as consolidation patterns. In particular, there is a pattern called the *wedge* and then there are two short-term configurations that go by the names of *flag* and *pennant*. The wedge, as a consolidation configuration, is illustrated in Figure 15. The pattern is somewhat similar to the triangular variety except that the trendlines move in the same direction. The *falling* wedge usually occurs in a major uptrend pattern. The slope of the trendlines indicates that the sellers may be aggressive but the buyers are relatively not as timid. This is indicated by the fact that the slope of the underlying trendline is not as great as the slope of the overhead downtrend line. In addition, as this short-term phase of profit-taking occurs, volume usually shows a marked decrease.

The flag and pennant formations are very short term in nature and indicative of a spritely market for the shares of the stock under observation. These patterns will most often occur early in an upward or downward trend. The flag is illustrated in Figure 14 and, as you can see, is made up of a few quick days of sharp moves which are then followed by a

FIGURE 16

Gaps

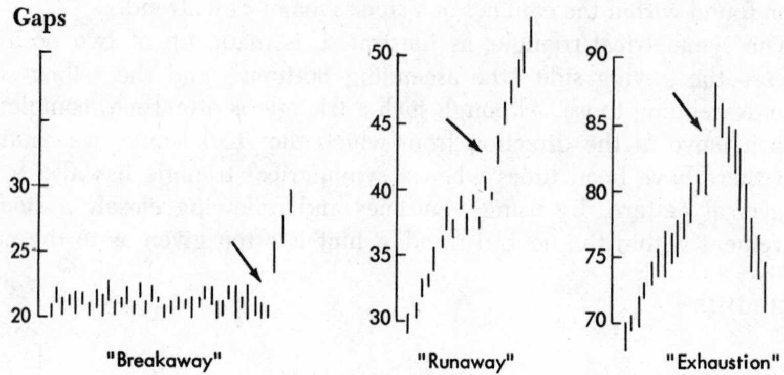

short-term phase of profit-taking. The stock will usually resume its upward trend. Years ago, someone called this price configuration a flag simply because it looked like one. On the other hand, the pennant formation is really nothing more than a small symmetrical triangle attached to a staff. It again is most often an illustration of short-term consolidation before resumption of the underlying trend in force occurs.

Perhaps no treatment of bar chart analysis would be complete without some explanation of the technical configuration known as a *gap.* Although there are a number of gaps readily formed within the marketplace, there are only three that the market technician is most concerned with in his work. These are the *breakaway gap,* the *runaway gap,* and the *exhaustion gap.*

Let us first point out that there is an old market legend that states: since nature abhors a vacuum, so does the stock market. Therefore, as the theory goes, a gap must be "filled." This is not necessarily true. By definition, a gap is a void of price action, only to be found on a bar chart, where a stock has opened at a level higher than the previous day's intraday high, and either maintains that opening level or, in fact, moves up and closes higher during the day's trading. Although some gaps are often filled and perhaps quickly so, one should not be wedded to the old belief that this will always occur.

As an example, a breakaway gap, by definition, is a void in price that occurs after a phase of consolidation. A stock will break away with vibrance from the consolidation zone and leave a gap in its wake. If, in fact, it is a true breakaway gap, it will not be immediately filled.

The runaway gap most often occurs within the framework of a trend in force. In an upward pattern, a runaway gap simply confirms that demand for the shares continues heavy.

The exhaustion gap carries such a connotation in its name because this gap will occur in the terminal phases of a stock's upward (or down-

FIGURE 17

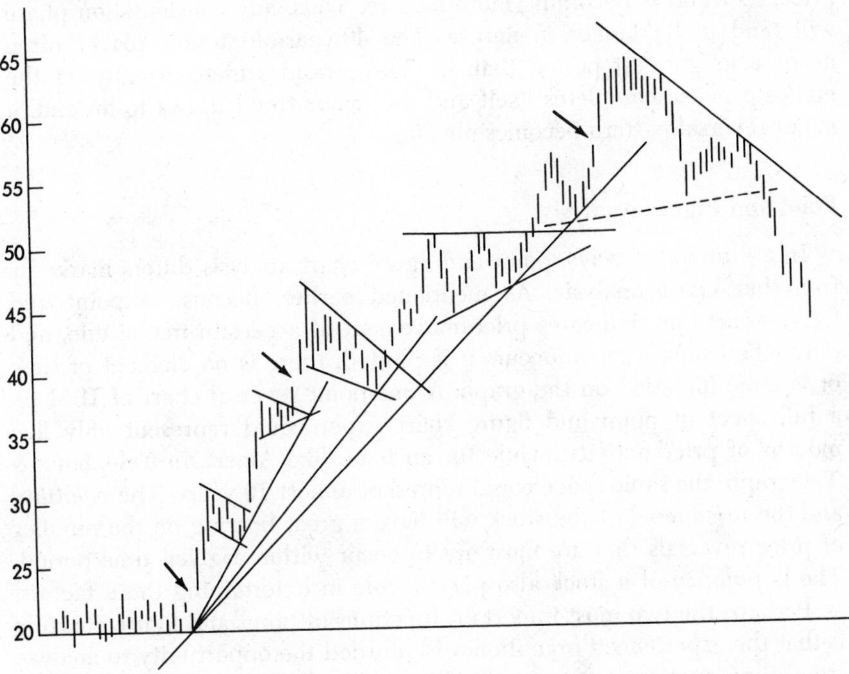

ward) trend. The exhaustion gap will be quickly filled by following price action thus indicating a marked reduction in the momentum of the stock's trend. Figure 16 illustrates the three gaps discussed.

We have reviewed a number of the basic tenets surrounding bar chart analysis. Space has dictated not getting too involved with an in-depth description as well as with a number of the other bar chart configurations; they are of less importance anyway. But, of those described herein, let us try to draw a chart of a stock's major trend (Figure 17) and insert where most frequently within that trend the patterns reviewed will most often occur.

The initial phase of consolidation is our point of departure. The stock breaks out and, in doing so, a breakaway gap is noticed. As the stock is in what could be called the discovery stage, demand for the shares is plentiful, thus two, three, or four days of rapid price advancement occurs. Only short-term profit-taking appears before the stock spurts upward again. It is in this phase of the stock's upward trend that a flag or a pennant formation will most often develop. Oftentimes, the initial trend of a stock is too steep to be sustainable. Therefore, if the shares invite some more serious profit-taking later on, the trend will obviously become less pronounced. That phase of profit-taking, which results in a more gradual trend, could take on the form of a wedge. Following the confirmation of a new recovery high, the next form of consolidation may well be that of a triangle. Obviously, as the stock moves up further in price, its trend is becoming more mature. Thus, any consolidation phase will tend to be longer in nature. The 40-year-old tennis player often needs a longer rest period than the 20-year-old athlete. Finally, as the mark-up phase completes itself and the major trend draws to an end, a major reversal pattern becomes obvious.

Point and Figure Analysis

In a number of ways, point and figure chart analysis differs markedly from bar chart analysis. As mentioned earlier, because a point and figure chart only indicates price movement of a certain magnitude, and only when such a move occurs it is plotted, there is no element of time or volume included on the graph. A one-point reversal chart of IBM on a full sheet of point and figure chart paper could represent only five months of price activity, while for an issue like American Telephone & Telegraph, the same space could represent almost 10 years. The *volatility* and the *price level* of the stock will have a great bearing on the number of price reversals that are most apt to occur within a given time period. The *popularity* of a stock also plays a role in determining these factors.

Perhaps the two most important functions of point and figure charting is that the experienced practitioner is afforded the opportunity to analyze from time to time—on a more discernable basis than a bar chart—whether or not a stock is (1) going through a distribution or accumulation phase while in fact the basic price trend is neutral. And, (2) by utilizing the point and figure "count" theory, a determination can oftentimes be made as to the extent of a price movement in either an upward or downward direction. Unfortunately, one cannot always project a time parameter for an impending move. In recent years this has been especially so with the great institutionalization of the marketplace that has occurred.

Like bar charts, point and figure charting affords the opportunity to analyze stock price *trends,* as well as *support* and *resistance* levels. In addition, there are certain technical price configurations such as the head and shoulders reversal, a rounding top or bottom, a *V* pattern, or a double or triple top that can be observed on a point and figure graph similar to the opportunities afforded by a bar chart. But as the bar chart has a number of its own peculiar formations such as the triangles, wedge, pennant, flag, and gap, so does the point and figure graph display its own peculiar patterns. Figure 18 illustrates some of these pattern formations by name.

When a stock is moving upward or downward, one need not be a technician to determine that the stock is being accumulated or distributed, respectively. On the other hand, when a stock is in fact going through a neutral phase, with neither an upward or downward bias

FIGURE 18

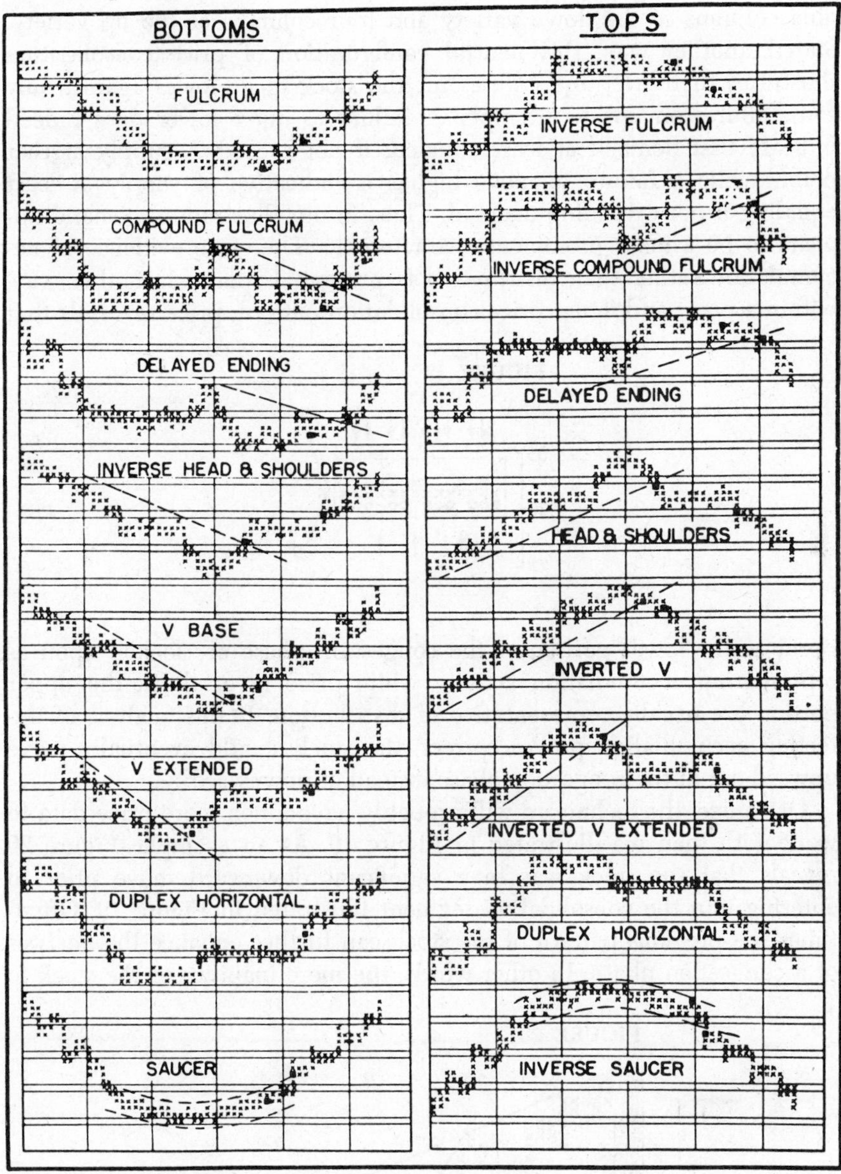

Courtesy: Morgan, Rogers, & Roberts, 150 Broadway, New York.

evident, it would be most helpful to arrive at some determination as to the direction of the next move. In many cases, point and figure charting lends itself to this type of analysis.

Figure 19 illustrates a typical consolidation phase as it might appear on a point and figure graph. You will note in our example that there are nine columns of the down variety and four columns of the up variety. Stated another way, this neutral configuration of price consolidation illustrates there are nine *failures* for the stock to go lower against only four failures on upside attempts. A failure to move lower does indeed indicate that demand at least equaled, if not exceeded, supply at that point, while a failure to move higher is indicative of supply at least equaling if not exceeding demand. Thus, in our illustration, demand appears to be a more prominent characteristic. Therefore evidence of accumulation rather than distribution is present. Explained another way, within a point and figure price consolidation pattern, price reversals that

FIGURE 19

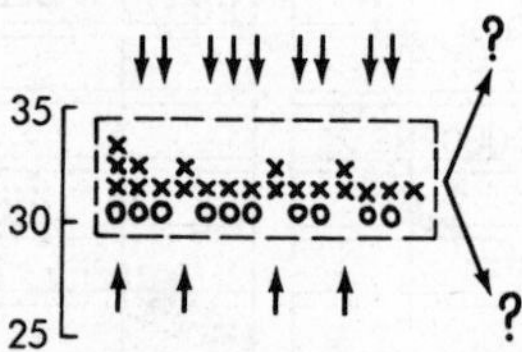

occur in the lower portion of the congestion phase are looked upon as representing accumulation activity while price reversals in the upper portion are usually representative of distribution. If this analysis of detecting accumulation proves correct, the stock should eventually move upward out of the congestion phase instead of downward.

Of course, the technician will probably have much more price data to work with than we illustrated in Figure 19. As an example, Figure 20 reveals that the stock was in a significant downward move prior to entering into the consolidation segment illustrated in Figure 19. Oftentimes the previous pattern of the stock can further enhance the analysis of a congestion phase. In other words, the mere inability of the stock to

FIGURE 20

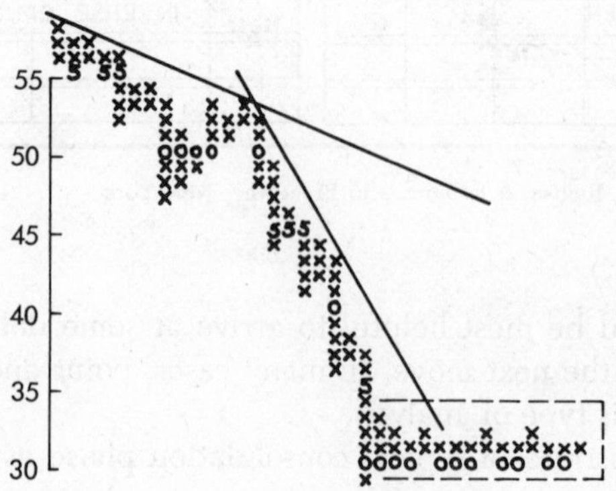

move lower following a prolonged downtrend implies basic accumulation, while the inability to continue higher after a significant uptrend would indicate distribution. Figure 21 illustrates the type of point and figure configuration that could very well follow a stock's upward trend.

In this regard, you will note the number of excessive failures in the up portion of the congestion pattern versus the reversals in the lower

FIGURE 21

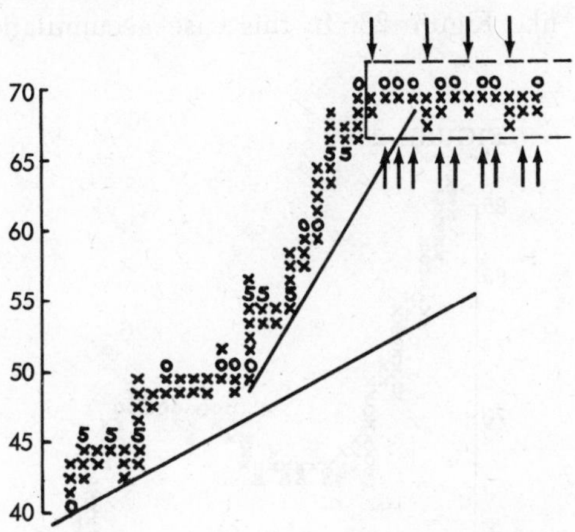

portion. This consolidation phase is in all likelihood a top reversal pattern. The resulting move from such a configuration would usually be downward.

Within the confines of a major uptrend, consolidation phases will, of course, occur. Figure 22 is a typical consolidation pattern in an upward trend. The trading range between 51 and 58 is considered to be the entire consolidation zone. But, note if you will, that the distinct phases of distribution and accumulation are quite evident in this pattern. At the 58 level, the stock refuses to move higher, thus giving evidence of en-

FIGURE 22

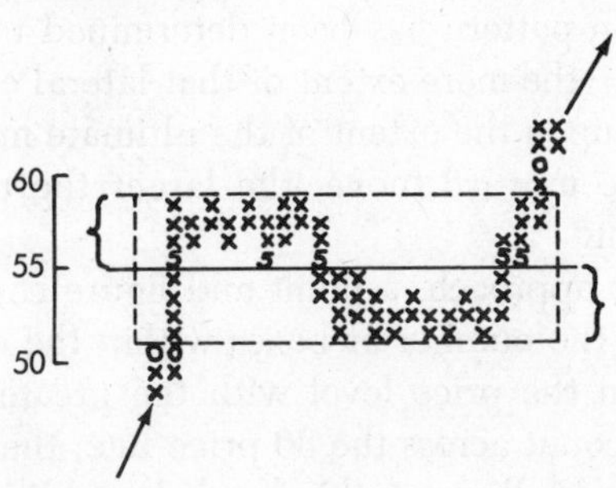

countering either resistance or supply. This is the distribution segment of the consolidation zone and should be followed by some type of a setback or profit-taking phase. This correction occurs as indicated by the decline to 51. But note how the issue ceases to decline any further at the 51–53 level. Evidence of demand equaling, if not exceeding supply, is again at hand as the stock *refuses to move lower.* A new upside move commences resulting in a breakout, and the consolidation pattern has been completed. Such a consolidation zone in a downtrend would appear something like Figure 23. In this case accumulation activity pre-

FIGURE 23

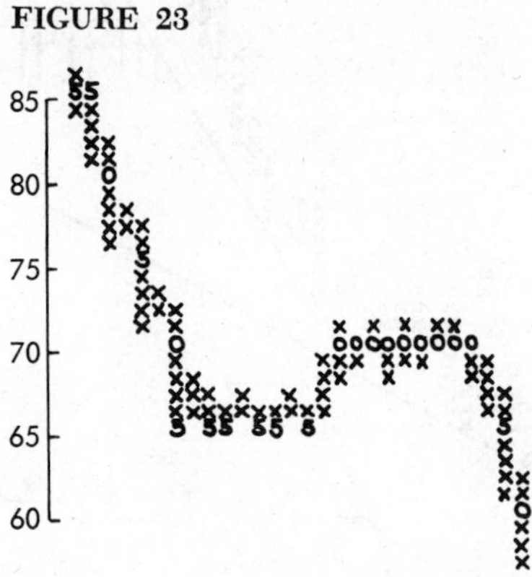

cedes distribution of the shares—just the opposite of the foregoing example.

The discussion above concerning the accumulation and distribution patterns obviously draws heavily upon our Assumption 2. The forthcoming dissertation is concerned with Assumption 3, as previously explained.

It stands to reason that the more supply that is eliminated from the marketplace (accumulation), the greater the impact should be on the following move (upward). Therein lies the logic or rationale behind the so-called point and figure *objective theory* (sometimes called the *count*). Once a consolidation pattern has been determined to be either distribution or accumulation, the mere extent of that lateral consolidation usually will have a bearing upon the extent of the ultimate move. The bigger the base, the bigger the upward move; the larger the top, the greater the downside adjustment.

According to one approach, a point and figure count is accomplished by merely counting the number of boxes within the consolidation phase, placing emphasis on the price level with the greater fill-ins. In Figure 24 this would be a count across the 36 price line; the example shows the greater number of *x*'s falling on this level. In addition, the 36 line also indicates the initiation point of the new upward trend phase (arrow).

In our illustration, a count of 21 points results, which added to the price level of 36 offers an upside price target of approximately 57.

Application of the point and figure count should, of course, be done with great caution and only after much experience. A stock's volatility or popularity in the marketplace can either enhance or degrade objective validity. For instance, a glamour stock in vogue at the time may tend to exceed projected price targets as market enthusiasm leads to greater extremes. On the other hand, to utilize the count theory for a utility stock would be more than foolhardy, as objectives of even greater than logical magnitude would no doubt result from apparent consolidation

FIGURE 24

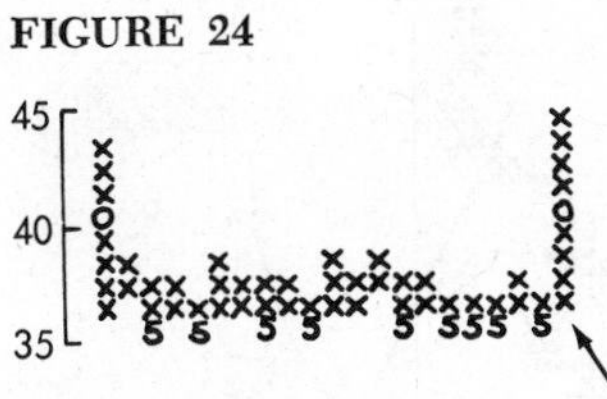

phases. It should be pointed out that the point and figure objective theory is simply another tool. Obviously, the type of market background will play a great role in the validity in the projected targets. A bull market will enhance upward objectives, and a bear market will usually be marked by a number of downside calculations. The count approach can also be used on the other reversal charts. On a three-point reversal chart, as an example, the number of lateral boxes in a consolidation phase would be multiplied by three to achieve an upside or downside objective potential. We caution, however, that objectives calculated off the three-point reversal chart should not be used as a primary input, but more or less as a confirmation to the one-point calculation. Figures 25A & B afford good examples of the count technique as it could have been applied to Bausch & Lomb, a glamour favorite of recent years.

Our description of bar chart and point and figure chart utilization has primarily focused on the more common aspects. By no means could a complete dissertation be accomplished in our allocated space. Technical students of the market will need to experiment for themselves with each of the two charting techniques to discover which one they would feel most comfortable with. Obviously, the use of both approaches would be most ideal for both short- and long-term stock analysis.

Stock Market Analysis

This section alone could, without difficulty, result in a 100-page text. Therefore, an assumption is made that the inquisitive market student will utilize the review contained herein to fertilize his thinking and then pursue a more complete investigation at a later date.

FIGURE 25A

Bausch & Lomb 1-Point Reversal

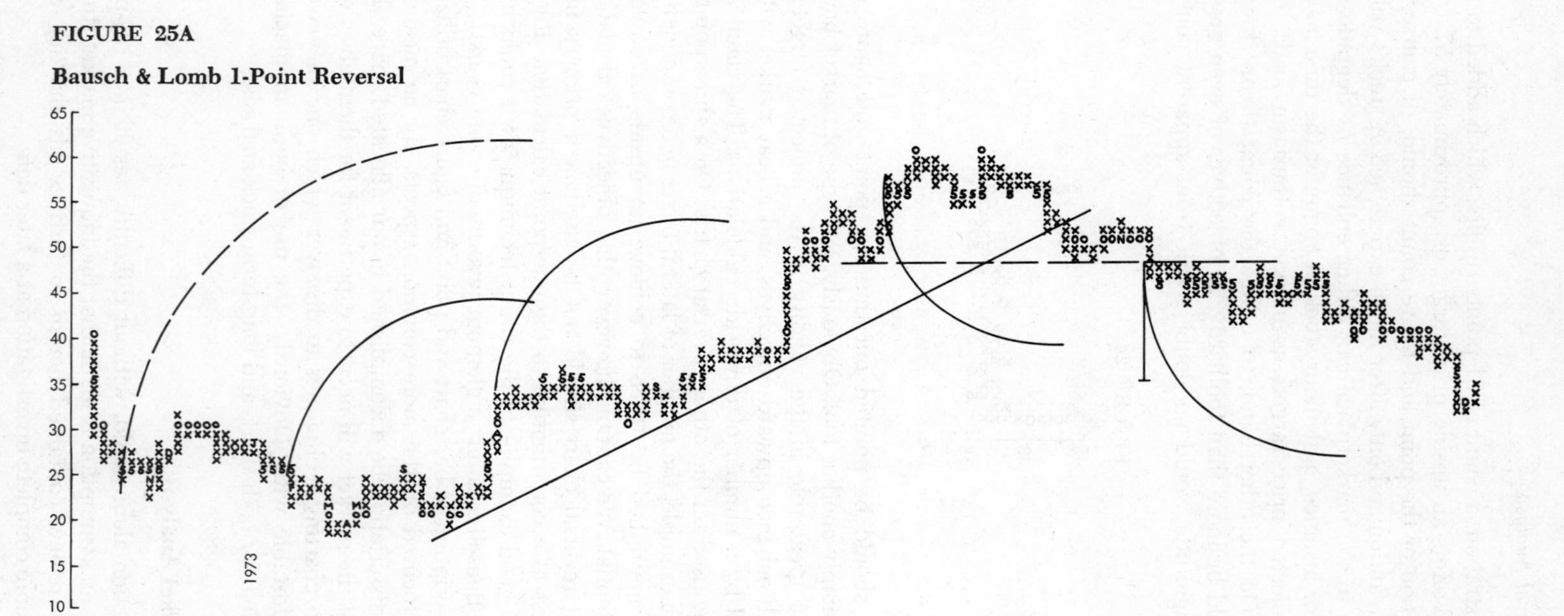

FIGURE 25 B

Bausch & Lomb 3-Point Reversal

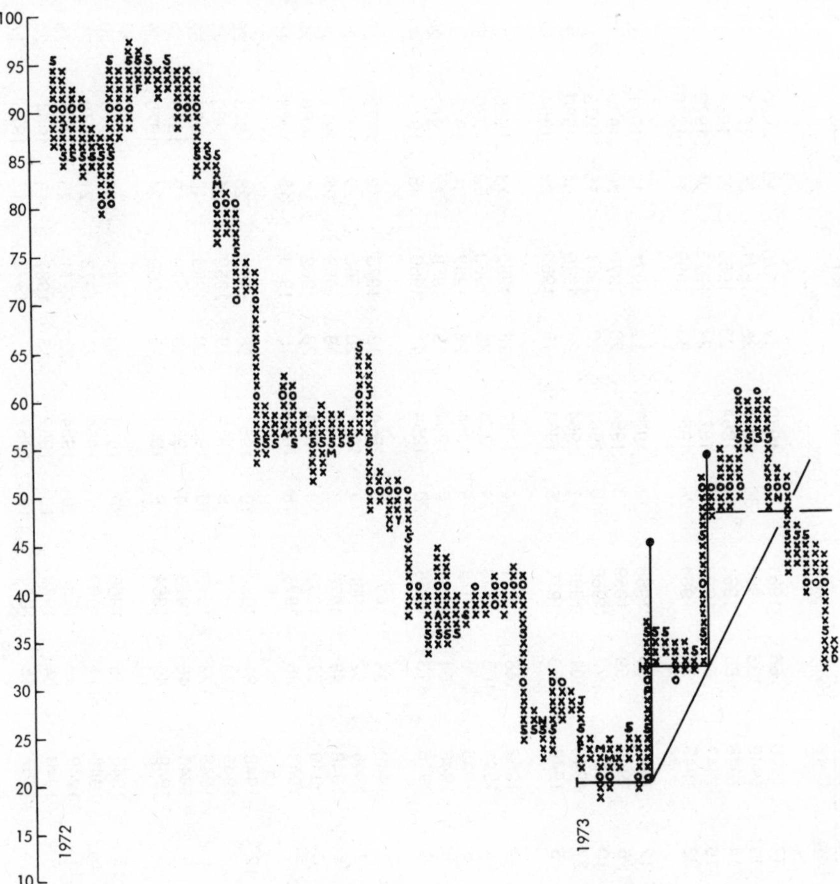

To start, there are a number of averages or yardsticks used to follow the stock market's trend. The oldest and most widely followed is the Dow Jones Industrial Average (D.J.I.A.). Debates pages long have centered upon the pros and cons of this indicator as a valid market measurement. In sum, its greatest weakness is that it only contains 30 stocks, but its greatest strength is its simplicity in computation and its obvious widespread utilization. As a straight and simple mathematical average, the higher priced component stocks do exert the greatest influence on the indicator's behavior. Respect for the D.J.I.A.'s mathematical makeup is paramount for a greater understanding of its potential. Suggestion is made, as an example, that one simply calculate the historic highs and lows for each component stock since World War II. Add these figures and divide by the Dow Jones divisor, which currently is 1.626.

FIGURE 26

D.J.I.A. Components	12/20/73 Recent Price	Post W.W. II Low	Date	High	Date	Approximate 20 Year Low		15 Year Low		10 Year Low		5 Year Low	
Allied Chemical	47	17	1970	66	1961	17	1970	17	1970	17	1970	17	1970
Aluminum Co. of Amer.	70	12	1949	133	1956	30	1954	36	1971	36	1971	36	1971
American Brands	33	14	1948	55	1961	14	1954	23	1959	27	1964	30	1970
American Can	24	19	1947	64	1967	24	1973	24	1973	24	1973	24	1973
American Telephone	51	23	1949	75	1964	26	1954	38	1959	41	1970	41	1970
Anaconda	24	12	1971	66	1968	12	1971	12	1971	12	1971	12	1971
Bethlehem Steel	31	6	1949	59	1959	13	1954	20	1970	20	1970	20	1970
Chrysler	15	10	1961	72	1968	10	1961	10	1961	15	1973	15	1973
DuPont	152	27	1948	261	1965	71	1954	94	1970	94	1970	94	1970
Eastman Kodak	112	5	1946	152	1973	5	1954	18	1959	29	1964	58	1970
Esmark	24	14	1957	45	1971	14	1957	16	1962	18	1966	21	1973
Exxon	91	11	1949	103	1973	24	1954	38	1960	50	1970	50	1970
General Electric	59	6	1948	75	1973	15	1954	28	1962	31	1970	31	1970
General Foods	23	5	1948	54	1961	8	1954	19	1959	22	1973	22	1973
General Motors	48	8	1946	113	1965	20	1954	41	1960	45	1973	45	1973
Goodyear	14	2	1949	35	1971	5	1954	13	1973	13	1973	13	1973
International Harvester	25	12	1946	52	1966	13	1957	20	1960	22	1970	22	1970
International Nickel	32	5	1948	48	1970	7	1954	18	1959	25	1971	25	1971
International Paper	50	6	1946	57	1973	19	1954	23	1962	24	1966	29	1970
Johns-Manville	16	8	1949	46	1971	15	1973	15	1973	15	1973	15	1973
Owens-Illinois	31	12	1948	81	1968	19	1954	28	1973	28	1973	28	1973
Procter & Gamble	92	7	1945	120	1973	9	1954	19	1959	31	1966	41	1970
Sears	84	5	1948	123	1973	10	1954	20	1959	45	1967	52	1970
Standard Oil California	32	6	1946	45	1973	14	1954	19	1970	19	1970	19	1970
Texaco	28	3	1949	46	1964	8	1954	16	1960	24	1970	24	1970
Union Carbide	31	15	1946	75	1965	30	1973	30	1973	30	1973	30	1973
United Aircraft	26	6	1946	111	1967	17	1954	21	1973	21	1973	21	1973
U.S. Steel	35	11	1949	108	1959	20	1954	25	1971	25	1971	25	1971
Westinghouse	33	6	1949	54	1972	13	1962	13	1962	15	1964	27	1970
Woolworth	17	12	1957	55	1971	12	1957	17	1973	17	1973	17	1973
D.J.I.A.	830	188		1506		316		450		514		556	

Table prepared December 24, 1973.

Such an exercise may provide an insight as to the specific price levels that may be needed so that the Dow itself could ever reach the extreme downside and upside projections that have been bandied about in recent years. (See Figure 26.)

The Standard & Poor's indicators are also weighted in the sense that price and capitalization are included in the calculation. Thus, an issue like IBM, where both a high price and a large capitalization are present, will tend to exert the greatest influence on the average's movement. Figure 27 is a computer run which ranks the percentage weight of each S & P's 500 component stock as of March 29, 1974. As you can note, the

FIGURE 27

	STOCK	PRICE	MARKET VALUE % OF 500	MARKET VALUE MIL
1	INTL BUSINESS MACHINES	236	6.66	34588
2	AMER TEL & TEL	50	5.34	27720
3	EXXON CORP	81	3.51	18217
4	EASTMAN KODAK CO	106	3.30	17148
5	GENERAL MOTORS CORP	50	2.74	14215
6	SEARS, ROEBUCK & CO	83	2.52	13075
7	GENERAL ELEC CO	54	1.90	9881
8	XEROX CORP	115	1.75	9102
9	MINNESOTA MNG & MFG CO	74	1.62	8398
10	DU PONT DE NEMOURS CO	165	1.53	7918
11	TEXACO INC	28	1.47	7613
12	PROCTER & GAMBLE CO	89	1.40	7277
13	COCA-COLA CO	110	1.27	6583
14	STANDARD OIL CO IND	93	1.25	6469
15	JOHNSON & JOHNSON	109	1.21	6256
16	AMERICAN HOME PRODS CP	39	1.18	6118
17	MERCK & CO INC	81	1.16	6010
18	DOW CHEMICAL CO	60	1.07	5538
19	WEYERHAEUSER CO	42	1.03	5351
20	STANDARD OIL CO CALIF	29	0.96	4968
21	LILLY ELI & CO	71	0.94	4856
22	MOBIL OIL CORP	46	0.89	4629
23	FORD MTR CO DEL	49	0.89	4615
24	GULF OIL CORP	23	0.86	4452
25	ROYAL DUTCH PETROLEUM	33	0.85	4389
26	ATLANTIC RICHFIELD CO	94	0.84	4386
27	PHILLIPS PETROLEUM	53	0.77	4020
28	PENNEY J.C. CO. INC	69	0.77	3994
29	BURROUGHS CORP	205	0.77	3982
30	SHELL OIL CO	59	0.76	3966
31	SCHLUMBERGER, LTD	104	0.73	3792
32	SCHERING PLOUGH CORP	70	0.71	3693
33	KRESGE SS CO	31	0.71	3683
34	CATERPILLAR TRACTOR	59	0.65	3373
35	AVON PRODS INC	54	0.60	3110
36	HALLIBURTON CO	153	0.57	2937
37	GENERAL TEL & ELECTRS	24	0.55	2877
38	WARNER LAMBERT CO	36	0.54	2822
39	PHILIP MORRIS, INC	99	0.53	2731
40	INTL NICKEL OF CANADA	36	0.51	2665

first 10 names equaled 30.87 percent of the Standard & Poor's 500 weight, the first 25, 47.30 percent. In other words, only 5 percent of the index's components exert almost one half the influence on the indicator's behavior.

Other broad-based market indicators that are of a weighted nature include the New York Stock Exchange Common Stock Index, the American Stock Exchange Market Value Index, and the NASDAQ Index.

In mid-1961, the Value Line Investment Survey started publishing an average that was *unweighted* in its makeup. This geometric compilation truly reflected the price movement of the majority of stocks, as each component issue carried the same weight regardless of its price or capitalization. In recent years, divergence in the marketplace has been most vividly pointed out by comparing the Value Line average with those indicators that are weighted in nature. The Indicator Digest Service has, for some years, also been publishing an unweighted index of New York Stock Exchange issues (IDA) and the American Stock Exchange (AIDA).

Different segments of the stock market are followed by the calculation of group averages or indices. Standard & Poor's is perhaps best known for its group statistics. Many market analysts have also developed their own particular price averages to further study different trends. Many years ago, as an example, a number of averages of so-called *glamour-growth stocks* came to the fore. Movement in this particular sector of the market could therefore be measured in relation to other areas. The use of growth stock averages was in part responsible for the discovery of the multitiered market of recent years. One such glamour-growth average is illustrated. The components of this average as of this writing are:

Avon Products
Baxter Laboratories
Burroughs
Coca Cola
Disney (Walt)
Int'l. Bus. Machines
Int'l Flav. & Fragrances
McDonald's
Minnesota Mining & Mfg.
Motorola
Polaroid
Simplicity Patterns
Sperry Rand
Texas Instruments
Xerox

This chart illustrates the trend of this average in recent years.

There are a number of other specific market averages that have, through the years, been available from various organizations. In this regard, we specifically cite the Dow Jones transportation and utility averages and Standard & Poor's rail and utility indexes. In addition to the NYSE Common Stock Index, which measures the market in dollars and cents, the exchange also prepares the industrial index, the transportation and utility indexes and, in addition, an index of financial stocks. Moody's publishes stock market indicators as does the Associated Press.

Before the advent of the more broad-based market statistics, there was a desire to study market movements in greater depth. Thus a number of decades ago, the *Advance/Decline Index* came into being. Unlike the price indicators, the Advance/Decline Index moves in a field unrelated to actual price changes. Its direction of movement is based upon participation or market breadth rather than the rate of change itself. The daily Advance/Decline indicator is a simple calculation. From sources of data available in most daily newspapers, the plus or minus differential between advancing and declining issues is simply accumulated each day. Any figure can serve as a starting point for this accumulation as the actual level of the Advance/Decline Index is not important, only its direction of movement. Advance/Decline statistics can be calculated for not only the New York Stock Exchange, but also for the American Stock Exchange and the over-the-counter markets, the latter making such data available in 1971.

Market analysts are most interested in distinguishing periods of divergence between, let us say, the D.J.I.A. and the daily Advance/Decline figures. The ideal situation is to see both sets of statistics moving in unison. Past instances of divergence in movement have generally been indications of an impending reversal of a trend. As our illustration reveals, an example of divergence in trends between the daily Advance/Decline and the D.J.I.A. was clearly given in late 1972. The Dow moved through to a historic peak above 1000, but the A/D index showed distinct evidence of not confirming the Dow's buoyancy. Further analysis on your behalf will result in additional examples of divergence in recent years.

As a measurement of internal stock market momentum, the daily and weekly high-low statistics are followed by a number of market analysts. Obviously, the order to judge internal participation during the market's downward and upward trends, breakouts to new highs or lows add perspective. The daily or weekly statistics are oftentimes smoothed by the use of a 10-day or 10-week moving average.

Depending upon the market trend in force, financial publications often are quoting market commentators with the statement that the market is greatly "oversold" or vastly "overbought." Simply stated, either condition means the stage is set for either a short-term rally or a short-term decline, respectively. The overbought/oversold (OB/OS) oscillators are used to indicate when the market appears to have reached a short-term extreme. Profit-taking may be overdone or demand for shares has occurred too quickly. The simple establishment of an oversold or overbought position does not in itself indicate that the market will *immediately* reverse its trend. As an example, in bear markets, an oversold condition can last for days or weeks, while in bull phases, an overbought status can prevail for a great length of time. The most common measurement of the OB/OS status, is a 10-day accumulation (sometimes called a moving average) of the daily differential between the advancing and declining stocks. A plus plurality will, of course, be added into the equation and later subtracted (on the 11th day), while the minus plurality will be initially subtracted from the equation and later added back. Thus, for any given 10-day period, the OB/OS statistic will reflect the actual total of the pluses and minuses for the preceding 10 days. Using this particular indicator, an overbought condition is usually present when the oscillator rises above a figure of +1600, while an oversold condition is usually indicated when the statistic falls below −1600.

Probably no discussion of stock market indicators would be complete without some reference to *odd-lot statistics*. For a number of years, odd-lot figures have been closely followed by market analysts with the thought in mind that the odd-lotter or small investor usually acts in an erroneous fashion. In other words, he is a significant buyer when stocks are going down, and a seller when stocks are advancing. Each day the financial press publishes daily odd-lot statistics as reported by the odd-lot brokerage firm of Carlisle & De Coppet & Co. And, as you are aware, there need not be an explicit buyer for every seller in the odd-lot arena, such as there is in the round-lot case. Thus, on a given day it is normal that odd-lot selling can be greater than odd-lot buying or vice versa. Market analysts are concerned with the *on-balance* activity that is evident on a given day. A word of caution should be added to this discussion. Using the past decade as an example, it is true that during the market decline of 1962 the odd-lotter was basically a buyer on balance, and when prices turned back up from 1962 through 1966, the odd-lotter returned to the sell side. In addition, it is further admitted that during the 1966 decline, the odd-lotter was a buyer on balance, and when the market turned up in late 1966, early 1967, he reversed to the sell side. But in the last couple of years, the odd-lotter's behavior appears to have shown some basic changes. Instead of being a preponderant buyer on balance during the 1969–70 market debacle, the odd-lotter did spend a great deal of time liquidating shares. And as our illustration indicates, he has also shown a rather astute ability to increase his buying significantly near a reversal low of some importance. This was particularly so in the summer of 1970. Furthermore, in the last few years, the odd-lotter has displayed an amazing ability to sell shares very heavily right at or near market peaks. See, as an example, the dramatic shift in selling that occurred in late 1972 as the Dow Jones did experience a false upside advance. We are not dismissing odd-lot activity as no longer having a valid place in stock market analysis, but we do feel it important that the recent change in behavior, which of course is marked by a shift in investing trends, should be recognized.

Lastly, concerning the odd-lot investor, there is one statistic that has not really changed in its meaning through all the years, that being the behavior of the small investor when he sells stocks *short*. Odd-lot shorting, although accomplished in different degrees, continues to show a remarkable tendency to expand at or near an important market low. In fact, in the summer months of 1970, on one day the odd-lotter shorted in excess of 40,000 shares. This was surpassed by only one other time in history—October 1966—when on one day the small investor shorted a record number of 57,000 shares. That period marked another important market bottom.

On a monthly basis there are a number of important statistics followed. The short interest ratio (S.I.R.) is an example. The S.I.R. is calculated by dividing the average daily trading volume for each reporting month into the monthly short interest as reported by the NYSE. The ratio is observed not so much because the shorts will be wrong, but because shorts outstanding represent a potential source of stock market demand, thus enhancing the potential of an advance in prices. Through the years the following S.I.R. levels have been looked upon as meaningful by market analysts: a short interest ratio of 2.0 or more (which indicates that the short interest for the month was equal to two or more days' average daily trading volume) has usually carried a *very* bullish connotation; a S.I.R. of 1.5 to 2 has been considered bullish; a ratio of 1.0 to 1.5, neutral; while a ratio of less than 1.0 has usually had unfavorable implications.

It is a known fact that in recent years mutual funds have declined in relative importance as influential market trend-setters. The rapid growth of bank trust departments and other pension fund management concerns has occurred, while concurrently investors have been basically redeeming their holdings in mutual funds. But the monthly mutual fund statistics are still followed primarily because they are readily available and are reported on a set schedule. As calculated by the Investment Company Institute, the trade organization of the mutual fund industry, numerous statistics concerning the funds are issued each month. In particular, the cash position of the funds, especially as a percentage of total assets, is watched carefully. In the past, a high cash position has coincided with a stock market low, while a more fully invested position has accompanied reversal peaks. In this regard, fund managers have often been criticized as behaving like odd-lotters, but we can never forget the retort to such a directed question given by a prominent mutual fund portfolio manager a few years ago. "Would you rather we be liquid so that we can take advantage of tomorrow's leaders or should we be fully invested in the favorites of the past?"

As stated in our opening commentary, we could go on and on describing the various market indicators used by technically oriented analysts. We have, quite frankly, only touched upon but a few of the

FIGURE 28

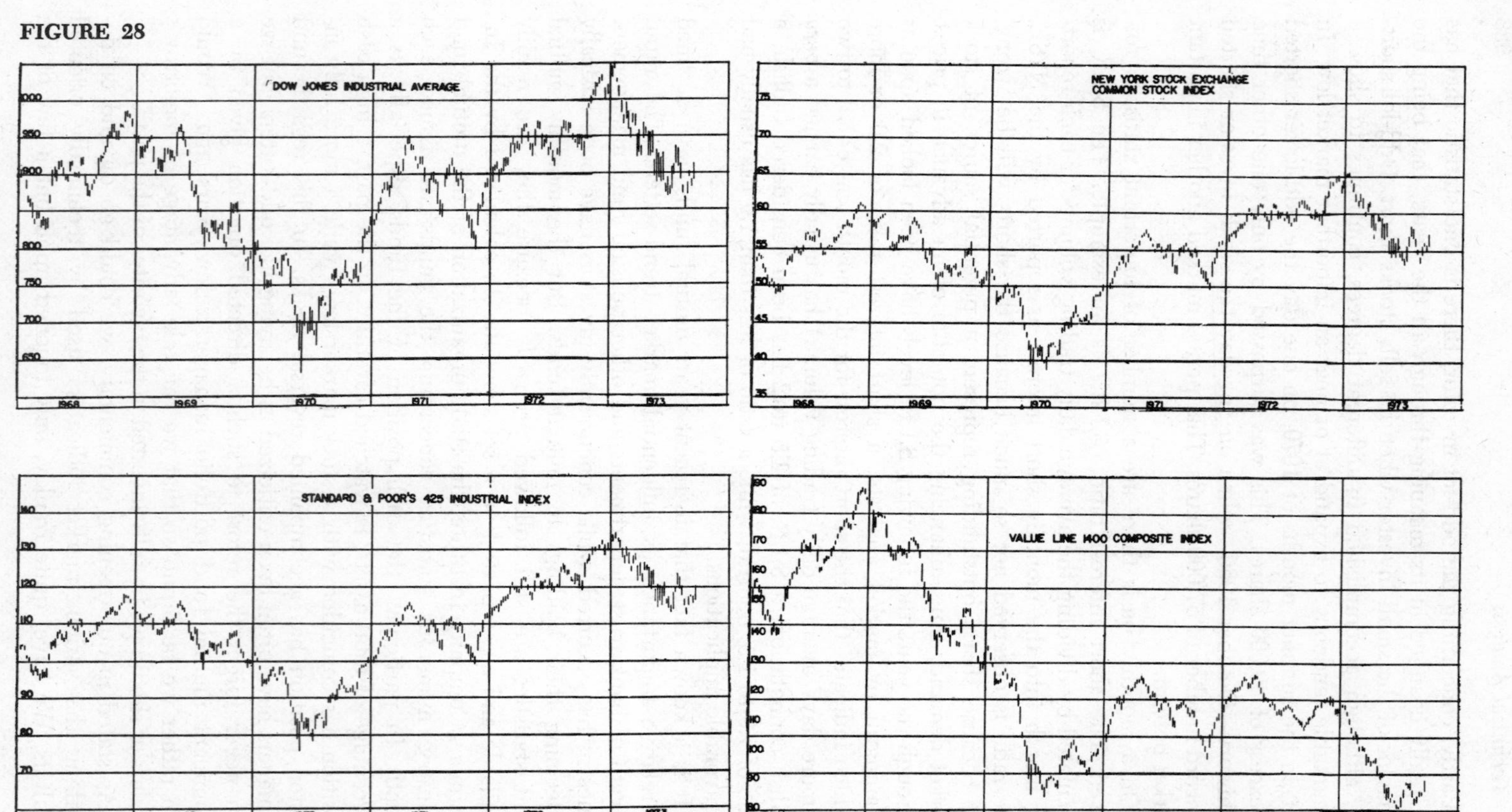
DOW JONES INDUSTRIAL AVERAGE
1000
950
900
800
750
700
650
1968
1969
1970
1971
1972
1973
NEW YORK STOCK EXCHANGE
COMMON STOCK INDEX
75
70
65
60
55
50
45
40
35
1968
1969
1970
1971
1972
1973
STANDARD & POOR'S 425 INDUSTRIAL INDEX
140
130
120
110
90
80
70
1968
1969
1970
1971
1972
1973
VALUE LINE 1400 COMPOSITE INDEX
180
170
160
140
130
120
110
100
90
80
1968
1969
1970
1971
1972
1973

FIGURE 28 (continued)

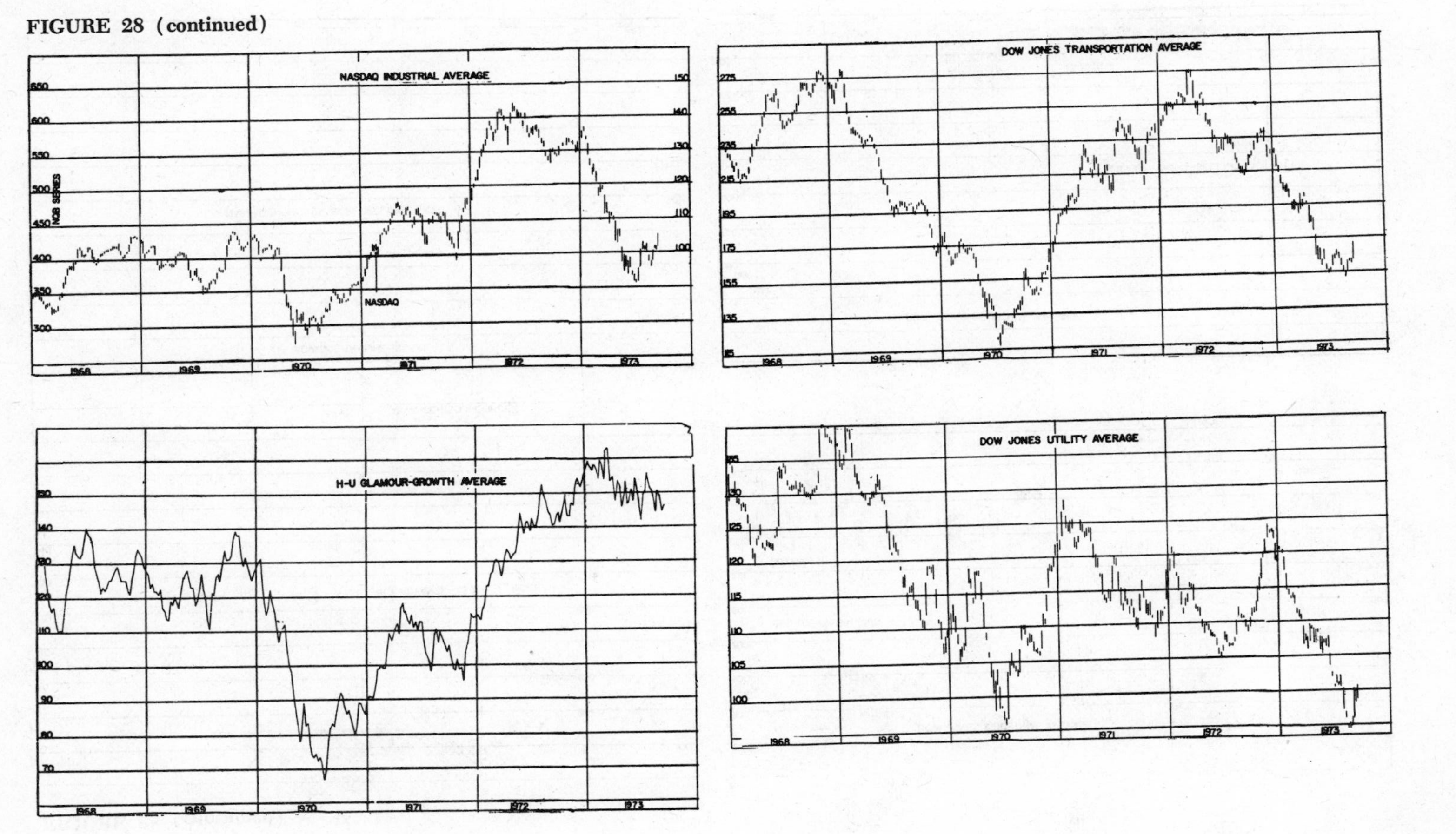

FIGURE 28 (continued)

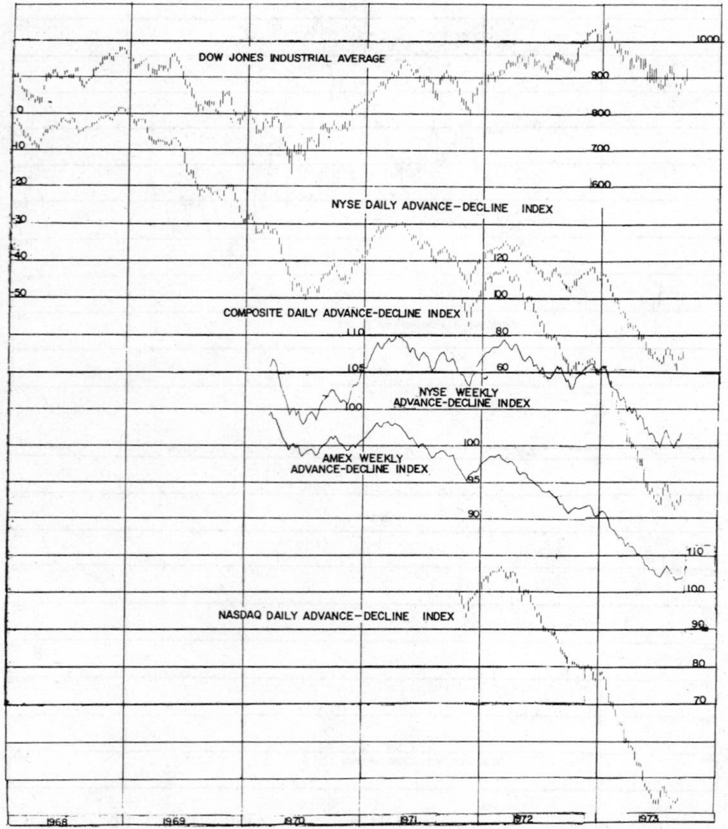

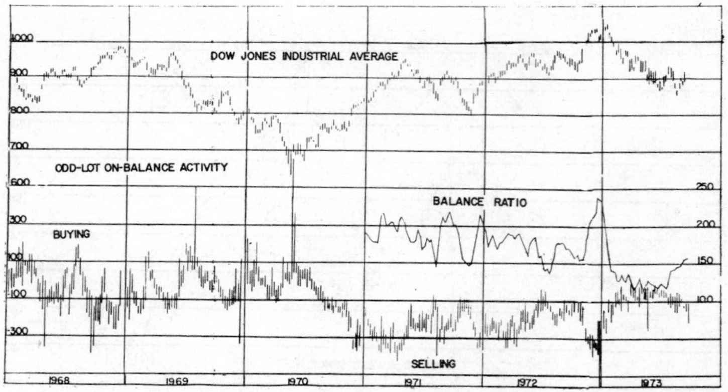

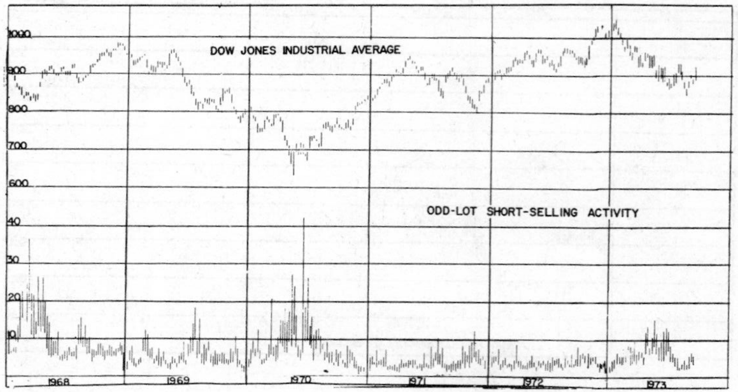

DOW JONES INDUSTRIAL AVERAGE

NYSE DAILY ADVANCE-DECLINE INDEX

COMPOSITE DAILY ADVANCE-DECLINE INDEX

NYSE WEEKLY ADVANCE-DECLINE INDEX

AMEX WEEKLY ADVANCE-DECLINE INDEX

NASDAQ DAILY ADVANCE-DECLINE INDEX

1968 1969 1970 1971 1972 1973

DOW JONES INDUSTRIAL AVERAGE

ODD-LOT ON-BALANCE ACTIVITY

BALANCE RATIO

BUYING

SELLING

1968 1969 1970 1971 1972 1973

DOW JONES INDUSTRIAL AVERAGE

ODD-LOT SHORT-SELLING ACTIVITY

1968 1969 1970 1971 1972 1973

FIGURE 28 (concluded)

many and vast statistics that serious analysts follow and observe. Oftentimes an analyst is asked which indicator does the best job or which one does he follow more closely. To be pragmatic, this question really cannot be answered. The analyst must assign different weights to his different inputs at different times. And these weights can shift dramatically depending on the market trend and environment being analyzed.

BIBLIOGRAPHY

Edwards, Robert D. and Magee, John. *Technical Analysis of Stock Trends.* New York: John Magee, Inc., 1966.

Gordon, William. *The Stock Market Indicators.* Investors Press, 1968.

Granville, Joseph E. *A Strategy of Daily Stock Market Timing for Maximum Profit.* Englewood Cliffs, New Jersey: Prentice-Hall, Inc. 1960.

Jiler, William L. *How Charts Can Help You in the Stock Market.* New York: Trendline, Inc., 1962.

Wheelen, Alexander H. *Study Helps and Point and Figure Technique.* New York: Morgan, Rogers and Roberts, 1971.

35

Calculation of Market Averages

SUMNER N. LEVINE, Ph.D.
State University of New York
Stony Brook, New York

DOW JONES AVERAGES are the most widely used and best known measures of market performance as indicated in the preceding section. Analysts interested in the detailed computation and structure of these indices will find the following description of value.[1]

Industrial Average

Dow Jones & Company first compiled an average consisting entirely of industrial stocks on May 26, 1896. Twelve stocks were used until 1916, when the list was increased to 20 and the new average was worked back to December 1914. On October 1, 1928, the list was increased to 30, where it has remained since, although substitutions have been made among the components from time to time.

Originally, the method of computation was simply this: When there were 12 stocks, the prices of the 12 were added together, and the total was divided by 12. When there were 20, their sum was divided by 20.

However, when some corporations whose stocks were in the list began splitting up their shares, this system would have produced distortions if adjustments had not been made. Here is an oversimplified example: Assume three stocks, selling at $5, $10, and $15. Their average price is $10. Now the $15 stock is split three for one, which would make the new shares sell at $5. The day this happens the market goes

[1] Quoted from information provided by Dow Jones Inc.

up, with the $5 stock closing at $6, the $10 one at $11, and the split stock at $6. Add up the three, and the total is 23 which, divided by 3 as before, would give an average of only $7.67—down sharply from the preceding day's average of $10 in spite of the fact the market actually went up.

The method used at first to obviate this distortion was to multiply the price of each split share by the amount of the split. In the example just given, the $6 price of the split stock would be multiplied by 3 before adding it to the other prices. The total of three stocks then would be 35 which, divided by 3, would give an average of $11.67, fully reflecting the market's rise from the average of $10 the day before.

In 1928 a new method was adopted. Again illustrating with our example from the above, here is how the method works:

The evening before the split takes place, after the average has been worked out for publication the same way as on preceding days, a theoretical calculation is made. The same stocks' prices are added up, but with the stock that is about to be split included as if the split had already taken place. In the simplified example, that would mean adding 5, 10, and one third of 15. Then this total, or 20, is divided by the actual average already calculated, which in this case was 10 (5 plus 10 plus 15 divided by 3). The result, in this example the figure 2, is the new divisor to be used in calculating the average beginning the next day.

On that next day, when the stocks close at 6, 11, and 6, their total of 23 is divided by the new divisor of 2, giving an average of 11.50, which gives reflection to the market's rise. This divisor is then used daily until another split, an issue of rights or other distribution takes place, or until it becomes necessary—as sometimes happens—to substitute one or more new stocks for one or more of the existing components.

Such substitutions are made upon the merger of one of the components in the averages into another company, or when a stock becomes too inactive, or when its movements, because of an extremely low price, become so small as to have little effect on the average, or when for some other reason a stock ceases to be representative of a substantial sector of American industry. When a substitution is made, the divisor is adjusted, just as when a split occurs. The same method of adjusting the divisor was also used in 1928, when the number of components in the Industrial Averages changed to 30 from 20. The divisor is not changed if the stock split, distribution, issue of rights, or substitution causes a distortion of less than five points in the Industrial Average.

Each day's change in each stock average is published by Dow Jones & Co., and in *The Wall Street Journal,* not only in points, but also in percentages. The purpose of doing this is to stress the fact that the use of a divisor other than 30 does not in any way affect the percentage change as long as the divisor remains the same. In the example used above, when the total of the three prices moves from 20 to 23, while the divisor remains at 2, the percentage gain in the average is 15 percent, and the percent gain in the total, from 20 to 23, is likewise 15 percent. Thus the published percentage figure reflects more accurately than any other just how the market for the 30 stocks moves from day to day. (There is a distortion in the percent movement on a day when the divisor must be changed, but the distortion is slight.)

When a component off the average does not sell on any day, its last previous closing price is used.

The current divisor will be found every day in *The Wall Street Journal,* under the tables on the next-to-last page giving the statistics of the averages.

Transportation Average

The earliest Dow Jones stock average on record, dating at least back to July of 1884, was primarily a transportation average—made up of nine railroads, one steamship line, and Western Union. An exclusively transportation average, made up of 20 railroad stocks, was first published on October 26, 1896. It continued as an all-railroad average until January 2, 1970, when it was modified to include other forms of transportation. The number of stocks in the average continues at 20.

Originally, quotations of stocks on the New York Stock Exchange were all in percentage of par value, which made no difference in the cases of stocks whose par was $100. But it did make a difference in the cases of the Pennsylvania, Reading and Lehigh Valley railroads, whose stocks were $50 par. For instance, if the Pennsylvania stock was bought at $40, it was quoted at "80" on the exchange. When an October 13, 1915, the exchange shifted to the present method of quoting in dollars, the average had to be calculated by multiplying the prices of such shares by 2 in order not to break the continuity of the figures. On August 8, 1930, Chesapeake & Ohio stock was split four for one and since then the rails' divisor has had to be adjusted from time to time in the same manner as that off the industrial average. The divisor is not changed if the stock split, distribution, issue of rights, or substitution causes a distortion of less than two points.

Public Utility Average

The Dow Jones utility average was first published on December 25, 1929, and was then worked back for the whole year. The original list consisted of 20 representative stocks. In figuring the average for the period prior to July 1, 1929, it was necessary to adjust the divisor, since quotations on Commonwealth & Southern and Niagara Hudson Power, which were in the July 1 list, were not available earlier. The total of the 18 available stocks was thus divided by 19.55 for the period May 27 to July 1. This divisor was determined by the same method as is used in computing the divisor for the industrial average. Prior to May 27, other divisors were used to compensate for various split-ups in the stocks. Five stocks were dropped from the list on June 2, 1938, and in subsequent years certain operating companies were substituted for holding companies. At present the average is based on 15 stocks. The divisor is not changed if the stock split, distribution, issue of rights, or substitution causes a distortion of less than two points in the utility average.

65-Stock Average

This average was begun November 9, 1933, as a simple arithmetical average of the 70 stocks comprising the Dow Jones industrial, railroad, and utility averages. It became a 65-stock average when five stocks were dropped from the utility average on June 2, 1938. No adjustments were made for substitutions in the 65-stock average until May 1945, since when its divisor has been adjusted whenever the divisor of any of the three component averages has been adjusted.

40-Bond Average

The Dow Jones bond averages were started in 1915. The 40-bond average represents the combined averages of 10 higher grade railroad bonds, 10 second grade railroad bonds, 10 public utility bonds, and 10 industrial bonds. In computing the bond averages, a simple arithmetic average of closing prices for each group is obtained. These four groups are then averaged to get the final average of the 40 bonds.

Railroad Income Bond Average

This average was started on January 2, 1947, to replace a former average of defaulted railroad bonds. It consists of income bonds of 10 important railroad systems.

Municipal Bond Yield Average

Each Monday, *The Wall Street Journal* publishes an average of yields on state and local municipal bonds; it was first published on January 2, 1928. This average is calculated in an unusual way because of a problem peculiar to such high-grade securities. The yields on these obligations vary not only with the condition of the market for long-term credit, but also with the number of years before they will be paid off.

The variations by years, however, are uniform on any given date. For instance, if a 10-year bond of Detroit sells to yield 2.60 percent and a 20-year bond of the same city yields 2.75 percent, a similar relationship will hold for bonds of the same maturities for any other well-regarded state or city. Therefore, an ideal average of municipal bond yields would be one composed entirely off bonds maturing the same number of years hence—say 20 years off. However, bonds actually are issued on many varying dates with many varying maturities, and obviously it is not possible to obtain a list of 20 bonds, each representing a different borrower, and all maturing 20 years hence.

To solve this problem *The Wall Street Journal* simply obtains each week, from the most reputable dealers in non-federal governmental securities, a set of 20 calculated figures, which are what the bonds of 20 state and city governments would yield if they all matured 20 years hence. These calculated figures are completely dependable, since they are arrived at by adding or subtracting the necessary number of percentage points to or from actual yields of actual bonds of the same local governments.

Once the individual yields are obtained, they are averaged simply by adding them together and dividing their total by 20.

List of Stocks and Bonds Used in Computing the Various Dow Jones Averages

30 Industrial Stocks

Allied Chemical	General Electric	Sears Roebuck
Aluminum Co. (Amer.)	General Foods	St'd Oil of Cal.
American Brands	General Motors	Exxon
American Can	Goodyear	Esmark
Am. Tel & Tel	Int. Harvester	Texaco
Anaconda	Inter. Nickel	Union Carbide
Bethlehem Steel	Inter. Paper	United Aircraft
Chrysler	Johns-Manville	U.S. Steel
DuPont	Owens-Ill.	Westinghouse Elec.
Eastman Kodak	Procter & Gamble	Woolworth

20 Transportation Stocks

American Air	Norfolk & West'n	Southern Pacific
Burlington Northern	Northwest Air	Southern Railway
Canadian Pacific	Pan Am World Air	Trans World Air
Chesapeake & Ohio	Penn Central	UAL Inc.
Consolid Freight	St. Louis-San Fran	Union Pac Corp
Eastern Air Lines	Sante Fe Indust	U.S. Freight Co.
McLean Trucking	Seaboard Coast	

15 Utility Stocks

Amer. Elec. Power	Consol. Nat. Gas	Panhandle E.P.L.
Cleveland E. Illum.	Detroit Edison	Peoples Gas
Columbia Gas Sys.	Houston Ltg. & Pow.	Philadelphia Elec.
Com'wealth Edison	Niagara Mohawk Pr.	Pub. Ser. E. & Gas Co.
Consol. Edison	Pacific Gas & El.	Sou. Cal. Edison

40 Bonds

10 Higher Grade Rails

Atchison Gen.	4s	'95	Northern Pacific	4s	'97
Ches. & Ohio "D"	3½s	'96	Penn Central	3½s	'97
Gt. Northern	3⅛s	2000	St. Louis Southwestern R.R.	4s	'89
L'ville & Nashville	2⅞s	2003	Southern Railway	5s	'94
Norfolk & Western	4s	'96	Virginian Rwy.	3s	'96

10 Second Grade Rails

Atl Coast L	4s	'80	Minneap & St L	6s	'85
Balt & Ohio	4s	'80	Mo Pac	4¼s	2005
Chicago Gt West	4s	'88	North Pacific	4s	'84
Chi Mil St P&P	4s	'94	St L S Fr	4s	'97
Louisville & Nash	7⅜s	'93	So Pac Oreg Lines 1st	4½s	'77

10 Public Utilities

Am T&T deb	2¾s	'75	Kansas City Pr & Lt	2¾s	'76
Central N.Y. Pwr	3s	'74	N.Y. Tel	4½s	'91
Com'l'th Edison 1st mtg	3s	'77	Ohio Edison Co 1st	3s	'74
Consumers Power	2⅞s	'75	Philadelphia Elec	2¾s	'74
Detroit Edison	9s	'99	Virginia Elec & Pwr Ser E	2¾s	'75

10 Industrials

Bath Steel Corp	6⅞s	'99	Nat'l Cash Reg	4⅜s	'87
Dow Chemical	4.35s	'88	Socony Mobil	4¼s	'93
Ford Motor	8⅛s	'90	St'd Oil of N.J	2¾s	'74
Gen'l Motors Acceptance	4½s	'85	Sun Oil Co	7¾s	'76
Inland Steel	3.20s	'82	Weyerhaeuser	5.20s	'91

Income Railroad Bonds

Chi & East Ill	5s	2054	Gulf Mobile & Ohio	5s	2015
Chi Gt Western	4½s	2038	Missouri Pacific	5s	2045
Chi Ind & Lville	4½s	2003	St Louis-San Fran	5s	2005
Chi Mil St P&P	4½s	2019	Western Pacific	5s	1984
Denver & R G West	4½s	2018	Wisconsin Central	4½s	2029

Municipal Bond Yield Average

Boston	4s	Milwaukee	4½s
Buffalo	3.90s	Minneapolis	4s
California	4s	Missouri	4s
Chicago	4s	New Orleans	4½s
Cleveland	4s	New York City	4s
Detroit	4½s	New York State	4s
Houston	4.65s	North Carolina	4½s
Illinois	4s	Pittsburgh	4½s
Kansas City	4s	St. Louis	4¼s
Los Angeles	4¼s	Seattle	4½s

Weighed Averages

Standard & Poor's averages like the New York Stock Exchange averages are examples of *arithmetically weighed indices* computed by an expression of the type shown below:

$$\text{Average} = \frac{\sum_{i}^{N} (\text{Current stock price}_i \times \text{Number of current shares}_i)}{f \sum_{i}^{N} (\text{Base period average price}_i \times \text{Number of shares}_i)} \times K$$

where f is an adjustment factor to account for the effects of increased capitalization. For the Standard & Poor's averages, the base period is the years 1941–43 and the constant K equals 10. For the New York Stock Exchange average, the base price is January 21, 1965, and K equals 50.

The above formula states that the average for N stocks is computed by multiplying the current price of each stock in the index by the current number of outstanding shares and then adding all N such products. This result is next divided by a similarly computed number for the base period and the result is multiplied by K.

The adjustment factor f corrects for changes in the number of shares outstanding for the issues making up the index and is given by:

$$f = \frac{\text{Total market value after capitalization change}}{\text{Total market value before capitalization change}}$$

The total market value is given by the sum of all issues of the products of the stock price and the quantity of stock. In some instances, such as stock splits or dividends, an increase in the amount of capitalization is generally offset by a proportionate decrease in the price stated so that f is unity and the base remains unchanged.

Standard & Poor's Averages. The currently used S & P's averages were introduced in 1957 though the company had calculated various other statistics since 1923. Among the S & P's averages are 425 industrials, 20 rails, 55 utilities, and the well-known composite of 500 stocks; the more important issues making up the latter were listed in the table given in the preceding article. Numerous special averages are also compiled by S & P.

Whereas the S & P's averages are computed in each case from a fixed list of companies, the New York Stock Exchange Composite Index is calculated for all issues traded on the exchange. The New York Stock Exchange also compiles averages of industrials, utilities, transportation, and finance companies; it began publishing its averages in 1966.

Geometric Averages. Value Line publishes geometric indices composed of 1297 industrials, 157 utilities, 18 rails, and a composite average for 1472 issues.

The formula for the Value Line averages is

$$\text{Current averages} = \Pi \left(\frac{\text{Current closing price}}{\text{Previous day's closing price}} \right)_i^{1/N} \times \text{Previous day's average.}$$

It will be noted that the prices in this formula are not weighed by the number of outstanding shares as was the case with the S & P's and NYSE averages.

The composite index, according to the above formula, is obtained as follows:

1. The closing price of each issue is divided by the preceding day's closing price.

2. The resulting quantities are multiplied and the Nth root obtained, where N is the number of issues.
3. The geometric average obtained in (2) is then multiplied by the average of the preceding day which was similarly calculated.

PART VI

Mathematical Aids

36

Compound Interest Calculations and Tables

SUMNER N. LEVINE, Ph.D.
State University of New York
Stony Brook, New York

THIS SECTION deals primarily with compound interest and return on investments calculations. Interest is the money paid for the use of money; to lenders it is a source of income and to borrowers it is the cost of a loan. The amount of money lent and upon which the interest is calculated is called the *principal.* The time period over which a given rate of interest is calculated is called the *unit of time* and may vary from days to a year.

More generally, interest received is merely a special case of return on investment. Thus, returns may also be realized from equity, hybrid investments (convertible bonds), and investments in options to purchase equity (warrants, rights, calls) or sell equity (puts). If the investment is productive, the accumulation of interest payments (return on investment) endows capital with a *time value* so that interest is sometimes referred to as the time value of invested money.

Interest rate is the ratio of the interest payable at the end of the time period to the money owned or invested at the beginning of the time period. Thus, if \$5 of interest is payable annually on a debt of \$100, the interest rate is $5/100 = 0.06$ per annum. An annual rate is understood unless some other time period is definitely stated.

In somewhat more general terms, the rate of return (i) is the total value realized from an asset at the end of a period of time, V_1, less the initial (V_0) value divided by the initial value:

$$i = (V_1 - V_0)/V_0.$$

Example. A stock with an initial cost of $10 appreciates during the year to $11 and pays a $1 dividend. The total *annual* rate of return is then:

$$i = (\$12 - \$10)/10 = 20\%.$$

Simple Interest. If interest is calculated only on the original principal or investment for the period during which the money is invested or borrowed, the interest is called *simple interest.* Let P be the original principal; i, the annual interest rate (expressed as a fraction); and n, the number of years, then I (the interest) is given by the formula: $I = Pni$.

Example 1. Find the amount of simple interest due at nine months if the annual interest rate is 6 percent.

$$I = \$28.00 \times 9/12 \times 0.06 = \$1.26$$

Example 2. A debt of $6,000 is to be repaid in semiannual installments of $400 with a simple annual interest of 6 percent on the outstanding principal. Find the total interest paid to discharge the debt.

Interest due with 1st payment	$= 6{,}000 \times \frac{1}{2} \times 0.06 =$	180
Interest due with 2d payment	$= 5{,}600 \times \frac{1}{2} \times 0.06 =$	168
Interest due with 3d payment	$= 5{,}200 \times \frac{1}{2} \times 0.06 =$	156
Interest due with 15th payment	$= 400 \times \frac{1}{2} \times 0.06 =$	12

The sums of all interest payments are given by:

$$S = 180 + 168 + 156 + \ldots + 12 = \$1{,}440.$$

Compound Interest. Interest is compounded when the interest each year is computed on the original principal plus the accumulated interest that has not been paid out. In other words, interest is paid on the retained interest plus principal. Let P be the original principal; n, the number of interest periods; i, the interest rate per interest period; and F, the sum of money at the end of the n compound interest paying periods, then:

End of 1st period:

$$F_1 = P + P_i = P(1 + i)$$

End of 2d period:

$$F_2 = P(1 + i) + iP(1 + i)$$

or

$$F_2 = P(1 + i)^2$$

End of 3d period:

$$F_3 = P(1 + i)^2 + iP(1 + i)^2$$

or

$$F_3 = P(1 + i)^3$$

In general, at the end of n periods:

$$F = P(1 + i)^n. \tag{1}$$

This formula gives the value of the sum of money due (F) at the end of n periods if an amount (P) is invested now at a compounded rate i. It is convenient to use the notation (F/P, i, n), the *future worth factor,* for the quantity $(1 + i)^n$ tabulated in the first column of the compound interest tables given at the end of this chapter, so that the above expression in the new notation is:

$$F = P(F/P,i,n). \tag{2}$$

The above formula can be transformed into the form:

$$P = F/(1 + i)^n.$$

The following notation will be used for the *present worth factor:*

$$1/(1 + i)^n = (P/F,i,n),$$

hence:

$$P = F(P/F,i,n).$$

The quantity ($P/Fi,n$) is also given in the tables.

The last formula permits us to calculate the amount which must be invested now, (P), at a compounded rate (i), if the sum of money (F) is desired at the end of n periods. The amount P is often referred to as the *present value* of a future amount (F). Clearly, in order to calculate the present value P corresponding to F we must know the time period (n) involved and the compound interest rate (i).

Example. If $1,000 is invested at 6 percent compounded, how much will be accumulated at the end of five years?

Solution.

$$F = P(F/P,i,n)$$
$$P = \$1{,}000,\ i = 0.06,\ n = 5,\ F = ?$$

It is often useful, particularly with complex situations, to represent the timing of the cash flows by means of a diagram in which disbursements (cash outlays) are represented by downward directed arrows and cash receipts by upward directed arrows. It will be assumed that the cash flows occur at the *end* of a given period, i.e., even though a cash flow may actually be occurring during a period of time, it is assumed for purposes of calculation that the cash flow occurs at the end of the period. For the above problem the cash flows are represented in Figure 1.

Turning to Table 11, labeled 6 percent, we find under the column headed ($P/F,i,n$) corresponding to $n = 5$, that:

$$(F/P,6\%,5) = 1.3382$$

Hence:

FIGURE 1

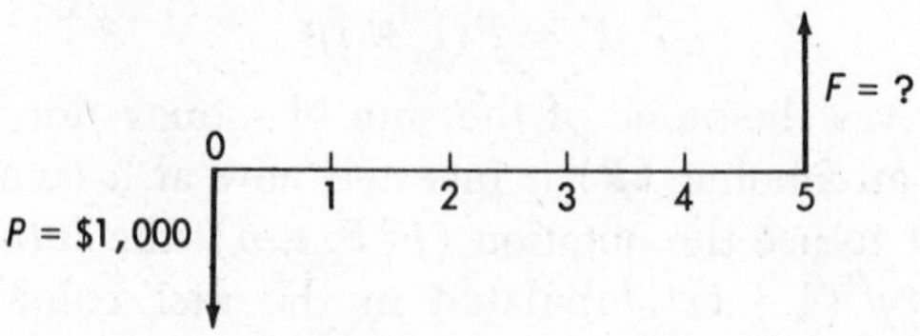

$$F = \$1,000\ (1.3382) = \$1,338.20$$

Example. An investment opportunity is available which provides a compounded annual rate of return of 12 percent. How much must be invested now in order to realize $100,000 at the end of 10 years?

Solution.

$$P = F(P/F,i,n)$$
$$F = \$100,000,\ i = 12\%,\ n = 10,\ P = ?$$

The cash flows are shown diagrammatically below:

FIGURE 2

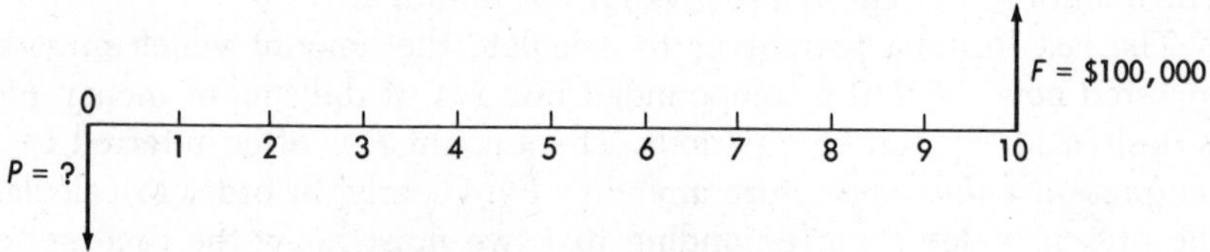

From table 16, labeled 12 percent, we find for $n = 10$:

$$(P/F,12\%,10) = 0.3220$$

Hence:

$$P = \$100,000\ (0.3220) = \$32,200$$

Thus, under the condition stated ($i = 12\%$, $n = 10$), the present value of $100,000 is $32,200.

Example. A portfolio is expected to appreciate at an annual rate of return of 10 percent. What lump sum must be invested now in order to permit a withdrawal of $10,000 at 5 years hence and a second withdrawal of $10,000 at 10 years from the present?

Solution.

The cash flow diagram is:

FIGURE 3

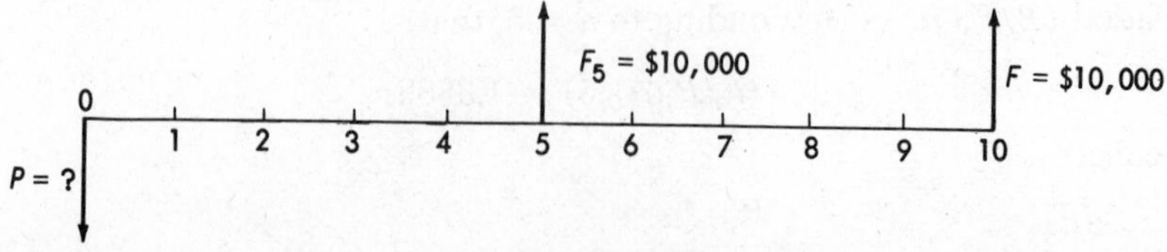

$$P = F_5(P/F,10\%,5) + F_{10}\,(P/F,10\%,10)$$
$$P = \$10{,}000\ (0.6209) + \$10{,}000\ (0.3855)$$
$$P = \$6{,}209 + \$3{,}855$$
$$P = \$10{,}064$$

Otherwise stated, the cash flows of $10,000 at 5 years and at 10 years from the time of the initial investment (at the stated compounded rate of return) has a present value of $10,064.

Calculation of the Rate of Return. The first formula given above can be used to calculate the compounded rate of return given the initial investment *P* and the return on the investment *F* realized after *n* years:

$$i = (F/P)^{1/n} - 1$$

The solution can be carried out using logarithms. However, a somewhat more convenient interpolation technique may also be used.

Example. A security costing $80 five years ago and was sold for $100. What was the compounded annual rate of return realized, neglecting taxes and commissions?

Solution.

$$n = 5,\ P = 80,\ F = 100,\ i = ?$$
$$i = (100/80)^{1/5} - 1 = (1.25)^{1/5} - 1$$
$$\log(1.25)^{1/5} = 0.09691/5 = 0.019382$$

so that

$$(1.25)^{1/5} = 1.0456$$
$$i = 1.0456 - 1 = 4.56\%.$$

A second method of solving the problem makes use of the compound interest tables and the formula:

$$F = P(F/P,i,n),$$

where:

$$n = 5,\ P = \$80,\ F = \$100,\ i = ?$$

so that $100/$80 = 1.25 = $(F/P,i,5)$.

Using the tables, we must seek a value of *i* which satisfies the expression given above. We note that:

$$(F/P,\ 4\%,\ 5) = 1.217 \text{ (from Table 9)}$$
$$(F/P,\ i,\ 5) = 1.250 \text{ (from problem)}$$
$$(F/P,\ 5\%,\ 5) = 1.276 \text{ (from Table 10)}$$

The first tabulated value is somewhat too small, and the second tabulated value is somewhat too large so that we must interpolate:

$$i = 4\% + 1\%(1.250 - 1.217)/(1.276 - 1.217) = 4.56\%$$

Uniform Series of Payments

Situations involving uniform (equal) series of receipts or payments sometimes arise in the analysis of investments. As an illustration, an investor may want to know the uniform amount that must be invested annually into a fund in order to realize a specified amount at some future time, i.e., say at retirement.

The cash flow diagram for a uniform series of payments of amount A each period into a fund providing a compounded rate of return i per period is shown below, for the case of four periods.

FIGURE 4

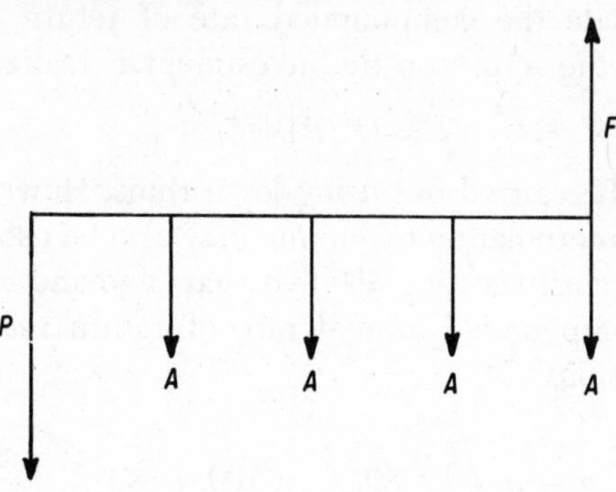

In the above diagram P is the present worth and F is the future worth of the uniform series.

Several situations may arise and the appropriate expressions for handling them are given below:

Given A to find F:

$$F = A\,\frac{(1+i)^n - 1}{i}$$

Given F to find A:

$$A = \frac{Fi}{(1+i)^n - 1} = F(A/F,i,n)$$

Given P to find A:

$$A = P\,\frac{i(1+i)^n}{(1+i)^n - 1} = P(A/P,i,n)$$

Given A to find P:

$$P = A\,\frac{(1+i)^n - 1}{i(1+i)^n} = A(P/A,i,n)$$

The various quantities, such as $(F/A,i,n)$ and $(A/P,i,n)$, appearing on the right side of the above expressions are tabulated in the compound interest tables at the end of the section.

Example. A series of uniform annual payments of $2,000 each are made to purchase shares of a portfolio expected to provide a 10 percent compounded annual rate of return. What is the value of the investment at the end of five years?

Solution. The cash flow diagram is:

FIGURE 5

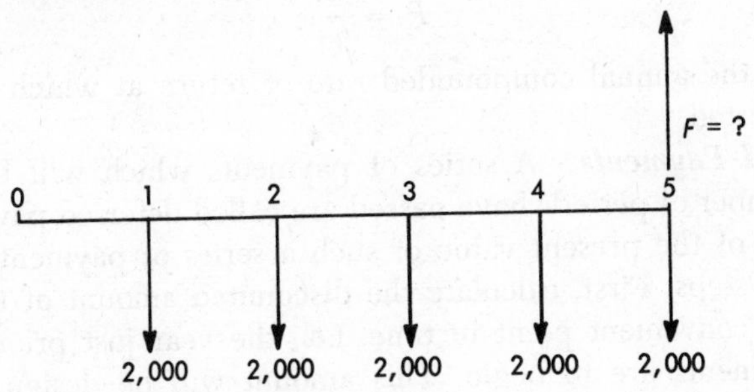

Notice that all payments are considered as having been made at the end of the year, starting with the first year and continuing to the fifth year. The solution is given by:

$$F = A(F/A,i,n)$$
$$A = \$2{,}000,\ i = 10\%,\ n = 5,\ F = ?$$

From the compound interest tables we have:

$$(F/A, 10\%, 5) = 6.105$$
$$F = \$2{,}000\ (6.105) = \$12{,}210$$

Example. What is the present worth of an annual annuity of $1,000 which will start at the end of the year and continue for six years? Assume that the money is worth 8 percent compounded per annum.

Solution. The cash flow diagram is:

FIGURE 6

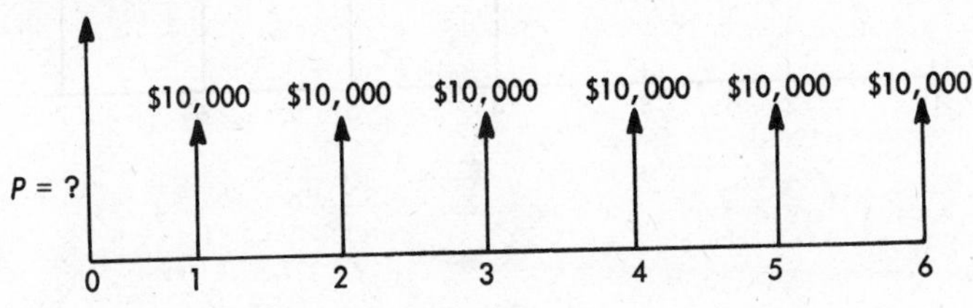

$$P = A(P/A,i,n)$$
$$A = \$1{,}000,\ n = 6,\ i = 8\%,\ P = ?$$
$$P = \$1{,}000(P/A,\ 8\%,\ 6)$$
$$P = 1{,}000\ (4.623)$$
$$P = \$4{,}623.$$

The significance of this calculation is that the investor should not pay more than $4,623 for the above annuity plan if he has alternative investments available yielding a compound annual rate of 8 percent.

Present Value of a Perpetual Annuity. The present value of an equal payment series (A) which continues without end and which commences at the end of the present period is:

$$P = \frac{A}{i},$$

where i is the annual compounded rate of return at which the income can be invested.

Deferred Payments. A series of payments which will become due after a number of periods have passed are called deferred payments. The calculation of the present value of such a series of payments is carried out in two steps. First, calculate the discounted amount of the uniform series at a convenient point in time, i.e., the year just prior to that at which payments are to begin. This amount will be designated as P_F. Secondly, the present value of P_F is determined using the expression:

$$P = P_F(P/F,i,n-1)$$

where n is the number of periods which must elapse before the first payment is due.

Example. Mr. X is planning for his son's college expenses estimated at $5,000 a year for four years. His son will enter college in five years. How much should Mr. X now invest in a fund providing a 10% compounded rate of return (neglecting taxes) in order to pay for his son's college expenses? Principal and appreciation are to be exhausted on completion of college.

Solution. The cash flow diagram is:

FIGURE 7

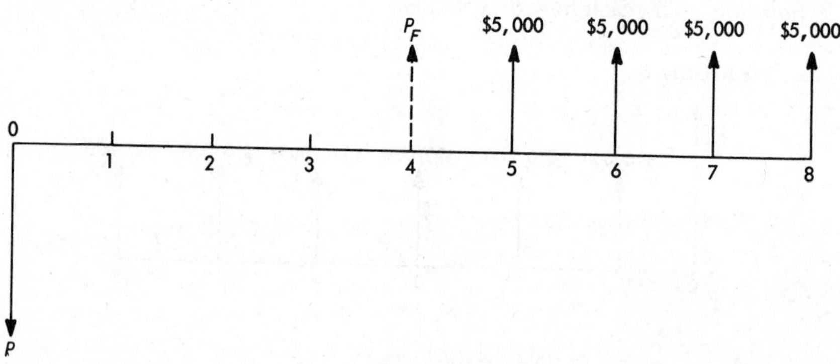

We first determine P_F at year 4 for the four equal payments which will start at year 5:

$$P_F = A(P/A,i,n)$$
$$A = \$5{,}000,\ i = 10\%,\ n = 4,\ P_F = ?$$
$$P_F = \$5{,}000\ (P/A,\ 10\%,\ 4)$$
$$P_F = \$5{,}000\ (3,\ 170)$$
$$P_F = \$15{,}850$$

This amount corresponds to a present investment into the fund given by:

$$P = P_F(P/F,i,n)$$
$$P_F = \$15{,}850,\ n = 4,\ i = 10\%,\ P = ?$$
$$P = \$15{,}850\ (0.6830)$$
$$P = \$10{,}778$$

Thus, $10,778 must be invested into the fund in order to meet the required disbursements.

Uniformly Increasing Gradient. Financial calculations frequently involve cash flows that increase each year by varying amounts. For example, because of inflation a retiree will require increasing annual payouts from his investments. We shall assume that the increases in the cash flow each period can be approximated by multiples of a fixed amount, G. Consequently, the cash flows that we shall consider here may be represented as shown in the following diagram:

FIGURE 8

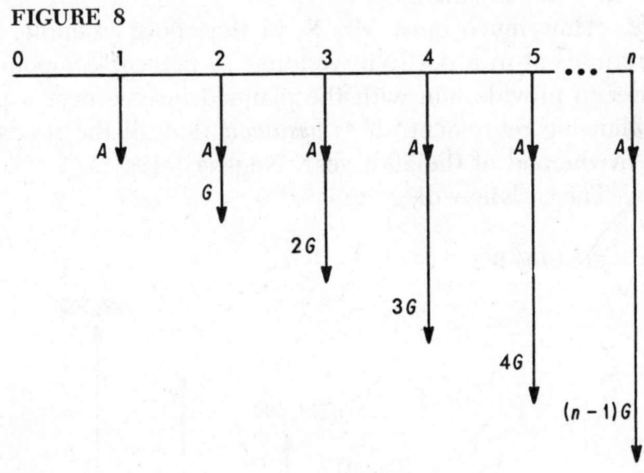

We see that the cash flows consist of two components: (*a*) a uniform component of amount *A* starting with the end of the first year and (*b*) an increasing component of amount $k\,G$ ($k = 1,2,3, \ldots$) starting at the end of the *second year.* We shall refer to G as the uniform gradient amount.

Example. Mr. X, a portfolio manager, is considering his retirement needs. He estimates that he will require $20,000 during the first year of retirement and, because of inflation, the following amounts in subsequent years:

Year	*Total*	*Uniform Series* (A)	*Gradient Series* (kG)
2	$20,500	$20,000	$ 500
3	21,000	20,000	1,000
4	21,500	20,000	1,500
5	22,000	20,000	2,000
...	...	...	...

Mr. X's financial needs can be represented by a uniform payment series of \$20,000 plus multiples of a uniform gradient amount G of \$500 which start at the end of the second year.

The problems of dealing with a uniform gradient series can be considerably simplified by converting the gradient series to a *uniform* series of amount A_g which starts at the end of the *first year.* After this conversion of the gradient series has been accomplished, then all of the earlier formulas (which apply to uniform series) can be used.

The factor for converting a gradient series to a uniform series is represented by the symbol $(A/G,i,n)$ and is compiled in the tables.[1] Thus, the uniform series of amount A_g per period is given by:

$$A_g = G(A/G, i, n),$$

where G is the gradient amount.

Example. How much must Mr. X, in the above example, have invested at retirement in a portfolio yielding 10 percent compounded per year in order to provide him with the planned income over a period of 20 years following retirement? *It is assumed* that all the funds will be consumed by the end of the 20th year. Neglect taxes.

Solution. The cash flow diagram is:

FIGURE 9

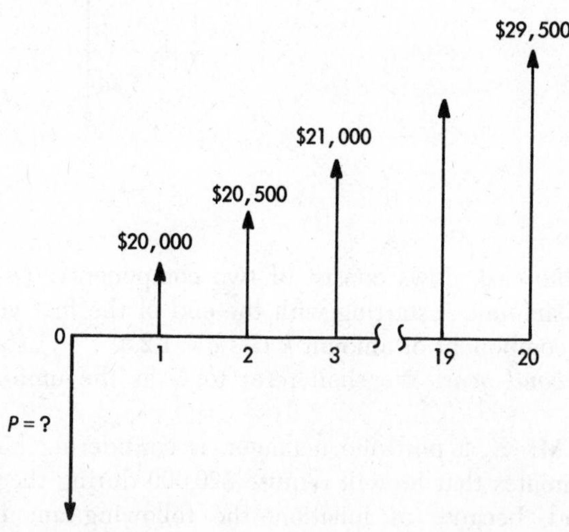

The cash payout consists of a uniform series A of amount \$20,000 plus a gradient series starting at the end of the second year with

[1] Mathematically it can be shown that:

$$(A/G, i,n) = \frac{1}{i} - \frac{n}{(1+i)^n - 1}$$

$G = \$500$. Convert the gradient series to a uniform series of amount A_g at the end of the first year:

$$A_g = G(A/G,i,n)$$
$$G = \$500,\ i = 10\%,\ n = 20 \text{ years},\ A_g = ?$$
$$A_g = \$500(A/G,\ 10\%,\ 20)$$
$$A_g = \$500(6.51) \text{ (from compound interest tables)}$$
$$A_g = \$3{,}255$$

The equivalent uniform series is $A + A_g$, i.e., the uniform series of \$20,000 plus \$3,255 or \$23,255.

$$P = A(P/A,i,n)$$
$$A = \$23{,}255,\ i = 10\%,\ n = 20,\ P = ?$$
$$P = \$23{,}255(P/A,\ 10\%,20)$$
$$P = \$23{,}255(8.514)$$
$$P = \$197{,}900$$

Thus, Mr. X's portfolio on retirement (P) should be \$197,900.

Nominal and Effective Interest Rates. Interest may be compounded more frequently than once a year, i.e., compounding may occur semi-annually, quarterly, or daily. Suppose that interest is compounded m times a year and the rate for each period is r, then the *annual nominal* interest rate is $R = mr$.

If one dollar is invested at the annual nominal rate R compounded m periods a year at the rate r per period, it will, at the end of the year, appreciate to the value F given by:

$$F = (1 + r)^m = (1 + R/m)^m = (F/P,r,m)$$

Example. Interest is compounded monthly at an annual nominal rate of 12 percent. If \$1,000 is invested for one year, what is the amount in the account?

$$F = P(F/P,r,m)$$
$$P = \$1{,}000,\ m = 12,\ r = 12\%/12 = 1\%,\ F = ?$$
$$F = \$1{,}000\ (1.1268)$$
$$F = \$1{,}126.80$$

Instead of compounding m times a year at an annual nominal rate R, it is possible to obtain the same interest by compounding only once a year at the annual *effective* rate i given by:

$$i = (1 + R/m)^m - 1 = (F/P,r,m) - 1$$

Example. What annual effective rate i (the rate compounded only once during the year) is equivalent to an annual nominal rate of 8 percent compounded quarterly?

Solution.

$$i = (F/P,r,m) - 1$$
$$r = 8\%/4 = 2\%,\ m = 4$$
$$i = (F/P,\ 2\%,\ 4) - 1$$
$$i = 1.0824 - 1 = 0.0824 = 8.24\%$$

Extensive tables are available for directly converting nominal rates to effective rates.

When comparing various nominal rates, it is usually desirable to convert them to effective rates.

CALCULATION OF RATE OF RETURN

In this section we discuss the calculation of an unknown internal rate of return given the cash flows associated with an investment, the *net present value.* The net present value (NPV) of an investment is obtained by subtracting the initial outlay of the investment C_0 from the present value of the subsequent cash flows resulting (or expected) from the investment, C_n:

$$NPV = \sum_{n=1}^{N} \frac{C_n}{(1+i)^n} - C_0$$

or in terms of our previous notation:

$$NPV = \sum_{k=1}^{N} C_n(P/F,i,n) - C_0$$

The number of time periods N over which the investment is considered is called the time *horizon* of the investment.

Clearly, the NPV depends among other things on the interest rate i used in the calculation. The larger the value of i in the above expression, the less the NPV. A negative value of NPV implies that the investment does not provide the desired rate of return i. Given a set of investment alternatives, that with the greater NPV would be selected.

Example. An investor buys a stock at \$100 per share. The expected annual dividend payout is \$10 per share. He plans to sell the stock at the end of the second year at an expected price of \$120. The investor expects a compounded rate of return (i) of 8 percent. What is the expected NPV of the stock to this investor?

Solution. The cash flows consist of an initial disbursement of \$100, followed by the expected receipt of \$10 at the end of the first year and of \$132 (the \$12 dividend and the \$120 from the sales of the stock) at the end of the second year.

$$NPV = C_1(P/F,i,1) + C_2(P/F,i,2) - C_0$$
$$C_0 = \$100,\ C_1 = \$10,\ C_2 = 132,\ i = 8\%,\ NPV = ?$$

Using Table 13 for the 8 percent compound interest factors, we have:

$$NPV = \$10(0.9259) + \$132(0.8573) - \$100$$
$$NPV = \$22.75 \text{ per share.}$$

Thus, the investment would return in excess of 8 percent. What is the actual rate of return? This may be found by calculating the internal rate of return as discussed next.

Internal Rate of Return. The internal rate of return i_0 is the compound interest rate i which gives a *NPV* of zero. This rate is usually calculated by trial and error using the cash flows and the tabulated $(P/F,i,n)$ functions.

The calculation can be systematized by using certain observations which are apparent from the graph of *NPV* versus i, as shown in Figure 10;

FIGURE 10
Net Present Value (NPV) versus Rate of Return (i)

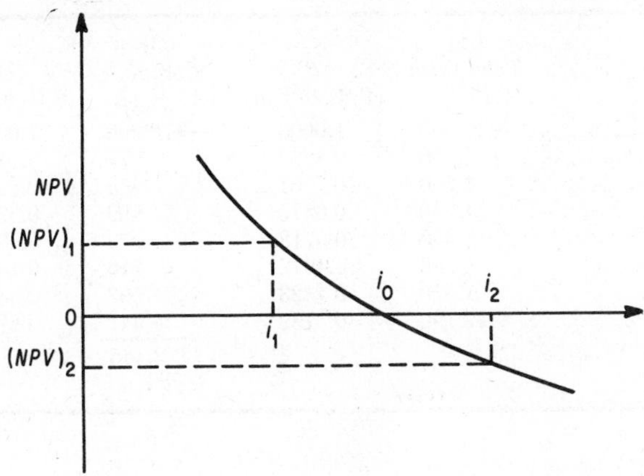

We see that *NPV* is positive for a choice of i less than i_0 and negative for a choice of i greater than i_0. To estimate i_0, we select, by trial and error, an i_1, giving a positive $(NPV)_1$ and for which the next greatest tabulated value i_2 gives a negative $(NPV)_2$ as shown in Figure 10.

We know that i_0 must lie between these two values so that i_0 may be estimated by interpolation using the formula:

$$i_0 = i_1 + \frac{(i_2 - i_1)(NPV)_1}{(NPV)_1 - (NPV)_2}$$

The closer i_1 and i_2 are in value the better will be the approximation.

Example. An investment of $10,900 was made in a portfolio which was held for seven years and then liquidated at a price of $21,190. Annual dividend and interest payments received during the seven years are tabulated below:

Year	*Portfolio Payout*
1	$1,000
2	1,250
3	1,230
4	1,350
5	1,440
6	1,370
7	1,000

Calculate the annual compounded rate of return on the investment before taxes.

Solution. By trial and error it was determined that a change in sign in the *NPV* occurred between 15 percent (i_1) and 20 percent (i_2). The trial-and-error calculation can be simplified by assuming that the payout occurred as a uniform cash flow of $1,200.

The detailed calculation is shown on the following work sheet:

Year	*(A)* *Total Cash Flow*	*(B)* (P/F,*15%*,n)	*(C)* *Column* (*A*) × (*B*)	*(D)* (P/F,*20%*,n)	*(E)* *Column* (*A*) × (*D*)
0	−10,900	1.0000	−$10,900	1.0000	−$10,900
1	1,000	0.8696	870	0.833	833
3	1,250	0.7561	945	0.6944	868
2	1,230	0.6575	809	0.5787	712
4	1,350	0.5718	772	0.4823	651
5	1,440	0.4972	716	0.4019	579
6	1,370	0.4323	592	0.3349	459
7	22,190	0.3759	8,341	0.2791	6,193
Total (*NPV*)			$ 2,145 $(NPV)_1$		−$ 605 $(NPV)_2$

The cash flow for year seven is the sum of the payout and the liquidation price of the portfolio. Interpolation between the two values gives a rate of return i_0 of 18.9 percent.

$$i_0 = 15\% + \frac{2145(20\% - 15\%)}{2750} = 18.9\%$$

BOND YIELDS

Definitions. Three types of bond yields should be distinguished:

1. The nominal or *coupon rate* is the rate based on the face value (par value) of the bond. Thus, a $1,000 par value bond issued with a coupon rate of 7 percent would pay $70 annually.

2. The *current yield* is calculated by dividing the annual interest by the current price of the bond:

Current yield = \$1,000 × Nominal rate/Market price.

3. *Yield to maturity* is the annual nominal rate of return if the bonds are held to maturity.

If a bond is sold at a price greater than par value (usually \$1,000), then it is said to sell at a *premium,* and if it sold at a price less than par value, it is said to sell at a *discount.*

Many bonds contain provisions permitting the issuer to redeem or call the bond after a specified date but prior to maturity at a premium over the offering price. The *yield to call* is the annual nominal rate of return if the bonds are held to the call date and redeemed at the call price.

In other words, the yield to maturity and the yield to call are simply the internal rates of return discussed previously and are therefore calculated by the same procedure.

It should be noted that bonds are usually purchased on an "and interest" basis, i.e., the buyer must pay the seller the proportional amount of interest accrued since the preceding interest date. The reason is that the buyer will receive the full interest on the next interest date, generally six months later.

Calculation of Yield to Maturity and Yield to Call

A bond paying A dollars interest semiannually is purchased at a price of P_0 (including the interest payment to the seller). The bond is held for n semiannual periods and redeemed at par \$1,000) on maturity or at a premium price on call represented by P_n (i.e., P_n is \$1,000 if the bond is redeemed at maturity or the call price if redeemed at call). The semiannual yield (i) is calculated from the familiar expression for the internal rate of return:

$$A(P/A,i,n) + P_n(P/F,i,n) - P_0 = 0$$

The *annual* nominal rate of return is $2i$.

Example. A bond bears an 8 percent per annum coupon and now sells at discount of 95(\$950) plus interest to the seller of \$20 and matures 10 years (20 semiannual interest periods) hence. What is the before-tax annual nominal yield to maturity?

Solution. The semiannual payments (A) are 1/2(0.08)(\$1,000), or \$40.

$$A(P/A,i,n) + P_n(P/F,i,n) - P_0 = 0$$
$$A = \$40,\ n = 20,\ P_n = \$1{,}000,\ P_0 = \$970,\ i = ?$$

In the following table, the present value factors $(P/A,i,n)$ and $(P/F,i,n)$, selected by trial and error, are shown in the columns labeled *PVF* and the cash flows are shown in the columns labeled *CF*.

Period	(A) CF	(B) PVF(4%)	(C) Columns (A) × (B)	(D) PVF(5%)	(E) Columns (A) × (D)
0	$ −970	1.0000	−970	1.000	−970
1–20	40	13.5900	543	12.462	498
20	$ 1,000	0.4564	456	0.377	377
Total			+ 29		− 95

Interpolation gives:

$$i = 4\% + \frac{29(1\%)}{124},$$

hence:

$$i = 4.2\%.$$

The *annual* nominal yield to maturity is 8.4 percent compounded semi-annually.

If the bond becomes callable after, say, three years and the call price is 105($1,050), then the yield to call is calculated in the same way with $n = 6$ and $P_n = \$1,050$.

RATE OF RETURN ON STOCKS

The annual compound rate of return on a stock is the value of (i) which satisfies the expression:

$$\sum_{k=1}^{n} D_k/(1+i)^k + P_n/(1+i)^n - P_0 = 0$$

where D_n is the dividend paid in the kth year, and P_0 is the purchase price of the stock, while P_n is the price at which the stock is sold at the end of year n.

If, instead of using annual dividends, we use quarterly dividends and time periods in the above equation, then the annual nominal rate of return is $4i$.

Payout Ratio. If R is the annual payout ratio given by:

$$R = \text{annual dividends/annual earnings},$$

and the fractional annual growth of earnings g is given by:

$$g = \Delta E/E,$$

where E is the annual earnings of the previous year and ΔE is the annual increase in earnings. If we assume g is constant, the kth year dividends are:

$$D_k = RE_0(1+g)^k,$$

where E_0 is the annual earnings at the time the stock is purchased.

Plowback Ratio. We note that the annual increase in retained earnings ΔS is given by:

$$\Delta S = E(1 - R) = Eb,$$

where:

$$b = 1 - R.$$

The quantity b is the *plowback ratio,* which is a measure of the proportion of the annual earnings retained in the business.

Return on Capital. The *return on stockholders' equity* (Y) is the ratio of annual earnings (E) to stockholders' equity (S):

$$Y = E/S$$

The *return on capitalization* (equity plus long-term debt, L) Y_C is

$$Y_C = \frac{E}{S + L}$$

The last expression may be written:

$$E = Y_C\,(S + L) = Y_C\,S(1 + L/S),$$

hence:

$$Y = Y_C\,(1 + L/S).$$

The quantity L/S is the *leverage* or the ratio of long-term debt to equity. *If the returns on equity and capitalization are given, the leverage may be calculated from:*

$$L/S = Y/Y_C - 1.$$

If we assume that the leverage remains constant, the increase in earnings is given by:

$$\Delta E = Y_C \Delta S(1 + L/S) = Y \Delta S.$$

Since $\Delta S = Eb$ we have:

$$\Delta E/E = bY = g,$$

so that the *fractional rate of earnings increase is simply the product of the plowback ratio and the return on equity.*

Modified Form of the Rate of Return Equation. Introducing the above definitions into the expression for the rate of return on investment we have:

$$\sum_{k=1}^{n} E_0(1 - b)\left[\frac{(1 + Yb)}{(1 + i)}\right]^k + \frac{P_n}{(1 + i)^n} - P_0 = 0$$

Long-Term Investments. For very long term investments, considerable simplification of the last equation is possible, since

$$\frac{P_n}{(1+i)^n}$$

approaches zero, and the summation term can be simplified using the algebraic result:

$$\sum_{k=1}^{\infty} Ar^k = Ar/(1-r) \qquad \text{(if } r < 1\text{)}$$

where

$$r = \frac{1+Yb}{1+i}$$

so that:

$$\frac{E_0(1-b)r}{1-r} = \frac{D_0 r}{1-r} = P_0$$

where $D_0 = E_0(1-b)$, the dividend at the time of purchase. Solving for i we find:

$$i \text{ (long term)} = \frac{D_0}{P_0}(1+g) + Yb = \frac{D_0(1+g)}{P_0} + g$$

Example. An investor is interested in purchasing a stock as a long-term holding which will provide a 10 percent compounded annual rate of return. Should he invest in universal Widget, a large well-established company with fairly constant debt to equity, payout, and return on investment ratios, given the data listed below?

Current price, $25 per share.
Current annual dividends (D_0), $1 per share.
Current annual earnings (E_0), $2 per share.
Return on equity (Y) = 0.12.
Return on capitalization (Y_C) = 0.18.

Solution.

$$i = \frac{D_0}{P_0}(1+g) + g$$

$$Y = 0.12$$
$$\text{Plowback ratio } (b) = \$1/\$2 = 0.5$$
$$\text{Earnings growth rate } (g) = bY = 0.5 \times 0.12 = 0.06$$
$$D_0 = \$1$$
$$P_0 = \$25$$

$$i = \frac{\$1}{\$25}(1.06) + 0.06$$

$$i = 0.102, \text{ or } 10.2\%$$

Hence, the long-term rate of return just about satisfies the investors requirements.

The debt-to-equity ratio (L/S) can be calculated from:

$$(L/S) = Y_C/Y - 1$$
$$(L/S) = 0.18/0.12 - 1 = 0.50$$

This moderately large ratio should be compared to similar companies in the industry. The debt provides favorable leverage, serving to raise the earnings per share. On the other hand, a substantial long-term debt imposes fixed charges which can become burdensome if earnings fall off substantially. The analyst should examine the earnings coverage of the debt charges and provisions for debt repayment.

TABLE 1

¼ % Interest Factors for Annual Compounding Interest

	Single Payment		Equal-Payment Series				
n	Compound-Amount Factor	Present-Worth Factor	Compound-Amount Factor	Sinking-Fund Factor	Present-Worth Factor	Capital-Recovery Factor	Uniform Gradient-Series Factor
	To Find F Given P F/P i, n	*To Find P Given F P/F i, n*	*To Find F Given A F/A i, n*	*To Find A Given F A/F i, n*	*To Find P Given A P/A i, n*	*To Find A Given P A/P i, n*	*To Find A Given G A/G i, n*
1	1.003	0.9975	1.000	1.0000	0.9975	1.0025	0.0000
2	1.005	0.9950	2.003	0.4994	1.9925	0.5019	0.4994
3	1.008	0.9925	3.008	0.3325	2.9851	0.3350	0.9983
4	1.010	0.9901	4.015	0.2491	3.9751	0.2516	1.4969
5	1.013	0.9876	5.025	0.1990	4.9627	0.2015	1.9950
6	1.015	0.9851	6.038	0.1656	5.9479	0.1681	2.4927
7	1.018	0.9827	7.053	0.1418	6.9305	0.1443	2.9900
8	1.020	0.9802	8.070	0.1239	7.9108	0.1264	3.4869
9	1.023	0.9778	9.091	0.1100	8.8885	0.1125	3.9834
10	1.025	0.9754	10.113	0.0989	9.8639	0.1014	4.4794
11	1.028	0.9729	11.139	0.0898	10.8368	0.0923	4.9750
12	1.030	0.9705	12.166	0.0822	11.8073	0.0847	5.4703
13	1.033	0.9681	13.197	0.0758	12.7753	0.0783	5.9651
14	1.036	0.9657	14.230	0.0703	13.7410	0.0728	6.4594
15	1.038	0.9632	15.265	0.0655	14.7042	0.0680	6.9534
16	1.041	0.9608	16.304	0.0613	15.6651	0.0638	7.4470
17	1.043	0.9585	17.344	0.0577	16.6235	0.0602	7.9401
18	1.046	0.9561	18.388	0.0544	17.5795	0.0569	8.4328
19	1.049	0.9537	19.434	0.0515	18.5332	0.0540	8.9251
20	1.051	0.9513	20.482	0.0488	19.4845	0.0513	9.4170
21	1.054	0.9489	21.533	0.0464	20.4334	0.0489	9.9085
22	1.056	0.9466	22.587	0.0443	21.3800	0.0468	10.3995
23	1.059	0.9442	23.644	0.0423	22.3242	0.0448	10.8902
24	1.062	0.9418	24.703	0.0405	23.2660	0.0430	11.3804
25	1.064	0.9395	25.765	0.0388	24.2055	0.0413	11.8702
26	1.067	0.9372	26.829	0.0373	25.1426	0.0398	12.3596
27	1.070	0.9348	27.896	0.0359	26.0774	0.0384	12.8485
28	1.072	0.9325	28.966	0.0345	27.0099	0.0370	13.3371
29	1.075	0.9302	30.038	0.0333	27.9401	0.0358	13.8252
30	1.078	0.9278	31.113	0.0322	28.8679	0.0347	14.3130
31	1.080	0.9255	32.191	0.0311	29.7934	0.0336	14.8003
32	1.083	0.9232	33.272	0.0301	30.7166	0.0326	15.2872
33	1.086	0.9209	34.355	0.0291	31.6375	0.0316	15.7737
34	1.089	0.9186	35.441	0.0282	32.5561	0.0307	16.2597
35	1.091	0.9163	36.529	0.0274	33.4724	0.0299	16.7453
40	1.105	0.9050	42.013	0.0238	38.0199	0.0263	19.1673
45	1.119	0.8937	47.566	0.0210	42.5109	0.0235	21.5789
50	1.133	0.8826	53.189	0.0188	46.9462	0.0213	23.9802
55	1.147	0.8717	58.882	0.0170	51.3264	0.0195	26.3710
60	1.162	0.8609	64.647	0.0155	55.6524	0.0180	28.7514
65	1.176	0.8502	70.484	0.0142	59.9246	0.0167	31.1215
70	1.191	0.8397	76.394	0.0131	64.1439	0.0156	33.4812
75	1.206	0.8292	82.379	0.0121	68.3108	0.0146	35.8305
80	1.221	0.8189	88.439	0.0113	72.4260	0.0138	38.1694
85	1.236	0.8088	94.575	0.0106	76.4901	0.0131	40.4980
90	1.252	0.7988	100.788	0.0099	80.5038	0.0124	42.8162
95	1.268	0.7888	107.080	0.0093	84.4677	0.0118	45.1241
100	1.284	0.7791	113.450	0.0088	88.3825	0.0113	47.4216

Source: Tables 1–22 are from W. J. Fabrycky and G. J. Thuesen, *Economic Decision Analysis*, © 1974, pp. 360–81. Reprinted by permission of Prentice-Hall, Inc., Englewood Cliffs, New Jersey.

TABLE 2

½ % Interest Factors for Annual Compounding Interest

	Single Payment		Equal-Payment Series				Uniform Gradient-Series Factor
n	Compound-Amount Factor	Present-Worth Factor	Compound-Amount Factor	Sinking-Fund Factor	Present-Worth Factor	Capital-Recovery Factor	
	To Find F Given P F/P i, n	*To Find P Given F P/F i, n*	*To Find F Given A F/A i, n*	*To Find A Given F A/F i, n*	*To Find P Given A P/A i, n*	*To Find A Given P A/P i, n*	*To Find A Given G A/G i, n*
1	1.005	0.9950	1.000	1.0000	0.9950	1.0050	0.0000
2	1.010	0.9901	2.005	0.4988	1.9851	0.5038	0.4988
3	1.015	0.9852	3.015	0.3317	2.9703	0.3367	0.9967
4	1.020	0.9803	4.030	0.2481	3.9505	0.2531	1.4938
5	1.025	0.9754	5.050	0.1980	4.9259	0.2030	1.9900
6	1.030	0.9705	6.076	0.1646	5.8964	0.1696	2.4855
7	1.036	0.9657	7.106	0.1407	6.8621	0.1457	2.9801
8	1.041	0.9609	8.141	0.1228	7.8230	0.1278	3.4738
9	1.046	0.9561	9.182	0.1089	8.7791	0.1139	3.9668
10	1.051	0.9514	10.228	0.0978	9.7304	0.1028	4.4589
11	1.056	0.9466	11.279	0.0887	10.6770	0.0937	4.9501
12	1.062	0.9419	12.336	0.0811	11.6189	0.0861	5.4406
13	1.067	0.9372	13.397	0.0747	12.5562	0.0797	5.9302
14	1.072	0.9326	14.464	0.0691	13.4887	0.0741	6.4190
15	1.078	0.9279	15.537	0.0644	14.4166	0.0694	6.9069
16	1.083	0.9233	16.614	0.0602	15.3399	0.0652	7.3940
17	1.088	0.9187	17.697	0.0565	16.2586	0.0615	7.8803
18	1.094	0.9141	18.786	0.0532	17.1728	0.0582	8.3658
19	1.099	0.9096	19.880	0.0503	18.0824	0.0553	8.8504
20	1.105	0.9051	20.979	0.0477	18.9874	0.0527	9.3342
21	1.110	0.9006	22.084	0.0453	19.8880	0.0503	9.8172
22	1.116	0.8961	23.194	0.0431	20.7841	0.0481	10.2993
23	1.122	0.8916	24.310	0.0411	21.6757	0.0461	10.7806
24	1.127	0.8872	25.432	0.0393	22.5629	0.0443	11.2611
25	1.133	0.8828	26.559	0.0377	23.4456	0.0427	11.7407
26	1.138	0.8784	27.692	0.0361	24.3240	0.0411	12.2195
27	1.144	0.8740	28.830	0.0347	25.1980	0.0397	12.6975
28	1.150	0.8697	29.975	0.0334	26.0677	0.0384	13.1747
29	1.156	0.8653	31.124	0.0321	26.9330	0.0371	13.6510
30	1.161	0.8610	32.280	0.0310	27.7941	0.0360	14.1265
31	1.167	0.8568	33.441	0.0299	28.6508	0.0349	14.6012
32	1.173	0.8525	34.609	0.0289	29.5033	0.0339	15.0750
33	1.179	0.8483	35.782	0.0280	30.3515	0.0330	15.5480
34	1.185	0.8440	36.961	0.0271	31.1956	0.0321	16.0202
35	1.191	0.8398	38.145	0.0262	32.0354	0.0312	16.4915
40	1.221	0.8191	44.159	0.0227	36.1722	0.0277	18.8358
45	1.252	0.7990	50.324	0.0199	40.2072	0.0249	21.1595
50	1.283	0.7793	56.645	0.0177	44.1428	0.0227	23.4624
55	1.316	0.7601	63.126	0.0159	47.9815	0.0209	25.7447
60	1.349	0.7414	69.770	0.0143	51.7256	0.0193	28.0064
65	1.383	0.7231	76.582	0.0131	55.3775	0.0181	30.2475
70	1.418	0.7053	83.566	0.0120	58.9394	0.0170	32.4680
75	1.454	0.6879	90.727	0.0110	62.4137	0.0160	34.6679
80	1.490	0.6710	98.068	0.0102	65.8023	0.0152	36.8474
85	1.528	0.6545	105.594	0.0095	69.1075	0.0145	39.0065
90	1.567	0.6384	113.311	0.0088	72.3313	0.0138	41.1451
95	1.606	0.6226	121.222	0.0083	75.4757	0.0133	43.2633
100	1.647	0.6073	129.334	0.0077	78.5427	0.0127	45.3613

TABLE 3

¾ % Interest Factors for Annual Compounding Interest

	Single Payment		Equal-Payment Series				Uniform Gradient-Series Factor
n	Compound-Amount Factor	Present-Worth Factor	Compound-Amount Factor	Sinking-Fund Factor	Present-Worth Factor	Capital-Recovery Factor	Uniform Gradient-Series Factor
	To Find F Given P F/P i, n	*To Find P Given F P/F i, n*	*To Find F Given A F/A i, n*	*To Find A Given F A/F i, n*	*To Find P Given A P/A i, n*	*To Find A Given P A/P i, n*	*To Find A Given G A/G i, n*
1	1.008	0.9926	1.000	1.0000	0.9926	1.0075	0.0000
2	1.015	0.9852	2.008	0.4981	1.9777	0.5056	0.4981
3	1.023	0.9778	3.023	0.3309	2.9556	0.3384	0.9950
4	1.030	0.9706	4.045	0.2472	3.9261	0.2547	1.4907
5	1.038	0.9633	5.076	0.1970	4.8894	0.2045	1.9851
6	1.046	0.9562	6.114	0.1636	5.8456	0.1711	2.4782
7	1.054	0.9491	7.159	0.1397	6.7946	0.1472	2.9701
8	1.062	0.9420	8.213	0.1218	7.7366	0.1293	3.4608
9	1.070	0.9350	9.275	0.1078	8.6716	0.1153	3.9502
10	1.078	0.9280	10.344	0.0967	9.5996	0.1042	4.4384
11	1.086	0.9211	11.422	0.0876	10.5207	0.0951	4.9253
12	1.094	0.9142	12.508	0.0800	11.4349	0.0875	5.4110
13	1.102	0.9074	13.601	0.0735	12.3424	0.0810	5.8954
14	1.110	0.9007	14.703	0.0680	13.2430	0.0755	6.3786
15	1.119	0.8940	15.814	0.0632	14.1370	0.0707	6.8606
16	1.127	0.8873	16.932	0.0591	15.0243	0.0666	7.3413
17	1.135	0.8807	18.059	0.0554	15.9050	0.0629	7.8207
18	1.144	0.8742	19.195	0.0521	16.7792	0.0596	8.2989
19	1.153	0.8677	20.339	0.0492	17.6468	0.0567	8.7759
20	1.161	0.8612	21.491	0.0465	18.5080	0.0540	9.2517
21	1.170	0.8548	22.652	0.0442	19.3628	0.0517	9.7261
22	1.179	0.8484	23.822	0.0420	20.2112	0.0495	10.1994
23	1.188	0.8421	25.001	0.0400	21.0533	0.0475	10.6714
24	1.196	0.8358	26.188	0.0382	21.8892	0.0457	11.1422
25	1.205	0.8296	27.385	0.0365	22.7188	0.0440	11.6117
26	1.214	0.8234	28.590	0.0350	23.5422	0.0425	12.0800
27	1.224	0.8173	29.805	0.0336	24.3595	0.0411	12.5470
28	1.233	0.8112	31.028	0.0322	25.1707	0.0397	13.0128
29	1.242	0.8052	32.261	0.0310	25.9759	0.0385	13.4774
30	1.251	0.7992	33.503	0.0299	26.7751	0.0374	13.9407
31	1.261	0.7932	34.754	0.0288	27.5683	0.0363	14.4028
32	1.270	0.7873	36.015	0.0278	28.3557	0.0353	14.8636
33	1.280	0.7815	37.285	0.0268	29.1371	0.0343	15.3232
34	1.289	0.7757	38.565	0.0259	29.9128	0.0334	15.7816
35	1.299	0.7699	39.854	0.0251	30.6827	0.0326	16.2387
40	1.348	0.7417	46.446	0.0215	34.4469	0.0290	18.5058
45	1.400	0.7145	53.290	0.0188	38.0732	0.0263	20.7421
50	1.453	0.6883	60.394	0.0166	41.5665	0.0241	22.9476
55	1.508	0.6630	67.769	0.0148	44.9316	0.0223	25.1223
60	1.566	0.6387	75.424	0.0133	48.1734	0.0208	27.2665
65	1.625	0.6153	83.371	0.0120	51.2963	0.0195	29.3801
70	1.687	0.5927	91.620	0.0109	54.3046	0.0184	31.4634
75	1.751	0.5710	100.183	0.0100	57.2027	0.0175	33.5163
80	1.818	0.5501	109.073	0.0092	59.9945	0.0167	35.5391
85	1.887	0.5299	118.300	0.0085	62.6838	0.0160	37.5318
90	1.959	0.5105	127.879	0.0078	65.2746	0.0153	39.4946
95	2.034	0.4917	137.823	0.0073	67.7704	0.0148	41.4277
100	2.111	0.4737	148.145	0.0068	70.1746	0.0143	43.3311

TABLE 4

1% Interest Factors for Annual Compounding Interest

n	Single Payment: Compound-Amount Factor, To Find F Given P F/P i, n	Single Payment: Present-Worth Factor, To Find P Given F P/F i, n	Equal-Payment Series: Compound-Amount Factor, To Find F Given A F/A i, n	Equal-Payment Series: Sinking-Fund Factor, To Find A Given F A/F i, n	Equal-Payment Series: Present-Worth Factor, To Find P Given A P/A i, n	Equal-Payment Series: Capital-Recovery Factor, To Find A Given P A/P i, n	Uniform Gradient-Series Factor, To Find A Given G A/G i, n
1	1.010	0.9901	1.000	1.0000	0.9901	1.0100	0.0000
2	1.020	0.9803	2.010	0.4975	1.9704	0.5075	0.4975
3	1.030	0.9706	3.030	0.3300	2.9410	0.3400	0.9934
4	1.041	0.9610	4.060	0.2463	3.9020	0.2563	1.4876
5	1.051	0.9515	5.101	0.1960	4.8534	0.2060	1.9801
6	1.062	0.9421	6.152	0.1626	5.7955	0.1726	2.4710
7	1.072	0.9327	7.214	0.1386	6.7282	0.1486	2.9602
8	1.083	0.9235	8.286	0.1207	7.6517	0.1307	3.4478
9	1.094	0.9143	9.369	0.1068	8.5660	0.1168	3.9337
10	1.105	0.9053	10.462	0.0956	9.4713	0.1056	4.4179
11	1.116	0.8963	11.567	0.0865	10.3676	0.0965	4.9005
12	1.127	0.8875	12.683	0.0789	11.2551	0.0889	5.3815
13	1.138	0.8787	13.809	0.0724	12.1338	0.0824	5.8607
14	1.149	0.8700	14.947	0.0669	13.0037	0.0769	6.3384
15	1.161	0.8614	16.097	0.0621	13.8651	0.0721	6.8143
16	1.173	0.8528	17.258	0.0580	14.7179	0.0680	7.2887
17	1.184	0.8444	18.430	0.0543	15.5623	0.0643	7.7613
18	1.196	0.8360	19.615	0.0510	16.3983	0.0610	8.2323
19	1.208	0.8277	20.811	0.0481	17.2260	0.0581	8.7017
20	1.220	0.8196	22.019	0.0454	18.0456	0.0554	9.1694
21	1.232	0.8114	23.239	0.0430	18.8570	0.0530	9.6354
22	1.245	0.8034	24.472	0.0409	19.6604	0.0509	10.0998
23	1.257	0.7955	25.716	0.0389	20.4558	0.0489	10.5626
24	1.270	0.7876	26.973	0.0371	21.2434	0.0471	11.0237
25	1.282	0.7798	28.243	0.0354	22.0232	0.0454	11.4831
26	1.295	0.7721	29.526	0.0339	22.7952	0.0439	11.9409
27	1.308	0.7644	30.821	0.0325	23.5596	0.0425	12.3971
28	1.321	0.7568	32.129	0.0311	24.3165	0.0411	12.8516
29	1.335	0.7494	33.450	0.0299	25.0658	0.0399	13.3045
30	1.348	0.7419	34.785	0.0288	25.8077	0.0388	13.7557
31	1.361	0.7346	36.133	0.0277	26.5423	0.0377	14.2052
32	1.375	0.7273	37.494	0.0267	27.2696	0.0367	14.6532
33	1.389	0.7201	38.869	0.0257	27.9897	0.0357	15.0995
34	1.403	0.7130	40.258	0.0248	28.7027	0.0348	15.5441
35	1.417	0.7059	41.660	0.0240	29.4086	0.0340	15.9871
40	1.489	0.6717	48.886	0.0205	32.8347	0.0305	18.1776
45	1.565	0.6391	56.481	0.0177	36.0945	0.0277	20.3273
50	1.645	0.6080	64.463	0.0155	39.1961	0.0255	22.4363
55	1.729	0.5785	72.852	0.0137	42.1472	0.0237	24.5049
60	1.817	0.5505	81.670	0.0123	44.9550	0.0223	26.5333
65	1.909	0.5237	90.937	0.0110	47.6266	0.0210	28.5217
70	2.007	0.4983	100.676	0.0099	50.1685	0.0199	30.4703
75	2.109	0.4741	110.913	0.0090	52.5871	0.0190	32.3793
80	2.217	0.4511	121.672	0.0082	54.8882	0.0182	34.2492
85	2.330	0.4292	132.979	0.0075	57.0777	0.0175	36.0801
90	2.449	0.4084	144.863	0.0069	59.1609	0.0169	37.8725
95	2.574	0.3886	157.354	0.0064	61.1430	0.0164	39.6265
100	2.705	0.3697	170.481	0.0059	63.0289	0.0159	41.3426

TABLE 5

1¼ % Interest Factors for Annual Compounding Interest

	Single Payment		Equal-Payment Series				
n	Compound-Amount Factor	Present-Worth Factor	Compound-Amount Factor	Sinking-Fund Factor	Present-Worth Factor	Capital-Recovery Factor	Uniform Gradient-Series Factor
	To Find F Given P F/P i, n	*To Find P Given F* P/F i, n	*To Find F Given A* F/A i, n	*To Find A Given F* A/F i, n	*To Find P Given A* P/A i, n	*To Find A Given P* A/P i, n	*To Find A Given G* A/G i, n
1	1.013	0.9877	1.000	1.0000	0.9877	1.0125	0.0000
2	1.025	0.9755	2.013	0.4969	1.9631	0.5094	0.4969
3	1.038	0.9634	3.038	0.3292	2.9265	0.3417	0.9917
4	1.051	0.9515	4.076	0.2454	3.8781	0.2579	1.4845
5	1.064	0.9398	5.127	0.1951	4.8178	0.2076	1.9752
6	1.077	0.9282	6.191	0.1615	5.7460	0.1740	2.4638
7	1.091	0.9167	7.268	0.1376	6.6627	0.1501	2.9503
8	1.104	0.9054	8.359	0.1196	7.5681	0.1321	3.4348
9	1.118	0.8942	9.463	0.1057	8.4624	0.1182	3.9172
10	1.132	0.8832	10.582	0.0945	9.3455	0.1070	4.3976
11	1.146	0.8723	11.714	0.0854	10.2178	0.0979	4.8758
12	1.161	0.8615	12.860	0.0778	11.0793	0.0903	5.3520
13	1.175	0.8509	14.021	0.0713	11.9302	0.0838	5.8262
14	1.190	0.8404	15.196	0.0658	12.7706	0.0783	6.2982
15	1.205	0.8300	16.386	0.0610	13.6006	0.0735	6.7683
16	1.220	0.8198	17.591	0.0569	14.4203	0.0694	7.2362
17	1.235	0.8096	18.811	0.0532	15.2299	0.0657	7.7021
18	1.251	0.7996	20.046	0.0499	16.0296	0.0624	8.1659
19	1.266	0.7898	21.297	0.0470	16.8193	0.0595	8.6277
20	1.282	0.7800	22.563	0.0443	17.5993	0.0568	9.0874
21	1.298	0.7704	23.845	0.0419	18.3697	0.0544	9.5450
22	1.314	0.7609	25.143	0.0398	19.1306	0.0523	10.0006
23	1.331	0.7515	26.457	0.0378	19.8820	0.0503	10.4542
24	1.347	0.7422	27.788	0.0360	20.6242	0.0485	10.9056
25	1.364	0.7330	29.135	0.0343	21.3573	0.0468	11.3551
26	1.381	0.7240	30.500	0.0328	22.0813	0.0453	11.8025
27	1.399	0.7151	31.881	0.0314	22.7963	0.0439	12.2478
28	1.416	0.7062	33.279	0.0301	23.5025	0.0426	12.6911
29	1.434	0.6975	34.695	0.0288	24.2000	0.0413	13.1323
30	1.452	0.6889	36.129	0.0277	24.8889	0.0402	13.5715
31	1.470	0.6804	37.581	0.0266	25.5693	0.0391	14.0087
32	1.488	0.6720	39.050	0.0256	26.2413	0.0381	14.4438
33	1.507	0.6637	40.539	0.0247	26.9050	0.0372	14.8768
34	1.526	0.6555	42.045	0.0238	27.5605	0.0363	15.3079
35	1.545	0.6474	43.571	0.0230	28.2079	0.0355	15.7369
40	1.644	0.6084	51.490	0.0194	31.3269	0.0319	17.8515
45	1.749	0.5718	59.916	0.0167	34.2582	0.0292	19.9156
50	1.861	0.5373	68.882	0.0145	37.0129	0.0270	21.9295
55	1.980	0.5050	78.422	0.0128	39.6017	0.0253	23.8936
60	2.107	0.4746	88.575	0.0113	42.0346	0.0238	25.8083
65	2.242	0.4460	99.377	0.0101	44.3210	0.0226	27.6741
70	2.386	0.4191	110.872	0.0090	46.4697	0.0215	29.4913
75	2.539	0.3939	123.103	0.0081	48.4890	0.0206	31.2605
80	2.701	0.3702	136.119	0.0074	50.3867	0.0199	32.9823
85	2.875	0.3479	149.968	0.0067	52.1701	0.0192	34.6570
90	3.059	0.3269	164.705	0.0061	53.8461	0.0186	36.2855
95	3.255	0.3072	180.386	0.0056	55.4211	0.0181	37.8682
100	3.463	0.2887	197.072	0.0051	56.9013	0.0176	39.4058

TABLE 6

1½ % Interest Factors for Annual Compounding Interest

n	Single Payment		Equal-Payment Series				Uniform Gradient-Series Factor
	Compound-Amount Factor	Present-Worth Factor	Compound-Amount Factor	Sinking-Fund Factor	Present-Worth Factor	Capital-Recovery Factor	
	To Find F Given P *F/P i, n*	*To Find P Given F* *P/F i, n*	*To Find F Given A* *F/A i, n*	*To Find A Given F* *A/F i, n*	*To Find P Given A* *P/A i, n*	*To Find A Given P* *A/P i, n*	*To Find A Given G* *A/G i, n*
1	1.015	0.9852	1.000	1.0000	0.9852	1.0150	0.0000
2	1.030	0.9707	2.015	0.4963	1.9559	0.5113	0.4963
3	1.046	0.9563	3.045	0.3284	2.9122	0.3434	0.9901
4	1.061	0.9422	4.091	0.2445	3.8544	0.2595	1.4814
5	1.077	0.9283	5.152	0.1941	4.7827	0.2091	1.9702
6	1.093	0.9146	6.230	0.1605	5.6972	0.1755	2.4566
7	1.110	0.9010	7.323	0.1366	6.5982	0.1516	2.9405
8	1.127	0.8877	8.433	0.1186	7.4859	0.1336	3.4219
9	1.143	0.8746	9.559	0.1046	8.3605	0.1196	3.9008
10	1.161	0.8617	10.703	0.0934	9.2222	0.1084	4.3772
11	1.178	0.8489	11.863	0.0843	10.0711	0.0993	4.8512
12	1.196	0.8364	13.041	0.0767	10.9075	0.0917	5.3227
13	1.214	0.8240	14.237	0.0703	11.7315	0.0853	5.7917
14	1.232	0.8119	15.450	0.0647	12.5434	0.0797	6.2582
15	1.250	0.7999	16.682	0.0600	13.3432	0.0750	6.7223
16	1.269	0.7880	17.932	0.0558	14.1313	0.0708	7.1839
17	1.288	0.7764	19.201	0.0521	14.9077	0.0671	7.6431
18	1.307	0.7649	20.489	0.0488	15.6726	0.0638	8.0997
19	1.327	0.7536	21.797	0.0459	16.4262	0.0609	8.5539
20	1.347	0.7425	23.124	0.0433	17.1686	0.0583	9.0057
21	1.367	0.7315	24.471	0.0409	17.9001	0.0559	9.4550
22	1.388	0.7207	25.838	0.0387	18.6208	0.0537	9.9018
23	1.408	0.7100	27.225	0.0367	19.3309	0.0517	10.3462
24	1.430	0.6996	28.634	0.0349	20.0304	0.0499	10.7881
25	1.451	0.6892	30.063	0.0333	20.7196	0.0483	11.2276
26	1.473	0.6790	31.514	0.0317	21.3986	0.0467	11.6646
27	1.495	0.6690	32.987	0.0303	22.0676	0.0453	12.0992
28	1.517	0.6591	34.481	0.0290	22.7267	0.0440	12.5313
29	1.540	0.6494	35.999	0.0278	23.3761	0.0428	12.9610
30	1.563	0.6398	37.539	0.0266	24.0158	0.0416	13.3883
31	1.587	0.6303	39.102	0.0256	24.6462	0.0406	13.8131
32	1.610	0.6210	40.688	0.0246	25.2671	0.0396	14.2355
33	1.634	0.6118	42.299	0.0237	25.8790	0.0387	14.6555
34	1.659	0.6028	43.933	0.0228	26.4817	0.0378	15.0731
35	1.684	0.5939	45.592	0.0219	27.0756	0.0369	15.4882
40	1.814	0.5513	54.268	0.0184	29.9159	0.0334	17.5277
45	1.954	0.5117	63.614	0.0157	32.5523	0.0307	19.5074
50	2.105	0.4750	73.683	0.0136	34.9997	0.0286	21.4277
55	2.268	0.4409	84.530	0.0118	37.2715	0.0268	23.2894
60	2.443	0.4093	96.215	0.0104	39.3803	0.0254	25.0930
65	2.632	0.3799	108.803	0.0092	41.3378	0.0242	26.8392
70	2.835	0.3527	122.364	0.0082	43.1549	0.0232	28.5290
75	3.055	0.3274	136.973	0.0073	44.8416	0.0223	30.1631
80	3.291	0.3039	152.711	0.0066	46.4073	0.0216	31.7423
85	3.545	0.2821	169.665	0.0059	47.8607	0.0209	33.2676
90	3.819	0.2619	187.930	0.0053	49.2099	0.0203	34.7399
95	4.114	0.2431	207.606	0.0048	50.4622	0.0198	36.1602
100	4.432	0.2256	228.803	0.0044	51.6247	0.0194	37.5295

TABLE 7

2% Interest Factors for Annual Compounding Interest

	Single Payment		Equal-Payment Series				Uniform Gradient-Series Factor
n	Compound-Amount Factor	Present-Worth Factor	Compound-Amount Factor	Sinking-Fund Factor	Present-Worth Factor	Capital-Recovery Factor	
	To Find F Given P F/P i, n	*To Find P Given F P/F i, n*	*To Find F Given A F/A i, n*	*To Find A Given F A/F i, n*	*To Find P Given A P/A i, n*	*To Find A Given P A/P i, n*	*To Find A Given G A/G i, n*
1	1.020	0.9804	1.000	1.0000	0.9804	1.0200	0.0000
2	1.040	0.9612	2.020	0.4951	1.9416	0.5151	0.4951
3	1.061	0.9423	3.060	0.3268	2.8839	0.3468	0.9868
4	1.082	0.9239	4.122	0.2426	3.8077	0.2626	1.4753
5	1.104	0.9057	5.204	0.1922	4.7135	0.2122	1.9604
6	1.126	0.8880	6.308	0.1585	5.6014	0.1785	2.4423
7	1.149	0.8706	7.434	0.1345	6.4720	0.1545	2.9208
8	1.172	0.8535	8.583	0.1165	7.3255	0.1365	3.3961
9	1.195	0.8368	9.755	0.1025	8.1622	0.1225	3.8681
10	1.219	0.8204	10.950	0.0913	8.9826	0.1113	4.3367
11	1.243	0.8043	12.169	0.0822	9.7869	0.1022	4.8021
12	1.268	0.7885	13.412	0.0746	10.5754	0.0946	5.2643
13	1.294	0.7730	14.680	0.0681	11.3484	0.0881	5.7231
14	1.319	0.7579	15.974	0.0626	12.1063	0.0826	6.1786
15	1.346	0.7430	17.293	0.0578	12.8493	0.0778	6.6309
16	1.373	0.7285	18.639	0.0537	13.5777	0.0737	7.0799
17	1.400	0.7142	20.012	0.0500	14.2919	0.0700	7.5256
18	1.428	0.7002	21.412	0.0467	14.9920	0.0667	7.9681
19	1.457	0.6864	22.841	0.0438	15.6785	0.0638	8.4073
20	1.486	0.6730	24.297	0.0412	16.3514	0.0612	8.8433
21	1.516	0.6598	25.783	0.0388	17.0112	0.0588	9.2760
22	1.546	0.6468	27.299	0.0366	17.6581	0.0566	9.7055
23	1.577	0.6342	28.845	0.0347	18.2922	0.0547	10.1317
24	1.608	0.6217	30.422	0.0329	18.9139	0.0529	10.5547
25	1.641	0.6095	32.030	0.0312	19.5235	0.0512	10.9745
26	1.673	0.5976	33.671	0.0297	20.1210	0.0497	11.3910
27	1.707	0.5859	35.344	0.0283	20.7069	0.0483	11.8043
28	1.741	0.5744	37.051	0.0270	21.2813	0.0470	12.2145
29	1.776	0.5631	38.792	0.0258	21.8444	0.0458	12.6214
30	1.811	0.5521	40.568	0.0247	22.3965	0.0447	13.0251
31	1.848	0.5413	42.379	0.0236	22.9377	0.0436	13.4257
32	1.885	0.5306	44.227	0.0226	23.4683	0.0426	13.8230
33	1.922	0.5202	46.112	0.0217	23.9886	0.0417	14.2172
34	1.961	0.5100	48.034	0.0208	24.4986	0.0408	14.6083
35	2.000	0.5000	49.994	0.0200	24.9986	0.0400	14.9961
40	2.208	0.4529	60.402	0.0166	27.3555	0.0366	16.8885
45	2.438	0.4102	71.893	0.0139	29.4902	0.0339	18.7034
50	2.692	0.3715	84.579	0.0118	31.4236	0.0318	20.4420
55	2.972	0.3365	98.587	0.0102	33.1748	0.0302	22.1057
60	3.281	0.3048	114.052	0.0088	34.7609	0.0288	23.6961
65	3.623	0.2761	131.126	0.0076	36.1975	0.0276	25.2147
70	4.000	0.2500	149.978	0.0067	37.4986	0.0267	26.6632
75	4.416	0.2265	170.792	0.0059	38.6771	0.0259	28.0434
80	4.875	0.2051	193.772	0.0052	39.7445	0.0252	29.3572
85	5.383	0.1858	219.144	0.0046	40.7113	0.0246	30.6064
90	5.943	0.1683	247.157	0.0041	41.5869	0.0241	31.7929
95	6.562	0.1524	278.085	0.0036	42.3800	0.0236	32.9189
100	7.245	0.1380	312.232	0.0032	43.0984	0.0232	33.9863

TABLE 8

3% Interest Factors for Annual Compounding Interest

	Single Payment		Equal-Payment Series				Uniform Gradient-Series Factor
n	Compound-Amount Factor	Present-Worth Factor	Compound-Amount Factor	Sinking-Fund Factor	Present-Worth Factor	Capital-Recovery Factor	
	To Find F Given P F/P i, n	*To Find P Given F P/F i, n*	*To Find F Given A F/A i, n*	*To Find A Given F A/F i, n*	*To Find P Given A P/A i, n*	*To Find A Given P A/P i, n*	*To Find A Given G A/G i, n*
1	1.030	0.9709	1.000	1.0000	0.9709	1.0300	0.0000
2	1.061	0.9426	2.030	0.4926	1.9135	0.5226	0.4926
3	1.093	0.9152	3.091	0.3235	2.8286	0.3535	0.9803
4	1.126	0.8885	4.184	0.2390	3.7171	0.2690	1.4631
5	1.159	0.8626	5.309	0.1884	4.5797	0.2184	1.9409
6	1.194	0.8375	6.468	0.1546	5.4172	0.1846	2.4138
7	1.230	0.8131	7.662	0.1305	6.2303	0.1605	2.8819
8	1.267	0.7894	8.892	0.1125	7.0197	0.1425	3.3450
9	1.305	0.7664	10.159	0.0984	7.7861	0.1284	3.8032
10	1.344	0.7441	11.464	0.0872	8.5302	0.1172	4.2565
11	1.384	0.7224	12.808	0.0781	9.2526	0.1081	4.7049
12	1.426	0.7014	14.192	0.0705	9.9540	0.1005	5.1485
13	1.469	0.6810	15.618	0.0640	10.6350	0.0940	5.5872
14	1.513	0.6611	17.086	0.0585	11.2961	0.0885	6.0211
15	1.558	0.6419	18.599	0.0538	11.9379	0.0838	6.4501
16	1.605	0.6232	20.157	0.0496	12.5611	0.0796	6.8742
17	1.653	0.6050	21.762	0.0460	13.1661	0.0760	7.2936
18	1.702	0.5874	23.414	0.0427	13.7535	0.0727	7.7081
19	1.754	0.5703	25.117	0.0398	14.3238	0.0698	8.1179
20	1.806	0.5537	26.870	0.0372	14.8775	0.0672	8.5229
21	1.860	0.5376	28.676	0.0349	15.4150	0.0649	8.9231
22	1.916	0.5219	30.537	0.0328	15.9369	0.0628	9.3186
23	1.974	0.5067	32.453	0.0308	16.4436	0.0608	9.7094
24	2.033	0.4919	34.426	0.0291	16.9356	0.0591	10.0954
25	2.094	0.4776	36.459	0.0274	17.4132	0.0574	10.4768
26	2.157	0.4637	38.553	0.0259	17.8769	0.0559	10.8535
27	2.221	0.4502	40.710	0.0246	18.3270	0.0546	11.2256
28	2.288	0.4371	42.931	0.0233	18.7641	0.0533	11.5930
29	2.357	0.4244	45.219	0.0221	19.1885	0.0521	11.9558
30	2.427	0.4120	47.575	0.0210	19.6005	0.0510	12.3141
31	2.500	0.4000	50.003	0.0200	20.0004	0.0500	12.6678
32	2.575	0.3883	52.503	0.0191	20.3888	0.0491	13.0169
33	2.652	0.3770	55.078	0.0182	20.7658	0.0482	13.3616
34	2.732	0.3661	57.730	0.0173	21.1318	0.0473	13.7018
35	2.814	0.3554	60.462	0.0165	21.4872	0.0465	14.0375
40	3.262	0.3066	75.401	0.0133	23.1148	0.0433	15.6502
45	3.782	0.2644	92.720	0.0108	24.5187	0.0408	17.1556
50	4.384	0.2281	112.797	0.0089	25.7298	0.0389	18.5575
55	5.082	0.1968	136.072	0.0074	26.7744	0.0374	19.8600
60	5.892	0.1697	163.053	0.0061	27.6756	0.0361	21.0674
65	6.830	0.1464	194.333	0.0052	28.4529	0.0352	22.1841
70	7.918	0.1263	230.594	0.0043	29.1234	0.0343	23.2145
75	9.179	0.1090	272.631	0.0037	29.7018	0.0337	24.1634
80	10.641	0.0940	321.363	0.0031	30.2008	0.0331	25.0354
85	12.336	0.0811	377.857	0.0027	30.6312	0.0327	25.8349
90	14.300	0.0699	443.349	0.0023	31.0024	0.0323	26.5667
95	16.578	0.0603	519.272	0.0019	31.3227	0.0319	27.2351
100	19.219	0.0520	607.288	0.0017	31.5989	0.0317	27.8445

TABLE 9

4% Interest Factors for Annual Compounding Interest

	Single Payment		Equal-Payment Series				
n	Compound-Amount Factor	Present-Worth Factor	Compound-Amount Factor	Sinking-Fund Factor	Present-Worth Factor	Capital-Recovery Factor	Uniform Gradient-Series Factor
	To Find F Given P F/P i, n	*To Find P Given F P/F i, n*	*To Find F Given A F/A i, n*	*To Find A Given F A/F i, n*	*To Find P Given A P/A i, n*	*To Find A Given P A/P i, n*	*To Find A Given G A/G i, n*
1	1.040	0.9615	1.000	1.0000	0.9615	1.0400	0.0000
2	1.082	0.9246	2.040	0.4902	1.8861	0.5302	0.4902
3	1.125	0.8890	3.122	0.3204	2.7751	0.3604	0.9739
4	1.170	0.8548	4.246	0.2355	3.6299	0.2755	1.4510
5	1.217	0.8219	5.416	0.1846	4.4518	0.2246	1.9216
6	1.265	0.7903	6.633	0.1508	5.2421	0.1908	2.3857
7	1.316	0.7599	7.898	0.1266	6.0021	0.1666	2.8433
8	1.369	0.7307	9.214	0.1085	6.7328	0.1485	3.2944
9	1.423	0.7026	10.583	0.0945	7.4353	0.1345	3.7391
10	1.480	0.6756	12.006	0.0833	8.1109	0.1233	4.1773
11	1.539	0.6496	13.486	0.0742	8.7605	0.1142	4.6090
12	1.601	0.6246	15.026	0.0666	9.3851	0.1066	5.0344
13	1.665	0.6006	16.627	0.0602	9.9857	0.1002	5.4533
14	1.732	0.5775	18.292	0.0547	10.5631	0.0947	5.8659
15	1.801	0.5553	20.024	0.0500	11.1184	0.0900	6.2721
16	1.873	0.5339	21.825	0.0458	11.6523	0.0858	6.6720
17	1.948	0.5134	23.698	0.0422	12.1657	0.0822	7.0656
18	2.026	0.4936	25.645	0.0390	12.6593	0.0790	7.4530
19	2.107	0.4747	27.671	0.0361	13.1339	0.0761	7.8342
20	2.191	0.4564	29.778	0.0336	13.5903	0.0736	8.2091
21	2.279	0.4388	31.969	0.0313	14.0292	0.0713	8.5780
22	2.370	0.4220	34.248	0.0292	14.4511	0.0692	8.9407
23	2.465	0.4057	36.618	0.0273	14.8569	0.0673	9.2973
24	2.563	0.3901	39.083	0.0256	15.2470	0.0656	9.6479
25	2.666	0.3751	41.646	0.0240	15.6221	0.0640	9.9925
26	2.772	0.3607	44.312	0.0226	15.9828	0.0626	10.3312
27	2.883	0.3468	47.084	0.0212	16.3296	0.0612	10.6640
28	2.999	0.3335	49.968	0.0200	16.6631	0.0600	10.9909
29	3.119	0.3207	52.966	0.0189	16.9837	0.0589	11.3121
30	3.243	0.3083	56.085	0.0178	17.2920	0.0578	11.6274
31	3.373	0.2965	59.328	0.0169	17.5885	0.0569	11.9371
32	3.508	0.2851	62.701	0.0160	17.8736	0.0560	12.2411
33	3.648	0.2741	66.210	0.0151	18.1477	0.0551	12.5396
34	3.794	0.2636	69.858	0.0143	18.4112	0.0543	12.8325
35	3.946	0.2534	73.652	0.0136	18.6646	0.0536	13.1199
40	4.801	0.2083	95.026	0.0105	19.7928	0.0505	14.4765
45	5.841	0.1712	121.029	0.0083	20.7200	0.0483	15.7047
50	7.107	0.1407	152.667	0.0066	21.4822	0.0466	16.8123
55	8.646	0.1157	191.159	0.0052	22.1086	0.0452	17.8070
60	10.520	0.0951	237.991	0.0042	22.6235	0.0442	18.6972
65	12.799	0.0781	294.968	0.0034	23.0467	0.0434	19.4909
70	15.572	0.0642	364.290	0.0028	23.3945	0.0428	20.1961
75	18.945	0.0528	448.631	0.0022	23.6804	0.0422	20.8206
80	23.050	0.0434	551.245	0.0018	23.9154	0.0418	21.3719
85	28.044	0.0357	676.090	0.0015	24.1085	0.0415	21.8569
90	34.119	0.0293	817.983	0.0012	24.2673	0.0412	22.2826
95	41.511	0.0241	1012.785	0.0010	24.3978	0.0410	22.6550
100	50.505	0.0198	1237.624	0.0008	24.5050	0.0408	22.9800

TABLE 10

5% Interest Factors for Annual Compounding Interest

	Single Payment		Equal-Payment Series				Uniform Gradient-Series Factor
n	Compound-Amount Factor	Present-Worth Factor	Compound-Amount Factor	Sinking-Fund Factor	Present-Worth Factor	Capital-Recovery Factor	
	To Find F Given P F/P i, n	*To Find P Given F P/F i, n*	*To Find F Given A F/A i, n*	*To Find A Given F A/F i, n*	*To Find P Given A P/A i, n*	*To Find A Given P A/P i, n*	*To Find A Given G A/G i, n*
1	1.050	0.9524	1.000	1.0000	0.9524	1.0500	0.0000
2	1.103	0.9070	2.050	0.4878	1.8594	0.5378	0.4878
3	1.158	0.8638	3.153	0.3172	2.7233	0.3672	0.9675
4	1.216	0.8227	4.310	0.2320	3.5460	0.2820	1.4391
5	1.276	0.7835	5.526	0.1810	4.3295	0.2310	1.9025
6	1.340	0.7462	6.802	0.1470	5.0757	0.1970	2.3579
7	1.407	0.7107	8.142	0.1228	5.7864	0.1728	2.8052
8	1.477	0.6768	9.549	0.1047	6.4632	0.1547	3.2445
9	1.551	0.6446	11.027	0.0907	7.1078	0.1407	3.6758
10	1.629	0.6139	12.587	0.0795	7.7217	0.1295	4.0991
11	1.710	0.5847	14.207	0.0704	8.3064	0.1204	4.5145
12	1.796	0.5568	15.917	0.0628	8.8633	0.1128	4.9219
13	1.866	0.5303	17.713	0.0565	9.3936	0.1065	5.3215
14	1.980	0.5051	19.599	0.0510	9.8987	0.1010	5.7133
15	2.079	0.4810	21.579	0.0464	10.3797	0.0964	6.0973
16	2.183	0.4581	23.658	0.0423	10.8378	0.0923	6.4736
17	2.292	0.4363	25.840	0.0387	11.2741	0.0887	6.8423
18	2.407	0.4155	28.132	0.0356	11.6896	0.0856	7.2034
19	2.527	0.3957	30.539	0.0328	12.0853	0.0828	7.5569
20	2.653	0.3769	33.066	0.0303	12.4622	0.0803	7.9030
21	2.786	0.3590	35.719	0.0280	12.8212	0.0780	8.2416
22	2.925	0.3419	38.505	0.0260	13.1630	0.0760	8.5730
23	3.072	0.3256	41.430	0.0241	13.4886	0.0741	8.8971
24	3.225	0.3101	44.502	0.0225	13.7987	0.0725	9.2140
25	3.386	0.2953	47.727	0.0210	14.0940	0.0710	9.5238
26	3.556	0.2813	51.113	0.0196	14.3752	0.0696	9.8266
27	3.733	0.2679	54.669	0.0183	14.6430	0.0683	10.1224
28	3.920	0.2551	58.403	0.0171	14.8981	0.0671	10.4114
29	4.116	0.2430	62.323	0.0161	15.1411	0.0661	10.6936
30	4.322	0.2314	66.439	0.0151	15.3725	0.0651	10.9691
31	4.538	0.2204	70.761	0.0141	15.5928	0.0641	11.2381
32	4.765	0.2099	75.299	0.0133	15.8027	0.0633	11.5005
33	5.003	0.1999	80.064	0.0125	16.0026	0.0625	11.7566
34	5.253	0.1904	85.067	0.0118	16.1929	0.0618	12.0063
35	5.516	0.1813	90.320	0.0111	16.3742	0.0611	12.2498
40	7.040	0.1421	120.800	0.0083	17.1591	0.0583	13.3775
45	8.985	0.1113	159.700	0.0063	17.7741	0.0563	14.3644
50	11.467	0.0872	209.348	0.0048	18.2559	0.0548	15.2233
55	14.636	0.0683	272.713	0.0037	18.6335	0.0537	15.9665
60	18.679	0.0535	353.584	0.0028	18.9293	0.0528	16.6062
65	23.840	0.0420	456.798	0.0022	19.1611	0.0522	17.1541
70	30.426	0.0329	588.529	0.0017	19.3427	0.0517	17.6212
75	38.833	0.0258	756.654	0.0013	19.4850	0.0513	18.0176
80	49.561	0.0202	971.229	0.0010	19.5965	0.0510	18.3526
85	63.254	0.0158	1245.087	0.0008	19.6838	0.0508	18.6346
90	80.730	0.0124	1594.607	0.0006	19.7523	0.0506	18.8712
95	103.035	0.0097	2040.694	0.0005	19.8059	0.0505	19.0689
100	131.501	0.0076	2610.025	0.0004	19.8479	0.0504	19.2337

TABLE 11

6% Interest Factors for Annual Compounding Interest

	Single Payment		Equal-Payment Series				Uniform Gradient-Series Factor
n	Compound-Amount Factor	Present-Worth Factor	Compound-Amount Factor	Sinking-Fund Factor	Present-Worth Factor	Capital-Recovery Factor	
	To Find F Given P F/P i, n	*To Find P Given F P/F i, n*	*To Find F Given A F/A i, n*	*To Find A Given F A/F i, n*	*To Find P Given A P/A i, n*	*To Find A Given P A/P i, n*	*To Find A Given G A/G i, n*
1	1.060	0.9434	1.000	1.0000	0.9434	1.0600	0.0000
2	1.124	0.8900	2.060	0.4854	1.8334	0.5454	0.4854
3	1.191	0.8396	3.184	0.3141	2.6730	0.3741	0.9612
4	1.262	0.7921	4.375	0.2286	3.4651	0.2886	1.4272
5	1.338	0.7473	5.637	0.1774	4.2124	0.2374	1.8836
6	1.419	0.7050	6.975	0.1434	4.9173	0.2034	2.3304
7	1.504	0.6651	8.394	0.1191	5.5824	0.1791	2.7676
8	1.594	0.6274	9.897	0.1010	6.2098	0.1610	3.1952
9	1.689	0.5919	11.491	0.0870	6.8017	0.1470	3.6133
10	1.791	0.5584	13.181	0.0759	7.3601	0.1359	4.0220
11	1.898	0.5268	14.972	0.0668	7.8869	0.1268	4.4213
12	2.012	0.4970	16.870	0.0593	8.3839	0.1193	4.8113
13	2.133	0.4688	18.882	0.0530	8.8527	0.1130	5.1920
14	2.261	0.4423	21.015	0.0476	9.2950	0.1076	5.5635
15	2.397	0.4173	23.276	0.0430	9.7123	0.1030	5.9260
16	2.540	0.3937	25.673	0.0390	10.1059	0.0990	6.2794
17	2.693	0.3714	28.213	0.0355	10.4773	0.0955	6.6240
18	2.854	0.3504	30.906	0.0324	10.8276	0.0924	6.9597
19	3.026	0.3305	33.760	0.0296	11.1581	0.0896	7.2867
20	3.207	0.3118	36.786	0.0272	11.4699	0.0872	7.6052
21	3.400	0.2942	39.993	0.0250	11.7641	0.0850	7.9151
22	3.604	0.2775	43.392	0.0231	12.0416	0.0831	8.2166
23	3.820	0.2618	46.996	0.0213	12.3034	0.0813	8.5099
24	4.049	0.2470	50.816	0.0197	12.5504	0.0797	8.7951
25	4.292	0.2330	54.865	0.0182	12.7834	0.0782	9.0722
26	4.549	0.2198	59.156	0.0169	13.0032	0.0769	9.3415
27	4.822	0.2074	63.706	0.0157	13.2105	0.0757	9.6030
28	5.112	0.1956	68.528	0.0146	13.4062	0.0746	9.8568
29	5.418	0.1846	73.640	0.0136	13.5907	0.0736	10.1032
30	5.744	0.1741	79.058	0.0127	13.7648	0.0727	10.3422
31	6.088	0.1643	84.802	0.0118	13.9291	0.0718	10.5740
32	6.453	0.1550	90.890	0.0110	14.0841	0.0710	10.7988
33	6.841	0.1462	97.343	0.0103	14.2302	0.0703	11.0166
34	7.251	0.1379	104.184	0.0096	14.3682	0.0696	11.2276
35	7.686	0.1301	111.435	0.0090	14.4983	0.0690	11.4319
40	10.286	0.0972	154.762	0.0065	15.0463	0.0665	12.3590
45	13.765	0.0727	212.744	0.0047	15.4558	0.0647	13.1413
50	18.420	0.0543	290.336	0.0035	15.7619	0.0635	13.7964
55	24.650	0.0406	394.172	0.0025	15.9906	0.0625	14.3411
60	32.988	0.0303	533.128	0.0019	16.1614	0.0619	14.7910
65	44.145	0.0227	719.083	0.0014	16.2891	0.0614	15.1601
70	59.076	0.0169	967.932	0.0010	16.3846	0.0610	15.4614
75	79.057	0.0127	1300.949	0.0008	16.4559	0.0608	15.7058
80	105.796	0.0095	1746.600	0.0006	16.5091	0.0606	15.9033
85	141.579	0.0071	2342.982	0.0004	16.5490	0.0604	16.0620
90	189.465	0.0053	3141.075	0.0003	16.5787	0.0603	16.1891
95	253.546	0.0040	4209.104	0.0002	16.6009	0.0602	16.2905
100	339.302	0.0030	5638.368	0.0002	16.6176	0.0602	16.3711

TABLE 12

7% Interest Factors for Annual Compounding Interest

	Single Payment		Equal-Payment Series				Uniform Gradient-Series Factor
n	Compound-Amount Factor	Present-Worth Factor	Compound-Amount Factor	Sinking-Fund Factor	Present-Worth Factor	Capital-Recovery Factor	
	To Find F Given P *F/P i, n*	*To Find P Given F* *P/F i, n*	*To Find F Given A* *F/A i, n*	*To Find A Given F* *A/F i, n*	*To Find P Given A* *P/A i, n*	*To Find A Given P* *A/P i, n*	*To Find A Given G* *A/G i, n*
1	1.070	0.9346	1.000	1.0000	0.9346	1.0700	0.0000
2	1.145	0.8734	2.070	0.4831	1.8080	0.5531	0.4831
3	1.225	0.8163	3.215	0.3111	2.6243	0.3811	0.9549
4	1.311	0.7629	4.440	0.2252	3.3872	0.2952	1.4155
5	1.403	0.7130	5.751	0.1739	4.1002	0.2439	1.8650
6	1.501	0.6664	7.153	0.1398	4.7665	0.2098	2.3032
7	1.606	0.6228	8.654	0.1156	5.3893	0.1856	2.7304
8	1.718	0.5820	10.260	0.0975	5.9713	0.1675	3.1466
9	1.838	0.5439	11.978	0.0835	6.5152	0.1535	3.5517
10	1.967	0.5084	13.816	0.0724	7.0236	0.1424	3.9461
11	2.105	0.4751	15.784	0.0634	7.4987	0.1334	4.3296
12	2.252	0.4440	17.888	0.0559	7.9427	0.1259	4.7025
13	2.410	0.4150	20.141	0.0497	8.3577	0.1197	5.0649
14	2.579	0.3878	22.550	0.0444	8.7455	0.1144	5.4167
15	2.759	0.3625	25.129	0.0398	9.1079	0.1098	5.7583
16	2.952	0.3387	27.888	0.0359	9.4467	0.1059	6.0897
17	3.159	0.3166	30.840	0.0324	9.7632	0.1024	6.4110
18	3.380	0.2959	33.999	0.0294	10.0591	0.0994	6.7225
19	3.617	0.2765	37.379	0.0268	10.3356	0.0968	7.0242
20	3.870	0.2584	40.996	0.0244	10.5940	0.0944	7.3163
21	4.141	0.2415	44.865	0.0223	10.8355	0.0923	7.5990
22	4.430	0.2257	49.006	0.0204	11.0613	0.0904	7.8725
23	4.741	0.2110	53.436	0.0187	11.2722	0.0887	8.1369
24	5.072	0.1972	58.177	0.0172	11.4693	0.0872	8.3923
25	5.427	0.1843	63.249	0.0158	11.6536	0.0858	8.6391
26	5.807	0.1722	68.676	0.0146	11.8258	0.0846	8.8773
27	6.214	0.1609	74.484	0.0134	11.9867	0.0834	9.1072
28	6.649	0.1504	80.698	0.0124	12.1371	0.0824	9.3290
29	7.114	0.1406	87.347	0.0115	12.2777	0.0815	9.5427
30	7.612	0.1314	94.461	0.0106	12.4091	0.0806	9.7487
31	8.145	0.1228	102.073	0.0098	12.5318	0.0798	9.9471
32	8.715	0.1148	110.218	0.0091	12.6466	0.0791	10.1381
33	9.325	0.1072	118.933	0.0084	12.7538	0.0784	10.3219
34	9.978	0.1002	128.259	0.0078	12.8540	0.0778	10.4987
35	10.677	0.0937	138.237	0.0072	12.9477	0.0772	10.6687
40	14.974	0.0668	199.635	0.0050	13.3317	0.0750	11.4234
45	21.002	0.0476	285.749	0.0035	13.6055	0.0735	12.0360
50	29.457	0.0340	406.529	0.0025	13.8008	0.0725	12.5287
55	41.315	0.0242	575.929	0.0017	13.9399	0.0717	12.9215
60	57.946	0.0173	813.520	0.0012	14.0392	0.0712	13.2321
65	81.273	0.0123	1146.755	0.0009	14.1099	0.0709	13.4760
70	113.989	0.0088	1614.134	0.0006	14.1604	0.0706	13.6662
75	159.876	0.0063	2269.657	0.0005	14.1964	0.0705	13.8137
80	224.234	0.0045	3189.063	0.0003	14.2220	0.0703	13.9274
85	314.500	0.0032	4478.576	0.0002	14.2403	0.0702	14.0146
90	441.103	0.0023	6287.185	0.0002	14.2533	0.0702	14.0812
95	618.670	0.0016	8823.854	0.0001	14.2626	0.0701	14.1319
100	867.716	0.0012	12381.662	0.0001	14.2693	0.0701	14.1703

TABLE 13

8% Interest Factors for Annual Compounding Interest

	Single Payment		Equal-Payment Series				
n	Compound-Amount Factor	Present-Worth Factor	Compound-Amount Factor	Sinking-Fund Factor	Present-Worth Factor	Capital-Recovery Factor	Uniform Gradient-Series Factor
	To Find F Given P F/P i, n	*To Find P Given F P/F i, n*	*To Find F Given A F/A i, n*	*To Find A Given F A/F i, n*	*To Find P Given A P/A i, n*	*To Find A Given P A/P i, n*	*To Find A Given G A/G i, n*
1	1.080	0.9259	1.000	1.0000	0.9259	1.0800	0.0000
2	1.166	0.8573	2.080	0.4808	1.7833	0.5608	0.4808
3	1.260	0.7938	3.246	0.3080	2.5771	0.3880	0.9488
4	1.360	0.7350	4.506	0.2219	3.3121	0.3019	1.4040
5	1.469	0.6806	5.867	0.1705	3.9927	0.2505	1.8465
6	1.587	0.6302	7.336	0.1363	4.6229	0.2163	2.2764
7	1.714	0.5835	8.923	0.1121	5.2064	0.1921	2.6937
8	1.851	0.5403	10.637	0.0940	5.7466	0.1740	2.0985
9	1.999	0.5003	12.488	0.0801	6.2469	0.1601	3.4910
10	2.159	0.4632	14.487	0.0690	6.7101	0.1490	3.8713
11	2.332	0.4289	16.645	0.0601	7.1390	0.1401	4.2395
12	2.518	0.3971	18.977	0.0527	7.5361	0.1327	4.5958
13	2.720	0.3677	21.495	0.0465	7.9038	0.1265	4.9402
14	2.937	0.3405	24.215	0.0413	8.2442	0.1213	5.2731
15	3.172	0.3153	27.152	0.0368	8.5595	0.1168	5.5945
16	3.426	0.2919	30.324	0.0330	8.8514	0.1130	5.9046
17	3.700	0.2703	33.750	0.0296	9.1216	0.1096	6.2038
18	3.996	0.2503	37.450	0.0267	9.3719	0.1067	6.4920
19	4.316	0.2317	41.446	0.0241	9.6036	0.1041	6.7697
20	4.661	0.2146	45.762	0.0219	9.8182	0.1019	7.0370
21	5.034	0.1987	50.423	0.0198	10.0168	0.0998	7.2940
22	5.437	0.1840	55.457	0.0180	10.2008	0.0980	7.5412
23	5.871	0.1703	60.893	0.0164	10.3711	0.0964	7.7786
24	6.341	0.1577	66.765	0.0150	10.5288	0.0950	8.0066
25	6.848	0.1460	73.106	0.0137	10.6748	0.0937	8.2254
26	7.396	0.1352	79.954	0.0125	10.8100	0.0925	8.4352
27	7.988	0.1252	87.351	0.0115	10.9352	0.0915	8.6363
28	8.627	0.1159	95.339	0.0105	11.0511	0.0905	8.8289
29	9.317	0.1073	103.966	0.0096	11.1584	0.0896	9.0133
30	10.063	0.0994	113.283	0.0088	11.2578	0.0888	9.1897
31	10.868	0.0920	123.346	0.0081	11.3498	0.0881	9.3584
32	11.737	0.0852	134.214	0.0075	11.4350	0.0875	9.5197
33	12.676	0.0789	145.951	0.0069	11.5139	0.0869	9.6737
34	13.690	0.0731	158.627	0.0063	11.5869	0.0863	9.8208
35	14.785	0.0676	172.317	0.0058	11.6546	0.0858	9.9611
40	21.725	0.0460	259.057	0.0039	11.9246	0.0839	10.5699
45	31.920	0.0313	386.506	0.0026	12.1084	0.0826	11.0447
50	46.902	0.0213	573.770	0.0018	12.2335	0.0818	11.4107
55	68.914	0.0145	848.923	0.0012	12.3186	0.0812	11.6902
60	101.257	0.0099	1253.213	0.0008	12.3766	0.0808	11.9015
65	148.780	0.0067	1847.248	0.0006	12.4160	0.0806	12.0602
70	218.606	0.0046	2720.080	0.0004	12.4428	0.0804	12.1783
75	321.205	0.0031	4002.557	0.0003	12.4611	0.0803	12.2658
80	471.955	0.0021	5886.935	0.0002	12.4735	0.0802	12.3301
85	693.456	0.0015	8655.706	0.0001	12.4820	0.0801	12.3773
90	1018.915	0.0010	12723.939	0.0001	12.4877	0.0801	12.4116
95	1497.121	0.0007	18701.507	0.0001	12.4917	0.0801	12.4365
100	2199.761	0.0005	27484.516	0.0001	12.4943	0.0800	12.4545

TABLE 14

9% Interest Factors for Annual Compounding Interest

	Single Payment		Equal-Payment Series				
n	Compound-Amount Factor	Present-Worth Factor	Compound-Amount Factor	Sinking-Fund Factor	Present-Worth Factor	Capital-Recovery Factor	Uniform Gradient-Series Factor
	To Find F Given P F/P i, n	*To Find P Given F P/F i, n*	*To Find F Given A F/A i, n*	*To Find A Given F A/F i, n*	*To Find P Given A P/A i, n*	*To Find A Given P A/P i, n*	*To Find A Given G A/G i, n*
1	1.090	0.9174	1.000	1.0000	0.9174	1.0900	0.0000
2	1.188	0.8417	2.090	0.4785	1.7591	0.5685	0.4785
3	1.295	0.7722	3.278	0.3051	2.5313	0.3951	0.9426
4	1.412	0.7084	4.573	0.2187	3.2397	0.3087	1.3925
5	1.539	0.6499	5.985	0.1671	3.8897	0.2571	1.8282
6	1.677	0.5963	7.523	0.1329	4.4859	0.2229	2.2498
7	1.828	0.5470	9.200	0.1087	5.0330	0.1987	2.6574
8	1.993	0.5019	11.028	0.0907	5.5348	0.1807	3.0512
9	2.172	0.4604	13.021	0.0768	5.9953	0.1668	3.4312
10	2.367	0.4224	15.193	0.0658	6.4177	0.1558	3.7978
11	2.580	0.3875	17.560	0.0570	6.8052	0.1470	4.1510
12	2.813	0.3555	20.141	0.0497	7.1607	0.1397	4.4910
13	3.066	0.3262	22.953	0.0436	7.4869	0.1336	4.8182
14	3.342	0.2993	26.019	0.0384	7.7862	0.1284	5.1326
15	3.642	0.2745	29.361	0.0341	8.0607	0.1241	5.4346
16	3.970	0.2519	33.003	0.0303	8.3126	0.1203	5.7245
17	4.328	0.2311	36.974	0.0271	8.5436	0.1171	6.0024
18	4.717	0.2120	41.301	0.0242	8.7556	0.1142	6.2687
19	5.142	0.1945	46.018	0.0217	8.9501	0.1117	6.5236
20	5.604	0.1784	51.160	0.0196	9.1286	0.1096	6.7675
21	6.109	0.1637	56.765	0.0176	9.2923	0.1076	7.0006
22	6.659	0.1502	62.873	0.0159	9.4424	0.1059	7.2232
23	7.258	0.1378	69.532	0.0144	9.5802	0.1044	7.4358
24	7.911	0.1264	76.790	0.0130	9.7066	0.1030	7.6384
25	8.623	0.1160	84.701	0.0118	9.8226	0.1018	7.8316
26	9.399	0.1064	93.324	0.0107	9.9290	0.1007	8.0156
27	10.245	0.0976	102.723	0.0097	10.0266	0.0997	8.1906
28	11.167	0.0896	112.968	0.0089	10.1161	0.0989	8.3572
29	12.172	0.0822	124.135	0.0081	10.1983	0.0981	8.5154
30	13.268	0.0754	136.308	0.0073	10.2737	0.0973	8.6657
31	14.462	0.0692	149.575	0.0067	10.3428	0.0967	8.8083
32	15.763	0.0634	164.037	0.0061	10.4063	0.0961	8.9436
33	17.182	0.0582	179.800	0.0056	10.4645	0.0956	9.0718
34	18.728	0.0534	196.982	0.0051	10.5178	0.0951	9.1933
35	20.414	0.0490	215.711	0.0046	10.5668	0.0946	9.3083
40	31.409	0.0318	337.882	0.0030	10.7574	0.0930	9.7957
45	48.327	0.0207	525.859	0.0019	10.8812	0.0919	10.1603
50	74.358	0.0135	815.084	0.0012	10.9617	0.0912	10.4295
55	114.408	0.0088	1260.092	0.0008	11.0140	0.0908	10.6261
60	176.031	0.0057	1944.792	0.0005	11.0480	0.0905	10.7683
65	270.846	0.0037	2998.288	0.0003	11.0701	0.0903	10.8702
70	416.730	0.0024	4619.223	0.0002	11.0845	0.0902	10.9427
75	641.191	0.0016	7113.232	0.0002	11.0938	0.0902	10.9940
80	986.552	0.0010	10950.574	0.0001	11.0999	0.0901	11.0299
85	1517.932	0.0007	16854.800	0.0001	11.1038	0.0901	11.0551
90	2335.527	0.0004	25939.184	0.0001	11.1064	0.0900	11.0726
95	3593.497	0.0003	39916.635	0.0000	11.1080	0.0900	11.0847
100	5529.041	0.0002	61422.675	0.0000	11.1091	0.0900	11.0930

TABLE 15

10% Interest Factors for Annual Compounding Interest

n	Single Payment		Equal-Payment Series				Uniform Gradient-Series Factor
	Compound-Amount Factor	Present-Worth Factor	Compound-Amount Factor	Sinking-Fund Factor	Present-Worth Factor	Capital-Recovery Factor	
	To Find F Given P F/P i, n	*To Find P Given F P/F i, n*	*To Find F Given A F/A i, n*	*To Find A Given F A/F i, n*	*To Find P Given A P/A i, n*	*To Find A Given P A/P i, n*	*To Find A Given G A/G i, n*
1	1.100	0.9091	1.000	1.0000	0.9091	1.1000	0.0000
2	1.210	0.8265	2.100	0.4762	1.7355	0.5762	0.4762
3	1.331	0.7513	3.310	0.3021	2.4869	0.4021	0.9366
4	1.464	0.6830	4.641	0.2155	3.1699	0.3155	1.3812
5	1.611	0.6209	6.105	0.1638	3.7908	0.2638	1.8101
6	1.772	0.5645	7.716	0.1296	4.3553	0.2296	2.2236
7	1.949	0.5132	9.487	0.1054	4.8684	0.2054	2.6216
8	2.144	0.4665	11.436	0.0875	5.3349	0.1875	3.0045
9	2.358	0.4241	13.579	0.0737	5.7950	0.1737	3.3724
10	2.594	0.3856	15.937	0.0628	6.1446	0.1628	3.7255
11	2.853	0.3505	18.531	0.0540	6.4951	0.1540	4.0641
12	3.138	0.3186	21.384	0.0468	6.8137	0.1468	4.3884
13	3.452	0.2897	24.523	0.0408	7.1034	0.1408	4.6988
14	3.798	0.2633	27.975	0.0358	7.3667	0.1358	4.9955
15	4.177	0.2394	31.772	0.0315	7.6061	0.1315	5.2789
16	4.595	0.2176	35.950	0.0278	7.8237	0.1278	5.5493
17	5.054	0.1979	40.545	0.0247	8.0216	0.1247	5.8071
18	5.560	0.1799	45.599	0.0219	8.2014	0.1219	6.0526
19	6.116	0.1635	51.159	0.0196	8.3649	0.1196	6.2861
20	6.728	0.1487	57.275	0.0175	8.5136	0.1175	6.5081
21	7.400	0.1351	64.003	0.0156	8.6487	0.1156	6.7189
22	8.140	0.1229	71.403	0.0140	8.7716	0.1140	6.9189
23	8.953	0.1117	79.543	0.0126	8.8832	0.1126	7.1085
24	9.850	0.1015	88.497	0.0113	8.9848	0.1113	7.2881
25	10.835	0.0923	98.347	0.0102	9.0771	0.1102	7.4580
26	11.918	0.0839	109.182	0.0092	9.1610	0.1092	7.6187
27	13.110	0.0763	121.100	0.0083	9.2372	0.1083	7.7704
28	14.421	0.0694	134.210	0.0075	9.3066	0.1075	7.9137
29	15.863	0.0630	148.631	0.0067	9.3696	0.1067	8.0489
30	17.449	0.0573	164.494	0.0061	9.4269	0.1061	8.1762
31	19.194	0.0521	181.943	0.0055	9.4790	0.1055	8.2962
32	21.114	0.0474	201.138	0.0050	9.5264	0.1050	8.4091
33	23.225	0.0431	222.252	0.0045	9.5694	0.1045	8.5152
34	25.548	0.0392	245.477	0.0041	9.6086	0.1041	8.6149
35	28.102	0.0356	271.024	0.0037	9.6442	0.1037	8.7086
40	45.259	0.0221	442.593	0.0023	9.7791	0.1023	9.0962
45	72.890	0.0137	718.905	0.0014	9.8628	0.1014	9.3741
50	117.391	0.0085	1163.909	0.0009	9.9148	0.1009	9.5704
55	189.059	0.0053	1880.591	0.0005	9.9471	0.1005	9.7075
60	304.482	0.0033	3034.816	0.0003	9.9672	0.1003	9.8023
65	490.371	0.0020	4893.707	0.0002	9.9796	0.1002	9.8672
70	789.747	0.0013	7887.470	0.0001	9.9873	0.1001	9.9113
75	1271.895	0.0008	12708.954	0.0001	9.9921	0.1001	9.9410
80	2048.400	0.0005	20474.002	0.0001	9.9951	0.1001	9.9609
85	3298.969	0.0003	32979.690	0.0000	9.9970	0.1000	9.9742
90	5313.023	0.0002	53120.226	0.0000	9.9981	0.1000	9.9831
95	8556.676	0.0001	85556.760	0.0000	9.9988	0.1000	9.9889
100	13780.612	0.0001	137796.123	0.0000	9.9993	0.1000	9.9928

TABLE 16

12% Interest Factors for Annual Compounding Interest

	Single Payment		Equal-Payment Series				Uniform Gradient-Series Factor
n	Compound-Amount Factor	Present-Worth Factor	Compound-Amount Factor	Sinking-Fund Factor	Present-Worth Factor	Capital-Recovery Factor	
	To Find F Given P F/P i, n	*To Find P Given F P/F i, n*	*To Find F Given A F/A i, n*	*To Find A Given F A/F i, n*	*To Find P Given A P/A i, n*	*To Find A Given P A/P i, n*	*To Find A Given G A/G i, n*
1	1.120	0.8929	1.000	1.0000	0.8929	1.1200	0.0000
2	1.254	0.7972	2.120	0.4717	1.6901	0.5917	0.4717
3	1.405	0.7118	3.374	0.2964	2.4018	0.4164	0.9246
4	1.574	0.6355	4.779	0.2092	3.0374	0.3292	1.3589
5	1.762	0.5674	6.353	0.1574	3.6048	0.2774	1.7746
6	1.974	0.5066	8.115	0.1232	4.1114	0.2432	2.1721
7	2.211	0.4524	10.089	0.0991	4.5638	0.2191	2.5515
8	2.476	0.4039	12.300	0.0813	4.9676	0.2013	2.9132
9	2.773	0.3606	14.776	0.0677	5.3283	0.1877	3.2574
10	3.106	0.3220	17.549	0.0570	5.6502	0.1770	3.5847
11	3.479	0.2875	20.655	0.0484	5.9377	0.1684	3.8953
12	3.896	0.2567	24.133	0.0414	6.1944	0.1614	4.1897
13	4.364	0.2292	28.029	0.0357	6.4236	0.1557	4.4683
14	4.887	0.2046	32.393	0.0309	6.6282	0.1509	4.7317
15	5.474	0.1827	37.280	0.0268	6.8109	0.1468	4.9803
16	6.130	0.1631	42.753	0.0234	6.9740	0.1434	5.2147
17	6.866	0.1457	48.884	0.0205	7.1196	0.1405	5.4353
18	7.690	0.1300	55.750	0.0179	7.2497	0.1379	5.6427
19	8.613	0.1161	63.440	0.0158	7.3658	0.1358	5.8375
20	9.646	0.1037	72.052	0.0139	7.4695	0.1339	6.0202
21	10.804	0.0926	81.699	0.0123	7.5620	0.1323	6.1913
22	12.100	0.0827	92.503	0.0108	7.6447	0.1308	6.3514
23	13.552	0.0738	104.603	0.0096	7.7184	0.1296	6.5010
24	15.179	0.0659	118.155	0.0085	7.7843	0.1285	6.6407
25	17.000	0.0588	133.334	0.0075	7.8431	0.1275	6.7708
26	19.040	0.0525	150.334	0.0067	7.8957	0.1267	6.8921
27	21.325	0.0469	169.374	0.0059	7.9426	0.1259	7.0049
28	23.884	0.0419	190.699	0.0053	7.9844	0.1253	7.1098
29	26.750	0.0374	214.583	0.0047	8.0218	0.1247	7.2071
30	29.960	0.0334	241.333	0.0042	8.0552	0.1242	7.2974
31	33.555	0.0298	271.293	0.0037	8.0850	0.1237	7.3811
32	37.582	0.0266	304.848	0.0033	8.1116	0.1233	7.4586
33	42.092	0.0238	342.429	0.0029	8.1354	0.1229	7.5303
34	47.143	0.0212	384.521	0.0026	8.1566	0.1226	7.5965
35	52.800	0.0189	431.664	0.0023	8.1755	0.1223	7.6577
40	93.051	0.0108	767.091	0.0013	8.2438	0.1213	7.8988
45	163.988	0.0061	1358.230	0.0007	8.2825	0.1207	8.0572
50	289.002	0.0035	2400.018	0.0004	8.3045	0.1204	8.1597

TABLE 17

15% Interest Factors for Annual Compounding Interest

	Single Payment		Equal-Payment Series				Uniform Gradient-Series Factor
n	Compound-Amount Factor	Present-Worth Factor	Compound-Amount Factor	Sinking-Fund Factor	Present-Worth Factor	Capital-Recovery Factor	
	To Find F Given P *F/P i, n*	*To Find F Given F* *P/F i, n*	*To Find F Given A* *F/A i, n*	*To Find A Given F* *A/F i, n*	*To Find P Given A* *P/A i, n*	*To Find A Given P* *A/P i, n*	*To Find A Given G* *A/G i, n*
1	1.150	0.8696	1.000	1.0000	0.8696	1.1500	0.0000
2	1.323	0.7562	2.150	0.4651	1.6257	0.6151	0.4651
3	1.521	0.6575	3.473	0.2880	2.2832	0.4380	0.9071
4	1.749	0.5718	4.993	0.2003	2.8850	0.3503	1.3263
5	2.011	0.4972	6.742	0.1483	3.3522	0.2983	1.7228
6	2.313	0.4323	8.754	0.1142	3.7845	0.2642	2.0972
7	2.660	0.3759	11.067	0.0904	4.1604	0.2404	2.4499
8	3.059	0.3269	13.727	0.0729	4.4873	0.2229	2.7813
9	3.518	0.2843	16.786	0.0596	4.7716	0.2096	3.0922
10	4.046	0.2472	20.304	0.0493	5.0188	0.1993	3.3832
11	4.652	0.2150	24.349	0.0411	5.2337	0.1911	3.6550
12	5.350	0.1869	29.002	0.0345	5.4206	0.1845	3.9082
13	6.153	0.1625	34.352	0.0291	5.5832	0.1791	4.1438
14	7.076	0.1413	40.505	0.0247	5.7245	0.1747	4.3624
15	8.137	0.1229	47.580	0.0210	5.8474	0.1710	4.5650
16	9.358	0.1069	55.717	0.0180	5.9542	0.1680	4.7523
17	10.761	0.0929	65.075	0.0154	6.0472	0.1654	4.9251
18	12.375	0.0808	75.836	0.0132	6.1280	0.1632	5.0843
19	14.232	0.0703	88.212	0.0113	6.1982	0.1613	5.2307
20	16.367	0.0611	102.444	0.0098	6.2593	0.1598	5.3651
21	18.822	0.0531	118.810	0.0084	6.3125	0.1584	5.4883
22	21.645	0.0462	137.632	0.0073	6.3587	0.1573	5.6010
23	24.891	0.0402	159.276	0.0063	6.3988	0.1563	5.7040
24	28.625	0.0349	184.168	0.0054	6.4338	0.1554	5.7979
25	32.919	0.0304	212.793	0.0047	6.4642	0.1547	5.8834
26	37.857	0.0264	245.712	0.0041	6.4906	0.1541	5.9612
27	43.535	0.0230	283.569	0.0035	6.5135	0.1535	6.0319
28	50.066	0.0200	327.104	0.0031	6.5335	0.1531	6.0960
29	57.575	0.0174	377.170	0.0027	6.5509	0.1527	6.1541
30	66.212	0.0151	434.745	0.0023	6.5660	0.1523	6.2066
31	76.144	0.0131	500.957	0.0020	6.5791	0.1520	6.2541
32	87.565	0.0114	577.100	0.0017	6.5905	0.1517	6.2970
33	100.700	0.0099	664.666	0.0015	6.6005	0.1515	6.3357
34	115.805	0.0086	765.365	0.0013	6.6091	0.1513	6.3705
35	133.176	0.0075	881.170	0.0011	6.6166	0.1511	6.4019
40	267.864	0.0037	1779.090	0.0006	6.6418	0.1506	6.5168
45	538.769	0.0019	3585.128	0.0003	6.6543	0.1503	6.5830
50	1083.657	0.0009	7217.716	0.0002	6.6605	0.1501	6.6205

TABLE 18

20% Interest Factors for Annual Compounding Interest

	Single Payment		Equal-Payment Series				Uniform Gradient-Series Factor
n	Compound-Amount Factor	Present-Worth Factor	Compound-Amount Factor	Sinking-Fund Factor	Present-Worth Factor	Capital-Recovery Factor	Uniform Gradient-Series Factor
	To Find F Given P *F/P i, n*	*To Find P Given F* *P/F i, n*	*To Find F Given A* *F/A i, n*	*To Find A Given F* *A/F i, n*	*To Find P Given A* *P/A i, n*	*To Find A Given P* *A/P i, n*	*To Find A Given G* *A/G i, n*
1	1.200	0.8333	1.000	1.0000	0.8333	1.2000	0.0000
2	1.440	0.6945	2.200	0.4546	1.5278	0.6546	0.4546
3	1.728	0.5787	3.640	0.2747	2.1065	0.4747	0.8791
4	2.074	0.4823	5.368	0.1863	2.5887	0.3863	1.2742
5	2.488	0.4019	7.442	0.1344	2.9906	0.3344	1.6405
6	2.986	0.3349	9.930	0.1007	3.3255	0.3007	1.9788
7	3.583	0.2791	12.916	0.0774	3.6046	0.2774	2.2902
8	4.300	0.2326	16.499	0.0606	3.8372	0.2606	2.5756
9	5.160	0.1938	20.799	0.0481	4.0310	0.2481	2.8364
10	6.192	0.1615	25.959	0.0385	4.1925	0.2385	3.0739
11	7.430	0.1346	32.150	0.0311	4.3271	0.2311	3.2893
12	8.916	0.1122	39.581	0.0253	4.4392	0.2253	3.4841
13	10.699	0.0935	48.497	0.0206	4.5327	0.2206	3.6597
14	12.839	0.0779	59.196	0.0169	4.6106	0.2169	3.8175
15	15.407	0.0649	72.035	0.0139	4.6755	0.2139	3.9589
16	18.488	0.0541	87.442	0.0114	4.7296	0.2114	4.0851
17	22.186	0.0451	105.931	0.0095	4.7746	0.2095	4.1976
18	26.623	0.0376	128.117	0.0078	4.8122	0.2078	4.2975
19	31.948	0.0313	154.740	0.0065	4.8435	0.2065	4.3861
20	38.338	0.0261	186.688	0.0054	4.8696	0.2054	4.4644
21	46.005	0.0217	225.026	0.0045	4.8913	0.2045	4.5334
22	55.206	0.0181	271.031	0.0037	4.9094	0.2037	4.5942
23	66.247	0.0151	326.237	0.0031	4.9245	0.2031	4.6475
24	79.497	0.0126	392.484	0.0026	4.9371	0.2026	4.6943
25	95.396	0.0105	471.981	0.0021	4.9476	0.2021	4.7352
26	114.475	0.0087	567.377	0.0018	4.9563	0.2018	4.7709
27	137.371	0.0073	681.853	0.0015	4.9636	0.2015	4.8020
28	164.845	0.0061	819.223	0.0012	4.9697	0.2012	4.8291
29	197.814	0.0051	984.068	0.0010	4.9747	0.2010	4.8527
30	237.376	0.0042	1181.882	0.0009	4.9789	0.2009	4.8731
31	284.852	0.0035	1419.258	0.0007	4.9825	0.2007	4.8908
32	341.822	0.0029	1704.109	0.0006	4.9854	0.2006	4.9061
33	410.186	0.0024	2045.931	0.0005	4.9878	0.2005	4.9194
34	492.224	0.0020	2456.118	0.0004	4.9899	0.2004	4.9308
35	590.668	0.0017	2948.341	0.0003	4.9915	0.2003	4.9407
40	1469.772	0.0007	7343.858	0.0002	4.9966	0.2001	4.9728
45	3657.262	0.0003	18281.310	0.0001	4.9986	0.2001	4.9877
50	9100.438	0.0001	45497.191	0.0000	4.9995	0.2000	4.9945

TABLE 19

25% Interest Factors for Annual Compounding Interest

	Single Payment		Equal-Payment Series				Uniform Gradient-Series Factor
n	Compound-Amount Factor	Present-Worth Factor	Compound-Amount Factor	Sinking-Fund Factor	Present-Worth Factor	Capital-Recovery Factor	
	To Find F Given P F/P i, n	*To Find P Given F P/F i, n*	*To Find F Given A F/A i, n*	*To Find A Given F A/F i, n*	*To Find P Given A P/A i, n*	*To Find A Given P A/P i, n*	*To Find A Given G A/G i, n*
1	1.250	0.8000	1.000	1.0000	0.8000	1.2500	0.0000
2	1.563	0.6400	2.250	0.4445	1.4400	0.6945	0.4445
3	1.953	0.5120	3.813	0.2623	1.9520	0.5123	0.8525
4	2.441	0.4096	5.766	0.1735	2.3616	0.4235	1.2249
5	3.052	0.3277	8.207	0.1219	2.6893	0.3719	1.5631
6	3.815	0.2622	11.259	0.0888	2.9514	0.3388	1.8683
7	4.768	0.2097	15.073	0.0664	3.1661	0.3164	2.1424
8	5.960	0.1678	19.842	0.0504	3.3289	0.3004	2.3873
9	7.451	0.1342	25.802	0.0388	3.4631	0.2888	2.6048
10	9.313	0.1074	33.253	0.0301	3.5705	0.2801	2.7971
11	11.642	0.0859	42.566	0.0235	3.6564	0.2735	2.9663
12	14.552	0.0687	54.208	0.0185	3.7251	0.2685	3.1145
13	18.190	0.0550	68.760	0.0146	3.7801	0.2646	3.2438
14	22.737	0.0440	86.949	0.0115	3.8241	0.2615	3.3560
15	28.422	0.0352	109.687	0.0091	3.8593	0.2591	3.4530
16	35.527	0.0282	138.109	0.0073	3.8874	0.2573	3.5366
17	44.409	0.0225	173.636	0.0058	3.9099	0.2558	3.6084
18	55.511	0.0180	218.045	0.0046	3.9280	0.2546	3.6698
19	69.389	0.0144	273.556	0.0037	3.9424	0.2537	3.7222
20	86.736	0.0115	342.945	0.0029	3.9539	0.2529	3.7667
21	108.420	0.0092	429.681	0.0023	3.9631	0.2523	3.8045
22	135.525	0.0074	538.101	0.0019	3.9705	0.2519	3.8365
23	169.407	0.0059	673.626	0.0015	3.9764	0.2515	3.8634
24	211.758	0.0047	843.033	0.0012	3.9811	0.2512	3.8861
25	264.698	0.0038	1054.791	0.0010	3.9849	0.2510	3.9052
26	330.872	0.0030	1319.489	0.0008	3.9879	0.2508	3.9212
27	413.590	0.0024	1650.361	0.0006	3.9903	0.2506	3.9346
28	516.988	0.0019	2063.952	0.0005	3.9923	0.2505	3.9457
29	646.235	0.0016	2580.939	0.0004	3.9938	0.2504	3.9551
30	807.794	0.0012	3227.174	0.0003	3.9951	0.2503	3.9628
31	1009.742	0.0010	4034.968	0.0003	3.9960	0.2503	3.9693
32	1262.177	0.0008	5044.710	0.0002	3.9968	0.2502	3.9746
33	1577.722	0.0006	6306.887	0.0002	3.9975	0.2502	3.9791
34	1972.152	0.0005	7884.609	0.0001	3.9980	0.2501	3.9828
35	2465.190	0.0004	9856.761	0.0001	3.9984	0.2501	3.9858

TABLE 20

30% Interest Factors for Annual Compounding Interest

	Single Payment		Equal-Payment Series				Uniform Gradient-Series Factor
n	Compound-Amount Factor	Present-Worth Factor	Compound-Amount Factor	Sinking-Fund Factor	Present-Worth Factor	Capital-Recovery Factor	Uniform Gradient-Series Factor
	To Find F Given P F/P i, n	*To Find P Given F* P/F i, n	*To Find F Given A* F/A i, n	*To Find A Given F* A/F i, n	*To Find P Given A* P/A i, n	*To Find A Given P* A/P i, n	*To Find A Given G* A/G i, n
1	1.300	0.7692	1.000	1.0000	0.7692	1.3000	0.0000
2	1.690	0.5917	2.300	0.4348	1.3610	0.7348	0.4348
3	2.197	0.4552	3.990	0.2506	1.8161	0.5506	0.8271
4	2.856	0.3501	6.187	0.1616	2.1663	0.4616	1.1783
5	3.713	0.2693	9.043	0.1106	2.4356	0.4106	1.4903
6	4.827	0.2072	12.756	0.0784	2.6428	0.3784	1.7655
7	6.275	0.1594	17.583	0.0569	2.8021	0.3569	2.0063
8	8.157	0.1226	23.858	0.0419	2.9247	0.3419	2.2156
9	10.605	0.0943	32.015	0.0312	3.0190	0.3312	2.3963
10	13.786	0.0725	42.620	0.0235	3.0915	0.3235	2.5512
11	17.922	0.0558	56.405	0.0177	3.1473	0.3177	2.6833
12	23.298	0.0429	74.327	0.0135	3.1903	0.3135	2.7952
13	30.288	0.0330	97.625	0.0103	3.2233	0.3103	2.8895
14	39.374	0.0254	127.913	0.0078	3.2487	0.3078	2.9685
15	51.186	0.0195	167.286	0.0060	3.2682	0.3060	3.0345
16	66.542	0.0150	218.472	0.0046	3.2832	0.3046	3.0892
17	86.504	0.0116	285.014	0.0035	3.2948	0.3035	3.1345
18	112.455	0.0089	371.518	0.0027	3.3037	0.3027	3.1718
19	146.192	0.0069	483.973	0.0021	3.3105	0.3021	3.2025
20	190.050	0.0053	630.165	0.0016	3.3158	0.3016	3.2276
21	247.065	0.0041	820.215	0.0012	3.3199	0.3012	3.2480
22	321.184	0.0031	1067.280	0.0009	3.3230	0.3009	3.2646
23	417.539	0.0024	1388.464	0.0007	3.3254	0.3007	3.2781
24	542.801	0.0019	1806.003	0.0006	3.3272	0.3006	3.2890
25	705.641	0.0014	2348.803	0.0004	3.3286	0.3004	3.2979
26	917.333	0.0011	3054.444	0.0003	3.3297	0.3003	3.3050
27	1192.533	0.0008	3971.778	0.0003	3.3305	0.3003	3.3107
28	1550.293	0.0007	5164.311	0.0002	3.3312	0.3002	3.3153
29	2015.381	0.0005	6714.604	0.0002	3.3317	0.3002	3.3189
30	2619.996	0.0004	8729.985	0.0001	3.3321	0.3001	3.3219
31	3405.994	0.0003	11349.981	0.0001	3.3324	0.3001	3.3242
32	4427.793	0.0002	14755.975	0.0001	3.3326	0.3001	3.3261
33	5756.130	0.0002	19183.768	0.0001	3.3328	0.3001	3.3276
34	7482.970	0.0001	24939.899	0.0001	3.3329	0.3001	3.3288
35	9727.860	0.0001	32422.868	0.0000	3.3330	0.3000	3.3297

TABLE 21

40% Interest Factors for Annual Compounding Interest

	Single Payment		Equal-Payment Series				
n	Compound-Amount Factor	Present-Worth Factor	Compound-Amount Factor	Sinking-Fund Factor	Present-Worth Factor	Capital-Recovery Factor	Uniform Gradient-Series Factor
	To Find F Given P F/P i, n	*To Find P Given F P/F i, n*	*To Find F Given A F/A i, n*	*To Find A Given F A/F i, n*	*To Find P Given A P/A i, n*	*To Find A Given P A/P i, n*	*To Find A Given G A/G i, n*
1	1.400	0.7143	1.000	1.0000	0.7143	1.4000	0.0000
2	1.960	0.5102	2.400	0.4167	1.2245	0.8167	0.4167
3	2.744	0.3644	4.360	0.2294	1.5889	0.6294	0.7798
4	3.842	0.2603	7.104	0.1408	1.8492	0.5408	1.0924
5	5.378	0.1859	10.946	0.0914	2.0352	0.4914	1.3580
6	7.530	0.1328	16.324	0.0613	2.1680	0.4613	1.5811
7	10.541	0.0949	23.853	0.0419	2.2628	0.4419	1.7664
8	14.758	0.0678	34.395	0.0291	2.3306	0.4291	1.9185
9	20.661	0.0484	49.153	0.0204	2.3790	0.4204	2.0423
10	28.925	0.0346	69.814	0.0143	2.4136	0.4143	2.1419
11	40.496	0.0247	98.739	0.0101	2.4383	0.4101	2.2215
12	56.694	0.0176	139.235	0.0072	2.4559	0.4072	2.2845
13	79.371	0.0126	195.929	0.0051	2.4685	0.4051	2.3341
14	111.120	0.0090	275.300	0.0036	2.4775	0.4036	2.3729
15	155.568	0.0064	386.420	0.0026	2.4839	0.4026	2.4030
16	217.795	0.0046	541.988	0.0019	2.4885	0.4019	2.4262
17	304.913	0.0033	759.784	0.0013	2.4918	0.4013	2.4441
18	426.879	0.0024	1064.697	0.0009	2.4942	0.4009	2.4577
19	597.630	0.0017	1491.576	0.0007	2.4958	0.4007	2.4682
20	836.683	0.0012	2089.206	0.0005	2.4970	0.4005	2.4761
21	1171.356	0.0009	2925.889	0.0004	2.4979	0.4004	2.4821
22	1639.898	0.0006	4097.245	0.0003	2.4985	0.4003	2.4866
23	2295.857	0.0004	5737.142	0.00018	2.4989	0.4002	2.4900
24	3214.200	0.0003	8032.999	0.00013	2.4992	0.4001	2.4925
25	4499.880	0.0002	11247.199	0.00010	2.4995	0.4001	2.4945
26	6299.831	0.0002	15747.079	0.00007	2.4996	0.4001	2.4959
27	8819.764	0.0001	22046.910	0.00006	2.4997	0.4001	2.4969
28	12347.670	0.0001	30866.674	0.00004	2.4998	0.4000	2.4977
29	17286.737	0.0001	43214.344	0.00003	2.4999	0.4000	2.4983
30	24201.432	0.0001	60501.081	0.00003	2.4999	0.4000	2.4988

TABLE 22

50% Interest Factors for Annual Compounding Interest

	Single Payment		Equal-Payment Series				Uniform Gradient-Series Factor
n	Compound-Amount Factor	Present-Worth Factor	Compound-Amount Factor	Sinking-Fund Factor	Present-Worth Factor	Capital-Recovery Factor	
	To Find F Given P F/P i, n	*To Find P Given F P/F i, n*	*To Find F Given A F/A i, n*	*To Find A Given F A/F i, n*	*To Find P Given A P/A i, n*	*To Find A Given P A/P i, n*	*To Find A Given G A/G i, n*
1	1.500	0.6667	1.000	1.0000	0.6667	1.5000	0.0000
2	2.250	0.4445	2.500	0.4000	1.1111	0.9000	0.4000
3	3.375	0.2963	4.750	0.2105	1.4074	0.7105	1.7369
4	5.063	0.1975	8.125	0.1231	1.6049	0.6231	1.0154
5	7.594	0.1317	13.188	0.0758	1.7366	0.5758	1.2417
6	11.391	0.0878	20.781	0.0481	1.8244	0.5481	1.4226
7	17.086	0.0585	32.172	0.0311	1.8830	0.5311	1.5648
8	25.629	0.0390	49.258	0.0203	1.9220	0.5203	1.6752
9	38.443	0.0260	74.887	0.0134	1.9480	0.5134	1.7596
10	57.665	0.0174	113.330	0.0088	1.9653	0.5088	1.8235
11	86.498	0.0116	170.995	0.0059	1.9769	0.5059	1.8714
12	129.746	0.0077	257.493	0.0039	1.9846	0.5039	1.9068
13	194.620	0.0051	387.239	0.0026	1.9897	0.5026	1.9329
14	291.929	0.0034	581.859	0.0017	1.9932	0.5017	1.9519
15	437.894	0.0023	873.788	0.0012	1.9954	0.5012	1.9657
16	656.841	0.0015	1311.682	0.0008	1.9970	0.5008	1.9756
17	985.261	0.0010	1968.523	0.0005	1.9980	0.5005	1.9827
18	1477.892	0.0007	2953.784	0.0003	1.9987	0.5003	1.9878
19	2216.838	0.0005	4431.676	0.0002	1.9991	0.5002	1.9914
20	3325.257	0.0003	6648.513	0.00016	1.9994	0.5002	1.9940
21	4987.885	0.0002	9973.770	0.00011	1.9996	0.5001	1.9958
22	7481.828	0.0001	14961.655	0.00008	1.9997	0.5001	1.9971
23	11222.741	0.0001	22443.483	0.00005	1.9998	0.5001	1.9980
24	16834.112	0.0001	33666.224	0.00004	1.9999	0.5000	1.9986
25	25251.168	0.0000	50500.337	0.00003	1.9999	0.5000	1.9990

37

Statistical Concepts

CHARLES P. BONINI, Ph.D.
Graduate School of Business
Stanford University
Stanford, California

and

WILLIAM A. SPURR, Ph.D.
Graduate School of Business
Stanford University
Stanford, California

ORGANIZATION OF DATA: RATIOS AND FREQUENCY DISTRIBUTIONS

AN EARLY STEP in any investigation is the collection and organization of data so that meaningful conclusions can be drawn. Two important tools for data analysis, ratios and frequency distributions, are treated in this section.

Ratios

A given number can often be better understood by comparing it to some other number in the form of a *ratio* or *rate*. The statement that 120,000 people were unemployed in a given state is less meaningful than to note the unemployment rate of 6.2 percent (the ratio of the number unemployed to the total work force). This rate can then be compared with the rate for other months or years to determine the trend of unemployment. Similarly, it often makes more sense to compare the costs for a business firm as a percentage of sales, rather than to examine the costs by themselves.

Ratios are computed from a numerator and a base (denominator). For a ratio to be meaningful, these may have to be adjusted or refined so as to exclude any extraneous factors that would obscure the direct relationship between them. For example, the base of the unemployment rate is not the total population; excluded are children, retired persons, and those not seeking employment such as housewives. As another example, consider the data shown in Table 1 which gives the trend of deaths in automobile accidents from 1950 to 1971.

Since the number of deaths increased by 63 percent from 1950 to 1972, one might conclude that the automobile menace is increasing. However, when this ratio is refined by appropriately relating deaths to motor vehicles or, better still, vehicle miles, the opposite conclusion is reached.

There are no set rules on how to refine a ratio to make it more meaningful. It is necessary to determine what extraneous factors can be misleading and to eliminate them from the numerator or base as appropriate, and this is ultimately a matter of judgment and common sense. Many

TABLE 1

Fatalities in Motor Vehicle Accidents, 1950 and 1971

	1950	*1972*	*Percent Change*
1. Persons killed in motor accidents	34,763	56,600	+63
2. Deaths per 100,000 population	23.0	27.2	+18
3. Deaths per 10,000 motor vehicles	7.1	4.66	−34
4. Deaths per 100,000,000 vehicle-miles	7.6	4.53	−40

Source: *National Safety Council*, Accident Facts, 1973, p. 59.

specific ratios have been identified for use in financial analysis, and their description is given elsewhere in this volume.

Frequency Distributions

Generally ratios are used for *attribute* data (attribute data are data that are sorted into groups, with a count made of each group). When data can be measured along an interval scale, they are called *variable* data, and the usual form of organization is to group the data by size into a *frequency distribution*. A frequency distribution is a device for summarizing an unwieldly number of figures, so that a maximum of information can be presented with a minimum of detail.

Variables may represent either discrete or continuous data. Discrete data have distinct values, with no intermediate points. Thus, the number of children in a family can be two or three, but not 2.7. Continuous data can have any value over a range, such as the exact heights of men. However, continuous data are often treated as being discrete, as when heights are rounded to the nearest inch.

The data under analysis should be *homogeneous*, i.e., sufficiently alike to be comparable for the purposes of the study. Thus in a study of stock prices, it might be appropriate to deal only with firms in a given industry (a homogeneous group) rather than to lump several industries together.

Grouping the Data into Classes. The idea of a frequency distribution is to take a large mass of data and reduce it into an understandable pattern. Consider, for example, the list of stock prices in the daily newspaper financial section. From this list it is easy to obtain the price of an individual stock, but the pattern of prices is not evident. The closing prices of a selected group of 170 stocks for a given day are grouped into the frequency distribution shown in Table 2. A graphic version of this frequency data, called a *histogram,* is shown in Figure 1.

TABLE 2

Frequency Distribution (closing prices of 170 selected stocks)

Closing Price	*Midpoint*	*Number of Stocks*	*Percent of Stocks*
0 and under $ 10	$ 5	37	21.8
$ 10 and under 20	$ 15	59	34.7
20 and under 30	$ 25	28	16.5
30 and under 40	$ 35	16	9.4
40 and under 50	$ 45	10	5.9
50 and under 60	$ 55	8	4.7
60 and under 70	$ 65	5	2.9
70 and under 80	$ 75	4	2.3
80 and under 90	$ 85	1	0.6
90 and under 100	$ 95	1	0.6
100 and under 110	$105	1	0.6
Total		170	100.0

In obtaining the frequency distribution in Table 2, it was necessary to decide upon the number of intervals or *classes* and the width of each interval. In general, it is advisable to divide the data into from 6 to 15 classes. If the number of classes is too small, important characteristics of the data may be concealed. The use of too many classes may show unnecessary detail, as well as a confusing zigzag of frequencies. Within these limits, the exact number of classes is determined by the width of the interval. This interval is usually selected as a convenient round number located so that if there are clusters in the data, they occur near the midpoint of the interval. Thus in Table 2, the interval selected was $10, resulting in 11 classes.

The class limits should be stated precisely to avoid ambiguity. Thus in Table 2, the interval was stated as $10 and under $20, not as $10 to $20, since a stock price of exactly $20 could fall into either of two classes.

All intervals in a frequency distribution should have the same width, if possible, because frequencies are easier to interpret and computations are facilitated. Intervals of varying width are confusing. However,

FIGURE 1

Histogram (closing price of 170 selected stocks)

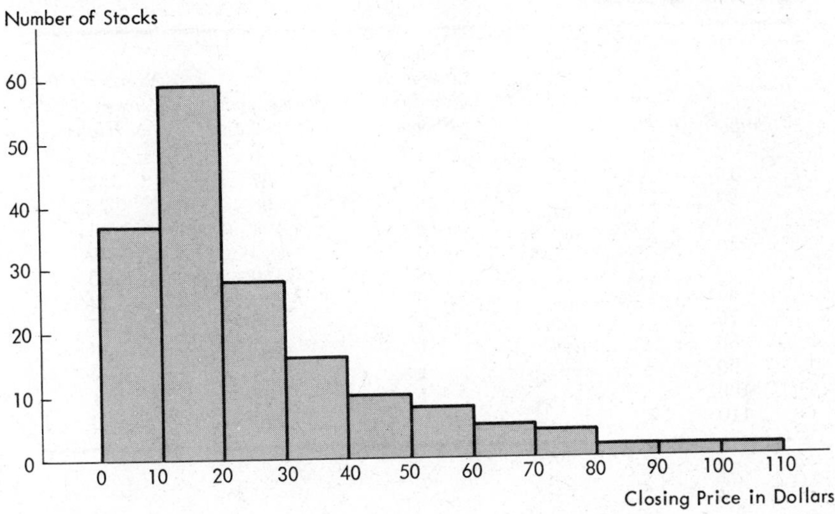

unequal intervals are sometimes necessary in order to cover a wide range of data.

Relative Frequency Distributions. It is often desirable to show each frequency as a relative part or percentage of the total, as shown in the last column of Table 2. This permits easy comparison of the frequencies in one interval with another on a common 100 percent base, and also comparison between one set of data and another (for example, stock prices in different industries).

Cumulative Frequency Distributions. It is sometimes convenient to express frequency data as the percent (or frequency) greater than or less than given amounts. The cumulative distribution for the stock price data is shown in Table 3 below and graphed in Figure 2. From the graph, the percentage or frequency of stocks above or below any given price can be easily read.

Shape of Frequency Distributions. Frequency distributions can have many shapes, and some of these are illustrated in Figure 3. Note that the curves in Figure 3 are smooth curves, called *frequency curves,* and could be obtained by smoothing out the histogram. The important bell-shaped *normal curve* is shown in panel A of Figure 3. This curve describes the distribution of many kinds of measurements in the physical, biological, and social sciences. In addition it reflects variations due to chance, and as such represents a curve for the measurement of sampling error. The two curves in panel B are symmetrical but differ from the normal curve. The curves in panels C and D represent distributions in

TABLE 3

Cumulative Frequency Distributions (closing prices of 170 selected stocks)

Closing Price	*Number in Class with Lower Limit Shown*	*Number with Price Less*	*Number with Price as High or Higher*
0	37	0	170
10	59	37	133
20	28	96	74
30	16	124	46
40	10	140	30
50	8	150	20
60	5	158	12
70	4	163	7
80	1	167	3
90	1	168	2
100	1	169	1
110	0	170	0

FIGURE 2

Cumulative Frequency Curves (closing prices of 170 selected stocks)

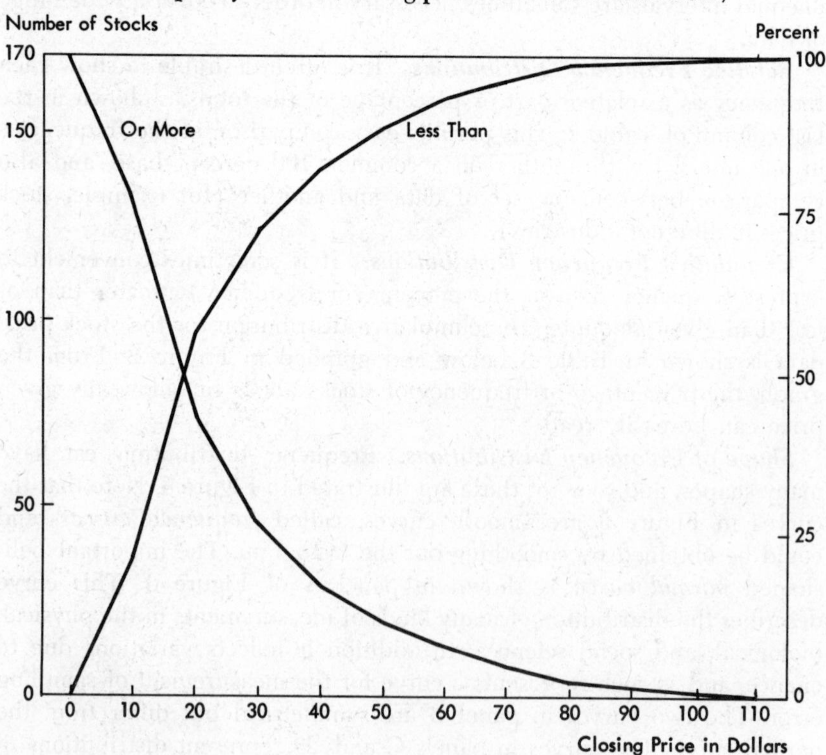

FIGURE 3

Types of Frequency Curves

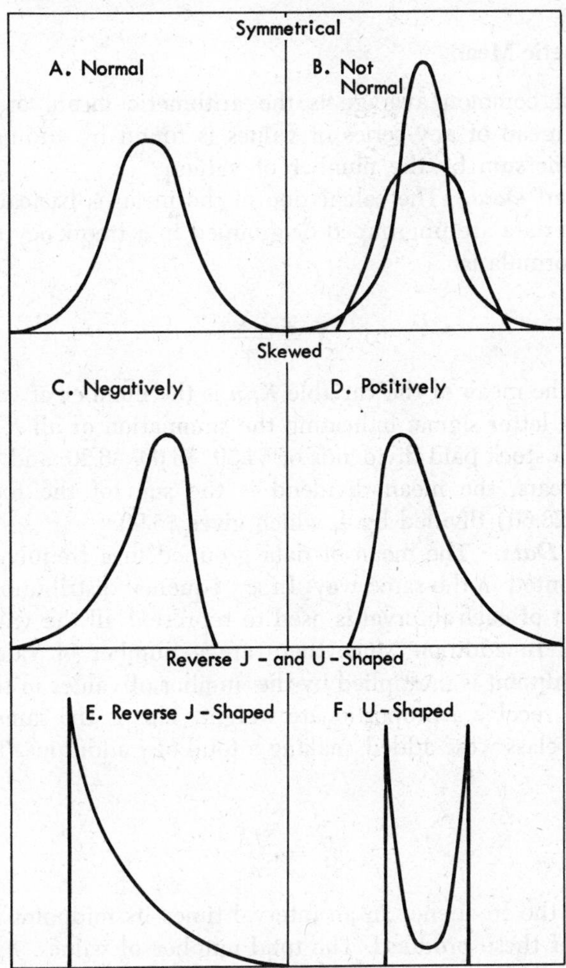

which the two branches of the curve are unequal or *skewed.* The panel C curve is skewed to the left or negatively skewed. The panel D curve is skewed to the right or positively skewed. Most economic data, including the example of stock prices in Figure 1, have the positively skewed shape of the curve in panel D. The shapes illustrated in panels E and F occur less frequently.

AVERAGES

Frequency distributions show the general shape of a set of data, but additional measures are usually needed. In particular, some summary measure of average or central tendency is most helpful in characterizing the data.

The Arithmetic Mean

The most common average is the arithmetic mean, or simply the mean. The mean of any series of values is found by adding them and dividing their sum by the number of values.

Ungrouped Data. The calculation of the mean is basically the same whether the data are ungrouped or grouped in a frequency distribution. The basic formula is:

$$\bar{X} = \frac{\Sigma X}{n}$$

where $\bar{X}$ is the mean of the variable X; n is the number of values; and Σ is the Greek letter sigma, indicating the summation of all X values. For example, if a stock paid dividends of \$4.50, \$6.00, \$6.20, and \$6.90 in the past four years, the mean dividend is the sum of the four amounts (which is \$23.60) divided by 4, which gives \$5.90.

Grouped Data. The mean of data grouped in a frequency distribution is computed in the same way. In a frequency distribution, however, the midpoint of each interval is used to represent all the values of X in the interval. In addition, since there are a number of values in each class, the midpoint is multiplied by the number of values in the class (f) so that they receive a proportionate weight. This is the same as if each value in the class were added, making a total of f additions. The formula is:

$$\bar{X} = \frac{\Sigma fX}{n}$$

where fX is the frequency in an interval times its midpoint X, and ΣfX is the sum of these products. The total number of values, n, is also the sum of the frequencies. The use of this formula is illustrated in Table 4, using the data on stock prices from Table 2. Note that ΣfX is 4130, and n, the number of stocks, is 170. Thus the mean price of the 170 stocks is:

$$\bar{X} = \frac{\Sigma fX}{n} = \frac{4130}{170} = 24.29$$

The mean computed from a frequency distribution is subject to a slight error of grouping, since all values are rounded to the nearest class midpoint.[1]

---

[1] Actually, in this example, there is an additional bias. Since stock prices are quoted in eights of a dollar, the class midpoint is, strictly speaking, one sixteenth less than the values used.

TABLE 4

Computing the Arithmetic Mean from a Frequency Distribution (closing prices of 170 selected stocks)

Closing Price	*Class Midpoint* X	*Number of Stocks (Frequency)* f	*Frequency* × *Midpoint* fX
0 and under $ 10	$ 5	37	$ 185
$ 10 and under 20	15	59	885
20 and under 30	25	28	700
30 and under 40	35	16	560
40 and under 50	45	10	450
50 and under 60	55	8	440
60 and under 70	65	5	325
70 and under 80	75	4	300
80 and under 90	85	1	85
90 and under 100	95	1	95
100 and under 110	105	1	105
Total		170	$4130

The Median

The median of any set of data is the middle value in order of size if n is odd, or the mean of the two middle items if n is even. The median is the middlemost value and is most often used as a descriptive measure when there are a few extreme items in a set of data. Thus, median family income is reported by the Census Bureau and is a better measure of average income than is the mean, which is somewhat higher because it averages in the incomes of very wealthy people.

The median can sometimes be found when other averages are not defined, such as when the items in a set of data are ranked in order rather than measured on a scale. For example, a group of employees may be ranked in order of merit. The median value can be found and measured.

Ungrouped Data. To determine the median in ungrouped data, it is first necessary to arrange the values in an array from highest to lowest (or vice versa). The median is not computed from a formula but is selected as the value whose rank or "order number" is $n/2 + 1/2$, counting from the lowest value. As an example, if we had the 6 numbers

$$2, 4, 6.8, 9.5, 10.2, 11.1,$$

the median would be the $6/2 + 1/2 = 3\ 1/2$th item, i.e., halfway between the third and fourth items, or $(6.8 + 9.5)/2 = 8.15$.

Grouped Data. When data are grouped in a frequency distribution, the median falls in the class interval whose frequency is the first to make the cumulative frequency greater than $n/2$. It is convenient to call this the median class. The median (Md) may then be located within the median class by means of the interpolation formula

$$\text{Md} = L + \frac{i(n/2 - F)}{f},$$

where L is the lower limit of the median class; i, its width; f, its frequency; F, the cumulative frequency below the median class; and n, the total number of values of X.

Using the data on stock prices from Table 2, the median can be calculated as follows. The median class is the one containing the 170/2 = 85th item in order. This item is in the second interval ($10 and under $20) which contains items from 38th through 96th. The lower limit of the class is $10, which is L; its frequency f is 59; the cumulative frequency below the class is 37 = F; and the interval width is $10 = i. The calculated median is thus:

$$\begin{aligned}\text{Md} &= L + \frac{i(n/2 - F)}{f}\\ &= 10 + \frac{10(170/2 - 37)}{59}\\ &= 18.14\end{aligned}$$

The Mode

The mode is the value which occurs most often or the value around which there is the greatest degree of clustering. The modal wage is the one received by the greatest number of workers. The modal interest rate for mortgages is the one that occurs more often than any other. The mode is ordinarily meaningful only if there is a marked concentration of values about a single point.

The mode can occasionally be determined directly from ungrouped data. When a large proportion of values are equal, no process of grouping could dislodge this value from its modal position. For example, if a bank charges the general run of its customers 9 percent, then 9 percent is the mode of interest rates, irrespective of what rates apply in special cases.

In grouped data, it is generally best to use the modal class, and not to consider the mode as a single number. Thus in the example of stock prices, the modal class is $10 and under $20. That is, more stock prices fall in the interval $10 and under $20 than in any other. The modal class is only a rough estimate, since it depends upon the choice of class limits.

Characteristics of Averages

The arithmetic mean, median, and mode have the same value in any symmetrical distribution. If the distribution is skewed, the mode remains under the highest point of the curve, the mean is pulled out in the direction of the extreme values, and the median tends to fall in between. This is shown in Figure 4, for positively skewed data, similar to that for the stock price example.

FIGURE 4

Relationship of Mean, Median, and Mode in a Positively Skewed Distribution

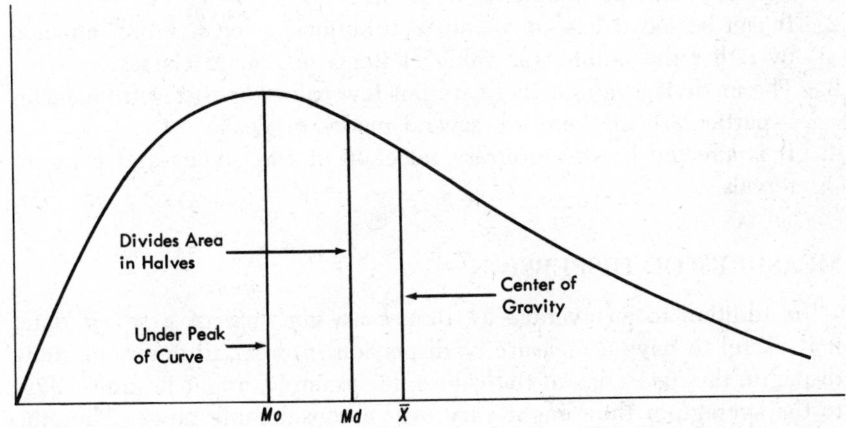

In summary, the characteristics of the individual averages are given below:

Arithmetic Mean

1. The arithmetic mean is the most widely known and widely used average.
2. It is, nevertheless, and artificial concept, since it may not coincide with any actual value.
3. It is affected by the value of every item, but
4. It may be affected too much by extreme values.
5. It can be computed from the original data without forming an array or frequency distribution, or from the total value and number of items alone.
6. Being determined by a rigid formula, it lends itself to subsequent algebraic treatment better than the median or mode.

Median

1. The median is a simple concept—easy to understand and easy to compute.
2. It is affected by the number but not the value of extreme items.
3. It is widely used in skewed distributions where the arithmetic mean would be distorted by extreme values.

4. It may be located in an open-end distribution or one where the data may be ranked but not measured quantitatively.
5. It is unreliable if the data do not cluster at the center of the distribution.

Mode

1. The mode can best be computed from a frequency distribution, unless one value predominates in an array.
2. It can be located in open-end distributions, since it is not affected by either the number or value of items in remote classes.
3. The mode is erratic if there are but few values or zigzag frequencies—particularly if there are several modes or peaks.
4. It is affected by the arbitrary selection of class limits and class intervals.

MEASURES OF DISPERSION

In addition to an average as a summary measure of a set of data, it is useful to have a measure of dispersion in order to determine how disparate the data are. All the values, for example, might be quite close to the average or they might vary over a considerable range. Thus the measure of dispersion can be used to gauge the reliability of an average. A second purpose for measuring dispersion is to determine the nature and causes of variation in order to control the variation itself. For example, in matters of health, variations in body temperature, pulse beat, and blood pressure are basic guides to diagnosis. Measures of dispersion include the range, the quartile deviation, the mean deviation, and the standard deviation.

The Range

The range is simply the difference between the largest and the smallest values of a variable. Sometimes the range is indicated merely by citing the largest and smallest figures themselves, as in daily stock quotations. If the high and low values are not widely separated from adjoining values, the range may be a fairly good measure of dispersion. However, if the two extremes are erratic, the range is unreliable and misleading because it gives no hint of the dispersion of the intervening values. For this reason the range is only used as a measure of dispersion in a few specific cases.

The Quartile Deviation

The quartiles are the three points which divide an array or frequency distribution into four roughly equal groups. That is, the first or lower quartile, Q_1, separates the lowest valued quarter of the total number of values from the second quarter; the second quartile, Q_2 (almost always called the median), separates the second quarter from the third quarter; and the third or upper quartile, Q_3, separates the third quarter from the top quarter. Consequently, the quartile range, $Q_3 - Q_1$, includes the middle half of the items. The quartile deviation, Q, is half this range. That is,

$$Q = \frac{(Q_3 - Q_1)}{2}$$

The quartiles are widely used as measures of dispersion. *Dun's*, for example, reports the medians and quartiles of 14 operating ratios in each of 22 types of retailers. Thus, the quartiles of net profits on net working capital of 144 grocery retailers in 1973 were 9 and 33 percent, compared with the median of 18 percent. This means that while the typical grocery retailer earned 18 percent on net working capital, about one fourth of the companies earned less than 9 percent and one fourth earned over 33 percent, indicating a wide spread of profitability in this field.

Ungrouped Data. The first and third quartiles are found in an array just as is the median, which is the second quartile. They are the values whose ranks or order numbers are $n/4 + 1/2$ and $3n/4 + 1/2$, respectively, counting from the lowest value. Fractional order numbers are interpolated between neighboring values in the array.

Grouped Data. The quartiles can be estimated for a frequency distribution in the same way as the median by these analogous formulas:

$$Q_1 = L + \frac{i(n/4 - F)}{f} \qquad Q_3 = L + \frac{i(3n/4 - F)}{f}$$

where L is the lower limit of the class containing the quartile, i is the class width, f is the frequency or number in that class, F is the cumulative frequency below that class, and n is the total number of values.

For the data on stock prices in Table 2, the first quartile, Q_1 is the $170/4 = 42\ 1/2$th item, and this falls in the second class ($L = \$10$; $f = 59$; $F = 37$); and Q_3 is the $(3)(170/4) = 127\ 1/2$th item, which falls in the fourth class ($L = \$30$; $f = 16$; and $F = 124$). Therefore,

$$Q_1 = 10 + 10(42.5 - 37)/59 = 10.93$$

and

$$Q_3 = 30 + 10(127.5 - 124)/16 = 32.19$$

The quartile range is then $32.19 - 10.93 = \$21.26$, and the quartile deviation is half this, or \$10.63.

The Mean Deviation

The mean deviation, sometimes called the average deviation, is simply the mean of the absolute deviations of all the values from some central point, usually the mean. The deviations are averaged as if they were all positive. The mean deviation is a concise and simple measure of variability that takes every item into account.

Ungrouped Data. The formula for the mean deviation (measured from the arithmetic mean) in a set of ungrouped data is

$$MD = \frac{\Sigma|X - \bar{X}|}{n}$$

where the blinkers | | mean that the signs are ignored. That is, the absolute deviations from the mean are added, and the sum (Σ) is divided by the number of values (n) to find the mean deviation (MD).

TABLE 5

Computation of Mean Deviation for Ungrouped Data (price-earnings ratios of five electronics stocks)

Common Stock	*Price-Earnings Ratio* (X)	*Deviation from Mean* |X − X̄|
A	19.6	0.4
B	17.3	2.7
C	19.2	0.8
D	14.0	6.0
E	29.9	9.9
Total	100.0	19.8
Mean	20.0 = X̄	4.0 = MD

The mean deviation is computed in Table 5 for the price-earnings ratios of five electronics stocks, whose mean is 20.0. That is,

$$MD = \frac{\Sigma|X - \bar{X}|}{n} = \frac{19.8}{5} = 4.0$$

Grouped Data. The mean deviation can be computed from grouped data by the formula

$$MD = \frac{\Sigma f|X - \bar{X}|}{n}$$

where $|X - \bar{X}|$ is the absolute deviation of the class midpoint (X) from the arithmetic mean, ignoring signs, and f is the frequency in that class. This formula will not be illustrated here.

The Standard Deviation

The standard deviation is found by (1) *squaring* the deviations of individual values from the arithmetic mean, (2) summing the squares,

(3) dividing the sum by $(n - 1)$, and (4) extracting the square root. Like the mean deviation, the standard deviation is based on the deviations of all values, but it is better adapted to further statistical analysis. This is partly because squaring the deviations makes them all positive, so that the standard deviation is easier to handle algebraically than the mean deviation. The standard deviation is therefore of such importance that it is, in fact, the "standard" measure of dispersion.

Ungrouped Data. The basic formula for the standard deviation of ungrouped data is

$$s = \sqrt{\frac{\Sigma(X - \bar{X})^2}{n - 1}}$$

where s is the standard deviation; $(X - \bar{X})$ is the deviation of any value of X from the arithmetic mean $\bar{X}$; $\Sigma(X - \bar{X})^2$ is the sum of the squared

TABLE 6

Computation of Standard Deviation for Ungrouped Data (price-earnings ratio of five electronics stocks)

(1)	(2)	(3)	(4)	(5)
		Direct Method		
Common Stock	*Price-Earnings Ratio* (X)	*Deviation from Mean* $(X - \bar{X})$	$(X - \bar{X})^2$	*Short-Cut Method* X^2
A	19.6	− .4	.16	384.16
B	17.3	−2.7	7.29	299.29
C	19.2	− .8	.64	368.64
D	14.0	−6.0	36.00	196.00
E	29.9	9.9	98.01	894.01
Total	100.0	0.0	142.10	2,142.10
Mean	20.0			

deviations; and n is the number of items in the sample. The square of the standard deviation (s^2) is called the *variance*.

The above formula for the standard deviation is for data that are considered a sample of some larger population. For the population itself, the formula for the standard deviation (small sigma or σ) is $\sigma = \sqrt{\Sigma(X - \mu)^2/N}$, where μ (small mu in Greek) is the population mean, and N is the number of values. Here the variance (σ^2) is simply the average of the squared deviations from the mean.

In the sample of five price-earnings ratios listed in Table 6, column 2, the deviations from the mean of 20.0 are shown in column 3 and the squares in column 4. Their sum, $\Sigma(X - \bar{X})^2$, is 142.10, and $n = 5$ stocks. The standard deviation is then

$$s = \sqrt{\frac{\Sigma(X - \overline{X})^2}{n - 1}} = \sqrt{\frac{142.10}{4}} = 6.0$$

Short-Cut Method. While the above formula describes the standard deviation succinctly, it may be easier to compute its value directly from the original data, without finding the deviations from the mean. The following formula gives the same result as the one above:

$$s = \sqrt{\frac{\Sigma X^2 - (\Sigma X)^2/n}{n - 1}}$$

In Table 6, column 5 shows the original X values squared for use in this formula; columns 3 and 4 are not needed. Then,

$$s = \sqrt{\frac{2{,}142.10 - (100.0)^2/5}{4}} = \sqrt{35.52} = 6.0$$

Grouped Data. In a frequency distribution the midpoint of each class is used to represent every value in that class. The basic formula for the standard deviation therefore becomes

$$s = \sqrt{\frac{\Sigma f(X - \overline{X})^2}{n - 1}}$$

where $(X - \overline{X})^2$ is the deviation of the class midpoint (X) from the arthmetic mean and f is the frequency in that class.

Relation between Measures and Dispersion

In a normal distribution there is a fixed relationship between the three principal measures of dispersion. The quartile deviation is the smallest, the mean deviation is next, and the standard deviation is the largest. In particular, when measured abound the mean of a normal population μ:

$\mu \pm Q$ includes 50 percent of the items.
$\mu \pm \text{MD}$ includes 57.51 percent of the items.
$\mu \pm \sigma$ includes 68.27 percent of the items.

These relationships are shown graphically in Figure 5. This figure also shows the proportion of items included within $\pm$ 2 and $\pm$ 3 standard deviations.

Characteristics of Measures of Dispersion

The characteristics of the individual measures of dispersion are summarized below.

FIGURE 5

Proportions of Area of Normal Curve Included in Intervals Based on Common Measures of Dispersion

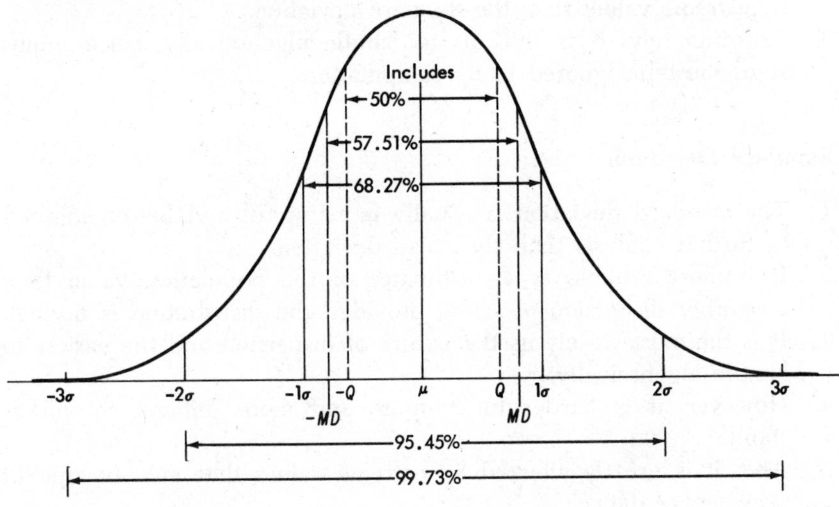

Range

1. The range is the easiest measure to compute and to understand. But,
2. it is often unreliable, being based on two extreme values only.

Quartile Deviation

1. The quartile deviation is also easy to calculate and to understand.
2. It depends on only two values, which include the middle half of the items.
3. It is usually superior to the range as a rough measure of dispersion.
4. It may be determined in an open-end distribution, or one in which the data may be ranked but not measured quantitatively.
5. It is also useful in badly skewed distributions or those in which other measures of dispersion would be warped by extreme values.
6. However, it is unreliable if there are gaps in the data around the quartiles.

Mean Deviation

1. The mean deviation has the advantage of giving equal weight to the deviation of every value from the mean or median.

2. Therefore, it is a more sensitive measure of dispersion than those described above and ordinarily has a smaller sampling error.
3. It is also easier to compute and to understand and is less affected by extreme values than the standard deviation.
4. Unfortunately, it is difficult to handle algebraically, since minus signs must be ignored in its computation.

Standard Deviation

1. The standard deviation is usually more useful and better adapted to further analysis than the mean deviation.
2. It is more reliable as an estimator of the population value than any other dispersion measure, provided the distribution is normal.
3. It is the most widely used measure of dispersion and the easiest to handle algebraically.
4. However, it is harder to compute and more difficult to understand.
5. And, it is greatly affected by extreme values that may be due to skewness of data.

PROBABILITY DISTRIBUTIONS

A probability is a number between 0 and 1 representing the chance or likelihood that an event will occur. A probability of zero means the event is impossible; a probability of one means that it is certain; and values in between, such as 0.5, indicate intermediate chances of occurrence.

An objective interpretation defines probability as the relative frequency of a certain event in a random process over a great number of trials. For example, assigning the probability of 0.5 to the event "heads" for a fair coin implies that 50 percent of a very large number of tosses would be heads. An alternative subjective interpretation defines the probability p of an event as an evaluation by a decision maker of its relative likelihood. It is his betting odds on the occurrence of the event.

Basic Definitions

A *simple* probability, written $P(A)$, is the probability that a single event A will occur. A *joint* probability, $P(A,B)$ is the probability that both of two events A and B will occur. A *conditional* probability is the probability that one event A will occur, given that another event B is known to have occurred, and is written $P(A|B)$. As an example, consider an urn that contains five balls, three red and two white. The probability of drawing a red ball on the first draw is a simple probability. The probability of drawing red balls on each of the first and second draws is a joint probability. And the probability of drawing a red ball on the second draw, after knowing that the first draw was red, is a conditional probability.

Two events, A and B, are defined to be statistically *independent* if $P(A|B) = P(A)$, that is, if the probability of A is not dependent upon whether or not event B has occurred. As an example, two flips of a coin are independent, since the outcome of the first does not affect the outcome of the second. On the other hand, if two balls are drawn from the urn described above (three red and two white balls) and the first is not replaced before the second is drawn, the events are *not* independent. Note that if the first is red (which has probability $3/5$), the probability that the second is red is $2/4 = 0.5$. And if the first drawn is white, the probability that the second is red is $3/4 = 0.75$. Hence there is not independence since the second outcome probability is influenced by the first outcome.

Rules for Dealing with Probabilities

Addition of Probabilities. For two events A and B, the probability of A or B occurring is:

$$P(A \text{ or } B) = P(A) + P(B) - P(A,B)$$

that is, the sum of the simple probabilities, minus the joint probability. If the two events are *mutually exclusive* (so that they cannot both occur), then the joint probability is zero and the rule is:

$$P(A \text{ or } B) = P(A) + P(B)$$

Multiplication of Probabilities. The joint probability that both events A and B occur can be written as:

$$P(A \text{ and } B) = P(A,B) = P(A)P(B|A)$$

that is, the product of the simple probability of A and the conditional probability of B given A. When the events are independent, $P(B|A) = P(B)$, and the rule is:

$$P(A,B) = P(A)P(B)$$

Random Variables

A probability function is a rule which assigns probabilities to each element of a set of events that may occur. If, in turn, a specific numerical value is assigned to the elements of a set of events, the function which assigns these values is called a *random variable*. For example, if the random variable X is the number of heads in three tosses of a fair coin, then the possible values of X and the corresponding probabilities are:

Possible Values of Random Variable X (Number of Heads in Three Tosses)	*Probability of X*
0	1/8
1	3/8
2	3/8
3	1/8
	1

A probability function, such as that illustrated above is called a *probability distribution* if the sum of the probabilities equals one. A probability distribution may be either *discrete* or *continuous.* In a discrete distribution, the random variable can take on only a specific set of values, often only integer values, and is sometimes called a *probability mass function.* In a continuous distribution, the random variable can take on any value within a range or within ranges. Examples of discrete and continuous distributions are given in Figure 6.

FIGURE 6

Examples of Probability Distributions Defined by Mathematical Equations

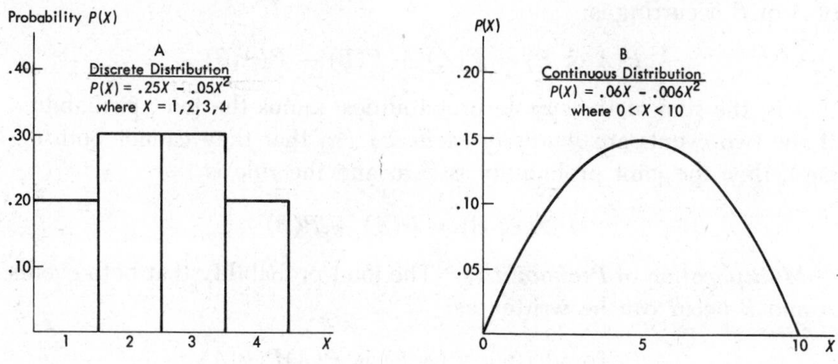

The Mean and Variance of a Random Variable. The mean or *expected value,* $E(X)$, of a discrete random variable X is defined as:

$$E(X) = \Sigma[X \cdot P(X)]$$

where $P(X)$ is the probability for each value of X.

The principal measure of dispersion for a probability distribution is the *variance* (the square of the standard deviation or σ^2) which is defined as: Variance $= \Sigma\{[X - E(X)]^2 \cdot P(X)\}$ in a discrete distribution. Similar formulas hold for the expected value and variance of continuous random variables.

Sums of Random Variables. The expectation of a sum of random variables is the sum of the expectations of those random variables. Thus the mean of the random variable $(X + Y + Z)$ is:

$$E(X + Y + Z) = E(X) + E(Y) + E(Z).$$

The expectation of a constant times a random variable is the constant times the expectation of the random variable:

$$E(cX) = cE(X),$$

where c is an arbitrary constant.

The variance of a sum of *independent* random variables is also the sum of the variances. Thus:

$$\text{Var}(X + Y + Z) = \text{Var}(X) + \text{Var}(Y) + \text{Var}(Z)$$

if X, Y, and Z are independent. Similarly, the variance of a constant times a random variable is the constant squared times the variance of the variable thus:

$$\text{Var}(cX) = c^2\text{Var}(X).$$

The Binomial Distribution

Certain specific probability distributions have been found particularly useful in business problems, and they are to be discussed briefly. The first is the binomial distribution, used when the random variable can take on only one of two values. Thus the distribution is used extensively in quality control (when a product is defective or not), in public opinion polls (for or against, candidate A versus B, Republican or Democrat), in auditing (an account is correct or not), and in many other instances.

The binomial distribution is a discrete distribution and is made up of n *independent* trials (items sampled or flips of a coin, for example), and on each trial the probability of a success (p) remains the same. A success is defined to be one particular outcome, such as the occurrence of heads in flipping a coin or the occurrence of a defective item in sampling from a production process.

The Binomial Probability Formula. In general, the probability of r successes in n trials is:

$$P(r) = {}_nC_r p^r q^{(n-r)}$$

where r is the number of successes (i.e., heads); n is the size of the sample (i.e., number of flips); p is the probability of a success (i.e., a head); $q = (1 - p)$ is the probability of a failure (i.e., a tail); and $P(r)$ = probability of exactly r successes (i.e., r heads). Also ${}_nC_r$ is the number of *combination* of n things taken r at a time and is defined as:

$${}_nC_r = \frac{n!}{r!(n-r)!}$$

where n factorial is $n! = 1 \times 2 \times 3 \times \ldots \times n$ and $0! = 1$ by definition.

Example. Probability of three heads and two tails using a bent coin that has a 0.6 chance for a head:

$$\begin{aligned} n &= 5 \text{ flips} \\ r &= 3 \text{ heads} \\ n - r &= 2 \\ p &= 0.6, \text{ the probability of a head} \\ q &= 1 - p = 0.4 \end{aligned}$$

$$P(r) = {}_nC_r p^r q^{(n-r)} = \frac{5!}{3!2!}(0.6)^3(0.4)^2 = 10 \times 0.034 = 0.34$$

The calculation of binomial probabilities is tedious work. Fortunately tables of the binomial distribution are included in most statistics tests. In addition, references to complete sets of tables are given at the end of this section.

The mean or expected value of the binomial distribution is $E(r) = np$, and the variance of the distribution is $\text{Var}(r) = npq$.

The Poisson Distribution

Another discrete distribution of some practical importance is the Poisson distribution. It is used to represent the number of random occurrences of some phenomenon per unit of measurement. Thus it might be used to represent the number of telephone calls arriving at a switchboard in a minute or the number of defective spots in a square foot of enameled plate. The Poisson distribution plays an important role in the theory of queues or waiting lines.

The random variable X (number of occurrences) for the Poisson distribution can take on only 0 or integer values. In addition, it assumes that the number of occurrences is independent from one unit of measurement to another. (The number of telephone calls arriving in one minute, for example, does not affect the number arriving in the next minute.) Finally, it assumes that the average rate of occurrences is the same over all units of measurement.

The Poisson probability function is

$$P(X) = \frac{e^{-m}m^X}{X!} \quad \text{for} \quad X = 0, 1, 2, \ldots$$

where X is the random variable, the number of occurrences per unit of measurement; m is the mean or average number of occurrences of X per unit of measurement; and e is a constant (the base of natural logarithms) with value of 2.718. . . .

As with the binomial distribution, tables of the Poisson distribution are widely available.

The Normal Distribution

By far the most important distribution in statistics is the normal distribution. This distribution was described briefly on pages 1043–45 as a continuous distribution represented by a symmetrical, bell-shaped curve (see Figures 3 and 5). The equation for the normal distribution is:

$$f(X) = \frac{1}{\sqrt{2\pi}\sigma} e^{-\frac{1}{2}\frac{(X-\mu)^2}{\sigma^2}}$$

where X is the random variable and μ and σ are the parameters. The constant π is 3.14159 . . . and e is 2.718. . . . For the normal distribution, the expected value or mean is $E(X) = \mu$ and the variance is σ^2. Normal distributions can take on many different shapes, depending on the values of these two parameters. Although this is so, the normal distribution includes the same percentage of values within $\pm$ any specific number of standard deviations. Thus:

$\mu \pm \sigma$ includes 68.27 percent of the values.
$\mu \pm 2\sigma$ includes 95.45 percent of the values.
$\mu \pm 3\sigma$ includes 99.73 percent of the values.

Tables of the area under a normal distribution are contained in any statistics text. To use these tables, it is necessary to calculate the *standard normal deviate z.* This represents the number of standard deviation units the random variable X is above or below the mean. The value of z is calculated as:

$$z = \frac{X - \mu}{\sigma}$$

The value of z can then be used in the table of the *standardized normal distribution,* with mean of 0 and standard deviation of 1.

Other Distributions. There are a number of other probability distributions which have some importance in applications in business. These include the *exponential* (used to represent the time between occurrences in a random process), the *beta,* the *gamma,* and others. The reader is referred to advanced texts.

Multivariate Probability Distributions

A multivariate probability distribution is a function expressing the joint probabilities for two or more random variables. For simplicity, the case of two random variables X and Y is considered. The expected values (μ_x and μ_y) and variances ($\sigma_x{}^2$ and $\sigma_y{}^2$) for the variables individually are exactly as defined earlier. However, there is an additional measure of variability called the *covariance,* which measures the degree to which the two variables tend to be related. The covariance is defined as:

$$\text{Cov}(X,Y) = E(X - \mu_x)(Y - \mu_y)$$

As an example, consider the joint distribution of the height and weight of men (let X be the height and Y, the weight). The covariance measures the degree to which height and weight are related, that is, the extent to which tall men tend to weigh more than average, and short men, less than average. Since the two characteristics do tend to move together, the covariance term would be large and positive.

If the covariance term is negative, it indicates that high values of one variable tend to be associated with low values of the other and vice versa. If the covariance term is zero, it indicates that the two variables are independent.

Another measure of the degree of dependence of the two variables is the *correlation coefficient.* This is defined as:

$$\rho = \frac{\text{Cov}(X,Y)}{\sigma_x \sigma_y}$$

The correlation coefficient can take on values from zero (if X and Y are independent) to plus or minus one. A correlation of plus or minus one indicates that the two variables vary exactly together.

In a general multivariate distribution, the covariance and correlation coefficient can be defined for any pair of variables.

SELECTED REFERENCES

Organization of Data, Averages, and Dispersion

CROXTON, FREDERICK E.; COWDEN, DUDLEY J.; and BOLCH, BEN W. *Practical Business Statistics.* 4th ed. Englewood Cliffs, N.J.: Prentice-Hall, 1969.

Chapters 2 to 5 provide a detailed treatment of ratios, frequency distributions, averages, and dispersion.

NETER, JOHN; WASSERMAN, WILLIAM; and WHITMORE, G. A. *Fundamental Statistics for Business and Economics.* 4th ed. Boston: Allyn & Bacon, 1973.

Includes analysis of relationships by cross-classification of data, as well as ratios and frequency distribution analysis.

SPURR, WILLIAM A, and BONINI, CHARLES P. *Statistical Analysis for Business Decisions.* Rev. ed. Homewood, Ill.: Richard D. Irwin, Inc, 1973.

Chapters 2 through 5 give a more detailed treatment of the material in this section of the volume.

YULE, G. UDNY, and KENDALL, M. G. *An Introduction to the Theory of Statistics.* 14th ed. London: Charles Griffin, 1950.

Chapters 5 to 7 provide a comprehensive treatment of frequency distributions, averages, dispersion, skewness, and kurtosis.

Probability Distributions

DRAKE, ALVIN W. *Fundamentals of Applied Probability Theory.* New York: McGraw-Hill, 1967.

A good, slightly more advanced treatment of probability and probability distributions is contained in Chapters 1, 2, and 4.

GOLDBERG, SAMUEL. *Probability, An Introduction.* Englewood Cliffs, N.J.: Prentice-Hall, 1960.

A detailed and systematic treatment of discrete probability.

Statistical Tables

BRACKEN, JEROME, and CHRISTENSON, CHARLES J. *Tables for use in Analyzing Business Decisions.* Homewood, Ill.: Richard D. Irwin, Inc., 1965.

BURINGTON, RICHARD S., and MAY, DONALD C. *Handbook of Probability and Statistics with Tables.* 2d ed. New York: McGraw-Hill, 1970.

NATIONAL BUREAU OF STANDARDS. *Tables of the Binomial Probability Distribution.* Washington, D.C.: U.S. Government Printing Office, Applied Mathematics Series No. 6, 1949.

38

Regression Analysis

ROBERT D. MILNE, C.F.A.
Partner
Boyd, Watterson & Co.
Cleveland, Ohio

REGRESSION ANALYSIS has become the most widely used technique in quantitative financial analysis as well as in general quantitative economics. The principles of regression analysis can be grasped firmly without reference to elegant mathematical proofs. The advent of the computer eliminated the mathematical drudgery involved with regression analysis. In fact, even some pocket calculators can perform the more basic elements of regression analysis. The purpose of this section will be to point out some of the situations where regression analysis might be helpful and also how to judge whether or not a regression equation represents a soundly based relationship. Any data can be fed into a regression program and used to generate a formidable series of equations and test statistics. A glance at a few of the test statistics will show whether the equations are simply nonsense or whether a meaningful relationship may be present. Unfortunately, test statistics are not infallible, and occasionally one may be led astray by regression analysis.

ECONOMIC MODELS FOR FINANCIAL ANALYSIS

The financial analyst will not be spending his time preparing elaborate models of the economy as a whole; instead, he will be mostly working with single equation models involving a variety of practical applications. The analyst is well prepared to develop single equation models. In fact, he probably uses such models all the time without formally defining them as models. For example, a tire industry analyst will relate prospective automobile tire sales to automobile production plus replacement demand related to the number of cars on the road. His formal model would be:

$$S = 5a + \alpha p$$

where:

S = Sales of auto tires.
a = Automobile production.
p = Automobile population at start of year.
α = Coefficient of replacement demand to be determined by regression analysis.

This is such a simplified model that the analyst might wonder why it might have any value. Actually, an important characteristic of any model is that it greatly oversimplifies the real world into a form that can be comprehended. A completely detailed description of tire demand broken down as to the number of tires ruined by broken bottles on local streets, by chuckholes, by careless driving, by underinflation, and so forth would so overwhelm the analyst that he would be hard pressed to make a forecast of next year's tire demand. By developing a model, the analyst has brought the problem into a form, which while it still has a logical basis in fact, can be comprehended. The testing of the model by regression analysis will determine the strength of the relationships—that is, how close the actual situation of the past compares with what seems to be the most probable relationships. Far too often, things are not quite what they seem and regression analysis may help the analyst to reconsider what he regards the major forces at work in an industry.

The analyst should be careful to make his regression studies on variables which are related to each other. In other words, he should specify his model beforehand; not simply investigate a large number of series and make his model from the series which appear to have the closest fit. Spurious "correlation" studies are frequent. For example, one might note that the decade of the 1960s was a decade of great growth in both the number of security analysts employed and in the number of auto thefts. It would be possible to come up with a fairly closely fitting regression equation indicating that auto thefts rose directly in line with the number of security analysts employed. The basic fallacy, of course, is that the two series are completely unrelated. Both series are reacting to other forces—it is just a coincidence that both were in a strong uptrend at the same time. In all types of analysis it is possible to be misled if one examines a large number of series. Oftentimes, the closest fit is obtained by use of factors which are not primarily related. However, the accident of close fit does not make the theory sound. In this era of easy computation it is necessary to be on one's guard against the temptation of "data mining" by examining a great variety of series. Just by chance, some regressions will show good results when measured against the past, but prove to be poor guides for the future.

While there are pitfalls along the way, regression analysis is a sound tool for the serious analyst. In addition to simple models, more sophisticated models can be developed easily. For example, if our tire analyst wished to construct a model to forecast the demand for radial tire replacement sales, he might come up with a model somewhat as follows:

$$S_r = \alpha P_r + \beta P_0$$

where:

S_r = Sales of radial tires in the replacement market.
P_r = Automobile population with radial tires.
P_0 = Automobile population with nonradial tires.
α,β = Coefficients to be estimated by regression analysis.

This is still a single equation model, although there are now two coefficients to be determined by regression analysis. While there is no limit to the number of coefficients that could be calculated, it is usually good practice to limit a single equation model to as few as possible—probably no more than three in most cases. The reason for this will be stated later.

USING REGRESSION ANALYSIS TO STUDY OTHER RELATIONSHIPS

Regression analysis can be helpful in studying all types of relationships where quantitative data are available. One of the many types of relationships where such data are often available is that of financial requirements. Determination of a growing company's future financial requirements is a crucial element of security analysis. Regression techniques will not give an unerring answer as to the amount of capital needed to finance a company's growth over the foreseeable future, but they can provide useful background for an analyst preparing for a field trip. Most of the categories on a balance sheet are related to sales. Certainly this is the case with receivables, inventories, fixed assets, and accounts payable. While these categories are directly related to sales, the relationships are by no means fixed constants. As time goes on, relationships change. To illustrate, the record of Eastman Kodak Company's inventories will be examined. At the close of 1970, Kodak's inventories amounted to $578 million or about $.21 for each dollar of the year's sales of $2,785 million. If inventories grow at exactly the same rate as sales, the analyst would expect to find that Kodak will require $.21 of added inventories for each dollar of added sales. However, Figure 1, which depicts the history

FIGURE 1

Eastman Kodak Co. Inventories and Sales (all figures in millions of dollars)

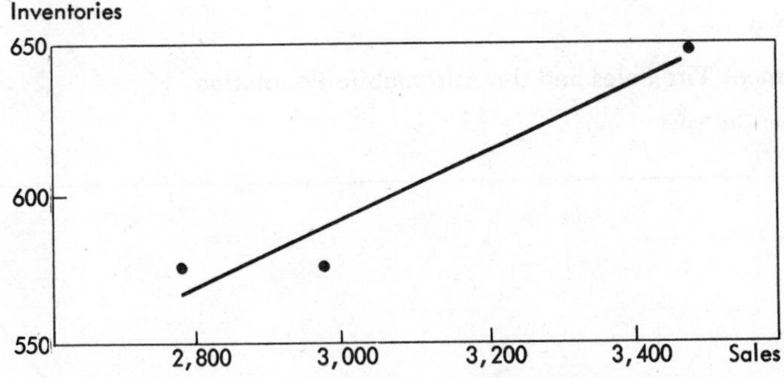

of the three years 1970–72, suggests that only $.11 of additional inventories are required for each added dollar of sales.

The analyst should review the inventory pattern when he interviews Kodak's management to see whether or not this recent trend can be continued. This same approach can be taken for the other main categories of financial assets and liabilities to gain an insight into the factors influencing future financing. These are presented merely as examples of some of the many ways in which regression analysis may be useful in seeking to interpret the meaning of a series of statistical data.

ESSENTIALS OF REGRESSION ANALYSIS

Computer programs for regression analysis frequently include a variety of test statistics, all of which have value. However, the most important elements to understand are:

1. What the regression equation means.
2. Is there a strong relationship between the factors; or only a weak, relatively meaningless relationship?
3. How precise are forecasts likely to be?

To illustrate, a regression line will be calculated to determine if there is a relationship between the demand for replacement tires and the population of cars on the road. Figure 2 depicts the actual results for the 10 years 1963–72 and the computed regression line.

The regression line looks as if it had been drawn freehand to fit in the middle of the dots, but actually it was calculated by least squares equations which resulted in the following coefficients for a straight line equation:

$Y = -71.3$ million $+ 2.31667X$.
Y = Replacement tire sales.
X = Automobile registrations at start of year.

FIGURE 2

Replacement Tire Sales and the Automobile Population

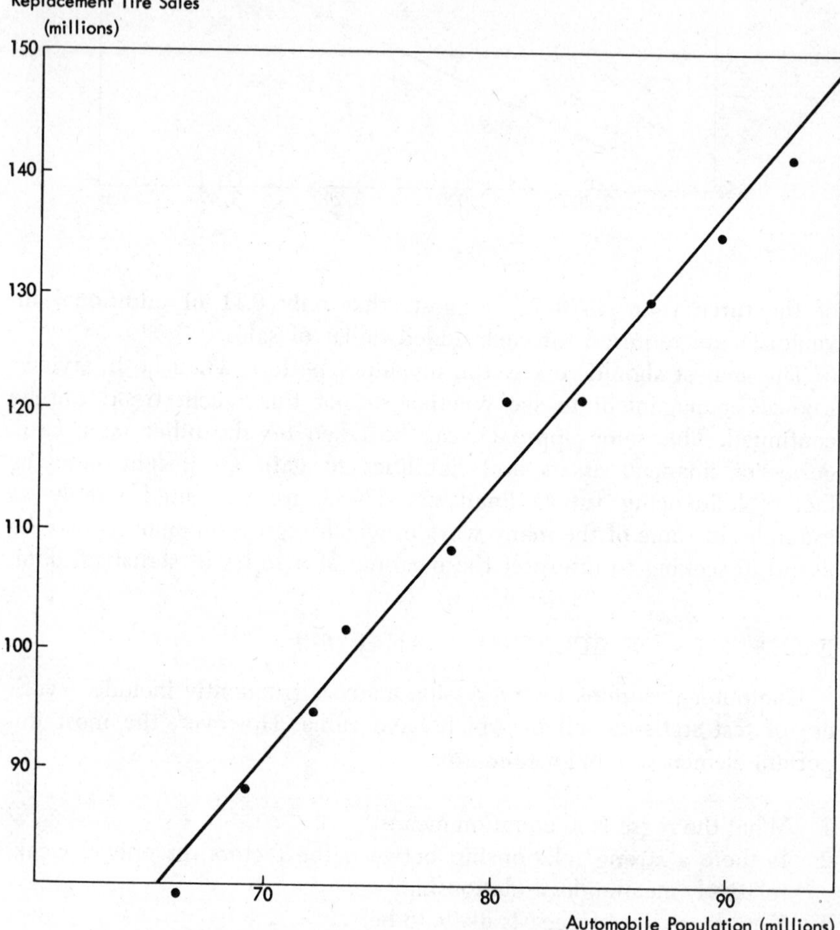

The relationship between the two series is thus reduced to a straight line. Replacement tire sales is termed the dependent variable and placed on the vertical axis (the Y-axis) since our hypothesis is that the level of replacement sales depends upon the number of automobiles on the road. Automobile registrations is thus the independent variable and placed on the horizontal axis (the X-axis). As the analyst varies the forecast for the independent variable, automobile registrations, the level of replacement tire sales changes accordingly at the rate of 2.3 tires per year for each additional automobile on the road at the start of the year.

The equation of a straight line can be expressed in the form: $Y = a + bX$. The term a in the equation indicates the point at which the regression line crosses the Y-axis. The term b in the equation indicates the slope of the regression line.

In any econometric equation, the true coefficients are defined in terms of Greek letters such as $Y = \alpha + \beta X$. The regression equations, however, do not result in true coefficients, but rather in estimates of the true coefficients and are therefore defined in normal roman letters such as: $Y = a + bX$.

In portfolio analysis, considerable emphasis is placed on the beta coefficients of stocks. These coefficients are computed in the same way that replacement tire sales were related to the automobile population. In beta analysis the price of the individual stock is placed on the Y-axis as the dependent variable, and the stock market index (often the S & P's 500) is placed on the X-axis as the independent variable. (The more sophisticated models make allowance for dividends and for the U.S. Treasury Bill rate as a proxy for the riskless rate of return in both series of data.) While the regression techniques in reality present only estimates of the true beta coefficients of the various stocks, they are generally referred to as beta coefficients. A beta coefficient of 1.0 would mean that a stock moves up and down at exactly the same rate as the market; a beta of 0.5 would mean that it would be more stable, moving up or down only half as fast as the market. In other words, the beta coefficient indicates the slope of the regression line for the individual stock.

GOODNESS OF FIT

A least squares regression line can be fitted to any two series of data, as indicated in the Appendix. When there is a strong relationship between the series, it makes sense to use the regression equation in interpreting the past and in forecasting the future. When there is only a weak relationship, the value of regression analysis is that it documents the futility of attempting to rely on simple projections of past relationships.

The most important test statistic is the one measuring *goodness of fit*, which is referred to as the *coefficient of determination*. This measures the amount of variance that is "explained" by the regression line. In the 10 years of data for replacement tire sales, the average annual volume was 112.1 million tires. Figure 3 illustrates the variance from the 112.1 million average that is "explained" by the regression line; the dashed lines leading to the actual values on Figure 3 depict the variance "unexplained" by the regression line.

A look at Figure 3 suggests that the regression line is a rather good fit, and this is documented by the following test statistics:

$$r = 0.992 \text{ (coefficient of correlation)}$$
$$r^2 = 0.985 \text{ (coefficient of determination)}$$

The r^2 value of 0.985 means that 98 percent of the variance is explained by the regression line. This is indeed a good fit and the regression line has passed an important test. The coefficient of correlation r serves as an intermediate step in the calculation of r^2. An r^2 of at least 50 percent would seem to be desirable before placing even minor reliance on the regression line.

Earlier in this chapter the reader was warned against the practice of data mining. A somewhat similar problem results when some of the variables excluded from the model in order to make a more workable

FIGURE 3

Replacement Tire Sales "Explained" Variance

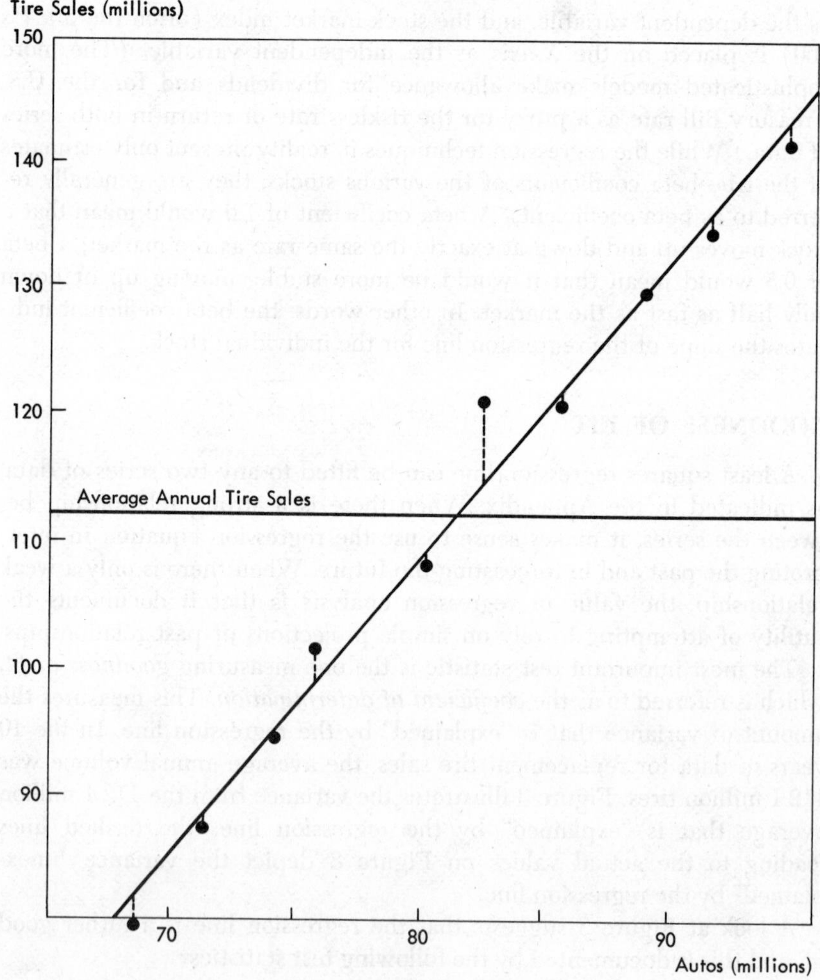

model are ones that have a strong effect on the variables included in the model. For example, if sales of General Motors cars were related to the total market for original equipment tires, there would probably be a good fit in the regression equation. However, the reason for the good fit would be due to the fact that total automobile sales have their impact on General Motors sales. Obviously the best measure is total auto production and not simply GM production alone. Thus, care in specifying the variables in the model is essential.

FORECASTING

In making practical forecasts, the analyst is especially interested in determining how accurate the forecasts are likely to be, assuming, of course, that the historical relationships persist in the future. The answer to this question is the standard error of the estimate, $S_{y,x}$, which for the replacement tire equation amounts to 2.75 million units. The standard error of the estimate is the standard deviation of the actual yearly figures for replacement tire sales around the regression line. Figure 4 depicts the regression line and dashed lines one standard deviation above the regression line and one standard deviation below the regression line. The standard error of the estimate means that 68 percent of the actual data would fall within plus or minus 2.75 million units about the regression line. Moreover, 95 percent of the actual data should be within two standard errors ($\pm 2S_{y,x}$) or within 5.5 million units. Thus, if the analyst makes a forecast of replacement tire sales for 1973, based upon an auto population of 96.4 million cars at the start of the year, the regression model provides a single figure estimate of 152.0 million replacement tires. He will be 95 percent certain that the actual figure for the year would be in the range of 146.5 million to 157.5 million tires.

PROBLEMS WITH RESIDUALS

The remainder of the test statistics found in computer generated regression analyses deal with problems which may arise from residuals or which relate to confidence limits. These test statistics are the result of highly sophisticated studies and are commended to the serious student of quantitative methods. However, there may be two test statistics which may be of at least moderate interest to the financial analyst who has access to them in his computer program.

A major problem for a financial analyst in using regression analysis is to identify when a fundamental relationship is changing. For example, the demand for replacement tires which has been extremely predictable in the past may become less so in the future if radial tires become standard equipment and if the energy crisis alters traditional driving patterns for speed and for miles driven per year. If patterns are changing,

FIGURE 4

Replacement Tire Sales—Standard Error of the Estimate $S_{y,x}$

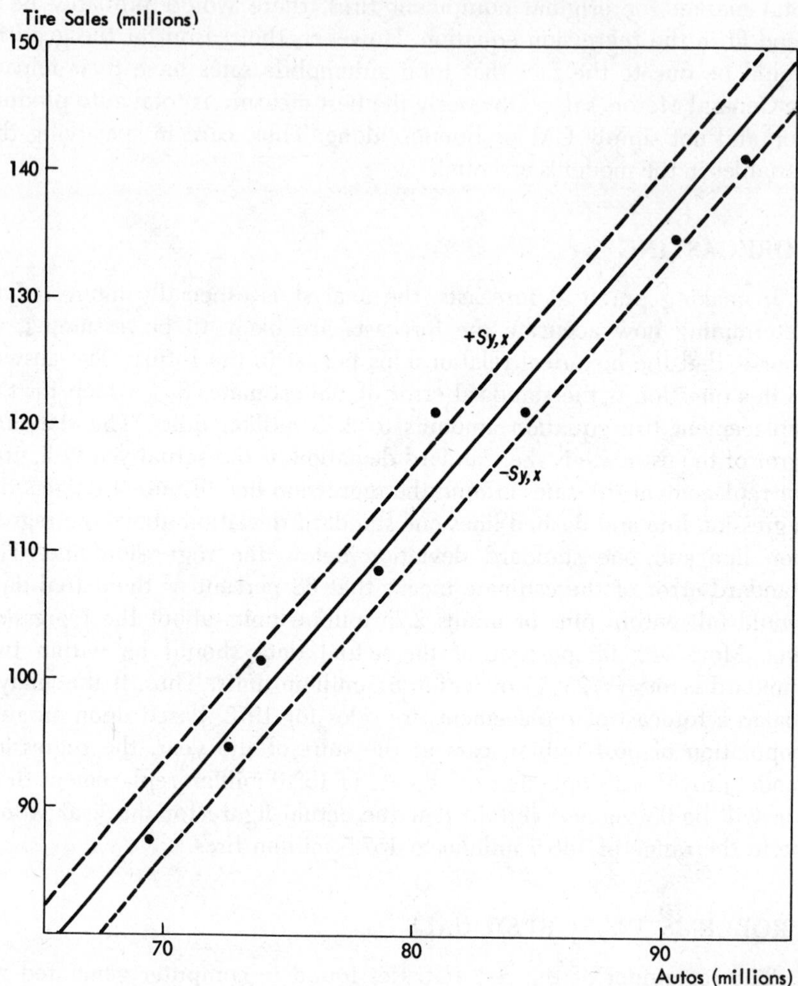

this can usually be noted from examination of a chart depicting the actual results for each year and the regression line. In order to show an exaggerated example of a changed pattern, Figure 5 shows a hypothetical company's earnings record with earnings rising from $1 per share in the first year to $2 in the second and $3 for each of the 12 remaining years in the series.

The least squares regression line represents the best fit for a straight line trend covering the 15 years of data, but quite obviously the regression line trend has no value as a predictor of future earnings growth. This is because the earnings trend has flattened out. Beyond its obvious draw-

FIGURE 5

Hypothetical Earnings Record

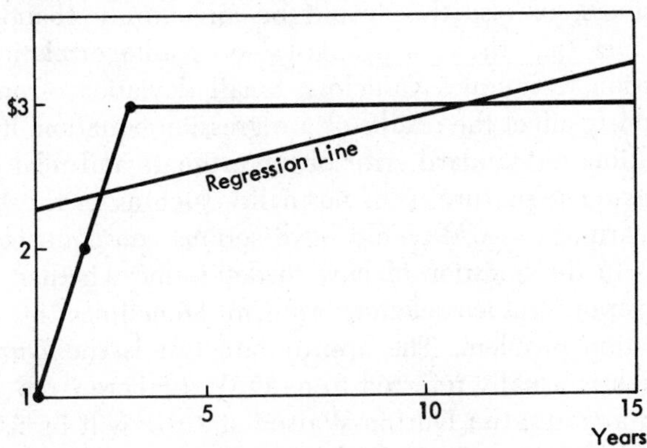

backs as a predictor, the least squares regression line is suspect since there is another force at work which has not been taken into consideration. The errors between the actual earnings figures and the trend values are not independent errors occurring at normally distributed intervals and of random size. In other words, the successive errors have a pattern of their own, each error is related to the previous one. If we tilt Figure 5 so that the trend line is horizontal, we can observe more readily the pattern of errors in this hypothetical example. This is illustrated in Figure 6.

The problem with our hypothetical illustration is termed *autocorrelation*—that is, the errors have a lagged correlation with their own past values—the error in year 3 influences the error in year 4 which influences the error in year 5 and so forth. This is not at all an uncommon occurrence. In fact, we would expect most economic series of interest to analysts to behave somewhat in this fashion. The price of a product one

FIGURE 6

Deviations from Regression Line

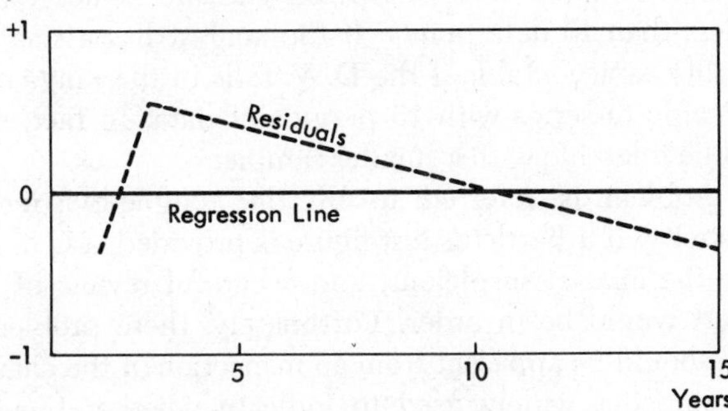

month has an influence on its price the next month; the amount of sales generated by the sales force one month does have an effect on next month's business; or else this would be an entirely chaotic economic world. The fact that there is probably some autocorrelation does not make regression techniques valueless. Small deviations from normality will not seriously affect the results of a regression equation, its coefficient of determination, its standard error of the estimate and related statistical tests; but greater departure from normality such as in the hypothetical case of the earnings record would have serious consequences.

This leads to the question of how to determine whether a particular series has a serious autocorrelation problem. Sometimes this is termed a serial correlation problem. The appropriate test is the *Durbin-Watson* statistic, which is usually referred to as D.W. If there is no autocorrelation at all in a series, the Durbin-Watson statistic will be 2.0. Thus the analyst should look for a D.W. fairly near the 2.0 mark—and in fact the great majority of series have D.W.s in the range between 1.5 and 2.5. In evaluation of a D.W., the following abbreviated table should serve in most instances:

Durbin-Watson Statistic Acceptability—5% Probability Level

Number of Data Points	*Clearly Reject*	*Clearly Accept*	*Clearly Reject*
15	1.08 or less	1.36–2.64	2.92 or more
25	1.29	1.45–2.55	2.71
50	1.50	1.59–2.41	2.50
100	1.65	1.69–2.31	2.35

The hypothetical example has a D.W. of 0.60, which is in the range of those clearly rejected. Thus the D.W. statistic efficiently brings this problem to the analyst's attention. It is then up to the analyst to determine how to adjust for the problem. Usually the best adjustment is to discard the earlier years of data and compute a regression line from the point the new forces seem to be at work. Before leaving this section, it might be noted that the Durbin-Watson statistic is not evaluated for samples of less than 15 data points. If the analyst has a smaller sample, it would qualify as acceptable if the D.W. falls in the range of 1.36–2.64 that is applicable to series with 15 periods of data. In fact, some wider range would be tolerable with a smaller sample.

Another problem is referred to by the tongue-twisting name of heteroscedasticity. If a Bartlett's test figure is provided, a Q of 4 or higher should make the analyst suspicious, and a careful review of the regression line chart would be in order. Fortunately, these problems are less common and should be apparent from an inspection of the chart.

Two test statistics widely used to indicate whether there is a true relationship or simply one which may have arisen by chance are the *t* statistic and the *F* statistic. The *t* statistic is easily interpreted. If it is 2 or more, the coefficient is significantly different from zero at the 5 percent level. This means that a *t* statistic of 2 would have arisen by chance in only 5 percent of a number of random series. The *t* statistic is useful in evaluating the coefficients in a multiple regression equation since it might identify which coefficients have value and which should be discarded in order to produce a more effective multiple regression equation.

The *F* ratio indicates whether or not it is likely that the regression equation could have arisen by chance. The *F* ratio is calculated by analyzing the variance of each observation from the mean value of its series and comparing it with the deviation about the regression line. The *F* ratio is calculated in many computer programs and even evaluated in a few. Generally, however, it is necessary to evaluate the *F* ratio by referring to a table. Most statistics texts have tables for determining the *F* ratio required to be considered significant at the 5 percent level and the higher *F* ratio required to be considered significant at the 1 percent level. The required *F* ratios vary with the size of the samples involved. The higher the *F* ratio, the more likely it is that the regression equation is meaningful and that the relationships between the two series did not arise solely by chance. If the *F* ratio is significant at the 5 percent level, this means that there is only a 5 percent chance that the relationship between the variables arose only by chance. Significance at the 1 percent level would mean that it could have arisen by chance in only one case out of 100. The 5 percent and the 1 percent levels are obviously arbitrary—and the *F* ratio might well be considered adequate by the analyst even if it did not quite meet the 5 percent level. The *F* ratio is a powerful and useful test of significance, worthy of its widespread use. It is also used in multiple regression in determining which are the strongest variables that can be used in the final equation, while weaker variables are discarded.

MULTIPLE REGRESSION

Simple regression is based upon the artificial assumption that the change in one variable—e.g., replacement tire sales—is entirely dependent upon changes in one other variable. Yet, in actual practice, most things are dependent upon a number of factors, not on one factor alone. This will require the use of multiple regression. The power of multiple regression is twofold:

1. The multiple regression equation should be a more accurate fit when compared with the actual data than in the case of a simple regression equation. In other words, there will be a lesser proportion of unexplained variance.

2. The relative importance of the various factors can be assessed and weak factors discarded.

To illustrate how multiple regression may be used to make a more effective regression equation, the following simple regression equation was calculated for a group of five fairly average electric utilities relating price/earnings ratios to the growth of the preceding five years:

$$p/e = 10.82 + 0.0027G$$

where G is the growth rate of the last five years expressed as a percentage.

This equation had a coefficient of determination of 69 percent, neither especially good nor especially bad. The coefficient for the growth rate suggests that this is only a minor influence in determining prices for electric utility stocks. However, if we add another factor, the estimated earnings growth for the coming year, the following multiple regression equation is produced:

$$P/E = 7.92 + 0.316G + 0.335G_e$$

where G_e is the estimated percent growth in the coming year.

This multiple regression equation has a multiple coefficient of determination of 98 percent, which is much improved as compared with the simple regression equation. This is illustrated by the following comparison of the theoretical P/E ratios which would have been calculated for each of the five utilities under both regression equations:

	Calculated P/E	
Actual P/E	*Multiple Regression*	*Simple Regression*
11.6	11.6	9.0
11.5	11.4	12.6
11.3	11.3	12.3
10.0	9.7	11.3
9.7	10.0	10.4

The multiple regression equation is also superior in indicating that the estimated growth in the coming year and the past growth record are both significant influences on the current valuations of the stocks.

P/E ratios are really not the most appropriate application of multiple regression analysis, but are simply presented as an illustration of the approach that might be taken to improve upon a simple regression equation in order to make it a better predictor of the future. Regression analyses should be performed for various combinations of the factors believed to influence a series. For example, if the variable to be forecast is known to be dependent upon factors A, B, and C, simple regressions could be computed for each of the three factors and multiple regressions could be computed for A and B, for A and C, and for B and C as well as for all three factors. Rates of change could also be calculated as well as partial correlations. The main idea, however, is to examine several plausible models in order to develop the most effective regression equation.

Before leaving multiple regression, it is necessary to warn against adding too many variables to the model in an attempt to improve the predictive capability of the regression analysis by raising the R^2 as high as possible. Each time an additional factor is added to a regression equation, there is a sacrifice of "degrees of freedom" which reduces the statistical significance of the regression equation. One could include a dozen factors in a multiple regression equation, but the resulting equation would probably be a poor forecasting tool. The fewer independent variables in the equation, the better. Sophisticated econometric models use a series of regression equations to come up with their final result, rather than attempting to string all of the variables in one equation. The analyst should find that he can accomplish much by using just one, two, three, or four independent variables in his equations.

SUMMARY

In simple regression it is assumed that Y is dependent upon the values for X plus an unknown random error. To make estimates of the parameters, Y is regressed on X with the residuals representing the random errors. In multiple regression it is assumed that Y is dependent upon the values for two or more factors, plus an unknown random error. Estimates are made of the coefficients for the various factors, with the residuals representing the random errors.

While the full ramifications of regression analysis are immense, the essential elements to be checked in every regression analysis are:

1. What does the regression equation mean? Values for the coefficients.
2. How much of the variance is explained? The coefficient of determination, r^2.
3. How accurate is the equation as a predictor? The standard error of the estimate.
4. Is the relationship significant or would it be likely that it arose merely by chance? Is the t statistic 2 or higher or the F statistic evaluated in a table?
5. Are there autocorrelation problems indicated by too low a Durbin-Watson statistic?

This section has covered only an introduction to the subject of regression analysis. If the analyst is working with a computer, a minicomputer, or even a sophisticated pocket calculator, the mechanics of regression analysis will be taken care of. There is no need to devise a new program for regression analysis—use the one supplied by the computer manufacturer. Attention to the five steps set forth above should keep one out of serious trouble with regression analysis. The interested analyst is referred to the following texts as starting points for delving into the world of regression analysis:

Christ, Carl F. *Econometric Models and Methods.* New York: John Wiley & Sons, 1968.

Kane, Edward J. *Economic Statistics and Econometrics.* New York: Harper & Row, 1965.

Valentine, J. L., and Mennis, E. A. *Quantitative Techniques for Financial Analysis.* Homewood, Ill.: R. D. Irwin, Inc., 1971.

APPENDIX
Simple Regression Calculations

SUMNER N. LEVINE

Regression analysis, as illustrated in the previous section, deals with the methods for deriving an equation by which one of the variables, the deepndent variable Y may be estimated from other variables, the independent variables X. In the case of simple linear regression it is assumed that the dependent variable is a linear function of only one independent variable:

$$Y = a + bX$$

Again, it must be emphasized that a regression relationship does not necessarily imply that a causal relationship exists.

Least Squares Method

Let Y_i be the observed value and Y be the value calculated by the reqression equation. As shown in Figure 7, the difference or error e_i between these values is

$$Y_i - Y = e_i$$
$$Y_i = a + bX_i + e_i.$$

The quantity e_i is considered to vary at random about the regression line with a mean value $E(e_i)$ of zero and with a constant variance $\sigma^2(e_i) = \sigma^2(y)$. The last assumption is referred to as *homoscedasticity.*

The problem is to find values of a and b in the above equation such that the sum of the squares of the error term is a minimum. This is accomplished by the *least squares method:* find an a and b such that

$$\Sigma(Y_i - a - bX_i)^2 = \sum_i e_i^2 = \text{Minimum.}$$

FIGURE 7

Regression Line, Data Points (X), and the Error (e_i) between the Data and Calculated Value.

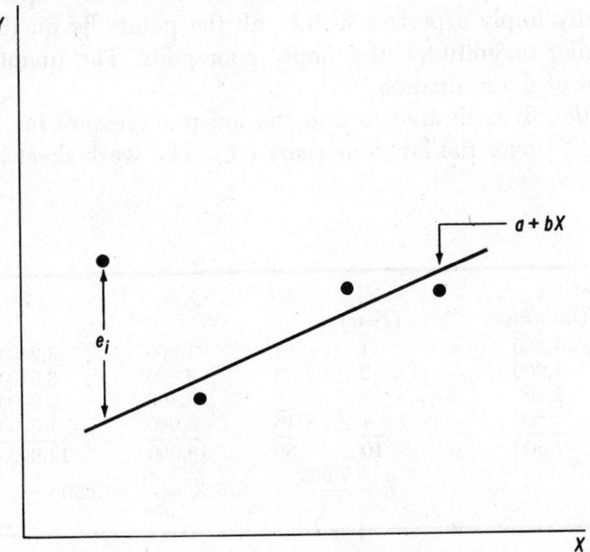

This condition is fulfilled by setting the derivative with respect to a and b of the sum equal to zero. The result is the two *normal* equations

$$\Sigma Y_i = na + b\Sigma X_i$$
$$\Sigma X_i Y_i = a\Sigma X_i + b\Sigma X_i^2.$$

These may be solved for a and b

$$a = \bar{Y} - b\bar{X}$$
$$b = \frac{\Sigma(X_i - \bar{X})(Y_i - \bar{Y})}{\sum_i (X_i - \bar{X})^2} = \frac{\text{Cov}(XY)}{\text{Var}(X)} = \frac{\Sigma X_i Y_i - n\bar{X}\bar{Y}}{\Sigma X_i^2 - n\bar{X}^2},$$

where:

$$\bar{X} = \frac{1}{n}\Sigma X_i$$
$$\bar{Y} = \frac{1}{n}\Sigma Y_i.$$

The last form on the right side is particularly convenient for purposes of calculation.

The question as to how well the regression line fits the data can be answered by means of the *correlation coefficient* defined by the expression

$$r = \frac{\Sigma X_i Y_i - n\overline{X}\overline{Y}}{[(\Sigma X_i^2 - n\overline{X})(\Sigma Y_i^2 - n\overline{Y})]^{1/2}}$$

where n is the number of observations. Values of r equal to plus or minus unity imply a perfect fit, i.e., all the points lie on the regression line. Smaller magnitudes of r imply poorer fits. The quantity r^2 is the coefficient of determination.

Example. It is desired to find the linear regression for a company's earnings (Y) over the last four years (X). The work sheet and data are given below:

Y_i (*Earnings*)	X_i (*Year*)	X^2	X_iY_i	Y^2
1,800	1	1	1,800	3,240,000
1,900	2	4	3,800	3,610,000
1,800	3	9	5,400	3,240,000
2,000	4	16	8,000	4,000,000
7,500	10	30	19,000	14,090,000

$$\bar{Y} = \frac{7{,}500}{4} = 1{,}875 \quad \bar{X} = \frac{10}{4} = 2.50$$

$$b = \frac{19{,}000 - (4)(1{,}875)(2.50)}{30 - (4)(2.50)^2} = 50$$

$$a = 1{,}875 - (50)(2.50) = 1{,}750$$

so that

$$y = 1750 + 50x$$

$$r = \frac{1{,}900 - 4(2.50)(1{,}875)}{\{[30 - 4(2.50)][(14{,}090{,}000) - 4(1{,}875)\}^{1/2}} = 0.6742$$

39

Time Series Analysis

EDWIN J. ELTON, Ph.D.
Graduate School of Business Administration
New York University
New York, New York

and

MARTIN J. GRUBER, Ph.D.
Graduate School of Business Administration
New York University
New York, New York

ONE ATTITUDE that has distinguished man from his fellow animals is his ability to record and learn from his past experience. While some of this past experience is qualitative in nature, much of it is quantitative. In this chapter we shall treat one set of techniques for extrapolating quantitative experiences into the future. The set of techniques we shall deal with are generally grouped under the title of time series analysis. The assumption made is that a series of numbers ordered over time represents the measurement of some process and that this process has inertia or continuity over time, e.g., that the pattern of past sales for a company is useful in forecasting future sales. This assumption often provides an excellent starting point for analysis. The techniques of time series analysis are simple and inexpensive to use. Nevertheless, the reader should be warned that they do not represent a replacement for human judgment. The techniques involved might have done an excellent job of forecasting buggy-whip sales prior to 1893, but they would not have been able to predict the invention of the automobile or the impact of its success on buggy-whip sales. One should think of these techniques as an inexpensive, fast, and efficient way of answering the question—what will the future be if it is a simple continuation of the past?

TIME SERIES ANALYSIS—AN INTRODUCTION

A time series is nothing more than a set of numbers ordered with respect to time. An ordered sequence of sales of a company is a time

TABLE 1

Quarterly Sales Data for a Hypothetical Department Store, 1971–75

Year	Quarter 1	2	3	4
1971	110	109	121	136
1972	118	108m	143	169
1973	119	133	156	181
1974	159	137	169	204
1975	166	150	183	230

Note: The observations are numbered 1 through 20 moving left to right, a row at a time. For example, the second quarter of 1972 is quarter 6.

series. A sequence of the quarterly earnings of a company is a time series. A time series of numbers can be described in two dimensions, one representing the numbers themselves, the other a time index indicating the order in which the numbers arose. A time series can be displayed in tabular form or in graphical form. For example, the sales for a hypothetical department store are presented in Table 1. The first date for which we have data is arbitrarily assigned the time index one and observations are consecutively numbered. A graph of the data shown in Table 1 is presented in Figure 1. A large part of this chapter shall be con-

FIGURE 1

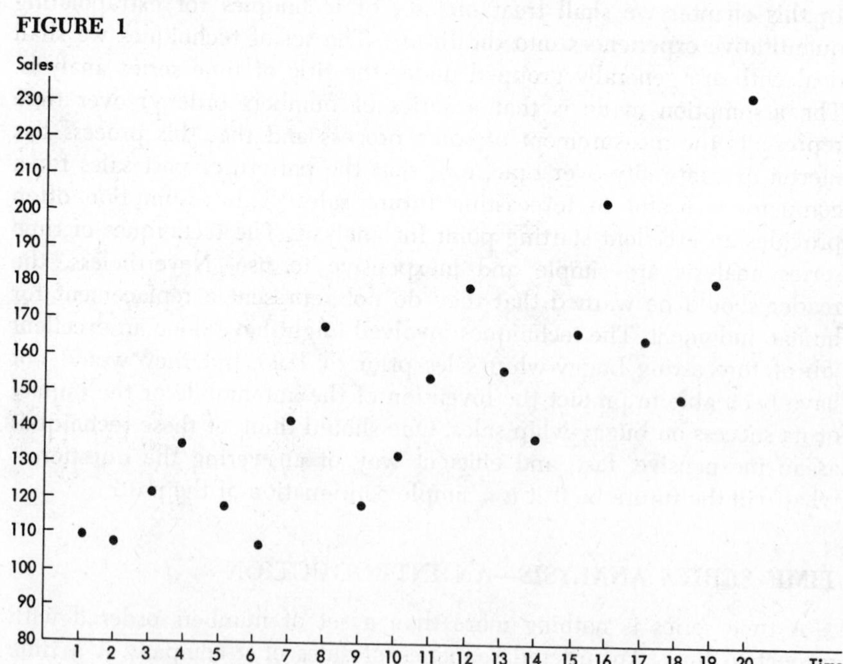

FIGURE 2

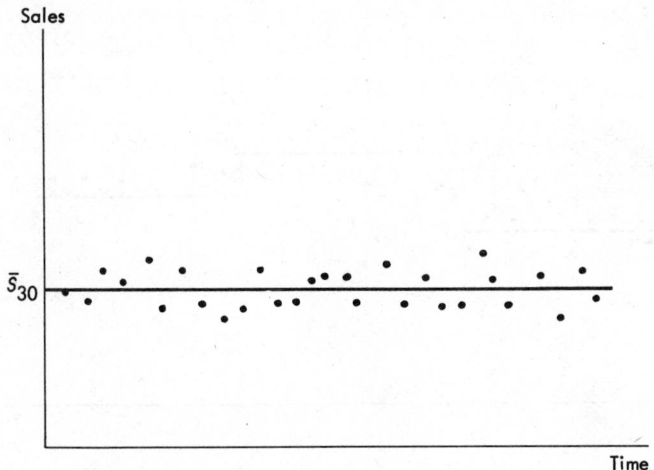

cerned with an analysis of this example, but to introduce the concept let us start out with some easier examples.

Let us assume that we wish to prepare a forecast for sales data as shown in Figure 2.[1] Notice that over time sales seem to fluctuate around a level $\bar{S}$. If one arbitrarily breaks the period up into shorter periods, the average level of sales in each of these shorter periods would be approximately the same. We can describe such a pattern as random fluctuations around a stable level of sales. For such a process deviations from the long-term average (mean) sales are unpredictable, so the best forecast we can make about any future level of sales is that they will be equal the mean value $\bar{S}$. Our problem then is to determine $\bar{S}$, the historical average level of sales. This is best done by simply averaging all past sales data. In this case:

$$\bar{S}_{30} = \sum_{i=1}^{30} \frac{S_i}{30}$$

where S_i is the yearly sales for year *i*. The more past data we have, the more sure we are about getting an estimate of $\bar{S}$ which is not affected by random noise. Since future sales are to be forecast as equal to S_{30} then,

$$\hat{S}_{30,\,T} = \bar{S}_{30}$$

where $\hat{S}_{30,\hat{T}}$ is the estimate of sales for period $30 + T$ made at time 30.

Now let us turn to a slightly more complex pattern for sales. Examine Figure 3. This figure represents a condition where sales fluctuate ran-

---

[1] The examples in this chapter deal with sales forecasts. The selection of sales rather than earnings, costs, or some other variable is simply a matter of convenience.

FIGURE 3

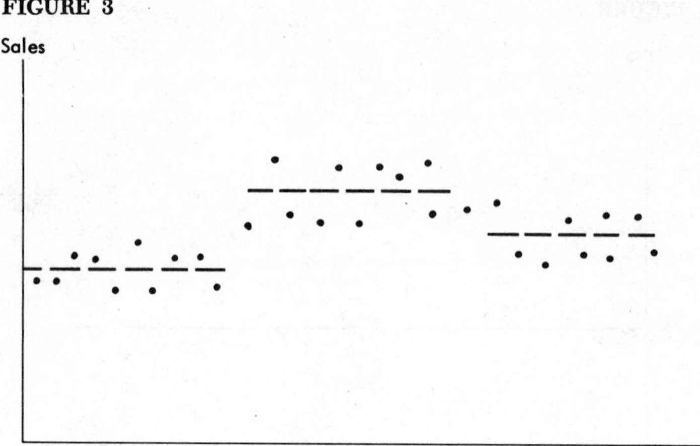

domly around a mean level but where this mean level shifts occasionally (and randomly) over time. In making a prediction, if one knew when the last shift in the mean level took place, one would estimate the future by averaging the data after the shift took place. However, when a prediction is to be made, one cannot usually differentiate between a shift in the mean and a random deviation from a stable mean. How then is one to capture shifts in the mean while still averaging out random deviations. Perhaps the most commonly used method is to employ a moving average of past data. That is, at any point estimate the future by averaging a limited amount of (rather than all) past data. Let us assume that we have decided to use a six-period moving average, then

$$\bar{S}_t = \frac{\sum_{i=t-5}^{t} S_i}{6}$$

For an n period moving average,

$$\bar{S}_t = \frac{\sum_{i=t-n+1}^{t} S_i}{n}$$

and

$$\hat{S}_{t,\,T} = \bar{S}_t.$$

That is, for an n period moving average we obtain an estimate of the future by simply averaging the last n observations on sales. As a new data point (sales level) becomes available, we simply drop the earliest observation included in the last average, add the new observation, and take a new average.[2]

An obvious question arises at this point. How do we decide on n or the length of the moving average? The choice of n involves the resolution of two conflicting goals. The larger n is the surer we are of eliminating random noise from our estimate of the average sales. However, the larger n is the longer it will take us to reflect, in our estimates, a fundamental shift in the average level of sales. If we knew how often shifts in the mean level of sales took place and how large they are relative to the random element in sales, we could resolve our difficulty. But we do not possess this knowledge and so we have to resolve the issue on empirical grounds. The procedure for doing so will be taken up in the section on the evaluation of forecasting techniques.

There is an alternative averaging technique which has found wide application in business problems—exponentially weighted averages. While a moving average places the same weight on each observation it includes, exponential smoothing places more weight on current observations than on past observations. The technique gets its name from the fact that the weights decline exponentially over time. The idea of placing more weight on current observations than past observations has great intuitive appeal. The future is expected to be more like the recent past than the far past. The exponential forecasting models evolved out of World War II research, where these models had great success in tracing and predicting the location of enemy aircraft. The exponential pattern of weights has appeal for an exponential pattern fits many real world phenomena. For example, radioactive material decays exponentially, people learn and forget in an exponential pattern.

The simplest exponential smoothing relationship is:

$$\bar{S}_t = \bar{S}_{t-1} + W_S(S_t - \bar{S}_{t-1}) \qquad (1)$$
$$\hat{S}_{t,\,T} = \bar{S}_t$$

where W_S is the weight placed on current compared to past sales ($0 \leqq W_s \leqq 1$). This model states that the best forecast of future sales is the last forecast of future sales plus some fraction of the error in the forecast. Thus, if $W_s = 0.2$, and we had forecast sales of \$100 which turned out to be \$110, our forecast for the future would be $\bar{S}_t = \$100 + 0.2(110\text{–}100) = \$102$.

Examining equation 1 it might appear that sales for only the periods t and $t-1$ are being considered. To see that this is not the case, the formula can be written as

[2] An equivalent way to update the moving average which saves computation time is to subtract $1/n$ times the earliest observation included in the test computation of the moving average from that computation and to add $1/n$ times the new observation.

$$\bar{S}_t = W_s S_t + (1 - W_s)\bar{S}_{T-1} \tag{2}$$

But

$$\bar{S}_{t-1} = W_s S_{t-1} + (1 - W_s)\bar{S}_{t-2}. \tag{3}$$

Substituting (3) into (2) yields

$$\bar{S}_t = W_s S_t + W_s(1 - W_s)S_{t-1} + (1 - W_s)^2\bar{S}_{t-2}.$$

Repetitive substitute yields

$$\bar{S}_t = \sum_{i=0}^{M-1} (W_s(1 - W_s)^i)S_{t-i} + (1 - W_s)^M S_s \tag{4}$$

where S_s represents the estimate of sales for period M.[3] An examination of equation (4) reveals that in computing $\bar{S}_t$ all past levels of sales are employed for they are embodied in $\bar{S}_{t-1}$. But note that to predict sales over time only one number $\bar{S}_t$ need be saved. All individual observation on past sales can be disregarded.[4]

So far we have ignored the question as to the proper choice for W_s. This choice is analogous to the choice of n in the simple moving average. To show this we have tabulated below the weights placed on past sales data from different periods for five alternative choices of W_s.

W_s	t	t-1	t-2	t-3	t-4	*All Previous Years*
1.0	1.0	0	0	0	0	0
0.8	0.8	0.1600	0.0320	0.0064	0.0013	0.0003
0.5	0.5	0.2500	0.1250	0.0625	0.0313	0.0157
0.2	0.2	0.1600	0.1280	0.1024	0.0819	0.0655
0.1	0.1	0.0900	0.0810	0.0729	0.0650	0.590

Notice that the smaller the W_s the more weight is placed on past data relative to recent data. Alternatively, the smaller the W_s the more likely we are to reduce the effect of random fluctuations in sales on our future forecast, but the slower we are to recognize a fundamental shift in the level of sales. As in the case of determining the optimal length moving average, the optimal exponential weight to use remains a matter of empirical investigation.

[3] To use an exponentially weighted smoothing model one has to have a starting estimate of the variable being forecast. Usually this starting estimate is obtained by averaging the first one third to one half of the data available. However, with any reasonable amount of data, forecasts will be very insensitive to the starting estimates.

[4] The ease of performing exponential smoothing, along with the limited data bank that is needed when employing this technique, has contributed greatly to its widespread use in industry as a forecasting technique.

TIME SERIES MODELS WITH SEASONAL AND TREND

Up to now we have assumed that the level of sales for a firm is stable over time except for random elements plus periodic changes in the level. But in practice most firms exhibit some long-term growth in sales, and many firms have a seasonal pattern to sales. Let us begin by examining Table 1 and Figure 1. Notice that in Figure 1 sales tend to move upward over time. This can be seen by analyzing the average quarterly sales for each of the five years. Average quarter sales are:

	1971	*1972*	*1973*	*1974*	*1975*
Sales	\$119.00	\$134.50	\$147.25	\$167.25	\$182.25

In each year average quarterly sales are higher than they were in the previous year, demonstrating the need for some type of adjustment for growth in making forecasts.

One would also expect to find some type of seasonal pattern in department store sales. Sales at and around Christmas are usually higher than at any other time of the year. Thus one would expect to see average sales for the fourth quarter higher than sales in any of the three previous quarters. Furthermore, third quarter sales should probably be higher than sales for either of the previous two quarters as pre-Christmas sales begin to build up. Such a pattern is found in the data under study. The average sales over the five years under study for each quarter are:

	Quarter			
	1	*2*	*3*	*4*
Average sales	\$134.40	\$127.40	\$154.40	\$184.00

If one were to predict sales for any quarter without considering the seasonal influence, one would overestimate sales in quarter 1 and 2 and underestimate sales in quarter 3 and 4.

We will first examine models that adjust for trend and then models that adjust for trend and seasonal.

Time Series Model with Trend

If the variable being forecast is expected to grow over time, a term to allow for this growth should be included in the forecasting model. While there are several patterns that growth might take, the two most popular patterns are that the variable grows by a constant amount each period (additive growth) or by a constant percent each period (multiplicative growth). For example, the following series illustrate additive growth.

	Period				
	1	*2*	*3*	*4*	*5*
Sales...............	\$100	\$110	\$120	\$130	\$140

The growth per period is simply \$10. If we wanted to forecast sales for period 6, the best forecast would be \$140 + \$10 = \$150. For period 7, \$140 + 2(\$10) = \$160, or for period 5 + n, \$140 + n(\$10).

The following series demonstrates multiplicative growth.

	Period				
	1	*2*	*3*	*4*	*5*
Sales..............	\$100.00	\$110.00	\$121.00	\$133.10	\$146.40

Sales grow by 10 percent per period. The best forecast of sales per period 6 would be \$146.40(1.10) = \$161.00. The best forecast of sales for period 5 + n would be \$146.40$(1.10)^n$.

The choice of the proper assumption concerning growth can often be made by an inspection of the data. Figure 4 shows the pattern that sales would follow for additive and multiplicative growth. Below we will examine time series that allow for growth.

Exponential Models. An exponential model incorporating an additive trend is quite simple to construct. To do so, define the following symbols:

S_t = The sales per share at time t.
$\bar{S}_t$ = The exponentially weighted average of past sales per share at time t.
$\hat{S}_{t,T}$ = The estimate of sales per share made at time t for period $t + T$.
W_s = The weight placed on current versus past sales per share, $0 \leq W_s \leq 1$.
$\bar{R}_t$ = The exponential weighted average of past growth at time t.
W_R = The weight placed on current versus past growth $0 \leq W_R \leq 1$.

In the absence of trend we said that

$$\bar{S}_t = \bar{S}_{t-1} + W_s(S_t - \bar{S}_{t-1}).$$

But if we have an additive trend the sales between periods are expected to grow by an amount $\bar{R}_{t-1}$. Thus sales at time t are expected to be $(\bar{S}_{t-1} + \bar{R}_{t-1})$ and the relevant error in the last forecast is

$$S_t - (\bar{S}_{t-1} + \bar{R}_{t-1}),$$

FIGURE 4

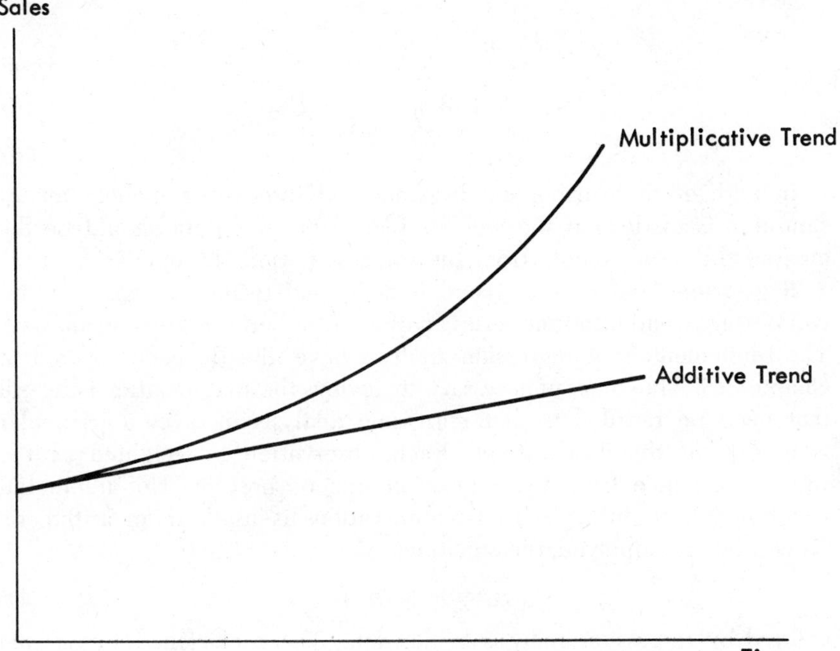

and the equation for arriving at S_t is

$$\bar{S}_t = (\bar{S}_{t-1} + \bar{R}_{t-1}) + W_s\,[S_t - (\bar{S}_{t-1} + \bar{R}_{t-1})] \quad (5)$$

This, like the earlier equation, simply states that we correct our latest estimate of average sales by some fraction of the error in our last forecast.

However, we now need an estimate of $\bar{R}_{t-1}$ or the amount of growth. Again we simply update our last estimate of $\bar{R}_{t-1}$ by how bad this estimate was, or

$$\bar{R}_t = \bar{R}_{t-1} + W_R\,[(\bar{S}_t - \bar{S}_{t-1}) - \bar{R}_{t-1}]. \quad (6)$$

Notice that a new smoothing coefficient W_R has been introduced. There is no reason why W_R should equal W_s. Methods for determining W_R and W_s will be discussed in a later section of this chapter.

To complete the model we need the following equation, which simply expresses the fact that sales in the future are expected to grow by an amount R_t per period, or

$$\hat{S}_{t,\,T} = \bar{S}_t + T\bar{R}_t. \quad (7)$$

The exponential model incorporating a multiplicative trend is directly analogous to the model incorporating additive trend. The difference is that R_t now stands for one plus the expected rate of growth in sales so that sales are expected to increase by R_{t-1} percent each period. Thus the model is

$$\bar{S}_t = \bar{S}_{t-1}\bar{R}_{t-1} + W_s(S_t - \bar{S}_{t-1}\bar{R}_{T-1}) \tag{8}$$

$$\bar{R}_t = \bar{R}_{t-1} + W_R\left(\frac{\bar{S}_t}{\bar{S}_{t-1}} - \bar{R}_{t-1}\right) \tag{9}$$

$$\hat{S}_{t,T} = \bar{S}_t(\bar{R}_t)^T \tag{10}$$

In both of these exponentially smoothed forecasting models, an assumption is made that the weights placed on past data should be decreased the more remote from the forecast period the data is.

Regression Models. A second widely used technique exists for incorporating trend into time series analysis: time series regression analysis. The fundamentals of regression analysis have already been covered in Chapter 18. Thus it is unnecessary to review the mathematics here. All that need be recalled is that regression analysis involves a particular weighting of the observations. Each observation is weighted as the squared distance from the regression line of best fit. No differential weighting of recent versus past observations is used. If an arithmetic growth rate is employed, the equation[5]

$$S_t = a + Rt + e \tag{11}$$

is fitted by regression analysis to the data. The coefficient R represents the dollar amount by which sales are expected to grow each period. A forecast for any period is made by computing the value of the dependent value (S) forecast by the regression equation for the appropriate period. Thus,

$$\hat{S}_{t,\,T} = a + R(t + T) \tag{12}$$

If multiplicative growth is assumed, then the appropriate regression equation is

$$\ell n\ S_t = a + R_t + e, \tag{13}$$

where $\ell n\ S_t$ represents the natural logarithm of S_t. Here R represents the rate of growth in sales per period.[6] The forecast of future sales is obtained by taking the antilog of this equation evaluated at the forecast date $t + T$, or

$$\ell n\ \hat{S}_{t,T} = a + R(t + T)$$

or

$$\hat{S}_{t,T} = e^{a+R(t+T)}. \tag{14}$$

[5] a is the intercept value, R is the slope coefficient, and e is the random error term.

[6] This can easily be demonstrated. Differentially, the equation with respect to t yields $\frac{\partial S_t/S_t}{\partial t} = R$ or the *rate* of change of S with respect to t equals R.

Up to this point we have ignored an important question. How much past data should we use in running the regression. Once again we are faced with the same type of problem we encountered when examining the length of the optimum moving average or the proper weights to use in the exponential smoothing models. The more data we use the more we smooth out random fluctuations but the more likely we are to miss a change in the underlying pattern of sales.

Having discussed the major time series forecasting models incorporating trend, let us now turn to an examination of seasonal influences.

Adding a Seasonal

Earlier we recognized that department store sales might be subject to seasonal influences. Another example of seasonal influences might be a firm engaged in the sale of ice cream. Here sales would reach their peak during the summer months and decline until the start of warm weather in the spring. The general pattern of seasonal influences can usually be specified by the forecaster. The type of data involved limits the type of seasonal influences which can be studied. For example, in our department store example, we have assumed that quarterly data was available, hence the data can reflect at most four seasonal influences. If monthly data had been available, the existence of 12 distinct seasonals could be checked. Now let us turn to the exponential models and to the regression models and see how seasonal influences can be incorporated.

Exponential Smoothing Models. The most widely used method of formulating exponentially smoothed forecasts with seasonals involves estimating the seasonal influence, removing the seasonal influence to estimate the smoothed sales series ($\overline{S}_t$), and then reintroducing seasonal influence when forecasting. There will be one seasonal adjustment factor for each season. For example, if there are L seasons to the year, we will have one seasonal factor for each of the L periods. Each seasonal is reestimated only when we observe data from that period. For example, the spring seasonal is reestimated only when spring sales are observed. Define F_{t-L} as the estimate of the seasonal factor as of period $t - L$. If there are L seasons to the year, and we are determining the seasonally adjustment factor for period t, the last estimate of the seasonal adjustment we will have is from period $t - L$. For example, if we are smoothing sales as of the spring quarter 1973, the last estimate we have of the seasonal factor for the spring quarter was calculated four quarters ago, in the spring of 1972.

Seasonal factors may enter a model either additively or multiplicatively. That is, each Christmas season we may expect sales to be up by the same dollar amount or by the same percentage of average sales. We present below models combining trend with both types of seasonal influence.

In order to incorporate a multiplicative seasonal into the models discussed earlier, one must modify the equation estimating normal sales and add an equation updating the seasonal. The equation for normal sales is modified by deseasonalizing actual sales. Since with a multiplicative seasonal, sales are some proportion of normal sales we deseasonalize sales by dividing by this proportion. If sales in a season are two times normal, we divide actual sales by two. If sales in a season are 0.5 normal, we divide by 0.5. For a multiplicative trend, the equation for normal sales becomes

$$\bar{S}_t = \bar{S}_{t-1}\bar{R}_{t-1} + W_s\left(\frac{S_t}{\bar{F}_{t-L}} - \bar{S}_{t-1}\bar{R}_{t-1}\right), \tag{15}$$

where F_{t-L} is the latest estimate of the proportion of normal sales which occur in the season which exists at time t. Notice that the subscript on F indicates that the latest estimate was obtained in the same season one year earlier. With an additive trend the equation for normal sales becomes

$$\bar{S}_t = (\bar{S}_{t-1} + \bar{R}_{t-1}) + W_s\left[\frac{S_t}{\bar{F}_{t-L}} - (\bar{S}_{t-1} + \bar{R}_{t-1})\right], \tag{16}$$

Having computed smoothed sales for period t, we can now update our estimate of smoothed seasonals and smoothed trend. The smoothed seasonal is simply our estimate of the smoothed seasonal one year earlier, plus some fraction (W_F) of how wrong this estimate was.[7]

$$\bar{F}_t = \bar{F}_{t-L} + W_F\left(\frac{S_t}{\bar{S}_t} - \bar{F}_{t-L}\right) \tag{17}$$

The equation updating the smoothed trend remains the same as it was in the nonseasonal model. That is, for a multiplicative trend, it is

$$\bar{R}_t = \bar{R}_{t-1} + W_R\left(\frac{\bar{S}_t}{\bar{S}_{t-1}} - \bar{R}_{t-1}\right), \tag{18}$$

while for an additive trend, it is

$$\bar{R}_t = \bar{R}_{t-1} + W_R[(\bar{S}_t - \bar{S}_{t-1}) - \bar{R}_{t-1}]. \tag{19}$$

Notice that S_t has been deseasonalized (has had seasonal influences removed). We want a forecast of sales for any future period to incorporate seasonal influences so that the sales forecasting equation becomes:

$$\hat{S}_{t,T} = \bar{S}_t\bar{R}_t{}^T\bar{F}_j \text{ (for multiplicative trend)} \tag{20}$$

$$\hat{S}_{t,T} = (\bar{S}_t + T\bar{R}_t)\bar{F}_j \text{ (for additive trend),} \tag{21}$$

[7] For more accurate results the model should contain a constraint to insure that the seasonal adjustments do not incorporate trend elements. The easiest way to do this is to constrain the sum of weights over any year to be equal to 1. Procedures for constraining seasonal weights can be found in [5]. (Note: Numbers in brackets refer to references given at the end of this chapter.)

where F_j represents our latest estimate of the seasonal influence for the season which occurs in period $t + T$.

In order to incorporate an additive seasonal in the models discussed earlier on, one must modify the equation estimating normal sales and add an equation updating the seasonal. With an additive seasonal, sales are normal sales plus the seasonal. Thus sales are deseasonalized by subtracting the seasonal. For a multiplicative trend, the equation for normal sales becomes:

$$\bar{S}_t = \bar{S}_{t-1}\bar{R}_{t-1} + W_s[(S_t - \bar{F}_{t-L}) - \bar{S}_{t-1}\bar{R}_{t-1})] \quad (22)$$

where F_{t-L} is the latest estimate of the number of units by which sales for the season which occurs at time t differ from normal sales. With an additive trend the equation for normal sales is:

$$\bar{S}_t = (\bar{S}_{t-1} + \bar{R}_{t-1}) + W_s[(S_t - \bar{F}_{t-L}) - (\bar{S}_{t-1} + \bar{R}_{t-1})]. \quad (23)$$

The seasonal component can be updated by

$$\bar{F}_t = \bar{F}_{t-L} + W_F[(S_t - \bar{S}_t) - \bar{F}_{t-L}], \quad (24)$$

and the trend is updated by either equation (18) or (19), depending on whether the trend is multiplicative or additive.

In forecasting, the seasonal factor should be reintroduced. Thus,

$$\hat{S}_{t,T} = \bar{S}_t + T\bar{R}_t + \bar{F}_j \text{ (for additive trend)} \quad (25)$$
$$\hat{S}_{t,T} = \bar{S}_t\bar{R}_t{}^T + \bar{F}_j \text{ (for multiplicative trend),} \quad (26)$$

where F_j is the latest estimate from the season that prevails at time $t + T$, the period for which the forecast is prepared.

Regression Models. The standard technique for incorporating seasonal influences into regression analysis is through the use of dummy variables. The previous regression equation we employed (for the additive trend case) was

$$S_t = a + R(t) + e.$$

In this expression, a represented the intercept or the value of expected sales at the first instant of time in the study, and R represented the slope coefficient or the amount that sales were expected to increase over each period. If seasonals are present, certain seasons would always fall above this line. Figure 5 illustrates a hypothetical two seasons' sales pattern for a product. If a regression is run ignoring the seasonal pattern, the solid line in Figure 5 would be obtained. The intercept a would be too large for the winter season and too small for the summer season. What we want is two separate intercepts, one for each season. This is obtained by introducing a dummy variable d_1 for the summer season. This variable takes on the value 1 for an observation for the summer season and is otherwise equal to zero. The regression equation then is

$$S_t = a' + R(t) + \alpha_1 d_1,$$

FIGURE 5

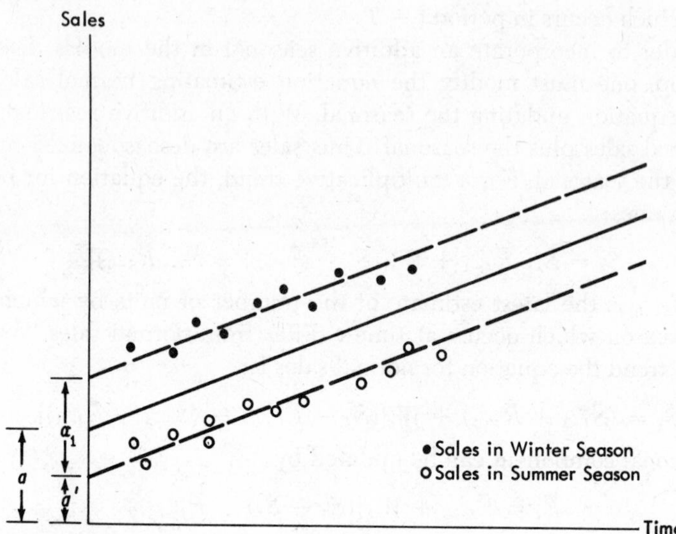

where a', R and α_1 are regression coefficients. The intercept for a summer month is then a (for $d_1 = 0$) and for a winter month, $a + \alpha_1$ (for $d_1 = 1$). The coefficient α_1 is the average difference between sales in the summer and winter months.[8] Notice that to incorporate two seasons we only have to use one dummy variable. This is because the intercept term itself, a', represents the intercept value for one season. Thus, in our present problem with four seasons the regression model becomes:

$$S_t = a' + Rt + \alpha_1 d_1 + \alpha_2 d_2 + \alpha_3 d_3 + e \tag{27}$$

To forecast for any period $t + T$, one simply computes $\hat{S}_{t,T} = a' + R(t + T) +$ correct α. If one were forecasting for the season associated with the second dummy variable, one would use[9]

$$S_t = a' + R(t + T) + \alpha_2.$$

The incorporation of a multiplicative seasonal with the multiplicative regression is directly analogous to the case just discussed. One simply uses

$$\ell n\, S_t = a' + Rt + \alpha_1 d_1 + \alpha_2 d_2 + \alpha_3 d_3 + e. \tag{28}$$

Before proceeding with a discussion of the implementation of these models, it seems appropriate to employ them to solve a simple example.

---

[8] If d_1 was assigned a value of 1 for the winter months, the model would hold. The results would be identical except that α_1 would be a negative number.

[9] Once again the association of a particular dummy variable with a particular season is totally arbitrary. All the researcher must do is be consistent in using the appropriate dummy variable when forecasting.

ILLUSTRATION OF TECHNIQUES

In this section we shall apply the techniques of exponentially smoothed moving averages and regression analysis to the simple example presented in Table 1 and Figure I in order to demonstrate their use. In illustrating the models, we shall use all available data for the regression technique and shall employ weighting coefficient of 0.3 for each weight in the exponential smoothing techniques.[10] For all techniques we will assume that we are attempting to estimate quarterly sales for 1976 as of the end of 1975.

Exponential Smoothing Model with Additive Trend and Seasonal

The three equations needed to compute the exponentially smoothed average of sales with an additive trend and seasonal are:

$$\bar{S}_t = \bar{S}_{t-1} + \bar{R}_{t-1} + W_s[(S_t - \bar{F}_{t-L}) - (\bar{S}_{t-1} + \bar{R}_{t-1})]$$
$$\bar{F}_t = \bar{F}_{t-L} + W_F[(S_t - \bar{S}_t) - \bar{F}_{t-L}]$$
$$\bar{R}_t = \bar{R}_{t-1} + W_R[(\bar{S}_t - \bar{S}_{t-1}) - \bar{R}_{t-1}]$$

In order to employ exponentially weighted averaging models, one must have starting estimates for S, R, and each of the four seasonals. These starting estimates are arrived at by simply averaging past data. Let us assume that the starting estimates for our problem are $\bar{S}_0 = 118$, $\bar{R}_0 = 2$, $\bar{F}_0 = +30$, $\bar{F}_{-1} = +5$, $\bar{F}_{-2} = -20$, $\bar{F}_{-3} = -20$.

We can then proceed to employ formulas starting with the first period for which we have data; period 1

$$\bar{S}_1 = \bar{S}_0 + \bar{R}_0 + 0.3[(S_t - \bar{F}_{-3}) - (\bar{S}_0 + \bar{R}_0)]$$
$$\bar{S}_1 = 118 + 2 + 0.3[(110 + 20) - (118 + 2)] = 123$$
$$\bar{F}_1 = \bar{F}_{-3} + 0.3[(S_t - \bar{S}_t) - \bar{F}_{t-L}]$$
$$\bar{F}_1 = -20 + 0.3[(110 - 123) + 20] = -17.9$$
$$\bar{R}_1 = \bar{R}_0 + 0.3[(\bar{S}_1 - \bar{S}_0) - \bar{R}_{t-1}]$$
$$\bar{R}_1 = 2 + 0.3[(123 - 118) - 2] = 2.9$$
$$\bar{S}_2 = 123 + 2.9 + 0.3[(109 + 20) - (123 + 2.9)] = 126.83$$
$$\bar{F}_2 = -20 + 0.3[(109 - 126.82) + 20] = -19.35$$
$$\bar{R}_2 = 2.9 + 0.3[(126.83 - 123) - 2.9] = 3.179$$

The results of the remaining calculations are shown in Table 2. In order to prepare forecasts for the future, the following values are needed: $\bar{S}_{20} = 188.87$, $\bar{R}_{20} = 4.85$, $\bar{F}_{17} = -12.10$, $\bar{F}_{18} = -22.51$, $\bar{F}_{19} = +3.71$, $\bar{F}_{20} = +31.25$.

The forecasting model that should be used with the additive model is:

$$\hat{S}_{t,T} = \bar{S}_t + R_t{}^T + \text{The appropriate seasonal.}$$

[10] The lengths and weights were selected on a completely ad hoc basis, merely to illustrate the techniques.

TABLE 2

Smoothed Sales, Trend, and Seasonal from an Exponential Smoothing Model with Additive Trend and Seasonal

Time Period (t)	S_t	R_t	F_t			
1.						
2.						
3.	125.81	1.92			2.06	
4.	121.21	0.04				25.44
5.	125.65	1.36	−14.83			
6.	127.11	1.39		−19.42		
7.	132.23	2.51			4.67	
8.	137.39	3.31				27.29
9.	138.64	2.69	−16.27			
10.	144.66	3.69		−17.09		
11.	149.24	3.96			5.30	
12.	153.35	4.01				28.63
13.	162.73	5.62	−12.51			
14.	164.07	4.33		−20.09		
15.	166.99	3.91			4.33	
16.	172.23	4.31				29.59
17.	177.13	4.49	−12.10			
18.	178.16	3.45		−22.51		
19.	180.73	3.14			3.71	
20.	188.87	4.85				31.25

Thus, the forecast for the first quarter of 1976 is

$$\hat{S}_{20,1} = 188.87 + 4.85 - 12.10 = 181.62$$

Furthermore,

$$\hat{S}_{20,2} = 188.87 + 2(4.85) - 22.51 = 176.06$$
$$\hat{S}_{20,3} = 188.87 + 3(4.85) + 3.71 = 207.13$$
$$\hat{S}_{20,4} = 188.87 + 4(4.85) + 31.25 = 239.52$$

Exponential Smoothing Model with Multiplicative Trend and Seasonal

The three equations needed to compute the exponential smoothed average of sales with a multiplicative trend and seasonal are

$$\bar{S}_t = \bar{S}_{t-1}\bar{R}_{t-1} + W_s\left(\frac{S_t}{\bar{F}_{t-1}} - \bar{S}_{t-1}\bar{R}_{t-1}\right)$$

$$\bar{F}_t = \bar{F}_{t-L} + W_F\left(\frac{S_t}{\bar{S}_t} - \bar{F}_{t-L}\right)$$

$$\bar{R}_t = \bar{R}_{t-1} + W_R\left(\frac{\bar{S}_t}{\bar{S}_{t-1}} - \bar{R}_{t-1}\right)$$

Let us assume starting estimates for the problem of $\bar{S}_0 = 118$, $\bar{R}_0 = 1.02$, $\bar{F}_0 = 1.25$, $\bar{F}_{-1} = 1.05$, $\bar{F}_{-2} = 0.85$, and $\bar{F}_{-3} = 0.85$. Again assuming values of 0.3 for all smoothing coefficients, we can then proceed to employ the model starting with the first period for which we have data, or

$$\bar{S}_1 = 118(1.02) + 0.3\left[\frac{110}{0.85} - 118(1.02)\right] = 123.10$$

$$\bar{F}_1 = 0.85 + 0.3\left[\frac{110}{123.1} - 0.85\right] = 0.863$$

$$\bar{R}_1 = 1.02 + 0.3\left[\frac{123.1}{118} - 1.02\right] = 1.027$$

$$\bar{S}_2 = 123.1(1.027) + 0.3\left[\frac{109}{0.85} - 123.1(1.027)\right] = 127.0$$

$$\bar{F}_2 = 0.85 + 0.3\left[\frac{109}{127} - 0.85\right] = 0.85$$

$$\bar{R}_2 = 1.027 + 0.3\left[\frac{127.0}{123.1} - 1.027\right] = 1.029$$

The calculations could be continued, producing a set of forecasts as in the additive case.

Regression Models

The first regression model we discussed involved an additive trend and could be represented as

$$S_t = a' + Rt + \alpha_1 d_1 + \alpha_2 d_2 + \alpha_3 d_3.$$

Letting $d_1 = 1$ for the second quarter, $d_2 = 1$ for the third quarter, and $d_4 = 1$ for the fourth quarter yields the following result when the model is fitted to our example.[11]

$$S_t = 98.57 + 3.98t - 10.98d_1 + 12.04d_2 + 37.66d_3$$

The forecasts for the future from this model are

$$\begin{aligned} S_{21} &= 98.57 + 3.98(21) &&= 182.15 \\ S_{22} &= 98.57 + 3.98(22) - 10.98 &&= 175.15 \\ S_{23} &= 98.57 + 3.98(23) + 12.04 &&= 202.15 \\ S_{24} &= 98.57 + 3.98(24) + 37.66 &&= 231.75 \end{aligned}$$

The forecasted results while close to those produced by the additive exponential model are different. The forecasts are higher for the first quarter but lower for the next three quarters.

The results yielded by the log regression model were[12]

[11] The coefficient of determination was 0.97. The authors wish to warn the reader that a high correlation coefficient for a model does not necessarily indicate that it is a good forecasting model. The seasonal coefficients were all significantly different from zero at the 0.10 level, indicating that seasonal influences are really present.

[12] The coefficient of determination was 0.976, and all the seasonals were statistically significant at the 0.01 level.

$$\ell n\, S_t = 4.648 + 0.026t - 0.74d_1 + 0.090d_2 + 0.234d_3.$$

The forecasts for the next four quarters from this model are:

$$S_{21} = e^{4.648+(0.026)21} = 181.91$$
$$S_{22} = 173.51$$
$$S_{23} = 209.85$$
$$S_{24} = 248.72$$

Once again there are differences in the forecasts produced by these techniques. This example has been included to demonstrate the use of these forecasting techniques. After a discussion of selecting optimum weights and methods of evaluating forecasts, we shall return to an evaluation of the use of the alternating time series models in a real problem—forecasting earnings.

THE PARAMETERIZATION OF THE MODELS

Earlier we raised the issue that in using any mechanical forecasting model one must resolve the dilemma that high weights or short time spans make the model responsive to fundamental shifts in the data but that they do a poor job of removing random noise. The tradeoff between the dampening out of random influences and the response of a model to long-term changes is a difficult one to make. If one understood the true nature of the process generating data, then the forecasting model could be an exact replica of this process. But because we almost never have this type of information, the dilemma must be decided on empirical grounds. The method which has worked best in forecasting several types of data is to find the length of moving averages, or regression, or the weights in an exponential smoothing model which do the best job of forecasting over some period for which we have results and assume that this same length or set of weights will continue to do the best job in the future.

For example, assume that using the simplest exponentially weighted moving average $\bar{S}_t = \bar{S}_{t-1} + W_s(S_t - \bar{S}_{t-1})$, we want to prepare a forecast for the year 1975 employing data through 1974. Also assume that data is available starting in 1960. We might then prepare forecasts for 1970 using all possible values for W_s on data through 1969, forecasts for 1971 using all possible values for W_s on data through 1970, and so on up to forecasts for 1974.[13] We could then examine which value of W_S had the smallest error in forecasting for the period 1970–74 and assume that that value was the best for forecasting 1975.[14] The assumption being

[13] Since W_s can take on all values between zero and one, there are an infinite number of values that can be tried. However, exponential smoothing models are reasonably insensitive to changes in weights in the optimum region, trying increments of 0.1 or at most 0.01 should prove efficient for almost all problems.

[14] The criteria for deciding on which forecast is best will be discussed in great detail in Section IV of this chapter. For now the reader can assume that we are using the minimization of the squared error as a criterion.

made here is that the mixture of random noise and fundamental shifts in the data is relatively constant over time so that the time span or weighing factor that did the best forecasting job in the past (represented the best compromise between these two elements) will do the best job in the future.

Parallel techniques can be used for all of the forecasting methods under discussion. For moving averages and regression techniques, one simply searches for the optimum length. For the exponential models, particularly those that employ trend and seasonal, one has to do a large search since there are three weights employed. Thus, for example, if a search is made at weight increments of 0.10, one has to try 1,331 sets of weights. However, a repetitive approximation technique has been found which reduces the number of calculations to a reasonable level.[15]

EVALUATION OF FORECASTING TECHNIQUES

The age of the computer has meant an information explosion. Most organizations are bombarded with forecasts from internal and external sources. It is increasingly difficult to intelligently analyze all information (much of which is contradictory) and come up with rational conclusions. In the light of this it has become even more important to systematically evaluate forecasting and forecasters. It has been our experience that such systematic evaluation will lead to a significant reduction in the amount of information that need be examined in the future.

A forecast or forecasting technique or source of forecasts can most meaningfully be evaluated on a comparative basis. An example presented in the last section of this chapter highlights the problem of trying to evaluate a set of forecasts in isolation. In Table 8 we present the results of three sources of analysts' forecasts along with time series forecasts for the same companies. A sample of financial institutions revealed that the firm labeled Investment Advisory Service was believed to produce one of the best sets of forecasts in the financial community. In fact, if we look at the errors in this company's forecasts we find that their analysts did in fact produce forecasts with lower errors than the other two institutions. However, when the forecasts of the analysts at these three companies were compared to a simple time series projection of past earnings, the analysts of the Investment Advisory Service did worse than the analysts at the other two institutions. In short, the Investment Advisory Service made their reputation by only following companies which had earnings' patterns that were easy to forecast. Once the mechanical time series forecasts had been introduced so that comparative analysis could be performed, this became clear.

---

[15] See Elton and Gruber [11] for a discussion of alternative techniques for deciding upon optimum weights.

The time series models presented in the first part of this chapter represent a good set of bench marks against which to compare the accuracy of other forecasting techniques. However, other more naïve techniques also represent a good standard of comparison. The simplest bench mark is the no change model. That is, forecast the future as the last observed value of the variable being forecast. A second bench mark is to forecast the future as the last observed value plus the last observed charge in the variable of interest. Still another good bench mark is to use a growth rate based on the economy average. For example, when evaluating forecasts of earnings growth rates, assume that earnings for each company will grow at the same rate as the economy grows. Finally, forecasts from a second source, such as forecasts purchased outside the firm, are a good bench mark. Having discussed some bench marks for comparative analysis, let us turn to the techniques for evaluating forecasts.

Geometric Analysis

One of the simplest and most effective ways to analyze forecast errors is to plot actual change versus predicted change in two dimensional space. An example of this graph is shown in Figure 6 for earnings per share. An estimate of the change in earnings per share is plotted against actual change in earnings per share.

An estimate for each firm's change in earnings per share can be plotted in this space. Its location in the space tells a great deal about

FIGURE 6

Diagram for Analyzing Forecasts

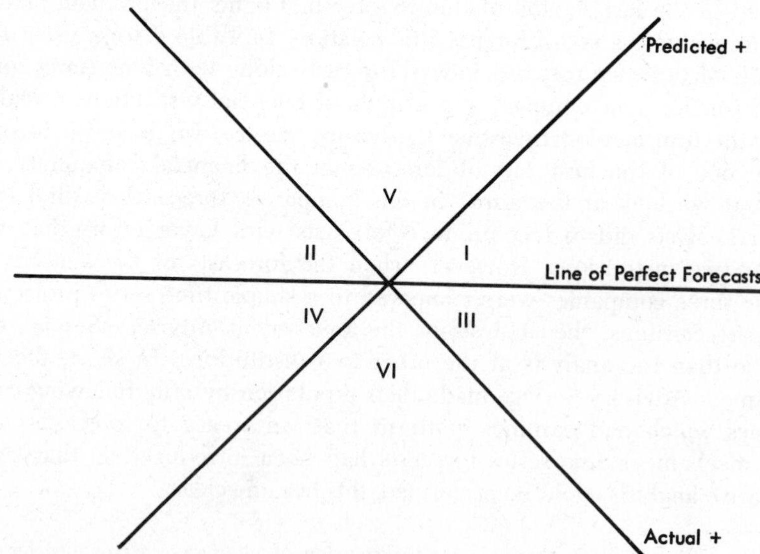

the type of error being made. For example, if an estimate lies in Section 1 of the graph, it indicates that the forecaster successfully predicted that earnings would increase but he overestimated the size of the increase. A point in Section 2 indicates that he correctly estimated a decrease in earnings but underestimated the size of the decrease. A point in Section 5 represents an estimate of an earnings increase when earnings actually decreased. The remaining three sections are analogous to those just discussed. Section 3 represents an underestimate of earnings change when earnings were growing; Section 4, an overestimate of a decrease in earnings; and Section 6, an estimate of a decrease in earnings when they were actually growing.

This graph can also be viewed as a diagrammatic representation of the level of earnings. A point in Section 1, 2, or 5 represents an overestimate of the level of earnings. A point in Section 3, 4, or 6 represents an underestimate. The further a point is from the horizontal axis, the worse the overestimate (or underestimate) is.

Examination of a group of forecasts on this graph can yield quite a lot of information about forecast accuracy and the sources of mistakes. Let us examine two examples.

Figure 7 presents the case of a firm where analysts are consistently overoptimistic. They tend to overestimate the change when the change in earnings is positive (Section 1) and either to underestimate the change in earnings (Section 2) or to actually predict a positive change (Section 5) when the change in earnings is negative.

FIGURE 7
Representation of Overoptimistic Forecasts

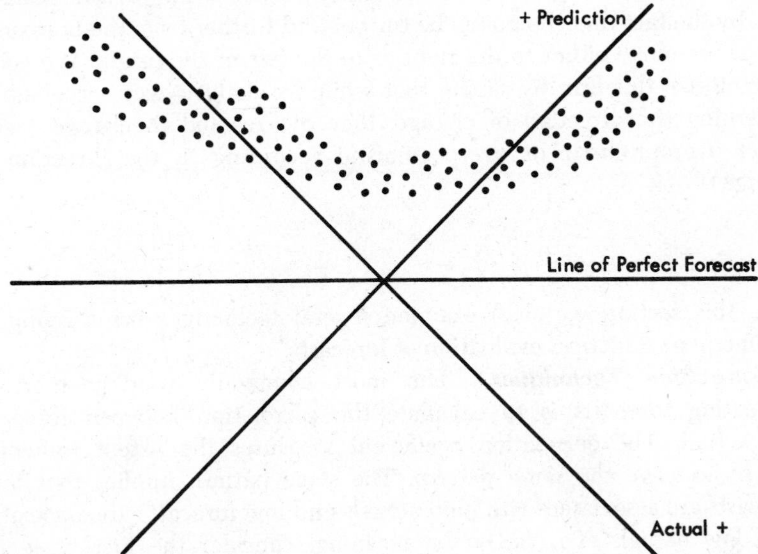

FIGURE 8
Representation of Overestimation of Change

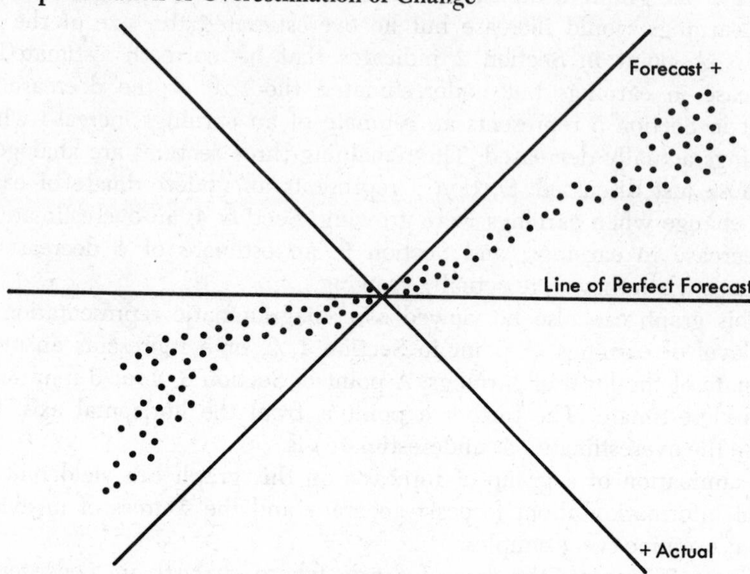

An alternative pattern for forecasting errors is shown in Figure 8. The fact that the points lie in Section 1 and Section 4 indicate that while the direction of change is correctly forecasted, the amount of change is constantly overestimated. Change is overestimated whether it is in the positive or negative direction. Furthermore, the tendency to overestimate change becomes more acute as the change itself is larger. This can be seen by the fact that the points lie further and further from the horizontal axis as we move either to the right or to the left of the origin. We could characterize this firm by saying that while its analysts were excellent at discerning the direction of change, they overreacted to change (were either overoptimistic or overpessimistic according to the direction of change).

Numeric Evaluation

In this section we shall examine several techniques for arriving at a numeric or statistical evaluation of forecasts.

Correlation Techniques. The most commonly used method of evaluating forecasts is to calculate the correlation between forecasts and actual. The correlation coefficient measures the extent to which two series have the same pattern. The same pattern implies that high forecasts are associated with high actuals and low forecasts are associated with low actuals. To clarify the meaning, consider the first three examples shown in Table 3. Forecast 1 and Forecast 2 have very similar patterns to the actual. However, with Forecast 1 deviations from actual tend to be random while with Forecast 2 low actuals are associated with underestimates and high actuals are associated with overestimates. The correlation coefficients of Forecast 1 and Forecast 2 with actual are very similar, 0.9986 and 0.9994, respectively. The pattern of Forecast 3 is very different than actual. The high forecasts are associated with both high and low actuals and the same is true for low forecasts. The correlation coefficient of Forecast 3 is 0.12.

TABLE 3

Some Alternative Forecasts

		Forecasts					
Company	*Actual*	*Technique 1*	*Technique 2*	*Technique 3*	*Technique 4*	*Technique 5*	*Technique 6*
1.	1.20	1.23	1.16	2.00	11.23	12.30	1.28
2.	1.31	1.28	1.28	1.75	11.28	12.80	1.31
3.	1.42	1.39	1.39	1.50	11.39	13.90	1.44
4.	1.55	1.58	1.58	2.50	11.58	15.80	1.53
5.	1.85	1.89	1.88	1.75	11.89	18.90	1.85
6.	3.00	2.96	3.04	2.00	12.96	29.60	2.92
Correlation.		0.9986	0.9994	0.12	0.9986	0.9986	0.9990

The correlation coefficient ranges from -1 to $+1$; $+1$ indicates that the forecasts have the same pattern as actual, -1 indicates that forecasts have exactly the opposite pattern as actual, and 0 indicates no similarity in patterns. Figure 9 shows an example of a correlation coefficient of -1, 0, 0.5, and $+1$. The correlation coefficient is calculated as follows:

$$\text{Correlation coefficient} = \rho = \frac{\sum_{i=1}^{N} (F_i - \bar{F})(A_i - \bar{A})}{\left[\sum_{i=1}^{N} (F_i - \bar{F})^2 \sum (A_i - \bar{A})^2\right]^{1/2}} \tag{29}$$

where:

1. F_i is the ith forecast.
2. $\bar{F}$ is the average forecast (i.e., $\bar{F} = \frac{1}{N}\sum_{i=1}^{N} F_i$). See Chapter 17 for a

   further discussion of the average or mean value.
3. A_i is the ith actual.
4. $\bar{A}$ is the average actual (i.e., $\bar{A} = \frac{1}{N}\sum_{i=1}^{N} A_i$).

FIGURE 9

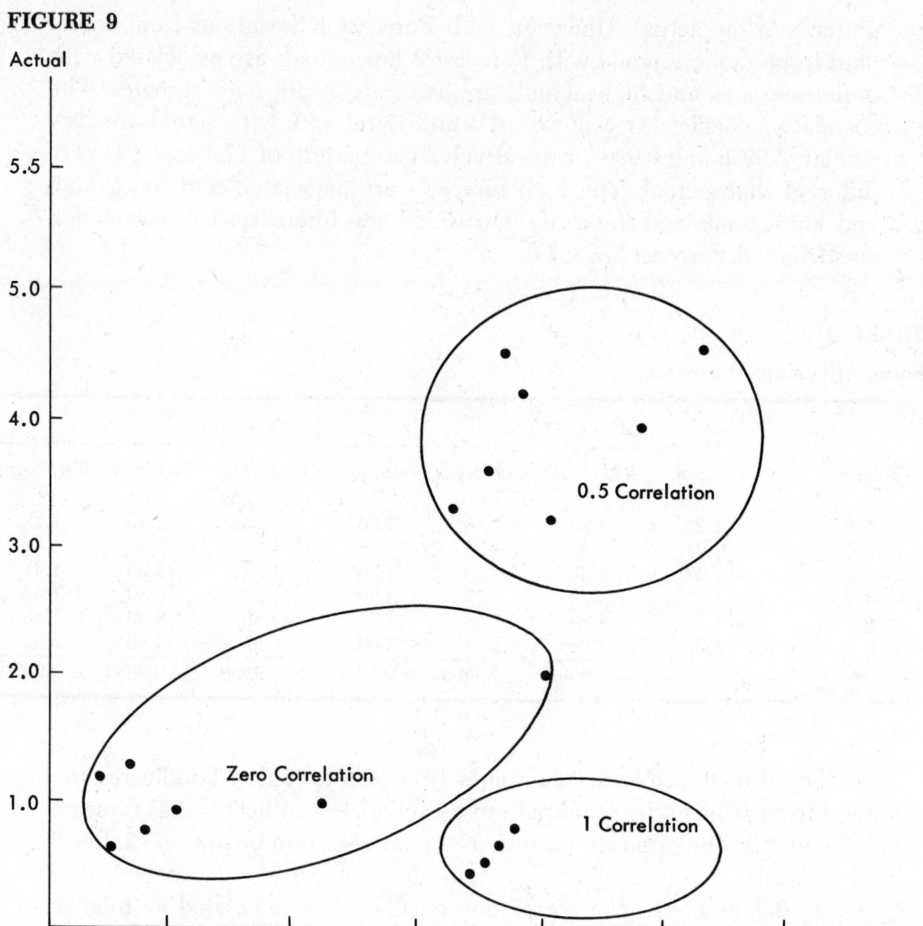

The calculations for Forecast 1 from Table 2 are contained in Table 4.

The correlation coefficient only measures similarity in pattern between forecast and actual. It does not measure the size of the error. For example, Forecast 1 in Table 3 was very similar to actual. Forecast 4 and 5 have exactly the same correlation coefficient, but they are very poor forecasts. Forecast 4 is Forecast 1 plus 10. Forecast 5 is Forecast 2 times 10. These examples can be generalized. The correlation coefficient is unaffected by multiplying each forecast by a positive constant or adding a constant to each forecast or both. Thus, very poor forecasts such as 4 and 5 can have high correlation coefficients. If the error is constant over time (i.e., the forecast is always 10 units too high or 10 times too much), then forecasts highly correlated to actual can be made into

TABLE 4

Calculation of Correlation Coefficient for Technique 1

Year	$(F_i - \bar{F})$	$(F_i - \bar{F})^2$	$(A_i - \bar{A})$	$(A_i - \bar{A})^2$	$(F_i - \bar{F}) \times (A_i - \bar{A})$
1	−0.49	0.2401	−0.52	0.2704	0.2548
2	−0.44	0.1936	−0.41	0.1681	0.1804
3	−0.33	0.1089	−0.30	0.0900	0.0990
4	−0.14	0.0196	−0.17	0.0289	0.0238
5	+0.17	0.0289	0.13	0.0169	0.0221
6	+1.24	1.5376	1.20	1.6384	1.5872
Total		2.1287		2.2127	2.1673

$$\rho = \frac{2.1673}{[(2.1287)(2.2127)]^{1/2}} = 0.9986$$

forecasts with small error by adjusting by this constant difference (subtracting 10 or dividing by 10). However, rarely is the error constant. Correlation has the property that high correlation can be associated with large error and low correlation with small errors, for it ignores differences in the average error produced by different techniques. Because of this it is argued that, despite its widespread use, correlation analysis is a poor way to evaluate forecasts.

Direct Analysis of Forecast Errors. An alternative to correlation is to examine the error directly. Table 5 is the same as Table 3, except it lists the error in the forecast rather than the forecast itself. One would not use the sum of the error to evaluate techniques since positive and negative errors would tend to cancel out. For example, the sum of the error for Forecast 3, a very bad forecast, is zero. There are a number of ways to eliminate the problem of positive and negative errors cancelling out. The simplest is to ignore the sign of the error and simply use its magnitude. Thus, for Forecast 1, the error would be stated as .03, .03, .03, .03, .04, .04. This is called the absolute value of the error.

TABLE 5

Forecast Errors

Actual	*Technique 1*	*Technique 2*	*Technique 3*	*Technique 4*	*Technique 5*	*Technique 6*
1.20	+0.03	−0.04	+0.80	10.03	11.10	0.08
1.31	−0.03	−0.03	+0.44	9.97	11.49	0.00
1.42	−0.03	−0.03	+0.08	9.97	12.48	0.02
1.55	+0.03	+0.03	+0.95	10.03	14.25	0.02
1.85	+0.04	+0.03	−0.10	10.04	17.05	0.00
3.00	−0.04	+0.04	−1.00	9.96	26.60	0.08
MAVE*	0.0333	0.0333	0.5617	10.00	15.495	0.0333
MSE†	0.0011	0.0011	0.4588	100.0011	268.5755	0.0023

* MAVE = Mean absolute value of error.
† MSE = Mean squared error.

The forecasting technique would be judged best by the lowest average or mean absolute error. Squaring a number also eliminates the sign so that all numbers become positive. In this case, with Forecast 1, the error would be stated as .0009, .0009, .0009, .0009, .0016, .0016. Using squared error the forecasting technique would be judged best by which had the lowest average or mean squared error.

The mean absolute error and the mean squared error for the six forecasting techniques are shown in Table 5. The difference in mean forecast error shown in Table 5 is interesting. It would be more useful, however, if it could be stated that the differences were not purely due to chance. This can be tested for a pair of techniques by determining the probability that differences in means (like any two shown in Table 5) could have arisen by chance when the true value of the means were in fact the same.[16] This is a problem in testing that the difference in two means is zero. The procedure to test for statistical significance must consider the fact that we have paired observations, that is, each technique is used to forecast for each firm and the errors in the two techniques in forecasting for a particular firm may be related.

We will describe the procedure for testing for statistically significant differences in squared error. The procedure for any other criteria function is analogous and can be obtained by substituting it (e.g., absolute error) wherever squared error is used in the discussion below. The basic idea is to calculate the difference in the mean squared forecast error and then to determine how many standard deviations away from zero the difference in mean squared error is. The probability of obtaining a difference in mean squared forecast errors x standard deviations away from zero, when the true difference between techniques is zero, is then determined from the table of the t distribution for small samples (approximately less than 30) and the normal distribution for large samples. The part of this procedure that requires special comment is how to determine the standard deviation of the mean difference in squared forecast errors. The standard deviation of the *mean* difference in squared forecast errors is the standard deviation of the differences in squared forecast error divided by the square root of N. Algebraically, the standard deviation of the difference in squared forecast errors is

$$\sigma = \left[\frac{\sum_{i=1}^{N} \left[\left[(F_{1i} - A_i)^2 - (F_{2i} - A_i)^2 \right] - D \right]^2}{N} \right]^{1/2}$$

where:

---

[16] It is necessary to initially test if all means in the table could be the same. This is done by using analysis of variance tests or the Friedman analysis of variance test. See Section VI for a further discussion.

1. F_{1i} = The forecast for firm i with technique 1.
2. F_{i2} = The forecast for firm i with technique 2.
3. N = Number of firms for which forecasts are prepared.
4. S_i = Actual for firm i.
5. $$D = \frac{\sum_{i=1}^{N}(F_{1i} - A_i)^2}{N} - \frac{\sum_{i=1}^{N}(F_{2i} - A_i)^2}{N}$$

The standard deviation of the mean difference in squared forecast errors is σ/N; an example of the procedure is as follows. Consider forecast 1 and 3 in Table 5. The difference in squared errors for these forecasts are −0.6301, −0.1927, −0.0055, −0.9016, −0.0084, −0.9984. The mean difference in squared error is −0.4561. The standard deviation of these differences in errors is 0.9978, and the standard deviation of the mean squared error is 0.4074. Therefore, the mean is 1.12 standard deviations from zero. Looking in the table for the t distribution shows that the probability that the actual mean difference is 1.12 standard deviations from zero, when the true difference is zero, is 0.16. Thus, it is possible that we would observe differences as large as this by chance, and it is possible that the two forecasting techniques are really not different.

Although the absolute value and squared error are the most commonly used criteria, there are a large number of other sensible possibilities. The choice is important because different forecasts are better under different valuation systems. Forecast 1 and Forecast 6 have the same absolute value of the error. However, Forecast 6 has a larger squared error since it has a few large errors rather than lots of small ones. Whether Forecast 1 and Forecast 6 are equivalent depends on whether an error of 0.08 is 4 times as costly as an error of 0.02 or 16 times as costly. Absolute value assumes the cost of the error depends strictly on the size of the error. Thus, an error of 0.08 counts four times as costly as an error 0.02. Squared error assumes that cost of an error depends on the square of the error. Thus, one large error is penalized more heavily than a series of small errors, the sum of which equals the large error. An error of 0.08 is penalized 16 times more heavily than an error of 0.02 $((0.08/0.02)^2)$.

The persons evaluating forecasts must decide what is the cost of an error and select the system that most closely reproduces this cost structure. There is no reason that underestimates and overestimates should be treated alike. If these costs are different, then they should be treated differently. For example, underestimates could be squared while overestimates are evaluated using absolute value. Furthermore, the evaluation of the errors need not be done by a simple formula. It is perfectly reasonable to tabulate the costs of various sized errors and for each forecasting technique utilize the table of costs to evaluate the forecast.

Although these variations are possible for most purposes, squared errors or absolute value of error are sufficiently close approximations to the true cost that one of these are chosen. The absolute value is chosen if costs are proportional to the size of the error, and squared error is chosen if the cost of a large error is much more than the cost of a series of small errors that sum up to the large error. Whatever the choice, it should be selected by choosing a technique that bears some relationship to the cost of the error.

Squared Error—Economic Decomposition. Before leaving this section, it is worthwhile to examine how the squared error can be decomposed into components for further analysis. This decomposition may help the analyst determine the sources of error and aid him in correcting them. There are two ways to decompose the error. The first is to base the decomposition on the basis of the characteristics of the earnings forecasts. It is

$$\frac{1}{N}\sum_{i=1}^{N}(P_i - A_i)^2 = (\bar{P} - \bar{A})^2 + (S_p - S_A)^2 + 2(1 - \rho)S_pS_A,$$

where:

1. $\bar{P}$ = Average P (i.e., $\bar{P} = \frac{1}{N}\sum_{i=1}^{N} P_i$).

2. $\bar{A}$ = Average A (i.e., $\bar{A} = \frac{1}{N}\sum_{i=1}^{N} A_i$).

3. S_p = Standard deviation of P.
   (i.e., $S_p = \left[\frac{1}{N}\sum_{i=1}^{N}(P_i - \bar{P})\right]^{1/2}$. For a more detailed discussion of the standard deviation, see Chapter 37.

4. S_A = Standard deviation of A (i.e., $S_A = \left[\frac{1}{N}\sum_{i=1}^{N}(A_i - \bar{A})^2\right]^{1/2}$

5. ρ = Correlation coefficient and is defined as in equation (29).

The first term is zero if the average prediction equals the average actual. Thus, this term is a measure of how well the forecasting technique predicted the average value for the population as a whole (e.g., all companies under study). For example, in predicting earnings the first term measures how well the forecaster estimated the average earnings in the next period. The second term is zero if the standard deviation of predictions is the same as the standard deviation of actuals. Deviations from zero measure the error in the forecaster's estimate of the variability of the variable being forecast. This would be large if the forecaster estimated the same value for each observation and the actual variation was quite large. The third term is zero if the correlation coefficient between predicted and actual is one. Thus, the third measures errors in the pattern of predictions compared to the pattern of actual (e.g., above-average predictions associated with above-average actuals, and so on). It is often useful to divide each term in the above equation by the mean squared error. This scales the right-hand side so that each term represents the proportion of error caused by each factor. In summary, the mean squared error can be decomposed into:

1. Error due to inability to predict overall average.
2. Error due to inability to predict the extent to which observations vary.
3. Error due to inability to predict the pattern of forecasts.

A second way to decompose the error is on the basis of universality of the error. Assume an analyst is forecasting earnings per share across a group of companies. One source of error could be due to misestimating the overall average because of general pessimism or optimism. A second source of error could be due to misestimating how some subgroup such as an industry would do. For example, errors could occur because the analyst incorrectly thought some industry would have spectacular performance and so adjusted all estimates in the industry upward. Finally, an error could occur because of misestimating company performance after accounting for economywide and industry influences. The formula for this breakdown is[17]

$$\frac{1}{N}\sum_{i=1}^{N}(P_i - A_i)^2 = (\bar{P} - \bar{A})^2 + \frac{1}{N}\sum_{i=1}^{N}[(\bar{P}_I - \bar{P}) - (\bar{A}_I - \bar{A})]^2 + \frac{1}{N}\sum_{i=1}^{N}[(P_i - \bar{P}_I) - (A_i - \bar{A}_i)]^2$$

where:

1. $\bar{P}$ = Mean value of P_i (i.e., $\frac{1}{N}\sum_{i=1}^{N} P_i$).
2. $\bar{A}$ = Mean value of A_i.
3. $\bar{P}_I$ = Mean value of predictor for each industry in turn.
4. $\bar{A}_I$ = Mean value of actual for each industry in turn.
5. P_i = A prediction.
6. A_i = An actual.

[17] This can be shown by substituting $\bar{P} + (\bar{P}_I - \bar{P}) + (P_i - \bar{P}_I)$ for P_i and noting that the cross-product terms cancel out.

The terms in this expression are: error due to misestimating the overall mean, error due to misestimating subgroup or industry movements, and error in company forecast given the industry and economy estimates. Once again, it is convenient to divide both sides by the mean squared error so that the right side shows the proportion of error due to the three causes.

Theil Inequality Coefficient. Theil has developed a variation of the squared error technique for evaluating forecasts. The Theil inequality coefficient is essentially the squared error divided by the sum of the squared actual changes (i.e., actual this year minus actual last year). Since the sum of the squared actual change is constant across techniques, the ranking will be the same as the mean squared error. The advantage of this over the mean squared error is that while there is no natural meaning to the magnitude of the squared error, there is when one scales the data in a form like the Theil inequality coefficient. Two values for the inequality coefficient have meaning. Zero corresponds to perfect forecast, and one corresponds to a forecast that is exactly as good as would be produced by the assumption that next year is the same as last year. For example, in forecasting earnings the value 1 means that the forecast is exactly as good as would be obtained if next year's earnings had been forecasted to be the same as last year's. The formula for the inequality coefficient is as follows:

$$\frac{\sum_{i=1}^{N} (F_i - A_i)^2}{\sum_{i=1}^{N} (A_i - B_i)^2}$$

where:

F_i is the forecast.
A_i is the actual.
B_i is the actual in the previous period, the base value.

Other Techniques. The techniques discussed above represent most of the common ways forecasts are analytically evaluated. There is another group of techniques that can be used less frequently, but are very powerful on occasions when they yield results. The fact that one set of forecasts has a lower mean squared error (or absolute error, and so forth) than a second source does not imply that each error is smaller. If each error from one technique was smaller than each error from a second technique, we could unequivocally reject one technique. Such an occurrence would be rare; however, a variant of this technique frequently yields results. If we rank the errors for each technique from largest to smallest, it is often the case that one technique always produces smaller errors than the second.[18] In this case, the technique that produces smaller errors is preferred to the second for almost all costs of errors.[19] For example, assume we evaluate two techniques for forecasting earnings by examining their forecasting ability on a sample of firms. If after ranking errors from highest to lowest, one technique always had lower errors, it would be preferred under almost all cost of error functions.

A Final Caveat. The alternate test of a forecasting technique is its value in the decision-making process. Two forecasts can be compared in the ways discussed previously, with one technique having superior performance, and yet have this statistical difference make no significant monetary difference. If one technique is more costly than a second, the statistically inferior method could potentially be preferred. For example, one set of earnings estimates could be statistically superior to a second and yet not be preferred since the second set is much cheaper and performs about as well in the security selection process. This could be the case if, for example, the more accurate source was purchased externally and the other source was an extrapolation of past values. A second example comes from the portfolio selection area. A number of years ago, the authors worked on techniques for providing estimates for inputs for portfolio selection. Some more costly and sophisticated techniques seemed to produce better estimates than the naive methods. Since the former were more costly, it was important to check to see that they produced significantly better portfolio selection or their use could not be justified.

THE ACCURACY OF TIME SERIES FORECASTS—A CASE STUDY

Up to this point we have presented a number of time series forecasting techniques and discussed methods of evaluating their accuracy. It seems appropriate to examine how well such models perform in a real forecasting situation. The problem that was selected was to forecast annual earnings per share for a group of industrial companies.[20] Since

---

[18] The cumulative frequency function of errors from one technique lie to the right of the cumulative frequency function of errors from a second technique.

[19] Exceptions include the case where the costs of an error depends on the particular unit on which it arose or the cost of an error is a different function of the size of the error over different size errors (e.g., underestimates are less costly than overestimates).

[20] The discussion in this section is based on a previously published article. See Elton and Gruber [11].

annual earnings were to be forecasted, models employing a seasonal adjustment were not employed. Instead the following eight models were used:

1 & 2. Two forms of moving average models—one in which the optimum length was set by looking at the forecast error for each company and choosing the lengths which minimized forecast error, and one where the length was set at four years.

3. An exponentially smoothed model with a multiplicative trend: equations (8), (9), and (10).

4. An exponentially smoothed model with an additive trend: equations (5), (6), and (7).

5 & 6. Models similar to 3 and 4 but where the trend was assumed to exhibit a trend.[21]

7. Linear regression—assuming an additive trend.

8. Log linear regression—assuming a multiplicative trend.

In addition, a naive forecasting model was introduced as a bench mark. The naive model forecast simply by predicting that next period's earnings would be equal to last period's earnings plus the previous year's change in earnings.

These nine models were all used to estimate earnings for the period 1962–67 on a stratified random sample of 180 firms selected from the Standard & Poor's Compustat Tape. In order to test the generality of the results from the 180-firm sample, these firms were divided into three

---

[21] There are a number of variations of exponential models that could be used. These are two of them. We have not discussed all of them because of space limitations and because the reader should be able to perform the modifications himself. The equations are:

Multiplicative Exponential with Trend in Trend

$$\bar{S}_t = \bar{S}_{t-1}\bar{R}_{t-1}\bar{D}_{t-1} + W_e[S_t - (\bar{S}_{t-1}\bar{R}_{t-1}\bar{D}_{t-1})].$$

$$\bar{R}_t = \bar{R}_{t-1}\bar{D}_{t-1} + W_R\left[\frac{\bar{S}_t}{\bar{S}_{t-1}} - (\bar{R}_{t-1}\bar{D}_{t-1})\right].$$

$$\bar{D}_t = \bar{D}_{t-1} + W_D\left[\frac{\bar{R}_t}{\bar{R}_{t-1}} - \bar{D}_{t-1}\right].$$

$$\hat{S}_{t,T} = \bar{S}_t\left[\pi_{i=1}^{T}\bar{R}_t(\bar{D}_t)^i\right].$$

Additive Exponential with Trend in Trend

$$\bar{S}_t = \bar{S}_{t-1} + \bar{R}_{t-1} + \bar{D}_{t-1} + W_e[S_t - (\bar{S}_{t-1} + \bar{R}_{t-1} + \bar{D}_{t-1})].$$

$$\bar{R}_t = \bar{R}_{t-1} + \bar{D}_{t-1} + W_R[(\bar{S}_t - \bar{S}_{t-1}) - (\bar{R}_{t-1} + \bar{D}_{t-1})].$$

$$\bar{D}_t = \bar{D}_{t-1} + W_D[(\bar{R}_t - \bar{R}_{t-1}) - \bar{D}_{t-1}].$$

$$\hat{S}_{t,T} = \bar{S}_t + \left[\sum_{i=1}^{T}(\bar{R}_t + i\bar{D}_t)\right].$$

random samples of 60 firms each.[22] In particular, the following forecasts were made:[23]

1. One-year forecasts for each of the years 1962–67.
2. Two-year forecasts for the years 1964 and 1966.
3. Three-year forecasts for the years 1964 and 1967.

The square of the forecast errors was the primary method used to judge the accuracy of forecasts. In addition, we also report a variation of the standard error of estimate in the form:

$$U = \frac{\Sigma_i\,(\text{Actual}_i - \text{Forecast}_i)^2}{\Sigma_i\,(\text{Actual}_i)^2}\,.$$

This statistic resembles the coefficient of variation and has the advantage of expressing the forecast error as a fraction of actual earnings.[24]

Performance of the Model—the One-Year Case. The accuracy of each model in making one-year estimates of earnings per share can be seen from Table 6. This table presents the value of U for each technique, derived from forecasts for all 180 companies in each of six years, and ranks the techniques on the basis of increasing U.

Evaluation of the relative performance of alternative forecasting techniques will be postponed to the next section where the statistical significance of differences in performance is discussed. However, at this time it is useful to mention some general conclusions which are more readily seen by examining Table 6. In comparing moving averages, an optimum length moving average which can take on different lengths for different companies seems to outperform a fixed length moving average for all companies. This conclusion is consistent with some earlier tests which

[22] The sampling procedure consisted of drawing 180 firms from the Compustat Tape in the following manner: select four-digit standard industrial classifications using a table of random numbers; select all firms with a suitable history within the four-digit industrial classification; continue to randomly select industrial classifications until 180 firms were sampled. (Our 180 firms represented 44 different four-digit industrial classifications). Two points need further clarification. Our sample is biased in favor of large stable firms, because in order to parameterize our models, we eliminated all firms with either an incomplete earnings history or negative earnings prior to 1962 (the year we start our forecasts). The rather unusual stratifying procedure was used in preparation for a parallel study which compared more sophisticated econometric models employing industry effects with the best techniques found in this study. See Elton and Gruber [9].

[23] Only two three-year forecasts were made in order to avoid overlapping forecasts within the six-year period under study. The two-year forecasts were designed to have the same base years (points of time at which the forecasts were made) as the three-year forecast. Fortunately, the results of the two- and three-year forecasts were so clear-cut that more replication seems unnecessary. All data used in forecasting were available at the time of the forecast. For example, in making the one-year forecast of earnings in 1964 we used data through 1963, and in making the three-year forecast for 1964 we used data through 1961.

[24] This statistic is based on Theil's U statistic as reported in [24].

indicated that a regression model which allowed the time span to vary between companies outperformed a regression model which employed the same number of years of data for all companies.

The comparison of all the additive models (models assuming earnings grow by a certain dollar amount each year) with their parallel multiplicative models (assuming earnings grow by a constant percent each year) reveals that the additive assumption is the better one. The linear regression outperforms the log linear regression; the additive exponential model with trend in trend outperformed the multiplicative exponential with trend in trend and the additive exponential with no trend in trend

TABLE 6

Relative Performance of Forecasting Techniques Based on Value of *U* (one-year forecast)

	Moving Averages			*Regressions*		*Exponentials*			
						Multiplicative		*Additive*	
	Fixed	*Optimum*	*Naive*	*Log Linear*	*Linear*	*Trend in Trend*	*No Trend in Trend*	*Trend in Trend*	*No Trend in Trend*
U	0.1230	0.0670	0.0622	0.1105	0.0595	0.0627	0.0500	0.0527	0.0498
Rank	9	7	5	8	4	6	2	3	1

outperformed the multiplicative exponential with no trend in trend. The difference in performance between the additive and the multiplicative models implies that the extrapolation of past rates of growth has a tendency to overestimate the extent of earnings change over the short run. It is interesting to note (as discussed later in the paper) that this is not true for longer run forecasts where the multiplicative model performs best. The introduction of a trend in trend in both the additive and multiplicative exponential leads to a deterioration in the forecasts. An examination of individual forecasts indicates that adding the trend in trend causes the forecasts for a small number of companies to deteriorate severely.

The ordering of the mechanical techniques should be of interest to management. Since differences in the cost of operating these techniques should be very small, the differences in performance are likely to be important.[25] It remains to be seen if management can have confidence in these results or if they could have arisen by chance alone.

[25] In fact, the technique which performed best should be one of the least costly techniques to operate.

Dominance among Forecasting Techniques. In this section, differences in the square of the forecast errors between different forecasting techniques are tested to see if they are statistically significant. Before testing differences between paired sets of forecasts (e.g., between the forecast error for the naive method and the log linear regression), however, it is necessary to determine whether all of the forecast errors could have come from the same population (whether all the methods may in fact yield the same result).

Because each firm appears as an observation for each technique, the samples of the square of the forecast errors for each technique are not independent, and the statistical tests must be appropriate for related samples. Under very stringent assumptions, namely that the standard errors are independently drawn from normally distributed populations, that the populations all have the same variance, and that the row and column effects are additive, analysis of variance tests would be employed. Because each of these assumptions appears unrealistic in this case, a nonparametric test, the Friedman two-way analysis of variance by ranks, is used.[26] Application of Friedman's test to the one-year forecasts reveals that the probability that all forecasting techniques did equally well is considerably less than one in a thousand. This highly significant result is also obtained when the sample is divided into three samples of 60 firms each.

Since significant differences exist in the forecasts produced by the mechanical techniques employed in this study, it is appropriate to undertake a detailed examination of the performance of each technique against all other techniques taken one at a time. In order to measure differences in performances, the frequency function of the differences in squared error between each pair of forecasting techniques is examined. For example, one observation determining the frequency function for technique A versus technique B would be the squared error in the forecast of company one by technique A minus the squared error in the forecast of company one by technique B. Repeating this for all possible companies produces one frequency function from which the comparative performance of techniques A and B can be judged. If the differences across all firms had the same sign, then this would indicate that technique A dominated technique B. Given the sample size, this would be unlikely to occur. What can and does happen is that some frequency functions have mostly positive or negative values and a mean significantly different from zero. When the mean is significantly different from zero, it is highly unlikely that the techniques being compared forecast equally well in terms of the square of the forecast errors, and it is appropriate to conclude that one technique is dominated by a second.

---

[26] See Siegel [23, pp. 166–72] for a discussion of this test.

From the central limit theorem, the distribution of the mean of these frequency functions is normally distributed with mean equal to the mean of the frequency function and standard deviation equal to the standard deviation of the frequency function divided by the square root of the number of observations.[27] Table 7 presents the results of a statistical test for the one-year forecasts.[28]

In this table, as in the ones that follow, the entries enclosed in parentheses are the ratios of differences in the squared error of any two forecasting techniques to the standard error of this difference. A minus sign indicates that the technique at the left of the table outperformed the technique listed at the top of the table. A plus sign indicates that the technique at the top performed better.

Perhaps the most striking result is that the additive exponential with no trend in trend outperforms every other technique at a statistically significant level. In fact, it outperforms every technique but two other exponentials and the naive model at the 0.01 level of significance.[29] Dominance is also apparent among other exponentials. For example, among the remaining exponential techniques, the multiplicative exponential with trend in trend is dominated by all exponential techniques at the 1 percent level. The remaining two exponentials do not show any statistically significant differences.

The next best group of techniques consists of the naive model and the optimum moving average. The naive model appears to do slightly better though the difference is not significant at the 0.10 level. The fixed moving average is clearly inferior to both of these techniques at the 0.01 level, and in fact is inferior to any other forecasting models selected.

The remaining techniques, the regression models, also differ in performance. The preferred technique is the linear regression, which outperforms the log linear regression at the 1 percent level.

In summary, the best exponential forecasting technique is the additive model with no trend in trend, the best moving average is the optimum moving average, and the best regression is the linear model. All of these differences are significant at the 0.05 level or better. Comparing these three models and the naive model shows that:

---

[27] That the frequency functions under question were derived from differencing two variables should not bother the reader. The central limit theorem states that as the number of observations increases, the distribution of the mean is normally distributed no matter what the original frequency function. The number of observations we used ranged from 120 to 1,080. A two-tailed test was used in testing significance since we were not willing to assert in advance which technique would dominate.

[28] To test the statistical significance of the mean when the standard deviation is unknown, one should use the t test. However, for samples as large as ours, this can be approximated by the normal.

[29] Identical ordering appears in each of the three smaller samples investigated, but the results are not always significant at the same level as in the larger sample.

TABLE 7

Relative Performance of the Forecasting Techniques* Based on Squared Error One-Year Forecasts

					Exponentials			
			Regressions		*Multiplicative*		*Additive*	
	Optimum Moving Average	*Naive*	*Log Linear*	*Linear*	*Trend in Trend*	*No Trend in Trend*	*Trend in Trend*	*No Trend in Trend*
Moving averages								
Fixed	0.2069 (8.68)†	0.2257 (5.55)†	0.0642 (1.38)	0.2061 (6.31)†	0.1115 (2.56)‡	0.2327 (6.46)†	0.2364 (6.80)†	0.2721 (8.79)†
Optimum	0.0	0.0187 (0.56)	−0.1427 (−3.57)†	0.0008 (0.03)	0.0954 (−2.39)‡	0.0257 (0.88)	0.0295 (1.12)	0.0652 (2.99)†
Naive	0.0	0.0	−0.1614 (−3.77)†	−0.0195 (−0.66)	−0.1142 (−3.07)†	0.0070 (0.24)	0.0108 (0.38)	0.0464 (1.69)§
Regressions								
Log linear	0.0	0.0	0.0	0.1419 (4.11)†	0.0473 (1.11)	0.1685 (4.59)†	0.1722 (4.65)†	0.2079 (5.63)†
Linear	0.0	0.0	0.0	0.0	−0.0946 (−2.70)‡	0.0266 (1.12)	0.0303 (1.47)	0.0660 (3.69)†
Exponentials								
Multiplicative								
Trend in trend	0.0	0.0	0.0	0.0	0.0	0.1212 (4.93)†	0.1249 (4.17)†	0.1606 (5.02)†
No trend in trend	0.0	0.0	0.0	0.0	0.0	0.0	0.0038 (0.23)	0.0394 (2.28)‡
Additive								
Trend in trend	0.0	0.0	0.0	0.0	0.0	0.0	0.0	0.0357 (2.70)‡
No trend in trend	0.0	0.0	0.0	0.0	0.0	0.0	0.0	0.0

* The top number in each cell is the difference in squared error between the technique listed at the left side of the table and the technique listed at the top of the table. Therefore, a minus sign indicates the technique at the left of the table performed best. The numbers in parentheses are the ratios of differences in the squared error of any two forecasting techniques to the standard error of this difference.

† Significant at 1 percent level.
‡ Significant at 5 percent level.
§ Significant at 10 percent level.

a. The additive exponential with no trend in trend dominates the other three techniques at a statistically significant level.

b. The ordering of the remaining techniques (from best to worst) are the naive model, the optimum moving average, and the linear regression. However, none of these differences is significant at the 10 percent level.

This demonstration of statistically significant differences in performance, combined with the fact that the technique which performed best should be among the least costly to operate, should be of use to management in the selection of a forecasting technique.

Comparison with Analysts. Having examined a large group of mechanical extrapolation techniques and determined the dominant technique, the next step is to compare this technique with some analysts' estimates of future earnings. Data on analysts' estimates were provided by three services: a large pension fund, a well-known investment advisory service, and a large brokerage house. Data were provided only for the latter three years (1964–66) for which forecasts had been made. Furthermore, no institution followed all of the stocks in this study's sample so that performance had to be judged across the stocks which were common to both the individual institution and our sample (resulting in a different sample for each institution).

These three institutions were not selected at random. In fact, one would expect them to be among those institutions that had produced the best earnings projections. The investment advisory service was selected after analysts in a number of financial institutions indicated that this was the service in whose projections they placed the greatest faith. Furthermore, the other two institutions were the only ones among those contacted who were willing to expose their forecasts to rigorous testing. Since such testing had potential repercussions within their own firms, it indicated some confidence in their projections. Another factor which might bias the results in favor of the analysts is that their estimates were made after the previous year's actual earnings were generally available. Thus analysts were able to incorporate actual data from the first two or three months of the forecast year rather than being restricted to only data available at the close of the fiscal year.

These biases, together with the fact that analysts have the opportunity to incorporate influences which may not be fully reflected in past earnings into their analysis, should lead one to expect analysts' estimates to outperform simple mechanical extrapolation techniques. Given a large cost differential between the preparation of earnings estimates by extrapolation techniques and by security analysts, the analysts' estimates must be a great deal better in order to justify the allocation of a large amount of their time to the preparation of earnings estimates.

The average squared forecast error for the analyst and the additive exponential model are reported in Table 8 along with the t value associated with the difference in performance.[30]

The average data show that the best mechanical technique outperforms the security analysts at one financial institution, but is outperformed by the analysts at two others. However, none of the three differences is significant at even the 20 percent level, and two of three differences are not even significant at the 35 percent level. In short, there is not statistically significant evidence to indicate that the forecasts made by analysts are different from those made by an exponentially weighted moving average employing an additive trend.[31] Insofar as better forecasts lead to better valuation models, the lack of such evidence

TABLE 8

Relative Performance of Security Analysts and Additive Exponential Model Based on Squared Error

	Investment Advisory Service	*Brokerage House*	*Pension Fund*
Sample size	213	177	84
Security analysts	0.0231	0.0342	0.0310
Additive exponential	0.0221	0.0352	0.0441
t value	+0.12	−0.34	−1.23

would seem to indicate that mechanical techniques exist which can provide valid inputs to financial models and that these techniques (given their low cost) should be employed at least as a bench mark against which to judge analysts' performance.[32]

Performance of the Model—The Two- and Three-Year Forecasts. The accuracy of the model in making both two- and three-year estimates of earnings can be seen from Table 9. This table presents the values of U derived from two forecasts for 180 companies.

The detailed analysis of these data will be presented below in a

[30] The t value represents the number of standard deviations the sum of the difference in the squared forecast error is from zero. A plus sign indicates that the mechanical technique has done better than the analyst. As we discussed earlier, the mean error should be normally distributed, and a two-tailed test is appropriate to test whether it is significantly different from zero.

[31] One must exercise care in generalizing these results, since, to the extent that the superior performance of the additive exponential was peculiar to our sample, the results may be biased against the analysts' performance. Cragg and Malkiel [6] in an earlier study reached a similar conclusion.

[32] It is interesting to note that the institutions which followed more stocks did a poorer job of forecasting, relative to the mechanical technique, than the institutions which followed a smaller number. This may indicate that mechanical techniques provide an efficient way of expanding the number of stocks an institution can follow.

discussion of statistical significance. However, it is useful to note that all of the exponential techniques appear to perform much better than any of the other techniques used for both the two-year and three-year forecasts. In fact, the exponential forecasts appear to do just about as well as they do in the one-year case, while all the other methods degenerate badly. For example, the difference in the *U* value for the exponential multiplicative with no trend in trend is less than 6 percent in going from a one- to a three-year forecast while the increase in *U* for the naive model is more than 300 percent.

As a first step in testing statistical significance, Friedman's test is again applied to see if differences exist in the forecasting ability of the

TABLE 9

Relative Performance of Forecasting Techniques Based on Value of *U*

	Moving Averages			*Regressions*		*Exponentials*			
						Multiplicative		*Additive*	
	Fixed	*Optimum*	*Native*	*Log Linear*	*Linear*	*Trend in Trend*	*No Trend in Trend*	*Trend in Trend*	*No Trend in Trend*
Two-year forecasts.......	0.2150	0.1522	0.2352	0.2232	0.1590	0.0523	0.0517	0.0673	0.0717
Three-year forecasts.......	0.3142	0.2022	0.4010	0.3985	0.2102	0.1058	0.0530	0.0563	0.0525

methods. For the two- and three-year forecasts, the likelihood that the techniques forecast equally well can be rejected at considerably better than the 0.001 level.[33]

Dominance among Techniques. For forecasts beyond one year the dominant techniques are the exponential forecasts. Each exponential technique dominates every other technique in both the two-year and three-year forecasts at the 0.01 level. When the 180-firm sample is split into three 60-firm samples, the dominance is also apparent. Each exponential technique dominates every other technique at the 0.01 level except for two of the samples for the two-year forecasts. In these samples there are a total of four cases where the exponential dominates the other techniques at the 0.05 level rather than the 0.01 level.[34]

It is difficult to choose among the exponential techniques. Although the multiplicative exponential with no trend in trend shows the best

[33] The same results hold in each of the three samples.

[34] In sample 1, the multiplicative exponential with trend in trend dominates the optimum moving average and the linear regression at the 5 percent level. In sample 2 the optimum moving average is only dominated by the additive exponentials at the 5 percent level.

performance for both two- and three-year forecasts, its performance is significant in only half the cases. It outperforms the two additive models at the 0.10 level for two-year forecasts, and it outperforms the other multiplicative model at the 0.10 level for three-year forecasts. Among the nonexponentials some definite patterns can be observed. Once again the optimum moving average dominates the fixed moving average, and the simple linear regression dominates the log regression. Comparing the optimum moving average and the linear regression indicates that the optimum moving average performs better.

Unlike the case of one-year forecasts, the naive model performs very poorly. It is dominated by every forecasting technique, although only at the 10 percent level in the case of log linear regression.

In summary, the order of performance for multiyear forecasts is:

1. The exponentials with the multiplicative exponentials with no trend in trend performing best.
2. The optimum moving average.
3. The linear regression.
4. The fixed moving average.
5. The log linear regression.
6. The naive model.

Generality of the Results. The sample of 180 firms was split into subsamples of 60 firms each, so that the generality of the results first reported could be examined.[35] If the forecasting technique that performed best varied a great deal between firms, one should find instability in their performance between samples and be unwilling to generalize the results beyond the 180-firm sample. The results of this sample splitting are very stable. At no time does technique A perform significantly better than technique B in one sample, and technique B significantly better than technique A in a second. There are reversals where the preferred technique changes between samples, but in these cases (and they were rare) neither technique shows a significant difference. There is a slight reduction in statistical significance when comparing the 60-firm samples to the 180-firm samples. For example, the 180-firm three-year forecasts have 25 cases of dominance at the 0.01 level, 2 at the 0.05 level, and 1 at the 0.10 level. In sample one, there are 22 cases of dominance at the 0.01 level, 3 cases of dominance at the 0.05 level and 1 case at the 0.10 level. The fact that statistical significance is in general maintained in the subsamples and that no major changes are found in the ordering of the mechanical techniques between samples indicates the generality of our results.

[35] While our results show statistical stability across our samples, the reader should realize that our sample may be biased as a representation of all firms. The firms in our sample are large, have a continuous earnings history, are industrial firms, and are heavily representative of a few industries. We can think of our data as an unbiased sample from firms with the above characteristics.

TABLE 10

Relative Performance of the Forecasting Techniques* Based on Squared Error Two-Year Forecasts

	Optimum Moving Average	Naive	Regressions: Log Linear	Regressions: Linear	Exponentials: Multiplicative: Trend in Trend	Exponentials: Multiplicative: No Trend in Trend	Exponentials: Additive: Trend in Trend	Exponentials: Additive: No Trend in Trend
Moving averages								
Fixed	0.2059	−0.2285	−0.0610	0.0942	0.6196	0.6300	0.5578	0.5569
	(4.47)	(−1.74)§	(−0.58)	(1.13)	(7.00)†	(7.73)†	(7.33)†	(7.41)†
Optimum	0.0	−0.4345	−0.2670	−0.1118	0.4136	0.4240	0.3519	0.3510
		(−3.52)†	(−2.97)†	(−1.66)§	(5.40)†	(6.26)†	(6.05)†	(6.45)†
Naive	0.0	0.0	0.1675	0.3227	0.8481	0.8586	0.7863	0.7855
			(1.27)	(2.62)‡	(7.42)†	(7.79)†	(7.32)†	(7.18)†
Regressions								
Log linear	0.0	0.0	0.0	0.1552	0.6806	0.6910	0.6188	0.6179
				(1.88)§	(6.76)†	(7.22)†	(7.15)†	(7.04)†
Linear	0.0	0.0	9.0	0.0	0.5254	0.5359	0.4636	0.4628
					(5.99)†	(6.70)†	(7.02)†	(7.05)†
Exponentials								
Multiplicative								
Trend in trend	0.0	0.0	0.0	0.0	0.0	0.0105	−0.0617	−0.0626
						(0.36)	(−1.27)	(−1.18)
No trend in trend	0.0	0.0	0.0	0.0	0.0	0.0	−0.0722	−0.0731
							(−1.83)§	(−1.86)§
Additive								
Trend in trend	0.0	0.0	0.0	0.0	0.0	0.0	0.0	−0.009
								(−0.05)
No trend in trend	0.0	0.0	0.0	0.0	0.0	0.0	0.0	0.0

* The top number in each cell is the difference in squared error between the technique listed at the left side of the table and the technique listed at the top of the table. Therefore, a minus sign indicates the technique at the left of the table performed best. The numbers in parentheses are the ratios of differences in the squared error of any two forecasting techniques to the standard error of this difference.

† Significant at 1 percent level.

‡ Significant at 5 percent level.

§ Significant at 10 percent level.

TABLE 11

Relative Performance of the Forecasting Techniques* Based on Squared Error Three-Year Forecasts

	Optimum Moving Average	Naive	Regressions: Log Linear	Regressions: Linear	Exponentials, Multiplicative: Trend in Trend	Exponentials, Multiplicative: No Trend in Trend	Exponentials, Additive: Trend in Trend	Exponentials, Additive: No Trend in Trend
Moving averages								
Fixed	0.1837 (3.92)†	−0.5803 (−3.26)†	−0.1809 (−1.34)	0.0523 (0.48)	0.9664 (7.73)†	1.0481 (8.80)†	1.0236 (9.32)†	1.0579 (9.73)†
Optimum	0.0	−0.7640 (−4.52)†	−0.3647 (−3.00)†	−0.1314 (−1.39)	0.7826 (6.70)†	0.8644 (7.85)†	0.8398 (8.24)†	0.8742 (9.04)†
Naive	0.0	0.0	0.3995 (2.17)‡	0.6327 (3.66)†	1.5467 (9.30)†	1.6285 (10.39)†	1.6039 (10.68)†	1.6383 (10.99)†
Regressions								
Log linear	0.0	0.0	0.0	0.2333 (2.12)‡	1.1473 (8.50)†	1.2291 (9.13)†	1.2045 (9.57)†	1.2388 (9.73)†
Linear	0.0	0.0	0.0	0.0	0.9140 (7.86)†	0.9958 (8.92)†	0.9712 (9.10)†	1.0056 (9.21)†
Exponentials								
Multiplicative								
Trend in trend	0.0	0.0	0.0	0.0	0.0	0.0818 (1.72)§	0.0572 (1.04)	0.0916 (1.37)
No trend in trend	0.0	0.0	0.0	0.0	0.0	0.0	−0.0246 −0.53	0.0098 (0.17)
Additive								
Trend in trend	0.0	0.0	0.0	0.0	0.0	0.0	0.0	0.0344 (1.01)
No trend in trend	0.0	0.0	0.0	0.0	0.0	0.0	0.0	0.0

* The top number in each cell is the difference in squared error between the technique listed at the left side of the table and the technique listed at the top of the table. Therefore, a minus sign indicates the technique at the left of the table performed best. The numbers in parentheses are the ratios of differences in the squared error of any two forecasting techniques to the standard error of this difference.

† Significant at 1 percent level.
‡ Significant at 5 percent level.
§ Significant at 10 percent level.

CONCLUSION

In this chapter we have presented some of the more commonly used time series forecasting techniques and have reviewed an application of these techniques to the problem of forecasting earnings. These techniques are relatively inexpensive to use and represent at least a good bench mark against which to judge subjective forecasts as well as the forecasts produced by more sophisticated econometric models. Because we believe that these techniques are most useful as an objective standard against which to evaluate other forecasts, we have included a large section on the evaluation of forecasts.

Before closing we should warn the reader that while we have covered the time series techniques which have received the greatest use in industry, we have not covered all of the modern literature on time series techniques. The mathematically sophisticated reader might find three additional techniques of interest.

1. Spectral analysis—see [13], [14].
2. Box Jenkins—see [3], [4].
3. Kalyman filters—see [16].

REFERENCES

[1] Ball, Ray, and Brown, Philip. "Some Preliminary Findings on the Association between the Earnings of a Firm, Its Industry and the Economy." *Empirical Research in Accounting: Selected Studies,* Supplement, *Journal of Accounting Research* 5 (1967): 55–77.

[2] Beaver, William. "The Information Content of Annual Earnings Announcements." *Empirical Research in Accounting: Selected Studies,* Supplement, *Journal of Accounting* 6 (1968).

[3] Box, G., and Jenkins, G. "Some Statistical Aspects of Adaptive Optimization and Control." *Journal of Royal Statistical Society, B24* (1962).

[4] ———. *Statistical Models for Forecasting and Control.* San Francisco: Holden Day, forthcoming.

[5] Brown, Robert G. *Smoothing Forecasting and Prediction of Discrete Time Series.* Englewood Cliffs, N.J.: Prentice-Hall, 1962.

[6] Cragg, John, and Malkiel, Burton. "The Consensus and Accuracy of Some Predictions of the Growth of Corporate Earnings." *Journal of Finance,* March 1968, pp. 67–84.

[7] Elton, Edwin J., and Gruber, Martin, J. "Estimating the Dependence Structure of Share Prices—Implications for Portfolio Selection." *Journal of Finance* 28, no. 5 (December 1973).

[8] ———. "Homogeneous Groups and the Testing of Economic Hypothesis." *Journal of Financial and Quantitative Analysis* 4 (January 1970): 581–602.

[9] ———. "Improved Forecasting through the Design of Homogeneous Groups." *Journal of Business* 44, no. 4 (October 1971), pp. 432–50.

[10] ———. "Security Evaluation and Portfolio Analysis." Englewood Cliffs, N.J.: Prentice-Hall, 1972.

[11] ———. "Earnings Estimates and the Accuracy of Expectational Data." *Management Science* 18, no. 8 (April 1972): B409–22.

[12] ———. "Clustering and Aggregation in Economics." In *Application of Management Science in Banking and Finance*. Edited by Samuel Eilon. London: Gower Press, 1972.

[13] Granger, C. W., and Hatanaka. *Spectral Analysis of Economic Time Series*. Princeton, N.J.: Princeton University Press, 1964.

[14] Jenkins, G., and Watts, D. *Spectral Analysis and Its Applications*. San Francisco: Holden-Day, 1969.

[15] Jones, R. H. "Exponential Smoothing for Multivariate Time Series." *Journal of Royal Statistical Society*, Ser. B28, pp. 286–93.

[16] Kalman, R. E. "New Methods in Wiener Filtering Theory." *Proceedings First Symposium on Engineering Applications of Random Function Theory and Probability*. New York: John Wiley & Son, 1963.

[17] Kirby, Robert. "A Comparison of Short and Medium Range Forecasting Methods." *Management Science*, December 1966, pp. 202–10.

[18] Malkiel, Burton. "The Valuation of Public Utility Equities." *The Bell Journal of Economics and Management Science*, Spring 1970, pp. 143–60.

[19] Mincer, Jacob. "Models of Adaptive Forecasting." *Economic Forecasts and Expectations, Analysis of Forecasting Behavior and Performance*. New York: National Bureau of Economic Research, 1969.

[20] Muth, John. "Optimal Properties of Exponentially Weighted Forecasts." *Journal of American Statistical Association*, June 1960, pp. 299–306.

[21] Nerlove, N., and Wage, S. "On the Optimality of Adaptive Forecasting." *Management Science*, March 1961, pp. 81–94.

[22] Rosenthal, M., ed. *Symposium on Time Series Analysis*. New York: John Wiley & Son, 1963.

[23] Siegel, Sidney. *Non-Parametric Statistics for the Behavioral Sciences*. New York: McGraw-Hill, 1956.

[24] Theil, Henri. *Applied Economic Forecasting*. Amsterdam, Netherlands: North-Holland Publishing Co., 1966.

[25] Whittle, P. *Prediction and Regulation by Least Squares*. London: English University Press, 1963.

40

Computers and Financial Data

FRANCIS A. MLYNARCZYK, JR.
Investment Officer
First National City Bank
New York, New York

THE FINANCIAL ANALYST, FINANCIAL DATA, AND COMPUTERS

THE FINANCIAL ANALYST is confronted with enormous amounts of financial data. An important function of the financial analyst is to decide which data are relevant for decision making in a set of circumstances, to assemble the data, and to organize the data intelligently. Computers can aid in assembling and performing computations upon data, but computers cannot decide which data are important nor how data should be organized.

Concept of Financial Data

The concept of financial data in the text that follows encompasses financial statement data, securities markets data such as security prices and trading volume, and economic data such as National Income and Product Account data. Also included in the concept are data not denominated in dollar terms, such as barrels of oil and number of automobiles, whose consideration can provide additional understanding of financial data behavior.

Use of Financial Data

In using financial data the analyst often assumes that some method of organizing a given set of data will produce useful information in the security trade decision process. A school of thought has developed over the past few decades that subscribes to the theory that all existing information is reflected in security prices at any point in time. Moreover, the theory holds, new information that comes to light becomes reflected in security prices extremely quickly, so it would be unlikely that a particular organization could consistently benefit, since it would be unlikely that that organization could develop or obtain new information consistently.

There is a considerable amount of validity to this theory over shorter time periods. The more important empirical tests of the theory generally support it; however, other important studies indicate some exception. In addition, a logical argument can be developed that organized and analyzed data can provide more information than raw data, and that more sophisticated analysis techniques can provide more information than less sophisticated techniques. An innovative organization can thus increase the probabilities that it will develop new information consistently by using financial data and more sophisticated analysis techniques. If the theory were completely valid, there would be little point to using and analyzing financial data to any great extent in the security trade decision process. Since the theory is not completely valid, opportunity does exist and should be pursued, albeit with caution and care, and close attention to the expenses involved.

Use of Computers

Any of the more sophisticated analysis techniques discussed in the previous chapters can be utilized without the aid of a computer. However, the use of a computer generally reduces the dollar cost and time cost of performing the required calculations by several orders of magnitude. A regression analysis problem that would take a man-day to do on a calculator can be done in seconds on a computer at less than a tenth the cost. Care must be taken even at the lesser cost, however, that the potential benefit outweighs the cost. To the initiated these words will seem hackneyed. To the newcomer to using computers for financial analysis purposes, these words may be the most important in this chapter.

Choosing a Computer-Use Philosophy

An organization contemplating the use of computers to analyze financial data generally has two alternatives from which to choose: use its own computers or use someone else's computers. In some instances, of course, it could make sense to select some combination of the two. The advantages and disadvantages of each alternative are a function of the type of problem to be solved and the technique used, and the personnel skills available to the organization. The alternative of using one's own computers is a concept that needs no elaborate discussion. The alternative of using someone else's computers is a concept that would benefit from a little background and perspective.

During the mid-1960s the computer time-sharing industry was born, and has evolved to specialize in providing computing power, financial data collection and maintenance services, and software and technical support services. The resources and pricing policies of this industry are such that an organization that wishes to use computers and financial data will usually find the services of this industry to be the most economical means of doing so. (A tabulation of companies and services offered by this industry is outlined in the appendix to this chapter.)

In broad outline, the characteristics and factors to consider in choosing the appropriate alternative appear in Figure 1.

FIGURE 1

Characteristics of Using Computers and Financial Data on Your Own Computers versus Someone Else's Computers

Hardware Resources	*Using Your Own Computers*	*Using Someone Else's Computers*
a. Computing power availability	Usually limited by the size of the organizations' recordkeeping requirements. The larger the organization, the larger the computer available. Computer system batch-processing oriented, turn-around time slow.	No limit on choice of computing power. Computer time-sharing vendors can be found that offer the availability of small to the very largest computers made. Turn-around time fast, due to on-line processing.
b. On-line storage availability	Usually none, which generally increases turn-around time.	Always, which generally reduces turn-around time.
c. Terminal input/output availability	Usually limited to batch input devices such as punched card and magnetic tape readers. Output usually produced on a high-speed printer.	On-line interactive typewriter-like terminals always supported, in addition to batch input devices. Terminal-to-computer link made by standard telephone. Output usually produced on the typewriter-like terminal instantly. Large amounts of output usually can be produced on a high-speed printer.
Software Resources		
a. Data base availability	Own raw data base must be maintained, requiring elaborate procedures to ensure data base integrity. This puts you in the raw data base maintenance business, and perhaps in the data collection business, too.	Some time-sharing vendors maintain extensive raw data bases at no or modest cost. This keeps you out of the large scale raw data base collection and maintenance business.
b. Program packages	Own program packages and systems must be created and maintained.	Own program packages and systems *can* be created and maintained. Extensive programs

FIGURE 1 (*continued*)

	Using Your Own Computers	Using Someone Else's Computers
		available which do not require knowledge of a programming language (such as BASIC, FORTRAN, or COBOL), at no or modest additional cost, to solve common classes of problems (e.g., regression analysis, time series analysis, etc.)
Personnel Resources		
a. Programmers	Must have own programming staff, or contract to have programming done for you.	Can and may need to have own programming staff.
b. Technical support	Must have access to own mathematicians, economists, etc., or to consultants.	Often can have access at no or modest cost to mathematicians, economists, etc., employed by time-sharing vendors.
Cost Characteristics		
a. Fixed costs	High. Must bear computer capital costs and relatively high personnel costs for programmers, data base maintenance staff. Incremental computer capital costs might not be significant, however.	Low. Interactive typewriter-like terminal cost is the bare minimum.
b. Variable costs	Low. Incremental computer costs negligible.	Moderate to high.
c. Total costs	Generally high. Primarily personnel costs.	Generally moderate. Primarily computer usage costs.

EXAMPLES OF COMPUTER AND FINANCIAL DATA USE

The availability of computers and financial data at moderate cost allows the financial analyst who has access to them to spend his time more productively. Instead of merely pondering occasionally about the impact of a change in aggregate economic activity on an industry or company of interest, the financial analyst can formulate a specific hypothesis, test it, and obtain the results with a very short turn-around time at modest cost. The analyst can also use the computer to sift through a large number of companies to search for companies with characteristics of interest as a prelude to doing in-depth analysis. The following sections discuss these and other uses of computers and financial data that would be of interest to the financial analyst.

Economic Forecasting

Macroeconomic Forecasting. Computer technology has permitted the development of large *macroeconomic models* that some business economists use in preparing forecasts of aggregate economic variables of the U.S. economy and, to a much lesser extent, economies of other major countries. These models are typically constructed by estimating average relationships among important economic variables by means of regression analysis. These average relationships, in the form of algebraic equations, along with some accounting identities, are then grouped and ordered according to the particular economist's view of how the U.S. economy is structured. This arrangement of equations constitutes the macroeconomic model.

In order to develop a "solution," i.e., a forecast, from the model, the minimum requirements are that the economist provides his own subjectively determined assumptions for a certain minimum number of economic variables, called *exogenous variables* (i.e., determined outside the model). The model can then be solved by simultaneous (all at the same time) equation solution techniques, or by recursive (one at a time) solution techniques, to produce forecasts for the variables that are not the exogenous variables. These other variables are called *endogenous variables* (i.e., determined within or by the model).

The existing (and commercially available) macroeconomic models are generally referred to as either Keynesian or monetarist, although purists would not entirely agree with these labels. Typically, the more important exogenous variables for a Keynesian model would be variables in the government expenditure sector of the economy, with the money supply as an endogenous variable (i.e., the Federal Reserve adjusts its monetary policy to economic activity rather than vice versa). In a monetarist model the reverse is generally the case (i.e., money supply growth is the more important determinant of aggregate economic activity).

Also, there is generally a difference in size between the two general classes of macroeconomic models. Keynesian models typically contain many more equations and accounting identities than do monetarist models. For example, the Data Resources, Inc. Model (Keynesian) contains over 300 equations and identities, while the St. Louis Federal Reserve Model (monetarist) contains around 10. This fact may or may not be of practical importance to the financial analyst. It simply means that a much finer breakdown of forecasts of National Income and Product Account variables is usually available from a Keynesian model. The analyst may not need the finer breakdown or may not develop confidence in the ability of the model to forecast a particular variable which is of interest.

An example of a macroeconomic forecast produced from a Keynesian model appears in Figure 2. Included is a partial listing of the exogenous and endogenous variables.

Microeconomic Forecasting. This kind of forecasting refers to making projections for industries and companies. Some commercially avail-

FIGURE 2

Example of Macroeconomic Forecasts
Data Resources Forecast of the U.S. Economy (billions of dollars—SAAR)

	73: 4	74: 1	74: 2	74: 3	74: 4	75: 1	75: 2	75: 3	75: 4	76: 1	76: 2	76: 3	76: 4	74	75	76
TOTAL CONSUMPTION	829.0	844.7	864.5	882.1	906.6	925.9	945.6	965.6	984.4	1005.5	1026.8	1049.4	1072.6	874.5	955.4	1038.6
DURABLES(TOTAL)	126.8	126.3	127.5	129.7	136.3	140.0	142.9	147.2	150.2	153.9	157.8	161.4	166.2	130.0	145.1	159.8
NONDURABLES	351.1	359.3	369.8	378.4	388.5	395.3	403.3	410.4	417.5	425.1	432.6	441.3	449.3	374.0	406.6	437.1
SERVICES	351.2	359.0	367.3	374.0	381.8	390.6	399.4	408.0	416.7	426.5	436.3	446.7	457.1	370.5	403.7	441.7
BUSINESS FIXED INVESTMENT	141.1	142.6	148.2	152.4	157.2	161.4	165.1	168.4	172.5	178.0	183.3	188.9	194.4	150.1	166.9	186.1
EQUIPMENT	90.0	93.2	97.2	99.3	102.2	104.6	107.3	110.0	112.9	116.4	120.3	124.2	127.9	98.0	108.7	122.2
NONRESIDENTIAL CONSTRUCTION	51.1	49.4	50.9	53.0	55.0	56.8	57.8	58.4	59.6	61.6	63.0	64.7	66.5	52.1	58.2	63.9
RESIDENTIAL CONSTRUCTION	54.2	48.2	47.6	49.9	53.8	56.7	58.6	59.9	60.8	62.2	64.5	66.6	67.4	49.9	59.0	65.2
INVENTORY INVESTMENT	15.9	8.4	9.7	8.7	7.8	9.1	9.0	9.2	9.2	9.3	9.5	9.7	9.9	8.6	9.1	9.6
NET EXPORTS	8.0	5.5	3.1	2.9	3.0	2.7	3.1	3.6	5.1	5.7	5.9	7.2	8.7	3.6	3.6	6.9
FEDERAL MILITARY	74.0	76.4	77.6	78.8	81.4	82.3	83.1	83.6	86.3	87.3	88.0	88.7	91.5	78.6	83.8	88.9
FEDERAL CIVILIAN	33.8	34.9	35.7	36.5	37.8	38.3	38.8	39.3	40.5	41.0	41.5	41.8	43.1	36.2	39.2	41.9
STATE AND LOCAL	178.0	182.6	188.2	194.2	200.1	206.0	212.2	218.0	223.9	228.8	234.3	240.1	246.1	191.3	215.0	237.3
GROSS NATIONAL PRODUCT	1334.0	1343.3	1374.5	1405.4	1447.7	1482.4	1515.5	1547.6	1582.7	1617.7	1653.8	1692.4	1733.7	1392.7	1532.1	1674.4
ANNUAL RATE OF CHANGE	9.4	2.8	9.6	9.3	12.6	9.9	9.3	8.7	9.4	9.1	9.3	9.7	10.1	8.1	10.0	9.3
REAL GNP (1958 DOLLARS)	844.1	835.8	840.7	846.6	858.9	868.6	877.4	885.7	894.8	904.9	915.2	926.3	938.2	845.5	881.6	921.1
ANNUAL RATE OF CHANGE	1.3	-3.9	2.4	2.8	5.9	4.6	4.1	3.9	4.2	4.6	4.6	5.0	5.2	1.0	4.3	4.5
IMPLICIT PRICE DEFLATOR (58=1)	1.580	1.607	1.635	1.660	1.686	1.707	1.727	1.747	1.769	1.788	1.807	1.827	1.848	1.647	1.737	1.817
ANNUAL RATE OF CHANGE	7.9	6.9	7.1	6.3	6.3	5.1	4.9	4.7	5.0	4.3	4.4	4.5	4.7	7.1	5.5	4.6
CONSUMER PRICE INDEX (67=1)	1.377	1.408	1.439	1.463	1.487	1.509	1.530	1.551	1.569	1.588	1.607	1.625	1.643	1.449	1.540	1.615
ANNUAL RATE OF CHANGE	10.3	9.4	9.0	6.8	6.7	6.2	5.8	5.5	4.9	4.8	4.8	4.6	4.6	8.9	6.3	4.9
WHOLESALE PRICE INDEX (67=1)	1.428	1.468	1.489	1.511	1.522	1.527	1.537	1.543	1.557	1.565	1.577	1.591	1.608	1.497	1.541	1.585
ANNUAL RATE OF CHANGE	10.7	11.5	5.8	6.1	2.9	1.5	2.5	1.7	3.6	2.2	3.1	3.5	4.4	10.5	2.9	2.9
INDUSTRIAL PRODUCTION (67=1)	1.270	1.245	1.245	1.248	1.270	1.289	1.308	1.323	1.339	1.357	1.376	1.398	1.421	1.252	1.315	1.388
ANNUAL RATE OF CHANGE	1.1	-7.5	-0.2	1.1	7.4	6.1	5.9	4.7	4.9	5.5	5.7	6.4	6.8	-0.1	5.0	5.5
HOUSING STARTS(MIL. UNITS)	1.566	1.456	1.642	1.801	1.938	1.974	2.014	2.030	2.050	2.113	2.172	2.172	2.149	1.709	2.017	2.151
UNEMPLOYMENT RATE (PERCENT)	4.7	5.3	5.7	5.9	6.0	5.8	5.7	5.7	5.6	5.6	5.6	5.5	5.4	5.7	5.7	5.5
FEDERAL SURPLUS(NIA)	3.5	-3.1	-7.1	-7.9	-6.0	-3.5	-1.6	1.2	1.7	0.7	3.4	6.6	8.2	-6.0	-0.6	4.7
NEW AA CORP. UTILITY RATE ($)	8.07	8.26	8.16	8.06	7.90	7.82	7.76	7.83	7.85	7.99	7.94	7.94	7.97	8.09	7.82	7.96
NEW HIGH-GRADE CORP.BOND RATE ($)	7.76	7.98	7.90	7.79	7.64	7.57	7.52	7.59	7.61	7.75	7.70	7.70	7.73	7.83	7.57	7.72
TREASURY BILL RATE (PERCENT)	7.50	7.25	6.16	5.94	5.74	5.67	5.57	5.65	5.74	5.86	5.79	5.85	5.95	6.27	5.65	5.86
PERSONAL INCOME	1079.2	1100.3	1125.2	1148.7	1179.2	1203.1	1228.6	1252.2	1278.0	1307.9	1335.1	1363.4	1393.3	1138.3	1240.5	1349.9
DISPOSABLE INCOME	918.0	936.4	957.8	977.5	1002.8	1022.1	1043.0	1062.4	1083.4	1109.7	1132.8	1156.8	1182.1	968.6	1052.7	1145.4
SAVING RATE (PERCENT)	6.9	7.1	7.1	7.1	7.0	6.8	6.7	6.5	6.6	6.8	6.8	6.8	6.8	7.1	6.7	6.8
CORP. CAP. CONS. ALLOW.	72.7	73.7	74.7	76.1	77.6	79.3	80.9	82.5	84.1	85.7	87.4	89.2	90.9	75.5	81.7	88.3
PROFITS BEFORE TAX	128.2	119.5	116.7	120.2	125.5	129.6	131.3	134.8	138.2	142.8	146.9	152.0	157.8	120.5	133.5	149.9
PROFITS AFTER TAX	71.0	66.8	65.3	67.2	70.2	72.4	73.4	75.4	77.3	79.9	82.2	85.0	88.3	67.3	74.6	83.8
ANNUAL RATE OF CHANGE	-3.0	-21.6	-8.8	12.5	18.9	13.5	5.3	11.3	10.5	14.2	12.1	14.5	16.2	-4.1	10.8	12.4
FOUR QTR. PERCENT CHANGE	17.7	-0.2	-8.9	-6.0	-1.1	8.5	12.4	12.2	10.1	10.3	12.0	12.8	14.3			
RET. UNIT CAR SALES-TOTAL	9.6	9.2	9.2	9.4	10.5	10.6	10.6	11.0	11.1	11.2	11.4	11.4	11.7	9.6	10.8	11.4

Source: Data Resources, Inc.

able macroeconomic models also offer a set of microeconomic models to forecast industry production, sales, profits, and other variables of interest. When the macroeconomic model is solved, the forecast values of the endogenous variables and, of course, the exogenous variables can serve as input to the set of microeconomic models. With some models the linkage between the macroeconomic forecast is direct, i.e., the macroeconomic forecast variables serve as exogenous variables for the industry models directly. With other models the linkage is made using an input/output matrix as a bridge in an attempt to make the linkage internally consistent with the historic physical flow of goods from one industry to another in the U.S. economy. An illustration of industry model output appears in Figure 3.

Experience with most of the industry forecasting microeconomic models indicates that the industry forecasts are useful but could be improved upon. To date, more value appears to lie in sensitivity analysis. The relative impact on changes in the industry forecasts for two or more different macroeconomic scenarios can be compared. An example of this appears in Figure 4.

An example of microeconomic forecasting at the company level is described in the next section.

Security Analysis

Statistical analysis and model building from empirical data can be very useful in helping the security analyst to understand how an industry or company is affected by aggregate economic activity. Because this is an area of considerable promise in using computers and financial data, a step-by-step description from start to finish of a real analysis problem encountered by the author in his capacity as a security analyst should be illustrative and informative.

Empirical Analysis: Problem. A security analyst is charged with the responsibility of analyzing the business prospects of a company whose major product line (65 percent of corporate revenues, between 65 percent and 75 percent of pretax corporate profits) is a national daily business publication. The other product lines are either relatively straightforward to analyze or not important profit contributors. Considerable concern has been voiced by the investment community with regard to the vulnerability of operating earnings of the national daily business publication to an economic decline, since during the 1969–70 downturn operating earnings for the company tumbled some 30 percent through 1971, only surpassing the 1969 level in 1973. How vulnerable are the company's earnings to an economic downturn?

Analytical Process. *Step 1—Formulate testable hypotheses.* Of the revenues of the national daily business publication, about 45 percent derive from circulation, the remaining 55 percent from advertising. The

FIGURE 3

Example of Industry Forecasts
Revenues and Costs from ATC Quarterly Financial Report

	Basic Chemicals									
	67	*68*	*69*	*70*	*71*	*72*	*73*	*74*	*75*	*76*
Sales	24.40	26.19	27.07	27.33	29.36	33.18	39.09	41.52	46.37	52.85
Less costs and expenses	21.68	23.12	24.05	24.82	26.61	29.71	34.64	37.56	42.01	48.10
Net profits from operations	2.71	3.07	3.02	2.50	2.75	3.47	4.45	3.96	4.36	4.74
Plus other income or deductions	− 0.03	−0.14	−0.12	− 0.21	−0.26	−0.34	−0.34	− 0.34	−0.34	−0.34
Net profit before taxes	2.68	2.93	2.90	2.29	2.49	3.13	4.11	3.62	4.02	4.40
Less Federal tax payments	1.08	1.27	1.29	0.95	1.04	1.31	1.73	1.48	1.65	1.81
Net profit after taxes	1.60	1.66	1.61	1.35	1.45	1.83	2.38	2.13	2.37	2.60
Less cash dividends	0.94	0.96	0.94	0.93	0.91	0.97	1.00	1.05	1.06	1.09
Retained earnings	0.67	0.70	0.68	0.42	0.54	0.86	1.38	1.09	1.31	1.51
Depreciation and depletion	1.65	1.76	1.79	1.87	1.99	2.15	2.27	2.99	3.03	3.41
Annual rates of growth										
Sales	3.6	7.4	3.4	0.9	7.4	13.0	17.8	6.2	11.7	14.0
Profit before taxes	−16.5	9.3	−1.1	−21.0	8.5	26.0	31.2	−12.0	11.2	9.5
Profit after taxes	−15.6	3.6	−2.7	−16.6	7.4	26.2	30.3	−10.3	11.2	9.5
Stockholders' equity	14.64	15.03	15.48	16.06	17.02	18.15	19.52	20.61	21.92	23.44
Operating ratios										
Rate of profit on equity										
Before taxes	18.3	19.5	18.7	14.3	14.6	17.3	21.1	17.6	18.3	18.8
After taxes	10.9	11.0	10.4	8.4	8.5	10.1	12.2	10.4	10.8	11.1
Profit as percent of sales										
Before taxes	11.0	11.2	10.7	8.4	8.5	9.4	10.5	8.7	8.7	8.3
After taxes	6.6	6.3	6.0	4.9	4.9	5.5	6.1	5.1	5.1	4.9

Source: Data Resources, Inc.

FIGURE 4

Sensitivity Analysis for Industry Forecasts
1974 Industry Forecasts under Three Alternative Economic Outlooks

	1974 Economic Outlook					
	Alternative Economic Outlook Sharp Recession—Moderate Recovery		*Cyrus J. Lawrence Economic Outlook Mild Recession—Moderate Recovery*		*Alternative Economic Outlook Stagflation*	
Industry	*Sales % Change*	*Profits* % Change*	*Sales % Change*	*Profits* % Change*	*Sales % Change*	*Profits* % Change*
1. Air transport—trunks	4%	−18%	6%	− 3%	9%	14%
2. Aluminum	0	− 1	4	6	6	12
3. Automobiles	−10	−50	− 5	−34	− 1	−39
4. Beverages—soft drinks	11	10	12	11	16	15
5. Broadcasters—network	2	−21	5	−13	9	− 2
6. Building materials—cement	− 3	−28	− 1	−20	0	−29
7. Chemicals—basic	− 4	−20	− 2	−14	1	−12
8. Computer—main frames	11	11	12	13	15	16
9. Electrical—diversified	6	− 3	7	1	10	0
10. Electrical—equipment	7	− 3	9	3	11	5
11. Electrical—household appliances	− 3	−34	0	−29	4	−20
12. Electronics—consumer	−30	−47	−23	−35	−16	−27
13. Electronics—semicond.	− 8	−22	1	− 7	8	4
14. Food—packaged foods	9	11	8	5	10	8
15. Forest products	− 6	− 8	− 2	1	3	13
16. Hand and power tools	1	− 9	4	− 3	11	6
17. Health care—beauty aids	7	7	8	8	9	10
18. Health care—hospital products	13	13	15	15	20	20
19. Health care—pharmaceutical	8	0	9	3	12	− 2
20. Machinery—const. and mat. hand.	9	1	12	8	15	8
21. Machinery—industrial	5	−11	9	− 2	10	4
22. Machine tools	5	−18	8	− 4	10	5
23. Oil—integrated international	27	30	28	35	29	39
24. Oil—integrated domestic	13	2	14	6	16	6
25. Paper	− 5	−29	− 3	−23	4	−11
26. Retail—conven. dept.	2	− 9	3	− 4	6	3
27. Retail—discount dept.	6	0	10	6	17	10
28. Retail—food chains	8	10	9	10	9	12
29. Retail—general merch.	2	− 2	4	− 2	8	14
30. Soap	3	3	5	5	7	7
31. Steel—major	−10	−48	− 4	−29	− 1	−33
32. Telephone cos.—bell	11	3	11	6	12	5
33. Textile—apparel	2	−17	6	− 7	13	− 1
34. Textile products	−11	−35	− 9	−25	− 3	−20
35. Tire and rubber goods	− 4	−21	− 1	−16	3	− 7
Average	2%	−10%	5%	− 4%	8%	1%

* Operating profits (sales less cost of goods sold and selling, general, and administrative expense).
Source: Cyrus J. Lawrence, New York.

circulation component is relatively predictable. The advertising component is the swing factor.

Advertising revenue changes can be split into changes in *linage* and changes in *rates*. While there is some demand elasticity for linage, it appears to have been negligible in the past. In addition, rate increases appear to have been tied to prior circulation increases. Linage analysis appears to be the key.

Hypothesis. Demand for advertising linage in this national publication is a function of some broad measure of the level of macroeconomic activity in the U.S. economy. In view of the steepness of the linage decline on an annual basis from 1969 through 1971, demand may also be a function of *change* in macroeconomic activity as well as the level of macroeconomic activity.

Step 2—Gather data. From commercially available data sources, broad measures of economic activity are available on-line on the same computers as statistical analysis programs capable of testing the hypothesis (and likely modifications of it). If these data were not available commercially, they could have been obtained easily (from the *Survey of Current Business* or *Business Conditions Digest* or *Economic Indicators,* all monthly U.S. government publications), but would have to be keyed into the computer and stored.

The major difficulty here is that no data are readily available on advertising linage for the daily business publication. This data availability problem is the single biggest problem faced by financial analysts who wish to use more powerful analysis techniques. Moreover, the company does not release this data, presumably for competitive reasons, on other than an annual basis. Unfortunately, economic fluctuations do not begin and terminate at the ends of calendar or fiscal years.

Fortunately, estimates of advertising linage for this publication can be developed, since the amount of news material per day in the publication does not change much over fairly long periods of time. As a result, linage estimates for a given day can be obtained by subtracting the number of news pages from the total number of pages published on that day. Unfortunately, this approach does not break out linage by major category, such as financial, retail, institutional, help-wanted, real estate, and other classified. These breakdowns could be obtained and analyzed separately with respect to economic fluctuations or other factors, but the data gathering cost of dissecting each day's linage, or a sample of days for a number of years, was judged to be prohibitive when compared to the prospective benefits from knowing how individual components behaved.

The procedure used to gather the data was to dispatch a statistical assistant to the New York Public Library to spin the microfilm reels of the eastern edition (about 50 percent of revenues for the publication) and to jot down the number of pages published each day from 1956 to the present. This period covers three recessions (1957–58, 1960–61, and 1969–70), and a mini-recession (1966–67). These daily data were then aggregated to a quarterly frequency to be consistent with the frequency of publication of National Income and Product Account data. The number of estimated news pages for the quarter were subtracted. The entire process took three man-days and produced the analyzable data required.

Step 3—Plot data. It is usually a good idea to plot the data to spot potential unusual behavior and possible data collection errors. The data can be entered into the computer, stored, and then plotted with commercially available plotting software, or can be plotted by hand. A plot of the raw data appears in Figure 5 on semilogarithmic (log/linear) scales.

Step 4—Examine data for seasonal behavior. As can be seen in Figure 5, quarterly advertising linage is highly seasonal, with the third calendar quarter seasonally low and the second and fourth seasonally high. It is thus necessary to smooth out these seasonal fluctuations by the process known as *seasonally adjusting* (see Chapter 39). This process

FIGURE 5

Plot of Raw Linage Estimate Data

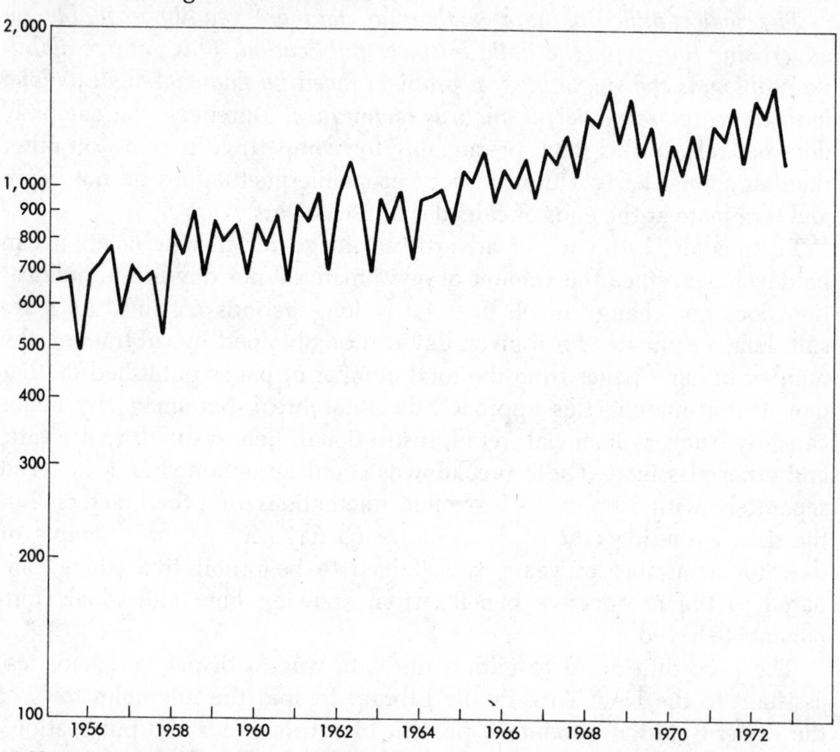

Vertical scale: Number of advertising pages.
Horizontal scale: Year.

is well-known to business economists but not widely used by financial analysts. It is generally necessary to seasonally adjust quarterly (or monthly) data in order to relate it to aggregate economic data, since most aggregate economic data are seasonally adjusted. Procedures to seasonally adjust data by computer were developed in the mid-1950s by Julius Shiskin, and these have been programmed in standard software packages available commercially on a number of time-sharing systems. Early versions of the computer program were commonly called the "X-11 program," and the name remains.

The data were thus seasonally adjusted, and the output of the seasonal adjustment program appears in Figure 6. The output contains the adjusted data, the historical seasonal factor for each quarter, and estimates of what the seasonal factors should be over the next four quarters, based on the past pattern of the data. The bottom of Figure 6 contains statistical information with regard to whether or not stable seasonality exists in the historical data. In this case it did exist. In other cases it may not, in which event further analysis along the lines to follow here is rendered more difficult, and often impossible.

The seasonally adjusted data appear in Figure 7, along with real gross national product data (i.e., GNP data in constant [1958] dollars). The periods of recession as defined by the National Bureau of Economic Research (NBER) are indicated, along with the mini-recession of 1966–67, a period of economic fluctuation which was not officially defined to be a recession by the NBER.

One point of the data sticks out like a sore thumb—the point for the first quarter of 1963. Rechecking the raw data did not indicate any obvious human error. A newspaper strike in New York City took place at that time, diverting linage to this publication and probably accounted for the anomaly. Since only one point stood out of the 70-odd points used, it was eliminated in subsequent analysis by a convenient statistical trick discussed later.

Step 5—Perform analysis to test the hypothesis. Testing the hypothesis, for all the statistical elegance that may be employed, to some extent remains an art form as it relates to being useful in financial analysis. This fact will become apparent in this section.

The test is begun by using the technique of linear regression analysis, which is described in another chapter, to relate the seasonally adjusted advertising linage estimates to a broad measure of economic activity. The broad measure of economic activity chosen was real GNP. Real GNP was chosen, vis-à-vis GNP in current dollars, because, like advertising linage, it is a real, i.e., nonmonetary quantity, unencumbered by the effects of inflation.

Test 1. The first test entails regressing (relating) linage upon (to) real GNP over the entire interval for which data are available, i.e., the first quarter of 1956 (56:1) through the second quarter of 1973 (73:2). To eliminate any bias that might arise from the unusual piece of data in the first quarter of 1963 (63:1), the statistical device of using a dummy variable is employed. The dummy variable takes the value of zero everywhere from 56:1 through 73:2 except in 63:1, where it takes the value of one.

The regression results for Test 1 appear in Figure 8. Depicted are the coefficients of the constant term, the real GNP term, and the dummy variable, along with their tests of statistical significance (t-tests). The actual values of seasonally adjusted linage and the values "fitted" by

FIGURE 6

Example of Seasonal Adjustment Program Output

X11Q SEASONAL ADJUSTMENT FOR W

FINAL SEASONALLY ADJUSTED SERIES

YEAR	Q1	Q2	Q3	Q4
56	640.047	615.683	606.320	642.433
57	689.929	707.684	715.222	667.850
58	639.222	630.080	643.124	775.515
59	728.919	826.255	831.767	805.192
60	778.996	773.673	827.257	784.654
61	776.792	804.257	825.025	852.690
62	849.601	893.433	863.247	896.734
63	1139.200	873.099	841.524	890.507
64	851.361	902.270	886.040	888.283
65	959.097	914.948	1014.930	1017.990
66	1029.380	1084.370	1085.960	1022.390
67	1018.190	1054.470	1094.760	1100.440
68	1138.400	1158.570	1205.830	1286.200
69	1353.980	1391.000	1413.760	1392.640
70	1213.020	1200.010	1139.430	1133.690
71	1101.680	1149.430	1182.910	1212.790
72	1288.420	1309.770	1298.140	1373.640
73	1413.720	1416.760		

FINAL SEASONAL FACTORS

YEAR	Q1	Q2	Q3	Q4
56	1.039	1.091	0.810	1.062
57	1.036	1.091	0.812	1.063
58	1.031	1.092	0.815	1.066
59	1.023	1.095	0.814	1.071
60	1.018	1.099	0.810	1.077
61	1.013	1.102	0.806	1.080
62	1.013	1.099	0.807	1.082
63	1.011	1.096	0.815	1.078
64	1.010	1.089	0.830	1.074
65	1.003	1.085	0.847	1.067
66	0.997	1.081	0.864	1.063
67	0.986	1.083	0.872	1.062
68	0.978	1.087	0.874	1.065
69	0.970	1.093	0.870	1.068
70	0.966	1.097	0.866	1.071
71	0.964	1.101	0.862	1.073
72	0.962	1.104	0.860	1.073
73	0.962	1.105		

SEASONAL FACTORS ONE YEAR AHEAD

YEAR	Q1	Q2	Q3	Q4
73			0.860	1.073
74	0.962	1.106		

STABLE SEASONALITY TEST

	SUM OF SQUARES	DEGREES OF FREEDOM	MEAN SQUARE	F
BETWEEN QUARTERS	6972.040	3	2324.010	148.154**
RESIDUAL	1035.310	66	15.686	
TOTAL	8007.350	69		

** PRESENCE OF STABLE SEASONALITY AT THE 1 PERCENT LEVEL

FIGURE 7

Plot of Seasonally Adjusted Linage and Real GNP Data

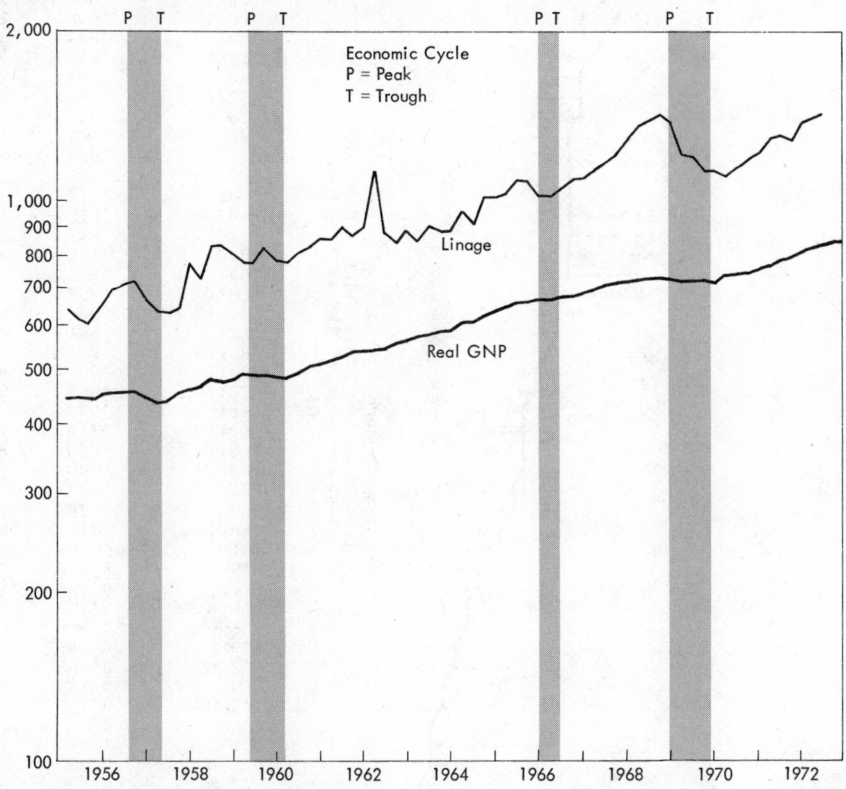

Vertical scale: Number of advertising pages.
Horizontal scale: Year.

(*a*) knowledge of the average relationship of linage to real GNP and (*b*) the value of real GNP and the dummy variable at each point from 56:1 to 73:2 also appear along with a plot of the actual and fitted values.

Indeed linage appears to be statistically related to real GNP, but some significant discrepancies between the fitted and actual linage values occur in several places, especially during the 1969–70 economic downturn. It appears that when a downturn occurs, actual linage declines faster than fitted linage and that when an upturn takes place, actual linage increases faster than fitted linage. The appearance of this fact suggests further testing.

Test 2. To the regression analysis in Test 1 can be added another variable to attempt to explain statistically more of the actual linage fluctuations. Because of the overshooting in both economic upturns and downturns, a plausible variable to include is some measure of

FIGURE 8

Regression Results: Linage and Real GNP, 56:1 to 73:2

```
ORDINARY LEAST SQUARES

FREQUENCY QUARTERLY
INTERVAL    56: 1 TO    73: 2
LEFT-HAND VARIABLE: DJAD
```

RIGHT-HAND VARIABLE	ESTIMATED COEFFICIENT	STANDARD ERROR	T-STATISTIC
CONSTANT	-138.388	44.2230	-3.12932
GNP58	1.85765	.721016E-01	25.7643

```
R-BAR SQUARED:   0.9057
DURBIN-WATSON STAT. (ADJ. FOR 0. GAPS):  0.7339
STANDARD ERROR OF THE REGRESSION:          72.3840
?SHOWNOW PLOT
```

PLOT: *=ACTUAL:+=FITTED

DATE	ACTUAL	FITTED
56: 1	640.0	685.7
56: 2	615.0	689.4
56: 3	606.0	687.3
56: 4	642.0	698.1
57: 1	690.0	703.9
57: 2	708.0	703.5
57: 3	715.0	707.2
57: 4	668.0	694.2
58: 1	639.0	674.3
58: 2	630.0	678.0
58: 3	643.0	698.9
58: 4	776.0	719.1
59: 1	728.0	732.1
59: 2	826.0	753.1
59: 3	832.0	744.0
59: 4	805.0	754.0
60: 1	779.0	772.2
60: 2	774.0	771.3
60: 3	827.0	766.8
60: 4	785.0	760.2
61: 1	777.0	758.1
61: 2	804.0	777.1
61: 3	825.0	793.2
61: 4	853.0	812.2
62: 1	850.0	826.7
62: 2	893.0	841.9
62: 3	863.0	852.5
62: 4	896.0	861.6
63: 1	1139.	867.0
63: 2	873.0	875.9
63: 3	841.0	892.0
63: 4	891.0	905.8
64: 1	851.0	922.5
64: 2	902.0	936.4
64: 3	886.0	949.8
64: 4	888.0	954.8
65: 1	959.0	979.2
65: 2	915.0	995.5
65: 3	1015.	1018.
65: 4	1018.	1044.
66: 1	1029.	1067.
66: 2	1084.	1078.
66: 3	1086.	1088.
66: 4	1022.	1103.
67: 1	1018.	1100.
67: 2	1054.	1109.
67: 3	1095.	1123.
67: 4	1100.	1132.
68: 1	1138.	1148.
68: 2	1159.	1172.
68: 3	1206.	1185.
68: 4	1286.	1193.
69: 1	1354.	1204.
69: 2	1391.	1210.
69: 3	1414.	1216.
69: 4	1393.	1209.
70: 1	1213.	1201.
70: 2	1200.	1203.
70: 3	1139.	1212.
70: 4	1134.	1198.
71: 1	1102.	1227.
71: 2	1149.	1237.
71: 3	1183.	1249.
71: 4	1213.	1272.
72: 1	1288.	1288.
72: 2	1309.	1321.
72: 3	1298.	1342.
72: 4	1373.	1371.
73: 1	1414.	1402.
73: 2	1417.	1411.

change in real GNP. However, what *kind* of change? Change from the previous quarter? From two quarters ago? There should be some logical causal reason for a particular choice. The choice made here is for a four-quarter change, with the rationale that advertisers look at their budgets in any quarter as compared to the expenditures actually made a year ago. This rationale is by and large consistent with actual practice.

The regression results for Test 2, which also covers 56:1 to 73:2, appear in Figure 9. The new variable, four-quarter change in real GNP, is also statistically significant. The fitted values of linage fall a bit closer to the actual values, at least through the economic fluctuations prior to 1969–70. However, an important period around 1969–70 is not satisfactorily accounted for by real GNP and changes in real GNP.

A close look at the problem period in Figure 9, which appears to begin around 68:2 and run through 70:4, indicates something indeed different had taken place. Recalling the turbulent financial market conditions through the better part of that period evokes images of a significantly greater than average number of proxy fights, tender offers, new issues, and employment affiliation changes in the financial community, all of which generate advertising linage. A check of the advertising content of the publication around that time confirms recollections. Full-page tender offer advertisements often appeared several days in succession. This analysis suggests another test.

Test 3. The structure of Test 2 is maintained, but the interval is changed from 56:1 through 73:2, to 56:1 through 68:2, with 68:2 being judged as about the beginning of the problem period.

The regression results appear in Figure 10. The fitted values are on-balance a bit closer to the actual values, and economic upturns and downturns are accounted for reasonably well. There appears to be some autocorrelation (serial correlation of errors [residuals] between fitted and actual values), as indicated both visually and by the Durbin-Watson statistic, which is somewhat below the 1.60 to 2.40 range that indicates a statistical lack of autocorrelation.

The hypothesis appears to stand up to the tests performed so far and cannot be rejected. An important question now is whether knowledge of this historical relationship from 56:1 to 68:2 is of any use in forecasting for a financial analyst in late 1973. A simple test should shed some light on this question.

Test 4. With the historical relationship from 56:1 through 68:2 that appears in Figure 10, forecasts can be made for linage for the 68:3 through 73:3 period by using the actual real GNP values that were recorded during that period. These forecasts of linage can be compared to the actual values of linage that prevailed during that period. This procedure will reveal how accurate forecasts could have been, as of mid-1968, for the ensuing five years if real GNP could have been forecast precisely on a quarterly basis over that period.

FIGURE 9

Regression Results: Linage, Real GNP, Change in Real GNP, 56:1 to 73:2

```
ORDINARY LEAST SQUARES

FREQUENCY QUARTERLY
INTERVAL     56: 1 TO    73: 2
LEFT-HAND VARIABLE: DOWSEA*

RIGHT-HAND        ESTIMATED       STANDARD        T-
 VARIABLE        COEFFICIENT       ERROR       STATISTIC

CONSTANT          -106.140        63.0915       -1.68233

GNP58              1.75345       0.143609        12.2098

CHNGGNP58*        0.595688       0.602894       0.988048

DUMMY631*          278.742        66.7125        4.17826
```

```
R-BAR SQUARED:    0.9221
DURBIN-WATSON STAT. (ADJ. FOR 0. GAPS):   0.5498
STANDARD ERROR OF THE REGRESSION:         66.0537
```

PLOT: *=ACTUAL;+=FITTED

TE	ACTUAL	FITTED
1	640.0	686.2
2	615.7	688.2
3	606.3	684.0
4	642.4	695.8
1	689.9	704.5
2	707.7	702.6
3	715.2	707.3
4	667.9	686.9
1	439.2	659.7
2	630.1	663.5
3	643.1	687.2
4	775.5	716.9
1	728.9	738.9
2	826.3	764.3
3	831.8	746.2
4	805.2	751.8
1	779.0	770.7
2	773.7	763.1
3	827.3	760.3
4	784.7	749.6
1	776.8	740.4
2	804.3	764.0
3	825.0	785.1
4	852.7	811.6
1	849.6	831.1
2	893.4	844.4
3	863.2	853.1
4	896.7	858.2
1	1139.	1139.
2	873.1	867.3
3	841.5	884.5
4	890.5	899.6
1	851.4	919.3
2	902.3	934.5
3	886.0	947.4
4	888.3	949.2
1	959.1	975.6
2	914.9	992.6
3	1015.	1016.
4	1018.	1049.
1	1029.	1072.
2	1184.	1083.
3	1086.	1090.
4	1022.	1101.
1	1018.	1089.
2	1054.	1096.
3	1095.	1111.
4	1100.	1119.
1	1138.	1144.
2	1159.	1174.
3	1206.	1187.
4	1286.	1194.
1	1354.	1204.
2	1392.	1206.
3	1414.	1212.
4	1393.	1200.
1	1213.	1189.
2	1200.	1188.
3	1139.	1196.
4	1134.	1181.
1	1102.	1224.
2	1149.	1238.
3	1183.	1249.
4	1213.	1280.
1	1288.	1291.
2	1310.	1328.
3	1298.	1352.
4	1374.	1387.
1	1414.	1425.
2	1417.	1434.

FIGURE 10

Regression Results: Linage, Real GNP, Change in Real GNP, 56:1 to 68:2

```
FREQUENCY QUARTERLY
INTERVAL     56: 1 TO     68: 2
LEFT-HAND VARIABLE:     W

RIGHT-HAND           ESTIMATED          STANDARD           T-
 VARIABLE           COEFFICIENT          ERROR          STATISTIC

CONSTANT             -27.0827           45.9176         -0.589811

GNP58                 1.57828          .946425E-01       16.6763

CHNGGNP58             1.48627          0.526950          2.82051

DUMMY                 279.863           44.4788          6.29206

R-BAR SQUARED:   0.9234
DURBIN-WATSON STAT. (ADJ. FOR 0. GAPS):   1.1073
STANDARD ERROR OF THE REGRESSION:               44.0239
?
```

DATE	ACTUAL	FITTED	PLOT: *=ACTUAL;+=FITTED
56: 1	640.0	696.2	
56: 2	615.7	691.4	
56: 3	606.3	678.0	
56: 4	642.4	689.4	
57: 1	689.9	703.1	
57: 2	707.7	699.5	
57: 3	715.2	707.3	
57: 4	667.9	677.2	
58: 1	639.2	639.8	
58: 2	630.1	646.2	
58: 3	643.1	677.6	
58: 4	775.5	721.4	
59: 1	728.9	758.7	
59: 2	826.3	790.4	
59: 3	831.8	758.7	
59: 4	805.2	759.1	
60: 1	779.0	778.7	
60: 2	773.7	760.4	
60: 3	827.3	760.3	
60: 4	784.7	741.2	
61: 1	776.8	723.3	
61: 2	804.3	755.3	
61: 3	825.0	785.5	
61: 4	852.7	822.1	
62: 1	849.6	847.7	
62: 2	893.4	857.6	
62: 3	863.2	862.2	
62: 4	896.7	862.0	
63: 1	1139.	1139.	
63: 2	873.1	861.9	
63: 3	841.5	880.0	
63: 4	890.5	895.4	
64: 1	851.4	918.7	
64: 2	902.3	934.6	
64: 3	886.0	943.7	
64: 4	888.3	941.0	
65: 1	959.1	967.7	
65: 2	914.9	983.6	
65: 3	1015.	1010.	
65: 4	1018.	1049.	
66: 1	1029.	1068.	
66: 2	1184.	1073.	
66: 3	1086.	1071.	
66: 4	1022.	1074.	
67: 1	1018.	1051.	
67: 2	1054.	1058.	
67: 3	1095.	1072.	
67: 4	1100.	1075.	
68: 1	1138.	1105.	
68: 2	1159.	1136.	

The results that appear in Figure 11 are interesting. After significantly underestimating actual linage for the quarters from 68:3 to 70:4, the forecasts come quite close to the actual for the rest of the period. The implications of these results are important:

1. It appears that a significant, unusual, and unsustainable change in mix of demand occurred in the 68:3 to 70:4 period.
2. If an analyst had perceived this at that time (hindsight is admittedly a wonderful thing), it would have been apparent that the odds were heavily in favor of a steep linage decline in the year 1970 from total linage in 1969, even if a robust economic environment had existed in 1970 instead of a recession.

FIGURE 11

Analysis of Forecasting Ability of a Historical Relationship

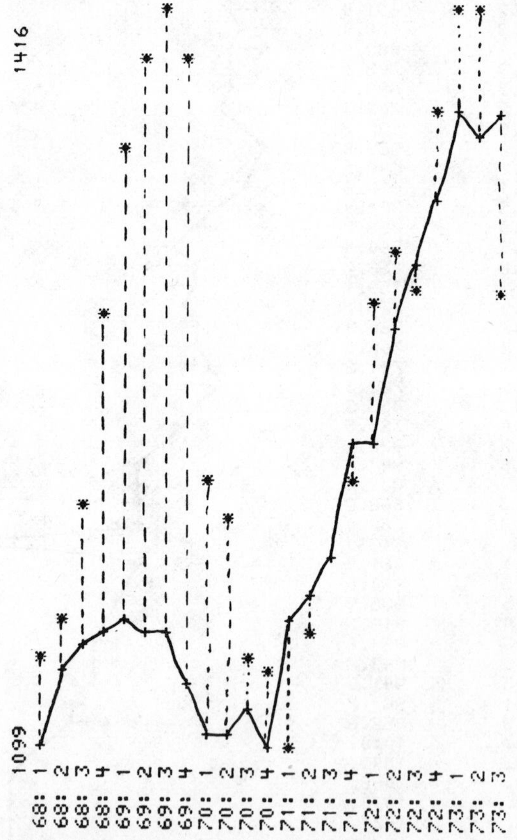

Vertical scale: Number of advertising pages.
Horizontal scale: Year.
Solid line: Forecast of quarterly linage (ad pages, eastern edition).
Asterisks: actual ad pages, quarterly (seasonally adjusted).
Relationships developed over period of 1956:1 through 1967:4.
"Forecast" based upon actual real GNP data from 1968:1 through 1973:3

3. It appears that the basic demand factors for advertising linage in this national business publication, on the average, have not changed perceptibly over the past five years from earlier periods.

These results, along with the Test 3 results, tend to support the hypothesis more by a "preponderance of evidence" than by cold statistics and provide useful grist for the financial analyst's mill. Even more interesting questions can now be addressed that bear upon the future.

Forecasting Process. The financial analysis that was just conducted produced results that give some degree of confidence that in this case past relationships may be useful in forecasting future eventualities. With the work just conducted in hand, the financial analyst may draw upon the expertise of an economist or a number of economists for a forecast of real gross national product on a quarterly basis.

The economist's real GNP forecast will dictate the forecast values for linage by the *forecasting model,* i.e., the equation in Figure 10. At this point the work of the economist is done, and it remains for the financial analyst to decide if he should adopt the forecast or modify it judgmentally up or down based on his own subjective feelings and his experience. The quantitative analysis helped in determining whether the financial analyst is on the right road and going in the right direction, but the financial analyst must interpret for himself the importance of the traffic signs and the road conditions in arriving at his destination.

The value of using more than one economist's views or more than one view of an economist is illustrated by the following *sensitivity analysis.* Two economic scenarios for the 1974 and 1975 period were envisioned to be relatively optimistic and relatively pessimistic with regard to how economic activity would proceed for the next two years. The numerical forecasts for real GNP and for the resulting linage forecasts appear in Figure 12. The graphs indicate the pattern of quarterly seasonally adjusted linage forecast. By taking the quarterly seasonally adjusted linage figures and multiplying the seasonal adjustment factors forecasted earlier, unadjusted linage forecasts can be obtained for each quarter, and these can be summed to obtain annual totals as illustrated in Figure 12. The linage forecasts can be combined with prospective rate increases and a revenue forecast for this product line can be developed, which, combined with the outlook for cost behavior, results in a profit forecast.

Caution cannot be thrown to the winds and the revenue forecasts embraced unconditionally at this point in history (year-end 1973) if the U.S. economy is indeed headed into a prolonged period of short supply. Advertising may become less necessary than in a demand constrained economy. The use of computers and financial data has helped the financial analyst in making his forecasts, but as usual, an important element of uncertainty remains.

FIGURE 12

Sensitivity Analysis for Linage Forecasts 1973:4 to 1975:4 (Seasonally Adjusted)

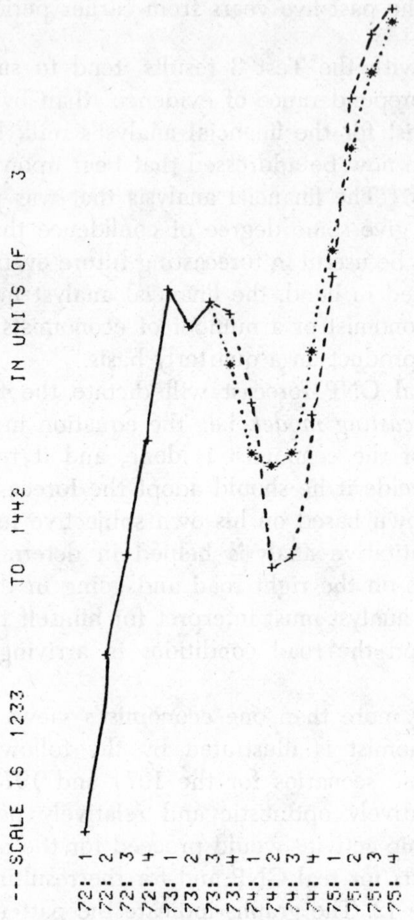

Forecasts

	Optimistic Outlook			*Pessimistic Outlook*		
	Real GNP	*Advertising Pages*		*Real GNP*	*Advertising Pages*	
Qtr.	*Seas. Adj. Ann. Rate*	*Seas. Adj. Qtrly Rate*	*Unadj. Qtrly*	*Seas. Adj. Ann. Rate*	*Seas. Adj. Qtrly Rate*	*Unadj Qtrly*
73:4	\$848.4	1365	1465	\$848.3	1365	1465
74:1	851.8	1351	1300	849.1	1342	1291
74:2	855.7	1355	1499	838.5	1302	1440
74:3	862.5	1365	1174	842.9	1305	1122
74:4	869.7	1377	1478	857.8	1341	1439
75:1	879.9	1403	1350	869.5	1375	1323
75:2	890.3	1429	1581	878.7	1419	1569
75:3	900.2	1449	1246	886.6	1437	1236
75:4	910.7	1482	1591	895.5	1442	1547
Year						
1974	\$859.9 +2.6%		5451 −0.3%	\$847.1 +1.0%		5292 −3.2%
1975	895.3 +4.1%		5768 +5.8%	882.6 +4.2%		5675 +7.2%

Vertical: Number of advertising pages.
Horizontal: Year.

Key: Solid line: Historical Estimate.
Dotted line: "Optimistic Macroeconomic Scenario.
Dashed line: "Pessimistic" Macroeconomic Scenario.

In addition to empirical analysis, deterministic and probabilistic analysis techniques can often be usefully employed in security analysis.

Deterministic Analysis. Financial statement projection software has been implemented by a few time-sharing vendors. Complete interlocking sets of income and funds-flow statements and balance sheets can be projected rapidly based on the users' assumptions. Projected sales and profitability data can be quickly translated into profits, capital expansion needs, and so on. Sets of such programs can be easily developed on a small scale by a knowledgeable programmer.

Probabilitistic Analysis. Subjective probability distributions can be formulated by an analyst for several financial variables that bear upon forecasting a key variable. These distributions can be combined quickly by simple computer simulation techniques to produce a probabilistic description of the key variable.

For example, probabilistic rate of investment return distributions can be developed by combining subjective probability distributions of earnings per share, earnings per share growth rates, relative price/earnings ratios, market price/earnings ratios, and dividend expectations, for a desired time horizon. These distributions can be computed for individual stocks or portfolios. The resulting investment return distribution can then be used to estimate risk, which can be defined as the probability of not achieving a desired investment return objective.

Screening

The availability of large financial data bases on computers permits rapid searching through or *screening* (sometimes called filtering) a large number of companies for those companies that possess a particular set of characteristics. As a result the financial analyst can be spared a great deal of tedious, unprofitable labor.

To run a screen it is necessary to write a computer program in a programming language such as FORTRAN to search a data base or to make use of commercially available screening software. The former procedure requires fairly extensive computer knowledge, the latter requires very little. Most financial analysts could learn to use commercially available screening software in less than an hour.

An example of the commands (instructions) that a financial analyst would have to enter into the computer to produce a list of companies in the drug industry with (*a*) market value greater than $500 million and (*b*) earnings growth over the past five years of 10 percent or more appears in Figure 13, along with the companies that satisfy the criteria. Further research can be performed on these companies to determine investment merit.

FIGURE 13

Example of Commands to Produce a Screen and Results of Screen

```
ffl
FFL VERSION 24
*pri rep drug
±NAME:DRUG;
±COLUMNS;
      10 Y73.M12.D31.CPRC"PRICE;
      20 Y72.SHS"SHARES";
      30 Y73.M12.D31.CPRC*Y72.SHS"MKT VAL";
      40 EPS.CGRW(Y67'TO'Y72)"EPS GRWTH";
      50 END;
±ROWS;
      10 $DRUGS;
      20 DISC:(EPS.CGRW(Y67'TO'Y72)'GT'15.0);
      30 SORT:(EPS.CGRW(Y67'TO'Y72));
      40 END;


*disp rep drug

ACCESSING DATA

REPORT "DRUG      "; PAGES:        1; ROWS:     4; COLUMNS:      4
OPTIONS? ±no
OUTPUT TO ±2741
----------------

INTERACTIVE DATA CORPORATION

                  PRICE       SHARES      MKT VAL    EPS GRWTH

JONSN-JNSN       112.75     56418.99   6361240.0         23.23
SCHERING          71.00     52589.99   3733889.0         19.32
LILLY ELI         74.13     68559.94   5082005.0         17.46
BAXTER LAB        48.13     29004.00   1395817.0         17.08
```

Equity Valuation

Attempts have been made to explain and/or forecast equity prices using advanced mathematical techniques and the computer. The approaches taken can be classified as either fundamental or technical. Some organizations that have done work in this area claim a degree of success, others do not. The cost to do this kind of work is generally high, requiring a great deal of computer time and considerable personnel skills—mathematical as well as programming, and an understanding of the investment business.

Fundamental. Work in this area focuses on relating equity prices or returns to *fundamental* variables such as earnings and earnings growth. Methodology employed can be classed as either descriptive or normative. Descriptive methodologies attempt to describe the equity markets as they are, in terms of the interrelationships among individual equities or classes of equities at a point in time and/or through time. The statistical technique used most frequently is linear regression analysis, although discriminant analysis and various cluster analysis procedures, such as factor analysis, are also used.

Normative methodologies attempt to describe equity prices as they should be and are usually based upon discounted cash flow techniques. A set of earnings or dividend growth rate assumptions, and discount rate assumptions usually based on some subset of the term structure of interest rates, are used to compute what the price of a stock should be. The computed price is then compared to the actual price. Alternatively, a set of discount rates or a single rate could be computed that would equate the actual price to the present value of the projected dividend or earnings stream. The computed rate(s) is then compared to some standard rate. Either way, significant discrepancies point to opportunities for further analysis.

Technical. Work in this area generally focuses upon behavior of equity price changes as related to past equity price changes and *technical* variables such as momentum, upside/downside volume, and so on. Statistical techniques employed range from arbitrary specification of the relationships among the variables to complex cluster analysis techniques.

Both fundamental and technical equity valuations can be and are performed on individual issues, groups or industry averages, or composite market indices.

Bond Valuation

An increasing amount of computer work is being done in the bond valuation area. This is primarily the case with nonconvertible, or *straight,* bonds, whose analysis is almost purely mathematical. Analysis of convertible bonds (and other convertible securities) also is mathematical, but to a lesser extent. With convertible securities, buy/sell decision criteria tend to be more subjective of necessity, because of the importance of judging the price appreciation prospects of the underlying equity.

Straight Bonds. Straight bonds are more nearly substitutes for one another than any other class of investment vehicles, except short-term money-market instruments. The concepts of yield to maturity, reinvestment yield, and realized yield developed in Chapter 36 can be computed instantly by computer. In fact, since the kind of calculations necessary recur so frequently, specialized programmable calculators and dedicated mini-computers are often used in place of, or in addition to, time-sharing computers, especially by market makers. Where investment analysis does not require explicit consideration of reinvestment, as often happens in personal trust account work, desk-top and hand-held financial calculators can be used to compute yields to maturity rapidly.

FIGURE 14
Convertible Bond Statistic Sheet

IN TWO SECTIONS
SECTION 1

LISTED CONVERTIBLE BONDS

Exch. Bd. Com.	Bonds Outstanding ($ Mil.)	COMPANY	Interest Dates	Accrued Interest	Coupon Rate (%)	Year Due	Year Exp.	Next Change (Mo./Day/Yr.)
NN	10.C	APL CORP	JD01	5.90	5 3/4	88	88	
NN	40.C	ARA SERVICES	JD15	2.95	4 5/8	96	96	
NN	25.C	A-T-O	JJ01	.84	4 3/8	87	87	
NN	31.7	AIR REDUCTION CO	FA15	15.39	3 7/8	87	87	
AA	2.1	ALASKA AIRLINES	JD01	7.06	6 7/8	87	87	
NN	8.3	ALASKA INTERSTATE	FA01	26.16	6.000	96	96	
NN	20.C	ALEXANDERS	JJ01	1.06	5 1/2	96	96	
AN	6.C	ALISON MORTGAGE INV	JD15	4.30	6 3/4	91	91	
AA	15.0	ALLEGHENY AIRLINES	AO01	15.49	5 3/4	93	93	
NN	5.7	ALLEGHENY LUDLUM	AO01	4.10	4.000	81	81	
NN	4.4	ALLEN GROUP	JJ01	1.16	6.000	87	87	
AA	2.8	ALLIED ARTISTS	MN15	12.88	8 3/4	90	90	
NN	3.4	ALLIED STORES	AO01	12.12	4 1/2	81	81	
NN	49.9	ALLIED STORES	MS15	14.12	4 1/2	92	92	
NN	19.5	ALLIED SUPERMKTS	JD01	5.90	5 3/4	87	87	
NN	125.0	ALUMINUM CO OF AMER	MS15	16.47	5 1/4	91	91	
NN	14.9	AMERACE CORP	MS01	17.63	5.000	92	92	
NN	12.5	AMERICAN AIR FILTER	MS01	21.16	6.000	90	90	
NN	166.0	AMERICAN AIRLINES	JJ01	.82	4 1/4	92	80	
AN	2.6	AMER CENTURY MTGE	AO01	18.85	7.000	90	90	
NN	10.2	AMER CENTURY MTGE	JD15	4.30	6 3/4	91	91	
NN	4.6	AMER HOIST&DERRICK	JD01	4.87	4 3/4	92	92	
NN	18.0	AMER HOIST&DERRICK	JD01	5.64	5 1/2	93	93	
NN	32.C	AMER MACH & FDRY	MS01	14.98	4 1/4	81	81	
NN	30.0	AMERICAN MEDICORP	JJ01	.97	5.000	97	97	
AA	5.7	AMER MOTOR INNS	FA01	23.98	5 1/2	91	91	
NN	35.0	AMERICAN MOTORS	AO01	16.16	6.000	88	88	
AA	2.4	AMER SAFETY EQUIP	JD01	5.90	5 3/4	83	83	
NN	35.0	AMFAC INC	MN01	9.77	5 1/4	94	94	
NN	60.0	AMPEX CORP	FA15	21.84	5 1/2	94	94	
NN	18.4	APCO OIL CORP	JJ15	24.02	5.000	88	88	7/15/78
NN	11.1	ARLEN REALTY&DEV	JD01	5.13	5.000	86	86	
NN	2.8	ARMOUR & CO	MS01	15.87	4 1/2	83	83	
NN	10.0	ARMSTRONG RUBBER	MS01	25.87	4 1/2	87	87	
NN	60.0	ASHLAND OIL	FA15	18.86	4 3/4	93	93	
NN	90.2	AVCO CORP	MN30	5.80	5 1/2	93	93	
NN	55.C	BALTIMORE&OHIO RR	JD01	6.41	6 1/4	97	97	
NN	10.9	BANGOR PUNTA	JJ01	1.60	8 1/4	94	94	
NN	20.C	BANK OF CALIFORNIA	MS15	20.39	6 1/2	96	96	
NN	62.1	BANK OF NEW YORK	MS01	22.04	6 1/4	94	94	
NN	30.C	BARNETT MORTGAGE	MS01	29.97	8 1/2	98	98	9/01/78
AA	5.3	BARTELL MEDIA	JD01	6.67	6 1/2	88	88	
NN	14.4	BAXTER LABORATORIES	MS01	14.10	4.000	87	87	
NN	60.0	BAXTER LABORATORIES	MS01	16.75	4 3/4	90	90	
NN	55.C	BAXTER LABORATORIES	MN01	8.14	4 3/8	91	91	
NN	25.C	BEAUNIT CORP	FA01	18.53	4 1/4	90	90	

CONVERSION TERMS PER $1,000 BOND									YIELDS			
No. of Shares	Conversion Price ($)	Com. Mkt. Price ($)	Conversion Value (%)	Bd. Mkt. Price (%)	Inv. Value (%)	Prem. CV (%)	Est. Risk (%)	Rating	Current Bond Yield (%)	Yield To Maturity (Approx.) (%)	Indicated Common Yield (%)	Footnotes (See Last Page)
36.90	27.10	6.62	24	58B		137		B-	9.91	11.93		
6.58	152.00	87.00	57	87	58	53	34	B	5.29	5.61	1.52	
17.09	58.50	5.50	9	48		411		B-	9.11	12.42	3.64	
32.00	31.25	13.75	44	61	61	40	1	B+	6.30	8.77	5.82	
132.98	7.52	5.00	66	86		30		C	7.93	8.51		
38.46	26.00	24.87	96	103B	68	8	34	B	5.83	5.75		
31.01	32.25	3.62	11	47		319		B	11.70	12.77	2.76	
36.36	27.50	20.25	74	70		0			9.57	10.42	14.91	
43.17	23.16	5.25	23	47		107		C+	12.23	13.54		
19.23	52.00	27.62	53	75	71	41	5	B	5.33	8.46	3.62	
37.17	26.90	7.00	26	61		134		B-	9.84	11.87	1.43	
222.22	4.50	3.25	72	92		27			9.51	9.73		
35.71	28.00	19.87	71	79	71	11	10	B	5.70	8.21	7.55	
22.47	44.50	19.87	45	58	54	30	7	B	7.73	9.23	7.55	
64.77	15.44	3.75	24	58		139		B	9.91	12.05		
11.76	85.00	73.00	86	98	72	14	227	B+	5.36	5.42	2.66	
27.03	37.00	17.75	48	65B		37		B+	7.63	8.80	6.76	
37.74	26.50	12.25	46	84B	72	82	14	B	7.14	7.75	3.59	
22.60	44.25	8.75	20	49	48	150	3	B	8.59	10.51		
47.62	21.00	9.12	43	67B		55			10.37	11.46	19.74	
35.71	28.00	9.12	33	63B		93			10.71	11.81	19.74	
63.86	15.66	13.12	84	81	58	0	29	B-	5.83	6.48	4.57	
47.92	20.87	13.12	63	72	63	15	12	B-	7.64	8.46	4.57	
16.89	59.19	18.62	31	74	72	135	3	B	5.74	9.29	5.80	
45.45	22.00	3.87	18	45		156			11.11	12.16		
31.25	32.00	7.12	22	55B		149			9.91	11.53	1.40	
87.11	11.48	8.75	76	87		14		B-	6.89	7.45		
88.89	11.25	4.87	43	72		66		B-	7.99	10.32		
22.90	43.67	12.00	27	61B	60	122	2	B	8.61	9.68	5.33	
21.74	46.00	3.37	7	42		475		B-	13.06	14.35		
33.78	29.60	12.12	41	60	60	47	1	B-	8.28	10.33		
52.63	19.00	3.00	16	54		242		B-	9.26	12.34		
63.53	15.74	14.62	93	87B	67	0	23	B	5.15	6.26	7.11	5
19.60	51.02	16.62	33	60B		86		B	7.42	9.79	9.63	
20.00	50.00	24.25	49	73	66	51	10	B+	6.51	7.37	5.36	
18.52	54.00	6.37	12	54	54	359	0	B	10.16	11.39		
17.47	57.25	56.50	99	97	70	0	28	B	6.44	6.50	6.37	53
18.87	53.00	4.75	9	76B		754		B-	10.78	11.20		
33.20	30.12	21.87	73	83		14			7.83	8.16	6.13	
26.67	37.50	30.12	80	89		11			7.02	7.28	6.64	
25.64	39.00	19.75	51	96		91			8.81	8.85	13.47	6
66.12	15.13	1.12	7	41		453		B-	15.85	18.09		
57.97	17.25	44.87	260	277B	65	7	77	B+	1.44		.38	
25.97	38.50	44.87	117	119B	68	2	43	B+	3.99	3.23	.38	
26.32	38.00	44.87	118	123	64	4	48	B+	3.56	2.73	.38	
35.96	27.81	13.12	47	50		6		B	8.48	10.78	7.62	7

Convertible Bonds. Commercially available data bases are drawn upon to provide prices for convertible bonds and their underlying equities. These price data are combined with constant data, such as conversion terms and dividend and coupon rates, to compute statistics than can be used for decision-making purposes. Such statistics include premium over conversion, break-even years, yield, and value as straight debt. This information must then be combined with subjective evaluations of appreciation prospects of the underlying equity. It is here that the decision-making process becomes less amenable to mathematical analysis. Figure 14 shows a sample of a convertible bond statistic sheet.

Portfolio Policy Analysis

Portfolio policy analysis involves simulating portfolio asset values for long time periods under different income, payout, funding, asset appreciation, and actuarial assumptions. To date this kind of analysis has been utilized by employee benefit funds and tax-exempt foundation funds more than by personal trust funds. A significant part of the value of this kind of analysis for an employee benefit fund derives from sensitivity analysis of funding requirements under various vesting, employee turnover, and employee age distribution assumptions for given realized investment return assumptions. In addition, portfolio policy analysis provides a better basis for communication between the investment managers and the funding organization, and conditions the expectations of both parties. An illustration of some of the structure and output from a portfolio policy analysis example appears in Figure 15.

Security Analyst Evaluation

Work in this area focuses on efficacy of investment recommendations and accuracy in earnings estimates for equities. It may come as a surprise that not many large investment management organizations employ formal quantitatively based analyst evaluation systems. Those that do are very cautious about how they utilize the statistics gathered in judging performance and determining compensation.

Important reasons for this situation include consideration of dependence of earnings forecasts on economic scenarios that do not come to pass and the length of the forecast period. The forecast period is usually one year, as few organizations insist that analysts forecast quarterly earnings in view of the considerable flexibility corporations have in reporting interim earnings. One observation per company per year does not constitute an abundance of data, but tentative conclusions can sometimes be drawn in cases where many companies are followed per analyst.

FIGURE 15

Portfolio Policy Analysis

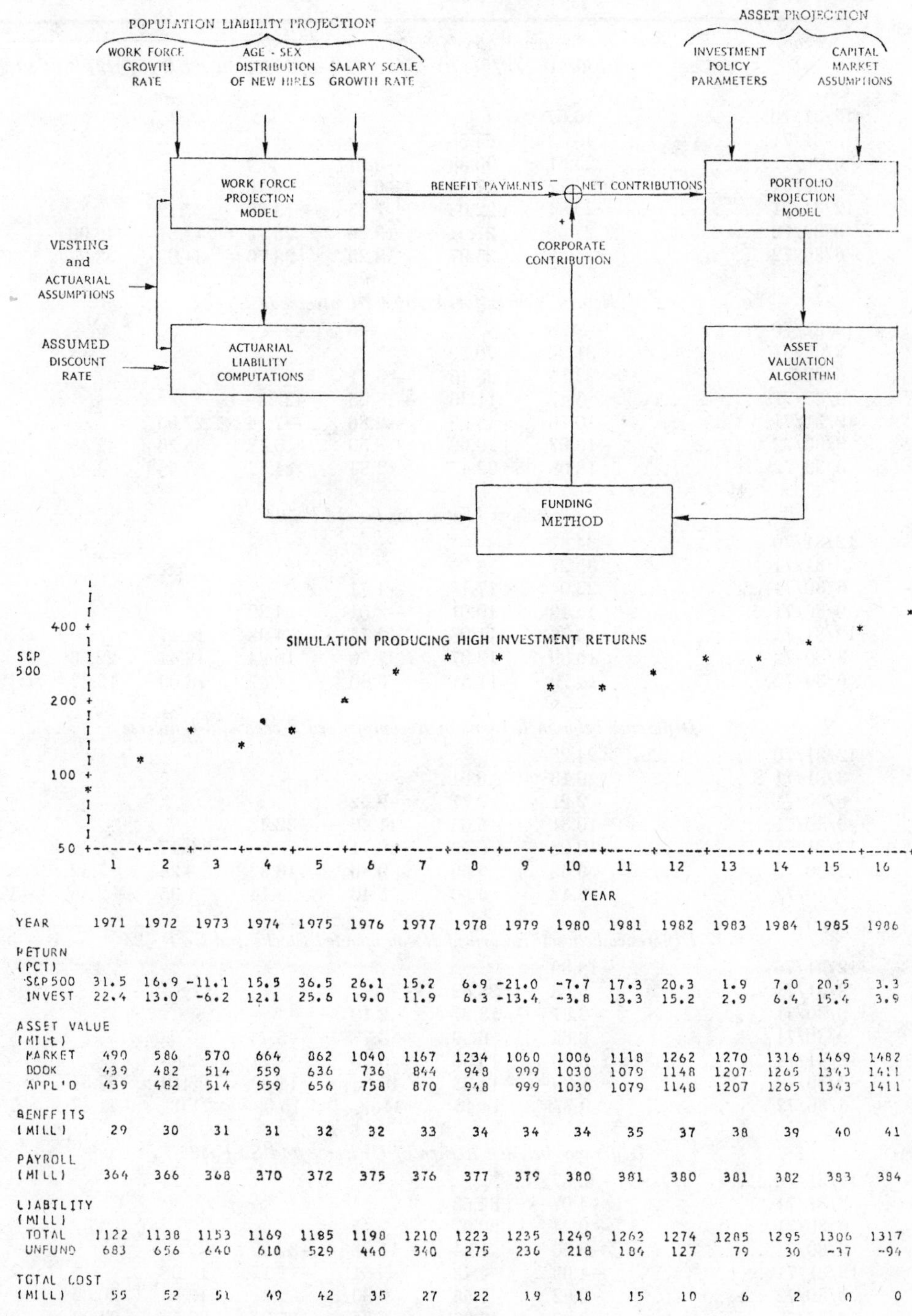

YEAR	1971	1972	1973	1974	1975	1976	1977	1978	1979	1980	1981	1982	1983	1984	1985	1986
RETURN (PCT)																
S&P500	31.5	16.9	-11.1	15.5	36.5	26.1	15.2	6.9	-21.0	-7.7	17.3	20.3	1.9	7.0	20.5	3.3
INVEST	22.4	13.0	-6.2	12.1	25.6	19.0	11.9	6.3	-13.4	-3.8	13.3	15.2	2.9	6.4	15.4	3.9
ASSET VALUE (MILL)																
MARKET	490	586	570	664	862	1040	1167	1234	1060	1006	1118	1262	1270	1316	1469	1482
BOOK	439	482	514	559	636	736	844	948	999	1030	1079	1148	1207	1265	1343	1411
APPL'D	439	482	514	559	656	758	870	948	999	1030	1079	1148	1207	1265	1343	1411
BENEFITS (MILL)	29	30	31	31	32	32	33	34	34	34	35	37	38	39	40	41
PAYROLL (MILL)	364	366	368	370	372	375	376	377	379	380	381	380	381	382	383	384
LIABILITY (MILL)																
TOTAL	1122	1138	1153	1169	1185	1198	1210	1223	1235	1249	1262	1274	1285	1295	1306	1317
UNFUND	683	656	640	610	529	440	340	275	236	218	184	127	79	30	-37	-94
TOTAL COST (MILL)	55	52	51	49	42	35	27	22	19	18	15	10	6	2	0	0

Source: O'Brien Associates, Inc., Santa Monica, California.

FIGURE 16

Price Forecast Data System

From: / To:	9/30/70	12/31/70	3/31/71	6/30/71	9/30/71	12/31/71	3/30/72
Return Matrix for Recommended Stocks							
12/31/70	16.07						
3/31/71	40.33	64.58					
6/30/71	25.61	30.38	−3.81				
9/30/71	16.77	17.00	−6.78	−9.76			
12/31/71	20.84	22.03	7.85	13.68	37.12		
3/30/72	25.68	27.61	18.36	25.75	43.51	49.90	
6/30/72	24.55	25.97	18.25	23.76	34.93	33.84	17.78
Return Matrix for Analysts' Universe of Stocks							
12/31/70	−8.20						
3/31/71	31.20	70.59					
6/30/71	22.70	38.15	5.71				
9/30/71	6.47	11.36	−18.26	−42.23			
12/31/71	10.76	15.50	−2.86	−7.14	27.95		
3/30/72	16.07	20.92	8.50	9.43	35.26	42.58	
6/30/72	18.08	22.47	12.84	14.62	33.58	36.39	30.20
Return Matrix for the S&P 425							
12/31/70	34.47						
3/31/71	35.27	36.06					
6/30/71	22.94	17.18	−1.71				
9/30/71	16.13	10.01	−3.01	−4.32			
12/31/71	15.76	11.08	2.75	4.98	14.27		
3/30/72	16.89	13.37	7.70	10.84	18.41	22.56	
6/30/72	14.79	11.51	6.60	8.67	13.00	12.37	2.17
Difference between Returns of Recommended Stocks and Universe							
12/31/70	24.28						
3/31/71	9.13	−6.01					
6/30/71	2.91	−7.77	−9.52				
9/30/71	10.31	5.65	11.48	32.48			
12/31/71	10.08	6.53	10.71	20.83	9.17		
3/30/72	9.62	6.69	9.86	16.32	8.25	7.32	
6/30/72	6.47	3.50	5.40	9.14	1.35	−2.55	−12.43
Difference between Return of Recommended Stocks and S&P 425							
12/31/70	−18.39						
3/31/71	5.06	28.52					
6/30/71	2.67	13.21	−2.10				
9/30/71	0.64	6.99	−3.77	−5.44			
12/31/71	5.09	10.96	5.10	8.71	22.85		
3/30/72	8.79	14.23	10.66	14.92	25.10	27.34	
6/30/72	9.77	14.46	11.65	15.09	21.93	21.47	15.60
Difference between Return of Universe and S&P 425							
12/31/70	−42.67						
3/31/71	−4.07	34.53					
6/30/71	−0.24	20.97	7.41				
9/30/71	−9.66	1.34	−15.25	−37.92			
12/31/71	−4.99	4.43	−5.61	−12.12	13.68		
3/30/72	−0.82	7.55	0.80	−1.41	16.85	20.02	
6/30/72	3.30	10.96	6.24	5.95	20.58	24.02	28.03

FIGURE 16—*Continued*

Summary of Individual Returns to Date

Recommended							
IBM	29.54	21.00	9.21	21.24	25.51	15.27	2.52
Xerox	54.82	55.55	35.22	26.20	26.85	18.53	6.33
Not recommended							
Sperry Rand	48.23	48.23	13.86	18.47	46.30	29.98	16.66
Burroughs	39.60	51.86	42.89	35.63	31.07	18.34	11.31
NCR	−28.26	−21.21	−31.76	−37.62	−7.96	7.79	0.0

Note: Returns and differences between returns in matrices are annualized; individual returns are not annualized.

Analysis of efficacy of investment recommendation price performance is somewhat easier than earnings accuracy analysis. The problem here is that recommendations typically take widely varying periods of time to work out. To expect a fair reading for judging the ability of each of a group of analysts every quarter or even every year is to be a bit optimistic. As a result, statistics must be used cautiously.

An illustration of a computer-based price forecast data system appears in Figure 16.

Portfolio Performance Measurement

Procedures to measure realized rates of return for judging performance were developed by the Bank Administration Institute (BAI) in the late 1960s. The BAI developed and has made available a computer program (called COMVEST) to calculate asset-weighted rates of return to measure portfolio performance and time-weighted rates of return to measure portfolio manager performance. The COMVEST program computes a risk measure, but the BAI does not advise how the risk measure should be used in evaluating performance. The COMVEST program is available in various form on commercial time-sharing systems.

A number of services have been developed to attempt to get at the risk measurement and risk-adjusted performance assessment problem. Considerable theoretical problems remain in this area, upon which research is being conducted at a number of universities.

Figure 17 contains an example of a portion of output from the COMVEST program.

Statistical Report Generation

Computers are commonly used to generate statistical reports. The reports may be more information oriented or more decision oriented. Information-oriented report generating software is supplied by some time-sharing vendors that can perform a variety of functions, such as portfolio accounting work, including asset statement and transaction

FIGURE 17

Example of COMVEST Program Output

IRR MATRIX — Dollar-Weighted Rates of Return

FROM TO	03/31/70	06/30/70	09/30/70	12/31/70	03/31/71
12/31/69	-25.02	-48.84	-21.39	-7.25	3.60
03/31/70		-64.98	-19.56	-0.65	11.99
06/30/70			81.18	64.19	62.48
09/30/70				49.19	54.09
12/31/70					59.16

TWR MATRIX — Time-Weighted Rates of Return

FROM TO	03/31/70	06/30/70	09/30/70	12/31/70	03/31/71
12/31/69	-24.95	-48.95	-21.68	-8.00	2.53
03/31/70		-65.13	-20.01	-1.66	10.73
06/30/70			81.82	64.21	62.52
09/30/70				48.31	53.56
12/31/70					59.12

All Returns Annualized

flow statement preparation. Decision-oriented reports are generally best designed by the user himself.

ECONOMICS OF COMPUTER USE

The major cost elements in using commercial time-sharing computers are equipment costs, computer time, and personnel costs. Generally, equipment costs are the least burdensome. Depending upon how a computer effort is organized, personnel costs may be more or less than computer time costs. A brief description of cost elements follows. Where possible, orders of magnitude or ranges of typical cost are given.

Terminal Rental Costs. The minimum equipment configuration for utilizing commercially available time-sharing computing and data base resources consists of a terminal about the size and appearance of a typewriter, which can be connected to the computer by means of an ordinary telephone. These terminals generally send and receive at rates of 10 to 30 characters a second. Some have wide carriages capable of printing up to about 130 characters a line. Some are portable. Most rent for $70 to $250 per month depending upon features desired.

Most time-sharing vendors support high-speed terminals capable of speeds up to 100 to 200 full lines of output per minute. These rent from around $500 to around $1,250 per month depending upon features desired. It is generally not necessary to use such large terminals in financial analysis work. If a large amount of output is needed from time to time, the vendor's own high-speed printer often may be used at nominal cost.

Contract Costs. Signing a contract with a time-sharing vendor to obtain access to computing resources may or may not require a minimum monthly or annual payment. Generally a minimum payment is credited against computer use charges for the month. De facto minimums can arise in the form of minimum on-line computer storage charges. Particulars vary considerably.

Usage Costs. Computer time-sharing usage costs vary considerably. Some vendors can be found that provide raw computing time for a flat $5 per hour, plus storage. If no programs or data are stored overnight, $5 per hour is the total cost. The charges of vendors who provide extensive on-line data bases for customer use generally charge rates for terminal connect time, computing power used, and data access that can easily total to an average of $40 to $50 per hour. Carefully done, an enormous amount of work can be performed in an hour. Usage cost elements generally consist of the following:

Terminal Connect Time. Users are always charged for the time when they dial into the computer and log-on until they log-off and hang up the telephone. Rates vary from around $4 per hour to around $15 per hour.

Central Processor Usage. A user may be connected to the computer, but he may not be using the computer to solve a problem. When he does use the computer he is charged according to a formula devised by the vendor. Some vendors charge nothing, making their money from terminal connect charges. Other vendors charge a lot. Comparison among those who do charge is difficult without running a test program on each computer.

On-line Storage. A user is customarily charged for storing his programs and data on-line. Rates vary considerably. A rough estimate would run from about $.20 to $.50 per thousand characters per month. To save money, users may store programs and data off-line on paper tape, punched cards, or magnetic tape, but must pay to reload the programs and data to use them.

Data Access. Time-sharing vendors that maintain large on-line financial data bases provide an important service to their customers by taking them out of the data collection and maintenance business and consequently minimizing their personnel costs. The vendors generally obtain revenue for this service by charging for each *piece* of data accessed. A piece of data may consist of one item, such as a closing stock price for one day, or a group of items such as daily closing prices for an entire month, depending upon how the vendor has structured the data base within the computer. Cost per piece of data ranges up to two cents, and many vendors offer concessions for overnight or off-peak-hour usage.

Software Access. Many time-sharing vendors offer specialized *data manipulation, data analysis,* and *modeling software.* Precise definitions have not evolved. Generally speaking, data manipulation software allows the user without any programming knowledge, among other things, to (*a*) display raw data from his own or a vendor's data base and/or (*b*) perform computations upon the data prior to display, and/or (*c*) sort and rank the data prior to display, and/or (*d*) screen out entities with undesired characteristics, prior to display, and/or (*e*) update the user's data base.

Data analysis software refers to programs that allow the user to perform various tests upon data, such as regression analysis, histogram preparation, cross-classification analysis, goodness of fit tests, and others.

Modeling software is taken here to mean software that allows a user to specify a set or collection of relationships, generally in the form of algebraic equations, and to solve the set of relationships to produce an internally consistent solution. Subsequent operation upon such a solution with data manipulation and analysis software allows the user with no programming knowledge to generate useful reports. Included in this concept of modeling software would be programs to perform diverse computations, such as bond swap analyses and generalized simulation problems. Charges, if any, are generally either on a per-program use basis or on a terminal-connect or central-processor use surcharge basis, and can run 20 to 50 percent extra.

ORGANIZING FOR COMPUTER USE

Some large organizations have centralized operations research departments. This kind of organization can work out well when the problems to be solved are complex and where the payoff is high. In most work in security analysis the payoffs do not justify elaborate projects. In addition, the response time required in security analysis is generally very fast. Consequently, it is usually advisable to consider a small group of computer trained analysts that understands the nuances and nature of financial analysis as it applies to typical problems encountered. One or two persons with the right skills can be more than adequate.

The better graduate schools are graduating persons, in some cases, well enough versed in computer applications to be able to utilize them immediately. Alternatively, undergraduate computer sciences schools have programs where a person can minor in a business field, and vice versa.

Finally, some time-sharing vendors employ staff specialists to assist users in solving problems, and self-employed consultants are available. These skills can be drawn upon to develop an organization's expertise in utilizing computers and financial data at minimum cost. The reader is again referred to Figure 1 for a quantitative summary of factors to consider.

APPENDIX

Below is a compilation of some commercially available time-sharing services, data bases, and econometric models that may be utilized by any organization willing to pay the attendant costs. No claim is made that the lists are exhaustive, but rather they are representative of the services available in the United States at the time of writing.

Time-Sharing Companies

Applied Logic, Princeton, New Jersey.
Computer Sciences, Los Angeles, California.
Comshare, Ann Arbor, Michigan.
Control Data, Minneapolis, Minnesota.
Cyphernetics, Ann Arbor, Michigan.
Data Resources, Lexington, Massachusetts.
General Electric, Baltimore, Maryland.
Interactive Data Corp., Waltham, Massachusetts.
National CSS, Norwalk, Connecticut.
On-Line Systems, Pittsburgh, Pennsylvania.
Rapidata, Newark, New Jersey.
Telstat, New York, New York.
Tymshare, Cupertino, California.
United Computing Systems, Kansas City, Missouri.

Data Bases

Type of Data	*Service*	*Description*
Security prices	IDSI	Daily price and volume data for 10,000 securities from the Associated Press price tapes, maintained by Interactive Data Services, Waltham, Mass.
	Telprice/70	Daily price and volume data, and latest dividend information for 15,000 securities from the AP tapes, maintained by Telstat, New York.
	CRSP	Historical pricing tapes covering NYSE common stocks for 45 years developed and maintained by the University of Chicago, Center for Research in Security Prices.
Corporate	Compustat	Quarterly and annual income statement and balance sheet data on 2,600 industrial companies, 150 utilities, and 100 banks developed and maintained by Investors Management Sciences, Denver, Colorado, available on-line from several time-sharing vendors.
	FUNDAC ADB-1	Quarterly and annual income statement and balance sheet ratios and annual spreadsheet data on 1,300 companies. Developed and maintained by Value Line Inc., New York.
	Command	Annual spreadsheet data on 1,200 companies, developed and maintained by First National City Bank, New York.
Economic	DRI Databank	Annual, quarterly, monthly, weekly, economic time series, including National Product and Income Account data, Federal Reserve System data, selected international data, and regional data. Over 10,000 series. Maintained by Data Resources, Inc., Lexington, Mass.
	IDC economic data base	Annual, quarterly, monthly, weekly, economic time series, including National Product and Income Account data, Federal Reserve System data. Over 6,000 series. Maintained by Lionel D. Edie for Interactive Data Corp., Waltham, Mass.
	NBER	Annual, quarterly, monthly, economic time series, including National Product and Income Account data, Federal Reserve System data. Over 2,000 series. Maintained by National Bureau of Economic Research, New York.
Census	Site	Housing and population data from 1970 Census, available from Tymshare, Cal.
	Censac	Housing and population data from 1970 Census, available from National CSS, Norwalk, Conn.
Earnings per share estimates	Catallactics	Individual- and summaries of earnings estimates made by brokerage firms for about 1,300 companies. Cattlactics Corp., Hinsdale, Ill.
	IBES	Summaries of earnings estimates made by brokerage firms for about 700 companies developed and maintained by Institutional Brokers Estimate System, New York.
	ADB-1	Estimates on 1,300 companies developed and maintained by Value Line, Inc., New York.

Investment company holdings	Spectrum	Holdings of all NYSE and AMEX and most NASDAQ companies by all registered investment companies with assets exceeding $7 million, developed and maintained by Computer Directions Advisors, Silver Spring, Md.
	ValueSpec	Summary of the purchases, sales, and holdings of 400 investment companies of over 1,500 common stocks, based in part on the Spectrum Data Base, developed and maintained by Value Line, Inc., New York.

Macroeconomic Models

Name	*Available Commercially on Time Sharing for Simulation*	*Industry Models or Detail Available*	*Comments*
Chase Econometrics—			
Macroeconomic model	Yes	Yes	Designed and maintained by Chase Econometrics Associates, Bala Cynwyd, Pa.
Monthly interest rate model	Yes		
Selected international models	Yes		
Data Resources—			
Quarterly model of the U.S. economy	Yes	Yes	Designed and/or maintained by Data Resources, Inc., Lexington, Mass.
Current quarter model	Yes		
Ten-year annual model	Yes		
Selected international models	Yes		
General Electric—			
MAPCAST	Yes	Yes	Designed and maintained by General Electric Company, New York.
St. Louis Federal Reserve Bank	Yes	No	Designed by St. Louis Federal Reserve Bank, St. Louis, Mo.
Wharton Econometric Forecasting Associates—			
Mark III quarterly model	Yes	Yes	Designed and/or maintained by Wharton Econometric Forecasting Associates, Inc., a nonprofit corporation owned by the trustees of the University of Pa., Philadelphia, Pa.
Annual and industry forecasting model	Yes		
MIT—Penn—SSRC model	No		
Fair model	No	No	Details of structure of model available in Ray C. Fair, *A Short-Run Forecasting Model of the United States Economy*, Lexington, Mass.: D. C. Heath, 1971.
Michigan Research Seminar in Quantitative Economics model	No	No	Details of structure of model and computer coding available from Michigan Research Seminar in Quantitative Economics, University of Michigan, Ann Arbor.

PART VII

Portfolio Management and Theories

41

The Investment Management Organization

W. SCOTT BAUMAN, D.B.A., C.F.A.
Executive Director
The Institute of Chartered Financial Analysts and
The Darden Graduate School of Business Administration
University of Virginia
Charlottesville, Virginia

THE INVESTMENT MANAGEMENT INDUSTRY is now a vitally significant element of the American capitalist system because of the growth of capital wealth, the development of organized securities markets, and the institutionalization of savings and investment. At no time in history has the American economy developed organized financial markets with publicly owned and publicly traded securities on such an enormous scale as exists today. The New York Stock Exchange alone has 19 billion shares of stock listed with a market value of over $800 billion. This compares with only $76 billion in 1949. With the concomitant growth in the investment management industry, over half of all marketable equity and debt securities are held by financial institutions or managed by professional investment advisors.

With the growth of the investment management industry, individual and institutional investors have a wide choice of possible professional investment managers with whom to entrust their investable funds. In turn, professional managers keenly compete for the business of investment clients. Inasmuch as the financial success and well-being of many millions of individual and institutional investors depend on the investment performance of professionally managed portfolios, considerable importance is placed on evaluations of prospective portfolio per-

---

This chapter is based on an occasional paper written by the author for The Financial Analysts Research Foundation, which grants its permission to use the content of that paper.

formance. The ability of investors to evaluate professional investment management organizations and the ability of investment managers to plan, organize, and control their performance will largely determine the extent to which an optimal future portfolio performance may be assured.

Because the investment operation has an important bearing on future portfolio performance, it is highly desirable to plan, organize, and evaluate the management system in order to determine the probabilities that it will achieve portfolio performance objectives. *The purpose of this chapter is to analyze and evaluate the investment system in the context of its ability to achieve portfolio performance objectives.* We will now proceed to an analysis of those characteristics and elements of the investment management system which are considered to contribute significantly to portfolio performance.

GENERAL CHARACTERISTICS OF THE ORGANIZATIONAL STRUCTURE

The basic characteristics of the structure of an organization, within which the investment management system operates, have both obvious and subtle influences on the type of portfolio performance which might be expected. The size, complexity, scope, and diversity of an organization have a bearing on the extent to which an investment management system successfully achieves portfolio performance objectives. Let us consider each of these facets.

Scope and Diversity of Functions

In evaluating the portfolio management system, the question is sometimes raised as to whether the system operates best in a specialized, single-purpose organization or in a diversified, multipurpose one.

Multipurpose Organization. Let us examine the case for the multipurpose organization. Examples of such organizations are commercial banks with trust departments, insurance companies, broker-dealer firms with investment advisory departments, employer organizations with a pension fund portfolio management department, and foundations and universities with an endowment fund portfolio management department.

One argument in support of the multipurpose or integrated organization is the reduction of total operating expenses achieved by having two or more different functions sharing common facilities and personnel. The trust investment division, for example, may be able to gather some of its economic, industry, and security market data for the investment management system at little or no cost from the bank's portfolio bond department, economics department, bond underwriting department, and correspondent banks. The bank's securities trading department may process security transactions for the trust department as well as for the bank's portfolio, correspondent bank portfolios, and the underwriting department. The bank's computer data processing system may maintain the portfolio records of the trust department and perhaps service the statistical and analytical requirements of investment research. The bank's legal and tax staff may render advice on tax problems for client portfolios. The marketing cost and effort in attracting new clients for the trust investment division can be shared with the trust department and commerical bank departments.

The investment research department in a broker-dealer firm could have its costs shared by the brokerage sales department, the underwriting department, as well as the portfolio management department. By sharing common costs, banks and brokerage firms are presumably able to provide clients with more or better services at the same or at a lower cost than otherwise.

Another advantage of some multipurpose organizations is the convenience to customers of having two or more needs met by the same organization. A bank, for example, can provide an investor with a wide range of services, including trust, estate, investment advisory, security custodial, record keeping, tax, checking account, and savings account services. In addition, the bank can service some of the client's business needs, such as corporate pension fund management and business credit. The customer can get to know the bank people better and save time by doing business with this one-stop financial service center rather than dealing with two or more separate organizations.

This same advantage might be said to apply to insurance companies where a customer's permanent life insurance policy, for example, provides for protection against the risk of premature death and provides for an income producing savings fund and a retirement income annuity. An insurance company may meet a number of other financial needs for a client, such as mutual funds, variable annuities, corporate group employee insurance and pension plans, variable life insurance, and separate accounts. If the customer has a small investment account or small portfolio to manage, the multipurpose organization may be willing to accept this unattractive account and to manage it well when the customer is using other services which are more profitable to the organization.

A third argument for the integrated multipurpose organization is that senior management may have greater control over the effectiveness of an in-house portfolio management system and may derive benefits at a lower cost than if these services were contracted from an outside organization. This argument is used by corporations, unions, and government agencies as justification for having their own in-house employee pension fund portfolio management department, by universities and foundations for managing their own endowment funds, and by insurance companies for managing their own insurance portfolios.

A fourth possible advantage of the multipurpose organization is the continuity and stability of support provided to the investment management system. For example, a diversified corporation is better equipped to transfer funds generated from strong and prospering units and to supply additional support to the investment management system if or when it is subject to the loss of key professional personnel, subject to severe competitive pressures, or subject to other temporary adverse conditions in the securities industry.

What might be the disadvantages of the multipurpose organization? Four potential disadvantages will be cited here.

First, in the multipurpose organization, the investment management system competes with other functions for support from the same budget source. The trust investment division competes with the rest of the trust department and the rest of the commercial bank for funds to support the investment management system. In insurance companies, the investment department competes with the underwriting and sales departments. The same is true of other in-house investment management departments, such as for a university's endowment fund portfolio, for a corporation's pension fund, and for a broker-dealer firm's investment management department.

In many multipurpose organizations, revenues generated by the investment management system can be identified or estimated. In addition, many direct expenses can be determined. However, senior management has the problem of determining what is a fair charge for overhead costs against the investment management function, what is a fair net return on the function, how much of this return should be plowed back, and how much of an outlay should be allocated by the organization to upgrade or expand the investment function. Given the competition for resources among the various functions of a multipurpose organization, such questions are not easy or simple for senior management to resolve. Because the investment management system may represent a relatively small component of a multipurpose organization, its requirements may be more easily neglected or overlooked.

The portfolio management system will likely have a high quality operation only if senior management assigns a proper priority to it, provides appropriate direction, and furnishes necessary support. One way to insulate the system from competition for resources within the multipurpose organization is to segregate it as a separate, autonomous department or subsidiary that is directly responsible to senior executive management. As a department it might not be insulated enough; on the other hand, as a subsidiary it may become too isolated in respect to tapping the benefits of a multipurpose organization.

A second possible problem, especially for horizontally integrated financial organizations, is a possible obligation to use the services available from other units in the organization regardless of their suitability or quality. The trust investment division, for example, may be expected to use services of the bank's economics department, correspondent bank relations, trading department, computer system, and marketing (new business development) department. Yet some of these services may be less suitable, more costly, or of less quality than services available to the investment division from outside the bank. In the case of the college endowment fund, the university portfolio management may be tempted to or be expected to accept the advise of professors of economics and finance regardless of their professional qualifications. In the case of the broker-dealer firm, the portfolio management department might be expected to use the facilities of its trading department and to use and accept the investment recommendations of industry research analysts in the securities research department or in the underwriting department, regardless of their quality or appropriateness.

Another possible disadvantage of the horizontally integrated financial organization pertains to the one-stop financial center concept. It is indeed fortunate for a customer to find that a single organization is well equipped to meet all his personal and business financial needs. An informed observer knows that a diversified firm may have product lines of different quality. However, the less informed prospective customer may not be aware of this. If the multipurpose organization, for example, has a poor reputation for certain services, this may unfairly cast an unfavorable image on the portfolio management service, or vice versa. Consequently, the quality of each service provided by a multipurpose organization should be evaluated on its own merits.

A fourth possible problem of the multipurpose organization is that senior management may not be adequately qualified to organize and properly control a high-quality, in-house portfolio management system. In some instances, senior management may hire incompetent portfolio managers or approve poor portfolio policies. In other instances, senior management may exert pressure or influence on the in-house investment management system which inadvertently impedes portfolio performance. Undesirable influence, conflicts of interest, or other pressures frequently occur, for example, in corporate, union, and government employee retirement funds and in college and foundation endowment portfolios. If these pressures cannot be deflected by adequate internal controls, then they might be minimized by contracting for the portfolio management service of one or more outside investment management firms, and by maintaining arms' length, professional, and business-like relationships with such firms.

Specialized Organization. Let us now consider the investment performance characteristics of the independent, specialized portfolio management organization. The term *independent* is used here to mean an organization which is a completely separate, legal entity, and is not a department or subsidiary of any other organization. Examples of single-purpose portfolio management organizations are ones which manage only investment counsel accounts, mutual funds, and closed-end funds.

An advantage frequently associated with the single-purpose portfolio management firm is the incentive of the organization to assign its full energies to the exclusive business of achieving portfolio objectives for its clients or fund shareholders. The management is not distracted by any other priorities, functions, or services. The success and reputation of the organization rests solely on meeting portfolio objectives and satisfying portfolio clients. Therefore, if management wants to retain existing clients, obtain referrals from satisfied clients, and attract new clients, it is vital, if not crucial, for management to have an effective portfolio management system which achieves a record of successful investment performance.

Another possible advantage is that the relationship between the organization and the client tends to be simple, clear-cut, objective, and business-like. The relationship need not be cluttered or complicated by other commercial, political, or personal arrangements which may exist with a multipurpose organization or with an in-house portfolio management system. The relationship can be established or terminated in a relatively short time. If he has sufficient funds, the client may diversify investment management by spreading his funds over two or more separate portfolio management organizations.

What are the possible disadvantages of the single-purpose organization? It is possible for the organization and the professional staff to become so specialized and to develop such a narrow perspective that the investment management system concentrates on daily events of only current interest and fails to recognize, analyze, and evaluate broad or diverse trends which are gradually unfolding in the broad business or social environment.

A second possible limitation is that the portfolio firm is dependent to a greater extent on the supporting services of outside organizations, such as industry and security research, information about economic and political developments, and legal, tax, and computer services. The firm is dependent on the existing quality and reliability of those services which are available to it. The cost of some of these external services may be higher than if they were in-house. On the other hand, the firm frequently has a wide choice of competing services from which to choose, and if or when such services become less attractive, there is no permanent obligation to continue them, so that they may be conveniently replaced with better ones.

From the standpoint of clients, a third possible disadvantage of the single-purpose firm is that the investment program and services are less integrated. For example, the bank trust department is able to offer trust executor and custodial services in conjunction with portfolio management. The insurance company is able to package death insurance benefits, savings, investment management, and annuity benefits together in an integrated contractual program, including variable annuities and variable life insurance. The client, who employs a single-purpose portfolio management firm, retains the responsibility of filling comprehensive needs by integrating, as best as he can, the financial services offered by two or more different specialized organizations.

A fourth possible problem is that the single-purpose firm may be inherently less entrenched and stable. If severe adverse forces impact on the investment management industry, such as occurred in the early 1970s for the mutual fund management business, this can lead to a more serious strain on the financial strength and operational effectiveness of a single-purpose portfolio management firm than on that of a diversified, multipurpose one. Conversely, if adverse forces affect one or more major lines of a multipurpose organization, this could lead to a reduction in support supplied to the portfolio management unit.

Finally, unlike multipurpose organizations, the senior professional staff of the single-purpose firm may not be subject to review or held accountable within the organization by a general executive management echelon. In a single-purpose firm, the occupational strength of the specialized professional staff is in management of portfolios rather than in the business management of an organization composed of personnel, budgets, office facilities, and equipment. The senior portfolio managers in many single-purpose firms, to be sure, have acquired the necessary skills to plan, organize, and control the operations effectively. However, in small, young, or rapidly growing organizations, the senior professional staff may not have gained the necessary skills to manage properly all aspects of the operations. In the absence of experienced business management, some employees may not be adequately trained or supervised, communications may break down, operating costs may get out of line, funds may not be properly controlled or safeguarded, and so on. Such organizational distractions could disrupt the performance of the professional staff.

Given the foregoing discussion, no clear conclusions can be drawn as to whether multipurpose firms as a class or single-purpose firms as a class have an inherently greater chance of providing an investment management system which will achieve portfolio objectives.

Structure of the Organization

In this section, we will consider the implications of organizational structure on portfolio performance in terms of four structural forms—the unitary system, the branch system, the correspondent system, and the parent-subsidiary arrangement. In the next section, we will consider the implications of organizational size.

The *unitary* organization is one which confines its whole investment management operations to offices in only one building location. Under such circumstances, all members of the professional investment staff are in one physical location rather than spread out in offices in different cities or communities. This arrangement tends to facilitate closer and frequent interaction and communication among members of the professional staff in regard to all aspects of the investment decision-making process, including investment research, formulation of portfolio policies, and review of client investment objectives and requirements. The professional staff in a unitary organization is able to be a closer knit group which can more fully share information and ideas from one another on a continuous and informal basis. With this type of interaction, each staff member has a greater opportunity of relating and tailoring his duties and responsibilities to the entire investment decision-making process. In addition, it is easier for senior management to monitor, evaluate, and control all functions of the investment management system.

On the other hand, the unitary operation tends to be more remote to clients and prospective customers who reside in cities some distance from the unit headquarters. This situation may impede the development of clientele outside the headquarters city, may hamper communications and a close working relationship with distant clients, and/or may increase the costs of communications with such clients. The latter may entail a greater commitment in time and travel cost for the professional staff in visits to faraway clients. On the other hand, such geographic barriers appear to be breaking down. Given the convenience of long-distance telephone service, of a fully developed, fast, jet airline network, and of modern highways and car rental arrangements, geographic distances are becoming less significant in terms of client relations. Depending on the volume of accounts and of travel involved, the total costs may be less than would be incurred in maintaining a branch system. Nevertheless, psychological, political, or competitive pressures sometimes necessitate having investment management representation residing in the same city or region as the client.

The *branch* type of investment management organization is utilized by investment counsel firms and to varying degrees by bank trust departments. Under this arrangement, certain functions are centralized in the head office, while others are decentralized in branch offices. Investment research and formulation of basic portfolio strategies with respect to economic and security market conditions are usually conducted under the direction of senior management and a staff in the head office. The final approval of policies and security transactions for individual portfolios are made either by the senior or specialized staff in the head office or by client account advisors in the branch office, depending on the organization's procedures.

With a branch system, the overhead of the specialized functions of investment research and basic portfolio policy formulation may be spread over or absorbed by a larger number of client accounts at widely dispersed geographic locations. This overhead cost per account may be less, or alternatively, this potentially larger number of accounts are able financially to support a higher quality or a more fully developed investment management system. In addition, the branch account advisor is able to have a closer relationship and more frequent two-way communication with his client because he is in the same geographic location.

What are the possible disadvantages of the branch system? Some disadvantages, as might be expected, are the possible advantages of the unitary system. The branch account advisor is moderately or significantly removed from the investment management operations in the head office. Consequently, his function or duties may not be as closely integrated in the total decision-making system. If the authority for portfolio decisions rests with branch advisors, then decisions might not fully reflect all of the expert resources available in the head office, and senior head office management might not have as much control over the quality and suitability of investment selections or portfolio policy decisions when they are being made in the field.

If, on the other hand, final authority for portfolio investment decisions resides in the head office, this centralization might create other problems. One result is awkward procedures and delays in implementation of portfolio changes at a time when speed of action is desirable, that is, two separate levels of the organization at two different locations (the branch account advisor and the head office staff) may need to concur with each portfolio change. If advisors in branch offices are relied on as the primary contact with clients, it is possible that the head office staff may be so isolated from clients that they develop a somewhat impersonal, standardized, or routine approach to meeting portfolio requirements of various clients. If the head office has final authority, some of the decisions may not fully reflect the personal financial considerations and portfolio performance objectives of clients. If the branch advisor is insulated from head office investment operations, then he may be less effective as a communicator or intermediary between the client and the investment organization.

From a cost standpoint, does each branch pay for itself? A branch operation is, of course, justified if the organization is able to gain a sufficient number of accounts that it would not otherwise have if there were no branch at that location.

The *correspondent* or affiliate system is, in a sense, one step removed from the branch system. The correspondent system is used by many bank trust investment divisions and by some investment counsel firms. A correspondent relationship is one in which one (usually a large) investment counsel firm or one (usually a large) trust investment division furnishes, for a consideration, investment research reports and portfolio policy suggestions to another (usually a smaller) counsel firm or trust investment division. Both parties to the correspondent relationship are usually, although not always, separate and independent organizations. A correspondent system has some of the characteristics of both the unitary and the branch systems. The small investment organization has the freedom of movement and compactness of a unitary organization, but has a measure of dependency on the investment expertise from an outside operation at a distant location. The effectiveness of the small organization depends on the quality of the local staff, the quality of the investment services of the correspondent, and the efficiency by which relevant information is transmitted between the two organizations.

The final type of organizational structure is the *parent company-subsidiary company* arrangement. A number of financial and industrial firms, as parent or holding companies, have acquired or formed subsidiaries which function as portfolio management organizations. These subsidiaries are wholly or partially owned by the parent corporation. Business corporations, such as a rubber company and a merchandising company, have acquired or formed portfolio management subsidiaries. Financial firms, such as life insurance companies, bank holding companies, and broker-dealer firms, have acquired or formed such subsidiaries. Such subsidiaries operate as investment counsel firms, mutual fund management companies, or both.

As to how much autonomy is exercised by the subsidiary's management depends on the arrangements with the parent company. Some of the potential strengths and weaknesses in the subsidiary-type organization correspond to those previously cited above for the multipurpose organization; however, because of the greater diversity of possible arrangements and combinations among different types of parent companies, fewer general comments can be made here. The opportunity for synergism of a life insurance company and a mutual fund management company combination is obvious where, for example, the same sales force may sell both life insurance and mutual funds; but the operational benefits are less for the combination of an industrial corporation with a mutual fund. Therefore, in evaluating the investment management system in a subsidiary organization, one must not only appraise the quality of the operations in the subsidiary but the nature of controls and quality of support provided by the parent organization.

Size of the Organization

The size of the investment management organization has several implications regarding portfolio performance. Is a large organization inherently best, or is the small one better? We will primarily discuss the advantages of each size organization. Factors considered advantages for larger organizations may, by inference, be considered as possible disadvantages for smaller organizations, and vice versa. The importance and relevance of these advantages and disadvantages to a given investor depend on his particular portfolio requirements and performance objectives. One size organization may possibly be better suited to achieve particular objectives than another size organization. It is possible that some investment management organizations are too small and restrictive; and it is equally possible that the size of some organizations has exceeded the optimum economies of scale, such that the excess size has a neutral or possibly even a negative effect on the performance of some portfolios.

Let us first examine the possible inherent advantages of the large portfolio management organization, followed by a consideration of the advantages of the smaller organization.

One advantage of the large organization is its greater degree of corporate or organizational stability, consistency of management, and continuity of services over an extended period of time. Some of the large bank trust departments, insurance companies, investment companies, and investment counsel firms have been prudently managing portfolios for over half a century. A large organization has a likelihood of having management in depth, that is, management echelons with staggered ages so as to provide an orderly and gradual succession of seasoned management over extended periods of time. If a highly productive executive is suddenly terminated from the large organization, the disruption in the long-term effectiveness of the portfolio management system can be negligible.

The large organization is able to support a complete or an elaborate system of review and control of the investment decision-making process by two or more levels of management so that each portfolio receives a consistent quality of supervision. This continuity of quality management over extended intervals of time is of special importance to certain clients. For example, it is ordinarily not feasible or extremely awkward for beneficiaries to replace trustees of irrevocable trusts and estates. Consequently such portfolios may be under the same management for decades. Many life insurance policyholders, beneficiaries, and annuitants are dependent on and financially committed to the same life insurance company portfolio for over a whole generation or two. Continuity of quality investment management is, therefore, important to all individual and institutional clients who are not in a position to replace the organization. Clients might not become aware in a timely fashion of a deterioration in the performance of a smaller management organization because the clients lack the time, interest, or ability to monitor closely on a continuing basis the portfolio management system. The professional relationship between the organization and client is sometimes difficult to terminate on a timely basis because of other personal, psychological, or political reasons which tend to lock in an account.

This situation frequently exists where the relationship involves an in-house portfolio management system, which involves relatives or close friends and other business or political connections. Confrontations with the problem of replacing a portfolio manager tend to be avoided when a large and stable management organization is able, over long periods of time, to achieve the investment performance objectives which the client had expected at the time the professional relationship was established.

A second advantage of the large organization is its ability to support a relatively complete investment system within a single organization. Because of the volume or scale of operations, the organization can support a large staff with a wide range of different specialized professional talents, a large library of research materials, an expensive and an elaborate computer research system and computer data bank, and a fully developed trading department system and can acquire considerable institutional brokerage house research through a large volume of soft-dollar commissions. With a large staff of professional specialists, the economy, government policies, international conditions, stock and bond market conditions, and many industries and companies can be analyzed and evaluated in depth. This research can be channeled to portfolio policy and strategy committees, account review committees, investment committees, bond committees, and others, where the research and portfolio recommendations can be carefully monitored and evaluated by a group of seasoned professionals. In short, the management of a large organization is in a position to plan, direct, and control a comprehensive and in-depth portfolio management system.

Let us now turn to the potential advantages of the smaller investment organization. The smaller organization has a simpler structure and is easier to operate, control, and evaluate. There is no elaborate system of specialized departments, committees, tiers of management, head office with branch offices, or affiliates or subsidiary units. The professional staff is close-knit like the unitary organization, only more so because of its small size. It is easier for senior managers to be intimately familiar with and to be a significant part of the organization's investment management system and to exercise closer control over the quality of the system. There is considerably less delegation of authority and diffusion of responsibility by the top management. If a member of the professional staff misunderstands his assignment or is not performing as expected, this can be more quickly detected and corrected.

Given this greater centralization of authority, decisions and actions can still be taken more rapidly than in some large organizations which are only partially decentralized. If portfolio performance objectives are based on strategies which sometimes require rapid decisions, then the small and simpler organizational system may be well equipped to execute such strategies.

The smaller organization has less problems with marketability. Because of the smaller amount of funds under management, the organization is able to accumulate or liquidate security portfolio positions in many of their accounts more rapidly and at a possible lower market transaction cost than other firms with large dollar holdings. Because the amount of funds is smaller, diversified portfolio positions can be taken in corporations with smaller capitalizations and possibly offering higher returns without adversely disturbing the market price. Consequently, a wider selection of different investments is available, and the portfolio management system has a higher degree of market mobility. This type of flexibility can easily enhance investment performance.

The quality and motivation of the professional staff at the smaller and younger organizations can be quite high. The key managers frequently are owners or otherwise share in the profits of the organization; consequently their financial rewards relate to the success of the organization and to attracting and retaining satisfied clients. Therefore, portfolio managers and security analysts who are ambitious and confident of their abilities frequently obtain their initial training and experience as employees in a large organization, and later gravitate to the smaller organization where their individual energies have a clearer and greater impact on the investment management system and where their efforts have a more direct and immediate result in professional satisfaction and personal compensation.

In contrast, some of the less industrious, less able or less confident professionals seek shelter in the large, stable, and more secure bureaucracies. To the extent that a large organization has a staff composed of both highly qualified and less qualified individuals, the chance exists that the input of those who are most competent will be diluted through the system of departments, review committees, and echelons such that the net output is of mediocre or average quality. And of course one reason good people sometimes go to a smaller organization is because their abilities are not fully recognized, appreciated, or used by the larger one. Consequently, a group of outstanding people in a small organization may be better able to produce a superior performance than they could in a large organization, given its inherent institutional constraints.

In the smaller organization, each client and each portfolio tend to be of greater importance and have less chance of being neglected or lost in the shuffle. This is especially relevant to clients with smaller portfolios because these are the ones which can be more easily neglected.

Many clients are attracted to large organizations because they are very well known, have been in business for a long time, and have established a reputation based on past achievements, sometimes in the distant past. Because of this large and apparent easy inflow of new funds, some organizations will overload their portfolio managers with too many accounts and their security analysts with too many different holdings to analyze and research.

Because the top executives of the smaller organization are frequently the portfolio managers and account representatives, the prospective client is better able to meet and personally evaluate those who have the authority and responsibility for portfolio decisions. Then after a relationship is established, a client will continue to have greater access to the senior managers. Consequently, the client is able to be kept informed on portfolio management matters directly from those who are making the decisions; and when his financial requirements change, the client is able to relay this directly to the portfolio manager for prompt action. This direct relationship with the portfolio manager, who is responsible for the account, increases the likelihood that the client will receive more individualized attention, that portfolio objectives will be more closely tailored to his specific requirements, and given this more personal relationship, that the manager will strive harder to achieve performance objectives.

The small portfolio management organization has some of the characteristics of the highly specialized organization cited previously. Both organizations lack a large staff of specialists with a diverse background of professional expertise.

The small organization can take the same steps to solve this problem as the specialized, single-purpose organization, namely to choose, on a selective basis, specialized professional services and research which are available from outside organizations and groups.

EVALUATION OF THE INVESTMENT MANAGEMENT SYSTEM

The purpose of this section is to raise several important questions and to provide a few insights which may be of use to both clients and investment managers in evaluating the effectiveness of investment management systems. It should be emphasized that there appears to be no single type of system which is best able to achieve all of the different kinds of portfolio performance objectives; and that two or more different types of systems may have an equal likelihood of achieving the objectives of the same kind of portfolio, i.e., the same end may be reached by different means.

Philosophies of the Organization and the Senior Administration

The true goals, direction, and future performance of an organization are frequently revealed in the philosophies, convictions, and ambitions as personally stated and executed by the senior management in the organization which has primary authority to formulate major plans, determine budgets, hire and fire the professional staff, and approve major portfolio policies and strategies and which has general responsibility over controlling the investment management system. Questions to be raised are the following: Are senior managers in close and frequent touch with the operations of the investment system, including developments in industry, in the financial markets, and in the economy? Does senior management have a strong administrative and professional background in the investment field? Do they have the desire and energy to manage a first class, highly competitive, successful organization with a reputation for good portfolio performance? Or are they trying to follow and keep up with the leadership exhibited by their competitors? Are they vitally interested in the investment management profession, in new developments in the investment environment, and in achieving client objectives? Or are they overly preoccupied with golf, club activities, social events, travel, civic and association activities, or looking forward to slowing down or to retirement?

What is the attitude and relationship between senior management and the rest of the professional staff? Do they cooperate, work closely together, and have a mutual respect and trust for one another? Is senior management interested in hiring a well-qualified staff of personnel with good promise, and does it develop the staff's potential, delegate responsibilities, evaluate the staff's work, reward good performance, and have the courage to penalize inferior performance?

Is senior management constantly on the alert to making improvements in the investment system, and does it have the imagination to initiate or readily accept changes in the system? On the other hand, does senior management make serious mistakes by being too quick to embrace new ideas which are highly experimental and unsubstantiated?

Evaluation of Portfolio Management Plans

One important responsibility of the investment management system is the development of appropriate performance objectives, strategies, and policy for each portfolio. For purposes of clarity, let us define several terms. *Performance objectives* give recognition to the amount of investment risk the client is willing and able to assume, and to the investment return the client expects to earn over a relevant time horizon. Portfolio *strategies* are the various plans which determine the types of investments and portfolio techniques which may be employed in a portfolio through which performance objectives are expected to be achieved. A portfolio *policy* is the *current* plan which decides what types of investments and portfolio techniques are to be employed in a portfolio at *a particular point in time* based on an appraisal of the current outlook for the investment environment. The *investment environment* encompasses the forces prevailing in the economic, monetary, political, social, industrial, and financial market systems which affect portfolio risks and returns.

Performance Objectives. The professional abilities of portfolio management may be reflected, in part, by the degree to which it formulates performance objectives which are suited to the investor based on his goals, requirements, and financial circumstances. Risk and return performance objectives should reflect an optimal combination (1) of what an investor wants or needs (2) with what is feasible in the investment environment and (3) with what the portfolio management system is capable of producing.

If portfolio management is unable to recognize what performance objectives are most suitable to its client and what risk and return policies are feasible based on a thoughtful appraisal of the opportunities and limitations prevailing in the investment environment, then doubts might be raised as to the competency of the investment management system in carrying out the objectives.

Clients are at times partly responsible for the suitability of performance objectives because of the influence exerted by investors on their portfolio managers. Investment management organizations are in the business of selling their services to investors. Because these organizations are not only in competition with one another but in competition with other saving and investment market channels, they have a task of attracting and retaining the funds of clients. Consequently, some managements are tempted to pursue objectives which might convey a currently favorable image but which are not strictly in the best long-term interests of clients. Like hair styles and hemlines, what a business is able to sell depends in part on what fashions are currently in demand. We are reminded of the optimistic investment objectives and aggressive policies in the 1920s dominated by such expressions as the "new era" and "pie in the sky." The popularity of such flamboyant policies suddenly terminated with the stock market crash and the Great Depression of the 1930s. With confidence shaken by the Depression and perpetuated by the upheaval of World War II, prudent and even ultraconservative investment policies were in fashion in the 1930s, 1940s, and early 1950s. Consequently, investment objectives and portfolios in that era needed to convey an image of pillars of strength. Portfolio strategies which were popular during a part of that era were associated with preservation of principal in dollar terms, adequate and stable income, balance between bonds and stocks, dollar cost averaging, formula timing, very extensive diversification, and portfolio window dressing with securities of large, entrenched companies having well-known names. Such major changes in policies over the past decades and the suitability of such investment objectives appear somewhat analogous to the farmer who locks the barn door after the horses are stolen or to the generals who prepare for the next war on the basis of successful strategies used in the previous war.

In the past 15 years, investment objectives have become gradually more ambitious and policies more aggressive as a result of the economic expansion, technological revolution, and inflation. Popular strategies in this era are associated with hedging against inflation, growth stocks, rapidly growing scientifically oriented industries, and small companies with new technologies. One of the newest concepts is the so-called *performance* portfolio objective which seeks to obtain a short-term return that exceeds the average return available in the stock market or that exceeds the return of other portfolios. Such an objective is associated with high portfolio turnover and security trading in anticipation of short-term market fluctuations. Some describe this policy as a sophisticated professional management approach, while others describe it as excessive short-term speculation. Nevertheless, some investors are exerting considerable pressure on portfolio managers to produce superior short-term profits. Whether this will be a lasting philosophy among a significant number of investors remains to be seen. Therefore, we should guard against inappropriate performance objectives which are either too ambitious or overly conservative.

Because the functions of portfolio objectives are to inform investors and portfolio managers alike as to what performance is to be expected and to be evaluated, performance objectives should be clearly stated and understood. Objectives are meaningfully stated in terms of risks and returns. Objectives of return could be stated in terms of size of expected rates of return, possibly broken down by income yield and capital growth, in terms of a distribution of probable returns, timing of returns within a stated time horizon, and the taxability or tax shelter of returns relative to long-term capital gains, ordinary income, and tax-exempt income. The level of risks to be assumed in the portfolio could be stated in terms of investment quality of securities, market risk (market price volatility), interest rate risk, and purchasing power risk.

Portfolio Strategies and Policies. The extent to which performance objectives are achieved is determined in part by which portfolio strategies and policies are chosen and by how skillfully they are employed. Consequently, these strategies and policies should be evaluated from the standpoint of their consistency with stated objectives and from the standpoint of achieving the objectives within the capabilities and limitations of the investment management system.

Based on past performance results, some strategies have been more successfully employed by portfolio managers in accomplishing objectives than other strategies. Also some strategies require greater skill to implement successfully than others do.

Two hypothetical examples of composite strategies and composite investors will be cited here for illustrative purposes. These composite illustrations represent several different types of investors and several different types of strategies all rolled into one.

The first hypothetical composite investor has a billion dollar portfolio, a long-term time horizon, wishes moderately to minimize investment risks associated with purchasing power and interest rate fluctuations and with business and security market uncertainties, and wishes to seek a conservative, somewhat reliable rate of return which is partially sheltered from high income tax rates. Such performance objectives call for the use of a conservative set of portfolio strategies which have a reasonable chance of success.

An appropriate strategy for such a portfolio is to have broad diversification of common stocks of strong, well-entrenched, growth companies which possess at least moderately large equity capitalizations. This strategy is consistent with the portfolio objectives and circumstances of the investor inasmuch as it minimizes purchasing power risk and business risks. Broad diversification in strong companies minimizes the size of specific business and market risks associated with individual stock issues, and coupled with investments in larger capitalizations, this provides a higher degree of marketability so that sizeable amounts of funds from this large portfolio may be used to buy and sell stocks within short time intervals without creating adverse market price fluctuations. Growth stocks tend to provide tax shelter because a larger portion of their total return is in the form of long-term capital gains as distinct from ordinary dividend income.

Additional strategies are to hold a portion of the portfolio in diversified holdings of high-quality municipal bonds with spaced maturities. The high quality minimizes the chance of a price decline due to the remote risk of technical insolvency of the issuer, the interest income is tax exempt, and the spaced maturities diversify or hedge against the risks of interest rate fluctuations. In addition, the bond portion minimizes exposure of the portfolio against the risks of business cycles and market risks associated with stock market cycles.

The strategies of making occasional and moderate portfolio shifts, such as between bonds and stocks, between long-term and shorter term bonds, and among different broad categories of stocks might be employed to take advantage of anticipated bond and stock price swings. The necessity for such strategies is marginal because the investor's profit performance objective is conservative and his risk exposure to market cycles is modest due to his long time horizon. The purpose of such strategies is to make portfolio shifts which will successfully enhance portfolio returns and reduce market losses. As to whether this is feasible depends importantly on the capability of the portfolio management system to reliable forecast changes in stock or bond prices. The historical record of many portfolio managers and analysts strongly suggests that this is very difficult to do.

The second hypothetical composite investor has a half-million dollar portfolio, has a strong personal financial position, has nerves of steel, is able and willing to assume above-average risks, and seeks above-average returns. These performance objectives permit the use of an aggressive set of portfolio strategies.

Strategies available for consideration are concentration of holdings (in contrast to diversification) and investment in riskier stocks and stocks of smaller companies. Concentration on a selective basis increases the likelihood that the portfolio's performance will exceed the average return available in the general market; however, it also tends to broaden the probability distribution of the portfolio's expected annual return which increases the chances that the return will more greatly diverge either above or below the general market return during subtime periods. If the investment management system is capable on average of selecting securities which provide better than average returns, then portfolio concentration will favorably capitalize on this superior selectivity over the long run. Because this is a smaller portfolio, it can more easily buy and sell the less marketable stocks of small companies. These stocks and other riskier ones selected for investment presumably will offer correspondingly higher rates of return. Because the performance of riskier companies is subject to larger and more sudden change, and because the market prices of these stocks tend to be much more volatile, it would be appropriate for these investments to be analyzed and reviewed more thoroughly and more frequently by the investment management system. Likewise, a portfolio with such holdings may be expected to have a higher turnover.

Additional strategies are concentration in and occasional major portfolio shifts between basic categories of securities in anticipation of forecasted changes in market prices. When the stock market is expected to go up, the portfolio could employ margin, shift funds from bonds to stocks, and shift funds from high-quality stocks to low-quality stocks (with high beta coefficients), reversing the process when the stock market is expected to go down. When the term structure of interest rates (the yield curve) is expected to go down, the portfolio could shift funds from short-term investments and stocks into long-term bonds, reversing the process when interest rates are expected to go up. By shifting and concentrating in specific categories of securities, the portfolio is concentrating in certain risks, is increasing its chances of producing a higher return if the timing is correct, is increasing its chances of realizing larger losses if its timing is poor, and in either event, is incurring larger transaction costs.

These aggressive strategies require a considerably greater skill in the investment management system in order to achieve performance objectives. As previously stated, the historical records of portfolio performance indicate that a significant number of portfolio managers and security analysts are not able to make consistently reliable and meaningfully precise forecasts of security price changes.

After it is determined as to what set of portfolio strategies is appropriate for the performance objectives and financial circumstances of a given investor, the portfolio manager needs to select and implement current portfolio policies which are consistent with these strategies and which conform to the outlook for the investment environment. For example, if a strategy of switching between long- and short-term bonds is to be employed, then the portfolio should have a current policy of concentration in short-term bonds if an analysis of the outlook for the investment environment suggests that current interest rates are low and that the term structure of interest rates will be rising in the near term future.

In conclusion, in evaluating portfolio management plans, it should be determined that performance objectives are clearly stated and conform with the financial goals and requirements of the investor; that the selected set of portfolio strategies are consistent with performance objectives and are feasible in terms of capabilities of the investment management system and its record of performance; and that current portfolio policies are consistent with plausible expectations based on an intelligent analysis of the outlook for the investment environment.

Investment Research System

Although we are primarily interested in the evaluation of portfolio management, the investment performance of portfolios is dependent to a considerable degree on the quality of the investment research system which is responsible for research of the investment environment, security markets, industries, companies, and securities. Portfolio managers must rely in part on research conducted by others inasmuch as they do not have the time personally to analyze in depth dozens of industries, hundreds of companies, and innumerable environmental forces. Therefore we will briefly discuss the investment research system in terms of the following two component parts:

1. Research of the investment environment including the analysis of security markets.
2. Research of industries, companies, and individual securities.

It was previously noted that the physical location of and the jurisdiction over these research functions vary among investment management organizations. Large nationwide organizations, for example, tend to perform these functions in their head office, while the small unitary management organizations tend to rely on the research services of several outside organizations that perform these functions. It is far from clear as to which of these organizational arrangements provide the best portfolio performance. Probably other variables are at least as important if not more important, such as: the time and effort devoted by and the abilities of the professional specialists who conduct this research; the efficiency by which this research information is properly integrated within the organization's entire decision-making process and is readily available to the portfolio managers; and the abilities of the investment management to analyze, comprehend, interpret, and evaluate the information furnished by these research services. Many investment management organizations, of course, utilized both internally and externally generated research.

In evaluating the research system, it is useful to know: how many people are conducting research in each subject area; what is their professional and specialized training, experience, and other qualifications; what is their reputation and past record of achievements; how long have they been with their present employer; and is there adequate breadth and depth of research coverage?

Is sufficient professional effort and manpower devoted to economic, monetary, political, social, industrial, and security market research and analysis? Is sufficient effort and manpower devoted to the analysis of all relevant or important industries, companies, and securities? Is each security holding being analyzed at sufficiently frequent intervals? If applicable, is sufficient effort devoted to the analysis of specialized markets and securities such as federal, municipal, corporate, foreign, and convertible bonds, and preferred stocks?

Is the organization constantly evaluating its research system and trying to improve it by testing new ideas, approaches, techniques, and sources of information? Is the system receiving adequate logistical support in terms of a clerical staff, library resources, statistical investment research models, computer data banks, programming assistance, and general computer support? Many of these questions are, of course, difficult to answer and to resolve satisfactorily; however, these elements vitally affect the performance of portfolios.

Another supporting system is the security trading operation of the organization. This operation can affect performance, especially of large portfolios, by how well it can quickly and easily process security orders once a decision is made. Does it obtain good transaction prices and effectively control transaction costs? In addition, the proper allocation of brokerage commissions is important in compensating for worthwhile brokerage services to the investment management organization such as for execution of security orders and research.

Portfolio Management Process

This section evaluates the methods by which portfolio plans are implemented and executed. Realizing satisfactory portfolio performance is dependent not only on the development of suitable objectives and feasible strategies, but on the effective execution of an investment program.

Because a client's objectives and financial requirements sometimes change, they should be periodically reviewed by the investment management organization so that portfolio strategies are compatible with the circumstances of the client.

Investment Environment. Investment management should adopt and implement portfolio policies based on justified and well-reasoned expectations derived from a broad and an intensive analysis of the outlook for the investment environment. In evaluating this process, we want to know about the quality, quantity, and availability of information, analyses, and relevant interpretations regarding the investment environment. Are these data transmitted quickly and at frequent intervals to those who make portfolio policy decisions? Is the quality of this information evaluated and is it screened so that portfolio policy makers are not deluged with mediocre and extraneous materials? Do policy makers have the ability to interpret these analyses properly in terms of selecting appropriate portfolio policies? When the investment environment outlook changes significantly, does investment management usually change policies correctly and in sufficient time to exploit profit opportunities and to minimize risks? Or do they seem to be changing portfolio policies either in the wrong direction or at the wrong time? How often are policies changed? Once every 25 years or 25 times a year? Can portfolio management clearly, plausibly, and convincingly explain the rationale for its policies, each change in policies, and its lack of change in policies? Is portfolio performance attributable to policy changes offset by transaction costs?

Security and Industry Analysis. The decisions as to which securities to buy, hold, or sell in a portfolio are presumably based on research regarding industries, companies, and securities. Therefore, we want to evaluate the quality of the security research information which is made available to the portfolio decision makers. Is the research conducted rigorously by competent industry specialists who have the ability to make intelligent projections of future corporate performance? Is the research on each portfolio holding conducted at frequent intervals, conducted in depth and based on field trips and management contacts? Is a sufficient number of industries and securities reviewed? Do the security analysis reports cover all major relevant points such as an appraisal of the profit outlook for the company, exposure to business and market risks, an estimate of the investment value, and so on?

Is this security research information transmitted rapidly, frequently, and in a meaningful form to the portfolio decision makers? When a significant change occurs in the performance or outlook of a corporation or industry of current interest, does portfolio management act on the change in an appropriate and timely fashion? Or is portfolio management slow to act or does it overreact to new information by generating excessive portfolio turnover? Insights may be gained by observing the market price changes preceding security sales and also by comparing the market price trend of securities after they are sold with the price trend of securities purchased as replacements.

Where appropriate, are the various kinds of securities, such as bonds of different maturities, preferred stocks, and convertible securities, being reviewed as intensively and as effectively as common stocks?

Similarity of Portfolio Accounts. The amount of time, effort, and abilities that a portfolio management organization can devote beneficially to one given portfolio is dependent in part on the size of that portfolio and on the number and size of other portfolios under management which have similar performance objectives. If the organization has only one large portfolio or has mostly one class of portfolios, such as private trusteed pension funds, then the management can concentrate its efforts on the development and implementation of one or closely similar portfolio policies. An ideal example of such efficiencies is a bank's common trust fund which is one portfolio that commingles the funds of many small trust accounts. If an organization receives a new account which has performance objectives that are similar to other existing accounts, then the investment management system presumably has the necessary experience and is already designed to manage this new account with a minimum of start-up effort. If this is the case, it might be revealing to the prospective client to know about the number and size of similar accounts, the number of years they have been under management, and their past portfolio performance. In addition, an evaluation of the organization by the prospective client might be facilitated if he were able to contact current clients for reference purposes.

Internal Interrelationship of the Professional Staff

The lines of authority, the lines of communication, the management style, and the roles played by the professional members vary considerable from one investment management organization to another. The nature of professional staff relationships in an organization is determined in part by management's attitudes and philosophy, characteristics of the clients, portfolio objectives and constraints, and qualities of the staff. Five variations of internal interrelationships will be identified and briefly described here.

The *chain of command* system is one in which investment decisions are the responsibility of department heads and other group administrators. This arrangement resembles that of a government, bureaucratic, or authoritarian organization. A junior portfolio analyst submits his analyses and recommendations to a senior portfolio manager for review and approval. Within certain prescribed limits, the senior portfolio manager may have the authority to effect a portfolio change. Decisions of greater importance are submitted by the senior portfolio manager to the head of the portfolio management division within which this portfolio is assigned. Within certain limits, the division head can authorize a portfolio action, otherwise he forwards a report with his recommendation to his superior, who may be the head of the department or of a group of divisions. If he has the authority, the recommendation is implemented when he approves it. If, however, it involved a major policy change, he needs approval from a senior executive. The advantages of such a system is that members of management maintain clear control over plans and decision making. The lines of communication and lines of authority and responsibility are clearly identified. If these administrators are good leaders, work closely with the people around them, and professionally are well qualified, good and timely decisions can be made. If these conditions are not present, if too much authority is centralized at the top, or if there are too many layers of management through which recommendations must be approved, then initiative and incentives among the professional staff can be stifled, and important decisions delayed too long.

A second type of management is the *committee* system. The number and extent of the responsibilities of committees in an investment organization can vary. An organization with a strong committee system can have many committees which are responsible for making decisions and for reviewing the decisions of other committees. The securities which are added to and dropped from the organization's approved list or buy list may be decided by a securities committee. Changes in common stock portfolio policies may be made by a common stock policy committee, changes in bond portfolio policy can be handled by a bond policy committee, and general investment policy may be made or reviewed by a senior investment committee. The portfolio policies and security holdings and changes thereto for each investment account may be reviewed and approved by an account review committee.

The strength of this system is that each decision receives the scrutiny and benefit of group deliberation. This is supported by the cliche that two heads are better than one, or that a whole group is greater than the sum of its individual parts. Undoubtedly, some committees and some committee meetings are very productive.

In evaluating the effectiveness of a committee, several questions are pertinent. How often does it meet? Does it meet often enough to deal with changes in a timely fashion? If significant new information suddenly becomes available which should be acted on promptly, can the committee be quickly assembled? If not, are certain individuals empowered to act? Is the committee encumbered by too many members? Are meetings well organized, or do they ramble on, absorbing a lot of valuable man-hours? What is the role of the committee? To exchange views and information, to review or critique previous staff decisions, or to make decisions? Certain committees are better suited to perform one role than that of another. Committees appear better suited for formulating policies, broad guidelines, and basic objectives, rather than for making rapid and frequent individual security decisions. If decisions are made by a committee, how are they made? By majority vote, by consensus, by the chairman, or by the senior members? Do the most able members have the greatest influence in the committee and do the best ideas have the greatest likelihood of being accepted? Or are decisions influenced by office politics, by people who have the greatest bureaucratic power, or by people who are the most articulate, manipulative, or vociferous? Depending on how the committee operates, it can draw out the best ideas of the individual members, it can procrastinate or lead to indecisive, confusing, or poorly compromised actions, or it can make mediocre decisions by averaging out the best and poorest ideas.

One variation to the chain of command and committee systems is the *rule system* in which the organization operates under a well-defined set of portfolio policies and investment rules. Under this arrangement, a portfolio manager is free to make investment and policy decisions in respect to a given portfolio account insofar as they are not inconsistent with the organization's approved portfolio policies and investment rules. The effectiveness of this system depends on the quality of the rules, how rigid or flexible they are, how much discretion or judgment is left up to the portfolio manager, how frequently the rules are reviewed, how easy it is to change them, and how easy it is to authorize exceptions to the rules. Carefully established policies and rules sometimes avoid investment decisions based on emotional impulses of the moment, on occasional poor judgment, or on superficial research.

A fourth approach is the *team system.* Each portfolio is assigned to a team of portfolio managers, usually consisting of a group of two to four people, in which one member of the team has primary responsibility for the assigned portfolio. The team is like a committee in the sense that the members exchange views and information and engage in friendly arguments. However, it differs from that of the usual committee. The working relationship of the team members is informal, with uninhibited give and take and close continual contact. Decisions are not formalized or finalized by the team as a whole. The team member who has primary responsibility for a portfolio has sole authority and responsibility for all decisions. If a significant development occurs which requires prompt action, and the primary manager is not available, then the team member with secondary responsibility takes the necessary portfolio action. The team can use or rely on research provided internally and/or from any external sources it wishes.

In comparison to the previous systems, the team approach provides greater simplicity, greater flexibility and freedom, and a framework within which to make decisions more rapidly. This system can be quite effective if the team members are well qualified, especially the primary member, they work cohesively, and the abilities of each member complement those of the other members such that the team is balanced and well rounded in background. If these conditions are not met, then this arrangement can be less satisfactory.

The fifth arrangement is the *decentralized system* which includes the so-called superstar system. The decentralized arrangement is one in which a portfolio manager has sole and complete discretion in the management of an assigned portfolio. As compared to the previous four systems, this one has the simplest and most flexible management arrangement. It is similar to the team system except that the portfolio manager does not work continually with other portfolio managers in reference to any one specific portfolio. In arriving at decisions, he is free to use whatever sources of research and other information he wishes.

This can be a satisfactory arrangement if the portfolio manager is highly proficient and conscientious, if he has ready access to and uses high-quality research information with sufficient breadth of coverage, and if he is familar with the portfolio performance objectives of the client. There should be a back-up system so that when the portfolio manager is away from the office on trips or because of illness or a vacation, another professional member of the organization is able to follow through with portfolio responsibilities.

The superstar system may be considered as one subtype under the decentralized system. The merits of the superstar arrangement have provoked considerable debate in the investment community. Under this system, one portfolio manager has sole authority over a portfolio account; in addition however, he is ordinarily expected (1) to achieve high short-term rates of return, (2) to achieve a short-term rate of return which is significantly above the average return in the stock market, or (3) to achieve a short-term rate of return which is above that of other selected portfolios. If he succeeds, he is subsequently and periodically rewarded by additional compensation, and/or his organization is assigned additional funds to manage. This system gained considerable popularity in the latter half of the 1960s particularly among corporate pension funds using split funding, among performance mutual funds, and hedge fund partnership types of accounts. This system seemed to succeed during the rising phase of stock market speculation, in part because a number of portfolios concentrated in stocks with volatile prices and with thin markets. With the stock market contractions, as experienced in the early 1970s, many superstared portfolios failed to outperform the market, while others underperformed the market by a considerable margin. The controversy surrounding the superstar system seems to focus on questions as to whether portfolio performance objectives were set too high and time horizons set too short, and whether portfolio managers were tempted or pressured into adopting speculative strategies which were unfeasible and inconsistent with the proper investment requirements of clients. Less acrimonious discussion is associated with the merits of the basic decentralized system.

In describing these five types of professional internal interrelations, many portfolio management organizations employ combinations of parts of two or more of these systems. Moreover, the success of these systems is dependent in part on the abilities of the professional staff and the willingness of the staff to make the system work effectively. Any carefully designed system will break down if key members of the organization abuse, resist, or fight the system. The system should be designed so that it is compatible with the particular requirements of the total portfolio management system, which includes performance objectives, strategies, and qualities of the professional staff.

Qualifications of the Portfolio Management Staff

In this section we are interested in evaluating the professional portfolio management abilities of the person or people who are directly responsible for the management of a given portfolio account. If the professional relationship between the client's portfolio and the organization is to be a long-term one, it should be recognized that the abilities of a portfolio manager may change over time and his investment philosophy may change over time or change with the ups and downs of the business and stock market cycles. In addition, the people who manage a given portfolio are occasionally replaced. Therefore, it is important to evaluate not only the current abilities of those who are managing the account but also to evaluate the organization's program for the professional development of its staff and the organization's plan for management succession.

In determining who and how many people we wish to evaluate depends on the internal interrelation of the professional staff in the organization. Our greatest concern in this section is the detailed evaluation of the portfolio manager (or managers) who is directly and primarily responsible for a particular portfolio account. To simplify our exposition here, we will refer to portfolio management as though it is one person regardless of the number of people who are directly responsible for the account.

In evaluating the portfolio manager, we wish to appraise all information about him (her) which provides some insight into his ability to achieve portfolio performance objectives. In evaluating his abilities, it may be helpful to identify those qualifications which he possesses as well as those which he does not possess. Let us now discuss those elements which are believed to have a bearing on the professional performance of a portfolio manager.

Knowledge and Education. Has he studied and mastered the body of knowledge which he needs to bring to bear in making effective portfolio policy and security decisions? Does he possess the necessary knowledge in the theories and practices in accounting, economics, investment analysis and management, security market operations and market psychology, corporation finance, investment legal requirements, mathematical and quantitative techniques, and other fields of business and industrial management? Exposure to and mastery of this knowledge is evidenced by a bachelor, master's, or doctor's degree in business administration, professional awards such as the Chartered Financial Analyst (C.F.A.) designation, participation in professional programs and conferences such as those sponsored by The Financial Analysts Federation (the Financial Analysts Seminar, Investment Management Workshop, and annual conferences), local financial analyst societies, and other professional groups and universities, as well as by his independent study of books, professional periodicals, and scholarly journals. Impressive evidence is reflected by scholarly awards, academic scholarships, high academic grades, membership in honorary societies, authorship of articles, papers, or books, speaking engagements at professional meetings, and appointments on committees and to boards of professional organizations. Educational and knowledge attainment is a reflection of intelligence, opportunity, and perseverance.

Intelligence. Intelligence is the mental capacity to be able to perform, whether or not this capacity is demanded or utilized. An individual cannot successfully accomplish a task if the task requires a level of intelligence which exceeds the capacity of the individual. Because successful portfolio management is considered by many to be intellectually challenging, a good level of intelligence is definitely useful. Intelligence is revealed in many ways, such as by the speed and effectiveness that a person can comprehend and retain complex and voluminous information, by the way he can quickly organize and clearly verbalize relevant thoughts orally and in writing.

There are different kinds of intelligence or aptitudes. Portfolio management places a stress on a research aptitude of gathering, absorbing, and retaining voluminous amounts of diverse items of information, of being able to identify relevant information, and of fitting it together in a logical coherent package. He should be able to recognize and understand cause and effect relationships in verbal and numerical terms. Such aptitudes are used to formulate portfolio performance objectives based on an appraisal of the client's financial requirements, to devise appropriate strategies, to select portfolio polices based on an appraisal of the investment environment, and to select securities based on these policies and based on the financial analyses of securities.

Experience and Training. Training and experience gained through the practice of investment research and management provide the manager with the necessary skills to organize his knowledge and apply his intelligence to the analysis of investment problems, to the formulation of solutions, and to the making of policy and investment decisions. These skills of application in investment management are developed by working on research projects, in study seminars, workshops, internships, on-the-job training, and by work experience in the investment field. The development of these skills and mature judgment are partly a function of a meaningful exposure to problems and problem solving tasks in the investment field as well as in life.

The portfolio manager's experience and seasoning is revealed by his age, by the number of years he has engaged in responsible investment research and management work, by the reputation of the people and organizations he has worked with, and by the professional reputation or technical record which he has established in the performance of his tasks. Is his reputation based on consistently good performance, or on one very lucky stock selection or on one market cycle? Insofar as experience in managing portfolios and a specialized type of account, it would be useful to know how many years experience he has had with primary portfolio responsibility, and the number and size of accounts, as well as the extent of his experience with other accounts which have the same or similar performance objectives as the particular account in question. Has he been successful in achieving the performance objectives of these portfolios? Are his clients satisfied?

Attitudes and Motivation. An important, though sometimes subtle, ingredient to personal professional performance is the portfolio manager's attitudes and motivation. Those who successfully achieve performance objectives frequently seem to have several desirable personality characteristics. They seem to be highly dedicated and stimulated by their work; they pride themselves in serving the best interests of their clients; they are energetic, ambitious, and strongly motivated to be competitive and have a determination to succeed; they seek new and challenging experiences; and they have a positive and constructive attitude. They seem to be self-disciplined and emotionally mature. The manager's degree of stability is sometimes revealed by how he reacts to important changes in the investment environment, changes in security prices, and changes in market sentiment. Does he overreact, make extreme or excessive changes in portfolio policies, have a high portfolio turnover, get swept away with the prevailing market psychology, or become preoccupied with minor daily news items? Signs of emotional maturity can be found elsewhere in his career and personal habits. For example, has he changed careers and jobs frequently for reasons other than advancement; has he relocated frequently; and does he have a stable personal and family life? If the portfolio manager has integrity and is honest, fair, and open in his discussions about performance with clients and superiors, then the reputation of the organization is protected, and the client's evaluation of portfolio performance is facilitated.

Support of the System. The performance of a portfolio manager is affected by the quality and quantity of logistical support furnished him by the investment management system. Does he have sufficient assistance so that he is free to devote a substantial portion of his time on the professional management of his portfolios, or is a significant amount of time spent on office administration, routine record maintenance, and internal organizational reports? Is he assigned other duties such as processing his security orders, being an industry research analyst, and hand holding clients in regard to routine and administrative details, rather than spending his time on portfolio review and policy formulation? Is the investment management system supplying him with sufficient high-quality and timely investment and portfolio policy research information?

What is the number, size, and type of other portfolio accounts for which he has primary responsibility? Does he have too many accounts and too much funds in order to give each account sufficient time and attention? Do these accounts have challenging performance objectives which should demand more of his time? Do many or most of these accounts have similar performance objectives, so that he can concentrate his time and effort on the formulation of similar portfolio policies and the research of similar portfolio holdings? If so, are the total amount of funds in all these accounts so large that simultaneous changes made by the portfolio manager in policies and holdings will have an adverse market affect on portfolio performance? In processing security orders, does the subject account have a fair priority in relation to other accounts?

What is the amount and basis of his compensation? Is it commensurate with his responsibilities and abilities? How is it determined? Is it a salary based on the value of his services, based on the short-term performance of his portfolio, or based on the profits of his organization? If the size or basis for determining compensation is too niggardly, this can stifle incentive; however, if it is heavily and generously weighted by short-term portfolio performance, this can encourage the adoption of highly speculative, ill-timed strategies.

Does the system give him sufficient portfolio management authority and freedom for him to use his professional talents productively? Likewise, does the system exercise sufficient supervision and control over his work in order to assure high-quality performance?

Interpersonal Skills. Because the functioning of the portfolio management system depends on the efforts of a number of people, it is desirable for the portfolio manager to have the personal skills to work effectively with these people in order that the portfolio may derive the greatest possible benefits from the talents offered by these people.

The portfolio manager is dependent on the services and cooperation of people who are at subordinate, superior, and lateral echelons within the organizations and of people who are outside the organization. These people help him carry out his tasks by supplying him with research information, by reviewing his work and making constructive suggestions, and by executing portfolio transactions. Therefore, if he has the skill to draw out the best talents of these people, individually and in groups and committees, who are sometimes working under stress conditions, then the performance of the portfolio can benefit. In addition, it is helpful for him to have a close and harmonious relation with the client. In this way, the portfolio manager may have a better insight into the financial requirements and temperament of the client which serve as a basis for the formulation of performance objectives, and the client will have greater confidence in the portfolio manager and a better understanding of what he is trying to do.

How well he gets along with others is suggested by how long he has worked for this and other organizations and is suggested by the reasons given for leaving previous employers, by how long he has worked with others around him, including clients, and by their opinions of him.

Evaluation of Portfolio Performance

The ultimate purpose of evaluating the portfolio management system is to ensure that portfolio performance objectives will be achieved. Because the past is the prologue for the future, a review of past portfolio performance of the investment management system may provide insights into what future performance might be expected. This subject will be discussed only briefly here because the evaluation and quantitative measurement of portfolio performance is a major topic in its own right.

Past performance should be measured over a sufficiently long period to represent different investment environments and different security market cycles. Some managers do better during bull markets, for example, while others do relatively better under adverse market conditions. Is past performance consistent with stated portfolio performance objectives and stated strategies?

Observe the composition of the portfolio near major market turning points. Does the portfolio structure correctly anticipate a change in market trend? Compare the portfolio composition between market bottoms and tops. Is performance being enhanced by timely portfolio shifts?

How does the past performance compare to other portfolios and to various stock indexes? How are differences explained? By differences in objectives, risks, luck, or portfolio management ability? Is management able to explain fully, rationally, and honestly questions raised about its past performance? If past mistakes occurred, has management taken intelligent remedial action? Is management constantly evaluating its own portfolio performance in order to minimize mistakes and to improve future performance? Are differences large in long-term performance among the various portfolio managers within the organization and, if so, has corrective action been taken to improve the performance of the worst managers?

THE INSTITUTIONAL CHARACTERISTICS OF DIFFERENT CATEGORIES OF INVESTMENT PORTFOLIO ACCOUNTS

Portfolio performance is importantly affected by or determined by institutional characteristics or constraints which are peculiar to different categories of investment accounts. We will briefly describe some of these important characteristics as they pertain to several major categories of portfolios of marketable securities.

Individual/Family-Type Investors

The seven classes of portfolios in this major category represent investment funds supplied separately by individual investors, families, or household units.

Advisory Account. Under this arrangement, an individual investor employs an investment advisor or advisory firm who furnishes him with investment recommendations as to what securities to buy and sell and as to when to buy and sell them. The advisor tailors his advice to the particular goals and requirements of each client's circumstances. For this advice the client pays a quarterly fee, usually determined as a percent of the portfolio's market value. He has the freedom of accepting and implementing the advice or not. If the client frequently does not follow the recommendations, the advisory relationship is usually terminated. The client retains the responsibility of placing security transaction orders with a brokerage firm. The minimum size account is usually $100,000 to $200,000. The portfolio goals and constraints vary widely among clients.

Investment organizations which provide this service are unincorporated and incorporated investment counsel firms, investment advisory departments of broker-dealer firms, financial publishing houses, and trust investment departments of banks.

Management Account. This account is quite similar to advisory accounts, described above, and indeed, even the titles used for such classes of accounts vary from one investment organization to another. The term *agency* account is sometimes used.

The primary difference between an advisory account and a management account is that in the latter case the investment organization acts more as a portfolio manager than as an advisor, in which the portfolio manager has complete discretion to make, implement, and execute portfolio decisions. Once the manager decides to make a portfolio change in a management account, he or his security trader places security orders directly with broker-dealers for execution, without the prior approval of the client. Obviously, the portfolio manager of a management account has inherently greater control over making investment decisions than an advisor of an advisory account. Because investment decisions are not reviewed and approved by the client prior to implementation in a management account, the client has in effect placed a higher level of confidence in the professional judgment of the portfolio manager. In the case of both management and advisory accounts, however, the client is kept informed regarding transactions and the status of the portfolio on a periodic basis. As in the case of advisory accounts, portfolio goals and constraints vary widely according to the circumstances of each client.

No-Load Mutual Fund. This class of portfolio and load mutual funds and closed-end funds described below are defined as investment companies. As such, their assets represent a portfolio of marketable securities, and their source of capital is primarily from individual investors who own securities, mostly common shares, which have been issued by the investment company. Portfolio objectives and policies vary widely among investment companies.

No-load mutual funds and load mutual funds described below are called open-end investment companies because their common stock capital structure is "open" in the sense that mutual funds are generally prepared to issue new common shares directly to new investors and to retire or redeem existing common shares directly from current shareholders during each business day. Consequently, these portfolios experience either a net cash inflow or a net cash outflow during any given time period depending on whether more shares or less shares are issued than old shares are redeemed. Because a net cash outflow may occur due to a net reduction of mutual fund shares outstanding, such a portfolio has a greater need for marketability and possibly liquidity as well.

An investor in most no-load mutual funds pays no sales charge (load or commission) when he purchases fund shares nor a redemption fee when he liquidates his shares. As a result, the investor does not purchase shares through a sales representative or a broker-dealer firm, but rather deals directly with the mutual fund home office or an affiliated distributor firm. Because a no-load mutual fund utilizes no sales forces, it usually generates fund share sales in one of three ways: (1) by advertising, (2) by being affiliated with an investment organization which has contact with the public such as a broker-dealer firm or an investment counsel firm, and/or (3) by its reputation in terms of portfolio performance.

In this last instance, large sales of fund shares sometimes result for a mutual fund with a substantial portfolio performance, because of wide publicity given by several financial publishers of mutual fund performance ratings. A portfolio management who attracts investors on the basis of performance publicity is economically motivated (or is under considerable pressure, when carried to an extreme) to achieve a successful future performance. A portfolio management which fails to deliver this expected performance will lose a source of new business and, possibly worse yet, may experience substantial share redemptions. The volume of redemptions in a no-load fund could be more volatile because individual shareholders incur virtually no direct transaction costs. Because the client tends to take the initiative to select and purchase the shares of a no-load fund, he tends to be more sophisticated or to take a more active interest in investment matters than the client of a load fund.

Load Mutual Fund. A load mutual fund is, of course, quite similar to no-load mutual funds, described above. The greatest difference is that investors pay a loading charge or sales commission, usually about 8½ percent of their investment when they purchase shares of a load fund. Usually no redemption fee or commission is charged when shares are liquidated by investors in a load or a no-load fund. The loading charge serves as an inducement or compensation for salesmen and dealers to solicit purchase orders from prospective mutual fund investors. It is difficult to generalize about the investment requirements of clients of load funds because there are so many funds with a wide range of different portfolio objectives and policies and they employ different appeals to attract and retain investors.

Closed-end Fund. A closed-end fund is an investment company. The major difference between a mutual (open-end) fund and a closed-end company is that the latter has a somewhat permanent capital structure. Its capital structure, therefore, resembles some of the characteristics of the capital structure of a typical corporation. The common shares of the fund are traded in the secondary market, either on an exchange or in the over-the-counter market. A few funds employ leverage in their capital structure by the use of preferred stocks and debt capital.

Some special purpose closed-end companies which emphasize investment in private placements and in small closely held growth-oriented companies are called *venture capital* funds. Some closed-end funds called *dual purpose* funds have two special classes of common stock type shares—income shares which are entitled to the net income from the total portfolio and capital shares which have a claim on the appreciation from the total portfolio.

Because of the closed capital structure, the portfolio of the conventional closed-end fund needs less marketability; likewise, the fund has inherently a stronger tenure of investment management which permits the portfolio management either to be more lax about performance or to place more emphasis on performance with a longer term time horizon. Portfolio policies tend to vary among closed-end funds. Because most of these funds have operated for several decades or more, their policies tend to be traditional in nature. Closed-end fund shares trade in the open market, frequently at discounts from their underlying asset values. The shareholders tend to be passive investors though sometimes more affluent than load fund shareholders.

Revocable Living Trust. A personal trust is an agreement made by a person called a trustor, creator, or grantor who also supplies assets, called the corpus, to a person or bank who administers the assets as trustee. The trustee ordinarily has custody of the assets, manages them, and disburses funds to beneficiaries. The agreement specifies when and over what period of time the income from the trust is to be disbursed and to whom it is to be paid. The recipient of the income is called the income beneficiary or life tenant. The government also specifies when the principal is to be disbursed and to whom it is to be paid. The recipient of the principal is called the remainderman or the beneficiary of the principal. As to portfolio objectives and policies, the trust agreement (1) may provide explicit instructions, (2) may grant full discretion to the trustee in regard to investment matters, or (3) may be silent. If it is silent, it is called a legal trust and the assets are to be invested in accordance with the laws of the state. The laws of some states specify a "legal list" which defines what investments are *legal* or permissible for legal trusts; however, the majority of states requires personal trusts to be invested in accordance with the *prudent-man rule.* In most modern trusts, the agreement grants the trustee full discretion, and the trustee is free to adopt investment objectives and portfolio policies which best meet the requirements of beneficiaries; however, to avoid difficulties, these investment policies must be ones which the courts consider to be prudent in accordance with the prudent-man philosophy.

Personal trusts may be classified into two major categories, testamentary trusts (discussed in the section below), and living trusts, sometimes called inter vivos trusts. Living trusts are established while the creator is alive. Living trusts are of two types, revocable and irrevocable. The irrevocable trust is one which cannot be voided or terminated by the creator; it will be discussed in the section below.

The revocable living trust is distinctive from most other personal trusts in that the creator retains the power, while he is alive, to terminate the trust agreement and repossess the corpus. Because the creator retains ultimate control, the tenure of investment management of the trustee is weaker. Clients usually have several reasons for creating revocable living trusts, such as to delegate the responsibilities of asset administration and investment management while they are living and to avoid probate. However, another possible reason for a revocable agreement is for the creator to evaluate the effectiveness of the trust arrangement and the effectiveness of the portfolio management. If he is not satisfied during his lifetime, the creator may revise the trust agreement or appoint a new trustee. Consequently, trustees and trust investment officers are usually sympathetically responsive, within reason, to the wishes of creators.

Irrevocable Personal Trust. A brief background description of personal trusts and living trusts was presented in the section above. This section deals with both irrevocable living trusts and testamentary trusts together because of a similarity of relationship between the trustee and the beneficiaries.

A testamentary trust becomes operational under the terms of the last will and testament upon the demise of the estate owner, who is called the testator. The trust receives its corpus from the estate when the estate is settled by probate court. Such a trust may be subject to federal personal income taxes as a separate entity.

An irrevocable living trust becomes operational when a trust agreement is approved by the creator or trustor and the trustee accepts the corpus. If the trustor permanently and fully relinquishes all control over the trust he has, in effect made a gift, such that the property may be subject to federal gift taxes, but not be subject to federal estate taxes in his estate upon his demise; in addition, the trust may be subject to federal personal income taxes as a separate entity.

When the irrevocable living trust and the testamentary trust become operational, both trusts become irrevocable inasmuch as the trust instructions or agreement cannot be changed except in extenuating circumstances, and only then by formal court proceedings. Consequently, the trustee and portfolio management is guided by the trust agreement, the law, and court orders. As stated in the section above, the trust agreement (1) may provide explicit instructions regarding investment objectives and portfolio policies, (2) may grant the trustee full discretion in such matters, or (3) may say nothing. If it says nothing, then it is a legal trust. Most modern trusts give the trustee full discretion in which case he is able to adopt legally prudent portfolio policies which hopefully will serve the best interests of the beneficiaries.

Within the confines of legally determined fiduciary constraints, the trustee holds a strong tenure of investment management. Because fiduciary constraints embrace a prudent philosophy and because of the strong tenure of the trustee, portfolio management of irrevocable personal trusts tends to be conservatively oriented. Beyond the confines of these constraints, the portfolio manager should adopt policies which seek to achieve a performance that satisfies the financial requirements of the beneficiaries. A trust may have two or more beneficiaries with different life tenants and remaindermen having conflicting financial interests and goals. Consequently, the investment management may find itself with one or more clients who want or need maximum income and one or more clients who want maximum growth. This frequently leads to a compromise in portfolio policy which fails to please fully any of the beneficiaries.

Formal Retirement Funds

Formal retirement funds consist of portfolios whose primary explicit purpose is to finance, partially or totally, the family consumption requirements of individuals or couples during their retirement years. Contributions into the most popular retirement fund programs are exempt from federal income taxes, as well as the income earned on the portfolio. Income taxes are normally paid by the pensioner when he receives cash disbursements; if he is retired, he usually pays a tax based on the lower progressive tax rates.

The beneficiary client is the current or future cash recipient from the fund and will be referred to simply as the pensioner. Perhaps because of the contemporary origin of group employee retirement funds, which under most plans are presently accumulating capital, no major investment policy distinction is usually made by investment management between gainfully employed (future) pensioners for whom current and previous contributions are retained in the fund (for later disbursement) and retired pensioners who are recipients of current cash benefits. The obligations of the portfolio differ between retired pensioners and future pensioners in terms of the investment time horizon and in terms of current financial dependency on the portfolio by the pensioner. That is to say, a young person faces a long time horizon and virtually no current financial dependency on the pension portfolio; however, the retired pensioner (he and his wife may be in their middle sixties) has a considerably shorter investment time horizon and possibly a very heavy dependency on the pension fund.

We frequently minimize the importance of this dependency on the pension portfolio because the employer (company or employment institution) or life insurance company is usually legally liable for pension payments and, in a growing or stable pension fund, new deposits and cash investment income are available to meet current pension disbursements. Nevertheless, if a pension fund program matures and the employer organization should decrease its work force and scale of operations, current pension disbursements may place an unexpected burden on the funds in the portfolio. More clearly in the case of variable annuities and mutual funds, adverse portfolio performance has a direct and relatively immediate effect on the size of cash payments or withdrawals and, in turn, on the consumption level of retired annuitants or shareholders with short time horizons, while the adverse effect on the consumption level of future pensioners is deferred and possibly averted with a cyclical market recovery.

Trusteed Pension. Trusteed pension programs are sometimes called noninsured plans because they are usually funded through a trust agreement in contrast to an insured annuity program which is funded through a life insurance company annuity policy contract.

As in the case of personal trusts discussed in the sections above, a considerable number of alternative terms and arrangements may be adopted in any given trusteed pension agreement. The parties to the agreement, as a minimum, are the employer organization, the employees, and the trustee. Trust administration includes the responsibilities for the receipt of contributions from the employer, disbursement of benefits to employee pensioners, maintenance of records, custody of trust assets, and quite often, portfolio management. Most of these functions may be performed by one organization, such as a bank, or they may be assigned to two or more different organizations, such as a management-employee committee, a bank, and an investment counsel organization.

Noninsured pension plans have become very popular. Because of the wide number of possible variations in these plans, we will discuss only the most common types of arrangements, giving emphasis to portfolio performance requirements.

Under the typical pension plan, the employer agrees to pay stipulated amounts at periodical intervals to individual employees, commencing at retirement and continuing for life. This employer liability is usually discharged by periodic employer pension contributions, by funds representing previous employer contributions, and by the profit performance of the pension portfolio. Ideally, the investment requirements of any given portfolio are satisfied by a risk and return performance in which the portfolio return minimizes the employer's future pension costs, and the portfolio risk level protects the interests of pensioners and, at the same time, does not exceed the client's risk tolerance level.

From the standpoint of pensioners, investment portfolio risk policies may be less constrained when the employer organization is in a relatively strong business and financial position, the pension fund is in an accumulation phase (i.e., employer pension contributions and investment income exceed pension benefit disbursements), and the pension fund is *fully funded* (i.e., fund assets equal the incurred liabilities for past services, actuarially discounted).

The investment management responsibility for a pension fund portfolio, as distinct from general pension trust administration, may be assumed by an employer or union pension committee, a bank trust investment department, an investment counsel firm, or other portfolio management organization. The portfolios of many noninsured pensions are managed by bank trust investment departments. The portfolios of larger pension funds are sometimes split among two or more investment management organizations for purposes of diversifying against the risk of mediocre portfolio performance. In order to gain the investment management benefits of a larger portfolio, the assets of small pension funds are sometimes commingled in a single portfolio managed by a bank, which is called a pooled pension common trust fund.

The investment management powers granted to the pension fund portfolio manager by the employer can vary. The instructions may grant complete investment discretion, may grant discretion limited to the prudent-man rule, may require that investment changes be approved in advance by an employer committee or officer, or may grant discretion within certain stipulations. Typically, portfolio managers have complete discretion in investment matters.

Pension portfolio performance requirements should stress a maximum long-term rate of return with less concern for the risk of principal volatility during the accumulation stage. Based on a rough rule of thumb, each percentage point of the annual rate of return earned on contributed funds is equivalent to 20 percent of the annual cost of pension benefits to the employer company.

Insurance Companies

Life Insurance Company Programs. These types of programs are perhaps the oldest and best known formal devices used to fund retirement. An individual saver or policy holder may purchase a deferred annuity or an immediate annuity from an annuity guarantor, which is a life insurance and annuity company. A *deferred fixed annuity* is a contract which guarantees to pay the policy holder or annuitant a fixed number of dollars each month or each year for life commencing at some future date, say when he retires at 65. An *immediate fixed annuity* is a contract which guarantees to pay the annuitant, who is usually already retired, a fixed number of dollars each month or each year for life, in which payments are now being disbursed to him.

Annuities may be purchased by an individual under a single policy or for a group of individuals (such as for an employee group) under a group policy contract. In either type of contract, the policy premium (annuity purchase price) and portfolio performance requirements are somewhat similar for the annuity company. The premium paid for a group contract may be less per annuitant than for a single contract because of administrative and marketing cost savings due to economies of large scale. Deferred annuities may be purchased by a single premium payment or by a series of monthly or annual premium payments made over a period of years.

Because the principles and purposes of annuities can be and frequently are intertwined with life insurance (more precisely called death insurance), annuities are sold by life insurance companies, and their features are commonly incorporated in life insurance contracts. In fact, all permanent life insurance policies (whole life, limited payment life, and endowment life insurance, but not term insurance) have annuity settlement or conversion options available to the insured (the person whose life is insured). The conceptual relationship between life insurance and annuity insurance might be tersely summarized thusly: life insurance financially protects those who are dependent on the insured against the risk of his dying too soon (premature death); while annuity insurance protects the annuitant and possibly his spouse against the risk of living too long, that is, outliving one's retirement savings. A portion of the cash premium payment for permanent life insurance provides for the gradual accumulation of assets, called cash surrender value (CSV), in the insurance company which are held for the future benefit of the insured. This portion of the life insurance premium is conceptually a premium for a deferred annuity contract. If the insured lives to retirement age, the policy matures, or may be cancelled. In either case, the CSV may be left on deposit with the insurance company or withdrawn in cash, or the policy may be converted to immediate annuity, in which case the CSV is used, in effect, as the purchase price (single premium) for the annuity.

Based on mortality experience and the law of large numbers (law of averages) an actuarially calculated minimum required rate of return on policyholder reserves is determined which, if realized, will meet the annuity obligations or policyholder liabilities of the insurance company. Because the portfolio performance requirement of our clients under a deferred fixed annuity (and CSV arrangements) is both fixed in terms of dollar amounts and long term, covering of a significant time span of human life, portfolio management seeks investments which provide assurance of meeting minimum long-term rate of return requirements in fixed dollar terms. From the standpoint of portfolio performance requirements, the investment time horizon is generally quite long for policyholder reserves of young, deferred annuitants. If the insurance company is mutual (owned by the policyholders) or the insurance contract is participating, then the benefits of superior portfolio performance accrue to the policyholders; otherwise such benefits accrue to the insurance company and its stockholders. In addition to client requirements, the general operations of insurance companies, including investment management, are subject to special and technical tax and legal constraints.

Immediate Fixed Annuity. Because of the fixed dollar nature of the contractual obligations to annuitants, the portfolio performance requirements of a life insurance and annuity insurer (company) in respect to immediate annuitants is quite similar to deferred annuitants. The primary difference is the timing of cash flows into and out of the annuity fund. In the case of immediate annuitants, cash benefits are currently being disbursed on a periodic basis during the lifetime of the beneficiaries. Therefore, sufficient liquid reserves need to be available to meet near-term disbursements. Because surplus reserves are usually small in comparison to annuity liabilities, little impairment of principal can be tolerated. Under participating annuity contracts (those issued by mutual insurers and participating contracts issued by stockholder owned insurers), annuity benefits may be increased above the guaranteed amount when the portfolio rate of return exceeds the assumed actuarial race of return. Under nonparticipating contracts, superior portfolio performance accrues to the benefit of the stockholders of the insurer.

Property and Casualty Portfolios. The primary business of a property and casualty insurance company is to insure policyholders against the risk of loss due to property damage, and to accidents and illnesses of individuals. This is the underwriting part of the insurance business. In the course of underwriting risks, underwriting premiums flow into the company which are used to pay operating expenses, and so on, and to purchase investments. The investment part of the insurance business can become a sizeable operation. The investment portfolio is available to meet insurance claims and expenses for processing claim settlements and to produce an investment return.

Insurance carriers are either mutual or stockholder owned companies. The underwriting and investment profits, if any, accrue to the benefit of policyholders who are owners of mutual companies, or they accrue to the benefit of stockholders in the case of stockholder owned companies.

In serving the interest of policyholders and stockholders, the portfolio performance requirements are to meet the short-term liquidity needs of insurance claim settlements, to minimize the risk of principal impairment which could jeopardize the interests of policyholders and stockholders, and to optimize investment returns for the benefit of the company owners. The need for liquidity and for marketability in the portfolio depends on the stability or predictability of aggregate insurance claims and on the ratio of policyholders' surplus (capital and surplus) to total liabilities. Portfolio objectives can be more aggressive given a larger ratio and/or greater predictability of underwriting losses. An insurance company is subject to the same federal income tax constraints as ordinary corporations, so that tax-exempt bonds and preferred stocks in the portfolio receive tax shelter.

Foundations, Endowments, and Charitable Trusts

Because the purposes and commitments of these types of funds vary, it is difficult to generalize about their portfolio performance requirements. Investment policies and performance are influenced in varying degrees by the policies of fund trustees, the articles of incorporation or trust agreement, investment instructions of donors, state fiduciary regulations, and Federal Internal Revenue regulations.

Because most of these funds support educational and charitable activities which, on the basis of financial need, tend to be open-ended or unlimited, a maximum rate of return is usually desired. Investment returns from these portfolios are characteristically used to support human services, such as scholarships and salaries of professional medical, welfare, religious, educational research, and student personnel. As the costs of these services increase with inflation, it is desirable for the portfolio return to increase likewise.

Confusion exists as to whether portfolio capital gains are to be treated as principal or income. Such a determination will decide whether capital appreciation is retained in the portfolio or whether all or a part of it is available for disbursement. This interpretation will obviously have important implications in formulating portfolio performance requirements relative to investment income yield and relative to total rate of return (which counts capital gains).

Need for stability of principal and investment income for a portfolio fund can vary depending on whether support is being provided to one-time projects or to recurring on-going programs, and whether disbursements of principal are used to support payments.

Conclusion

A reliable evaluation of portfolio management is accomplished by a comprehensive study of the characteristics of the investment management organization and of the elements of the investment management system. No one facet should be examined to the exclusion of other significant criteria. For example, a study of only past portfolio performance can be deceptive, inasmuch as portfolios which produce outstanding results in one period sometimes produce dismal results in a succeeding time interval.

42

An Integrated Approach to Portfolio Management

EDMUND A. MENNIS, Ph.D., C.F.A.
Senior Vice President and Chairman of the Investment Policy Committee
Security Pacific National Bank
Los Angeles, California

FOR THE PAST 30 years, the volume of funds under the management of large institutional investors (such as banks, insurance companies, pension funds, and mutual funds) has been increasing substantially. Institutional investors are now significant shareholders of many corporations and institutional trading activity represents the overwhelming proportion of trading on the New York Stock Exchange. The methods used to manage these large funds vary, but they are all designed to handle either sizable sums of money, many accounts with varying investment objectives, or both. The management problems involved are quite different from those for a relatively small individual portfolio. The resources utilized for such management, similarly, are ordinarily far beyond the reach of the individual investor.

The purpose of this chapter is to describe an integrated, logical, and structured system for portfolio management applicable to a large institutional investor. This approach has as its objective that of achieving a rate of return moderately better than that of the market and with a portfolio risk level equal to, or slightly higher than, that of the market. It is assumed that funds are available to obtain the staff necessary to perform the functions to be described and also that experienced economists, security analysts, and portfolio managers are available to develop the inputs needed. This approach would have limited applicability to managing a single investor's portfolio because of the substantial expense that would be involved.

In succeeding sections the information required to manage institutional portfolios will be described. Among the basic inputs necessary are economic projections, interest rate projections, projections of corporate profits and estimates of earnings, and judgments of appropriate multiples of earnings to be applied to stock market averages. In addition, industry studies and company analyses and valuations must be provided, either by an internal staff or from external sources such as brokerage firms or consulting organizations. In addition to these basic inputs, policy decisions are required regarding the economic and security market environment, the investment objectives for the types of portfolios to be managed, the mix of the portfolios between fixed and variable income securities, and finally, industry diversification of the equity portion of the portfolio into various groups such as basic, moderate-growth, and high-growth industries.

With this information available, the portfolio manager must establish the objectives and risk assumptions for each account, structure the diversification of the account within policy guidelines, select and time the purchase and sale of particular investments, and monitor the performance of the portfolio to take corrective action if necessary (see Figure 1). Each of these items will be discussed in the sections that

FIGURE 1

The Investment Decision Process

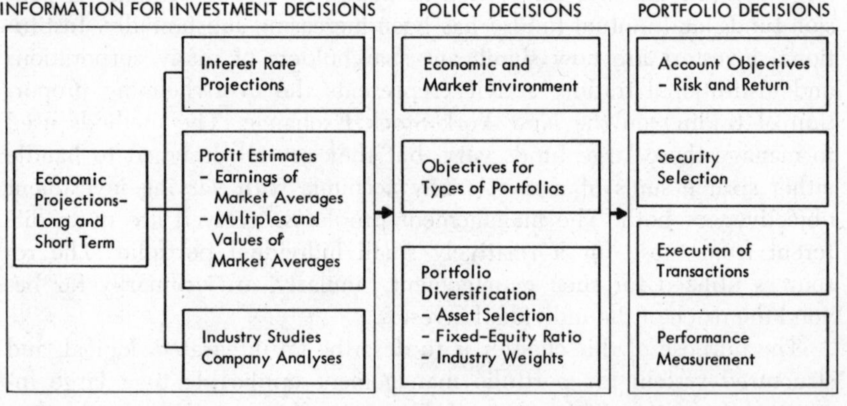

follow, and finally, a discussion will contrast the approach described herein with the portfolio management approaches advocated in recent years in the academic literature.

ECONOMIC PROJECTIONS

Economic projections are the foundation of any effective investment management process. They are used to provide a consistent framework for the comparative selection of investments. The projections needed are of two types: long term and short term. Long-term projections are critical for portfolio planning in that they provide an estimate of the future investment climate in which portfolios are to be managed and permit an evaluation of the returns from alternative types of investments. Long-term projections are also needed to enable security analysts to estimate the trends of earnings of companies to be reviewed for inclusion in or exclusion from a portfolio. Short-term projections are the basis for deciding on portfolio strategy and also for determining the near-term attractiveness of individual securities for inclusion in the portfolio.

The projections should be of two types. Near-term projections should cover about eight calendar quarters. The long-term projections need not be in quarterly detail but should cover estimates for a high employment year about five years away from the most recent year for which current data are available. Going beyond five years is considered of limited usefulness because the difficulties in making reasonable projections increase as the time span lengthens. Moreover, a reasonable time span over which to measure the effectiveness of a portfolio manager is ordinarily three to five years, and portfolio planning can be done effectively for this period. On the other hand, making a long-term projection for less than five years involves the problem of associating the projected year with the present cyclical status of the economy and the path to the year projected. By divorcing the long-term projection from the current position of the economy, a better estimate of long-term normalized earnings and long-term normalized market values can be obtained.

Economic Information Needed

The content of the projections should include the following:

1. Assumptions about the phase and duration of the business cycle, and fiscal and monetary policy during the forecast period.
2. Gross national product and its components from the demand side in current and constant dollars.
3. Personal income, disposable income, and personal savings.
4. Unemployment rate.
5. Federal Reserve Board index of industrial production and its major components.
6. Other economic data, such as automobile production and sales, construction activity, and business spending plans.
7. Price indexes, including the major components of the wholesale price index and the consumer price index as well as the GNP deflator.

Once these projections are made, a continuing review of them is necessary. As current economic data become available, it may be necessary to shade or even significantly change assumptions. It is most fruitful to conduct an intensive review each quarter when the information on gross national product and its components is released by the Department of Commerce. In interpreting the data, the political and international environment must not be overlooked. Political decisions can have a far-reaching impact on economic assumptions and on the path of the economy. International developments, particularly in the political and monetary area, also can substantially alter the economic environment in which investments are made.[1]

DERIVATIONS FROM ECONOMIC PROJECTIONS

The economic projections described above can best be made by a trained economics staff or by an individual economist. In order to maximize the usefulness of these projections, however, certain additional information must be derived, which ordinarily should be done jointly by someone with skill and experience in the investment area together with a trained economist.

Interest Rates

Interest rate projections should be prepared in the same disciplined fashion as the preparation of economic projections. The information should include estimates for both the near and longer term on long-term and short-term interest rates. The estimates found most useful are for AAA seasoned long-term bonds, AA new issue utility bonds, municipal bond rates (The Bond Buyer index), the treasury bill rate, commercial paper rates, and the bank prime rate. Estimates for the level of rates for these types of fixed income obligations will also require the discipline of determining the yield spreads between the various types of fixed income issues.

Interest rate projections are needed in portfolio management for a variety of purposes. The most obvious is the determination of the relative attractiveness of bond versus stock investment. In addition, the level of short-term rates will indicate the return that can be obtained on any cash reserves held in an account. Interest rate projections are useful in the evaluation of financial stocks and other industries such as utilities that are sensitive to movements in interest rates. Bond yields may also be compared with the yields available from stocks where current income is an investment consideration.

---

[1] For a further discussion, see Edmund A. Mennis, "Economics and Investment Management," *Financial Analysts Journal* 22, no. 6 (November–December 1966): 17–23.

Profits and Stock Values

A crucial link between economic projections and investment decisions is the impact of economic developments on profits. Consequently, the second major piece of information derived from the economic projections should be estimates of profits for both the near and the long term. These profits should be those reported in the national income accounts, and projections can be derived from projections of gross national product.[2]

From these profits, earnings can be estimated for the Dow Jones industrial average (Table 1) and Standard & Poor's 425 and 500 stock indexes (Table 2). To these earnings estimates, an appropriate multiple can be applied to derive reasonable value estimates for the stock averages for both the near and the long term.[3] The multiple to be used can be derived from historical levels adjusted for current and expected conditions and then checked against the bond yield assumptions made to insure internal consistency.[4] Of course, these value estimates are not a prediction of the prices of these indexes. Prices will undoubtedly range above and below these values. However, these estimates provide a valuable bench mark against which current prices can be compared, and thereby give important direction to investment planning and policy.

Industry Expectations

The third major use of the economic projections is to determine the sales and earnings outlook for various industry areas. This information will indicate the direction for research emphasis and also suggest portfolio diversification schedules by industries. Industry analysis is the appropriate link between economic projections and company analysis. Nevertheless, it is one of the more neglected areas of security analysis.

---

[2] For a description of a technique found useful in such profits projections, see Edmund A. Mennis, "Forecasting Corporate Profits," a chapter in *Methods and Techniques of Business Forecasting*, ed. by William Butler, Robert A. Kavesh, and Robert Platt, 2d ed. (Englewood Cliffs, N.J.: Prentice-Hall, Inc., 1974): 517–42.

[3] For a description of a methodology using long- and short-term economic projections to derive estimates of profits and then estimates of earnings on the Dow Jones and Standard & Poor's averages together with an appropriate multiple, see Sidney Cottle, Edmund A. Mennis, and Mary Schuelke, "Corporate Earnings—Long Term Outlook and Valuation," and Edmund A. Mennis and Sidney Cottle, "Corporate Earnings—Short Term Outlook and Valuation," *Financial Analysts Journal*, 27, no. 4 (July–August 1971): 22–25, 50–64.

[4] For example, assume that the yield on the Dow Jones Industrial Average should be at least 50 percent of the AAA bond yield. If AAA bonds yield 8 percent, the DJIA should yield 4 percent. If the payout of the DJIA is 57 percent and the yield required is 4 percent, the implicit price earnings multiple is 14.25. (The ratio of dividends to earnings, or the payout ratio, divided by the ratio of dividends to price, or the yield, will give the ratio of price to earnings, or the multiple.)

TABLE 1

Dow Jones Industrial Average

			Price Range			Year-end		12 Months			
Year	Earnings	Dividend	High	Low	Average	Closing Price	Book Value	Average Price	Average P/E	Average Yield	Average S/B Yld. Ratio*
1945	$10.56	$ 6.69	195.82	151.35	173.59	192.91	$122.74	169.82	16.1X	3.9%	157.17%
1946	13.63	7.50	212.50	163.12	187.81	177.20	131.40	191.65	14.1	3.9	161.10
1947	18.80	9.21	186.85	163.21	175.03	181.16	149.08	177.58	9.4	5.2	205.90
1948	23.07	11.50	193.16	165.39	179.28	177.30	159.67	179.95	7.8	6.4	236.92
1949	23.54	12.79	200.52	161.60	181.06	200.13	170.12	179.48	7.6	7.1	282.51
1950	30.70	16.13	235.47	196.81	216.14	235.41	194.19	216.31	7.0	7.5	301.14
1951	26.59	16.34	276.37	238.99	257.68	269.23	202.60	257.64	9.7	6.3	233.68
1952	24.78	15.43	292.00	256.35	274.18	291.90	213.39	270.76	10.9	5.7	197.78
1953	27.43	16.11	293.79	255.49	274.64	280.90	224.26	275.97	10.1	5.8	190.04
1954	28.18	17.47	404.39	279.87	342.13	404.39	248.96	333.94	11.8	5.2	190.45
1955	35.78	21.58	488.40	388.20	438.30	488.40	271.77	442.72	12.4	4.9	163.65
1956	33.34	22.99	521.05	462.35	491.70	499.47	284.78	493.01	14.8	4.6	140.08
1957	36.08	21.61	520.77	419.79	470.28	435.69	298.69	475.71	13.2	4.5	120.30
1958	27.95	20.00	583.65	436.89	510.27	583.65	310.97	491.66	17.6	4.1	112.08
1959	34.31	20.74	679.36	574.46	626.91	679.36	339.02	632.12	18.4	3.3	76.72
1960	32.21	21.36	685.47	566.05	625.76	615.89	369.87	618.04	19.2	3.4	82.04
1961	31.91	22.71	734.91	610.25	672.58	731.13	385.82	691.55	21.7	3.3	77.97
1962	36.43	23.30	726.01	535.76	630.89	652.10	400.97	639.76	17.6	3.6	88.30
1963	41.21	23.41	767.21	646.79	707.00	762.95	425.90	714.81	17.3	3.3	79.36
1964	46.43	31.24	891.71	766.08	828.90	874.13	417.39	834.05	18.0	3.7	87.80
1965	53.67	28.61	969.26	840.59	904.93	969.26	453.27	910.88	17.0	3.1	71.44
1966	57.68	31.89	995.15	744.32	869.74	785.69	475.92	861.86	14.9	3.7	73.11
1967	53.87	30.19	943.08	786.41	864.75	905.11	476.50	879.83	16.3	3.4	63.19
1968	57.89	31.34	985.21	825.13	905.17	943.75	521.08	903.47	15.6	3.5	56.86
1969	57.02	33.90	968.85	769.93	869.39	800.36	542.25	873.47	15.3	3.9	56.28
1970	51.02	31.53	842.00	631.16	736.58	838.92	573.15	756.27	14.8	4.2	53.85
1971	55.09	30.86	950.82	797.97	874.40	890.20	607.61	883.05	16.0	3.5	48.88
1972	67.11	32.27	1,036.27	889.15	962.71	1,020.02	642.87	954.20	14.2	3.4	46.85

* DJIA/S&P Ind.

S&P 425 Industrials

Year	Earnings	Dividend	Price Range High	Price Range Low	Price Range Average	Year-End Closing Price	Book Value	12 Months Average Price	12 Months Average P/E	12 Months Average Yield	12 Months Average* S/B Yld. Ratio
1945	$0.82	$0.61	17.06	12.97	15.02	16.79	NA	14.72	17.95X	4.14%	165.21
1946	0.92	0.66	18.53	13.64	16.09	14.75	11.19	16.48	17.91	4.00	165.38
1947	1.59	0.82	15.83	13.40	14.62	15.18	12.49	14.85	9.34	5.52	218.90
1948	2.33	0.91	16.93	13.58	15.26	15.12	14.53	15.34	6.58	5.93	220.02
1949	2.42	1.14	16.52	13.23	14.88	16.49	15.17	15.00	6.20	7.60	302.08
1950	2.93	1.53	20.60	16.34	18.47	20.57	16.77	18.33	6.26	8.35	337.22
1951	2.55	1.45	24.33	20.85	22.59	24.24	18.66	22.68	8.89	6.39	235.38
1952	2.46	1.44	26.92	23.30	25.11	26.89	20.15	24.78	10.07	5.81	201.63
1953	2.59	1.47	26.99	22.70	24.85	24.87	20.76	24.84	9.59	5.92	192.50
1954	2.89	1.57	37.24	24.84	31.04	37.24	22.09	30.25	10.47	5.19	189.09
1955	3.78	1.68	49.54	35.66	42.60	48.44	25.09	42.40	11.22	3.96	133.56
1956	3.53	1.78	53.28	45.71	49.50	50.08	26.35	49.80	14.11	3.57	108.18
1957	3.50	1.84	53.25	41.98	47.62	42.86	29.44	47.63	13.61	3.86	102.50
1958	2.95	1.79	58.97	43.20	51.09	58.97	30.66	49.36	16.73	3.63	99.88
1959	3.53	1.90	65.32	57.02	61.17	64.50	32.26	61.45	17.41	3.09	72.38
1960	3.39	2.00	65.02	55.34	60.18	61.49	33.74	59.43	17.53	3.37	79.60
1961	3.37	2.08	76.69	60.87	68.78	75.72	34.85	69.99	20.77	2.97	70.45
1962	3.87	2.20	75.22	54.80	65.01	66.00	36.37	65.54	16.94	3.36	81.63
1963	4.24	2.38	79.25	65.48	72.37	79.25	38.17	73.39	17.31	3.24	78.48
1964	4.83	2.60	91.29	79.74	85.52	89.62	40.23	86.19	17.84	3.02	70.75
1965	5.51	2.85	98.55	86.43	92.49	98.47	43.50	93.48	16.97	3.05	70.12
1966	5.89	2.98	100.60	77.89	89.25	85.24	45.59	91.08	15.46	3.27	65.19
1967	5.66	3.01	106.15	85.31	95.73	105.11	47.78	99.18	17.52	3.03	55.77
1968	6.15	3.18	118.03	95.05	106.54	113.02	50.21	107.49	17.48	2.96	48.62
1969	6.17	3.27	116.24	97.95	107.10	101.49	51.70	107.15	17.37	3.05	44.28
1970	5.36	3.24	102.87	75.58	89.23	100.90	52.65	91.29	17.03	3.55	45.79
1971	5.97	3.18	115.84	99.36	107.60	112.72	55.28	108.36	18.15	2.93	41.20
1972	6.80	3.22	132.95	112.19	122.57	131.87	58.46	122.47	18.01	2.63	36.76

* S&P 500/S&P AAA Ind.

It is often overlooked that industry profits are strongly influenced not only by internal factors but also by the economic environment in which that industry must operate. Moreover, as will be discussed below, portfolio diversification by industry is considered one of the critical determinants of successful investment performance.

INPUT FROM SECURITY ANALYSIS

As a part of the investment decision process, two contributions from the security analysis staff should be required: industry studies and company analyses.

Industry Studies

These studies should provide both the near- and long-term outlook for selected industry groups within the economic assumptions given. The analysis should include a review of the supply and demand forces affecting the industry, the price structure, the patterns of labor and nonlabor costs, the resultant estimates of profits, and then the stock market evaluation of these profits, both historical and projected. The focus should be to determine those factors that are critical to the movement of profits in the industry, which may include not only those internal to the industry itself but also external forces, such as economic, political, and international developments.[5] These studies should also highlight the most attractive segments within the industry as well as the companies most exposed to these segments.

Company Reports

The research staff should also provide reports on specific companies. It is not necessary for analysts to project stock prices, set price targets, make purchase and sale recommendations, or even display their formidable knowledge of the minutiae of a particular industry. The main purpose of these studies is to provide the portfolio manager with estimates of near- and long-term values of particular stocks upon which he can base an investment decision.

Within the economic and industry context made available, the analysis of a company should include the position of the company in its industry, near- and long-term sales and profits estimates, an analysis of rates of return on total capital and on common stock equity, and a

---

[5] For a discussion of the blending of economic and security analysis in the preparation of industry forecasts, see Gary M. Wenglowski, "Industry Profit Forecasting" and Roy E. Moor, "Aggregate Profits vs Company Profits," in *Business Economics*, no. 1 (January 1972): 61–69; and Robert B. Platt, "Forecasting Industry Profits," in *Business Economics*, no. 1 (January 1974): 47–50.

projection of near- and long-term values of the stock compared with historical valuations of that stock relative to some market index. Earnings and value estimates are most useful if stated in probabilistic ranges rather than single point estimates. The ranges will thus provide an essential measure of the risk involved in the selection of a particular security.

Other Information from Research

The security research function should supply two cross-checks on the security analyses prepared. The first should include a comparison of internal earnings and value estimates with comparable estimates from outside sources, such as major institutional brokerage firms, in order to ascertain differences in expectations. Profit opportunities are greatest in those areas when one's expectations are different from those generally held and these expectations prove correct. If estimates for a particular stock are widely held and are reasonably accurate, the stock probably is properly priced, and it is unlikely that any incremental profit can be obtained in purchasing it in the market.

The second type of information that can be provided from research is an aggregate of individual company earnings and values by industry and by a total of all of the companies followed to insure consistency of the earnings estimates with the economic and market projections that have been made. This will avoid the paradox of an economic projection indicating a slowing in economic activity and a reduction in corporate profits on the one hand and an aggregate of earnings estimates prepared by the research staff indicating a significant increase in profits on the other.

INPUTS FROM INVESTMENT POLICY

In most large investment institutions broad policy guidelines are ordinarily established by a group of experienced senior investment executives, with the portfolio managers given individual responsibility for specific account management within established policy. Some of the decisions described below may be performed by a portfolio manager, but generally speaking these types of decisions are best made by a group rather than by an individual.

Economic and Market Assumptions

The first policy decision required is the review and approval of the economic and securities markets assumptions prepared by the economics and analytical staff. Probabilities should be assigned to alternative expectations. A cross-check should be made with views held by other economists and major investors in order to evaluate whether the assumptions adopted represent a majority or minority viewpoint.

An important part of this policy review is an understanding of the structure of the stock market and current participants in it. Ordinarily, large institutional investors will have as an objective investment performance better than some stock market average, such as the Standard & Poor's 500 stock average. A disaggregation of this average into industries and broad industry groups and an analysis of the relative performance of each of these industries and groups can be very revealing in indicating what areas of the market have been performing well or badly and what areas can be expected to perform well under the given broad economic and market assumptions. Moreover, a change in the major participants in the market can have a significant impact on the performance of particular types of stocks. Purchases of individual investors and many mutual funds are frequently different in character than those of large banks and pension funds, and the relative availability of investable funds from these different types of investors can have an important impact on the price movement of particular stocks and industry groups.

Portfolio Objectives

A second policy decision required is a classification of portfolios by investment objectives. Many institutional investors manage only one or a few portfolios where the objectives are similar and clearly defined. These portfolios ordinarily have a total return (income plus appreciation) objective, with little consideration given to tax consequences of portfolio activity. By contrast, a bank trust department may have literally thousands of accounts with varying objectives, and the diverse interests of income beneficiaries and remaindermen can make a significant difference in investment policies to be followed. For this latter type of organization, a suggested classification of portfolios might be along the following lines:

1. Taxable portfolios.
   a. Income-oriented accounts with a long time horizon (three to five years).
   b. Accounts in which both income and appreciation are important. Such accounts may have a shorter time horizon (12 to 18 months).
   c. Accounts in which appreciation is the primary objective. These accounts may either have a long or a short time horizon, depending on the investor's objectives. However, better investment results can be obtained if the time horizon is as long as possible.

2. Tax-exempt accounts.
   a. These accounts stress total return regardless of whether it comes from income or appreciation. Ordinarily such accounts have a high total return objective with results measured over a short time period (12 to 18 months).

Most investment managers should prefer the luxury of a longer term horizon, say three to five years, because over this period the fundamentals of earnings, growth rates, and stock values will assert themselves over the shorter term technical and psychological aberrations of the stock market. However, many customers are more short term oriented in their expectations for investment results. A 12- to 18-month time horizon is considered the minimum time over which the fundamental factors affecting stock prices can be expected to operate; to adopt a shorter term horizon requires an investment approach quite different from that discussed in this chapter.[6]

Stocks to be Analyzed

The third type of policy decision to be made is the types of stocks to be analyzed for use in portfolios. For large institutions, considerations of marketability, quality, and risk suggest that ideally analysis should be limited to approximately 200 diversified stocks. Although nearly all of the stocks listed on the security exchanges and traded in the over-the-counter market are potential investments, in a large organization problems of the liquidity of large holdings and the managerial capability of supervision suggest that about 200 stocks are the reasonable maximum that any one organization can follow closely.

Some organizations also manage high-risk portfolios with above-average appreciation objectives. Several bank trust departments have developed commingled funds for this purpose. Managing these types of portfolios requires a special type of analytical coverage and a different approach to portfolio management. However, discussion of this type of investment operation is outside the bounds of this chapter.

Portfolio Mix

The fourth policy decision to be made is the portfolio mix guidelines for each general type of portfolio. Portfolio assets may be broadly classified into cash reserves, investments with a fixed contractual return, and investments with a variable return. Ordinarily, portfolios contain primarily short-term debt instruments, bonds, and stocks, although other types of investments may be included in appropriate categories. Based

[6] For an excellent discussion of this subject, see Frank E. Block, "Time Horizon," *Financial Analysts Journal* 28, no. 5 (September–October 1972): 30–31, 60–62.

on the estimated total return for each type of investment, the expected development of the business and market cycles, the appropriate time horizon for each type of portfolio, and the degree of risk the investor is willing to assume, the recommended diversification of the portfolio into these major categories can be determined.

The recommended diversification shown in Table 3 indicates how different types of accounts can have different bond-stock ratios and cash reserves under a given economic and market outlook.

For an income account, no specific allocation between fixed income and equity securities can be made because bonds are the most appropriate vehicle for the production of income, and the percent allocated to bonds must be a function of the income required and the funds available for investment. To the extent possible, equities can be used to provide the opportunity for increased income through rising dividends. For accounts with appreciation as the sole objective, a total commitment to equities seems desirable. For accounts with a shorter time horizon, some bond investment is recommended in view of the high yields available and the potential for appreciation as yields fall. Some cash reserve may be indicated from time to time, depending upon the economic outlook.

Industry Diversification

The fifth policy decision is the industry diversification of the equity portion of the portfolio.

If the objective of the equity portion of the portfolio is to outperform the "market" (ordinarily defined as the Standard & Poor's 500 stock average), a careful analysis of this index should be made. The Standard & Poor's index is a value weighted index, with the weight of each stock determined by the number of shares outstanding multiplied by the market price of the stock at any particular point in time. Consequently stocks with a large capitalization have an important influence

TABLE 3

Recommended Portfolio Diversification by Type of Account

	Taxable Portfolios			*Tax-Exempt Portfolios*
	Income A/C	*Income and Appreciation A/C*	*Appreciation A/C*	*Total Return A/C*
Maximum percent of portfolio in equity securities	*	75%	100%	75%
Reserve position as percent of portfolio	0%	10%	0%	15%

* In an income-oriented account, bonds should be used as the primary income source. To the extent possible, equities should be used to provide inflationary protection through the potential for increased dividends.

on the movement of the index. Some 25 stocks account for about half of the weight of the index, and therefore certain industry groups that include these stocks strongly influence the index's performance. This factor is of critical importance in the allocation of funds by industry in a portfolio, because significant weightings contrary to market weightings expose the portfolio to potential risk as well as reward.

Another matter to be considered is the number of industries included in the index. Standard & Poor's has classified the index into about 100 industry groups, which may be difficult to manage when portfolio diversification rather than market performance measurement is the objective. Experience has indicated that somewhere between 40 and 50 industry classifications are easier to handle. A suggested industry classification and the weighting of each industry in the total index are shown in Table 4.

The results of the next two steps in the analysis are also shown in Table 4. The first step is to determine the expected performance relative to the market of each of the industries for the two time horizons selected for the model accounts—12 to 18 months and three to five years. Although an economics and securities research staff can make important contributions to this analysis, the final judgment regarding the industry outlook is best made by senior investment officers.

Having determined both the expected performance and the weight of each industry, the next policy decision is the allocation of equity investments by industry. Experience has indicated that it is useful to approach this task first by dividing industries into three broad categories:

1. Basic: cyclically oriented, volatile, usually the ternd of earnings growth projected at or below average.
2. Moderate growth: relatively insensitive to business cycles, moderate earnings growth projected.
3. High growth: relatively insensitive to business cycles, above-average earnings growth projected.

The policy approach will then be to allocate equity funds in the portfolio depending on:

1. The outlook for the economy and stock market, including the present and expected state of the business and market cycle.
2. The outlook for each industry group and industry.
3. The weight of each industry group and industry in the Standard & Poor's index.

A market weighting of 0–2 percent suggests that an investment in that industry is optional; investments are required in industries where a minimum number is shown. It is not recommended that these weightings be significantly different from market weightings unless a high degree of confidence is held about the expected industry performance.

TABLE 4

Industry Relative Market Expectations and Recommended Diversification

	S & P Weights	Market Expectations 12-18 Months	Market Expectations 3 - 5 Years	Recommended Diversification Income A/C	Recommended Diversification Income and Appreciation A/C	Recommended Diversification Appreciation A/C	Recommended Diversification Total Return A/C
Basic Industries	26.25%			10%	20%	15%	20%
Aerospace	0.73	-	-	0	0	0	0
Automobiles	4.31	0	-	0-2	2-4	0-2	1-3
Automobile parts	0.69	0	-	0-2	0-2	0-2	0-2
Air transportation	0.45	+	-	0-2	1-3	0-2	1-3
Building materials	1.11	+	0	0-2	0-2	0-2	1-3
Forest products	1.25	0	0	0-2	0-2	0-2	0-2
Chemical & allied products	3.88	+	0	3-5	4-6	3-5	5-7
Containers-metal & glass	0.40	-	-	0	0	0	0
Electrical equipment	3.09	+	+	4-6	4-6	4-6	4-6
Conglomerates	0.62	-	0	0-2	0-2	0-2	0-2
Household appliances	0.62	0	+	0-2	0-2	1-3	0-2
Machinery-general	2.14	-	+	0-2	0-2	1-3	0-2
Metals & mining	3.24	-	-	0	0	0	0
Paper & paper containers	1.08	0	-	0-2	0-2	0-2	0-2
Publishing	0.24	-	0	0-2	0-2	0-2	0-2
Textiles & apparel	0.65	-	-	0	0	0	0
Tire & rubber goods	0.61	-	-	0	0	0	0
Transportation	1.16	-	-	0	0	0	0
Moderate growth industries	34.27%			35%	35%	35%	35%
Banks-major	0.00	+	+	2-4	2-4	2-4	2-4
Banks-regional	0.00	+	+	1-3	1-3	1-3	1-3
Finance companies	0.86	+	+	0-2	1-3	1-3	1-3
Food & allied products	2.69	0	+	2-4	2-4	2-4	1-3
Insurance-life	0.00	+	+	2-4	2-4	2-4	2-4
Insurance-l & c	0.00	0	0	0-2	0-2	0-2	0-2
Oils-international	9.05	0	-	2-4	3-5	2-4	3-5
Oils-domestic	4.86	+	+	5-7	6-8	6-8	6-8
Retail-department stores	4.98	+	+	4-6	3-5	4-6	3-5
Retail-grocery stores	0.38	0	+	0-2	0-2	0-2	0-2
Retail-miscellaneous	0.31	0	+	0-3	0-3	0-3	0-3
Utilities-electric	4.21	0	0	3-5	3-5	3-5	3-5
Utilities-natural gas	1.26	+	+	2-4	2-4	2-4	2-4
Telecommunications	5.68	+	+	5-7	5-7	5-7	5-7
High growth industries	39.48%			55%	45%	50%	45%
Soft drinks	1.98	0	+	1-3	1-3	1-3	1-3
Brewers & distillers	0.97	+	+	0-2	1-3	0-2	2-4
Pollution control	0.00	0	+	0-2	0-2	0-2	0-2
Cosmetic & toiletries	1.76	+	+	2-4	2-4	2-4	2-4
Drug & medical supplies	8.32	+	+	6-9	6-9	6-9	6-9
Electronics	1.46	+	+	0-2	2-4	2-4	3-5
Leisure time	0.98	+	+	0-2	1-3	1-3	1-3
Tobacco & allied prods.	1.16	+	+	1-3	1-3	1-3	1-3
Office equipment	11.60	+	+	12-14	13-16	13-16	13-16
Soaps	2.34	+	+	2-4	2-4	2-4	2-4
Photography	4.52	0	+	3-5	3-5	3-5	3-5
Machinery-oil well	1.60	+	+	0-2	2-4	2-4	2-4
Hotel-motel & restaurants	0.87	0	+	0-2	1-3	1-3	1-3
Miscellaneous	1.93	+	+	2-4	2-4	2-4	2-4

* + = Better than market performance expected.
0 = About market performance expected.
− = Worse than market performance expected.

If only moderate differences are suggested for particular industries, the cumulative effect for the entire portfolio can nevertheless be significant.

As an example, in Table 4 the industry allocations reflect a number of economic uncertainties and consequently a somewhat defensive stock posture. The exposure in basic industries is below a market weighting, and greater emphasis is placed on moderate and high growth industries. Although the reader may disagree with several of the indicated industry weightings, the important point is the discipline of the allocation. Regular review will also indicate a shift in emphasis from time to time. However, this discipline will focus the attention of a portfolio manager, his superiors, and the customer on the risks taken in a portfolio and require an awareness of the positions taken contrary to the market.

FUNCTION OF THE PORTFOLIO MANAGER

It is assumed that the policy decisions described above are provided by an investment committee, although some or all of them may be performed by the portfolio manager himself. Certain tasks, however, clearly are best performed by the individual portfolio manager.

Account Objectives

At the outset, the portfolio manager should determine, in consultation with the customer, the objectives of the account he manages with respect to income required and appreciation objectives. He should also attempt to determine the customer's attitude toward risk, usually in terms of aversion to capital loss and the portfolio stability relative to the market. Agreement should be reached on the time over which performance is to be measured. It is strongly recommended that these objectives be mutually agreed upon and committed to writing, in order to avoid subsequent misunderstanding.

Stock Selection

The second task, using the portfolio diversification and industry guidelines appropriate for the account, is to select individual securities to meet the account's objectives. The selection and timing of individual purchases and sales are best done by one individual rather than by a committee, which is rarely effective for this purpose. Moreover, if the responsibility for investment performance rests with the portfolio manager, he should be given opportunity and responsibility to exercise judgment in this area.

In this connection the use of so-called guidance or buy lists prepared by many institutions seem of questionable value. The underlying assumption in preparing such lists is that a security can be rated as a buy or sell and that such a decision is universally applicable to all portfolios under management. A moment's reflection will indicate that some securities might be quite appropriate for one particular type of account but totally unsuited for another. Consequently, it is suggested that this decision of the suitability of the security be left to the portfolio manager based on the information inputs given to him from the research staff and his own knowledge of the objectives of the account.

Executions

The portfolio manager, working with the trader of his organization, must then put his recommendations into action through efficient executions. Regardless of the work that leads to the selection and timing of purchases and sales, it is vital to have good executions in order to make these decisions the reality of a portfolio. Close cooperation between the portfolio manager and the trader is essential, and the trader's insight into what can realistically be done is frequently an important contributor to portfolio performance.[7]

Performance Evaluation

An important part of portfolio management is the evaluation of the performance of the portfolios managed. This measurement of performance is ordinarily done in two parts: first, an external report for customer purposes and, second, an internal report for control purposes.

It seems almost unnecessary to say that performance of a portfolio should be evaluated over a relatively long time span (three to five years) in order to determine whether the account's objectives have been met. The customer should be made constantly aware of the fact that short-term performance is not a true measure of a portfolio manager's effectiveness. Stress on short-term results requires trying to outguess the immediate movement and psychological aberrations of the stock market, a task that no portfolio manager has been able to do consistently over a long period of time.

However, for internal purposes more frequent reports (preferably monthly) are necessary, at least for major accounts, in order to see the results of investment decisions and to detect problems at an early stage. This monitoring may indicate areas where a reevaluation of the fundamental analysis and assumptions should be made.

---

[7] The importance of the trading function in institutional portfolio management and an excellent discussion of the techniques used is presented in Carter T. Geyer, "A Primer on Institutional Trading," *Financial Analysts Journal* 25, no. 2 (March–April 1969): 16–25.

The contents of such an internal evaluation report should include the following:

1. Both time-weighted and dollar-weighted rates of return. This information can be shown in absolute terms and may also be shown relative to market indexes. The time-weighted rate of return is, of course, the best measure of the portfolio manager's capability, because it makes adjustments for uneven flow of cash contributions and distributions. The dollar-weighted rate of return is important to the customer because it indicates to him what the returns of his portfolio have been. A comparison of the two may indicate a change in the method by which contributions and distributions are made.

2. An analysis of the absolute and relative performance of each of the industries and securities in the portfolio in order to evaluate the contribution (or lack thereof) of each to the total return achieved.

3. An analysis of purchases and sales in order to determine the effectiveness of portfolio changes.

4. A measure of portfolio turnover.

5. An analysis of portfolio volatility as well as projected volatility by means of weighted portfolio betas in order to see whether the portfolio risk exposure is consistent with the market assumptions used.

Reviews of these reports should be made not only by the portfolio manager but also by the investment policy committee. This procedure will not only insure detection of problems and monitor results of portfolio managers but will also reflect to the policy group the particular areas where policy decisions have been successful or unsuccessful.

TRADITIONAL VERSUS ACADEMIC PORTFOLIO THEORY

The approach described in this chapter contrasts to portfolio management approaches advocated in recent years in the academic literature. Theoretical debate on this subject is not in keeping with the purpose of this chapter. Such debate has been conducted elsewhere and may be read with profit by those interested.[8] However, departures from the approach taken herein from so-called modern portfolio theory should be mentioned.

Briefly summarized, current theory holds that the stock market is efficient and that stock prices reflect fully and virtually instantaneously what is knowable about the prospects of companies whose stocks are traded. Consequently, it is useless to attempt to select securities con-

[8] A well-written statement of the academic research in this area is contained in James H. Lorie and Mary T. Hamilton, *The Stock Market—Theories and Evidence* (Homewood, Ill.: Richard D. Irwin, Inc., 1973), especially Section 3. A critique of this approach is J. L. Valentine, *Financial Analysis and Capital Market Theory* (Charlottesville, Va.: Financial Analysts Research Foundation, 1974).

sidered undervalued because current price reflects value. Therefore, the portfolio manager should construct a well-diversified portfolio, and the securities in the portfolio should be selected from those having a greater or less than market risk depending on his view of the market and the customer's willingness to accept risk. In the strictest academic presentation, the percent of the portfolio committed to the market as a whole is varied as market and risk assumptions vary, borrowing or lending at the risk-free rate as necessary. Risk is measured by the historical volatility of a stock relative to the market, or its beta value. Successful portfolios are therefore achieved by diversifying away specific risk and exposing the portfolio only to the market risk.

The approach described in this chapter seeks to expose the portfolio to specific risks rather than diversifying these risks away. The specific risks are primarily those of the industry and secondarily those of the particular companies within the industry. The key to successful portfolio performance is correct judgments on industry diversification at variance with the industry diversification of a market index. Company selection within appropriate industries should provide a further incremental return.

What then of market risk as measured by the beta of individual securities and the weighted beta of a portfolio? After the steps described in this chapter have been taken, it may be useful to compute the weighted beta of the portfolio to see whether it conforms to the market expectations held and the degree of risk the customer is willing to assume. However, beta analysis has certain limitations. The betas of individual stocks are unstable, and frequently insufficient attention is paid to the amount of a stock's fluctuations that is peculiar to that stock itself rather than to the market. Betas become meaningful only when applied to a well-diversified portfolio; betas of large, inefficient (i.e., poorly diversified) portfolios are unstable. Computations of betas should also encompass a relatively long time period (8–10 years of monthly fluctuations) and be applied to future relationships over a relatively long time period (several years rather than several months or quarters). Nevertheless, beta analysis may provide some cross-check on expected portfolio volatility, but it is considered a supplementary tool rather than a primary technique in constructing portfolios.

CONCLUSION

Long-term portfolio performance using the methods described above will depend to a great extent upon how skillfully these methods are applied. However, this disciplined and structured approach should lead to consistently better than market performance over time and also should permit the prompt detection of significant errors so that corrective action can be taken. Such errors can be attributed to incorrect economic assumptions, inaccurate market forecasts, improper industry weightings, or poor stock selection, and periodic review of policy and performance should uncover the causes of the difficulties. Following the approach recommended will not lead to dramatic variances from market performance, but it should result in consistent results equal to or moderately better than the market. The cumulative results over a period of years should produce a performance that will be sufficiently favorable to result in reasonably satisfied customers or, perhaps put more appropriately, the satisfaction of reasonable customers.

43

Efficient Markets and Random Walk

CHARLES D. KUEHNER, Ph.D., C.F.A.
Director-Security Analysis and Investor Relations
American Telephone and Telegraph Co.
New York, New York

INTRODUCTION

In the past dozen years, both the academic world and the financial community have focused a great deal of attention on the *efficiency* of the securities markets. By efficiency they did not mean how efficiently stock certificates were moved from seller to buyer, or how promptly customers' bills were collected. Rather, they meant how efficient stock prices are in reflecting value.

> Efficiency in this context means the ability of the capital markets to function so that prices of securities react rapidly to new information. Such efficiency will produce prices that are "appropriate" in terms of current knowledge, and investors will be less likely to make unwise investments. A corollary is that investors will also be less likely to discover great bargains and thereby earn extraordinary high rates of return.[1]

The idea that market prices embody what is knowable and relevant for judging securities and adjust rapidly to such information "was considered bizarre in 1960 but by 1970 was very generally accepted by academicians and by many important financial institutions."[2] The

[1] James H. Lorie, "Public Policy for American Capitol Markets," (Washington, D.C.: U.S. Dept. of Treasury, 1974), p. 3.

[2] James H. Lorie and Richard Brealey, *Modern Developments in Investment Management* (New York: Praeger, 1972) p. 101.

practical significance of the efficient market hypothesis to investors is simply this: To do unusually well in selecting investments, one must have superior insight and abilities to see into the murky future better than other investors.

As the efficient market concept has developed, there has been a noticeable movement of the academicians into the fold, the so-called true believers. To be sure, there were a number of exceptions. For example, Downes and Dyckman stated that several studies exist "whose results are not consistent with the efficient markets hypothesis in, at most, its semi-strong form. Unfortunately, these studies have been largely ignored by summarizers of the efficient markets literature."[3] In the main, practicing security analysts and portfolio managers, the nonbelievers, have been seemingly unconvinced of the merits of the efficient markets hypothesis. On the other side of the coin. Fouse, an advocate of the efficient market concept and an investment officer of a very large bank, stated that "it is high time" for investment management to evaluate its theoretical basis, and that "in my opinion our industry has drifted to a point close to conceptual and logical bankruptcy."[4] Indeed, the growing interest in *index funds* reflects pessimism concerning the ability of conventional money managers to perform as well as the market. In this environment, it was quite natural that a vast outpouring would ensue in the academic journals, financial periodicals, and textbooks, as well as on convention platforms.

The objective of this chapter is to examine some of the writings relative to the efficient markets dialogue. By doing so it is hoped that the reader will be able to form an independent judgment with respect to the merits of the numerous issues involved.

REQUIREMENTS FOR AN EFFICIENT MARKET

Black, Fama, Francis, Lorie, and others have set forth various requirements for an efficient market. They include:

1. Effective Information Flow. This means that news is disseminated quickly and freely across the entire spectrum of actual and potential investors. Thus, they can react appropriately to new information as it develops. SEC requirements concerning full disclosure of material information are embodied in this concept.

2. Fully Rational Investors. This means investors must be "able to recognize efficient assets so that they will want to invest their money

---

[3] David Downes and Thomas R. Dyckman, "A Critical Look at the Efficient Market Empirical Research Literature as It Relates to Accounting Information," *The Accounting Review,* April 1973, pp. 300–17.

[4] William L. Fouse, "Practical Applications of Economic, Market, and Portfolio Theory," Stanford University Graduate School of Business, 1972 Investment Management Program, July 1972, p. 2.

where it is needed most—that is, in assets with relatively high return."[5]

3. Rapid Price Change to New Information. "Such changes are sometimes considered to constitute excessive volatility . . . when price changes are in response to new information, public policy should facilitate, rather than impede them."[6] "It is worth emphasizing again that price continuity or stability is not in itself a desirable characteristic of an efficient market. It is both undesirable and unprofitable for a specialist or market marker to resist changes in the price of a stock."[7]

4. Low Transaction Cost. Sales commissions and taxes on securities should be low enough so as not to impede either potential buyers or sellers from implementing their investment decisions.

5. Continuous Trading. The investor who desires to buy or sell can do so immediately. This focuses on the viability of the market and the close proximity of "bid" and "ask" prices. Consequently, the execution of a small trade should not ordinarily change prices significantly, if at all. "The bid and ask prices for large purchases and sales may be far apart, however, and execution of such orders may cause all 'bid' and 'ask' prices to shift substantially."[8]

Black holds that the market should be structured in a way that large investors are not disadvantaged in dealing with many small investors. Specifically, he opines that the trading cost to the large investor should be the same for a given size transaction, whether he is trading with one large investor or many small investors. Admittedly the cost of handling the latter would be higher. However, Black contends that the extra cost of handling many small orders should be borne by the small investors who are responsible for such costs.

In commenting on some of the preconditions for efficiency, Fama notes that these "are not descriptive of markets met in practice" but that "these conditions, while sufficient for market efficiency, are not necessary." For example, he states that as long as transactions take account of all available information, even large costs do not necessarily mean that when transactions do occur, prices will not fully reflect available information. Also, "even disagreement among investors as to the significance of given information does not imply market inefficiency unless some investors are consistently able to make better evaluation of such information than is implicit in market prices."[9]

---

[5] Jack Clark Francis, *Investment Analysis and Management* (New York: McGraw-Hill, 1972), p. 53. Used with permission of McGraw-Hill Book Company.

[6] Lorie, "Public Policy," p. 3.

[7] Fischer Black, "Toward a Fully Automated Stock Exchange," *Financial Analysts* Journal, July–August 1971, p. 35.

[8] Ibid., p. 31.

[9] Eugene F. Fama, "Efficient Capital Markets: A Review of Theory and Empirical Work," *Journal of Finance*, May 1970, pp. 383–417.

SITUATION PRIOR TO EMERGENCE OF THE EFFICIENT MARKET CONCEPT

It would be helpful, before proceeding with a review of empirical research on the question of the efficient markets hypothesis to delineate it from the two basically different schools of stock price evaluation into which random walk emerged in the early 1960s.

Technical Analysis

Technical analysis is *internally* oriented. In this, technicians endeavor to predict future price levels of stocks by examining one or many series of past data *from the market itself.*

> The basic assumption of all the chartist or technical theories is that history tends to repeat itself, i.e., past patterns of price behavior in individual securities will tend to recur in the future. Thus the way to predict stock prices (and, of course, increase one's potential gains) is to develop a familiarity with past patterns of price behavior in order to recognize situations of likely recurrence.
>
> The techniques of the chartist have always been surrounded by a certain degree of mysticism, however, and as a result most market professionals have found them suspect. Thus it is probably safe to say that the pure chartist is relatively rare among stock market analysts.[10]

Pinches states that technical analysts "believe that the value of a stock depends primarily on supply and demand and may have very little relationship to any intrinsic value."[11] He summarizes a general statement of technical analysis, including:

1. Market prices are determined by supply and demand.
2. At any moment, supply and demand reflect hundreds of rational and irrational considerations: facts, opinions, moods, and guesses about the future.
3. Disregarding minor fluctuations, market prices move in trends which persist over an appreciable length of time.
4. Changes in trend represent a shift in balance between supply and demand. However caused, these shifts are detectable "sooner or later in the action of the market itself."

As we will see below, chartists assume that successive price changes in individual securities are *dependent.* This means that future stock prices are importantly dependent upon patterns of past price changes

[10] Eugene F. Fama, "Random Walks in Stock Market Prices," *Financial Analysts Journal,* September–October 1965, pp. 55–59.

[11] George E. Pinches, "The Random Walk Hypothesis and Technical Analysis," *Financial Analysts Journal,* March–April 1970, pp. 104–10.

reflecting the shift between supply and demand. Among the many techniques used by technical analysts are:

1. Charting—past prices, e.g., Dow theory.
2. Determining—major trends (the tides), intermediate corrections (the waves), and minor fluctuations (ripples).
3. Share volume trends—rising–falling, and so on.
4. Combined volume and price charts.
5. Point and figure charts—channels, wedges, head and shoulders, triple tops, triple bottoms, and so on.
6. Support areas versus resistance levels.
7. Breadth of market—advance–decline lines.
8. Odd lots—purchases versus sales.
9. Odd-lot volume related to round-lot volume.
10. Odd-lot short sales.

Buckley and Loll concluded that:

> On the basis of these technical theories, many have endeavored to forecast the future course of the stock market. Some have been moderately successful, but the woods are full of people who have lost money trying to forecast the future of the stock market. It is believed that the averages are useful and interesting in showing the course of the market and for measuring changes but not for forecasting the future.[12]

Cohen, Zinbarg, and Zeikel stated that

> we can understand the characterization of technical analysis as "crystal ball gazing." But we consider this characterization to be rather unfortunate, for it casts aside the good with the bad. The more scholarly and sophisticated technical analyst uses his tools with a proper sense of proportion . . . if a stock looks attractive to him on technical grounds he probes into its fundamentals . . . he is certainly not unmindful of earnings growth, of values, or of the impact of business cycles.[13]

The broad consensus of several different technical indicators may be helpful in understanding market psychology for whatever value that nebulous term might have. Roberts states:

> Perhaps no one in the financial world completely ignores technical analysis—indeed, its terminology is ingrained in market reporting—and some rely intensively on it. Technical analysis includes many approaches, most requiring a good deal of subjective judgment in applica-

---

[12] Julien G. Buckley and Leo M. Loll, Jr., *The Over-the-Counter Securities Market* (Englewood Cliffs, N.J.: Prentice-Hall, 1967), p. 130.

[13] Jerome B. Cohen, Edward D. Zinbarg, and Arthur Zeikel, *Investment Analysis and Portfolio Management* (Homewood, Ill., Richard D. Irwin, Inc., 1973), p. 554.

tions. In part these approaches are purely empirical; in part they are based on analogy with physical processes, such as tides and waves.[14]

Fundamental Analysis

Fundamental analysis is *externally* oriented. "The fundamentalist never measures the attractiveness of a stock by the fickle standards of the market place, but rather determines the price at which he is willing to invest and then turns to the market place to see if the stock is selling at the required price."[15] The fundamental analyst focuses on the intrinsic value of a stock.

> The assumption of the fundamental analysis approach is that any point in time an individual security has an intrinsic value (or in the terms of the economist, an equilibrium price) which depends on the earnings potential of the security. The earning potential of the security depends in turn on such fundamental factors as quality of management, outlook for the industry and the economy, etc.
>
> Through a careful study of these fundamental factors the analyst should, in principle, be able to determine whether the actual price of a security is above or below its intrinsic value. If actual prices tend to move toward intrinsic values, then attempting to determine the intrinsic value of a security is equivalent to making a prediction of its future price; and this is the essence of the predictive procedure implicit in fundamental analysis.[16]

Fundamental analysis embraces many facets of a company in developing an evaluation of intrinsic value. Among the factors considered are:

1. Growth: revenues, expenses, net income, earnings per share, assets.
2. Management: record, innovation, motivation, plans long-range objectives, and philosophy.
3. Earnings rates: on total capital, on equity capital, objectives.
4. Capital structure: policy, credit ratings, debt ratio objectives, fixed charge coverage.
5. Dividends: payment policy, past growth, percent pay out.
6. Accounting policies: reserves, inventory policies, depreciation policies, tax normalization versus flow through.
7. Ratios: acid test ratio, quick ratio, current assets to current liabilities.
8. Marketing: market share, short- and long-term strategy, competition.

---

[14] Harry V. Roberts, "Stock Market Patterns and Financial Analysis: Methodological Suggestion," *Journal of Finance,* March 1959, pp. 1–10.

[15] Frank E. Block, "The Place of Book Value in Stock Evaluation," *Financial Analysts Journal,* March–April 1964, p. 29.

[16] Fama, "Random Walks," pp. 56–57.

9. Labor: labor relations policies and environment, labor cost trends, labor intensity.
10. Economic environment: sensitivity to business cycles, long-term trends of industry, raw materials situation.
11. Technology: research and development, plant obsolescence, patent protection.
12. Social and political environment: government regulatory environment, tax situation, geographic decentralization.
13. Earnings per share: growth rates, stability, outlook.
14. Market price per share: growth, volatility, P/E multiple.
15. Per share: cash flow, book value, intrinsic value.

THREE FORMS OF THE EFFICIENT MARKET–RANDOM WALK HYPOTHESIS

We have already touched upon the efficient market concept and its preconditions, i.e., the requirements for its efficiency. In its present stage of development (1974), the efficient market hypothesis takes three different forms: weak, semistrong, and strong. Each form stems from a different level of information or knowledge concerning a stock:

The Weak Form

This is the oldest statement of the hypothesis. It holds that present stock market prices reflect all known information with respect to past stock prices, trends, and volumes. Thus, it is asserted, such past data cannot be used to predict future stock prices.

Reflecting the historical development of this form, which focused on various statistical tests for random movement of successive stock prices, it has also been characterized as the *random walk hypothesis.* The weak form implies that knowledge of the past patterns of stock prices does not aid investors to attain improved performance. Random walk theorists view stock prices as moving randomly about a trend line which is based on anticipated earnings-power.[17] Hence they contend that (1) analyzing past data does not permit the technician to forecast the movement of prices about the trend line and (2) new information affecting stock prices enters the market in random fashion, i.e., tomorrow's news cannot be predicted nor can future stock price movements be attributable to that news.

In its present context, the weak form of the efficient market hypothesis is a direct challenge to the chartist or technician. It was the earliest focus of interest and has received by far the greatest attention in the literature.

---

[17] Sidney Robbins, *The Securities Markets* (New York: Free Press, 1966), pp. 44–47.

The Semistrong Form

This form holds that current market prices *instantaneously* reflect all publicly known information. Consequently, it holds that such data cannot be analyzed successfully to achieve superior investment results.

This form of the efficient market hypothesis reflects a substantially greater level of knowledge and market efficiency than the weak form. The second stage, or level, of information content includes all knowledge which is available from such publications as annual reports, quarterly reports, press releases, and news flashes on "the broad tape," i.e., the Dow-Jones news wire service. The semistrong form holds that, since such public information is already embedded, i.e., fully discounted, in current stock prices, analyzing such data cannot produce superior investment performance.

The shift from the weak, i.e., random walk, form to the semistrong form of the efficient market hypothesis represented a quantum jump.

> This stronger assertion has proved to be especially unacceptable and unpalatable to the financial community, since it suggests the fruitlessness of efforts to earn superior rates of return by the analysis of all public information. Although some members of the financial community were willing to accept the implications of the weaker assertion about the randomness of price changes and thereby to give up technical analysis, almost no members of the community were too willing to accept the implications of the stronger form and thereby to give up fundamental analysis.[18]

It is crystal clear that the semistrong form represents a direct challenge to traditional financial analysis based on the evaluation of publicly available data.

The Strong Form

This form holds that present market prices reflect all information that is *knowable* about a company, including all relevant information that might be developed by exhaustive study, including interviews with corporate managements, by numerous fully competent institutional security analysts. Hence, this form holds that consistently superior investment performance is not possible.

The strong form ratcheted the efficient market hypothesis up to a still higher level of information and knowledge. In large measure, the strong form reflects the intense competition that exists among the nation's leading financial institutions. These institutions have staffs of security analysts who are top graduates of the nation's leading business schools, are highly motivated, and are held to high standards of professional

---

[18] James H. Lorie and Mary T. Hamilton, *The Stock Market—Theories and Evidence* (Homewood, Ill.: Richard D. Irwin, Inc., 1973), p. 81.

performance. Security analysts who can outperform their peers in this environment move to higher positions in the investment analysis and management hierarchy. Those who fail to meet these lofty standards tend to move to other pursuits.

> . . . even if half of the professional money managers outperform the market as a whole, the market conforms to the strong form of efficiency as long as they do not generate superior results consistently. That is, in a strong form market, up to half of the time money managers could outperform the market as a whole, if only during the remainder of the time their performance was inferior to the general market.[19]

The strong form of the random walk hypothesis constitutes a direct challenge to the most knowledgeable segment of the investment community: the institutional investor.

This concludes our capsule review of the efficient market—random walk hypothesis. Its significance to the practicing security analysts is pointed up in the words of Lorie and Brealey, two founding fathers of the efficient market hypothesis, who summarize their views in these words:

> It is extremely unlikely, in principle, that the efficient market hypothesis is strictly true, particularly in its strongest form. For example, as long as information is not wholly free, one might expect investors to require some offsetting gain before they are willing to purchase it. Nor does the empirical evidence justify unqualified acceptance of the efficient-market hypothesis even in its weakest form. The important question, therefore, is not whether the theory is universally true, but whether it is sufficiently correct to provide useful insights into market behavior. There is now overwhelming evidence to suggest that the random walk hypothesis is such a close approximation to reality that technical analysis cannot provide any guidance to the investment manager. When one turns to the stronger forms of the hypothesis, the evidence becomes less voluminous and the correspondence between theory and reality less exact. Nevertheless, the overriding impression is that of a highly competitive and efficient marketplace in which the opportunities for superior performance are rare.[20]

THE WEAK FORM OF THE EFFICIENT MARKET-RANDOM WALK HYPOTHESIS: SURVEY OF EVIDENCE

Overview

The earliest documentation in this century of the efficient market–random walk model was recorded in 1900 by Bachelier in his Ph.D.

[19] See Dan Dorfman, "Why Can't Research Directors Hold Their Jobs?" *Institutional Investor,* October 1973, pp. 48–50 ff.

[20] James H. Lorie and Richard Brealey, *Modern Developments in Investment Management* (New York: Praeger, 1972) p. 102.

dissertation, written under the guidance of the world-famous French mathematician, H. Poincaré.[21] Bachelier's work dealt primarily with commodity prices and government bonds, but the principles are readily adaptable to other securities such as stocks. Bachelier concluded that past price patterns provided no basis for predicting future price changes.

Except for the endeavors of Working of Stanford University on commodity prices and Cowles and Jones on stock prices, the efficient market–random walk concept was largely neglected until the mid-1950s.[22]

The first work reviewed in this chapter is that of Kendall, written in 1953. Kendall focused on serial correlation in an effort to determine whether weekly changes in stock market prices could be predicted from past data. His findings were essentially negative. Subsequently, Weintraub tested serial correlation over shorter periods, i.e., daily price changes. Weintraub concluded that, under certain assumptions used in his study, serial correlation did indeed exist. Contrariwise, Osborne, a distinguished astronomer at the United States Naval Research Laboratory in Washington, D.C., applied computer techniques to daily stock price changes and determined that stock prices changes comport to "Brownian movement of small particles suspended in liquid."

Granger and Morgenstern attacked the serial correlation question with a sophisticated new tool, spectral analysis. They likewise found that the simple random walk model obtained for most time bands. However, there were some indications of nonrandom behavior in time spans of 24 months or longer.

Fama, one of the most diligent students of the efficient market–random walk hypothesis, also tested serial correlation of stock price changes over a period ranging from 1 to 10 days. His extensive work confirmed the negative findings of the earlier researchers. Roberts pioneered an interesting approach: constructing hypothetical stock price charts from random numbers. He found that the Dow-Jones index of 30 industrial stocks could be quite closely replicated from random numbers.

Cheng and Deets also tested the Dow-Jones 30 industrials for successive price changes, using a portfolio "rebalancing" strategy. However, they concluded that the random walk theory is not supported by the evidence, since their rebalanced portfolios exceeded random portfolios by a substantial margin.

Additional tests of the efficient market–random walk hypothesis were conducted by Fama using daily runs, i.e., successive price changes in a similar direction. Using the 30 individual stocks in the Dow Jones Industrial Index, he found overwhelming evidence of the random distri-

---

[21] Louis Bachelier, "Theory of Speculation," in Paul Cootner, *The Random Character of Stock Market Prices* (Cambridge: MIT Press, 1964) pp. 17–78.

[22] Holbrook Working, "A Random—Difference Series for Use in the Analysis of Time Series," *Journal of the American Statistical Association,* March 1934, pp. 11–24; and Alfred Cowles and Herbert F. Jones, "Some a Posteriori Probabilities in Stock Market Action," *Econometrica,* July 1937, pp. 280–94.

bution of price changes. Shiskin also tested runs in the Standard & Poor's 500 stock price index, using monthly data. He concluded that the evidence does not support the random walk theory.

Alexander pioneered trading rules or *filters* for daily price changes and determined that prices were affected by something other than a random walk. Cootner also tested filters and found that stock prices behaved as a random walk with reflecting barriers.

Levy tested the random walk theory, using a *relative strength* strategy for 200 New York Stock Exchange (NYSE) stocks. He concluded that "the theory of random walks has been refuted." Jensen and Bennington used the same approach for all NYSE stocks for a longer period and found to the contrary. Jen evaluated both of these relative strength studies. While essentially sympathetic to the random walk in the longer run, Jen declared that relative strength did capture the essence of market imperfections in shorter time spans.

Kruizenga and Boness made interesting digressions into the options arena as a proxy for common stock price studies. The former found price changes for 90-day options reasonably close to random, but this was not the case for six-month options for several individual companies. The latter judged the evidence to support the random walk theory.

Analysis of Studies

Kendall—Serial Correlation: The Next Move

Kendall tested the independence of weekly closing market prices of 22 indices of British industry groups, e.g., oil, iron, and steel, for the 1928–38 period. He determined that it was preferable not to attempt to eliminate long-term trends and examine only the residuals. He found that, broadly speaking, random changes from one week to the next "are so large as to swamp any systematic effect which may be present," and that "such serial correlation as is present in these series is so weak as to dispose at once of any possibility of being able to use them for prediction."[23] He noted, however, that

> it may be, of course, that a series of *individual* share prices would behave differently; the point remains open for inquiry. But the aggregates are very slightly correlated and some of them virtually wandering. Investors can, perhaps, make money on the Stock Exchange, but not apparently by watching price movements and coming in on what looks like a good thing. But it is unlikely that anything I say or demonstrate will destroy the illusion that the outside investor can make money by playing the markets, so let us leave him to his own devices.

Kendall ranked the various series according to the magnitude of first serial correlation—as a measure of internal correlation of each series.

[23] Maurice G. Kendall, "The Analysis of Economic Time-Series—Part 1: Prices," *Journal of the Royal Statistical Society* 96, (1953): 11–25.

He noted that the "aggregate series," e.g., all classes of stock, total distribution, total manufacturing, had greater internal correlation and significantly greater serial correlation than the constituent series, i.e., the several piece-parts. In part, Kendall found that this could be attributed to lag correlations between different series in the aggregate series: "Whatever the reason, the existence of these serial correlations in averaged series is rather disturbing. The so-called "cycles" appearing in such series may not be due to endogenous elements or structured features at all, but to the correlations between disturbances acting on the constituent parts of the aggregative series."

Weintraub—Serial Correlation: The Next Move

Weintraub, employing serial correlation, used Kendall's concept of "the next move," in part, but applied it to a variable time period within the next day. Weintraub noted that professional traders earned such substantial incomes from speculating on short-term price movements that seats for floor traders were valued at several thousand dollars. This he found difficult to reconcile with the random walk hypothesis. "These men, in effect, earn their incomes by betting *against* the applicability of the random walk hypothesis to price moves of less than 5 percent."[24]

The specific techniques used by Weintraub may be explained by the following example. If a stock price moved up from the closing price on Monday to the closing price on Tuesday, the next move (on Wednesday) was assumed to be up (+). Conversely, if the Monday to Tuesday closing price showed a downtrend, the next move was assumed to be down (−). However, in an effort to match the real world speculator's opportunities and avoid the mechanical approach of using daily closing prices, Wednesday's prices were either the *highest* during the day if the Monday-Tuesday trend was up (+) or the *lowest* during the day on Wednesday if the Monday-Tuesday prices were down (−).

Thus, speculators betting on the existence of trends would buy at Tuesday's close when the Monday-Tuesday was up (+) and sell during the day on Wednesday at a higher price, hopefully the day's high. Alternatively, if they believe in a zig-zag pattern, they would sell short on Tuesday and cover during the day on Wednesday, hopefully at the day's low price.

Table 1 depicts data for one of the time periods cited by Weintraub. Weintraub summarized his results as follows:

1. Using Kendall's definition of the next move, serial correlation of 0.31 was found.
2. Using the definition of the next move that would be employed by

[24] Robert E. Weintraub, "On Speculative Prices and Random Walks: A Denial," *Journal of Finance*, March 1963, pp. 59–66.

speculators betting on a zig-zag pattern, i.e., against the trend, serial correlation was −0.61.

3. Using the definition of the next move that professional traders would use betting on a monotonic trend, serial correlation was 0.69.

Weintraub concluded:

> One of the implications of my results is that speculators have opportunity to make capital gains. A corollary implication is that it is an error to infer, as many have done, from the lack of lagged serial correlation between first differences of closing prices that speculations have little or no opportunity to win. Instead, it would appear that this lack of serial correlation between first differences of closing prices simply means that speculators who are supposed to smooth out price movements over time are doing their job well.[25]

Osborne—Brownian Motion

Osborne investigated whether stock price changes comport to Brownian movement. This is a law of the physical sciences governing movements of small particles suspended in liquids. He analyzed changes in daily closing prices of all NYSE stocks and found them nearly normally distributed. Osborne concluded that "it may be a consequence of many independent random variables contributing to the changes in values."[26] This he attributed to the tradeoff of seller and buyer, with both making logical decisions in the market. He also tested price changes of stocks over longer periods: weekly, monthly, and so on, up to 12 years. He concluded that price changes were randomly distributed.

He then examined Cowles' stock price data, some of it going as far back as 1831. Osborne postulated a certain linkage in price changes for stocks akin to earlier studies of changes in commodities:

> To put it another way, the NYSE is a market for money in exactly the same sense that it is for the securities of any given corporation. Certainly for the era covered in the Cowles' data, a dollar represented a share in the assets of Fort Knox in exactly the same sense that a stock certificate of General Motors represented a share in the assets of that corporation. Under conditions of trading at statistical equilibrium, why should these changes in value not diffuse in the same way.[27]

Granger and Morgenstern—Spectral Analysis

Granger and Morgenstern used spectral aanlysis, a highly sophisticated statistical technique, to test the random walk hypothesis. They

---

[25] Ibid., p. 66.

[26] M. F. M. Osborne, "Brownian Motion in the Stock Market," *Operations Research*, March–April 1959, pp. 145–73.

[27] Ibid., p. 165.

TABLE 1

"The Next Move" Calculated from Dow Jones Industrials (30 Common Stocks) Daily Prices for June 1–July 31, 1962

				"The Next Move"		
					For Speculators' Betting	
Date	*High*	*Low*	*Close*	*Under Kendall's Definition*	*On Trend*	*Against Trend*
June						
1	616.54	603.58	611.07	− 2.31*	—	—
4	608.82	591.37	593.68	−17.37	−19.68	2.23
5	603.37	584.12	594.96	1.28	− 9.56	9.69
6	611.82	595.50	603.91	8.95	16.86	0.54
7	608.14	599.27	602.20	1.71	4.23	− 4.64
8	607.30	598.64	601.61	−00.59	− 3.56	5.10
11	603.20	592.66	595.17	− 6.44	− 8.95	1.59
12	593.83	580.11	580.94	−14.23	−15.06	− 1.34
13	586.42	572.20	574.04	− 6.90	− 8.74	5.48
14	579.14	560.28	563.00	−11.04	−13.76	5.10
15	579.90	556.09	578.18	15.18	− 6.91	16.90
18	583.08	567.05	574.21	− 3.97	4.90	−11.13
19	575.21	566.59	571.61	− 2.60	− 7.62	1.00
20	574.59	561.28	563.08	− 8.53	−10.33	2.98
21	561.87	549.15	550.49	−12.59	−13.93	− 1.21
22	551.99	537.56	539.19	−11.30	−12.93	1.50
25	541.24	524.55	536.77	− 2.42	−14.64	2.05
26	548.61	533.46	535.76	− 1.01	− 3.31	11.84
27	539.28	528.73	536.98	1.22	− 7.03	3.52
28	559.32	541.49	557.35	20.37	22.34	4.51
29	569.06	555.22	561.28	3.93	11.71	− 2.13
July						
2	576.63	557.31	573.75	12.47	15.35	− 3.97
3	582.99	570.53	579.48	5.73	9.24	− 3.22
5	586.30	577.39	583.87	4.39	6.82	− 2.09
6	582.58	571.28	576.17	− 7.70	− 1.29	−12.59
9	582.28	569.65	580.82	4.65	− 6.52	6.11
10	599.02	583.50	586.01	5.19	18.20	2.68
11	590.94	580.36	589.06	3.05	4.93	− 5.65
12	596.59	586.68	590.27	1.21	7.53	− 2.38
13	592.99	583.87	590.19	− 0.08	2.72	− 6.40
16	591.23	582.41	588.10	− 2.09	− 7.78	1.04
17	588.77	576.59	577.85	−10.25	−11.51	0.66
18	577.39	568.02	571.24	− 6.61	− 9.83	− 0.46
19	578.68	568.98	573.16	1.92	− 2.26	7.44
20	579.86	570.78	577.18	4.02	6.70	− 2.38
23	582.24	574.50	577.47	0.29	5.06	− 2.68
24	579.31	572.02	574.12	− 3.35	1.84	− 5.45
25	576.55	568.10	574.67	0.55	− 6.02	2.43
26	582.87	574.08	579.61	4.94	8.20	− 0.59
27	586.80	577.14	585.00	5.39	7.19	− 2.47
30	593.03	583.87	591.44	6.44*	8.03	− 1.13
31	601.15	591.78	597.93	6.49*	9.71	0.34

* The first number in this column, −2.31, is not a number in the series termed "The Next Move under Kendall's Definition". But this number is the first number in the previous trend series. Conversely, the last number in this column, 6.49, is not a number in the previous trend series but is the last number in the series termed "The Next Move under Kendall's Definition." The last number in the previous trend series is the next to last number in this column, 6.44.

Source: After Weintraub, "On Speculative Prices," p. 65, Table 2.

examined some 700 weeks of SEC price series for various industries, e.g., motor vehicles, utilities, air transport, for years 1939–61; American Tobacco, General Foods, American Can, Woolworth, Chrysler, and U.S. Steel for the period 1946–60; the S & P's 500 Stock Index 1915–61 and the Dow Jones industrials for 1915–61.

Their work indicated that, after eliminating trend, the simple random walk model is upheld "for the large majority of the frequency bands." However, "it thus seems that the model, although extremely successful in explaining most of the spectral shape, does not adequately explain the strong long run (24 months or more) components of the series. Nothing definite can be said about the business cycle component of these series as they cover too short a time span."[28]

In pursuing the business cycle question further, S & P's index was analyzed for the 1875–1952 period and the Dow Jones index for 1915–58. A small business cycle component was seen at 40 months, but was not found to be statistically significant. They also noted that "The whole problem of studying business cycle indicators (impact on stock prices) is bedeviled with the vagueness of the concept of the business cycle movement of the economy and the huge inaccuracies known to exist in many series used to indicate cycles."[29]

It was also pointed out that,

> To the extent that stock prices perform random walks, the short term investor (ignoring transaction costs) engaged in a fair gamble, which is slightly better than playing roulette, since that game is biased in favor of the bank. For the long term investor, i.e., one who invests at the very minimum for a year, the problem is to identify the phases of the different long run components of the overall movement of the market. The evidence of "cycles" obtained in our studies is so weak that "cyclical investment" is at best only marginally worthwhile. Even this small margin will rapidly disappear as it is being made use of.[30]

Fama—Serial Correlation: 1 to 10 Days Lag

Fama tested the independence of successive price changes by measuring serial correlation for the 30 individual stocks in the Dow-Jones Industrial Index in the five years ending 1962.[31] Thus, if a company's data showed a high degree of correlation, it would suggest systematic dependence and might be used to predict future prices. Contrariwise, a low correlation coefficient would indicate that prior price changes

---

[28] Clive W. J. Granger and Oskar Morgenstern, "Spectral Analysis of New York Stock Market Prices," *KyKlos*, 1963, pp. 1–27.

[29] Ibid., p. 16.

[30] Ibid., p. 30.

[31] Eugene F. Fama, "The Behavior of Stock Market Prices," *Journal of Business*. January 1965, pp. 34–105.

cannot successfully be used to predict future prices. Table 2 summarizes coefficients of correlation between sucessive price changes for each of the 30 companies.

Column 1 of Table 2 shows that the correlation coefficients are generally close to zero and in eight cases out of 30 it is negative. Since the successive one-day price changes were unrelated, Fama also tested for possible lagged correlation. Thus, the correlation for each day's price change with that following by two days is shown in Column 2; the three-day lag, in Column 3; up to a lag of 10 days—shown in Column 10. Statistically there is virtually no relationship in these daily price changes. The average serial correlation coefficient shown in the bottom of the table ranges from −.04 to .03.

Fama tested correlation of price changes for adjacent periods of 1,

TABLE 2

Correlation Coefficients: Daily Price Changes versus Lagged Price Changes for Each Dow Jones Industrial Company

	Lag in Days									
Stock	*1*	*2*	*3*	*4*	*5*	*6*	*7*	*8*	*9*	*10*
Allied Chemical	.02	−.04	.01	−.00	.03	.00	−.02	−.03	−.02	−.01
Alcoa	.12	.04	−.01	.02	−.02	.01	.02	.01	−.00	−.03
American Can	−.09	−.02	.03	−.07	−.02	−.01	.02	.03	−.05	−.04
AT&T	−.04	−.10	.00	.03	.01	−.01	.00	.03	−.01	.01
American Tobacco	.11	−.11	−.06	−.07	.01	−.01	.01	.05	.04	.04
Anaconda	.07	−.06	−.05	−.00	.00	−.04	.01	.02	−.01	−.06
Bethlehem Steel	.01	−.07	.01	.02	−.05	−.10	−.01	.00	−.00	−.02
Chrysler	.01	−.07	−.02	−.01	−.02	.01	.04	.06	−.04	.02
DuPont	.01	−.03	.06	.03	−.00	−.05	.02	.01	−.03	.00
Eastman Kodak	.03	.01	−.03	.01	−.02	.01	.01	.01	.01	.00
General Electric	.01	−.04	−.02	.03	−.00	.00	−.01	.01	−.00	.01
General Foods	.06	−.00	.05	.00	−.02	−.05	−.01	−.01	−.02	−.02
General Motors	−.00	−.06	−.04	−.01	−.04	.−01	.02	.01	−.02	.01
Goodyear	−.12	.02	−.04	.04	−.00	−.00	.04	.01	−.02	.01
Int'l. Harvester	−.02	−.03	−.03	.04	−.05	−.02	−.00	.00	−.05	−.02
Int'l. Nickel	.10	−.03	−.02	.02	.03	.06	−.04	−.01	−.02	.03
Int'l. Paper	.05	−.01	−.06	.05	.05	−.00	−.03	−.02	−.00	−.02
Johns Manville	.01	−.04	−.03	−.02	−.03	−.08	.04	.02	−.04	.03
Owens Illinois	−.02	−.08	−.05	.07	.09	−.04	.01	−.04	.07	−.04
Procter & Gamble	.10	−.01	−.01	.01	−.02	.02	.01	−.01	−.02	−.02
Sears	.10	.03	.03	.03	.01	−.05	−.01	−.01	−.01	−.01
Standard Oil (Cal.)	.03	−.03	−.05	−.03	−.05	−.03	−.01	.07	−.05	−.04
Standard Oil (N.J.)	.01	−.12	.02	.01	−.05	−.02	−.02	−.03	−.07	.08
Swift & Co.	−.00	−.02	−.01	.01	.06	.01	−.04	.01	.01	.00
Texaco	.09	−.05	−.02	−.02	−.02	−.01	.03	.03	−.01	.01
Union Carbide	.11	−.01	.04	.05	−.04	−.03	.00	−.01	−.05	−.04
United Aircraft	.01	−.03	−.02	−.05	−.07	−.05	.05	.04	.02	−.02
U.S. Steel	.04	−.07	.01	.01	.01	−.02	.04	.04	−.02	−.04
Westinghouse	−.03	−.02	−.04	−.00	.00	−.05	−.02	.01	−.01	.01
Woolworth	.03	−.02	.02	.01	.01	−.04	−.01	.00	−.09	−.01
Average	.03	−.04	−.01	.01	−.01	−.02	.00	.01	−.02	−.01

Source: After Fama, "Behavior of Stock Market Prices."

TABLE 3

Correlation Coefficients for 1-, 4-, 9- and 16-Day Interval Price Changes for Each Dow Jones Industrial Company

	Interval in Days			
Stock	*1*	*4*	*9*	*16*
Allied Chemical	.02	.03	−.09	−.12
Alcoa	.12	.10	−.11	−.04
American Can	−.09	−.12	−.06	.03
AT&T	−.04	−.01	−.01	−.00
American Tobacco	.11	−.18	.03	.01
Anaconda	.07	−.07	−.13	.20
Bethlehem Steel	.01	−.12	−.15	.11
Chrysler	.01	.06	−.03	.04
DuPont	.01	.07	−.04	−.06
Eastman Kodak	.03	−.01	−.05	−.02
General Electric	.01	.02	−.00	.00
General Foods	.06	−.01	−.14	−.10
General Motors	−.00	−.13	.01	−.03
Goodyear	−.12	.00	−.04	.03
Int'l. Harvester	−.02	−.07	−.24	.12
Int'l. Nickel	.10	.04	.12	.04
Int'l. Paper	.05	.06	−.00	−.01
Johns Manville	.01	−.07	−.00	.00
Owens Illinois	−.02	−.01	.00	−.02
Procter & Gamble	.10	−.01	.10	.08
Sears	.10	−.07	−.11	.04
Standard Oil (Cal.)	.03	−.14	−.05	.04
Standard Oil (N.J.)	.01	−.11	−.08	−.12
Swift & Co.	−.00	−.07	.12	−.20
Texaco	.09	−.05	−.05	−.18
Union Carbide	.11	.05	−.10	.12
United Aircraft	.01	−.19	−.19	−.04
U.S. Steel	.04	−.01	−.06	.24
Westinghouse	−.03	−.10	−.14	.07
Woolworth	.03	−.03	−.11	.04
Average	.03	−.04	−.05	.01

Source: After Fama, "Behavior of Stock Market Prices."

4, 9, and 16 days each. Table 3 shows that there is no evidence of significant linear dependence of price changes between these days. The average serial correlation coefficients are −.04, −.05 and +.01. He notes that "Looking hard, though, one can probably find evidence of statistically significant linear dependence in the table. But, with 1,200–1,700 observations per stock on a daily basis, statistically significant deviations from zero covariance are not necessarily a basis for rejecting the efficient market model."[32] He noted that, with a standard error of approximately .03, a correlation of .06 implies that a linear relationship explains only .36 percent of the variation in price changes.

[32] Eugene F. Fama, "Efficient Capital Markets: A Review of Theory and Empirical Work," *Journal of Finance*, May 1970, pp. 383–417.

Roberts—Random Numbers

Roberts noted that:

> Technical analysis includes many different approaches, most requiring a good deal of subjective judgment in application. In part these approaches are purely empirical; in part they are based on analogy with physical processes, such as tides and waves. . . . it seems curious that there has not been widespread recognition among financial analysts that the patterns of technical analysis may be little, if anything, more than a statistical artifact. . . . one possible explanation is that the usual method of graphing stock prices gives a picture of successive *levels,* rather than of *changes,* and levels can give an artificial appearance of pattern or trend.[33]

Using a series of random numbers, Roberts developed random price changes for data with a mean of plus 0.5 and a standard deviation of 5.0. This represents a hypothetical year's price changes, i.e., data for 52 weeks were developed and plotted on Figure 1.

FIGURE 1

Simulated Price Changes Based on Random Numbers

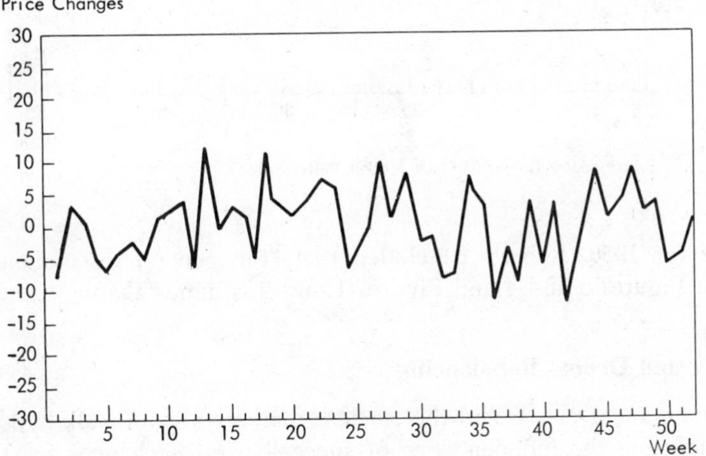

Source: After Roberts, "Stock Market Patterns."

The numbers were then cumulatively added, starting from a level of 450—relatively close to the range of the Dow Jones Industrial Index at that time. This is shown in Figure 2. To a casual observer of the stock market, Figure 2 is quite realistic even to the head-and-shoulders top.

Figures 3 and 4 give the actual data for the Dow Jones Industrial

---

[33] Harry V. Roberts, "Stock Market Patterns and Financial Analysis: Methodological Suggestions," *Journal of Finance,* March 1959, p. 1.

FIGURE 2

Simulated Dow Jones Industrial Index Based on Random Numbers

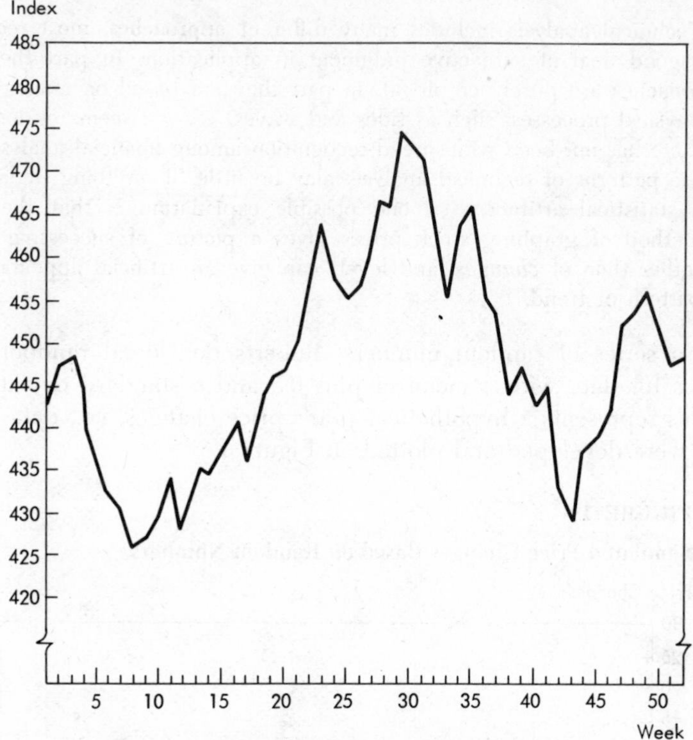

Source: After Roberts, "Stock Market Patterns."

Index for 1956. Roberts concluded that "the general resemblance between Figures 3 and 4 and Figures 1 and 2 is unmistakable."

Cheng and Deets—Rebalancing

Cheng and Deets tested the efficient market–random walk hypothesis by analyzing the independence of successive price changes for the 30 companies in the Dow Jones Industrial Index.[34] To do this, they compared the portfolio return under the buy and hold strategy (B & H) with the portfolio return under rebalancing strategy (RB) over a 31-year period 1937–69.

Under the B & H strategy, a fixed portfolio is purchased at the beginning of the period and held until the terminal period. Under RB strategy, a portfolio is purchased at an initial period and rebalanced at the end of each one-week holding period. Rebalancing means the selling

[34] Pao L. Cheng and M. King Deets "Portfolio Returns and the Random Walk Theory," *Journal of Finance,* March 1971, pp. 11–30.

FIGURE 3

Actual Price Changes Dow Jones Industrial Index

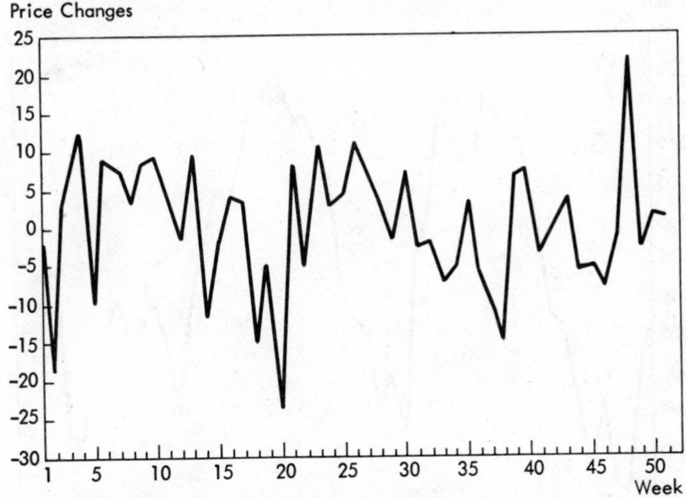

Source: After Roberts, "Stock Market Patterns."

of some portion of the securities that have experienced superior performance and replacing them in the portfolio with securities that have experienced a relatively inferior return. Thus, when rebalanced each of the 30 stocks will again constitute 1/30 of the total portfolio's value. As in Fama's earlier study (1972), Cheng and Deets assumed no taxes or transaction costs "in order not to bias in favor of either strategy."

As shown by Table 4, they find that $1.00 equally distributed among the 30 Dow Jones industrial stocks in 1937 would have grown to $9.52 in 1969. However, with weekly rebalancing, the $1.00 would have grown to $22.76 in the same period. They concluded that:

1. The random walk theory is not supported by the evidence.
2. The buy and hold strategy is "overwhelmingly inferior to the rebalancing strategy."
3. There is a tendency for performance to improve as the frequency of rebalancing increases.
4. "In summary, the fact that rebalancing yields greater return than buy and hold indicates security prices are not independent."[35]

Fama—Runs

Correlation coefficients may be dominated by a few unusual or extreme price changes. Hence, Fama designed a series of tests which

[35] Ibid., p. 30.

FIGURE 4

Dow Jones Industrial Index 1956

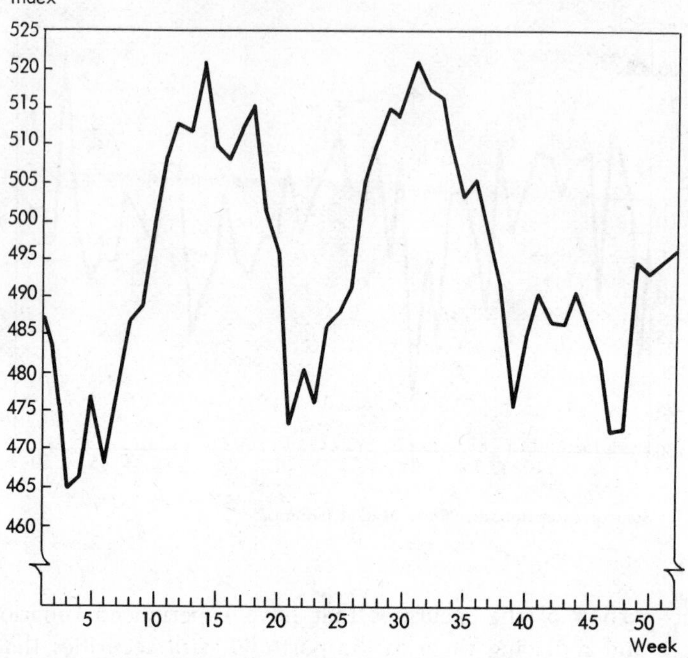

Source: After Roberts, "Stock Market Patterns."

TABLE 4

Return on Buy and Hold versus Rebalancing: 30 Dow Jones Industrial (1,625 weeks: 1937–69)

Frequency of Rebalancing	*Weeks Holding Period*	*Portfolio Policy* Buy and Hold	*Portfolio Policy* Rebalancing	*Portfolio Policy* Difference
1,625	1	$9.52	$22.76	−$13.24
812	2	9.87	14.49	− 4.62
541	3	9.87	15.25	− 5.38
406	4	9.87	13.40	− 3.53
325	5	9.52	10.69	− 1.17
270	6	9.62	11.97	− 2.35
232	7	9.87	11.73	− 1.86
203	8	9.87	12.49	− 2.62
180	9	9.62	12.42	− 2.80
162	10	9.62	10.31	− 0.69
108	15	9.62	9.89	− 0.27
81	20	9.62	10.17	− 0.55
54	30	9.62	9.92	− 0.30
40	40	9.31	9.44	− 0.13
27	60	9.62	10.16	− 0.54
18	90	9.62	9.36	+ 0.26

Source: After Cheng and Deets, "Portfolio Return."

focused on the directional signs of successive price changes to see if runs tended to persist.[36] In this series he used the 30 individual companies in the Dow Jones Industrial Index; daily price changes were designated as +, 0, or −, regardless of the amount of the change. For example: +++−−−++0−− constitutes five runs. If successive price runs are found, i.e., if price changes tend to persist, the average length of runs will be longer and the number of runs will be less than if the series were random.

Table 5 summarizes Fama's data; the first column in the table, i.e., the actual daily runs for each company are compared with the second column showing the number of runs that would obtain with a perfectly random distribution. The data indicate a very slight tendency (760 versus 735) for the one-day runs to persist. As the test is extended for successive runs of 4, 9, or 16 days, the persistence disappears, and on average, the actual total conforms precisely with a random distribution.

Shiskin—Runs

Shiskin made a test of the systematic nature of stock prices comparable to that used in economic series.[37] He noted that the *average duration of run* is a generally accepted test of the systematic nature of economic series to determine whether month-to-month movements depart significantly from randomness. This concept focuses on the number of consecutive months of change in the same direction. It takes into account only the direction of the change: +++−+− and so on, not the amplitude. Shiskin stated that, for a purely random series, the expected average duration of runs is 1.5 (months, quarters, or whatever time unit is used). "For a random series of 120 observations, i.e., 10 years in monthly data, the average duration of run should be within the range of 1.36 to 1.75 about 95 percent of the time."

Shiskin examined the average duration of run for the S & P's 500 stock price index for 120 months. He found

> The average duration of run for stock prices is 2.37, well above the limits for a random series. Since stock prices had a pronounced upward trend from 1948 to 1966, the average duration of run was also computed for the series after the trend was eliminated. It proved to be 2.30, also well above the limits for a random series.[38]

Alexander—Filters

Alexander prioneered trading rule techniques or *filters* for daily average closing prices to test independence of stock price changes. For

---

[36] Eugene F. Fama, "Behavior of Stock Market Prices," in Lorie and Hamilton, *The Stock Market*.

[37] Julius Shiskin, "Systematic Aspects of Stock Price Fluctuations," University of Chicago, Seminar on the Analysis of Security Prices, May 1968.

[38] Ibid., p. 6.

TABLE 5

Runs of Consecutive Price Changes in Same Direction: Actual versus Expected for Each Dow Jones Industrial Company

	Daily Changes		*4-Day Changes*		*9-Day Changes*		*16-Day Changes*	
Stock	*Actual*	*Expected*	*Actual*	*Expected*	*Actual*	*Expected*	*Actual*	*Expected*
Allied Chemical	683	713	160	162	71	71	39	39
Alcoa	601	671	151	154	61	67	41	39
American Can	730	756	169	172	71	73	48	44
AT&T	657	688	165	156	66	70	34	37
American Tobacco	700	747	178	173	69	73	41	41
Anaconda	635	680	166	160	68	66	36	38
Bethlehem Steel	709	720	163	159	80	72	41	42
Chrysler	927	932	223	222	100	97	54	54
DuPont	672	695	160	162	78	72	43	39
Eastman Kodak	678	679	154	160	70	70	43	40
General Electric	918	956	225	225	101	97	51	52
General Foods	799	825	185	191	81	76	43	41
General Motors	832	868	202	205	83	86	44	47
Goodyear	681	672	151	158	60	65	36	36
Int'l. Harvester	720	713	159	164	84	73	40	38
Int'l. Nickel	704	713	163	164	68	71	34	38
Int'l. Paper	762	826	190	194	80	83	51	47
Johns Manville	685	699	173	160	64	69	39	40
Owens Illinois	713	743	171	169	69	73	36	39
Procter & Gamble	826	859	180	191	66	81	40	43
Sears	700	748	167	173	66	71	40	35
Standard Oil (Cal.)	972	979	237	228	97	99	59	54
Standard Oil (N.J.)	688	704	159	159	69	69	29	37
Swift & Co.	878	878	209	197	85	84	50	48
Texaco	600	654	143	155	57	63	29	36
Union Carbide	595	621	142	151	67	67	36	35
United Aircraft	661	699	172	161	77	68	45	40
U.S. Steel	651	662	162	158	65	70	37	41
Westinghouse	829	826	198	193	87	84	41	46
Woolworth	847	868	193	199	78	81	48	48
Averages	735	760	176	176	75	75	42	42

Source: After Fama, "Behavior of Stock Market Prices."

example, with a 5 percent filter, if the price rises by 5 percent: buy; if it declines by 5 percent: sell. He used daily closing prices for the S & P's 425 industrials for the 1928–61 period.

According to Alexander, "the filter approach rather closely resembles, at least in spirit, the Dow Theory. Stripped of its qualifications, the Dow Theory consists of selling when the averages are a certain point off peak and buying when they are a certain distance up from the trough. The filter scheme can be described in precisely the same words."[39]

[39] Sidney S. Alexander, "Price Movement in Speculative Markets: Trends or Random Walks," in Cootner, *Random Character of Stock Market Prices* (Cambridge, Mass.: M.I.T. Press, 1964), pp. 338–72.

Alexander's filters, however, differ from the Dow theory in that under the filter scheme, a certain distance is to be defined as X percent which is set in advance. Under the Dow theory a certain distance is determined by inspection of charts showing prices from swing to swing and at any point the key is the trough or peak of the preceding swing.

As shown below, Alexander found that brokerage commissions had a serious impact on the profitability of filters:

> If a commission of 2 percent on each turnaround transaction had to be paid, however, the smallest filters would have incurred such substantial losses as to wipe out the initial capital. . . . Only the larger filters (21.7 percent or greater) show sizeable gains over commissions so as to approach "buy and hold," and only the very largest (over 40 percent) beat buy and hold by any substantial margin if commissions are deducted.
>
> . . . I should advise any reader who is interested only in practical results, and who is not a floor trader and so must pay commissions, to turn to some other source for advice on how to beat buy and hold. . . . I maintain that neither commissions nor profits from "buy and hold" are relevant to the random walk issue. The case for exclusion of commissions is straightforward. Suppose that in a game of coin tossing, the bet is $1.00 a throw on heads, with the "house" charging a commission of 2¢ a throw . . . if after 10,000 bets you find you are $200 behind, it would be unreasonable to complain that the coin was not fair.
>
> . . . As to the comparison with buy and hold—how is that relevant to the issue of whether stock prices follow a random walk? Buy and hold will be profitable when there is an upward movement of prices. If the uptrend is generated by a random walk with independent steps, there would be a certain expectation of profit from any given filter. It is a comparison of "observed" with "expected" profits that is relevant, rather than a comparison with buy and hold. For if, as we shall later see, from 1928–1961 the filters were substantially more profitable than to be expected on a random walk hypothesis but sometimes more, sometimes less, profitable than buy and hold, we can still conclude, as I do, that something other than a random walk was at work.
>
> The significant data of Table 6 may therefore be taken to be the terminal capital assuming no commissions. Even the least profitable filter yielded a terminal capital 2.1 times the initial capital. Of course the number of transactions decline with increasing size of filter, so that the statistical reliability of the measure of profitability of the larger filters must be weaker, based as they are on 8 or 12 transactions rather than the 1730 of the 1 percent filter. On the other hand, for "buy and hold" we have only one transaction, hence one observation.[40]

The basic data are shown in Table 6.

Alexander conducted several other filter tests and concluded with these remarks, "Taken all together the evidence runs strongly against

[40] Ibid., pp. 351–52.

TABLE 6

Filter Profitability 1928–61

Filter Size	*Number of Transactions*	*Terminal Capital as Multiple of Initial Capital*		
		If No Commissions	*With Commissions*	*Buy and Hold*
1.0%	1730	41.3	0.0	5.1
4.0	418	10.7	0.0	5.1
8.2	142	14.8	0.9	5.1
12.5	88	4.0	0.7	5.1
17.0	54	2.1	0.7	5.1
21.7	32	6.4	3.4	5.1
29.5	20	5.3	3.6	5.1
34.6	16	4.8	3.5	5.1
40.0	12	6.2	5.0	5.1
45.6	8	10.6	9.2	5.1

Source: After Alexander, "Price Movement in Speculative Markets."

the hypothesis that from 1928–1961 the movement of the S & P Industrials is consistent with a random walk with drift. . . . maybe there just is a wee bit of persistence in the movement of stock price averages."

Cootner—Random Walk with Barriers

Cootner commented that

> You can see why the idea (of a random walk) is intriguing. Where else can the economist find that ideal of his—the perfect market. Here is the place to take a stand if there is such a place.
>
> Unfortunately, it is not the right place. The stock market is not a random walk. A growing number of investigators have begun to suspect it and I think I have enough evidence to demonstrate the nature of the imperfections. On the other hand, I do not believe the market is grossly imperfect. . . . Even more interesting, is that my model is perfectly compatible with much of what I interpret Wall Street chart reading to be all about. Like the Indian folk doctors who discovered tranquilizers, the Wall Street witch doctors, without the benefit of scientific method, have produced something with their magic, even if they can't tell you what it is or how it works."[41]

Cootner set forth the idea that, if professional investors held an idea of what was going to happen in the future, stock prices would behave as a random walk with reflecting barriers. Figure 5 shows how this concept operates.

Thus, starting with the intrinsic value of 54, the hypothetical stock fluctuates randomly between 53 and 55. Subsequently, as new informa-

[41] Paul H. Cootner, ed., *Random Character of Stock Market Prices,* pp. 231–52.

FIGURE 5
Reflecting Barrier Concept

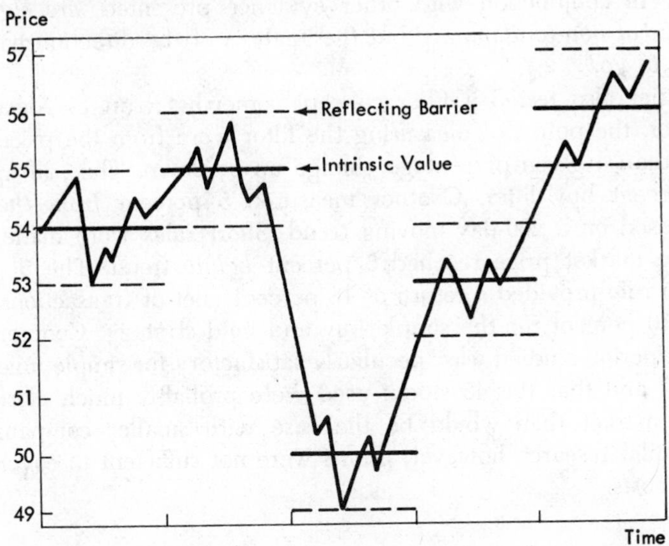

tion is received, the stocks intrinsic value rises to 55, then down to 50, up to 53 and 56. The reflecting barriers, in part, express the fact that, because of transaction cost and so on, prices tend to move randomly about a central value. Cootner also noted that these barriers may be "soft and rubber like" since not all professionals held the same expectations. Also, that there is no reason to expect changes in the price expectation of professionals should occur in other than a random manner over the time dimension. Thus, over any substantial period of time, stock prices would be composed of a random number of trends each of which is a random walk within the reflecting barrier. Cootner notes that this concept has much random behavior, and it also has some implications which are strikingly different.

Cootner then noted that over *longer periods of time*, other factors, which may be relatively unimportant in the case of weekly changes, become much more significant. This is based on the assumption that stocks may have trends, or several trends, over longer periods of time, each with a reflecting barrier. This he contends implies that stocks would not be "as free to wander" as if the series were a random walk.

On this basis, Cootner studied 45 NYSE stocks, 5 of which had weekly price data for 10 years and 40 of which had data for 5 years, 1956–60. All data were adjusted for cash dividends, stocks splits, and so on. He found that each of the 45 companies had at least one trend of a year or more, most had at least one longer trend and "very few stretches without a trend." He concluded that "It would seem as if the lengths of the trends involved in the price series studied, especially in conjunction with other evidence presented, *are significant evidence of non-randomness,* but the analysis of the direction has much further to go."

Cootner also tested a filter concept somewhat akin to Alexander's. However, the points of measuring the filter were from the price *trend,* rather than a given percentage change up or down. Thus, in applying a 5 percent buy filter, Cootner measured 5 percent *from the trend line*—based on a 200-day moving trend. Short sales were made whenever the market price reached 5 percent *below* trend. The 5 percent decision rule provided a return of 18 percent (net of transactions costs) versus 10 percent for the simple buy and hold strategy. Cootner noted that the period studied was "peculiarly satisfactory for simple investment policies" and that the 45 stocks used were probably much closer to a perfect market than would be the case with smaller companies. As with similar research however, profits were not sufficient to cover transactions costs.

Levy—Relative Strength: 200 Stocks

Levy tested the random walk hypothesis using several different strategies based essentially on relative strength. His basic data were 200 NYSE stocks covering a 200-week period from 1960 to 1965. Stocks were selected from the S & P's 425 Industrial Stock Index with representative sampling from each industry group. All stock price data were adjusted for splits, dividends, and rights. Three different inputs were computed:

1. *Relative Strength Data.* Computed for each stock using the formula: $C/A26$; or $C/A4$, in which C equals current week's price; $A26$ is average price over preceding 26 weeks; and $A4$ is average price over prior 4 weeks. These ratios were computed for each stock and ranked highest to lowest.
2. *Volatility Ranks.* Calculated for each set of prices using ratio of standard deviation to arithmetic means, i.e., the average closing price for the prior 26 weeks.
3. *Weekly Geometric Average.* For all 200 stocks to serve as the random portfolio. This has "the virtue of continually equalizing the dollars invested in each component stock."

The investment strategy was to use historical, i.e., 26- or 4-week average relative strength. Thus, upgrading continuously eliminated the weaker stocks from the portfolio and reinvested the proceeds in the strongest stocks. For example, under a 10 percent relative strength strategy, equal amounts were invested in each of the 20 strongest stocks. The portfolio would, however, not be changed until one or more stocks had declined in relative strengths to say rank 160 (from the top). Turnaround transactions costs of 2 percent were assumed.

Table 7 summarizes the data for several different cast-out rank strategies. It will be noted that the highest returns, i.e., the 21.8 percent gross or 19.1 percent net annual returns, are in the range of 150 cast-out rank. The random portfolio annual return was 10.6 percent, but this portfolio had a better, i.e., lower standard, deviation of four-week returns.

TABLE 7

Result of Portfolio Upgrading with 10 Percent Relative Strength Selection and Trades Based upon Relative Strength Cast-Out Ranks

	Cast-Out Ranks						
Gross Results (%)	*020*	*050*	*100*	*150*	*180*	*195*	*Geometric Average*
Annual return..............	14.20	20.30	21.10	21.80	19.30	13.80	10.60
Average of 4-week returns...	1.08	1.47	1.54	1.59	1.45	1.09	0.83
Standard deviation of 4-week returns..................	4.79	4.85	4.35	4.39	4.53	4.60	3.52
Net Results (%)							
Annual return..............	−3.20	11.10	16.30	19.10	17.80	13.20	10.60
Average of 4-week returns...	−0.19	0.86	1.22	1.41	1.35	1.05	0.83
Standard deviation of 4-week returns..................	4.87	4.90	4.39	4.41	4.55	4.61	3.52

Source: Levy, "Random Walks."

Other strategies were tested, such as 10 stocks, i.e., 5 percent of 200 stocks, different relative strength selection, and different cast-out ranks. Additionally "balancing" of portfolios which had become too volatile was accomplished by introducing a bond component on a flexible basis. Thus, Levy's strategy called for movement out of bonds into stocks when the stock market was becoming relatively stronger and vice versa. The data indicate that this strategy permitted both a higher annual return on the relative strength portfolio than the random portfolio and a lower risk as measured by the standard deviations of the four-week returns.

Levy concluded that

> the profitability of portfolio upgrading variable ratio strategies over the 1960–1965 period has been completely and reliably proven. Moreover, the large returns can be attained by incurring no more risks than would be incurred if a random investment strategy were pursued. . . . stock prices follow discernible trends and patterns which have predictive significance; and the theory of random walks has been refuted. . . .

Of course, the empirical results presented herein must be interpreted in light of the specific time frame investigated. Therefore, an obvious extension of the study would be the performance of similar tests for different periods of time.[42]

Jensen and Bennington—Relative Strength: All NYSE Stocks

Jensen and Bennington endeavored to further test Levy's relative strength trading role.[43] They divided the years 1930–65 into seven nonoverlapping periods, e.g., 1930–35, . . . , 1960–65. Using all NYSE securities, they composed 29 separate samples of 200 stocks with an equal dollar amount invested in each, with dividends reinvested. Their results are shown in Table 8. Thus, before allowing for transaction costs, the 5 percent or 10 percent trading rules outperformed simple buy and hold, but failed to do so if such costs were included.

TABLE 8

Average Compound Returns—All Periods and All Portfolios

	Average Annual Return	
	Gross	*Net of Transaction Costs*
Buy and hold	11.1%	10.7%
10% rule	12.5	10.7
5% rule	12.4	9.3

Source: After Jensen and Bennington, "Random Walks and Technical Theories."

Jensen and Bennington also examined variations attributable to differences in risk calculated on the basis of difference in the standard deviation of monthly returns. Measures of systematic risk for each of the portfolios generated by the trading rules or buy and hold policy were reflected by comparison of the market return and the "riskless return." The latter measured by yield to maturity of U.S. government bonds due in five years, i.e., the portfolio holding period. They stated: "After explicit adjustment for the level of risk, it was shown that net of transaction costs the two trading rules (5 percent or 10 percent) as tested earned an average −3 percent and −2.4 percent less than the equivalent risk buy and hold policy."

Different portfolios were tested over several different time periods, including the 1961–65 period originally studied by Levy. Results for the latter are shown in Table 9.

[42] Robert A. Levy, "Random Walks: Reality or Myth," *Financial Analysts Journal*, November–December 1967, pp. 69–77.

[43] Michael C. Jensen and George A. Bennington, "Random Walks and Technical Theories: Some Additional Evidence," *Journal of Finance*, May 1970, pp. 460–82.

Jensen and Bennington compared their own results with the 20–26 percent returns reported by Levy and conclude that "Levy's original high returns were spurious and probably attributable to selection bias." The authors attribute the latter to differences such as: their five portfolios included all stocks listed on the NYSE at the beginning of the period, whereas Levy's portfolio consisted of 200 stocks that were listed during the entire 1961–65 period. They also noted significant differences in risk, as reflected in the portfolio beta coefficients,

TABLE 9
Average Compound Returns—1961–65 Buy and Hold versus 10 percent Trading Rule

	Gross	*Net of Transaction Costs*	*Beta*
Buy and hold	10.1%	9.6%	0.96
Portfolio #1	14.6	12.9	1.09
2	10.5	8.7	0.96
3	12.0	10.1	1.30
4	8.1	6.3	1.09
5	12.3	10.3	1.02
Average portfolio	11.5	9.7	1.09

Source: After Jensen and Bennington, "Random Walks and Technical Theories."

> Since the trading rules portfolios were, on the average, more risky than the buy and hold portfolios. This simple comparison of returns is biased in favor of the trading rules. . . . After explicit adjustment for the level of risk, it was shown that, net of transaction costs, the two trading rules (5 percent and 10 percent) we tested earned an average −0.3 percent and −2.4 percent less than the equivalent risk buy and hold policy.[44]

Jen—Relative Strength: Long Term versus Short Term

Another viewpoint was expressed by Jen who wrote

> . . . I am sympathetic to Jensen & Bennington's basic position that the random walk hypothesis will hold in a long run. J. & B should, however, recognize that Levy's strategy may not be a statistical quirk, but actually represent a trading rule that works for a short period of time because the rule captures the essence of market imperfection at that period of time. On the other hand, the usefulness of Levy's rule is limited to small traders only because a mutual fund of substantial size operating on Levy's 10 stocks ($X=10$ percent) and 20 stocks ($X=5$ percent) will most probably find that the market prices of the stocks

[44] Ibid., p. 481.

will shift so much that the rules will no longer produce better returns.[45]

Jen also took exception to Jensen and Bennington's use of

> the yield to maturity on five-year government bonds at the beginning of the period as the measure of riskless rates in their regressions. While government bonds are recognized traditionally as riskless bonds, they are only risk-free in a default sense, not in a price sense.

Jen concluded with the comment that:

> As many writers including J & B have pointed out, most empirical evidence supporting the random walk hypothesis are of two kinds. The first kind is purely statistical in nature, that is, statistical procedures are applied to demonstrate that successive price changes over a short run in individual common stocks are very nearly independent for a long price series. The inference is then made that the market is efficient. The second kind of empirical tests involves the use of simple mechanical trading rules such as filters. While the evidence is largely consistent with the random walk hypothesis, it is again based on a long price series. Both kinds of tests can be criticized on the ground that the statistical procedure used cannot disprove the hypothesis that, for a *limited* period of time, price changes are not random for certain stocks or even a significant part of the market in response to some new information. Nor can they disprove the hypothesis that price changes are random for a long period but actually either mean or variance, or both, have shifted within that period in response to some new information.[46]

Kruizenga and Boness—Options

Cootner stated that "The richest field of application of the random walk theory has been at the determination of the value of such derivative assets as puts, calls, warrants and convertible bonds. These assets, which are options to buy or sell shares of common stock, obtain their price from the price of the underlying shares."[47] As noted below, the evidence from different studies can best be described as "mixed."

Kruizenga examined the results of investing in put and call options for some 500 weeks in the 1946–56 period.[48] He found that, for both the 90-day and 6-month periods, call premiums on average were lower than their actuarial values, i.e., their value in terms of the movement of stock prices and cash dividends during this period. He used an average price for options of eight broadly held and traded companies: Anaconda Copper, Bethlehem Steel, Chrysler, General Motors, New York Central,

[45] Frank C. Jen, "Discussion," *Journal of Finance,* May 1970, pp. 495–99.

[46] Ibid., p. 498.

[47] Paul H. Cootner, "The Statistical Analysis of Option Prices," *Random Character of Stock Market Prices,* p. 373.

[48] Richard J. Kruizenga, "Profit Returns from Purchasing Puts and Calls," in Cootner, *Random Character of Stock Market Prices,* pp. 392–411.

FIGURE 6

Logarithmic Probability Graph of Data: U. S. Steel, Six-Month Gains

Source: Kruizenga, "Profit Returns."

Republic Steel, Southern Pacific, and U.S. Steel. He found that for the period as a whole, "for the 8-stock average, steady purchases of calls yielded an average profit on 90-day options of about 9 percent on the cost of the calls and about 35 percent on the 6-months calls." He concluded, "This is contrary to the general presumption which has prevailed that option buyers pay more for options than they are worth."

The data indicate that price changes of 90-day options were reasonably close to random. However, price changes on the six-month options did not appear to be random, and this is more pronounced in the individual company. For example, the logarithmic probability graph of U.S. Steel six-month options is reproduced in Figure 6. If the data has been distributed in a perfectly random, i.e., normal, manner the "curve" would have been a straight line.

Boness examined some 500 customer transactions in put and call options at two brokerage firms in the 1958–60 period.[49] Annual rates of

[49] A. James Boness, "Some Evidence on the Profitability of Trading in Puts and Calls," in Cootner, *Random Character of Stock Market Prices,* pp. 475–96

return were calculated for options held for 1,2,3,4,5, and 6 months. In contrast to the finding outlined in Figure 6, Boness determined that, recognizing brokerage costs and transfer taxes, both buyers and sellers of options lost money in the period. And, perhaps reflecting on the efficiency of the market: "Buyers of options lose money and lose it more rapidly on short term options than on long term options."

Examining option transactions relative to changes in the S & P's 500 index, Boness concluded that

> These findings tend to show that the buyers of puts and calls act as if they believe in turning points in the stock market such as are rationalized in the Dow theory. The findings also tend to show that buyers of puts and calls would have improved the returns on their investments if they had acted instead as if they believed in the random walk theory of stock price changes.[50]

THE SEMISTRONG FORM OF THE EFFICIENT MARKET–RANDOM WALK HYPOTHESIS: SURVEY OF EVIDENCE

Overview

This form of the efficient market–random walk hypothesis centers on how rapidly and efficiently market prices adjust to new publicly available information. This matter has received relatively less attention in the literature.

Fama, Fisher, Jensen, and Roll tested the efficiency of the market prices in reacting to the announcement of over 900 stock splits involving NYSE listed firms. They ascertained that there is strong evidence that the market efficiently anticipates dividend increases. Ball and Brown conducted similar tests of the market's ability to correctly anticipate changes in earnings per share and likewise found that the market efficiently anticipates earnings changes of companies with rising earnings as well as those that decline.

Niederhoffer and Regan tested the promptness of news dissemination for 50 NYSE stocks experiencing the sharpest increase in earnings as well as the 50 with the sharpest declines. Their work revealed that news lags in reporting sharp earnings declines raises questions as to the efficient dissemination of significant news. Zeikel examined the efficiency of individual company stock prices in adjusting to new, significant information. His work suggests that market price reactions are not instantaneous, but may lag over a several month period.

Scholes tested the stock market's efficiency in absorbing secondary

[50] Ibid., p. 483.

distributions. He analyzed some 345 secondaries and concluded that the market operates quite efficiently in adjusting to the news and that the size of the offer had no impact on market prices. He also demonstrated that secondary sales have different impacts on stock prices according to the type of institution or individual effecting the sale. Kraus and Stoll made similar studies for block trades. Their data largely confirm market efficiency. However, they did find some evidence that the size of the distribution tended to have an impact on stock prices.

Analysis of Studies

Fama, Fisher, Jensen, and Roll—Splits

Fama, Fisher, Jensen, and Roll conducted a test of the speed and accuracy of the market's reaction to the announcement of stock splits.[51] The tests embrace 940 splits of NYSE stocks in the 1927–59 period where the split increased shares outstanding by 25 percent or more. One objective of their study was to test the oft-heard theme that a stock split increases the total value of the share outstanding because investors are more inclined to purchase lower price shares.

Their analysis centered upon each stock's behavior in the period 30 months before and after the split. The way in which each stock price changed in relation to the overall market (eliminating the period adjacent to the split) was measured. Thus, one stock might, over the long run, have a tendency to rise 5 percent faster than the market and another stock to decline 5 percent relative to the market per year, and so on. Accordingly, the relationship of each stock's trend to that of the market during the period under study was eliminated. This would permit an unbiased calculation of whether prices of split stocks went up or down more than would rationally be expected by the split itself.

Figure 7 summarizes the price performance of all 940 stocks 30 months before and after each split. From the sharp upward trend of market prices prior to the split, it is suggested that the market was efficient in anticipating the pending split. Other data indicate that the mere fact a stock's price is rising sharply could have directly or indirectly been a causative factor in the split itself, i.e., most splits occur in rising markets and relatively few in depressed markets. After the 940 stock splits, prices on average did not change relative to the general market.

Another aspect of market efficiency is reflected in Figure 8. It shows the record of 672 stock splits where dividends were raised by an above-

[51] Eugene F. Fama; Lawrence Fisher; Michael C. Jensen; and Richard Roll, "The Adjustment of Stock Prices to New Information," *International Economic Review*, February 1969, pp. 1–21.

FIGURE 7

Relative Performance of 940 Stocks over the Period of a Split

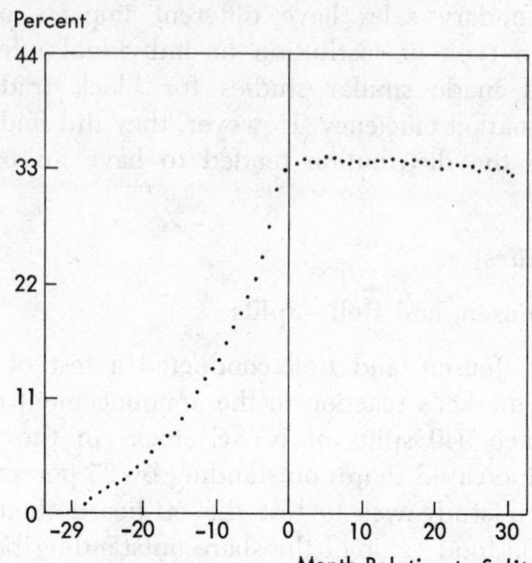

Source: Fama, Fisher, Jensen, and Roll, "Adjustment of Stock Prices."

average amount within one year after the split. Prices did improve moderately in the several months following the split after which a generally flat pattern was evident.

Figure 9 traces the performance of 268 stock splits where no relative

FIGURE 8

Relative Performance of 672 Stocks for Which a Split Was Succeeded by a Relative Increase in the Dividend

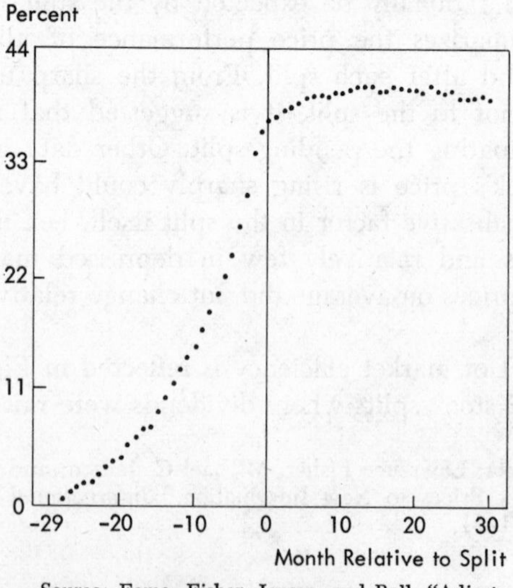

Percent
44
33
22
11
0
-29 -20 -10 0 10 20 30
Month Relative to Split

Source: Fama, Fisher, Jensen, and Roll, "Adjustment of Stock Prices."

FIGURE 9

Relative Performance of 268 Stocks for Which a Split Was Not Succeeded by a Relative Increase in the Dividend

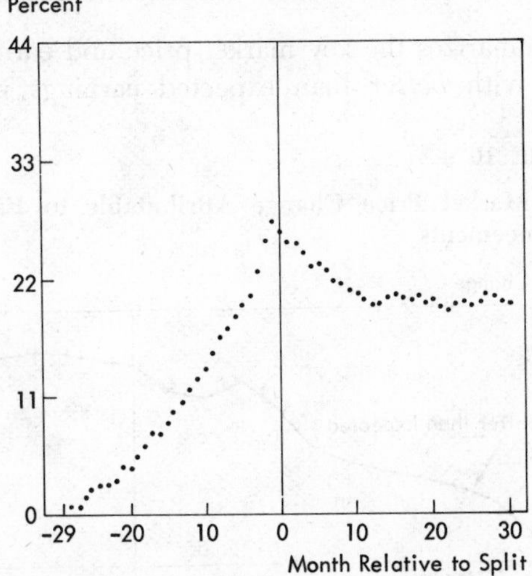

Source: Fama, Fisher, Jensen, and Roll, "Adjustment of Stock Prices."

increase in dividends occurred. Prices weakened in the several months after the split and then trended sideways relative to the market as a whole. Fama et al. concluded that the market reflected disappointment in the dividend policy and prices drifted downward.

In conclusion, the authors cite these data as strong evidence that the market is efficient both in anticipating the dividend increases and in subsequently adjusting to dividend increases that were greater than the market generally. Fama et al. conclude "On the average the market makes unbiased dividend forecasts for split securities, and these forecasts are fully reflected in the price of a security by the end split of the month."

Ball and Brown: EPS Announcements

Ball and Brown conducted a test of the stock market's ability to correctly anticipate changes in annual earnings per share well in advance of the actual announcement of the news.[52] They selected 261 large firms with complete earnings data available in the S & P's Compustat tapes and complete information in the University of Chicago's monthly price and dividend tapes. Prices were adjusted for the general trend of the market. Each firm's actual earnings per share were then compared

[52] Ray Ball and Philip Brown, "An Empirical Evaluation of Accounting Income, Number 5," *Journal of Accounting Research,* Autumn 1968, pp. 159–78.

to the forecast of earnings per share with the companies arranged in two groups:

1. Firms with "increased" earnings relative to forecast
2. Firms with "decreased" earnings relative to forecast.

Figure 10 summarizes the key market price and earnings data. Stock prices of firms with *better* than expected earnings increased in the

FIGURE 10

Stock Market Price Change Attributable to Earnings Announcements

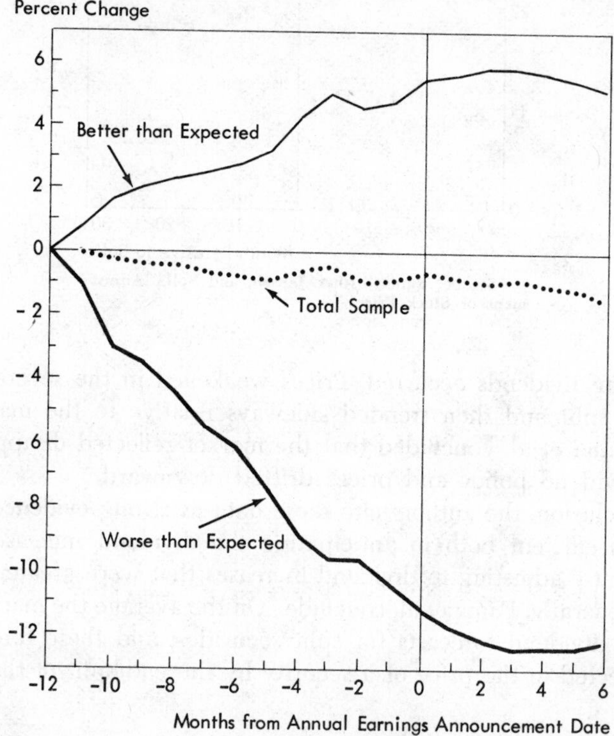

Source: After Ball and Brown, "Empirical Evaluation of Accounting Income."

12 months prior to the annual earnings announcement data and plateaued for the next 6 months. Stock prices of firms with *worse* than expected earnings declined in the 12 months prior to the announcement and then drifted essentially sideways.

Ball and Brown conclude that "most of the information contained in reported annual earnings is anticipated by the market before the annual report is released." In fact, the anticipation is so accurate that the announcement of the actual earnings does not appear to cause any unusual jumps in price relative to the market in the announcement month. They state that about 85–90 percent of the content of the annual earnings announcement is anticipated in advance of its announcement by other media, such as interim reports.

Neiderhoffer and Regan—News Reporting Lag

The efficient market concept depends importantly on prompt and widespread dissemination of all important news—good or bad. Neiderhoffer and Regan studied this question and found evidence which suggests that bad news is not reported as promptly as good.[53] They examined the time reporting interval for the 50 NYSE stocks that had the sharpest yearly increase in earnings as well as the 50 companies which had the sharpest declines in earnings. The data are summarized in Figure 11.

FIGURE 11

Time Lag in Reporting Good News versus Bad News

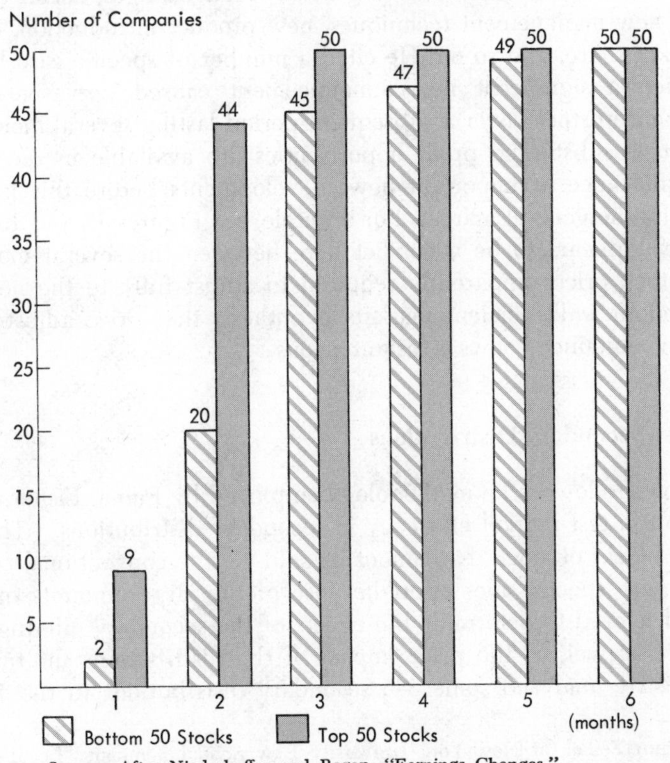

Source: After Niederhoffer and Regan, "Earnings Changes."

[53] Victor Neiderhoffer and Patrick J. Regan, "Earnings Changes, Analysts Forecasts and Stock Prices," *Financial Analysts Journal,* May–June 1972, pp. 69–74.

Some 88 percent of the top earning 50 companies reported their earnings within two months of the end of the fiscal year. In contrast, only 40 percent of the 50 bottom earning companies did likewise. Perhaps this underscores the old adage that "good news travels fast." However, it also raises questions with respect to market efficiency. For example, does the lack of earnings news convey a message of bad news to come? If so, do investors who act on that assumption gain an advantage over those who wait for the news?

Zeikel—Adjusting to New Information

Zeikel examined the efficiency of the stock market in adjusting to new information. He stated that "Every industry, company and economic sector responds to a different set of business phenomenon, forces and critical factors. Every sound analytical approach requires that those factors be identified, isolated and followed on a consistent basis".[54]

Zeikel notes that critical factors are not confined to short-term movements, but include slower moving basic trend changes, social developments, new management techniques, new product introduction, changes in market share, and so on. He cited a number of specific case histories in which a significent new announcement caused pervasive market movement in stocks over a subsequent period lasting several months. He noted that substantial profit opportunities are available in recognizing the significance of important news developments before this is appreciated by the general market. For example, see Figures 12 and 13.

There appears to be a conflict here between the several months of price stock prices apparently required to adjust fully to the news and the random walk–efficient markets hypothesis that price adjustment to publicly announced news is instantaneous.

Scholes: Secondary Distributions

Scholes followed the methodology employed by Fama, Fisher, Jensen, and Roll to test market efficiency in secondary distributions.[55] These are sizable blocks of stock that cannot be sold via the conventional channels but require special sales effort because of the large amounts involved. He endeavored to determine the effects of the secondary offering per se on price as well as the price impact of the distributions informational content. He analyzed some 345 secondary distributions in the 1961–65

---

[54] Arthur Zeikel, at New York University Law School Seminar, "Legal Implications of Random Walk Hypothesis," in February 1974.

[55] Myron G. Scholes, "A Test of the Competitive Market Hypothesis, the Market for New Issues and Secondary Offerings," Ph.D. dissertation, University of Chicago, 1969; and Richard A. Brealey, *Security Prices in a Competitive Market* (Cambridge, Mass.: MIT Press, 1971).

FIGURE 12

Curtiss-Wright Corp.

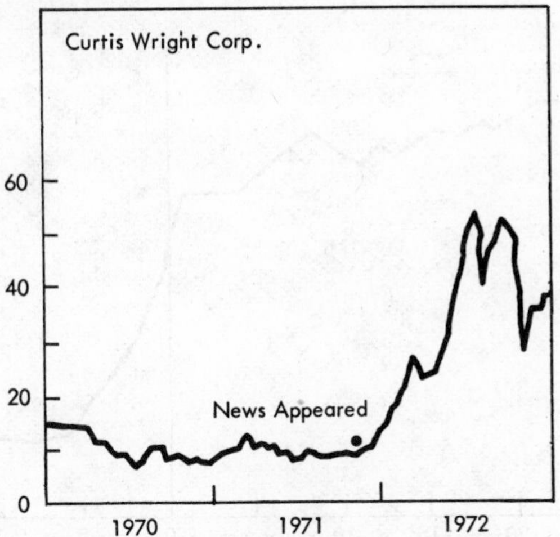

• = Several articles in *New York Times* and other publications in December 1971 concerning its interest in U.S. development of the Wankel engine.

period. Scholes adjusted the prices of each security involved in a secondary distribution for the normal relation of its price movement to the general market.

Figure 14 summarizes the relative price action of the 345 stocks in the 40-day period surrounding the distribution.

FIGURE 13

American Broadcasting Company

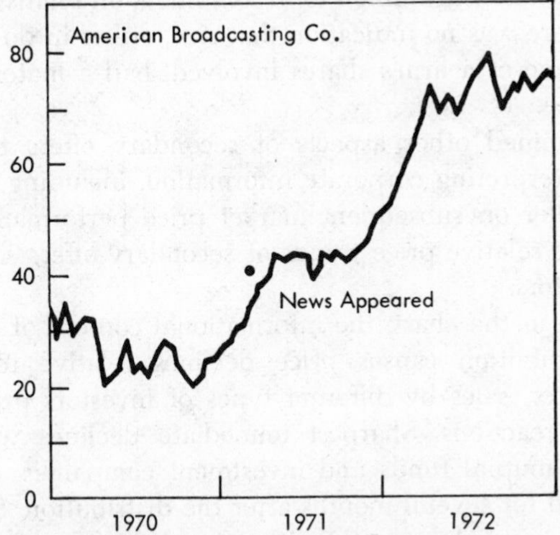

• = Article in *Wall Street Journal,* March 1971, and other periodicals concerning sudden surge in TV advertising demand and higher prices in prime time.

FIGURE 14

Stock Price Change Relative to Market

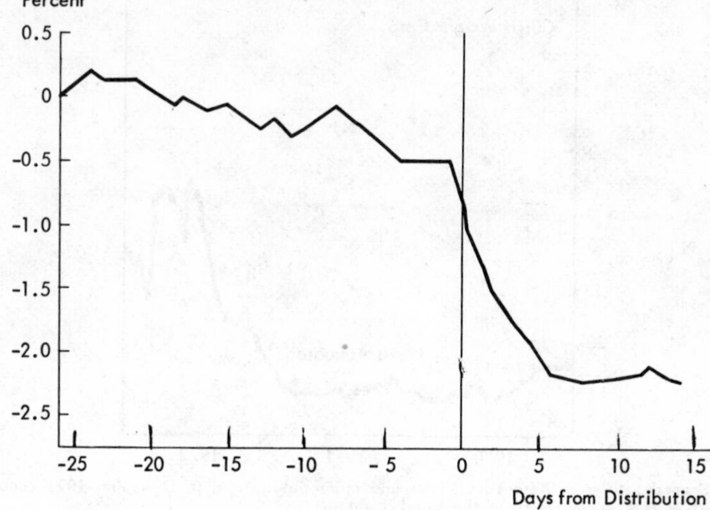

Source: After Scholes, "Test of Competitive Market Hypothesis"; and Brealey, *Security Prices*.

Scholes' data show that prices declined about 1 percent in the 26 days prior to the actual distribution with an approximately equal decline within six days after the distribution was effective. Scholes pointed out that the SEC does not require full identification of a secondary vendor until six days after the distribution and that the decline in the six-day period indicated that the market anticipated this information in an efficient manner. Scholes also tested the impact of offering size, which ranged from less than $1 million to $100 million, on relative market price movement. There was no indication that size, either in dollar amount or in the percentage of a firm's shares involved, had a material impact on the market price.

Scholes examined other aspects of secondary offers to test market efficiency in interpreting corporate information, including the impact of the type of seller on subsequent market price performance. Figure 15 summarizes the relative price trends of secondary offers sold by various classes of investors.

As indicated in the chart, the informational content of the news of a secondary distribution causes price declines relative to the general market. However, sales by different types of investors experienced different market reactions. Sharpest immediate declines were made by shares sold by mutual funds and investment companies, and these declines continued for several months after the distribution. Shares sold by firms or officers reacted promptly with price declines, and this continued through most of the subsequent 18 months. Shares sold by individuals

FIGURE 15

Stock Price Change Relative to Market

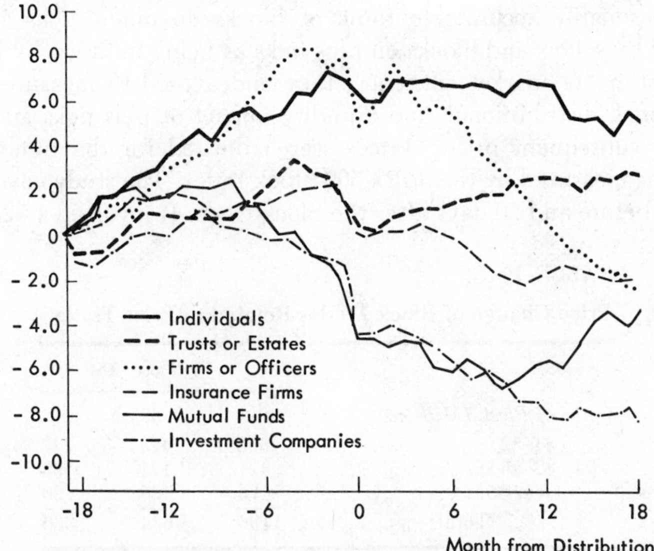

Source: After Scholes, "Test of Competitive Market Hypothesis"; and Brealey, *Security Prices.*

or for trust and estates had relatively less of an immediate price decline and, over the longer term, exhibited relatively less pressure than shares sold by institutions.

Many plausible interpretations can be made of these data. For example, the market may recognize that sales by individuals or trusts and estates are frequently made to meet cash needs or to meet requirements for taxes in settling estates. Hence, this is not interpreted as bad news. Another interpretation is that mutual funds and investment companies, which have among the highest share turnovers of all institutions, may tend to sell shares promptly when bad news develops. Additionally, sales by corporate officers might signal to the market a concern by individuals who are rather well informed of a corporation's future outlook. Scholes thus concludes that price action is not attributable to the size of an offer as much as to the informational content of the sale. He cites this as further support for the efficient market hypothesis.

Kraus and Stoll—Block Trades

Kraus and Stoll also tested market efficiency—but on block trades.[56] These are blocks of 10,000 shares or more that can be traded in the

[56] Alan Kraus and Hans R. Stoll, "Price Impact of Block Trading on the New York Stock Exchange," *Journal of Finance,* June 1972, pp. 569–88.

normal course of a day's trading. They studied 2,199 block trades involving over $1 million each on the NYSE from July 1968 to September 1969. Basic data relative to these trades are shown in Table 10. Based on discussion with institutional traders, Kraus and Stoll concluded that it is "reasonably accurate to think of blocks on minus ticks as being initiated by sellers and blocks on plus ticks as being initiated by buyers."

In testing for market efficiency, they endeavored to measure the informational, distributional, and liquidity impact of plus ticks and minus ticks on subsequent prices. Prices were adjusted for the trend of the market as measured by the S&P's 500 Stock Index. The study covered the 20 days before and 20 days after the block trade. It involved 1,121 minus

TABLE 10

Price Change of Block Trades Related to Prior Trade

	Tick		
Value of Block (Millions)	—	*0*	+
$1–$2	603	425	247
$2–$5	421	171	99
Over $5	175	38	20
Total	1199	634	366

Source: After Kraus and Stoll, "Price Impact of Block Trading."

ticks and 345 plus ticks trades. Figure 16 summarizes data for minus ticks trades.

As Figure 16 indicates, closing prices on day zero averaged 2 percent below prices 20 days earlier. Also, a new (lower) level of prices tends to be established with a slight recovery by 10 days after the block trade with little shift thereafter.

Figure 17 points up price action, relative to the market, for 345 blocks on plus ticks. Closing prices on day zero averaged 5 percent above prices 20 days before the block trade. Also, prices tended to establish new higher levels.

Kraus and Stoll concluded that

> . . . these results do not show evidence of a change in rate of return subsequent to the block, reflected in a subsequent rise or fall of prices, that would support the existence of a distribution effect. Prices seemed to have experienced a once-and-for-all rise or fall depending on whether the block was purchased or sold. Such a pattern is consistent with the information hypothesis. However, further tests tend to support the liquidity cost version of the distribution hypothesis.[57]

[57] Ibid., p. 582.

FIGURE 16

Relative Price Performance for 1,121 Blocks on Minus Ticks

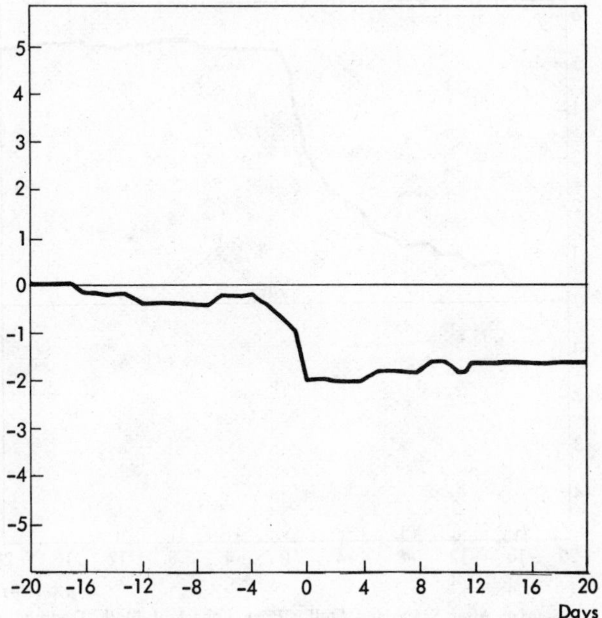

Source: After Kraus and Stoll, "Price Impact of Block Trading."

In examining the latter, Kraus and Stoll tested the size of a block offered upon subsequent market price. If different securities are imperfect substitutes, relatively larger price changes would be associated with larger trades. Separate regressions were run for minus tick blocks and plus tick blocks relating size of block and size of price effect. The results show that:

1. Minus tick blocks had a heavier *negative* price impact as the size of the block increased.
2. Plus tick blocks had a corresponding *positive* price effect.

The results indicate that an increase of $1 million in block size had a price effect of 0.13 percentage points. For example, if a 20,000 share block of a $50 stock were increased to 100,000 shares, the price effect would be $0.25 per share.

The authors conclude that, while the evidence is not uniformly strong, for trades on minus ticks the data indicated some form of distribution effect. This appears to be contrary to the findings of Scholes who found no relationship between size of secondary offering and price movement. In part, Kraus and Stoll concluded that this could be due to

FIGURE 17

Relative Price Performance for 345 Blocks on Plus Ticks

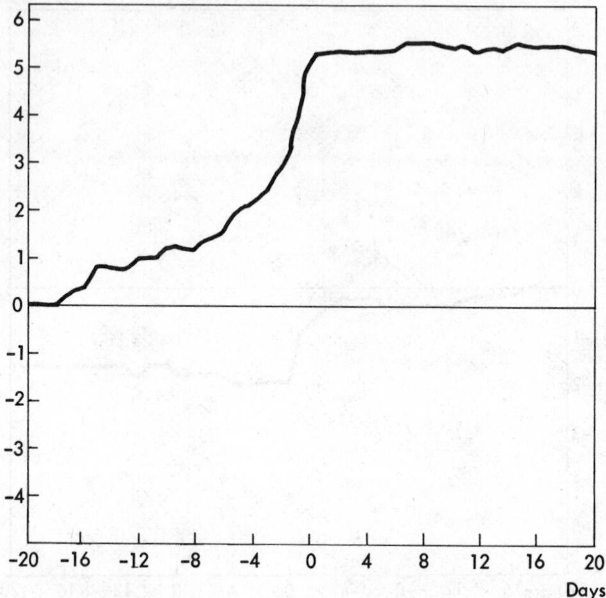

Source: After Kraus and Stoll, "Price Impact of Block Trading."

different institutional arrangements, such as commissions, for secondary distributions and block trades.

THE STRONG FORM OF THE EFFICIENT MARKET–RANDOM WALK HYPOTHESIS; SURVEY OF EVIDENCE

Overview

The strong form of the efficient market–random walk hypothesis holds that even highly sophisticated research cannot produce consistently superior investment performance because present stock prices embody all that is known or knowable about a company.

Miller tested this question by analyzing low P/E stock portfolios versus high over a 17-year period for over 300 companies. The evidence suggests that some bias exists in favor of low P/E companies, i.e., the market was not correctly evaluating their prospects for superior market performance in the test period. Breen performed a similar test, using low P/E stocks and randomly selected portfolios. He also found that low P/E stocks produce superior performance over a 14-year period.

The accuracy of security analysts' forecasts was analyzed by Diefenback, who examined over 1,200 specific buy or sell recommendations of institutional research firms. The results caused him to question whether institutional research performs better than random selection, or whether the market somehow reacts in anticipation of publication of institutional research reports. Niederhoffer and Regan analyzed the change in stock prices relative to earnings changes which were significantly higher or lower than those forecasted. They found substantial evidence of drastic price changes in cases where security analysts' earnings forecasts were wide of the mark.

Friend, Blume, and Crockett analyzed the performance of 136 mutual funds versus randomly selected portfolios of NYSE stocks with corresponding betas. They found mixed evidence with mutual funds being outperformed by the random portfolios with lower betas, and mutual funds outperforming the random portfolios with higher betas. Black tested the performance of the Value Line stock-ranking system covering some 1,400 stocks. He concluded that traditional methods of security analysis are superior to random selection. Kaplan and Weil also tested stock performance, but used beta as the control rather than the Value Line expected performance ranking. They concluded that the performance of their high beta portfolios supported the efficient market–random walk hypothesis.

Wallich focused on the wide stock price gyrations in the 1968–70 period and found such market swings were a challenge to the efficient market thesis that stock prices are efficiently determined. Kuehner found similar evidence for the 30 companies in the Dow Jones Industrial Index during the 1971–73 period.

Morton examined the relationship between risk and realized investor yields for some 400 companies. His data suggested that, using stock price fluctuations as a measure of risk, stocks with high risk showed no evidence of providing higher realized returns. Edesess tested the relationship between beta and total return for some 75 managed equity portfolios. He concluded that there was no reward for assuming higher risk or that historical beta was not a measure of risk. Fouse expressed the desirability of integrating conventional financial analysis with the efficient market theory for 500 companies. He found that in a 28-month test period, beta deciles did not predict returns, and he attributed this to the impact of relatively high interest rates. In a more recent 12-month period, however, there was a relatively strong relationship between realized yield and risk as reflected by beta.

Analysis of Studies

Miller—Low P/E Portfolios versus High

Miller focused on low P/E multiple stocks versus high P/E multiple stocks.[58] His study raises questions about the efficiency of the market

[58] Paul F. Miller, Jr., *Institutional Service Report—Monthly Review* (Philadelphia: Drexel & Co. Inc., November 1965).

with respect to discounting future prospects. It covered annual data for the 1948–64 period for all companies in the S & P's Compustat tapes having sales over $150 million per year in any given year. The number of companies grew consistently in the period from 110 in 1948 to 334 in 1964.

P/E multiples were computed by using year-end stock market prices and calendar year (or fiscal year) earnings. The companies were ranked in five groups or quintiles for each year end. Table 11 summarizes the data and shows a strong tendency for price performance to vary inversely with the P/E multiple.

TABLE 11

Average Price Increase per Year

P/E Quintile	*Price Increase*
1st (high P/E)	7.7%
2d	9.2
3d	12.0
4th	12.8
5th (low P/E)	18.4

Source: After Miller, *Institutional Service Report.*

The lowest P/E quintile group had an average price performance which ranked first in 12 of the 17 years. In contrast, the highest P/E quintile group ranked last, i.e., fifth in 8 of the 17 years or 47 percent of the time. Distribution of the yearly results is shown in Table 12.

TABLE 12

Price Performance in Subsequent Year of Stock Ranked by Year-end P/E Multiple Quintiles (1948–64)

	Yearly Price Performance Ranking				
P/E Quintile	*1st*	*2d*	*3d*	*4th*	*5th*
1st (high P/E)	1	3	2	3	8
2d	1	1	2	11	2
3d	1	5	7	1	3
4th	2	7	4	2	2
5th (low P/E)	12	1	2	0	2
	17	17	17	17	17

Source: After Miller, *Institutional Service Report.*

Similar results were obtained for all three-year and five-year periods in the 1948–64 span. Miller concluded

> We think that the results of this study support our contention that price-earnings ratios are indeed an important consideration in portfolio management and research direction. However, much further work needs to

be done to determine why this bias has been so consistently present in favor of low price-earnings ratio groups.[59]

Breen—Low P/E Portfolios versus High

Breen investigated performance of low price-earnings ratio stock portfolios against randomly selected portfolios, using the 1,400 company S & P's Compustat data for the 1953–66 period.[60] After eliminating all stocks with less than 10 percent compound growth in earnings per share for the prior five years, two test groups of 10 stocks each were selected each January and sold the following January, i.e., a one-year holding period was used.

Return consisted of market price appreciation and dividends. Portfolio 1 consisted of the 10 stocks with the lowest P/E multiples relative to the entire market. Portfolio 2 consisted of the 10 stocks having the lowest P/E multiples in their respective industries. A control portfolio was made up of 10 randomly selected stocks. The results are given in Table 13.

TABLE 13
Compound Return from Low P/E Portfolios (1953–68)

	Low P/E Relative to Market		*Low P/E Relative to Industry*	
Year	*Compound Return*	*Percentage Random Portfolio with Lower Return*	*Compound Return*	*Percentage Random Portfolio with Lower Return*
1953	19.3%	95%	13.3%	95%
1954	57.5	95	92.8	95
1955	45.2	95	35.5	95
1956	19.4	90	7.7	65
1957	−9.9	45	−15.6	20
1958	112.6	95	72.6	95
1959	102.9	95	61.1	95
1960	13.7	90	12.1	90
1961	155.2	95	36.1	70
1962	−4.2	95	−19.8	35
1963	25.5	75	33.8	90
1964	26.1	80	26.7	80
1965	50.5	80	22.0	15
1966	3.4	85	6.1	90
Average	37.5	—	23.9	—

Source: After Breen, "Low Price-Earnings Ratios."

Breen concluded that "low price earnings multiples measured either relative to the whole population, or to industry classification, when com-

[59] Ibid., p. 5.

[60] William Breen, "Low Price-Earnings Ratios and Industry Relatives," *Financial Analysts Journal*, July–August 1969, pp. 125–27.

bined with a control on average past growth in earnings, give portfolio performance which in most years is superior to the performance of randomly selected stocks."[61]

Diefenback—Research Advice versus Performance

Diefenback examined the one-year market performance of stocks previously recommended by the institutional research departments of 24 brokerage and advisory firms.[62] Some 1,200 specific buy recommendations received in the November 1967–May 1969 period were evaluated by measuring market performance over the subsequent 52 weeks relative to the S & P's Industrial Index. See Table 14.

TABLE 14

52-Week Market Performance of Buy Recommendations Received in November 1967–May 1969 Period

Broker or Investment Advisor	*Number of Buy Recommendations*	*Mean Price Change*	*Percentage Out-performing S&P's 425 Industrials*	*Mean Performance Differential from S&P's 425 Industrials*
A	12	+24.6%	75%	+25.9%
B	11	+ 6.7	36	+13.8
C	26	+ 1.8	54	+13.7
D	5	− 1.6	60	+11.8
E	12	+ 8.9	50	+11.6
F	288	+10.8	56	+ 9.8
G	49	+ 3.5	51	+ 6.9
H	192	+ 5.8	47	+ 5.9
I	13	+ 0.7	38	+ 5.7
J	91	+ 3.2	48	+ 4.3
K	59	+ 7.2	53	+ 4.0
L	24	− 1.5	50	+ 0.1
M	21	− 8.0	48	− 0.2
N	39	−13.9	46	− 1.6
O	147	−11.1	39	− 4.0
P	67	− 9.6	43	− 4.5
Q	39	−11.4	36	− 4.9
R	33	−10.7	39	− 6.3
S	14	−18.7	21	−11.1
T	23	−21.6	35	−11.7
U	9	−25.5	11	−13.4
V	8	−26.0	0	−19.3
W	9	−29.5	22	−21.3
X	18	−38.8	17	−25.3
Aggregate: All sources	1,209	− 0.3	47	+ 2.7

Source: After Diefenback, "How Good Is Institutional Brokerage Research?"

[61] Ibid., p. 127.

[62] Robert E. Diefenback, C.F.A., "How Good Is Institutional Brokerage Research?" *Financial Analysts Journal*, January–February 1972, pp. 55–60.

Diefenback concluded

> it is apparent that this group of investment recommendations did not in the aggregate provide a useful universe from which to select investment ideas. Whether or not these recommendations performed statistically better or worse than random selection is not demonstrated; but there would certainly seem to be little to choose between this group of recommendations and a random selection process.[63]

He also examined the relatively scarce number of sell recommendations received, which are summarized in Table 15. He also examined six

TABLE 15
52-Week Performance of Sell Recommendations Received in November 1967–May 1969 Period

Broker or Investment Advisor	*Number of Sell Recom-mendations*	*Mean Price Change*	*Percentage Out-performing S&P's 425 Industrials*	*Mean Performance Differential from S&P's 425 Industrials*
H.	4	−39.4%	0%	−28.1%
O.	11	−27.4	9	−19.6
S.	3	−24.4	0	−14.2
P.	14	−16.6	36	− 9.1
D.	3	−31.1	67	− 3.7
F.	11	− 3.9	45	− 0.6
Aggregate: All sources. . . .	46	−18.7%	26%	−11.2%

Source: After Diefenback, "How Good Is Institutional Brokerage Research?"

months' performance in the strong bull market of early 1968 and found buy recommendations averaged 16.5 percent better than the S & P's 425. In contrast, buy recommendations averaged 2.6 percent in the six months ending in the market trough of May 1969.

Diefenback raised some fundamental questions, including:

> 1. Are the random walk theorists correct? Is it not possible to obtain above-average performance results by applying a sound sense of values, strong reasoning power and a well-disciplined mind to relevant facts?
> 2. Does the time required to prepare a good investment idea for market permit recognition to spread to the point where no value remains in the idea when it finally appears in finished form?[64]

---

[63] Ibid., p. 56.
[64] Ibid., p. 60.

Niederhoffer and Regan—EPS Forecasts versus Market Price Changes

Niederhoffer and Regan state that "In their search for the philosopher's stone, security analysts have found that stock price fluctuations are closely linked to earnings changes."[65] This was brought out forcefully by Niederhoffer and Regan's examination of the 1970–71 market performance of 1,253 NYSE common stocks to test the linkage between EPS changes and market price changes. The 50 best and 50 worst companies in market price performance in 1970 are listed in Tables 16 and 17. The tables also show actual 1969 EPS and estimated EPS for 1970. The latter was the median forecast of leading financial institutions as published in S & P's "Earnings Forecaster."

Niederhoffer and Regan concluded that the most important factor separating the best from the worst performers in market price was profitability, i.e., EPS changes. They noted that security analysts "consistently *underestimated* the earnings gains of the top 50 and just as consistently *overestimated* the same data for the bottom 50."

As shown in Figure 18, the security analysts' consensus had forecasted growth in earnings per share for the top 50 companies averaging 8 percent versus an actual increase of 21 percent. A subsequent rise in market price of 48 percent was recorded. The forecasts for the bottom 50 companies called for 15 percent growth in EPS versus an actual change of −83 percent. Market prices declined by 57 percent.

Tables 16 and 17 show the specific data for each of the 50 companies in the top group and the bottom group. In order to analyze the data on a more comparable basis and avoid statistical problems such as occur when the base year is small, the estimated EPS changes and actual EPS changes were normalized by price. Thus, earnings changes were expressed per $1 of market price. Hence, a rise of $.50 in EPS would be $.10 per $1.00 of price for a $5.00 stock but only $.01 for a $50.00 stock. Niederhoffer and Regan concluded that stock price changes were strongly influenced by EPS changes, both in absolute terms and relative to the consensus of security analysts' forecasts and that "it is clear that an accurate earnings forecast is of enormous value in stock selection."

Friend, Blume, and Crockett—Mutual Funds versus Random Portfolios

Friend, Blume, and Crocket analyzed the performance of 136 mutual funds in the 1960–68 period in comparison with hypothetical portfolios made up of NYSE listed stocks.[66] The latter were selected randomly

[65] Victor Niederhoffer and Patrick J. Regan, "Earnings Changes, Analysts' Forecasts and Stock Prices," *Financial Analysts Journal*, May–June 1972, pp. 65–71.

[66] Irwin Friend, Marshall Blume, and Jean Crockett, *Mutual Funds and Other Institutional Investors*, a Twenty Century Fund Study (New York: McGraw-Hill, 1970). Used with permission of McGraw-Hill Book Company.

TABLE 16

Fifty Best Percentage Price Changes in 1970

	Earnings Per Share					
	Actual 1969	Est. 1970	Actual 1970	Change Per $ of Price Est.	Change Per $ of Price Actual	Stock Price, Actual % Change
1. Overnight Transportation	$1.47	$1.47	$2.58	+ .000	+ .092	+125.0%
2. Coca Cola Bottling, N. Y.	1.08	1.18	1.30	+ .007	+ .015	+ 84.2
3. Bates Manufacturing	.02	NA	1.28	NA	+ .163	+ 72.6
4. General Cigar	2.24	2.30	3.01	+ .003	+ .041	+ 70.5
5. Texas East. Transmission	2.40	2.50	2.70	+ .003	+ .009	+ 70.5
6. Credithrift Financial	1.07	NA	1.15	NA	+ .007	+ 63.6
7. Green Shoe Mfg.	1.93	2.20	2.60	+ .014	+ .035	+ 63.6
8. Pittston Co.	1.11	1.67	2.20	+ .021	+ .040	+ 63.6
9. Campbell Red Lake Mining	.73	.65	.48	− .005	− .014	+ 62.3
10. Blue Bell	3.13	3.70	3.81	+ .017	+ .021	+ 60.0
11. Collins & Aikman	2.47	2.50	2.61	+ .001	+ .006	+ 59.2
12. Gamble-Skogmo	2.66	2.60	3.08	− .003	+ .019	+ 57.1
13. Amerada Hess	2.41	2.55	3.22	+ .005	+ .027	+ 56.0
14. Giant Portland Cement	.71	NA	1.07	NA	+ .042	+ 55.1
15. AMF, Inc.	1.85	2.00	2.05	+ .008	+ .011	+ 54.7
16. Rubbermaid, Inc.	1.28	1.40	1.44	+ .005	+ .007	+ 54.2
17. Cone Mills Corp.	.97	1.20	1.51	+ .017	+ .039	+ 53.6
18. Graniteville Co.	1.29	1.30	2.07	+ .001	+ .051	+ 52.5
19. Keebler	2.01	2.10	2.95	+ .002	+ .024	+ 51.8
20. Interco	3.13	2.80	3.31	− .012	+ .007	+ 51.6
21. M. Lowenstein & Sons	2.69	2.75	2.58	+ .003	− .005	+ 51.2
22. Maytag	1.62	1.70	1.70	+ .004	+ .004	+ 51.1
23. Cabot Corp.	2.75	2.95	3.33	+ .007	+ .019	+ 49.6
24. MAPCO	1.72	1.80	1.97	+ .005	+ .015	+ 48.9
25. Dr. Pepper	.50	.60	.61	+ .003	+ .004	+ 48.4
26. Pacific Intermt. Express	1.05	1.25	.94	+ .013	− .007	+ 48.4
27. International Utilities	1.80	NA	2.40	NA	+ .025	+ 47.2
28. U. S. Tobacco	1.69	1.95	2.04	+ .014	+ .019	+ 46.4
29. Russ Togs	1.02	1.30	1.47	+ .019	+ .030	+ 46.3
30. American Ship Building	1.10	1.25	1.42	+ .008	+ .017	+ 45.3
31. Liggett & Meyers	2.92	3.00	3.86	+ .002	+ .029	+ 45.2
32. Genuine Parts	1.40	1.57	1.73	+ .007	+ .013	+ 45.0
33. General Portland Cement	1.36	1.40	1.40	+ .002	+ .002	+ 44.9
34. Cudahy	1.77	NA	2.01	NA	+ .019	+ 44.1
35. Cleveland Cliffs Iron	3.81	3.90	4.73	+ .002	+ .023	+ 43.8
36. Getty Oil	5.20	5.00	5.20	− .004	.000	+ 43.8
37. American Water Works	1.11	NA	1.29	NA	+ .019	+ 42.7
38. Lone Star Gas	1.58	1.75	1.99	+ .009	+ .022	+ 42.5
39. Broadway Hale Stores	1.99	2.40	2.04	+ .010	+ .001	+ 42.3
40. Kings Dept. Store	.73	.73	.85	.000	+ .013	+ 41.9
41. Northwest Industries	d .23	1.40	2.21	+ .132	+ .197	+ 41.4
42. Weyerhaeuser	2.11	2.35	1.87	+ .006	− .006	+ 41.4
43. Quaker State Oil	1.42	1.65	1.67	+ .009	+ .010	+ 41.1
44. Bucyrus Erie	1.84	1.70	1.72	− .007	− .006	+ 40.1
45. Louisiana Land & Explor.	2.80	2.90	2.93	+ .002	+ .003	+ 40.0
46. Copeland Refrigeration	2.30	2.40	3.50	+ .003	+ .031	+ 38.7
47. Philip Morris	2.58	3.00	3.36	+ .012	+ .022	+ 38.5
48. Kaufman & Broad	.80	1.00	1.12	+ .004	+ .007	+ 37.7
49. Helmerich & Payne	1.55	1.70	1.72	+ .009	+ .011	+ 37.5
50. Safeway Stores	2.01	2.10	2.70	+ .004	+ .028	+ 37.4

NA = not available. d = deficit.

Source: Victor Niederhoffer and Patrick J. Regan, "Earnings Changes, Analysts Forecasts and Stock Prices," *Financial Analysts Journal*, May–June 1972, p. 66, Table 1.

from NYSE stocks with betas corresponding to those in each of the mutual funds. Table 18 summarizes some of the key data from this extensive investigation.

The equally weighted portfolio assumes an equal dollar amount invested in each security included. Portfolio variant #1 was selected on the basis of each stock's probability of inclusion being proportional to the aggregate dollar amount of its shares outstanding. In one sense, this was a market-weighted portfolio because once selected, each stock was apportioned an equal amount of dollar investment. Variant #2 corresponds to #1 in selection of the securities. But, once selected, the amount invested was proportional to each stock's total market value.

TABLE 17

Fifty Worse Percentage Price Changes in 1970

	Earnings Per Share			Change Per $ of Price		Stock Price,
	Actual 1969	Est. 1970	Actual 1970	Est.	Actual	Actual % Change
1. Penn Central	$ .18	$2.00	$d 13.67	+.064	−.490	−77.9%
2. University Computing	2.58	NA	d 1.28	NA	−.040	−77.7
3. Electronic Mem. & Mag.	.93	1.05	d 2.12	+.003	−.075	−76.9
4. Fairchild Camera	.23	1.00	d 4.40	+.008	−.050	−74.7
5. Scientific Resources	d .78	NA	d 1.40	NA	−.050	−72.7
6. Transcontinental Invest.	.60	1.30	d .62E	+.029	−.051	−72.5
7. FAS International	.92	1.10	.39	+.008	−.023	−71.1
8. Republic Corp.	1.48	2.75	.23	+.046	−.045	−68.2
9. Sonesta	.27	NA	d 1.17	NA	−.112	−68.0
10. Automation Industries	.81	1.20	.22	+.032	−.049	−62.9
11. GAC Corp.	3.22	4.00	1.62	+.013	−.026	−62.9
12. Sprague Electric	.43	.75	d 1.78	+.012	−.083	−61.8
13. Memorex	1.87	2.50	.83	+.004	−.007	−61.0
14. Ward Foods	1.84	NA	.40	NA	−.053	−60.6
15. Whittaker Corp.	1.51	1.25	.28	−.014	−.067	−59.2
16. Ling-Temco-Vought	d .05	NA	d 12.73	NA	−.500	−59.1
17. Dictaphone	1.09	1.15	d .74	+.003	−.079	−58.4
18. MEI Corp.	d .19	NA	d .05	NA	+.012	−58.3
19. Smith International	1.63	1.75	.98	+.010	−.016	−58.2
20. Standard Pressed Steel	.73	.70	d 1.10	−.002	−.139	−58.1
21. High Voltage Engr.	.21	.25	d 1.00	+.002	−.057	−57.4
22. Palm Beach Co.	1.01	NA	.10	NA	−.046	−57.2
23. Bourn's Inc.	1.46	1.55	1.01	+.004	−.019	−57.1
24. Copper Range	6.80	10.00	4.07	+.050	−.042	−56.9
25. North American Philips	2.49	2.65	1.00	+.003	−.027	−56.4
26. Deltec International	.96	NA	d 1.24	NA	−.198	−56.2
27. Control Data	3.08	2.50	d .40	−.005	−.030	−56.1
28. Faberge, Inc.	1.67	1.70	.41	+.001	−.038	−56.1
29. Hamilton Watch	.68	NA	d 5.52	NA	−5.82	−55.8
30. Dillingham Corp.	1.15	1.25	d .51	+.004	−.063	−55.5
31. Berkey Photo	1.13	1.00	.41	−.007	−.041	−55.4
32. Fuqua Industries	1.90	2.02	1.48	+.004	−.015	−54.8
33. Equity Funding	1.91	NA	2.21	NA	+.005	−54.7
34. Kentucky Fried Chicken	1.24	1.70	1.24	+.011	.000	−53.8
35. Seaboard World Air.	d .43	NA	d .32	NA	+.007	−52.8
36. Electronic Associates	d .85	NA	d 1.95	NA	−.110	−52.5
37. Athlone Industries	3.31	NA	1.33	NA	−.072	−52.1
38. Crowell-Collier	1.35	1.44	.55	+.003	−.031	−51.9
39. Microdot, Inc.	1.95	2.05	1.14	+.004	−.030	−51.9
40. Arlan's Dept. Stores	1.43	1.40	d 4.40	−.002	−.315	−51.4
41. National Cash Register	2.11	2.25	1.37	+.002	−.009	−51.1
42. Varian Associates	.93	1.00	.68	+.002	−.009	−51.1
43. Diversified Industries	1.33	1.80	.01	+.026	−.072	−50.7
44. Norlin Corp.	3.31	NA	2.20	NA	−.043	−50.7
45. Budget Industries	.96	1.50	d .41	+.016	−.040	−50.0
46. HCA Industries	d .15	NA	d 1.88	NA	−.204	−50.0
47. Boeing	.47	2.00	1.02	+.054	+.020	−49.3
48. Lionel	.21	.80	.08	+.066	−.015	−49.3
49. Callahan Mining	.11	NA	d .06	NA	−.009	−49.1
50. Interstate Stores	1.70	2.00	.25	+.011	−.054	−49.1

NA = not available. d = deficit. E = preliminary earnings report.

Source: Victor Niederhoffer and Patrick J. Regan, "Earnings Changes, Analysts Forecasts and Stock Prices," *Financial Analysts Journal*, May–June 1972, p. 68, Table 2.

FIGURE 18

Median Changes: Forecasted Earnings, Actual Earnings, and Stock Market Prices

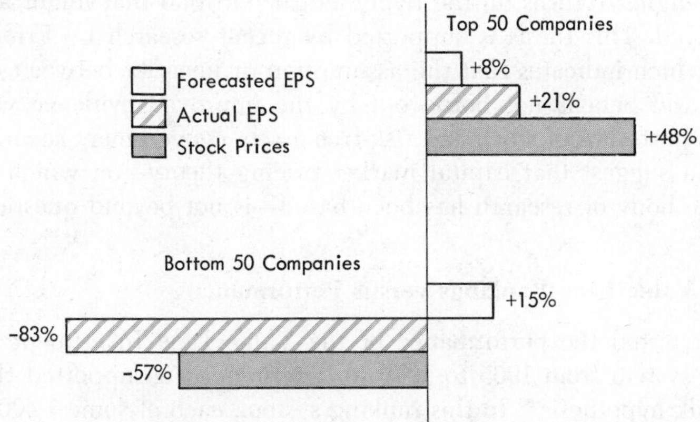

Source: After Niederhoffer and Regan, "Earning's Changes."

This was, thus close to a market-value portfolio.

Among the key findings of this study were:

1. Low risk (beta 0.5–0.7). The randomly selected portfolios outperformed the mutual funds in all categories.
2. Medium risk (beta 0.7–0.9). Mutual funds outperformed two of the three random portfolios.
3. High risk (beta 0.9–1.1). Mutual funds outperformed two of the three random portfolios.

On balance the evidence of mutual funds outperforming randomly selected portfolios differs from a number of earlier studies. To a large extent, such earlier studies were based on caiptal market theory which endeavors to equilibrate differences in risk—as measured by beta—as

TABLE 18

Return from Dividends and Market Appreciation Mutual Funds versus Random Portfolios (1960–68)

			Random Portfolios		
				Proportionately Weighted	
Risk Class	*Beta Coefficient*	*Mutual Funds*	*Equally Weighted*	*Variant #1*	*Variant #2*
Low	0.5–0.7	9.1%	12.8%	11.6%	10.1%
Medium	0.7–0.9	10.6	13.1	9.7	8.4
High	0.9–1.1	13.5	13.7	10.3	9.2

Source: Friend, Blume, and Crockett, *Mutual Funds.*

between the actual and hypothetical portfolios through the assumption of ending borrowing *risk-free* funds at the risk-free rate, i.e., government bonds. This assumption embodies an element of unreality and tends to achieve higher returns on the hypothetical portfolio that might actually be attained. This thesis is supported by recent research by Friend and Blume which indicates that the assumption of linearity between ex post returns and beta is not borne out by the improved evidence with respect to portfolios of stock and risk-free assets (government securities).[67] The data suggest that capital market pricing theory—on which a considerable body of research has been based—is not beyond question.

Black—Value Line Rankings versus Performance

Black tested the performance of the Value Line Investment Survey ranking system from 1965 to 1970 to determine if it supported the random walk hypothesis.[68] In this ranking system, each of some 1,400 stocks is ranked according to expected performance for the next 12 months. Each stock is assigned a rank from I thru V as shown in Table 19.

TABLE 19
Distribution of Stocks by Expected Performance Ranking Group

Expected Performance Ranking Group	*Approximate Number of Stocks*
I—Best	100
II—Above average	300
III—Average	600
IV—Below average	300
V—Poorest	100
Total	1,400

Source: Black, "Tests of Value Line Ranking System."

The rankings are based on a fundamental analysis of each company, including an evaluation of 10 years of data in regard to earnings and market prices. Black noted that the rankings tend to assign high ranks to stocks with:

1. Low P/E ratios relative to past averages and to the markets' current P/E ratio.
2. Quarterly earnings having "upward momentum" relative to the market.
3. Upward price momentum.

[67] Irwin Friend and Marshall Blume, "A New Look at the Capital Asset Pricing Model," *Journal of Finance*, March 1973.

[68] Fischer Black, "Yes, Virginia, There Is Hope: Tests of the Value Line Ranking System," University of Chicago, Center for Research in Security Prices, May 1971.

Relative weights assigned each of the three factors are based on a cross-sectional regression of past data. Using time-series tests to evaluate consistency of performance, Black found that Group I performed better than Group V in each of the five years and that "the probability of this happening by chance is one in 32."[69]

Additional tests were made of the data on a monthly basis. This involved constructing portfolios of all stocks in each ranking group weighted equally. Then, at the end of each month, a portion of all stocks that had gone up were sold, while portions of stocks that had declined were purchased.

Revising the portfolio on a monthly basis produced about 10 percent better return for Rank I than annual revisions and some −10 percent less for Group V. A statistical test of significance (*t* test) indicated that "The possibility that this could have occurred by chance is one in 10,000 . . . the success of the rankings was very consistent over time." Interestingly, the average betas for the groups were Rank I: 1.11; II: 1.03; III: 0.98; IV: 0.96; and V: 1.03.

Black states

> In conclusion, it does appear that there is hope that traditional methods of portfolio management and security analysis can succeed. However, I must continue to maintain that it is a rather small hope. The Value Line Ranking System is one of only two or three clear examples I have seen that show significant performance over a reasonable period of time.

Figure 19 reflects the record of the five Value Line ranking groups in the 1965–73 period.

Kaplan and Weil—Beta versus Value Line Performance

Kaplan and Weil tested the beta risk measurement concept against the conventional performance concept in the Value Line stock selection contest.[70] The Value Line conducted a contest in which contestants selected a portfolio of 25 stocks from the Value Line List of 1,400 stocks. Contestants' portfolios were rated on the basis of the average percentage price increase of their 25 stocks in the six months ending in February 1973.

Kaplan and Weil said

> As believers in the efficient market theory, we did not think we can pick a portfolio of 25 stocks that will significantly and consistently outperform other portfolios of equal risk. . . . Therefore, we chose to enter the contest with two portfolios, one from each end of the risk spectrum.

[69] Ibid., p. 4.

[70] Robert S. Kaplan and Roman L. Weil, "Risk and the Value Line Contest," *Financial Analysts Journal,* July–August 1973, pp. 56–61.

FIGURE 19

Record of Value Line Ranks for Next 12 Months Performance 1965–73

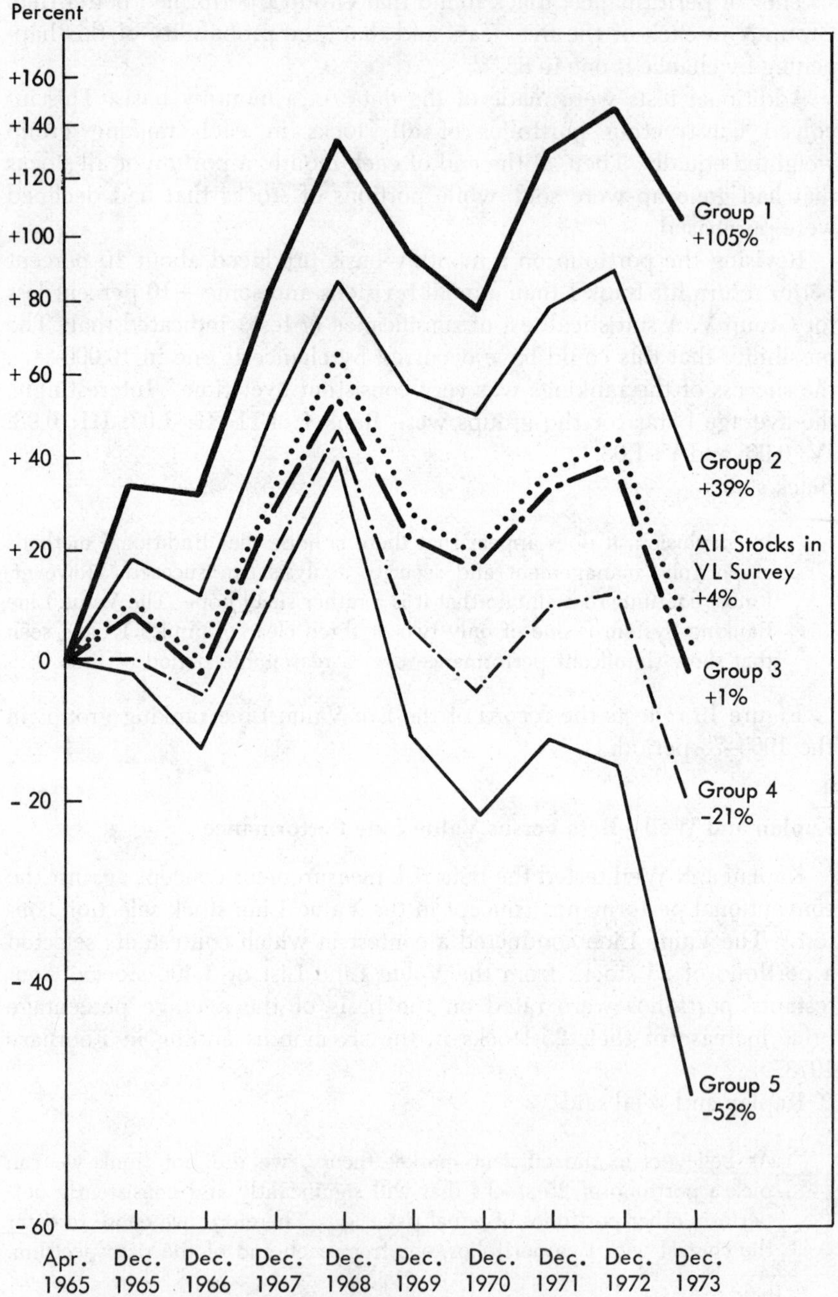

Source: Value Line "Selection and Opinion," January 25, 1974.

They reasoned that the high-beta portfolio should increase faster in a rising market. Conversely, if stock prices generally declined, the low beta portfolio would do relatively well. Kaplan and Weil's two portfolios were distributed as seen in Table 20.

TABLE 20

Expected Performance of Companies in High Beta and Low Beta Portfolios

Value Line Expected Performance Ranking Group	*High Beta*	*Low Beta*
I	1	2
II	7	7
III	10	9
IV	4	6
V	3	1
Total	25	25
Average ranking	3.04	2.88
Average beta	2.13	0.21

Source: After Kaplan and Weil, "Risk and Value Line Contest."

During the six month's contest period, the Value Line Index of some 1,400 stocks declined 8.8 percent. The Kaplan-Weil *low* beta portfolio increased 3.8 percent which placed it in the top 2.3 percent of the more than 89,000 contest portfolios. The *high* beta portfolio declined 22.9 percent and was in the lowest 0.6 percent of all portfolios.

TABLE 21

Performance versus Betas

Betas by Quintile	*Average Beta*	*Average Price Change*
1st	0.48	+ 1.4%
2d	0.79	− 2.8
3d	1.02	− 6.6
4th	1.29	−10.5
5th	1.82	−15.0

Source: After Kaplan and Weil, "Risk and Value Line Contest."

Kaplan and Weil noted that systematic risk is also reflected in the overall performance of all portfolios as shown in Table 21. They concluded

> that the performance of these five portfolios is consistent with their differing risks and the realized market return over the contest period. . . . Detailed investigation of individual securities does not appear to pay off. While such investigation may turn up stocks that appear to be mildly under- or overvalued, the overall performance of a diversified

portfolio of stocks is dominated by the systematic risk of the portfolio and market movements.[71]

Wallich—Stock Price Gyrations versus Intrinsic Values

Wallich expressed concern relative to the wide fluctuations in stock market prices in recent years. He noted that

> recent experience is a challenge to the "dart throwing" theory. It is an experience that confirms the wisdom of traditional investment policies, as I believe these policies are practiced by trust officers all over the country. . . . Recent extreme gyrations of some stocks, in my view, seriously question the assertion of the "dart throwing theory" that stocks always are valued at the price that the best analysis suggests.[72]

In reference to the 1968–70 price debacle, Wallich stated "on the contrary, such extreme gyrations seem to show that these stocks were not correctly valued and that the application of wisdom and good sense could discover this."

Kuehner noted that more recent evidence in support of Wallich's thesis is found in market gyrations in the 1971–73 period. The 30 companies included in the Dow Jones Industrial Index are among the world's largest with assets and sales in the hundreds of millions up to several billions of dollars. These firms are widely held and closely followed. Thus, under the efficient market hypothesis, one might assume that prices of these stocks at any given time would provide valid evidence of each firm's "intrinsic value." Data in Table 22 raise question as to the market's ability to do so with any degree of stability. The table shows the price spread from low to high for each stock. Thus, if a stock's price ranged from a low of 30 to a high of 40, its price spread would be 33 percent. Price spreads in the table range from a minimum of 19 percent (General Motors in 1972) to a maximum of 173 percent (Chrysler in 1973). In 34 of the 90 cases, price fluctuations exceeded 50 percent and 80 of the 90 price fluctuations were 25 percent or more. This raises the question, Did the underlying value of these well-known and established securities really fluctuate in accord with the gyrations in their market prices?

Morton—Relationship between Risk and Investor Returns

Morton tested the efficiency of the market in discounting returns on individual stocks over a future period of 1, 2, and 3 years.[73] For this

[71] Ibid., p. 60.

[72] Henry C. Wallich, "Traditional vs Performance Stock Valuation," *Commercial and Financial Chronicle*, February 18, 1971, pp. 1–5. Used with permission from Commercial and Financial Chronicle, 110 Wall St., New York, NY 10005

[73] Walter A. Morton, "Market Price, Risk and Investor Return," *Commercial and Financial Chronicle*, June 3, 1971, pp. 1–5.

TABLE 22

Price Spread: Low to High Dow Jones 30 Industrials (1971–73)

	1971	*1972*	*1973*
Allied Chemical	48%	29%	72%
Alcoa	94	47	68
American Can	55	36	45
AT&T	32	30	21
American Brands	34	24	51
Anaconda	107	40	70
Bethlehem Steel	51	37	45
Chrysler	36	49	173
DuPont	22	28	40
Eastman Kodak	39	61	47
Esmark	57	31	95
Exxon	23	31	23
General Electric	43	25	38
General Foods	42	54	40
General Motors	24	19	89
Goodyear	29	26	155
Int'l. Harvester	47	51	76
Int'l. Nickel	86	25	40
Int'l. Paper	43	27	73
Johns-Manville	26	52	128
Owens Illinois	62	35	59
Procter & Gamble	45	48	35
Sears Roebuck	41	28	58
Standard Oil of Cal	28	52	37
Texaco	34	34	73
Union Carbide	30	24	77
United Aircraft	84	71	123
U.S. Steel	44	27	43
Westinghouse	16	43	95
Woolworth (F.W.)	57	56	102

Source: Charles D. Kuehner, at New York University Law School Seminar, "Legal Implications of Random Walk Hypothesis," in February 1974.

purpose he studied 400 of the S & P's 425 industrial companies for which complete data were available over the 12-year period 1956–68.

For the 10-year period 1956–66, an index of high-low market price fluctuations was calculated as a measure of instability or risk. Thus, a stock with a low average market price of 5 in 1958 and a high average market price of 10 in 1963 was assigned an index of 2, a high of 30 and a low of 10 was given an index of 3, and so on. Realized investor yields were measured by market appreciation and dividends over the 1965–68 period in six combinations of 1-, 2-, or 3-year holding periods.

Figure 20 shows the relationship between average realized yield and market price instability for each of the 400 S & P's companies. Morton observed that

> the proposition that wide fluctuations mean high returns has no substance in theory or in fact. Investors must still rely on their knowledge

FIGURE 20

Realized Investor Yields versus Market Price Fluctuation for 400 S & P's Industrial Companies

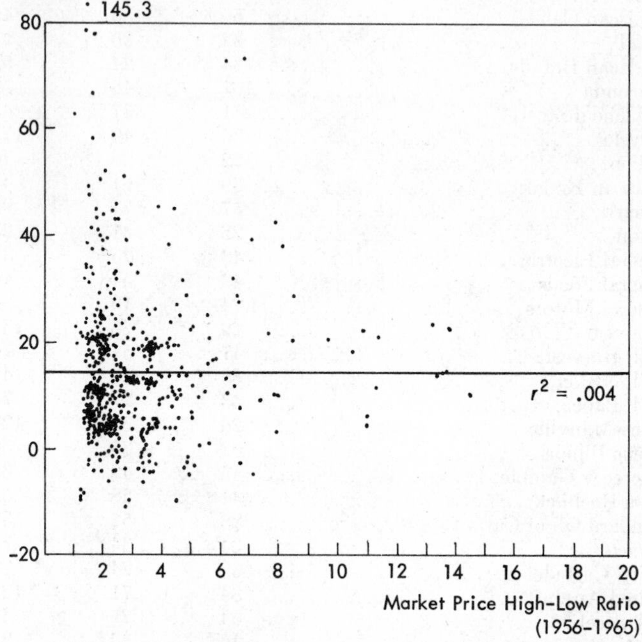

Source: Morton, "Market Price."

and judgment about the reasonably expected dividends and capital gains for individual stocks based on their analysis of the firm and the industry. . . . The source of the error that high risks will yield high returns is an elementary intellectual confusion between the relation of risk to *ex ante,* or expected return, and relation of risk to *ex post,* or realized return. The first proposition that an investor does not take large risks unless he *expects* a large return is a matter of common observation confirmed by fact, logic and data. But the second proposition that the *actual* return realized by investors is necessarily commensurate with the risk taken is an elementary error unsupported by fact, logic or data.[74]

Edesess—Beta versus Portfolio Performance

Edesess noted that the Capital Asset Pricing Model holds that the expected portfolio return is linearly related to expected market returns, with the coefficient of market return in the linear equation expressed

[74] Ibid., p. 15.

as beta.[75] However, he stated that estimates of beta which use data from more than one time period assume the validity of some form of the random walk theory. Being mathematically precise in using the capital asset pricing model, according to Edesess, tells "how to maximize expected *instantaneous* returns for a given value of the statistical variance of the *instantaneous* returns. That's all."

Edesess raised two basic questions with regard to the capital asset pricing model.

1. The assumption that risk, which has many nuances and meanings, can be adequately measured by the statistical variance of the instantaneous return, or by beta.
2. The assumption that beta is constant over time.

He contends that investment management has not come to grips with the problem. Instead, Edesess said, it has "taken a leap to an abstract statement of the problem and, having leaped, we routinely accept our new situation as the starting point for all further work." He concluded that a major task facing investment management is to retreat from that leap.

Edesess studied 75 managed pension funds with regard to total return and historical beta over the 1962–72 period, which constitutes three market cycles (Figure 21), and 145 managed pension funds over the 1966–72 period, covering two market cycles (Figure 22).

Edesess concluded that based on both parametric and nonparametric tests of correlation there was "no evidence of correlation whatsoever" between beta and rate of return. Also he stated that "there was no reward for having had a higher historical beta." He added that either (1) there was no reward for assuming higher risk or (2) historical beta was not a proxy for risk.

Fouse—Integrating Fundamental Security Analysis with Efficient Market Theory

Fouse focused on practical applications of economic, market, and portfolio management theory.[76] He noted that economic theory holds that the value of a security is the discounted value of a future stream of dividends and that the widely used P/E model is a formulation of the traditional dividend model since the P/E is a function of EPS growth rate, payout ratio, and the appropriate discount rate. Fouse cited the

---

[75] Michael Edesess, "Resolved that the Capital Asset Pricing Model Has Little Practical Value," University of Chicago, Seminar on the Analysis of Security Prices, October 1973.

[76] William L. Fouse, "Practical Applications of Economic, Market, and Portfolio Theory," Stanford University Graduate School of Business, 1972 Investment Management Program, July 1972.

FIGURE 21

Managed Equity Portfolios: Total Returns versus Betas 1962–72 (three cycles)

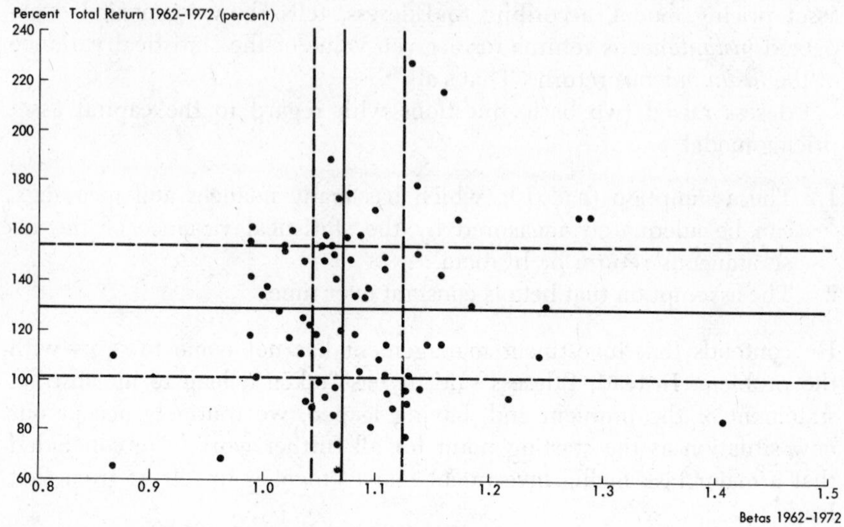

Source: After Edesess, "Resolved that Capital Asset."

need to reconcile conventional financial analysis with the efficient market theory: Given the consensus forecast for the stream of future dividends, common stocks will be efficiently priced in the market relative to the risk-free return plus a premium for risk that cannot be diversified away in portfolios. On this basis and using different proportions of risk, or a combination of stocks plus borrowing, "the market should tend to be so arbitraged that no net expected advantage should exist for one strategy over another."

In this arbitrage process, Fouse stated, the market, which is made up of a large number of well-informed buyers and sellers acting in their own best interest, discounts the future at an efficient rate. And as risk increases, these well-informed investors demand greater returns. On this basis he holds, given consensus expectations of the future, capital market theory provides a quantitative way to estimate market risks—historical beta is used as a proxy for future beta.

Working from this theoretical construct, security analysts in the Wells Fargo Financial Analysis Department were asked to classify stocks as to risk developed from fundamental analysis. These ratings were arranged in eight groups from lowest to highest risk. Fouse found "a perfect match" between these risk ratings and the average betas of each group. Thus, it was concluded that traditional analysis, or accounting measures of risk, are embedded in the market price based risk measure, i.e. beta.

FIGURE 22

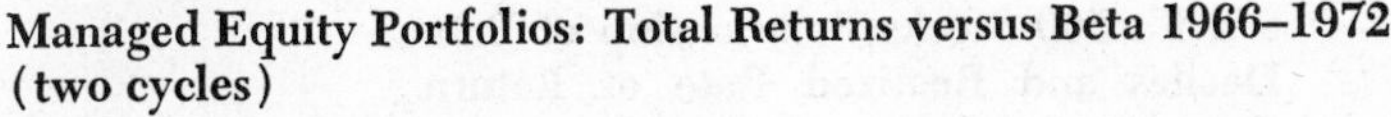

Managed Equity Portfolios: Total Returns versus Beta 1966–1972 (two cycles)

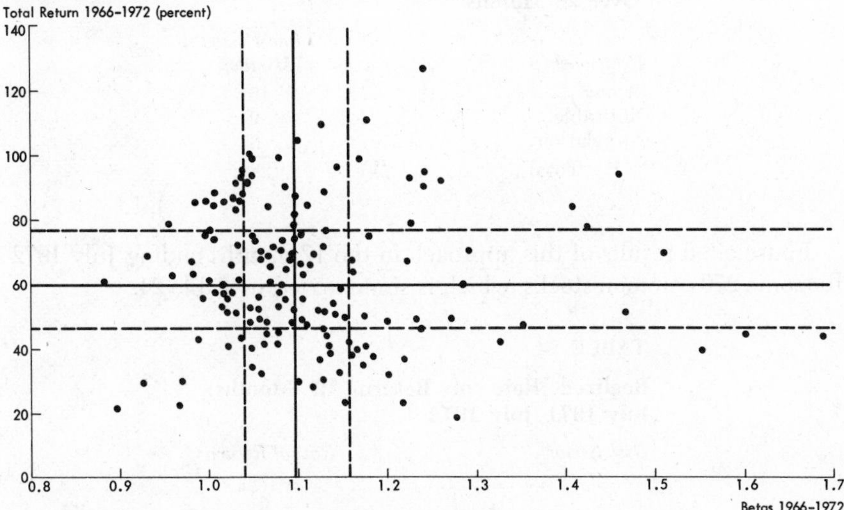

Source: After Edesess, "Resolved that Capital Asset."

As a next step to incorporate this concept into portfolio management, a "market line" was developed to reflect the investors' required discount rate for each risk class. Thus, if the efficient market hypothesis is correct, there is a logical correspondence between implied earnings growth rates and actual forecast. Fouse tested the data for 25 major stocks, using growth estimates provided by a dozen large Wall Street firms. The five-year growth rates implied by the model averaged 10.4 percent. The Wall Street composite was 10.5 percent. R^2 was 0.90. On this basis, an ex ante market line was developed. Fouse pointed out that the realized return on each security would depend upon changes in perceived risk, changes in the market's price for risk, and changes in the consensus forecast of a security.

The concept was tested for 28 months using the beta deciles of the S & P's 500. The relationship between the beta deciles and realized rate of return is shown in Table 23.

"However, for the 28 month period as a whole," Fouse stated, "beta deciles did not predict return. We think because excess return in stocks over borrowing rates [during this time span] were too small for Beta to assert itself." The adoption of this concept by Wells Fargo has meant that "in the area of security analysis we have returned to fundamentals with a vengeance." Careful long-range forecasts are integrated into the market line, and conventional security analysis thereby has a direct interface with modern capital theory.

TABLE 23

S & P's 500 Stocks Relationship of Beta Deciles and Realized Rate of Return Over 28 Months

Relationship	*Time Period (Months)*
Strong	16
Noticable	9
No relation	3
Total	28

Fouse cited results of this approach in the 12 months ending July 1972 for some 270 common stocks, which is summarized in Table 24.

TABLE 24

Realized Rate of Return 12 Months: July 1971–July 1972

Risk Sector	*Rate of Return*
1	+ 7%
2	+ 9
3	+ 7
4	+15
5	+28

Source: Fouse, "Practical Applications."

Friend, Baumol, Murray, and Treynor—Efficiency Revisited

Friend stated "to much of the public, the stock market seems to be a legalized gambling casino. To many economists, the stock market seems endowed with an almost mystical degree of efficiency, even if what is meant by efficiency is not always clear."[77] Which of these two extreme views is correct? Or does neither accord with reality, and the answer lie somewhere in between?

A broad overview of the past half century suggests that there have been numerous occasions when large bodies of investors have been emotionally affected by fads and fashions in Wall Street. Turning back the clock to late October 1929, one might have difficulty in asserting that, at that time, stock market prices were efficiently discounting the future. The same might have been said in March 1932 after the market had plunged by some 80–90 percent.

More recently, in early 1962, stock market ebullience even surpassed that of 1929, but it was relatively short lived. On May 28 a selling panic occurred with share volume reaching the highest level since 1929, thereby wiping out some $21 billion of market values in one day. Shares of many

[77] Irwin Friend, "The Economic Consequences of the Stock Market," *American Economic Association Papers and Proceedings*, May 1972.

of the nation's leading firms dropped by one quarter to one third of their value in less than a week. Even a month later, after the dust had settled and stock prices had stabilized, market volumes reflected widespread disinterest in purchasing even the bluest of the Blue Chips at relative bargain prices.

A similar scenario occurred during the growth stock craze of 1967–68. At that time it was said that stock prices were not only discounting the future—they were discounting the hereafter as well. New issues of relatively unseasoned companies were eagerly gobbled up with prices doubling and tripling or even more during the first week of trading. Many investors—large and small—operated on "the greater fool theory," i.e., to sell the shares later to other investors—whoever they might be. But this did not happen. In the ensuing 18 months, the stock market was hit by wave after wave of selling, much of it reaching panic proportions. As a result, by May of 1970, a pervasive state of disenchantment obtained. As before, shares of many of the nation's leading corporations were discounting not the hereafter but Armageddon. Within a year later most of these same securities were selling 25–50 percent higher and some even more.

This short overview has focused on only a few of the broad price swings that have engulfed the market as a whole. When we look at specific industries or companies the record is even more extreme. How might we explain this apparently irrational behavior of a reputedly rational, all-efficient market?

Friend noted that "one important attribute of an efficient market in which investors are not indifferent to risk is that the risk as perceived by the investor when he is making his decision should correspond fairly closely to the risk which actually materializes." But he also observed that while such measures of risk as the relative stability of return on a stock tend to be reasonably invariant over time and that the empirical evidence generally points to a positive relationship between risk and return, "the results are by no means uniform or strong." After considering several other facets of the problem Friend concludes "it seems clear that no convincing case can be made for the position held by many economists that the stock market possesses a high degree of allocational efficiency, though the market does appear to transmit information rather rapidly."[78]

Baumol noted that "we have all seen cases where the behavior of prices on the stock market has apparently been capricious or even worse, cases where hysteria has magnified largely irrelevant events into controlling influences.[79] Baumol also stated that while most analysis would doubtless agree that the price of a security should be determined,

---

[78] Ibid., p. 218.

[79] Reprinted by permission of the publisher from William J. Baumol, *The Stock Market and Economic Efficiency* (New York: Fordham University Press, 1965) Copyright © 1965 by Fordham University Press, pp. 36–38.

ultimately, by the companies' prospective earnings, "It is not clear, however, how closely the value of future earnings and share prices correspond in practice."

Noting that there is not a sharp and well-defined conflict between two extreme types of influences which account for stock prices, Baumol offers two possible explanations:

1. One explanation gives stock prices as being set systematically and rationally by an economic process which leads prices to approximate the economic value of the shares.
2. Another explanation envisions stock prices as essentially "a speculative and anticipatory phenomenon" in which stock prices are what they are only because of what purchasers and sellers expect them to be."

Murray offered another essentially psychological explanation, "the financial community has a pervasive and highly developed talent for rationalizing its aberrations. When greed overcomes prudence, the arrival of a new era is proclaimed . . . concepts become a substitute for earning power. The compound interest table is banished as earnings growth is projected into the hereafter.[80]

Treynor attributed errors in investment judgment to faulty analysis,

> if investors disagree on the value of a security even when they have the same information, their differences of opinion must be due to errors in analysis. . . . If all—or even a substantial fraction—of these investors make the *same* error, then the independent's assumption is violated, the market consensus can divert significantly from "true" value, and the market ceases to be efficient in the sense of pricing information correctly. Influences that encourage large numbers of investors to make the same error abound.[81]

Implications, Challenge, and Conclusion

In 1970, after the random walk–efficient market hypothesis had been debated for over a decade, Granger stated

> there is still a great deal of controversy over the random walk model of stock market price movement. On the one hand, statisticians continue to provide evidence in favor of the model and, on the other hand, economists and financial analysts continue to state that they do not believe in the correctness of the model.[82]

[80] Roger F. Murray, "Institutionalization of the Stock Market," *Financial Analysis Journal,* March–April 1974, p. 18.

[81] Jack L. Treynor, "Efficient Markets and Fundamental Analysis," *Financial Analysts Journal,* March–April 1974, p. 14.

[82] C. W. J. Granger, "What the Random Walk Model Does NOT Say," *Financial Analysts Journal,* May–June 1970, pp. 91–93.

Granger stated that this problem highlights

> the lack of contact between many of the academic workers and real financial analysts or market operators. One gets an impression of mistrust, partly due to the barrier formed by the different technical languages used by both sides. It is to be hoped that this gap will decrease as each side recognizes the advantages of closer cooperation.

He continued that the output of the academics often have important implications for analysts but that it must be properly understood and assimilated. On the other hand, he indicated that academics need to concentrate more on the actual problems of importance to analysts.

In this chapter an effort has been made to delineate the different points of view and sharpen up the thrust of the arguments on all sides of the spectrum. Regardless of whether one subscribes to the random walk–efficient market hypothesis, we must agree that the dailogue has served a useful purpose. Namely, it has helped to bring the academic and financial communities into closer appreciation of each other's points of view. It has also forced both the technician and the fundamentalist to rethink their premises and methods of evaluating securities. It has likewise posed certain implications and challenges for both.

Implications

Lorie and Hamilton, strong proponents of the efficient market–random walk hypothesis, summarize its implications in three different areas:[83]

1. Value of the Analyst. "The most general implication of the efficient market hypothesis is that most security analysis is logically incomplete and valueless." They asserted that for "true believers in efficient markets" an analyst's recommendation to buy or sell must be predicated on a significant difference between the analyst's views and those of other investors whose opinions have established the stock's current market price.

2. Economics of Scale in Security Analysis and Portfolio Management. The question of efficient allocation of human resources is also stepped up by increasing competition. Analysis of securities "costs about the same whether the amount available for investment is $1,000 or $1 billion." Thus if such endeavors could produce superior returns of, say, 0.5 percent, they state this would produce "additional returns of $5 on the investment of $1,000 and of $5 million on the investment of $1 billion." On this basis they conclude that security research "might make sense for large financial institutions having billions of dollars to manage, while it would not make sense for investors with smaller sums."

3. Consistently Superior Performance. Another implication of the efficient markets theory is "the extreme unlikelihood that one can con-

[83] Lorie and Hamilton, *The Stock Market.*

sistently earn superior rates of return by analyzing public information in conventional ways." Thus, Lorie and Hamilton suggest that "the only hope for superiority in results like in seeking unique ways of forming expectations about the prospects for individual companies."

Challenge to Security Analysis

Another leading advocate of the efficient market–random walk hypothesis has specified two challenges to conventional security analysts:

1. Challenge to the Chartist. Fama states that

> if the random walk model is a valid description of reality, the work of the chartist is of no real value in stock market analysis . . . the only way the chartist can vindicate his position is to show that he can *consistently* use his techniques to make better than chance predictions of stock prices. It is not enough for him to talk mystically about patterns that he sees in the data. He must show that he can consistently use these patterns to make meaningful predictions of future prices.[84]

2. Challenge to the Fundamental Analyst. Fama also suggests that "if the random walks theory is valid and if security exchanges are 'efficient' markets, then stock prices in any point in time will represent good estimates of intrinsic or fundamental values." On this basis, he concludes that additional fundamental analysis is of value only when the analyst has information or new insights not already embedded in a stock's current market price. Thus, "if the analyst has neither better insights nor better information, he may as well forget about fundamental analysis and choose securities by some random selection procedure."[85]

Malkiel—A Middle Road

Malkiel has a slightly different point of view, "I walk a middle road. While I believe that investors must reconsider their faith in Super-Analysts, I am not as ready as many of my academic colleagues to damn the entire field. . . . I am also cautious because the random walk theory rests on several fragile assumptions."[86] Malkiel specified three basic problems with the random walk–efficient market theory:

1. Perfect Markets. Malkiel commented that the random walk theory holds that at any time stocks sell at the best estimates of their intrinsic values . . . the problem is that this line of reasoning is uncomfortably close to that used by proponents of the greater-fool theory." He further noted there has been ample evidence that stocks sometimes are not

---

[84] Eugene F. Fama, "What Random Walk Really Means," *Institutional Investor*, April 1968, p. 40.

[85] Ibid.

[86] Burton G. Malkiel, *A Random Walk Down Wall Street* (New York: W. W. Norton, 1973) p. 170.

priced on estimates of actual value "but are often swept up in waves of frenzy."

2. Speed of News Dissemination. He likewise took issue with the semistrong form. "News does not travel instantaneously, as the random walkers suggest . . . moreover, the random walk theory implies that no one possesses monopolistic power over the market and that stock recommendations based on unfounded beliefs do not lead to large buying."

Malkiel asserted that neither assumption accords with reality in today's markets. "Brokerage firms specializing in research services to institutions wield enormous power in the market and can direct tremendous money flows in and out of stocks." On this score he stated that many speculators, or even fund managers, may buy and sell a stock simply because they believe an influential brokerage house may recommend buying or selling it. Consequently, he concluded that it is entirely possible that "erroneous beliefs about a stock by some professionals can, for a considerable time, be self-fulfilling."

3. Evaluation of Information. Malkiel also commented on different levels of expertise in security analysis. He noted the enormous difficulty of converting information of a stock into specific estimates of true value.

> We have seen that the major determinants of a stock's value concern the extent and duration of its growth path far into the future. Both the estimation of the growth path from known information and the translation of the growth path into a value estimate require art as much as science. In such an environment there is considerable scope for an individual to exercise the superior intellect and judgment to turn in superior performance.
>
> But while I believe in the possibility of superior professional investment performance, I must emphasize that the evidence we have thus far does not support the view that such competence in fact exists; and while I may be excommunicated from some academic sects because of my only lukewarm endorsement of the random walk, I make no effort to disguise my heresy in the financial church. It is clear that if there are exceptional financial managers they are very rare.[87]

Molodovsky—Needed: A Good Idea

Perhaps this was all foreordained many years ago by Nicholas Molodovsky the late and great editor of the *Financial Analysts Journal* when he said "we are living in a new age of security analysis. We are now at the point where we have all the numbers you could possibly want. Moreover you can now do quickly anything you want to do with numbers. This never happened before. What is needed now, and perhaps this is a constant through time, is a good idea."[88]

---

[87] Ibid., p. 172.

[88] Nicholas Molodovsky, "It's Good to Own Growth Stocks," *Financial Analysts Journal,* March–April 1963, p. 99.

44

An Introduction to Risk and Return: Concepts and Evidence[1]

FRANCO MODIGLIANI, Ph.D.
Sloan School of Management
Massachusetts Institute of Technology
Cambridge, Massachusetts

and

GERALD A. POGUE, Ph.D.
Baruch College
City University of New York
New York, New York

1. INTRODUCTION

PORTFOLIO THEORY deals with the selection of optimal portfolios by rational risk-averse investors: that is, by investors who attempt to maximize their expected portfolio returns consistent with individually acceptable levels of portfolio risk. Capital markets theory deals with the implications for security prices of the decisions made by these investors: that is, what relationship should exist between security returns and risk if investors behave in this optimal fashion. Together, portfolio and capital markets theories provide a framework for the specification and measurement of investment risk, for developing relationships between expected security return and risk, and for measuring the performance of managed portfolios such as mutual funds and pension funds.

The purpose of this article is to present a nontechnical introduction to portfolio and capital markets theories. Our hope is to provide a wide class of readers with an understanding of the foundation upon which the modern risk and performance measures are based. We will present the main elements of the theory along with the results of some of the more important empirical tests. We are attempting to present not an ex-

[1] Reprinted with permission of the *Financial Analysts Journal.*

haustive survey of the theoretical and empirical literature, but rather the main thread of the subject leading the reader from the most basic concepts to the more sophisticated but practically useful results of the theory.

The presentation is organized as follows. Section 2 develops a number of commonly used measures of investment return—the arithmetic, time-weighted, and dollar-weighted average returns. Section 3 introduces the concept of portfolio risk. We will suggest that the standard deviation of portfolio returns is a useful measure of total portfolio risk. Section 4 deals with the impact of diversification on portfolio risk and introduces the concepts of systematic and unsystematic risk. Section 5 deals with the contribution of individual securities to portfolio risk. The nondiversifiable or systematic risk of a portfolio is shown to be a weighted average of the systematic risk of its component securities. Section 6 presents a theoretical relationship between security systematic risk (designated as "beta") and expected return. The model is known as the Capital Asset Pricing Model. Section 7 discusses procedures for measuring the systematic risk factors for securities and portfolios. Section 8 presents a review of empirical tests of the Capital Asset Pricing Model. The purpose of these tests is to see how well the model explains the relationship between risk and return observed in the securities market. Finally, Section 9 discusses how we can use the results of the theory to measure investment performance.

2. INVESTMENT RETURN

Measuring historical rates of return is a relatively straightforward matter. We begin by showing how investment return during a single interval can be measured, and then present three commonly used measures of average return over a series of such intervals.

Single-Interval Portfolio Return

The return on an investor's portfolio during a given interval is equal to the change in value of the portfolio plus any distributions received from the portfolio expressed as a fraction of the initial portfolio value. It is important that any capital or income distributions made to the investor be included, else the measure of return will be deficient. Equivalently, the return can be thought of as the amount (expressed as a fraction of the initial portfolio value) that can be withdrawn at the end of the interval while maintaining the principal intact. The return on the investor's portfolio, designated R_P, is given by

$$R_P = \frac{V_1 - V_0 + D_1}{V_0}, \tag{1a}$$

where

V_1 is the portfolio market value at the end of the interval.
V_0 is the portfolio market value at the beginning of the interval.
D_1 is the cash distributions to the investor during the interval.

The calculation assumes that any interest or dividend income received on the portfolio securities and not distributed to the investor is reinvested in the portfolio (and thus reflected in V_1). Further, the calculation assumes that any distributions occur at the end of the interval, or are held in the form of cash until the end of the interval. If the distributions were reinvested prior to the end of the interval, the calculation would have to be modified to consider the gains or losses on the amount reinvested. The formula also assumes no capital inflows during the interval. Otherwise, the calculation would have to be modified to reflect the increased investment base. Capital inflows at the end of the interval, however, can be treated as just the reverse of distributions in the return calculation.

Thus given the beginning and ending portfolio values, plus any contributions from or distributions to the investor (assumed to occur at the end of the interval), we can compute the investor's return using equation (1*a*). For example, if the XYZ pension fund had a market value of $100,000 at the end of June, capital contributions of $10,000, benefit payments of $5,000 (both at the end of July), and an end-of-July market value of $95,000, the return for the month is a loss of 10 percent.

The Arithmetic Average Return

The arithmetic average return is an unweighted average of the returns achieved during a series of such measurement intervals. For example, if the portfolio returns (as measured by equation [1*a*]) were −10 percent, 20 percent, and 5 percent in July, August, and September, respectively, the average monthly return is 5 percent. The general formula is

$$R_A = \frac{R_{P1} + R_{P2} + \cdots + R_{PN}}{N}, \qquad (1b)$$

where

R_A is the arithmetic average return.
R_{PK} is the portfolio return in interval k, $k = 1, \ldots, N$.
N is the number of intervals in the performance-evaluation period.

The arithmetic average can be thought of as the mean value of the withdrawals (expressed as a fraction of the initial portfolio value) that can be made at the end of each interval while maintaining the principal intact. In the above example, the investor must add 10 percent of the principal at the end of the first interval and can withdraw 20 percent and 5 percent at the end of the second and third, for a mean withdrawal of 5 percent of the initial value per period.

The Time-Weighted Rate of Return

The time-weighted return measures the compound rate of growth of the initial portfolio during the performance-evaluation period, assuming that all cash distributions are reinvested in the portfolio. It is also commonly referred to as the *geometric* rate of return. It is computed by taking the geometric average of the portfolio returns computed from equation (1*a*). For example, assume the portfolio returns were −10 percent, 20 percent, and 5 percent in July, August, and September, as assumed above. The time-weighted rate of return is 4.3 percent per month. Thus one dollar invested in the portfolio at the end of June would have grown at a rate of 4.3 percent per month during the three-month period. The general formula is

$$R_T = [(1 + R_{P1})(1 + R_{P2}) \ . \ . \ . \ (1 + R_{PN})]^{1/N} - 1, \qquad (1c)$$

where

R_T is the time-weighted rate of return.
R_{PK} is the portfolio return during the interval k, $k = 1, \ . \ . \ . \ , N$.
N is the number of intervals in the performance-evaluation period.

In general, the arithmetic and time-weighted average returns do not coincide. This is because, in computing the arithmetic average, the amount invested is assumed to be maintained (through additions or withdrawals) at its initial value. The time-weighted return, on the other hand, is the return on a portfolio that is varying in size because of the assumption that all proceeds are reinvested.

The failure to coincide is illustrated in the following example. Consider a portfolio with a $100 market value at the end of 1972, a $200 value at the end of 1973, and a $100 value at the end of 1974. The annual returns are 100 percent and −50 percent. The arithmetic and time-weighted average returns are 25 percent and 0 percent, respectively. The arithmetic average return consists of the average of $100 withdrawn at the end of Period 1, and $50 replaced at the end of Period 2. The compound rate of return is clearly zero, the 100 percent return in the first period being exactly offset by the 50 percent loss in the second period on the larger asset base. In this example the arithmetic average exceeded the time-weighted average return. This is always true, with the exception of the special situation where the returns in each interval are the same, in which case the averages are identical.

The Dollar-Weighted Return

The dollar-weighted return measures the average rate of growth of all funds invested in the portfolio during the performance-evaluation period—that is, the initial value plus any contributions less any distributions. As such, the rate is influenced by the timing and magnitude of the contributions and distributions to and from the portfolio. The measure is also commonly referred to as the *internal rate of return.* It is important to corporations, for example, for comparison with the actuarial rates of portfolio growth assumed when funding their employee pension plans.

The dollar-weighted return is computed in exactly the same way that the yield to maturity on a bond is determined. For example, consider a portfolio with market value of $100,000 at the end of 1973 (V_0); capital withdrawals of $5,000 at the end of 1974, 1975, and 1976 (C_1, C_2, and C_3); and a market value of $110,000 at the end of 1976 (V_3). Using compound interest tables, the dollar-weighted rate of return is found by trial and error to be 8.1 percent per year during the three-year period. Thus each dollar in the fund grew at an average rate of 8.1 percent per year. The formula used is

$$V_0 = \frac{C_1}{(1 + R_D)} + \frac{C_2}{(1 + R_D)^2} + \frac{C_3}{(1 + R_D)^3} + \frac{V_3}{(1 + R_D)^3}, \qquad (1d)$$

where R_D is the dollar-weighted return.

What is the relationship between the dollar-weighted return (internal rate of return) and the previously defined time-weighted rate of return? It is easy to show that under certain special conditions both rates of return are the same. Consider a portfolio with initial total value V_0. No further additions or withdrawals occur and all dividends are reinvested. Under these special circumstances all of the C's in equation (1*d*) are zero so that

$$V_0 = \frac{V_0(1 + R_{P1})(1 + R_{P2})(1 + R_{P3})}{(1 + R_D)^3},$$

where R_P's are the single-period returns. The numerator of the expression on the right is just the value of the initial investment at the end of the three periods (V_3). Solving for R_D we find

$$R_D = [(1 + R_{P1})(1 + R_{P2})(1 + R_{P3})]^{1/3} - 1,$$

which is the same as the time-weighted rate of return R_T given by expression (1*c*). However, when contributions or withdrawals to the portfolio occur, the two rates of return are not the same. Because the dollar-weighted return (unlike the time-weighted return) is affected by the magnitude and timing of portfolio contributions and distributions (which are typically beyond the portfolio manager's control), it is not useful for measuring the investment performance of the manager. For example, consider two identical portfolios (designated A and B) with year-end 1973 market values of $100,000. During 1974 each portfolio has a 20 percent return. At the end of 1974, portfolio A has a capital contribution of $50,000 and portfolio B a withdrawal of $50,000. During 1975, both portfolios suffer a 10 percent loss resulting in year-end market values of \$153,000 and \$63,000, respectively. Now, both portfolio managers performed equally well, earning 20 percent in 1974 and −10 percent in 1975, for a time-weighted average return of 3.9 percent per year. The dollar-weighted returns are not the same, however, due to the different asset bases for 1975, equaling 1.2 percent and 8.2 percent for portfolios A and B, respectively. The owners of portfolio B, unlike those of A, made a fortuitous decision to reduce their investment prior to the 1975 decline.

In the remainder of this article, when we mention rate of return, we will generally be referring to the single interval measure given by equation (1*a*). However, from time to time we will refer to the arithmetic and geometric averages of these returns.

3. PORTFOLIO RISK

The definition of investment risk leads us into much less well explored territory. Not everyone agrees on how to define risk, let alone measure it. Nevertheless, there are some attributes of risk which are reasonably well accepted.

If an investor holds a portfolio of treasury bonds, he faces no uncertainty about monetary outcome. The value of the portfolio at maturity of the notes will be identical with the predicted value. In this case the investor bears no monetary risk. However, if he has a portfolio composed of common stocks, it will be impossible to exactly predict the value of the portfolio as of any future date. The best he can do is to make a best guess or most-likely estimate, qualified by statements about the range and likelihood of other values. In this case, the investor does bear risk.

One measure of risk is the extent to which the *future* portfolio values are likely to diverge from the expected or predicted value. More specifically, risk for most investors is related to the chance that future portfolio values will be less than expected. Thus, if the investor's portfolio has a current value of \$100,000, and an expected value of \$110,000 at the end of the next year, he will be concerned about the probability of achieving values less than \$110,000.

Before proceeding to the quantification of risk, it is convenient to shift our attention from the terminal value of the portfolio to the portfolio rate of return, R_p, since the increase in portfolio value is directly related to R_p.[2]

---

[2] The transformation changes nothing of substance since

$$\begin{aligned}\tilde{M}_T &= (1 + \tilde{R}_p)M_0 \\ &= M_0 + M_0\tilde{R}_p,\end{aligned}$$

where $\tilde{M}_T$ is the terminal portfolio value and $\tilde{R}_P$ is the portfolio return. Since $\tilde{M}_T$ is a linear function of $\tilde{R}_P$, any risk measures developed for the portfolio return will apply equally to the terminal market value.

A particularly useful way to quantify the uncertainty about the portfolio return is to specify the probability associated with each of the possible future returns. Assume, for example, that an investor has identified five possible outcomes for his portfolio return during the next year. Associated with each return is a subjectively determined probability, or relative chance of occurrence. The five possible outcomes are:

Possible Return	*Subjective Probability*
50%	0.1
30	0.2
10	0.4
−10	0.2
−30	0.1
	1.00

Note that the probabilities sum to 1 so that the actual portfolio return is confined to take one of the five possible values. Given this probability distribution, we can measure the expected return and risk for the portfolio.

The expected return is simply the weighted average of possible outcomes, where the weights are the relative chances of occurrence. The expected return on the portfolio is 10 percent, given by

$$\begin{aligned} E(R_p) &= \sum_{j=1}^{5} P_j R_j \\ &= 0.1(50.0) + 0.2(30.0) + 0.4(10.0) \\ &\quad + 0.2(-10.0) + 0.1(-30.0) \\ &= 10\%, \end{aligned} \tag{2}$$

where the R_j's are the possible returns and the P_j's, the associated probabilities.

If risk is defined as the chance of achieving returns less than expected, it would seem to be logical to measure risk by the dispersion of the possible returns below the expected value. However, risk measures based on below-the-mean variability are difficult to work with, and furthermore are unnecessary as long as the distribution of future return is reasonably symmetric about the expected value.[3] Figure 1 shows three probability distributions: the first symmetric, the second skewed to the left, and the third skewed to the right. For symmetrical distribution, the dispersion of returns on one side of the expected return is the same as the dispersion on the other side of the expected return.

[3] Risk measures based on below-the-average variation are analytically difficult to deal with. Markowitz, in Chapter 9 of [18], develops a semivariance statistic which measures variability below the mean and compares it with the more commonly used variance calculation. (Note: See bibliography at the end of this chapter for full references.)

FIGURE 1

Possible Shapes for Probability Distributions

Symmetric Probability Distribution

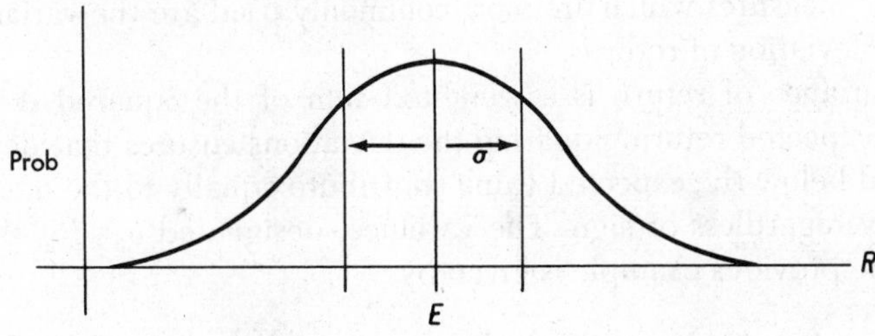

Probability Distribution Skewed to Left

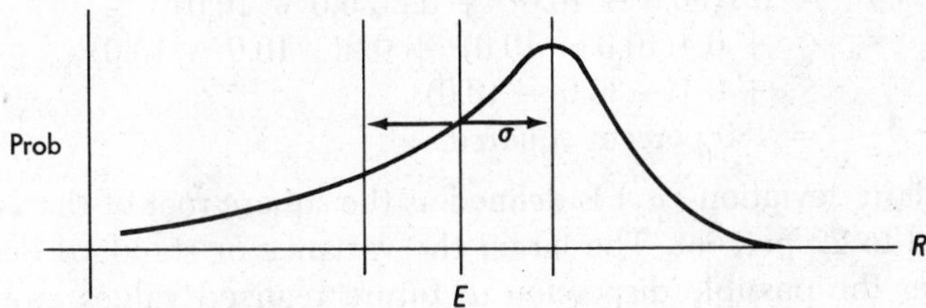

Probability Distribution Skewed to Right

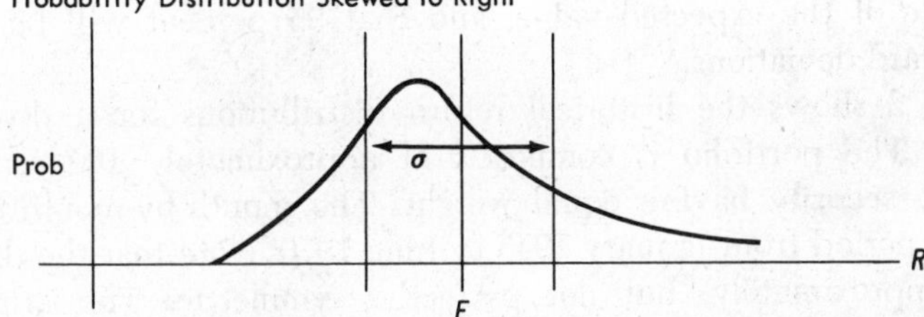

Empirical studies of realized rates of return on diversified portfolios show that skewness is not a significant problem.[4] If future distributions are shaped like historical distributions, then it makes little difference whether we measure variability of returns on one or both sides of the expected return. If the probability distribution is symmetric, measures of the total variability of return will be twice as large as measures of the portfolio's variability below the expected return. Thus, if total variability is used as a risk surrogate, the risk rankings for a group of portfolios will be the same as when variability below the expected return is used. It is

[4] See for example Blume [2].

for this reason that total variability of returns has been so widely used as a surrogate for risk.

It now remains to choose a specific measure of total variability of returns. The measures which are most commonly used are the variance and standard deviation of returns.

The variance of return is a weighted sum of the squared deviations from the expected return. Squaring the deviations ensures that deviations above and below the expected value contribute equally to the measure of variability regardless of sign. The variance, designated σ_p^2, for the portfolio in the previous example is given by

$$\sigma_p^2 = \sum_{j=1}^{5} P_j(R_j - E(R_p))^2$$

$$\begin{aligned} &= 0.1(50.0 - 10.0)^2 + 0.2(30.0 - 10.0)^2 \\ &\quad + 0.4(10.0 - 10.0)^2 + 0.2(-10.0 - 10.0)^2 \\ &\quad + 0.1(-30.0 - 10.0)^2 \\ &= 480 \text{ percent squared.} \end{aligned}$$

The standard deviation (σ_p) is defined as the square root of the variance. It is equal to 22 percent. The larger the variance or standard deviation, the greater the possible dispersion of future realized values around the expected value, and the larger the investor's uncertainty. As a rule of thumb for symmetric distributions, it is often suggested that roughly two thirds of the possible returns will lie within one standard deviation either side of the expected value, and that 95 percent will be within two standard deviations.

Figure 2 shows the historical return distributions for a diversified portfolio. The portfolio is composed of approximately 100 securities, with each security having equal weight. The month-by-month returns cover the period from January 1945 to June 1970. Note that the distribution is approximately, but not perfectly, symmetric. The arithmetic average return for the 306-month period is 0.91 percent per month. The standard deviation about this average is 4.46 percent per month.

Figure 3 gives the same data for a single security, National Department Stores. Note that the distribution is highly skewed. The arithmetic average return is 0.81 percent per month over the 306-month period. The most interesting aspect, however, is the standard deviation of month-by-month returns—9.02 percent per month, more than double that for the diversified portfolio. This result will be discussed further in the next section.

Thus far our discussion of portfolio risk has been confined to a single-period investment horizon such as the next year. That is, the portfolio is held unchanged and evaluated at the end of the year. An obvious question relates to the effect of holding the portfolio for several periods—say for the next 20 years: Will the one-year risks tend to cancel out over time? Given the random walk nature of security prices, the answer

FIGURE 2

Rate of Return Distribution for a Portfolio of 100 Securities (equally weighted) January 1945–June 1970

	RANGE		FREQ.	. . 1 . . .5 . . .10 . . .15 . . . 20. . .25. . .30. . .35. . .40. . . 45. . .50 .
1	-13.6210	-12.2685	1	*
2	-12.2685	-10.9160	2	**
3	-10.9160	-9.5635	2	**
4	-9.5635	-8.2110	3	***
5	-8.2110	-6.8585	8	********
6	-6.8585	-5.5060	9	*********
7	-5.5060	-4.1535	17	*****************
8	-4.1535	-2.8010	18	******************
9	-2.8010	-1.4485	27	***************************
10	-1.4485	-0.0960	28	****************************
11	-0.0960	1.2565	30	******************************
12	1.2565	2.6090	50	**
13	2.6090	3.9615	35	***********************************
14	3.9615	5.3140	33	*********************************
15	5.3140	6.6665	18	******************
16	6.6665	8.0190	14	**************
17	8.0190	9.3715	4	****
18	9.3715	10.7240	2	**
19	10.7240	12.0765	2	**
20	12.0765	13.4290	3	***

Average return = 0.91 percent per month.
Standard deviation = 4.46 percent per month.
Number of observations = 306.

to this question is no. If the risk level (standard deviation) is maintained during each year, the portfolio risk for longer horizons will increase with the horizon length. The standard deviation of possible terminal portfolio values after N years is equal to $\sqrt{N}$ times the standard deviation after one year.[5] Thus, the investor cannot rely on the "long run" to reduce his risk of loss.

A final remark before leaving portfolio risk measures. We have im-

[5] This result can be illustrated as follows. The portfolio market value after N years, $\tilde{M}_N$, is equal to

$$\tilde{M}_N = M_0[(1 + \tilde{R}_{p1})(1 + \tilde{R}_{p2}) \ldots (1 + \tilde{R}_{pN})],$$

where M_0 is the initial value, and R_{pt} $(t = 1, \ldots, N)$ is the return during year t (as given by equation [1*a*]). For reasonably small values of the annual returns, the above expression can be approximated by

$$\tilde{M}_N = M_0[1 + \tilde{R}_{p1} + \tilde{R}_{p2} + \cdots + \tilde{R}_{pN}].$$

Now, if the annual returns, $\tilde{R}_{pt}$, are independently and identically distributed with variance σ^2, the variance of $\tilde{M}_N$ will equal $(M_0)^2 N\sigma^2$, or N times the variance after one year. Therefore, the standard deviation of the terminal value will equal $\sqrt{N}$ times the standard deviation after one year. The key assumption of independence of portfolio returns over time is realistic since security returns appear to follow a random walk through time.

A similar result could be obtained without the restriction on the size of the $\tilde{R}_{pt}$ if we had dealt with continuously, as opposed to annually, compounded rates of return. However, the analysis would be more complicated.

FIGURE 3

Rate of Return Distribution for National Department Stores January 1945–June 1970

	RANGE		FREQ.	1...5...10...15...20...25...30...35...40...45...50.
1	-32.3670	-29.4168	1	*
2	-29.4168	-26.4666	0	
3	-26.4666	-23.5163	0	
4	-23.5163	-20.5661	1	*
5	-20.5661	-17.6159	1	*
6	-17.6159	-14.6657	3	***
7	-14.6657	-11.7155	13	*************
8	-11.7155	-8.7653	11	***********
9	-8.7653	-5.8151	39	***************************************
10	-5.8151	-2.8649	47	***
11	-2.8649	0.0853	45	***
12	0.0853	3.0355	34	**********************************
13	3.0355	5.9857	28	****************************
14	5.9857	8.9359	25	*************************
15	8.9359	11.8861	17	*****************
16	11.8861	14.8363	17	*****************
17	14.8363	17.7865	9	*********
18	17.7865	20.7366	8	********
19	20.7366	23.6868	5	*****
20	23.6868	26.6370	2	**

Average return = 0.81 percent per month.
Standard deviation = 9.04 percent per month.
Number of observations = 306.

plicitly assumed that investors are risk averse, i.e., that they seek to minimize risk for a given level of return. This assumption appears to be valid for most investors in most situations. The entire theory of portfolio selection and capital asset pricing is based on the belief that investors on the average are risk averse.

4. DIVERSIFICATION

When one compares the distribution of historical returns for the 100-stock portfolio (Figure 2) with the distribution for National Department Stores (Figure 3), he discovers a curious relationship. While the standard deviation of returns for the security is double that of the portfolio, its average return is less. Is the market so imperfect that over a long period of time (25 years) it rewarded substantially higher risk with lower average return?

Not so. As we shall now show, not all of the security's risk is relevant. Much of the total risk (standard deviation of return) of National Department Stores was diversifiable. That is, if it had been combined with other securities, a portion of the variation in its returns could have been smoothed or cancelled by complementary variation in the other securities. The same portfolio diversification effect accounts for the low standard deviation of return for the 100-stock portfolio. In fact, the portfolio standard deviation was less than that of the typical security in the portfolio. Much of the total risk of the component securities had been eliminated by diversification. Since much of the total risk could be eliminated simply by holding a stock in a portfolio, there was no economic requirement for the return earned to be in line with the total risk. Instead, we should expect realized returns to be related to that portion of security risk which cannot be eliminated by portfolio combination (more on risk-return relationships later).

Diversification results from combining securities which have less than perfect correlation (dependence) among their returns in order to reduce portfolio risk. As noted above, the portfolio return being simply a weighted average of the individual security returns is not diminished by diversification. In general, the lower the correlation among security returns, the greater the impact of diversification. This is true regardless of how risky the securities of the portfolio are when considered in isolation.

Ideally, if we could find sufficient securities with uncorrelated returns, we could completely eliminate portfolio risk. Unfortunately, this situation is not typical in real securities markets where returns are positively correlated to a considerable degree. Thus, while portfolio risk can be substantially reduced by diversification, it cannot be entirely eliminated. This can be demonstrated very clearly by measuring the standard deviations of randomly selected portfolios containing various numbers of securities.

In a study of the impact of portfolio diversification on risk, Wagner and Lau [27] divided a sample of 200 NYSE stocks into six subgroups based on the Standard and Poor's stock quality ratings as of June 1960. The highest quality ratings (A+) formed the first group, the second

TABLE 1

Risk versus Diversification for Randomly Selected Portfolios of A+ Quality Securities June 1960–May 1970

Number of Securities in Portfolio	*Average Return (percentage/month)*	*Standard Deviation of Return (percentage/month)*	*Correlation with Market*	
			R	R^2
1	0.88	7.0	0.54	0.29
2	0.69	5.0	0.63	0.40
3	0.74	4.8	0.75	0.56
4	0.65	4.6	0.77	0.59
5	0.71	4.6	0.79	0.62
10	0.68	4.2	0.85	0.72
15	0.69	4.0	0.88	0.77
20	0.67	3.9	0.89	0.80

Source: Wagner and Lau [27], Table C, p. 53.

FIGURE 4

Standard Deviation versus Number of Issues in Portfolio

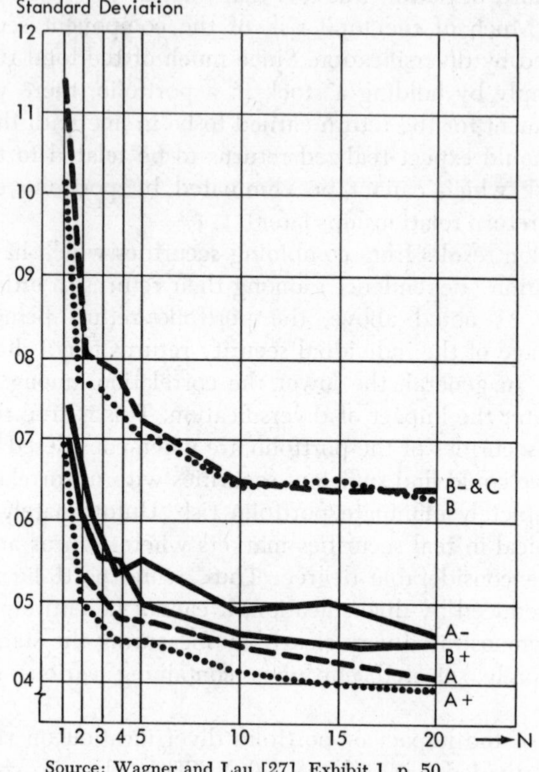

Source: Wagner and Lau [27], Exhibit 1, p. 50.

highest ratings (A) the next group, and so on. Randomly selected portfolios were then formed from each of the subgroups, containing from 1 to 20 securities. The month-by-month portfolio returns for the 10-year period through May 1970 were then computed for each portfolio (portfolio composition remaining unchanged). The exercise was repeated 10 times to reduce the dependence on single samples. The values for the 10 trials were then averaged.

Table 1 shows the average return and standard deviation for portfolios from the first subgroup (A+ quality stocks). The average return is unrelated to the number of issues in the portfolio. On the other hand, the standard deviation of return declines as the number of holdings increases. On the average, approximately 40 percent of the single security risk is eliminated by forming randomly selected portfolios of 20 stocks. However, it is also evident that additional diversification yields rapidly diminishing reduction in risk. The improvement is slight when the number of securities held is increased beyond, say, 10. Figure 4 shows the results for all six quality groups. The figure shows the rapid decline in total portfolio risk as the portfolios are expanded from 1 to 10 securities.

Returning to Table 1, we note from the second last column in the table that the return on a diversified portfolio follows the market very closely. The degree of association is measured by the correlation coefficient (R) of each portfolio with an unweighted index of all NYSE stocks (perfect positive correlation results in a correlation coefficient of 1.0).[6] The 20-security portfolio has a correlation of 0.89 with the market. The implication is that the risk remaining in the 20-stock portfolio is predominantly a reflection of uncertainty about the performance of the stock market in general. Figure 5 shows the results for the six quality groups.

FIGURE 5

Correlation versus Number of Issues in Portfolio

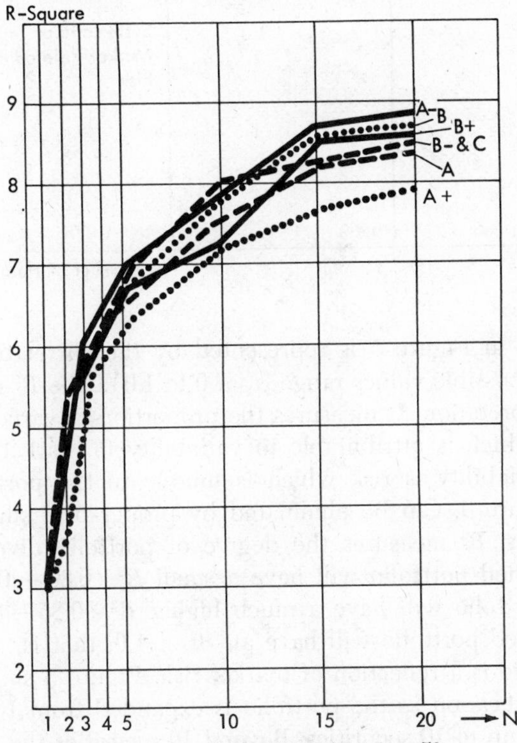

Source: Wagner and Lau [27], Exhibit 2, p. 50.

[6] Two securities with perfectly correlated return patterns will have a correlation coefficient of 1.0. Conversely, if the return patterns are perfectly negative correlated, the correlation coefficient will equal −1. Two securities with uncorrelated (i.e., statistically unrelated) returns will have a correlation coefficient of zero. The average correlation coefficient between returns for NYSE securities and the S & P's 500 Stock Index during the 1945–70 period was approximately 0.5.

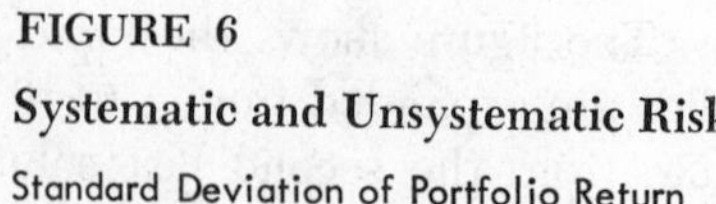

FIGURE 6

Systematic and Unsystematic Risk

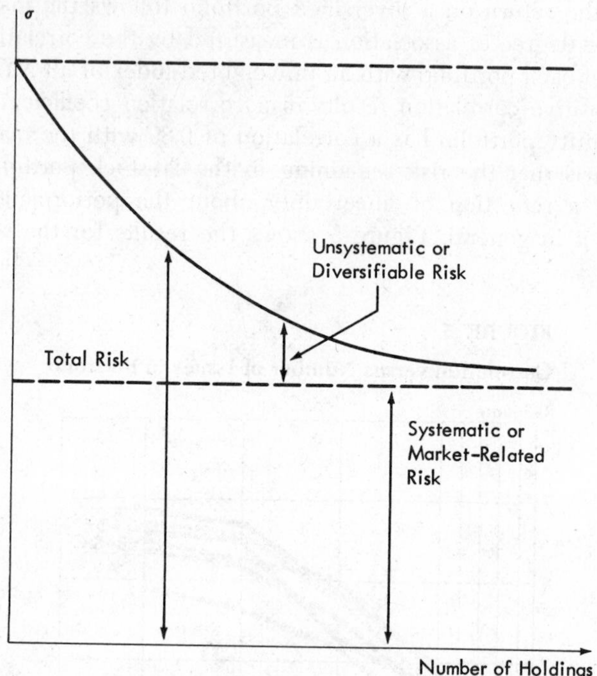

Correlation in Figure 5 is represented by the correlation coefficient squared, R^2 (possible values range from 0 to 1.0). The R^2 coefficient has a useful interpretation. It measures the proportion of variability in portfolio return which is attributable to variability in market returns. The remaining variability is risk which is unique to the portfolio and, as shown in Figure 4, can be eliminated by proper diversification of the portfolio. Thus, R^2 measures the degree of portfolio diversification. A poorly diversified portfolio will have a small R^2 (0.30 – 0.40). A well-diversified portfolio will have a much higher R^2 (0.85 – 0.95). A perfectly diversified portfolio will have an R^2 of 1.0; that is, all the risk in such a portfolio is a reflection of market risk. Figure 5 shows the rapid gain in diversification as the portfolio is expanded from 1 security to 2 securities and up to 10 securities. Beyond 10 securities the gains tend to be smaller. Note that increasing the number of issues tends to be less efficient at achieving diversification for the highest quality A+ issues. Apparently the companies comprising this group are more homogenous than the companies grouped under the other quality codes.

The results show that while some risks can be eliminated via diversification, others cannot. Thus we are led to distinguish between a security's "unsystematic" risk which can be washed away by mixing the security with other securities in a diversified portfolio, and its "systematic" risk which cannot be eliminated by diversification. This proposition is illustrated in Figure 6. It shows total portfolio risk declining as the number of holdings increases. Increasing diversification gradually tends to eliminate the unsystematic risk, leaving only systematic, i.e., market-related risk. The remaining variability results from the fact that the return on nearly every security depends to some degree on the overall performance of the market. Consequently, the return on a well-diversified portfolio is highly correlated with the market, and its variability or uncertainty is basically the uncertainty of the market as a whole. Investors are exposed to market uncertainty no matter how many stocks they hold.

5. THE RISK OF INDIVIDUAL SECURITIES

In the previous section we concluded that the systematic risk of an individual security is that portion of its total risk (standard deviation of return) which cannot be eliminated by combining it with other securities in a well-diversified portfolio. We now need a way of quantifying the systematic risk of a security and relating the systematic risk of a portfolio to that of its component securities. This can be accomplished by dividing security return into two parts: one dependent (i.e., perfectly correlated) and a second independent (i.e., uncorrelated) of market return. The first component of return is usually referred to as *systematic*, the second as *unsystematic* return. Thus we have

$$\text{Security return} = \text{Systematic return} + \text{Unsystematic return}. \tag{4}$$

Since the systematic return is perfectly correlated with the market return, it can be expressed as a factor, designated beta (β), times the market return, R_m. The beta factor is a *market sensitivity index*, indicating how sensitive the security return is to changes in the market level. The unsystematic return, which is independent of market returns, is usually represented by a factor epsilon (ϵ'). Thus, the security return, R, may be expressed

$$R = \beta R_m + \epsilon'. \tag{5}$$

For example, if a security had a β factor of 2.0 (e.g., an airline stock), then a 10 percent market return would generate a systematic return for the stock of 20 percent. The security return for the period would be the 20 percent plus the unsystematic component. The unsystematic component depends on factors unique to the company, such as labor difficulties, higher-than-expected sales, and so on.

The security returns model given by equation (5) is usually written in a way such that the average value of the residual term, ϵ', is zero. This is accomplished by adding a factor, alpha (α), to the model to represent the average value of the unsystematic returns over time. That is, we set $\epsilon' = \alpha + \epsilon$ so that

$$R = \alpha + \beta R_m + \epsilon, \tag{6}$$

where the average ϵ over time is equal to zero.

The model for security returns given by equation (6) is usually referred to as the *market model.* Graphically, the model can be depicted as a line fitted to a plot of security returns against rates of return on the market index. This is shown in Figure 7 for a hypothetical security.

The beta factor can be thought of as the slope of the line. It gives the expected increase in security return for a 1 percent increase in market return. In Figure 7, the security has a beta of 1.0. Thus, a 10 percent

FIGURE 7

The Market Model for Security Returns

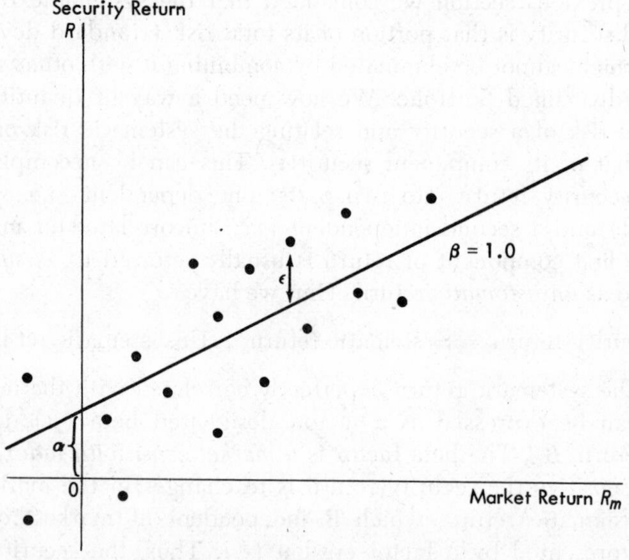

Beta (β), the market sensitivity index, is the slope of the line.
Alpha (α), the average of the residual returns, is the intercept of the line on the security axis.
Epsilon (ε), the residual returns, are the perpendicular distances of the points from the line.

market return will result, on the average, in a 10 percent security return. The market-weighted average beta for all stocks is 1.0 by definition.

The alpha factor is represented by the intercept of the line on the vertical security return axis. It is equal to the average value over time of the unsystematic returns (ϵ') on the stock. For most stocks, the alpha factor tends to be small and unstable. (We shall discuss alpha later.)

Using the definition of security return given by the market model, the specification of systematic and unsystematic risk is straightforward—

they are simply the standard deviations of the two return components.[7]

The systematic risk of a security is equal to β times the standard deviation of the market return.

$$\text{Systematic risk} = \beta\sigma_m \tag{7}$$

The unsystematic risk equals the standard deviation of the residual return factor ϵ.

$$\text{Unsystematic risk} = \sigma_\epsilon \tag{8}$$

Given measures of individual security systematic risk, we can now compute the systematic risk of portfolio. It is equal to the beta factor for the portfolio, β_p, times the risk of the market index, σ_m.

$$\text{Portfolio systematic risk} = \beta_p\sigma_m \tag{9}$$

The portfolio beta factor in turn can be shown to be simply an average of the individual security betas, weighted by the proportion of each security in the portfolio, or

$$\beta_p = \sum_{j=1}^{N} X_j\beta_j\,, \tag{10}$$

where

X_j is the proportion of portfolio market value represented by security j.
N is the number of securities.

Thus, the systematic risk of the portfolio is simply a weighted average of the systematic risk of the individual securities. If the portfolio is composed of an equal dollar investment in each stock (as was the case for the 100-security portfolio of Figure 2), the β_p is simply an unweighted average of the component security betas.

The unsystematic risk of the portfolio is also a function of the unsystematic security risks, but the form is more complex.[8] The important

[7] The relationship between the risk components is given by

$$\sigma^2 = \beta^2\sigma_m{}^2 + \sigma_{\epsilon'}{}^2.$$

This follows directly from equation (5) and the assumption of statistical independence of R_m and ϵ'. The R^2 term previously discussed is the ratio of systematic to total risk (both measured in terms of variance).

$$R^2 = \frac{\beta^2\sigma_m{}^2}{\sigma^2}$$

Note also that the R^2 is the square of the correlation coefficient between security and market returns.

[8] Assuming the unsystematic returns (ϵ'_j) of securities to be uncorrelated (reasonably true in practice), the unsystematic portfolio risk is given by

$$\sigma^2(\epsilon'_p) = \sum_{j=1}^{N} X_j^2\sigma^2(\epsilon'_j),$$

point is that with increasing diversification this risk can be reduced toward zero.

With these results for portfolio risk, it is useful to return to Figure 4. The figure shows the decline in portfolio risk with incerasing diversification for each of the six quality groups. However, the portfolio standard deviations for each of the six groups are decreasing toward different limits because the average risks ($\bar{\beta}$) of the groups differ.

Table 2 shows a comparison of the standard deviations for the 20-stock portfolios with the predicted lower limits based on average security systematic risks. The lower limit is equal to the average beta for the quality group ($\bar{\beta}$) times the standard deviation of the market return (σ_m). The standard deviations in all cases are close to the predicted values. These results support the contention that portfolio systematic risk equals the average systematic risks of the component securities.

TABLE 2

Standard Deviations of 20-Stock Portfolios and Predicted Lower Limits June 1960–May 1970

(1) *Stock Quality Group*	(2) *Standard Deviation of 20-Stock Portfolios* $\sigma \cdot$ *%/mo.*	(3) *Average Beta Value for Quality Group* $\bar{\beta}$	(4) *Lower Limit** $\bar{\beta} \cdot \sigma_m$ *%/mo.*
A+	3.94	0.74	3.51
A	4.17	0.80	3.80
A−	4.52	0.89	4.22
B+	4.45	0.87	4.13
B	6.27	1.24	5.89
B− & C	6.32	1.23	5.84

* σ_m is 4.75 percent per month.
Source: Wagner and Lau [27], p. 52, and Table C, p. 53.

The main results of this section can be summarized as follows. First, as seen from Figure 4, roughly 40 to 50 percent of total security risk can be eliminated by diversification. Second, the remaining systematic risk is equal to the security β times market risk. Third, portfolio systematic risk is a weighted average of security systematic risks.

The implications of these results are substantial. First, we would ex-

---

where $\sigma^2(\epsilon'_j)$ is the unsystematic risk for stock j. Assume the portfolio is made up of equal investment in each security and $\bar{\sigma}^2(\epsilon')$ is the average value of the $\sigma^2(\epsilon'_j)$. Then, $X_j = 1/N$ and

$$\sigma^2(\epsilon'_p) = \frac{1}{N}\bar{\sigma}^2(\epsilon'),$$

which (assuming $\bar{\sigma}^2(\epsilon')$ is finite) obviously approaches zero as the number of issues in the portfolio increases.

pect realized rates of return over substantial periods of time to be related to the systematic as opposed to total risk of securities. Since the unsystematic risk is relatively easily eliminated, we should not expect the market to offer a "risk premium" for bearing it. Second, since security systematic risk is equal to the security beta times σ_m (which is common to all securities), beta is useful as a *relative* risk measure. The β gives the systematic risk of a security (or portfolio) relative to the risk of the market index. Thus, it is often convenient to speak of systematic risk in relative terms (i.e., in terms of beta rather than beta times σ_m).

6. THE RELATIONSHIP BETWEEN EXPECTED RETURN AND RISK: THE CAPITAL ASSET PRICING MODEL

We have now developed two measures of risk: one is a measure of total risk (standard deviation), the other a relative index of systematic or nondiversifiable risk (beta). The beta measure would appear to be the more relevant for the pricing of securities. Returns expected by investors should logically be related to systematic as opposed to total risk. Securities with higher systematic risk should have higher expected returns.[9]

The question of interest now is the form of the relationship between risk and return. In this section we describe a relationship called the Capital Asset Pricing Model (CAPM), which is based on elementary logic and simple economic principles. The basic postulate underlying finance theory is that assets with the same risk should have the same expected rate of return. That is, the prices of assets in the capital markets should adjust until equivalent risk assets have identical expected returns.

To see the implications of this postulate, consider an investor who holds a risky portfolio[10] with the same risk as the market portfolio (beta equal to 1.0). What return should he expect? Logically, he should expect the same return as that of the market portfolio.

Consider another investor who holds a riskless portfolio (beta equal to zero). The investor in this case should expect to earn the rate of return on riskless assets such as treasury bills. By taking no risk, he earns the riskless rate of return.

Now consider the case of an investor who holds a mixture of these two portfolios. Assume he invests a proportion X of his money in the risky portfolio and $(1 - X)$ in the riskless portfolio. What risk does he bear and what return should he expect? The risk of the composite port-

[9] From this point on, *systematic risk* will be referred to simply as risk. *Total risk* will be referred to as total risk.

[10] We use the term *portfolio* in a general sense, including the case where the investor holds only one security. Since portfolio return and (systematic) risk are simply weighted averages of security values, risk-return relationships which hold for securities must also be true for portfolios, and vice versa.

folio is easily computed. Recall that the beta of a portfolio is simply a weighted average of the component security betas, where the weights are the portfolio proportions. Thus, the portfolio beta, β_p, is a weighted average of the beta of the market portfolio and of that of the risk-free rate. However, the market beta is 1.0, and that of the risk-free rate is 0. Thus,

$$\begin{aligned} \beta_p &= (1 - X) \cdot 0 + X \cdot 1 \\ &= X. \end{aligned} \qquad (11)$$

Thus, β_p is equal to the fraction of his money invested in the risky portfolio. If 100 percent or less of the investor's funds are invested in the risky portfolio, his portfolio beta will be between zero and 1.0. If he borrows at the risk-free rate and invests the proceeds in the risky portfolio, his portfolio beta will be greater than 1.0.

The expected return of the composite portfolio is also a weighted average of the expected returns on the two-compound portfolios; that is,

$$E(R_p) = (1 - X) \cdot R_F + X \cdot E(R_m), \qquad (12)$$

where $E(R_p)$, $E(R_m)$, and R_F are the expected returns on the portfolio, the market index, and the risk-free rate. Now, from equation (11) we know that X is equal to β_p. Substituting into equation (12), we have

$$E(R_p) = (1 - \beta_p) \cdot R_F + \beta_p \cdot E(R_m),$$

or

$$E(R_p) = R_F + \beta_p \cdot (E(R_m) - R_F). \qquad (13)$$

Equation (13) is the Capital Asset Pricing Model. It is an extremely important theoretical result. It says that the expected return on a portfolio should exceed the riskless rate of return by an amount which is proportional to the portfolio beta. That is, the relationship between return and risk should be linear.

The model is often stated in *risk-premium* form. Risk premiums are obtained by subtracting the risk-free rate from the rates of return. The expected portfolio and market risk premiums—designated $E(r_p)$ and $E(r_m)$, respectively—are given by

$$E(r_p) = E(R_P) - R_F \qquad (14a)$$

$$E(r_m) = E(R_M) - R_F. \qquad (14b)$$

Substituting these risk premiums into equation (13), we otbain

$$E(r_p) = \beta_P \cdot E(r_m). \qquad (15)$$

In this form, the Capital Asset Pricing Model states that the expected risk premium for the investor's portfolio is equal to its beta value times the expected market risk premium.

We can illustrate the model by assuming that the short-term (risk-free) interest rate is 6 percent and the expected return on the market is 10 percent. The expected risk premium for holding the market portfolio is just the difference between the 10 percent and the short-term interest rate of 6 percent, or 4 percent. Investors who hold the market portfolio expect to earn 10 percent, which is 4 percent greater than they could earn on a short-term market instrument for certain. In order to satisfy equation (13), the expected return on securities or portfolios with different levels of risk must be as follows.

Expected Return for Different Levels of Portfolio Beta

Beta	*Expected Return*
0.0	6%
0.5	8
1.0	10
1.5	12
2.0	14

The predictions of the model are inherently sensible. For safe investments ($\beta = 0$), the model predicts that investors would expect to earn the risk-free rate of interest. For a risky investment ($\beta > 0$), investors would expect a rate of return proportional to the market sensitivity (β) of the investment. Thus, stocks with lower-than-average market sensitivities (such as most utilities) would offer expected returns less than the expetced market return. Stocks with above-average values of beta (such as most airline securities) would offer expected returns in excess of the market.

In our development of the CAPM we have implicitly made a number of assumptions which are required if the model is to be established on a rigorous basis. These assumptions involve investor behavior and conditions in the capital markets. The following is a set of assumptions which are sufficient to allow a simple derivation of the model.

a. The market is composed of risk-averse investors who measure risk in terms of standard deviation of portfolio return. This assumption provides a basis for the use of beta-type risk measures.

b. All investors have a common time horizon for investment decision making (e.g., one month, one year, and so on). This assumption allows us to measure investor expectations over some common interval, thus making comparisons meaningful.

c. All investors are assumed to have the same expectations about future security returns and risks. Without this assumption, the analysis would become much more complicated.

d. Capital markets are perfect in the sense that all assets are completely divisible, there are no transactions costs or differential taxes, and borrowing and lending rates are equal to each other and the same for all investors. Without these conditions, frictional barriers would exist to the equilibrium conditions on which the model is based.

While these assumptions are sufficient to derive the model, it is not clear that all are necessary in their current form. It may well be that several of the assumptions can be substantially relaxed without major change in the form of the model. A good deal of research is currently being conducted toward this end.

While the CAPM is indeed simple and elegant, these qualities do not in themselves guarantee that it will be useful in explaining observed risk-return patterns. In a later section we will review the empirical literature on attempts to verify the model.

7. MEASUREMENT OF SECURITY AND PORTFOLIO BETA VALUES

The basic data for estimating betas are past rates of return earned over a series of relatively short intervals—usually days, weeks, or months. For example, in Tables 3 and 4 we present calculations based on month-by-month rates of returns for the periods January 1945 to June 1970 (security betas) and January 1960 to December 1971 (mutual fund betas). The returns were calculated using equation (1*a*).

It is customary to convert the observed rates of return to risk premiums. As described in Section 6, risk premiums are obtained by subtracting the rates of return that could have been achieved by investing in short-maturity risk-free assets, such as treasury bills or prime com-

TABLE 3

Regression Statistics for 30 Randomly Selected Securities*
(January 1945–June 1970)

SECURITY	(1) NOBS	(2) ALPH	(3) SE.A	(4) BETA	(5) SE.B	(6) SE.R	(7) R**2	(8) ARPJ	(9) SD.R	(10) CRPJ
1 City Investing Co.	306.00	0.30	0.53	1.67	0.14	9.20	31.43	1.45	11.09	0.87
2 Foster Wheeler	306.00	-0.12	0.49	1.57	0.13	8.36	32.98	0.96	10.20	0.46
3 Pennsylvania Dixie	306.00	-0.20	0.47	1.40	0.12	8.15	29.33	0.77	9.67	0.33
4 National Gypsum Co.	306.00	-0.18	0.32	1.38	0.08	5.45	47.29	0.77	7.49	0.50
5 Radio Corp. Of America	306.00	0.02	0.38	1.35	0.10	6.60	37.02	0.95	8.30	0.62
6 Fox Film Corp.	306.00	-0.04	0.53	1.31	0.14	9.15	22.35	0.87	10.36	0.38
7 Intercontinental Rubber	306.00	0.69	0.64	1.28	0.17	10.95	16.13	1.58	11.94	0.92
8 National Department	306.00	-0.05	0.45	1.26	0.12	7.73	27.05	0.81	9.04	0.41
9 Phillips Jones Corp.	306.00	0.36	0.44	1.25	0.12	7.54	27.89	1.22	8.86	0.85
10 Chrysler Corp.	306.00	-0.26	0.37	1.21	0.10	6.29	34.12	0.58	7.73	0.28
11 American Hide & Leather	306.00	0.55	0.66	1.16	0.17	11.36	12.78	1.35	12.14	0.67
12 Adams Express	306.00	0.11	0.23	1.16	0.06	3.93	54.87	0.91	5.84	0.75
13 Caterpillar Tractor	306.00	0.43	0.32	1.14	0.08	5.45	38.09	1.22	6.92	0.99
14 Continental Steel Co.	306.00	0.21	0.36	1.12	0.10	6.22	31.31	0.99	7.50	0.72
15 Marland Oil Co.	306.00	0.06	0.29	1.11	0.08	4.99	40.69	0.82	6.47	0.62
16 Air Reduction Co.	306.00	-0.59	0.29	1.08	0.08	4.98	39.73	0.16	6.41	-0.05
17 National Aviation	306.00	0.22	0.39	1.04	0.10	6.71	25.15	0.94	7.74	0.65
18 NA Tomas Co.	306.00	0.28	0.63	1.01	0.17	10.88	10.72	0.98	11.50	0.37
19 NYSE Index	306.00	0.0	0.0	1.00	0.0	0.0	0.0	0.69	3.73	0.62
20 American Ship Building	306.00	0.31	0.52	0.99	0.14	9.01	14.53	0.99	9.73	0.54
21 James Talcott	306.00	0.33	0.42	0.98	0.11	7.23	20.43	1.01	8.09	0.68
22 Jewel Tea Co. Inc.	306.00	0.21	0.32	0.95	0.08	5.42	30.14	0.87	6.47	0.66
23 International Carrier	306.00	0.34	0.26	0.93	0.07	4.39	38.41	0.98	5.58	0.83
24 Keystone Steel & Wire	306.00	0.18	0.30	0.84	0.08	5.19	26.90	0.76	6.05	0.58
25 Swift & Co.	306.00	-0.09	0.30	0.81	0.08	5.08	26.08	0.47	5.89	0.30
26 Southern California	306.00	0.00	0.22	0.77	0.06	3.77	36.60	0.53	4.72	0.42
27 Bayuk Cigars	306.00	-0.04	0.39	0.71	0.10	6.76	13.49	0.45	7.26	0.19
28 First National Store	306.00	-0.08	0.31	0.67	0.08	5.33	18.01	0.38	5.88	0.21
29 National Linen Service	306.00	0.61	0.33	0.63	0.09	5.75	14.50	1.04	6.20	0.86
30 American Snuff	306.00	0.17	0.25	0.54	0.07	4.33	17.74	0.54	4.77	0.43
31 Homestake Mining Co.	306.00	0.16	0.38	0.24	0.10	6.60	1.77	0.33	6.65	0.11
32 Commercial Paper	306.00	0.0	0.0	0.0	0.0	0.0	0.0	0.28	0.17	0.28
...Mean Sec. Values	306.00	0.13	0.39	1.05	0.10	6.76	27.25	0.86	7.88	0.54
...Standard Deviations	0.0	0.28	0.12	0.31	0.03	2.10	11.85	0.33	2.13	0.26

* Based on monthly data, regression results sorted by beta (column 4). Notations are on page 1320.

TABLE 4

Regression Statistics for 30 Randomly Selected Securities*
(January 1960–December 1971)

SECURITY	(1) NOBS	(2) ALPH	(3) SE.A	(4) BETA	(5) SE.B	(6) SE.R	(7) R**2	(8) ARPJ	(9) SD.R	(10) CRPJ
1 McDonnell Fund	144.00	0.58	0.82	1.50	0.22	9.76	25.18	1.13	11.24	0.67
2 Value Line Spec. Sit.	144.00	0.02	0.40	1.48	0.11	4.78	57.62	0.57	7.32	0.30
3 Keystone S-4	144.00	0.03	0.28	1.43	0.08	3.38	71.77	0.55	6.34	0.35
4 Chase Fund of Boston	144.00	0.11	0.33	1.42	0.09	3.94	64.78	0.63	6.61	0.41
5 Equity Progress	144.00	-0.54	0.41	1.26	0.11	4.85	48.89	-0.08	6.77	-0.31
6 Oppenheimer Fund	144.00	0.42	0.24	1.23	0.06	2.89	72.16	0.88	5.46	0.73
7 Fidelity Trend Fund	144.00	0.79	0.29	1.23	0.08	3.52	63.39	1.24	5.80	1.07
8 Fidelity Capital	144.00	0.41	0.24	1.20	0.06	2.81	72.17	0.85	5.31	0.71
9 Keystone K-2	144.00	0.08	0.22	1.17	0.06	2.63	73.90	0.51	5.13	0.38
10 Delaware Fund	144.00	0.18	0.19	1.15	0.05	2.32	77.62	0.60	4.90	0.48
11 Keystone S-3	144.00	0.18	0.19	1.14	0.05	2.32	77.50	0.60	4.88	0.48
12 Putnam Growth Fund	144.00	0.21	0.19	1.13	0.05	2.25	78.19	0.62	4.80	0.51
13 Scudder Special Fund	144.00	0.39	0.28	1.12	0.07	3.33	61.93	0.80	5.37	0.66
14 Energy Fund	144.00	0.06	0.18	1.10	0.05	2.18	78.39	0.46	4.67	0.35
15 One William Street	144.00	0.13	0.22	1.06	0.06	2.66	69.33	0.52	4.78	0.41
16 The Dreyfus Fund	144.00	0.17	0.14	1.04	0.04	1.69	84.40	0.55	4.26	0.46
17 Mass. Investors Gr. Stk.	144.00	0.15	0.16	1.03	0.04	1.96	79.65	0.52	4.34	0.43
18 Windsor Fund	144.00	0.18	0.16	1.03	0.04	1.95	79.87	0.56	4.33	0.47
19 Axe-Houghton Stock	144.00	0.39	0.30	1.02	0.08	3.62	52.96	0.76	5.26	0.62
20 S&P 500 Stock Index	144.00	0.0	0.0	1.00	0.0	0.0	0.0	0.37	3.76	0.30
21 T. Rowe Price Gr. Stk.	144.00	0.05	0.14	0.98	0.04	1.72	82.08	0.41	4.06	0.32
22 Mass. Investors Trust	144.00	-0.02	0.14	0.97	0.04	1.72	82.07	0.34	4.04	0.26
23 Bullock Fund	144.00	0.09	0.19	0.96	0.05	2.32	71.10	0.44	4.29	0.35
24 Keystone S-2	144.00	0.04	0.12	0.96	0.03	1.45	86.12	0.39	3.89	0.31
25 Eaton & Howard Stock	144.00	-0.05	0.13	0.95	0.03	1.52	84.75	0.30	3.89	0.23
26 The Colonial Fund	144.00	0.06	0.19	0.95	0.05	2.27	71.24	0.41	4.23	0.32
27 Fidelity Fund	144.00	0.15	0.11	0.95	0.03	1.31	88.08	0.50	3.79	0.43
28 Invest. Co. of America	144.00	0.26	0.20	0.95	0.05	2.40	68.79	0.61	4.29	0.51
29 Hamilton Funds - HDA	144.00	-0.12	0.23	0.93	0.06	2.73	62.55	0.22	4.44	0.12
30 Affiliated Fund	144.00	0.08	0.10	0.90	0.03	1.22	88.55	0.41	3.59	0.34
31 Keystone S-1	144.00	0.03	0.10	0.88	0.03	1.21	88.18	0.35	3.51	0.29
32 Axe-Houghton Fund B	144.00	0.01	0.20	0.86	0.05	2.44	63.68	0.32	4.03	0.24
33 American Mutual Fund	144.00	0.20	0.20	0.85	0.05	2.38	64.35	0.51	3.97	0.43
34 Pioneer Fund	144.00	0.24	0.16	0.84	0.04	1.88	73.85	0.55	3.67	0.48
35 Chemical Fund	144.00	0.57	0.25	0.83	0.07	3.03	51.50	0.88	4.33	0.79
36 Stein R&F Balanced Fd.	144.00	0.06	0.10	0.79	0.03	1.21	86.05	0.35	3.22	0.30
37 Puritan Fund	144.00	0.19	0.15	0.78	0.04	1.79	72.89	0.48	3.43	0.42
38 Value Line Income Fd.	144.00	0.07	0.17	0.78	0.04	2.01	67.96	0.36	3.54	0.29
39 Geo. Putnam Fd. Boston	144.00	0.07	0.10	0.77	0.03	1.18	85.75	0.35	3.12	0.30
40 Anchor Income	144.00	-0.03	0.13	0.74	0.04	1.60	75.24	0.24	3.21	0.19
41 Loomis-Sayles Mutual	144.00	0.05	0.10	0.74	0.03	1.22	83.96	0.32	3.04	0.27
42 Wellington Fund	144.00	-0.12	0.13	0.72	0.03	1.54	75.60	0.14	3.11	0.09
43 Massachusetts Fund	144.00	0.04	0.11	0.72	0.03	1.26	82.16	0.30	2.98	0.26
44 Nation-Wide Sec.	144.00	-0.32	0.15	0.67	0.04	1.78	66.45	-0.08	3.07	-0.12
45 Eaton & Howard Bal. Fd.	144.00	-0.07	0.12	0.62	0.03	1.46	71.62	0.16	2.74	0.12
46 American Business Shares	144.00	0.12	0.09	0.53	0.02	1.10	76.96	0.31	2.28	0.29
47 Keystone K-1	144.00	0.01	0.11	0.53	0.03	1.32	69.59	0.21	2.39	0.18
48 Keystone B-4	144.00	0.12	0.13	0.30	0.03	1.51	35.82	0.23	1.88	0.21
49 Keystone B-2	144.00	0.05	0.10	0.16	0.03	1.16	22.03	0.11	1.31	0.10
50 Keystone B-1	144.00	-0.08	0.10	0.07	0.03	1.21	4.43	-0.06	1.23	-0.07
51 30 Day Treasury Bills	144.00	0.0	0.0	0.0	0.0	0.0	0.0	0.34	0.12	0.34
...Mean Sec. Values	144.00	0.12	0.19	0.93	0.05	2.32	69.25	0.46	4.25	0.36
...Standard Deviations	0.0	0.22	0.12	0.30	0.03	1.42	17.50	0.27	1.64	0.23

* Based on monthly data, regression results sorted by beta (column 4). Notations are on page 1320.

mercial paper. This removes a source of noise from the data. The noise stems from the fact that observed returns may be higher in some years simply because risk-free rates of interest are higher. Thus, an observed rate of return of 8 percent might be regarded as satisfactory if it occurred in 1960, but as a relatively low rate of return when interest rates were at all-time highs in 1969. Rates of return expressed as risk premiums will be denoted by small *r*'s.

The market model of equation (6), when expressed in risk-premium form, is the basic equation used to estimate beta. The market model in risk-premium form is given by

$$r = \alpha + \beta r_m + e. \qquad (16a)$$

Description of Columns in Tables 3 and 4

Column Number	*Symbol*	*Description*
1	NOBS	Number of monthly returns
2	ALPHA	The estimated alpha value
3	SE · A	Standard error of alpha
4	BETA	Estimated beta coefficient
5	SE · B	Standard error of beta
6	SE · R	Standard error of the regression—an estimate of the unsystematic risk
7	R**2	R^2 expressed in percentage terms
8	ARPJ	Arithmetic average of monthly risk premiums
9	SD · R	Standard deviation of monthly risk premiums
10	CRPJ	Geometric (time-weighted) average of monthly risk premiums

The use of risk premiums instead of returns as in equation (6) simply changes the interpretation of alpha, leaving beta unchanged. In the return form, the expected value of alpha as given by the CAPM is $R_F(1 - B_p)$; compare equations (6) and (13). In the risk-premium form, the expected value of alpha is zero; compare Equations (15) and (16*a*). In the latter case, measured values of alpha different from zero can thus be interpreted as an *excess return* earned by a stock or portfolio beyond the return predicted by the CAPM given the assets beta value (more on the interpretation of alpha in Section 9).

Beta for a security is calculated by regressing the observed security risk premiums, r, on the observed risk premiums on the market, r_m. By this procedure we are, in effect, estimating the parameters of the market model of equation (16*a*). The equation of the fitted line is

$$r = \hat{\alpha} + \hat{\beta} r_m + \hat{\epsilon}, \tag{16b}$$

where $\hat{\alpha}$ is the intercept of the fitted line and $\hat{\beta}$ represents the stock's systematic risk. The $\hat{\epsilon}$ term represents variation about the line resulting from the unsystematic component of return. We have put hats (^) over the $\hat{\alpha}$, β, and $\hat{\epsilon}$ terms to indicate that these are estimated values. It is important to remember that these estimated values may differ substantially from the true values because of statistical measurement difficulties. However, the extent of possible error can be measured, and we can indicate a range within which the true value is almost certain to lie.

Figure 8 shows a risk-premium plot and fitted line for National Department Stores. The market is represented by a weighted index of all NYSE securities. The plot is based on monthly data during the period January 1945 to June 1970.

The estimated beta is 1.26 indicating above-average systematic risk.

FIGURE 8

Risk Premiums on National Department Stores versus NYSE Index (January 1945–June 1970)

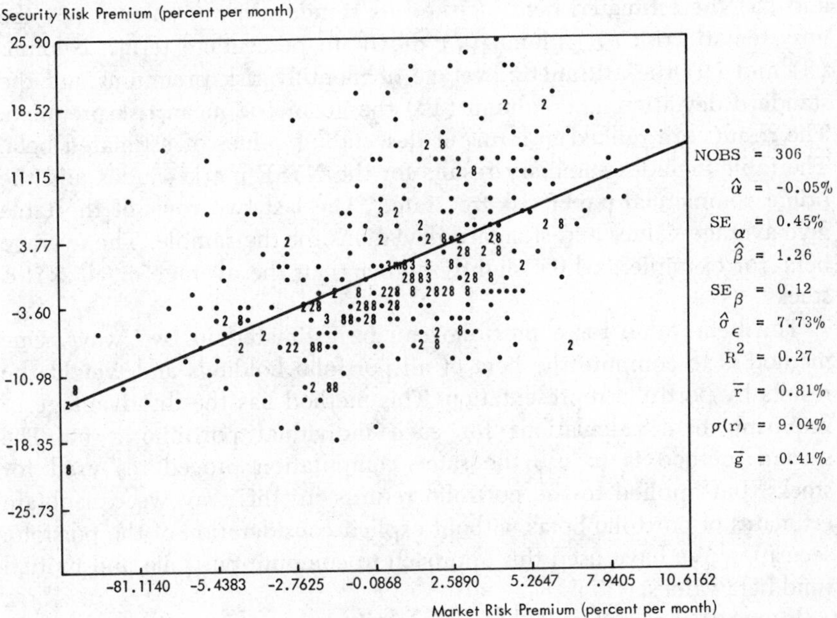

The estimated alpha is −0.05 percent per month, indicating that the excess return on the security averaged −0.60 percent per year over the 25-year period. The correlation coefficient is 0.52; thus, 27 percent of the variance of security returns resulted from market movements. The remainder was due to factors unique to the company.

Our interpretation of the estimated alpha and beta values must be conditioned by the degree of possible measurement error. The measurement error is estimated by *standard error* coefficients associated with alpha and beta.

For example, the standard error of beta is 0.12. Thus, the probability is about 66 percent that the true beta will lie between 1.26 ± 0.12, and about 95 percent between 1.26 ± 0.24 (i.e., plus or minus two times the standard error). Thus we can say with high confidence that National Department Stores has above-average risk (i.e., true beta greater than 1.0).

The standard error for alpha is 0.45, which is large compared with the estimated value of −0.05. Thus, we cannot conclude that the true alpha is different from zero, since zero lies well within the range of estimated alpha plus or minus one standard error (i.e., −0.05 ± 0.45).

Table 3 presents the same type of regression results for a random collection of 30 NYSE stocks.[11] The table contains the following items: Column (1) gives the number of monthly observations, columns (2) and (3) the estimated alpha $(\hat{\alpha})$ and its standard error, columns (4) and (5) the estimated beta $(\hat{\beta})$ and its standard error, column (6) the unsystematic risk σ_ϵ, column (7) the R^2 in percentage terms, columns (8) and (9) the arithmetic average of monthly risk premiums and the standard deviation, and column (10) the geometric mean risk premium. The results are ranked in terms of descending values of estimated beta. The table includes summary results for the NYSE market index and the prime commercial paper risk-free rate.[12] The last two rows of the table give average values and standard deviations for the sample. The average beta, for example, is 1.05, slightly higher than the average of all NYSE stocks.

The beta value for a portfolio can be estimated in two ways. One method is to compute the beta of all portfolio holdings and weight the results by portfolio representation. This method has the disadvantage of requiring beta calculations for each individual portfolio asset. The second method is to use the same computation procedures used for stocks, but applied to the portfolio returns. In this way we can obtain estimates of portfolio betas without explicit consideration of the portfolio securities. We have used this approach to compute portfolio and mutual fund beta values.

Figure 9 shows the plot of the monthly risk premiums on the 100-stock portfolio against the NYSE index for the same 1945–70 period. As in the case of National Department Stores, the best-fit line has been put through the points using regression analysis. The slope of the line reduction in the standard error term compared to the security examples. $(\hat{\beta})$ is equal to 1.10, with a standard error of 0.03. Note the substantial reduction in the standard error term compared to the security examples. The estimated alpha is 0.14, with a standard error of 0.10. Again, we cannot conclude that the true alpha is different from zero. Note that the points group much closer to the line than in the National Department Store plot. This results, of course, from the fact that much of the unsystematic risk causing the points to be scattered around the regression line in Figure 8 has been eliminated. The reduction is evidenced by the R^2 measure of 0.87 (versus 0.27 for National Department Stores). Thus, the market explains more than three times as much of the return variation of the portfolio than for the stock.

---

[11] The sample was picked to give the broadest possible range of security beta values. This was accomplished by ranking all NYSE securities with complete data from 1945–70 by their estimated beta values during this period. We then selected every 25th stock from the ordered list. The data was obtained from the University of Chicago CRSP (Center for Research in Security Prices) tape.

[12] The commercial paper results in Table 3 are rates of return, not risk premiums. The risk premiums would equal zero by definition.

FIGURE 9

Risk Premiums on 100 Stock Portfolio versus NYSE Index (January 1945–June 1970)

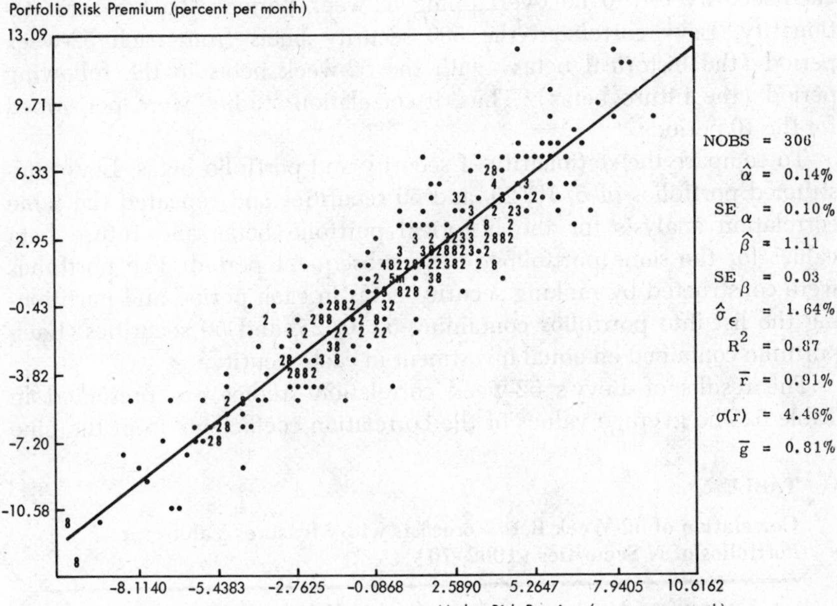

Table 4 gives regression results for a sample of 49 mutual funds. The calculations are based on monthly risk premiums for the period January 1960 to December 1971. The market is represented by the Standard & Poor's 500 Stock Index. Average values and standard deviations for the 49 funds in the sample are shown in the last two rows of the table. The average beta value for the group is 0.93 indicating, on the average, the funds were less risky than the market index. Note the relatively low beta values of the balanced and bond funds, in particular, the Keystone B1, B2, and B4 bond funds. This result is due to the low systematic risk of the bond portfolios.

Up to this point we have shown that it is a relatively easy matter to estimate beta values for stocks, portfolios, and mutual funds. Now, if the beta values are to be useful for investment decision making, they must be predictable. Beta values based on historical data should provide considerable information about future beta values if past measures are to be useful. How predictable are the betas estimated for stocks, portfolios of stocks, and mutual funds? Fortunately, we have empirical evidence at each level.

Robert A. Levy [13] has conducted tests of the short-run predictability (also referred to as stationarity) of beta coefficients for securities and unmanaged portfolios of securities. Levy's results are based on weekly returns for 500 NYSE stocks for the period December 30, 1960, through December 18, 1970 (520 weeks). Betas were developed for each security for 10 nonoverlapping 52-week periods. To measure stationarity, Levy correlated the 500 security betas from each 52-week period (the historical betas) with the 52-week betas in the following period (the future betas). Thus, 9 correlation studies were performed for the 10 periods.

To compare the stationarity of security and portfolio betas, Levy constructed portfolios of 5, 10, 25, and 50 securities and repeated the same correlation analysis for the historical portfolio betas and future beta values for the same portfolios in the subsequent period. The portfolios were constructed by ranking security betas in each period and partitioning the list into portfolios containing 5, 10, 25, and 50 securities. Each portfolio contained an equal investment in each security.

The results of Levy's 52-week correlation studies are presented in Table 5. The average values of the correlation coefficients from the nine

TABLE 5

Correlation of 52-Week Beta Forecasts with Measures Values for Portfolios of N Securities (1962–70)

Forecast for 52 Weeks Ended	*Product Moment Correlations:* N =				
	1	*5*	*10*	*25*	*50*
12/28/62	.385	.711	.803	.933	.988
12/27/63	.492	.806	.866	.931	.963
12/25/64	.430	.715	.825	.945	.970
12/24/65	.451	.730	.809	.936	.977
12/23/66	.548	.803	.869	.952	.974
12/22/67	.474	.759	.830	.900	.940
12/20/68	.455	.732	.857	.945	.977
12/19/69	.556	.844	.922	.965	.973
12/18/70	.551	.804	.888	.943	.985
Quadratic Mean	.486	.769	.853	.939	.972

Source: Robert A. Levy [13], Table 2, p. 57.

trials were 0.486, 0.769, 0.853, 0.939, and 0.972 for portfolios of 1, 5, 10, 25, and 50 stocks, respectively. Correspondingly, the average percentages of the variation in future betas explained by the historical betas are 23.6, 59.1, 72.8, 88.2, and 94.5.

The results show the beta coefficients to be very predictable for large portfolios and progressively less predictable for smaller portfolios and individual securities. These conclusions are not affected by changes in market performance. Of the nine correlation studies, five covered forecast periods during which the market performance was the reverse of the preceding period (61–62, 62–63, 65–66, 66–67, and 68–69). Notably, the betas were approximately as predictable over these five reversal periods as over the remaining four intervals.[13]

The question of the stability of mutual fund beta values is more complicated. Even if, as seen above, the betas of large unmanaged portfolios are very predictable, there is no a priori need for mutual fund betas to be comparatively stable. Indeed, the betas of mutual fund portfolios may change substantially over time by design. For example, a portfolio manager may tend to reduce the risk exposure of his fund prior to an expected market decline and raise it prior to an expected market upswing. However, the range of possible values for beta will tend to be restricted, at least in the longer run, by the fund's investment objective. Thus, while one does not expect the same standard of predictability as for large unmanaged portfolios, he may nevertheless be interested in examining the extent to which fund betas are predictable.

Pogue and Conway [21] have conducted tests for a sample of 90 mutual funds. The beta values for the period January 1969 through May 1970 were correlated with values from the subsequent period from June 1970 through October 1971. To test the sensitivity of the results to changes in the return measurement interval, the betas for each subperiod were measured for daily, weekly, and monthly returns. The betas were thus based on very different numbers of observations, namely 357, 74, and 17, respectively. The resulting correlation coefficients were 0.915, 0.895, and 0.703 for daily, weekly, and monthly betas, respectively. Correspondingly, the average percentages of variation in second-period betas explained by first-period values are 84, 81, and 49, respectively. The results support the contention that historical betas contain useful information about future values. However, the degree of predictability depends on the extent to which measured errors have been eliminated from beta estimates. In the Pogue-Conway study, the shift from monthly to daily returns reduced the average standard error of the estimated beta values from 0.11 to 0.03, a 75 percent reduction. The more accurate daily estimates resulted in a much higher degree of beta predictability, the correlation between subperiod betas increasing from 0.703 to 0.915.[14]

Figure 10 shows a Pogue-Conway plot of the first-period versus second-period betas based on daily returns. The figure illustrates the high degree of correlation between first- and second-period betas.

---

13 Correlation studies of this type tend to produce a conservative picture of the degree of beta coefficient stationarity. This results from the fact that it is not possible to correlate the true beta values but only estimates which contain varying degrees of measurement error. Measurement error would reduce the correlation coefficient even though the underlying beta values were unchanged from period to period.

14 These results are consistent with those found by Mains [16] in a later study. Mains correlated adjacent calendar-year betas for a sample of 99 funds for the period 1960 through 1971. The betas were based on weekly returns. The average correlation coefficient for the 11 tests was 0.788, with individual values ranging from a low of 0.614 to a high of 0.871.

FIGURE 10

Interperiod Beta Comparison: Daily Data for 90 Mutual Funds

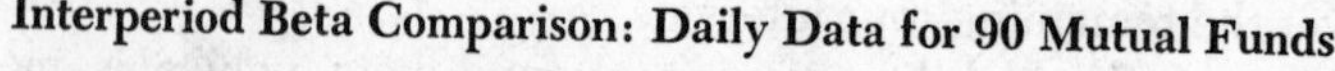

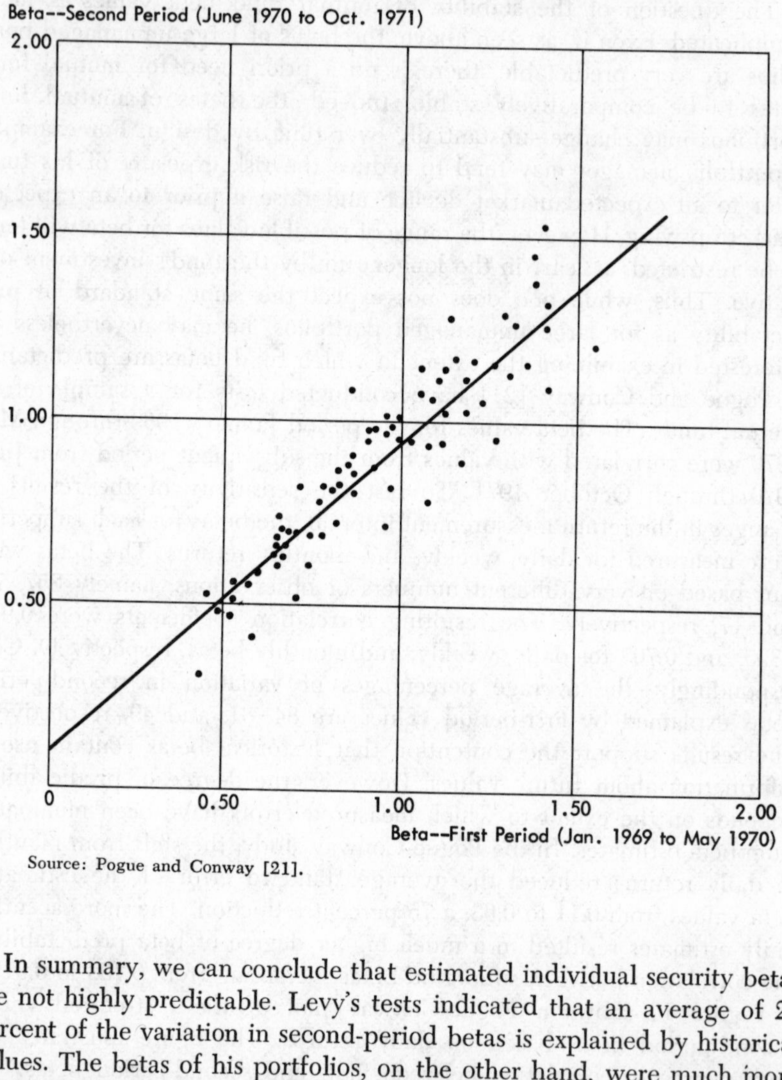

Source: Pogue and Conway [21].

In summary, we can conclude that estimated individual security betas are not highly predictable. Levy's tests indicated that an average of 24 percent of the variation in second-period betas is explained by historical values. The betas of his portfolios, on the other hand, were much more predictable, the degree of predictability increasing with portfolio diversification. The results of the Pogue and Conway study and others show that fund betas, not unexpectedly, are not as stable as those for unmanaged portfolios. Nonetheless, two thirds to three quarters of the variation in fund betas can be explained by historical values.

Further, it should be remembered that a significant portion of the measured changes in estimated beta values may not be due to changes in the true values, but rather the result of measurement errors. This observation is particularly applicable to individual security betas where the standard errors tend to be large.

8. TESTS OF THE CAPITAL ASSET PRICING MODEL[15]

The major difficulty in testing the Capital Asset Pricing Model is that the model is stated in terms of investors' expectations and not in terms of realized returns. The fact that expectations are not always realized introduces an error term which, from a statistical point of view should be zero *on the average,* but not necessarily zero for any single stock or single period of time. After the fact, we would expect to observe

$$R_j = R_f + \beta_j(R_m - R_f) + \epsilon_j, \tag{17a}$$

where R_j, R_m, and R_f are the realized returns on stock j, the market index, and the riskless asset; and ϵ_j is the residual term.

If we observe the realized returns over a series of periods, the average security return would be given by

$$\bar{R}_j = \bar{R}_F + \beta_j(\bar{R}_M - \bar{R}_F) + \bar{\epsilon}_j, \tag{17b}$$

where $\bar{R}_j$, $\bar{R}_M$, and $\bar{R}_F$ are the average realized returns on the stock, the market, and the risk-free rate. If the CAPM is correct, the average residual term, $\bar{\epsilon}_j$, should approach zero as the number of periods used to compute the average becomes large. To test this hypothesis, we can regress the average returns, $\bar{R}_j$, for a series of stocks ($j = 1, \ldots, N$) on the stocks' estimated beta values, $\hat{\beta}_j$, during the period studied. The equation of the fitted line is given by

$$\bar{R}_j = \gamma_0 + \gamma_1\hat{\beta}_j + \mu_j, \tag{18a}$$

where γ_0 and γ_1 are the intercept and slope of the line, and μ_j is the deviation of stock j from the line. By comparing equations (17b) and (18a), we infer that if the CAPM hypothesis is valid, μ_j should equal $\bar{\epsilon}_i$ and hence should be small. Furthermore, it should be uncorrelated with $\hat{\beta}_j$, and hence we can also infer that γ_0 and γ_1 should equal $\bar{R}_F$ and $\bar{R}_M - \bar{R}_F$, respectively.

The hypothesis is illustrated in Figure 11. Eeach plotted point represents one stock's realized return versus the stock's beta. The vertical distances of the points from the CAPM theoretical line (also called the "market line") represent the mean residual returns, $\bar{\epsilon}_j$. Assuming the CAPM to be correct, the ϵ_j should be uncorrelated with the $\hat{\beta}_j$ and thus the regression equation fitted to these points should be (1) linear, (2)

[15] The material in this section was also prepared as an appendix to testimony to be delivered before the Federal Communications Commission by Stewart C. Myers and Gerald A. Pogue.

FIGURE 11

Relationship between Average Return ($\bar{R}_j$) and Security Risk (β_j)

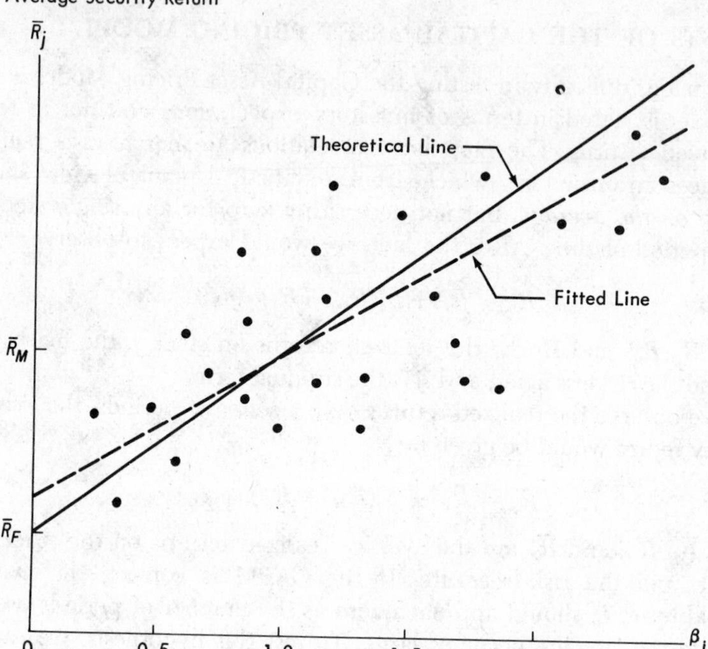

upward sloping with slope equal to $\bar{R}_M - \bar{R}_F$, and (3) pass through the vertical axis at the risk-free rate.

Expressed in risk-premium form, the equation of the fitted line is

$$\bar{r}_j = \gamma_0 + \gamma_1 \hat{\beta}_j + \mu_j, \tag{18b}$$

where $\bar{r}_j$ is the average realized risk premium for stock j. Comparing equation (18*b*) to the CAPM in risk-premium form, equation (15), the predicted values for γ_0 and γ_1 are 0 and $\bar{r}_m$, the mean market risk premium ($\bar{R}_M - \bar{R}_F$). Thus, shifting to risk premiums only changes the predicted value for γ_0, but not for γ_1.

Other Measures of Risk

The hypothesis just described is only true if beta is a complete measure of a stock's risk. Various alternative risk measures have been proposed. The most common alternative hypothesis is that expected return is related to the standard deviation of return—that is, to a stock's total risk, which includes both systematic and unsystematic components.

Which is more important in explaining average observed returns on securities, systematic or unsystematic risk? The way to find out is to fit an expanded equation to the data:

$$R_j = \gamma_0 + \gamma_1\hat{\beta}_j + \gamma_2(S\hat{E}_j) + \mu_j \tag{19}$$

Here $\hat{\beta}_j$ is a measure of systematic risk and $S\hat{E}_j$, a measure of unsystematic risk.[16] Of course, if the Capital Asset Pricing Model is exactly true, then γ_2 will be zero—that is, $S\hat{E}_j$ will contribute nothing to the explanation of observed security returns.

Empirical Tests of the Capital Asset Pricing Model

If the Capital Asset Pricing Model is right, the empirical tests would show the following:

1. On the average, and over long periods of time, the securities with high systematic risk should have high rates of return.
2. On the average, there should be a linear relationship between systematic risk and return.
3. The slope of the relationship (γ_1) should be equal to the mean market risk premium ($\overline{R}_M - \overline{R}_F$) during the period used.
4. The constant term (γ_0) should be equal to the mean risk-free rate ($\overline{R}_F$).
5. Unsystematic risk, as measured by $S\hat{E}_j$, should play no significant role in explaining differences in security returns.

These predictions have been tested in several recent statistical studies. We will review some of the more important ones. Readers wishing to skip the details may proceed to the summary at the end of this section.

We will begin by summarizing results from studies based on individual securities. Then we will turn to portfolio results.

Results for Tests Based on Securities

The Jacob Study. The Jacob study [9] deals with the 593 New York Stock Exchange stocks for which there is complete data from 1946 to 1965. Regression analyses were performed for the 1946–55 and 1956–65 periods, using both monthly and annual security returns. The relationship of mean security returns and beta values is shown in Table 6. The last two columns of the table give the theoretical values for the coefficients, as predicted by the Capital Asset Pricing Model.

The results show a significant positive relationship between realized

---

[16] $S\hat{E}_j$ is an estimate of the standard error of the residual term in equation (17*a*). Thus, it is the estimated value for $\sigma(\epsilon_j)$, the unsystematic risk term defined in equation (8). See column (6) of Tables 3 and 4 for typical values for securities and mutual funds.

TABLE 6

Results of Jacob's Study

$\bar{r}_j = \gamma_0 + \gamma_1\hat{\beta}_j + \mu_j$

(tests based on 593 securities)

Period	Return Interval	Regression Results*			Theoretical Values	
		$\hat{\gamma}_0$	$\hat{\gamma}_1$	R^2	$\gamma_0 = 0$	$\gamma_1 = \bar{R}_M - \bar{R}_F$
46–55	Monthly..........	0.80	0.30 (0.07)†	0.02	0	1.10
	Yearly..........	8.90	5.10 (0.53)	0.14	0	14.40
56–65	Monthly..........	0.70	0.30 (0.06)	0.03	0	0.80
	Yearly..........	6.70	6.70 (0.53)	0.21	0	10.80

* Coefficient units are: monthly data, percent per month; annual data, percent per year.
† Standard error.
Source: Jacob [9], Table 3, pp. 827–28.

return and risk during each of the 10-year periods. For example, in 1956–65 there was a 6.7 percent per year increase in average return for a one-unit increase in beta. Although the relationships shown in Table 6 are all positive, they are weaker than predicted by the Capital Asset Pricing Model. In each period $\hat{\gamma}_1$ is less and $\hat{\gamma}_0$ is greater than the theoretical values.

The Miller-Scholes Study. The Miller-Scholes research [19] deals with annual returns for 631 stocks during the 1954–63 period. The results of three of their tests are reported in Table 7. The tests are (1) mean return versus beta, (2) mean return versus unsystematic risk $(S\hat{E}_j)^2$, and (3) mean return versus both beta and unsystematic risk.

TABLE 7

Results of the Miller and Scholes Study

$\bar{R}_j = \gamma_0 + \gamma_1\hat{\beta}_j + \gamma_2(S\hat{E}_j)^2 + \mu_j$

Annual Rates of Return 1954–63 (tests based on 631 securities)

Regression Results*				Theoretical Values		
$\hat{\gamma}_0$	$\hat{\gamma}_1$	$\hat{\gamma}_2$	R^2	γ_0	γ_1	γ_2
12.2 (0.7)†	7.1 (0.6)		0.19	2.8	8.5	0
16.3 (0.4)		39.3 (2.5)	0.28	2.8	8.5	0
12.7 (0.6)	4.2 (0.6)	31.0 (2.6)	0.33	2.8	8.5	0

* Units of coefficients: percent per year.
† Standard error.
Source: Miller and Scholes [19], Table 1B, p. 53.

The results for the first test show a significant positive relationship between mean return and beta. A one-unit increase in beta is associated with a 7.1 percent increase in mean return.

The results for the second test do not agree with the Capital Asset Pricing Model's predictions. That is, high unsystematic risk is apparently associated with higher realized returns. However, Miller and Scholes show that this correlation may be largely spurious (i.e., it may be due to statistical sampling problems). For example, a substantial positive correlation exists between beta and $(S\hat{E}_j)^2$. Thus, even though unsystematic risk may be important to the pricing of securities, it will appear to be significant in tests from which beta has been omitted. This sort of statistical correlation need not imply a causal link between the variables.

Test number (3) includes both beta and $(S\hat{E}_j)^2$ in the regression equation. Both are found to be significantly positively related to mean return. The inclusion of $(S\hat{E}_j)^2$ has somewhat weakened the relationship of return and beta, however. A one-unit increase in beta is now associated with only a 4.2 percent increase in mean return.

The interpretation of these results is again complicated by the strong positive correlation between beta and $(S\hat{E}_j)^2$, and by other sampling problems.[17] A significant portion of the correlation between mean return and $(S\hat{E}_j)^2$ may well be a spurious result. In any case, the results do show that stocks with high systematic risk tend to have higher rates of return.

Results for Tests Based on Portfolio Returns

The security tests clearly show the significant positive correlation between return and systematic risk. Tests based directly on securities, however, are not the most efficient method of obtaining estimates of the magnitude of the risk-return tradeoff. Tests based on securities are inefficient for two reasons.

The first problem is well known to economists. It is called "errors in variables bias" and results from the fact that beta, the independent variable in the test, is typically measured with some error. These errors are random in their effect—that is, some stocks' betas are overestimated and some are underestimated. Nevertheless, when these estimated beta values are used in the test, the measurement errors tend to attenuate the relationship between mean return and risk.

By carefully grouping the securities into portfolios, much of this measurement error problem can be eliminated. The errors in individual stocks' betas cancel out so that the portfolio beta can be measured with much greater precision. This in turn means that tests based on portfolio returns will be more efficient than tests based on security returns.

---

[17] For example, skewness in the distributions of stock returns can lead to spurious correlations between mean return and $S\hat{E}_j$. See Miller and Scholes [19], pp. 66–71.

The second problem relates to the obscuring effect of residual variation. Realized security returns have a large random component, which typically accounts for about 70 percent of the variation of return. (This is the diversifiable or unsystematic risk of the stock.) By grouping securities into portfolios, we can eliminate much of this noise, and thereby get a much clearer view of the relationship between return and systematic risk.

It should be noted that grouping does not distort the underlying risk-return relationship. The relationship that exists for individual securities is exactly the same for portfolios of securities.

Friend and Blume Studies. Friend and Blume [3, 8] have conducted two interrelated risk-return studies. The first examines the relationship between long-run rates of return and various risk measures. The second is a direct test of the Capital Asset Pricing Model.

In the first study [8], Friend and Blume constructed portfolios of NYSE common stocks at the beginning of three different holding periods. The periods began at the ends of 1929, 1948, and 1956. All stocks for which monthly rate-of-return data could be obtained for at least four years preceding the test period were divided into 10 portfolios. The securities were assigned on the basis of their betas during the preceding four years—the 10 percent of securities with the lowest betas to the first portfolio, the group with the next lowest betas to the second portfolio, and so on.

After the start of the test periods, the securities were reassigned annually. That is, each stock's estimated beta was recomputed at the end of each successive year, the stocks were ranked again on the basis of their betas, and new portfolios were formed. This procedure kept the portfolio betas reasonably stable over time.

The performance of these portfolios is summarized in Table 8. The table gives the arithmetic mean monthly returns and average beta values for each of the 10 portfolios and for each test period.

For the 1929–69 period, the results indicate a strong positive association between return and beta. For the 1948–69 period, while higher beta portfolios had higher returns than portfolios with lower betas, there was little difference in return among portfolios with betas greater than 1.0. The 1956–69 period results do not show a clear relationship between beta and return. On the basis of these and other tests, the authors conclude that NYSE stocks with above-average risk have higher returns than those with below-average risk, but that there is little payoff for assuming additional risk within the group of stocks with above-average betas.

In their second study [3], Blume and Friend used monthly portfolio returns during the 1955–68 period to test the Capital Asset Pricing Model. Their tests involved fitting the coefficients of equation (18*a*) for three sequential periods: 1955–59, 1960–64, and 1965–68. The authors

TABLE 8

Results of Friend-Blume Study (returns from a yearly revision policy for stocks classified by beta for various periods)

	Holding Period					
	1929–69		*1948–69*		*1956–69*	
Portfolio Number	*Beta*	*Mean Return Percentage*	*Beta*	*Mean Return Percentage*	*Beta*	*Mean Return Percentage*
1	0.19	0.79	0.45	0.99	0.28	0.95
2	0.49	1.00	0.64	1.01	0.51	0.98
3	0.67	1.10	0.76	1.25	0.66	1.12
4	0.81	1.28	0.85	1.30	0.80	1.18
5	0.92	1.26	0.94	1.35	0.91	1.17
6	1.02	1.34	1.03	1.37	1.03	1.14
7	1.15	1.42	1.12	1.32	1.16	1.10
8	1.29	1.53	1.23	1.33	1.30	1.18
9	1.49	1.55	1.36	1.39	1.48	1.15
10	2.02	1.59	1.67	1.36	1.92	1.10

Monthly arithmetic mean returns.
Source: Friend and Blume [8], Table 4, p. 10.

also added a factor to the regression equation to test for the linearity of the risk-return relationship.[18]

The values obtained for γ_0 and γ_1 are not in line with the Capital Asset Pricing Model's predictions, however. In the first two periods, γ_0 is substantially larger than the theoretical value. In the third period, the reverse situation exists, with γ_0 substantially less than predicted. These results imply that γ_1, the slope of the fitted line, is less than predicted in the first two periods and greater in the third.[19] Friend and Blume conclude that "the comparisons as a whole suggest that a linear model is a tenable approximation of the empirical relationship between return and risk for NYSE stocks over the three periods covered."[20]

Black, Jensen, and Scholes. This study [1] is a careful attempt to reduce measurement errors that would bias the regression results. For each year from 1931 to 1965, the authors grouped all NYSE stocks into 10 portfolios. The number of securities in each portfolio increased over the 35-year period from a low of 58 securities per portfolio in 1931 to a high of 110 in 1965.

Month-by-month returns for the portfolios were computed from

---

[18] Their expanded test equation is

$$\bar{R}_j = \gamma_0 + \gamma_1\hat{\beta}_j + \gamma_2(\hat{\beta}_j)^2,$$

where, according to the Capital Asset Pricing Model, the expected value of γ_2 is zero.

[19] Table 1, p. 25, of Blume and Friend [3] presents period-by-period regression results.

[20] Blume and Friend [3], p. 26.

January 1931 to December 1965. Average portfolio returns and portfolio betas were computed for the 35-year period and for a variety of subperiods. The results for the complete period are shown in Table 9. The average monthly portfolio returns and beta values for the 10 portfolios are plotted in Figure 12. The results indicate that over the complete 35-year period, average return increased by approximately 1.08 percent per month (13 percent per year) for a one-unit increase in beta. This is about three quarters of the amount predicted by the Capital Asset Pricing Model. As Figure 12 shows, there appears to be little reason to question the linearity of the relationship over the 35-year period.

TABLE 9

Results of Black-Jensen-Scholes Study

$\bar{R}_p = \gamma_0 + \gamma_1\hat{\beta}_p + \mu_p$

1931–65

(tests based on 10 portfolios, averaging 75 stocks per portfolio)

*Regression Results**			*Theoretical Values*	
$\hat{\gamma}_0$	$\hat{\gamma}_1$	R^2	$\gamma_0 = \bar{R}_F$	$\gamma_1 = \bar{R}_M - \bar{R}_F$
0.519 (0.05)†	1.08 (0.05)	0.90	0.16	1.42

* Units of coefficients: Percent per month.
† Standard error.
Source: Black, Jensen, and Scholes [1], Table 4, p. 98, and Figure 7, p. 104.

Black, Jensen, and Scholes also estimated the risk-return tradeoff for a number of subperiods.[21] The slopes of the regression lines tend in most periods to understate the theoretical values, but are generally of the correct sign. Also, the subperiod relationships appear to be linear.

This paper provides substantial support for the hypothesis that realized returns are a linear function of systematic risk values. Also, it shows that the relationship is significantly positive over long periods of time.

Fama and MacBeth. Fama and MacBeth [6] have extended the Black-Jensen-Scholes tests to include two additional factors. The first is an average of the β_j^2 for all individual securities in portfolio p, designated $\hat{\beta}_p^2$. The second is a similar average of the residual standard deviations ($S\hat{E}_j$) for all stocks in portfolio p, designated $S\hat{E}_p$. The first term tests for nonlinearities in the risk-return relationship, the second for the impact of residual variation.

The equation of the fitted line for the Fama-MacBeth study is given by

$$\bar{R}_p = \gamma_0 + \gamma_1\hat{\beta}_p + \gamma_2\hat{\beta}_p^2 + \gamma_3 S\hat{E}_p + \mu_p, \tag{20}$$

[21] Figure 6 of Black, Jensen, and Scholes [1], pp. 101–03, shows average monthly returns versus systematic risk for 17 nonoverlapping two-year periods from 1932 to 1965.

FIGURE 12

Results of Black, Jensen, and Scholes Study (1931–65)

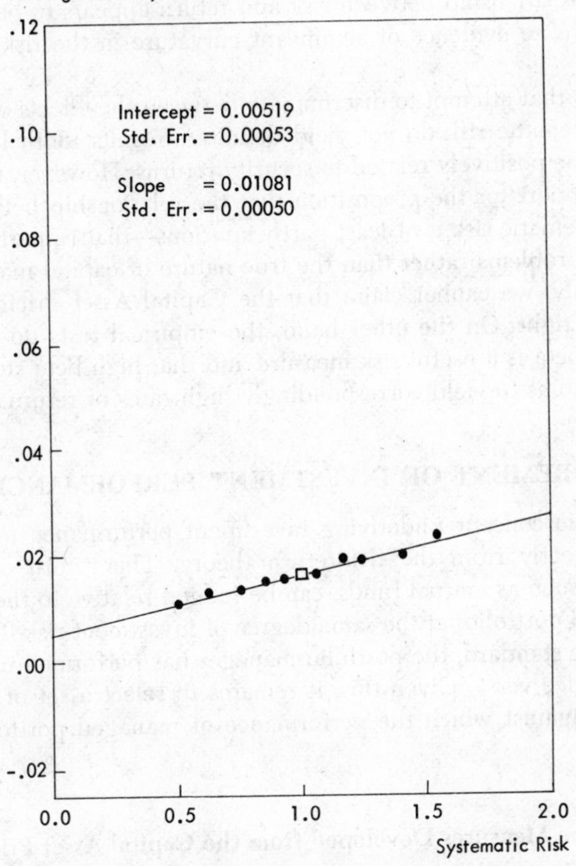

Average monthly returns versus systematic risk for the 35-year period 1931–65 for 10 portfolios and the market portfolio.
Source: Black, Jensen, and Scholes [1], Figure 7, p. 104.

where, according to the CAPM, we should expect γ_2 and γ_3 to have zero values.

The results of the Fama-MacBeth tests show that while estimated values of γ_2 and γ_3 are not equal to zero for each interval examined, their values tend to be insignificantly different from zero. Fama and MacBeth also confirm the Black-Jensen-Scholes result that the realized values of γ_0 are not equal to $\bar{R}_f$, as predicted by the Capital Asset Pricing Model.

Summary of Test Results

We will briefly summarize the major results of the empirical tests.

1. The evidence shows a significant positive relationship between

realized returns and systematic risk. However, the slope of the relationship ($\hat{\gamma}_1$) is usually less than predicted by the Capital Asset Pricing Model.

2. The relationship between risk and return appears to be linear. The studies give no evidence of significant curvature in the risk-return relationship.

3. Tests that attempt to discriminate between the effects of systematic and unsystematic risk do not yield definitive results. Both kinds of risk appear to be positively related to security returns. However, there is substantial support for the proposition that the relationship between return and unsystematic risk is at least partly spurious—that is, partly reflecting statistical problems rather than the true nature of capital markets.

Obviously, we cannot claim that the Capital Asset Pricing Model is absolutely right. On the other hand, the empirical tests do support the view that beta is a useful risk measure and that high beta stocks tend to be priced so as to yield correspondingly high rates of return.

9. MEASUREMENT OF INVESTMENT PERFORMANCE

The basic concept underlying investment performance measurement follows directly from the risk-return theory. The return on managed portfolios, such as mutual funds, can be judged relative to the returns on unmanaged portfolios at the same degree of investment risk. If the return exceeds the standard, the portfolio manager has performed in a superior way, and vice versa. Given this, it remains to select a set of benchmark portfolios against which the performance of managed portfolios can be evaluated.

Performance Measures Developed from the Capital Asset Pricing Model

The Capital Asset Pricing Model provides a convenient and familiar standard for performance measurement; the benchmark portfolios are simply combinations of the riskless asset and the market index. The return standard for a mutual fund, for example, with beta equal to β_P is equal to the risk-free rate (R_F) plus β_P times the average realized risk premium on the market $R_M - R_F$). Thus, the return on the performance standard (R_S) is given by

$$\bar{R}_S = \bar{R}_F + \beta_P(\bar{R}_M - \bar{R}_F), \tag{21}$$

where $\bar{R}_M$ and $\bar{R}_F$ are the arithmetic average returns on the market index and riskless asset during the evaluation period. The performance measure, designated α_p, is equal to the difference in average returns between the fund and its standard; that is,

$$\alpha_p = \bar{R}_P - \bar{R}_S, \tag{22}$$

where $\overline{R}_P$ is the arithmetic average return on the fund. Under the CAPM assumption, the expected values of $\overline{R}_P$ and $\overline{R}_S$ are the same; therefore, the expected value for the performance measure α_p is zero. Thus, managed portfolios with positive estimated values for α_p have outperformed the standard, and vice versa. Estimated values of alpha ($\hat{\alpha}_p$) are determined as discussed in Section 7 by regressing the portfolio risk premiums on the corresponding market risk premiums.

The interpretation of the estimated alpha must take into consideration possible statistical measurement errors. As discussed in Section 7, the standard error of alpha (SE_a) is a measure of the extent of the possible measurement error. The larger the standard error, the less certain we can be that the measured alpha is a close approximation to the true value.[22]

A measure of the degree of statistical significance of the estimated alpha value is given by the ratio of the estimated alpha to its standard error. The ratio, designated as t_a, is given by

$$t_\alpha = \frac{\hat{\alpha}_{\hat{p}}}{SE_{\hat{\alpha}}}\,. \tag{23}$$

The statistic t_a gives a measure of the extent to which the true value of alpha can be considered to be different from zero. If the absolute value of t_a is large, then we have more confidence that the true value of alpha is different from zero. Absolute values of t_a in excess of 2.0 indicate a probability of less than about 2.5 percent that the true value of alpha is zero.

These methods of performance measurement were originally devised by Michael Jensen [10, 11] and have been widely used in many studies of investment performance, including that of the recent SEC Institutional Investor Study [22].

A performance measure closely related to the Jensen alpha measure was developed by Jack L. Treynor [24]. The Treynor performance measure (designated TI) is given by[23]

$$TI = \frac{\alpha}{\beta} \tag{24}$$

The difference between the α and TI performance measures is simply that the fund alpha value has been divided by its estimated beta. The

---

22 See columns 2 and 3 of Table 4 for typical mutual fund $\hat{\alpha}$ and SE_a values.

23 Treynor's work preceded that of Jensen. In a discussion of Jensen's performance measure [26], Treynor showed that his measure (as originally presented in [25]) was equivalent to

$$TI = R_F - \frac{\alpha}{\beta}$$

Since R_F is a constant, the TI index for ranking purposes is equivalent to that given in equation (24).

FIGURE 13

Relationship between the Jensen and Treynor Measures of Investment Performance

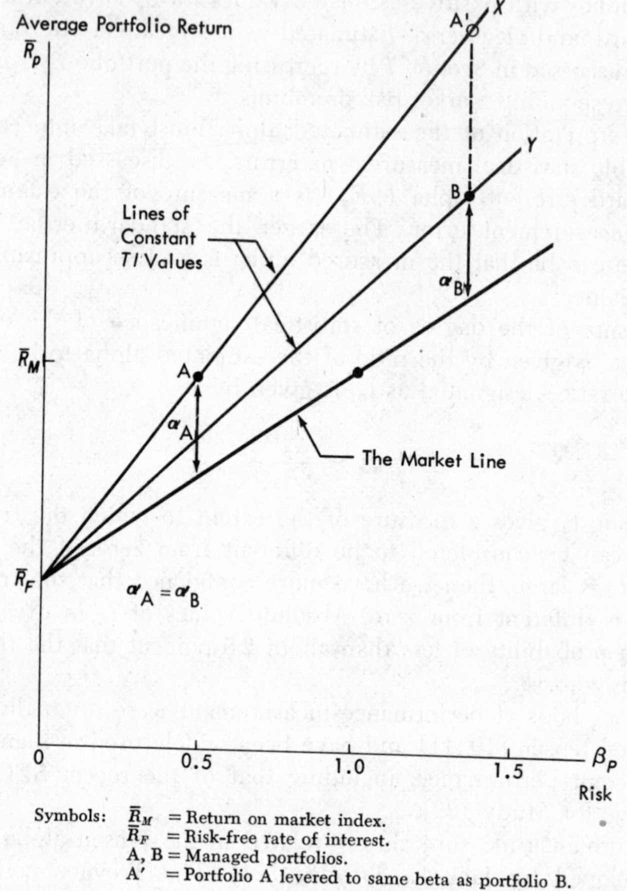

Symbols: $\bar{R}_M$ = Return on market index.
$\bar{R}_F$ = Risk-free rate of interest.
A, B = Managed portfolios.
A′ = Portfolio A levered to same beta as portfolio B.

effect, however, is significant, eliminating a so-called leverage bias from the Jensen alpha measures. This is illustrated in Figure 13.

Funds A and B in Figure 13 have the same alpha values. (The alphas are equal to the vertical distance on the diagram between the funds and the market line.) By combining portfolio B with the riskless rate (that is, by borrowing or lending at $\bar{R}_F$), any return-risk combination along line *Y* can be obtained. But such points are clearly dominated by combinations along line *X*—attainable by borrowing or lending combined with fund A. As can be seen from Figure 13, the alpha for fund A, when levered to the same beta as fund B (Point A′), dominates the latter's alpha value.

The Treynor measure eliminates this leverage effect. All funds which lie along a line (such as X or Y) have the same TI value. Thus, borrowing or lending combined with any fund outcome will not increase (or decrease) its performancme measure. The Treynor measure thus permits direct performance comparisons among funds with differing beta values.

Problems with the Market Line Standard

The tests of the Capital Asset Pricing Model summarized in Section 8 indicate that the average returns over time on securities and portfolios tend to deviate from the predictions of the model. Though the observed risk-return relationships seem to be linear, they are generally flatter than predicted by the CAPM, implying the tradeoff or risk for return is less than predicted.

FIGURE 14

Measurement of Investment Performance: Market Line versus Empirical Standard

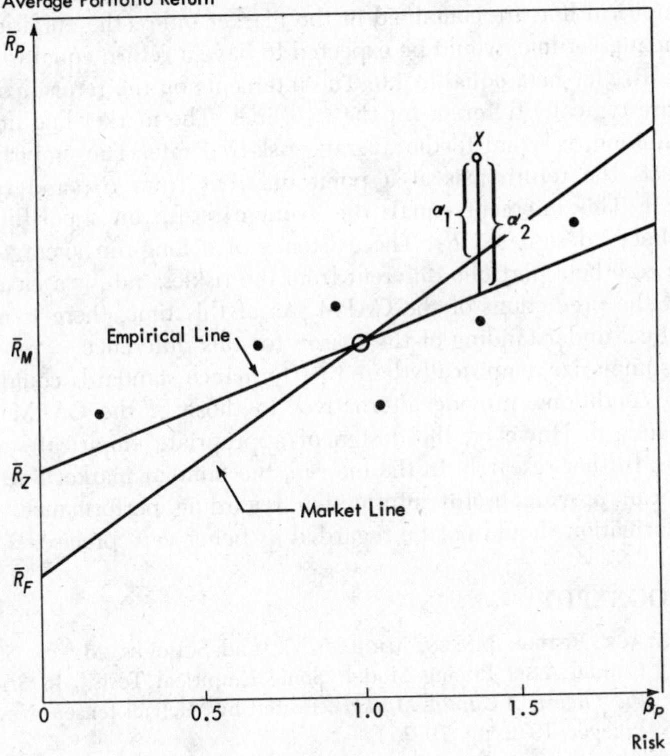

Symbols: $\bar{R}_M$ = Return on market index.
$\bar{R}_Z$ = Return on zero beta portfolio.
$\bar{R}_F$ = Risk-free rate of interest.
X = Investment portfolios.
O = Market index.

This evidence raises some question as to whether the CAPM market line provides the best benchmark for performance measurement and suggests instead that other benchmark portfolios may be more appropriate. For example, under certain conditions, the empirical risk-return lines developed by Black, Jensen, and Scholes [1] and others would seem to be a reasonable alternative to the CAPM market line standard. This might be the case if the portfolio for which performance is being measured were restricted to exactly the same set of investment options used to create the empirical standard, that is, the portfolio were fully invested in common stock and could not use leverage to increase its beta value. For such a portfolio it would seem appropriate to measure performance relative to the empirical line, as opposed to the market line.

A comparison of these standards is illustrated in Figure 14. The market line performance measure (designated as α_1 in Figure 14) is equal to the vertical distance from the portfolio to the market line. The empirical line measure (designated α_2) is the vertical distance from the portfolio to the empirical line. Since ideally all the stocks used to develop the empirical line are contained in the market index, the empirical line, like the market line, would be expected to have a return equal to market return, $\bar{R}_M$, for beta equal to 1.0. The intercepts on the return axis, however, are typically different for the two lines. The market line intercept, by definition, is equal to the average risk-free rate. The empirical line intersects the return axis at a point different from $\bar{R}_F$, and typically above it. This intercept equals the average return on a portfolio with "zero beta," designated $\bar{R}_Z$. The existence of a long-run average return on the zero beta portfolio different from the riskless rate is a clear violation of the predictions of the CAPM. As of this time, there is no clear theoretical understanding of the reason for this difference.

To summarize, empirically based performance standards could, under certain conditions, provide alternatives to those of the CAPM market line standard. However, the design of appropriate empirical standards requires further research. In the interim, the familiar market line benchmarks can provide useful information regarding performance, though the information should not be regarded as being very precise.[24]

BIBLIOGRAPHY

[1] BLACK, FISHER; JENSEN, MICHAEL C., and SCHOLES, MYRON S. "The Capital Asset Pricing Model: Some Empirical Tests." In *Studies in the Theory of Capital Markets*. Edited by Michael Jensen. New York: Praeger, 1972, pp. 79–121.

[24] There are a number of excellent references for further study of portfolio theory. Among these we would recommend books by Richard A. Brealey [4], Jack Clark Francis [7], and William F. Sharpe [24]. For a more technical survey of the theoretical and empirical literature, see Jensen [12].

[2] Blume, Marshall E. "Portfolio Theory: A Step toward Its Practical Application." *Journal of Business* 43 (April 1970): 152–73.

[3] Blume, Marshall E., and Friend, Irwin. "A New Look at the Capital Asset Pricing Model." *Journal of Finance* 28 (March 1973): 19–33.

[4] Brealey, Richard A. *An Introduction to Risk and Return from* Common Stocks. Cambridge, Mass.: MIT Press, 1969.

[5] Fama, Eugene F. "Components of Investment Performance." *The Journal of Finance* 27 (June 1972): 551–67.

[6] Fama, Eugene F., and MacBeth, James D. "Risk Return and Equilibrium: Empirical Tests." Unpublished working paper no. 7237 University of Chicago, Graduate School of Business, August 1972.

[7] Francis, Jack C. *Investment Analysis and Management*. New York: McGraw-Hill, 1972.

[8] Friend, Irwin, and Blume, Marshall E. "Risk and the Long Run Rate of Return on NYSE Common Stocks." Working paper no. 18–72. Wharton School of Commerce and Finance, Rodney L. White Center for Financial Research.

[9] Jacob, Nancy. "The Measurement of Systematic Risk for Securities and Portfolios: Some Empirical Results." *Journal of Financial and Quantitative Analysis* 6 (March 1971): 815–34.

[10] Jensen, Michael C. "The Performance of Mutual Funds in the Period 1945–1964." *Journal of Finance* 23 (May 1968): 389–416.

[11] ———. "Risk, the Pricing of Capital Assets, and the Evaluation of Investment Portfolios." *Journal of Business* 42 (April 1969): 167–247.

[12] ———. "Capital Markets: Theory and Evidence." *The Bell Journal of Economics and Management Science* 3 (Autumn 1972): 357–98.

[13] Levy, Robert A. "On the Short Term Stationarity of Beta Coefficients." *Financial Analyst's Journal* 27 (November–December 1971): 55–62.

[14] Lintner, John. "The Valuation of Risk Assets and the Selection of Risky Investments in Stock Portfolios and Capital Budgets." *Review of Economics and Statistics* 47 (February 1965): 13–37.

[15] ———. "Security Prices, Risk, and Maximal Gains from Diversification." *Journal of Finance* 20 (December 1965): 587–616.

[16] Mains, Norman E. "Are Mutual Fund Beta Coefficients Stationary." Unpublished working paper. Investment Company Institute, Washington, D.C., October 1972.

[17] Markowitz, Harry M. "Portfolio Selection." *Journal of Finance* 7 (March 1952): 77–91.

[18] ———. *Portfolio Selection: Efficient Diversification of Investments.* New York: John Wiley and Sons, 1959.

[19] Miller, Merton H., and Scholes, Myron S. "Rates of Returns in Relation to Risk: A Reexamination of Recent Findings." In *Studies*

in the Theory of Capital Markets. Edited by Michael Jensen. New York: Praeger, 1972, pp. 47–78.

[20] MODIGLIANI, FRANCO, and POGUE, GERALD A. *A Study of Investment Performance Fees.* Lexington, Mass.: Heath-Lexington Books, 1974.

[21] POGUE, GERALD A., and CONWAY, WALTER. "On the Stability of Mutual Fund Beta Values." Unpublished working paper. MIT, Sloan School of Management, June 1972.

[22] SECURITIES AND EXCHANGE COMMISSION. *Institutional Investor Study Report of the Securities and Exchange Commission.* Chapter 4, "Investment Advisory Complexes," pp. 325–47. Washington, D.C.: U.S. Government Printing Office, 1971.

[23] SHARPE, WILLIAM F. "Capital Asset Prices: A Theory of Market Equilibrium under Conditions of Risk." *Journal of Finance* 19 (September 1965): 425–42.

[24] ———. *Portfolio Theory and Capital Markets.* New York: McGraw-Hill, 1970.

[25] TREYNOR, JACK L. "How to Rate the Management of Investment Funds." *Harvard Business Review* 43 (January–February 1965): pp. 63–75.

[26] ———. "The Performance of Mutual Funds in the Period 1945–1964: Discussion." *Journal of Finance* 23 (May 1968): pp. 418–19.

[27] WAGNER, WAYNE H., and LAU, SHEILA. "The Effect of Diversification on Risk." *Financial Analyst's Journal* 26 (November–December 1971): pp. 2–7.

45

The Analyst's Role in Portfolio Management

JACK L. TREYNOR
Editor
Financial Analysts Journal
New York, New York

IT IS OFTEN ASSERTED that security selection is a matter of balancing risk against reward (see Chapter 44). But which reward? And which risk? It is obvious the cumulative effect of individual selection decisions determines overall portfolio policy parameters such as: level of systematic risk, degree of diversification, turnover rate, and number of securities held. It is not always clear, however, how

1. these portfolio policies should be determined. To what extent are they truly independent, rather than different measures for the same thing?
2. these policies bear on the individual selection decision.

The computer approaches described by Markowitz make certain simplifications, but even so they suggest that portfolio selection is in principle a complicated process. The approach described here manages to be only slightly more complicated than the seat-of-the-pants approach, while making only one or two simplifications in the Markowitz approach.[1] The result is an approach which, while faithful to the main features of the real problem, is simple enough for any portfolio manager to use—without the benefit of a computer.

The key simplification is one now made quite commonly. Covariability among securities is assumed entirely explained by a general market

[1] Jack L. Treynor and Fischer Black, How to Use Security Analysis to Improve Portfolio Selection, in *Journal of Business,* Vol 46, pp. 66–86.

performance index. Any uncertainty surrounding future returns not explained by a market index is assumed to result from the statistical independence of one security from another. The terms *unique* and *specific risk* are often applied to the portion of total uncertainty not explained by the market.

In general, the individual security will have elements of both kinds of risk, i.e., market and specific. When balancing risk against reward it is crucially important to distinguish between the two kinds of risk. They play very different roles in portfolio selection. There is, however, at least one asset available to the portfolio manager which entails only one of the two kinds of risk. This is the market asset—i.e., an investment in the market as a whole.

A share in the market as a whole is hardly a practical portfolio investment. On the other hand, *approximations* to the market asset—i.e., assets with minimal, though not zero unique risk—are surprisingly easy to come by. It is convenient to refer to well-diversified proxies for the market portfolio as *passive* portfolios. The objectives for such portfolios are merely (1) a high degree of diversification and (2) maintenance of a specified level of market sensitivity. Both objectives can normally be met with a minimum of trading, hence the name passive.

The importance of the market asset in portfolio selection is that, in principle, its easy availability makes the degree of market risk in a security irrelevant when the portfolio manager is weighing risk against return in the selection decision. Suppose, for example, that the portfolio manager has decided—for whatever reason—that, as a matter of overall policy, his portfolio should have a level of systematic, or market, risk of 1.5—meaning that the portfolio's sensitivity to market fluctuations will be such that, on average, when the market goes up (down) 10 percent, the portfolio's value goes up (down) 15 percent.

If the average level of market sensitivity (β_M) in the equity portfolio is 2.0, then mixing with riskless treasury bills in the proportions of three parts equity (X_M) to one part treasuries (X_f) will achieve the desired overall level of sensitivity ($\beta_p = 1.5$):

$$\beta_p = (1 - X_f)\beta_M$$

or

$$1.5 = (1 - X_f)(2.0),$$

hence

$$X_f = 1/4;\ X_M = 3/4$$

or

$$X_M/X_f = 3/1,$$

since

$$X_M + X_f = 1.$$

If, on the other hand, a low sensitivity stock is sold out of the equity portfolio and replaced with a high sensitivity stock, the proportions of equity in the overall portfolio will have to be diluted further to sustain the desired overall sensitivity level (1.5). If the portfolio manager is free to displace the passive portfolio with money-fixed claims or vice versa, he can usually strike the complement to his active portfolio that achieves the desired level of market risk overall. Thus the inclusion of a particular equity in the portfolio has no necessary implications for the sensitivity of the overall portfolio.

Specific risk, however, is a horse of a different color. Unless the specific return for one security is perfectly correlated (or perfectly anticorrelated) with the specific return for another, there is no way to realize on one's expectations for the first security without exposing the final portfolio to the associated specific risk.

Lintner has defined the difference between return on the risky asset and the riskless rate of interest as "excess return."[2] Sharpe proposed a measure of fund performance that incorporated the ratio of excess return to the standard deviation of return.[3] We shall accept Sharpe's measure of performance and use it with slight modifications as an objective in seeking optimum portfolio selection. The modifications are the substitution of expected future return for average retrospective return, and dealing with the square of Sharpe's measure of goodness, rather than with the measure itself. (Although retrospectively excess portfolio returns may be negative, prospectively no rational set of portfolio holdings will lead to negative excess portfolio return.)

We call the square of Sharpe's measure the Sharpe ratio. The Sharpe ratio is unaffected by borrowing or lending at the riskless rate. It can be shown that the Sharpe ratio depends only on (1) the ratio of expected independent return, squared, to the variance of independent return; and (2) the balance between specific risk (i.e., the variance of independent return) and market risk (i.e., the variance of market return); and (3) the ratio of expected return on the market, squared, to the variance of market return.

The third number is simply a market constant, unless the portfolio manager is attempting to time the market. But in any case, the second and third numbers have nothing directly to do with individual securities. On the other hand, the first number, involving as it does independent returns, has everything to do with individual securities. We shall call a portfolio selected purely with regard to maximizing the ratio of expected abnormal return, squared, to variance of unique return an *active* portfolio. (Because the only justification for exposing a portfolio to

---

[2] J. Lintner, "Security Prices, Risk and Maximal Gains from Diversification," *Journal of Finance*, Dec. 1965, pp. 587–615.

[3] W. F. Sharpe, Mutual Fund Performance, *Journal of Business*, Jan. 1966, Vol. XXXIX, pp. 119–38.

specific risk is abnormal return, and because the abnormal return on a security persists only until the motivating investment insight is fully discounted, the residence in this portfolio of any specific security is likely to be temporary—hence the name *active.*)

Since market and specific risk are independent, the combination offers an excellent opportunity for diversification. The practical consequence is that the portfolio with the highest Sharpe ratio will rarely be either perfectly diversified (all market risk and no specific risk) or perfectly hedged (all specific risk and no market risk).

If, to achieve the highest Sharpe ratio, the active portfolio is supplemented by a long position in the market, the active portfolio's abnormal return will of course be diluted in the overall portfolio. But if the supplemental position is well diversified, the ratio of abnormal return, squared, to variance of unique return, will remain unaffected. Thus the value of this ratio obtained for the active portfolio determines its value for the overall portfolio; we call it the *appraisal ratio.*

Conceptually portfolio balancing can be viewed as a three-stage process: (1) using security analysis to achieve the highest possible appraisal ratio on the active portfolio, (2) buying the selling a passive portfolio to achieve the optimum blend between market risk and specific risk (that is, the blend that maximizes the Sharpe ratio), and (3) borrowing or lending to tailor the risky portfolio with the maximum Sharpe ratio to the ability and willingness of the investor in question to bear risk. Consideration of independent returns on specific securities arises only at the first of these three stages. The critical determinant of risk-adjusted performance in an equity portfolio is the value of the appraisal ratio for the active portfolio. Maximizing this ratio is the sole purpose of securities research.

The question naturally arises: Under the simplified model assumed here, what set of individual security holdings in the active portfolio maximizes the appraisal ratio? Let the fraction of the investor's equity devoted to the *i*th security be h_i, the expected abnormal return be $\bar{z}_i$, and the unique variance (i.e., the variance of the unique return) be $\bar{\sigma}_i^2$. Then the optimal holding is

$$h_i = \lambda \frac{\bar{z}_i}{\bar{\sigma}_i^2},$$

where λ is a number expressing in appropriate terms the investor's aggressiveness.

A similar expression gives the optimal holding of the market proxy:

$$h_m = \lambda \frac{\bar{z}_m}{\bar{\sigma}_m^2}.$$

The explicit position in the market proxy is, of course, the difference between the optimal position and the accumulated market exposure implicit in the active portfolio holdings; the latter number is given by

$$\sum_i h_i\beta_i .$$

The easiest way to understand how the necessary input variables $\bar{z}$ and $\bar{\sigma}^2$ are generated is in terms of a two-variable regression model relating actual z to the security analyst's opinion, μ. If there is no correlation between μ and z, then his opinion conveys no useful investment information. If there is a correlation, then there is also a set of regression coefficients relating z to μ:

$$\begin{aligned} z &= a + b\mu + \nu \\ &= \bar{z} + \nu, \end{aligned}$$

where ν is the forecast error between actual return z and the best estimate based on the analyst's opinion, μ.

The square of the correlation coefficient ρ^2 is the fraction of the variance in z anticipated by the analyst's opinions. If the correlation is perfect, all the variance is anticipated; there are no surprises, and there is no unique risk to the investor who takes positions in the security based on the opinions of that analyst. More generally, the relevant measure of risk is that fraction of the variance σ^2 in z not anticipated by the analyst's opinions. We have

$$\begin{aligned} \bar{\sigma}_i{}^2 &= (1 - \rho_i{}^2)\sigma_i{}^2, \\ h_i &= \lambda \frac{\bar{z}_i}{(1 - \rho_i{}^2)\sigma_i{}^2} . \end{aligned}$$

When $\rho^2 = 0$, the relevant risk is the variance of z; the entire unique return is surprise. Of course, the regression coefficient will then also be zero, and the only possible expectation of the unique return is zero. There is no justification for holding such a security in the active portfolio.

On the other hand, as the correlation—and its square, the coefficient of determination—improves, (1) unbiased forecasts $\bar{z}$ of z will take on larger absolute values, and (2) the relevant risk $\bar{\sigma}^2 = (1 - \rho^2)\ \sigma^2$ will grow smaller. The result will be larger positions in the security in absolute terms (for fixed λ), hence greater departures from perfect diversification (i.e., from an equity portfolio consisting purely of a market proxy) and more trading (turnover).

The above equation contains in one simple relationship all the traditional elements entering into an intuitive investment decision:

1. The investor's willingness to bear risk (λ).
2. His forecast of future return ($\bar{z}_i$).
3. The intrinsic, or "total ignorance" risk unique to a position in that security (σ_i^2).
4. His confidence in his forecasting ability (ρ_i^2).

It is frequently necessary to make some judgment about the economic value of an analyst's work. It is also necessary from time to time to make decisions about the allocation of research effort among securities. Many practical considerations, including specifically human considerations, will of course enter into such judgments and such decisions. Greater consistency across securities and across time is possible, however, if one has a framework for relating them to a common goal. The equations discussed here provide such a framework.

When the expected unique returns $\bar{z}_i$ and unanticipated variances in unique returns $\bar{\sigma}_i^2$ are known, the appraisal ratio, at optimum balance, takes the form

$$\text{Appraisal ratio} = \sum_i \frac{\bar{z}_i^2}{\bar{\sigma}_i^2} = \sum_i \frac{\bar{z}_i^2}{(1 - \rho_i^2)\sigma_i^2},$$

where, in principle, the sum runs over all the securities in which the investor has research information. (As noted, at any given point in time, some of these securities will contribute terms with negligible value.)

When we talk about the value of an analyst, or about how well a given portfolio is managed, we abstract from knowledge of a specific set of return forecasts. We are talking, in effect, about *long-run* expectations of the appraisal ratio, or of terms in the appraisal ratio corresponding to specific securities. Since the value of this ratio will vary over time, as investment opportunities present themselves (when the true future value of z is zero, the good analyst's opinion will imply a return forecast of zero, and the security in question will make no contribution to the appraisal ratio in that period), a plausible common goal in securities research is maximizing the *expectation* of the appraisal ratio, taking into account the frequency with which potential opportunities present themselves. In this case the contribution of research in the *i*th security to the appraisal ratio becomes

$$\frac{E[\bar{z}_i^2]}{(1 - \rho^2)\sigma^2} = \frac{\rho_i^2}{1 - \rho_i^2},$$

and the expectation of the appraisal ratio is

$$E\left[\sum \frac{\bar{z}_i^2}{\bar{\sigma}_i^2}\right] = \sum \frac{\rho_i^2}{1 - \rho_i^2}.$$

It is clear that the long-run contribution of the *i*th security to the appraisal ratio of the portfolio depends only on ρ_i^2. It is also clear that $\rho_i^2/1 - \rho_i^2$ is the measure of the economic contribution of research on the *i*th security.

The object of allocating research effort is maximizing

$$\sum_i \frac{\rho_i^2}{1 - \rho_i^2},$$

subject to some constraint on total effort. Let w_i be the effort devoted to researching the ith security. Allocation of research effort is optimal only if for securities i and j among the set researched we have

$$\frac{\frac{\partial}{\partial w_i}(\rho_i^2)}{(1-\rho_i^2)^2} = \frac{\frac{\partial}{\partial w_j}(\rho_j^2)}{(1-\rho_j^2)^2},$$

for all i and j. In other words, the marginal improvement in the fraction of the variance of the unique return anticipated will stand in the same ratio to the square of the fraction of the variance not anticipated for every security. For securities not researched, this ratio should of course be smaller than for those researched.

Numerical Example

To demonstrate the application of the principles developed above, we provide a sample problem. The problem is finding a risky portfolio containing these two assets—the market and the single security—with the highest expected return for specified level of variance. The problem is both exaggerated and simplified. It is simplified in that no ability to forecast the market is assumed and in that forecasting ability is confined to a single security. It is exaggerated in that the forecasting ability far exceeds that normally encountered in practice.

The ability to forecast the independent return on the single security is measured in terms of the correlation coefficient between forecast return and subsequent actual return. In practice the straightforward way to estimate this correlation coefficient is to collect forecasts and subsequent returns and compute the historical correlation coefficient between them. The correlation coefficient may for a variety of reasons not be stationary, and in such cases the correlation coefficient computed from an actual forecast sample returns can be misleading. It still represents a place to start, however, in forming a subjective judgment about the value of the correlation coefficient that will apply over the holding period for which the portfolio is being formed.

Table 1 displays the historical track record from which the correlation coefficient employed in our problem is calculated. The column headed u contains forecasts of independent return (i.e., return net of market effect) for the security in question, month by month; and the column headed z contains the subsequent actual returns. In addition to these two columns, it is convenient to list the values of u^2, z^2, and the product, uz. The sums of all five columns are then computed. From these sums we can compute the values of the correlation coefficient, the regression coefficient, and the variance of the independent return. Using the formulas provided in Chapter 38, the value of the correlation coefficient is 0.52. The coefficient of determination, the square of the correlation

TABLE 1

Month	u	z	u²	z²	uz
1	10	20	100	400	200
2	8	10	64	100	80
3	5	11	25	121	55
4	0	−8	0	64	0
5	−2	12	4	144	−24
6	−8	−15	64	225	120
7	−2	−5	4	25	10
8	−5	8	25	64	−40
9	0	4	0	16	0
10	−2	−11	4	121	22
11	2	−2	4	4	−4
12	5	−12	25	144	−60

coefficient, is therefore 0.276. The value of the regression coefficient is 1.13, implying that the forecaster in this case is underestimating the absolute value of both good returns and bad returns. The variance of the actual (independent) returns is 118. (The values of u and z in Table 1 are percentage returns. The variance is a kind of average of squares of these returns. Thus the percentage effect is itself squared when the variance is expressed in these terms).

Let us assume for definiteness that the return variance for our optimal portfolio is stipulated to equal the return variance for the market as a whole. Let us further assume that the expected excess return (that is, the return in excess of the riskless rate—here assumed to be 4 percent) for the market asset is 5 percent per annum, and that the variance around this return is 15 percent squared.

The formulas previously developed contain a factor of proportionality, λ, which expresses a desired balance between risk (expressed as the variance of return) and expected return. The algebraic development below provides one way of obtaining its value in practical problems. In the formulation below, λ^2 is expressed as a function of the desired portfolio variance σ_P^2 and the Sharpe ratio for the universe of assets from which the portfolio is to be constructed.

$$\lambda^2 = \frac{\sigma_p^2}{\sum_i \frac{\bar{z}_i^2}{\bar{\sigma}_i^2}}.$$

The market ratio under the assumptions stated above is computed as follows:

$$\frac{\bar{z}_m^2}{\sigma_m^2} = \frac{(0.05)^2}{(0.15)^2} = 0.111.$$

It is arbitrarily assumed that for the holding period for which we are attempting to engineer the optimal portfolio balance, the raw forecast of independent return for the individual security is 3 percent. Using the regression coefficient and intercept value obtained from regressing actual returns against forecast returns, we compute the expected return as follows.

$$\bar{z}_i = -0.13 + 1.13(3.0) = 3.26\ (\%).$$

Together with the coefficient of determination ρ_i^2 and variance σ_i^2 of the independent return previously calculated, this number enables us to compute the appraisal ratio for the security:

$$\frac{\bar{z}_i^2}{\bar{\sigma}_i^2} = \frac{\bar{z}_i^2}{(1 - \rho_i^2)\sigma_i^2} = \frac{0.0326^2}{(1 - 0.276)(0.0118)} = 0.124.$$

The sum of the market ratio and the appraisal ratio for individual securities (in this case there is of course only one) is the Sharpe ratio for the portfolio. Its value is

$$0.111 + 0.124 = 0.235.$$

The value of the Sharpe ratio together with the stipulated level of portfolio risk enables us to calculate the value of the proportionality constant, λ.

$$\lambda = \frac{\sigma_p}{\sqrt{\sum_i \frac{\bar{z}_i^2}{\bar{\sigma}_i^2}}} = \frac{0.15}{\sqrt{0.235}} = 0.309$$

Substituting the expected return and variance for the market asset and the individual security, respectively, into the formula for optimal holding, page 1346, we have for the respective holdings

$$h_m = 0.687$$
$$h_i = 1.178,$$

expressed as fractions of the investor's equity. Weighting these holdings by the expected excess returns for the respective assets and summing, we have the expected excess return for the portfolio

$$\text{Expected portfolio return} = 0.04 + 0.687(0.05) + 1.18(0.0326) = 0.113.$$

Table 2 displays the contributions of the market asset and the individual security to the Sharpe ratio, the portfolio variance, and the expected portfolio return for the respective assets. In principle the ratio, asset to asset, of these three numbers should be the same.

At the same level of portfolio risk (variance), the addition of (the independent return on) a security which for the holding period ahead is only slightly more attractive than the market asset raises expected portfolio return by 2.3 percent.

If the individual security has a market sensitivity (beta) of 0.5, then

TABLE 2

	Sharpe Ratio	*Variance*	*Expected Return*
Market	0.111	0.0106	0.0343
Security	0.124	0.0119	0.0385
Ratio	1.116	1.1220	1.1220

the optimal holding implies an exposure to market risk equivalent to devoting 0.589 (1.178(0.5) = 0.589) of the investor's equity to the market asset. The difference between the optimal holding of the market asset (0.687) and the exposure incidental to the optimal holding of the individual security (0.589) is the necessary explicit investment in the market (again, expressed as a fraction of the investor's equity): 0.687 − 0.589 = 0.098.

46

Application of Linear Programming to Financial Planning

ABRAHAM CHARNES, Ph.D.
Center for Cybernetic Studies
University of Texas at Austin
Austin, Texas

WILLIAM W. COOPER, Ph.D.
School of Urban and Public Affairs
Carnegie Mellon Institute
Pittsburgh, Pennsylvania

MARTIN A. KEANE, Ph.D.
Research Laboratories
General Motors Corporation
Warren, Michigan

THIS CHAPTER deals with linear programming in financial planning. Generally speaking, a linear program optimizes a linear form subject to linear inequality constraints. A mathematical statement of this is:

$$\text{minimize} \quad \sum_{j=1}^{n} c_j x_j$$

(1.1)

$$\text{subject to:} \quad \sum_{j=1}^{n} a_{ij} x_j \geq b_i \quad \text{for} \quad i = 1, 2, \ldots, m$$

$$x_j \geq 0,$$

where the c_j, a_{ij}, and b_i are known constants and the x_j are decision variables. The a_{ij} might represent the per unit return at period i from investment j; the b_i, amounts of cash required at period i, x_j the amount to be invested in j and the c_j might be factors used to translate all investments to comparable units, perhaps present value dollars. For instance, this might represent a situation in which we desire an annuity that returns at least b_i in period i. (There are m such value constraints.) We then want to obtain this annuity at minimum cost, as noted in the objective function, where c_j represents the cost of investing in the jth security, which yields the indicated return of a_{ij} in period i. The following then is a possible application of linear programming: "Find the set of non-negative investments with minimal cost which will return at least the amount b_i in period $i = 1, 2, 3, \ldots, m$."

PRIMAL DUAL RELATIONS

Associated with the linear program (1.1), is a second problem involving the same parameters, c_j, a_{ij}, b_i, called its dual:

$$\text{maximize} \quad \sum_{i=1}^{m} y_i b_i$$

$$(1.2) \qquad \text{subject to:} \quad \sum_{i=1}^{m} y_i a_{ij} \leq c_j,\ j = 1, 2, \ldots, n$$

$$y_i \geq 0.$$

There is a basic theorem known as the "Dual Theorem of Linear Programming" that asserts, among other things, that when (1.1) and (1.2) both have finite solutions, then the values of these solutions are equal, i.e., if x^* and y^* are optimal solutions to (1.1) and (1.2), respectively, then

$$(1.3) \qquad \sum_{j=1}^{n} c_j x_j^* = \sum_{i=1}^{m} y_i^* b_i .$$

Of importance to our present discussion is the use of the dual solution y^*, as "prices" or "evaluators" of the b_i in the primal constraints. This is possible if y is optimal not only for the original dual objective function but also for a slight perturbation of b_i to $b_i + \Delta b_i$. This is usually the case. When this is so the equation (1.3) provides the incremental increase in the new optimal investment policy,

$$\sum_{j=1}^{n} c_j \bar{x}_j$$

associated with the additional cash need, Δb_i, at period i. This is simply $\Delta b_i y_i^*$. For example, if y_{10} is .9 present value dollars per dollar in period 10 then .9 more present dollars must be optimally invested to increase the return at period 10 by 1 dollar.

In practice a simple model is unable to encompass all possible investment alternatives but is restricted to those which are most likely. The dual evaluators can then point toward investments that may have been excluded from the initial problem formulation. It might be in our simple example that there exists, outside the model framework, an investment that will return \$1 in period 10 for \$.85 invested today. The optimal dual variable $y_{10}^* = .9$ implies that the latter is preferable to any investment within the model.

Complementary slackness is a second important result relating dual programs. Also called "the theorem of the alternative"—see [3], p. 185—this states that if x and y are optimal solutions to (1.1) and (1.2) then

$$x_j > 0 \text{ implies } \Sigma y_i a_{ij} = c_j,$$
$$y_i > 0 \text{ implies } \Sigma a_{ij} x_j = b_i,$$

i.e., we optimally invest a positive amount in j, ($x_j > 0$) only if its present value calculated with the internal "discount factors," y_i, is equal to the external discount factor, c_j.

The following example is based on a simple buying, selling, and storage problem drawn from [8], the articles which first showed how linear programming, including its duality theory, could be used to deal with financial planning problems, including determining internal yield or discount rates, and so on. For purposes of illustration we set $n = 5$ periods as the "planning horizon," and let j be the period index, $j = 1,2,3, \ldots 5$. We also let B = fixed warehouse capacity (in units of the single product we will consider in this example) and A = initial inventory. Finally, we let p_j and c_j be the respective unit sales and purchase price in period j, and x_j and y_j the amounts bought and sold in period j. Given A, B, p and c, the firm wishes to select a program, i.e., a set of purchases, x, and sales, y, that will maximize its profit. Such a program must, of course, be feasible, which is here interpreted to mean: (1) the amount of inventory on hand must never exceed the warehouse capacity, and (2) all sales must be made from inventory.

This problem can be represented by the following mathematical model:

$$\text{maximize} \quad \sum_{j=1}^{5} p_j y_j - \sum_{j=1}^{5} c_j x_j$$

$$\text{(1.4)} \qquad \text{subject to:} \quad -\sum_{j=1}^{i} y_j + \sum_{j=1}^{i} x_j \leq B - A$$

$$\sum_{j=1}^{i} y_j - \sum_{j=1}^{i-1} x_j \leq A, \; i = 1, 2, \ldots, 5$$

$$x_j, y_j \geq 0, \; j = 1, 2, \ldots, 5.$$

where the first $i = 1, \ldots, 5$ constraints refer to condition (1) and the next $i = 1, \ldots, 5$ constraints refer to condition (2). We next adjoin financial constraints reflecting a fixed line of credit or a cash fund, limited to a maximum amount, M, and use the dual solution to deduce de facto interest rates, etc. These financial constraints

$$\text{(1.5)} \qquad \sum_{j=1}^{i} c_j x_j - \sum_{j=1}^{i-1} p_j y_j \leq M, \qquad 1 = 1, 2, \ldots, 5,$$

reflect the fact that all purchases are made in cash and the proceeds of a sale are realized one period later. For definiteness we restrict our attention to the numerical example of Table 1. This primal problem and its dual are presented, with optimal solutions, in Table 2.

TABLE 1

Data for Warehousing Model with Simple Financial Constraints: One-Period Lag

j = *Period*	*Unit Cost* = c_j	*Unit Sales Price* = p_j
1	25	20
2	25	35
3	25	30
4	35	25
5	45	50

A = 100 = opening inventory } "Tons" or equivalent units
B = 125 = warehouse capacity }
M = 500 = minimum cash balance
n = 5 = number of "periods"

The dual evaluators may be analyzed period by period, or cumulatively. We first examine the latter via

$$T \equiv t_1 + t_2 + t_3 + t_4 + t_5 = \$25$$

and

$$U \equiv u_1 + u_2 + u_3 + u_4 + u_5 = \$60$$

The cumulant, T = \$25, evaluates the worth of an additional unit to B, the warehouse capacity. This value is the amount which can be obtained from employing this additional unit of capacity optimally with the data of Table 1. Turning next to the amount of opening inventory, A, we observe that it appears in both buying and selling constraints in Table 2. Hence we must combine its evaluators into (U-T) = (\$60–25) = \$35. An additional unit of opening inventory increases opportunities for additional accumulations by U = \$60, on the one hand, but, on the other hand, it simultaneously reduces other opportunities by utilizing an additional ton of warehouse space. Hence, an additional unit of inventory adds only \$35 to the sum that can be accumulated over this $n = 5$ period horizon. Of course, if both inventory and warehouse capacity are *simultaneously* increased, then the entire \$35 + \$25 = \$60 can be secured.

The financial evaluators shown in Table 2, *viz.*,

TABLE 2

Solution to the Warehousing Example of Table 1

Dual	*Direct* x: 20 0 125 0 0	*Direct* y: 0 120 0 0 125	*In-equality*	*Stipu-lation*
$0 = t_1$	x_1	$-y_1$	< 25	
$0 = t_2$	$x_1 + x_2$	$-y_1 - y_2$	< 25	
$10 = t_3$	$x_1 + x_2 + x_3$	$-y_1 - y_2 - y_3$	$= 25$	*B—A*
$15 = t_4$	$x_1 + x_2 + x_3 + x_4$	$-y_1 - y_2 - y_3 - y_4$	$= 25$	
$0 = t_5$	$x_1 + x_2 + x_3 + x_4 + x_5$	$-y_1 - y_2 - y_3 - y_4 - y_5$	< 25	
$0 = u_1$		y_1	<100	
$0 = u_2$	$-x_1$	$y_1 + y_2$	$=100$	
$10 = u_3$	$-x_1 - x_2$	$y_1 + y_2 + y_3$	$=100$	*A*
$0 = u_4$	$-x_1 - x_2 - x_3$	$y_1 + y_2 + y_3 + y_4$	<100	
$50 = u_5$	$-x_1 - x_2 - x_3 - x_4$	$y_1 + y_2 + y_3 + y_4 + y_5$	$=100$	
$0 = v_1$	c_1x_1		$=500$	
$2/5 = v_2$	$c_1x_1 + c_2x_2$	$-p_1y_1$	$=500$	
$0 = v_3$	$c_1x_1 + c_2x_2 + c_3x_3$	$-p_1y_1 - p_2y_2$	<500	*M*
$0 = v_4$	$c_1x_1 + c_2x_2 + c_3x_3 + c_4x_4$	$-p_1y_1 - p_2y_2 - p_3y_3$	<500	
$0 = v_5$	$c_1x_1 + c_2x_2 + c_3x_3 + c_4x_4 + c_5x_5$	$-p_1y_1 - p_2y_2 - p_3y_3 - p_4y_4$	<500	
Direct Costs	−25 −25 −25 −35 −45 (−c)	20 35 30 25 50 (p)	*Direct Price*	

$$V = v_1 + v_2 + v_3 + v_4 + v_5 = 2/5$$

are of special interest. This cumulant, $V = 2/5$, is the opportunity cost associated with the balance, $M = \$500$, which this business wants to maintain at all times. Setting $W = 1 + V$ we obtain the value of the "compounding factor" $w = 7/5$, which means that an added dollar invested in this constraint will accumulate to \$1.40. Alternatively, W may be used to discount the other dual evaluators as in $T/W = \$17\ 6/7$ or $(U\text{-}T)/W = \$25$ if a comparison with alternative uses of funds is wanted. Figures 1, for example, shows how a parent company might consider allocating available funds between two subsidiaries F_1 and F_2 by reference to the V value associated with an amount $M = M_1 + M_2$. Starting with $M_1 = \$0$ for F_1, one may vary it parametrically either separately for each firm (as is done here) or together in one, more comprehensive, model—the latter is preferred if there are opportunities for trade or joint endeavors between F_1 and F_2—to obtain the graphs depicted in Figure 1. Holding M fixed one may regard F_2 as the source of funds for F_1 or if one regards these as flows per unit time then F_1 and F_2 may be regarded as demand and supply curves with an intersection at M_1^* (or somewhere in the half-open interval to its right) at which the remnant value $M_2 = M - M_1$ would remain with F_2. And, of course, one may also add a third dimension to study analogous variations in the value of M, the total funds availability which limits the range of variation for M_1 (hence M_2) in Figure 1.

The analysis to this point was restricted to the case in which only the whole $n = 5$-period horizon was of interest. Turning to the values associated with the dual evaluators written in lower case letters in Table 2, however, we can deal with subdivisions in this total time-

FIGURE 1

Supply and demand for Funds or Graphs of V Values for $M_1 = M - M_2$

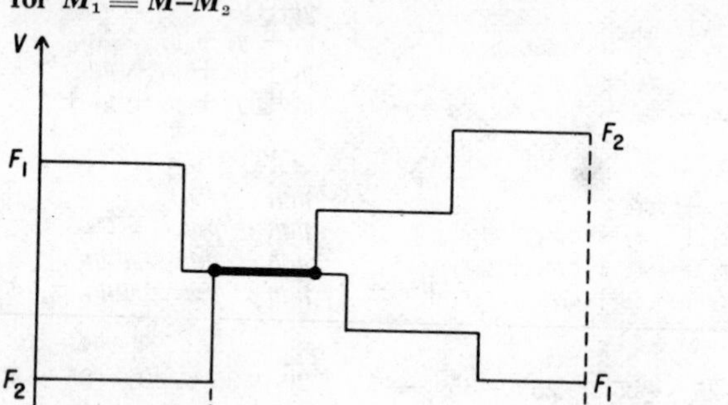

interval. Observe, for instance, that $v_3 = v_4 = v_5 = 0$. This means that after the purchases and sales realizations of periods 1 and 2, no further accumulation opportunities are available and funds may be diverted elsewhere at no cost due to lost opportunities here if everything else, e.g., warehouse capacity, remains fixed. Similar remarks apply to the t_j and u_j values so that the assets with which they are associated may also be diverted in or out of this business at the indicated times, if this is possible, and a more refined time-dimensional analysis is thus available via these lower case evaluators. See [8] for their further development. See also [15].

The structure of the matrix of Table 2 leads to efficient computational algorithms described in [3]. It also suggests an alternate formulation as a capacitated cash-commodity exchange network (Fig. 2), which can be used as a prototype for effecting analogue or other computations to analyze financial plans relative to other company operations. (Only the segment involving the cash "amplifier," $p_1 = \$35$, resulting from a sale in period 2 and the "deamplifier" $1/c_1 = 1/\$25$ resulting from a period 2 purchase, as obtained from Table 1, is shown.) This network type of model can also be extended to handle many commodities subject to a single liquidity constraint. The cash axis role as medium of exchange in

FIGURE 2

Network Model of Single Commodity Liquidity Constraint Warehouse Model

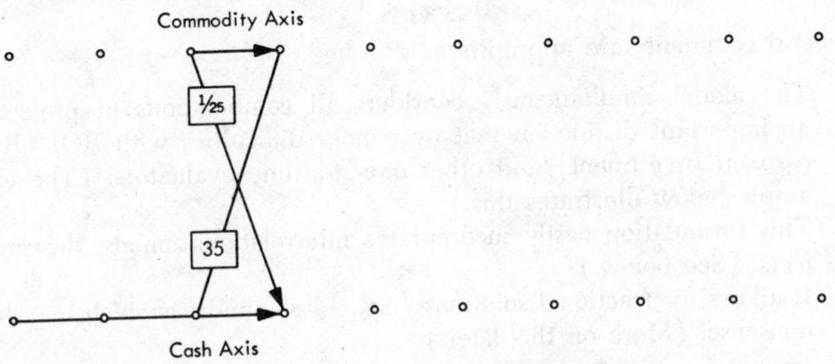

this multicommodity model (Fig. 3) and the potential, or potential drops, of currents and voltages across the various branches can be associated with the more refined time-dimensional analysis for the dual variables and direct flows, as was discussed at the end of the preceding paragraph.

LINEAR PROGRAMMING FORMULATIONS OF CAPITAL BUDGETING PROBLEMS

We turn now to the use of linear programming in business budgeting where we focus on capital budgeting under rationing—i.e., when investment choices must be made without access to external sources of funds. This problem as first stated by Lorie and Savage [11] for a business with a limited amount of funds for investment, can be restated as an LP (i.e., linear programming) problem. Briefly this problem is:

> A set of n projects exists, indexed by $j = 1, 2, \ldots, n$; project j has a present value to the firm of B_j. The costs associated with these projects are incurred over a T-year horizon indexed by $t = 1, 2, \ldots, T$, with c_{tj} denoting the cost of the jth project in the tth year. The capital budget for year t is C_t. An optimal choice of projects is one with maximum present value that does not require more cash than is available in the capital budget.

Letting x_j = the fraction of project j undertaken, we can restate this as

$$\text{maximize} \quad \sum_{j=1}^{n} B_j x_j$$

(3.1)

$$\text{subject to:} \quad \sum_{j=1}^{n} c_{tj} x_j \leq C_t, \qquad t = 1, 2, \ldots, T$$

$$0 \leq x_j \leq 1 .$$

Several comments are appropriate:

1. The model simultaneously considers all combinations of projects, an important distinction that overcomes difficulties with ROI (Return on Investment) and other one-at-a-time evaluators. (The example below illustrates this.)
2. This formulation easily incorporates interrelations among the projects. (See below.)
3. It allows for fractional solutions (e.g., ½ a foundry) which may be nonsense. (More on this later.)

In what had seemed to be a very "natural" extension of classical economic theory, Joel Dean (9) had sought to deal with capital budgeting within a firm by ROI or present worth rankings. In fact, however, the Lorie-Savage formulation resulted when it was discovered that the indicated extensions of ROI or discounted present value did not work because of various interrelations between prospective projects and budgets across time. The approach of Lorie-Savage did not prove completely satisfactory. Shortly thereafter, however, H. M. Weingartner [27] saw the possibilities of extending the dual evaluators as internal discount factors, which had previously been developed in [8] and thus got better

FIGURE 3

Network Model of Two-Commodity Liquidity Constraint Warehouse Model

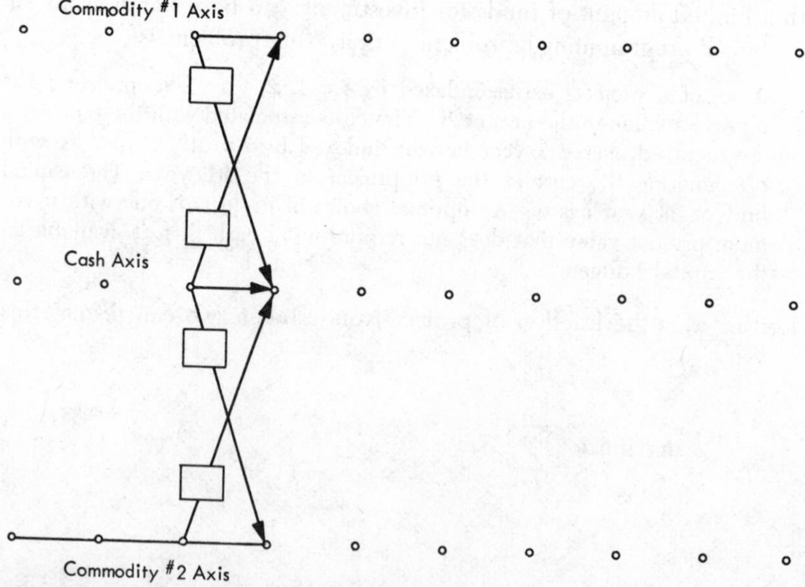

than was asked by Dean, or Lorie and Savage—i.e., Weingartner was able not only to address the problem of investment selection but, via the dual evaluators, he was also able to obtain capital discount rates for evaluating the resources available for such investments. Finally, he was able also to include additional conditions of a technological or economic variety (e.g., complementarity of assets) as we shall now illustrate.

Following Weingartner we make these definitions:

> A set of projects are "mutually exclusive" if acceptance of one from the set makes it undesirable or impossible to choose any of the others. A project j is "contingent on" another project k if acceptance of j presupposes that k is also accepted.

We can also incorporate these conditions in the programming formulation. If J is the set of mutually exclusive alternatives, we need only append the constraint:

$$0 \leq \sum_{j \epsilon J} x_j \leq 1, \tag{3.2}$$

where "$j \epsilon J$" means that the indexes j are in the set of mutually exclusive alternatives. It is assumed that the x_j will take only the integer values 0 or 1 which means that *at most* one of the set J can be accepted via (3.2). If *exactly* one of the projects from the set J must be accepted, we replace the inequality in (3.2) with an equality.

If j is contingent on k we can require

$$x_j \leq x_k \tag{3.3}$$

Constraints of both types are incorporated implicitly in (3.1). For simplicity we omit them from explicit treatment in our discussion of its dual, which is

$$\begin{aligned} &\text{minimize} \quad \sum_{t=1}^{T} w_t C_t + \sum_{j=1}^{n} u_j \\ &\text{subject to:} \quad \sum_{t=1}^{T} w_t c_{tj} + u_j \geq B_j,\ j = 1, 2, \ldots, n \\ &\qquad w_t,\ u_j \geq 0 \end{aligned} \tag{3.4}$$

From the dual theorem (Equation 1.3) we see that the optimal w_t are internal discount factors evaluating C_t in period t; i.e., we can increase the present value of the projects we accept by \$$w_t$ for each dollar increase in C_t. The u_j are interpreted via the complementary slackness conditions. If x,w,u are a dual optimal pair and $x_j > 0$, i.e., project j is accepted, then the corresponding dual inequality is tight. Recalling that B_j in (3.1) is the present value of project j using external (market) discount factors, the condition

(3.5.1) $$x_j > 0 \text{ implies } u_j = B_j - \sum_{t=1}^{T} w_t\, c_{tj}$$

which allows us to interpret u_j, the evaluator of the jth project as the excess of the present value of project j as calculated with external discount factors, over its costs discounted by the internal opportunity discount factors, the w_t. For the projects that are fractionally accepted a second application of complementary slackness gives

(3.5.2) $$x_j < 1 \text{ implies } u_j = 0$$

so that if also $x_j > 0$ then

$$B_j = \sum_{t=1}^{T} w_t\, c_{tj}$$

Such projects are marginal, in that their present value just balances their internally discounted cost.

The reverse implication of the complementary slackness relations

$$x_j = 0 \text{ implies } u_j > B_j - \sum_{t=1}^{T} w_t\, c_{tj}$$

is true when the solution to the dual and primal program is unique. We can, by perturbation if necessary, assure that this is true and draw the conclusion: if project j is not accepted,

$$x_j = 0 \text{ implies } u_j > B_j - \sum_{t=1}^{T} w_t\, c_{tj},$$

and since $x_j < 1$ implies $u_j = 0$ and therefore if j is not accepted $\Sigma\, w_t\, c_{tj} > B_j$. All technological and other interrelations as formally incorporated in the primal problem are taken into account in these evaluations. See Weingartner [27] for more extended discussion.

The following example is intended to serve two purposes: (1) fix the previous discussion in concrete terms, and (2) shows the deficiency of one-at-a-time evaluation methods. Consider a firm facing the capital budgeting decision summarized in Table 3. The projects there are arranged in decreasing order of the ratio

$$B_j / \sum_{t=1}^{T} c_{tj}$$

and a naive approach might select projects from the top down, in the indicated order, until one of the budget constraints is violated. See (27), pp. 9 ff. Table 3, however, contains optimal values for both primal and

TABLE 3

Multi Period Capital Budgeting Example

Data

Project	Net Present Value B_j	Present Value of Outlays, c_{tj} Period t = 1	Period t = 2	Period t = 3	Ratio $B_j / \sum_{t=1}^{3} c_{tj}$
1	16	12	10	2	.67
2	19	14	8	12	.56
3	11	8	6	6	.55
4	20	24	16	6	.43
5	24	16	20	24	.40
6	7	13	8	0	.33
7	18	18	18	20	.32
8	4	1	6	9	.25
9	4	6	4	7	.24
10	4	4	6	8	.22

Solutions

Primal	Dual
$x_1 = 0$	$u_1 = 0$
$x_2 = 0$	$u_2 = 0$
$x_3 = 0.375$	$u_3 = 0$
$x_4 = 0$	$u_4 = 0$
$x_5 = 1.0$	$u_5 = 2.0$
$x_6 = 0$	$u_6 = 0$
$x_7 = 0$	$u_7 = 0$
$x_8 = 1.0$	$u_8 = 2.625$
$x_9 = 0$	$u_9 = 0$
$x_{10} = 0$	$u_{10} = 0$

Budget

Ceilings	$C_1 = 20$	$C_2 = 30$	$C_3 = 40$
Evaluations	$w_1 = 1.375$	$w_2 = 0$	$w_3 = 0$

dual programs formulated from the data of Table 3 which will enable us to explore these projects in varying combinations as well as one at a time. The primal problem formed from the data of Table 3 is

$$\begin{aligned} \text{maximize } & 16x_1 + 19x_2 + \cdots + 4x_{10} \\ \text{subject to: } & 12x_1 + 14x_2 + \cdots + 4x_{10} \le 20 \\ & 10x_1 + 8x_2 + \cdots + 6x_{10} \le 30 \\ & 2x_1 + 12x_2 + \cdots + 8x_{10} \le 40 \\ & 0 \le x_1, x_2 \ldots, x_{10} \le 1. \end{aligned}$$

The dual to this problem, formulated by reference to the same data, is

$$\begin{aligned} \text{minimize } & 20w_1 + 30w_2 + 40w_2 + u_1 + u_2 + \cdots + u_{10} \\ \text{subject to: } & 16 \le 12w_1 + 10w_2 + 2w_3 + u_1 \\ & 19 \le 14w_1 + 8w_2 + 12w_3 + u_2 \\ & - - - - \\ & 4 \le 4w_1 + 6w_2 + 8w_3 + u_{10} \end{aligned}$$

and

$$0 \leq w_1, w_2, w_3; u_1, u_2, \ldots, u_{10}.$$

The solutions for the above pair of problems are given in Table 3. That these are solutions may be verified by observing that all constraints are satisfied. That they are optimal may also be verified by substituting these values in the objectives and observing that

$$11x_3 + 24x_5 + 4x_8 = 32.125$$
$$20w_1 + u_5 + u_8 = 32.125,$$

so that equality obtains for the values of primal and dual functionals. See (1.3) above.

Evidently x_3, which has a fractional value for $0 \leqq x_3 \leqq 1$, is marginal since $u_3 = 0$. Incrementing $x_3 = 0.375$ by an amount Δ will not add anything to the primal objective, whereas incrementing $x_5, x_8 = 1$ will.

If these latter values exhaust their investment possibilities (at 100 percent) then, of course, the indicated increments are not physically meaningful. Even graver difficulties occur if these primal variables must be integers ($x_j = 1$ means "accept" and $x_j = 0$ means "reject" are the only possibilities). A more recondite analysis must then be used and our interpretation of the dual variables as evaluators must be seriously modified if ambiguity and possible error is to be avoided. See pp. 135–37 in [2].

The requirement that solutions must be in integers leads into topics such as special methods which have been devised for solving such problems. These cannot be dealt with here. See [11]. Computer codes for problems in which all or some of the variables must take only integer values are available. This means that other ways of securing evaluations are available by altering data (sensitivity analysis and parameterization) or by adjoining new constraints or variables in different periods. See pp. 145–53 in [3]. This section now closes with the following very limited discussion of some of the computer codes available for solving ordinary linear programming problems.

The MPSX code of IBM and the OPTIMA code of CDC are proprietary, large scale, general purpose linear programming systems made available for a fee to users of the machines of these manufacturers. The maximum problem size that can be handled is determined by the amount of high speed storage available. Problems with over 4,000 constraints and virtually an unlimited number of variables can be solved on present day machines. Advanced starts are possible to reduce computing cost by taking advantage of any "good" solution that may be available, e.g., one obtained from prior solutions of a similar problem. The MPSX code is also capable of handling problems in which some of the variables are constrained to take on only integer values (mixed-integer programming problems).

Besides these efficient, larger scale proprietary codes, almost all computer manufacturers have available non-proprietary codes suitable for "student" type problems of several hundred constraints and generally written for ease of use instead of computational efficiency.

These codes, and others, too, all provide values of primal and dual variables as part of the solution and have other features as well. This includes routines for exploring data variations and sensitivity analyses by means of which upper and lower bounds can be established for direct and dual variables. Other codes are available with still other features not only from other computer manufacturers but also from commercial service bureaus and consultants. Some of these are further specialized by industry or model structure—such as the code written by Bonner and Moore for the UNIVAC 1108 block diagonal models, e.g., the blending type models which are often encountered in refinery operations. Among these codes are certain especially efficient ones for use on network and transportation-type models which may prove attractive for use in financial planning and analyses by virtue of the remarks made at the end of the preceding section. See [12] and [26].

PORTFOLIO SELECTION

The ability to deal simultaneously with combinations of projects suggests possible uses in portfolio selection and other areas where diversification offers a way to deal with certain aspects of risk-return relations. This may be illustrated by reference to concepts and formulations introduced by H. Markowitz (19). The variance of the returns associated with any portfolio may be represented

$$V(x) = \sum_{j=1}^{n} \sum_{i=1}^{n} x_i \sigma_{ij} x_j,$$

where x_j is the amount invested in the jth security and σ_{ij} is the covariance between the returns on securities i and j. The value of this variance $V(x)$ may be considered a measure of risk (e.g., the variability of returns) associated with each choice, x, of a portfolio.[1] An investment objective might then be to minimize this risk subject to securing a specified expected return as in

$$\text{minimize} \sum_{i=1}^{n} \sum_{j=1}^{n} x_i \sigma_{ij} x_j$$

(4)

$$\text{subject to:} \sum_{j=1}^{n} \mu_j x_j = \mu$$

[1] Markowitz also introduces the idea of semi-variance as a measure of unfavorable variations—i. e., variations below the expected returns.

$$\sum_{j=1}^{n} x_j = 1$$

where x is the proportion of the total portfolio utilized for the jth security and μ_j the known (expected value) of its return. Here then the problem is to select a portfolio which will minimize the risk of securing a specified overall return, μ.

This involves a quadratic function in the objective and hence is a problem in quadratic programming. The ordinary (Lagrangean) conditions for an optimum, however, result in a set of linear constraints. When adjoined to the constraints of [4], above, a new enlarged set of linear constraints is obtained. A number of readily available artifacts may then be employed to bring the indicated optimization within reach of the computer programs described above. See [31], p. 684. Finally, the condition[2] $x_j \geq 0$ may also be accommodated by a slight variation of the standard solution procedures so that these, too, may be regarded as having achieved the status of being equivalents to linear programming models—by virtue of the indicated algorithmic alteration. See [5] for further discussion of this way (and others as well) of achieving equivalences as part of a model-making strategy.

Now suppose that by one device or another we vary μ, and for each such value we obtain the minimum variance, V—or equivalently, the standard deviation $\sigma = \sqrt{V(x)}$ and the portfolio associated with it. This leads to the idea of an "efficient portfolio," as one for which the risk is minimized for each possible level of return, μ.[3]

We illustrate by means of the following data

$$\begin{aligned} \mu_1 &= 0.1;\ \mu_2 = 0.2;\ \mu_3 = 0.3;\ \mu_4 = 0.4, \\ \sigma_{11} &= \sigma_{22} = \sigma_{33} = \sigma_{44} = 0.01 \\ \sigma_{ij} &= 0 \text{ for all } i \neq j. \end{aligned}$$

A graph of the resulting efficient portfolios is plotted in Figure 4. To illustrate the computations we single out portfolio a for which we have

$$x_1 = x_2 = x_3 = x_4 = 0.25.$$

This gives

$$\mu = 0.1x_1 + 0.2x_2 + 0.3x_3 + 0.4x_4 = 0.25$$

and

$$\begin{aligned} \sigma &= \sqrt{x_1{}^2\sigma_{11} + x_2{}^2\sigma_{22} + x_3{}^2\sigma_{33} + x_4{}^2\sigma_{44}} \\ &= \sqrt{(.25)^2(.04)} = 0.05 \end{aligned}$$

by reference to the above data.

---

[2] This may be interpreted as a condition or security issues.

[3] An alternate formulation is one which maximizes the expected return for a given (prescribed) risk. Either formulation may be used to define efficiency, but it seems better to proceed as we do here, if only because many persons may find it difficult to think in terms of prescribing a risk-variance quantity initially.

FIGURE 4

Efficient Portfolios for a Four Security Market Example

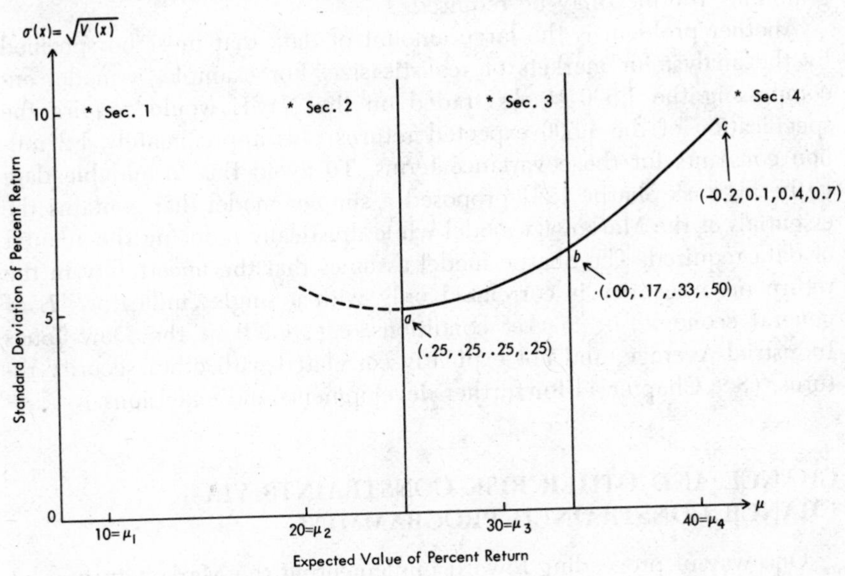

The other portfolios are calculated in analogous fashion so that we can evidently comment as follows:

1. The value of diversification is strikingly demonstrated by portfolio *a* with an expected return of 25% and a standard deviation of return of 5%—½ that of any of the constituents of the portfolio.
2. The minimum standard deviation over all unit portfolios is 5% so there is no reason to accept less than 25% expected value of return.
3. The efficient portfolios to the right of *b* require short selling of security 1 which may be unacceptable to some investors.

We can also observe that none of the individual securities, held alone, is efficient since the * with which they are associated all have a $\sigma_{ij} = 0.01$ and lie above the indicated curve of efficient portfolios. Finally, we may remark that the familiar Lagrange multipliers can be assigned the role of dual variables with a value $w_1 = .05 + 0.2\mu$ associated with the first constraint in (4)—as a rate of change of $V(x)$ with the associated change in μ—and a value of $w_2 = .015 - .05\mu$ associated with the second constraint. Note now, however, that the values of these dual variables now vary with each change in the value of μ so that the unusual feature of a clean break for ranging Δ values, as in ordinary linear programming, is not available here.

In general, realistic portfolio problems are not as simply stated as (4). Typically, constraints are placed on the composition of the portfolio; e.g., no short selling, $x_j \geq 0$, or no more than ½ the portfolio in securities 3 and 4, so that $x_3 + x_4 \leq \frac{1}{2}$ must apply, and so on. When these constraints are added to (4), then a recourse to quadratic programming routines may be required.

Another problem is the large amount of data that must be specified by the analyst for markets of realistic size. For example, a model encompassing the 1,500 stocks traded on the NYSE would require the specification of the 1,500 expected returns plus approximately 1.2 million constants for the covariance terms. To avoid this formidable data gathering task Sharpe [22] proposed a simpler model that contains the essentials of the Markowitz model while drastically reducing the amount of data required. The Sharpe model assumes that the uncertainty in the return on a security is correlated only with a single "indicator," *I*, of general economic or market conditions, e.g., GNP or the Dow Jones Industrial Average, and not explicitly correlated with other security returns. (See Chapter 44 for further developments and extensions.)

CHANCE AND OTHER RISK CONSTRAINTS VIA CHANCE CONSTRAINED PROGRAMMING

One way of proceeding toward implementing the Markowitz type of approach to risk has just been indicated. More remains to be done, however, especially as one proceeds from the security (and other relatively liquid) markets toward the more involved problems of business budgeting (e.g., capital budgeting) and financial planning. The latter are likely to involve far more constraints, technological and otherwise, than these approaches can accommodate.

As a start toward considering some of these problems we might refer back to (1.1) and assume that the a_{ij}, c_j, and b_i now take the form of random variables instead of being merely constants, as before. In other words our problem is now one in which we are to choose values for the decision variables, x_j, without exact knowledge of the returns and costs. A variety of approaches for dealing with these kinds of problems have been developed, and one of them called chance constrained programming will be illustrated here.

Consider, for instance, the following quotation from a recent study [21] of the motives of a selected sample of financially sophisticated investors. "Risk, as alluded to [by some of these investors] is not dispersion [or variance] or returns *per se*, but the possibility of not receiving a desired positive return." In terms of chance constrained programming, then one might write

$$(5.1) \qquad Pr\left[\sum_{j=1}^{n} a_{ij}x_j \geq a_i\right] \geq \alpha_i, \quad i = 1, \ldots, m$$

where the a_{ij} are random variables, with known probability distributions, and a_i a constant, is the desired positive return for period (or portfolio) i. Here Pr stands for probability and $1\text{-}\alpha_i$ with $0 \leqq \alpha_i \leqq 1$ serves as a measure of the "risk" that such an investor is willing to take of not receiving at least the indicated level, a_i. The x_j as decision variables must then be selected in a way that satisfies the indicated inequalities.

Of special interest are the "posture constraints" which one may impose on liquidity or other balance sheet items, which thus represent desired postures, at specified times within a planning horizon. Such a constraint imposed at the end of a planning period is further distinguished as a "horizon posture constraint." The reason for effecting this distinction is that such a horizon posture constraint can be used to establish bounds—i.e., upper and lower limits—for evaluating opportunities *beyond* the horizon by reference to its effects on opportunities *within* the planning period covered by the model. A widely used example of such a posture constraint is the so-called payback period constraint, which is almost ubiquitously employed for marketing new products in consumer packaged goods, and other products, too, where substantial investments and large uncertainties—e.g., for the development of other new products—are encountered. The potential for lost opportunities which may occur while funds are tied up in marketing a new product makes it desirable to have some such means for reducing these uncertainties to corresponding risk equivalents within the horizon indicated by a payback period. See [6]. On the other hand, it is also possible to relax the perhaps overly stringent requirements of a product-by-product payback period constraint by means of a single constraint imposed on a *portfolio* of such investments. See references under [21].

The presence of risk, uncertainty, and like conditions (e.g., ignorance or the absence of knowledge), also sharpens the need for considering a variety of possible objectives—and, of course, an alteration in objectives will generally also alter the evaluation values. Alternative objectives which have already received attention are the so-called E (or expected value) and V (minimum variance) models with associated chance constraints. Another alternative is the so-called P-model with an objective that may be written

$$\text{(5.2)} \qquad \text{maximize} \quad Pr\left(\sum_{j=1}^{n} b_j x_j \geq b\right).$$

This might also be called an "aspiration-level model" by virtue of the way it reflects the idea of an aspiration level, b, which is set at a level that one might "realistically" hope to achieve by x_j choices. This construct from social psychology was subsequently generalized by H. A. Simon [23] who referred to it as "satisficing," which he believed was more likely behavior than the "optimizing" posited by economists (among others). See [24]. This, too, has also been accorded a chance-constrained formulation, which can be used to illuminate this construct (satisficing) and the nature of the generalization involved. Suppose, in particular, that one of the constraints in (5.1) is the same as (5.2) with a prescribed probability, β, for its achievement. That is, we are supposing

$$Pr\left(\sum_{j=1}^{n} b_j x_j \geq b\right) \geq \beta \tag{5.3}$$

forms one of the constraints. Note, in particular, that the prescribed $0 \leqq \beta \leqq 1$ may exceed the *maximum* attainable via (5.2). When that occurs it then becomes necessary either to (1) abandon the effort (e.g., *any* investment alternative offered by the market) associated with the model or (2) revise the aspiration level, b, or the risk, $1 - \beta$, of not attaining it.

There are also various formalized rules (called decision rules) for choosing the x_j values in chance-constrained programming. Some classes of these rules are dynamic (or adaptive) and some are not. The zero-order rules are examples of the latter class in that, under these rules, all of the x_j values are chosen in advance. See the references noted in [1]. Other rules prescribe only some choices and withhold others until additional data, along with the consequences of preceding choices, are available. The latter includes the general class of linear decision rules and extends to still other classes which prescribe even the nature of the observations which are to be taken and how they are to be estimated and evaluated in the model. See [7].

The case of linear decision rules with normal distributions has been explored in [4] and corresponding deterministic equivalents delineated for the *E*, *V*, and *P* models. This means that all elements of the resulting models are deterministic—i.e., contain no random elements. They are nevertheless equivalent to the corresponding chance-constrained models —which do contain random terms—in that the x_j values obtained from these deterministic models also optimally satisfy the corresponding chance constraints.

In conclusion we may observe that the portfolio models explored in the preceding section are deterministic. They are also static, involving only "one-shot" choices for the portfolios which presumably then satisfy the risk and risk-preference conditions for investors in the markets where these choices are effected. Chance constrained programming formulations provide one route for generalizations to more dynamic models with explicit delineation of the conditions of risk (or uncertainty) and investor risk-preferences. It is not the case, however, that deterministic equivalents and analytic (closed-form) solution procedures will always be available. Recourse to other approaches such as simulation, etc., may be required. Finally, even an availability of deterministic equivalents may still require the development of new computer codes and solution routines as witness [4], for instance, where the deterministic equivalents involve quadratic constraints.

We can conclude with this last remark since its further pursuit would take us into topics like nonlinear programming and related solution procedures. See [10], and note only that we can also assign decision variables y and t to b and β in (5–3) to replace risk-preferred relations.

BIBLIOGRAPHY

[1] Byrne, R. F., A. Charnes, W. W. Cooper, and K. O. Kortanek. "Some New Approaches to Risk." *The Accounting Review* 43, no. 1, January 1968, pp. 18–37.

[2] Byrne, R. F., A. Charnes, W. W. Cooper, O. A. Davis, and Dorothy Gilford, eds. *Studies in Budgeting*. Amsterdam-London: North Holland Publishing Co., 1971.

[2.1] Byrne, R. F., A. Charnes, W. W. Cooper, and K. O. Kortanek. "A Chance-Constrained Approach to Capital Budgeting with Portfolio Type Payback and Liquidity Constraints and Horizon Posture Controls." pp. 71–90.

[2.2] Hillier, F. S. "A Basic Approach to the Evaluation of Risky Interrelated Investments." pp. 3–43.

[2.3] Naslund, B. "A Model of Capital Budgeting under Risk." pp. 3–43.

[2.4] Weingartner, H. M. "Some New Views on the Payback Period and Capital Budgeting Decisions." pp. 138–56.

[3] Charnes, A., and W. W. Cooper. *Management Models and Industrial Applications of Linear Programming*. New York: John Wiley and Sons, Inc., 1961.

[4] Charnes, A., and W. W. Cooper. "Deterministic Equivalents for Optimizing and Satisficing under Chance Constraints." *Operations Research* 11, no. 1, January–February, 1963, pp. 18–39.

[5] Charnes, A., and W. W. Cooper. "Elements of a Strategy for Making Models in Linear Programming." Chapter 26 in R. E. Machol et al., *System Engineering Handbook*. New York: McGraw-Hill Book Co., Inc., 1965.

[6] Charnes, A., W. W. Cooper, J. K. DeVoe, and D. B. Learner. "DEMON: A Model for Marketing New Products." *California Management Review* 11, no. 1, Fall 1968, pp. 31–46.

[7] Charnes, A., W. W. Cooper, and M. J. L. Kirby. "Optimal Decision Rules in Conditional Probabilistic Programming." *Rendiconti della Classe di Scienze Fisichi Mathematiche e Naturali* (Rome: Accademia Nazionale dei Lincei) fasc. 5 serie 8, vol. 45, November 1969, pp. 231–35.

[8] Charnes, A., W. W. Cooper, and M. H. Miller. "Applications of Linear Programming to Financial Budgeting and the Costing of Funds."

Journal of Business of the University of Chicago 32, no. 1, January, 1959, pp. 20–46.

[9] DEAN, J. *Capital Budgeting.* New York: Columbia University Press, 1951.

[10] FIACCO, A. V., and G. P. MCCORMICK. *Nonlinear Programming.* New York: McGraw-Hill, Inc., 1969.

[11] GARFINKEL, R. S., and G. L. NEMHAUSER. *Integer Programming.* New York: John Wiley & Sons, Inc., 1972.

[12] GLOVER, F., D. KARNEY, D. KLINGMAN, and A. NAPIER. "A Computation Study of Start Procedures, Basis Change Criteria and Solution Algorithms for Transportation Problems." *Research Report CCS93,* Center for Cybernetic Studies, University of Texas at Austin, September 1972.

[13] HAMILTON, W. F., and M. A. MOSES. "An Optimization Model for Corporate Financial Planning." *Journal of the Operations Research Society of America,* May–June, 1973.

[14] HILLIER, F. S. *The Evaluation of Risky Interrelated Investments.* London-Amsterdam: North Holland Press, 1969.

[15] JAASKELEINEN, V. *Optimal Financing and Tax Policy of the Corporation.* Helsinki Research Institute, 1967.

[16] LORIE, J. H., and L. J. SAVAGE. "Three Problems in Rationing Capital." *Journal of Business* 28 No. 4, October, 1955, pp. 229–39.

[17] LUTZ, F., and V. LUTZ. *The Theory of Investment of the Firm.* Princeton: Princeton University Press, 1951.

[18] MAO, J. C. T. *Quantitative Analysis of Financial Decisions.* London: Macmillan and Co., 1969.

[19] MARKOWITZ, H. M. *Portfolio Selection.* New York: John Wiley & Sons, Inc. 1959.

[20] ORGLER, Y. E. *Cash Management: Methods and Models.* Belmont, Calif.: Wadsworth, Inc., 1970.

[21] POTTER, R. E., and R. S. HOOKE. "The Objectives of Stock Investment of a Group of Financial Analysts." *University of Pittsburgh Business Review,* July–August 1973.

[22] SHARPE, W. F. *Portfolio Theory and Capital Markets.* New York: McGraw-Hill, Inc., 1970.

[23] SIMON, H. A. *Models of Man.* New York: John Wiley & Sons, Inc., 1957.

[24] SIMON, H. A. "Theories of Decision Making in Economics and Behavioral Science." *American Economic Review* 49, no. 3, 1959.

[25] SRINIVASAN, V. "A Transshipment Model for Cash Management Decisions." *Management Science* 20, no .10, June 1974, pp. 1350–63.

[26] SRINIVASAN, V., and G. L. THOMPSON. "Benefit-Cost Analysis of Coding Techniques for the Primal Transportation Algorithm." *Journal of the Association for Computing Machinery* 20, 1973, pp. 194–213.

[27] WEINGARTNER, H. M. *Mathematical Programming and the Analysis of Capital Budgeting Problems.* Englewood Cliffs, N.J.: Prentice-Hall, Inc., 1962).

47

Management of Individual Portfolios

PETER L. BERNSTEIN
Peter L. Bernstein, Inc.
New York, New York

IS THERE A DIFFERENCE BETWEEN PERSONAL AND INSTITUTIONAL PORTFOLIO MANAGEMENT?

When institutional holdings of common stocks were much less than they are today, the professionals who managed the security portfolios of individuals also took on the task of managing institutional accounts. Today, however, the functions are separate in most organizations, with portfolio managers specializing in either one area or the other, but the twain seldom meet.

While this gives one the impression that somehow the investment problems are unrelated and that each requires different types of understanding, experience, and skill, the essential principles of portfolio management are in fact identical. Of course, portfolios differ widely in their requirements, time horizons, risk thresholds, and cash flows. The objective of portfolio management is to reconcile these variables in such a manner as to minimize risk and maximize return, but the goal and the process of reconciling the variables is the same regardless of who happens to own the assets in question.

Admittedly, individual accounts frequently differ from institutional accounts in two areas: (1) many individuals are unable to add fresh cash to their investment portfolio in a systematic and predictable fashion—indeed, some individuals consume capital rather than accumulate it; and (2) many institutional portfolios are exempt from income and capital gains taxes. As we shall see, however, these are just two of the many variables that enter into the construction of an investment program, but in all cases the theoretical considerations are the same.

All portfolios share one objective: to provide the largest possible pool of assets from which the owner can finance expenditures now or at some future date. Since the future is uncertain, however, we can never know precisely what the value of the assets will be over time, and we know even less about what their purchasing power will be. The degree of risk that we take should therefore vary in each case, based on the time horizon within which we have to work and the likelihood that the portfolio will enjoy a net cash inflow or will be subject to cash withdrawals. The art of portfolio management consists of nothing more than selecting securities that fit within the time and cash flow constraints of the client: the application of this process to differing portfolios is only a variation on a constant theme.

DEFINING INVESTMENT OBJECTIVES

Conventionally, portfolio managers differentiate among three goals: maximum income, capital appreciation, and preservation of capital. If we look at the matter rationally, however, all investors should want to achieve all three of these goals: obviously, no one wants to lose money, while everyone wants to have as much as possible.

The problem is that most of the time circumstances deny us the opportunity to achieve all three goals simultaneously. The search for capital gain is never assured of success, so it inevitably involves risk of loss of capital; assured income is seldom available with opportunities for capital gain; high income is frequently associated with high risk. Consequently, when the time horizon is short or when the investor has to face cash withdrawals from the portfolio, we lean toward those assets with greatest certainty of income and capital value; while when the time horizon stretches out into the future and when the investor is adding to rather than withdrawing principal, we can live more comfortably with uncertainty.

Nevertheless, leaving tax considerations aside for more detailed discussion later on, the temptation to look at income and principal as separate pools of money can frequently lead to poor decisions. Admittedly, income is more certain than capital appreciation and therefore seems a more appropriate objective for the investor whose risk threshold is low. On the other hand, what he really wants is money, or, perhaps more accurately, purchasing power. If his income is high relative to his expenditure requirements, he will be able either to minimize his capital withdrawals or, in fact, to add to his capital. On the other hand, if his capital grows, he can draw on it to supplement his income or will have more money available to finance outlays at a later date.

As a result, the relatively new concept of *total return* is a refreshing addition to the terminology of portfolio management. It emphasizes that the objective of investment is to have the largest possible pool of money to finance outlays either now or later, that money is money no matter what its source, and that the search for income and for capital gain are only variations on the basic theme of maximizing return and minimizing risk.

Thus, generous income can allow an individual or a pension fund to accumulate assets at a time when the opportunities for capital appreciation seem limited. On the other hand, when the opportunities are right, capital appreciation can also increase the size of the assets or finance a higher level of expenditure. Exclusive focus on one or the other may lead to minimizing returns or maximizing risks (or both) when market considerations as well as the requirements of the portfolio might lead to a different set of decisions. And all of this applies with equal significance to institutional and individual portfolios.

HOW SHOULD RISK BE CONSIDERED?

Risk essentially means the degree of certainty or uncertainty regarding the outcome of a decision. When we buy a U.S. government bond, we know precisely what our income will be and precisely how much money we will have at a specified date in the future; when we drill for oil, no one can tell us precisely how much income or principal we will have at any date in the future. When we buy stock in a company selling consumable products to millions of customers and with a strong proprietary position in its market, the chances of unpleasant surprises are smaller than when we buy stock in an armament manufacturer with only one big customer or in a company operating in a fiercely competitive field. Similarly, projecting future earnings is more certain for a company without debt than for one that is highly leveraged.

Risk varies in degree from the chance of *total* loss of capital—such as drilling for oil or a new and untried venture—to its more benign aspect of *variability* of capital value rather than total loss. The risk considerations involved in most of the assets that go into a conventional investment portfolio usually take the latter form, although even here they can be real enough: the shrinkage in equity values from 1929 to 1932 ran to 90 percent on the average, and the investor who bought in 1929 had to wait about 25 years to break even on capital values. Even in October 1973, U.S. Steel was selling below its level of 1959.

Thus, for most investment decisions, the major uncertainty is the probable volatility in the price of the asset and, in particular, its volatility relative to the prices of all similar types of assets. The term *beta* refers to the degree to which any individual common stock fluctuates relative to the fluctuations in the stock market as a whole, as discussed in Chapter 44.

Assets that are closest to cash—that is, assets like savings accounts or very short-term securities, whose dollar value fluctuates either not at all or only in a negligible range—obviously have a high degree of certainty as to their value in the future. Assets like long-term debt instruments may fluctuate widely between purchase date and maturity but will clearly fluctuate within a narrowing range as their maturity date approaches. Meanwhile, the investor does know precisely what his income will be and what the value of the security will be at a specified date in the future. Equities, on the other hand, have no maturity date and therefore have no limit to their possible price swings between infinity and zero.[1]

Investors will rationally choose assets with less certainty as to their future value only if they expect such assets to provide a higher return than assets with more limited volatility. But what we are really saying here is that the investor who seeks higher returns has a greater probability of losing money than the investor who settles for lower returns. Since everyone obviously wants to make as much money as possible, the determining question in structuring a portfolio is the *consequence of loss*. This is far more important than the *chance* of loss. Even if the chance of loss is small (such as the probability of dying at the age of 35), the consequences can be so serious that the individual must either avoid the risk altogether or must insure against it if he is unable to avoid it.

This is why the widow is conventionally viewed as an investor unable to take much risk. Because she typically has neither the life expectancy nor the earning power outside her portfolio to provide the opportunity to recoup losses, any diminution in her capital or income may immediately impact her standard of living. Her mythological opposite, the aggressive young businessman, on the other hand, has sufficient earning power to sustain his living standard and also has many years in which to recoup his losses. At an even further extreme, the consequences would be virtually minimal for a young man who will inherit millions from aging parents.

But is this the end of the matter? If the degree of risk that we are willing to take is a function of the consequences of loss, loss is nevertheless an unpleasant possible outcome to *any* investment decision, no matter how small the consequences. In other words, we should also ask some questions about the consequences of *gain*. To what extent would an increase in capital or income significantly improve the living standard of the investor? A widow with less than $100,000 to invest might lead an entirely different life if it were $200,000, while the multimillionaire (and his heirs) might live precisely the same whether his assets never changed in value or whether they doubled.

[1] An interesting corollary of this is that cold arithmetic automatically stacks the cards in the investor's favor: he can lose only 100 percent but can gain an infinite amount.

Two cases of actual investors serve to emphasize this point. One, whose company had just gone public and put him in the multimillionaire class, stated without qualification, "Just remember you don't have to try to make me rich—I am rich!" The other, a man in his mid-50's, had lost his job two years earlier with only $15,000 to his name. He realized that if he lost the whole $15,000 playing the market, his family would be broke just one year sooner than if he had used the money to cover their living expenses, so he margined the $15,000 to the hilt, bought three of the hottest stocks in the market, and parlayed the $15,000 into $200,000 after paying off the margin debts.

In other words, the apparent *ability* to sustain losses frequently fails to go hand in hand with the *necessity* to take risks to maximize gains. The consequences of gain and the consequences of loss seldom fit in such a way that the risk exposure of the portfolio is easy to determine. In many instances, this is a subjective decision: some people never feel rich enough, while others would rather take the chance of going broke next year than this year, but the more rational approach to this question is illustrated by the two clients I have just described.

The principles involved here illustrate clearly the identity of basic considerations in individual and institutional portfolio management. A pension fund whose contributions will exceed its benefit payments for the indefinite future is surely in an ideal position to take big risks, because both time and net cash inflow provide full opportunity to recoup losses. On the other hand, since actuarial calculations can provide a precise projection of how much it must earn to meet its ultimate objectives, why should it take the risk of falling short of those objectives when low-risk assets such as long-term bonds may readily do the job?[2]

HEDGING AGAINST RISK

Experience tells us that, *on the average,* the greater the risk, the greater the probable return. Even investors who are risk-averse for one reason or another should want to take advantage of profitable opportunities that fit within the risk constraints of the portfolio.

The implications of this statement are crucial for successful portfolio management. Indeed, the statement highlights what portfolio management is all about. Portfolio management is not stock selection, which is the task of security analysis. Portfolio management is the adjustment of the overall risk exposure of the portfolio to the needs of the client. To put it another way, good portfolio management enables the client to seek the higher returns implicit in higher risk without exceeding the total amount of risk that the client wants to take.

Seen from this viewpoint, much of the common practice of portfolio

[2] Of course, beating the actuarial requirement would permit either higher benefits to beneficiaries or lower cost to the employer.

management falls short of its potential. Traditionally, some types of securities are considered appropriate for widows, and entirely different securities are considered appropriate for the aggressive businessman's account. Some are used in institutional portfolios and others in individual accounts.

But this is irrational. At all times, the process of security analysis and stock selection should designate those securities whose risk/reward ratio is most promising at any particular moment. If the most attractive stock the portfolio manager knows happens to be a highly volatile one, why should his widow clients miss the opportunity to enjoy the rewards he expects from it? If no volatile stocks appear attractive, why should the aggressive businessman take the risk of owning them when his prospective total return might be greater in the tax-exempt bonds the manager is buying for his widow clients?

All securities that appear attractive to the manager are appropriate for all clients; no issues of lesser attractiveness are appropriate for any client. The crucial question is the *proportion of the total portfolio* that he concentrates in securities of one type or another. The overall volatility of a widow's account should in all likelihood be low, which means that the volatile sector should be small and offset by larger holdings of low volatility—but that is different from saying that the manager should never buy volatile stocks for that account. On the other hand, the client mentioned above with $15,000 who decided to shoot the moon would have defeated his purpose if he had concentrated his portfolio in anything other than highly volatile stocks.

Thus, portfolio management turns out to be a process of hedging against the risks that the investor must take if the outcome is to be a successful one. Hedging against risk has nothing to do with avoiding risk. Rather, it is an effort to reduce the probabilities of loss that are implicit in every risk-taking decision. While part of this effort is obviously involved in limiting the overall volatility of the portfolio, as we have just seen, the other crucial aspect of it is to avoid involuntary liquidation of assets at depressed prices.

This is why the conventional wisdom of portfolio management places so much emphasis on the resources the investor owns in addition to his volatile assets. A steady job with good earning power in a sound company, comfortable balances in the savings bank to cover emergency needs, and adequate life insurance all provide *staying power*—the ability to hold depressed securities until they recover in price or until they can be sold and the proceeds used to purchase securities with more promise.

The investor who has no liquid resources to meet the emergencies of life or to cover other needs unrelated to his investment program will always face the unpleasant necessity to dip into his portfolio to raise cash for these external purposes. No one can have any preordained guarantee that the moment for such sales will be precisely the most appropriate one. In fact, loss of a job, appeals for help from other members of the family, or margin calls have the uncomfortable habit of coinciding with depressed security prices.

Any investment program will be disrupted if decisions to sell depend upon anything other than investment considerations. Unless the investor has liquid reserves over and above his security portfolio, in fact, he may have to be selling early to be sure he has cash reserves when, in a properly hedged program, he could hold out longer and take the risk of greater price fluctuations in his portfolio.

Thus, although most people look at the investor's outside resources as a device to protect the investor himself, we should really look at them as a means of protecting his portfolio *from him!*

A CASE STUDY

The following case study is a true story that illustrates most of the principles analyzed above, even though the situation was a most unusual one.

Late in 1959, a young man was referred to us after he had sustained a hideous accident. Although the accident had deprived him of any chance of earning a decent living and, in all probability, of getting married, it left him with a normal life expectancy of 50 years or so. To make matters worse, he had been the sole support of aging and ailing parents. The insurance company had just presented him with a check for $200,000.

Here was a case where invasion of capital was perilous, for the $200,000 was going to have to take care of him for many years. On the other hand, the maximum income available from quality securities at that time—primarily from bonds yielding less than 5 percent—was insufficient to provide for the family's needs, to say nothing of the inflation risk inherent in putting all one's resources into bonds. Here was a case where the investor simply had to take some risks, even though his capability to absorb losses was clearly limited.

We solved the problem by putting about three quarters of the account into bonds and the remainder into what appeared at the time to be pretty aggressive investments, such as IBM, MMM, American Hospital Supply, and a small highly speculative mutual fund. Thus, individual items in the portfolio had high volatility, but the portfolio as a whole had the low volatility that was appropriate to this particular individual. The income we sacrificed by buying these low-yielding stocks would, hopefully, be more than compensated for by capital appreciation, but in any case, the income sacrifice was small relative to the total picture.

While the success of this program speaks for itself, the important point is that this man never would have gone broke even if the stock selections had been a less fortunate. Furthermore, since the bonds had less volatility than the stocks, the bonds were available to cover capital withdrawals if the stocks were depressed; this provided the staying power to hold the stocks until they recovered. As it happened, things went the other way, so that the appreciated values of the stocks were used to meet capital withdrawals, which both kept the overall volatility of the account down and also enabled the portfolio manager to avoid liquidating the bonds when they were depressed.

This example is a good illustration of the factors involved in determining overall volatility, in establishing staying power, and in using the concept of total return. Even though this particular individual's circumstances were unusual, they differ hardly at all from the considerations that must be faced by the portfolio manager of a mutual fund who may be faced with a continuous flow of net redemptions. Here, too, he must attempt to preserve and enhance the assets of those stockholders who are holding rather than redeeming, at the same time that he must avoid liquidating assets at depressed prices when redemptions come in. Furthermore, given the necessity to limit the overall volatility of the portfolio and therefore the probabilities of large total capital gains for the portfolio as a whole, he must instead try to increase the stockholder's return by generating a higher level of income.

TAX CONSIDERATIONS

Taxes are just one more external factor that should not interfere with rational investment decision making. When taxes dominate the investment decision, investors frequently end up regretting it. Indeed, taxes frequently lead people to make moves that they would never make under any other circumstances and that are therefore irrational.

In the first place, many individual investors tend to exaggerate the impact of the capital gains tax. The tax on capital gains is taken at one half the investor's top bracket on regular taxable income, with a maximum of 25 percent on the first $50,000 of long-term gains and up to about 35 percent on the balance. This means that the tax will be equal to 25 percent or more of the capital gain only when it pushes the investor's top bracket up to the 50 percent area. On single returns, this is now at $32,000 of taxable income; on joint returns, it is at $44,000 of taxable income. Many investors, particularly those who live only on the income from their securities, have taxable incomes that fall well short of those figures and will therefore pay capital gains taxes of less than 25 percent.

Furthermore, since the tax falls on the gain only, it will have a major impact on the proceeds only when the gain is unusually large. Thus, on a gain equal to 50 percent of the cost price, the tax is at most going to be

35 percent of one third of the proceeds, or less than 12 percent of the total amount realized from the sale; many stocks fluctuate much more than that in the course of a year or even a few months. In general, suppose that a stock is purchased at a price P and it appreciates to nP. If T is the capital gains rate, then the capital gains tax as a percentage of the sales price is $T\frac{(n-1)}{n}$. Since the ultimate outcome of establishing a long-term gain rests as much with the new security that might be purchased as with the action of the security that might be sold, and since no one can guess with any accuracy the double movements involved, reluctance to sell stock A to buy stock B simply because of tax considerations is likely to be the cause for ultimate regret.

In addition, since under present law, the only way to avoid the capital gains tax is to hold a security until it declines to a point where the gain is wiped out, which is obviously irrational, or until one dies. Experience tells us over and over that no company's fortunes are precisely predictable for a period of more than a few years at a time, so the decision to hold something until death is equally irrational unless the investor's life expectancy is shrinking rapidly; even the greatest companies of one era have been known to fade from glory in a later era, for reasons that no one could foresee.

Even then, the investor may tend to exaggerate the impact of the capital gains tax and be unnecessarily reluctant to make portfolio shifts that he would make under any other circumstances. The ultimate impact of the estate tax should always enter into the calculations of an older investor.

Take the case of a wealthy investor whose capital gains tax bracket will be 35 percent but whose top estate tax bracket will be 40 percent. Let us assume he holds a security worth $30,000 with a cost basis of $10,000. Assuming also that the security remains unchanged in price from the moment when he might have sold it until the moment he dies, his estate will pay no capital gains tax but it will pay an estate tax of 40 percent of $30,000, or $12,000. If he sells it and pays the capital gains tax of 35 percent of $20,000, or $7,000, his estate will be worth $7,000 less but the estate tax will be diminished by 40 percent of $7,000, or $2,800. If we offset the $2,800 estate tax saving against the $7,000 capital gains tax, the true impact of the tax was only $4,200—only 21 percent of the gain and only 14 percent of the proceeds, which are amounts that might well justify a portfolio switch that made sense from a strict investment viewpoint.

But investors become infatuated with taking losses as much as they fear taking gains. Here, too, they frequently fail to do the arithmetic needed to arrive at rational decisions that they would otherwise make if free of tax considerations.

Except on very large transactions, brokerage eats up about 3 percent of the proceeds if the investor sells one stock and buys another. Furthermore, he usually sells on the bid and buys on the offer. If the transaction is large, the sale will depress the price of one stock, while the purchase will push up the price of the other; this spread is likely to more than offset any savings in brokerage. Consequently, the investor should calculate the size of the tax saving in relation to the transaction cost. For example, consider an investor in the 35 percent capital gains tax bracket with a stock that cost $30 and is now selling for $20. He would save $3.50 in taxes by establishing the loss but would incur about $1.50 in brokerage plus the spread between bid and offer. Would a saving of less than two points, or about 6 percent of the price of the stock, justify making the sale on pure investment considerations? If he were in a 20 percent capital gains tax bracket, the transaction cost would substantially wipe out the tax saving.

If a little arithmetic will protect the investor from selling a depressed security that fundamental investment considerations would otherwise induce him to hold, he should be equally rational in selecting a security to substitute for the one on which he has established a loss. Many investors want to replace one security with another at the same price, or equally depressed, or in the same industry, or even all three where possible. They thus often end up buying something they would never have bought under any other circumstances. They should realize that the proceeds of a sale consists of cash and that cash should be used to purchase the most attractive security they can find at that moment, which may only coincidentally be an equally depressed security in the same industry.

One final point is worth remembering. The rule that taxes are paid on capital gains only when the gains are realized in effect means that the investor who avoids paying a capital gains tax has in effect an interest-free loan from the government. But, unless he holds a security until he dies, it is still a loan. If he offsets a gain with a loss and uses the proceeds of the security on which the loss was taken to buy something else that then appreciates, he may well ultimately have to pay the capital gains tax on the new security in any case. Establishment of losses, in other words, may postpone the payment of the tax but seldom avoids it.

PROFESSIONAL CONSIDERATIONS

Professional portfolio managers in recent years have increasingly insisted upon discretionary authority in the management of individual portfolios. While this obviously makes life simpler for the portfolio manager, it also should work out to the benefit of the client.

The client should—and must—participate in the determination of the overall strategy for the account. The consequences of loss or gain in many instances are as much a subjective consideration as an objective one and are properly as much the client's problem as the advisor's. The risk exposure and game plan for the portfolio should be worked out jointly, explicitly set forth in writing, and reviewed on regular occasions.

Within the limitations of the overall strategy, however, the portfolio manager should have full authority for security selection. If the client must approve all moves, then it is ultimately the client who is managing the portfolio. Furthermore, he will be the victim of the manager's salesmanship, which may or may not coincide with the manager's best judgment. The manager will tend to make only those suggestions to which he expects the client to agree and will refrain from making suggestions that will result in argument and disagreement—even if the advisor's better judgment would favor the latter set of moves. This is hardly the basis for rational portfolio management.

The use of discretionary authority, however, should in no way reduce the portfolio manager's responsibility to maintain communication with the client, to keep him informed of the progress of the portfolio, and to advise the client of the advisor's uncertainties as well as his expectations. Full and honest communication, particularly when things are going less well than anticipated, is the surest way to keep the client's confidence and sustain a mutually profitable relationship.

One final matter deserves some comment. Many advisors like to select the broker through whom transactions are placed, either to facilitate good executions or to receive research services. Most clients will agree to this arrangement if the reasons for it are set before them and they understand that it is for their benefit. On the other hand, research generated through one client's brokerage is frequently used to make portfolio changes for another client, so the manager has an explicit responsibility to make certain that some sort of equitable relationship exists between any one client's brokerage costs and the research applied to his security holdings. Conflicts of interest are occasionally less apparent and more complex than many people believe!

APPENDIX—QUANTITATIVE ASPECTS

Sumner N. Levine, Ph.D.

Quantitative considerations which may be useful in the management of portfolios are presented in this section. The quantitative approach given below has the merit that it compels the investors to focus on the specifics of their needs and expectations. In so doing it helps provide the investor with an overall perspective as well as guidelines.

By way of illustration, consider a 40-year-old man who has begun to accumulate a retirement investment, the income from which is intended to supplement other incomes expected at his retirement at an age of 65 years. The time horizon for accumulating the investment income is thus 25 years. He must also set a time horizon for the retirement period, say 15 years. Monthly retirement needs are estimated at $2,500 (before tax estimates are used for the sake of simplicity), and he estimates his incomes from pensions, social security payments, insurance, and sources other than that from the investment to be $2,000 per month, so that the basic income from his investments must be $500 per month or $6,000 per year. In addition, let us assume that he requires that the income from his investment provide an additional amount of, say, $500 a year to compensate for inflation. Thus, on retirement his investment income would be $6,000 the first year, $6,500 the second year, $7,000 the third year, and so on. Both distributions and principal will be utilized during the retirement period so that at the end of 15 years no residual investment is expected to remain.

During the retirement period preservation of principal is a prime consideration. The retirement portfolio might consist of a large portion of high-grade bonds and some shares in an income-oriented mutual fund which provides some opportunity for capital appreciation. The overall rate of return (i_R) can be calculated given the monetary proportion (X_B) of the investment in bonds and the bond yield R_B as well as the proportion in equities (X_E) and the expected equity rate of return R_E. The expression is

$$i_R = X_B R_B + X_E R_E.$$

Note that in this case $X_B + X_B = 1$. Beta enthusiasts can calculate the overall beta (B) from the expression for the beta of the bonds B_B and that of the equity B_E:

$$B = X_B B_B + X_E B_E.$$

We assume that an appropriate level of volatility has been selected and that the resulting retirement investment is expected to yield 8 percent per annum compounded. The rate of return of the retirement portfolio will be presented by i_R (8 percent).

The first problem to be considered is that of establishing the size of the accumulated investment (P_F) at the time of retirement which will provide the basic extra yearly income (A_R) of $6,000 and a yearly inflation increment (G_R) of $500 over a time period ($n_R$) of 15 years. The formula for P_F is (see Chapter 36)

$$P_F = [A_R + G_R(A/G, i_R, n_R)](P/A, i_R, n_R),$$

where $(A/G,i,n)$ and $(P/A,i,n)$ are quantities tabulated in Chapter 36.

In the present case we have

$$P_F = [\$6{,}000 + \$500(5.59)](8.56)$$
$$P_F = \$75{,}285.$$

Thus the investor should have accumulated $75,285 at age 65 in a portfolio yielding 8 percent in order to realize the above stated objectives on retirement.

The next problem is that of determining the amount the investor must deposit (A_I) each year over the 25 years prior to retirement so as to accumulate the above amount at age 65. This accumulation will occur during a time when the investor is employed and is in a position presumably to undertake the greater risks associated with higher returns. Suppose he invests in a well-managed, growth-oriented fund expected to provide an average 10 percent annual compounded return. Representing this return on the accumulation investment by i_I and the time period by n_I, here 25 years, we next calculate the amount that must be invested annually (A_I) to accumulate the amount P_F (here $75,285). The formula is, using the tabulated values given in Chapter 36:

$$A_I = P_F(A/F, i_I, n_I),$$

which gives the result

$$A_I = \$75{,}285\ (0.010) \text{ per year}$$
$$A_I = \$752 \text{ per year.}$$

Thus the investor must invest $752 per year if he wishes to realize the specified retirement objectives. The value of these calculations should be clear from the above example; namely, that the estimates serve to spell out the investment obligations associated with a given set of objectives. Thus the investor must consider whether he is in a position to set aside $750 annually from his discretionary income. If not, then less ambitious retirement goals must be accepted.

Another type of calculation is useful. Instead of beginning the calculation by specifying the retirement income to be derived from the investment, the investor first decides on how much he can afford to invest (A_I) at a rate of return i_I during the accumulation period (n_I). At retirement his total investments (P_F) is given by

$$P_F = A_I(F/A, i_I, n_I).$$

Having calculated P_F, the basic annual expected income (A_R) from the retirement investment, yielding i_R over n_R retirement years, is given by the expression

$$A_R = P_F(A/P, i_R, n_R).$$

Comments

Tax-Exempt Issues. Tax-exempt bonds may appeal to investors in the higher income tax brackets (rate R). The tax-exempt yield (TE) is related to the taxable yield (T) by the formula

$$T = \frac{TE}{1 - R}.$$

Thus for an investor in the 60 percent bracket ($R = 0.6$) at 4.5 percent tax-exempt yield is equivalent to a 11.2 percent taxable yield.

Return to be Expected from Mutual Funds. Achieving an average annual gain of 10 percent or better over the long term is not an easy matter. Bearing in mind that a 10 percent compounded rate of return over seven years would result in an appreciation of 100 percent, the table below shows that only 14 major funds out of hundreds managed to show an average gain of 10 percent or better over the nearly seven-year period January 1967 to September 1973. The table is based on the assumption that all returns are reinvested.

Mutual Fund	*Percentage Change since January 1, 1967*	*Percentage Change in Nine Months to September 28, 1973*
International Investors	+245.35	+47.59
Scudder International Investors*	+109.92	+ 3.54
Templeton Growth	+269.55	+ 2.84
Pioneer Fund	+ 99.32	+ 2.22
David L. Babson Investors*	+106.21	− 0.70
Canadian Fund	+ 99.56	− 0.72
Istel Fund	+110.86	− 3.41
Chemical Fund	+110.20	− 3.60
Putnam Investors	+128.63	− 5.95
Neuwirth Fund	+441.82	− 2.35
Ivy Fund	+101.71	−14.96
Mathers Fund*	+112.97	−14.32
Founders Special	+111.95	−17.10
Rowe Price New Horizon*	+174.90	−22.31

* No load.

During the 1973 period with one exception (International Investors, a fund specializing in gold stocks), none of these select funds provided a significant return and four experienced substantial losses. However, for most investors with limited time and means, well-managed mutual funds are a popular and easy way of providing diversification and continuous management.

Index

Index

A

All page numbers printed in boldface type refer to Volume II.

All page numbers printed in boldface type refer to Volume II.

All page numbers printed in boldface type refer to Volume II.

All page numbers printed in boldface type refer to Volume II.

All page numbers printed in boldface type refer to Volume II.

All page numbers printed in boldface type refer to Volume II.

All page numbers printed in boldface type refer to Volume II.

All page numbers printed in boldface type refer to Volume II.

All page numbers printed in boldface type refer to Volume II.

All page numbers printed in boldface type refer to Volume II.

All page numbers printed in boldface type refer to Volume II.

All page numbers printed in boldface type refer to Volume II.

All page numbers printed in boldface type refer to Volume II.

All page numbers printed in boldface type refer to Volume II.

All page numbers printed in boldface type refer to Volume II.

All page numbers printed in boldface type refer to Volume II.

G

All page numbers printed in boldface type refer to Volume II.

All page numbers printed in boldface type refer to Volume II.

All page numbers printed in boldface type refer to Volume II.

All page numbers printed in boldface type refer to Volume II.

All page numbers printed in boldface type refer to Volume II.

All page numbers printed in boldface type refer to Volume II.

O

All page numbers printed in boldface type refer to Volume II.

All page numbers printed in boldface type refer to Volume II.

All page numbers printed in boldface type refer to Volume II.

All page numbers printed in boldface type refer to Volume II.

All page numbers printed in boldface type refer to Volume II.

All page numbers printed in boldface type refer to Volume II.

All page numbers printed in boldface type refer to Volume II.

All page numbers printed in boldface type refer to Volume II.

All page numbers printed in boldface type refer to Volume II.

All page numbers printed in boldface type refer to Volume II.

All page numbers printed in boldface type refer to Volume II.

All page numbers printed in boldface type refer to Volume II.

All page numbers printed in boldface type refer to Volume II.

All page numbers printed in boldface type refer to Volume II.

All page numbers printed in boldface type refer to Volume II.